P9-EEM-143

Univ. of Colorado
Fall 1977

960 S Miller Way
Lakewood, Col.
988-5771

# Culture,
# Disease,
# and
# Healing

*In reality, if medicine is the science of the healthy as well as of the ill human being (which is what it ought to be), what other science is better suited to propose laws as the basis of the social structure, in order to make effective those which are inherent in man himself? Once medicine is established as anthropology, and once the interests of the privileged no longer determine the course of public events, the physiologist and the practitioner will be counted among the elder statesmen who support the social structure. Medicine is a social science in its very bone and marrow. ...*

**Rudolph Virchow**
*Die Einheitsbestrebungen,* 1849


*I should perhaps briefly state the reasons that have progressively led me—a microbiologist not trained in medicine—to explore some of the biological and social implications of man's response to his total environment. My concern with such problems emerged from an increasing awareness of the fact that the prevalence and severity of microbial diseases are conditioned more by the ways of life of the persons afflicted than by the virulence and other properties of the etiological agents. Hence the need to learn more of man and of his societies in order to try to make sense of the patterns of his diseases.*

**René Dubos**
*Man Adapting,* 1965

# Culture, Disease, and Healing

## Studies in Medical Anthropology

*Edited by*
# David Landy

*Macmillan Publishing Co., Inc.*
NEW YORK

*Collier Macmillan Publishers*
LONDON

*To the memory of six*
*who pioneered in*
*medical anthropology*

WILLIAM CAUDILL
ANN FISCHER
JOHN P. GILLIN
A. IRVING HALLOWELL
W. H. R. RIVERS
HENRY E. SIGERIST

Copyright © 1977, David Landy

Printed in the United States of America

All rights reserved. No part of this book may be reproduced or transmitted in any form or by any means,
electronic or mechanical, including photocopying, recording, or any information storage and retrieval system,
without permission in writing from the Publisher.

Macmillan Publishing Co., Inc.
866 Third Avenue, New York, New York 10022

Collier Macmillan Canada, Ltd.

Library of Congress Cataloging in Publication Data

Main entry under title:

Culture, disease, and healing.

   Bibliography: p.
   1. Medical anthropology—Addresses, essays, lectures.
   2. Medicine, Primitive—Addresses, essays, lectures.
   3. Social medicine—Addresses, essays, lectures.
   I. Landy, David. [DNLM: 1. Social medicine.
   2. Culture.   3. Disease.   WA30 C968]
GN296.C84            362.1            76-2013
ISBN 0-02-367390-7

Printing: 1 2 3 4 5 6 7 8          Year: 7 8 9 0 1 2 3

# Contributors

**Erwin H. Ackerknecht,** Professor Emeritus of the History of Medicine, Medizinhistorisches Institut, Universität Zurich, Switzerland.

**Alexander Alland, Jr.,** Professor of Anthropology, Department of Anthropology, Columbia University.

**George J. Armelagos,** Associate Professor of Anthropology, Department of Anthropology, University of Massachusetts, Amherst.

**John Cassel,** Professor of Epidemiology, Department of Epidemiology, School of Public Health, University of North Carolina.

**T. Aidan Cockburn,** Medical Director, City of Detroit, Michigan, and Research Associate, Division of Physical Anthropology, Smithsonian Institution.

**Alfred Worcester Crosby, Jr.,** Associate Professor of History, Department of History, Washington State University.

**René Dubos,** Professor Emeritus of Microbiology and Pathology, The Rockefeller University.

**Don E. Dumond,** Professor and Head of Anthropology, Department of Anthropology, University of Oregon.

**Frederick L. Dunn,** Professor, Department of International Health, School of Medicine, University of California, San Francisco.

**Robert B. Edgerton,** Professor of Anthropology and Psychiatry, Department of Anthropology and Neuropsychiatric Institute, University of California, Los Angeles.

**Charles J. Erasmus,** Professor of Anthropology, Department of Anthropology, University of California, Santa Barbara.

**Horacio Fabrega, Jr.,** Associate Professor of Psychiatry and Anthropology, College of Human Medicine and Department of Anthropology, Michigan State University.

**\*Ann Fischer,** Professor of Anthropology, Newcomb College and Research Associate, School of Public Health, Tulane University.

**John L. Fischer,** Professor of Anthropology, Department of Anthropology, Tulane University and Professor of Anthropology, Department of Anthropology, University of Pittsburgh.

**Reo Franklin Fortune,** Wolfson College, Cambridge, England.

**Charles O. Frake,** Professor of Anthropology, Department of Anthropology, Stanford University.

**Judith Friedlander,** Assistant Professor of Anthropology, Department of Anthropology, State University of New York, Purchase.

**Clifford Geertz,** Professor of Anthropology, Institute for Advanced Studies, Princeton, New Jersey.

**Leonard B. Glick,** Professor of Anthropology, Hampshire College, Amherst, Massachusetts.

**Harold A. Gould,** Professor of Anthropology, Department of Anthropology and Associate

\*Deceased.

V

Director, Center for Asian Studies, University of Illinois, Urbana-Champaign.

**Zachary Gussow,** Associate Professor of Anthropology, Department of Psychiatry and Behavioral Science, Louisiana State Medical Center, New Orleans.

*****A. Irving Hallowell,** Professor of Anthropology, Department of Anthropology, and Curator of Social Anthropology, University Museum, University of Pennsylvania.

**Irene Hamer,** Social Worker, Children's Aid Society, Western Manitoba, Canada.

**John H. Hamer,** Professor of Anthropology, and Head, Department of Sociology and Anthropology, Brandon University, Manitoba, Canada.

**Don Handelman,** Lecturer in Anthropology, The Hebrew University of Jerusalem, Israel.

**Alan Harwood,** Associate Professor of Anthropology, Department of Anthropology, University of Massachusetts, Boston.

**Ivor H. Jones,** First Assistant, Department of Psychiatry, Melbourne University, Australia.

**John G. Kennedy,** Associate Professor of Anthropology and Psychiatry, Department of Anthropology and Neuropsychiatric Institute, University of California, Los Angeles.

**Malcolm A. Kidson,** Senior Lecturer, Department of Psychological Medicine, Monash University, Melbourne, Australia.

**R. S. Khare,** Professor of Anthropology, Department of Anthropology, University of Virginia.

**David Landy,** Professor of Anthropology, Department of Anthropology, University of Massachusetts, Boston.

**Sarah Langley,** Assistant Professor of Anthropology, Eastern Connecticut State College, Willimantic.

**William S. Laughlin,** Professor and Chairman, Laboratory of Biological Anthropology, Department of Biobehavioral Sciences, University of Connecticut.

**Takie Sugiyama Lebra,** Associate Professor of Anthropology, Department of Anthropology, University of Hawaii.

**Charles M. Leslie,** Professor of Anthropology, Department of Anthropology, New York University.

*Deceased.

**Claude Lévi-Strauss,** Professor of Social Anthropology, Collège de France, Paris.

**Barbara W. Lex,** Research Anthropologist, Alcohol and Drug Abuse Research Center, McLean Hospital, Belmont, Massachusetts.

**Richard W. Lieban,** Professor of Anthropology, University of Hawaii, Honolulu.

**Michael H. Logan,** Assistant Professor of Anthropology, Department of Sociology and Anthropology, East Carolina University, Greenville, North Carolina.

**Frank Mahony,** Programme Director, Social Development, South Pacific Commission, Noumea, New Caledonia.

*****William Morgan,** Psychologist and Physiologist, Harvard University.

**Mary Louie New,** Consultant, Department of Behavioural Science, Faculty of Medicine, University of Toronto, Canada.

**Peter Kong-ming New,** Professor of Sociology, Department of Behavioural Science, Faculty of Medicine, University of Toronto, Canada.

**Marshall T. Newman,** Professor of Physical Anthropology, Department of Anthropology and Adjunct Professor, Institute for Environmental Studies, University of Washington.

**Ethel Nurge,** Associate Professor of Anthropology, Department of Human Ecology and Community Health, University of Kansas Medical Center, Kansas City.

**Seymour Parker,** Professor and Chairman of Anthropology, Department of Anthropology, University of Utah.

**Benjamin D. Paul,** Professor of Anthropology, Department of Anthropology, Stanford University.

**Irwin Press,** Associate Professor of Anthropology, Department of Sociology and Anthropology, University of Notre Dame.

**Ronald A. Reminick,** Assistant Professor of Anthropology, Department of Anthropology, Cleveland State University.

**Lola Romanucci-Ross,** Assistant Professor of Community Medicine and Director of Muir Interdisciplinary Studies, School of Medicine, University of California, San Diego.

**Arthur J. Rubel,** Professor of Anthropology, Department of Anthropology and College of Human Medicine, Michigan State University.

*Henry E. Sigerist, Professor of the History of Medicine, Institute for the History of Medicine, Johns Hopkins University.

Robert F. Spencer, Professor of Anthropology, Department of Anthropology, University of Minnesota.

Melford E. Spiro, Professor of Anthropology, Department of Anthropology, University of California, San Diego.

George S. Tracy, Assistant Professor of Sociology, Department of Sociology, Louisiana State University, Baton Rouge.

Paul R. Turner, Professor of Anthropology, Department of Anthropology, University of Arizona.

Victor W. Turner, Professor, Committee on Social Thought and Professor of Anthropology, Department of Anthropology, University of Chicago.

Douglas Uzzell, Assistant Professor of Anthropology, Department of Anthropology, Rice University.

Edward Wellin, Professor of Anthropology, Department of Anthropology, University of Wisconsin, Milwaukee.

Beatrice Blyth Whiting, Lecturer in Educational Anthropology, School of Education and Department of Anthropology, Harvard University.

R. G. Willis, Lecturer in Social Anthropology, Department of Social Anthropology, Edinburgh, Scotland.

B. Berthold Wolff, Research Associate Professor of Clinical Psychology and Chief, Pain Research Group, Department of Psychiatry, New York University Medical Center, New York City.

*Pow Meng Yap, Professor of Psychiatry, Hong Kong Psychiatric Centre.

*Deceased.

# Acknowledgments

As the reader will find in the introductory chapter, this book emerged from many years of teaching medical anthropology. Along the way I have been educated by students and colleagues in more ways than I can name, and if I thank them here collectively I hope they will not think I am not in their debt individually. I should like to thank most warmly all those authors who have permitted me to include their work here. In every case I invited each author to make any changes he or she wished in his published writing though I reserved the right to abridge the work in the interest of saving space. In many cases, authors took advantage of the occasion to correct, simplify, expand, and otherwise modify the published versions of the papers and books. Where they did so, I have acknowledged the fact in the credit line of each selection. I also wish to thank the publishers who permitted the reprinting of material to which they held the copyright; most have been cooperative and helpful. To the large number of colleagues whose work I had selected originally for inclusion and formally accepted, only later to be forced to excruciating decisions to exclude because of space limitations and ballooning publishing costs, my deepest apologies and appreciation for their understanding, tolerance, and initial permission to reprint.

For various suggestions regarding the book and for help in locating authors or materials, and in other ways, I should like to express my deep gratitude to George J. Armelagos, Golamreza Fazel, Michael F. Gibbons, Jr., Leonard Glick, Lucille N. Kaplan, Bernard M. Kramer, Louise F. Landy, Charles M. Leslie, W. H. Lo, Margaret Mead, Peter Kong-ming and Mary Louie New, Benjamin D. Paul, Richard Lieban, Ailon Shiloh, and Gretel Pelto. In the case of deceased authors I want to convey my warm thanks to the following: Virginia Chang for permission to publish the paper by her late husband, Pow Meng Yap; John L. Fischer for permission to publish the paper co-authored with his late wife, Ann Fischer; Nora Sigerist Beeson for permission to publish the paper by her late father, Henry E. Sigerist; Maude F. Hallowell for permission to publish the paper by her late husband, A. Irving Hallowell. I was unable to locate survivors or heirs of William Morgan but I am most grateful for information about Dr. Morgan furnished by John O. Brew, Scott Miyakawa, Elizabeth Nottingham, Stephen Williams, and Leland C. Wyman.

For rather extensive rewriting of their published materials at my request in order to adapt them to the purposes of this book I am grateful to Alan Harwood, Charles M. Leslie, and Peter Kong-ming New. My gratitude goes also to Edward Wellin for rewriting his original essay especially for this volume, and to Zachary Gussow and George S. Tracy for reworking their paper to our mutual satisfaction.

Kenneth J. Scott, senior editor at Macmillan, has been consistently understanding and supportive. Finally, I should like to offer my warmest appreciation to Jeanne Ryan, secretary of the Department of Anthropology, University of Massachusetts, Boston, for her arduous and dedicated labors in typing large portions of the manuscript and for her other help far beyond the call of duty; and to Marie Gaudet and Valerie Goldman, student assistants and anthropology majors, for persevering with me through the devilish task of integrating, collating, and typing the bibliography.

**David Landy**

*Newton Highlands, Massachusetts*

# Contents

# III
## Ecology and Epidemiology of Disease

# IV
## Medical Systems and Theories of Disease and Healing

# V
## Divination and Diagnosis

# VI
## Sorcery and Witchcraft in Sickness and in Health

# VII
## Public Health and Preventive Medicine

# VIII
## Anatomy, Surgery, and the Medical Knowledge of Preindustrial Peoples

# IX
## Obstetrics and Population Control

# X
## Pain, Stress, and Death

Contents

# XI
## Emotional States and Cultural Constraints

# XII
## The Patient: Status and Role

# XIII
## The Healers: Statuses and Roles

# XIV

## Healers and Medical Systems in Social and Cultural Change

# Introduction: Learning and Teaching Medical Anthropology

Humans everywhere, at all times and places, and under all forms of social organization and cultural design, have had to deal with the threat of disease and illness. Insults and injuries to the human organism have always challenged the ingenuity of human individuals and groups to devise means and forms toward their prevention, control, and treatment. Disease did not begin with man, but in a sense, as Sigerist has noted, disease is part of life itself; that is, a manifestation of life under altered conditions. It is likely that most of the diseases that afflict *Homo Sapiens* were inherited from earlier hominid ancestors; the latter, in turn, no doubt acquired them as part of their primate heritage.

The precise role of disease in human evolution has yet to be clearly understood, but paleopathologists (anthropological and medical) are convinced that this role was a critical one. The relations between disease and human evolution were transactional, that is, disease shaped man's evolution and man's continuing and varied evolutionary adaptations, in turn, influenced the course and history of disease. What happened to people in prehistory and history was in part a function of the diseases that attacked human groups, and the fate of a disease in a group was a function not only of the collective group biology but its habitat, social relations, value patterns, technology, and views of the universe as well.

In other words, there is an intimate and inexorable linkage between disease, medicine, and human culture. In part, cultures are the responses made by human groups to obstacles placed by sickness and trauma in the path of successful adaptation. Theories of disease (scientific or religious), including etiology, diagnosis, prognosis, treatment, and amelioration or cure, all are part of the cultural repertory and equipment of human groups. These differ as cultures differ; they are similar as human cultures resemble each other as universal problem-solving, adaptive organizations and technologies. The various theories of disease cannot be studied or understood apart from an understanding of the culture and social structure of the groups holding them.

The study of human confrontations with disease and illness, and of the adaptive arrangements (that is, medicines and medical systems) made by human groups for dealing with these ever-present and panhuman dangers, has come to be known as *medical anthropology*. This book attempts to present a representative selection of studies in that field and thus to sample something of its vast scope. The approach and orientation of the editor is at once ecological, evolutionary, historical, and

1

structural-functional; it is also epidemiological in that a knowledge of the distribution and incidence of a disease provides important clues to the shape of a particular social order. In effect, the ecology and epidemiology of disease in a society become a portrait of the strengths and weaknesses, the resistances and vulnerabilities of the culture and social system of that society. And the characteristics of disease, in turn, become critical clues and corollaries to its patterning and scatter on the demographic map.

Many aspects of the transactions between human illness, medicine, and culture have not been included in this volume. This is in part a function of the limitations of space and perhaps also of my personal orientation and predilections. Some aspects were eliminated not because I considered them unimportant, but because a number of anthologies have appeared in recent years dealing with these phenomena, for example, the cultural use of various medicinal substances, or the whole area of the relationships between the use of alcohol, drugs, hallucinogens, and trance states, and cultural imperatives and social pressures. What should be patently clear is that the field of medical anthropology is indeed wide in scope, and if any single anthology attempted to fling a net over the whole the resulting catch would probably capsize the vessel. Students and teachers may wish to add their own modifications in the form of additional readings to the ones included herein, either to expand the scope of the book, or to read more intensively within the areas that are represented. But it is heartening to realize that the literature directly and indirectly bearing on medical anthropology forms a vast pool of work of increasingly high caliber into which student and professional anthropologist will want to dip frequently, though with appropriate caution.

## How This Book Came into Being

In 1960 in the Department of Anthropology at the University of Pittsburgh I began to teach a course which I then called "Primitive and Folk Medicine." Simultaneously, at the Graduate School of Public Health at the same institution I began to offer a course entitled "Social and Cultural Factors in Health and Disease." The objective of the latter course was to introduce graduate students in public health, representing a wide spectrum of professionals in that field (physicians, nurses, sanitation engineers, epidemiologists, social workers, and nutritionists, among others) to knowledge and ideas in the social sciences that were relevant to the conceptualization and understanding of the kinds of collective behavioral phenomena and problems that face the public health worker. I hoped to help train these vital agents of social control and social change in complex, industrialized society to see the linkages between the manifestations of health and disease and social institutions and cultural values, and thus effectively to frame alternative courses of action in the prevention and control of illness and injury on a societal scale. This was essentially applied anthropology, or, perhaps more properly, applied behavioral science, with an emphasis on public health programs.

The objective of the former course, though in some respects complementary, was quite different. It was an attempt to begin to delineate a field of study within anthropology in which the focus was on the medical aspects of culture and the cultural aspects of medicine. This was a slowly emerging interest then among a small number of anthropologists, and it was partially glimpsed in the early survey by Caudill (1953), "Applied Anthropology in Medicine," especially in one section of that article with the somewhat redundant subtitle of "Primitive Medicine in Non-Literate Societies." My interest then, quite unlike that of the orientation of the public health course, was in carving out and defining a topical field within

2

anthropology that was analogous to such other topics as religion, economics, social organization, psychological anthropology, and the like.

It became increasingly necessary in my course to develop the concept of medical systems (defined subsequently in Section IV) as parts of social and cultural systems. I began to call the course "Comparative Medical Systems," bringing it into line with other courses then being taught in Pittsburgh's anthropology department such as "Comparative Political Systems" and "Comparative Economic Systems." Then, for two years, it was called "Medical Systems in Cultural Perspective," and finally, in 1968, "Medical Anthropology."

For my purposes, the course provided the magnet for coalescing what proved to be an enormous but scattered body of relevant—but not always focussed—literature in a stunning array of anthropological, medical, and other journals and books. I was aided in this task by materials from an earlier course, "Health and Illness in Cross-Cultural Perspective," taught at Harvard University in the early 1950s by several anthropologists including Benjamin D. Paul and the late William Caudill in which I had participated as a graduate student and teaching fellow. To those students then interested in medical anthropology the course was enormously stimulating and we applied to it the humorous but affectionate acronym, "the Hiccup seminar."

My own course had undergone considerable change and development as I learned from experience, expanding knowledge, and especially the reactions and contributions of my students, first at the University of Pittsburgh, then at the University of Massachusetts in Boston. In part, this was also a function of the changes that were taking place in anthropology generally as it emerged from its own paleolithic era. For example, it became increasingly apparent to me as to many anthropologists that the terms *primitive* and *folk* were hoary with tradition, confusion, and obfuscation, in and out of anthropology. Despite an occasional attempt to resuscitate and ennoble the term *primitive* (for example, Diamond 1963), it had become identified not only as "early" or "primal" (in which case it is at least etymologically accurate) but as "less evolved," "less advanced," and "inferior" (Montagu 1962). It hearkens back to a type of straight-line thinking about human evolution, biological and cultural, which presumed that the culture practiced by certain Mediterranean and Anglo-Saxon peoples was the end point in a chain of "progress" and the cultures of other peoples of the world—mainly European-dominated colonial dependencies—were essentially "backward," "savage," and "primitive." From about 1963 onward, I have reserved the concept of primitive to refer only to the level of technological development of a society, but not to its religion, social organization, or other of its cultural elements. When the reader encounters such terms as *backward, savage,* or *primitive*, in the selections herein, caution should be exercised as to their precise meaning and interpretation. Such terms are dropping out of the lexicon of anthropology but have not yet disappeared. Similarly, terms that signify, however unwittingly, invidious comparisons by sex will crop up in some selections, though they, too, as our collective consciousness is raised, will tend to depart from anthropological description. Anthropology surely no longer can be described simply as the science of man (even though the term refers to the species, it retains sexist overtones), but as the science of people, or the study of humankind. No doubt with time our linguistic ingenuity will engender the creation of a new, more euphonious and appropriate term.

## A Brief Historical Perspective

Permit me to recollect briefly the state of knowledge in what we now call medical anthropology at the time I began to teach the subject in 1960. It was ironic to realize at that time that, despite the fact that every human society faces critically and daily the often life-and-death questions of health and disease, coverage of institutional means of coping with these vital problems in most ethnographic reports had been generally unsystematic, often handled in a casual, fragmentary, and even confusing manner, and in some cases almost completely neglected. Of course, some classic ethnographies did include substantial accounts of the medical aspects of the cultures observed, but these were distinguished by their rarity. Despite W. H. R. Rivers' (1927) pioneering theoretical classic, *Medicine, Magic, and Religion* in which that British anthropologist-physician-psychologist began to conceptualize and define an anthropological concentration on medicine as a cultural system, thus foreshadowing the present field of medical anthropology, only a few anthropologists began to follow his important leads. I recall discussing the possibility of the course with colleagues in 1960 and being told that such medicine as there was in the world's non-Western cultures was mainly subsumed under religion, was indistinguishable from religion, or was mainly psychological and, therefore, to be included as part of the data of culture-and-personality or psychological anthropology. Although I had been drawn into medical considerations from my own research and interest in psychological anthropology and ethnopsychiatry, I soon realized that the general neglect of medicine by anthropologists betrayed, however unwittingly, an ethnocentric bias toward the very societies with which they were the most familiar.

It had begun to become clear that Rivers' book in many ways represented the symbolic totem of medical anthropology as a field of study. He conceptualized medicine, magic, and religion not as static concepts but as "three sets of social processes ... so closely interrelated that the disentanglement of each from the rest is difficult or impossible; ... man's attitude towards disease [is] identical with that which he adopts towards other classes of natural phenomena" (Rivers 1927:1). Medicine should be defined, in Rivers' view, as "... a set of social practices by which man seeks to direct and control a specific group of natural phenomena, viz., those especially affecting man himself, which so influence his behavior as to unfit him for the normal accomplishment of his physical and social functions—phenomena which lower his vitality and tend towards death" (Ibid.:4). Although, as Wellin suggests in Chapter 4, Rivers' conception of culture was somewhat rigid, Rivers did lay down vigorous strictures against the loose labeling by anthropologists of many medical practices and beliefs as simple magic rather than more properly as religious activity. I do not, incidentally, agree with Wellin's assertion that Rivers insisted that a medical practice must be *either* magical or religious. In fact, Rivers used the compound "magico-religious" to show their close connection. He *was* concerned with discovering "... the nature of the concept of disease among those who fail to distinguish medicine from magic and religion." Without opening this argument further, I would state simply that a useful distinction can be made between magic and religion and between them and medicine. For now, I refer the reader to my definition of medicine in the introduction to Section IV and to Rivers' own words which, more than half a century later, are still a salutary corrective.

Rivers was the first to conceptualize the medical beliefs of "primitive" peoples as "theories of disease" and "theories of disease causation," with an internal logic of their own, and not to be dismissed lightly as bizarre, esoteric, illogical, and irrational bits and pieces of belief and behavior in exotic cultures. Rivers interpreted theories of disease causation as consisting mainly of three classes of agents: human, spiritual or supernatural, and natural, and he showed how similar categories exist in the medical beliefs of contemporary Western culture. He dealt in some detail with much more in medical anthropology than we have the space to recapitulate, but his contributions were extremely significant and still too little known or recognized by medical anthropologists. Wellin's piece helps to place Rivers where he properly should be, an early explorer along the then largely unexplored frontier of medical anthropology.

Before 1960, not a single book in anthropology after Rivers had been devoted to the topic *as a theoretical concern*. Two books came closest to this need, in my opinion. *Social Science in Medicine* by Leo Simmons (anthropologist) and Harold Wolff (physician) (1954) drew heavily on ethnographic reports, anthropological concepts, and the data of medicine, especially psychosomatic medicine, to explore a number of exciting propositions linking medical symptomatology to behavioral phenomena and sociocultural systems. *Culture, Psychiatry, and Human Values* by Marvin Opler (anthropologist) (1956) drew together the fields of culture-and-personality in anthropology and psychiatry in medicine to synthesize a social psychiatry. The book was later enlarged and improved as *Culture and Social Psychiatry* (Opler 1967). Opler (1959a) also edited an excellent anthology, *Culture and Mental Health*. Also in the 1950s the Russell Sage Foundation (which published the Simmons and Wolff volume) sponsored two first-rate books related to applied medical anthropology: *Cultural Difference and Medical Care* by Lyle Saunders (1954), an account of the problems of bringing "Anglo" medical care to Spanish-speaking peoples in the United States Southwest, and, one year later, *Health, Culture, and Community*, edited by Benjamin D. Paul (1955), a collection of case studies of efforts to bring public health programs to mainly non-Western societies, written by anthropologists and others. The latter work is still unexcelled for the task it set for itself, namely, demonstrating how a knowledge of the internal dynamics of social and cultural systems that public health teams were attempting to influence to accept programs in community health and medical care could have prevented what were mainly failures at medical innovation and change.

A number of other books were published, mainly in social psychiatry, that drew upon anthropology and other social sciences, but they were concerned primarily with practical problems in the care and treatment of psychiatric patients, and the contributions *to* anthropology were limited. From the viewpoint of medical anthropology, a landmark event in the same decade was the appearance in 1951 of the first volume of a projected eight-volume *History of Medicine* by the illustrious medical historian, Henry E. Sigerist (1951). Subtitled "Primitive and Archaic Medicine," this was the first comprehensive attempt by anyone to draw together the cross-cultural materials then at hand in a more or less consistent fashion. The book also contained summaries of such topics as the historical approach to medicine, the geography of disease, and superb original syntheses of Egyptian and Mesopotamian medicine. Whatever its limitations, this work brought into focus for the first time, so far as I am aware, a fully developed notion of a field that could only be called medical anthropology (though Sigerist did not use the term).

In the 1960s a number of works emerged of interest to medical anthropology. Two that I have found particularly helpful are *Magic, Faith, and Healing*, edited by an anthropologically oriented psychiatrist, Ari Kiev (1964), and *Magic, Witchcraft, and Curing*, edited by an anthropologist, John Middleton (1967). The first work, though oriented essentially around psychiatric illness and therapy, lay clearly within the province of medical anthropology; the second, though containing a number of fine papers, was only partially within the field.

In 1970, a welcome first attempt to provide a theoretical framework via evolutionary and game theory for medical anthropology was published by Alexander Alland, Jr. (1970), *Adaptation in Cultural Evolution: An Approach to Medical Anthropology*. Neither a textbook nor an attempt fully to cover the subject matter, this small volume nevertheless provides a useful conceptual framework for the study of medical anthropology, and a series of cross-culturally testable theoretical propositions, pointed and relevant to a host of vital questions. This book, along with Alland's (1966; reproduced in this volume) earlier paper and one by Steven Polgar (1964), "Evolution and the Ills of Mankind," represent the first serious attempts to articulate the biological, social, cultural, and demographic concerns of medical anthropology, thus bringing it broadly into the scope of general anthropology. Indeed, from this point of view, medical anthropology may be viewed as providing a critical articulating nexus for linking the subdisciplines of general anthropology, a point also made recently by Hasan (1975).

Outside of anthropology, the sister discipline of sociology previously had become increasingly concerned with the many common junctures of that field with medicine and public health. As early as 1927, Bernhard Stern, a pioneer scholar in medical sociology, had published *Social Factors in Medical Progress*, and his seminal papers of several decades ago presaged many of the later concepts and focuses of that field (see the posthumous volume of his selected writings: Stern 1959). Stern was also trained in anthropology, did anthropological field research, and made significant contributions to that field, and most of his writings were informed by anthropological knowledge and perspective. Of great importance also to the development of medical anthropology were the conferences and published volumes of the New York Academy of Medicine through two decades, organized and edited by a physician, Iago Galdston, who had a broad, Renaissance-like interest in, and urge to bring together, individuals from the medical and behavioral sciences so as to explore and identify the points of mutual concern. See, for example, *Man's Image in Medicine and Anthropology* (Galdston 1963), and *Medicine and Anthropology* (Galdston 1959). Also critical in organizing some of the literature and providing some categorical and theoretical foci were a series of important papers by Steven Polgar (1962, 1963, 1964) dealing with both the applied and theoretical aspects of the developing field. Summaries and assessments of continuing research and writing in the field have appeared in the *Biennial Review of Anthropology* from time to time (Fabrega 1972, Scotch 1963), and now in the *Annual Review of Anthropology* (Montgomery 1973, Colson and Selby 1974). Since the historical development of medical anthropology is treated briefly in Chapter 1 of this book in the paper by Richard Lieban, no more will be said of it here.

## The Design of the Book

Selecting the pieces for this anthology has been a complex and perplexing task because in some areas of medical anthropology the literature is sparse and difficult to locate (and not always to my liking even so), whereas in others, the plethora of material raises bedeviling problems of typicality. Furthermore, although many valuable nuggets are buried in the papers and monographs of an earlier day, the equally numerous anachronisms and discarded theories and concepts could unreasonably litter the landscape of readers for whom this book may serve as an introduction to the subject. Many historians, physicians, and anthropologists have written first-rate papers and books that lie partially or wholly within the field and made a number of signal contributions. Still, one can only be astounded at the antique notions that prevailed a few decades ago. For example, in his stimulating and often-quoted paper, "Problems of Primitive Medicine," Ackerknecht (1942), while rightly pointing out the error of a simplistic, unilinear evolutionary approach to "primitive" medicine, can still refer to "folk" medicine as a "strange mixture of true primitive traits with degenerate high cultural elements," and he can make, among others, the following sweeping generalizations:

The primitive's treatment is deeply embedded in the whole magico-religious system, hence his extreme traditionalism, conservatism and conformity. Everything new is resented as highly dangerous, and fear, the kernel of primitive man's faith, makes him cling so closely to rules and customs. This traditionalism on the other hand makes him surprisingly insensible to experience.

It will be apparent to the reader that the studies in this book, especially those of more recent vintage, do not support such a conclusion. Preindustrial and non-Western peoples of the world do not hold a monopoly on cultural conservatism and those of the Western industrial societies, Marx to the contrary notwithstanding, are not, even in their proletariats, inevitably inclined toward change, much less revolution. Nevertheless, it is a grievous error to throw away or ignore the earlier studies in medical anthropology. Rather one must mine the rich veins of earlier scholarship while at the same time being extremely cautious about the ethnocentric bias that frequently informed both conceptualization and interpretation of ethnographic data. The same could be said for studies in physical anthropology (excepting the dead end of anthropometry). I have included some of these still valuable older writings since each makes a unique contribution toward the goal of this book, and it is well to recognize our debt to our predecessors.

My selection has been directed mainly, though not exclusively, to accounts of those peoples who traditionally have caught the attention of anthropologists: the prehistoric, historic, and contemporary non-Western, largely preindustrial societies of the world. The cultures of these societies lie largely outside the mainstream of Euro-American culture and include the indigenous and mestizo communities of North, Middle, and South America, and the Great and Little Traditions of Old and New World cultures. Although I am keenly aware of the growing interest of anthropology with contemporary urban populations, especially in America and Europe, the medicines and medical systems of these people are too vast and complex to come within the boundaries of this single volume. Actually the ground has already been broken and well cultivated by medical sociologists, physicians, other medical scientists, historians, and others, and in any case would require rather different treatment from that applied here.

The body of literature relevant to medical anthropology has become too huge for any single individual fully to keep abreast of more than selected portions. By 1970, I had accumulated a working bibliography that I distributed to my students running to nearly 70 pages but with no pretension to completeness. My tests for the inclusion of material in the present volume were several: (1) the article or book excerpt had to fall fairly directly within anthropology rather than the behavioral sciences more broadly speaking; (2) the theoretical or conceptual findings and conclusions had to rest on an ethnographic or cross-cultural data base and not float bodiless in the thin atmosphere of pure abstraction; (3) the problem or topic area had to deal fairly directly with medicine, disease, and/or healing (many fine papers on witchcraft and sorcery, for example, could not be considered for inclusion because their medical concerns were either peripheral or absent); (4) the selections singly and as a whole should contribute toward providing one view of the still emerging field of medical anthropology, of a sampling of its scope and the kinds of topics that attract the efforts of a variety of scholars within and outside of anthropology.

Implicit in the plan of the book is one way of structuring and ordering the data and theories of this area of study. It pretends neither to completeness nor exhaustiveness, yet I would claim for it a measure of representativeness. But medical anthropology is growing so rapidly on so many fronts that a decade hence I am sure that such a book will have to be organized quite differently. And this certainty on my part only emphasizes the excitement and vitality of the subject.

No doubt many, perhaps all, readers of this book will conceive of different selections and a quite different way to organize the ones presented here. Each of us has his favorite selections, and indeed, hundreds of my own had to be eliminated. Not only a different arrangement, but different topics could be suggested. The 14 broad sections into which the selections have been placed each constitute a separate category of concern to medical anthropologists (there are, of course, ever so many more!).

A word should be said about the quality of the material in the field, both the more traditional and the more contemporary. It is my happy impression that quality and, significantly, quality control, have greatly increased over the past two decades. Much of the work by scholars today is not only more systematic than that of their forebears, but conceptually and theoretically, it is richer and more exciting. Some recent work alas, still bears the scars and disabilities of an earlier day, not only in not adhering to the canons of scientific research and assessment but even, however unwittingly, by using concepts (such as *primitive* and others mentioned earlier) that cast the groups with which they deal in an invidious light. One must still read portions of the published corpus, especially (though not exclusively) that of nonanthropologists, with care and caution.

I have also sought broad ethnographic representation of societal types and cultural levels, except for the world's industrialized societies. With a few exceptions, I have also endeavored not to reprint articles already heavily anthologized. Because of space restrictions, most of the selections here have been abridged, although I have been extremely careful not to distort or lose the major meaning and significance of any study. As a colleague, the contributors whose selections were shortened will know that I have tried to be keenly sensitive to the need not to destroy a piece in order to save it for the anthology. Naturally, scholars interested in the complete statements of such selections will want to consult the original versions.

Since the selections were taken from a variety of sources, it was necessary to change many of them to conform with the uniform style used herein. The present format follows pretty much the forms and conventions used in major anthropological journals in the United States. Because of space limitations, all footnotes have been eliminated. In a few articles I incorporated some footnotes into the text where they seemed essential to the author's argument. Most illustrations have been omitted as well as certain tables, maps, and the like, most of which may be consulted in the original sources. All references have been retained in order to ensure documentation of the points made by the writers but have been integrated into a single bibliography that appears at the end of the volume.

Another aim, through the selection and organization of these studies (however they may be rearranged by others), is to show that medical anthropology has begun to come of age. Feeding into what we may consider the main currents of medical anthropological thought and research flow contributions from a number of subfields of anthropology (I can hardly think of one that does not contribute in some fashion) and from many related and adjacent disciplines. In the studies presented here the reader will note contributions from other social sciences; from history, especially the history of medicine and of epidemic and contagious diseases; from demography, both contemporary and historical; from biology, including many of its subdisciplines; from medicine and public health in too many ways to list here; and from anthropologists representing a broad spectrum of theoretical postures, specialties, interests, and ethnographic experience. Although what is presented here is not meant to stand for a complete introduction to a field of study still characterized by uncertainty and problems of identity, I believe that each section of the book represents an important segment of the field.

I take a perhaps more optimistic position that those colleagues who in attempting to delineate and describe medical anthropology usually conclude that the field is really just a branch of applied anthropology, or applied behavioral science, or that there is too little agreement in the field to call it one (taking refuge in such hopeless statements as "medical anthropology is what medical anthropologists do"), or that it suffers from a paucity of theory. I believe that a number of conceptual and theoretical contributions have already been made, though perhaps not always with the direct intention of aiding medical anthropology as such, as I think this volume will show. It must be admitted that anthropology has always suffered from a poverty of theory, or at any rate this has been its self-image and that bestowed upon it gratuitously by members of other behavioral sciences. In any event, anthropology has not hesitated to borrow from (some would say cannibalize) other fields. The very scope of a science of culture and humankind makes frequent contact with other fields mandatory and certainly does not preclude borrowing concepts and theories. I happen to believe that we anthropologists have contributed as much as we have received.

*       *       *

By the early 1960s the term *medical anthropology* had come to be used increasingly by anthropologists working in and around problems in health and disease in human societies. A Society for Medical Anthropology was established, which in 1975 claimed more than a thousand members, and distributed a quarterly newsletter. The Society is a recognized affiliate of the American Anthropological Association. Courses in the subject are now being taught in many colleges and universities. These courses and the members of the Society for Medical Anthropology have stimulated a growing number of undergraduate and graduate students to begin to work on problems in the field.

A number of universities offer Master's degrees in the subject and in 1976 doctoral programs in medical anthropology involving collaboration between anthropology departments and medical schools were launched in at least two major universities: University of California (Berkeley-San Francisco) and Michigan State University. Most encouraging was the heartening recent appearance of an introductory anthropology textbook (Pelto and Pelto 1976) with a chapter on medical anthropology and a whole section devoted to related topics, thus for the first time introducing the new student to the field as a basic subfield within general anthropology.

Equally important, many students outside of anthropology, but in related fields—medicine, nursing, psychology, sociology, the biological and physical sciences, social services, and so on—have been exposed to the conceptual perspectives and wealth of ethnographic knowledge of anthropology in ways that are germane to their own interests. It is my hope that, thus informed, these future practitioners will broaden and deepen their own clinical, service, and scientific contributions, since the anthropological view, once experienced, is not easy to ignore. It perforce wrenches away the blinders of parochialism and narrow interest, and presses toward the casting of medical and social problems within the framework of human culture and universal humanity.

Finally, in the most immediate pragmatic sense, I must confess a heretofore unrequited longing for easily accessible teaching materials. This was a prime mover in the evolution of this book and I plan to make use of it in my own teaching. My fervent wish is that it will prove to be a useful tool not only for students but for colleagues who require, as I have, a volume that provides both a notion of the nature and breadth of medical anthropology and a sampling of its treasures.

# I
# The Field of Medical Anthropology

## Anthropological Approaches to the Study of Human Adaptation to Health and Disease

Recently, George Foster (1974) performed a useful service by comparing and contrasting medical anthropology and medical sociology in order to distinguish between them. He concluded that these disciplines have certain real differences, mainly that the anthropologist is more interested in culture and cultural phenomena and the sociologist is more oriented toward society and social phenomena. Perhaps his most important conclusions are that

Both approaches are valid; both are important. From the two together we learn more than from either one singly. And this, it seems to me, is the rationale for separate but allied medical behavioral specializations. Precisely because we ask different questions, seek out different data, and come to conclusions that reflect our professional biases, our total understanding of medical and health phenomena is richer and more varied than if the task were left to a single discipline. We are in complementary, and not competitive, lines of work. We learn from each other and we teach each other. Our society needs both of us (Foster 1974:5).

I am in general agreement with the notion of the complementarity of the two disciplines, and, as is apparent in the readings in this volume, I am keenly aware of the many contributions to medical anthropology and to general anthropology that have come from sociology. However, I do not think that the interests of the two disciplines can be divided sharply along the concepts of culture and society, since, as will be seen subsequently herein, both concepts are important to medical anthropology and of equal interest to both in the kinds of problems investigated and the questions raised. The differences are perhaps sharpest, it seems to me, and Foster includes these also in his statement, in the more holistic view of medical anthropology, its constant awareness of cultural context as a point of reference for everything that comes under its scrutiny, and for the participant-observer technique of the anthropologist as contrasted with the more particularistic, less personal, less intimate, and generally more formalized techniques of the sociological investigator. Even these distinctions today are more in tendency than in actuality, and it is no longer rare for a sociologist to become a participant observer and for the anthropologist to use the formal, systematic, quantitative techniques of the sociologist—each using these in addition to, rather than as substitutes for, his own traditional approaches.

I do, however, differ with certain aspects of Foster's notion of what constitutes medical anthropology. As Hasan (1975) has noted, Foster's assertions "... on the relationships between sociological and anthropological approaches to the study of health and medicine were essentially exercises in answering the age old question: What are the differences and similarities between *social anthropology* and sociology?" Hasan goes on to show that not only is medical anthropology much broader than envisaged by Foster but that its antecedents are rather more venerable than the relatively recent ones indicated by Foster (though, of course, not necessarily *as* medical anthropology). The roots of medical anthropology are probably as ancient as anthropology itself, since the earliest accounts often contain some attention to medical phenomena (although usually fragmentarily and unsystematically, as I indicated in my introductory chapter and as Wellin shows in his essay in this section). Ethnographic accounts of medical–cultural data extend to well over a century ago. One may find in the writings of Sir James Frazer, Edward Tylor, and others in nineteenth-century anthropology some interest in such matters as illness and curing, shamanism, divination, and the like. And studies in paleopathology, involving physical anthropology, archeology, and medicine possess a quite archaic heritage beginning with the earliest fossil discoveries.

Most importantly medical anthropology includes interests and contributions from *all* the branches of anthropology. Without this broad, biocultural approach, the use of the ecological framework, already so promising in other subdisciplines of anthropology and which has made an initial impact in the medical anthropological area, will not be utilized. Or, if this approach is attempted, it will not be as effective and appreciated. This encompassing approach has other advantages as Hasan (1975:9) shows:

> Anthropology combines in one discipline the approaches of the biological sciences, the social sciences, and the humanities. Thus, the biological and ecological approaches are common to anthropology, medicine, and health and provide valuable grounds for collaboration between medical scientists, health professionals, and anthropologists.

As Wellin suggests, and as others demonstrate in this book, the ecological approach holds great promise for anthropology and especially for medical anthropology. In one sense, the traditional ethnographic approach, particularly in American anthropology, has always been ecological. But the new ecology, deriving in part from the new biology, is a much sharper, more systematic, and more theoretically fruitful method than the rather static organization and desultory methodology of the past.

As Wellin concludes, the ecological approach did not just emerge spontaneously upon the anthropological scene, but builds upon its predecessors. Thus, while offering clear advances over all that has gone before, the ecological approach also

> ...accommodates Rivers' fundamental insight that medical beliefs and practices are part of culture. It even resurrects Clements' use of the single trait as a unit of study and analysis but on a more viable conceptual and methodological basis. It incorporates Ackerknecht's insistence on the cultural patterning of medical belief and behavior and the functional interrelatedness of medicine with other parts of the cultural whole. It makes use of Paul's system approach and interest in change. However, previous insights are accommodated within a new framework. To be sure, cultural variables are seen to count, and to count heavily, but in terms of their interplay with biologic factors in multivariate ecological systems.

Thus, the use of the concept of ecology—and not just cultural ecology—carries with it the implication of *evolutionary* theory: humans in adapting to environmental conditions are constantly evolving new forms of society and culture to meet changing ecological conditions and in the process modifying their environments. In addition, it requires, depending, of course, upon the questions asked, an

12

awareness of history and at times an *historical* (diachronic) approach, and an awareness of the need to understand the dynamic equilibrium achieved by a population and culture under study, that is, a *structural-functional* (synchronic) approach. For despite the apparently undying disputations in some professional anthropological circles, I find that for specified purposes all four approaches—ecological, evolutionary, historical, and structural-functional—are useful, productive, and, for the "whole picture," indispensable. The selections in every section of this book illustrate this statement.

To illustrate some approaches in anthropology to the study of human adaptation to health and disease, we present first a brief overview of the present state of research and thinking in medical anthropology preceded by an even briefer historical sketch of developments leading up to the formation of this field. This is followed by a statement on the concepts of health and disease and some of their biological, cultural, and social determinants from a medical-ecological perspective. Then we find a seminal statement on the place of medical anthropology within general anthropology with a demonstration of how it can serve as a mediating nexus between biological and cultural aspects of anthropology in the study of human adaptation. This is followed by a much-needed analysis of the theoretical orientations of a series of medical anthropologists from Rivers to contemporary ecologically oriented scholars. The section concludes with an approach to the ethnographic study of medicine and medical system in a culture within an ecological framework, but incorporating both an *emic* and *etic* position on the assumption that both an "inside" and an "outside" view are required for the total medical ethnography.

# 1 The Field of Medical Anthropology

## Richard W. Lieban

This first selection by Richard Lieban provides a convenient. overview of the field of medical anthropology. It begins with a brief historical perspective. The author then proceeds to discuss four major areas of medical anthropology: (ecology and epidemiology, ethnomedicine, medical aspects of social systems, and medicine and culture change). There is a decided emphasis in these discussions upon the applied features of medical anthropology, but the basic scientific problems in these areas are nevertheless brought into sharp focus. Many of the problems and

Reprinted with abridgments from Richard W. Lieban, 1974, "Medical Anthropology," Chapter 24 in John J. Honigmann, ed, *Handbook of Social and Cultural Anthropology*, copyright © 1973 by Rand McNally College Publishing Company, with permission of the author and Rand McNally College Publishing Company, Chicago, pp. 1031–1072.

concepts that are summarized in this selection are illustrated in various places throughout the present volume. Lieban states that he is deliberately eschewing some aspects of medical anthropology that are covered elsewhere in the handbook from which this paper is adapted. Even so, my own tendency is to view the scope of medical anthropology rather more extensively than does Lieban, although this in no way detracts from the value of this quite useful review and organization of the literature. Lieban is admittedly selective but the novice will begin to learn, as he reads this and the succeeding selections in this book, that the concerns of medical anthropology articulate with all subdisciplines and topical areas of interest in general anthropology. In fact, one objective of the present anthology is to illustrate, at least partially, that very assumption.

## INTRODUCTION

Health and disease are measures of the effectiveness with which human groups, combining biological and cultural resources, adapt to their environments. The fact that health and disease are related to cultural as well as biological factors underlies the convergence of medical and cultural anthropological interests.

Modern medicine has had a primarily biological orientation (Jaco 1958), but basic concern with social and cultural aspects of the maintenance of health and the etiology of disease is deeply rooted in medical history. Ever since the earliest medical systems of which we have historical knowledge, variations in health have been connected with variations in social circumstances and habit patterns. (For example, see Rosen 1963, Dubos 1965, Veith 1966.) Interest in social and cultural dimensions of illness reached a peak in the West during the nineteenth century, stimulated by public health problems associated with the Industrial Revolution (Dubos 1959). This was the period of an impressive development of social medicine, led by such figures as Villerme in France and Virchow in Germany (Dubos 1959, 1965; Rosen 1963). Virchow and others conceived of medicine as a social science, both in a basic and an applied sense. That is, they not only emphasized the need for scientific investigations of the impact of social and economic conditions on health and disease, but they also stressed that a society had the obligation to assure the health of its members, and they advocated social intervention to promote health and combat disease (Rosen 1963). In that perspective, Virchow referred to politics as "nothing but medicine on a grand scale."

Beginning in the latter part of the nineteenth century, modern medicine came to be increasingly preoccupied with specific microorganic agents as the causes of disease (Galdston 1963, Dubos 1959, Polgar 1968). With attention concentrated so heavily on direct, immediate causes of disease, such as the effect of microbes on body tissue, interest in the social and cultural context of medicine declined (Galdston 1959). In recent years, however, this has changed, and there has been a marked upsurge in research by both medical and social scientists on social and cultural aspects of health and disease.

In anthropology this development has been stimulated by problems connected with Western medical programs in developing areas and by current trends in Western medicine itself (Scotch 1963). Undoubtedly changes that have occurred in the relative importance of certain threats to health have increased the need for medically related research in anthropology and other social sciences. Galdston (1963) discusses the point: "The infectious diseases have been all but 'conquered.' Now there is emergent a new pathodemography. The disorders and diseases now dominant are due not to specific pathogens, but rather to economic, social, political, and cultural factors. The resultant pathology is manifest in physiological, functional, behavioral, and psychological disorders." Under the circumstances, Galdston sees the need for more anthropological knowledge in medicine, which will be "increasingly confronted by pathogenic forces that are ecological, social, and cultural in nature."

Much of the development of medical anthropology has occurred since World War II. The beginnings of major anthropological involvement in medical problems were cogently reviewed by Caudill (1953) in his landmark paper on applied anthropology in medicine. Prior to that time, descriptions of etiological beliefs and medical practices in simpler societies had been important components of certain ethnography (e.g., Evans-Pritchard 1937, Gillin 1948), and Rivers (1924) and Clements (1932) had produced substantial works on the worldwide distribution of etiological concepts. But even in 1945 Ackerknecht could write about the serious neglect of medicine in much of the ethnographic literature available up to that time, and when Caudill (1953) wrote his review, involvement of anthropologists and other social scientists in health programs and medical research and education was still something of a novelty. Since then the situation has changed considerably, and there has been a marked increase in work by anthropologists and other social scientists in medicine and medically related areas. A good idea of the scope and volume of research during what might loosely be considered the first decade of substantial growth in medical anthropology can be gained from excellent review articles by Polgar (1962) and Scotch (1963). A cogent summary and analysis of developments in subsequent years is provided by Fabrega (1972).

The rapid emergence of substantial interest in social and cultural aspects of medicine among anthropologists of diverse training, theoretical and methodological orientations, and particular problem interests has created something of an identity problem for medical anthropology. The field has been viewed from a wide range of perspectives. For example, Weaver (1968) sees it as a branch of applied anthropology; Alland (1966, 1970) emphasizes its potential contribution to basic research on human evolution. One way of approaching a definition could be on a purely operational basis, in terms of what those who consider themselves engaged in medical anthropology do. A spectrum of activities could be spelled out, such as those represented by various

14

committees of the recently organized Society for Medical Anthropology, including anthropology and epidemiology, community medicine, medical education, nursing, pediatrics, population planning, and traditional medical systems (*Medical Anthropology Newsletter* 1969). But a circular definition of this kind avoids epistemological issues that go beyond the question of what's in a name, and it is these issues that concern us at this point. In considering them, let us return momentarily to the basis for the intersection of medical and anthropological interests.

Physicians and anthropologists have intersecting interests because health and disease are related not only to biological factors, but also to people's cultural resources and the social behavior that utilizes these resources. As Ackerknecht (1947) defines the situation, "disease and its treatment are only in the abstract purely biological processes ... such facts as whether a person gets sick at all, what kinds of disease he acquires and what kind of treatment he receives depend largely on social factors."

In the junction of physicians' interests with those of anthropologists, the physician's primary concern is likely to be with the ways in which human behavior affects the maintenance of health and the occurrence and control of disease (Roemer 1959). Medical anthropologists have a major involvement in research on these problems, primarily in applied anthropology and etiological and epidemiological studies. But there is another side of the picture, in which problems are defined not by the effects of human behavior on the states of health and disease, but by the indications about human behavior that can be discerned in responses to the states of health and disease. Health and disease are fundamentally connected with the reproduction, quality, preservation, and loss of life. In view of the significance of these phenomena for human societies, it is not surprising that an anthropological study of health and the occurrence and means of coping with disease can involve one deeply in the manner in which people perceive their world, in the characteristics of human social systems, and in social values. In this perspective, medical anthropology is not only a way of viewing the states of health and disease in society, but a way of viewing society itself. ...

... Thus the anthropological study of social and cultural influences on health and disease includes not only subjects of immediate therapeutic relevance, but phenomena that have special interest because of their effects on human ecology and the

course of human evolution; and it is not only medical personnel that is the subject of medical anthropology, but society at large, as it relates to health and medical problems.

... The same behavior, pivotal from the standpoint of medical anthropology, can be studied as it affects the state of health or disease in a society, and as a response to a medical situation that is revelatory of the attitudes, beliefs, and customary actions of a group.

Indications are that the stressful reactions of individuals who are convinced that they are the victims of sorcery, witchcraft, or axiomatic punishment for violations of taboos can lead to their illness and death (Cannon 1942, Lester 1972). In such cases, culture is pathogenic. And regardless of the causes of an illness, once it is attributed to magical attack, this diagnosis can determine such matters as the kind of practitioner who will be consulted for treatment and the therapy that will be used (Lieban 1967). In these respects, behavior based on certain cultural beliefs can be studied in relation to its effects on the medical situation. But such behavior can also be studied for its wider social implications.

When members of a society regard illness as a sanction, for example, attributions of incidences of illness to the work of enemies or to punishment for deviation from norms reflect strains and conflicts in the social system (Evans-Pritchard 1937; Middleton and Winter, eds., 1963; Marwick 1965). And such attributions can indicate deficiencies in or the absence of other sanctions when strains and conflicts occur (B. Whiting 1950, Swanson 1960, Lieban 1967). Here medical phenomena become the means of understanding social phenomena rather than vice versa.

In such cases, the wider ramifications of medical phenomena may illustrate human behavior under conditions of conflict and inadequate social sanctions. But in cases of this kind the findings of medical anthropology are more than illustrative. For the ways in which medical phenomena are linked to behavior in these social circumstances, and the reasons they are linked as they are, are in themselves significant aspects of such behavior.

Medical anthropology, then, encompasses the study of medical phenomena as they are influenced by social and cultural features, and social and cultural phenomena as they are illuminated by their medical aspects. These distinctions may be seen as two facets of a set of interrelated phenomena. But depending on the nature of the study and the interests of the investigator, one or the other at times may receive greater emphasis or be the focus of attention.

I shall not try to provide an exhaustive survey of the voluminous literature pertinent to medical anthropology within the limited scope of this chapter (useful bibliographies may be found in Caudill 1953, Rosen and Wellin 1959, Polgar 1962, Pearsall 1963, Simmons 1963, Scotch 1963, Mechanic (1968), and Fabrega (1972). Rather than attempt the very condensed synthesis that such a strategy would require, I shall discuss somewhat selectively four major areas of medical anthropology, ecology and epidemiology, ethnomedicine, medical aspects of social systems, and medicine and culture change—the problems encountered in these areas, approaches to these problems, and relevant research findings. . . .

## ECOLOGY AND EPIDEMIOLOGY

In the study of medical aspects of the adaptation and maladaptation of human groups to their environments, cultural factors are of major importance. Consider Jacques May's (1960) experience as an epidemiologist in a village in China before World War II. May observed that some of the villagers were seriously affected by a heavy infestation of hookworm, while others were not. An investigation showed that almost all the hookworm patients were rice growers; there were no rice cultivators among those not ill with the malady. The rice cultivators worked in mud mixed with night soil, which helped explain the infestation of hookworm larvae. The other villagers were engaged in silkworm farming, and spent their working days on ladders tending mulberry leaves. Here disease boundaries and cultural distinctions virtually coincided. In a case such as this, the effects of culture on the prevalence of disease are striking, but it is also apparent that the hookworm infestation was part of a complex ecosystem involving relationships between human and nonhuman organisms and their environments. (The influence of culture on occurrences of disease in ecosystems that include human beings is contingent on a variety of factors with which culturally oriented behavior is linked.) An interesting exploration of the intricacies of such linkages is provided by John Whiting's (1964) analysis of the parts that postpartum sexual taboos and late weaning may play in protecting infants against kwashiorkor. Whiting notes that kwashiorkor is largely confined to areas of high temperatures and humidity, conditions conducive to the growing of root and fruit crops low in protein. In societies dependent on such foods, he observes, a lactating mother may help prevent the reduction of the already low protein values of her milk—a reduction that could lead to illness for her nursing child—so long as she avoids another pregnancy.

He also points out that the prevention of pregnancy in such societies, without alternative means of contraception, generally is accomplished by abstinence from sexual intercourse. In essence, as Whiting sees it, in these circumstances prolonged postpartum taboos are cultural practices that could have the effect of reducing the frequency of kwashiorkor both by prolonging the nursing period and by ensuring that the protein content of the lactating mother's milk is not lowered below the danger point. Here cultural practices are seen as prophylactic in an ecological situation produced by the interrelationship of certain cultural, biological, and physical variables.

The ecological approach, characterized by comprehensive attention to the mutual relations between organisms and their environment, brings to medicine and public health a concern with multiple causes (Gregg 1956, Gordon 1958). It also focuses attention on multiple effects of human actions that alter the relationship between people and their environment, often with important medical consequences. This, of course, is a central contemporary issue in industrial societies, where various forms of environmental modification threaten health. It also can be a paramount consideration in assessing the net value of economic growth projects in developing societies. The construction of new irrigation systems in arid areas such as Egypt has augmented food production, but it also has increased the incidence of schistosomiasis (bilharziasis), a disease carried by a waterborne fluke (Read 1966, Dubos 1965, Alland 1966). Schistosomiasis has been endemic in the Nile Valley for centuries, and in view of the opportunity for spread of the disease afforded by the new irrigation works, it has been predicted that the new Aswan High Dam may prove to be a liability rather than an asset (van der Schalie 1969).

Health ramifications are important criteria of the effects of cultural practices on the adaptation of human groups to their environments. The adaptive value of human behavior is not determined simply by assessing the advantages this behavior offers a population in its relationship with its environment,

16

but also by looking for detrimental consequences of the behavior and weighing gains against losses (Alland 1966, 1967, 1970). Health figures significantly when such an ecological balance sheet is calculated, as the spread of schistosomiasis associated with the spread of irrigation agriculture in certain areas has shown. (For other examples of increases in the prevalence of disease as the results of development, see Hughes and Hunter 1970.)

Changes in the relationship between human populations and disease parasites have been brought about by a combination of cultural and biological processes. Concentrated populations, for example, are more vulnerable to epidemics than dispersed ones (Alland 1969, 1970; Kunstadter 1969). It seems unlikely that parasites capable of producing epidemics could have maintained themselves with man as their sole host before the development of agriculture, since in relatively small, scattered hunting and gathering societies there would be few, if any, potential hosts available once the disease had run its course within a group (Polgar 1964). The development of agricultural communities, accompanied by an increase in trade, greatly enlarged the supply of potential victims. A related example is to be found in unbroken tropical forests, which offer an inhospitable environment for the malaria vector, *Anopheles gambiae*, since the mosquito cannot breed in very shaded water. The introduction of agriculture into West Africa necessitated clearing the tropical forest, and the consequent open swamps afforded breeding places for malarial mosquitoes, with a resulting increase in disease incidence (Livingstone 1958). And cultural developments that led to the concentration of populations in preindustrial cities and intercontinental contacts between peoples also provided the opportunity for widespread epidemics (Polgar 1964, Armelagos 1967).

Through their effects on changes in the relationship between human populations and disease parasites, cultural evolutionary developments such as these can be linked to biological evolutionary changes in both hosts and parasites. A number of observers have pointed out that since parasites require hosts, parasites deleterious enough to threaten elimination of hosts also threaten to eliminate themselves (Dubos 1959, 1965; Polgar 1964; Gordon 1958; Alland 1966). Under these circumstances, when a highly virulent parasite is introduced into a human population, there are selective pressures on the parasitic population to produce a less destructive strain able to live in

accommodation with its hosts while serving its own needs (Dubos 1959). As far as evolutionary changes in the host population are concerned, exposure to the parasite will exercise selective pressure in favor of genetic endowments resistant to pathogens. Livingstone (1958) has impressively analyzed a case in point, relating the increase of malaria in West Africa, discussed above, to the spread of the sickle-cell gene among populations of the area, since the heterozygote for this gene is resistant to falciparum malaria. In a later analysis of data from sixty societies in both East and West Africa, Wiesenfeld (1967) found that increased dependence on agriculture, accompanied by increased exposure to malarial parasitism, was associated with rising frequency of the sickle-cell trait.

Some individuals homozygous for the sickle-cell gene die young from sickle-cell anemia, but in malarial areas this pernicious effect of the gene on a population's adaptation to its environment is offset by the immunity to malaria that heterozygous individuals possess (Medawar 1960). When malaria is eradicated, however, the advantage of the gene for the population that possesses it is lost, while for those homozygous for the gene the negative consequence, sickle-cell anemia, remains.

The loss of selective advantage of genes under changed environmental conditions is a problem that has interested the geneticist Neel (1962), who believes it likely that in this respect the gene (or genes) responsible for diabetes mellitus has undergone effects similar to those of the sickle-cell gene. Neel calls the genotype for diabetes "thrifty" because there is evidence that in the early years of life the diabetes genotype is exceptionally efficient in the intake and/or utilization of food. Neel feels that such a genotype would have been advantageous when all human groups consisted of hunters and gatherers whose supply was variable, since in times of temporary abundance of food it would enable individuals who had it to store up extra adipose reserve against periods of acute food shortage. (Recent data on contemporary hunter-gatherers indicate that Neel may have overestimated earlier food supply fluctuations (Dunn 1968).) Neel sees indications that this capability of the diabetic genotype is due to the fact that it is distinguished at the outset by greater than normal availability of effective circulating insulin at some stage in the cycle of responses that follow food intake. He then asks, "How to reconcile this with the relative insufficiency of later years?" His

17

hypothesis is that the normal metabolism of glucose balances insulin and anti-insulins.

In keeping with the usual mechanisms operative in physiologic balances, we may theorize that in the individual predisposed to diabetes, the postulated increased ability in the early years of life to release insulin provokes in time a relative overproduction of its antagonist. There is initially in those genetically predisposed to diabetes a balance between increased insulin production and an increased production of antagonist. Not until this balance is overcome by excessive antagonist production does clinical diabetes develop.

In Neel's view, civilization has brought an increased frequency of diabetes associated with increased mean caloric intake and/or decreased physical activity, resulting in increased stimulation of insulin and its antagonist. According to this hypothesis, then, cultural evolution has had the effect of transforming a genetic advantage into a serious liability (see Smith 1970).

## Social and Cultural Aspects of Epidemiology

... Epidemiology is essentially devoted to selective distributions of disease and their meanings (Francis 1959). Epidemiological units of investigation are populations and samples of populations rather than clinical samples (Mechanic 1968). Epidemiology is both descriptive and analytic (Scotch 1963), and the field has become increasingly concerned with the origin and cause of disease rather than with its distribution alone (Suchman 1968). In this connection, some observers feel that the significant contributions made by epidemiology have stemmed from analytical rather than descriptive studies, and they are critical of the dichotomy made by some between "epidemiological" and "etiological" investigations (Cassel, Patrick, and Jenkins 1960).

Epidemiology has a close relationship to ecology. ... Social and cultural factors, then, may help determine disease etiology and distribution through their influence on the relationship between a human population and its natural environment, or through their direct influence on the health of the population.

Social and cultural distinctions associated with differences in age, sex, occupation, class, ethnicity, and community can have significant effects on epidemiological phenomena.

### AGE DIFFERENCES

The incidence of numerous acute infections is highest in childhood, indicating that as people grow older they develop immunities that decrease their vulnerability to these diseases (Francis 1959). Death rates are clearly related to age; they are relatively high in infancy, low between the ages of five and fourteen, begin rising in the age period of fifteen to nineteen, and continue to increase with age after that (Mechanic 1968). Obviously these epidemiological patterns reflect biological variations in vulnerability to sickness and death associated with age differences, but the patterns are also subject to social and cultural influences, as exemplified by significant group contrasts in infant mortality rates (Anderson 1958), depending on such factors as nutrition, sanitation, and medical care.

### SEX DIFFERENCES

Indications are that biological factors play a large part in sexual differences in mortality, with females having longer life expectancy. ...

The picture with respect to morbidity differences between the sexes is complex. ... But if male and female role distinctions can influence differences in response to illness, they can also influence differences in the development of illness as well, particularly if the culture emphasizes such role distinctions. Read (1966), for example, points out that osteomalacia, a disease characterized by softening of the bones and caused by a lack of sunshine, or a deficiency of vitamin D in the diet, occurs with greater frequency in parts of the world where sunshine is abundant. Speaking of the Bedouin area of Niger, she says, "These Bedouins live in black tents made of goat hair. Men, youth and children go freely, but married women spend most of their lives in tents, wearing a white shawl indoors, but outside a heavy black cloak completely covering head and body, leaving a merest slit for the eyes." The diet of the Bedouins is poor in vitamins A and D and in calcium, and osteomalacia is mainly found "among child-bearing women, who are sometimes immobilized by their pains, need a cane for support in walking and cannot mount or ride a donkey."

### OCCUPATIONAL DIFFERENCES

Studies of the effects of occupation on disease have been an important part of the epidemiological literature since the nineteenth century, when studies of social aspects of pathology indicated that susceptibility to disease varied in accordance with means of gaining a livelihood. When Snow (1936) investigated the occurrence of cholera in the area of the Broad Street pump in London in 1854, he discovered that the incidence of cholera was high among workers in a percussion cap factory where water from the Broad Street pump was drunk, while workers at the Broad Street brewery, where beer was served instead of water, were not similarly affected.

... Occupations that entail a good deal of social psychological stress and relatively little physical activity have been linked in some studies with a relatively high occurrence of coronary heart disease (Morris 1964). Severe occupational stress among tax accountants was shown to be associated with increases in both serum cholesterol and blood clotting time (Friedman, Rosenman, and Carroll 1958; Friedman and Rosenman 1959). Although a number of investigations have shown correlations between emotional factors and cardiovascular diseases (for useful reviews of such studies, see Syme and Reeder 1967), several cautionary notes seem to be in order. First, as King (1963) points out, such diseases probably can be accounted for only by a compound etiology, involving the interaction of diet, stress, exercise, and hereditary factors. Second, while the study of tax accountants apparently indicated that specific increases in stress preceded specific physiological reactions, it is sometimes difficult to disentangle correlations from causal evidence. It has been noted that when attempts are made to establish associations of occupation with coronary artery disease, "both the disease and the occupational choice could logically result from a third variable, e.g., personality type" (Wardwell, Hyman, and Bahnson 1964).

Hughes (1963) points out that although there has been considerable research on occupational hazards to health in the epidemiology of industrial society, similar studies among primitive groups have been relatively rare. ...

STATUS AND ETHNIC DIFFERENCES

A substantial part of epidemiological research has been devoted to the influence of social stratification and ethnic differences on disease prevalence and etiology. This influence can be particularly significant in nutritional maladies and in certain infectious diseases whose spread is affected by the material conditions of life. The following figures on numbers of deaths per million population during an outbreak of plague in India, which reflect caste differences in combination with ethnic differences, graphically illustrate the point: low-caste Hindus, 53.7; Brahmans, 20.7; Moslems, 13.7; Eurasians, 6.1; Jews, 5.2; Parsees, 4.6; Europeans, 0.8 (Sigerist 1961).

As the importance of infectious diseases has decreased, epidemiological interest in the effects of socioeconomic differences on the prevalence and etiology of degenerative diseases has grown. But here the influence of socioeconomic variables is not so readily apparent, and in some cases, such as studies of the relationship between social class and coronary heart disease, research findings have been contradictory (Graham 1963; Wardwell, Hyman, and Bahnson 1964). ...

Differences in disease rates of ethnic groups have been an important problem in epidemiology, and a number of studies have explored possible relationships between ethnic styles of life and degenerative pathologies. Various forms of cancer have been investigated in this light, and intergroup variations in prevalence have been found. In comparing groups in Hawaii, for example, Quisenberry (1960) found the highest frequency of cancer of the stomach among the Japanese, primary cancer of the liver among Filipino men, cancer of the breast among white women, cancer of the intestines among whites, cancer of the nasopharynx among Chinese, and cancer of the uterine cervix among Hawaiian women. But while such differences in prevalence exist, etiological explanations for them must still be speculative. Disease rates for cancer of the cervix are a case in point. They are especially low for Jewish women, and this seems to be uniform in various areas of the world (Wynder et al. 1954). The rates are also low among Moslem and Parsee women. Male circumcision is practiced by all these peoples, and much attention has been given to this factor in attempts to account for the low prevalence of the disease among women of these groups. Graham (1963) points out that when hygiene is poor, uncircumcised males may introduce a substance, smegma, into contact with the cervix, and since smegma has been found to be carcinogenic to the cervix of mice, the possible relationship between circumcision, smegma, and prevalence rates for cancer of the human cervix have attracted epidemiological interest. However, as Graham notes, studies investigating the problem have not produced mutually consistent results, and he questions methods employed in the research. Graham also raises the possibility that a genetic factor may be involved in differential group rates for cervix cancer.

COMMUNITY DIFFERENCES

Associations of disease frequency with contrasting community settings have formed another focus of epidemiological interest. As part of this interest, social correlates of rural-urban distinctions and their implications for health have been significant problems for investigation. Scotch (1960, 1963) found that when rural and urban Zulu were compared, high blood pressure was found to occur more frequently among the urbanites, regardless of sex or age. Scotch observes that urban Zulu are subject to greater frequency and severity of social stress than rural Zulu, and he sees this stress as an important factor in the difference in rates of hypertension between the two populations. He points out that while acculturation proceeds slowly in the countryside, a considerable breakdown of traditional Zulu culture has occurred in the city; yet "acculturation to European modes of life is blocked except for piecemeal adoptions of simpler European technologies" (Scotch 1960). In his analysis, Scotch emphasizes that he does not regard urbanization in itself, or even culture change in general, as stressful enough to have a significant effect on hypertension; it is social conditions conducive to behavior that is not adaptive to the demands of urban living that do the damage.

Thus the urban hypertensive was likely to live in an extended family, have a lower income, resort to bewitchment to explain illness and misfortune, retain traditional religious beliefs, and have a large number of children. In general the reverse was true of the nonhypertensive. In addition, the nonhypertensive was likely to attend the European clinic more frequently, and for women, to belong to the Christian church, both adaptive patterns.

Scotch's analysis is consistent with the view of Cassel, Patrick, and Jenkins (1960) that a culture adapted to rural life may increase rather than decrease stress in an urban situation because of the incongruity between the culture of the migrant and the social situation in which he lives. But there are also indications that the persistence of traditional cultural traits in situations of change need not exacerbate stress and actually may ameliorate it or its effects. For example, Jahoda (1961) found relatively little mental illness in Ghana under the stresses accompanying change there, and attributed this situation to the influence of traditional healers and similar institutions that have adapted to new circumstances. In general, there is substantial evidence that old cultural patterns are not necessarily incompatible with new institutions (see Abegglen 1958, Dore 1958, Geertz 1963, Lloyd 1968). Studies such as those of Scotch (1960) and Jahoda (1961) raise the problem of identifying circumstances when old cultural patterns are

adaptive to new conditions and when they are not, and the implications of this difference for health.

## ETHNOMEDICINE

### Modern vs. Traditional Practices

The domain of ethnomedicine is indigenous medical features, those to which Hughes (1968) refers as "not explicitly derived from the conceptual framework of modern medicine." This does not mean that traditional medical systems are impervious to the influence of modern medicine. In the Philippines, for example, it is not unusual to hear local healers refer to "TB" or "germs." But despite such accretions, distinctive traditional qualities persist in these systems; and even when modern medical features are borrowed, they function in an alien context and can carry different connotations than they do in modern medicine (Lieban 1967; see also Halpern 1963).

In addition to "ethnomedicine," various other terms have been used to refer to the domain under discussion or parts of it: "folk medicine," "popular medicine," "popular health culture," "ethnoiatry" (Scarpa 1967), "ethnoiatrics" (Huard 1969).

Polgar (1962) has distinguished the "professional health culture" of medical practitioners from the "popular health culture" of unspecialized lay practitioners. He would include folk healers among health professionals so long as they are recognized as specialists by others in their society.

Leslie (1967) contrasts professional and popular health cultures on a different basis. He has taken a special interest in highly sophisticated indigenous medical systems that are rooted in ancient civilizations, particularly those of South Asia, and which persist today alongside modern medicine. He uses "professional health culture" to refer to the realms of practitioners in both systems, but would not include the medical sphere of folk specialists:

A distinction should be made at the outset between *professional health cultures* and *popular health cultures*. The first term refers to the institutions, roles, values, and knowledge of highly trained practitioners of the indigenous medical systems of South Asia, as well as practitioners of cosmopolitan scientific medicine. *Popular health cultures* include the health values and knowledge, roles and practices of laymen, of specialists in folk medicine, and of laymen-specialists such as the avocational practitioners of homeopathic medicine.

Leslie also points out that while these sophisticated indigenous medical systems appeal to ancient texts, they combine modern institutional forms —hospitals, colleges and schools of medicine, pharmaceutical companies, and so on—as well as certain modern medical concepts with those of traditional civilizations. And in a later paper (1969b) Leslie observes that students of the modernization process have neglected indigenous scientific traditions, "apparently assuming that the only scientific knowledge and institutions relevant to modernity are Western."

Leslie's point about the distinction between great and little medical traditions in societies such as India and China, which are the present heirs of major ancient civilizations, is well taken. (Polgar [1963] also notes the significance of this distinction.) But in view of the connections between great and little traditions generally (see, for example, Redfield 1956 and Marriott 1955b), it does not seem unreasonable to consider their medical aspects as contrastive but interdependent manifestations of indigenous medicine. My use of the term "modern medicine" is not intended to belittle traditional practices; I use it simply to refer to medical concepts and practices that are based on modern developments in the sciences.

## Disease Classifications

Modern medicine classifies diseases in terms of a single taxonomy of universal categories. From the standpoint of this taxonomic system, a recognized disease retains its identity wherever it occurs, regardless of the cultural context. Therefore, as the use of the system has spread, it has increasingly served as a transcultural reference for diagnosis of disease.

In contrast, the disease classifications of indigenous medical systems, much more limited in the reach of their influence, tend to be confined within cultural boundaries, and in ethnomedicine there is often marked variation in disease entities recognized from culture to culture.

To begin with, in some instances phenomena considered to be symptoms of disease by some groups may be regarded as signs of health or without medical significance by others. A classic case in point is *pinta* (dyschromic spirochetosis), which is so common among northern Amazonian Indians that those whose skins are blotched with the disease are regarded as normal; a similar situation obtains with respect to yaws among the Mano of Africa (Ackerknecht 1946). Read (1966) quotes an Egyptian physician to the effect that since Egyptian villagers believe that illness must be associated with pain, bilharziasis and certain other

parasitic infections are not considered to be illnesses or to require treatment. Intestinal worms are so endemic among the Thonga of Africa that they consider them necessary for digestion (Ackerknecht 1946). The same is true of Yap islanders (Saunders 1954). Some Mayan Indians in Guatemala regard worm infestation as an unpleasant but fairly normal condition, recognizing it as a problem that requires treatment only when the worms emerge through the esophagus and cause vomiting or choking (Adams 1953).

These examples do not mean that diagnosis in indigenous medical systems in general is less sensitive to or less concerned about signs of morbidity than modern medical diagnosis. It may be more or less, depending on the phenomena perceived and the significance attached to them in a particular cultural context. In his elegant analysis of disease categories among the Subanun of the southern Philippines, Frake (1961) describes a system that in some respects makes finer discriminations between symptoms of skin disease than modern medicine. The Subanun often make significant distinctions between lesions on the hands and feet and those on other parts of the body, and when it comes to certain skin diseases that they regard as extremely disfiguring, lesions hidden by clothing are categorized differently than those visible on a clothed body. . . .

## Ethnomedical Therapy

Therapy in ethnomedicine is a vast subject that can be touched on only lightly here. It includes both magico-religious and mechanical and chemical procedures. Laughlin (1963) has made the point that the success of the human species is in no small measure due to the ability to cope with medical problems; and an assessment of indigenous medical systems, including those of nonliterate societies, shows an impressive array of practices that demonstrate empirical therapeutic knowledge, including trephining, bonesetting, removal of ovaries, obstetrics including caesarean section, laparotomy, uvulectomy, comparative anatomy, autopsy, cautery, inoculation, baths, poultices, inhalations, laxatives, enemas, ointments, and cupping (Ackerknecht 1942, Simmons 1955, Laughlin 1963, Huard 1969). . . .

The pharmacopoeia of ethnomedicine is copious and includes such proven drugs as quinine, opium, coca, cinchona, copaiba, curare, chaulmoogra oil, ephedrine, and rauwolfia. Quisumbing (1951) lists more than eight hundred known medicinal plants in the Philippines alone, including flora efficacious

21

in the treatment of a number of maladies, such as asthma, diarrhea, dysentery, malaria, diabetes, and kidney ailments, to mention only a few.

As the great medical traditions of the Mediterranean, South Asia, and China developed, they became based on secular scientific theories (Sigerist 1961, Leslie 1969b, Croizier 1968, Needham and Lu 1969), and simpler indigenous medical systems appear to vary in the extent to which they depend on magic and religion. Laughlin (1963) finds a relative minimization of magic in the pragmatic orientation of Eskimo-Aleut culture, yet in many cultures medical practices and religious practices are often fused (Glick 1967); and even when mechanical or chemical therapy is employed, magico-religious elements may also be an essential part of the prescription, or the treatment may be regarded as incomplete without attention to mystical factors involved in the etiology of the illness. . . .

### PREVENTIVE MEASURES

Although preventive medicine has been seen as less important in most traditional medical systems than in modern medicine (e.g., Foster 1962), studies such as that of Colson (1969) indicate how significant preventive measures can be in a traditional medical system, and the literature shows that prophylactic practices are widely prevalent in indigenous medicine. These include both mechanical and magico-religious measures, such as bathing, massage, and rapid rewarming to prevent hypothermia, dietary restrictions, surgery, inoculation, incantations, amulets, and prayers at shrines (Laughlin 1963, Hughes 1963).

In indigenous medical systems as in modern medicine, prophylaxis is geared to etiology. Thus in many areas of the world, including Latin America and South and Southeast Asia, one finds prevalent notions, derived from Hippocratic humoral theory or comparable ideas of Indian medicine, that health depends in part on a proper balance between "hot" and "cold" (Foster 1953, 1967; Jelliffe 1956; Polgar 1962; Nash 1965; Hart 1969). (For interpretations relating this etiology in Mexican communities to the social outlook of peasants, see Foster 1967 and Ingham 1970.) Associated with this theory is the prescription of detailed precautions to maintain the equilibrium of health, such as measures to prevent chilling in a Guatemalan Mayan community: keeping oneself covered, avoiding cold water and foods that are classified as "cool," and not getting caught in the rain (Adams 1953).

Vulnerability to illness may be shielded in many ways. Thus, in some groups the name of a child is changed after someone in the family has suffered a deadly affliction, in the belief that a new name will disguise the soul of the child against attack by spirits who cause disease (Hughes 1963). With the idea that the evil eye is drawn to what is attractive, Turkish villagers protect their children by hanging unattractive objects on their clothing (Oztürk 1964). While the health value of mechanical procedures such as these may be readily apparent on an empirical basis, undoubtedly in many situations magical resources may also be prophylactically effective. In a society where belief in magical attacks may induce severe stress that can lead to illness and death (Cannon 1942), reliance on the protection of an amulet may be psychically hygienic.

### ETHNOMEDICAL SPECIALISTS

When illness occurs, it may be ignored, or treated without the help of a specialist (Polgar 1962). If treatment is sought from a medical practitioner, various types of specialists may be available, including herbalists, diviners, shamans, midwives, and masseurs (e.g., Nurge 1958, Lieban 1962b, Maclean 1969). Therapists may specialize in only one type of skill or calling, or they may combine several in their practice (Lieban 1962b). While there is considerable material on distinctions among traditional therapists based on variation in specialization, there is relatively little regarding distinctions based on variation in reputation for therapeutic success. Yet this factor, as well as the perceived appropriateness of the specialization for the illness to be treated, plays an important part in determining the choice of therapists. Romano (1965) finds that some folk healers have achieved considerable fame and devoted followings among Mexican-Americans of southern Texas, while other folk healers practice in comparative obscurity. Blum and Blum (1965) describe a comparable situation with respect to folk healers in Greece. In one Philippine city, healers differ significantly in the number of patients they attract, and the most successful among them may treat up to a hundred patients a day (Lieban 1967).

Qualifications for folk medical roles vary considerably. In some cases, no formal training may be required for practitioners (Metzger and Williams 1963); in others, a long apprenticeship may be customary (Maclean 1969). In the great medical traditions of Asian civilizations, with a sophisticated literature going back beyond the beginning of the Christian era, training was comprehensive. In India the student of Ayurvedic medicine entered into a spiritual relationship with his guru; he learned how to diagnose illness by observing his teacher, and he memorized medical texts that were explicated by the guru (Leslie 1969a). In China the teaching of medicine under state supervision goes back at least to the seventh century (Huard and Wong 1968), perhaps to the fifth century (Needham and Lu 1969). Chinese medicine spread to Japan in the early centuries of the Christian era, and by the eighth century a medical program was established by the Japanese. "Seven years of training was required for medicine, five years for pediatrics and surgery, and four years for eye, ear, nose and throat, or dentistry" (Bowers 1965).

Spiritual accreditation is frequently an attribute of indigenous medical roles. But this does not necessarily mean that spiritual backing obviates medical knowledge. They tend to be interrelated, as in the case of Tzeltal practitioners in Chiapas, Mexico (Metzger and Williams 1963). These practitioners are principally distinguished by their ability to "pulse," a skill that comes to the curer only as a "gift of God." Curers as a class are divided into two groups, "master curers" and "junior curers." One of the ways in which the two differ is in extent of knowledge. It is said of the junior curer that "not all is given into his hands by God," of the master curer that "all is given into his hands."

## Cultural Aspects of Ethnomedicine

Up to this point we have discussed characteristics of indigenous medical systems, but we have not yet concentrated our attention on ways in which medical beliefs and behavior relate to and illuminate the cultural contexts in which they appear. The relationship between medicine and the rest of culture has been noted by Ackerknecht (1942), who said, "Medicine is nowhere independent and following its own motivations. Its character and dynamism depend on the place it takes in every cultural pattern; they depend on the pattern itself."

Concepts of disease are cultural classifications of adversity. They do not, of course, cover the whole range of misfortune a society may face, but they can reflect its members' view of misfortune in a general sense (Maclean 1969), or their specific outlook on disease and its place in their lives. Thus Frake (1961), in discussing the problem of why finer distinctions are made between certain folk disease categories than others, offers the hypothesis that "the greater the number of distinct social contexts in which a particular phenomenon must be communicated, the greater the number of different levels of contrast into which that phenomenon is classified. ..."

The reactions of an ill person to his symptoms may express important cultural values of his society. Clark (1959) found that men in a Mexican-American community tend to be especially Spartan in responding to illness. "A man who admits to illness is not *macho* (tough and rugged). ... Relatives and friends commend him for endurance and sometimes criticize him when he yields to an infirmity before it becomes acute." Although the relationship between responses to pain and cultural factors has been a relatively neglected subject in anthropology, work that has been done on it indicates that ethnic groups do vary in their reactions to pain, and the differences appear to reflect cultural contrasts (Wolff and Langley 1968). The work of Zborowski (1952, 1969) has been of special interest. In a well-known study (1952) he found that Jews, Italians, and "Old Americans" differed in their reactions to pain. ...

### ETIOLOGY AND DIAGNOSIS OF DISEASE

The etiology of disease is central to any discussion of the connection between medical phenomena and their cultural settings. To begin with, in most indigenous medical systems the primary consideration in the diagnosis of disease is its cause (Glick 1967; see also Adams 1953, Alland 1964). And causality in these systems usually is sought in the relationship between the victim of illness and his surroundings as this relationship is culturally interpreted. While traditional etiologies may attribute illness to mechanical and emotional as well as magical and religious causes (Polgar 1962), and, as I have mentioned previously, the great medical traditions of ancient civilizations underwent secularization, in general magic and religion play important parts in indigenous explanations of the occurrence of disease (Hughes 1968), and in many indigenous medical systems ideas about illness and religious beliefs are all but inseparable (Glick 1967). Numerous etiologies illustrate the significance of magic and religion in traditional medical systems. ... Since etiology is so inextricable from its sociocultural context, explanations of the occurrences of illness are at the same time representations of the world as it is experienced and comprehended by members of the society.

Thus far, I have been discussing etiologies as emic phenomena; that is, as they are perceived by the members of a group who utilize them to explain why illnesses occur. But etiological interpretations linking the causes of illness to the culture of the group in which they occur may also be etic, made by observers who see connections between phenomena that are not necessarily perceived by anyone in the group studied. For example, Rubel (1964) has offered a hypothesis concerning the etiology of a syndrome frequently known as *susto*, which occurs among Indians and non-Indians in Latin America and among Spanish-speaking peoples of the United States. ...

## MEDICAL ASPECTS OF SOCIAL SYSTEMS

### Illness as Sanction

The belief that illness is a punishment for wrongdoing is widespread in human society. Where it occurs, the social order is identified with the moral order of a universe in which health depends on virtue.

The attribution of illness to misconduct may have been a very early form of social control in the development of human society (Hallowell 1963), and in Paul's view perhaps the most important latent purpose of indigenous concepts of etiology and curing is to provide sanction and support for moral and social systems (Paul 1963). The idea of punitive sickness is, of course, no stranger to Western traditions; it has been a feature of Judeo-Christian beliefs concerning the consequences of sin (Polgar 1968, Crombie 1969). And today in many non-Western societies illness is a major social sanction.

Where illness is a sanction, etiology is a stringent guide to social expectations. Hospitality, for example, is an important value in Ojibwa society, and this is underscored by the belief that failure to share generously with guests exposes the host to the threat of illness (Hallowell 1963). Among the Ganda of East Africa there is a belief that a disease called *obuko*, the symptoms of which are swelling of the cheeks, limbs, and genitals and body tremor, is caused by the violation of certain taboos (Bennett and Mugalulu-Mukiibi 1967). In this society, social proscriptions such as those forbidding parents-in-law to share prepared food with their children-in-law, or a boy to touch his female cousin, are linked to the etiology of disease. Among the Irigwe of Nigeria, men who preside over shrine houses have important authority and ritual obligations upon which Irigwe welfare depends. These obligations are also related to the etiology of disease, for it is believed that if the shrinekeepers do not fulfill their obligations, they will provoke the displeasure of

ancestors and nature spirits and be subject to illness and untimely death (Sangree 1970). In this case, there are epidemiological data that can be related to etiology. Sangree was told of numerous men who had become shrinekeepers and died shortly afterward, supposedly because they had mishandled one or another ritual and had been killed by spirits. He also had access to an earlier medical survey of sleeping sickness that showed that its prevalence was highest among males in the southern part of the Irigwe territory, where Irigwe lineages that have the major ritual responsibilities are located. The survey report stated that this distribution of the disease was probably due to women's exclusion from sacred groves, which were the main areas of tsetse fly infestation, and in which a large number of southern Irigwe men were obliged to hold rituals. Given this combination of epidemiology and Irigwe etiology, the prevalence of disease would have the effect of showing how dangerously exacting the shrinekeeper's role is, and demonstrating the failings of men.

Since the belief in punitive sickness is a traditional sanction of traditional social roles, it is frequently a force for conservatism when societies are subject to pressures for change (Messing 1958, Lieban 1962a, Adams and Rubel 1967). And in situations where etiologies defend the existing social system, they also indicate where there are strains on the system under the impact of change. ...

In discussing punitive sickness, it is well to point out that victim and transgressor need not be one and the same person. Thus Clark's (1959) study of a Mexican-American community describes how a husband who abuses his pregnant wife may be accused of subjecting his unborn child to *susto* by his actions. The individual who violates Ojibwa food taboos endangers not only his own health, but that of his family as well (Hallowell 1963). Among the Ixil of Guatemala, displeased ancestral spirits may cause illness, and Colby and van den Berghe (1969) describe how a young man's cramps were ascribed to the fact that his mother had had an argument with his grandmother ten or more years earlier. Adams and Rubel (1967), discussing diagnosis in some Middle American Indian communities, report that if the patient himself has not been guilty of any social or ritual misdemeanor, the lives of his parents and even grandparents will be explored. An etiology of this kind, which states that others may suffer punishment for one's own transgressions, fosters the value of social interdependence. Beyond that, it widens the range of incidences of illness that are potentially attributable to proscribed conduct and thereby increases the applicability of this kind of sanction.

The notion that the actions of one individual may result in illness or death for another can function as a sanction on the behavior of both persons in societies that subscribe to belief in sorcery and witchcraft. Kluckhohn (1962) points out that in Navaho society, a troublemaker tends to be talked about as a probable witch. The fact that the individual who "acts mean" may be accused of being a witch acts as a deterrent to hostile acts, as does its corollary: an offended person may use witchcraft to avenge himself. Similarly, Hallowell (1963) has shown how aggression in Ojibwa society is constrained by the prospect of retaliation through sorcery.

Recourse to the risk of illness as a sanction seems to carry with it certain implications about the availability or effectiveness of other means of social control in a society. The problem may be looked at in relation to cross-cultural comparative studies of witchcraft and sorcery. In an analysis of the prevalence of witchcraft in primitive societies, Swanson (1960) sees the frequent use of witchcraft in a society as indicative of a serious lack of legitimate means of social control and moral bonds. He offers the hypothesis that witchcraft will be prevalent in situations where there are intimate but "unlegitimate" social relations, "situations in which people must interact closely with one another for the achievement of common ends" and "in which the relations among people were not developed with the consent, tacit or explicit, of all concerned; or in which persons with conflicting objectives cannot resolve their differences through commonly agreed upon means such as the courts or community councils." Swanson finds strong statistical confirmation of his hypothesis in a sample of forty-nine societies. Consistent with these findings are the results of a cross-cultural study of sorcery in societies with coordinate and superordinate social controls (B. Whiting 1950). Societies with coordinate controls lack special authorities to settle disputes or punish offenders, so that the primary means of social control is retaliation by peers; in societies with superordinate controls, certain individuals possess authority to settle disputes and enforce punishment. Whiting hypothesizes that sorcery as a means of retaliation will be more important in societies with coordinate rather than superordinate social controls, and her hypothesis is statistically confirmed in a comparison of fifty non-Western societies.

These studies provide evidence that the relative prevalence of attributions of illness to magical attacks is an indicator of a society's capacity to avoid disputes and settle them when they arise through legitimate authority. Whiting approaches the problem structurally and provides important evidence that the development of political authority with jurisdiction over disputants is associated with a reduction in the importance of sorcery. But the existence of such institutionalized authority in itself does not necessarily obviate or mitigate reliance on sorcery as an explanation of illness. The effectiveness of the authority must also be considered. ...

When illness is interpreted as a sanction, medical diagnosis is frequently also a diagnosis of the relationship of patients with those believed to be responsible for attacks against them. And if restoration of health is believed to be contingent on removing the ultimate cause of the illness, medical therapy can consist of social repair. ...

In situations of this kind, the practitioner plays a key role in the influences of the medical system on social control. For if a medical case reveals that the risk of illness has not been an effective sanction in preventing or ameliorating social difficulties, the intervention of the healer to influence the outcome of the illness can still be a persuasive social sanction.

### Illness as Deviance

We have seen that when illness is considered a social sanction, its occurrence is a sign that someone has deviated from social norms. But illness can also be seen as a form of deviance in its own right.

The position that in certain respects illness may be viewed as a type of deviance subject to social control is especially associated with the work of Parsons (1951, 1953, 1958, 1964; Parsons and Fox 1952). He points out that a high incidence of illness is dysfunctional for a social system. Therefore, a society has a functional interest in exercising whatever controls it can to minimize illness. This would be true even if illness were in no sense an expression of motivated behavior. But in fact in various ways motivation is involved in the etiology of numerous illnesses and in receptivity to therapeutic influence. This fact increases the significance of illness for the social system, which requires its members to have the capacity and be motivated to perform social roles that may be necessary for the maintenance or development of the system. Although Parsons (1958) has tended to emphasize mental or psychosomatic illnesses as forms of deviance, he has also made it clear that his thesis is applicable to other illnesses as well: "As we have already emphasized, illness is very often motivational in origin. Even in those instances where the *etiology* of the disorder is primarily physiochemical, the nature and severity of symptoms and the rate of recuperation are almost invariably influenced by the attitudes of the patient."

Parsons has particularly directed his attention to the "sick role" in the United States, which he sees defined by the following characteristics: (1) The incapacity is interpreted as involuntary; the patient is not held responsible for his condition. (2) The incapacity is regarded as a legitimate basis for exempting the sick individual from normal role obligations. (3) This waiving of obligations is conditional; it depends on recognition by the sick person that to be ill is undesirable and that he has an obligation to try to get well. (4) The sick person and those responsible for his welfare have an obligation to seek competent assistance, principally the assistance of a physician.

Parsons' approach to illness as a form of deviance and to reactions of society to the sick person has been the subject of criticism that will be considered shortly. However, he provides a valuable theoretical framework for the analysis of facets of the relationship between illness and social control, and his thesis appears to be consonant with behavior that occurs in certain kinds of medical situations. ...

Parsons (1958) sees the complexity of life produced by the development of modern industrial society as making great demands on the capacity of the individual. As a consequence, "the motivation to retreat into ill health has been accentuated and with it the importance of effective mechanisms for coping with those who do retreat."

The favorable reception of Parsons' analysis of the sick role by Western European writers indicates that it makes sense in terms of middle-class European experience (Freidson 1961–1962), and Fox (1968) points out that in at least one respect—the threat posed by dependence and the retreat from obligations and tasks—the concept of the sick role has particular pertinence for the Soviet Union, where maximum effort and productivity are expected at all times to meet the needs of collective industrial and agricultural development, as well as for the United States, with its emphasis on values of responsibility, activity, achievement, and independence. The problem of malingering in the Soviet Union, the severe sanctions that have been enforced against it, and the strategic role of the

Soviet physician in legitimating illnesses of persons absent from their jobs are instructive (Field 1957).

Yet although the sick role as conceptualized by Parsons is obviously a useful tool for analyzing medical aspects of social control in certain contexts, its applicability, as Parsons recognizes, is variable. ...

It is apparent that socioeconomic factors can have an important influence on readiness and opportunity to play the sick role as Parsons defines it. Freidson (1961–1962), who has emphasized the limitations of Parsons' thesis when the broad range of behavior surrounding illness is considered, finds it of little relevance to illnesses such as those not considered serious enough to warrant a significant reduction in activity; those considered incurable and adjusted to as such; those that do not lead the sick person to consult a physician; and those that occur among working-class, peasant, and non-Western populations, among at least some of which being ill in a socially acceptable manner does not require professional legitimation or consultation.

**Illness as an Indicator of Social System Performance**

In a good part of our discussion so far we have seen how illness and responses to it can be related to the structure and maintenance of a social system, a system of interactions among the members of a society and a system that is linked to its environment. But medical phenomena also can be indicative of the performance of a social system.

The health of its population is one significant test of the effectiveness with which a society functions. Certain philosophers of the ancient world believed that physicians would not be in great demand in a society that was well governed, and Plato considered the need for many hospitals and doctors as a sign of a bad city (Dubos 1959). Soon after the Russian Revolution, when a typhus epidemic severely threatened people weakened by hunger and without soap and fuel, Lenin told the Seventh Congress of the Soviets, "Either the louse defeats socialism or socialism defeats the louse" (Field 1957). Contemporary approaches to the problem of social indicators in the United States, indexes of the state of American society, include health as one of the major areas of pertinent evidence (e.g., Bauer 1966; U.S. Department of Health, Education, and Welfare 1969).

The use of health as a gauge of a society's effectiveness in meeting the needs of its members confronts major conceptual problems. The World

Health Organization (1946) defines health as "a state of complete physical, mental and social well-being and not merely the absence of disease or infirmity." The highly abstract criteria of this definition are difficult to operationalize. More specific, measurable criteria, such as life expectancy or morbidity, may be used to determine the state of health in a society. But this does not obviate complex questions of value. For, as Bates (1959) points out, health connotes an optimal state, and this may differ in accordance with one's goal. Is the goal length of life, maximum happiness, or maximum productivity? Beyond this there are cognitive problems, as similar mental or physical states can have dissimilar health significance for people of different groups or in different circumstances.

Given these difficultues, adequate utilization of health as a social indicator appears to be a complex, long-range objective. But steps in this direction are needed as part of a general effort to improve the means of evaluating the performance of social systems. Short of that, attention to the problem of such evaluation in its health dimensions can in itself provide a useful cross-cultural perspective for viewing "supernatural" and "natural" etiologies of illness. For when the prevalence of illness is attributed to the action of spirits, sorcerers, witches, or the manifestation of some other extraordinary power, this belief may be seen as a mystical interpretation of a society's shortcomings, the supernatural counterpart of natural interpretations that also perceive the prevalence of illness as reflective of deficiencies of the social system.

## MEDICINE AND CULTURE CHANGE

Under the impact of modern technology, and the industrial societies dependent on it, profound cultural changes are taking place throughout the world. In the developing areas, modern health and medical practices have been among the most important changes introduced. Yet despite the increasing utilization of modern medicine in these areas, with consequent reduction in morbidity and mortality, traditional medical systems still persist and exert a significant influence on the state of health and on medical decisions and outcomes in developing societies.

The fact of the matter is that modern medicine generally has been established in these societies not so much by displacing indigenous medicine as by increasing the medical options available to their populations. ...

In these pluralistic medical situations, one medical system may be influenced by the other. White medical beliefs have been incompletely assimilated into the medical system of the eastern Cherokees, and in some cases the older Cherokee beliefs and modern white disease theory show some fortuitous correspondence, providing reinforcement for Cherokee beliefs (Fogelson 1961). I have previously mentioned other examples of the influence of modern medicine on indigenous medical systems. It has been argued that modern medicine can more effectively serve populations in developing areas by utilizing certain of the resources of indigenous medical systems (e.g., Shiloh 1965, Kiev 1966). Yet for the most part both practitioners and the population at large dichotomize the medical situation in developing societies; competition between local healers and physicians is often intense, invidious distinctions abound, and differences that people perceive in the two kinds of medical systems can have a significant effect on the medical choices they make. Knowledge of the reasons for these choices not only has practical value for efforts to improve local, regional, and world health, but also can contribute to a general understanding of human behavior in relation to culture changes.

### Cognitive Influences on Choice of Medical Treatment

#### DEFINITION OF DISEASE

One cognitive approach to the problem of alternation between modern medicine and indigenous medicine has emphasized the importance of the type of disease as an influence on the choice made. Observers have pointed out that people in developing areas tend to distinguish the kinds of illnesses that can be cured by the physician from those that will respond only to the therapy of local healers (e.g., Erasmus 1952; Simmons 1955; Foster 1958, 1962; Goodenough 1963). ...

There is ample evidence that people who utilize both modern and indigenous medical systems tend to place illnesses in two broad categories: those more likely to be cured by a physician and those more likely to respond to the ministrations of a healer. But considerable allowance must be made for flexibility in such perceptions. The course of an illness, the outcome of previous treatment for the same condition, and a variety of other factors may cause the patient to redefine it and shift from one medical system to the other (Lieban 1967). While it is true that modern and indigenous disease names are guides to the sort of practitioner a patient will consult, a label is not necessarily fixed for the duration of an illness. The patient may begin to doubt that he really has whatever it was he thought he had, and the label of the illness may be changed if the practitioner is changed. Thus Erasmus (1952) observes that in poorer districts of Quito, Ecuador, people have more confidence in a physician's treatment of illnesses with modern names, but they do not always classify their symptoms according to those names until a physician is consulted at an advanced stage of the illness.

### GRATIFICATIONS OF TREATMENT

Another cognitive approach to the utilization of modern and indigenous medicine emphasizes the contrastive but complementary gratifications the two types of systems may offer to patients. Gonzalez (1966) distinguishes two categories of healing techniques: medicines and practices. She defines medicine as "any substance applied to or introduced into the body, which is believed by some specialist and/or the sick person to change the existing state of the body in the direction of better health," while a medical practice is "any act undertaken by either the sick one or someone else, which may or may not directly involve the body, but which is believed to have an effect on the health." In Gonzalez' view, people in developing or nonwestern areas have utilized modern therapy primarily for the effectiveness of its medicines, which are widely recognized as superior to indigenous medicines. But such Western therapeutic practices as rest, exercise, exposure to fresh air or a change of climate, and reduced smoking or drinking seem either inappropriate or unconvincing to people in these areas. At the same time, Gonzalez points out that indigenous medical practices, in which ritual usually plays a key role, still have considerable popular appeal. Gonzalez (1966) finds that in the Guatemalan groups she has studied, people very often seek help for the same illness from both the indigenous curer and the physician.

It is not so much a question of either/or, as it is *what* shall be sought from each specialist. I strongly believe that the power of scientific medicine in relieving symptoms is what is sought from the doctor, while the practices suggested by the curer for relieving the basic cause of the disease, plus the hope he gives the patient, lead the ill to him.

... Gonzalez' point about the importance of ritual in the persistence of indigenous medicine appears to be well taken, and her ideas are consistent with the widespread observation that people will utilize modern medicine on the basis of its

demonstrated successes while still retaining their traditional beliefs about disease causality (Simmons 1955; Erasmus 1952, 1961; Newell 1957; Foster 1958). With its emphasis on the complementary services that modern medicine and indigenous medicine offer patients, Gonzalez' thesis is more applicable to cases of illness that are taken to both kinds of practitioners than to cases of illness that are treated throughout their duration exclusively by physicians or by healers.

### THE INFLUENCE OF TRADITION

As I have mentioned before, the prevalence of indigenous medical beliefs has not prevented the utilization of modern medicine where its effectiveness has been shown. This fact has been particularly accentuated by Erasmus (1961) as part of his theory of culture change, including its medical facets. Erasmus has stressed that traditions are not blinders that keep individuals from seeing advantages in changing their behavior, and he has been highly critical of the weight that some writers have given to prior cultural conditioning as an impediment to modernization. In his words, "... even uneducated and illiterate people are not simple tradition-bound puppets of their culture. Given adequate opportunity to measure the advantages of a new alternative, they act to maximize their expectations. ..."

Positions similar to Erasmus' have been maintained by public health personnel. Roemer (1954) states that some anthropologists tend to exaggerate the grip of tradition and to underestimate the receptivity of people to change in their medical behavior if they experience new measures that help them. ...

But while demonstrated therapeutic advantages of modern medicine have gained it widespread and growing adherence in developing areas, it is also true that the personal experiences of many people prevent them from perceiving these advantages, and in these circumstances, their traditions may dominate what they see and do. Although Erasmus (1961) emphasizes people's readiness to discard their old customs for new ones if they can readily perceive the benefit of doing so, he also points out that when cognitive situations are not conducive to such perceptions, it is not surprising that people continue their traditional activities, or add new practices while still retaining their old ones. This has perhaps particular relevance for medical situations, in which appearances can so frequently be deceptive, and Foster (1958) notes that convincing demonstration is relatively more difficult in health programs than in other forms of technical aid. Perception of medical realities can be obfuscated by a number of factors in situations where modern medicine is effective and/or indigenous medicine is not.

1. Most illnesses eventually end in spontaneous recovery (Beck 1961). When this occurs and the patients have been treated by local healers, confidence in indigenous medicine may be bolstered by cures with which it is only fortuitously connected. (For a specific example, see Kiev 1966.)

2. When therapy for an illness is sought from both a physician and a healer, the physician may cure the patient and the healer get the credit. (Again, see Kiev 1966.)

3. Purposes as well as results of modern medicine may be misperceived. Measures that the physician may take to diagnose an illness are often thought to be the treatment; the patient may believe he should expect to see results as soon as a blood sample has been taken (Lebeuf 1955).

When the advantages of modern medicine are not convincingly apparent, traditional medical beliefs provide a ready frame of reference. These beliefs are linked to other ideas and patterns of behavior (Firth 1959). They are particularly interwoven with magic, religion, and traditional social values, and they serve multiple cognitive functions (Hughes 1968). They can also focus multiple cognitive sources of resistance to change in medical behavior. . . .

**Other Influences on Medical Behavior**

FATALISTIC ATTITUDES TOWARD ILLNESS

Medical efforts may be impeded if an individual believes that the outcome of his illness is inevitable, unalterable by any human action (Foster 1958, Erasmus 1961). However, a distinction should be made here between passive reactions to morbid signs that the sick person does not regard as marks of illness (Read 1966) and reactions to symptoms that are perceived as manifestations of illness but are believed to be beyond human ability to affect. In addition, in some cases fatalistic views may be only *post factum* explanations of the outcomes of illnesses; they may not necessarily persuade the sick person that remedial action would be futile while the illness is in progress (Lieban 1966).

SYMBOLIC SIGNIFICANCE OF MEDICAL PHENOMENA

People may respond to medical systems on the basis of what they represent as well as what they do.

Different associations may be contradictory in their effects. On the one hand, utilization of modern medicine is often regarded as enlightened or sophisticated behavior, and this fact can be an inducement when social status is a consideration (Foster 1958, 1962; Lieban 1967). On the other hand, when ethnic pride comes into play, traditional medical beliefs and practices can be valued as distinctive resources of the group (Halpern 1963). "Loyalty" may even be shown to certain illnesses considered beyond the competence of modern medicine (Schwartz 1969). In contemporary China and India, considerable intellectual and political support has been given indigenous medical systems, not only because of their therapeutic accomplishments, but also as manifestations of cultural creativity and the national identity of these countries (Crozier 1968; Leslie 1967, 1969b).

THERAPEUTIC STYLES

The manner of therapy as well as its substance may influence people's choice of practitioners. Marriott (1955a) found that in a rural community of northern India, Western medical practice was handicapped by the villagers' perceptions of such things as its emphasis on privacy and individual responsibility, its utilization of written prescriptions, and the democratic nature of its expectation of interpersonal trust—all features incongruent with village experience and attitudes. Marriott argues that a distinction must be made between "Western" and "scientific" medicine, and that medical practices could be divested of many Western cultural accretions to make them more compatible with the local scene without impairing their technical effectiveness. . . .

There is ample evidence to show that certain Western medical procedures are not necessarily based on logico-empirical considerations, or may contravene them (e.g., Roth 1956, 1957). Sorting out what is intrinsically therapeutic from what is not and distinguishing features that can be variably modified to make medicine more responsive to views, wants, and needs of patients is a problem in both basic and applied science. Attention to this problem can help balance the tendency of some public health scientists to emphasize consumers rather than providers of health services (see Hochstrasser and Tapp 1970).

SOCIAL FACTORS

The importance of knowledge of social organization to effective intercultural health programs has been stressed by British social anthropologists

(Firth 1957; Freedman 1956, 1957). Freedman (1956) notes that for the health worker this means both "a clear picture of the structure of the community in which he has to carry out his duties and the study of health workers and institutions in relation to the public they set out to serve."

The effects on medical behavior of social relationships within groups being served by health and medical programs are found in such factors as patterns of power and authority, which permit those in dominant positions to facilitate or impede acceptance of medical changes by others (Freedman 1956, Lewis 1955, Foster 1958); class and caste differences, which affect access to and utilization of health and medical facilities (Simmons 1958, Foster 1958, Erasmus 1961, Lieban 1967); factionalism, which can have a differentiating effect on responses of antagonists to health and medical programs (Foster 1958); and family, kinship, and other solidary social factors, which in themselves can influence or link people in medical decisions: for example, Kunstadter (1960) found that the stronger the bond of solidarity between Mescalero Apache parents and their children (twenty years and older), the greater the likelihood of similarity in their use of the Public Health Service clinic. Weaver (1970) describes a general pattern among Spanish-Americans of the southwestern United States: when illness occurs, members of the nuclear family of the afflicted individual are the first to perceive and validate the situation; after that, if the symptoms are severe and/or persistent, the family turns for consultation and minor medication first to the kin group, then to neighbors and important persons of the community, and only after that to an indigenous healer or scientifically trained practitioner.

Much of the literature on social relationships between medical personnel and the groups they serve has emphasized the effects of the social distance that separates modern medical professionals from patients of lower status, both in developing and in industrial societies (Simmons 1958, Foster 1958). Simmons states that mutual trust, respect, and cooperation vary inversely with the social distance between practitioner and patient, and various observers find that difficulties of rapport between the two can hamper utilization of modern medicine (Polson and Pal 1956, Freedman 1956, Clark 1959, R. J. Wolff 1965). Yet professional behavior that may be regarded as intimidating or supercilious and may disaffect patients in some cultural settings can be the expected and approved model in others. ...

It seems apparent that in social situations in which deference to authority is stressed, maintenance of social distance may enhance rather than diminish confidence in the practitioner.

### SOCIOECONOMIC AND TECHNICAL FACTORS

In developing societies, as in our own, the state of health is pervasively affected by social inequalities and associated privations. The impact of socioeconomic conditions on nutrition and health of underprivileged peoples in Latin America has been emphasized by Bonfil Batalla (1966) in a critique of applied anthropology. He criticizes what he calls the "psychological emphasis" in applied anthropology's concentration on such subjects as ideas and beliefs about health and illness and communication problems due to differences in cultural traditions, with relative neglect of basic causes of public health and malnutrition problems. He states that it is such factors as basic social structure and inadequate technology that underlie health problems in Latin American societies, and that improvement of life conditions depends on their alteration rather than concern with local ideas about health, welfare, and the causes and treatment of illness, which he regards as psychological manifestations of a problem rather than its causes.

Bonfil Batalla's argument is, of course, pertinent to areas other than Latin America, and there is no gainsaying the fundamental importance of the factors he cites. The risk of disease is greater for the poor than for others, and generally good medical care is less accessible to them (Kosa, Antonovsky, and Zola, eds., 1969). Even when they receive effective therapy, their living conditions combined with their limited medical knowledge may defeat the purposes of treatment. Parasitosis, for example, is endemic in the slums of Bogotá, Colombia; according to an outpatient physician, the poor take their medicine with polluted water and pathology persists (Press 1969).

But while poverty is the matrix of many serious health problems, and general improvement in health in developing countries is basically contingent on improvement in the living standard of the majority of the population, in several respects the other factors we have been discussing also play very important roles in both the current and the future health status of these societies. In the first place, improved health and medical practices do exist and do reach the poor. Such efforts are relatively limited in their range and effectiveness under present social and economic conditions, but they have significantly reduced morbidity and mortality in many areas. Therefore, factors that induce people to utilize the facilities, personnel, and practices of modern medicine now available can and do reduce suffering and save lives. Second, increased understanding of medical realities can motivate as well as result from social change. Growing awareness by the poor of the health implications of their standard of living, and of the advantages of expanding the availability of modern medicine, can increase pressures for social change that would make improvement possible. Taylor and Hall (1967) point out that successful health programs are inclined to produce recognition that change is possible, and improvements in health and other social and economic changes tend to be synergistic. The point is that health can be an aspiration of people, as well as a consequence of social process. Increased awareness of ways to improve it can contribute constructively to social action.

COMPLEXITIES OF TECHNOLOGICAL
DEVELOPMENT

We have been concerned here with what is essentially a distributional problem: factors that facilitate or impede utilization of modern medicine. In developing societies the benefits of such utilization are fairly clear-cut: lowered morbidity and mortality rates among groups with substandard health. But in areas where modern medicine is most highly developed, it has become apparent that new technical achievements in medical science make the relationship between the utilization of modern medicine and the welfare of human populations increasingly complex.

This complexity is clearly seen in problems with which physicians increasingly must deal: weighing the prolongation of the life of the aged and ailing or the hopelessly injured against the hardships this may entail for the patient and others (Dubos 1965, Solomon 1969); deciding who among those needing it to stay alive will receive therapy such as renal dialysis when funds, the number of machines, and staff to operate them are limited (Hubble 1969); deciding precisely when death has occurred for potential transplant donors—a situation in which timing is crucial (Solomon 1969).

Dubos (1965:427) finds modern medicine facing a paradox unprecedented in history:

On the one hand, science can eventually solve the technical aspects of almost any medical problem. On the other hand, the application of medical knowledge to the prevention and treatment of disease will be necessarily limited by economic and other social factors. Choices

have to be made among all the possibilities for medical care and disease prevention, but there is no agreement as to the social or ethical bases on which to make choices.

And the situation promises to become even more complicated in the years to come. Prospective developments in curative and preventive medicine through "genetic engineering" presage not only dramatic new medical achievements but also new questions concerning society's response to increasing opportunity for human control of biological processes (Lederberg 1970). It is apparent that medicine, in its social, cultural, and biological dimensions, will continue to share in the central problem of our age: how to use our rapidly expanding knowledge wisely and humanely.

# 2 Determinants of Health and Disease

## René Dubos

This selection by the noted microbiologist René Dubos sets forth in a clear and cogent fashion the social, cultural, and psychological dimensions of the states of health and disease. Dubos even attempts to define these elusive terms. (If the reader has any illusion, let him attempt to invent definitions that will be satisfactory for most medical professionals, anthropologists, and laymen.) Dubos sketches some of the cultural factors—"mechanisms of adaptation"—involved in the medical systems of non-Western, preindustrial peoples, shows how disease patterns change over time in different historical epochs even within the same cultural tradition, and indicates how these patterns are influenced by the types of societies and cultures in which they occur. Finally, Dubos tells us how the same mechanisms of adaptation that man has evolved to combat disease, in turn, provide their own hazards to human societies. Thus, the social arrangements and cultural techniques devised in human societies to maintain health and treat sickness create, for the same populations they were designed to serve, a whole new host of problems and may, in themselves, be implicated in the etiology of diseases in a given medical system. These mechanisms are spelled out in greater detail in the small volume from

Reprinted with abridgments from René Dubos, 1968, "Determinants of Health and Disease," Chapter 4, in *Man, Medicine, and Environment*, New York: Mentor Books, New American Library, pp. 87–113, with permission of the author, Praeger Publishers, Inc., and Phaidon Press, Ltd. (London).

which this selection was taken and his earlier, superb work, *Man Adapting* (Dubos 1965).

## HEALTH AND DISEASE DEFINED

The difficulty of defining disease is implied in the very structure of the word: "dis-ease." So many different kinds of disturbances can make a person feel not at ease and lead him to seek the aid of a physician that the word ought to encompass most of the difficulties inherent in the human condition. Generally, especially among the lay public, disease implies some serious organic or psychic malady such as cancer or insanity. Modern medicine in practice is broadening this concept to refer to any state, organic or psychic, real or imaginary, that disturbs a person's sense of well-being. In this sense, disease may threaten life or simply interfere with its enjoyment; it may prevent the sick person from functioning as a normal human being or simply from reaching his self-selected goals. Physicians now realize that in dealing with the problems of the "dis-eased" person subjective and social factors may be as important as the objective organic lesions or behavioural disturbances recognized by the pathologist or the psychiatrist.

It seems reasonable at first sight to define health as the absence of disease. ... The preamble of the charter of the World Health Organization attempts to convey this utopian ideal in the following words: "Health is a state of complete physical, mental, and social well-being and not merely the absence of disease or infirmity." Health so defined is a utopian state indeed.

Health will be considered in the following pages from a more practical point of view, not as an ideal state of well-being achieved through the complete elimination of disease, but as a modus vivendi enabling imperfect men to achieve a rewarding and not too painful existence while they cope with an imperfect world. ... Their goals determine the kind of vigour and resistance required for success in their own lives. ...

## HEALTH AND DISEASE AMONG PRIMITIVE PEOPLES

In the course of evolution, as his characteristic structural, physiological, and mental equipment gradually emerged, ancient man developed the fitness to resist environmental threats, those dangers, emanating from cosmic forces, food shortages, microbial parasites, wild animals, or human competitors.

Most of the skeletal remains found in Paleolithic and Neolithic sites are of vigorous adults essentially free of organic diseases at the time of death. Human remains of more recent origin provide further evidence of primitive man's ability to resist harsh natural conditions, at least until he is exposed to the influences of Western civilization. A large burial ground from a period preceding Captain Cook's discovery of the Hawaiian Islands was recently excavated in Honolulu; the skeletons recovered from the site had healthy teeth and strong bones with powerful muscle attachments. Apparently life on the Hawaiian Islands was compatible with health and vigour even under the primitive conditions of pre-European settlements. Similar discoveries made in other parts of the world validate the legend of the healthy, happy savage appearing in accounts of primitive life written by 17th- and 18th-century explorers.

Recent medical surveys of contemporary African, American Indian, and Australian tribes give us even more convincing evidence that health and vigour can be achieved under primitive conditions in extremely harsh climates. During the 1960's, Western physicians, biologists, and anthropologists studied the Meban Negroes of East Africa and the Chavanté Indians of the Brazilian Mato Grosso in their own undisturbed environments. The Meban and Chavanté tribes live in isolated primitive villages, with limited food resources, under difficult climatic conditions and out of contact with Western technology or medicine. Men in both tribes were found to to be extremely vigorous and of magnificent physique. They were essentially free from dental caries, high blood pressure, cancer, and other degenerative diseases so common in civilized, prosperous countries.

The medical and social picture seen by modern scientists in these two primitive tribes parallels in many respects the description of Eskimo life during the early decades of this century published by various explorers. Modern findings in this regard are also reminiscent of 18th-century descriptions by voyagers in Oceania and in the Americas. Granted the likelihood that early explorers and contemporary medical investigators failed to detect many disease problems common among the primitive people they observed or studied, their testimony makes clear nevertheless that health and vigour can be achieved in the absence of modern sanitation and without the help of Western medicine. Man has in his nature the potentiality to reach a high level of physical and mental well-being even without nutritional abundance or physical comfort. . . .

[Nevertheless] very few of the prehistoric skeletons discovered so far are of human beings who were old at the time of death. Judged from information available at present, ancient man rarely lived much beyond the age of fifty. The medical study of the Chavanté Indians mentioned above has led to a similar conclusion. Although the men of this tribe are in general vigorous and healthy, seemingly only a small percentage of them reach old age. These concordant findings have been explained away by the hypothesis that death among primitive people comes not from disease or senility but from violent causes such as accidents or homicide. As yet unproven, this hypothesis does not preclude the possibility that pathological processes still unrecognized are responsible for the short life-span of many people living under primitive conditions.

Several investigators have recently called attention to the scarcity of cancers, vascular disorders, and other degenerative diseases among the most carefully studied primitive populations. Unfortunately, so few old people existed in most of these populations that the significance of such findings is unclear. Since neoplastic, vascular, and degenerative disorders become prevalent only in late adulthood, few men and women in primitive populations live long enough to become victims of them. Also, as we shall again emphasize later, the health, vigour, and resistance of primitive people is often almost an artifact resulting from the selective processes. The unfit are weeded out, and only those members of the tribe endowed with great innate resistance survive. Life under primitive conditions helps human beings become stronger and tougher, but it is obvious that those who are seen and counted are the favoured ones who have survived precisely because they had the innate attributes to become strong and tough.

Finally, a vigorous and healthy appearance does not necessarily imply the absence of disease. Resistant as they had to be in order to survive, ancient populations nevertheless experienced many of the dieases that afflict mankind today. . . .

It is almost impossible to establish with certainty whether mental diseases existed among the most ancient people, but descriptions of abnormal behaviour and illustrations of hysteria in early Greek literature and art leave no doubt that disorders of the mind have long been accompaniments of human life. Many forms of mental disease are frequent also among primitive populations today.

The problem of health and disease among primitive peoples thus presents itself under two different aspects. Prehistoric remains and ancient history strongly suggest that disease has been coexistent with human life; other kinds of anthropological evidence indicate that life under the most primitive conditions is compatible with a high level of health. This incompatibility of evidence is more apparant than real. Disease can occur occasionally in one person without affecting his group as a whole. Recognition of a particular disease in a Paleolithic or Neolithic skeleton does not signify its prevalence in prehistoric communities.

Equally important, the achievement of a healthy state depends in large part upon man's ability to become well adapted to a stable environment. At the time of their discovery by white men, the societies of Polynesians, American Indians, Eskimos, and other primitive peoples were in a state of arrested civilization. For long periods of time they had lived in fairly stable physical and social environments almost out of contact with the rest of mankind. They had achieved an equilibrium with their limited world and learned to utilize its natural food resources and to protect themselves against its threats. In particular, they had developed a high level of immunity against the microbial agents of disease prevalent in their communities. . . .

## SOCIAL UPHEAVALS AND DISEASE CAUSATION

From historical experience, we know that all primitive peoples fall prey to many forms of disease when they come into contact with Western civilization. The details of this increased susceptibility to disease are complex, but the general pattern quite simple.

Whenever European explorers entered a newly discovered country, they unwittingly introduced a host of microbes they harboured in their bodies. These microbes, little harming the Europeans who had built up resistance to them, proved highly virulent for the primitive peoples who had had no prior contact with them. Not only did the Europeans introduce new infectious agents but their arrival and continued presence suddenly and profoundly disturbed the nutritional habits and ancestral ways of life of the primitive tribes. These social disturbances further lowered general resistance to disease. Such a constellation of unfavourable circumstances readily accounts for the immensely destructive character of the diseases that afflicted the Polynesians, the American Indians, and the Eskimos during the 18th, 19th, and 20th centuries. (Parenthetically, the reverse process is also true. That is, many Europeans who go to primitive areas commonly encounter infectious agents to which they have no acquired resistance and to which they fall prey. It is thought, though not proven, that syphilis came to Europe by this process following the New World explorations of Columbus.)

In Europe and America, all periods of social upheaval have been accompanied by a marked increase in the incidence of disease and, more strikingly, by a change in the relative incidence of various kinds of diseases. During the 19th century, the circumstances surrounding the Industrial Revolution brought on an explosive aggravation of many pathological states with a resulting deterioration of the general health, especially among the labouring classes. Within a few decades, millions of men and women migrated from rural districts into mushrooming industrial cities where they had to live under physiologically deplorable and totally strange conditions. We shall later mention specific factors acting as direct causes of disease; it will suffice here to emphasize that the industrial environment per se constituted the primary disturbing factor. Because it was unhealthy and different from anything experienced before, it imposed on the immigrants recently arrived from rural areas, especially from foreign countries, excessive adaptive demands that they could not meet successfully.

Whatever their nationality, the citizens of prosperous countries have by now become fairly well adapted to the kinds of environment emergent from the first Industrial Revolution. This does not mean, however, that failures of adaptation are no longer important in the causation of disease among Westernized people. Environmental conditions change constantly and rapidly, partly because we manipulate them in an attempt to control the external world and more perhaps because each technological and social innovation has unpredictable consequences. These unforeseen effects alter many aspects of our lives, often in an unfavourable manner. The more dynamic the society, the more rapid and profound are the modifications in environment and ways of life. As many persons fail to meet successfully the adaptive requirements created by these rapidly changing conditions, numerous and varied pathological states emerge despite an increase in comfort and prosperity. ...

## THEORIES OF DISEASE CAUSATION

The reader consulting an encyclopaedia about the cause of a particular disease is likely to receive an equivocal answer. And surprising as it may seem, he may not obtain more definite information from professional textbooks of medicine, for, in most cases, there is no simple answer. Much is known of the anatomical and functional abnormalities behind the signs and symptoms of disease, but information is often lacking on the causative circumstances initially associated with these changes. The common cold illustrates how conceptual difficulties with the very meaning of the word "cause" can compound the scientific task of identifying specific causation. ...

Recent experiments, designed to show that a condition similar to the common cold can be produced by spraying suspensions of certain viruses into the nostrils of human volunteers, have substantiated the microbial theory of cold causation. According to present evidence, numerous strains of virus can cause these symptoms, a finding obviously and disturbingly pointing to the existence of a multiplicity of microbial causative agents. To complicate the microbial theory further, many volunteers fail to develop a cold even though they have been heavily contaminated with virus suspensions known to cause the disease in other persons. Other experiments have revealed still more complexities. The chance of contracting a cold is not appreciably increased when volunteers wearing wet socks in a drafty, cold room, conditions assumed by both physicians and laymen to enhance susceptibility, are exposed to the implicated viruses.

Exposure to one of several viruses is a *necessary* condition for the development of the common cold but not a *sufficient* condition. Exposure results in disease only when the exposed person is in a receptive state. This receptivity is in turn affected by the season, the weather, and almost certainly by a host of other ill-defined factors, such as fatigue, probably acting to decrease general resistance to infection.

The puzzle of the common cold, and of its multifactorial determinants, has its counterpart in most important diseases. Indeed, multifactorial etiology is the rule rather than the exception, and apparently conflicting theories of disease causation can be reconciled. ...

In almost all cases, several determinant factors must therefore act in concert to produce a detectable pathological state; moreover, the manifestations of any given agent differ profoundly from one person to another. Thus, causality and specificity are much less readily demonstrated in natural clinical situations than they are in experimental laboratory models. Admittedly, a few acute infectious processes and nutritional deficiencies present such a characteristic clinical picture that there is no difficulty in identifying them and in attributing them to specific causes. Few diseases present such a simple picture. What the patient experiences and what the physician observes constitute generally a confusing variety of symptoms and lesions rather than a well-defined entity. In most cases, a complex syndrome such as anemia, cardiac insufficiency, gastric disturbance, or depression is more in evidence than the unique and clear-cut pathological manifestations of a specific etiological agent.

In common experience, a traumatic accident that would be fatal to an aged person may have only trivial consequences for a young healthy adult. More generally, the character and severity of the damage caused by any given deleterious agency will differ from one situation to another. The pulmonary disease that our 19th-century ancestors called a decline, consumption, or phthisis was unquestionably pulmonary tuberculosis; but it was usually much more severe than the kind of tuberculosis most commonly seen in our communities today. Evidence indicates that the virulence of tubercle bacilli has not changed; what has changed is the response of Western man to tuberculous infection. Many other examples could be quoted to illustrate that the severity of a microbial or toxic disease is determined as much by the intensity of the body response as it is by the characteristics of the microbe or toxin involved.

Noxious agents differing widely in nature can elicit similar reactions from the body, complicating still further an understanding of disease causation. Congestion of the nasal mucous membranes and their hypersecretion can be caused by many unrelated agencies such as: viral and bacterial infections; inhalation of smoke, dust, allergens or cold air; migraine of vascular origin; the administration of certain drugs; sorrow and tears. Likewise, urticaria can result from contact with wool, from consumption of many types of foods and drugs, from emotional disturbances, or from exposure to agents as different as sunlight and cold. Bacterial endocarditis in man and mastitis in cows used to be caused almost exclusively by streptococci. Now that streptococcal infections can be successfully treated with penicillin, other microbial species commonly establish themselves in the heart lesions of human beings or in the mammary lesions of cows; they thus give a new microbial causation to these ancient diseases.

The body is capable of only a limited range of reactions. Its response to assaults of very different origin and nature is consequently rather stereotyped. Intestinal lesions mimicking those of typhoid fever can be produced by introducing into the mesenteric nodes of animals almost any irritating substance, even a rose thorn. Stimulation of the neurovegetative system can produce severe lesions not only in the viscera directly affected but also in others with indirect and distant anatomical connections. So much uniformity in the lesions and hormonal responses caused by various types of noxious stimuli has been observed that the blanket expressions "stress response" and, more technically, "General Adaptation Syndrome" have been coined to include them all. Such informity of response seems incompatible with the doctrine of specific causation. Were it only for this reason, there is need for a new formulation of the etiologial theory.

The activities of various hormones influence all of the human organism's responses to noxious agencies. The secretion of these hormones is in turn affected by psychological factors and by the symbolic interpretation the mind attaches to environmental agents and stimuli. This individual interpretation is so profoundly conditioned by the experiences of the past and by the anticipations of the future that the physicochemical characteristics of noxious agents rarely determine the character of the pathological processes they set in motion. These facts also point to the need and the possibility of reformulating theories of disease causation. ...

Like living organisms, theories can survive only by adapting themselves to new demands and by continuously evolving. If the doctrine of causality were restricted to its classical formulation, it would wither away or at best become mummified. Thomas Huxley, in his statement that new truths commonly begin as heresies but all too often end as superstitions, pungently expressed this danger one century ago. Fortunately, the doctrine of specific etiology is acquiring new life and becoming even more fruitful of understanding because its scope is being widened. At first focused on a few noxious factors of the external world, it is now taking cognizance of a multiplicity of internal mechanisms when body and mind attempt to respond adaptively to environmental stimuli and stresses.

Failure of such adaptive efforts accounts for a large percentage of diseases. Seen from this broader point of view, the docrine of specificity will stimulate the development of methods for the study of the whole human organism's response to the presence of any noxious agent. It will thus permit a more comprehensive analysis of the multifarious mechanisms involved in disease causation. "Science," Pasteur wrote, "advances through tentative answers to a series of more and more subtle questions which reach deeper and deeper into the essence of natural phenomena."

## CHANGING PATTERNS OF DISEASE

As we have seen, diseases most prevalent in modern industrialized nations also afflicted prehistoric man and exist today in all primitive societies; diseases have unchangeable and universal characters because man's nature has remained essentially the same for some 100,000 years. The relative prevalence of the various diseases, however, has changed from one historical period to another and differs today among geographical areas and social groups. Differences in the total environment and in the ways of life make for this diversity.

Many kinds of documents testify to spectacular change in the prevalence and severity of diseases during historical times. The classical texts from India, Greece, or Rome contain numerous and accurate descriptions of the signs and symptoms of advanced pulmonary tuberculosis, a disease almost rampant in ancient urban civilizations. In contrast, neither the Old nor the New Testament contains references to tuberculosis, probably because these texts constitute the lore of pastoral peoples whose ways of life made them resistant to this disease. Countless paintings and drawings illustrating the manifestations and ravages of plague document the frequent occurrence of this disease in Europe from the 14th to the 17th century. Boccaccio's *Decameron* and Daniel Defoe's *A Journal of the Plague Year* underscore the severity of bubonic plague during that period in Europe. Plague practically disappeared thereafter from Europe, though it is still today a destructive scourge in many parts of Asia. ...

If ever man lived under conditions completely removed from the state of nature dreamed of by Rousseau and his followers, it was the English proletariat of the 1830's. Public-minded citizens came to believe that, since disease always accompanied want, dirt, and pollution, the best and perhaps the only way to improve health was to bring back to the multitudes pure air, pure water, pure food, and pleasant surroundings. As we shall see later, this point of view relates directly to the problems of disease being created in the modern world by the second Industrial Revolution, and to their control by social improvements.

In 19th-century Europe, the sanitary ideal developed at first without any support from laboratory science. It emerged from the conviction that with the correction of filth, dirt, crowding, and other social ills, high rates of disease and death could be prevented also. Simple as was this concept, it would not have become a creative force in medicine and in public health if it had not been publicized and implemented by intensely dedicated social reformers. Their crusade brought about a true sanitary revolution resulting unquestionably in the practical control of many diseases, especially those affecting the multitudes. Nothing demonstrates more vividly the profound changes that can occur within a few generations in the health of a people. One has only to contrast the sickly proletariat described by Engels and the tall, husky men now typical of the working classes in prosperous Western countries to appreciate what miracles can be wrought in a short time. ...

Disease presents itself simultaneously with so many different faces in any given area that it is usually impossible to attribute one particular expression of it to one particular set of environmental circumstances. Nevertheless, some generalizations appear justified. Without question, nutritional and infectious diseases account for the largest percentage of morbidity and mortality in most underprivileged countries, especially in those just becoming industrialized. Undernutrition, protein deficiency, malaria, tuberculosis, infestation with worms, and a host of ill-defined gastrointestinal disorders are today the greatest killers in these countries, just as they used to be in the Western world one century ago. In contrast, the toll taken by malnutrition and infection decreases rapidly wherever and whenever the living standards improve, but other diseases then become more prevalent. In prosperous countries at the present time, heart diseases constitute the leading cause of death, with cancers in the second place, vascular lesions affecting the central nervous system in the third, and accidents in the fourth. Increasingly also, persons who are well fed and well sheltered suffer from a variety of chronic disorders, such as arthritis and allergies, that do not destroy life but often ruin it.

## DISEASE AS AFFECTED BY THE WAYS OF LIFE

... Epidemics and other disease manifestations have been interpreted since ancient times as punishment for collective or individual sin. The well-documented cases of death by suggestion in primitive tribes when a man broke a taboo or some other tribal regulation can be traced to this ancient belief. In all probability, voodoo death is but an extreme form of body response to fear or panic and has its counterpart in even the most advanced communities. In the minds of many persons everywhere disease is still associated with guilt.

The outbreak of Manchurian plague at the turn of this century constitutes a well-documented example of the role of living patterns in disease causation. The plague bacillus is widely distributed among the wild rodents of Asia. Manchurian marmots normally harbour this microbe, but they do not suffer from the infection under usual circumstances. Around 1910, a change in women's fashions in Europe suddenly created a large demand for the fur of the Manchurian marmot, and a number of inexperienced Chinese hunters began to hunt this wild rodent. Until then it had been hunted only by Manchurians who had a taboo forbidding them to hunt sick animals. In contrast, the inexperienced Chinese trapped every animal within reach, especially the sickest who were slower and easier to catch. As it turned out, the sick marmots were suffering from plague, and many Chinese hunters contracted the infection from them. When the hunters met in the crowded and ill-ventilated Manchurian inns, those who had caught the microbe spread it to their neighbours, thereby initiating a widespread epidemic of pneumonic plague. A change in women's fashions in Europe thus indirectly caused an epidemic of pneumonic plague in Manchuria. ...

Porphyria, an affliction which damages the red blood cells, illustrates how modern innovations can result in new forms of disease. This hereditary disorder originated with a Dutch woman who migrated to South Africa in 1686. As far as is known, the gene for porphyria has been transmitted ever since to all her descendants; although these are now numerous, the disease itself has become a problem only during recent years. Under ordinary conditions, the porphyria gene manifests itself only by the production of mild neurological symptoms and minor skin blemishes usually overlooked. However, violent reactions often culminating in death are likely to occur if the porphyric person takes certain modern drugs such as sulfas and barbiturates. The normally mild signs and symptoms of this genetic disorder are converted suddenly into severe and often fatal responses by modern drugs otherwise considered lifesaving. ...

Some geneticists have postulated that obesity, correlated in our prosperous communities with great susceptibility to disease and a short life expectancy, may have constituted a genetic advantage in the distant past when the supply of food was erratic and when man often had to depend on his bodily reserves for survival. This hypothesis finds no convincing evidence, but its merit is to illustrate that in all cases the deleterious manifestations of a gene are profoundly conditioned by environmental influences.

## THE DISEASES OF CIVILIZATION

Cancer, heart disease, and disorders of the cerebral system are commonly referred to as diseases of civilization. Strictly speaking, the designation is incorrect, since these diseases occur also among the primitive peoples. Such chronic and degenerative conditions are so much more frequent among prosperous peoples than among primitive or economically deprived groups that it is justifiable to speak of "diseases of civilization." The very use of the phrase is tacit acknowledgment that our ways of life may have nefarious effects and that affluence, like poverty, can constitute a cause of disease.

Experiments with animals and observation of human beings have established beyond doubt that cancer can be produced by agencies as different as viruses, ionizing radiations, tar products, and a multiplicity of unrelated chemical substances. The precise mechanisms through which these agencies bring about uncontrolled neoplastic growths are still obscure. Granted this uncertainty, the conclusion is inescapable: many types of neoplastic disease can be traced to several different kinds of environmental factors. While all human beings can develop cancers, the incidence of various types of this disease exhibits spectacular differences from one country and one social group to another. Lung cancer is the most common cause of cancer death among men in the United States, England, Wales, and several other Western countries, but it is much less frequent in Iceland. In contrast, stomach cancer accounts for 50 percent of cancers among men in Iceland and Japan but for only 10 percent in the United States and for even less in Indonesia. Liver cancer causes half of all cancer deaths among the Bantus in Africa but less than 4 percent in Europe and North America. Breast cancer is over eight times more common among women in Israel than among women in Japan. Cancer of the cervix accounts for half of all cancer deaths among Hindu women.

Local differences also exist within a given country. Skin and lip cancers are proportionately twenty times more common among white people living in the southern half of the United States than among those living in the northern half. In the U.S.S.R., they are five to six times more common in the south than in the north and are particularly frequent on the coast itself. One is reminded here of Hemingway's character in *The Old Man and the Sea* with his precancerous lesions on the face. These peculiarities in cancer distribution cannot be explained in terms of the race or colour of the peoples involved. All evidence points rather to the ways of life as the responsible agents—perhaps simply extensive exposure to sunshine. The rapid increase in the incidence of lung carcinoma in our communities and the concomitant decrease in the incidence of stomach cancer leave no doubt that, while all human beings are potentially susceptible to neoplastic disease, environmental factors primarily determine its frequency and manifestations.

A similar conclusion can be reached from the study of the prevalence of vascular diseases. Enormous geographical and social differences exist in the distribution of deaths caused by vascular disorders, but it is now certain that racial factors are not involved. Differences in frequency are at least as great among the various economic strata of a given race in a given country as they are among national groups. ...

Whereas microbiological pollution of water used to be responsible for much disease among our ancestors, chemical pollution of the air is now becoming a great public health problem. Chemical fumes from factories and motor vehicle exhausts are causing a variety of pathological disorders that threaten to increase in frequency and gravity. They may create widespread and serious health handicaps in the near future. There is reason to fear that various types of ionizing radiation will soon add their long-range and unpredictable effects to this pathology of the future. ...

Who could have dreamed a generation ago that hypervitaminoses (conditions arising from an excess of certain vitamins) would become a nutritional disease in the Western world; that the introduction of detergents and various other synthetics would increase the incidence of allergies; that advances in chemotherapy and other therapeutic procedures would create new forms of microbial disease; that patients suffering from toxicities induced by drugs would occupy such a large number of beds in modern hospitals; that cigarettes, air pollutants, and ionizing radiations would be held responsible for the increase in certain types of cancer; that some maladies of our times could be referred to as "pathology of inactivity" and "occupational hazards of sedentary and light work"?

It can be taken for granted that, while man's nature will remain fundamentally the same as it has been since Paleolithic times, the pattern of his diseases will continue to change because his physiological responses to changing environmental situations will not adapt him rapidly enough to the new conditions. Change itself may constitute a cause of disease. Once man is adapted to certain kinds of food, weather, housing, microbes, and social habits, he commonly finds it unpleasant and traumatic to be uprooted suddenly and forced to live under new conditions even though these appear more favourable to the outsider. As Hippocrates wrote 2,500 years ago, "It is changes that are chiefly responsible for diseases, especially the greatest changes, the violent alterations both in the seasons and in other things."

## MECHANISMS OF ADAPTATION

... Man began to migrate extensively and to colonize most of the globe during the Late Paleolithic period. As he dispersed away from the conditions of his biological origins, he underwent many deep-seated anatomical and physiological adaptive changes, and the progressive emergence of the several human races took place. Migrations on a large scale, and successful settlement in remote areas, became possible only after man had mastered certain technologies and social procedures permitting him to survive and to function effectively under profoundly altered climatic conditions. The success of man as a species is a consequence of his ability to call into play a wide range of adaptive potentialities.

For man, as for other living things, the word "adaptation" connotes fitness to a particular environment or the possession of attributes making it possible to function effectively and to reproduce abundantly in this environment. Adaptation, however, is often bought at a high price, and its consequences may be unfavourable in the long run. Therein lies the reason for one of the most paradoxical aspects of human life. On the one hand, it is certain that the diversity and immensity of man's achievements stem in large part from his lack of biological specialization and his gift for adaptation, the greatest among mammals. On the other hand, these same attributes create many of his biological and social difficulties. ...

In the course of time, and probably even before he had completed his biological evolution, man learned to function in complex social groups and to use fire, tools, clothing, and shelter. He was thus able to supplement his genetic mechanisms with social procedures. Naturally, he long remained threatened by certain dangers, especially those resulting from infection and shortages of food. Wherever the environment is harsh, the food resources limited, and the ways of life unsanitary, a large percentage of the population dies during infancy, childhood, and early adulthood. Under such conditions, today as in the past, the constant weeding out of those most suceptible to malnutrition and to infection naturally brings about selective breeding for a high degree of native resistance to certain forms of infectious and nutritional disease.

Genetic mechanisms of resistance to disease have their drawbacks, however. Natural resistance acquired through genetic selection is effective chiefly, if not entirely, for the conditions under which it is selected; it is of little value in another environment or when the ways of life change. Genetic resistance to one type of disease may entail greater susceptibility to another. In many parts of Africa and around the Mediterranean, certain genetic peculiarities affecting the composition of the blood pigment hemoglobin are associated with greater resistance to malaria and therefore are advantageous wherever this disease is endemic. What is an asset where malaria is endemic, however, becomes a handicap in the United States where it has been almost eradicated. The defect in hemoglobin mentioned above may express itself in the form of a serious disease, sickle-cell anemia. ...

While genetic and physiological mechanisms of adaptation continue to operate in man, the control of the environment through technology progressively decreases their importance and in some cases appears to make them obsolete. Control of water and food supplies, better ventilation of dwellings, and various procedures of sanitation have greatly reduced the spread of many killing infectious agents and have almost eliminated the role of infection as a selective force in human evolution. Poor eyesight is less and less a biological handicap because it can be corrected by glasses. Insulin enables diabetics to live as long as other persons and to have as many children. Even phenylketonuria, a genetic disease resulting a few years ago in death or gross mental disability, can now be partially controlled by proper dietary management. Modern man can so manipulate his environment and the conditions of his life to minimize the effects of genetic abnormalities and postpone death from the diseases they cause. Needless to say, such manipulations interfere with or prevent altogether the operation of natural selective processes.

Environmental control also decreases the need for physiological adaptations. Man finds it more convenient to air-condition his dwellings than to adapt physiologically to heat or cold; wherever possible, he uses mechanical devices instead of depending on his muscles; he invents learning aids to decrease mental effort; he takes drugs as a substitute for mental discipline in resisting pain and overcoming fatigue. Almost universally, man tries to eliminate the unpleasant effects of environmental forces instead of making the greater effort required to cope with them through his own adaptive physiological resources.

Man's control of the environment has gone further than his biological adaptabilities toward eliminating many forms of suffering; it has thus constituted one of the most influential determinants of civilization. Yet, it is a dangerous error to believe that disease and suffering can be wiped out altogether by raising still further the standards of living, increasing our mastery of the environment, and developing new therapeutic procedures. The less pleasant reality is that, since the world is ever changing, each period and each type of civilization will continue to have its burden of diseases created by the unavoidable failure of biological and social adaptation to counter new environmental threats.

### THE DANGERS OF ADAPTATION

... Unfortunately, fitness achieved through constant medical care has distressing social and economic implications for the future. Medicine will certainly continue to progress, but at the same time the cost of medical care will continue to soar. Each new discovery tends to increase the demand for specialized skills and for expensive equipment and products. There is certainly some limit to the percentage of technical and financial resources that society can or will devote to the prevention and treatment of disease.

Technological advances can also exert deleterious nongenetic effects at first unnoticed. Environmental pollution illustrates how many of the adjustments that facilitate life in a hostile environment commonly express themselves later in disease and human misery. The inhabitants of the industrial areas of northern Europe behave as if they had made a successful adjustment to massive air pollution. For more than a century they have functioned effectively and successfully despite irritating substances in the atmosphere they breathe. However, their adaptation is less satisfactory than might be supposed. The lining of their respiratory tracts registers the insult of air pollution. The cumulative effects of years of constant exposure to various pollutants have resulted in widespread chronic bronchitis and other forms of irreversible respiratory disease.

Chronic respiratory disease is now the leading cause of disability among adults in all the industrialized parts of northern Europe and is becoming increasingly prevalent in the United States. This condition provides a model for the kind of medical problems likely to arise in the future from all forms of environmental pollution in industrial communities. Paradoxically, control over the quality of air, water, and food is in many cases sufficiently strict to prevent the most obvious kinds of toxic effects. Neither the acute toxicity nor the nuisance value of environmental pollution is great enough to be immediately disabling and to interfere seriously with social and economic life. Public attention is not alerted to the hidden danger of repeated exposure to levels of toxic and irritating agents so low as to remain unnoticed. Like chronic bronchitis, cancer, and many other types of pathological manifestations, the multifarious effects of environmental pollutants may not be detected until several decades after the initial exposure. Many technological innovations certainly exert a variety of unfavourable effects long remaining unnoticed because they are delayed and indirect.

As in the case of environmental pollution, apparently successful adjustments to emotional stresses caused by competitive behaviour and crowding can result in delayed organic and mental disease or at least in behavioural disturbances. Through the experience of social intercourse, man learns to control the outward manifestations of his emotional responses. He usually manages to conceal his impatience, irritations, and hostile feelings behind a mask of civil behaviour. Inwardly, however, he still responds to emotional stimuli by means of physiological mechanisms inherited from his Paleolithic ancestry and from his animal past. The ancient fight and flight response still operates in him, calling into play through the autonomic nervous system various hormonal mechanisms that generate useless and potentially dangerous physiological reactions.

The most disturbing aspect of the problem of adaptation is paradoxically that human beings *are* so adaptable. They can become adjusted to conditions and habits that will eventually destroy the values most characteristic of human life. If only for this reason, it is dangerous to apply to human beings the concept of adaptability in a purely biological sense. Biological adaptability often leads to the passive acceptance of conditions in the long run undesirable; the lowest common denominators of existence tend to become the accepted criteria in social and individual life merely for the sake of a gray and anonymous state of peace or tranquillity. There is real danger that the ideal environment will come to be regarded as one in which man is physically comfortable while he progressively forgets the values that constitute the most precious and unique qualities of human life. ...

Medical problems posed by the environmental stimuli and insults of modern civilization have acquired a critical urgency; most technological and social changes now achieve their full effects in a very short time and affect simultaneously almost all parts of the world and all economic classes. Until recently the rate of change was generally so slow as to allow time to make the proper conscious or unconscious adjustments. Many individuals suffered when conditions changed for the worse, but the bulk of mankind slowly and almost unconsciously adapted. The genetic endowment of the population became progressively altered; phenotypic modifications helped each person to function in his particular niche; and, especially, most human beings slowly learned to achieve better fitness to their milieu through technological and social innovations without entirely sacrificing the past or jeopardizing the future. Now, the rate of change is so rapid that there may not be time for the orderly and successful operations of these conscious and unconscious adaptive processes. For the first time in the history of mankind, the biological and social experience of the father is almost useless to his son.

# 3   Medical Anthropology and the Study of Biological and Cultural Adaptation

*Alexander Alland, Jr.*

The work of Alexander Alland was alluded to briefly in my introductory statement, in the preceding paper by Lieban, and in the next one by Wellin in discussing the proponents of the ecological approach in medical (and general) anthropology. Alland's two important theoretical statements, in addition to his reports on his field research and his volumes on human evolution, are contained in this article and are expanded and elaborated in his subsequent book (Alland 1970), the first work to offer a clear and explicit model for the study of medical anthropology. Since Wellin presents a more complete statement of appreciation for Alland's ecological approach, I shall comment only on a few points here. Alland in this essay successfully endeavors to connect biological and cultural anthropology through the junction of medical anthropology. In doing so, here and in his later volume, Alland places the study of medical anthropology solidly within evolutionary theory and provides a chronological, dynamic framework within which to organize the field and approach some of the several problems of research that he adumbrates. Though his broad approach is evolutionary, Alland suggests that studies of health and disease in human societies should be examined as investigations in human ecology. Not only should such an approach permit medical anthropologists to obtain a better purchase on the problems they study but the data of medical anthropology, in turn, should be of immense benefit to students of human ecology and human evolution.

In its short history medical anthropology has served primarily as an adjunct to applied anthropology and public health. While there are obvious and good reasons for combined research in these subjects it seems to me that there is a vast area for medically oriented research within the main stream of anthropological theory. In fact it shall be my

Reprinted with abridgments from Alexander Alland, Jr., 1966, "Medical Anthropology and the Study of Biological and Cultural Adaptation," *American Anthropologist*, **68**:40–51, with permission of the author and the American Anthropological Association.

contention in this paper that medical anthropology may serve as a major link between physical and cultural anthropology, particularly in the areas of biological and cultural evolution.

A good deal of recent research has shown that the evolution of man's sapient form has been an interactive process between cultural and physical development (cf. Spuhler 1959, Washburn, 1959, Dobzhansky 1962). Simpson (1962) has suggested that culture itself is an adaptive process of biological evolution. While most physical anthropologists accept the role of culture in physical development many of those interested in cultural evolution have tended to bypass the biological aspect of cultural development. They have concentrated instead on the cumulative aspect of the evolutionary process. No one can deny that biological evolution is cumulative in the two senses that there has been a proliferation of species through time and that greater complexity of the nervous system has been a constant of phylogenetic development. Nor can one deny that functional interrelationships exist between specific ecological niches and different levels of cultural complexity. Primary focus on these, however, has led researchers away from the main tenets of Darwin, variation and selection, the latter reflected in selective fertility and selective mortality. In fact Leslie White (1959) has stated that the theory of cultural evolution owes more to Spencer than to Darwin.

Sahlins and Service (1960) have applied an analogue model of the Darwinian theory to problems of culture, but in their system there are no measurable biological variables and no generalizations may be made from established biological laws.

Even the multilineal evolutionists, virtuous in their attention to environmental factors, have tended to overcategorize their material in premature attempts to show orderly levels of development within particular ecological niches. But while the development of complexity may well be a long term effect of evolution, it is not itself a determinant in the process, and the study of complexity is not particulay germane to an understanding of process.

I think that everyone would agree with the proposition that the extension of Darwin's theory to cultural phenomena is good science in that it would add to the generalizing power of that theory and place more material on human development within the mainstream of biology. The question that must be raised is: Can the Darwinian model of evolution be applied to cultural evolution and if so, to what extent and how? Before an attempt can be made to answer these questions, certain theoretical points associated with the organization and analysis of data must be clarified.

First of all it must be emphasized that the unit of such studies is a human population characterized by a configuration of biological and cultural traits and occupying a specific ecological space. The term culture shall be reserved to denote traits which are shared by a significant number of individuals and which are transmitted through the learning process. This should help us to avoid the tendency toward typological thinking which too often accompanies the use of the term culture to describe human societies and facilitate the study of cultural and biological variables as interacting factors in the adaptive process.

Second, it must be understood that what is to be studied is neither a teleological nor a unidirectional process. Traits which have adaptive value do not necessarily arise as a response to need. Thus there is no question of causality in the analysis. This is in keeping with the theory of evolution which provides functional explanations for the fixation or loss of random events (mutations) within a defined system (a population). Factors responsible for mutation may be investigated independently, just as factors responsible for the origin of particular cultural traits may be investigated independently, but these are not our major concern.

Traits which have survival value may be sorted out in a process which may well be, though it need not be, independent of the individuals involved. This is not to say that all cultural traits are adaptive, but the proposition that many of them are is not a new one. What is new is the proposed investigation of the biological adaptability of such traits within a given environment.

Lastly I must emphasize that medically oriented studies are only one means of pursuing research in the field of human evolution. Adaptive environmental exploitation and adaptive forms of social structure are, of course, of extreme if not major importance, but I think that medical studies will provide units of analysis which are more directly measurable and which may reveal more readily the relationships between biological and cultural variables.

It is often pointed out that the major difficulty in applying Darwinian evolution to so-called cultural adaptation is the fact that culture traits are extra-somatic and therefore not bound to genetic mechanisms. Hence it is said, quite correctly, that different rules govern their transmission. They are not only passed from generation to generation through a learning process, but may easily transgress societal boundaries without concomitant interbreeding. But how important is this difference? As I have pointed out above, adaptation is the major concern here, not the origin of traits nor the mechanism of their transmission. The relationships between traits and environments have the same effect on adaptation whether the traits are biological or cultural, and adaptation in human groups is bound to be the result of combined biological and cultural forces.

As far as methodological orientation is concerned, most biologists accept the fact that careful studies on the microevolutionary level are essential to an understanding of the mechanisms of evolution. If we accept the principle that microevolutionary studies are a necessary prerequisite for this type of research, then it becomes possible to discuss specific lines of attack on those areas which are subject to biological measurement. Generally speaking these measurements are fertility and fecundity, morbidity and mortality. The material to be examined falls into two groups. First, those relationships between culture and biological variables which affect the distribution and frequency of genes, and second, those relationships between culture and biological variables which directly affect disease frequency, disease outcome, and fertility. The first group reflects primarily the effects of culture on physical development, but changes in genes may well feed back to culture. The second group is concerned specifically with cultural development as it is affected by biological variables. Where genes are concerned we have the added measure of gene frequency.

Before presenting a general outline for research in medical anthropology, I should like to cite a series of articles which reflect the major theme of this paper. Although I have reservations about some of the ideas presented, they are not offered here for critical review, but rather as a series of studies which, taken together, help form the basis and direction for further investigation.

Livingstone's brilliant paper on sickle cell anemia (Livingstone 1958) has opened a vast field of research into the relationships among genes, disease, and cultural practices. In this paper Livingstone has correlated the distribution of the vector in West Africa for Falciparum malaria with the introduction of agriculture to this area. The increase in vector population is related to an increase in disease incidence and the increase of disease incidence to the development of an adaptive polymorphism based on the resistance of heterozygotes for the sickle cell trait to a highly fatal form of malaria.

It is unfortunate that further research of this type has not been pursued, although there is data in the literature on the genetics of disease resistance and susceptibility (cf. Schull 1963, Blumberg 1962, Buettner-Janusch 1959). Cultural factors which act to increase the frequency of disease organisms in particular ecological areas or which act to reduce or increase resistance will have an effect on the genetic constitution of populations.

A recent paper by Lambrecht (1964) on the evolution and ecology of the tsetse fly and trypanosomiasis provides much material of anthropological interest. While Lambrecht does not investigate the genetics of disease resistance to trypanosomiasis in present human populations, he does relate the distribution of various species of carrier and disease organism to both environmental and cultural factors. This paper is interesting also because the author raises the question of relationships between primate and hominid evolution and the incidence of disease. To quote his summary paragraph: "Exposure to and invasion by parasitic organisms may play an important part among many other intrinsic factors that guide the evolution of animal forms. Trypanosomes, two species of which cause African sleeping sickness today, are blood parasites of great antiquity. Their presence in Africa at the time of the first stages of human evolution may have been of great consequence, at first acting as a discriminating agent between resistant and nonresistant types of hominids, and later also in shaping migration routes and settlement patterns. As a possible clue as to why man arose in Africa, the author postulates that trypanosomes may have precluded the development of certain ground-dwelling faunas, allowing certain more resistant primates to fill the empty ecological niches" (Lambrecht 1964:22).

The suggestion that disease has been a factor in primate evolution has also been made by Schultz (1950:53). "I feel that this question could be answered by a geneticist (is there a relaxation of Natural Selection in variable species?) together with some pathologist, since disease is the most potent selective factor in anthropoids."

It is interesting to note in this respect that Macques will drive sick animals away from their territory and thus protect the group from an increased frequency of disease organisms. Thus disease may well have played a selective role in the evolution of certain primate behavioral traits as well.

A phenomenon observed in chickens and rabbits that may have implications for certain human populations is the existence of variance in the thermoregulatory processes which has been related to disease resistance and the function of phagocytes. To quote Hutt (1963:202–203):

"Evidence of a similar relationship in a mammal between superior control of thermoregulatory processes and resistance to infection was found by Locke who studied resistance of rabbits to virulent pneumonococci. He could not measure the degree of control over body temperature as easily or as nicely as we could (*using chickens*). He measured it by what he called the warming time, i.e., the number of minutes needed for rabbits to get the body temperature back to normal after they had been chilled by immersion in cold water. Those with short warming time proved more resistant than others."

Now if this relationship exists or existed in man we should expect to find it in groups with primitive technology inhabiting areas which have cold periods either seasonably or diurnally, or in populations which for subsistence reasons have prolonged body contact with cold water. At least two population groups for which these conditions exist and for which there is evidence of thermoregulatory processes may be found. These are the Indians of Tierra del Fuego and the Australian aborigines. Although there are indications that the Alacaluf and Yahgan suffered disastrous consequences from diseases introduced by Europeans, the possibility remains that these populations and populations like them are resistant to certain diseases, particularly those caused by bacteria and which are attacked by phagocytes. The Tierra del Fuegans were wiped out primarily by virus infections.

If the relationship which obtains in lower animals applies to these groups, it would certainly suggest that such an adaptive mechanism may once have been widespread in human populations and that cultural advances served to relax selection pressure. Furthermore it is very possible that variation in thermoregulation may exist as a polymorphic trait in more highly developed cultures, including our own, and that disease remains the selective mechanism. The frequency of the adaptive trait may be related to cultural factors influencing the incidence of specific diseases.

A hypothesis relating culture traits to biological adaptation has been offered by Whiting (1964) who suggests that long post partum sexual taboos and consequent late weaning may be related to the incidence of kwashiorkor in certain areas of the world. Late weaning is often associated with long post partum sexual taboos and late weaning is adaptive in the face of kwashiorkor which is assumed to be a form of protein malnutrition. Even under extreme protein deficiency mother's milk is believed to remain at a relatively constant protein level and of major importance in baby diets in protein deficient areas. Whiting has correlated a host of other traits with post partum sex taboos. Many of these may be non-adaptive, at least as far as disease is concerned, but the hypothesis states that a biologically adaptive culture trait lies at the base of the entire sequence.

There have been few adequate field studies of fertility, but Nag (1962) in his cross cultural analysis points out that venereal disease is a major factor in both sterility and fertility. Gonorrhea and granuloma venereum cause tubal obstruction in women and syphilis is known as a cause of congenital abnormalities and miscarriages. Social patterns associated with marriage and sexual license are important cultural factors in the distribution of disease organisms. Rosman (personal communication) has informed me that among the Kanuri of Northern Nigeria upper class men tend to marry virgins, while lower class individuals rarely do. Thus rich men and their wives are less likely to be infected by venereal organisms (the commonest is syphilis) and their fertility is significantly higher than other social groups within the culture.

The role of sexual selection in groups with genetic deformity and/or high incidence of chronic diseases such as leprosy and tuberculosis may well affect the reproductive potential of such victims of disease and insulate at least part of the population from frequent contact with particular disease organisms or debilitating genetic traits. Intermarriage within sub-groups showing a high frequency of a recessive trait will increase the expression of such a trait within such groups by raising the coefficient of inbreeding, but it will also tend to restrict the distribution of the trait in the population at large and weed out the higher frequency of homozygous individuals. There is no mention of such breeding patterns in the literature, but the possibility that they exist should certainly be investigated.

Laughlin (1963) presents an interesting hypothesis regarding the effect of longevity on cultural complexity. He suggests that in pre-literate societies where longevity is high for a significant portion of the population the "faculty-student ratio" is increased, leading to an increase in accumulated knowledge. This is an interesting idea, although the process must be somewhat circular, i.e., other things being equal, cultures with a greater accumulation of knowledge may have higher longevity due to better nutrition as well as more effective medical practice. Still, the circularity of the process does not negate the possibility that disease has played an indirect but non-genetic role in slowing down the process of cultural evolution in isolated populations in adverse environments. The entire question of longevity and culture is one which may be studied both in the field and archeologically, and I hope that the field of medical anthropology will stimulate more skeletal analysis of age at death as well as paleopathology, particularly for those cultures whose members thoughtfully provided the archeologist with graveyards and thus good sample populations.

Another little understood area of possible direct relationship between disease and cultures is stress, particularly overcrowding. In a delightful article on the cause of lemming migrations Deevey (1960:581) suggests a connection between overcrowding, stress and hypoglycemia. Deevey quotes J. J. Christian from the August 1950 issue of the Journal of Mammalogy:

"We now have a working hypothesis for the die off terminating a cycle. Exhaustion of the adrenopituitary system resulting from increased stress inherent in a high population, especially in winter plus the late winter demands of the reproductive system, due to increased light or other factors, precipitates population-wide death with the symptoms of adrenal insufficiency and hypoglycemic convulsions."

Stress, no doubt, has bearing upon morbidity in terms of lowered resistance to infective agents as well as its possible effects on fertility. Factors which tend to expose or protect individuals from stress conditions are certainly important in the general investigation of cultural epidemiology. The negative effect of stress may well act as an adjustive mechanism to decrease population when a level of adaptive saturation is achieved. One of the major problems in stress research is the lack of good definitions and measuring devices. Such problems should be the concern of the anthropologist as well as the physiologist.

Analysis of the direct relationship between culture and specific diseases presents a fertile field for research of the type suggested above. In these studies the adaptive value of traits may be measured against comparative mortality and morbidity rates for specific diseases in the same or similar ecological zones.

## GENERAL PROBLEMS FOR RESEARCH IN MEDICAL ANTHROPOLOGY

Although there are obvious difficulties it may be possible to measure the overall adaptation of a population group in terms of size and general measurements of fertility, morbidity, and mortality. Studies of this type may be controlled for economic and other factors as well as for environmental variables. A society transected by caste differences would be an ideal laboratory for such research. Each caste would be treated as a subunit of society to be investigated independently for relationships between disease and culture. The combined ecological picture presented by the caste village as a single unit would also have to be included in such a study.

It would also be interesting to investigate those situations in which a society appears to be expanding at the expense of neighboring peoples. This is not to suggest that health levels and ecological adjustments to disease will be the only or even the major factor in such expansions, but they may well play some part in the vitality of the dominant culture. Relationships between disease and culture should be examined along with technology and social structure as possible determinants of adaptation.

In my field study in West Africa the dominant group in the area, the Abron of the Ivory Coast, were strikingly superior to their subject peoples in relation to political organization and health as measured by morbidity statistics. The health factor was related to superior hygiene practices.

Population size, density, and total distribution are probably the best measures of evolution (these reflect reproductive success and the widening of environmental niches) but there are situations in which expanding population would be nonadaptive. Insular populations must certainly require some measure of control for optimum adjustment. In crowded areas one would expect various functional disorders and lowered vitality to occur in high frequency as a result of stress and factors related to the ecology of disease organisms. In such situations there may be some sort of self-regulating mechanism which acts to keep population at an optimum level, although we may have recently outsmarted ourselves with the invention of the germ theory.

In most cases an expanding population must eventually increase its living space. The expansion of a group across certain ecological boundaries may be inhibited, however, by an inability to cope with new health problems. European expansion into parts of Africa was partially limited by a combination of low genetic resistance to many of the prevalent diseases such as yellow fever and malaria and by cultural practices which made adjustment difficult.

The framework within which disease and culture traits are related is extremely complex, and many factors must be taken into account. Among these are:

1. The mutual adjustment between host and parasite.

   The introduction of a new parasite of high virulence into a population creates a genetic sieve through which non-resistant individuals are rapidly selected out. At the same time natural selection will tend to operate on the parasite population to produce a strain of lowered virulence since a parasite benefits most by living in accommodation with its host. The death of an infected individual creates the problem of transfer for the disease organism, and while natural selection also works to refine the mechanisms associated with viable transfer, low grade infection is usually advantageous to the parasite population.

2. Cultural practices which indirectly affect health and fertility levels.

   a) Long term adjustments. Practically all behavior patterns will affect disease incidence in some way. Not all of these will be adaptive epidemiologically since adjustment to disease is only one of several problems faced by a population. It is likely that minimax situations develop through time such that benefits are matched, at least crudely, against harmful situations. The use or non-use of human excrement as a fertilizer may be an example of just such an adjustment. The practice increases soil fertility, but also increases contact with, and spread of, disease organisms. In areas where land is plentiful the practice has little to recommend it, but in over-populated areas it becomes almost an economic necessity. The distribution of this trait throughout the world reflects such a situation.

   It is my conclusion from a hasty perusal of the literature that the eating of carrion resulting from the natural death of domestic animals is restricted to areas in which animal husbandry is a difficult pursuit and where live cattle are rarely slaughtered. This is certainly true for the area of West Africa in which I did field work. People living in an environment well-suited for cattle raising will not eat diseased animals, while those living in more marginal areas will. The eating of carrion is, of course, a somewhat risky business as far as disease is concerned, but carrion is also a source of protein.

While the examples given are cases of adoption or non-adoption of a trait, there must be situations in which strategies based on compromise between profit and loss develop. Any study of ecological adaptation as systematic adjustment should, I would think, view the process in terms of such accommodations. The type of game theory analysis offered by Davenport (1960) may shed light on this aspect of ecology, although problems of quantification are obviously severe.

b) The introduction of new technology. Almost any technological change is bound to upset the ecological adjustment which developed in times of relative stability. In addition to creating problems in the economic order which may themselves be reflected in disease incidence due to increased stress, technological innovations may change the environment sufficiently to create new and advantageous opportunities for disease organisms or their carriers. Livingstone's example of agricultural development in West Africa is one example, the development of irrigation systems and the spread of schistosomiasis is another.

3. Ethnomedicine.

a) Drugs. All societies have means of treating disease. Many of these treatments involve the use of effective drugs. The result of effective medicinal knowledge feeds back to the prevalence of disease organisms and the incidence of disease.

b) The cognitive system as it relates to disease theory. The way in which disease is viewed by members of a society affects what individuals do about it, and this of course feeds back to the total ecological situation. Symptom categories may increase or decrease the effectiveness of treatment. The general attitude towards disease may orient therapy in the direction of symptoms, cause, or a total condition, and affect the success or failure of therapy in relation to specific disorders.

c) The medical practitioner. The role of treatment sources in a society and the methods they employ must also be considered. Strategies which are based on the analysis of the patient's complaint, for example, should be more effective than those which ignore the patient and make appeal to supernatural revelation.

4. Introduction of new diseases through contact.

Genetic and cultural adjustments are both upset with the introduction of new disease organisms. The general level of resistance in the population may be affected so that other diseases which have been brought under control may once again become a problem. Like any other change in environmental conditions the introduction of new disease organisms upsets the existing ecological relationships.

5. Acculturation.

A change in significant cultural practices by even a few members of the community may provide new avenues for the invasion of disease organisms. Social breakdown as a result of acculturation may affect only a minority of individuals and still create new situations for disease organisms to invade the entire population. The loyalty of conservative members of the community to traditional norms may break down as they themselves become victims of disease even though they refuse initially to change their traditional behavior.

## SUMMARY: METHODS, TECHNIQUES AND PROBLEMS FOR STUDY

At the beginning of this paper I asked the question: Can the Darwinian model of evolution be applied to cultural evolution and, if so, to what extent and how? I have attempted to answer the first part of this question in the affirmative by relating evolutionary studies to disease ecology and by suggesting areas for further research. What we should study is not biological or cultural evolution but evolution as a total process. Human evolution as a process is based on the interaction of cultural and physical variables. Medical anthropology clearly offers us an opportunity to study existing populations in terms of these factors and, as such, is a valuable area for research. But what are the limitations of such an approach, particularly in those situations in which genetic change is not a variable? I have no doubt that increasingly sophisticated environmental exploitation and innovation in social organization are major factors in the increase and spread of human populations and that except under special conditions disease is a somewhat less pervasive factor. But I am also convinced that any good theory of evolution must be Darwinian with biological variables as major factors in process and with population as the constant measuring device. If this is indeed the case, then medical anthropology has its place in such studies. The basic method is ecological with the focus on cultural and biological parameters. The theoretical basis of such research is the biological theory of evolution with the assumption that there are areas of culture which are open to investigation on the biological level. Reductionism in this sense is not to be feared. Specific studies may be carried out on a variety of levels but should include the following:

1. Studies of culture traits associated with presence or relative absence of specific diseases (functional, genetic, nutritional, and infectious).
2. Studies of population size in relation to fertility, and health levels as measured by mortality and morbidity in specific ecological niches.
3. Historical and paleopathological studies of disease distribution and its effects on population size and distribution.
4. Comparative studies of populations and behavioral systems in culture areas located in epidemic and endemic centers of disease.
5. Studies of the relation between types of stress and disease as well as fertility.
6. Studies of disease ecology in situations of culture change.

All studies of medical ecology require careful attention to demographic details. Population size, age pyramids, and sex ratios are all important sources of data. In addition to these, overall death rates, mortality, morbidity, fertility, and fecundity statistics are essential with breakdowns for each related to specific disorders. Problems related to genetics, of course, require adequate genealogical material as well as the appropriate biological techniques associated with the gathering of physiological samples. In addition to these techniques specific problems may require training in paleopathology and historical epidemiology. These in turn require training in ethnohistorical methods and biology.

Where vectors are part of a disease cycle an entomological survey may be a prerequisite.

A basic understanding of ethnographic techniques and biological ecology is essential for all research in the area described. This calls for training which goes beyond the traditional fields of anthropology, although it includes them. Teamwork is one way of dealing with the requirement of specialized knowledge but it is desirable and, I would hope, not impossible to train medical anthropologists to work with a minimum of aid. The major area of necessary cooperation is between anthropology and medicine, but in the long run the anthropological overview will be necessary to derive generalizations from data.

# 4 Theoretical Orientations in Medical Anthropology: Continuity and Change Over the Past Half-Century

## Edward Wellin

As I remarked in the introduction, and as Edward Wellin notes in this essay, the field of medical anthropology, as its parent discipline of general anthropology, has not yet been distinguished for the sharpness, precision, or even originality of its concepts and theories. Indeed, as Wellin suggests, in the strict sense "we don't have much theory in anthropology generally or in medical anthropology specifically." "What we do have," Wellin goes on to say, "are theoretical orientations, broad postulates that involve ways of selecting, conceptualizing, and ordering data in response to certain sorts of questions." This depends, of course, upon what one decides to settle for as "theory." I do not take as cloudy a view of theory in anthropology as do many of my colleagues, as I noted in the introduction to this book, and I feel that anthropology, and in particular medical anthropology, already has a sizable body of theory and data in which it may take a certain pride. It is a snare and a delusion to chase after the wraith of ultraprecise theory in the behavioral sciences, expending great quantities of time, money, and energy to pursue the muse of

Written in this version especially for this book by the author from Edward Wellin, "Theoretical Orientations in Medical Anthropology from Rivers to the Present," a paper presented at a Symposium on the Theoretical Foundations of Medical Anthropology, Annual Meetings of the American Anthropological Association, Mexico City, November 1974.

theoretical models designed after those of the physical sciences, seemingly oblivious to the differences in the nature of human behavior as compared with the behavior of atoms or cells.

Be that as it may, Wellin proceeds in this exceedingly needed exercise to tease out the conceptual and theoretical "models" of a number of anthropologists and others who have strongly influenced the origins and growth of medical anthropology. I do not quibble with whether these concepts and formulations represent theories or theoretical orientations. I recognize that Wellin's analysis mightily helps to place the work of these anthropologists and other scientists in their proper frame insofar as their significance for a medical anthropology is concerned. This should enhance our understanding of the works of these scholars and of their place in our discipline, and, therefore, should assist in advancing the efforts of the discipline itself. Like Alland's preceding paper, Wellin's essay represents another step in placing the infant subdiscipline of medical anthropology within the historical development of anthropology as a whole.

Although the term medical anthropology was not in general use before Scotch (1963), work in many of the areas associated with the term has a considerably longer history. The task of this paper is to examine the succession of theoretical orientations in medical anthropology over the past five or six decades, to ascertain what each approach has tried to explain, and to trace both the shifts and continuities in theoretical emphasis. Our aim, in other words, is not to review the substance of developments in medical anthropology—this has been amply done in a series of summaries and syntheses by Caudill (1953), Polgar (1962, 1963), Scotch (1963), Hughes (1968), Fabrega (1972), Lieban (1973), Colson and Selby (1974), and Foster (1974)—but, rather, to identify and compare the major conceptual models that have served to underlie and frame substantive work in the field.

First, the continuities. To be sure, the historic roots of medical anthropology are diverse (Foster 1974), and its current orientations and problem interests are varied (Lieban 1973). Nonetheless, one can identify a limited number of commonalities that serve and have served as points of consensus around which medical anthropology, for all its varied facets, has developed. These commonalities consist of *three empirical generalizations*, that is, of certain repeatedly observed regularities in nature, one or more of which have been reference points for medical-anthropological study over the years. The three empirical generalizations, formulated in various ways by, among others, Ackerknecht (1945),

Caudill (1953), Scotch (1963), Polgar (1963), and Hughes (1968), may be stated as follows:

1. *Disease* in some form is a universal fact of human life; it occurs in all known times, places, and societies.
2. All known human groups develop *methods* and allocate *roles*, congruent with their resources and structures, for coping with or responding to disease.
3. All known human groups develop some set of *beliefs, cognitions, and perceptions* consistent with their cultural matrices, for defining or cognizing disease.

Both the strength and weakness of medical anthropology lie in its basic empirical generalizations. Their strength is anchored to the fact that they summarize and order a large number of specific time-place-people observations; thus, they provide a rich empirical base and many points of departure for medical-anthropological research. Their weakness, one that is inherent in all empirical generalizations, is that they can describe observed regularities in nature but cannot explain them. We shall return to the empirical generalizations.

Throughout we refer not to theories but to theoretical orientations. The distinction is deliberate. Merton (1967) observes that *theory* has to do with formulations that specify determinate relationships between particular variables. Following Merton, a theory constitutes a set of logically interconnected propositions from which one derives specific hypotheses that are prescribed by the theory and whose empirical testing must lead to confirming, modifying, or rejecting the theory. Stated differently, *a theory must attempt to explain something*, and a well-formulated theory tries to explain the something in terms of a causal sequence of interrelated variables capable of generating hypotheses that can put the theory to an empirical test. In this sense, we do not have much theory in anthropology generally or in medical anthropology specifically.

What we do have, as Kaplan and Manners note (1972), are *theoretical orientations*—broad postulates that involve characteristic ways of selecting, conceptualizing, and ordering data in response to certain sorts of questions. To cite two examples, the "functional" orientation leads one to look at society as a relatively integrated organization of mutually related and interdependent parts, whereas the "cognitive" orientation calls attention to the modes of categorizing and structuring experience that are characteristic of carriers of different cultures and speech communities. Each of the foregoing provides a general context for inquiry, identifies certain types of relevant variables, and serves to inspire hypotheses that are congruent with the given orientation. Whereas either approach can generate theories, neither *is* a theory but, rather, a broad theoretical orientation. In the same sense, the various approaches discussed in this paper are best viewed as theoretical orientations, not theories.

As we examine theoretical approaches in medical anthropology, our core question is: what has each of them tried to explain? More specifically, on what sorts of *dependent variables* have the different theoretical orientations attempted to shed light? Further, what explicit or implicit models have served as the frameworks of inquiry?

We proceed chronologically, starting with the work of W. H. R. Rivers, and go on to analyze the orientations and models in the contributions of Forrest Clements, Erwin Ackerknecht, Benjamin Paul, and of a number of recent "ecological" scholars, considered as a group. Although all the foregoing workers have influenced the thinking and research of other anthropologists, their selection here is not meant to imply that they are the only or the most outstanding figures in medical anthropology over the past 50 years. They are selected, rather, because each typifies a distinct and important theoretical orientation, with each orientation representing a significant modification over that employed by the preceding worker.

## RIVERS: NATIVE MEDICINE AS
## PART OF CULTURE

William Hallam Rivers (1864–1922) is perhaps better known for his contributions to ethnography and social organization (1900, 1906, 1914a, 1914b) than for his work related to medical anthropology. He was originally trained as a physician and, in fact, practiced medicine at various stages of his career. His primary legacy to medical anthropology consists of *Medicine, Magic and Religion* (1924) and portions of *Psychology and Ethnology* (1926), both published posthumously.

Although Rivers was by no means the first anthropologist to report on the medical beliefs and practices of nonliterate peoples, he was a pioneer in attempting systematically to relate native medicine to other aspects of culture and social organization. His enduring theoretical contribution to medical

anthropology lies in a two-part proposition that animates his work—first, that primitive medical *practices* follow from and make sense in terms of underlying medical *beliefs*, and, secondly, that both are best conceived not as quaint folklorisms but as integral *parts of culture*. As Rivers states it, native medical practices:

> are not a medley of disconnected and meaningless customs ... [but rather] ... are inspired by definite ideas concerning the causation of disease (1924:51).

Further, native medical practice and belief, taken together, constitute a:

> social institution ... [to be studied in terms of the same] ... principles or methods found to be of value in the study of social institutions in general (1926:61).

On the basis of his general proposition, Rivers attempts to formulate a set of general statements concerning the nature of primitive medicine. In line with one of the preoccupations of early twentieth-century anthropology, this revolves around efforts to classify manifestations of primitive medicine as *either* magical *or* religious.

Rivers' basic conceptual model consists of three sets of variables. His dependent variable, whose range of manifestations he seeks to explain, has to do with observed or reported behavior, specifically, the practices of native peoples in coping with disease. His independent or causal variable, and he recognizes only one, is what Rivers calls the group's "attitude toward the world," or what modern workers might term "world view." Derived from, or a subclass of, the latter is a derivative variable, that is, the society's beliefs regarding the nature and causes of disease. Rivers further specifies his model by defining three types of world view and associated belief-systems and three corresponding modes of behavior. Putting this in diagrammatic form, we have a model as conceptualized in Figure 1.

Rivers confines himself largely to the first two world views, magical and religious, defining them essentially in Frazer's terms (1890). The magical outlook involves belief in man's ability to manipulate forces in the universe, whereas the religious world-view has to do with belief in the control of events by the will of some supernatural power. Rivers deals only lightly with the third world-view, the "naturalistic." Defining it as the outlook that views phenomena as "subject to natural laws," he sees it as characteristic of the West and of modern medicine, not of primitive peoples. Although he

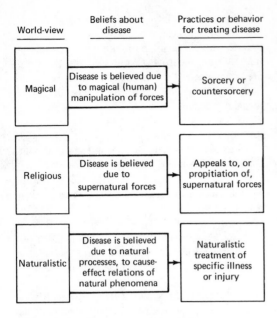

| World-view | Beliefs about disease | Practices or behavior for treating disease |
|---|---|---|
| Magical | Disease is believed due to magical (human) manipulation of forces | Sorcery or countersorcery |
| Religious | Disease is believed due to supernatural forces | Appeals to, or propitiation of, supernatural forces |
| Naturalistic | Disease is believed due to natural processes, to cause-effect relations of natural phenomena | Naturalistic treatment of specific illness or injury |

**Figure 1.** Rivers' conceptual model.

acknowledges the occurrence among native groups of empirical, and ostensibly naturalistic, curing practices, Rivers decides not to regard the latter as naturalistic within his terms of reference, on the grounds that they are embedded in magical or religious matrices of belief.

Rivers also attempts to relate type of disease-related belief and behavior to an associated curer-role. Thus, he sees the *sorcerer* as playing the key role where magic and sorcery predominate, the *priest* where religious and supernatural explanations rule, and, where the emphasis is on empirical techniques, it is the *leech* (proposed by Rivers as a generic term for traditional empirical curers). However, this aspect of Rivers' scheme is wholly circular—he defines the type of medical belief-practice on the basis of role-type and the role-type on the basis of the prevailing set of disease-related beliefs and practices.

Although Rivers' model is essentially a static one, he does allow for change. He does so by placing the primary elements of his model on a change-gradient, with the *world views* of native societies relatively fixed and unchanging, *beliefs* about the nature and causes of disease somewhat less impervious to modification, and medical *practices* most susceptible to change. He sees alterations in practices as occurring primarily through two processes—diffusion, or cultural increments brought about through contact, and degeneration,

that is, culture loss, produced largely through cultural isolation.

Within Rivers' outlook, primitive and modern medicine constitute wholly separate universes of discourse. By focusing on world view and its linkages with belief and behavior, Rivers can find no way to accommodate magico-religious *and* naturalistic-scientific world views within the same domain of inquiry. As a result, Rivers' model precludes consideration of Western medicine and is limited to medicine among primitive groups.

Rivers deals with culture as though it were a closed system, in which cultural facts can be explained only by recourse to other cultural facts, with ultimate explanations to be sought in psychology. Despite his training as a physician, Rivers is indifferent to biological factors and allows no place in his model for them. Nor is he interested in adaptations to environment. In his model, behavior is treated not as adaptive but as the product of beliefs that are, in turn, derived from world view.

Despite Rivers' constant and futile pre-occupation with classifying manifestations of primitive medicine as either magical or religious, he provides an insight of fundamental and enduring significance, in viewing the elements of primitive medicine not as shreds and patches of inexplicable behavior but as constituting a "social institution," one as worthy of study as any of a people's institutions. In short, the essence of Rivers' contribution was to set the stage for medical anthropology by pointing to the interrelationships between native medical practice and belief and viewing both as integral parts of culture.

## CLEMENTS: PRIMITIVE MEDICINE AS ATOMIZED TRAITS

Forrest Clements' monograph, *Primitive Concepts of Disease* (1932), involves what is sometimes called a "culture-trait" approach. More precisely, its conceptual model is that of an atomistic historical particularism. Despite the work's conceptual and methodological muddiness, it is often cited as one of the classical studies in medical anthropology.

On an *a priori* basis, but without acknowledging that substantially the same classification had already been offered by Rivers (1924), Clements classifies disease-causation concepts among primitive peoples into five categories—sorcery, breach of taboo, intrusion by a disease object, intrusion by a spirit, and soul loss. He then proceeds to carry out two aims—charting the worldwide distributions of the separate traits as reported in the literature and, on the basis of charted distributions, inferring relative time sequences and routes of spread for each of the several traits.

Although references to Clements' scheme continue to turn up in the literature without critical comment, it should be noted that his classification of disease-causes is a conceptual morass. To be sure, it includes two traits that can be categorized as causes—sorcery and breach of taboo. However, the remaining three—disease-object intrusion, spirit-intrusion, and soul loss—are not causes but *mechanisms*; each is a result or effect attributed to human, supernatural, or other causative action.

The heart of Clements' study consists of a lengthy tabulation of each of the five etiologic concepts according to the region, tribe, or local group for which one or more of the concepts have been reported. In all, about 300 groups are listed. He then presents a series of world-maps summarizing the distribution of the separate traits. Clements interprets the spatial distributions as indicating that some manifestations of sorcery go very far back in time, whereas others may be relatively recent; the next oldest is object-intrusion, followed by soul loss, then spirit-intrusion, and, most recent, breach of taboo.

However, one must be cautious about accepting some of the details of either Clements' trait-distributional data or his interpretations of time-relationships and routes of spread. Years before Clements' work, Sapir had posed the same general question that Clements attempted to address: "How [are we to] inject a chronology into this confusing mass of purely descriptive fact?" (Sapir 1916, *in* Mandelbaum 1949:392). Sapir pointed out a series of conceptual hazards and methodological cautions in charting the spatial distributions of traits and in making temporal inferences from them. As far as one can tell, Clements ignored most of Sapir's admonitions.

Let us turn to Clements' frame of reference. Three assumptions that inform and underlie his entire study are implicit; they are not explicated. The first and most fundamental is that were it not for the operation of diffusion brought about through geographic-historic factors (spatial propinquity, migration, and other modes of contact or spread), the distribution of traits would be essentially random. The second is that there are no functional relationships among any of the five traits, and that the reported presence of two or more traits in the same society is a chance or

happenstance event. The third is that there are no necessary functional relationships between any of the traits and the economic, religious, sociopolitical, ecological, or other features of the societies in which they occur.

On the basis of these implicit assumptions, Clements constructs his conceptual model. It holds that, other things being equal, diffusion and/or other historic-geographic events produce given profiles of distribution for each disease-concept, and that relative time-sequences and routes of spread—his dependent variable—can be inferred from the mosaics of distribution. When the spatial occurrence of a trait is such as to make diffusion an implausible explanation, that is, when other things seem not to be equal, Clements invokes the possibility of independent invention to account for the trait's presence. In essence, the universe generated by Clements' conceptual model is one in which isolated culture traits enjoy time-place itineraries governed by little more than culture contact or propinquity and are largely unaffected by the cultural milieus or adaptive needs of their host peoples.

Despite Clements' unfruitful conceptual model, he does make a positive contribution to the anthropology of medicine. This has to do with his efforts in documenting the worldwide distribution of disease-concepts, that is, with attempting to buttress the third of the previously discussed empirical generalizations—that societies everywhere develop some set of cognitions for defining disease.

## ACKERKNECHT: PRIMITIVE MEDICINE AS CULTURALLY PATTERNED AND FUNCTIONALLY INTERRELATED ELEMENTS WITHIN A CONFIGURATION

The first shaping of medical anthropology as a modern subfield of the discipine is the result of the work of Erwin H. Ackerknecht. His considerable contributions to medical anthropology are embodied in a series of publications extending over three decades, beginning in 1942 (1942, 1942a, 1943, 1943a, 1945, 1945a, 1945b, 1946, 1947, 1948, 1949, 1958, 1965, 1971); during the same span, he has also written extensively on a variety of topics in the history of medicine. Like Rivers, he was first a physician and later an anthropologist; unlike Rivers, he has done little or no firsthand field research among non-Western peoples. His research has been primarily in libraries and with museum collections.

Ackerknecht (1942a, 1971) publicly acknowledges intellectual debts to the British functionalists, to several American workers representing various facets of the Boasian tradition, and, in particular, to "the theoretical and personal influence of Ruth Benedict" (1971:9). In a series of papers during the 1940s (1942, 1942a, 1945, 1946), Ackerknecht presents his theoretical orientation, expressing it in the form of five generalizations. His five generalizations and some of the views with which they take issue are:

1. The significant unit of study in medical anthropology is *not the single trait* but the *total cultural configuration* of the society and the place that the "medical pattern" occupies within that totality. This is also a rejection of trait-list and non-contextual approaches, as typified by Clements.

2. There is *not one* primitive medicine, but *many* primitive medicines, perhaps as many as there are primitive cultures. This extends Benedict's cultural relativism and her insistence on the uniqueness of each culture into the study of native medical patterns. It also counters the view of Garrison (1914, 1933), one of the most influential medical historians during the first third of the century, that all forms of primitive medicine are identical.

3. The parts of the medical pattern, like those of the entire culture, are *functionally interrelated*, although the degree of functional integration of elements at both levels varies from one society to another. Ackerknecht's latter qualification is a mild and implicit corrective for what he construes as Benedict's extreme position regarding the internal integration and consistency of a culture's parts.

4. Primitive medicine is best understood largely in terms of *cultural belief and definition*, that is, without consideration of biologic, epidemiologic, environmental, or, for that matter, material-culture factors. He poses the question as to the determinants or causes of native medical patterns only to explicitly reject what he calls the "... great temptation to explain the causal necessity of things in terms of psycho-biology, environment or material culture ..." (1942a,574). Ackerknecht's view—that what non-Western peoples do and think about disease are relatively unaffected by the nature and distribution of disease or by considerations of adaptations to habitat but are governed only or primarily by degree of fit with prevailing custom and belief—strongly shaped medical-anthropological inquiry during the 1940s and 1950s.

5. Finally, paralleling Rivers' explicit and Clements' implicit contentions, Ackerknecht insists that the varied manifestations of primitive medicine—however they differ and regardless of the acknowledged empirical efficacy of many primitive drugs and curing techniques—*all constitute magic medicine*. Ackerknecht denies the possibility of considering the medical patterns of primitive and of modern-Western societies within a single universe of discourse on the grounds that "... primitive medicine is primarily magico-religious, utilizing a few rational elements, while our [modern-Western] medicine is predominantly rational and scientific employing a few magic elements" (1946:467).

Ackerknecht's conceptual model for dealing with primtive medicine is a sharply restricted one. He limits himself to two variables. His dependent variable is the complex of medical belief and behavior, that is, the prevailing medical pattern. He attempts to explain or account for it in terms of a single global independent variable—the society's overall cultural configuration. Ackerknecht's model also includes the postulate that the parts of the medical pattern stand in some degree of functional relationship to each other and to the total culture.

Essentially, Ackerknecht's orientation represented an explicit effort to integrate the two primary theoretical currents in the social-cultural anthropology of the time. These were American historicalism and cultural relativism, especially Benedict's configurational approach, and British functionalism.

Ackerknecht's model undoubtedly has been fruitful. By focusing on the importance of the *culture-whole* in shaping the society's medical elements, directing attention to the *patterning* of medical belief and behavior, and emphasizing the *functional interrelationships* among the parts of the medical pattern and between the latter and the total culture, his orientation stimulated the development of medical-anthropological inquiry within the mainstreams of social-cultural anthropology of the 1940s and early 1950s. At the same time, despite his recognition that phenomena of health and disease were *both* cultural and biological (1945), his approach helped to confine medical-anthropological study to a virtually exclusive focus on cultural parameters until the late 1950s.

## PAUL: SYSTEM AND SYSTEM-CHANGE

The formulations of Rivers, Clements, and Ackerknecht address essentially "basic" rather than "applied" issues. In contrast, *Health, Culture and Community* (1955), edited by Benjamin D. Paul, is designed primarily as a contribution to applied anthropology and public health. The volume is both a reflection of and stimulus for the international public health movement of the late 1940s and 1950s. Paul's central concern is not to advance basic research or theory but to examine "... the immediate situation where medicine and community meet" (1955:4). To do so, Paul utilizes a model that differs from those of his predecessors, one oriented around the concept of *system*.

The term *system* receives no special emphasis in Paul's volume, and the concept is not among those elucidated in a summary review of key concepts. Nonetheless, system constitutes Paul's strategic and integrating conceptual model. This is manifest if, following Riley (1963:10–11), we adopt a minimal definition of system as (a) an *entity*, which is (b) made up of *identifiable parts*, which are (c) *mutually interdependent*, such that each part tends to influence and be influenced by other parts, and (d) together the *several parts and their interrelationships form the system as a whole*. Exemplifying the focus on system and system-change are two of Paul's integrative and interpretive statements:

> The habits and beliefs of people in a given community are not separate items in a series but elements of a cultural system. The elements are not all equally integrated, however; some are central to the system, others peripheral. Hence, some cultural elements can be altered or replaced with little effort, others only by applying great force (1955:15).

> One way to learn what a particular organ contributes to the functioning of the whole organic system is to see what happens when that organ is altered or removed. The same method applies in the study of social systems (1955:325).

Paul departs from Ackerknecht not in rejecting the latter's ideas, but in taking them a step further. He does so by posing a set of questions that Ackerknecht had never addressed. That is, viewing culture as a system and the medical pattern as one of its subsystems, *what happens to the system and subsystem when they are disturbed, that is, when new health-related elements are introduced?* Further, *what happens to newly introduced elements in the context of a given sociocultural system?*

Two propositions are fundamental to Paul's approach:

a. The responses of a given sociocultural (and medical) system to the introduction of new elements are to be explained not solely by the nature of the system nor alone by the nature and mode of introduction of new elements but by the complex interaction of both.

b. Reciprocal or feedback processes occur. That is, the introduction of new health-related elements can be expected to affect the host sociocultural (and medical) system; in turn, the latter will also affect (shape or reinterpret) the new elements.

Figure 2 embodies Paul's primary variables and basic propositions.

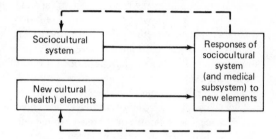

**Figure 2.** Paul's model of system and system-change.

In at least two respects, Paul's model represents an important departure from the outlooks of Rivers, Clements, and Ackerknecht. For one, conceptual limitations in the models of his predecessors restrict medical-anthropological inquiry to traditional or relatively simple societies; in contrast, Paul's system-model removes this constraint and permits the medical systems of modern or complex communities to be as appropriate for study as those of traditional groups. For another, despite differences in theoretical orientation among his three predecessors, the latter are similar in that they employ essentially *static* models—they dissect native medical systems at rest. Paul's orientation, on the other hand, requires a *dynamic* model, one that can deal with the nature and consequences of change.

In one respect, however, Paul's system-model retains a significant feature from the outlooks of Rivers, Clements, and Ackerknecht. This has to do with his treatment of culture as though it were essentially a closed system, and the exclusion from his model of factors of biology and environmental pressure. Although Paul acknowledges the fact and importance of broader ecological considerations, they are dealt with largely as background, and their interrelationships with social and cultural variables are explored only lightly.

We now turn to the final and most recent theoretical orientation, one that not only incorporates Paul's system-approach but comprehends factors of biology and environmental exigency as well.

## ECOLOGICAL APPROACH WITH CULTURAL AND BIOLOGICAL PARAMETERS

Until about the 1960s, theoretical orientations in medical anthropology revolved exclusively around the ideas of scholars who were closely identified with a single sector of anthropological interest—the social-cultural. However, the expositors of an orientation that developed rapidly during the 1960s are more closely associated with *biological*, rather than social-cultural, anthropology. This approach cannot readily be delineated by reference to a single author; its most explicit and vigorous theoretical statement has been offered by Alland (1966, 1970), and some of its best-known empirical contributions have been made by Livingstone (1958), Wiesenfeld (1967), Dunn (1968), McCracken (1971), and others.

The orientation—for convenience, let us call it the "ecological"—is broadly concerned with dimensions of *disease*. The latter is often treated as a dependent variable, that is, how do factors of biology, culture and/or environmental pressure influence the process or distribution of disease? Sometimes, however, it is an independent variable—what are the sociocultural, including the cognitive, consequences and concomitants of given diseases in particular groups? Anthropologists have given the approach various labels— "dynamics of health status," "ecology," "medical ecology," "epidemiology," "social epidemiology" (see Polgar 1962, Scotch, 1963, Fabrega 1972, Lieban 1973, Colson and Selby 1974). Alland (1966) refers to the orientation with precise but unwieldy terms as "ecological with the focus on cultural and biological parameters." The relative newness of the ecological orientation may be gauged by Scotch's observation as recently as the early 1960s (1963) that with some exceptions the area of sociocultural aspects of disease has been "neglected and disdained in anthropological research and theory."

The root source of the ecological orientation was essentially a "scientific revolution" (see Kuhn 1970) in evolutionary biology that erupted along a broad front of biological disciplines during the 1940s and laid the necessary theoretical foundations for dealing with human evolution and adaptation as the complex interaction of cultural and biological factors under given environmental conditions. It is by no means fortuitous that biological, more than social-cultural, anthropologists have been centrally associated with the ecological approach in medical anthropology. It is because of the nature of the scientific revolution and to the understandable consequence that its impact on anthropology was most immediate in the discipline's biological sector.

Until about the 1940s, as Dobzhansky (1951) observes, each biological science tended to produce ideas and conclusions about evolution that were distinct from, and often inconsistent with, those of other biological fields. Although workers from genetics, systematics, embryology, comparative anatomy, ecology, paleontology, zoology, botany, and other disciplines were interested in evolutionary problems, some closely related, they did not have a common language and many did not share planes of discourse. Work in evolutionary biology tended to follow three primary lines, each involving a different and seemingly incompatible theoretical orientation—natural selectionist, Mendelian geneticist, and mutationist.

By the early 1940s, it became evident to a growing number and variety of biological scholars that the three orientations and a host of separate developments among many biological fields were not only compatible but could shed more light on evolutionary processes in combination than was possible for any one approach or field alone. With relative suddenness during the decade, the scientific revolution occurred, that is, the three competing paradigms were synthesized into a new, single, comprehensive paradigm—the so-called "synthetic" theory of evolution.

The theory proceeds on the proposition that *populations*—not genes, individual organisms, or species—are the basic units of evolutionary change, and it relies on the statistics of population dynamics as a primary tool for the study of evolutionary processes. The theory might be briefly stated as follows. Any population of life-forms has a pool of hereditary characteristics and occurs in an environment. Hereditary variation in the population is produced by two means. One is *genetic combination and recombination*, essentially according to Mendelian laws of inheritance. The other is *mutation*, especially of the small and virtually imperceptible variety. The keystone evolutionary process is Darwinian *natural selection*, in which environmental exigencies result in differential selection of a population's hereditary characteristics, promoting or conferring advantage on some at the expense of others. No one of the processes singly is *the* cause of evolution; rather, evolution proceeds by the intricate interaction and complementarity of all three.

Within this broad frame, humans are seen as evolutionarily unique, utilizing and transmitting culture as a prime and highly efficient instrument for adapting to and controlling their environments. Fundamentally, however, human adaptation, always with reference to given environmental parameters, is a mutually interactive cultural and biological process. As Alland succinctly puts it (1970): "Man changes his environment, often drastically, through the adaptive mechanisms of culture, and this changed environment then acts as a selective agent on man's physical structure as well as on his behavior."

Drawing on the synthetic theory of evolution, Alland presents a general statement of the interrelatedness of culture, biology, environment, and disease in the adaptive process:

> In general, the incidence of disease is related to genetic and nongenetic factors. Any change in a behavioral system is likely to have medical consequences, some of which will produce changes in the genetic system. On the other hand, disease-induced changes in the genetic structure can affect the behavioral system. Such effects may be the result of population restructuring or the emergence of new immunological patterns which alter the possibilities for niche exploitation. In addition, induced or natural alterations in the environmental field provide new selective pressures relating to health and disease which must be met through a combination of somatic and nonsomatic adaptations (1970: 49–50).

The ecological model conceptualizes health and disease, more or less in Lieban's terms, as "... measures of the effectiveness with which human groups, combining biological and cultural resources, adapt to their environments" (1973:1031). The model also views health and disease in their feedback effects on culture, biology, and response to environment.

Figure 3 is a highly generalized depiction of the ecological model. It does not describe any one piece of research with any specificity but attempts to set forth the broad and generic framework underlying much recent medical-anthropological research within the ecological approach.

The place of the "medical system" in the adaptive equation varies evolutionarily. That is, in primitive and technologically simple societies, past and present, their medical theories and specific therapeutic procedures had and have less direct impact on the control of disease than those customs and behaviors outside the medical system that, whatever their rationale, serve to prevent or minimize disease through positive feedback from the environment (*vide* Alland 1970). However, among populations that possess advanced technology, full-time health practitioners, and a more or less systematic body of codified medical knowledge, the medical system comes to play an increasingly independent and significant therapeutic and preventive role in the total adaptive picture.

As noted, empirical research in medical anthropology utilizing the ecological approach was first contributed by workers with primary interests in biological problems and human evolution, for example, Livingstone (1958), Wiesenfeld (1967), Dunn (1968), McCracken (1971), and others. Thus, Livingstone's classic study (1958) relates the distribution of the sickle-cell trait in West Africa to factors of cultural and biological evolution and their interplay under given environmental conditions. He attempts to account for the trait's differential frequencies by recourse to the operation of multiple and interrelated variables— diffusion of new technology and crops, modification of tropical forest habitats, population increase, spread of malarial mosquitoes, and effects of malaria on populations and of the sickle-cell gene on malaria.

Subsequently, Wiesenfeld (1967) refines Livingstone's findings. Analyzing data from 60 societies in both East and West Africa, Wiesenfeld finds that the particular type of agricultural system significantly affects rates of the sickle-cell trait and of malaria. Specifically, he reports that reliance on the root and tree crops that go with the "Malaysian agricultural complex" (Murdock 1959) creates a more malarious environment, leading to selective advantage for individuals with the sickle-cell trait and to changes in the population's gene-pool over time. He presents a hypothesis of "human biology and culture interacting and differentiating together in a stepwise fashion," that is, given the intensely malarious environment and the given agricultural innovation, biological change in the gene-pool helps maintain the cultural change that previously had led to the new cellular environmental change; the biological change allows further development of the cultural adaptation: the latter in turn

55

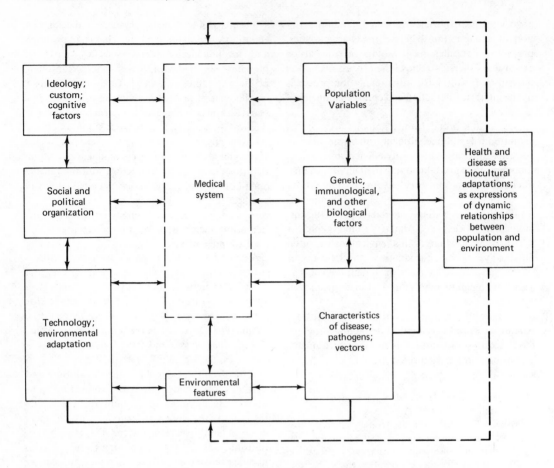

**Figure 3.** Ecological model with cultural and biological parameters.

increases the selective pressure to maintain the biological change.

Dunn (1968) combines limited data with reasoned speculation about morbidity and mortality in relation to the ecology of hunter-gathering life and raises significant issues regarding diseases as agents of natural selection and as dependent and independent variables affecting population size and stability.

McCracken (1971) recasts in broad ecological terms a problem that anthropologists had formerly defined solely as one in cultural conditioning—the fact that some peoples have an aversion to milk. Testing the hypothesis that distaste for milk is not simply a cultural, but a biocultural, trait, McCracken attempts to explain differentials in the worldwide distribution of lactase deficiency (or lactose intolerance). He postulates that lactase deficiency was the normal and universal adult condition prior to animal domestication and dairying, and that the introduction of lactose into adult diets in certain cultures generated selective pressures among the populations concerned favoring the genotype for adult lactose tolerance. To be sure, McCracken's evidence supports the notion that the long-term experience of populations with the production and consumption of milk is closely related to lactase deficiency rates; however, whether the data confirm McCracken's *genetic* hypothesis is still an open question. In any event, McCracken's effort to relate cultural evolution and cultural practices to the distribution of a biological trait is a provocative example of ecologically framed research on the interrelationships between cultural and biological variables.

In addition to medical-anthropological research related to evolutionary or diachronic issues, increasing attention is also being given to synchronic, cross-sectional, and contemporary problems within broad biocultural frameworks. Fabrega (1972) and Colson and Selby (1974) review some of the latter work, and Montgomery (1973) provides a succinct summary of recent research on ecological aspects of health and disease in local populations. Indeed, Montgomery's review indicates that the two things that Bates (1953) called for more than 20 years ago—greater emphasis on the study of disease as an environmental factor influencing human development as well as the combining of medical and anthropological interests in single investigators or working teams—are now occurring. Other recent instances of the latter are Boyden (1970) and Bahnson *et al.* (1974), in which medical workers and anthropologists (and other social scientists) deal with the interplay between disease and culture and do so within broadly similar ecological frameworks.

It is of more than passing significance that the broad ecological approach brings the *single trait* back into medical anthropology for the first time since Clements' work in the 1930s. Ackerknecht had argued forcefully in the 1940s that single traits have no meaning outside the context of their organization and patterning into larger wholes; within the terms of his cultural-pattern-and-configuration model, Ackerknecht was right. However, modern workers (for example, Livingstone, Wiesenfeld, McCracken, Gadjusek [1963], and others) have been finding it conceptually and methodologically advantageous to focus on the frequencies and distributions of specific biological traits, relating them to more or less specific cultural practices and usages, always within the frames of broad ecological models.

It will be of great interest to observe how the combining of cultural and biological variables develops in medical anthropology in the years to come. Several workers view the prospects as highly promising. Alland (1966) contends that, given the broad ecological approach, "medical anthropology may serve as a major link between physical and cultural anthropology, particularly in the areas of biological and cultural evolution." Katz and Wallace (1974) predict that "biological and cultural anthropologists will soon deal with problems of behavior and disease in the same ecological framework ... [involving the] ... interactions of biology, the sociocultural system, the environment (living and nonliving), and population size and structure as continuously interacting and essential variables with various degrees of independence and dependence."

## DISCUSSION

There have been both continuities and shifts in theoretical orientations in medical anthropology over the past half-century. As noted, the common point of departure for the field over the years has consisted of three empirical generalizations—(1) the universality of disease as part of the human condition, (2) the fact that all human groups develop methods and roles for coping with disease, and (3) the fact that all human groups develop beliefs and perceptions for cognizing disease. All three generalizations have been recognized for a long time, but until relatively recently only the second and third ones—those dealing with sociocultural dimensions—have provided the subject matter for research, whereas the first— involving biological parameters—has been held constant and thereby excluded from the purview of medical-anthropological study.

Thus, Rivers, prior to 1920, employed cultural practices or methods as his dependent variable and sought to explain the latter as a function of either magical or religious belief. Clements, in the early 1930s, focused on certain cultural beliefs— primitive concepts of disease-causation—and, treating them as isolated culture traits, endeavored to chart their spatial distributions and relative time sequences. Ackerknecht, largely in the 1940s, built on Rivers by conceiving both belief and practice as components of a people's medical pattern and attempted to account for the latter in terms of its functional and historical linkages with the larger culture-whole.

Although Ackerknecht's theoretical contribution dwarfed those of his predecessors, the orientations of Rivers, Clements, and Ackerknecht shared certain important similarities. Each of the three viewed primitive and modern medicine in dichotomous terms, conceived the former as essentially magical or religious, focused on it to the virtual exclusion of modern or "rational" medicine, and dealt with it in conceptually static terms.

Paul's model, in the 1950s, ignored Clements but represented both continuity with and departure from the approaches of Rivers and Ackerknecht. Paul proceeded cumulatively from Rivers by viewing health-related belief and practice as part of culture and also utilized Ackerknecht's postulates regarding the cultural patterning of medical elements and their functional interrelationships with other parts of the cultural totality. However, Paul diverged from his predecessors in accommodating their approaches to a system-model and was thereby able to eliminate the conceptual gulf between primitive and modern medicine and to deal with problems of change. At the same time, Paul followed the antecedent workers in holding relatively constant factors of biology and environmental exigency and in limiting his parameters to cultural variables.

The final orientation reviewed here, an ecological approach involving cultural and biological parameters, differs from previous orientations in several respects. Whereas earlier approaches were derived from concepts in social-cultural anthropology and the social sciences, the ecological model, by contrast, owes its basic lineaments to revolutionary theoretical syntheses in the biological sciences, specifically in evolutionary biology. Moreover, the most important initial contributions based on this orientation have been made not by social-cultural anthropologists but by workers interested in biological and human-evolutionary problems.

This approach departs strikingly from previous models in that it comprehends biologic variables, viewing health and disease (whether as dependent or independent variables) as expressions of dynamic relationships between populations, their cultures, and their environments. Thus, the scope of the ecological model includes societies *and* populations, the behavior of human groups *and* of microbiota, perceptions of the environment *and* primary environmental features, definitions of disease *and* disease itself, ethnomedicine (and traditional medical systems) *and* modern medicine.

At the same time, the ecological orientation enjoys definite continuity with and builds on preceding approaches. It accommodates Rivers' fundamental insight that medical beliefs and practices are part of culture. It even resurrects Clements' use of the single trait as a unit of study and comparison but on a more viable conceptual and methodological basis. It incorporates Ackerknecht's emphasis on the cultural patterning of medical belief and behavior and the functional interdependence of medicine with other parts of the total culture. And it embodies Paul's system approach and interest in change. However, previous insights are accommodated within a new framework. To be sure, cultural variables are seen to count, and to count heavily, but in terms of their interplay with biologic factors in multivariate ecological systems.

# 5 Medicine as an Ethnographic Category: The Gimi of the New Guinea Highlands

## *Leonard B. Glick*

The theorists whose contributions were discussed by Wellin in the preceding chapter were concerned in one way or another with some of the theoretical and conceptual problems of medical anthropology. But none was concerned, at least in his published writings, with methodological problems. In this paper Leonard Glick addresses himself to a fundamental methodological question: how does the ethnographer, so often castigated in the past by medical anthropologists for neglecting medical features of cultures, approach the problem of categorizing this order of data? This requires the assumption that any approach will have to be applicable not to a unique medical system but to *all* so that cross-cultural research and analysis may be done according to consistent criteria and a common baseline, and therefore be truly transculturally comparative. In seeking to organize his own data on the medicine and medical system of the Gimi of the New Guinea Highlands the author "attempts to find a middle road between the requirements of ethnology and the strictures of the ethnoscience approach to ethnography." He concludes that the proper ethnographic study of medical systems may be operationalized best by identifying the loci of power and the ways by which it is distributed, handled, controlled, manipulated, resisted, and experienced as it relates to ideas and behavior about illness. Whether or not one agrees with this approach, the author is making, it seems to me, a critical (if obvious to some) statement: to analyze and understand a viable, functioning medical—or any other cultural—system, one needs to use both the *etic* ("objective," imposed by the observer) and *emic* ("subjective," imposed by the culture's practitioners) approaches. Another application of the emic method is found in Charles Frake's paper on the diagnostic system of a Philippine society in Chapter 20 of this book.

... Introducing the term "medicine" into an ethnography entails certain methodological considerations. First, there is the question of whether one has arrived at a definition of "medicine," and

Reprinted with abridgments and with changes by the author from Leonard B. Glick, 1967, "Medicine as an Ethnographic Category: The Gimi of the New Guinea Highlands," *Ethnology*, **6**:31–56, with permission of the author and *Ethnology: An International Journal of Cultural and Social Anthropology*.

an ethnographic method corresponding to that definition, applicable not only to the data at hand but perhaps to a number of other medical systems as well. Second, and closely tied to the preceding, there is the larger question of whether the assumptions underlying any such definition are still acceptable in anthropology—in other words, whether it is still feasible to try to establish ethnographic categories for which one claims even partial cross-cultural validity.

The second question may be answered immediately. Although this paper is confined to a single cultural domain, it is predicated on what would seem to be the truism that generalizations in any ethnographic domain are impossible unless one ventures definitions comprehensive enough to apply to a number of individual situations. This is not to deny the principle that one should present a people's world as nearly as possible in their own terms, even though it seems plain that any attempt to formulate cross-cultural categories must begin by compromising that principle. In brief, it must be made clear from the start that the paper attempts to find a middle road between the requirements of ethnology and the strictures of the ethnoscience approach to ethnography. It aims to achieve, for a single ethnographic domain, a method offering a measure of ethnological promise with minimal sacrifice of ethnographic (i.e., "ethnoscientific") fidelity. Put simply, the question it seeks ultimately to answer is: In an ethnography, what should be the subject of a chapter entitled "Medicine"?

In many ethnographies "medicine" is implicitly defined according to Western criteria, with the result that all sorts of seemingly irrelevant, contradictory, and paradoxical observations intrude. One is confronted, for example, with so-called medicines that have nothing to do with illness, that may in fact be used to cause illness (cf. Nadel 1954:132ff). One reads of curers who cause illness as often as they cure it (hence the term "witch-doctor"); indeed at times a man may cure the very illness he has caused. One finds only occasional associations of particular illnesses and treatments, the more common premise being that whatever cures, cures everything. And so on, until the paucity of meaningful correspondences is so obvious that the ethnographer is reduced to placing many of his key terms—medicine, treatment, doctor, diagnosis—in quotation marks. Related to this is the frequent practice of collecting medicinal substances for pharmacological analysis, to ascertain whether or not their use passes inspection before the court of Western rationalism.

Moreover, although it seems reasonable to expect that responses to illness (treatments) would be the logical outcome of ideas about illness (diagnoses), seldom does one find this relation spelled out; it is not made apparent that ideas and action are complementary facets of a cultural system. Treatments in particular are often presented as though they were a phenomenon unto themselves. This failure to think about medicine as a coherent cultural system is related to uncertainty about its ontological status, hence about its place in an ethnography. I have in mind especially the relationship between medicine and religion; one appears to be part of the other (cf., for example, Nadel 1954: ch. v; Murphy 1958: ch. iii), or closely related to the other (Field 1937), although everyone knows that whereas some treatments are plainly associated with supernatural causes and magical cures, others seem incontestably empirical and down-to-earth.

## MEDICINE, RELIGION, AND THE IDEA OF POWER

As a start toward resolution of these problems, I suggest that we abandon conventional ideas about "medicine" and phrase our initial question as: What is a medical system? And for the time being I would answer this with a simple working definition: A medical system is a patterned set of ideas and practices having to do with illness. If this sounds so straightforward as to be disappointing, it should be noted that its validity hinges on how one defines "illness," on whether one can demonstrate patterned relationships, and on whether one can isolate a system or subsystem having to do with illness and with nothing else.

To employ the definition only as an opening wedge, it is common knowledge that, in many cultures, ideas and practices relating to illness are for the most part inseparable from the domain of religious beliefs and practices. Illnesses are said to be caused by gods, ghosts, angry ancestors, demons, spirits, and other so-called supernatural beings; or they may be attributed to human beings who are in some way able to mobilize unusual powers— witches, sorcerers, evil shamans. Likewise, curing may involve visions, guardian spirits, invocations, sacrifices, manipulation of sacred objects, and so on. The association is by no means alien to our society; Christian Science and the many forms of faith healing are all predicated on

59

the essential interdependence of medical practice and religious belief. It would appear, then, that we must think about how and where "medicine" fits into "religion." To reduce the question to practical terms: In an ethnography of a religious system, where does the description of the medical system belong; and how does it relate to the remainder?

The answer, as I see it, depends on whether one can single out some aspect of the total domain of religious ideas as crucial to the lesser domain comprising ideas about illness. What we require, in other words, is an idea around which a specific kind of ethnographic information can be organized—an idea more comprehensive and less culture-bound than, say, "the supernatural," one that will make it possible to meet standards of ethnographic fidelity without sacrificing all possibility of ethnological comparison.

I suggest that these requirements are most adequately met by the idea of *power*—not diffuse unattached power, but power existing as a manifest attribute of persons and of objects in their environment. I am aware that in an imprecise sense this concept has been part of anthropology since at least the time of Codrington (1891), but I am proposing that we reassess it. First of all, there is no need, it seems to me, for becoming entangled in arguments about what particular words—Polynesian *mana* or Algonkian *manitu*—"really mean." Recently, both Hallowell (1960:44–45), supporting Radin (1957:12–13), and Evans-Pritchard (1965:110), citing Firth (1940) and others, have reasserted that, however these terms are translated, it is fallacious to equate them with ideas of diffuse power. We may accept this particular argument as settled; indeed, if this has any consequences for the present discussion, it is supportive of the point of view I am developing. In any event, attempts at ethnological comparison of ideas must begin with the premise that particular words in particular places cannot serve as more than guides or clues; whatever ideas an ethnologist compares must transcend definitions of individual words. Second, we need not become involved in discourses on religious ontology; we need not be concerned with whether power or any other idea is the "essence" of religion (cf. Van der Leeuw 1938), at the "threshold" of religion (cf. Marett 1914), or the essential "dynamic" in anyone's world view (cf. Wax and Wax 1964, Goldenweiser 1922:200–201). I am willing that it be considered simply as a heuristic device that may advance our ability to generalize about "medicine" with minimal distortion of ethnographic detail.

Where power resides in a particular sociocultural system is a question for the ethnographer to answer. Obviously the answers will not be the same everywhere, but that is where comparison enters in. Likewise, how power is controlled—how it may be mobilized, counteracted, neutralized, or otherwise resisted—will also vary cross-culturally; again, that is what one compares. But these unavoidable (indeed, from the ethnologist's viewpoint, indispensable) variations in belief and practice must be organized at a level of generality sufficient to make comparison feasible. As I shall eventually try to demonstrate in this paper, fitting specific ethnographic information into a framework centered on the idea of power makes it possible to present potentially comparable data without submerging ethnographic detail or violating the canons of the culture in question. Even where people have no word for power or do not discuss events in this frame of reference, the ethnographer is not precluded from using the concept as a means to ordering information and relating theory and practice. Here I am thinking of power as an ethnographic category comprising more than just medical beliefs and practices; but for the ethnography of medical systems in particular this approach would, I believe, represent an advance on the great bulk of studies which beg the question altogether by implicitly equating "medicine" with what Western physicians do.

How does this work out in practice? To begin, the ethnographer, whether or not the medical system is his main concern, will be interested, on the one hand, in people's ideas about loci of power and, on the other, in their ways of controlling it. Specifically, he will need to answer the following questions. In this particular society, who or what is said to be powerful—potentially either beneficial or harmful, or both? How is this power controlled? Can one, for instance, mobilize nonhuman sources of power to serve human purposes? Can harmful sources be effectively resisted or overcome? Further specific questions come to mind, but all of them can be subsumed under two fundamental headings: locus and control. One must learn where people believe power to reside or inhere; and one must learn — how they endeavor to put it to their own uses. Note that this information will not necessarily relate only to illness or the medical system; it may have to do with agriculture, aspects of social control, and so on. But if, for the time being, we concentrate on the possibilities of such an approach for the study of the medical system alone, we find that answers to questions about locus and control correspond to what are ordinarily signified by the terms diagnosis and treatment. A diagnosis involves ideas about sources of disease-causing power, and treatment involves attempts to overcome that power.

## DIAGNOSIS: IDEAS ABOUT CAUSES OF ILLNESS

A diagnosis is a kind of classification: a diagnostic statement about a condition declares it to be an illness and assigns it to a particular category of illnesses. Since diagnoses are classification, we may expect to find diagnostic systems differing in two respects. First, they may comprehend different categories; they may recognize different kinds of illness and may group them in a variety of ways. Second, they may not all employ the same criteria; that is to say, from the total array of signs and symptoms that might be taken as evidence for significant illness (with some emphasis on "significant"), people may differ in what they select for attention and in how much weight they assign to one kind of evidence as against another. Therefore, one must keep several questions in mind. First, in this culture what constitutes an illness? Second, what kinds of illness are recognized? And, finally, what criteria underlie diagnosis?

In answer to the first question, an illness is any situation evoking a response that can be identified as part of the medical system. A fuller definition of "medical system" must be developed as we go along; here it will suffice to note that an ethnographer who concentrates exclusively on what he considers to be illness may emerge thoroughly confused if (as is likely to be the case) his subjects' ideas differ sharply from his own. Subtle considerations enter here. Thus apparent agreement or disagreement about whether something is an illness may have to be rephrased as agreement or disagreement about whether it is a significant illness, for people often distinguish plainly between illnesses having significant causes and demanding cooperative responses from the sick individual's social group and what might better be labeled "ailments"—conditions having no significant cause and requiring no treatment other than what might be called "remedies" (cf. Nadel 1954:145–146). Once ailments have been identified in a particular culture, I would exclude them and their remedies from consideration as part of the medical system proper. If, for example, an infected insect bite is looked upon as purely the concern of

the individual, as having no socially significant cause, and as requiring no treatment other than a leaf plaster or perhaps just patience, I would not call it illness and would not include matters relating to it in a chapter on medicine. This argument should become clearer as we proceed.

The second and third questions must be answered together because, in contrast to Western medical thought, the most important fact about an illness in most medical systems is not the underlying pathological process but the underlying cause. This is such a central consideration that most diagnoses prove to be statements about causation, and most treatments, responses directed against particular causal agents. To be more explicit, any diagnostic statement about illness may take into consideration three dimensions, which I call evidence, process, and cause. Each dimension may support a system, or part of a system, of diagnostic terms. I would argue that the third is always present as a critical consideration and, moreover, is of central importance to comparative studies.

*Evidence* is whatever is taken as empirical indication of the existence of an illness. It is what our physicians call "signs and symptoms"; but in Western medicine signs and symptoms are never in themselves diagnoses, they are only clues to diagnosis. Lung cancer or lobar pneumonia, for example, may both cause coughing, but they are not formally grouped together, at least by physicians, as "coughing illnesses."

*Process*, or what is actually happening to produce evidence of illness, is the local concern in Western medicine. Pathology, the study of disease processes, is the foundation of our system of medical classification; illnesses are grouped together because they are understood to represent related pathological processes. Identification of these processes is for the most part dependent, of course, on the technology, investigative capacities, and, most important, cognitive orientation characteristic of modern medical science. To our way of thinking, then, pathological process is the fundamental dimension of illness; but it is often precisely this dimension that other medical systems bypass altogether.

*Cause*, the third dimension in diagnosis, is the one to which I want to draw particular attention. When a Western physician establishes a cause for an illness, this becomes part of his diagnosis, supplementary (although not necessarily secondary) to the statement about process: e.g., lobar pneumonia (process) due to *Diplococcus pneumoniae*

61

(a bacterial cause), or cerebrovascular hemorrhage (process) due to hypertensive cardiovascular disease (a physiological cause, but itself a process with determinable causes). Other cultures also have ideas about the causes of illness, but they bear no resemblance to these. The ethnographer who asks what causes illnesses is not likely to hear about bacteria or disordered physiology: instead he hears about competition, jealousy, greed, and lust; witches, sorcerers, and demons; mothers' brothers and grandfathers recently deceased. In brief, whereas in Western medicine causation has no essential relationship to socio-cultural context, in most other medical systems causation and context are so intimately linked as to be the ethnographer's principal concern. Moreover, in the absence of understanding of disease processes, diagnosis may resolve into conclusions about causation inferred from evidence; that is, the dimension of process may be overlooked altogether, or it may be relegated to strictly secondary significance. In any event, in contrast to our own medical system, in such systems as we are now discussing a statement about process can never be more than a partial diagnosis, whereas a statement about causation may stand alone.

Thus the ultimate significance of illness in folk medical systems is so much a part of the victim's socio-cultural identity and experience that a diagnosis cannot be made or understood in any other terms. Causes may turn out to be as invisible as viruses, but never as impersonal. Instead, illnesses are caused by *agents* who in some way bring their powers to bear against their victims. Such agents may be human, "superhuman" (Spiro 1966:91), or nonhuman; but always they are conceived as willful beings, who act not indifferently but in response to consciously perceived personal motives. For this reason it is misleading to cite "disease object intrusion" as a cause of illness on a par with "sorcery" (Clements 1932; cf. Caudill 1953:772). Sorcerers are *efficient* causes of disease—agents whose actions are explainable. Disease objects are *instrumental* causes; sorcerers may employ them in producing illness, but it is sorcerers and their motives, not the objects they insert, that require ethnographic explanation (cf. Hallowell 1935).

In line with our theme, it may be noted now that power may also reside in plants, artifacts, or objects of any sort (again it is for the ethnographer to discover specific loci), and that when a sorcerer uses such objects, e.g., a "poisonous" packet combining plant and animal materials with human exuviae, he is tapping this power. The distinction drawn by Evans-Pritchard (1937:21, 387) between witchcraft and sorcery calls attention to the difference between persons possessing inherent power to harm—witches—and those who harm by tapping outside power—sorcerers.

Soul loss (another of Clements' "disease concepts"), whether spontaneous or attributable to an agent, involves loss of vital internal power; but the result is the same, and, as will be seen, the same concepts of treatment apply.

An instrumental cause is what is done or what is used; an efficient cause, who does it or uses it. The latter, the agents of illness, are, with a few arguable exceptions, persons; they are part of the same socio-cultural system as the sick individual, and they demand consideration in this wider context. Gaining an understanding of why they act, of what induces them to bring on illnesses, leads the ethnographer beyond the medical system proper and into the realm of *ultimate* causes—kinship and political relations, property and inheritance disputes, jealousy, envy, rancor, and spite.

## TREATMENT: RESPONSES TO ILLNESS

It will be apparent to anyone who reads ethnographies that the number of treatments people employ is virtually infinite, so that unless one imposes some form of organization on the plain ethnographic facts, the ethnology of systems of treatment resolves into little more than "comparative" lists of potions and ointments. But there are more appealing possibilities. As a first step, I suggest that we put aside for a moment the tabulation of botanical remedies and ask whether people's responses to illness everywhere are perhaps formally, even though not substantively, comparable. I think it can be shown that treatments are formally comparable, by continuing along the line of thought we have now established. Treatments are responses to illness reflecting ideas expressed in diagnostic statements about illness. If diagnoses are statements about malevolent sources of power, we may expect that treatments will be designed in some way to restore the "balance of power" between antagonist and victim. This presents two possibilities; either one tries to weaken the antagonist, or one tries to strengthen the victim. (Often, of course, people try both.)

First, we may consider attempts to weaken, neutralize, or eliminate malevolent sources of power. These might be called "negatively directed," in that they are intended to negate the powers of antagonists or of the objects and substances they control. The patient may not even be present, for treatment is here conceived as essentially a struggle on his behalf against external forces. For example, a curer may magically retrieve and destroy a packet in which a sorcerer has combined poisons with his victim's refuse. Or he may remove from his patient's body a poisonous object which a sorcerer has inserted. The sufferer's kinsmen and friends may perform rituals of invocation, perhaps accompanied by sacrifice, asking or ordering a ghost, a god, or a demon to cease torturing its victim. Homeopathic principles may be employed: The Gimi sometimes leave tasty food parcels where vicious disease-causing forest trolls are likely to nibble them; the sick individual then eats the remains of the parcel and is thereby "immunized" against the powers of his antagonist. The list might be extended, but the same point would remain: such treatments are ways of opposing harmful sources of power.

In contrast, a second class of treatments is "positively directed" in that it comprises attempts to augment or restore the personal power of the victim himself. The foremost representative of this kind of treatment is the consumption of medicines. Ethnographers seem uncomfortable with this word; often they enclose it in quotes, apparently to indicate that what is being called "medicine" is not really medicine (cf. Middleton and Winter 1963:3). In this paper the term means any substance used as part of a response to illness in the expectation that some of its power will augment that of the patient. Note that this definition restricts medicine to the medical system but does not remove the possibility that the same or similar substances may at other times be applied to any number of situations having something to do with power but not with illness, e.g., improving an arrow's effectiveness or stimulating the growth of crops.

Medicines are often plants or parts of plants. But by now it should be evident that efforts to link up particular plants with particular illnesses may prove futile, for people are not unlikely to take the common-sense view that if a substance is therapeutic for one illness it is probably therapeutic for another. (Think of our ideas about vitamins, tonics, chicken broth, and tea.) An adequate ethnographic statement on this point might resolve, then, into the simple assertion that many plants are potential sources of therapeutic power. The plants should, of course, be identified by native names and taxonomic domains (Conklin 1962), and also botanically identified if possible, but it is

essential to add that there may not be a finite number of items to be discovered, and that a complete record of the native "pharmacopoeia" may be misleading if people are using plants with uninhibited catholicity and have only vague notions about the value of particular plants for particular illnesses.

Plants are, of course, not the only sources of medicine. Flesh, blood, fat, pigments, fumes, and ritually empowered substances or objects of any sort may all be eaten, drunk, inhaled, rubbed, or blown into and onto the body in the quest for restored health. An important source of power is the shaman or curer himself. He may rub or massage his patient, blow breath or smoke on him, or manipulate his body—all practices designed to impart power. These same persons, as is well known, may become sorcerers when offended. This is not a reversal of role; it is simply another way of using power.

In summary, the second class of treatments includes all procedures designed to strengthen the victim and increase his personal capacity to resist whatever or whoever is afflicting him. Just as diagnosis is understandable as ideas about malevolent sources of power and how they make people ill, treatment is understandable as a reflection of ideas about how benevolent sources can be mobilized to make them well again.

## THE GIMI MEDICAL SYSTEM

To illustrate how all this works out in practice, I shall now describe in some detail a medical system known to me at first hand, that of the Gimi, of the Eastern Highlands of New Guinea. The Gimi are horticulturalists and pig raisers living in the relatively isolated Labogai subdistrict south and southwest of Mount Michael (see map in Watson 1964:307). They reside in villages and hamlets, loosely grouped into communities but essentially autonomous, strung out along the ridges and sides of the steep mountains which dominate the environment. Villages are ideally the homes of patrilineal, patrilocal descent groups, but in fact there is considerable moving about, and, as elsewhere in the Highlands, residence emerges as the key to social organization (Langness 1964). Relations among villages comprise all there is of political organization; from the viewpoint of any one village, other villages are the homes of either consanguineal kin, affinal and avuncular kin, or enemies. These relations shift over time, so that today's enemies may be tomorrow's affines. But the day-to-day life of a Gimi man is predicated on the assumption that social identity and social relations are timeless and ineradicable; he himself is loyal to his home village to the point of fierce chauvinism and is ready to believe anything about men in other villages.

Prior to the imposition of Australian control less than fifteen years ago, intervillage fighting was endemic and seems to have been heartily enjoyed. Now everyone is formally at peace, but basic attitudes have not changed; men still look upon the residents of other villages, including their distant or putative consanguines, affines, and matrilateral kin, as people to be manipulated, exploited when possible, and actively opposed whenever the home village's interests are in the balance (cf. Read 1954:22; Berndt 1964). These elementary aspects of Gimi social life are the essential background to Gimi medicine (cf. Glick 1963).

### Gimi Diagnosis

How do the Gimi diagnose illness? First, it must be noted that many afflictions that seem on first consideration to belong in this discussion are what I prefer to call ailments, and are thus not part of the medical system as defined in this paper. For example, sprains, fractures, minor burns, skin ulcers, rashes, infected insect bites, and so on, all elicit some response among the Gimi at least some of the time; they may have names denoting what I have called evidence and perhaps, in a limited sense, process; but nothing that is said or done about such conditions suggests that people attribute them to identifiable causes. "Chance" or "accident" are the only causes I could cite in this connection, but these are not Gimi concepts and have no place in a Gimi ethnography. I conclude, therefore, that ailments— relatively minor and temporary afflictions lacking significant socio-cultural antecedents or consequences—are a separate category of experience in Gimi life, standing in contrast to true illnesses, which have named socio-culturally relevant causes and require culturally defined and socially mediated responses. The descriptive account that follows is concerned only with illness in this strict sense.

Gimi diagnostic statements center on the premise (so integral to their world view as not to receive overt expression) that what matters most about an illness is its cause. Although one encounters names for some illnesses that seem to refer principally to evidence or perhaps, in a loose sense, to processes, the foremost consideration in any illness, named or not, is always the same: Who or what brought this on? In trying to answer this question, the Gimi make an implicit distinction between severe (*adabu*) illnesses and those marked by an element of the weird or peculiar (*neki*). The great majority of severe illnesses are attributed to sorcerers (of whom there are two kinds, "poison sorcerers," *rubeseke bana*, and "assault sorcerers," *rukabi bana*), while the great majority of peculiar illnesses are attributed to vicious little troll-like creatures called *nekina*, "weird beings."

Two infrequently encountered exceptions are convulsive illnesses and insanity. The former are caused by creatures called *amora bana*, "demonic beings." The word *bana*, which it will be noted also appears in the terms for sorcerers, is most simply translated "man" (or "men"), and for this reason I include convulsive illnesses with sorcery-caused illnesses in the category of severe illnesses attributable to human (*bana*) or human-like antagonists. Conversely, insanity fits appropriately into the category of peculiar (*neki*) illnesses. A mentally disturbed or psychotic person is called *neki bana* and is said to be ill because a ghost (*kore*) has entered his body and interfered with his capacity to behave sensibly and respond appropriately. Table 1 summarizes the above information in the form of a simple paradigm for Gimi diagnosis.

**Table 1** Paradigm for Gimi Diagnosis

| Evidence | Cause (Agents) |
| --- | --- |
| *Severe Illness* | *Human Antagonists* |
| Insidious and tenacious | "Poison sorcery" |
| Violent and bizarre | "Assault sorcery" |
| Convulsions | "Demonic beings" |
| *Peculiar Illness* | *Nonhuman Antagonists* |
| Deformity, destructive lesions, severe illness in children | "Weird beings" |
| Insanity | "Ghosts" |

*Severe Lingering Illness: Poison Sorcery.* Most severe illnesses are attributed to sorcery. In this domain, however, there are two possibilities: some illnesses are due to "poison sorcery" (*rubesekena*), others to "assault sorcery" (*rukabina*). Poison sorcery is associated with illnesses that are marked by an insidious onset, perhaps seeming even trivial at first but then proving to be tenacious, progressive, and eventually crippling or fatal. Such illnesses are called *kio*, "lingering illness." There are special names for its more noteworthy varieties, not necessarily mutually exclusive since they refer to both causes and evidence. ...

What a sorcerer is believed to have done bears, of course, on how his victim is treated, but a more important consideration, especially if the latter dies, is placing blame for the deed. It is always assumed that the sorcerer is a resident of some other village, usually one in a state of chronic enmity with that of the victim. He is seldom if ever identified by name, and indeed people disagree as to what kind of man is most likely to be responsible; some maintain that only puny second-rate men (*foipa bana*, "worthless men; *aru bana*, "shabby men") would ever stoop to sorcery, while others say that it is the most forceful and impressive men (*fakeke bana*, "competent men") who know best how to kill other men. But the sorcerer's individual identity hardly matters anyway; what matters is the identity of the village, his own or another, that induced him to carry out the act. The Gimi seldom if ever conceive of sorcery as an act of personal vengeance; rather it is planned aggression by one village against another, sometimes for revenge, sometimes simply to weaken the opposition by eliminating a valued man or woman.

(It may be noted here that, with a very few questionable exceptions, sorcerers are always males, and that there are no witches of either sex. I think this is because women are for the most part believed to be too ignorant, erratic, and irresponsible to control forces as momentous as those involved in sorcery. They may, however, be sorcerers' victims, for as workers and bearers of children they are by no means without value to their husbands and the men of their husbands' villages.)

*Violent Illness: Assault Sorcery.* The term *rukabina*, literally translatable as "violence," may refer to nothing more serious than a family squabble; indeed any man who enjoys fighting may be called a *rukabi bana*. But in the particular sense intended here, open assault is combined with magical actions to leave a victim both mutilated and poisoned. Because it demands boldness and aggressiveness, *rukabina* is not work for a weakling. In fact, it is said that in former times one way for young men to demonstrate their virility was by participating in these assaults, which once again took the form of aggression by one village against another. ...

*Convulsions: Demonic Beings.* Despite their name, *amora bana*, the "demonic beings" who control storms and lightning, are aloof from the realm of human relationships. People express only vague ideas about their appearance but seem to conceive them as creatures monstrous in size and capacity, indifferently destructive, and utterly unapproachable. They are said to strike their victims during lightning storms, leaving them dying or else subject to repeated convulsions thereafter. With all this power they are still mortal, for, although their bodies are never seen, in certain locations high up on mountainsides men sometimes encounter their bones. These bones (called *amora adapu*) are so potent that not every man is willing to risk taking them, but they are valuable therapeutic aids, particularly in the treatment of convulsions. Sorcerers may also use them to induce convulsions or, worse, to cause lightning to strike a victim.

*Peculiar Illnesses: Weird Beings.* The word *neki* stands for whatever is weird, peculiar, irregular, or unnatural in the Gimi world. The term *neki bana* (or *neki badaa* for a woman) may refer to anyone who is unable to perceive (*fe-*) and respond adequately to speech (*kaina*). The phrase *neki bana miri, kaina kafei*, "he is a *neki* man, he doesn't perceive [understand] speech," may refer to someone whom we would identify as either deaf, mentally defective, psychotic, or perhaps just plain foolish. In the Gimi view, all such people are in some way peculiar; normal persons are social beings, but *neki* people are in some way crippled for social roles. Animals, places, and things may also bear *neki* qualities. Frogs and lizards, for instance, are considered so ugly and disgusting as to be the model for people's ideas of what *nekina*, "weird beings," are like.

It will be remembered that *nekina* are the troll-like creatures that cause certain kinds of peculiar illnesses. Few people claim to have seen them. The evidence for their existence lies in the illnesses they cause when offended, illnesses marked by a *neki* quality that betrays their origin. Wherever land is distinguished by some topographical or vegetational peculiarity, and particularly wherever ponds and swamps are found (for in this mountainous environment, with its rushing streams and treacherous whirlpools, still waters are, in a sense, a peculiar phenomenon), *nekina* congregate and claim the location as their own. Such a place is a *neki maa*, "weird land," and everything it contains—not only the *nekina* but all other plants and animals living there, even the very soil—bears a *neki* quality spelling danger for human intruders. Trouble comes whenever someone behaves disrespectfully or arrogantly in *neki* territory, e.g., chops down a tree, pulls out a plant, kills an animal, or—even more foolishly—urinates, defecates, spits, or tosses away food scraps. If the *nekina* can get hold of some such refuse (*asakikina*), they are able to attack the offender (or more likely his or her children) through exuvial magic. Serious childhood illnesses, especially in previously healthy children, are often explained this way; a child falls ill, for instance, and its father recalls that he recently urinated in a *neki maa*.

Diseases leading to destruction or distortion of body parts are similarly explained. The story was told of a pregnant woman who chopped up and ate a snake in a *neki* place with the result that her son was born with a stump in place of one arm. Another woman removed taro from a plot of *neki* land; later some of the taro rotted, and her infant son developed a destructive disease of the genitals. A boy cut a vine growing near a pond in a *neki* locale, and as the vine grew again, the flesh over his left eye grew until it was little more than scar tissue. Children are the most frequent victims of encounters with *nekina* and *neki maa*, but adults are not altogether immune. Young men who copulate in such places, for instance, and leave semen behind, may develop fatal illnesses.

*Psychotic Behavior: Ghosts.* Men or women who are *neki* in the sense of being deaf, mentally defective, or somewhat silly are not usually considered ill, although such an affliction suddenly befalling a previously vigorous man would no doubt be looked upon as an illness with a significant cause. A *neki* person who is unquestionably ill, however, is the one who is acutely psychotic. Psychotic behavior is attributed to possession by a ghost which enters the body and sets up a whirring or buzzing noise in the victim's head so that he cannot "hear" properly (*kaina kafei*). For a few days after a death the ghost (*kore*) of the deceased wanders about in search of a weak victim, perhaps a child, whom it can carry off as company. Occasionally an adult is accosted by a ghost who flaps about and tries to carry him away, but without success. One such episode, as related to me soon afterward, was rather ludicrous and ended with the intended victim, a youth of seventeen or so, batting off his oppressor and running away. After a few days of this sort of behavior, the ghost sinks into the grave to join its corporeal counterpart, and there it remains, unable to participate in the affairs of men unless someone is unfortunate enough to be possessed. . . .

*Illness as Sanction.* A number of taboos, prohibitions, and injunctions are sanctioned by the expectation that violation will lead to illness. Boys may be told, for example, that eating certain foods in the years between initiation and adulthood will cause stunted growth, weakness, or the like. Prohibitions against contact with women are a more important case in point. Gimi men take every opportunity to express distaste for females and things feminine. There can be little question that their reactions to women are grounded in fear of contamination from menstruation, which they do not even superficially understand but associate only with a female essence, called *araka*, believed to be "in the air" when a woman menstruates. Young men and boys are warned to avoid women, especially menstruating women, lest they become scrawny, sickly, and pimply-faced. The point to be noted here is that, when illnesses actually occur, the Gimi do not turn to such explanations but think rather of causes beyond personal control—or sorcerers, *nekina, amora bana*, and ghosts. Diagnosis is a retrospective judgment. Breaches of taboo and contamination lead only to hypothetical illnesses, but what might be called prospective diagnosis; they do not explain real illnesses.

## Gimi Treatment

Gimi diagnoses are statements about causative agents based on kinds of evidence associated with each agent. In the Gimi environment these agents, and the substances they sometimes use, are loci or sources of power, in this case power applied to malevolent ends. How to resist such power—how to neutralize or destroy it, how to strengthen its victims—is the problem to which treatment must be directed. Gimi treatment techniques are ways of mobilizing, negating, or otherwise controlling power.

*Medicines.* We may begin with the "positive" aspects of treatment, with ways of strengthening sick persons, increasing their powers of resistance, through the use of medicines. The Gimi attribute therapeutic potential to many more substances than we would ordinarily call medicines—not only expectable items like leaves, barks, and other parts of plants, but also meat, blood, fat, salt, tobacco smoke, pandanus oil, human bones, and more. With a few exceptions these are not categorically related to particular illnesses, and never are they said to be cures for specific disease processes; they are substances with the power to strengthen and renew anyone who is ill. The curative properties of most plants, for instance, are so nonspecific, and so much a matter of individual judgment, that it would be quite impossible to compile a finite list of

Gimi "medicinal plants." ... To try to explain their use by pharmacological analysis—to determine whether or not they are "really" therapeutic—would be to leave the principles of Gimi medicine far behind.

The same can be said for all other medicines. Although leaves and bark may be consumed alone, they more often form part of a therapeutic meal (very likely to be shared by the patient's kinsmen and friends) consisting also of pork, edible greens, salt, and ginger, all of which (with the probable exception of the greens) are credited with therapeutic properties of their own. Pork and pig blood, for instance, are full of the power of pigs, which are said to have *iuna*, "vital powers," similar to those of men (see *aona* below). ...

*Counteracting Malevalent Power.* In addition to treatments designed to strengthen an individual's capacity to resist illness, a considerable proportion of Gimi treatments are primarily intended to weaken whoever or whatever is causing the illness. In this class of treatments we encounter four kinds of activity: ritual retrieval and destruction of exuvial sorcery packets, disease object extraction, procedures employing homeopathic principles to neutralize the power of "demonic beings" (*amora bana*) and "weird beings" (*nekina*), and ritual injunctions to combat unidentified agents causing individual or epidemic illnesses.

Although no one among the Gimi is a full-time specialist in curing, and although curing is in a sense the province of every mature person, when someone falls seriously ill and sorcery seems the most likely diagnosis, people turn for help to certain specially endowed men called *aona bana*, "men of power," who are credited with curative abilities considerably beyond the ordinary. The word *aona* might be translated "soul," "shadow," "vital force," or "familiar spirit," for it has each of these meanings depending on context. But *aona* is not exclusively the property of men, for animals, plants, rocks, whirlpools, lightning, and a host of other phenomena are at times credited with a vital component. When someone dreams of an animal or object in the natural environment, it is an *aona* that has become manifest. Having once experienced such encounters, individuals anticipate repeated contact, in dreams, throughout life. Mystical bonds are thereby established between the *iuna* (plural of *aona*) of humans and those of their nonhuman familiars, such that the qualities of one are transmitted to the other. A man who has encountered the *aona* of a wild pig, for example, can be identified (for he would not announce this himself) by his physical endurance and by his speed and elusiveness in battle.

Men turn to their *iuna* for information about puzzling situations or forthcoming events, working themselves into a trance-like state by smoking quantities of tobacco or chewing a special bark (*Himantandra belgraeveana*). An occasional individual has an *aona* of power sufficiently beyond the ordinary to enable him to combat sorcerers and other agents of disease, and in recognition of this special capacity such men are singled out as *aona bana*. This term might be translated "man with a powerful familiar spirit" or "man with superior vital force," but I think it is not a distortion to translate *aona* simply as "power" and to call the man who cures a "man of power. ..."

Disease object extraction is an infrequent mode of treatment, applied mostly to illnesses of questionable severity and not necessarily requiring an *aona bana*. Attention seems to be directed entirely to the object itself, and only in a limited sense can the procedure be interpreted as a contest between rival powers. In the community where I worked, in fact, the man who was said to be especially talented at disease object extraction was a mild ineffectual soul who would certainly not be considered as *aona bana*, and I doubt that anyone would have turned to him for treatment of a serious illness.

A number of interesting treatment procedures employ homeopathic principles in attempts to neutralize the malevolent power of "demonic beings" (*amora bana*), "weird beings" (*nekina*), and "weird places" (*neki maa*). Lightning is demonic power in its extreme form and is said to be under the control of the *amora bana*. The association between lightning and *amora bana* on the one hand, and convulsions on the other, is not clearly formulated, but, as noted earlier, the general belief seems to be that convulsive episodes are evidence that the victim has been struck (*fa-*, to strike or kill) by a demonic being. The treatment for convulsions is thus aimed at neutralizing *amora bana* power through homeopathic principles, by feeding a patient, or applying to his body, substances bearing some relationship to *amora bana* themselves. The most valuable items in this regard are their "bones," the aforementioned *amora adapa*. In appearance these are not unlike the bones of ordinary men, but they contain vestiges of the power of their demonic owners. In the past a man could increase his fighting abilities by tying an *amora* bone to his war shield, but nowadays the bones are valued principally for their medicinal properties. Bits of the bone may be added to a therapeutic meal (pork, medicinal plants, etc.), or the bone may be immersed in water which is then drunk by the victim or (if he is unable to drink) poured over him. ...

Similar principles emerge in the treatment of illnesses caused by trespassing or misbehaving in a "weird place" (*neki maa*). The patient's kinsmen bind bits of meat or sugar cane and some therapeutic leaves into a small packet (called *mutana*, "detoxifier") designed to seduce the *nekina* into participating in the cure of its own victim. They take the packet to the *neki maa* near where the violation occurred, and lay it at the edge of a pond in the hope that the *nekina* will encounter it. If the venture is successful, they return later to find their bait partly nibbled away; the *nekina* has in effect left behind his own refuse and with it some of his own essence. The men blow smoke over the bait, presumably to lessen the danger of contact with something now so intimately connected with an agent of illness. Then it is brought to the victim, to be eaten or rubbed over his body, thereby enabling him partly to incorporate the very power that made him ill.

A *neki* plot of land is itself credited with power to cause illness, as is evidenced by treatment procedures aimed at neutralizing the actual site of a violation. One such procedure consists simply of pouring pig blood over the site. An elderly village headman was said to have shot an arrow into a tree in a *neki maa* when he was a young man, and to have fallen ill soon thereafter. His father poured blood of a freshly killed pig over the tree, and the victim recovered. (Note that the young man sat off to the side, so to speak, while his father and a pig fought the battle for him.)

A related technique combines the principles of homeopathic counteraction and positive therapy: water collected from a *neki maa* pond is placed in a ceremonial flute and poured over the sick individual. Flutes are objects of central importance in Gimi ritual; they symbolize all that Gimi men hold dear: continuity, social solidarity, male dominance (Glick 1963:81–86; cf. Read 1952). Used in a medical context, they transmit some of their own therapeutic power along with that of the homeopathic pond water.

To warn away trespassers from privately owned land, Gimi men sometimes drape pieces of a fern called *fuba* in the branches of trees. The name of the fern and the term for a trespass warning are the same; one says, *fuba arome arai*, "he cut and placed a warning." The same phrase appears in reference to certain kinds of treatments designed to combat

unknown agents of illness by ritual warnings and injunctions to release their victims. ...

During May, 1962, several children died in an epidemic in the Gimi community of Mekino (Mengino). To combat this visitation the people erected a barrier, again called *fuba*, across the main path leading into the community. This was plainly a symbolic device: three poles entwined with leaves (unfortunately not identified) and tied to form a rickety squared arch. People explained: "We made and placed a warning" (*fuba ome maraune*). ...

## Responses to Death: Divination and Revenge

An illness ending in death, particularly that of an able adult male, is a genuine blow to his village. The survivors, convinced that only a sorcerer could have brought on such a catastrophe, and that ultimate responsibility rests, therefore, with the men who instigated the sorcery, feel it incumbent on themselves to identify the guilty party and gain revenge. Prior to Australian hegemony this meant warfare—killing in return, at times to the point of massacre. Now warfare is no longer possible, but there remain subtler ways of gaining satisfaction.

First, however, we need to consider the matter of identifying the responsible agents. People's thoughts turn first to their traditional enemies, and what follows is more often than not an attempt to verify suspicions that are already firmly rooted. Identification procedures are predicated on the expectation that the ghost (*kore*) of the deceased will disclose to his kinsmen the identity of his murderers, either by revealing their names, leading searchers to their village, or singling them out in groups of visitors who are invited for just that purpose. ...

Failure to visit an ostensibly friendly village after a death has occurred there is itself suggestive of guilt, so that men make a practice of appearing before suspicions have time to mature. Again this probably seldom holds true now, but in the recent past they came prepared to submit to guilt detection tests. For example, each visitor might be expected to touch the corpse's toe; should the guilty man do so, the body would twitch. (One man remarked that it might also defecate.) Or a cord might be tied from the corpse's finger to a house rafter, and each visitor expected either to loop his thumb and index finger around it or to place an extended hand just beneath it; if the cord vibrated, the jittery, and thus presumably guilty, individual might be attacked. ...

If a sorcerer and, most important, those who encouraged him to act could be identified, the obvious response was overt counteraggression. But for those who were perhaps uncertain or not strong enough to risk open attack, and nowadays for anyone who fears administrative reprisals, there are counterattack techniques that operate at long range and entail no risk. First, the sorcerer himself can be made to suffer and die by a procedure known as *kapari funa*, "stinger blowing." The *kapari* is an unidentified bush or tree bearing barbs on its stems. In *kapari funa* the barbs are burned on a low fire, then one blows the ashes into the air, whereupon they magically seek out the sorcerer and fly up into his anus. Although he may realize nothing at the time, he is from then on a stricken man; soon some form of disaster—severe injury or illness, death in a quarrel—overtakes and destroys him. Second, it was said that those who sought vengeance against all of a sorcerer's kinsmen and cohorts might shoot flaming arrows, with tufts of the dead man's hair attached, in the direction of suspected villages. Apparently the intent was not to burn a village at once but to induce the guilty village to burn in the future.

## Summary of the Gimi Medical System

The Gimi medical system has essentially nothing to do with medicine as we ordinarily understand this term, for the Gimi do not share our understanding of disease processes. When a Gimi individual falls seriously ill, people deduce from the signs and symptoms of his illness—the evidence—a probable cause, and this constitutes their diagnosis. But causation has several dimensions, not all of equal importance. First, there is the relatively minor question of how an illness was brought about (what I call the instrumental cause); then there is the much more compelling question of who was the responsible agent (the efficient cause); and finally one encounters more extensive explanations for why agents act as they do (ultimate causes), at which point one has moved beyond the realm of the medical system and into such considerations as social and political competition, intra-familial disputes, quarrels, conflicts, and crimes.

The diagnostic paradigm (Table 1) stresses efficient causes because that is what concerns the Gimi. This principle, insofar as I can judge, would also apply to the medical concepts of many or most of the people whom anthropologists study. Instrumental causes are of relatively little importance because as explanations for illness they are incomplete; they tell nothing about who acted or why. It might be added that, taken out of context and considered as "culture traits," they are entirely

inadequate for ethnological purposes, because they are so widespread and nonspecific as to be useless for characterizing a particular medical system or comparing it with others.

Causative agents, human or nonhuman, bring alien power to bear against their victims. Gimi treatments can all be understood as attempts to resist such power, either by tapping additional power for the victim or by neutralizing or destroying the power of his antagonist. Like most people, the Gimi look to plants especially for therapeutic help, but they depend also on substances whose potential is fully understandable only in the context of Gimi culture: the flesh, blood, and fat of pigs; water and blood poured from ceremonial flutes.

Finally, it must be emphasized that the Gimi do not face illness alone or respond to illness as a phenomenon independent of the personal identity of its victim. An illness has meaning for a community, not just for an individual, and this is what is expressed each time a man or woman's kinsmen and friends gather to establish a diagnosis or to cooperate in a treatment procedure. But the most striking social response follows death, when the survivors must decide who is ultimately responsible so that they can gain revenge. The conviction that most severe illnesses are ultimately attributable to aggression on the part of other villages is perhaps the most distinctive feature of the Gimi theory of illness, but the idea that causative agents are the central consideration in diagnosis and treatment is something that Gimi culture shares with many others.

## CONCLUSION

Although the idea of "universal categories" of culture has held little currency in anthropology in recent years, there is lately discernible some reawakening of interest in what looks very much like universal categories, albeit not under that label. For example, the introduction by Burling (1962) of the idea of maximization into economic anthropology is grounded in the conviction that one can isolate universal principles of human behavior. A parallel example is the recent definition of religion advanced by Geertz (1966:4): "a system of symbols which acts to establish powerful, pervasive, and long-lasting moods and motivations in men by formulating conceptions of a general order of existence. ..."

Work of this kind represents movement in two directions. First, long entrenched ethnographic categories are being subjected to critical examination and redefinition. The question is whether or not such categories, as conventionally defined, belong in ethnographies, and, if so, what they should contain. Second, these authors have ventured definitions that are more comprehensive, more abstract, and at the same time less rooted in Western conceptions and biases. With the accumulated wisdom of some fifty years of detailed ethnographic work by their predecessors at their command, quite a few anthropologists seem not so sensitive to the possibility of being labeled "Frazerian." Their work reveals a shift in emphasis not only toward rather bold generalizations of the kind just cited, but also toward more intensive attention to the ideas, principles, and symbolic correspondences underlying the concrete actions and behavior to which we have for a long time been adjured to confine ourselves (cf. Leach 1961; Turner 1964, 1966).

In opposition to this point of view, although seldom explicitly, anthropologists engaged in what has been called "the new ethnography" (Sturtevant 1964) have advanced the argument that ethnographic categories must be indigenously derived, that they must reflect without distortion the categories of the people whom that particular ethnography is about. ... Although it is unfashionable to dispute this position (but see Berreman 1961), it seems to me that unqualified adoption of such a course would steer us still farther from all possibility of significant accomplishments in ethnology. On one level, therefore, this paper may be read as an attempt to achieve, within the context of a single ethnographic category, a course somewhere between those associated with ethnoscience and ethnology. For the particular problem set here, I have suggested that the idea of intrinsic power—where it is found, how it is controlled—offers a focal point around which certain ethnographic materials can be organized so as to be potentially comparable. It would appear that similar themes or concepts can and should be isolated and tested for other categories.

But first and foremost this paper is intended to be read as a contribution to the ethnography of medical beliefs and practices. Compared to the sophistication and organization of ethnographic accounts of social and political systems, even of religious systems, descriptions of that body of beliefs and practices called "medicine" lag far behind. I have tried to demonstrate that by approaching this subject as a system, in which behavior reflects belief, we may be able to put ideas in order, present comparable materials, and show how a people's medicine relates to other dimensions of their experience.

How then do I suggest that we proceed in the ethnography of medical systems? By beginning with the idea of power and asking: Where in this culture are the loci of power? How is it mobilized, resisted, and otherwise controlled? How does it enter into the various domains of a people's experience, such as subsistence practices, social control, and religious belief? Finally, how do ideas about the loci and control of power relate to ideas about illness and responses to illness? The answers to this final question rightly constitute the subject matter of a chapter on "Medicine."

# II
# Paleopathology

## Disease in Early Humans and Their Societies

The study of disease and trauma in the early hominids and societies now extinct is known as *paleopathology*. Because the major—but not the only—source of evidence has been the fossilized remains of people and other animals, it is a field that from time to time has attracted the attention of both anthropologists and physicians, and sometimes their efforts have yielded inaccurate data and unwarranted conclusions and interpretations (see, for example, Calvin Wells' [1967] useful compilation of many such sins and errors). Anthropologists who would work in this area need to have clinical training as well as biological and sociocultural training, according to Wells (1964) in his excellent book summarizing some major aspects of the field, *Bones, Bodies and Disease*. This is quite acceptable but it should also be granted that physicians ought to be well grounded in anthropology, and especially in archeology and biological anthropology.

Interest in paleopathology waned between the 1920s and 1950s, but began then to accelerate and the field now draws upon a number of workers in anthropology, medicine, biology, and the related fields of geology, chemistry, and physics. In addition to Wells' book, other recent works that attempt to collect the evidence and synthesize the results in this field include Brothwell and Sandison's (1967) extensive survey, *Diseases in Antiquity*, Jarcho's (1966) survey based on a symposium, and Jannsens' (1970) small volume. Also useful is a lengthy bibliography compiled by Armelagos, Mielke, and Winter (1971). It can be expected that the quality of findings will improve rapidly with the great outpouring of effort now being invested in this important scientific enterprise. Current research is already yielding rich results, frequently utilizing teams of scientists from a variety of disciplines using complicated techniques and methodologies. Illustrative of this interdisciplinary approach is the recent report by Cockburn et al. (1975) on the extensive analysis of an Egyptian mummy, which has already yielded unexpectedly fruitful discoveries and may take as long as a decade to complete.

The major assumptions underlying the investigation of disease in extinct populations are well described by Wells (1964:17):

The pattern of disease or injury that affects any group of people is never a matter of chance. It is invariably the expression of stresses and strains to which they were exposed, a response to everything in their environment and behaviour. It reflects their genetic inheritance (which is their internal environment), the climate in which they lived, the soil that gave them sustenance and the animals or plants that shared their homeland. It is influenced by their daily occupations, their habits of diet, their choice of dwelling and clothes, their social structure, even their folklore and mythology.... Disease and injury mirror... the haps and mishaps imposed by the vagaries of life and the struggle to survive. If we seek the genetic affinities of an individual or group, details of normal anatomy and physiology are usually our most rewarding study; for the more intimate knowledge of how people have responded to the aggression of their environment pathology is a surer guide.

Paleopathology has produced a number of findings of significance to medical anthropology. Perhaps the most important of these is that most diseases that now afflict humans also menaced our earliest ancestors, and indeed most of these diseases preceded humankind, as demonstrated by evidence of our distant primate relatives. This finding also adds support to the idea of Virchow, based on microbiology, that disease is not something necessarily abnormal but an expression of life under changed or changing conditions. A recent report by a microbiologist-epidemiologist may cause an eventual qualification in the foregoing. Black (1975) presents some interesting data from anthropology and the epidemiology of infectious diseases that lead him to conclude that

Diseases that infect only man fall into two distinct categories. Those which can persist in an individual for a prolonged period are highly endemic, but those which are infectious only in the acute phase die out quickly after introduction. The suggestion is made that the latter diseases could not perpetuate themselves before the advent of advanced cultures and did not exert selective pressures on the human genetic constitution until relatively recently (Black 1975:518).

Black suggests that such factors as isolation and small populations encouraged some diseases but provided a sterile environment for others. The findings of Black and others whose work he draws upon undoubtedly will stimulate research into this important problem in the study of diseases in early human societies.

# 6 Paleopathology

## Erwin H. Ackerknecht

I have not been able to find a fully satisfactory and succinct statement within the space of a single article of the approach and major methods and findings of paleopathology. Perhaps the closest approximation to a brief treatment that explains the nature of the field, as well as the varieties of evidence, is this one by Ackerknecht written for the massive "inventory" of anthropology in 1953, *Anthropology Today*. For this reason, although it was by design cursory, I have included this still useful paper here. For discussions of recent research, methods, and methodological problems the reader is referred to the references in the introduction to

Reprinted from Erwin A. Ackerknecht, 1953, "Paleopathology," *Anthropology Today*, ed. A. L. Kroeber, University of Chicago Press, pp. 120–126, with permission of the author and the University of Chicago Press. Copyright 1953 by the University of Chicago Press.

this section. As with other aspects of medical anthropology, paleopathology contributes more than knowledge of the diseases and injuries that afflicted extinct societies. As Ackerknecht says, *"The pathology of a society reflects its general conditions and growth and offers, therefore, valuable clues to an understanding of the total society"* [his emphasis]. The two following articles by Armelagos and Cockburn are excellent examples of more recent work.

Paleopathology deals with the pathology of prehistoric animals and of man in prehistoric and nonliterate societies. The only documents at its disposal for reconstructing the pathological picture are bones, and sometimes works of art and mummies. The methods of paleopathology have been also occasionally applied with success to "historical" periods where insufficient written documents exist.

The first observations on a pathological fossil bone were published by Esper in 1774 ("sarcoma"—actually healed fracture—in the cave bear, that Job of Paleopathology). Slowly material accumulated first on animals, then on man. These studies gained great impetus in the second half of the nineteenth century, the period of Broca and Virchow. The field became a special discipline during the first thirty years of the twentieth century through the accomplishments of Sir Armand Ruffer (who introduced the name "paleopathology"), Grafton Elliot Smith, Wood Jones, H. U. Williams, Roy L. Moodie, L. Pales, and others. The latter two published treatises on paleopathology (1923 and 1930) with extensive bibliographies. The bibliography after 1930 is given by H. E. Sigerist in Appendix IV of the first volume of his *History of Medicine* (New York, 1951). This period is characterized by the successful use of such technological aids as the X-ray machine and the microscope.

The last twenty years have brought important new detailed knowledge on tumors, prehistoric tuberculosis, etc., although the work has, regrettably enough, not been carried on with the same intensity as before. The main progress during this period lies in the increasing realization that paleopathology gives more than important medical data. *The pathology of a society reflects its general conditions and growth and offers, therefore, valuable clues to an understanding of the total society.* Pioneer work in this direction has been done by Todd, Hooton, Vallois, Ad. Schultz, L. Angel, and others. We have witnessed the first steps from a paleopathology of individuals to a paleopathology of groups and societies. It is to be hoped that, when this point of view is fully assimilated, increased activity in the field will result. In the following survey of the results of this young science, emphasis will be laid on human material. Animal material will be mentioned only occasionally.

## THE BONE RECORD

### Traumatism

The first healed fractures of animals as evidenced by callus are found in Permian reptiles. A healed fracture was also found in the Neanderthal man. The evidence of healed fractures becomes very extensive in the European Neolithic and in early Egypt. That well-healed fractures alone are no proof for fracture treatment was already maintained by Baudouin and was definitely shown by Ad. Schultz's work on gibbons.

Head injuries are found in *Sinanthropus*, Neanderthal men, Cro-Magnon men, the European Neolithic, and the American pre-Columbian, especially in Peru. The latter prevalence might be due

to the use of special weapons like maces. A certain number of the Neolithic and old Peruvian trephinings were apparently provoked by skull fractures. Whether this was the sole reason for trephining is doubtful. Trephining itself is part of paleomedicine, not paleopathology, and therefore is not discussed further here.

Numerous arrowheads have been found in the European Neolithic and in pre-Columbian America, imbedded especially in vertebrae and extremities.

The famous exostosis of Dubois's *Pithecanthropus* might be of traumatic origin.

### Malformation

Evidence of dwarfism, achondroplastic and cretinistic, has been found in Egypt, in skeletons and statues. Also an anencephalic mummy has been described. The congenital perforated sternum has been observed in material stemming from Neolithic Europe and from Peru. In the same places evidence of spina bifida was discovered. Other congenital anomalies of the vertebral column have been reported from Peru. Congenital hip luxation was diagnosed in skeletons from Neolithic Europe, pre-Columbian North America, and Peru.

Congenital clubfoot (talipes equinovarus) has been found repeatedly in Egyptian mummies and works of art. G. E. Smith regarded the clubfoot of King Siptah (Nineteenth Dynasty, around 1225 B.C.) as a congenital clubfoot. Slomann interpreted it rather as an aftereffect of *poliomyelitis*. The same interpretation was given by J. K. Mitchell to the shortened femur of a mummy dated about 3700 B.C.; the deformation on the stele of the priest Ruma (Copenhagen) offers itself to the same interpretation. Rolleston diagnosed a Neolithic skeleton from Cissbury as postpoliomyelitic.

Hydrocephalus has been reported from Roman Egypt as well as copper-age Turkey, Peru, and ninth-century Germany.

### Inflammation (Nonspecific)

If we are to believe the bone record, bacterial infection was a rather early event, and the multicellular organism reacted to this as to other irritations by inflammation that is a combination of necrosis and formation of new tissue.

Periostitis ossificans was first described in Permian reptiles, later in early mammals (especially the cave bear), and eventually in Neolithic man. Osteitis is particularly often represented in the form of *sinusitis* (pre-Columbian North American, Peru, Neolithic France) and mastoiditis (pre-Columbian North American, Peru, Egypt).

The first known cases of osteomyelitis in Permian reptiles were apparently sequels to infected fractures; osteomyelitis again was very prevalent in cave bears. It is found in European Neolithic and ancient Peruvian bones.

Myositis ossificans was found to be common in fossil animals but rare in human remains.

**Specific Inflammation (Syphilis, Tuberculosis)**

The pre-Columbian existence of syphilis in either hemisphere has been debated heatedly for about four hundred years. It was hoped that paleopathology would eventually decide the question. Starting with Parrot in France in 1877 and with Joseph Jones in North America in 1876, numerous prehistoric bone lesions have been described as syphilitic. Many of these interpretations have been discarded. New suspect specimens have appeared.

There are always two great difficulties to overcome in making a definite diagnosis of pre-Columbian syphilis in a bone: (a) Is the bone actually pre-Columbian? (b) Were the bone changes actually produced by the *Spirocheta pallida* or by some other infectious agent?

The latter question seems not answerable unless a positive serological reaction or other proof of specificity can be obtained. Such proof has not been produced so far. It should always be remembered by those deciding the case on mere morphology that Virchow was able to demonstrate in the tibia of a cave bear the same changes that are usually attributed to syphilis in human bones.

H. U. Williams, who surveyed the question last in 1932, came to the conclusion that certain bones from Pecos, Paracas, Tennessee Mounds, etc., are beyond any doubt both pre-Columbian and syphilitic. These bones are morphologically strongly suggestive of syphilis. But hardly more so than, e.g., the Neolithic material from Petit Morin in the Museum of St. Germain, from Iran (Krogman), from eleventh-century Russia, from Japan (Adachi), which Williams, with the characteristic fervor of an "American-origin" partisan, disregarded. The safest conclusion seems still to give to none of these inflammatory bone changes the definite label of syphilis.

Some of these bones have meanwhile been claimed as specimens of Paget's disease (osteitis deformans).

The problem is subjectively and objectively somewhat simpler in the case of *tuberculosis*. There is at least one tuberculous affection of the bone, the so-called "Pott's disease," in the vertebral column which it is hard to mistake for any other type of infection. On the basis of numerous cases of Pott's disease the antiquity of tuberculosis seems now established in both hemispheres. Cases of Pott's disease have been described from predynastic Egypt (300 B.C.), and from the end of the third millennium in Nubia. A particularly convincing case was described by Smith and Ruffer in the mummy of a priest of Ammon (about 1000 B.C.), where the characteristic psoas abscess also was found. The finding of clay sculptures, picturing the typical hunchback in Pott's disease, reinforce these diagnoses. Tuberculous changes in the hip joints of children (dated 2700 and 1900 B.C.) have also been reported from Egypt.

Only one (controversial) case of Pott's disease has been described from the European Neolithic. Pales feels confident as to the tuberculous nature of a Neolithic hip and an ankylosed foot.

In North America not completely convincing pre-Columbian specimens of Pott's disease have been described by Whitney, Means, and Hrdlička. The findings of Hooton (Pecos) and especially of W. A. Ritchie (New York State) leave little doubt concerning the pre-Columbian existence of tuberculosis in North America. The same can be said for South America after the work of Requena and Garcia Frias. Hunchbacked clay figurines again reinforce the diagnosis in the Western Hemisphere.

A parasitism of a much cruder nature may be mentioned at this point. The hair of Egyptian as well as Peruvian mummies is frequently decorated with the eggs of lice.

**Osteoarthritis and Spondylitis**

Spondylitis is here treated together with osteoarthritis, as it is actually the osteoarthritis of the vertebral column. Osteoarthritis is not subdivided in the following into its rheumatoid and osteoarthritic forms, as this subdivision is at present primarily of clinical interest. Suffice it to say that the material reported below shows both forms of chronic arthritis. If, however, it could be shown that, as suggested by T. D. Stewart, the rheumatoid form is less prevalent in some periods and regions, this would throw an important light on the whole rheumatism problem.

Next to traumatism, arthritis is the oldest and most widespread pathological lesion reported in paleopathology. In the animal kingdom it starts with the dinosaurs of the Comanchian and is continuously found up to the present. In the hominids it has been observed everywhere since Neanderthal man. Egyptian material showing it has existed since 4000 B.C.

Spondylitis, arthritis of the vertebral column, which often transforms the finely structured vertebral column into one solid bony mass, is one of the most frequent and most extensive arthritic lesions. Spondylosis is already present in dinosaurs (*Diplodocus*) of the Secondary. The man of La Chapelle-aux-Saints, a Neanderthal, shows spondylitis of the cervicodorsal and the lumbar parts of the vertebral column. Cro-Magnon men suffered from it. Spondylitis is very frequently seen in European Neolithic, the early Egyptian, and the pre-Columbian American. An interesting feature of spondylitis is the changing seat of the lesion along the vertebral column in animals and men. Different subdivisions of the vertebral column are involved. In early man and primitives, lumbar spondylitis is frequent, while dorsal and cervical are rare (the ancient Egyptians are an exception, with frequent dorsal involvement). In modern man cervical involvement is often found. As similar differences exist between the wild horse and the riding horse (the former shows more dorsal, the latter more lumbar, involvement) or between different species of vertebrates, the conclusions seem legitimate that, *on the one hand, these localizations have something to do with areas of stress and strain and that, on the other hand, conclusions can be drawn from pathological areas as to living, conditions and posture of the material under examination.*

Chronic arthritis of the hip joint has so far been observed only in man, not in animals. Here again it begins with the Neanderthalian Homme de la Chapelle, is found in the European Neolithic, frequently in ancient Egypt, and, for unknown reasons, even more frequently in ancient Peru. Pales has suggested that subluxations of the joints form the basis for many of these cases.

Temporo-maxillary arthritis was found in the Neanderthal man of Krapina, but not in other European skeletons. It is rare today in Western countries. It is, on the other hand, fairly frequent among the pre-Columbian North and South Americans, and among present-day West Africans and Melanesians, especially in the New Hebrides and in New Caledonia. Pales explains the puzzling fact by the combined action of predisposing racial anatomical structure and particularly coarse food.

Numerous other joints—for instance, of the phalanges—have been found to be affected, e.g., in mosasaurs, cave bears, Neanderthal man, upper Paleolithic men like Cro-Magnon, Neolithic Europeans, ancient Egyptians, Peruvians, and other pre-Columbian Amer-indians. The Patagonians show arthritis only in the joints of the upper extremities. Here we again encounter the problem of selective localization, probably connected with zones of particular functional stress.

The universality of arthritis in bones at all periods, climates, and places does not confirm climatic theories of the disease (moist or cold climate). The existence of osteoarthritis in dinosaurs, cave bears, etc., is not in favor of alcohol or tobacco as causative factors.

**Rickets and Symmetrical Osteoporosis**

Rickets, an avitaminosis and a bone disease extremely prevalent during the last three hundred years, has been found in a giant Pleistocene wolf and in a domesticated Egyptian ape, but, in general, not in early man. No rickets in the tens of thousands of Egyptian skeletons examined, none in the extensive pre-Columbian material (this is consistent with findings in primitives). Only from the Scandinavian Neolithic and from Indochina (?) has evidence of rickets been reported. Two cases of osteomalacia, a disease often confounded with rickets, have been seen in Peru.

On the other hand, abundant proof of a bone disease that is practically nonexistent among present-day whites and that might be an avitaminosis—symmetrical osteoporosis—has been found in ancient Egypt (Nubia) and ancient Peru. Pecos also offers several examples, and it is supposed to have occurred often among the ancient Maya. Like rickets, symmetrical osteoporosis, which produces the so-called "cribra parietalia" and "cribra orbitalia"—lesions called syphilitic by older authors—is primarily a disease of childhood. Several anemias of childhood and scurvy produce similar pictures. The disease is very rare among Neolithic Europeans and North American pre-Columbians but is common in many present-day non-European populations (African Negroes, Malays, Chinese, Japanese, etc.). Besides avitaminosis, mechanical causes (like skull deformation) have been suggested.

**Tumors**

Bone tumors in prehistoric men and animals, especially malignant ones, are surprisingly rare, as compared to findings in present-day men and animals. The oldest osteomas are found in mosasaurs. They occur in the European Neolithic and rather frequently in ancient Peru, especially as osteomata of the auditory duct. To differentiate osteomata—true tumors—from exostoses—mere reactional growth—is not always simple. Other benign tumors—hemiangiomata—have been described in dinosaurs.

Osteosarcomata have been found in the cave bear and perhaps the Pleistocene horse. Human osteosarcomata have been described by Smith and Dawson from the Fifth Dynasty (*ca.* 2750 B.C.) in Egypt. Recently, sarcomatous meningiomata have been described in Egyptian skulls of the First Dynasty (3400 B.C.). Osteosarcomata occur also in ancient Peruvian skulls. Moodie has interpreted some of these Peruvian cranial tumors as residuals of meningiomata.

Bone defects, especially of the skull basis and the sacrum, in Neolithic and ancient Peruvian materials might have been caused by neighboring cancers of the soft parts of their metastases. Such erosions might, of course, also be produced occasionally by aneurysm.

Multiple myeloma has been reported from Neolithic France and pre-Columbian North America.

### Dental Pathology

Pyorrhea appears in the animal series with the mosasaurs, among hominids with the Neanderthals. It is found in ancient Europe, Egypt, Peru, Hawaii, etc. Abscess resulting from pyorrhea is described first in an oligocene rhinoceros. In man it starts with the Neanderthal man. Caries, though seen in mosasaur and cave bear, seems to have appeared later on a large scale in man. First clear evidence for it dates from the Neolithic, especially in Scandinavia. In ancient Egypt it struck supposedly only the wealthy. A number of dental malformations are also on record.

## SOFT PARTS

Only a small percentage of diseases leave their mark on the bones. In mummies, fortunately, the soft parts are preserved to a certain extent. Mummification can be spontaneous in very dry climates like that of Arizona. Artificial mummification, supported by a dry climate, was practiced on a large scale in ancient Egypt and Peru. Study of mummies has greatly extended our knowledge of prehistoric disease conditions.

One of the most striking findings in Egyptian mummies (by direct inspection and by X-ray) was that of *arteriosclerosis*. It was first described in the aorta of Merneptah (1225–1215), the Pharaoh of the Exodus. Arteriosclerosis has also been demonstrated in Peruvian mummies.

The *lungs* of mummies have shown the following conditions: silicosis (Basketmaker), anthracosis (Egypt, Basketmaker), pneumonia (Egypt, Basketmaker; one of the Egyptian pneumonias contained bacilli resembling plague bacilli), pleurisy (Egypt).

*Kidneys* of mummies have presented congenital atrophy (Egypt), multiple abscesses (Egypt), stones (Egypt, Basketmaker). In a mummy of the Twentieth Dynasty (1250–1000) the eggs of *Bilharzia* have been demonstrated. Schistosomiasis, caused by *Bilharzia,* which is still one of the main Egyptian health problems, already existed, apparently, 2000 years ago. Vesicovaginal fistula has been observed in female Egyptian mummies, together with other evidence of difficult birth.

Egyptian mummies have, furthermore, contained gallstones, liver cirrhosis, and chronic appendicitis. Skin changes in one case have strongly suggested smallpox, in another one leprosy. Large spleens have been thought of as possible signs of malaria. Prolapsus of rectum and of female genitalia has been seen.

Ruffer, who did the largest amount of microscopic work in paleopathology and demonstrated a large number of structures, could not find traces of any blood corpuscles. This has unfortunately brought about a somewhat defeatist attitude in the search for the latter, in spite of the fact that G. E. Wilson (1927, Basketmaker) and H. U. Williams (1927, Peruvian mummies) were able to demonstrate red blood corpuscles. Krumbhaar (1936) even found not only erythrocytes but monocytes and polymorphonuclear leukocytes in a pre-Columbian tibia from Peru. Great progress in what we might call "paleophysiology" was achieved when Canela (1936) developed a technique to type blood groups from skeletal material. Wyman and Boyd (1937) followed with important work on blood-grouping in mummies.

## ART OBJECTS

Art objects from both hemispheres have already been referred to above in the cases of poliomyelitis, Pott's disease, and dwarfism. In the case of the paleolithic sculptures of obese women it is not clear whether we are dealing with actual representations of the artist's wishful thinking or whether such conditions were spontaneous and pathological or artificially produced. Closer scrutiny of the greatly increased volume of paleolithic art might still yield important discoveries.

Peruvian pottery is particularly rich in pathological representations. The outstanding findings are those of verruga Peruviana (Carrion's disease), uta (leishmaniasis), and sand-flea lesions on the soles of feet.

## INTEGRATION

The last twenty years have produced specialized findings of great interest as to the prehistory of, e.g., tuberculosis, tumors, blood corpuscles, etc. Much remains to be done in this field. Important biological hypotheses on the age of infectious diseases like those of the late Charles Nicolle remain still to be integrated with the work of paleopathologists. Certain medical conclusions as to the great age of disease and of certain diseases (tuberculosis, poliomyelitis), the legendary character of ideas of the "healthy wild animal" and the "healthy savage," and the identity of basic disease mechanisms throughout time can be safely made today.

Yet, as mentioned above, another task, even more important than its purely medical implications, faces paleopathology today—the task of integrating its data with other types of information, e.g., from archeology or paleoanthropology, in such a way that it realizes its potentialities for an illumination of human society and its dynamics. On the other hand, all those co-operating in such a synthesis will have to pay more attention to the data of paleopathology than has been done in the past.

Pioneer work in integrating the data of paleopathology was undertaken by Todd (1929), when he reconstructed the duration of life in medieval and in primitive communities from bone material. Vallois did the same for early man (1932).

The most important effort in this direction was made by Hooton in his splendid monograph on Pecos in 1930, when, on the basis of the bone record, he reconstructed the life-history of the settlement, utilizing the archeological findings and his exhaustive study of Pecos paleopathology. Hooton found arthritis, traumatism, sinusitis, mastoiditis, osteomyelitis (syphilis?), osteoporosis, Pott's disease, cancer, etc. That he found so much is probably due less to a particularly high morbidity in Pecos than to his sustained interest in the problem. Hooton set a shining example, unfortunately isolated so far. If a few more sites had been handled with the same thoroughness, we would probably have achieved far greater progress in our

field. Bone material should always be studied beyond the traditional examination for its racial nature and *should receive at least the type of attention that is given to material in legal cases.* Physical anthropology has contributed valuable techniques to legal medicine. It could, in turn, profit from adoption of some techniques of legal medicine and other medical technology.

It is no accident that one of the most significant and brilliant recent contributions in integration has come from a pupil of Hooton, J. L. Angel, in his work on the anthropology of the early Greeks. Angel found the growth of Greek culture between 800 and 500 B.C. connected with such phenomena as an increase in body size, life-span, and population volume and a decrease in arthritis, dental pathology, osteoporosis, and infant mortality. He noticed again a decrease in health after 400 B.C. The fact that the one or the other conclusion of Angel might be based on too small a sample does not detract from the value and interest of his studies as a whole. Sigerist has recently integrated in a similar way cultural and paleopathological data on Egypt in the first volume of his *History of Medicine.*

Another important recent contribution has been the work of Ad. Schultz on Primate pathology. We have already mentioned his work on fractures in gibbons. When, besides the lesions we are familiar with in early man and in mummies, he found a high degree of infestation with plasmodia, filaria, and trypanosoma, the conclusion seems legitimate, in view of biological relationships, that man's ancestors were affected in a similar way.

# 7 Disease in Ancient Nubia

## *George J. Armelagos*

How does a paleopathologist go about making inferences from his findings? This paper by George Armelagos not only presents important data on disease in this site of earlier Old World cultures but is instructive in indicating how the findings are interpreted and the methods used for research and interpretation. The

Reprinted with abridgments from George J. Armelagos, 1969, "Disease in Ancient Nubia," *Science,* **163**:255–259, with permission of the author and the American Association for the Advancement of Science. Copyright 1969 by the American Association for the Advancement of Science.

study is a good example of contemporary paleo-pathology that is population-based rather than drawn from individual specimens in undefined populations, as in the past. It also demonstrates that the use of a population of skeletal material permits an epidemiological approach to the study of disease in ancient societies, an approach called for by Ackerknecht in the preceding paper and praised by Cockburn in the following one. An obvious advantage to the paleopathologist and archeologist working in the part of the world studied by Armelagos is the relatively excellent state of preservation of both biological and cultural materials made possible by the arid climate, making the task of biological and cultural reconstruction a good deal more feasible and fruitful. One interesting conclusion is that all three post-Mesolithic populations "demonstrated the classic survival curve characteristic of an agricultural society. Mortality was high among infants, leveled off slightly among young adults, and increased sharply among older adults."

## PROBLEM AND APPROACH

The study summarized here is an attempt to analyze the skeletal lesions found in populations from three archeological horizons in the Wadi Halfa area of Lower Nubia in the Republic of the Sudan (Figure 1). Specifically, the analysis focused on populations from the Meroitic, X-Group (term coined during first Aswan Project at turn of the century; letters were used to designate various cultural horizons), and Christian populations (Table 1), which Greene has shown, on the basis of genetically determined dental characteristics, to be biologically similar (Green 1967). In view of Greene's study, the possibility of elucidating, in prehistoric populations, differences in disease processes which result from cultural differences became another objective.

In this study I have attempted to overcome some of the shortcomings of the individualistic approach of the early studies through use of the paleoepidemiological method, which entails study of the host, the disease, and the environment (Roney 1966). One of the most important aspects of paleopathology is study of the culture of the populations concerned. For knowledge of the culture we are dependent primarily on archeological investigations, which place the population in the proper position chronologically and provide information necessary for reconstructing the life pattern of the people. In some cases the reconstruction of cultural patterns may reveal stresses which affected

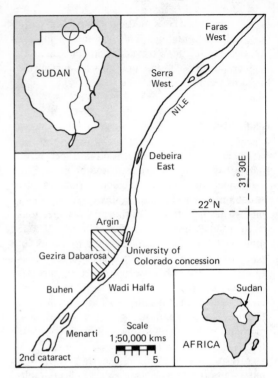

**Figure 1.** The Wadi Halfa area of Lower Nubia. Note the relationship of the University of Colorado concession area (where all the sites discussed, except for NAX and 2413, are located) to other sites in the Sudan. In the insert at upper left, the small circle indicates the Wadi Halfa area.

biological processes; in other instances, an examination of the pathological conditions may provide insights into the cultural practices.

Lower Nubia is hot and extremely dry, and the dry heat helps to preserve the burials. Many of the

**Table 1**  Chronological Sequence of Archeological Horizons in Sudanese Nubia.

| Group and Sites (in parenthesis) | Sample Size (No. of individuals) | Dates |
|---|---|---|
| Christian (6B13, 6G8, Meinarti) | 403 | A.D. 550–1300 |
| X-Group (2413, NAX) | 218 | A.D. 350–550 |
| Meroitic (6B16) | 129 | 350 B.C.–A.D. 350 |
| Mesolithic (6B36) | 39 | 7000 B.C. |

skeletons examined in the study still had tissue adhering to them, although there was no evidence of embalming. The major causes of infrequent damage were the high water table and gnawing by insects; portions of some of the specimens showed evidence of such damage.

The nearly 800 skeletons analyzed in this study span the Mesolithic, Meroitic, X-Group, and Christian cultural periods—some 8000 years (Table 1). They included 39 fossilized human skeletons discovered in a Mesolithic site, which provided information on preagricultural adaptation in Nubia (Greene, et al. 1967, Green, et al. 1972). Reconstruction of the Meroitic, X-Group, and Christian cultural horizons is hampered by the fact that the published reports on many of the sites excavated in recent years are only now beginning to appear (Adams 1964, 1965). The people belonging to these cultural groups were basically agriculturists who practiced irrigation farming. There is variation in cultural development among the three groups, which can be explained in part in terms of the fluctuation of the Nile and of pressures applied by foreign groups.

The picture which has emerged indicates that the Meroitic phase (350 B.C.–A.D. 350) was a period in which a native Nubian culture attained one of its highest peaks. The center of the culture was far to the south, in Meroë; it is thought that the Wadi Halfa area of Lower Nubia enjoyed a degree of cultural development similar to that of the groups in the center of Meroitic development.

The X-Group period (A.D. 350–550) is thought to have been a time in which Nubian culture declined from the development characteristic of the Meroitic period. During the X-Group period the populations broke up into local groups, which were ruled independently.

The Christian period (A.D. 550–1300) saw the religious reunification of Nubia and was a period of cultural growth. The archeological evidence reveals long periods of stability, like the stability of the Meroitic development. The growth of villages and the development of writing and of art which were independent of Egyptian influence are all evidence of this cultural growth. Even after the Muslim conquest of Egypt, in A.D. 640–42, the Christians in Nubia maintained their independence. During the classic period of Christianity there was an elaboration of church architecture and the first evidence of urbanization, with concentration of population in large centers and in monastic communities. Nubia was an important center of Christianity at this time.

## PATHOLOGICAL CONDITIONS

An investigation of pathologies in prehistoric populations is usually restricted to examination of the skeletal system. The excellent state of preservation of the Nubian material made it possible to study many other conditions. For example, the hair was examined for evidence of parasitic infestation, since there had been reports of lice in ancient material (Ewing 1924). Forty percent of the scalp and hair samples from the X-Group series were infested with head lice, *Pediculus humanus capitis*. Lice are known to be vectors for diseases such as relapsing fever, but any suggestion concerning the role of lice in the disease pattern of the prehistoric population of Nubia would be pure speculation.

In many instances the interpretation of skeletal lesions is difficult, whereas in other cases the cause is obvious. For example, the occurrence of hydrocephaly, osteochondroma, and endochondromas in the Nubian series presented no problem of interpretation. Other lesions, such as those of Legg-Calvé-Perthes disease (aseptic necrosis of the head of the femur), were much more difficult to interpret. Other conditions rarely seen in skeletal populations, such as carcinoma, sarcoma, and hyperostosis frontalis, were found. The lesions were unusual; apart from this study, only four instances of hydrocephaly, 12 of malignant neoplasm (Brothwell 1961), one of hyperostosis frontalis (Moore 1955), and possibly three of Legg-Calvé-Perthes disease (Goff 1954, Anderson 1963) have been reported in the archeological literature. There were also evidences of intentional mutilation—decorative scarification, tattooing, and pierced earlobes—such as are rarely found in archeological material. Discovery and identification of these pathological conditions in a series from a limited area and in such a small sample is unusual.

Study of the more frequently occurring pathological lesions provides insights for interpreting cultural behavior. It is from the frequency of occurrence of these lesions that inferences concerning cultural stresses are drawn. For example, the frequency of trauma resulting from aggressive action gives insights into the cultural behavior of a population which may not be attainable from examination of the artifactual remains.

In order to facilitate comparisons. I used broad categories in studying the Nubian material —categories such as congenital abnormalities; trauma; infectious, inflammatory, and degenerative lesions; neoplastic and metabolic diseases; and lesions

79

resulting from artificial interference such as mutilation.

The incidence of traumatic lesions in a population provides a broad index of another form of stress in the culture. Since traumatic injuries are not necessarily due to aggressive behavior, they must be analyzed with care. For example, some fractures of the ulna or radius may be due to falls in which one or both bones in the forearm are fractured as the individual attempts to "break" the fall. On the other hand, a "parry fracture" most commonly occurs when an individual raises his arm to protect himself from a blow.

It is difficult to distinguish intentional cranial injuries from accidental ones; however, many of the cranial lesions were in locations such that they could hardly have resulted from an accidental fall, and it is assumed that most of them were probably the result of intentional blows. In the samples from the sites, the percentages of craniums with traumatic lesions were as follows: Meroitic, 14.2; X-Group, 13.2; Christian, 13.4. Seventeen individuals (56.1 percent) in the combined sample with cranial injuries are male, 13 (42.9 percent) are female.

Analysis of postcranial lesions, on the other hand, is more difficult, since intentional injury is suggested only in certain instances of multiple injuries and in lesions such as the "parry fracture." The percentages of individuals with postcranial lesions show a variation with culture group which was not apparent in the case of cranial lesions. The percentages are as follows: Meroitic, 5.6; X-Group, 3.1; and Christian, 11.3.

In the combined Nubian series, there seems to be a correlation between frequency of occurrence of postcranial lesions and sex. Of 12 individuals with postcranial injuries, ten (83 percent) are males, two (17 percent) are females. The two females with postcranial injuries were from a Christian cemetery. Although generalization from such a small sample would be unwarranted, the pattern of traumatic lesions does show an increase during the Christian period both in injuries from aggression and in those resulting from accidents.

For revealing stress, some of the most informative pathological conditions are the degenerative lesions such as those of arthritis. In some of the Nubian populations, arthritis involved 10 percent of the vertebrae, while osteophytosis (lipping of the vertebral body) was found in 50 percent of the population. The frequency of occurrence of arthritic lesions is fairly constant throughout the Nubian series. For example, in the Meroitic sample there were arthritic lesions on 2.1 percent of the

articular surfaces of the long bones; for the X-Group samples the average was about 3.0 percent; and for the two Christian samples the average was 3.1 percent. There was variation among the three groups in the extent of involvement of the mandibular condyle and the occipital condyle.

Arthritic lesions of the articular facets of the vertebrae were found in 0.6 percent of the specimens from site 6B16 (Meroitic); in 4.1 percent of those from site 24I3 (X-Group); in .7 percent of those from site 6B13 (Christian); and in 3.8 percent of those from site 6G8 (Christian). Part of the variation may be due to differences in the average age at death for the different populations. For the site 6G8 (Christian) population, for example, the average age at death for adults (15 years or older) is 35.6 years; for the site 24I3 (X-Group) population the figure is 29.7 years, and for the site 6B16 (Meroitic) population, 26.3 years.

The frequency of occurrence of osteophytosis also reflects, in part, the differences in life-span. The percentages of osteophytosis for the three cultural groups are as follows (values in parentheses are average age at death for adults): 6B16 (Meroitic), 5.8 (26.3); 24I3 (X-Group), 10.3 (29.7); 6B13 (Christian), 10.1; 6G8 (Christian), 24.9 (35.6). I feel that a major factor in the increase in osteophytosis was probably an increase in longevity. In other words, when people live longer the vertebrae are subject to stress for a longer period. There is an apparent inconsistency here, since the increase in longevity is evidence of a reduction in selective pressure yet there is an increase in the frequency of occurrence of this minor pathological condition.

The rate of occurrence of osteoporosis as a function of age was determined in prehistoric samples for the first time in a study undertaken by John Dewey (1968). Dewey obtained quantitative measurements of bone involution through direct measurement of the thickness of femoral cortical bone. The results of this study indicated a sex difference with respect to the rate of involution. The females in the Nubian series show a rapid and statistically significant loss of bone (Figure 2) compared to the loss in males. There appears to be no significant cultural difference with respect to bone loss. The females in the 22-to 31-year age group show a 6.3-percent decrease in thickness of femoral cortical bone, whereas males in this age group show an increase in bone thickness. The bone loss in females increases to 18 percent in the 32-to 41-year group and to 23.4 percent in the last age group (42 to 50+). The total loss in males from age 32 to 50+ is 13.8 percent.

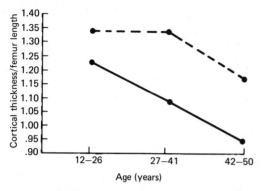

**Figure 2.** Bone involution of the femur (ratio of thickness of femoral cortical bone to length of femur) in the combined Meroitic, X-Group, and Christian populations. Number of males in sample, 71; number of females, 107. Bone loss in males (dashed line) is not significant, bone loss in females (solid line) is significant ($p > .001$).

Since differences in stature may obscure differences in bone loss among populations of different cultures, a method of normalization had to be developed; the ratio

(thickness of femoral cortical bone)/(length of femur)

was used to correct for such differences in stature. In addition to showing a statistically significant loss of bone in the Nubian females, the normalization of data indicated that this ratio does differ for the Meroitic, X-Group, and Christian populations. Normalized data had not been used in earlier studies of bone involution; Dewey's analysis of the prehistoric material indicates that normalization of bone loss in modern series may be methodologically necessary.

Rates of bone involution in the prehistoric Nubian series and in modern series indicate that the ancient populations started losing bone at an earlier age and lost it more rapidly than modern populations. The bone loss in 51-year-old females in the Nubian series is as great as that in 60-year-old females in modern series (Bartley 1967).

## DENTAL PATHOLOGY

The analysis of dental pathologies was limited to analysis of macroscopic lesions such as caries, missing teeth, apical abscessing, crowding, dental attrition, and alveolar recession. Analysis of carious lesions in archeological populations is always a problem. Since sampling biases may be introduced

by tooth loss (Krogman 1935) and since missing teeth may be the result of any of several causes unrelated to the carious process, a comparison of the frequencies of occurrence of caries for the total sample of teeth from different populations may not reveal important differences that do in fact exist. On the other hand, comparison by tooth classes will reveal these differences.

The analysis of carious lesions in the Nubian series shows an increase in frequency of occurrence from 1 percent in Mesolithic times to 18 percent in Christian times. The cause cannot be specified, but it is suggested that the higher proportion of agricultural products in the Nubian diet was a contributing factor.

There are other factors which have been frequently overlooked in the study of dental carious lesions in ancient populations. For example, the study of the Nubian series showed that the increase in dental attrition was followed by an increase in occlusal carious lesions (Figure 3). Abrasion of the enamel gives cariogenic agents easy access to the vital tissues. Attempts to find evidence of similar factors in the frequency of occurrence of interproximal and gingival carious lesions have been unsuccessful.

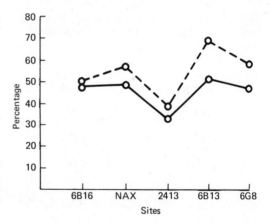

**Figure 3.** Percentages of (dashed line) maxillary occlusal caries and (solid line) maxillae with stage-3 and stage-4 dental attrition (cusps abraded to expose dentine) for various populations.

A final point which should be made concerning dental pathology is the relationship of dental attrition to alveolar recession; the Nubian series shows an inverse relationship. Mastication inhibits alveolar recession. Although not unexpected, demonstration of this relationship in an ancient population is important (Figure 4).

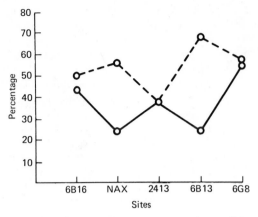

Figure 4. Percentages of (dashed line) mandibles with stage-3 and stage-4 dental attrition and (solid line) maxillae displaying alveolar recession.

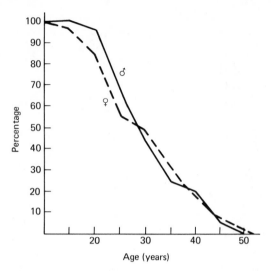

Figure 5. Survival curve for the adult population from the Christian site of Meinarti (A.D. 1050 to 1100) (N = 160).

## MORTALITY DATA

The Nubian series reveals both general and specific survival patterns comparable to those of other populations. For example, the Meroitic, X-Group, and Christian samples all demonstrated the classic survival curve characteristic of an agricultural society. Mortality was high among infants, leveled off slightly among young adults, and increased sharply among older adults.

Comparison of survival rates for males and females indicates an increase in mortality for females during the childbearing years with a shift near, or shortly after, the 30th year, at which time there is a relative increase in the mortality rate for males (Figure 5).

## SUMMARY

A study of the paleopathology of the Meroitic, X-Group, and Christian populations of Lower Nubia has provided information that is important in delimiting chronologically and geographically the distribution of a number of diseases. The finding of such conditions as carcinoma, endochondromas, sarcoma, hyperostosis frontalis, Legg-Calvé-Perthes disease, hydrocephaly, tattooing, and intentional scarification—all rare in skeletal material—is in itself an important contribution to our knowledge. In addition, evidence of infestation with head lice was found in some of the skeletal material.

The increased frequency of occurrence of traumatic postcranial lesions is due in part to intentional injury. The highest percentages of such lesions occur in the Christian series—populations which, on the basis of the mortality data, appear to have been under less stress than the cultural groups that preceded them. A similar pattern is manifested by degenerative lesions such as those of arthritis. The higher percentages of arthritic lesions may be in part due to increased longevity; the Christians were living longer than earlier populations, and degenerative lesions would be an expected consequence.

Another pathological condition whch increases with age is osteoporosis. Although this is a well-known clinical entity in modern medicine, it had not previously been studied in a prehistoric population. The Nubian series provided an opportunity to study small homogeneous groups. In females, osteoporosis was shown to be correlated with age; in males, the bone loss was not statistically significant. It was also shown that normalization of the data [through use of the ratio (thickness of femoral cortical bone)/(length of femur)] is an important method of controlling for differences in stature. The rate of bone involution was higher than the rate in modern populations and demonstrated that prehistoric populations were losing as much bone by age 51 as modern populations lose by age 60.

The frequency of occurrence of carious lesions in the Nubian series has increased since Mesolithic times. Inclusion of more soft foods in the diet is undoubtedly a factor; dental attrition, cusp number, and fissure patterns may also have played a role. The analysis also demonstrated the need to analyze dental lesions by specific classes of teeth, since sampling bias may otherwise obscure some relationships.

The treatment of mortality data provided one of the most useful tools in the study of cultural growth.

The results of pathological analysis and mortality patterns suggest that the X-Group may not have experienced the cultural decline suggested by the archeological record, and that the X-Group period may have been one of cultural growth relative to the earlier, Meroitic period in Lower Nubia.

# 8 Infectious Diseases in Ancient Populations

## *T. Aidan Cockburn*

A more recent paper than Ackerknecht's previous selection is this fine review of the possible evolution of certain infectious diseases in early human populations. It provides a stimulating summary of a tremendous mass of data and thus will serve to extend the earlier statements of Ackerknecht. Cockburn makes passing reference to the classic data of paleopathology but, as Ackerknecht himself notes, until recently so much work was not population-based and, therefore, generalization from such idiosyncratic or unknown-based findings will perforce be severely limited. Using an evolutionary paradigm, Cockburn constructs a series of hypotheses to indicate the *probable* development and routes of transmission of a number of infectious diseases in prehominid and hominid populations. He depends heavily upon analogy from living peoples but the study of ancient disease in this fashion seems reasonably and cautiously undertaken here and Cockburn is aware of the potential pitfalls of his approach. Despite the appearance of Figure 1, it is apparent that Cockburn does not view the evolution of *Homo Sapiens* or of the infectious diseases that beset this species as a unilinear or simplex process. What such studies show is not only that the course of human evolution

Reprinted with abridgments from T. Aidan Cockburn, 1971, "Infectious Diseases in Ancient Populations," *Current Anthropology*, **12**:45–62, with permission of the author and *Current Anthropology* and the University of Chicago Press. Copyright 1971 by the Wenner-Gren Foundation for Anthropological Research.

has influenced the development of many diseases, but that, as Cockburn says elsewhere, "the history of mankind has been shaped to a considerable degree by infectious disease."

Although many of Cockburn's assertions are in the nature of informed guesses, my own belief is that progress in a still rudimentary reconstructive science such as paleopathology requires such hypotheses from time to time, both as inventories of existing knowledge and as pointers toward the areas where more intensive research is required. The reader is referred to the original source of this article for informative commentaries and additional information (and criticism). Also of interest is the study by Dumond, in Chapter 33 of this book, which suggests that voluntary individual and cultural decisions and methods of population control may have been more crucial than disease in limiting the size of human populations.

Infectious diseases result from the interplay of three main factors: the host, the parasite, and the environment. The matter is highly complex, since each of these factors can vary in many ways and many differing diseases can result. In this review, attention will be concentrated on two of these factors: the prehuman and human hosts and their environments during the periods of man's evolution from the earliest days to the present. A number of distinct eras can be discerned: those of the primate precursors of man, early man, agricultural man, industrial man, and the man of one world. The first three of these eras will be discussed here.

### THE PRECURSORS OF MAN

The Primates are assumed to have descended from an insectivorous mammal somewhat resembling the modern tree shrew. This animal is presumed to have had certain parasites and infections, and it is further presumed that some of these parasites and infections still exist, perhaps in somewhat modified forms, in its descendants of today. However, its descendants are now scattered over the world and live in many varying ecologic niches (Cockburn 1963, 1967; Cameron 1956; Ruch 1959; Dunn 1966; Fiennes 1967). Some of the ancestral parasites and infections probably failed to survive in certain host genera or species, owing to the differing conditions under which their hosts lived. On the other hand, some host lines would acquire new parasites and infections after branching off from the main phylogenetic tree, and these would continue to exist only in their descendants. This process is depicted in Figure 1.

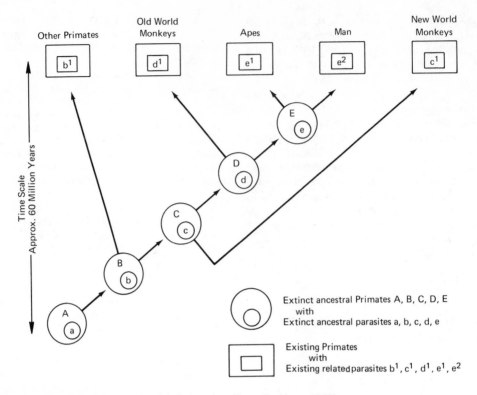

**Figure 1.** Evolution of Primates and their parasites (from Cockburn 1967).

In a previous work (Cockburn 1963), I have suggested that this is the explanation of the distribution of many parasites and infections common to man and other primates. For example, no fewer than 13 of the intestinal protozoa of man are found also in apes and monkeys, according to the findings of Dobell (1926), Kessel (1928), and Hegner and Chu (1928, 1930). This is difficult to explain on any grounds except that these intestinal protozoa were passed down to all these primates from a common ancestor.

Similarly, of 34 genera of parasitic helminths in the Hominoidea, man is known to be host to 20, *Pan* to 26, *Pongo* to 13, and *Hylobates* to 14. Seven genera, *Trichuris, Strongyloides, Oesophagostomum, Ascaris, Dipetalonema, Dirofilaria,* and *Bertiella,* have been reported from all four primate genera (Dunn 1966). The distribution of helminths is apparently related to the phylogenetic relationships of the primate hosts.

Other parasites include lice of the genus *Pediculus,* malaria parasites, the scabies mite, *Acarus,* herpes virus, infectious hepatitis virus, and numerous other viruses now being discovered. The monkey equivalent (*Herpes simiae*) of the human herpes virus is now recognized as a common

infection (Wood and Shimada 1954, Keble *et al.* 1958, Hull and Nash 1960). Infectious hepatitis virus has not yet been isolated with certainty, but the numerous instances of transmission of the disease from chimpanzees to their keepers leave little doubt that the infection is a natural one among chimpanzees (Hillis 1961, Communicable Disease Center 1965). Reviews of the literature on parasites of primates have been made by Ruch (1959), Dunn (1966), and Fiennes (1967). A summary of the viral infections is given by Andrewes (1964). Reviews of malaria parasites in monkeys and apes have been given recently by Coatney (1968), Eyles (1963), Bruce-Chwatt (1965), Bray (1963), and Garnham (1963).

Syphilis and other treponematoses (cf. Hudson 1963, 1965)—among them yaws, pinta, bejel, irkinja, etc.—may also have come down from a nonhuman primate ancestor (see Cockburn 1959, 1961*a*, 1963, 1967). The possibility that apes and monkeys share these infections has been argued for more than 50 years. Trappers have reported that apes in nature have a yaws-like disease (Raven 1950). A yaws-type lesion called groundou is not uncommon in monkeys (Marchoux and Mesnil 1911, Mouquet 1929, 1930, Bouffard 1909, Secques

1929), although some authorities, such as Ruch (1959), have denied that the condition has anything to do with yaws. Fribourg-Blanc and his colleagues (1963; also personal communication, 1967) tested large samples of sera from many species of ape and monkey and found many of the African, but not the Asian, ones to be serologically positive. This finding was confirmed by the U.S. Public Health Service Communicable Disease Center (personal communication), which tested 220 chimpanzees and found 10 percent of them positive. The French workers went on to recover treponemes from the popliteal glands of baboons. This is strong evidence in support of the theory that the treponemal infections have existed in man and his ancestors for many millions of years, possibly as far back as the Miocene. Although syphilis itself was "discovered" only when Columbus reached the New World, other diseases of the treponemal group would have existed before then on both sides of the Atlantic.

It seems generally accepted that our original ancestors were tree-living creatures. The primates of South America maintained a strictly arboreal life. On the other hand, many Old World primates, including the ancestors of man, learned to live either partially or entirely on the ground.

This basic difference in ecology must have had a marked effect on the infections to which the primates were exposed. A primate whose living is basically arboreal is exposed to arthropod vectors different from those on the ground. The most obvious of these is the type of mosquito which feeds and breeds in a canopy, unlike those feeding and breeding at ground level. Many more bloodsucking arthropods are found on the ground than in the treetops, the ticks and mites being notable examples. Furthermore, a ground-living primate is very much more exposed to parasitic infections from the feces of other animals. The water drunk by the monkey in a hole halfway up a tree is much more likely to be uncontaminated than that of the streams and lakes used by terrestrial primates. Wherever there are water snails in tropical Africa, there is always the hazard of *Schistosoma* infections; tree-living primates would not be faced with this hazard to anything approaching the same extent (Paoli 1965, Nelson 1960, Strong *et al.* 1961). Incidentally, the classic studies of Jane Goodall among the chimpanzees of East Africa have shown that these primates prefer to drink running water and avoid standing pools. This behavior could be important in reducing exposure to schistosomes. Mobility or lack of it can have substantial effects on the parasites and infections maintained in a

"herd." Washburn (1965:89) has said that if we look at the behavior of all the nonhuman primates,

> we find that these creatures are incredibly restricted in the area that they occupy. Only the gorilla and the baboon have ranges as great as fifteen square miles; while in the majority of the nonhuman primates, an animal spends virtually its entire life within two or three square miles—a tiny area.

Just when early man or his immediate ancestors adopted the roving way of life we do not know. However, it seems that by the time early man appeared in the Olduvai Gorge some 2,000,000 years ago, he was already mobile.

A static group of animals becomes infected over and over again with the same lines of parasites. Because the ground or trees on which they live are soon contaminated with their feces, there is an almost direct route from one intestine to another. There is little contact with other groups of animals, so that parasites are apt to develop high degrees of adaptation to their hosts. The mosquitoes and other arthropods that feed on these animals can breed nearby in the certainty of finding food with very little effort. This tends to produce strains of arthropods with preference for the particular host's blood and, in turn, infection and reinfection of the host by the same strains of parasites.

In a mobile animal like man, these factors disappear, and highly specific parasites have very little chance of surviving unless they can travel along with the man. On the other hand, a mobile band of primates would be exposed to numerous new infections in areas into which it migrated, and some of these might establish themselves as permanent infections. Perhaps the schistosomal infections of the Far East arose in this fashion. Primates leaving Africa would free themselves automatically from the schistosomes of that continent, since the snails needed for continued transmission would be missing in their new homes. On arriving in the Far East, however, they would encounter a new form already established in many kinds of animals and would come to be included in its ecology. When man first evolved, he must have been a comparatively rare creature, living in small bands of not more than 200–300 persons. His total population in the world was probably no greater than that of the chimpanzees today. It is obvious, therefore, that those specifically human infections which can live only by rapid transmission from one host to another and which do not form "carrier" associations could not have survived. This matter is discussed in more detail later; it will suffice to state here that it is improbable that infections like measles, smallpox, and mumps were present in those early days. However, one school of thought is of the opinion that very few viruses specific to man could have existed. This idea has been put forward most strongly by Burnet (1946:30–31), who states:

It is generally considered that in the early stages of human evolution primitive man and his subhuman progenitors existed in small wandering groups of at most a few families, and that these groups only rarely came into contact one with the other. Under such circumstances it would be virtually impossible for a pathogen to evolve as a specifically human parasite unless, as is the case with herpes simplex, the period over which a person remained capable of transferring infection was of the order of a generation. . . .

To return to the question of the specifically human virus disease: we have given reasons for believing that in the early phase of human existence, from the beginning of the Pleistocene up to about 10,000 years ago, infectious disease due to micro-organisms specifically adapted to the human species was almost nonexistent. The herpes virus could have persisted with very much its present type of activity, but the viruses producing brief infection with subsequent immunity—measles, mumps, and the like—could obviously not have survived in anything like their present form.

Much has happened in the field of primate virology since Burnet expressed his views. The adoption of tissue culture for the laboratory growth of viruses led in the 1950's to the development of vaccines against diseases like poliomyelitis. This in turn resulted in large-scale commercial production of these vaccines, often using substantial amounts of monkey and ape tissues. These procedures activated latent viruses in the tissues. It soon became apparent that monkeys and apes are hosts to a great many viruses, the existence of which had previously gone unsuspected.

For many types of naturally occurring virus infections in humans, there are equivalent ones to be found in nonhuman primates. Except for those transmitted by arthropods, the differences between monkey viruses and human ones are slight; indeed, when a human infection like polio virus is found in a primate colony, the first conclusion is that it was acquired from some human carrier. Our knowledge of infections in the wild is very incomplete; reports of isolations from animals in captivity must be handled with the greatest of caution (Andrewes 1964, Guilloud 1965, Hahon 1961, Hull *et al.* 1958, Strode 1951, Arbovirus studies in Bush-Bush Forest, Trinidad 1968, Bhatt *et al.* 1966).

Since monkeys and apes have many apparently specific viral infections today in spite of their comparatively small numbers, the arguments of Burnet and his fellow thinkers become invalid. Therefore, emerging and early man may also have had many specific viral infections, perhaps as many as the monkeys and apes of today.

## EARLY MAN

Two million [or possibly 3.5–5 million—Ed.] years ago, man was a terrestrial creature probably no more numerous than the chimpanzees of today. He lived in small bands and ate whatever he could gather, kill, or find as carrion. Some of his infections were those handed down from his non-human primate ancestor and were probably much the same as those of the apes of his time living in the same environment. These infections have been outlined above. Among the other infections to which he was exposed would be parasites acquired by eating raw many kinds of insects, fish, birds, and mammals. He would also have been vulnerable to what are today called the zoonoses, infections of other animals transmitted to man by ticks, mites, mosquitoes, and other biting arthropods. Two zoonoses that probably occurred are anthrax and botulism.

Anthrax might have occurred in early man under conditions similar to those I witnessed when, in 1943, I was asked by the Colonial Government of the Gold Coast (Ghana) to help in an outbreak of disease in a village in the Northern Territories. On arrival, I found the village quarantined by Africans from the neighboring villages armed with spears. No one was being allowed to leave. The disease was anthrax. The villagers had killed and eaten a cow with a sore on its leg, having decided that the lesion was a snake bite and the cow therefore fit to eat. Thirty-seven people were very ill, and all who had eaten the flesh died from the disastrous intestinal form of the disease.

Endemic Type E botulism is not uncommon among Eskimos and Indians today and presumably occurred in similar fashion in times past. Dolman (1964) lists 18 outbreaks, evenly divided between Alaska and Labrador, between the years 1945 and 1962, in which 52 cases and 28 deaths were caused by eating marine animals.

The chief vehicle in the Alaskan outbreaks was *muktuk,* an Eskimo delicacy prepared by cutting the skin and underlying blubber or flippers of a beluga into chunks or strips and hanging them on a rack or over a pole outdoors for some days to dry. These pieces are then cured several weeks, or even months, in the comparative warmth of a hut. Mouthful-sized pieces of the matured *muktuk* are sliced off as needed. Two or three such pieces have been known to kill a hardy Eskimo male. Deaths from botulism have also been attributed to the *utjak* of the Eskimos of Labrador, prepared by letting seal flippers stand in oil, usually near a stove, for several days, until the skin falls loose and they are ripe for consumption.

Dolman also lists numerous outbreaks from another kind of botulogenic vehicle, variously called "salmon-egg cheese" and "stink eggs," traditionally popular among the salmon-eating Indians of the Northwest Pacific Coast. This concoction, usually eaten raw, has been responsible since 1940 for 14 authenticated outbreaks of botulism involving 34 persons, of whom 19 died. During the 23 years since the condition was first recognized there have no doubt been many other unreported outbreaks. Previously an indeterminate number of botulinic deaths and serious illnesses were presumably attributed to accidental or homicidal poisoning.

Tuberculosis in the early days of man was most probably a zoonotic infection. Man may have had a specific mycobacterial infection of his own, but this most likely was leprosy and was associated with his ancestors over vast periods of time. (If this reasoning is correct, then the apes of today probably also have a form of leprosy.) There are several forms of tuberculosis. The human variety of *Mycobacterium* is associated chiefly with pulmonary disease in urban populations long exposed to it and with an acute progressive glandular type in nonurban peoples such as Africans and Eskimos. The earliest evidence of human pulmonary tuberculosis comes from the writings of Hippocrates. The disease probably arose after the invention of agriculture (Cockburn 1963). The bovine *Mycobacterium* is responsible for most of the bone lesions in man. The skeletons, pictures, and clay pots giving evidences of spine disease and hunchbacks in ancient times must reflect infections acquired from cattle via infected milk or flesh. Tuberculosis of avian origin can cause human tuberculosis much like that of the specific human type, but does not spread rapidly from person to person. It is not uncommon in the southern states of the U.S.A. today. Fish tuberculosis can cause skin lesions in man. Several outbreaks associated with swimming pools have been reported.

Modern theory states that *Homo erectus* wandered from his place of origin in Africa to most parts of the Eurasian land mass suitable for occupation. Climatic and geographical conditions in his times were much different from those of today; for much of the time, large sections of the northern parts of the territory were covered with sheets of ice. On leaving Africa, man must have taken with him all those parasites that were transmitted directly person to person, leaving behind those that required vectors found only in Africa. These vectors would include those of filaria, schistosomiasis, trypanosomiasis, many arboviruses, mite-and tick-borne rickettsias and spirochaetes, and malaria. (Of course, we cannot say how the distribution of these vectors and intermediate hosts differed in those times from today.) Temperature would have been an important factor here. All vector-borne infections require certain temperatures for the extrinsic reproduction of the parasite. In the northern limits of the newly occupied territories it would have been too cold to permit the establishment of many infections.

On the other hand, *H. erectus* would have encountered many new infections in his new locations. The animals already established there would have had numerous forms of viruses, intestinal pathogens, and helminths that would be readily transmitted to him in a variety of ways.

The first men to arrive in Australia would have encountered a completely new fauna, the marsupials. The infections of these marsupials would have differed considerably from those of the animals of the Asian area, although unfortunately there is little data on this point. As a result, the zoonotic infections acquired through contact with the marsupials would have been kinds man had not previously experienced.

It would be the same story in the Americas, with the first migrants moving down from the north into a strange land filled with unusual animals. At that time, prehistoric forms of elephants and bison still roamed the prairies, and increasing evidence is being found to show that man hunted them. As man moved south, conditions changed. In the southern continent of the Americas he found an extremely wide range of habitats, with conditions ranging from the almost impassable rain forest of the Amazon to the high mountains of the Andes, the dry coastal plains of Chile, the wide pampas of Argentina and the cold and bleak coasts of Patagonia. In each of these, the infections of the animals would differ, and so of course would those acquired by man. The biting insects of the rain forest would transmit new forms of arboviruses, protozoa, and filaria; in drier regions man would acquire new kinds of leishmaniasis and, perhaps most serious of all, the American form of trypanosomiasis carried by *Triatomata*.

## AGRICULTURAL MAN

Agriculture probably had a more significant effect on man than any other factor from his first appearance to the present time of scientific revolution. For the first time, not only was there plenty of food for all, but it was of a kind that could be stored for periods of shortage. Man lost his mobility and became tied to his land, and many animals moved into his ecological niche to be supported by him, willingly or otherwise. Population increased and spread, bringing long-separated human groups into contact. All of these changes, as well as the agricultural practices themselves, tended to increase certain infectious hazards.

### Loss of Mobility

Man's loss of mobility meant that various parasites could now establish themselves under conditions which permitted constant reinfection of the host. The hookworms and ascarids could maintain themselves in situations in which the host excreted the eggs and through reinfection became the unwilling host of the larvae that hatched from them. The stage was now set for the massive infections seen only too commonly in children in underdeveloped countries today. The feces of the family are either dropped indiscriminately around the home or in fixed places in the fields to which the members go daily. Either practice makes the continued transmission of the worms inevitable.

### Addition of Animals to Ecological Niche

The anchoring of man to his fields led many animals to move in beside him—not only those which he domesticated, such as the cow, pig, sheep, cat, dog, and goat, but many that were unwanted, such as the rat and mouse, English sparrow, tick, flea, and mosquito. So long as man was a wanderer, it would be rare for a mosquito to develop a preference for human blood; but now it was possible for mosquitoes to breed near man's home or even inside it and be close at hand for a meal when this was required. In this fashion special strains of *Aedes aegypti* and *Anopheles gambiae* would be selected, and they would be excellent

transmitters of infections such as yellow fever, dengue, and malaria. Later, man tamed a number of birds, such as the pigeon, jungle fowl, and duck and goose, and they also joined the community centered on man's habitation.

Each of these animals would be infected with its own collection of pathogens. The community living in which they participated would ensure that these pathogens would be spread readily among all its members, and that man would receive samples of them all. Among them would be all the intestinal bacteria, protozoa, helminths, viruses, and, as well, most of the parasites from other tracts of the body. Many of these would be unable to invade him successfully, but occasionally one would succeed. If this one could be transmitted from man to man, then the stage would be set for the evolution of a new specifically human pathogen.

### Agricultural Practices

Agricultural practices by themselves do not create new infections, but some can accentuate those already present or convert what was previously an occasional event into a major hazard to health. The subject is a vast one that cannot be covered in this review. It includes the influences of draining swamps on malaria, of the slave trade in transmitting parasites like those of schistosomiasis and filaria from one region to another, of the slash-and-burn type of farming on malaria, of the cutting of undergrowth on trypanosomiasis (which it helps to suppress), and of many other interesting practices. Here, only two main agricultural practices will be discussed: the use of feces and urine as fertilizer, and various techniques of irrigation.

Spreading feces among crops can be a hazardous business. The possibilities of contamination with pathogenic organisms by those handling the material is obvious, but even more serious are the chances of transmission by the food plants fertilized in this way. There are many instances of typhoid epidemics originating in this fashion, and probably many helminths and cyst-forming bacteria are similarly spread. The eggs of *Ascaris* (roundworm) and the cysts of *Entamoeba histolytica* (amoebic dysentery) are especially suited for this form of transmission. People walking barefooted on ground so fertilized are particularly vulnerable to massive infection with hookworm. (The South Korean Government has just announced that it is taking action on the use of feces for fertilizer. About 75 percent of all feces in the country is used for this purpose; 90 percent of the population have intestinal parasites, the commonest being roundworms and whipworms in that order.)

The Chinese have carried the use of excreta to the extreme, employing it not only on the ground but also to support the growth of plants and fish in artificial ponds or canals. Since numerous snails are present in such places, this practice has caused the population to be heavily infected with a number of flukes. These flukes were present in the areas before the immigration of man, the hosts being various carnivorous and herbivorous animals, and the intermediate transmitters snails and fish, crustaceans, or plants. On arrival in the Orient, man became involved incidentally by eating raw the infected fish or crab or, in the case of the intestinal fluke *Fasciolopsis buski,* certain bulbs or fruits of edible water plants. The development of fish and water-plant cultivation,using feces as nutrient, converted what was an incidental infection into a major one. In all instances, the eggs of the flukes are excreted in the feces; when these are added to the water, miracidia hatch out and invade the snails present; after an interval, cercariae leave the snails and then encyst in various ways according to the species of fluke. *Fasciolopsis buski* encyst on almost any aquatic plant, although caltrops, water hyacinths, water chestnuts, and bamboos usually serve as "transfer hosts." As many as 1,000 metacercariae have been found on a single water chestnut; if kept moist, most will live for a year. Since it is common practice to peel off the outer skin of water chestnuts with the teeth, infection takes place readily. The mature flukes develop in the intestine within a month.

*Clonorchis sinensis,* the liver fluke, has much the same cycle except that the cercariae penetrate into fish and the cysts they form are swallowed when the fish is eaten raw or undercooked. Drying, salting, or pickling the fish does not necessarily kill the parasites. *Paragonimus,* the lung fluke, differs from the others merely by using various freshwater crustaceans for the third stage in its life cycle. Infection occurs when these are eaten raw or partially cooked. The fluke develops in the human lung and the eggs are passed out in the sputum, which is often swallowed so that the eggs appear in the feces.

The numbers of persons in the Orient with these flukes are enormous (some populations are 50 percent infected); much of this must be blamed on using feces in the water farming of fish and water plants.

Irrigation must have been invented very early in the history of agriculture. As far back as recorded history goes, the civilizations of the Chinese, Egyptians, Sumerians, and Incas were based on the production of crops supported by irrigation. Unfortunately, the artificial use of water in this fashion tends to accentuate infections in the same way as does the use of feces, and here again, a fluke, as well as certain insects, is involved.

The liver fluke *Schistosoma* has a cycle of transmission involving snails, just as have the others mentioned above, but because the cercariae are capable of penetrating the unbroken human skin man is infected merely by wading or swimming in water containing them. The eggs are excreted in either the feces or the urine. The snails can live in vast numbers in irrigation canals and rivers; one of the world's greatest health problems today is the spread of these snails to new areas being opened up by the vast dam-building and irrigation projects of Asia and Africa. After malaria and tuberculosis, schistosomiasis is probably the greatest cause of morbidity in much of Asia and Africa and will become even more prominent after malaria disappears and as irrigation extends.

Insects readily take advantage of certain aspects of irrigation practices, especially where leaky canals and uneven fields form small ponds of water, or where large lakes are formed behind dams. *Anopheles* mosquitoes, which transmit malaria, can breed in either the small pools or the lakes, according to the species. Because of this, malaria became a major problem in the artificial lakes of the Tennessee Valley Authority, and may have been a factor in the breakdown of the old civilization in Ceylon. *Culex* mosquitoes transmit filaria and viruses; they are often directly linked with irrigation. For example, *Culex tarsalis* in irrigated areas of the Missouri River Valley Authority has caused several epidemics of encephalitis.

**Increase in Population**

In previous works (Cockburn 1963, 1967) I have theorized that many infections require minimum host populations for permanent maintenance; if the sizes fall below the threshold levels, the infections die out. There are many diseases in which the infectious stages are brief and which exist entirely by rapid transmission of the agents from one host to another. Obviously, this can only happen if large numbers of susceptibles are present to support such a chain of transmission. These have been referred to as the acute community infections; they include rubella, cholera, smallpox, mumps, measles, and chickenpox. Such infections are specific to man and have no animal host other than man.

The effect of the introduction of an acute infection, measles, into a small isolated community was first studied in 1846 by Panum, who collected much valuable data about disease in a small "herd" on the Faroe Islands off the northern coast of Scotland (Panum 1940). In 1846, when the population was 7,782, measles was imported and attacked nearly everyone. A previous epidemic in 1781 had also infected almost the whole population, but the disease had disappeared completely afterward, presumably owing to a lack of susceptible persons. This also happened in 1846, for, after some 95 percent of the population had been attacked, the disease disappeared again.

Even pathogens that can live in their hosts like commensals for months find it difficult to survive if the population is too small. Bodian (1955) has said that poliomyelitis dies out in small communities after a certain time, even though carriers can excrete the virus for many months.

In a very small population with few susceptible persons, the survival of a pathogen depends on its ability to exist until new hosts appear. Natural selection will, therefore, favor those pathogens that can live in a kind of commensal relationship with their hosts and those that can continue to live away from their hosts. In a small population there would be no infections like measles, which spreads rapidly and immunizes a majority of the population in one epidemic, but many like typhoid, amoebic dysentery, pinta, trachoma, or leprosy, in which the host remains infective for long periods of time, and many like malaria, filaria and schistosomiasis, where the infection not only persists in the host for a long time but also has an outside vector or intermediate host to serve as an additional reservoir.

There is little in the way of precise and well-documented data on the infections of small groups of people living in isolation under the conditions of a hunting economy. It is difficult now to find such groups that have not already been infected through contact with larger civilizations. About three decades ago, what was known about the infections of the Australian Aborigines was written up by Cleland (1928) and Basedow (1932); more recently, Mann (1957) has published work on the eye infections of these people. As would be expected, most of the infections reported are of a chronic nature, such as trachoma, malaria, irkinja (a form of yaws), and roundworms. However, the influence of colonists and traders is obvious. An outbreak of smallpox, for instance, was reported within a year of the first British settlement. It was said to have crossed the continent from the north and possibly was started by Malay fisherman. Even trachoma may have been introduced by the white traders, as maintained by Mann (1957), although others think that Dampier, the first British explorer to reach Australia, was indeed describing the disease when he said that the natives had to throw their heads back to see straight ahead. Tuberculosis is apparently found predominantly only among those natives living in close association with white men.

In Africa, Jelliffe and his colleages (1962) have studied the infections of the Hadza, a hunting people of northern Tanganyika, about 800 in number, who live an isolated life in the tsetse area of the savannah. The Hadza are very mobile, especially in wet weather. They eat almost anything they can get, including baboon, vulture, and hyena, but not tortoises. The food is usually barbecued. An examination of 62 children showed them to be well nourished and with good teeth. Malaria parasites were present in 27 percent. In the stools, four children had *Taenia,* probably from the wart hogs they ate, and three had *Giardia.* Conjunctivitis was found in 30 percent; many had ringworm. There was no roundworm or hookworm, presumably because constant moving prevented transmission. In other words, the only infection found was that which could survive in a small population always on the move. Other infections, such as measles, rubella, and chickenpox, come to the Hadza only as introduced infections from populations large enough to support them on a permanent basis.

Neel and his associates (1964, 1968) have reported on the infections of the Xavante Indians of Brazil. Tests for various zoonoses were positive. No evidence was found of tuberculosis or treponemal infections, but there were high percentages of positives for measles, poliomyelitis, whooping cough, and malaria. Unfortunately, these tribes are not completely isolated from the outside world. They had trade articles; these articles could reach them, so could infectious diseases. The only form of trade that cuts transmission to a minimum is that of "silent barter," where the persons exchanging goods do not come into personal contact with each other. Even in that instance, smallpox can be passed on through infected blankets, as some tribes of North American Indians found to their sorrow.

The matter of population size leads us to the interesting question of the threshold sizes needed to support the acute community infections. If some 7,000 people on the Faroes were not enough to support measles indefinitely, would it have taken ten times, 100 times, or even 1,000 times that number of people?

In Greenland today, the population is about 30,000 people; until recently it was very isolated. Measles was unknown until 1951, when a sailor brought the infection from Denmark. As a result, practically every susceptible person in the area contracted the disease, and then it disappeared. The same pattern was repeated in 1955, in 1959, and in 1962. The spread of the infection was greatly speeded by the introduction of air travel (Bech 1962, 1965). Presumably the population was too small to support the disease indefinitely.

It is obvious that in large urban populations, such as Greater New York City and Greater London, with their many millions of people, measles can continue to exist throughout the year without breaking the chain of transmission. The threshold size for measles must, therefore, be somewhere between the populations of the Faroe Islands and Greenland and those of Greater New York City and London.

The population of the city of Cincinnati is 503,000 people. If the suburbs and neighboring towns are included, there are a little over a million people living in Greater Cincinnati. In 1961, the City Health Department was invited to take part in a program to test measles vaccine organized by the United States Public Health Service Communicable Disease Center, and for the next two years a careful watch was kept on the measles situation in the city (Guinee *et al.* 1963). More than 1,000 children took part in an experiment in which one-half were given vaccine and one-half were given placebos. The surveillance programs showed that measles could not be detected for two approximately four-month periods in the latter parts of the years 1962 and 1964. During those periods, cases reported to the Health Department by physicians proved either not to be measles or to have been acquired outside the city. As far as could be determined, the findings support the concept that the chain of transmission during the four-month periods of 1962 and 1964 had, in fact, failed. It may be that in an American city like Cincinnati a population of about 1,000,000 is near the threshold required to support measles as an endemic infection (Cockburn 1967).

Populations of the size needed to support the acute community infections did not exist on earth until the agricultural revolution had progressed to a substantial degree. These infections could not have evolved earlier than 10,000 years ago. Even

for some time after this, no single community had a population of a million people. In Iran, India, and China, however, there were civilizations with cities of 100,000–200,000 people, and if a half-dozen of these cities were linked closely enough by trade to permit the interchange of infections, the stage would be set for the acute community infections. That these infections did originate in the Old World seems quite clear. When intercontinental travel opened up the world to the interchange of infections, the natives of the newly discovered areas reacted very severely to the acute community infections of the newcomers, thus demonstrating that they had not experienced them before (Hirsch 1883, Cummins 1939, Stearn and Stearn 1945, Ashburn 1947).

In several instances the sources of the organisms causing these new diseases probably were the animals living in close relationship with man. For example, smallpox virus is very similar to a range of viruses found in domestic animals, the closest being cowpox virus (Hahon 1961); measles virus belongs to a group containing dog distemper and the cattle rindepest viruses; influenza virus is very closely related to viruses found in domestic animals, particularly that of the hog (Andrewes 1964, Meenan *et al.* 1962, Kilbourne 1968).

## Differential Resistance to Infection

There are three main types of resistance to infection: active immunity, in which the body reacts specifically against the invader; passive immunity, in which antibodies are passed from the mother to the offspring via the placenta, milk, or egg; and genetically inherited nonspecific resistance. The existence of this latter kind of immunity, which will be discussed here, cannot be doubted although its mode of action is usually obscure.

Infection with a pathogen reduces the survival capacity of the host and, all other factors being equal, the host with the most resistance is the one most likely to survive. If this resistance is inherited, then natural selection can be expected to produce a population more and more resistant to the prevalent pathogens, and in time a benign host-pathogen relationship will be established. The earliest expression of this idea I can find is contained in a paper read by W. C. Wells (cited in Darwin 1906) before the Royal Society in 1813, entitled "An Account of a White Female, Part of Whose Skin Resembles That of a Negro." In this paper Wells distinctly recognized the principle of natural selection. He stated that of the accidental varieties of man which occurred among the first few and scattered inhabitants of the middle regions of Africa, one would have been better fitted than the others to withstand the diseases of the country. This race would consequently have multiplied; the others would have decreased, not only because of their inability to sustain the attacks of the disease, but also because of their incapacity to contend with their more vigorous neighbors (cf. Darwin 1958).

The existence of genetically controlled nonspecific resistance has been debated for more than 30 years, chiefly by two teams of workers, one in the United States led by Webster and another in England under Topley and Greenwood. Webster (1932) showed that mice varied in their resistance to infection with *Salmonella* species and that selective breeding would produce, from a strain of mice 40 percent susceptible to infection, strains that were either 10 percent or 90 percent susceptible. In 1935, Greenwood and his colleagues summarized their results by saying that the available experimental data appeared to have established quite clearly the existence of significant differences in resistance among strains of mice or rats. Even in the most favorable records, however, there was no instance in which animals of the selected strain were uniformly resistant to bacterial infection, even when the test was resistance to infection by the bacteria concerned in a dose that failed to kill 100 percent of the unselected controls.

This deficiency was made up by Sabin in 1952, when he found a strain of mice 100 percent resistant to a dosage of yellow fever virus that was 100 percent lethal to standard test animals. By crossmating on Mendelian lines, he was able to show that this resistance was inherited according to Mendel's laws.

These reports have been paralleled by similar findings for mouse typhoid (Gowan 1948, 1951), the rat cysticercus disease due to the cat tapeworm, *Taenia taeniaeformis* (Curtis *et al.* 1933), and, at the cellular level, virus infections (Morgan 1960).

The natural selection pressures from infectious diseases can be very intense. Perhaps the best-known instance is the relationship between malaria and the abnormal hemoglobin that causes sickle cell anemia. The latter condition can be lethal, but the abnormal hemoglobin has the big advantage of protecting against the much more serious malaria. Natural selection in malarious areas has apparently favored persons with the sickle cell trait (Allison 1954, Livingstone 1967). Yellow fever is frequently lethal to Europeans, but the African living in an endemic area is naturally immune (Strode 1951). Conversely, the European is little affected by measles, but populations not previously exposed react disastrously when the virus reaches them. The introduction of measles to America by the Spaniards caused many catastrophes among the Indians.

The intensity of the pressures can be illustrated by the example of smallpox. Until the end of the 18th century, practically everyone in Europe was infected sooner or later. In London about 1750, where half those born were dead before the age of three, there were nearly 20,000 cases of smallpox a year. Haygarth (1793) quotes French estimates that one in ten of all children born died of smallpox and cites Baron Dimsdale, Dr. Percival, and other authorities as stating that the proportion of births to deaths from smallpox in London was $6\frac{1}{4}$ to one, in Manchester $6\frac{1}{2}$ to one, in Liverpool $5\frac{1}{2}$ to one, and in Chester $6\frac{2}{3}$ to one.

The contrast between the reactions to smallpox of Europeans and American Indians became evident early in the colonization of the New World. Diaz (1956) wrote:

Let us return now to Narvaez and a Negro he brought with him who was full of smallpox, and a very black dose it was for New Spain, for it was because of him that the whole country was stricken, with a great many deaths. According to what the Indians said, they had never had such a disease, and as they did not understand it, they washed themselves very often, and because of that, a great number of them died, so that black as was the luck of Narvaez, still blacker was the death of so many people who were not Christians.

The Spaniards were not affected, for they already had had the disease in childhood. So common was it in Spain to suffer from smallpox as a child that Ruy Diaz de Isla remarks that he knew a man that did not have it until his 20th year.

Perhaps more significant was the experience in Massachusetts. When smallpox broke out in the Plymouth Plantation, many were ill but only 20 persons died, including both young and aged. Yet when the Indians of Connecticut were attacked by the disease, nearly all died. Although the English nursed the sick Indians, none caught the disease (Bradford 1928).

That infectious disease can cause severe damage in a population not previously exposed to it has often been documented. This has led many workers to wonder if some of the ancient civilizations might not have been destroyed in this way. Did malaria lead to the downfall of the Singhalese cultures of 2,000 years ago? Could some infection have been the factor that caused the abandonment of the cities of central Mexico, or the dwellings of Mesa Verde?

Undoubtedly, some local groups or tribes have been brought to near extinction by some pathogens. In addition to the instances involving smallpox just mentioned, one thinks of the reports that whole tribes of Eskimos died in Alaska during the influenza pandemic of 1918–19 and the estimate that worldwide the disease killed 20,000,000 people in that period. Again, sleeping sickness depopulated wide areas of Africa; malaria was so severe in such localities as the Pontine marshes near Rome and parts of northern Greece that only a handful of people could live there; and the Black Death is judged to have killed a quarter of the population of Europe.

One must conclude, nevertheless, that so far there is no good evidence that any single significant culture was ever wiped out by an infection. In theorizing on any particular culture in this fashion, one must ask what specific organism could have produced the disaster. As far as America is concerned, it is my opinion that the acute community infections, such as measles and smallpox, and possibly malaria and yellow fever as well, were introduced after the Spanish invasion. I cannot think of any infection present before that time in the Americas that could have caused morbidity or mortality of such a scale as to result in the breakdown of a civilization. It is a different story in other parts of the world; but even the Black Death or the epidemic in Athens described by Thucydides (MacArthur 1958) did not destroy the civilizations in question. The matter remains an interesting speculation, but nothing more.

## STUDIES OF THE EVIDENCE

The importance of infectious disease in the control of populations demands that more attention be given to the study of the available evidence of infections in early man. This evidence is found primarily in fossil specimens, but ancient writings (Hoeppli 1959, Guerra 1964), paintings, sculptures, poetry, pottery, and folklore are also valuable sources. Analogies can often be made between primitive societies existing today and those of the past; such analogies lead to a better understanding of the societies of early man. Cultural patterns, civilizations, trade routes, occupations, and population sizes are all of great importance.

Geographic alterations, climatic fluctuation, and changing distributions of insect vectors must all be considered.

Paleopathology came of age in Egypt in the first decade of the 20th century. At that time, a new dam at Aswan threatened a number of sites of great importance in archaeology, so several investigators attempted to study the materials available before they were lost to science. Over 8,000 mummies were examined and much pathology found (Ruffer 1921, Ruffer and Smith 1910, Ruffer and Ferguson 1911, Smith and Wood Jones 1910, Morse, Brothwell, and Ucko 1964). It was found possible to reconstitute, to a surprising extent, the preserved soft tissue of the mummies and to demonstrate bacteria in sections of skin and various organs, such as the lungs and kidneys. The finds included a mummy with the calcified eggs of *Schistosoma haematobium* in the kidney, one with a psoas abscess, another with poliomyelitis, and yet another with possible smallpox lesions.

Since then, a great deal of work has been done in the field of the study of ancient human remains for evidence of disease; for reviews of the literature, see Moodie (1923), Pales (1930), Sigerist (1951), Brothwell (1961), Goldstein (1963), Ackerknecht (1965), Jarcho (1966), and Brothwell and Sandison (1967). There are still, however, sharp limitations to investigations of human relics. Usually, only diseases that produce pathologies in bones can be recognized. This limits diagnoses of infectious diseases to those that produce abscesses in bones or deformities such as those resulting from leprosy, tuberculosis, and syphilis.

The soft tissues are of most importance in infectious diseases, and all relics with any tissues still attached demand special attention. The largest groups are still, of course, the Egyptian mummies; these deserve a fresh study using methods that were not available to Ruffer and his colleagues. Their pioneering attempts to reconstitute the soft tissues need reexamining, and better techniques should be devised. The reports that bacteria could be seen in sections should be followed up and attempts made to identify the bacteria. If chickenpox, warts, or molluscum contagiosum existed in those days the scars might be detectable on the skin. Guinea worm was almost certainly present (was it the fiery serpent that afflicted the Israelites in the desert?) and would leave a scar on the ankle. The eggs of lice might still be present on the hairs of the head and pubis. Containers in which intestines were preserved should be examined for parasite eggs or cysts.

A naturally mummified body of 4,000 years ago found in a cave in South America has provided the earliest record of head lice infestation (Ewing 1926); some of the hair was still attached, and on it were found head louse eggs. An even more valuable find was the frozen body of an Inca child found in a small stone building on a mountain near Santiago, Chile at an elevation of 17,658 ft. It was a remarkably well-preserved specimen, estimated as that of a boy eight-to-nine-years old who had died about 450 years ago. Contents of the rectum showed numerous eggs of *Trichuris trichiura* and some unidentifiable cysts of *Entamoeba* (Pizzi and Schenone 1955).

A very exciting find has been made in Russia (Artamonov 1965). In the Altai mountains of that country, many tombs of the Scythians, dating back to 400 B.C., have been excavated, revealing the frozen bodies of the people and their horses. Apparently, the Scythians dug deep holes in the ground for burials and then roofed the tombs with tree trunks. Since the ground was very cold, the water of condensation which fell on the bodies froze, encasing everything in the tomb in ice. Some of the bodies are in an excellent state of preservation and appear as though buried just yesterday. According to Artamonov (personal communication), no medical inspections of the bodies have yet been made, but obviously all kinds of skin lesions should be discernible, and possibly parasites and their eggs may still exist in the parts of alimentary tracts that remain.

The single most promising field at the moment is the study of ancient feces. Very large quantities are available already, and if special attention were given in the field much more would be forthcoming. The few studies of ancient feces already reported make it quite clear that parasite eggs in good condition can survive in recognizable forms for long periods of time.

Biddle (1967:58) gives this account of British studies:

The best work so far comes from Winchester, England. The first report of parasite eggs from archaeological excavations in Britain is that of Taylor (1955) who identified large numbers of eggs of the nematodes *Ascaris lumbricoides* and *Trichuris trichiura* and of the fluke *Dicrocoelium dendriticum* (Rud.) in soil from a medieval timber-lined cess-pit on a site at Middle Brook Street, Winchester. In 1964 Dr. H. H. Williams and Mr. A. W. Pike of the Commonwealth Bureau of Helminthology, alerted by Taylor's publication, took further samples from a second pit in Lower Brook Street (Biddle 1965, pp. 245–46). Pike has since confirmed the presence of very

large numbers of helminth eggs of the nematodes *Ascaris* sp., *Trichuris* sp. and of the fluke *Dicrocoelium dendriticum* at average concentrations of 450, 2,300, and 216 per gramme respectively (Biddle and Pike 1966). All the eggs were in an excellent state of preservation and were easily recognizable, even the remains of the embryo within the egg being visible.

The possibility of eggs surviving in recognizable forms for perhaps thousands of years is suggested by a study on fecal material of about 3000 B.C. from Peru. The specimens consisted of coprolites that had been rapidly desiccated in the very dry atmosphere and material collected from the abdomen of a skeleton. The specimens were soaked in a 0.5 percent aqueous solution of sodium triphosphate for 72 hours, after which the mixture was sedimented and the precipitate examined for food particles and parasite eggs. The procedure was so successful that remains of plant and sea foods could be readily recognized and sometimes even the smell was recreated. The eggs of a species of *Diphyllobothrium*, a fish tapeworm common in carnivores in South America today, were identified (Callen and Cameron 1960).

Samuels (1965) examined feces from the Wetherill Mesa cliff dwellings. In one specimen he discovered eggs of the pinworm *Enterobius vermicularis* in which the larvae inside were still clearly visible. Numerous microorganisms were seen but not identified.

The statistical analysis of adequate samples of relicts could be a powerful tool in studies of diseases of ancient populations. As long ago as 1910, Smith and Wood Jones showed that the distribution of fractures in Nubian skeletons differed from that of a modern population. More recently, Brothwell (1961) has shown a probable difference in the susceptibility to osteoarthritis in modern and ancient British populations. The time has come when it is no longer enough for a fieldworker to select a few bones with obvious pathologies and ignore the remainder. Fortunately, several workers have undertaken the tedious procedure of examining *all* the material of a find with significant results. According to Roney (1959), Hooton's (1930) work on the Indians of Pecos Pueblo is an early example of the statistical study of evidences of disease in ancient populations. Roney also cites the work of Krogman (1940), Angel (1946), Goldstein (1957), Vallois (1937), and Todd (1927). More recent works along these lines are those of Angel (1967), Roney (1959) on a California archaeological site, Warwick (1964) at a Roman cemetery in York, England, and Anderson

(1963) in an Iroquois ossuary. In all of these studies, there is emphasis upon studying a population sample, upon relating disease to age, sex, and race, upon observing temporal trends in disease, and upon relating disease to cultural factors. This approach is, therefore, epidemiological, concerning itself with host and environmental factors in diseases occurring in a population sample.

## SUMMARY

1. Most of man's specific infections are descended from those acquired from his prehuman ancestors. The apes and monkeys of today received infections from the same source.

2. Every change in the environment or culture is reflected in the patterns of the infectious diseases of the population. In particular, the invention of agriculture and the domestication of animals had a profound effect on the evolution of new infections and increased hazards from some previously existing ones.

3. Natural selection results in a population increasingly resistant to a pathogen to which it is exposed; and a population exposed to a pathogen to which it has not developed resistance may be devastated by it.

4. Since infectious disease is one of the most important factors controlling populations, more attention should be given to the study of the available evidence of infections of early man. The soft tissues that are found in a state of preservation are of particular importance, and special care should be taken of them. Feces are also an important and promising source of information. A statistical approach to the evidence of disease in ancient populations can be a powerful research tool.

# III
# Ecology and Epidemiology of Disease

## Adaptation to Disease and Its Distribution in Human Populations

In writing on the ecology of human disease and adaptation to disease by human groups, Alland (1970:52–113) provides a useful summary of the major dimensions involved and places these subjects in an anthropological perspective. Among the many factors in human disease ecology, Alland notes the size, density, and mobility of human populations, the organism's environment outside the human host, mode of infection, viability and type of vector and carrier, immunity, symptoms, incubation period, nutrition, and stress. He also provides a useful model of adaptation analyzed as "behavior strategies developed in response to pathology" and shows how these strategies on the part of human groups may succeed or fail as they provide the group with the capability to deal with these factors: acute versus chronic disease; complexity of the route of infection; reservoir versus nonreservoir; degree of severity; endemic versus epidemic; degree of prevalence and incidence; discreteness of symptomology; and degree of contagion (Ibid.: 89ff). The selections that follow deal with several of these factors, although for completeness the reader would do well to read the Alland volume and also consult textbooks in epidemiology and medical ecology, especially works dealing with the adaptive aspects of disease and stress (for example, Burnet 1963, Burnet and White 1972, Burton and Smith 1975, Dubos 1965, Fox, Hall, and Elveback 1970, Hobson 1965, Mausner and Bahn 1974, Paul 1964).

That society is more likely to survive that is capable of designing cultural techniques, or behavioral strategies in Alland's conception, for preventing infections of its members, healing members once they are infected, and minimizing possibilities for contagion. This requires attention to factors connected with the potentially lethal organisms and micro-organisms that inhabit human internal and external environments (knowledge of which, in many societies, may be rudimentary, inaccurate, or nonexistent). Some heed must be paid to the requirements of sanitation and conditions of living. Therefore, all ecological techniques, from house types to methods of preparing foods, from systems of social control to medical systems, are critical factors in determining the fate of a group with regard to disease (infectious and noninfectious, acute and chronic). Furthermore, as we see in the following chapters, not only do a society's ecology, history, culture, and collective biological traits largely determine the course of a disease in that population, but the course and characteristics of a disease, in turn, influence the demography, biology, and, at times, the culture of a society. The social organization, cultural values and traditions, and general modes of existence of a human group are fundamental factors in the epidemiology of any disease. Thus, in human evolution, in the continuing complex transactions among the biological and social-cultural components of populations, disease may play a decisive role. These factors, in turn, as we see in this section and throughout the book, play a vital part in the history and development of disease.

The ecology of a disease is intertwined with its epidemiology, that is, its spread in time and space. Epidemiology has been defined as "the study of the distribution and determinants of disease and injuries in human populations" (Mausner and Bahn 1974:3). The pertinence of epidemiological studies for medical anthropology is fundamental, since it represents a type of investigation that is based on populations and groups within populations, and upon all the environmental, biological, social, cultural, and historical elements characteristic of such agglomerations that bear upon the distribution and causal linkages of disease. As Mausner and Bahn (Ibid.:4) say, "This implies that disease is not randomly distributed throughout a population, but rather that subgroups differ in the frequency of different diseases." As an example let us turn to the horrendous and strange disease, *kuru*, which was taking a devastating toll among the Fore people of New Guinea. It is a progressive, degenerative impairment of the central nervous system, and almost invariably fatal. Two anthropologists, Ann and John Fischer (1961), examined the ethnographic materials on the Fore and the medical-biological studies being conducted by teams of scientists trying to discover its etiology. From these the Fischers constructed an epidemiological picture and tested the various theories against the facts. The Fischers considered the prevalent theories, especially that the disease was genetic (and which was held by many investigators) and decided that the evidence failed to support them. They suggested that the explanation had to be largely social-cultural, although it was likely to involve an infectious agent. They said, "If *kuru* is passed by a viral or other infectious agent, such an agent must be one which is in more contact with women and children than with men. The Fore culture presents a clear-cut opportunity for such an agent in the separate dwellings of men and women" (Fischer and Fischer 1961:24). They also suggested that the Fore practice of cannibalism could well be implicated.

Ultimately, medical investigators (Alpers 1970, Zigas and Gadjusek 1957, Gadjusek 1963) were able to demonstrate that the disease was caused by a slowly developing virus with a long latency period and that it attacked women and adolescent males and females, but seldom adult males. These were precisely the groups practicing ritual cannibalism. And as cannibalism was outlawed the rate of *kuru* infection decreased and today is marked by a disappearing incidence.

The idea of including environmental and social-cultural factors in studying the distributions and etiologies of diseases is not new. According to Fox, Hall, and Elveback (1970:20) the first epidemiologist was also the first systematic medical clinician, Hippocrates. Whatever its origins, the discipline of epidemiology has become a highly useful method, or cluster of methods and methodologies, for understanding how diseases are distributed among populations and for understanding the paths they take in the causal sequence. To this study anthropology may make its contribution as epidemiology may contribute to it. As Fox, Hall, and Elveback (Ibid.:15–16) state,

Epidemiology is more method than a body of knowledge. In investigating disease causation, it depends heavily on knowledge and skills drawn as needed from many other sciences. These include clinical medicine. microbiology, pathology, zoology, demography, anthropology, sociology, and, almost universally, statistics.

Anyone familiar with the history of anthropological theory will know that anthropology is itself no stranger to the practice of drawing from other fields of knowledge. To the listing just stated should perhaps be added another discipline, that of history, and in particular the skills of the medical historian, as the paper in this section on the history of syphilis will show. For a subject of interest both to medical anthropology and epidemiology is that of the origin and spread of disease. Just as a knowledge of the evolution of human groups and their contacts with each other may throw light for the medical historian upon the origin and spread of a pestilence, a knowledge of the latter, in turn, may aid the anthropologist in illuminating the evolution, modes of adaptation, and distribution of human societies and cultures. Such studies demonstrate the need not only for the talents of the historiographer but for knowledge of the biological characteristics of the disease itself.

The methods of ethnohistory may also come into play to investigate certain epidemiological questions, as well as those of historical demography. For example, a study by a historian and a physician in the journal *Ethnohistory*, "The 'Intermittent Fever' Epidemic of the 1830's on the Lower Columbia River" (Taylor and Hoaglin 1962), investigates the depopulation of several large groups of American Indians in the American Northwest and solves the mystery of the malady described in early documents as "intermittent fever" (which turned out to be epidemic influenza). A somewhat different problem of the implication of disease in the depopulation of indigenous peoples is found in the paper on malaria by Friedlander later in this section. Another recent ethnohistorical study of interest to medical anthropologists is the account of a smallpox epidemic on the Six Nations Reserve of Canadian Iroquois Indians (Weaver 1971). Here the relative mildness of the infection and the feelings of invidiousness on the part of the reservation governing council (because of the perception of threat by the surrounding white community) combined to increase the strength of external political authority, weaken the hold of internal power, and create indifference to the epidemic, thus facilitating its spread.

# 9 Health and Disease in Hunter-Gatherers: Epidemiological Factors

## Frederick L. Dunn

In their introductory chapter to the ground-breaking review and stock-taking of hunter-gatherer cultures, *Man the Hunter*, Lee and DeVore (1968:3) state:

Cultural man has been on earth for some 2,000,000 years [more recent estimates would

Reprinted with abridgments and with changes by the author from Frederick L. Dunn, 1968, "Epidemiological Factors: Health and Disease in Hunter-Gatherers," from *Man the Hunter*, eds. Richard L. Lee and Irven DeVore, Chicago: Aldine Publishing Co., with permission of the author and Aldine Publishing Co. Copyright 1968 by the Wenner-Gren Foundation, Inc., for Anthropological Research, Inc.

double that figure—Ed.]; for over 99 percent of this period he has lived as a hunter-gatherer. Only in the last 10,000 years has man begun to domesticate plants and animals, to use metals, and to harness energy sources other than the human body. *Homo Sapiens* assumed an essentially modern form at least 50,000 years before he managed to do anything about improving his means of production. Of the estimated 80 billion men who have ever lived out a life span on earth, over 90 percent have lived as hunters and gatherers; about 6 percent have lived by agriculture and the remaining few percent have lived in industrial societies. To date, the hunting way of life has been the most successful and persistent adaptation man has ever achieved.

This mode of adaptation, now and in the ancient past, has always been a topic of fundamental interest to anthropology. Even as the remaining hunter-gatherer peoples are moving toward cultural change—or extinction—so that this mode of existence may disappear completely on this planet, anthropologists, working with other scientists, have begun to discover that perhaps man the hunter might really be better termed woman the gatherer. Estimates as to the actual proportion of food of such groups yielded through foraging range as high as 50 percent (Kolata 1974), so that hunting's other functions (social and symbolic) may have been more essential than those of diet and subsistence (at least in those environments permitting such yields). Be that as it may, the health and disease of such societies are matters of great importance about which we still know relatively little. This paper by Frederick Dunn from the Lee-DeVore survey is a much-needed endeavor to bring together some of the facts and factors involved and to present them in an ecological context. It is a prolegomenon to a line of research that is greatly needed both in medical and general anthropology. Disease is seen by Dunn as one, but only one, variable in the regulation of size and stability of human populations. Since hunter-gatherer societies live in such close interdependent communion with their physical and biological environments, Dunn shows how a comparison of ecosystems may initiate the formulation of principles for the study of environmental limitations and possibilities with regard to humans and their transactions with internal and external biological friends and enemies. In connection with this paper the reader will want to refer to other selections in this volume by Dumond (Chapter 33) and Cockburn (Chapter 8).

## INTRODUCTION

A series of generalizations concerning health, disease, and mortality in hunter-gatherers are reviewed and discussed in this paper. Some are long-established and widely accepted; others are proposed in the light of certain considerations of ecological diversity and complexity. I shall refer particularly to the published record for health and disease in the Bushman, the Australian aborigine, the Eskimo, the African Pygmy, and the Semang (Malayan Negrito). In the course of the discussion some epidemiological or "medical ecological" issues will be raised which pertain to the study of diseases: (1) as agents of natural selection, and (2) as dependent or independent variables influencing size and stability of human populations. I shall emphasize the role of disease in population regulation rather than in selection, but much that will be said relates to both areas of inquiry. Disease—particularly parasitic and infectious disease—has attracted considerable attention from human geneticists and anthropologists in recent years (Livingstone 1960; Motulsky 1960; Neel *et al.* 1964; World Health Organization, 1964) but the role of disease in population regulation has been somewhat neglected.

Whether one's concern may be the destiny of the modern hunter-gatherer or the reconstruction of prehistoric hunting and gathering conditions, hunter-gatherer studies are really urgent today. This urgency is emphasized in a succinct World Health Organization report, "Research in population genetics of primitive groups" (1964), which also outlines research needs, procedures, and the kinds of demographic, ethnographic, genetic, and biomedical data whose collection is so essential. These procedural matters need not be discussed here, but a brief review of the means available for gathering data and developing a picture of disease patterns in prehistoric hunter-gatherers may be useful. Only four approaches come to mind:

1. We may study health and disease in modern hunter-gatherers and project these findings into the past. This approach assumes that disease patterns in populations still removed from substantial contact with outsiders are to some extent similar to ancient disease patterns. The extensive pilot study of the Xavante Indians of the Brazilian Mato Grosso by Neel and his colleagues (1964) is a good example. Their report provides some tentative hypotheses of human genetic and evolutionary interest; many indications exist that additional studies along the same lines may also provide data of value in the interpretation of prehistoric populations and demographic conditions.

2. We may review first-contact records—historical and ethnographic within this century—for information about specific diseases and conditions of health. Much of our knowledge of aboriginal health conditions in the Americas has been built up in this way (Cook 1955, for example).

3. We may make use of increasing refinement of archeological technique and extensive multidisciplinary collaboration in archeological investigations, which are beginning to provide extraordinary dividends in knowledge of the prehistoric environment. Paleoecological studies now make it possible to assess prehistoric environmental potentials for transmission of infectious and parasitic agents of disease. Paleopathological investigations are becoming increasingly sophisticated, and coprolite studies, which also provide valuable dietary and ecological information, have opened the way to epidemiological assessment of intestinal helminthiases in prehistoric populations (Callen and Cameron 1960; Samuels 1965). Recently, in collaboration with Dr. Robert Heizer of the University of California I have had the opportunity to study a series of more than fifty coprolites from Lovelock Cave in Nevada. We found no eggs or

larvae of parasitic helminths, but because of the extraordinary state of preservation of certain pseudoparasites—mites and nematodes—we were able to conclude, with a fair degree of certainty, that the ancient people represented by these specimens were in fact free of a whole series of intestinal helminths, including flukes, tapeworms, and important nematodes such as hookworm and *Ascaris*. This conclusion was not altogether surprising in the light of our knowledge of helminthiasis in modern Bushmen and other hunter-gatherers of arid regions.

4. We may finally approach the study of prehistoric patterns of disease in man through the study of disease patterns in non-human primates today in a variety of ecological settings, some of which are shared with modern hunter-gatherers (Dunn MS-1, MS-2). In this relatively unexplored field we can only expect to discern broad patterns of similarity for man and other primates. I shall return briefly to this approach when I discuss ecological complexity and diversity.

## DISEASE IN THE POPULATION EQUATION

To examine the role of disease in a human population, we may refer to the "equation of recruitment and loss" of Wynne-Edwards (1962), defining the variables contributing to the condition of population stability:

Recruit- + Immi-  = Uncon-  + Emi-  + Social
ment        gration    trollable    gration    Mor-
Arising              Losses                        tality
from Re-
production

In this equation, "uncontrollable losses" are identified as the independent variable and include losses due to predation, parasitism (infectious and parasitic diseases), accidents, starvation and old age (chronic diseases, diseases associated with aging). Social mortality comprises that mortality arising from "social stress": strife, stress diseases, cannibalism, infanticide, war, homicide, suicide, etc. Wynne-Edwards, with an acknowledgement to Carr-Saunders (1922), discusses population stability in hunter-gatherer and subsistence agriculturalist societies in terms of this equation. Births and immigration are balanced by emigration and two kinds of mortality, the socially controllable (social mortality) and the socially uncontrollable (losses due to independent variables). Within the realm of

controllable (sometimes even "acceptable") mortality is population regulation by abortion and infanticide, by reduction in numbers (sacrifice, cannibalism, head-hunting and other forms of warfare, geronticide, and even homicide and suicide), and by territoriality (rules regulating the utilization of space and resources, land tenure, marriage regulations, etc.). In a brief discussion of mortality due to predation and disease, Wynne-Edwards points out that neither of these variables can be considereed wholly density-dependent or density-independent. Predation not only contributes to uncontrollable loss but is also density-dependent insofar as the prey may "cooperate" in making its surplus members available to predators. Similarly, infectious and parasitic diseases may be either uncontrollable or density-dependent, as socially stressed individuals are selected out by disease because of their "depressed" physiological state. Thus, as variables contributing to mortality, predation and disease due to parasitism are to some extent controllable and density-dependent, to some extent uncontrollable and independent. The disease variable is obviously important in the regulation of human population but its impact is constantly modified by sociocultural and ecological factors. Other variables in the demographic equation—notably accidents, predation, and certain forms of social mortality—may affect population size more profoundly than disease in certain settings.

## MORTALITY AND DISEASE IN HUNTER-GATHERERS

Some of the characteristics of the hunting and gathering way of life (as seen today and in historic times) that may influence the prevalence and distribution of various diseases and other causes of mortality are these: the size of the social group is small, and contact between groups is limited, in part because of the relatively large area needed to support each small population unit; the group utilizes environmental resources intensively but with minimal permanent disturbance of the environment; the individuals are well adapted to the conditions of the ecosystem in which they belong; the individual lives in intimate contact with his fellows and the environment; the group is characteristically mobile, within certain territorial limits; dwellings are often rudimentary or temporary; the dietary range is relatively wide, at least potentially—less desirable foods are available as a reserve for times of hardship; in general the diet may be said to be well balanced in the sense that minimal nutritional requirements are apparently met; in the tropics and subtropics the vegetable component of the diet normally exceeds the animal component in quantity if not in quality; in the arctic and in certain maritime and riverine settings the animal component may bulk larger than the vegetable; occupational specialization except along lines of age and sex is relatively slight.

With these characteristics in mind we may consider some generalizations about health, disease, and mortality in hunting and gathering peoples (prehistoric, precontact, or isolated modern population).

1. *Patent (and perhaps even borderline) malnutrition is rare.* We should expect this in stable, well-adapted hunter-gatherer populations, modern or prehistoric. Dietary resources, even in arid environments, are diverse: typical sampling of these resources by modern hunter-gatherers in ecosystems relatively undisturbed by outsiders seems to provide at least the minimal protein, carbohydrate, fat, mineral, and vitamin requirements. Many workers have commented on the relatively good nutritional status of hunter-gatherers in comparison with neighboring agriculturalists or urban dwellers (for example: Ackerknecht 1948; Maingard 1937; Turnbull 1965b; Woodburn 1959). Neel (1962) postulated a dramatic gorging-and-fasting way of life for hunter-gatherers through "99 percent of hominid existence" in developing his hypotheses of the "thrifty" diabetic genotype. In the light of recent studies of the Bushman (Lee 1965), this portrayal of major fluctuations in the quantity and quality of the hunter-gatherer diet is probably somewhat exaggerated.

2. *Starvation occurs infrequently.* While hunter-gatherers are rarely exposed to *relative* dietary deficiencies leading to malnutrition, they may, exceptionally, be faced with *gross* deficits. In tropical and temperate regions of moderate to heavy rainfall, starvation has undoubtedly been the exception, occurring only in individuals incapacitated for other reasons (Turnbull 1965b). In the arid tropics only an unusually prolonged drought may be expected to imperil the food supply, but failure of the water supply may select out the aged and sick before gross food shortages can have their effect. In the arctic and subarctic winter, on the other hand, starvation has probably always been a relatively important cause of death (Ackerknecht 1948). In general it seems that agriculturalists, more or less dependent on one or several staple crops, are more liable to food supply failure and

famine than are hunters and gatherers. Famine risk may even be increased as the effects of dry seasons are exaggerated through agricultural modification of the natural vegetational cover.

3. *Chronic diseases, especially those associated with old age, are relatively infrequent.* Birth rates are high, but the population pyramid for hunter-gatherers is broad only at the base because life-expectancy at birth is low for males and even lower for females (Ackerknecht 1948; Krogman 1939; Krzwicki 1934; Neel *et al.* 1964; Polunin 1953; Roney 1959). Shorter female life expectancies presumably reflect maternal losses in childbirth, stresses associated with multiple pregnancies and deliveries, and in certain cultures male-female dietary disparities. Although life expectancies of hunter-gatherers are low by modern European or American standards, they compare favourably with expectancies for displaced hunter-gatherers, many subsistence agriculturalists, and impoverished urbanized people of the tropics today (Ackerknecht 1948; Billington 1960; Duguid 1963; Dunn MS-1; Maingard 1937; Polunin 1953). Few hunter-gatherers survive long enough to develop clinical cardiovascular disease or cancer, major causes of mortality in America and Europe today. These diseases do occur infrequently, however, and preclinical manifestations of cardiovascular disorder may be detected in such populations (Mann *et al.* 1962). Occasional writers have claimed that certain primitive populations are "cancer-free" or "heart disease-free," but sound evidence to support such contentions is lacking, and evidence to the contrary has been steadily accumulating. Chronic diseases of early onset, including genetic disorders, do of course occur regularly in all human populations; upon survey the more severe of these appear less frequent in hunter-gatherers, probably because prolonged survival of incapacitated individuals is less likely in mobile than in settled situations. Such persons have sometimes been abandoned or killed, particularly in the Arctic (Ackerknecht 1948).

4. *Accidental and traumatic death rates vary greatly among hunter-gatherer populations.* It is sometimes said that accidents constitute a major cause of death in hunting and gathering societies. Although this is indeed the case for certain peoples, it is not universally true for all hunter-gatherers, past and present. Deaths due to drowning, burns, suffocation, exposure, and hunting accidents have probably always weighed heavily in the population equation for Eskimos and other peoples of polar and subpolar regions (Ackerknecht 1948; Hughes

1965; World Health Organization 1963). The Australian aborigines and Bushmen, on the other hand, cannot often drown or suffocate or fall from trees, and are physiologically tolerant of an environment that is climatically "constant" compared to that of the Eskimo. Turnbull (1965b) has recently commented on the low incidence of accidental injuries and deaths among the Mbuti Pygmies. He recorded falls from trees, falls into campfires, attacks by animals, falling on a spear, bee stings, and snakebites as Congo forest hazards. Similarly, Billington (1960) noted the infrequent occurrence of trauma among "settled" aborigines in Arnhem Land. Paleopathologists have nevertheless demonstrated abundant traumatic pathology in skeletal series for certain hunters and agriculturalists; most of these series have been recovered from archeological sites outside the tropics.

5. *Predation, excluding snakebite, is a minor cause of death in modern hunter-gatherers; predation may have been relatively more important in the past.* Haldane (1957) and Motulsky (1960) suggest that through much of hominid evolution predation and other selective agencies were far more important than infectious and parasitic diseases, which became major agents of natural selection only after the introduction of agriculture with its concomitant increases in population density, community size, and community contact. Livingstone (1958) has provided an interpretation of sickle cell gene distribution in West Africa that supports such an hypothesis, but little other evidence is available at this time to assist us in evaluating Haldane's suggestion. We cannot rule out the possibility (a strong probability, in my opinion) that some infectious and parasitic diseases were important selective agencies in prehistoric hunting and gathering populations, as they undoubtedly are and have been in modern hunter-gatherer societies. Other parasites and microorganisms have undoubtedly become important in selection only in recent millenia in response to culturally induced environmental change. We do not know the relative importance of predators at various points in human evolution, although common sense suggests that predators constituted a greater hazard for early man than for modern hunter-gatherers. Accurate predation data for the great apes would be of interest in this connection, but it would be rash to utilize these data in generalizing about predation in early hominid life. In reviewing some of the literature on health in hunter-gatherers, I have come upon occasional references to snakebite fatalities, which were apparently particularly frequent in Australia (Cleland 1928), but references to animal attacks have been few, even for the Arctic (Ackerknecht 1948; Turnbull 1965b).

6. *Mental disorders of hunting and gathering peoples have been so little investigated that no generalizations about incidence can be justified.* Descriptions I have encountered of presumed mental disorder have been presented in terms of the psychological norms of the observer-recorder (for example, Cleland 1928; Basedow 1932). Ackerknecht (1948) and others have suggested that the rates for phobias and hysteria were higher for the precontact Eskimo than for other societies; discussions of mental disorder in other hunter-gatherers usually emphasize that mental health was good, at least in the aboriginal state. Facts to support such statements are essentially nonexistent. Cawte and his colleagues in Australia are pioneering in their ethnopsychiatric investigations of acculturated and unacculturated aborigines. A few limited psychological investigations of Bushmen and Pygmies have been cited by Doob (1965).

7. *Ample evidence is available that "social mortality" has been and is significant in the population equation for any hunting and gathering society.* Cannibalism, infanticide, sacrifice, geronticide, head-hunting, and other forms of warfare have largely disappeared today, but the early contact records provide abundant evidence of the importance of these practices in many societies (for example, Ackerknecht 1948; Krzwicki 1934; Neel *et al.* 1964; Radcliffe-Brown 1933). Other forms of social mortality, such as homicide, suicide, and stress diseases, were apparently less frequent prior to contact; today they are replacing the old forms and increasing in frequency in displaced and acculturated hunter-gatherers as in so many other human societies (Doob 1965; Duguid 1963; Hughes 1965; Polunin 1953; World Health Organization 1963).

8. *Parasitic and infectious disease rates of prevalence and incidence are related to ecosystem diversity and complexity. Although many of these diseases contribute substantially to mortality, no simple, single generalization is possible for all hunter-gatherers.*

A. *Introductory comments: Infection.* Infections by microorganisms and parasites may be classified for epidemiological purposes in two primary subdivisions: *asexual infections* (organisms reproducing asexually) and *sexual infections* (organisms with some form of sexual reproduction; Macdonald 1965). Each subdivision may be further divided into *direct* and *indirect* categories. An indirect infection requires some development outside the definitive host in normal transmission. This type of infection is therefore partially dependent upon conditions of environmental temperature and humidity; many but not all are specifically tropical.

Asexual infections may be introduced into a population by a single dose in a single individual. Multiplication in the community occurs most readily if the agent is *rare* in that community, and particularly if that agent has not circulated in the community previously. Malaria and yellow fever, whose agents are arthropod vector-transmitted, are good examples of indirect asexual infections. Direct asexual infections are numerous; they include many of the common viral and bacterial infections of mankind (measles, smallpox, diphtheria, etc.). Asexual infections often produce partial and sometimes complete acquired immunity to repeated infection.

Sexual infections cannot normally be introduced into new populations by single doses. The agents multiply and maintain themselves in the population more readily if they occur in large numbers in a high proportion of available hosts—that is, if the prevalence rate is high in the community and if the intensity of infection in the individual is great. Indirect sexual infections include many of the helminthiases: schistosomiasis, filariasis, hookworm infection, etc. Direct sexual infections are not numerous, but include such well-known parasitic helminths as the pinworm. Sexual infections stimulate poor to partial acquired immunity at best.

B. *Introductory comments: Ecological diversity and complexity.* The concepts of ecological diversity and complexity are well known to ecologists (Holdridge 1965; Odum 1959) but little attention has been paid to their epidemiological implications until recently. The starting point for discussion is the climax tropical rainforest, which is characterized by many species of plants and animals per unit area and by few individuals per species in the same unit area. A one-hectare plot in the Brazilian tropical rainforest, for example, contained 564 trees (greater than 10 cm. diameter at chest height) belonging to 60 species. Even the commonest species was represented by only 49 individuals, and 33 species were represented by single individuals (Dobzhansky 1950). I need not stress the contrast with the tree species/individual relationships in boreal forest. As Dobzhansky (1950) has said, where diversity of inhabitants is great, the environment is rich in adaptive opportunities. This diversity in climax rain forest applies not only to trees,

and to other plants, but of course also to birds, snakes, insects, mammals, and many other forms of life, not omitting potential or actual vectors, intermediate hosts, and alternative hosts for infective organisms. We are now beginning to see that this diversity also extends to parasites and microorganisms.

The ratio between the number of species and the number of individuals per species has been called the *diversity index* (Odum 1959). In the tropical rain forest the diversity index is high; wherever man disturbs this forest the index is lower; wherever physical factors are severe and limiting, as in the Arctic, the desert, or at high altitude, the diversity index is very low—few species but large numbers of individuals per species. At an "edge," that is, the line of contact between a forest and a field, the diversity index may be somewhat higher than on either side of the line. Wherever man has substantially altered the environment, and the diversity is accordingly low, some of the species represented by large numbers of individuals are commonly called "weeds." Actually all plants and animals (including man) are weeds in such circumstances.

The *complexity index* recently developed by Holdridge (1965) provides a measure of vegetation complexity (and secondarily of other biological complexity), but should not be confused with the diversity index. The complexity index is based on height of forest stand, basal area of stand, number of trees, and number of tree species, but it does not take into account the number of trees per species. Holdridge has recently published a useful classification of world plant formations; it provides complexity indices for many of these formations (Holdridge 1965).

C. *Infection and Ecological Diversity and Complexity: Hypothetical Conditions.* We may now contrast two "ideal" and undisturbed ecosystems including human populations of similar group sizes, similarly dispersed (Table 1). One is complex—with high diversity and complexity indices; the other is simple—with low indices.

D. *Generalizations: infectious and parasitic disease in hunter-gatherers.* The ideal conditions outlined in Table 1 for a *complex* ecosystem are believed applicable in any consideration of infection in unacculturated, undisplaced Congo forest Pygmies or Malayan Negritos (Semang). The conditions for a *simple ecosystem* are presumably applicable to the Eskimo, the Bushman, or the Australian aborigine. These conditions should also be relevant in any epidemiological study of

**Table 1**  Infection in Ecosystems of Contrasting Diversity and Complexity

| Complex Ecosystem (example: tropical rain forest) | Simple Ecosystem (examples: subpolar tundra, desert bush, thorn woodland) |
|---|---|
| —*Many* species of plants and animals | —*Few* species of plants and animals |
| —*Few* individuals per species | —*Many* individuals per species |
| —*Many* species of parasitic and infectious organisms (in man and in other animals) | —*Few* species of parasitic and infectious organisms (in man and in other animals) |
| —*Many* species of potential vectors, intermediate hosts, and alternative hosts (to man) for parasitic and infectious organisms | —*Few* species of potential vectors, intermediate hosts, and alternative hosts (to man) for parasitic and infectious organisms |
| —*Low* potential transmission efficiency for indirect infections | —*High* potential transmission efficiency for those few indirect infections occurring in this ecosystem |
| —Sexual infections: *many* kinds due to many species of organisms | —Sexual infections: *few* kinds |
| —Sexual infections: *low* intensities of infection—*low* worm burdens—light infections | —Sexual infections: *greater* intensity of infection—*heavier* worm burdens |
| —Asexual infections: *many* kinds due to many species of organisms | —Asexual infections: *few* kinds |
| —Direct asexual infections producing good partial or permanent immunity: appearing in human population units at long intervals | —Direct asexual infections producing good partial or permanent immunity: appearing in human population units at long intervals |
| —Direct asexual infections producing little or no immunity: *low* prevalence | —Direct asexual infections producing little or no immunity: *high* prevalence |
| —Indirect asexual infections (except those producing substantial immunity): *low* prevalence | —Indirect asexual infections (except those producing substantial immunity): *high* prevalence |
| —(Also: many species but few individuals of venomous and noxious arthropods and reptiles = *low* incidence of bites) | —(Also: many individuals of a few species of venomous and noxious arthropods and reptiles = *high* incidence of bites) |

**Table 2**  Parasitic Helminths and Protozoa in Four Hunting and Gathering Peoples (summarizing all available records)

| | Bushman Africa | Australian Aborigine Entire Continent | Central Australia | Semang Malaya | Pygmy Africa |
|---|---|---|---|---|---|
| Plant Formation | Desert Desert Bush Thorn Woodland | Primarily: Desert Desert Bush Thorn Woodland | Desert Desert Bush | Tropical, Premontane and Lower Montane Rain-Forest | Tropical and Premontane Rain-Forest |
| Complexity Index (Holdridge) | 5.6 or less | primarily less than 5.6 | 5.6 or less | 270–405 | 270–405 |
| No. Species Helminths | 2 | 6 | 1 | 10 | 11 |
| No. Species Intestinal Protozoa | — | 1 | — | 9 | 6 |
| No. Species Blood Protozoa | 1 | 2 | — | 3 | 3 |
| Total No. Species | 3 | 9 | 1 | 22 | 20 |

105

infection in non-human primates: in the more or less arboreal rain-forest species on the one hand, and in the more or less terrestrial open-country species on the other. I have recently reviewed records for parasitism in African primates, setting the findings against the conditions outlined above. The results are consistent with these conditions (Dunn, MS-2). The epidemiological record for infection in hunter-gatherers is of course considerably "contaminated" by contact with outsiders, introductions of infections, environmental disturbances, and displacements. Careful study of historical and ethnographic records will probably provide additional data for examination against the hypothesized conditions. At the moment, however, I can offer only limited supporting data on helminthic and protozoan parasite species numbers in four hunting and gathering peoples (Table 2). Records for the Bushmen, Australians, and Pygmies have been extracted from the literature (primarily: Billington 1960; Black 1959; Bronte-Stewart et al. 1960; Casley-Smith 1959; Cleland 1928; Crotty and Webb 1960; Heinz 1961; Maingard 1937; Mann et al. 1962; Price et al. 1963). Records for intestinal protozoa are probably incomplete; in other respects the records appear adequate. All available records for the Australian continent, representing a variety of habitats (mainly arid), are shown in one column; findings for one nomadic and isolated population in Central Australia are also shown separately. Semang data are based primarily upon my own surveys in 1962–64 (Dunn and Bolton 1963), and on the work of Wharton et al. (1963) and Polunin (1953). A few species of helminths and intestinal protozoa in modern acculturated, semi-urbanized Eskimos have been recorded, but I have not so far encountered any records of parasitological survey for truly isolated Eskimo populations.

E. *Summary.* The complexity and diversity of the ecosystem must influence—perhaps profoundly—the patterning of infection and disease in hunter-gatherer populations. Prevalence, incidence, intensity, distribution, transmission efficiency, vector abundance, intermediate or alternative host variety and abundance are all affected by these ecological factors. For some hunter-gatherers many kinds of parasitic and infectious diseases may be responsible for moderate rates of morbidity and mortality; for others only a few kinds of disease may be responsible for much morbidity, and even mortality; some diseases appear at long intervals, causing high mortality; others are ever present, causing more or less morbidity and mortality depending on a complex array of ecological and cultural factors. If diseases caused by parasites and microorganisms serve as agents of natural selection and population regulation, then any patterning of these diseases will mirror, or be mirrored by, similar patterning of disease-related selection pressures and population-regulating mechanisms.

## CONCLUSION

The hunter-gatherer is an element in an ecosystem and cannot isolate himself from his environment. Little or no buffering stands between him and the other components of the system. His relationship to the land, to its flora and fauna, and to his fellow man is intimate. Although he is never perfectly adapted to the conditions in his environment, there is a degree of adaptive stability—of ecological conservatism—which does not exist in a modern urban setting. When forces of change appear, however, rapid and profound destabilization may follow. The medical sphere today provides many examples of this destabilization among the surviving hunting peoples as they encounter outsiders, lose their lands to agricultural and pastoral encroachment, and even suffer permanent displacement from these lands. "New" diseases and disorders appear, endemic diseases either disappear or become more prevalent and more damaging as social and ecological change enhances their transmissibility, and former causes of mortality are displaced by new causes.

Hunters today do not live in wholly aboriginal or "prehistoric" states of health, and historic or ethnographic records offer little data upon which to base speculations about prehistoric conditions of health. We can, however, take note of the *patterning* of present-day health problems among the surviving hunters. This patterning is inevitably affected by the ecological setting of the hunting group, for, as I have previously noted, the hunter lives in a truly intimate relationship with his surroundings. If we can determine and understand the factors that contribute to patterning of diseases and causes of death in modern peoples who live in an unbuffered relationship to their environment, we can apply this understanding to the interpretation of the prehistoric and evolutionary record, even in the absence of knowledge about which (specific) diseases may or may not have been present in an ancient population.

A discussion of epidemiological patterning for the infectious and parasitic diseases has been presented; this patterning is linked to ecological factors, including diversity and complexity. Elsewhere in this review I have mentioned striking differences in incidence for predation, accidents, and other causes of death for hunter-gatherers in various geographical settings. A few ecologically linked patterns of morbidity and mortality have emerged; others will no doubt be added as old information is screened and new data become available. The findings already emphasize the fallacy in generalizing about "hunter-gatherers" as though they were some kind of homogeneous cultural-genetic-ecological unity. They are *diverse*, their hunting territories are diverse, and so are their diseases and ways of death.

# 10 The Early History of Syphilis: A Reappraisal

*Alfred W. Crosby, Jr.*

An epidemiological controversy has existed for literally hundreds of years regarding the origin of venereal syphilis. Until a few decades ago historians were divided as to whether the dreaded disease was of Old World provenance brought by Columbus and his crew to the New World where it devastated the indigenous populations as did so many other Old World maladies, or whether the Old World first experienced it when it was carried back by Columbus' crew who were infected in the New World. This paper by a historian of medicine reviews the arguments for both sides.

A few decades ago, a theory appeared (Hudson 1965) that a single disease, treponematosis, appeared in different forms in various parts of the world long ago and followed human peregrinations in one guise or another everywhere. Hudson, a physician, suggested that the disease has existed since hominids first emerged in evolution and may very well have predated hominids in earlier primate forms, and has afflicted humankind on a global scale, though in varying degrees of intensity. Some types of treponematosis, (some epidemiologists prefer the plural, treponematoses, to indicate possible species differences in the several varieties) finally evolved into venereal syphilis, according to Hudson's "Unitarian" hypothesis. Given the facts of human evolution, Hudson assumes that syphilis, or a syphilislike type of disease, probably originated in the Old World, say, East Africa, and, therefore, was brought to the New World not by

Reprinted from Alfred W. Crosby, Jr., 1969, "The Early History of Syphilis: A Reappraisal," *American Anthropologist*, **71**:218–227, with permission of the author and the American Anthropological Association.

Columbus' aides but by the Asians who first populated this part of the planet.

The following paper argues that rather than treponematosis being at its inception one disease, it has evolved into many different—though related—forms in various regions, and that the variety developed in the Americas was venereal syphilis whence it was transported to Europe by America's "discoverer." Crosby's argument has great cogency, but some would argue with his conclusion that there is no convincing evidence for its appearance in the Old World until 1500 (see Ashburn 1947, Hudson 1965). But both Crosby's and Hudson's hypotheses are provocative and instructive for medical anthropology. It is significant that both chose to publish their views in the *American Anthropologist*. Crosby documents his case more thoroughly in a recent monograph (Crosby 1972), *The Columbian Experience: Biological and Cultural Consequences of 1492*.

In the writings of Desiderius Erasmus, one can find mention of nearly every significant figure, event, crusade, fad, folly, and misery of the decades around 1500. Of all the miseries visited upon Europe in his lifetime, he judged few more horrible than the French disease, or syphilis, as we would call it. He reckoned no malady more contagious, more terrible for its victims, more difficult to cure . . . or more fashionable! "It's a most presumptuous pox," exclaims one of the characters in his *Colloquies*. "In a showdown, it wouldn't yield to leprosy, elephantiasis, ringworm, gout or sycosis" (Erasmus 1965:401, 405).

The men and women of Erasmus' generation were the first Europeans to know syphilis, or at least so they said. The pox, as the English called it, had struck like a thunderbolt in the very last years of the fifteenth century. But unlike most diseases that appear with such abruptness, it did not fill up the graveyards and then go away, to come again some other day or perhaps never. Syphilis settled down and became a permanent factor in human existence.

The French disease has a special fascination for the historian because, of all mankind's most important maladies, it is the most uniquely "historical." The beginnings of most diseases lie beyond the ken of man's earliest rememberings. Syphilis, on the other hand, has a beginning. Many men, since the last decade of the fifteenth century, have insisted that they knew almost exactly when syphilis appeared on the world stage, and even where it came from. "In the yere of Chryst 1493 or there aboute," wrote Ulrich von Hutten (1540), one of Erasmus' correspondents, "this most foule and most grevous dysease beganne to sprede amonge the people" (1540:1). Another contemporary, Ruy Díaz de Isla, agreed that 1493 was the year and went on to say that "the disease had its origin and birth from always in the island which is now named Española" (1542:iii; translation mine). Columbus had brought it back, along with samples of maize and other American curiosities (Bloch 1901:306–307).

Since the third decade of the sixteenth century the most popular theory of the origin of syphilis has been this Columbian theory, but popularity has not saved it from disputation. In fact, the matter of the origin of syphilis is doubtlessly the most controversial subject in all medical historiography. It would take months of labor merely to assemble a full bibliography of the subject.

Until the most recent decades there were only two widely accepted views of the provenance of syphilis: the Columbian and its antithesis, the theory that syphilis was present in the Old World long before 1493. Now the Unitarian theory has appeared, which postulates that venereal syphilis is but one syndrome of a multifaceted worldwide disease, treponematosis. But before we examine this newest challenge to the veracity of Ulrich von Hutten, Díaz de Isla, and the other Columbians, let us deal with the older argument: was venereal syphilis present on both sides of the Atlantic in 1492, or only on the American?

The documentary evidence for the Old World seems clear—at least to this author. No unequivocal description of syphilis in any pre-Columbian literature of the Old World has ever been discovered. Description of diseases that might be the pox have been uncovered, but they might also be descriptions of leprosy or scabies or what-have-you. It is especially noteworthy that, in spite of Chinese worship of the ancients and the tradition of quoting from the classics whenever possible, no Chinese writer "has ever described syphilis as being mentioned in ancient literature" (Wong 1936:218). Galen and Avicenna and other medical writers of ancient and medieval times knew nothing of germ theory or antibiotics, but they were accomplished clinicians and could describe the surface symptoms of a disease as well as any modern physician. If a disease is not mentioned in their writings, we may assume that it had a different character in their time or that they never saw it (Pusey 1933:12). This assumption is particularly safe when we are searching for mention of a disease that spreads as widely as syphilis does in any society exposed to it.

The physicians, surgeons, and laymen of the Old World who wrote on venereal syphilis in the sixteenth century recorded, with few exceptions, that it was a new malady; and we have no reason to believe they all were mistaken. From Díaz de Isla to Wan Ki—Spaniards, Germans, Italians, Egyptians, Persians, Indians, Chinese and Japanese—agreed that they had never seen the pox before (Huard 1956). It is very unlikely that they were all mistaken on the same subject at the same time.

Even if no direct statements on the newness of syphilis to the inhabitants of the Old World existed, there is enough linguistic evidence to support that contention. The variety of names given it and the fact that they almost always indicate that it was thought of as a foreign import are strong evidence for its newness. Italians called it the French disease, which proved to be the most popular title; the French called it the disease of Naples; the English called it the French disease, the Bordeaux disease, and the Spanish disease; Poles called it the German disease; Russians called it the Polish disease, and so on. Middle Easterners called it the European pustules, Indians called it the disease of the Franks (western Europeans); Chinese called it the ulcer of Canton, that port being their chief point of contact with the west; the Japanese called it the Tang sore—Tang referring to China—or more to the point, the disease of the Portuguese. A full list of the early names for syphilis covers several pages, and it was not until the nineteenth century that Girolamo Fracastoro's word "syphilis" minted in the 1520s, became standard throughout the world (Huard 1956; Wong 1936:217; Elgood 1951:378; Pusey 1933:378; Pusey 1933:7–8; Bloch 1901:297–305; Hendrickson 1934; Díaz 1542:iii).

Another proof of the abrupt appearance of the pox is the malignancy of the disease in the years immediately after its initial recognition in Europe. The classic course of a new disease is rapid spread and extreme virulency, followed by a lessening of the malady's deadliness. The most susceptible members of the human population are eliminated by death, as are the most virulent strains of the germ, in that they kill off their hosts before transmission to other hosts occurs. The records of the late fifteenth century and early sixteenth century are full of lamentations on the rapid spread of syphilis and of the horrible effects of the malady, which often occurred within a short time after the initial infection: widespread rashes and ulcers, often extending into the mouth and throat; severe fevers and bone pains; and often early death. The latter is a very rare phenomenon in the initial stages of the disease today, and most who do die of syphilis have resisted the disease successfully for many years. Ulrich von Hutten's description of syphilis in the first years after its appearance indicates a marked contrast between its nature then and its "mildness" today:

There were byles, sharpe, and standing out, hauying the similitude and quantite of acornes, from which came so foule humours, and so great stenche, that who so ever ones smelled it, thought hym selfe to be enfect. The colour of these pusshes [pustules] was derke grene, and the sight thereof was more grevous unto the pacient then the peyne it selfe: and yet their peynes were as thoughe they hadde lyen in fire [1540:2–2r].

This extreme manifestation of the disease, he tells us, "tarryed not long above the vii yere. But the infyrmytie that came after, which remayneth yet, is nothynge so fylthy" (Hutten 1540:2–2r; Fracastoro 1935:8; Morton 1966:27, 87).

The most convincing of all evidence for the abrupt arrival of the French disease in the Old World in approximately 1500 is from the physical remains, the bones of the long dead. No one has ever unearthed pre-Columbian bones in the Old World that display unequivocal signs of syphilitic damage. Paleopathologist Elliot Smith tells us that

after examining something like 30,000 bodies of ancient Egyptians and Nubians representing every period of the history of the last sixty centuries and from every part of the country, it can be stated quite confidently that no trace whatever, even suggesting syphilitic injuries to bones or teeth, was revealed in Egypt before modern times [Barrack 1956].

It is nearly certain that if syphilis were present in pre-Columbian Europe, and likely that if it were present in any of the high civilizations of the Old World engaged in long-distance commerce before 1493, one of the bodies examined by Smith would have shown syphilitic lesions (Henschen 1966:124–126).

Several anti-Columbian theorists have brushed aside all the above arguments by hypothesizing that syphilis had existed in a *mild* form in the Old World prior to the 1490s, but that the causative organism then mutated into the deadly *Treponema pallidum,* and syphilis began to affect the deep body structures and became a killer. This hypothesis cannot be disproved, and it comfortably fits all the facts, but it cannot be proved either. Microorganisms simply do not keep diaries, so the only way we can "prove" the validity of the mutation theory is by the process of elimination. We must

disprove all the other hypotheses, which brings us to a direct consideration of the Columbian theory.

Where did syphilis come from? If it came from America, then we may be nearly certain that it came in 1493 or shortly after. Let us consider the physical evidence first. Is there a contrast here between the Old and New Worlds? The answer becomes more and more unequivocally affirmative as the archeologists and paleopathologists disinter from American soil an increasing number of pre-Columbian human bones displaying what is almost surely syphilitic damage (Henschen 1966:124; Jarcho 1964; Anderson 1965). According to one researcher, the deformation of the forehead bones in some of these skeletons is as unambiguously syphilitic in origin as a positive Wasserman reaction (Sigerist 1951:55).

Documentary evidence supporting the Columbian theory is quite impressive: some of the most trustworthy physicians and historians of the sixteenth century insisted that Columbus must bear the blame for bringing the pox to Europe. But the certainty with which they spoke must be weighed against the fact that none of them insisted on the American origin of syphilis until a generation after the first Columbian voyages. One would think that if a relationship existed between the sensational discovery of the New World and the sensational new disease, that relationship would have been emphasized over and over again in the 1490s and early 1500s. No mention of the connection between the two, however, appears until guaiacum, a decoction of a West Indian wood, became widely popular as a sure cure for the French disease. According to the logic of the time, God always arranged for a disease and its remedy to originate in the same locality. "Our Lorde GOD would from whence this euill of the Poxe came, from thence would come the remedy for them" (Monardes 1577:10r). To reverse the logic, if American guaiacum cured syphilis, then syphilis must be American. What could be more sensible? Many historians have judged, therefore, that the Columbian theory is based on the source of guaiacum and not on the actual origin of syphilis in the West Indies (Munger 1949; Morison 1942;[2]:199–200; Dennie 1962:30).

Even more discomforting for the Columbians is the fact that neither syphilis nor anything resembling it is mentioned at all in the documentation of the Columbian voyages written prior to the first epidemic of the pox in Europe. It certainly would have been advantageous to Columbus to omit any such mention from his reports, but it is strange that one of the other eye witnesses did not do so. Nor do we find any contemporary reports of syphilis in Spain or Portugal in the months and years between the return of the ships of the 1492 and 1493 voyages to America and the first recorded epidemic of syphilis in Europe, which began in Italy in 1494 or 1495. Such reports do exist, but they were written years after the alleged events.

But we cannot be sure that syphilis was not prevalent simply because it is not mentioned in contemporary documents. The documentation is too sparse. For example, we know little or nothing about what happened aboard the Pinta on the first voyage, for she spent much of the time in the West Indies and the last half of the return trip far beyond the sight and knowledge of Columbus, the only chronicler of that voyage. Nor do we know much about the condition of the Indians, who may well have been latently syphilitic, brought back in 1493 and 1494. Furthermore, it was to the interest of many involved in Columbus' schemes, some in high places, to suppress negative reports about the New World. There may be an even simpler explanation for the absence of the mention of the pox from the early documentation. Many of the documents of this period have been lost forever. Others undoubtedly still lie buried in European archives, unread for four hundred years (Morison 1942 [2]: 193–218).

Let us examine the written evidence supporting the Columbian hypothesis. The first mention of Europeans with syphilis in the New World is found in the biography of Columbus by his son, Ferdinand. It is a work of immense value, but unfortunately we have only an Italian translation of it. The original Spanish version is lost, and we cannot be sure that the Italian translation is absolutely accurate. Be that as it may, Ferdinand tells us that when his father arrived in Española on his 1498 voyage he found that "Part of the people he had left were dead, and of the survivors more than one hundred and sixty were sick with the French sickness" (1959:155). This unfortunately proves nothing beyond the fact that the colonists were a very active lot, because syphilis was already widespread in Europe by 1498.

Also contained in this book is the "Relation of Fray Ramón Concerning the Antiquities of the Indians, Which He, knowing Their Language, Carefully Compiled by Order of the Admiral," written, according to Ferdinand, in the mid-1490s. This relation tells practically all we know of the cosmogony of the Arawack people of Española. Their great folk hero, according to the good friar,

"had great pleasure" with a woman, "but soon had to look for many bathhouses in which to wash himself because he was full of those sores that we call the French sickness" (Columbus 1959: 191). Humans are very slow to change their folklore, and so it seems unlikely that the Arawacks would have altered their legends so as to give a new disease to their Achilles, their Beowulf, so soon after the arrival of the Europeans.

The two most important historians of the early Spanish empire, Bartolomé de las Casas (1876) and Gonzalo Fernández Oviedo (1851), both state that Columbus brought syphilis back from America to Europe. Their accounts differ somewhat in detail and taken together are not clear as to which of the first fleets returning from America brought syphilis to Europe. The difference in detail does not necessarily indicate a lack of veracity: such an importation would be very difficult to pinpoint chronologically. Both Las Casas and Oviedo were certainly qualified by personal experience and access to those who sailed with Columbus to make their statements on the origin of the pox. Las Casas was in Seville in 1493 when Columbus came to that city with his report on his discoveries and with his Indian captives. Las Casas' father and uncle sailed with Columbus in 1493, and he must have known many others of the early voyagers, as well. Las Casas himself came to the New World in 1502 and spent most of the rest of his life working for and with the Indians (Las Casas 1876 [5]: 349).

Oviedo was attached to the Spanish court in the 1490's and even met Columbus before his 1492 epochal voyage. Oviedo was quite friendly with the great explorer's sons and with members of the Pinzon family, which figured so importantly in the first voyages to America. A number of his friends, who he asked to bring him back detailed reports, sailed with Columbus in 1493 (Oviedo 1851 [1]: 55). Oviedo was even on hand in Italy for the initial European syphilis epidemic, about which he wrote, "Many times in Italy I laughed, hearing the Italians speak of the French disease, and the French call it the disease of Naples; and in truth both would have had the name better, if they called it the disease of the Indies" (Oviedo 1959:xi, xiii, 88–90). In 1513 he sailed to the Indies, where he spent the bulk of the rest of his life. No one can claim that Las Casas and Oviedo did not have full opportunity to know all there was to know about the origin of the pox.

Las Casas personally asked the Indians if they had known the disease before the coming of the Europeans, and was answered, yes, that they had suffered from it beyond all memory. Both the historians report the medically significant fact that the disease was much less dangerous for the infected Indians than for the Spaniards, a contrast one would expect if the former race had had long contact with the malady and the latter none at all (Sauer 1966:38–39).

The third charter member of the Columbian theorist school was a physician, Ruiz Díaz de Isla, who claimed in a book first published in 1539 that he had treated some of Columbus' men who had contracted syphilis in 1492 in America and that he had observed its rapid spread through Barcelona. He did not know what the disease was at the time but later realized that he had been witness to the arrival of syphilis. He called it *Morbo Serpentino,* for, as the snake "is hideous, dangerous and terrible, so the malady is hideous, dangerous and terrible" (Díaz 1542:iii).

One either accepts his account and becomes a Columbian, or one must reject it completely. It is certain that he was no quack. He was one of the most accomplished clinicians of his time and even his most vehement twentieth century detractor, R. C. Holcomb, admitted that "he was the greatest syphilographer. His historical errors do not affect my opinion of him as a surgeon in the slightest" (Holcomb 1944). Indeed, it took scientists immeasurably better equipped than Díaz four hundred years to appreciate properly his shrewd guess that a high fever, such as that caused by malaria, tends to arrest syphilis (Dennie 1962:16).

At the present stage of research we have no documents specifically confirming what Díaz tells us. Perhaps one day we will. It is lucky that we have even his book, which apparently caused little stir when it first appeared. Then, in contrast, for instance, to the writings of Paracelsus, it almost completely disappeared from scholarly concern until Jean Astruc consulted it in the eighteenth century. It again dropped out of sight, for all practical scholarly purposes, until rediscovered by Montejo y Robledo in the 1880s. A very rare book today, few researchers would have a chance to read it but for microfilm. All in all, the saga of Díaz's book is a very good object lesson for any who would place a great deal of confidence in negative evidence when dealing with the documentation of the sixteenth century (Holcomb 1936:277–280).

The only evidence we have that even tends to directly corroborate Díaz's statements was taken down a generation after the initial voyage to the West Indies and pertains to the obscure death of the commander of the Pinta, Martín Alonso Pinzón. In Díaz's original manuscript, *but not in the published book,* he says that one of the seamen who came back from America in 1493 suffering from syphilis was "a pilot of Palos called Pinzón" (Morison 1942[2]:204). At least two members of the Pinzón family of Palos sailed with Columbus in 1492, and all authorities agree that Martín Alonso died very shortly after his return to Spain. Díaz tells us that the ailing sailors attributed their new illness to "the toils of the sea, or other causes according as they appeared to each one" (Díaz 1542:iii). In testimony taken in the 1530's and 1540's, witnesses of the return of the Pinta to Palos agreed that Martín Alonso was sick upon arrival and that he died a few days later of an illness brought on by the exhaustion and hunger he had undergone during the voyage (Jos 1942). This testimony corroborates in part what Díaz says. Even though he may have misinterpreted the facts, he did have them, and we may be sure that he was no writer of pure fiction.

The documentary evidence for the Columbian provenance of venereal syphilis is obviously shaky, nor can we say that the evidence provided by the paleopathologists is utterly decisive, but when the two are combined—when archive and grave diggers join hands to claim that America is the homeland of the *Treponema pallidum*—it becomes very difficult to reject the Columbian theory. Or, at least, it would be very difficult to do so if the argument on the history of syphilis was still being fought over the same ground as it was a generation ago. But the scene of battle has changed. All the arguments, pro and con, touched on in this paper thus far may not be wrong so much as merely irrelevant!

Is venereal syphilis a separate and distinct disease, once endemic to only one part of the world, or is it merely a syndrome of a disease that has always been worldwide but happens to have different symptoms and names in different areas? Those who accept the Unitarian theory, as it is called, claim that what is called syphilis, when transmitted venereally, is really the same malady as the non-venereal illnesses called yaws in the tropics, bejel in the Middle East, pinta in Central America, irkinja in Australia, and so on. The manner in which this ubiquitous disease, named treponematosis by the Unitarians, manifests itself in man is somewhat different in different areas because of climatic and cultural differences, but it is all one disease. If this is true, then all the squabble about deformation of forehead bones here and not there, ulcers on the sex organs now and not then, etc., is completely irrelevant. As E. H. Hudson, the foremost champion of the Unitarian theory puts it, "Since treponematosis was globally distributed in prehistoric times, it [is] idle to speak of Columbus' sailors bringing syphilis to a syphilis-free Europe in 1493" (Hudson 1965b:738).

Perhaps the best way to present the Unitarian theory is to summarize E. H. Hudson's version of that theory. His arguments are not accepted universally even by all the Unitarians, but they will serve to introduce the reader to the basic ideas of the proponents of this hypothesis. The organism that causes treponematosis is an extremely delicate one. It needs the moisture and the warmth of the body of a host to survive more than a few minutes, and normally it is carried by man alone among the animals (Morton 1966:69; Hackett 1963:21). Thus it is very sensitive to differences in climate and human habits, and, in its Darwinian adaptations to these differences, appears as "different" diseases. Hudson theorizes that man first acquired the treponema causing these maladies in moist, sub-Saharan Africa, where the climate allowed it to live on the surface of the body, many thousands of years ago. The disease was originally manifested as yaws, an infection that, initially, at least, affects only the surface layers of the body. Then, as man migrated into drier areas, the organism retreated into the bodies of its hosts and became a kind of non-venereal syphilis, a disease of childhood, transmitted by close contact under very unhygienic conditions. This manifestation is called bejel in the Middle East. As cities developed and the general level of civilization rose, more careful personal hygiene, cleaning of eating utensils, separation of sleeping individuals, etc., robbed the treponemas of most of their avenues of transmission from human to human and threatened their existence everywhere on the surface of the bodies of their hosts. Therefore, they retreated even deeper into the human body, into the bones and arteries and nervous system, and utilized the only avenue of transmission left open to them by modern man: the one extremely intimate contact with another human that modern man has not given up and in which he indulges in many times over, sexual intercourse. Thus, venereal syphilis appeared (Hudson 1964, 1965a, 1965b).

A great deal of scientific evidence has accumulated to support the Unitarian theory. The syndromes of the several "different" diseases of the trepanematosis group are not sharply contrasted one from the other. Rather, there seems to be a continuum of at least partial similarity from the surface lesions of pinta, on one extreme, to the deep body-structure damage caused by venereal syphilis,

on the other extreme. The recognition of these similarities is not new (Jeanselme 1931:227–228). Thomas Sydenham, the great British physician of the seventeenth century, believed venereal syphilis to be a variation of yaws, brought to both Europe and America on the slave ships (Isenberg 1940). In the book *Every Man His Own Doctor or The Poor Planter's Physician,* popular in Britain's American colonies around 1730, the suggested cure for yaws is also recommended for syphilis; "because the Symptoms are much the same, it is very probable, the one was the Graft of the other" (Lane 1920).

The organisms that cause the various treponematoses have different names—*Treponema pallidum, Treponema pertenue, Treponema cuniculi*—but they cannot be differentiated visually, no matter what the power of the microscope used. The antibodies created within the body of the host by one serve to immobilize the others, too; so acquired immunity to one of the treponematoses seems, in many cases, to confer immunity to all of them. All, or at least very many, of their victims react positively when given the Wasserman test, which was specifically created as a test for venereal syphilis alone. At present, the only way to differentiate between the several allegedly different treponemas is to infect laboratory animals with them and then check the symptoms. The symptoms thus created are different, but the contrast is by no means a sharp one. And the symptomatic differences observed in one animal, rabbits, are not always identical to those found in another, hamsters (Hackett 1963; Weisman 1966; Guthe 1960; Manson-Bahr 1966: 42–43, 69).

All this is very disconcerting for the Columbians, but not necessarily disastrous for their hypothesis. The scientific evidence certainly indicates a very close relationship between the various treponemas, but it has not been proved that they are all the same. Most experts either withhold final decision on the matter or continue to consider them as separate kinds of organisms. Perhaps our current means of distinguishing between these organisms are too crude and one day soon a more discriminating test will be invented. After all, smallpox and cowpox are closely related maladies symptomatically, immunity to one is immunity to both, and the organisms that cause these diseases appear to be nearly identical under the electron microscope. But no one would claim that the two illnesses are the same (Rhodes and van Rooyen 1962:156, 167, 173, 174).

If we accept the Unitarian theory we have two possible explanations for the appearance of venereal syphilis in Europe during the lifetime of Columbus: (1) the practice of improved hygiene in the cities had risen to such a level as to bring about, by the process of elimination of the less adaptable treponemas, a venereal strain of treponematosis. This seems unlikely because it would have been a gradual process, and the contemporaries agreed upon the abrupt appearance of venereal syphilis. Or, (2) in the 1490's the treponemes living in the bodies of Europeans suddenly mutated, producing a new and deadly version of an old disease. This explanation fits nearly all the facts we have, but, as said before, is not susceptible to proof or disproof. It is a scientifically acceptable explanation, but remains distasteful.

In fact, such is the paucity of evidence come down to us from the fifteenth and sixteenth centuries that the Unitarian theory is no more satisfactory than the Columbian. We simply do not know, and may never know, much about the world distribution of the treponemas in the 1490's. The field is nearly as wide open for theorizers today as in that terrible decade when many Europeans blamed the pox on the conjunction of Saturn and Mars and on "the unholsom blastes of the ayre" (Hutten 1540:2r–3).

There are only two things of which we can be sure. First, the only pre-Columbian bones clearly displaying the lesions of treponematosis or one of that family of diseases are American. The infections that affect only the surface or viscera would, of course, leave no trace on bones, no matter how deadly the disease, but that does not necessarily prove that yaws or pinta or what-have-you did exist in the Old World in 1492. It only means that we do not know and perhaps never will. Two, several contemporaries in a position to know did record the return of venereal syphilis with Columbus. Their testimony cannot be shrugged off. They may have been confused, but they were not fools or liars, and they were all in Spain in the mid-1490's.

The Columbian theory is still viable. Even if it is unequivocally proved that all the treponematoses are one, the Columbians, if their nerve holds, can simply claim that treponematosis was exclusively American in 1492. There is no unquestionable evidence that any of the treponematoses existed in the Old World in 1492. For instance, sub-Saharan Africa is usually thought of as the homeland of yaws, but we really do not know this as a fact. We know practically nothing about the medical situation in Africa in Renaissance times (Barrack 1956).

It is not impossible that the organisms causing treponematosis arrived from America in the 1490's in Lord-knows what form, mild or deadly, and breeding in the entirely new and very salubrious environment of European, Asian, and African bodies, evolved into both venereal and nonvenereal syphilis and yaws. If this is true, then Columbus ranks as a villain with the serpent of the Garden of Eden.

A less presumptuous theory is that the treponematoses were one single disease, but many thousands of years ago. Then, as man changed his environment and habits, and especially when he crossed the Bering Straits into the isolation of the Americas, the differing ecological conditions produced different types of treponematosis and, in time, closely related but different diseases. This pattern of divergent evolution has affected more than one of man's parasites. For example, body lice, certainly ancient companions of man, have become adapted to the differences among the races. Oriental, Caucasian, and American Indian lice are all different, and African lice are just what you would expect they would have to be to survive: black (Cockburn 1961).

This theory of the origin of the treponematoses squares with all Mr. Darwin tells us about evolution and allows the American Indians and Columbus the dubious honor of incubating and transporting venereal syphilis. It is this hypothesis which, in the current state of medical and historical research, seems to hold the most promise as a vehicle for future inquiry and speculation.

# 11 Malaria and Demography in the Lowlands of Mexico: An Ethno-Historical Approach

*Judith Friedlander*

The task of the ethnohistorian, as of the archeologist, is to solve a riddle, or series of riddles that lie beneath

Reprinted with abridgments and minor changes by the author from Judith Friedlander, 1969, "Malaria and Demography in the Lowlands of Mexico: An Ethno-Historical Approach," *Proceedings of the American Ethnological Society*, Seattle: University of Washington Press, pp. 217–233, with permission of the author and the American Ethnological Society.

significant problems and questions in anthropology. The medical ethnohistorian, as the medical historian (see the preceding paper by Crosby on syphilis), works somewhat as a detective, though insofar as documents are available, there are apt to be rather more direct and reliable clues than those presented to the archeologist. Medical ethnohistory is very much an undeveloped field of study and the following paper, written when its author was still a graduate student (it was awarded the Elsie Clews Parsons prize of the American Ethnological Society in 1969), is a fine example of the painstaking archival and primary and secondary documentary research required for answering the kinds of questions posed. Even more, the paper shows the careful deductive reasoning required for the task. But because this study addresses itself to a medical problem, it also requires research on data provided by physicians, biological anthropologists, and demographers. A number of tables and maps not included here should be consulted in the original article for documentation of many of the key assertions made by the author.

Judith Friedlander raises a large question: Why did more Indians die of malaria in the Mexican lowlands than in the highlands, given that African slaves were present in large numbers in both regions? Using many lines of evidence, she concludes that Black slaves, selected for their strength and health, were brought into the New World by the Spanish to fill a labor shortage, that they brought with them genetic immunity as malaria parasites were transported in the blood of European slavers, that the nonimmune Indians were slaughtered in large numbers by malaria (they were already highly vulnerable to other Old World diseases), and that the lowlands became depopulated of indigenous peoples as more Blacks were imported to fill the heavy labor demands and so came, with the Europeans, to dominate this region of Mexico. Of interest to the readers of this selection is the recent study by Wood (1975) which introduces experimental evidence in favor of a late introduction of malaria into the New World, and which aroused strong commentaries both for and against this conclusion (appended to the end of the article in *Current Anthropology*).

The purpose of this paper is to offer an explanation for the presence of a relatively high Black and surprisingly low indigenous population in the lowlands of Mexico during colonial times. Almost immediately after the Spanish conquest, the Indians throughout Mexico started to die off in great numbers, causing a severe labor shortage which threatened the Spanish economic system. These deaths were in large part caused by Old World diseases which were introduced by the colonizers and against which the Indians had no resistance. African slaves were therefore imported, proving healthier and more suited to the strenuous work than the Indians.

Even after the arrival of the African slaves, the Indians' mortality rate remained high. In fact they very nearly disappeared entirely in the lowlands and during the early years of colonization the Indians were dying off twice as fast in the lowlands as in the highlands. The Black slaves, on the other hand, who came primarily from the tropics of Africa, seemed better adapted to the hot humid lowlands of Mexico than did the original inhabitants. Thus while the Indians were vanishing from everywhere and African slaves were being used throughout Mexico, it was in the lowlands where the Indians' death rate was most dramatic and where the Black slaves were in greatest demand. It should be kept in mind that sugar, one of Mexico's most lucrative exports, was grown and processed in the lowlands; therefore as sugar became increasingly important, the plantations and mills required larger and larger labor forces, which, for lack of Indians, depended almost entirely on African slaves.

Such being the case, we are faced with the following questions: (1) why should proportionately more indigenous peoples have died in the lowlands than in the highlands? (2) Did the African slaves serve to increase further the mortality of the Indians in the lowlands and if so, why did they not affect the Indians in the highlands as well, for Black slaves were numerous there too? The answers, we suggest, are in part related to the role played by one particular disease, malaria, and the differential immunity to it afforded to the two populations under discussion. Malaria is primarily a lowland disease and its impact was only felt in the lowland areas of Mexico.

We argue that the Indians suffered greater losses in the lowlands than in the highlands because of the deleterious effects of this imported disease, while the African thrived, for significant numbers of them had a genetically inherited immunity to malaria. We further postulate that the introduction to Mexico of the malarial parasites coincides with that of the Black slaves who came from some of the most malaria-ridden regions of Africa. In Mexico, the *Anopheles* mosquitoes, the necessary vector, fed on the infected blood and thus passed on this disease to the Indian and white peoples who were not immune. As to why the Indians suffered more than the White men will be clarified below.

Unlike many of the other imported diseases that ravaged Mexico after the conquest, malaria does not hit just once, killing large numbers, perhaps, but leaving those who survive immune; rather it attacks the individual repeatedly, wearing down one's general resistance to other diseases as well as causing pregnant women to abort. Malaria, therefore, very easily could have dealt a severe blow to the indigenous population. Once introduced into an area, it could have taken a continuing yearly toll of non-immune Indians, either by being directly responsible for their deaths, by inhibiting normal reproduction, or by making them more susceptible to any disease that might have passed through the region. Epidemics of greater intensity than malaria came and went, leaving many dead, but those who survived were immune; while malaria continued year in and year out, constantly draining the people, never permitting the Indians to recover numerically, even to the meager extent they so succeeded in doing in the highlands. Although the Europeans suffered from malaria also, at least their systems were partially protected against the other diseases which were introduced into the area, for these were primarily of Old World origin. As for the Africans, they suffered neither from the periodic Old World epidemics to any great extent, nor from the omnipresent malaria. Thus the Black slave seemed to be the perfect labor substitute for the disease-ridden lowlands of Mexico; however, this solution to the problem was complicated by the fact that with the Blacks came malaria, the very disease, we suggest, which caused the further demise of the Indian population. . . .

## I. EVIDENCE FOR THE IMMUNIZATION TO MALARIA OF SIGNIFICANT NUMBERS OF AFRICANS

The Blacks' relative immunity to malaria has been the subject of great speculation among both biological anthropologists and medical doctors for years. Recently it has been suggested that there might be a positive correlation between the comparatively high incidence of certain blood deficiencies, most notably sickle-cell anemia and glucose-6-phosphate-dehydrogenase (abbreviated G-6-P-D) deficiency and the fact that the populations in which these are found are living in highly malarial regions. Since the evidence for G-6-P-D deficiency is rather suspect, according to specialists at Billings Hospital at the University of Chicago (Bowman 1967 and Powell *et al.* 1966), we will restrict this discussion to sickle-cell anemia alone.

Sickle-cell anemia (Singer 1962 unless otherwise noted) which is found primarily among Black or Black mixed-blood populations, is caused by the presence of an abnormal hemoglobin in the blood of the individual. This is only phenotypically evident when the person is homozygous for this trait, that is, when he inherits a gene for the abnormal hemoglobin from both of his parents. The heterozygote sometimes suffers as well when under great stress. In other words, under most circumstances, it is only the homozygous individual who suffers from this disease. When a person does have sickle-cell anemia, he is not expected to live long enough to have children.

With such an extremely high mortality rate among anemic victims, it would be expected that the incidences of the sickle-cell gene would be selected out of a population. However, this is not the case in malarial regions. It seems that those individuals who are heterozygous for the sickling trait, having inherited the gene from only one of their parents, and who do not usually suffer from the anemia, are favored in such environments. This means that these heterozygous individuals are reproducing at a greater rate than those who do not have this sickling trait at all in areas with malaria; thus the number of sickle-cell anemia cases remains constant, the death of the homozygotes being balanced by the higher fertility of the heterozygotes. The explanation for this offered by Neel, Allison and others is that those individuals heterozygous for the sickle-cell trait have a selective advantage over non-sicklers in malarial regions. In simpler terms, heterozygotes do not usually suffer from malaria, a disease which, among other things, is known to cause miscarriages and they are therefore reproducing more rapidly.

. . . The areas in Africa with the greatest incidence of the sickle-cell trait . . . are West Africa, Angola, the Congo and the Sudan. These are also the most intensive malarial zones.

Since findings of paleo-pathologists indicate that malaria is not indigenous to the New World (Dunn 1965), we suggest that it was transported to Mexico along with the African slaves. It is, however, unlikely that the parasite could have entered Mexico in, let us say, the blood of the "infected," but "unaffected" Black slaves; for according to one fairly well-accepted hypothesis, individuals with the sickling trait do not suffer from malaria precisely because, for the parasite, this abnormal hemoglobin is an unfavorable medium in which to develop, hence it dies. On the other hand, it does seem reasonable to postulate that malaria could have been contracted by the White slavers who transported the slaves from Africa to Mexico and thus the disease accompanied the slaves to the New

World. Another carrier of malaria could have been the large number of Spanish soldiers who served in Italy before coming to the New World, for Italy at that time was seriously plagued by malaria (Sauer 1966:204).

## II. AFRICAN SLAVES IN MEXICO; THEIR ORIGIN; THEIR NUMBERS; AND WHERE THEY WORKED

The slaves sent to Mexico came primarily from Cape Verde during the sixteenth century and from Angola in the seventeenth (Aguirre Beltrán 1946:245). There was also a large number coming from the Sudan as well. As can be observed on the maps, these areas have populations with some of the highest occurrences of the sickle-cell trait today and are highly endemic for malaria. We are assuming that these regions were at least as concentrated during the sixteenth and seventeenth centuries as now.

...As early as 1570, there were as many as 20,569 Africans and 2,435 Afro-Mestizos in Mexico according to the information quoted by Aguirre Beltrán. By 1742, there were 20,131 Africans and 249,368 Afro-Mestizos, which implies a sizable population of Blacks and Black mixed bloods.

We are left, then, with the problem of establishing that there was a large Black population in the lowlands areas of Mexico. The bishopric (obispado) of Tlaxcala, which consistently has one of the highest African and African mixed populations in Mexico, is an area which includes the present-day states of Tabasco and Veracruz (Priestly 1923:104), which do have lowland sections. However, the indigenous and European populations are also high in the bishopric. We might assume that the Indians lived in the highlands and the Blacks in the lowlands, but working from these figures alone, that would be mere conjecture. On the other hand, to support such a speculation, Aguirre Beltrán states that by the end of the sixteenth century, the city of Veracruz, for one, had 200 Spaniards, more than 500 Blacks and virtually no Indians, either in the city or in the surrounding lowland region (1946:192). Furthermore, since the crown as early as 1609 proclaimed that Indian labor could not be employed for certain jobs, such as sugar processing (Harris 1964:15), and sugar was one of the most important exports, as well as the fact that the Indians were dying off at a more drastic rate in the lowlands than in the highlands, it does stand to

reason that slaves would be more in demand here than elsewhere and would therefore be found in greater numbers. With no figures to support his statement, Harris maintains just this (1964:17).

## III. EVIDENCE THAT THE INDIANS WERE DYING AT A MORE DRASTIC RATE IN THE LOWLANDS THAN IN THE HIGHLANDS

The best information on the population decline in Mexico after the conquest comes from the work of the demographers, Borah and Cook. According to their latest tabulations, the aboriginal population in 1519 was between 20 and 28,000,000 (Borah and Cook 1963:88). These figures are considered extremely high for the aboriginal population on the eve of the conquest by prehistorians and are questioned on the grounds that prehispanic agricultural techniques could not have supported such a large population (Armillas 1968:personal communication). However, everybody agrees that the population loss was catastrophic. Without giving specific numbers, Wolf suggest that 6/7 of the pre-conquest population of Middle America was wiped out (Wolf 1959:195). Since in this paper we are not concerned with exact figures, rather with overall patterns, it is enough merely to alert the reader to the fact that the above totals for 1519 are debatable; for there is no question about the fact that the population loss was dramatic. By 1532, the population had dropped to 16,800,000; by 1548, to 6,300,000; by 1580, to 1,900,000; by 1595, to 1,375,000 and by 1605, to 1,075,000.... By 1568, only 7.44 percent of the 1532 population was left in the lowlands and 19.85 percent in the highlands. African slaves began to be imported in substantial numbers by 1528 (Scelle 1910:1619). After 1580, however, the decline was faster in the highlands than in the lowlands and by 1605, the population was hardly declining at all in the lowlands. At the same time, the rate in the highlands was also abating, but not as quickly. Thus in the earlier years, the rate of population decline in the lowlands was greater than that in the highlands and after 1580, the trend was reversed. When the figures.... are averaged over the years, however, they suggest that "the rate of population decline was nearly twice as great in the lowland regions as in the highland ones" (Cook and Borah 1960:52).

Many factors would account for this sudden

leveling off of the mortality rate in the lowlands: the disappearance of epidemic diseases, the improvement of the diet and the migration of highland Indians to the lowlands (Cook and Borah 1960:56), although the latter was against the law—the New Laws of 1542 (Humboldt 1811, Vol. 2:168). As to why the highland Indians' mortality rate was more constant and hence became greater than the lowlands during the latter fifth of the sixteenth century and into the seventeenth before it too began to level off, is a complex question which we will not attempt to answer fully here. Let us suggest in passing, however, that the highland region had a long history of famines before the Spanish conquest, as is reported in the Nahuatl Codices (Carter 1931:96) and such food shortages remained a serious problem, for although the Spaniards improved the agricultural techniques, they permitted fewer Indians to attend to farming and irrigation than had formerly been the case because they needed large labor forces to work in the mines. Thus food shortages undoubtedly remained a serious problem, continuing to weaken the Indians even after many of the more dangerous epidemics disappeared. The humid lowlands, on the other hand, with its fertile land and sparser population always had abundant food, a situation which lured the Aztecs to conquer the region during pre-hispanic times.

Cook and Borah's statistics for the lowlands are compatible with the argument which is being presented in this paper. As we have stressed earlier, malaria is not necessarily a killer, but causes one to be more susceptible to other diseases by wearing down the individual's general resistance. It follows, therefore, that if the other major epidemics should disappear, malaria would lose some of its force as a lethal catalyst. As Curtin has pointed out, the most numerous immunities to diseases are acquired, not inherited (Curtin 1968:197). Many diseases, when experienced during childhood are far less likely to be lethal at that time. When the child recovers, he is conferred with a life-long immunity to the disease. "In general, then, the individual will be safest if he stays in the disease environment of his childhood" (Curtin 1968:197). Now the Indians' disease environment was radically altered by the Europeans and Africans who were carriers, though often not sufferers of the Old World diseases; hence the fully grown and unimmune Indians fell victim to epidemic after epidemic. During these first sixty years (up to 1580), however, it is perfectly conceivable that a new equilibrium was being defined. In other words, by 1580 or so, the majority of the Old World

diseases had already been introduced and were now a part of the Indians' childhood disease environment and therefore new generations of young Indians were growing up having acquired, during childhood, immunities to these other Old World diseases. Thus, although malaria was still present, for one cannot acquire an immunity to it but must be born with it, this disease no longer posed the same lethal threat that it did before.

By the time the lowland Indian population started to level off, however, the number of indigenous people left was so low and they were so culturally fragmented as a result of the thorough infiltration of the hispanic plantation way of life (Harris 1964:IV), that they never regained their cultural identity, even to the meager extent they succeeded in doing so in the highlands where their numbers, in absolute terms, never dropped so low. There are of course exceptions, most notably the Yucatan, which will be discussed later, and a few pockets of Indian communities in other lowland areas. In the Costa Chica area, for one, we will see that these "Indians" have mated with Blacks.

To look at one specific lowland region more closely, we find that the following demographic changes took place between 1519 and 1580 in the environs of the city of Veracruz: at Cempoala, two leagues to the north, there were 20,000 people, by 1580, fewer than 30 houses remained; at Rinconada, five leagues to the west, there were 10,000 Indians, dropping to fewer than 50 houses; other towns left no trace at all aside from their names (letter written by Alonso Hernandez Diosado to Viceroy Don Martin, 1580. In Pasquel 1960:188).

## IV. EVIDENCE THAT THERE WAS MALARIA IN THE LOWLANDS DURING COLONIAL TIMES AND THAT THERE WAS A DIFFERENTIAL IMMUNITY TO THIS DISEASE

The cause of malaria was not understood during colonial times. However, the disease was recognized and was thought to have been the result of inhaling the putrid air which came from swamps, hence its name, "malaria"—"mal aria" or "bad air" in Italian (Prothero 1965:7). The current Spanish term for the disease is "el paludismo" coming from the same root as the adjective "paludosa," *marshy*.

Contemporary accounts of the area describe a malarial environment, which is convincing both in terms of the colonial conception of the disease conditions as well as our own. Diosado pointed out that the region around Veracruz was particularly unhealthy because there were many "ponds, rivers and marshes and other wet and swampy places from which the aforementioned winds collect the thick and putrid vapors which are blown over the city causing no small inconveniences to those who live there...." (Pasquel 1960, Vol 1:91). A Jesuit priest described the city in similar terms: "The port of the city is very hot and humid, plagued by mosquitoes to such a degree that hardly any light gets through to the homes and what made [sic] this port more uncomfortable was it being infested with diseases..." (Aguirre Beltrán 1946:191). ("El puerto de la ciudad es muy caliente y húmedo, molestado de mosquitos en tanto grado que apenas permiten tener luz en los aposentos y lo que hacía más desacomedado este puerto era el ser poco favorable e infestado de enfermedades.")

In sum, it is fairly clear that malaria was a serious problem by at least 1580. That the Blacks were able to withstand this disease is supported by statements such as the royal proclamation of 1778 which said: "In view of the fact that the malaria epidemic has laid up the majority of the Granada Infantry Regiment, give arms to the companies of Blacks and Black mixed-bloods" (Aguirre Beltrán 1946:195) ("En vista de la epidemía de tercianas [malaria] que tiene postrada a la mayor parte de los soldados del Regimiento de la Infantería de Granada, póngase sobre las armas a las companías de morenos y pardos"), for they alone were healthy enough to perform military duties. Furthermore, as recently as seventy years ago, it was still held that only the Blacks were able to withstand tropical diseases, that the Indians and Europeans were not meant to live in such places (Murphy 1958:183); yet the Indians did live quite comfortably in these lowland regions before the onslaught of Old World diseases, particularly malaria.

Black slaves were regarded as Herculean in strength; one Black was thought to be as strong as four Indians (Murphy 1958:181). Aguirre Beltrán points out that those slaves who arrived in the New World were undoubtedly some of the most physically fit Blacks available, for they had to undergo several screenings before they set foot in the Western Hemisphere. Most important, they were chosen in Africa for their superior strength and health (this implies those who were not suffering from malaria).

## V. EVIDENCE OF TRACES OF THIS IMMUNITY IN MODERN BLACK POPULATIONS IN THE MALARIAL REGIONS OF PRESENT-DAY MEXICO

Under the direction of Ruben Lisker of the Department of Hematology in the Instituto Nacional de la Nutricion in Mexico, studies have been conducted to determine the prevalence of the sickle-cell trait among the present-day populations of Mexico. His work in the Costa Chica of the Pacific coast (present-day Guerrero) area shows that the population has a significant amount of the sickle-cell trait, directly linked to the Blacks in the area and that furthermore, the trait seems to have been positively selected for in the area which is highly endemic for *vivax* malaria and, to a lesser extent, for *falciparum* malaria (Lisker *et al.* 1965:184–185). When we say a "significant" number of individuals have this trait, we are talking about 10 percent of the population in the town of Cuajincuilapa, known for having many Black inhabitants, Blacks having been in this area since the seventeenth century, approximately 4 percent in Ometepec, 3 percent in San Pedro Mixtepec and virtually no incidence in Pochutla. These villages are listed in order of proximity to Cuajinculapa. Since for Africa, Livingstone considers similar statistics meaningful in determining the genetic resistance of those populations to malaria (Livingstone 1967), then the figures in the New World are all the more outstanding when we remember that the peoples in the Costa Chica region are the descendents of the inter-mating of three races, two of which (the Indians and the whites) do not have the abnormal hemoglobin S.

Aside from Lisker's work, virtually no studies have been conducted in Mexico which have tested for the sickle-cell trait. Until Lisker or others do more of the kind of work already done in the Costa Chica region, we will not know whether the trait is prevalent throughout the lowlands and whether it might have played a significant role in the demographic changes in the entire coastal region. At this time we can only say the following: the fact that the Blacks coming to Mexico were primarily from malarial parts of Africa whose populations today exhibit a high incidence of the sickle-cell trait and the fact that the historical literature emphasizes the superiority of the Blacks and the Black mixed-bloods' resistance to malaria which was ravaging the area, both seem to support the hypothesis that the Blacks' immunity to the disease was genetically based and could very well be linked with the sickle-cell trait. In any case, their general immunity was common enough to merit considerable comment.

There is, of course, the very important qualification to be made, namely that most of the research on the sickle-cell trait has been done in correlation with *falciparum* and not *vivax* malaria. Although both exist in Mexico, Lisker's studies have been conducted in an area more seriously threatened with the latter. It is true that one of the major objectives of his article was to suggest that the sickle-cell trait afforded production against *vivax* malaria as well, but this is a very recent hypothesis. Therefore, in order to substantiate the role this genetic immunity played in protecting the Black slave in Mexico, we must determine what form of malaria existed in the area in question and validate the fact that the sickle-cell trait serves as an immunization to it. If we are correct in assuming that malaria accompanied the ostensibly healthy Blacks to the New World, i.e., that malaria came from those areas of Africa where the slaves were sold to the White slavers, it then follows that the African slaves were immune to the species imported. For even if the slaves had been captured by Black slavers far from the ports where they were ultimately transferred to the White slavers, these slaves could not have remained healthy in the port towns had they not also been immune to the particular species of the area.

## VI.  CONCLUSIONS

The ecological implications for this malaria hypothesis are interesting. It happens that with the advance of agriculture, man has provided the perfect environment for malaria. By cutting down the forests in Africa, the necessary open ground and open stagnant pools were produced, permitting the spread of the *Anopheles* mosquitoes and hence malaria (Singer 1962:158). The same situation could have taken place in the lowlands of Mexico as well, for the plantation economy opened up much more land in this area and with the sugar plantation came the Blacks and malaria. Furthermore, it is suggested that certain of the drier parts of the "tierra caliente" near Veracruz, such as Rinconada, which were opened for agriculture in pre-Columbian times by the introduction of irrigation (Sanders 1953) would have undoubtedly proved to be an ideal environment for breeding *Anopheles* mosquitoes in an area which would not ordinarily have suffered from these insects and subsequently from malaria.

In addition, it is interesting to note that the Yucatan lowlands have no malaria (Carter 1931:115), the reason being that the soil is extremely calcareous and thus very porous, not permitting stagnant water to collect on the surface of the ground. Coincident with this is the fact that unlike the other lowland areas which were ravaged by malaria, the Yucatan was not only free from malaria, but had and has a proportionately higher indigenous population than other lowland regions.

In sum, it has been suggested that as a result of a severe native labor shortage, the Spaniards imported Black slaves to fill the gap. They were essential in the lowlands to work on the sugar plantations and in the sugar mills. Selected for their superior strength, the healthiest representatives were sent to the Americas; this implies those who were not suffering from malaria at the time they were chosen. Among these slaves, a large number might very likely have had a genetically inherited protection against the disease. Malaria, however, accompanied the Blacks to the New World in the blood of the White slavers and was then spread to the unimmune Indians by the aboriginal *Anopheles* mosquitoes to the Indians and European colonists. This disease served as an extra catalyst to wear down the already ailing Indians and to help cause the greater indigenous mortality in these regions than in the malaria-free highlands and the Yucatan. As the Indians continued to die out, the Blacks became progressively more in demand and soon, by default, they and the Europeans dominated this area of Mexico numerically. As to whether the sickle-cell trait was diffused among the native and White populations to a great enough extent to fortify the progeny of Afro-Indian and Afro-European unions in the area against malaria is still uncertain; however, Lisker's work suggests such a possibility.

# 12  The Epidemiology of a Folk Illness: *Susto* in Hispanic America

## Arthur J. Rubel

This article by Arthur J. Rubel represents a significant and original contribution to medical anthropology. It proposes to select a folk illness, in this case

Reprinted with abridgments from Arthur J. Rubel, 1964, "The Epidemiology of a Folk Illness: *Susto* in Hispanic America," *Ethnology, 3*: 268–283, with permission of the author and *Ethnology, An International Journal of Cultural and Social Anthopology.*

the malaise produced by fright and resulting in "soul loss" known in Latin America as *susto, espanto*, and by other names, and to subject this illness to the same kind of careful examination that is usually reserved for those illnesses for which names and textbook descriptions have been written in European and American medicine. In so doing, Rubel's essay goes a long way toward rescuing these disturbances, quaint and strange as they may appear to the Western-oriented mind, from the limbo of exotica (into which even some anthropological accounts seem to have consigned them) and place their study within the realm of science. The same principles that are used in the epidemiological study of such contagious diseases as measles, tuberculosis, and syphilis should be applied, Rubel suggests, to the study of these illnesses, which are perceived as real by the societies in which they occur and which have, to repeat W. I. Thomas' famous dictum, real consequences.

Rubel suggests a useful operational definition of the concept of folk illness as "syndromes from which members of a particular group claim to suffer and for which their culture provides an etiology, diagnosis, preventive measures, and regimens of healing." Under this rubric we may subsume all so-called ethnic illnesses about which, as Rubel shows, we know much bizarre symptomatology, but, from a medical and epidemiological point of view, little else. Even those ethnosemantic studies of folk illnesses that are useful in demonstrating how illness and diagnosis are framed in native cognitive systems "do not inform us which components of the population do in fact become ill, nor under what circumstances illness occurs, nor what course the illness follows when it does manifest itself." Rubel describes several of the difficult problems of methodology in such research, and using the symptom cluster that appears in the literature under many different terms as generically *susto* ("magical fright"), he presents the characteristics and epidemiology of the illness through ethnographic case histories. Rubel then derives a theoretical model to explain the epidemiology of *susto*, demonstrating in this manner that it "may be understood as a product of a complex interaction between an individual's state of health and the role expectations which his society provides, mediated by aspects of that individual's personality." In this connection see also in this volume Chapter 39 by Parker and Chapter 38 by Yap.

This exploratory article seeks to assess the extent to which folk illness may be subjected to epidemiological studies, as are other illnesses. It is a working assumption of this paper that, in general, folk-illness phenomena are indeed amenable to such investigation if one is aware of special methodological problems which are concomitants of such research. A presentation of some of these general problems is followed by an examination of the

Hispanic-American folk illness which I refer to as *susto*.

## METHODOLOGICAL PROBLEMS

A work which has as its announced goal the description, distribution, and etiology of folk illness faces a number of methodological problems. Not the least of these is an acceptable definition of folk illness. In these pages "illness" refers to syndromes from which members of a particular group claim to suffer and for which their culture provides an etiology, diagnosis, preventive measures, and regimens of healing. I apply the prefix "folk" to those illnesses of which orthodox Western medicine professes neither understanding nor competence—a definition which, although somewhat cumbersome, has the value of subsuming a number of seemingly bizarre syndromes which are reported in anthropological, medical and psychiatric literature from many areas of the world.

Another problem of basic importance is that, when modern epidemiologists or research-oriented physicians engage in systematic research on folk health phenomena, they find it difficult to agree with the population that a health problem indeed exists; furthermore, they tend to disagree with their patients on even the most fundamental premises about health and illness. The two groups perceive the same condition from premises which are fundamentally divergent. The problem is compounded by the fact that the health professional must elicit medical history and descriptions of the discomfort from people who hold an opposing point of view.

In recent years anthropologists have elucidated the underlying logic whereby a number of folk peoples understand illness, diagnosis, and healing, e.g., the work of Frake (1961) among the Subanun, of Metzger and Williams (1963) on the Tzeltal, and of Rubel (1960) among Mexican-Americans. These are steps along the way, but such studies do not inform us which components of the population do in fact become ill, nor under what circumstances illness occurs, nor what courses the illness follows when it does manifest itself. Investigations of folk illness are presently at a stage where we can assert with some degree of confidence only that certain syndromes appear to be confined to particular cultural or linguistic groups, e.g., Algonkians, Eskimos, or Mexican-Americans, and do not appear among others. That is to say, if one may divide the study of folk illness into two complementary areas of achievement—illness as a culture complex and the epidemiology of folk illness—then I submit that the first of these represents our present state of knowledge.

Monographs, articles, and more casual reports on exotic cultures abound with allusions to certain seemingly bizarre notions about illness. Sometimes these descriptive writings discuss the folk concept in some detail, but more often they do not. Often such reports titillate the reader by providing a few clinical case histories which reflect cultural beliefs about health and illness, but only in rare instances is one provided detailed descriptions about an individual patient's medical history, his or her response to the onset of the folk illness, or close observations of the course which the illness follows. Even more rarely does the reader encounter an extensive corpus of cases assembled either from published sources or from field observations.

The large collections of library data on the basis of which Parker (1960) and Teicher (1960) discuss the folk illness known as *wiitigo* are extremely valuable. The scrupulous attention paid by these scholars to the intricacies of a folk illness points up some of the more pressing problems faced by researchers who utilize library resources to derive epidemiological inferences as to causality. For example, the case materials on the *wiitigo* illness are reported by such diverse observers as anthropologists, explorers, missionaries, trappers, and Indians. Moreover, in these as in other instances, the descriptive reports often span years or even centuries of time and define the population involved in only the grossest terms. In the absence of precise chronological, social, or cultural parameters it is hazardous to attempt to infer rates of prevalence or incidence of a folk illness, much less the relationships which obtain between these rates and such demographic variables as age, sex, or marital status. Yet it is precisely from such inferences and associations that we may hope to gain an understanding of the nature of folk illness.

The methodical field worker who seeks cases of folk illness within a precisely delimited locale and time span is confronted by the problem of defining beforehand what it is that he seeks. Oftentimes, though the symptoms of presumed patients remain constant from place to place, the labels by which a disability is identified vary considerably. For heuristic and practical purposes I suggest that, in the present state of the study of folk illness, when several symptoms regularly cohere in any specified population, and members of that population respond to such manifestations in similarly patterned ways, the cluster of symptoms be defined as a disease entity. For, as Leighton (1961:486) has commented, it will prove profitable to fasten our attention first on "the distribution of selected types of human patterns, and only later ask what the functional effect and consequences of these are. The determination of pathology is the last thing to be done rather than the first" (cf. also Blum 1962).

## SUSTO IN HISPANIC AMERICA

The general problems in the study of folk illness, to which we have alluded, apply equally to the investigation of a condition, here called *susto*, which is reported from many regions of the Spanish-speaking New World. Though variously called *susto, pasmo, jani, espanto, pédida de la sombra*, or other terms in different localities, the reference in this paper is always to a syndrome, rather than its variant labels, and for purposes of exposition this particular cluster of symptoms and its attendant beliefs and behaviors will be arbitrarily designated as *susto*.

Those who suffer from *susto* include Indian and non-Indian, male and female, rich and poor, rural dwellers and urbanites. In the United States it is endemic to the Spanish-speaking inhabitants of California, Colorado, New Mexico, and Texas (Clark 1959; Saunders 1954; Rubel 1960). In Hispanic America *susto* is often mentioned in the writings of anthropologists and others. In contrast to other well-known folk illnesses such as *wiitigo* and arctic hysteria, however, it is not confined uniquely either to the speakers of a single group of related languages or to the members of one sociocultural group. Peoples who speak unrelated aboriginal languages, e.g., Chinantec, Tzotzil, and Quechua, as well as Spanish-speaking non-Indians, appear to be equally susceptible to this syndrome.

From the point of view of cultural analysis, the *susto* syndrome reflects the presence in Hispanic America of a trait complex which also occurs elsewhere in the world—a complex consisting of beliefs that an individual is composed of a corporeal being and one or more immaterial souls or spirits which may become detached from the body and wander freely. In Hispanic America, as elsewhere, these souls may leave the body during sleep, particularly when the individual is dreaming, but among peasant and urban groups they may also become detached as a consequence of an unsettling experience. The latter aspect of spirit separation from the corporeal being has attained such importance in Hispanic America as to justify being described as a cultural focus (Honigmann 1959: 128–129). I shall speak of it, together with its associated behavioral traits, as the *susto* focus. It is clearly distinct from the more widely diffused trait of soul separation. It is on the behavioral, rather than the cultural, nature of this focus that this paper concentrates.

Local embellishments on the basic cohering symptoms of *susto* make this entity appear far more inconstant than is really the case. When one concentrates on the constants which recur with great consistency among the various groups from which *susto* is reported, the basic syndrome appears as follows: (1) during sleep the patient evidences restlessness; (2) during waking hours patients are characterized by listlessness, loss of appetite, disinterest in dress and personal hygiene, loss of strength, depression, and introversion (Sal y Rosas 1958; Gillin 1945).

A number of basic elements recur in the folk etiology of *susto*. Among Indians the soul is believed to be captured because the patient, wittingly or not, has disturbed the spirit guardians of the earth, rivers, ponds, forests, or animals, the soul being held captive until the affront has been expiated. By contrast, when a non-Indian is diagnosed as suffering from soul loss, the locale in which it occurred, e.g., a river or forest, is of no significance nor are malevolent beings suspected. In many though not all cases a fright occasioned by an unexpected accident or encounter is thought to have caused the illness.

The curing rites of the groups in which this syndrome manifests itself as a significant health phenomenon likewise share a number of basic features. There is an initial diagnostic session between healer and patient during which the cause of the particular episode is specified and agreed upon by the participants. The soul is then coaxed and entreated to rejoin the patient's body; in the case of Indians those spirits who hold the soul captive are begged and propitiated to release it, and in both Indian and non-Indian groups the officiant shows the soul the direction back to the host body. During healing rites a patient is massaged and often sweated, both apparently to relax him, and he is "swept" or rubbed with some object to remove the illness from his body. In the Peruvian highlands a guinea pig is utilized for the therapeutic rubbing, whereas some Guatemala Indians use hens' eggs, and in south Texas and parts of Mexico medicinal brushes are employed for the same purpose.

## CASE HISTORIES

The fullest account of a case of *susto* (Gillin 1948) describes the condition of a Pokomam Indian woman from San Luis Jilotepecque in eastern Guatemala. The 63-year-old woman shared with neighbors a belief that her soul had been separated from the rest of her body and held captive by sentient beings. The capture of her soul was believed to have been precipitated when she discovered her husband philandering with a loose woman of the village. As a consequence of her discovery, the patient upbraided her husband, who retaliated by hitting his wife with a rock. When Gillin (1948: 348) encountered the woman,

she was in a depressed state of mind, neglected her household duties and her pottery making, and reduced her contact with friends and relatives. Physical complaints included diarrhea, "pain in the stomach," loss of appetite, "pains in the back and legs," occasional fever. Verbalizations were wheedling and anxious; she alternated between moods of timorous anxiety and tension characterized by tremor of the hands and generally rapid and jerky movements, and moods of profound, though conscious, lethargy. Orientation was adequate for time and place and normal reflexes were present.

The next case (Rubel 1960) is from a small city in south Texas. The patient, Mrs. Benitez, was a non-Indian who had been born in Mexico but had resided in Texas for many years. She was in her middle thirties and was the mother of five children, all girls. Her husband had deserted his family more than five years before. During our acquaintance the patient was irregularly employed as an agricultural field laborer, but most of her family's income was in fact derived from welfare agencies. She was extraordinarily thin and wan and appeared much older than her years. She had had a long history of epileptoid attacks, involving the locking of her jaw and involuntary spasms of her legs, but she claimed not to be able to recall what had occurred during such seizures. She expressed a feeling of constant tiredness and of complete social isolation, and she maintained that she had suffered recurrently from soul loss. . . .

The next case involved Antonio, a young married man about 25 years of age, likewise a native-born American citizen who could neither read, write, nor communicate in English. He and his family before him were laborers employed in harvesting cotton and vegetables in south Texas and migrating every spring and summer to the north-central states for similar field labor. To all outward appearances Antonio seemed an outgoing fellow contented enough with his lot. He lived with his wife and children in a homemade shack with an earth-packed floor, walls of corrugated paper, and a roof of tin. There was, of course, no indoor plumbing, but Antonio and the owner of the lot on which his shack stood had fashioned a shower and water closet in an outhouse which both families used. Unlike her husband, Antonio's wife came from a hamlet in northeastern Mexico. She neither spoke nor understood English, but she was able to write Spanish by using self-taught block letters. Despite the family's impoverished condition she, too, seemed a cheerful and untroubled person.

On one occasion Antonio was sent to a hospital with a diagnosis of double pneumonia. His fever was successfully controlled, and he was placed in a ward for a recuperative period. One night he noticed a change in the condition of a wardmate, became alarmed, and tried to communicate his concern to the attendants, but for some reason he was unsuccessful. Some time later they discovered that the wardmate had died and removed the corpse from the room. Antonio was much upset by the incident. He became fitful, complained of restless nights, and exhibited little interest in his food or surroundings. Moreover, he found his body involuntarily "jumping" on the bed while he lay in a reclining position. After leaving the hospital he went home and asked that his mother, who lived in Mexico, be brought to his side. When she arrived she immediately began to coax his soul back to his body by means of a traditional cure (see below).

A woman from Laredo, Texas, suffered *susto* on at least two occasions, several years apart. Each instance occurred during the course of her family's seasonal migration for field labor in the north. Mr. Solís, the patient's husband, was a highly excitable and apparently alienated person who conceived of himself as earning a living "by the honest sweat of my brow" in face of the restricting regulations of the local and federal government and of the outright malice of his employers. His lack of other than agricultural skills and the absence of year-round employment in south Texas left the family no choice except migratory labor and precluded the children's regular attendance at school despite the family's strong motivation toward education and their manifest aspirations toward a better way of life. Mrs. Solís, though probably only in her middle forties, was constantly sickly, felt weak, and had no desire to eat anything, not even when she awoke in the morning. Moreover, she felt listless during the

day and did not like to move about. She claimed she had suffered this condition for two years but had not brought it to a physician's attention.

The first episode of *susto* afflicted Mrs. Solís during her family's stay in an Indiana migrant labor camp. It occurred after she had unwillingly and helplessly witnessed an attack on a peaceable member of her husband's crew by drunken and bellicose members of another crew in which the victim was slashed in the abdominal region and removed to a hospital. Several years later, when she was pregnant, Mrs. Solís helplessly watched the family truck overturn, carrying with it the fruit of the crew's labor. As a consequence of this disturbing event she suffered a miscarriage and was again afflicted with *susto*.

In the cases of soul loss presented thus far—one from an Indian community in Guatemala and the remainder from non-Indian groups in south Texas—it has been possible to present relevant data on the patient's personality, on the family contexts, and on the causes presumed by the people involved to have precipitated the soul loss and illness. The following cases are less complete because all the relevant data are not available.

One case involved a young Chinantec Indian schoolboy from San Lucas Ojitlán in Oaxaca, Mexico. According to the boy's teacher, it was necessary one day to punish him for talking in class. The lad was instructed to stand by his desk with his hands outstretched and his palms up, and the teacher then slapped one upturned palm with a small wooden ruler. According to the instructor's account, the blows were not hard enough to have hurt the boy in a physical sense. Nevertheless, the illness which resulted from this chastisement was so serious as to keep the lad out of school for two weeks. During this period he was unable to eat and manifested considerable apathy. The child's mother recognized from these signs that her son's soul had left his body and had been captured by the spirit of the earth, and she took corrective steps which will be related later.

The following two cases are reported by Diaz de Solas (1957) from the Tzotzil-speaking Indians of San Bartolomé de Los Llanos in the Mexican state of Chiapas. In the first case an Indian mother seated her four-year-old son on a stone wall from which he could watch her while she gardened in the family corn field. After a while the child lost his balance and fell to the ground. Although he cried, he seemed to have been uninjured by the accident, nor was it thought that he had suffered *susto* as a result. The mother, however, lost her soul—a condition which the community considered to have been precipitated by her helplessness as she watched her child's fall.

The second case from San Bartolomé involved a man who suffered a *susto* as a result of an accident he was unable to prevent. This Indian was leading his heavily laden horse home from market, a trip which required the fording of a swiftly flowing steam. As they crossed the stream, the pack animal was swept downstream by the current. The owner saved himself, and was finally able to retrieve his horse, but the valuable load was lost. Subsequently the Indian sickened, and his condition was diagnosed as *susto*; his soul was presumed to have been taken captive by the spirit of the locale in which the accident occurred. In both the cases from San Bartolomé it was thought that the illness would continue until the annoyance suffered by the spirits, respectively of the earth and the river, had been expiated.

A very similar case occurred in another Tzotzil municipio, San Andrés Larrainzar, in the Chiapas highlands (cf. Guiteras-Holmes 1961:269–275). An Indian was driving a horse laden with corn on a trip from one section (*paraje*) of San Andrés to another, and in the course of his journey they were forced to cross the Río Tiwó. The man drove his animal into the river whilst he himself crossed over a small bridge. The horse was carried away by the current until it finally came to rest against a fallen tree trunk. Although the owner was able to rescue his horse, his load was lost. He felt very sad about his loss, and then he suffered an *espanto* (note the sequence!). At the end of a month the patient felt sad and sick, and had no desire to eat anything; as a consequence of these symptoms a curer was called into the case. . . .

The examples of *susto* reported in the preceding pages represent only a few of the references to the illness which were discovered in the literature. They have been selected for inclusion herein because they describe with some amplitude the circumstances surrounding the onset of a specific case of *susto* or because they provide some of the social or personality characteristics of the patients.

## HEALING RITES

I now move to a discussion of the curing rites associated with the syndrome of *susto*. I shall first describe those utilized to heal some of the patient: in the cases already presented and shall then refer to some generalized, but detailed, descriptions of

healing procedures provided by the psychiatrist Sal y Rosas (1958) and the anthropologists Tschopik (1951), Weitlaner (1961), and Carrasco (1960).

In the case from San Luis Jilotepecque, Guatemala, described by Gillin (1948), the patient for whom the healing ceremonies were intended was the wife who had suffered from a philandering husband. The essentials of the treatment may be divided into several stages. During the first stage, that of diagnosis, the native curer pronounced to the patient a clear-cut and authoritative diagnosis of *espanto* or soul loss. Later the woman was required to consider and "confess" the actual events which had led up to the particular episode of soul loss (she had had a previous history of similar episodes). During the second stage, that of the actual healing rites, a group of persons who were socially significant to the patient was organized to attend a nocturnal ceremony. Some of them joined the patient and the healer in offering prayers to the Catholic saints of the village. Hens' eggs were then passed over the patient to absorb some of the illness. They were later deposited at the place where the soul loss had occurred, along with a collection of gifts to propitiate the spirits who held the patient's soul and who were now requested to release it. Following prayers and libations to the spirits, a procession was formed. It led from the place of the accident back to the woman's home, the healer making noises to indicate to the soul the appropriate direction. Finally, the patient was undressed, "shocked" by cold liquor sprayed from the mouth of the curer, then massaged, and finally "sweated" on a bed placed over a brazier filled with burning coals.

The essentials of the Pokomam ceremony, with the exception of certain details in the expiation rites, are found widely dispersed in Hispanic America among Indians and non-Indians alike. In the case involving the Chinantec schoolboy, for example, the healing rites were as follows. The boy's mother proceeded to the schoolhouse, taking with her the shirt her son had worn on the day he had been punished. Inside the building she moved directly to the desk alongside of which her son had been chastised. She took his shirt, rolled it up, and proceeded to wipe the packed earth flooring, meanwhile murmuring:

I come in the name of curer Garcia who at this time is unable to come. I come in order to reunite the spirit of my boy, José, who is sick. I come this time and this time only. It surely was not your intention to dispossess him of his spirit. Goodbye, I will return in four days to advise you as to his condition and to do whatever is necessary.

The mother then removed from her clothing a bottle of liquor mixed with the herb called *hoja de espanto* and sprayed some of this liquor from her mouth on the shirt, as well as on the earthen floor on which the desk rested, meanwhile crossing herself and making the sign of the cross over the wet shirt. She then picked up the shirt and excavated a little earth, which she carried home. Here her son donned his shirt, and the earth was placed in a receptacle containing liquor set beside the boy's cot. The mother next called on the services of a professional curer, who poured liquor from the receptacle into his own mouth and sprayed the patient on his face, chest, crown, and the back of his neck. The child was then placed on his cot, rolled in blankets, and a brazier of hot coals was placed under the cot to sweat him. Following the child's recovery, the curer went himself to the school-house, where he offered thanks to the earth for releasing the child's soul and then ceremoniously bade it farewell. . . .

In the non-Indian cases reported from Texas the cures, though similar in many respects, involved neither expiation nor propitiation. The major problem a Texas curer confronts is to induce the soul to return to the patient's body; it is not compounded by the conception of malevolent captors. In Antonio's case his mother placed him on the dirt floor of his shack, with his arms outstretched but his legs together so that he formed a human cross. She then dug a hole at the base of his feet, another above his head, and one at each of his extended hands, filling them with a liquid composed of water and medicinal herbs. Then she began to "sweep" the illness out of her son's body via the extremities, using a broom constructed of a desert bush with medicinal qualities. She and her son then prayed, entreating his lost and wandering soul to rejoin his body, after which she blew a spray of liquid from her mouth directly into her son's face, and Antonio sipped some of the medicinal liquid which his mother had scooped from the holes in the dirt floor.

Among the most meticulous descriptions of cures for *susto* are those provided by Sal y Rosas (1958:177–184). In the main, his data pertain to the Quechua Indians of the Callejon de Huaylas region of Peru, but a number of his observations refer to other parts of that country as well. After diagnosis, according to Sal y Rosas, a patient reclines on a cot or on a blanket stretched on the floor, and alongside him is placed a mixture of various flower petals, leaves, and wheat or corn is placed beside him. The curer blesses the mixture

and distributes it over the patient's body, commencing at his head and moving down to the legs and then the feet. Later the curer's helper carries the mixture, wrapped in the patient's clothing, to the locality where the illness was precipitated, scattering on his way a trail of petals, leaves, and flour to indicate to the soul the path by which it is to return to the body. He also leaves an offering of liquor, cigarettes, and coca leaves at the site as an inducement to the soul to return. He then holds up the patient's shirt and shakes it in the air to attract the soul's attention. Returning to the patient's house, the helper carefully follows the trail of petals, leaves, and flour and holds the shirt in plain sight so that the soul will encounter no trouble in finding its way. (In more serious cases of soul loss, the patient is rubbed with a live guinea pig, which is then taken and left as a gift to the spirits of the locality where the illness occurred, in exchange for the captive soul.)

Reports by Weitlaner (1961) and Carrasco (1960:103–105, 110) of symptoms, etiology, and curing rites among Nahuatl-speaking and Chontal-speaking groups in western Mexico indicate that soul capture and its concomitant syndrome are remarkably similar to those reported among aboriginal groups with very very different linguistic affiliations. Among these Chontal and Nahua groups the loss and capture of a soul is believed to be precipitated by a fall on a road or pathway, by slipping or falling near a body of water, or by a sudden encounter with animals, snakes, or even a corpse. Diagnosis and healing include the elicitation by a healer of the date, place, and other pertinent circumstances of the event the patient presumes to have brought on the illness. This is followed by expiation for the annoyance caused the spirit guardians of the locale and by propitiation of these being in exchange for the captive soul. The healer then attempts to coax and lead the absent soul back to its host body. Unlike other groups previously discussed, the Nahua and Chontal adorn their healing rites with elaborate symbolism in which ritual colors, numbers, and directions play important parts. Nevertheless, beneath these local embellishments, one quickly discerns the fundamentals of the widespread *susto* complex and the associated healing rites which these Indians share with the other groups mentioned.

## SUMMARY OF DESCRIPTIVE DATA

One of the most noteworthy aspects of the *susto* phenomenon is the fact that a basic core of premises and assumptions—symptoms, etiology, and regimens of healing—recur with remarkable constancy among many Hispanic-American groups Indian and non-Indian alike. In general, the following symptoms characterize victims of this illness: (1) while asleep a patient evidences restlessness, and (2) during waking hours he manifests listlessness, loss of appetite, disinterest in costume or personal hygiene, loss of strength and weight, depression, and introversion. In one unique instance, a Texas patient (Mrs. Benitez) subsumes under *susto* her epileptoid seizures in addition to the more usual loss of strength, depression, apathy, listlessness, and introversion. However, it should be noted that, when this victim of *susto* describes her own condition, she stresses the post-spasmodic depressive and introversive emotional states rather than the seizure itself.

Although Indian and non-Indian populations appear to be equally subject to *susto,* there are significant differences between them with respect to the nature of the causal agents. Unlike non-Indians, Indian groups conceive of the separation of the soul from the body as precipitated by an affront to the spirit guardians of a locality— guardians of the earth, water, or animals—although the offense is usually caused unwittingly by the victim. Intentional or not, however, the mischief must be expiated and the spirits of the site propitiated before they will release the captured soul.

There are also other features of the precipitating events which recur with remarkable constancy. Thus one salient feature of all the cases cited is role helplessness. Significantly, however, a victim's helplessness appears in association with only some kinds of problems in role behavior, but not with others. In none of the instances cited, for example, do we discover a victim helpless in the face of role conflicts or expectations which are products of his or her cultural marginality or social mobility. In other words, *susto* appears to communicate an individual's inability to fulfill adequately the expectations of the society in which he has been socialized; it does not seem to mark those role conflicts and uncertainties Indians confront as they pass into Ladino society or the problems posed to upwardly mobile Mexican-Americans in the process of being assimilated into the Anglo-American society of Texas.

In cases of soul capture, a healing specialist visits the site at which the mishap occurred, where he propitiates the spirits and then coaxes the released soul back to the body of the victim along a path clearly indicated by the healer. Sickness which has "entered" the victim's body is removed either by sweeping it out by means of medicinal branches or by passing hens' eggs, a fowl, or a guinea pig across the body of the victim in such a manner as to absorb the illness, removing it from the victim. Inasmuch as non-Indian groups neither attribute soul loss to malevolent sentient beings nor consider the site at which a mishap occurred to be important, it follows that neither expiation nor propitiation occur in their healing rites. Finally, the rites of both groups share such other elements as medicinal "sweeping" to remove internalized illness, recollection and verbalization by the patient of the event precipitating the separation of his soul from the body, simulation of the "shock" which was the immediate cause of that separation, and entreaties directed to a soul to return to the victim. The constancy with which similar precipitating events, symptoms, and healing methods recur among a variety of groups in Hispanic America makes the syndrome amenable to systematic epidemiological investigation.

## AN EPIDEMIOLOGICAL MODEL

Epidemiology has been described by Wade Hampton Frost as "something more than the total of its established facts. It includes their orderly arrangement into chains of inference which extend more or less beyond the bounds of direct observation" (Maxcy 1941:1). In what follows I shall attempt to order the descriptive data into such "chains of inference." Let me first make clear that it is not my intent to investigate the truth of informants' statements as to whether or not those who complain of illness associated with a presumed loss of soul are really ill. It has been my experience (one which I share with others who write of this phenomenon) that individuals who claim to suffer an *asustado* condition are characterized by, if nothing else, a distinctive absence of well-being—the minimal criterion for defining illness.

It is hoped that my conceptual model and the hypotheses it generates will result in a later test of those hypotheses and their verification, modification, or rejection as may be required. Underlying this model is an assumption which holds that the *susto* syndrome is a product of the interaction between three open systems, each linked with the others (Caudill 1958:4–7). The three systems in question are (1) an individual's state of health, (2) his personality system, and (3) the social system of

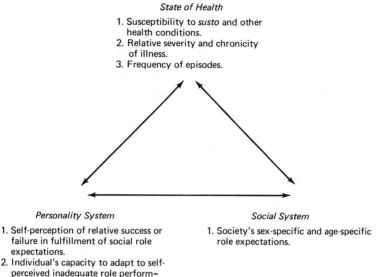

**Figure 1.**   Conceptual model for the epidemiological study of a folk illness.

which he is a member. The interaction between these three linked open systems is portrayed in the above simple diagram (see Cassell *et al.* 1960).

Finally, I proffer the following tentative hypotheses:

I. A *susto* syndrome will appear only in social situations which victims perceive as stressful. The syndrome is the vehicle by means of which people of Hispanic-American peasant and urban societies manifest their reactions to some forms of self-perceived stressful situations, but not others. People in these societies not only choose to assume the sick role but also elect the kinds of symptoms by which to make manifest to others an absence of well-being (cf. Parsons and Fox 1952; Weinstein 1962).

II. The social stresses which are reflected in the *susto* syndrome are intra-cultural and intra-societal in nature. Stresses occasioned by conflict between cultures or by an individual's cultural marginality or social mobility will be symbolized by symptoms of illness other than *susto*. In other words, the frustration or alienation which often result from efforts to identify with, and to be accepted by, members of a society or social stratum distinct from that into which one has been socialized will not be reflected by *susto*.

III. In Hispanic-American societies, the *susto* syndrome will appear as a consequence of an episode in which an individual is unable to meet the expectations of his own society for a social role in which he or she has been socialized.

Corollary 1: Because these societies differentially socialize males and females, and because society's expectations of male and female children differ from those held for mature men and women, it is expected that girls and women will be afflicted by *susto* and its concomitants as a consequence of experiences different from those which jeopardize the health of boys and men of the same society. For example, girls are socialized to be demure, dependent, and home-oriented, whereas boys are trained to show aggressiveness, independence, and orientations toward occupational and public responsibility roles. I should not expect many girls or women in these societies to manifest *susto* under circumstances where the society has no reason to expect a female to fulfill a responsibility successfully. Neither should one expect a young man to suffer ill effects from his inability to carry out successfully a task usually assigned to females. If, for example, a girl of the same age as the Mexican-American boy, Ricardo, refused to enter the water because of timidity, it is my belief that the soul-loss syndrome would not have appeared. The girl's timidity would have been a demonstration of appropriate female behavior,

127

whereas Ricardo's behavior was a far cry from the expectations which Mexican-Americans hold for boys and men.

Corollary 2: Since Hispanic-American societies attach greater importance to the successful accomplishment of some tasks than of others, the more importance which socializers attach to a particular task, the greater the likelihood will be that *susto* will occur in association with failure to perform that task adequately. It follows that, although females and males both risk illness as a consequence of failure adequately to perform sex-specific and age-specific tasks, not all such tasks are equally risky.

IV. Although all persons in a society may believe in the concept of soul loss and its attendant illness, not all members of that society will actually fall victim to this kind of illness. It is hypothesized that individual personalities act as contingency variables. That is, if two members of a society, matched for age and sex, fail to meet adequately the society's role expectations, one may respond to his self-perceived inadequacy by electing the sick role, i.e., *susto*, whereas the other may adapt in a different manner, e.g., by an expression of generalized anger or by displacement of hostility. Moreover, among those who do elect the *susto* syndrome, the severity, chronicity, and frequency of episodes will vary systematically with respect to personality and societal variables. The points which are of interest to us, of course, are (1) that some cultures provide *susto* as an adaptive mechanism to self-perceived social inadequacies, whereas others do not, and (2) that some but not all individuals with these cultural beliefs elect *susto* symptoms to indicate an absence of well-being.

Briefly, these hypotheses propose that *susto* illness in societies of Hispanic America may be understood as a product of a complex interaction between an individual's state of health and the role expectations which his society provides, mediated by aspects of that individual's personality.

## SUMMARY

In this exploration of the health phenomenon which I call *susto*, I have sought to assess the extent to which this folk illness is amenable to epidemiological analysis. Despite localized embellishments on a general theme of soul-loss illness, there recurs in many societies a hard core of constant elements which lead one to conclude that this phenomenon is indeed subject to orderly description and analysis. Moreover, inferences of causality drawn from ethnographic data offer great potential for understanding the nature of folk illness and some facets of the relationships which obtain between health and social behavior. Finally, if one folk illness, *susto*, proves amenable to such investigation, other seemingly bizarre notions of illness demand the attention of epidemiologists and research physicians working in collaboration with anthropologists (see Fleck and Ianni 1958).

# IV
## Medical Systems and Theories of Disease and Healing

## Medical Systems in Transcultural Perspective

Two key concepts found in this section and throughout this book deserve some effort at definition: *medicine* and *medical system*. Before offering these definitions we first give a nod of recognition toward some other central notions, especially *health* and *disease*. René Dubos considers these terms at the beginning of his selection in Section I. At a minimum, a state of *health* refers to a condition of an organism that permits it to adapt to its environmental situation with relatively minimal pain and discomfort (but not their absence), achieve at least some physical and psychic gratifications, and possess a reasonable probability of survival. A state of *disease* is a condition of the organism that seriously obtrudes against these adaptive requirements and causes partial or complete disablement and physical and/or behavioral dysfunction. But these are necessarily relative terms, and especially so when they are applied to the human animal. No individual human is ever completely healthy. As the medical ecologist and epidemiologist Jacques May (1960:789) writes:

> A famous French playwright once quipped: "A healthy person is nothing but an unrevealed patient." I have a great fondness for this definition, and I think there is much more to it than meets the eye. I like it because it stresses the fact that what we call health is nothing but a struggle between mysterious forces that occur below the horizon. Nothing happens in the visible field that does not stem from deep, invisible, and unknown roots. It has been said that one of the traits that distinguishes man from animals is that man suspects there is another value to the appearance of what he observes. . . . Thus the French playwright's remark implies that some day the challenges of the environment will reveal the strength and the weakness of the person and give us a measure of his ability to adjust to this environment.

An anthropologist would take May's statement a further step to say that the ability of the person to adjust to his environmental challenges is a function not only of his genetic "hidden traits," as May says elsewhere in the same paper, but also a function of the strategies, devices, and organizational arrangements evolved in, and by, his society for coping with pestilence and other environmental threats. For if, as I noted previously, cultures represent, in part, the ways in which human societies deal with sickness and trauma as challenges to successful adaptation, they also, as Dubos (Section I) has shown, become themselves threats to human adaptation and survival, and indeed may be pathogenic or situationally iatrogenic. The same practices, methods, techniques, substances, places, and personnel that are designed by a culture to combat disease, as we see time after time in the studies in this anthology, themselves may become the cause of disease and death. And this is not confined to non-Western nonliterate societies but applies to "civilized" societies of the West as well. With all the glittering, overwhelming technological apparatus into which patients are fed in our Western hospitals, these treatment institutions are unsafe places to be. The probability of infection (not to mention other hazards, including maltreatment, mistreatment, and sheer neglect) is far greater for people in hospitals than out of them. Thus, the ironic paradox, which encompasses not only illness and treatment but all other aspects of human life as well, that cultures are always potentially maladaptive though their *raison d'être* is human adaptation.

The reader who judges the medical systems and medicines of the societies considered herein as "barbaric," "primitive," or "underdeveloped" will be sobered by the knowledge that not only are our own medical system and medicine, though little short of miraculous in so many ways, themselves fraught with hazards (for example, antibiotics and other broad-spectrum drugs, radiation treatment, major surgery), but that our own recent forebears possessed medicines and therapies that are not greatly different from, and perhaps even less effective than, those of so-called "primitive" and "folk" medicine. It may be worth noting that at the end of the eighteenth century in 1799, at the age of 67, George Washington died within a few days of an illness for which the diagnosis today seems uncertain (earlier it was said to be laryngitis, diphtheria, and quinsy, and more recently and retrospectively, a laryngeal streptococcic infection). But attended first by his aide and servants, and then by three reputable physicians, the Father of Our Country was repeatedly bled, blistered, and purged until he expired. Although this treatment subsequently received much criticism, the historical evidence indicates that Washington's physicians were probably acting according to the best advice of their day. Two of them had been trained at one of the world's great medical schools at the University of Edinburgh. These methods practiced on Washington were used extensively through the nineteenth centruy, and purging, at least, continued to be used well into the present century (Carroll and Ashworth 1957:617–631, 637–647).

A recent interesting study by a medical historian on the use of hydropathy in nineteenth-century America makes the following statement:

> At its best, medicine in the nineteenth century was to a large degree still speculative and theoretical, and many "regular" practitioners were easily led astray by new "irregular" innovations. The plain man, too poor to take advantage of the best practices in medical science, resorted to homemade nostrums.
>
> Many of the aberrations in medical thinking achieved the status of cults or schools of medical doctrine, generally as a direct reaction to the excessive medication which character-ized the practice of many regular physicians. Dr. Thomas L. Nichols wrote in 1864 of the physicians in every school: "There are allopaths of every class in allopathy; homeopaths of high and low dilutions; hydropaths mild and heroic; chronothermalists, Thompsonians, spiritualists with healing gifts, and I know not what besides. What is worse, perhaps, is the fact that there is no standard—no real science of medicine—no absolute or acknowledged authority."
>
> With the arising sects, it was difficult to judge who was a "regular" physician and who was "irregular." At times, sectarians seemed to be larger in numbers, and often they practiced with more sense and science than did the "regular." So keen became the competition between these cults and the orthodox practitioners, and so popular were they, that the "regular" doctor was often forced to adopt their methods or lose his practice (Legan 1971:267–268).

Thus it has been scarcely a century ago that Western medicine began to become rigorously scientific. Indeed, as Shryock (1947) sees it, the early and middle 19th century was a period of widespread disenchantment with American and European medicine. The profession was held in profound contempt by much of the public for

An illuminating clue to the psychological significance of disease situations interpreted as a result of the causes just cited is obtained if we follow Freud's differentiation of what he terms a *traumatic* situation from a simple *danger* situation. He introduces this distinction by asking what the kernel of the danger situation is (Freud 1936:149). He finds that it revolves about the estimation of our strength in relation to the danger. If we feel a sense of helplessness in the face of it, an inability to cope with it, then he calls the situation *traumatic*. This is precisely the differentiation that applies to those disease situations among the Saulteaux where the cause of the illness is uncertain and obscure. In these situations, the quality of the anxiety aroused is different from that where illness is faced in the same way any danger situation is faced. It is disease situations of this *traumatic* type that operate as a social sanction.

The qualitative aspects of the anxiety aroused emerge from the combination of two determinants. The first is purely objective: ordinary medical treatment of the sick person has failed to produce improvement. The symptoms persist or the person gets worse. It is at this point that the situation becomes serious. Prior to this, the illness may not even have been considered dangerous,but when the medicine does not work, the situation rapidly becomes traumatic. This is because the suspicion is aroused in the patient or his associates that the cause of the illness is hidden. It may be a penalty for something done in the past. It may be due to bad conduct or witchcraft. But who knows? Yet if this is so, his very life is in jeopardy. Consequently, a feeling of helplessness arises which can only be alleviated if the precise cause of the sickness is discovered. Otherwise, appropriate measures cannot be undertaken. Meanwhile, the source of the danger remains uncertain and obscure; further suffering, even death, menaces the patient.

Thus, while from an objective point of view we often may have displayed what seems to be a "disproportionality of affect" in disease situations, at the same time the definition of such situations in terms of Saulteaux beliefs presents dangers that are not comparable to those we would recognize in similar situations. This is an important qualitative difference. The affective reactions of the Saulteaux are a function of this difference (Mowrer 1939).

It would also appear that there are some analogies, although by no means an identity, between the anxiety created in some of these traumatic disease situations among the Saulteaux and neurotic anxiety. This is true, at least, in the cases where the danger that threatens is believed to have arisen out of the patient's own acts, so there is the closest integral relation between inner and outer danger as in neurotic anxiety, but there are no substitute formations in the individual which project the danger outwards, as in animal phobias, while the real source of danger remains unknown. Nevertheless, it is true that the impulses of the individual become the sine qua non of the external danger, just as in neurotic anxiety. Consequently, these impulses are the ultimate source of the danger itself. The disease is not considered to be impersonal and objective in origin and for this reason it cannot be faced in the same terms as other kinds of illness or other objective hazards of life. The real source of danger is from within and, like neurotic anxiety, it is connected with forbidden acts.

Take the case of an Indian who believes himself bewitched, for example. At the first appearance of his illness, he may not have been worried because he may have thought that there was some other cause of his trouble, but as soon as he believes he is the victim of a hostile attack, he gets anxious. Why? Because he believes his illness is in retaliation for some previous act of aggression he has perpetrated. The assertion of these aggressive impulses on his part has led to a feeling of guilt and the illness from which he is suffering has aroused anxiety because he senses danger. His very life may be threatened. What this man fears is that he had endangered his life by acting as he did. He is afraid of the consequences of his own impulses. The source of the outwardly sensed danger lies in his own hostile impulses.

So far I have tried to explain how anxiety is integrated in disease situations among the Saulteaux and why it is that the emotion generated has qualitative features which suggest neurotic anxiety. I hope that I have made it clear, however, that these features are only analogies deduced from the manner in which the belief system of the Saulteaux compels the individual to interpret the objective aspects of disease situations under certain conditions. What we actually appear to have exhibited in these cases is an affective reaction on a fear-anxiety continuum that lies somewhere between true objective anxiety and real neurotic anxiety (Freud 1936:148). That this is indeed the case is supported by the fact that, on the one hand, we can point to occurrences of real anxiety in danger situations among the Saulteaux and, on the other, to cases of neurotic anxiety.

The point I wish to emphasize particularly is that at both extremes of the fear-anxiety continuum the main function of the affect has reference to the individual alone. This is true whether he runs away from some objective danger or develops phobias which are reaction formations in self-defense against some instinctual danger. The anxiety associated with disease situations among the Saulteaux, on the other hand, has a social function insofar as it motivates individuals to avoid the danger (disease) by comforming to the dictates of the social code. This is accomplished by forcing the individual to reflect upon disapproved acts under the stress of the anxiety aroused by a disease situation or to anticipate possible discomfort through a knowledge of the experience of others. In either case, the disease sanction encourages the individual to be responsible for his own conduct.

The full implications of the social function of anxiety in Saulteaux society can best be exposed, however, if we return to the traumatic disease situation and inquire what steps are taken to reduce anxiety in the individual. I have already pointed out that, in such situations, the cause of the disease is at first problematical though the suspicion is aroused that the patient himself or some other person is responsible for the illness. This means that the true cause of the trouble must be sought before the disease can be alleviated. Once the cause of the illness is discovered, the disease situation loses some of its traumatic quality because the danger can be squarely faced like any other danger and some action taken to meet it. The therapeutic measures employed can be looked upon as anxiety-reducing devices.

Now one of the distinctive features of the Saulteaux belief system is this: if one who is ill because of "bad conduct" *confesses* his transgression, the medicine will then do its work and the patient will recover. This notion is the most typical feature of the operation of the disease sanction in cases where the penalty threatened is automatically induced. In fact, it adds considerable force to the sanction so far as the individual is concerned. It means that deviant conduct may not only lead to subsequent illness but that in order to get well one has to suffer the shame of self-exposure involved in confession. This is part of the punishment. Since it is also believed that the medicine man's guardian spirits (*pawáganak*) will inform him of the cause of the trouble, there is no use withholding anything. At the same time, confession provides the means of alleviating the guilt and anxiety of the individual, because, if a feeling of helplessness or being trapped is an intrinsic factor in these traumatic situations (or in any severe anxiety situation), confession

provides a method of escape according to both Saulteaux belief and sound psychological principle.

From the standpoint of Saulteaux society as a whole, confession is also a means by which knowledge of confessed transgressions is put into social circulation. Confession among the Saulteaux is not equivalent to confession to a priest, a friend, or a psychoanalyst in Western culture. In our society, it is assumed that what is exposed will be held in absolute confidence (Petazzoni 1931), but among these Indians the notion is held that the very secrecy of the transgressions is one of the things that makes them particularly bad. This explains why it is that when one person confesses a sexual transgression in which he or she has participated with a second person, the latter will not become ill subsequently or have to confess. Once the transgression has been publicized, it is washed away or, as the Saulteaux phrase it, "bad conduct will not follow you any more."

Perhaps this attitude towards what is secret is connected with the lack of privacy that is intrinsic to the manner in which these people live. Anything that smacks of secrecy is always suspect. There is even an aura of potential menace about such things, fortified no doubt by the covert practice of magic and sorcery. Consequently, in disease situations where any hidden transgression is thought to be the cause of the trouble what is in effect a public exposure is a necessary step to regaining health.

In actual practice, this works out in a very simple way. When anyone is sick, there is no isolation of the patient; on the contrary, the wigwam is always full of people. Any statement on the part of the patient, although it may be made to the doctor, is not only public but also very quickly may become a matter of common gossip. Where conjuring is resorted to, in cases where all other efforts have failed to reveal the hidden cause of the malady (Hallowell 1942a) almost the whole community may be present en masse. Under these conditions, to confess a transgression is to reveal publicly a secret "sin." Consequently, the resistance to self-exposure is very great and the shame experienced by the individual extremely poignant. In terms of our own society it is as if the transgressions committed were exposed in open court or published in the newspapers so that everyone knew that Jerry had slept with his sister or that Kate had murdered her child. Among the Saulteaux, however, it is only after such a confession is made that the usual medicine can do its work and the patient can recover. In one case, three children of a married couple were all suffering from a discharge of mucous through the nose and mouth. They had been treated by a native doctor who was also a conjurer but his medicine had done no good. Finally, a conjuring performance was held. Despite the fact that the woman's husband, who was present, had threatened her with death if she ever told, she broke down in a flood of tears and confessed to everyone that he had forced fellatio upon her.

This public aspect of confession is one of the channels through which individuals growing up in Saulteaux society and overhearing the gossip of their elders *sense*, even though they may fail to understand fully, the general typology of disapproved patterns of behavior. Children do not have to be taught a concrete panel of transgressions in Saulteaux society any more than in our own. Nor does it have to be assumed that they have been present on numerous occasions when transgressions have been confessed. Even if they are present, they may not always understand what is meant. Yet some feeling is gained of the *kind* of conduct that is disapproved. The informant who told me about the case of fellatio was present at the conjuring performance when this was confessed. She was about ten years old at the time and did not understand what was meant until later when her stepmother enlightened her.

In actual operation, the disease sanction among the Saulteaux does not completely deter individuals from committing socially disapproved acts but it functions as a brake by arousing anxiety at the very thought of such conduct. Functionally viewed, a society can well tolerate a few breaches of the rules if, through some means such as confession, a knowledge of dissocial conduct is publicized with the result that a large majority of individuals follow the approved types of behavior.

These deductions are by no means theoretical. That individuals in Saulteaux society actually are deterred from acting in forbidden ways by the disease sanction is illustrated by the following story (Mowrer 1939:558). In this case, illness did not follow incestuous intercourse. Perhaps this was because it occurred only once. In fact, this may be the moral of the story from the point of view of the Saulteaux themselves. At any rate, it gives a very clear picture of the conscious conflict between the impulses of the individual and socially sanctioned modes of conduct.

An unmarried woman had "adopted" her brother's son, a boy who was already a fairly good hunter. They were camping by themselves alone in the bush. The boy

had shot some meat and they were drying it. One night after they both lay down to sleep, he began to think about his *kīsʌgwas*. After awhile he spoke to her. "How's chances?" he said. "Are you crazy," she replied, "to talk like that? You are my brother's son." "Nothing will happen to us," the boy said. "Yes, there will," said his aunt, "we might suffer." "No we won't. Nothing will happen," her nephew replied.

Then he got up, went over to where she was lying and managed to get what he wanted. After he had finished, he went back to his own place and lay down again. He could not go to sleep. He began to worry about what he had done to his father's sister.

In the morning he said to her, "I'm going now." "Where?" she asked. "I'm going to live somewhere else. I'm ashamed of what I did. I'm going away. If I starve to death, all right." "No! No! Don't go," said his aunt. "If you leave who is going to make a living for me? I'll starve to death. It's not the first time people did what we did. It has happened elsewhere."

But the young man was much worried and determined to go. "No, you can't leave me," said his aunt. "I've brought you up and you must stay here." "I'll go for awhile, anyway," the boy said. "All right," said his aunt "just for a short time. No one knows and I'll never tell anyone. There might come a time to say it, but not now."

So the young fellow went off. He came to a high rock and sat down there. He thought over what he had done. He was sorry that he did it. He pulled out his penis and looked at it. He found a hair. He said to himself, "This is *nīsʌgwas*, her hair." He threw it away.

That night he camped by himself, half thinking all the time that he would go back to his aunt. In the morning, he did go back to where they had their camp. He arrived at sundown.

All during the night he was away his aunt had been crying. She was so very glad to see him now. He said to her, "I wonder if it would be all right if we lived together, just as if we were man and wife." "I don't think so," the woman said. "It would not look right if we did that. If you want a woman you better get one for yourself and if I want a man I better get one."

The trouble was this young man had tasted something new and he wanted more of it. He found a girl and got married in the spring. He and his wife lived with his aunt. Later his aunt got married, too.

The narrator commented that the boy's aunt was a sensible woman. They just made one slip and then stopped. This may explain why nothing happened to them, i.e., neither one got sick and had to confess.

Among the Saulteaux, then, desire for *pīmädʌz-īwin* can be assumed to be a major goal response. Everyone wants to be healthy, to live long, and to enjoy life as much as possible. In order to achieve this aim, certain kinds of conduct should be avoided, not only for one's own sake, but for the sake of one's children. If one does commit transgressions and then falls ill, or if one's children become ill, it is better to suffer shame than more suffering or even death. This is the setting of confession and its individual motivation (Petazzoni 1931:151–152). Confession, in turn, by making public the transgression committed permits the individual to recover. This is its ostensible purpose. But confession has a wider social function. It makes others aware of disapproved types of conduct which act as a warning to them. At the same time, since patients who confess usually recover, the publicity given to such cases supports both the native theory of disease causation on which the sanction rests, and the efficacy of confession itself. So while most individuals are motivated to avoid the risk of illness, there is consolation in the fact that even if one's sins find one out, there still is a means of regaining health.

In some traumatic disease situations where witchcraft is thought to be the cause of the illness, the anxiety of the patient and his associates is relieved by the removal of a material object from the patient's body by the doctor. This type of therapy is based upon the belief that it is possible to project material objects into the body of a person that will cause illness. Once the object is removed the patient is supposed to recover. The sociopsychological reverberations of cases diagnosed as due to witchcraft are much the same, however, as those in which confession has occurred. This follows because the same factors are involved: (a) a disease situation that requires explanation in terms of some previous behavior on the part of the patient; (b) the selection, perhaps with the help of the doctor, of some offensive act that is brought forward because the patient feels guilty about it; (c) the dissemination of the cause of the illness through gossip about the case; (d) the resulting publicity given to socially disapproved types of conduct that act as a warning to others.

We can see, then, how the therapeutic measures utilized by these Indians in traumatic disease situations have the social function of anxiety reduction, although this is not their ostensible purpose from the standpoint of the Saulteaux themselves. We can likewise understand how it is that in a society where so much anxiety is associated with disease the persons who specialize in curative methods are individuals who enjoy the highest prestige. In psychological terms, this prestige accrues to those who are instrumental in reducing anxiety.

It is impossible to discuss here all the further ramifications of the functional aspects of anxiety, but we may point out that the whole magico-religious apparatus of the Saulteaux is a complex anxiety-reducing device (Willoughby 1935).

In summary, the thesis developed here is that, by its very nature, disease may arouse "normal" or objective anxiety, but among the Saulteaux, native theories of disease causation invest certain disease situations with a traumatic quality which is a function of the beliefs held rather than of the actual danger threatened by the illness itself. The quality of the anxiety precipitated in the individuals affected by such situations suggests neurotic rather than objective anxiety because the ultimate cause of the disease is attributed to the expression of dissocial impulses. The illness is viewed as a punishment for such acts and the anxiety is a danger signal that heralds the imminence of this penalty. Insofar as individuals are motivated to avoid dissocial acts because of the penalty anticipated, the pseudo-neurotic anxiety aroused in disease situations has a positive social function. It is a psychic mechanism that acts as a reinforcing agent in upholding the social code. Thus, in a society with such a relatively simple culture and one in which formalized institutions and devices for penalizing the individual for dissocial conduct are absent, the utilization of anxiety in connection with disease is an extremely effective means for supporting the patterns of interpersonal behavior that make Saulteaux society a going concern.

# 14 Etiology of Illness in Guinhangdan

## Ethel Nurge

In this Philippine fishing-agricultural village, the medical system and the concepts of illness and causes of illness are an amalgam of traditional Tagalog and Spanish terms, which may be explained by the fact that the islands were under Spanish occupation and rule for four centuries. Although some persons living in this village know of Western-style medicine, it is a treatment of last resort when all else in the traditional system has been tried and found wanting. It is interesting to

Reprinted with abridgments from Ethel Nurge, 1958, "Etiology of Illness in Guinhangdan," *American Anthropologist*, 60:1158–1172, with permission of the author and the American Anthropological Association.

note that one category of illness-causing spirits are the *cahoynon*, or tree-spirits, who take the form of Filipinos and Europeans—and it is the latter who are the focus of major interest. Symptomatology is of minor interest; what is important is the diagnosis and whether the sickness is caused by displeased *encantos* (spirits), or by *asuangs* (witches). The system also boasts of a number of specialists in the various types of disease, and especially whether the disease is spiritually or "naturally" caused. Ethel Nurge concludes in this study that disease entities are of no interest to the villagers as they might be either to the practicing physician or observing anthropologist. It is the fact that they are miserable, hurting, and possibly incapacitated that disturbs them. As Nurge says, "It is not measles or bronchitis or tuberculosis but an unhappiness and a dis-ease which the patient brings to specialists and which the curer or M.D. defines for the patient." She suggests that even highly trained medical specialists have difficulty in identifying disease entities from symptoms. What the villager knows is his own system of beliefs and what to do about them.

... This paper is a study of a theory of disease causation and treatment in a society undergoing transition. The aim is to illuminate the social and cultural factors in beliefs about (a) the nature of disease, (b) agents which cause disease, (c) media for disease transmission, and (d) qualifications and role of therapists and curers. To a lesser degree, the paper deals with modifications in the indigenous theory of disease and therapy which are due to Western influence.

## THE VILLAGE

The materials presented were gathered in a small agricultural-fishing village in eastern Leyte, Philippine Islands. The population, numbering 1,200, lives in houses which for the most part are made of bamboo and raised on stilts. Tha natives of Guinhangdan derive their subsistence from fishing in the ocean and, to a lesser degree, in the river which flanks the village on the west and north. Rice and coconuts are raised in fields west and south of the river, and a familiar part of the village picture is the pigs and chickens which wander freely around, in, and under the homes. The people are nominally Catholics, for the islands as a whole began to feel Catholic influence some 400 years ago. Individual commitment to the precepts and practices of Catholicism is tempered by allegiance to a pantheon of spirit-gods who are older in the area than are the supernaturals of the Catholic hierarchy.

For ten years the Philippines have been a free and democratic nation. Prior to that time they were successively under American rule, Japanese rule, American rule, and earliest of all in historic times, several centuries of Spanish rule and influence. The Spaniards had different emphases in their plans for these people than did succeeding rulers, and it is only in the last 50 years that any concerted efforts have been made to introduce formal elementary education. These have been accompanied by an attempt to introduce sanitary practices and to teach modern concepts of disease. Despite 50 years of the presence of elementary educational institutions and continued but intermittent efforts to teach hygiene and sanitation, most people in Guinhangdan have no knowledge of—or at least little understanding of—the germ theory of disease and the nature of contamination. They are not without their own theory of disease, however, and only through a knowledge of the nature of this theory and its similarities and dissimilarities to modern theory can educators hope to be effective in inaugurating change through the teaching of scientific concepts and practices.

The recognition of specific sickness as it is known and understood by Western medical personnel or by the Western lay population is a rare phenomenon among the village folk. There are a few educated women and men who have been exposed to, and who have understood, the tenets of hygiene and health education. Such women will talk about whooping cough, measles, chicken pox, and colds. Other illnesses are described vaguely with a disinterest in the description per se. Seemingly, everyone who is ill has fever and aches and pains; a little less frequently the symptoms are itchiness, swelling, and little red spots. A mother will report that a child has slightly loose, or very loose, bowels but she does not look for, or understand the need to look for, related symptoms. To her, the nature of the excreta and the child's frequent bowel movements are the illness, and she speculates no further than about what the child might have been eating. Irritability may be a sign of illness, but again it may not. Significantly, it is recognized that some irritability in a baby may be a stage of presickness, and a potion is administered while waiting for the sickness to develop.

No matter what the ailment, it will be considered slight when it is first noticed. A mother rarely seeks aid or gives treatment on the initial appearance of symptoms. The gravity of the sickness will impress itself only as the patient suffers more and more. If one mentions pain or great itching, that is one stage of malaise. If the irritation continues over a considerable time, the length of time is in itself unimportant, but if the duration is coupled with increasing intensity, the sickness assumes greater gravity in the minds of patient and family. If the patient takes to his bed instead of continuing with his daily routine, this is another distinct stage of severity. The surest indicator of severity of suffering (and automatically more serious illness) comes when the patient cries. All are moved to pity and attempt to do what they can within the limited range of their belief and knowledge to alleviate his discomfort.

Related to the belief that illness is not serious in its initial manifestations is the practice of not seeking aid in the early stages of the illness. When a child first has fever or a rash of some kind, the mother hopes passively that it will disappear. A mother reported that her child died in one day of illness; he started to vomit in the morning and was dead by afternoon. This swift collapse allowed no more than the administration of an aspirin and consultation with neighbors and friends. If the malady persists for some time, there will be recourse to the home remedies in one's own repertory and that of friends. Everybody has some knowledge of leaves prepared in such and such a manner which cured old X when he had exactly the same trouble, and such possibilities must be exhausted before the curer is called. Many and strange are the treatments that are tried in this experimental frame of mind. Most are harmless and some undoubtedly help the sufferer mentally or physically, but occasionally the attempted cure leads to dangerous complications. One schoolteacher applied gun powder and coconut oil to an open blister on her heel.

Home remedies failing, the family of the patient discusses the nature of the illness and decides to whom they should turn for help. They diagnose the case as probably being within the province of one or another of the curer-specialists, who is then requested to visit the home of the sufferer—or the patient, if ambulatory, may go to the house of the curer. If the ministrations of the first curer fail, a different type of specialist will be called.

## THERAPISTS

In the minds of the people, an important distinction as to the nature of illness has to do with the categorization of various afflictions, and this distinction is best understood in terms of the practitioner who treats the cases. Specialists among the curers and healers of the village include the midwife or *partira* who gives prenatal care when it is requested, assists at delivery, and routinely gives postnatal care. In most instances she will be called if the neonate becomes ill, and she will be consulted until the baby has passed the infant stage at about one-and-a-half years of age. She is thus the obstetrician and pediatrician of the village. In addition, she treats painful menstrual cases. The masseuse or masseur, the *hilot*, attends to sprains, dislocations, and broken bones. His special province is the skeleton and such ills as the bones are heir to. If a person falls, twists an ankle, or has aches and pains near protuberant bones, he will call the hilot. The *parasona*, who may also be male or female, is consulted if one has been bitten by a centipede or a snake, or has been hurt by the spiny fins of a fish. There are two remaining classes of practitioners, the *haplasan* and *tambalan*; both treat skin diseases, infections, debilitating and fatal diseases, and the multitudinous vague aches and pains that are the lot of mankind. However, the haplasan treats only by anointing while the tambalan has a series of varied treatments. The tambalan is also reputed to be much more powerful, for his knowledge of agents of disease and treatment is more extensive.

There are, then, five types of practitioners: the midwife, the masseur, the parasona, the haplasan, and the tambalan. The qualifications for any one of these callings are interesting. To become a midwife, one must be a female and must demonstrate interest and skill in midwifery. Both midwives who live in Guinhangdan deny having received any instruction in their art but they both had borne a child or two before they began assisting at births. One may become a midwife, then, if one is of the proper sex, has given birth to a child, and has the inclination. The same is not true with the masseur and masseuse, for their qualification for their profession comes at birth or not at all: they must have been born feet first. There are five hilots in the village studied, and all were so born; the single parasona was also born feet first. In addition, she learned the rudiments of her practice from her mother and husband. The requisite experience for haplasan or tambalan comes in adulthood and either males or females may receive the call. In order to become a haplasan or tambalan a person must have a dream experience, in which a supernatural comes to him and instructs him in the use of a magical potion. He is told what leaves or roots to use and how to prepare and apply them. There are fewer haplasans and tambalans than midwives or masseurs; in Guinhangdan there is but one of each. Practitioners from other villages may be called upon and two tambalans who were born in Guinhangdan but who no longer live there are sometimes consulted at their homes some distance up the river.

## CLASSES OF MALAISE AND ILLNESS

The natural causes of illness include indigestible foods, sudden changes in temperature, strong winds and vagrant breezes, and the vapor that arises from the ground when the sun comes out after a prolonged rain. Blood or air may be "trapped" in the body. Birth and falls resulting in injury are in the category of the natural; the supernatural enters into causation rarely, as, for example, when a newly delivered mother who is weak and defenseless is visited by an evil spirit. Correspondingly, the midwife and the masseur are assumed to have little understanding or knowledge of supernatural causation and no need of it. The parasona's patients come to her as a result of injury from natural causes and she, too, has little dependence on, or control over, the supernatural. She may invoke a Catholic deity if her patient fails to respond to her ministrations or she may refer him to one of the curers who are versed in the lore of the spirits. In contrast, most cases about which the haplasan or tambalan are consulted are considered to be in the province of the supernaturals.

Among the natural incapacitations which women are subject to are *guindudugoan*, which is bleeding during pregnancy of hemorrhage in delivery, and *guinaawakan* or miscarriage. *Bangnan* and *sigpit* are difficulties in delivery caused by obstructions in the birth canal. Among the natural digestive disorders most common to babies and children are *nagooro-oro* or frequent bowel movement and watery feces due to the eating of indigestible foods. *Inpatso* is caused by the curdling or souring of the mother's milk. *Guintutubol*, or constipation, is also thought of as a digestive upset. *Watihon*, or hookworm, is recognized by worms in the stool and is believed by most mothers to be caused by eating too much fish. Sprains, fractures, and dislocations of bones are thought of as naturally caused; so, too, is hernia. Snake or centipede bites, *kinagat*, and puncture from a fish spine, *nahabisol*, are caused by natural forces.

Among the supernaturally caused incapacitations are a group of illnesses called *pasma*. There is a pasma of hunger, of sleeplessness, of drinking too much, and of crossing a stream of warm water. Another group of illnesses are *dahura* which are recognized by itchiness, spots, aches, and pains. Dahura are caused by annoyed spirits. Sorcerers cause various forms of illness including yaws, leprosy, and some mental disturbances. Milder unnatural powers are possessed by a sorcerer who can give stomach ache, *nahaawog*, to those who pilfer his protected fruit trees.

Sorcerers and witches operate across family lines. Within the family three kinds of illness may result from human-to-human relationships. The tie between parent and child is considered so firm that what happens to the former will influence the latter; what the father does when he is away from home may affect his offspring. If he is startled, frightened, or unfaithful, his child will have a tendency to be easily frightened, will jerk his head backwards, and, in serious cases, will have convulsions. This is known as *calas*. One informant reported that the symptoms following marital infidelity begin in a child, the moment the father begins illicit intercourse. Theoretically, such a tie also exists between the mother and the child of either sex, but all the cases of illness traceable to this parent-child closeness were through the father.

The strength of the familial tie is shown by the illness a person may suffer while away from home for an extended period. This is known as *hinamindang*. The symptoms are excessive perspiration, fever, and weakness; it is caused by a spouse or a sibling who wraps and heats the clothes of the absentee. This is considered to be playing a trick; the coercive intent of the act is rationalized or overlooked.

Harshness on the part of a parent who slaps or beats a child more frequently than is considered normal may result in *buntog*; the symptoms are described as extreme nervousness, falling down, and foaming at the mouth. It is interesting to note how the values of stable family ties both between spouses and between parents and children are emphasized in the expected punishment for infidelity, leaving home, or being unduly stern with children.

## AGENTS OF DISEASE

Spirit-gods, witches, and sorcerers are deemed responsible for most illnesses which are not natural. In the mythology as it is now expounded, the *encantos*, spirit-gods, were the fallen angels who were doomed to follow Lucifer when he was expelled from Heaven. The encantos fell into the trees, the river, and onto the earth. Earth beings are the *tunanon*, river and ocean spirits are the *tubignon*, and tree spirits are the *cahoynon*. In Guinhangdan only the cahoynon are present, although if one goes further afield one may meet the other types.

Cahoynon rarely live in the village or town but there are still a few old trees which are reputed to house a population of them. Guinhangdan had such a tree on the school grounds. The school principal ordered it cut down and replaced by a shade or fruit tree. Soon afterwards, she acquired a rash (probably hives) which she became convinced was due to her untimely order. Cahoynon characteristically inhabit the remote farms, uncultivated lands, and relatively untraveled strips of the river. They live in families in houses and cultivate fields. In appearance they are like mortals except that they are very beautiful, rich, and well dressed. There are cahoynon who resemble Filipinos and some who resemble Europeans but the ones most frequently discussed are the latter—the fair-haired, white-skinned beings. To mortal eyes, cahoynon homes look like trees and their fields look like weeds and grass.

While cahoynon are invisible to mortals they have the power to become visible. They are reported to mix with people in the market place, in buses, and in the theater, but they do not become known unless it is their intention to do so. Most people from Guinhangdan have never seen, nor imagined they have seen, an encanto, but this has no bearing on the belief in their existence. Millions of people have never seen germs, but their belief in their existence is unquestioned.

Most cahoynon leave human beings alone. On occasion cahoynon may help humans, but generally any contact between the two which offends or injures the cahoynon results in illness for the human. When one is in the habitat of cahoynon, one should move lightly and slowly and be ever aware that a harsh word or an abrupt act may irritate the unseen ones. What appears to be merely a tree may be the home of the cahoynon and the shady area beneath may be their kitchens; weeds or grass in the path or the field may be their crops. To disturb these supernaturals in their habitat is to invite their anger. When one has offended a cahoynon the consequences may or may not be immediate and recognizable to the layman. If a man is cutting down a tree and the bolo slips and nicks him, or some of the sap of the tree spurts on him and causes itchiness or pain, he knows he is in the vicinity of the cahoynon. On the other hand one may have offended the invisible people but remain unaware of the offense for hours or days until a tambalan or haplasan makes the diagnosis. An ill person will always suspect that dysphoria is the result of some failure to observe the precautions necessary to maintain good health, and accordingly search his memory for such lapse. The probability is very high that he has been in the fields or working in the nipa palm along the river. He therefore goes to the specialist, if his illness is serious enough for therapy and aid in propitiation of the offended spirits.

Tubignon live primarily in the deep seas, though they may also inhabit the rivers and ponds. Their upper body is human and the nether portion is fish. Tubignon causes illness and death if one angers them by failing to seek their permission to navigate or fish. Failure to observe the proprietary control may be minimally punished with a poor catch.

The tunanon live in the ground; their lower torso is imprisoned by the earth while the upper portion is free. From this uncomfortable position they are briefly delivered about dusk to seek their food. The tunanon are the most irritable of all the encantos because they are imprisoned so much of the time while the humans around them enjoy freedom. There is danger of hitting or kicking them almost any time of the day except dusk. Tunanon are both mischievous and dangerous. They may play tricks such as hiding an article of clothing, blocking off a path, or they may cause illness. They cannot cause as many sicknesses as the cahoynon and tubignon and cannot cure all sicknesses they cause.

A special class of the tunanon is the *agta*, who are small black people with long black hair all over their bodies and on their faces. Agtas are reported to be rare in Guinhangdan but many are believed to be in Tanauan and on the west coast of Leyte. The agta differ from all other encantos in that they are completely malevolent and cause illnesses which cannot be cured. Unlike other encantos, they never become enamored of a human being and never perform benevolent acts such as providing a good catch, a better harvest, or imparting to a curer the knowledge of how to treat an illness. Their lesser acts are mischievous tricks (the same as with the tunanon) such as misplacing the hat a man has hung on a bush while working, or causing a path to disappear.

The cahoynon and the tunanon transmit illness by throwing sand, bits of dirt, insects, or small stones at their victims. If the victim suffers a slight illness, he is said to be dahura; if the illness is grave, he is considered to be *guindarahogan*, or seriously punished. The extent of injury depends not upon the size of the missile but rather upon the intent of the mischievous or avenging encanto. The tubignon wreak their misfortune on intractable humans by controlling the winds, waves, and schools of fish. The agta hits his victim with an arrow released from a bow.

While the encantos are supernaturals who can assume human form, the *asuangs*, or witches, are another class of beings who were originally human and who acquire and develop supernatural powers. In his human shape the asuang lives among his neighbors, undifferentiated and undistinguishable in appearance and behavior from others. An asuang may be either male or female. If a person is suspected of being an asuang, his neighbors will continue to treat him with normal courtesy and cordiality; they will accept, but not eat, any food prepared or offered by him. At present there is one female asuang resident in the village; in recent years there were two men so termed. When desiring a nonhuman guise, the asuang often transforms himself into a cat, dog, pig, or bird, such transformation usually takes place about dusk and often near the residence of a sick person. Asuangs do not cause sickness but prey on those who are already sick or who are weak and vulnerable for other reasons, e.g., mothers who have just delivered babies or the babies themselves. They may grasp the mother's vagina and crumple it, and she will die; or they may pull the umbilical cord of the infant and he will die. They may scratch or bite and they are considered to find the patient's bowel contents particularly delectable, although they are not interested in voided excreta.

Asuangs may be slightly or highly developed, that is, they may be newly infused with their evil powers and consequently not very adept in their use, or they may have been practicing asuangs for a long time and therefore be more dangerous and more difficult to exorcise. Asuangs can be cured of their evil proclivities and once again assume their place among innocuous human beings.

No sorcerers live in Guinhangdan. A sorcerer is a human who cannot change his shape, who may possess unusual powers of locomotion, and who has a limited and specialized power to cause illness. A sorcerer, a *daotan*, uses a hair from the whorl point on the top or back of the head or some clothing of the intended victim as the media for causing illness. A *palakodan* is a sorcerer who uses oils and roots rather than hair or clothing to cause sickness and death. The power of sorcerers may be used or bought to inflict illness on unwilling or unfaithful lovers, and on enemies. . . .

## PREVENTION AND CURE

One way to stay healthy and to insure the well-being of one's family is to obey the cultural mores, both as they relate to interaction with the supernatural and with other humans. The most effective defense against any supernatural is to stay out of his province. If a person knows the habitat of a family of tree spirits, the surest (but not an infallible) technique for remaining healthy is not to enter the enchanted area. But total avoidance of the habitations of supernaturals is both impractical and unlikely. In the first place, encantos may live in the middle of residential sections, cultivated fields, or coconut groves, which people cannot indefinitely avoid. As the supernaturals are invisible, an individual may inadvertently step on them or hit them. If one is in the supposed abode of tree spirits, the approved precaution is to speak and walk quietly and slowly and not to laugh. If one must disturb the tranquillity of the area by such an act as chopping down a tree, the permission of the cahoynon should first be sought. Further, some supernaturals such as the cahoynon and the water spirits may aid and reward humans, and this possible blessing may draw a person to the area. Of the three classes of spirits, the water spirits receive the most offerings. Their permission must be sought by verbal request and an accompanying food offering before one may build a fish corral. They, like the cahoynon, may benefit or harm humans according to their whim, but with the earth spirits, little is to be gained; they are almost unrelievedly malevolent. In defense against them a man may carry bits of sacred articles, *relicios*, which are obtained from the priest.

How distressing must be the teaching about the Christian supernaturals. As a class they have no fixed abode, and the formal teachings of the church emphasize the omnipresence and omnipotence of God. Fortunately, the Christian pantheon are not looked upon as a disease agent. No ailment was ever reported to be a visitation from God as a punishment for sin or as a trial of one's faith, ideas prominent in some Christian circles.

Avoidance of powerful and potentially malevolent humans is also desirable but impossible. Thus the asuang lives among her fellow villagers and is treated as naturally as possible, in order not to arouse her anger. Defense against the asuang has two aspects. One cannot with impunity eat any food offered by an asuang since the evil spirit and power enters in this way. Prepared foods which have been allowed to grow cold and meat (whether cold or hot) are especially dangerous. Sick or otherwise vulnerable persons must be protected from the preying asuang; thus men armed with sharpened bamboo poles will stand guard over a dying person or the newly delivered mother and babe. The dead are not guarded since they are no longer considered likely victims.

The efficacy of some sorcery is dependent on physical proximity and these sorcerers can be avoided or contact with them minimized. Others may operate from a distance and no precautions avail. In the unavoidable presence of a sorcerer, quiet conciliatory behavior is expedient. "The best way is not to argue with someone who has *palakod*. Even if his ways are all lies, just listen, don't argue. Just praise him. Abide with him." If one becomes bewitched, the sorcerer must be appeased through an intermediary who seeks assurance that the symptoms will be dispelled.

Diagnosis, treatment, and patient education differ somewhat from specialist to specialist, but certain common notions are held by all. It is believed that treatment should be repeated three times, and preferably at the same time of day as during the first meeting. The most common forms of treatment are rubbing and massaging, ritual anointment with coconut oil accompanied by prayer, dry and wet poultices, and herbal additions to the drinking or bath water. No curer practices sucking or manual extraction. Nothing is injected into the body and pills are not prescribed. Dried roots, dried leaves, and scrapings of branches are popular medicinal ingredients, and coconut oil is ubiquitous. Specific leaves are required for specific ailments. For instance, a midwife treats constipation in children under five by placing tomato leaves on their stomachs; older children require "stronger" leaves. While the kind of leaf required is specific, the curer need not do the collecting. The parasona plants and tends a small patch of herbs which she uses in her therapy, a unique instance of a planned and conserved pharmacopoeia.

Diagnosis of malaise is arrived at by looking at the patient and by asking questions. A mother is guided by a fever or a dry tongue. The masseuse considers temperature and swelling. The parahaplas has an exotic diagnostic technique. She ritually anoints the patient with coconut oil and has him lie down on large leaves, covers him with the same kind of leaves and lets him perspire for about an hour. When he is uncovered, the leaves are examined for the missiles which the annoyed encantos have presumably shot into him or at him. Bits of hair, sand, or part of insects are "proof" of the disease causation. The tambalon examines his patient and then awaits an inspirational diagnosis; the knowledge "just comes to him."

Incantation to spirits and prayer to Christian deities are used by all practitioners, and the tambalon also observes a perpetual novena to an encanto ancestor; failure to observe daily devotions would cause him to become ill. Occasionally, a lay person with a persistent malady will vow to a saint to make an offering or to perform a particular action if he is cured.

When success follows a treatment, curers are modest and generally attribute the recovery to the help and intervention of supernaturals, both God and the encantos. Failures are rationalized as being due to faulty diagnosis, lack of cooperation on the part of the patient, the advanced state of the sickness when the curer was called, or the omnipotence of God or the power of the encanto. Curers are paid modest fees ranging from 20¢ to 50¢. A few curers may be given as much as $2.50. Most healers disclaim any desire for a fee and explain that people force the minuscule sums upon them; in some instances the patient's family claims that the cure will not work if the healer does not accept payment.

Little mention has been made of patent medicines, antibiotics, or any other paraphernalia of present-day therapy. The products of the pharmacist's shop and the services of an M.D. are not totally lacking in Guinhangdan, but they are accepted with but slight modifications of the old theories of disease. Some individuals who are both adherents to the old ways and timid advocates of the new, show ingenuity in their resolution of conflicts between the two theories and the divergent practices. Some fail to effect a compromise and vacillate between the M.D. and the local curer. Some feel that the sphere of influence and competence of a local curer can be distinguished from the sphere of influence of a medical doctor, and this is a belief in which contemporary M.D.'s who were born and raised in a village are apt to concur....

## DISCUSSION

A system of beliefs about the nature of disease causation, the natural and supernatural agents of transmission, and the practices of defense and cure have been considered. Beliefs about sickness, and trust and confidence in treatment and therapists are seen to be systematically patterned; the belief systems are coherent and logical in the light of the mythology.

In recent years, when consideration of an indigenous theory of disease has gone beyond mere description, it has often been focused on the admixture of the scientific and magical, or rational and nonrational, aspects of theory and practice. It is hypothesized that magic and "real knowledge" are often intertwined, may be indistinguishable, and that the individual oscillates between the two and resorts to both quite indiscriminately (Hsu 1952:8). Evidence for this hypothesis has been convincingly presented by Hsu and is further strengthened by the material presented here. Furthermore, Hsu says that such practice is not confined to primitives or to peoples of underdeveloped areas, but is part of the way of life of societies everywhere, although the proportions of magic and science in a given society vary.

Another hypothesis that has been advanced is that villagers can and do differentiate, perhaps unconsciously, between minor and incapacitating diseases and, on the basis of this distinction, can and do seek Western therapy for cases of greater incapacitation (Gould 1957:508). Of 30 cases in a village in north India (whose size and population are not mentioned), Gould finds that the greater number of incapacitating diseases were treated by the M.D. and the greater number of minor ailments by native curers. Erasmus (1952:417) suggests that the folk look up to the M.D. for his greater ability to cure serious illnesses. No evidence in support of these hypotheses has been presented here. A point in need of amplification is the nature of individual knowledge of disease. Diseases do not exist as categories which can be identified, named, and brought for treatment according to the classification. This may seem obvious, but it must be kept in mind that, especially to the layman, symptoms are confusing, are interpreted naively, and are subject to frequent reinterpretation. A particular malaise is not quickly and accurately identified by either a villager or anthropologist. For that matter, professional curers in any society have recurrent difficulties in diagnosis. The fact that reasonably frequent accurate identification of a disease requires extensive training and experience raises some problems about techniques of investigation on the part of the social scientist. For instance, one must question the value of administering questionnaires to schoolchildren, naming 22 diseases and asking them to check the ones which

they would treat at home, the ones for which they would consult a folk curer, and the ones for which they would go to a doctor (Erasmus 1952:416; Gould 1957:514f). In Guinhangdan, at least, the individual does not grapple with a disease, but with a discomfort or malaise which he may describe as being itchy, disturbing, or painful. It is not measles or bronchitis or tuberculosis but an unhappiness and a dis-ease which the patient brings to specialists and which the curer or M.D. defines for the patient. Again, the validity of answers of folk curers who were asked who should treat diphtheria, tuberculosis, venereal disease, and appendicitis (Erasmus 1952:416) is debatable when these words are just labels for which clear and precise referents seldom exist in our own society. The carriers of another culture are at still greater disadvantage. What is missing is a series of stable referent points and a frame of reference commonly understood.

Erasmus has also addressed himself to the question of the degree to which preliterate people think differently. To what extent are their knowledge and beliefs less empirical in nature than our own? He finds that:

> ...folk beliefs in themselves are offering no resistance to modern medical practices in so far as those practices may be judged by the folk on an empirical basis. Preventative medicine, however, is being resisted because its comprehension is largely at a theoretical level that does not readily lend itself to empirical observation (Erasmus 1952:418f).

Simmons (1955:71) concurs. I would not quarrel with this conclusion. However, it should be added, in the interest of applying the generalization to public health practices, that very few of the procedures of a therapist can be judged on a reliable and valid basis either by the folk or by their city cousins. For instance, the relationship between a treatment and its effect is usually far from obvious, is often obscure, and at best is amazingly complex. This refers both to the Filipino who is anointed with oil and whose red spots disappear, and to the American who faithfully follows the regimen prescribed by a competent M.D., after which his symptoms disappear. What is empirical knowledge here? The cause-treatment and the effect-cure noted by the patient? Or an observable, describable, verifiable relationship defined not by the patient but by the trained specialist? Both Filipinos and Americans have trained specialists who observe and describe the relationship. The tambalan, after a lifetime of study and thought, "knows" where families of encantos live. He has charted the provenance of daotan in western Leyte and Samar. He is convinced and he is convincing about his own empirical observations, as is the doctor. However, Erasmus notes (1952:423), as does Hsu (1952:122), that while both the folk and the Western urbanites individually may be unable to differentiate between statistically probable relationships and unrelated but co-existing phenomena, the urbanite is fortunate in that the society in which he lives has made it more probable that he will be dealing with the former.

# 15 Curing, Sorcery, and Magic in a Javanese Town

## Clifford Geertz

Published a decade and a half ago, Clifford Geertz's ethnographic study of *The Religion of Java* still has no peer as an anthropological descriptive analysis of an endlessly intricate religious system. Many otherwise good ethnographies or anthropological studies of religion manage nevertheless to slight the medical system. Not so Geertz, who applies to the medical system the same depth of perceptive reporting as he does to the market system and other important phases of life in Modjokuto, the town in east Central Java which is the site of his study. Though nominally Moslem, the religion in Javanese village culture "commonly consists of a balanced integration of animistic, Hinduistic, and Islamic elements, a basic Javanese syncretism which is the island's true folk tradition, the basic substratum of its civilization...." But Geertz tells us that in this semirural, semiurban tributary of the Javanese mainstream, the *abangan* religious tradition is still only part of a very complex whole. This Great Tradition consists of at least three variants: "*Abangan*, representing a stress on the animistic aspects of the overall Javanese syncretism and broadly related to the peasant element in the population; *santri*, representing a stress on the Islamic aspects of the syncretism and generally related to the trading element (and to certain elements of the peasantry as well); and *prijaji*, stressing the Hinduistic aspects and related to the bureaucratic element...." The medical system within the *abangan* variant is the one described in this section, though, as Geertz says, "belief and disbelief in their powers, as well as actual

Reprinted with abridgments from Clifford Geertz, 1960, *The Religion of Java*, New York: The Free Press, Chap. 8, "Curing, Sorcery, and Magic," pp. 86–111, with permission of the author and Macmillan Publishing Co. Inc. Copyright 1960 by The Free Press of Glencoe, a Corporation.

practitioners of the art, are spread throughout Javanese society, among *prijajis* and *santris* as well as *abangan*."

Central to the operation of the medical system, including its theories of disease causation, diagnosis, and treatment, is the role of the *dukun*, a multifaceted one that may and often does combine in one person the roles of sorcerer (or agent of illness), diagnostician, curer, and ritual specialist. Geertz's analysis focuses mainly on the *dukun bijasa* or "common" *dukun*, a general practitioner capable of several specialities at once, and to a lesser extent, on the *dukun tiban* or possessed *dukun*. The latter is female, the former male, and they differ as well in most other respects.

I hope that the flavor of Geertz's study has not been dissipated through the omission of a wealth of ethnographic examples here, but, in any case, the full context will require a reading of the whole superb monograph. What will come through immediately is that in this rich, complex, ancient culture the number of religious and medical alternatives open to the individual are many and varied. Indeed one of the main thrusts of Geertz's whole study of the religion of Java is that it is varied, complex, and full of conflict and compromise, and yet with a depth of gratification that provides a full-bodied cultural system of belief and spirituality for the Javanese people.

If spirit beliefs and *slametans* are two of the most general subcategories of *abangan* religion, the complex of curing, sorcery, and magic centering around the role of the *dukun* makes up a third. Strictly speaking, restricting *dukuns* to the *abangan* context is not correct, for belief and disbelief in their powers, as well as actual practitioners of the art, are spread throughout Javanese society, among *prijajis* and *santris* as well as *abangan*. But both their greater frequency and their greater everyday importance, and probably a generally greater belief in them, among the *abangans* can justify their being considered here as a predominantly *abangan* phenomenon, with *santri* and *prijaji dukuns* being taken as secondary variations.

## THE *DUKUN*: CURER, SORCERER, AND CEREMONIAL SPECIALIST

There are all kinds of *dukuns*: *dukun baji*, midwives; *dukun pidjet*, masseurs; *dukun préwangan*, mediums; *dukun tjalak*, circumcisors; *dukun wiwit*, harvest ritual specialists; *dukun temantèn*, wedding specialists; *dukun pétungan*, experts in numerical divination; *dukun sihir*, sorcerers; *dukun susuk*, specialists who cure by inserting golden needles under the skin; *dukun djapa*, curers who rely on spells; *dukun djampi*, curers who employ herbs and other native medicines; *ḍukun siwer*, specialists in preventing natural misfortune (keeping the rain away when one is having a big feast, preventing plates from being broken at the feast, and so on); *ḍukun tiban*, curers whose powers are temporary and the result of their having been entered by a spirit.

Usually one man is several kinds of *ḍukun*; he may be everything but a midwife, a status reserved to women. Some types—*ḍukun temantèn*, for example—are not true specialties, usually being taken on rather casually for the particular occasion by any older person who commands the necessary knowledge of tradition. A man who is able in several of these specialties at once is called a *ḍukun bijasa*—"common *ḍukun*"—or just *ḍukun* without a qualifier, and it is he who is the most important. He is the general magical specialist in the traditional society, useful for all that ails one physically or psychologically, predictor of future events, finder of lost objects, insurer of good fortune, and usually not unwilling to practice a little sorcery if that is what one desires.

This type of practitioner is in the typical case the son of a similar practitioner. To be a *ḍukun* is thought to be dangerous to the individual, for the extraordinary power with which he traffics can destroy him if he is not spiritually strong. Since madness is a typical outcome for people who attempt too much along these lines, it is a help to be a descendant of a man with proven ability to support such power, for then is also likely to have the necessary spiritual resources. But this is not necessarily so. One *ḍukun* I interviewed said that his father had originally tried to teach his specialty to each of the informant's two older brothers, but both of them fell ill, showing that they were not strong enough for it; and so he, the third brother, got his chance to become a *ḍukun*.

Further, although the capacity to be a *ḍukun* is at least in part inherited, the actual ability is not; it is a learned skill. Just what is learned varies somewhat from *ḍukun* to *ḍukun*. *Prijaji ḍukuns* tend to emphasize ascetic discipline—extended fasts and long periods of wakeful meditation—and to claim that their power is entirely spiritual. *Santris* usually employ chanted passages from the Koran interpreted mystically, or magic bits of carefully drawn Arabic script chewed up and swallowed, or the like; and some *santris* claim that whatever curing "real Moslems" do is based on scientific medical knowledge included in the Koran hundreds of years before it was "discovered" in the West. *Abangan ḍukuns*, finally, tend more to emphasize specific techniques, amulets, spells, herbs, and the like. Admittedly, however, these lines blur; most *ḍukuns* employ something of all these techniques, and some sort of spiritual preparation is necessary in any case. ...

Whatever it is that the practitioner learns, he learns from another *ḍukun*, who is thus his *guru* (teacher); and whatever he learns he and others call his *ilmu* (science). *Ilmu* is generally considered to be a kind of abstract knowledge or supernormal skill, but by the more concrete-minded and "old-fashioned" it is sometimes viewed as a kind of substantive magical power, in which case its transmission may be more direct than through teaching. ...

What a man can do with his *ilmu* more or less depends upon what kind it is. Some *ilmu* is quite specific. There is *ilmu* for causing people in a house one is robbing to sleep soundly, for finding lost objects (some *ilmu* enables one to tell where the object is exactly, other *ilmu* just tells one in which direction it lies), for getting rich, for seeing what is going on in other places, and for becoming invulnerable. This latter *ilmu* was very popular during the revolution. At the time of the battle against the British in Surabaja about a hundred young men setting off to fight were first each given a small glass of tea over which one of Modjokuto's leading *ḍukuns* had chanted a spell which was supposed to render them invulnerable. There is also *ilmu* for telling where to drill a well so the water will not be foul, where to build a house so the occupants will not sicken, for attracting the affections of someone else's spouse. There is even *ilmu* for predicting world events. ...

Other *ilmu* is quite general and consequently rarer, enabling one to do almost anything—fly, disappear, turn into a tiger—but somehow the really powerful practitioners of this sort seem always to have existed in the past, there being a rather general belief that so far as *ilmu* is concerned people are not so skilled as they once were. ...

Today the leading *ḍukuns* in Modjokuto are all at least middle aged, but none is really old. Of the really well-known ones, three are *abangans*; one is a *santri*, and one, the subdistrict officer, a *prijaji*. All but the subdistrict officer are sons of *ḍukuns*, and all but him are also small landholders (from one-half to about two acres) who either rent their land to sharecroppers in order to be free to cure or (in one case) work it themselves. Thus no one in Modjokuto makes a living entirely from being a *ḍukun*; it is at best a part-time specialization. None of the leading *ḍukuns* is extremely poor, and none, again excepting the subdistrict officer, is particularly well off. All are members of that peculiar economic category the Javanese call *tjukupan*—they "have enough."

As to personality, nothing seems to set the leading *dukuns* off from their neighbors. They show no unusual character traits and no obvious neurotic behaviors, nor are they considered peculiar by others. With one possible exception there is little sign that these *dukuns* chose their vocations because of frustrated prestige or power drives, for they are not the type of men to whom the normal channels to power and prestige are closed; and, in fact, the *dukun* role, although it carries some prestige, also tends to draw suspicion, for some people always suspect the *dukun* of either fakery or sorcery. All in all, it is hard to escape the impression that within the *abangan* context the *dukun* role is a fairly straightforward one which people adopt for fairly understandable reasons: it brings a certain monetary reward, although seemingly not an extremely great one; it carries some prestige, although this is ambivalent at best; and they believe in their own skills and enjoy practicing them successfully.

The impression of "normality" in the *dukun's* role is strengthened by the consideration that, in addition to the five fairly well-known *dukuns*, there are literally dozens much less well-known—mostly *abangans*—whose powers are considered much less but who nevertheless draw part of their income from curing, seeking lost objects, practicing sorcery, and the like. In each neighborhood there always seems to be some man, usually a little older and somewhat more intelligent than the rest, to whom people look for help in the event of illness, theft, and so on, turning to the better known *dukuns* only rarely and in more serious cases. In fact, since almost every adult male knows at least a few spells and may be called upon to try his hand at curing a neighbor, finding a lost ring, or attracting a girl's affections, the role of the *dukun*, although a professional specialty, shades off at the edges into an irregular amateurish practice. If one stays in Modjokuto long enough one will hear just about every man in town referred to as a *dukun* at one time or another, although it will be clear that only certain people are really considered to be very good as *dukuns* and spend very much time at this practice....

Finally, there is the problem of the belief in *dukuns*. A partial skepticism about *dukuns* and their ability to do the things they claim to do is nearly universal. Nearly everyone with whom I spoke about the matter in Modjokuto believed in *dukuns* in general, in their possibility; but opinions about the powers of any one given *dukun* living in the area varied tremendously. I heard opinions expressed about each of the leading *dukuns* which ranged from absolute belief to outright accusation of fraud, but I never heard a denial that at least some *dukuns* were good, honest, and miraculously powerful.

Also, the concept of *tjotjog*—fittingness—which is so important in numerical divination plays a crucial role here too. A particular *dukun* may be very powerful and very clever, but he still may not *tjotjog* with one. There may be no question of his skill—for example, in a case of illness, he may have cured far more difficult cases but if the patient and he do not *tjotjog*, there will be nothing he can do and the patient will remain sick. So, when a man is ill, he tries one *dukun* after another until one cures him, never concerning himself about the reasons for their failure, and not necessarily holding it against them that they were unable to help him. It is just the same with Western-trained doctors. People would say earnestly to me: "Sometimes they *tjotjog* and cure you and sometimes they do not. The only difference is that you have to pay a doctor even if you die in his hands, while a good *dukun* expects payment only if he succeeds."

## CURING TECHNIQUES

Despite all the wonderful things really powerful *dukuns* can do, their real forte, and the basis of their prestige, is their curative powers. As does any medical practice, the *dukun's* treatment has two main aspects or stages: first, diagnosis and selection of the appropriate method of treatment. Diagnosis can be based on any one of three main methods or any combination of them: numerology (*pétungan*), intuitive insight through meditation, analysis of symptoms.

The general *pétungan* process has already been described. Suffice it to say in this context that the usual method is to take the day on which the individual was born in connection with the day on which he fell sick and by various calculations come up with a number which then corresponds to a form of treatment (usually an herb medicine) and in some cases indicates the cause of the disease as well. This is the most common method of diagnosis, especially among second-rank *dukuns*, for it is the quickest and easiest to apply.

The method of intuitive insight through meditation is more difficult, for it takes years of practice. Both cases of it which I encountered were among *prijaji ḍukuns*. The *ḍukun* meditates, going into a near trance and clearing his mind entirely of any "pictures" until he gets an abstract and formless feeling which tells him what the disease is and what the cure should be. Despite the lack of mental pictures, however, the diagnosis and cure may be quite concrete. . . .

Analysis of symptoms is particularly appropriate to more specific illnesses with well-defined disease pictures and rests on a categorization of such pictures at once elaborate and, seemingly, quite accurate, which is widely diffused among the populace generally. One boy, not a *ḍukun*, listed 47 separate diseases for me, each with a special name and symptom pattern, in the space of a half hour; and four other informants did almost as well. Among diseases commonly listed are: fever, chills, rheumatism, headache, red eyes with and without pus, boils, infected wounds, pimples on face and hands of adults and adolescents, white blotches on the skin, toothache, running nose, venereal diseases, paralysis, old age, rash (itchy or painful), yaws, smallpox, upset stomach, dysentery (with or without blood in the stools), short breath, gasping breath, tuberculosis (marked by continual coughing and extreme weakness), unclear eyesight, simple-mindedness, insanity (violent or nonviolent), measles, convulsions, malaria (called by that name; alternating fevers and chills), menstruation, frequent urination, tumors (external or at least perceivable to the touch), goiter, piles, swollen jaw, swelling in the groin, broken bones, and burns.

For each of these there are appropriate herbs (which are appropriate to which illnesses differs somewhat from informant to informant and *ḍukun* to *ḍukun*), mechanical methods of manipulation (massage, rubbing glass on the skin, bone setting), and specialized techniques such as the insertion of gold needles under the skin or the administration of mercury to be swallowed. The herb pharmacopoeia is very large and elaborate. . . . However, as all the informants said, which medicine you use depends on the one that "fits" you, and if one doesn't work, you try another. "Doctors have only two medicines—pills and injections; Javanese have thousands."

When one goes to a *ḍukun* one gets not only a herb but a spell with it. The *ḍukun* holds the herb in his hand and chants over it—in Arabic if he is a *santri ḍukun*, in Javanese if an *abangan*—and then either spits on it or blows on it when treating a child for worms. . . .

As it is the spell, or more exactly the spiritual power, of the *ḍukun* which counts, he does not necessarily have to use an herb if he is powerful enough; and, in fact, perhaps the most common medicine dispensed by *ḍukuns* is just plain tea over which they have chanted and into which they have spat. This tea is then drunk by the patient or perhaps rubbed on his navel, for many *ḍukuns* conceive of their function as calling back to the patient the two guardian spirits who were born with him in the amniotic fluid and his umbilical cord. It is these who cure, they argue, by chasing off spirits, not the *ḍukun*; and the latter's only function is to enable the patient to get in touch with his invisible twin guardians, which he cannot do unaided and which the *ḍukun* accomplishes for him through his concentration, his chanting, and his application of the tea to the navel. Instead of tea, liquid concoctions made of egg yolk, coconut juice, or mashed vegetables are often used. It is of perhaps some interest that the word for the sipping of such a liquid medicine is the same for suckling at the breast: *mik*.

Finally, one of the most common curing techniques is the massage or *pidjet*. The massage may be a simple secular massage with no mystical overtones of any sort, but it may also be accompanied by a spell and a spitting. . . .

Many other curing techniques are used. For example, Hadji Rasid was a specialist in what one might call metallic medicines. He gave people mercury to swallow for syphilis, iron filings pounded into a dust for general strengthening, and egg burned black and rubbed with silver for dysentery; but the technique for which he was most famous was *susuk*: injecting small slivers of gold under the skin. These slivers—the Hadji said he had about sixty or so of them in himself, and I knew dozens of people who had been injected by him, the slivers often still being visible under the skin—are injected where the pain is. . . .

In sum, there are three elements in the curing process: the medicine, the spell, and what Malinowski used to call "the condition of the performer"—in this context the spiritual strength of the *ḍukun*, his ability to so concentrate his mind that the spell reaches the ears of either God or the patient's twin guardian spirits. In Trobriand curing and sorcery Malinowski found the spell the essential part and so called them "magical practices"; among the Azande, Evans-Prichard emphasized the medicine as basic and held the other two aspects secondary. It is of interest that in Java the third, the condition of the performer, is the crucial element. . . .

Each of the three elements—medicine, spell, and condition of the performer—may be used separately. Medicines may be employed in the home with or without the advice of a *dukun*. Individuals may be cured simply through meditating on their problems and giving them advice to move the toilet, rebury their child's umbilical cord, or sleep with their head at the other end of the bed, without any spells or medicines at all. People may be massaged and chanted over with no medicines and no particular power of concentration necessary on the part of the masseur. But more commonly all three are employed as interdependent parts of a unitary curing method in which the spell and the medicine are energized by the spiritual abilities of the *dukun*. The spell the *dukun* chants reaches God or the guardian twins because the curer's intense mental concentration drives it into their consciousness, and then they act in response to the spell's plea back through the *dukun* as he spits into the medicine to make it really powerful. So each element lends to the others some of its own efficacy, but it is the state of superior spiritual strength in the *dukun*, a state conceived of in psychological terms, upon which the process as a whole depends.

**THEORY OF DISEASE AND CURING**

. . . There are several factors clustering around the psychological relationship between the *dukun* and his patient which seem to account for the ambivalent attitude most people show toward *dukuns*, for the fact that they regard them both as supportive figures and as threatening ones. The first is the problem of the uncertain outcome of treatment, the essential contingency of the curative process involving as it does the possibility that one's hopes for well-being will be frustrated. The second is the degree to which the *dukun* may become involved in his patient's personal life and the necessity from the *dukun*'s point of view for the careful handling of this problem. And the last is the inherent ambiguity of the *dukun*'s power, trafficking as he does both with God and with devils, able to sicken people as well as to cure them, and engaging both in devout supplications to a high God and in dubious contracts with less elevated spirits—*ndukuni* ("to *dukin* someone") means

both to cure a person of a disease and to sorcerize a person into having one. . . .

*Dukuns* are quite aware, at least peripherally, that much of their power is psychological; and all Javanese seem to hold that there are two main kinds of disease: one kind, with discoverable physical causes, which is amenable to treatment by Western doctors; and a second kind in which there are no medical findings but still the person is ill, the latter type being the kind *dukuns* are peculiarly competent to cure. Thus Pak Parman said that he was at his best on convulsions and temporary insanity. But if the person with convulsions or the insane man came from parents who were also liable to convulsions or were mentally ill he very rarely could help them and usually refused even to try. All *dukuns* emphasize the necessity for absolute trust and belief in the *dukun* and ascribe many of their failures to the fact that the patient had inner reservations about the curer's ability. The psychological causation of physical illness is a commonplace. . . .

The connection between emotional stability and physical health is usually put in more concrete form, especially by *abangans*. If one is upset, startled, or severely depressed, one becomes confused and disoriented, and one's soul is then empty and easily entered by the spirits. . . .

Among the specialists themselves, particular psychological stresses may be explicitly connected to particular physical symptoms. One *dukun*, something of a *prijaji* actually, said he treated two kinds of diseases: specific ones, such as toothaches, broken bones, upset stomach, and dysentery; and general all-over ones, of which latter type there were four main varieties: dirty blood (*darah kotor*), a shortage or lack of blood (*kurang darah*), an empty soul, perhaps entered by spirits but not necessarily (*dijwa kotong*), and air, "heat," or some other foreign substance inside the body, sometimes induced there magically through sorcery.

The first, dirty blood, he said could be caused in one of two ways. Eating bad food—spoiled or too peppery, or merely food which one is not used to eating—which "startles" your stomach and so makes you upset in the "heart" will dirty your blood. Secondly, continual anger, greed resulting in frequent frustration of your wishes, or secreted emotions like envy or jealousy will upset your "heart" and dirty your blood. The symptoms of dirty blood are general sluggishness, perhaps a rash or boils, alternation between fevers and chills and a "dark mind"—i.e., confused and suspicious thought, liability to sudden thrusts of passion.

Lack of blood the *ḍukun* traced to nagging fear, anxiety, or depression without an obvious cause. This thins out one's blood, leading to a shortage of it. Symptoms are paleness, weakness and general lassitude of mind—one just lies around and does nothing all day. Lack of blood may also follow as a second stage after dirty blood.

An empty soul, on the other hand, is due to a lack of spiritual discipline—a failure to exercise the soul by fasting, staying awake, and meditation—which leaves one very liable to sudden startle and prey to marauding spirits. The general symptoms are: if a spirit has entered, intellectual disorientation, delirium, strange behavior—in a word, "insanity"; and, if no spirit has yet entered, a general inability to persist in an activity, indirection, aimlessness, and so forth—a kind of loss of inward strength quite often ascribed by older Javanese to younger ones of the rising generation. . . .

Finally, the last variety of general disease is caused either by air entering the body, by heat entering it, or by foreign objects—nails, glass, human hair—introduced into the stomach by means of sorcery. Air in the body (*masuk angin*) produces symptoms much like our "cold"—coughing, sneezing, and general aches. Heat in the body (*panas mlebu*) leads to somewhat more localized pains. The symptoms of a disease due to sorcery are more violent: vomiting blood, convulsions, and the like. Again, those most liable to sorcery are those who are weak spiritually, but anyone may have air or heat enter merely by sitting in a draft or in wet clothes. . . .

## THE POSSESSED CURER: *DUKUN TIBAN*

If the common *ḍukun* is protected against the inevitable ambivalence with which the public views the curer of souls in any culture by the social "normality" of his role, by the regularity of the traditionalized procedures he employs, by the strictness of his discipline and the breadth of his learning, by his insistence that he cures only with the aid of God, by his pseudoparental status, and by his own usually sound enough civic reputation—these "bourgeois virtues" balancing off the morally equivocal forces with which he deals and the possibilities for doing evil with which he is presented—the *ḍukun tiban* has no such protection. He exchanges the social acceptability of the common *ḍukun*'s practice for the greater power possible in a more simple, direct, and

uncircumspect approach to the darker powers.

The roles of the *ḍukun bijasa* and the *ḍukun tiban* differ in almost every particular. Where the power of the former is based on learning plus, sometimes, an inherited factor, that of the latter comes suddenly, without any preparation on his part, by "divine stroke" (*tiban* means "fallen," "fallen as a wonder from the skies"). Where almost all of the former are men, perhaps a majority of the latter are women. Where the former seem usually to be psychologically stable and economically secure, the latter are said usually to be at least somewhat unbalanced and to come from among the economically depressed. Where the power of the former is continuing and, relatively speaking, moderate, the power of the latter disappears as suddenly as it comes (usually within a year, almost always within three) and is of much greater intensity while it lasts. Where the former are numerous everywhere, the latter are rare and occur only sporadically (most informants said one seemed to turn up somewhere around Modjokuto about once every five years or so). And where there is at most only a mild skepticism about either the effectiveness or the morality of the practices of the former, there is sharp disagreement concerning both the reality and the ethical character of the forces upon which the *tiban* calls . . . .

## SECONDARY CURING METHODS: MAGIC, DRUGS, AND WESTERN MEDICINE

In addition to the *ḍukuns*, *tiban* or common, to whom they have access, Modjokuto Javanese have two other possible sources of help in the face of disease: home curing and the more or less scientific Western-type medical care provided by the two hospitals in town.

The home curing methods are several. There are various kinds of amulets, such as small daggers worn inside the belt or pebbles strung around one's neck. There are packaged medicines of the "good for all that ails you" type, which traveling salesmen are forever hawking in the market or the town square. There are Chinese drugs, such as ground dragon's tongue, which can be purchased at the local Chinese drugstores (while one waits they are mixed up by the druggist (*singsèh*), to whom one has described his symptoms). There are the special time-honored techniques for specific diseases (e.g., polliwogs rubbed on the skin for measles). And there are the peculiar, all-purpose protectors the

Javanese call *djimats*. Commonly, *a djimat* is a written amulet, usually in Arabic and often made by the more old-fashioned Koranic scholars for their followers. They not only cure but also may be worn, like amulets generally, as invulnerability charms or as instruments of sorcery. The term *djimat* also tends to be used for a "snips and snails" kind of medicine in which otherwise repulsive substances, particularly waste products from one's own body, are ingested, worn, or hung over the doorway....

The patent medicines, with their supposed scientific legitimacy, their appeal to the Javanese conviction that the West, whatever its spiritual drawbacks, has discovered the technological key to all the material problems of life, and the extreme simplicity of applying them ("take two spoonfuls for tuberculosis, three for indigestion"), stand halfway between the indigenous curing system and the intrusive system of Western-type medical care institutionalized in the town's two hospitals, its three Western-trained doctors, and its group of locally trained male nurses (*mantri*). Patent medicines are advertised in the newspapers and sold in the stores, but the most vivid hawking of them is by the traveling medicine men who can be found three or four times a week at the center of a large crowd in the town square and almost every day in the market....

The three doctors and two hospitals in the small town of Modjokuto are certainly not typical for Java. It is rather the accidental result of three circumstances. One of the two main East Java hospitals of the *Handelsvereniging Amsterdam* (HVA), the huge prewar Dutch plantation concern, happens to be located in Modjokuto. Mainly because a building was available, the government hospital for the whole of the Bragang area comprising four districts and hundreds of thousands of people happens to be located in Modjokuto rather than in Bragang, the capital city of the area, as it normally would be. And the man who was the government doctor is now past retirement age and has been replaced in the hospital itself by an imported Austrian doctor, but, owing to the shortage of doctors in Indonesia generally, continues to travel around the rural areas holding clinics and still maintains some of his private practice within the town itself. As a result, Modjokuto is something of a medical center; but for most *abangans* this can hardly be said to be of much importance in their life, except insofar as it provides them with jobs as launderers, janitors, gardeners, and ambulance drivers.

Only a few of the higher-status people of some wealth go to the HVA hospital in any case, unless they happen to be employees of the company, for the fees for private patients are exorbitant. The government's hospital maintains a daily clinic for a flat fee of one-half rupiah, and many people in the town itself (but relatively few outside of it) go to it each day; but the patient-doctor ratio is so extremely large and the financial resources of most people with which to pay for any extended medical care so sharply limited that only minimal treatment is possible. As a result, the main contact that most people in the Modjokuto area have with the hospitals and with rational scientific medicine is through the male nurses called *mantri*.

Generally trained for simple laboratory work or pharmacy, the *mantris* are forbidden by law to dispense medicines, but as a matter of fact they do so quite freely. For many people, going to a *mantri* has replaced or supplemented going to a *dukun*, with the result that the *mantris* are carrying a rather striking amount of the medical load in Java these days and have become a modernized version of the traditional curing specialist. Where the *dukun* has spells and herbs, the *mantri* has pills and injections, and there is apparently little greater scientific understanding of illness in the latter case than in the former. The *mantri* has become the agent for the Javanese reinterpretation of Western medicine and has simply been added to the traditional armory of curing means available to the average Javanese.

People everywhere tend to face a crisis such as illness with all the cultural resources upon which they can call and to interpret what they are doing in terms of the categories which they learned as children; and so the Javanese flails at his health difficulties with any stick his culture gives him and sees imported methods as but new elements in an age-old pattern. *Dukuns*, herbs, patent medicines, *mantris*, and doctors—all get called into play in a desperate attempt to alter an impossible situation, but somehow in the end the vivid word pictures of the *dukun* give him an edge on his new-fangled competitors....

## SORCERY

There is an underside to everything, and so far as Javanese curing and magical practices are concerned the underside is sorcery. Sorcery, like curing, is largely in the hands of specialists. If one wants to sorcerize someone, one has to hire a *dukun* to do it. Most *dukuns* will deny that they practice sorcery, but evidently it is not hard to find one who will do it if the price is right—about a hundred rupiahs for visiting someone not too far away with a relatively severe sickness, and up to several hundreds for a death. The only defense against sorcery is to get a better *ḍukun*, one whose spiritual strength is greater than that of the *ḍukun* one's enemy has employed against him. A struggle between *ḍukuns*, on a mystical plane of course, then takes place, and if one's *ḍukun* is indeed stronger than his adversary's, he will turn the latter's magic back upon him, and the enemy will fall ill with the disease he has wished on one. In either case, the *ḍukuns*, like contending lawyers in a civil suit, remain unharmed.

There are several different types of sorcery, all of which bear a family resemblance one to the next, but true witches, able to harm others as a result of a purely natural ability and without ritual manipulation, seem not to exist among the Javanese. The general term for sorcery is *sikir* or *sihir*, and the three most virulent varieties are *tenung*, *djènggès*, and *santèt*.

The symptoms of *tenung* sorcery are such as vomiting blood, violent sickness in the stomach, or a raging fever, without any traceable cause. The *ḍukun*'s performance (an informant told me; with one exception I have never seen witchcraft performed) consists of a kind of Black-Mass mock *slametan*. The *ḍukun* sits chanting spells in the center of a half-circle of *sadjèns*—food offerings for the evil spirits—pleading for the destruction of his victim. The *sadjèns* consist of unbroken pieces of incense and opium mostly, although various other things of which *sétans* are especially fond, such as mirrors, may be added. If one intends to kill the victim rather than merely sicken him, one must break the incense into small bits and wrap it in white muslin tied in three places as though it were a corpse, and one can chant a little *tahlil* (the chanting one does at funerals) if he wishes.

In *djènggès* a similar rite is performed, except that objects such as nails, hair, broken glass, and pieces of iron and needles are added to the *sadjèns*. The *ḍukun* spells his spell and concentrates upon his evil intent and by so doing is able to persuade the spirits to induce the objects into the stomach of the victim, who will hear a sudden explosion all around him and then fall dreadfully sick. Sometimes a long piece of wire may be employed which is induced into the victim's arm or leg, thereby paralyzing him. This seems to be the most common form of serious sorcery, and observed cases of it were reported to me by about a half-dozen people,

including one of the town doctors (the Javanese). He said a seriously ill woman came into the hospital only a year or so before, but he could find nothing wrong with her. The X-ray revealed bits of glass, metal, and hair in her stomach, which were then removed by a stomach pump and which are still in the hands of the police. The woman had refused to marry a young man to whom her parents had betrothed her, and she accused him of the sorcery. The doctor said that his Western training had made him skeptical of sorcery, and in 30 years or so of practice all over Indonesia he had not seen a case until this one, but now he had changed his mind and felt perhaps it was possible after all.

The term *santèt* is also sometimes used for inducing foreign objects into the stomach of the victim, but, strictly speaking, it refers to the kind of sorcery in which the *ḍukun* must actually approach the victim and rub pepper grains (or something of the sort) against him while repeating a spell soundlessly in his mind. The victim then contracts incurable diarrhoea.

Agreement on terms is far from complete, but other kinds of sorcery—all on a similar pattern—include being able to make a person come to a set place against his will (*gendam*) and various sorts of love magic (one man outlined four types of increasing strength to me) to attract reticent men (or women) to one's bed (*guna*)....

Accusations of witchcraft are common enough, but they are never made openly and directly against anyone; they are only whispered to others as malicious gossip or discussed rather abstractly as hypotheses to account for peculiar behaviors. Thus a woman whose third marriage to the same man had just ended the same way the first two had—with his losing all their money at cards—when asked why on earth she had married him again anyway said matter-of-factly that she supposed she had been sorcerized. When the first village-chief election in my village was declared invalid by the government, many people ascribe it to the successful employment of a *ḍukun* by the losing candidate. One man told me that two years after his wife had died suddenly he discovered that an old enemy of his had sorcerized her. When I asked if he were now going to sorcerize the culprit in return or do anything else to him, he said, no, that was all in the past now. His main interest in the sorcery notion seemed to be mainly as an explanation of something for which he could not otherwise account.

In many instances the immediate suffering from sorcery is psychologically real and the accusations fervent. A young man whose proposal of marriage had been turned down blamed his very severe depression over the matter on the fact that the girl had not been content just to turn him down but had got a *ḍukun* after him as well; and he spent a few weeks eating in the pitch dark, praying for three hours every night (he was a *santri*) and, I suspect, getting a *ḍukun* friend of his to send out a few counterimprecations against the girl. Even in cases of this sort where the hurt is real and immediate, accusations are never expressed directly to the assumed culprit, nor is a public charge made; gossip to all one's neighbors is the typical pattern....

Sorcery, then, as the Javanese conceive of it, tends to be practiced on neighbors, friends, relatives, and other acquaintances fairly close at hand. Of course, the *ḍukun* employed may be a distant one and so be attacking someone far away from where he is performing his rite, but the actual instigator of the deed is always someone near at hand. Unlike some other peoples, Javanese do not accuse outsiders of sorcery: "The enemies of the people in Tebing live in Tebing," I was told when I asked a man who had told me that there was much sorcery in this nearby town if the people there ever sorcerized the people in Modjokuto.

Secondly, sorcery is always practiced for a specific reason, never for sheer malevolence. It seems to follow no definite kin or class lines, but instead there seems to be a tendency for a man to accuse another of sorcerizing him if he, the victim, conceives of himself as having either frustrated the wishes of the attacker or angered him in some way.

Finally, there is no way in which sorcery can be established as a public crime or even a tort. In all the cases of sorcery of which I heard, I never discovered a case in which direct confrontation by the victim of the accused took place or where any general open accusation was made or any claim for punishment or damages instituted even informally—there being no formal procedures for doing so in any case. Sorcery is a mystical act to be mystically combatted. Although one may gossip about it and make secret accusations to one's heart's content (which will in most cases get back to the accused in one fashion or another), any open attempt to organize public opinion against an accused sorcerer would be almost certain to fail. Similarly, one finds no private individuals in Modjokuto with a wide reputation for instigating sorcery. Although some *ḍukuns* are suspected as all-too-willing agents, even these are in no way socially ostracized....

# 16  Totemism and Allergy

## John L. Fischer, Ann Fischer, and Frank Mahony

In their fine book *Social Science and Medicine*, Simmons and Wolff (1954) devote a chapter to "Links Between Stress and Disease" much of which is derived from data on psychosomatic research. These writers believe that a fuller understanding of psychosomatic disease in sociocultural context suggests that the term *sociosomatic* might be appropriate. One of the most interesting and clinically puzzling groups of such diseases is the allergies. In this ingenious paper, the authors compare allergic reactions that are common in the United States to those resulting from violations of totemic food taboos in Ponape, one of the Caroline Islands. In interpreting the data, the authors call upon several theories of the etiology of allergies by allergists. Is the reaction to the violation of a totemic food taboo caused by chemical properties of the food or to psychological and/or cultural attributions made about the food? A personal communication from one of the authors (J. L. Fischer) is instructive:

> Lévi-Strauss has cited this paper as evidence that allergy-like reactions to totemic food may be purely cultural or psychogenic, but I consider that the fact that the violation of the "runt" taboo does *not* lead to allergy-like symptoms suggests that there is an interaction between culture and allergy: that potentially allergenic foods are chosen as totems and that these allergies can become emotionally activated by guilt over taboo violation.

The "runt" taboos to which Fischer refers are an interesting totemic variant in which the totem consists of the runts of any animal or vegetable species. For the rest of the argument, read the paper!

The purpose of this paper is to discuss some similarities between certain disorders attributed to allergies in the United States and the symptoms attributed to violations of totemic food taboos in Ponape, Caroline Islands. We suggest that a study of totemic taboos, violations of these taboos, and concomitant symptoms may help illuminate the operation of physiological and psychological factors in such disorders as hives (urticaria), angioneurotic oedema, contact dermatitis, etc.

Reprinted with abridgments from John L. Fischer, Ann Fischer, and Frank Mahony, 1959, "Totemism and Allergy," *International Journal of Social Psychiatry*, 5:33–40, with permission of the authors and the *International Journal of Social Psychiatry*.

We are by no means the first to raise the question of a connection. Some time ago, for instance, Frazer noted that the belief is common that eating one's totem causes skin disorders (Frazer 1922:548). Buck specifically noted the belief that urticaria is a punishment for eating the totem in parts of Polynesia, and suggested that the choice of a totem animal and associated food taboos originated in the allergic reaction of an ancestor to a food (Buck 1932:214).

The island of Ponape, which we shall discuss below, is about 12 miles in diameter and was traditionally organized into five petty feudal states, which were cross-cut by a number of matrilineal clans and sub-clans. In general the clans or their component sub-clans (or in some cases both clans and sub-clans) have one or more totemic animal or plant. When an entire clan shares totems the ancestress of the clan is often believed to have been an animal of the most important totemic species. The sub-clan totems and some other lesser totems are often believed to be species of animals which have assisted an ancestor or are in some other way connected with some exploit of an ancestor (for further details see J. L. Fischer 1957).

When the totem is an edible species there is most often a specific food taboo for the members of the matri-clan or sub-clan and the children of the men of the clan, while persons unrelated to the clan are allowed to eat the food freely. However, while most of the tabooed totemic animals are eaten freely by "outsiders", some edible totemic animals, such as the shark, fresh water eel, and sting ray, are rarely eaten by most Ponapeans.

The fact that most, though not all, of the mythical animal ancestors are female and that one shares the same totem as one's mother, may be thought to contradict Freud's theory in *Totem and Taboo* that the totem animal represents primarily an ancestral father. However a strong connection of totems with males on Ponape in spite of matrilineal descent is indicated (to our surprise) by Mahony's finding on questioning 24 men and 13 women, that the father's (matrilineal) totem was more respected and regarded more dangerous to eat than one's own totem (which is also one's mother's). Some individuals respected their fathers' totems even though the fathers themselves did not. Moreover, he found three individuals who observed taboos on their father's father's totem as well, and two of these did not respect their own totem.

In addition to the extension of the taboo to father's totem, J. L. Fischer was also told that the

taboo applied also to spouses of members of the clan, but Mahony's more extensive check failed to confirm this as a general practice. We cannot say definitely whether observance of spouses' taboos was formerly general and is now obsolescent, or whether it has always been sporadic and confined to individuals who perhaps felt especially inhibited about expressing aggression towards their spouses.

Violating the totemic taboo has in Ponape the meaning of forbidden behaviour toward a blood relative or close family. One informant who ate his father's totem fish reported that his father had compared the act to sib incest (*kilikileng-sued*, literally "evil looking"). This was in spite of the fact that the marriage of a man with his father's sister's daughter or other female member of the father's matrilineage is not forbidden on Ponape, and is somewhat encouraged among people of high rank for purposes of inheritance of political titles and property.

Ponapeans believe that a variety of symptoms result from the violation of totemic taboos. According to some informants, severe illness or even death may result from the consumption of one's totem. However, very frequently some lesser symptom is thought to result, and the offender's connection with the totem is emphasized by making him resemble it in some way. Ponapean informants say that a person who has the *sawi*, a kind of fish, as his totem will acquire sores similar to the fish's spots on eating the fish. Violation of a taboo on eating turtle is thought to make a person liable to shortness of breath, which causes him to gasp for air like a turtle, or to acquire roughened skin like a turtle's skin; or, according to one informant, to be subject to a compulsion to flap his arms like a turtle's flippers. An informant, whose sib totem was the eel, reported that his cheeks swelled up like an eel's gills when he violated his taboo. Slightly different, but still showing the basic principle of emphasizing totemic connections, is a taboo on runts of any kind for the *Soun Marakei* sib. Members of this sib may not eat the runt of a litter of dogs or pigs, the smallest hand of bananas on a stalk, small, deformed breadfruit, etc. The penalty for violating this taboo is the birth of a deformed child to the violator.

Of course, if the taboos were carefully observed we would have no way of knowing whether any of these symptoms do, in fact, result from violations of totemic taboos. It seems obvious that in some cases totemic beliefs are invoked after the fact to explain physical symptoms and other misfortunes. For instance, if a member of the *Soun Marakei* sib has a deformed child, other members of the sib will conclude that this person must have violated the sib taboo. However, there has been a considerable amount of acculturation over the last century, and totemic observances have, in fact, lapsed in varying degrees. Some individuals do not even know their totemic taboos, while others know them but do not observe them, and still others have violated them occasionally, and perhaps less than half have never violated them. Among those who have knowingly violated their totemic taboos there appears to be a fair proportion who have experienced culturally appropriate physical symptoms, in view of data collected by the Fischers in 1953 and more recently by Mahony in 1958. Mahony provided statistical data as to the incidence of certain behaviour connected with totemic taboos in a survey of 48 men and women. This and other data are summarized in Table 1.

Not all of the physical symptoms reported by informants could be plausibly interpreted as allergic. Thus one man who reported symptoms after eating his totem showed Mahony a patch of roughened skin around his temples, which Mahony judged to be possibly fungus. The man attributed this to a past violation of his taboo, although it had been a number of years since he had eaten his totem. A woman told Mahony that her teeth hurt after she had eaten her totem. While it may be psychologically appropriate for pain to afflict the offending organ, tooth decay is fairly common among the Ponapeans and toothache would not be an unusual symptom. A man who ate his father's totem fish, a *sawi*, (Plectropomus?) (Elbert 1947), said he could not walk afterwards. Muscle weakness and numbness of the extremities is sometimes a symptom of non-allergic fish poisoning, but it is difficult to evaluate this symptom from the informant's report alone.

The symptoms of the remaining individuals who reported trouble after eating their own or their father's totem could plausibly be explained in Western medical terms as allergic reactions. Thus one man who had two totem fish, *iomo* and *sara* (Holocentrus leo) (Bascom 1946), and had eaten both of them had vomited on these occasions. He said that one of these times he did not find out he was eating a totem until after he had vomited. When he inquired, the Japanese who had prepared the food told him the identity of the fish. However, conceivably he may have subliminally recognized the odour of the fish before eating it. Two other informants mentioned that they had learned to recognize the peculiar odour of their totem fish

**Table 1**  Behaviour of Some Ponapeans Toward Their Totems

| A.  Own (Mother's) Totem | | | |
|---|---|---|---|
| | *Male* | *Female* | *Total* |
| Never ate edible totem | 8 | 9 | 17 |
| Never harmed inedible or seldom eaten totem | 4 | 3 | 7 |
| Ate at least once, got sick, stopped eating | 2 | 4 | 6 |
| Ate, got sick; kept eating, sickness stopped | 1 | — | 1 |
| Ate continuously in spite of symptoms | — | 1 | 1 |
| Ate once; disliked taste, stopped eating | 1 | — | 1 |
| Ate regularly, no symptoms | 6 | 1 | 7 |
| Didn't care if harmed inedible totem | — | 1 | 1 |
| Didn't know own totem | 4 | 3 | 7 |
| Total | 26 | 22 | 48 |

| B.  Father's Matrilineal Totem | | | |
|---|---|---|---|
| | *Male* | *Female* | *Total* |
| Never harmed or ate | 12 | 3 | 15 |
| Ate at least once, got sick, stopped eating | 1 | 2 | 3 |
| Ate, got sick, kept eating, sickness stopped | — | 1 | 1 |
| Ate regularly | 4 | 5 | 9 |
| Didn't care if harmed inedible totem | 1 | — | 1 |
| Didn't know father's totem | 6 | 2 | 8 |
| Total | 24 | 13 | 37 |

from smelling it when cooked by other people. This man ate his other totem during the war when food was hard to get. He continued to eat it in spite of the vomiting, and eventually the symptom disappeared.

Two women described symptoms to Mahony, which sounded like urticaria. Another woman complained of redness in her eyes, another plausible allergic symptom, as a result of eating her totem, but she ate it whenever available nevertheless. Three women who ate their father's totem fish, a *samwei*, reported that they developed "sores" on the palms of their hands and soles of their feet.

John Fischer did not conduct a systematic study, but recorded four males who reported physical symptoms after eating a totem fish, including vomiting, headache, swelling and skin spots.

While informants' reports alone without direct observation leave something to be desired, they are sufficient to indicate that a sizeable proportion of the actually experienced reactions to violations of totemic food taboos on Ponape consist of symptoms which in the United States would often be attributed by physicians to food allergy.

To what extent may there be parallels between Ponapean behaviour towards totemic foods and Western behaviour toward foods which produce allergic symptoms? In the United States, individuals do not as a rule have any total prohibitions on foods considered edible (before the development of allergic symptoms). However, numerous partial taboos exist in the sense of marked parental restrictions in childhood on the quantity of certain kinds of food which may be considered harmful, hard to digest, excessively expensive or luxurious, or safe only for adults. Some allergists have noted that allergenic foods are often the patient's favourite foods, and that patients often eat the food "as symbolic resistance of the authority of a restrictive parent surrogate" (Kaufman 1952:314). Presumably the patients may have acquired the original longing for these foods as a result of childhood restrictions by parents on the consumption of these or other comparable foods.

Foods that have become associated with forbidden activities also have been observed to produce allergic reactions. For example, Kaufman notes the case of a man who repeatedly drank martinis whenever he had sexual relationships with his fiancée. This man developed an allergic reaction to vermouth. He associated the rash he developed with the biblical passage about the sins of the fathers and with venereal disease as a punishment for illegitimate sexual relations (Kaufman 1954). This recalls the Ponapean association of eating the totem animal with sib incest, another illegitimate sexual activity.

Some allergists have speculated about the meaning of the symptom in allergic reactions. Two meanings of interest, aside from the punishment of having the symptom, are riddance and the physiological expression of shame or guilt. In vomiting and diarrhoea, we might see an attempt to undo the crime of eating the forbidden food. In the wheals of urticaria, psychologically oriented investigators have seen the meaning of a blush (Saul and Bernstein 1948:424).

By no means all allergists are agreed as to the importance of psychological situations in producing what have been often regarded as allergic reactions. There are all shades of opinion, from those who consider that a disturbed emotional state is the principal cause of so-called allergic symptoms, to those who consider that the prime cause is some specific chemical to which some tissue of the body becomes sensitized. One adherent of the latter school has stated, for example, that an occasional patient can become so sensitive to eggs that mere presence in the same room with them is enough to bring on an allergic attack (Tuft 1949:175). On the other extreme investigators in one study of thirty urticaria patients found that no evidence of any special allergic cause for the attacks could be discovered, and that, on the contrary, the connection of the attacks with psychological stress was clear, and that incipient or in some cases full-fledged urticaria could be produced simply by bringing up certain painful topics in psychiatric interviews (Graham, Wolf and Wolff 1950).

Theories of allergy also exist which allow for the combination of biochemical and behavioural or emotional factors. For one thing, individuals who are aware of their allergies may eat allergenic foods to test or evoke their reactions. Some masochistic individuals may eat allergenic foods when they wish to punish themselves, while others may eat the foods in an attempt to prove their invulnerability and deny their allergy, and still others may regard the medical prohibition on an allergenic food as a denial of pleasure which they insist on retaining (Kaufman 1954). Of course these attitudes are not necessarily exclusive. The view has also been advanced that the timing and quantity of food consumed is important in developing allergic sensitivity, and that foods which are consumed only occasionally but in large quantities at the time are especially likely to produce allergic symptoms. The consumption of some seasonal foods would fall in this category, but so might luxury foods or any food on which there was some sort of restriction of consumption. A further view which also involves the quantity of the offending substance to which the organism is exposed is that in certain individuals under emotional stress the intestinal wall becomes more permeable, allowing an abnormal amount of the allergen to enter the bloodstream, provoking an excessive defensive reaction of the affected tissues. Another view allows for the influence of emotional disturbance on allergic sensitivity through hormones which are said to contribute to immunologic responses generally —and allergies are widely regarded as a special kind of exaggerated immunologic response (White 1950).

In citing these various theories we do not intend to pass final judgment on them, nor are they all mutually exclusive. We do wish to note, however, that at least theoretically there are a number of ways in which psychological and biochemical factors might contribute to the development of allergic symptoms in individuals, and that in the present state of knowledge we are not forced to dichotomize all allergic symptoms into psychological or chemical, although extreme cases probably exist on both sides.

## CONCLUSIONS

While a further more intensive field study should yield more conclusive results, our data do suggest some implications for theories of urticaria and other physical reactions to food. A psychological factor, specifically, guilt about violating prohibitions established by one's parents on sexual and aggressive behaviour, appears to be involved in producing physical symptoms resembling allergies in a fair proportion of those Ponapeans who violate totemic food taboos. According to Mahony's investigation, individuals who ate the totemic animal (usually fish) of a clan other than their own or their father's rarely, if ever, experienced allergic symptoms, so it would appear that any explanations based purely on the alleged allergenic qualities of the food are insufficient.

Buck's theory, mentioned above, that totemic taboos are simply the embroidered memory of an ancestor's allergy, fails to account for the sizable number of contemporary cases, although it may well be satisfactory as an explanation for the initial choice of many of the clan totems.

At the same time, the data contain implications that a chemical factor may be involved in many, perhaps most of the taboos. Most of the totems are species of fish or shellfish, and these are widely regarded by allergists as being especially allergenic. Some of the totem species are shared by more than one unrelated sub-clan, which would suggest, under Buck's theory, that those species may contain allergens which affected several individuals in the past. The fact that eels and sharks are rarely eaten even when not actually taboo may also be due partly to allergenic properties, although their appearance must also be taken into consideration.

Perhaps the most interesting bit of evidence for a chemical factor is in the nature of the traditional punishments for violation of the taboos. Most of the traditional punishments consist of or include symptoms that could be interpreted as allergic, and these punishments are specific to a single totemic species—getting spots like the fish's, etc. A convincing demonstration of the purely psychogenic nature of these symptoms could be made if a group could be found with a "cross totem" (a totem containing individuals or parts of individuals from a variety of species) which also had the traditional allergic punishments. In an attempt to make this demonstration Mahony was asked to investigate the traditional penalty for violating of the *Soun Marakei* totem, which, it will be recalled, consists of runts of any species—coconuts, breadfruit, bananas, dogs, etc. Presumably there would be no biochemical difference, certainly no consistent one across animal and vegetable species, between runts and normal sized individuals and any "allergic" reaction to eating runts would be clearly psychogenic. However the traditional penalty for this violation is not, as previously mentioned, interpretable as an allergic symptom but is rather the birth of a deformed child. We may infer from this the proposition that where the totem is a clearly defined allergenic species the traditional punishment will usually include allergic symptoms, but where the totem is defined to cut across many species allergic symptoms will be lacking as punishment. Further data bearing on this point, either from Ponape or other totemic societies, would be of great interest.

A number of other questions about the development of allergies might be considered in the light of the Ponapean data. For instance, according to allergic theory the excessive reaction to the allergen can occur only after the individual has been previously sensitized by an earlier exposure. But according to Ponapean theory and informants' reports, the first consumption of an allergic food produces symptoms which are as severe as any later time, or even more so. In fact some informants reported the gradual vanishing of symptoms as they repeatedly violated the taboo. Another complaint regarded by Western physicians as allergic in origin is asthma. Dr. Eugene MacDonald, who has served over a decade in the positions of Public Health Director for Ponape District and later, the entire Trust Territory of Micronesia has stated it as his clinical impression that the incidence of asthma appears to be greater in Ponape District of the Trust Territory. Hospitalization figures available to us decisively support this statement. The native theory of asthma is unclear to us at this date but might well repay investigation.

If we look back for a moment on our own culture the Ponapean data on totemic food taboos raise the question as to whether the production of some allergic symptoms in Westerners may not involve a similar socio-psychological situation. The eating of a tabooed or restricted food, or eating a food which has become associated with a tabooed activity, is symbolic of hostility toward loved but rejecting parents from whom one had longed to receive approval. "Adult foods" which are those most usually tabooed completely or partially to children in our culture, often cause allergic reactions in adults, e.g., coffee and liquor. In Ponape the parents are identified with their matrilineages, all members of which are treated as equivalent in a number of respects, so the breaking of the taboo can express hostility towards one's own or one's father's matrilineal relatives in general, as well as towards one's parents. Among persons subject to food allergies in our country, the basic meaning of expressing hostility toward a loved but rejecting parent may be quite similar, but because of differences in social structure the extensions of the hostile feelings from the parents ought to be not to lineage mates, but to non-kin authority figures such as employers, doctors, officials, and the like. Increases in hostile feelings might bring out both an increased tendency to eat forbidden foods and an increased tendency to react to them.

Anthropologists will be interested in the problem of the traditional punishments for violating totemic food taboos for the light shed on the operation of clans. However, investigation of this problem could also, it is hoped, provide evidence relevant to various medical and psychiatric theories of the origin of allergic symptoms among members of our own society. The cultural stereotyping of the symptoms on Ponape and the native belief that symptoms are connected with only a relatively small number of natural species might lead an investigator to ignore some cases of genuine (immunological) allergy, but at the same time these limitations in the data bring out the socio-psychological aspects of the problem all the more clearly, and would justify the concentration on reactions to a small sample of the potential allergens.

# V
# Divination and Diagnosis

## Divination and Diagnosis as a Sociocultural Process

The train of events from the time a person first experiences a serious discomfort or dis-ease to the final outcome of that experience may be viewed as a purely biological process in which one or more types of organisms are seen as causing stress in another organism; a psychological process in which the behavior and feelings of the affected person are highlighted; a social-psychological process in which the focus becomes the transactions between the patient and relevant others; or a sociocultural process in which an afflicted individual is implicated in complex transactions between himself, relevant others, and the social and cultural networks that they share. If measures taken by the stricken person or those immediately around him do not bring melioration the help of a specialist or professional is sought. Sometimes the same professional attempts to divine—or diagnose—the condition of the patient and also undertakes the cure. Sometimes the person making the diagnosis is primarily a diviner who, having made a decision as to the nature of the illness, then prescribes a remedy and makes a referral to the appropriate healing specialist.

This event-series, from first perception of a malaise to the final resolution of the pain and menace, is an exceedingly intricate transaction in those societies of the world where the individual's social networks are intimately concerned not only with the person's health but also with the gains and losses from his behavior and relationships vis-à-vis all the individuals and groupings to whom the afflicted person affiliates. The decision-making process in divination, which in preindustrial and non-Western societies is called into play with the occurrence of serious illness and other anxiety-provoking events, has social, economic, political, as well as psychological consequences and functions. The aim of this section is to present some selections that examine and analyze diagnosis and divination as a medical, economic, political, and social process as well as a psychological one. The selections structure the diagnostic process as one with grave consequences both for the individual and his social system. The aim of the diagnosis reaches beyond such questions as "What is wrong with this person?" "What label shall be placed upon this condition?" "What remedy should be sought and from whom?" In addition, the diagnosis seeks to discover and identify the ruptures in the

161

relationships between the patient and his spiritual and social relatives and associates and, beyond this, the rents in the general social fabric resulting in the vulnerability of this particular member of the society. The prescription for treatment and the prognosis for the patient will also simultaneously function to repair the damage to the social structure, to restore social harmony (and, in the case of the affected gods, human-spiritual harmony), and to reaffirm, where it is involved, the authority of the power structure. As George K. Park (1963) states in his seminal paper, "Divination and Its Social Contexts." "...divination has as its regular consequence the elimination of an important source of disorder in social relationships." And as Park (1963: 197) further postulates,

> For it is the peculiar property of the diviner's role that he is able, in the public conscience, to remove the agency and responsibility for a decision from the actor himself, casting it upon the heavens where it lies beyond cavil and beyond reproach.... The diviner in effect provides a legitimating sanction upon a process of structural realignment which, depending as it does upon a voluntary act, would be difficult indeed to sanction in any remarkably different manner.

In a frequently cited paper, O. K. Moore (1957) suggests that one function of divination, at least in the case of hunting, is to randomize a group's hunting territory and thereby increase the probability of success in the hunt by aiding the hunters in not exhausting repeatedly the resources of the same area. Moore cites the dependence of the Naskapi Indians of Labrador upon scapulimancy in determining their hunting routes, thus in effect, according to Moore, providing themselves with "a functional equivalent of a table of random numbers" (Moore 1957: 73). Park tends to disagree with this "probability theory" of divination (his phrase), not only because most ethnographic evidence, in Park's opinion, would not support such "objectivity" in the divination process but because apparent techniques of chance used in divination are neither universal nor even accepted as random where they do exist. Furthermore, even if they should be so used, Park asks, "Is it useful or not to scatter accusations of witchcraft?" Park contends that even an apparently randomizing device is used mainly to deflect any malign prior aim of the diviner's client (except to be relieved of his misfortune), and is, therefore, "suited by its apparent impartiality and its association with prescience to the task of rendering a decision with exceptional authority." Indeed, Park goes on, "Paradoxically, divination appears to have a derandomizing function; establishing a consensus, it renders action more predictable and regular" (Park: 199–200).

A study by Austin J. Shelton (1965), "The Meaning and Method of Afa Divination Among the Northern Nsukka Ibo," which appeared on the heels of Park's (1963) theoretical essay, is of interest not only as an empirical sequel to Park's formulations but because it presents an actual patterned analysis of *afa* or divination by casting. Interestingly to me, in light of my previous discussion of Park's formulations, Shelton seems to misinterpret Park's position regarding divination as a system of chance or probability-based. In any event, Shelton's case is an interesting one whether or not the reader is prepared to accept his or Park's formulations regarding the "objectivity" or "nonobjectivity" of the divination process. An excellent recent article (Werbner 1973) on domestic divination among the Kalanga of Botswana observes and records a part of the divination process that is only sparsely covered in other studies, that of the patterning and process of communication between the diviner and his clients. Although, like Shelton, Werbner offers a careful accounting of an actual séance, he is less concerned with the "objectivity" of the process, but very much with accountability and control of the diviner. He concludes (Werbner 1973: 1438–39):

> A local diviner gives his services in the hire of a specific client. Yet he is highly accountable and subject to control by his neighbors; he represents the informed opinions of intimates or neighbors, and at issue in his divination may even be moral evaluation of his personal

conduct, apart from séances. He and his congregation must collaborate, together they must revise understandings of their past and modulate retrospective knowledge, if he is to define a course of action about a certain complaint, such as a patient's illness requiring a ritual remedy. There are various devices which he may use in reasoning with his congregation about contextually troublesome implications of the divining lots. These devices play on configurations and continuities of evidence which the diviner can stress selectively. The devices include, among others, inference from a sequence in a series of actual outcomes—the continuity from an initial one or from a mesh of excluded or hypothetical outcomes. There are also other devices of rhetoric, such as ellipsis or compression of verse, which the diviner can use to make outcomes imply a dominant message. He and his congregation convey both manifest and intimated meanings, at once, through highly stylized rhetoric, rich in metaphors. They must consider moral duties and acts of occult significance, but they need not acknowledge fully, and with detailed reference to particular persons, the troublesome suspicions underlying their discourse. Indeed, a thoroughgoing ventilation of grievances is what much domestic divination dodges.

Thus, if, as many anthropologists allege, divination has as a major function the uncovering (and remediation) of individual grievances and interpersonal conflict, clearly, as Werbner shows, the process must be kept within bounds, or else it could become itself, like witchcraft, a source of social discord.

The methods, techniques, paraphernalia, and personnel of divination are multitudinous and various, although some seem to have broad, nearly universal appeal. A useful survey of divining methods and techniques in parts of Africa may be found in Barrie Reynold's (1963:100–127) monograph *Magic, Divination and Witchcraft Among the Barotse of Northern Rhodesia.* Several examples are noted in the selections that follow.

# 17 Navaho Treatment of Sickness: Diagnosticians

## William Morgan

The concern and preoccupation of the Navaho Indians of the Southwestern United States with religion and healing have been a source of fascination and attention on the part of anthropologists for generations. The present study is exemplary in several ways for it demonstrates that nearly a half-century ago ethnographic data that was specifically focused on the medical features of a society and its culture were being collected systematically, sensitively, and carefully. William Morgan tells us that his interviews were conducted directly in the very difficult Navaho language to preclude the problems inherent in using translators; in fact, these were not so much interviews as exchanges of medical information between Morgan and his informants.

Morgan draws a clear distinction between the diagnostician and what he calls the *shaman* or, perhaps more accurately, the singer or other healer. (His is one

Reprinted with abridgments from William Morgan, 1931, "Navaho Treatment of Sickness: Diagnosticians," *American Anthropologist, 33*:390–402, with permission of the American Anthropological Association.

of the earliest uses of the Western technical term *diagnostician* for medical diviners, thus aiding to rescue Navaho medicine from the ethnographic swamps of "primitive" medicine.) There are three types of divining: hand-trembling, star-gazing, and listening, and of these the first is probably the most frequently used. For the first two forms of diagnosis the diviner goes into a trance state and may experience auditory or visual illusions (hallucinations?). Sickness caused by dreaming is perhaps the major etiological class. Diagnosticians can be either male or female, and whereas women appeared to be decreasing in number, I would hypothesize that in earlier epochs they were more numerous and generally stronger in influence. Several years after this paper was published, another study of Navaho diagnosticians appeared (Wyman 1936), but although certain differences were noted, doubtlessly because of local variations over the huge range of Navaho territory, the findings mainly paralleled those of Morgan. Refreshingly for his time, Morgan also attempts to bring a theoretical orientation to his discussion. Although contemporary scholars may differ with his formulations based on Jungian psychology, the attempt is laudable. At the end, Morgan issues a call for what can only be interpreted as research toward a medical anthropology.

When the "family remedies" of a Navaho Indian give no relief, he consults a diagnostician, of whom there are three kinds: men (or women) "with motion-in-the-hand," stargazers, and listeners. These diagnosticians are consulted about sickness, dreams, and any unusual happening; they are asked to provide means of warding off dangers, and are summoned to advise about the recovery of lost horses, sheep, and money. [In the following account, Navaho informants = capital letters, white informants = lower case—Ed.]

A definite distinction must be made between shamans and diagnosticians. The Chants conducted by shamans comprise the religion of the Navaho. Legends about these Chants are transmitted orally from generation to generation among the shamans. These legends describe how the gods revealed the Chants to the Navaho and sometimes contain specific instructions about the preparation of ceremonial paraphernalia and sand paintings. Diagnosticians do not use sand paintings or masks, nor do they possess tribal legends about their work. The collecting of medicines and the preparation of material ("cigarettes," kethawns, etc.) for a Chant is an extremely complicated procedure. A diagnostician may or may not observe similar restrictions according to his own inclination. During a Chant, the words of a song and the ritual treatment of a patient on a particular sand painting may not be altered; whereas, the diagnostician may make his own songs and minor rituals and may vary them at will. The shaman has no technique for discovering the cause of an illness, and wherever the cause is obscure, the shaman will not know the cure. A diagnostician, however, will reveal the cause and will prescribe the cure. C, a shaman, consulted two diagnosticians about a recurrent dream which was making him sick. The diagnosticians told him the particular gods who were causing the dream, and why they caused it, and what Chant would remedy his condition. The apprenticeship of a shaman's assistant may last fifteen years, depending on his ability to memorize verbally and visually. A diagnostician's apprentice may be ready to practice in a few months. A shaman must not cut his hair and must be fully initiated into the tribe. Neither of these conditions is required of a diagnostician. These are the most important distinctions between shamans and diagnosticians.

In cases of sickness the diagnostician is called upon to give the cause of the sickness and to say what ceremony will cure it, and what shaman can give that ceremony. If the sickness is not serious, the diagnostician will undertake to cure it himself. The ability to diagnose is not inherited, but must be proved during an apprenticeship, and psychological abnormalities do not qualify an individual for this work. [E, B, K, t, i.]

The cause of a sickness is revealed when the diagnostician is in a trance, therefore diagnosticians must first prove their ability to trance and then serve an apprenticeship under a practicing diagnostician. From him they become familiar with his medicines and learn his songs, prayers, and short rituals. [C, E, P, t, d.]

From the point of view of the everyday life of the Indians, too much interest should not be centered upon the shamans and their ceremonies, which may take from one to two hundred hours according to the desire and especially the pocketbook of the patient. When it is realized that three hundred and fifty dollars will support a family of five in comparative comfort for one year [t], the cost of a "serious" sickness is also a serious financial burden upon patient, relatives, and friends because a nine-night ceremony will cost a minimum of eight hundred dollars. A Night Chant cost t fifteen hundred dollars, and A paid a similar amount for his Mountain Chant. On the 25,000 square miles of the Reservation, it is doubtful if the "40,000" Navaho hold more than thirty of these nine-night ceremonies between the first frost and the first thunder.

Before proceeding further, it should be stated that the writer did not use an interpreter. One trial with a friend who "knew Navaho before he could speak English," demonstrated that it was impracticable. There is a curious concentration on the interpreter, and toward him each person is oriented. Notes taken on such a conversation resemble interchanges of telegrams. An interpreter can get parcels of specific information but the presence of a third person blocks the development of a personal conversation. And it must be understood that the writer did not "interview" an Indian. The writer gave as much information as he received. In other words he "swapped" white men's dreams, visions, trance material, superstitions, customs, rituals, and certain "treatments" commonly used by white doctors.

The following is a preliminary description of the three diagnostic techniques and a discussion thereof.

The first description is a paraphrase of E and P. P is a practitioner of motion-in-the-hand, whose father was a shaman and whose brother is a stargazer [t]. The man with motion-in-the-hand enters the hogan of the patient. Friends and relatives are present and the sickness is discussed.

(These discussions are important in order to estimate their effect upon the prognosis.) The diagnostician seats himself facing the patient. He closes his eyes. He holds out his arm. He thinks of all the possible causes of the illness. When the "correct" cause "comes to his mind," his arm involuntarily shakes (Matthews 1902).

When the diagnostician's arm has shaken, he lowers it. He then tells the cause of the sickness to the patient. Sometimes it is necessary to locate where the sickness is in the body. When his arm is extended toward the "correct" part it will shake. This is a skeleton of the procedure. Other details should be noted which vary with each diagnostician. He smooths the sand between himself and the patient, and sits down. On the sand he makes signs. From one of his buckskin or calico bags, he takes out reeds, or stones, or sticks. He may paint them in various designs with colored clays. He orders these on the sand in front of him. He may sprinkle them with corn pollen or corn meal. He may arrange on the ground certain stones or arrowheads which he has previously prayed or chanted over. He holds in his extended hand a special stone, pollen, object, or corn meal. He may chant or pray. Then with his arm outstretched he closes his eyes and enters a trance state. Through the mind of a man with motion-in-the-hand runs a series of visualizations of the illness and of the cause of the illness, whereas the listeners receive auditory manifestations. These men believe in their ability to diagnose, because the trance-state seems unusual and real, the more so in that the visions come to them when they are oblivious of external stimuli. Such visions carry the usual conviction of truth....

These, then, are diagnoses almost sure to be accepted by the patient. And such diagnoses are commonly used by "mediums" among white men who describe the person who is communicating a message in such general terms that members of the audience can readily supply specific details and identify the person as a friend or relative. These comments tend to show that this diagnosis was not done by means of a trance. I am not prepared to deny this. A brief critique of P is relevant. This man is approximately fifty years old, is married, has three children and is a university graduate. He is of medium height, stout, and careless about his clothes. He is readily fluent in speech, both Navaho and English. This deterred me from asking questions which would give him a chance to expand his answers. For example, I suspected that if I asked him what a man with motion-in-the-hand did when

called to diagnose, he would reply with a description of what he himself did, including therein all that he had ever seen or heard from other diagnosticians as well as stargazers and listeners. He watched me closely and was sensitive to my reactions. This confirmed t's warning that he would tell me what he thought I wanted to hear. The result was that I increased my attitude of indifference and asked specific questions. Shifting the conversation from one phase of diagnosis to another, or from one type of dream to another type lessened the chance of his manufacturing an answer. Nevertheless some suspected dramatic fictions were deleted from memory before his conversations were privately recorded. He takes an active part in the Mountain Chant dances. His levity does not extend to his work. Occasionally in a diagnostic trance he has seen a man or woman, but too vaguely to identify them. This vagueness of identity is characteristic of the controlled white man's trance, where human figures are invariably generalized and impersonal. The diagnostician assumes that the man or woman of the trance has caused the illness of the patient by witchcraft, and it is therefore important to identify this person. With the help of the patient, family, and friends, this usually is not difficult. Some believe that when the patient by means of a ceremony is freed from the witch's spell, this influence will return to the witch and cause him or her to be sick. [P, i.] P states that twice he has had the patient get well and the bewitchers have died within ten days, and in a third case death has come after a longer period; "the bewitcher usually dies of heart trouble and generally from a hemorrhage." If true, these should not be dismissed at once as coincidences. Psychological phenomena produce in the Indian extensive physiological affects, as they do in the white man.

The technique of the stargazer as given below is a close paraphrase of E's description and corresponds essentially to those of P and t who has a moving picture of part of the procedure.

A man is sick. A stargazer is called in. He comes into the hogan (Mindeleff 1898). The patient is there. Others are there. He talks to the patient and others. They discuss the illness. The fire is put out. The stargazer chants, then he says, "Everyone must close his eyes. No one must move or speak. Everyone must concentrate on the illness and try to see something." The stargazer takes a man from the hogan, and walks away some distance. He performs movements with his body. Any horses or sheep are frightened away. When there is no noise, the stargazer places a crystal or stone on his hand.

He chants. He prays to the Gila monster. He does not pray to a lizard, but a lizard beyond the lizards, a larger one. Then the stargazer holds out his arm and hand in line with the moon or some star, and gazes unwinking at the crystal. Soon he sees something. He closes his hand upon what he has seen in the crystal. Also there may seem to be a line of light which is "lightning" from the star to the crystal or to the ground around him so that the ground appears light. The stargazer sees the hogan and the sick man, even though his back is turned to it. [P asserted, without being questioned, that when the patient was seen in a trance he was naked, whereas in reality the patient was sitting fully clothed in the hogan. This is a familiar phenomenon of white men's trance imagery.] He sees a man, or a bear, or a coyote, or perhaps the head of a coyote, or perhaps the bear is biting the patient. Then he goes back to the hogan. The fire is lighted. He asks what the others have seen. This is talked about. He tells what he has seen. Maybe it is a man. Maybe the man is a witch and is making the illness. He must find out who the man is. Maybe it is a coyote. The stargazer puts marks on the floor of the hogan. He lays down a handkerchief. He lays a piece of turquoise, maybe a special stone, maybe a bit of pearl, on the handkerchief. He makes a bag of the handkerchief. He chants and prays. He gives the bag to a man. He tells him to go in a certain direction until he finds a coyote track. He must see how fresh it is, what the coyote was doing, what direction he went. He must open the bag and lay it on the tracks and carefully arrange it in order. Then he must return to the hogan. If the coyote track led away from the hogan, the patient will get well. If the illness is serious the stargazer will prescribe a ceremony and the shaman who can give it....

The third group of diagnosticians, the listeners, apparently are less common on the Reservation, though the Winds, as bearers of messages, are frequently mentioned in the Chants and Origin Legend (Washington Matthews). Their methods resemble the stargazers except that, when they leave the hogan and take up a position, the diagnosis which comes to them is auditory. [t, P, E, i, d.]. . . .

From the foregoing, the trance appears to be the only constant of Navaho diagnostics. Comment is therefore relevant because the word "trance" is vague and tainted in western civilization. A relative idea of the trance may be gained from the following sequence of manifestations which show the participation of increasing increments of consciousness: dreams, certain hallucinations and delusions, hypnagogic visions, certain involuntary visions, trances, phantasies, and day-dreams. A woman's self-diagnosis might be interpreted as an involuntary vision. Having been present when she described it, I find reason to believe that she exaggerated. The blackness, the sudden vision, suggests loss of consciousness. Anything revealing itself under such conditions would be more highly valued because of its mysteriousness than in the usual controlled trance during which the diagnostician is aware of the equilibrium of his body. On the other hand, all my information concerning listeners seems to imply the occurrence of mere auditory hallucinations which were translated by the mind into plausible "hunches." Listeners are uncommon but presumably some exist who receive verbal messages. It should be noted that none of the diagnosticians lie down when trancing. Hypnagogic visions are thus forestalled, but there is tense concentration upon the patient and his sickness. Innumerable have been the attempts to elucidate trances. Two references are here sufficient: one from the Irish Free State, "The Candle of Vision," by "AE"; and one quotation from Tibet (Wentz 1929),

May the consciousness undistractedly be kept in its natural state;
Grasping the true nature of dreams, may I Train myself in the clear Light of Miraculous Transformation. . . .

Such references are unsatisfactory, to say the least. The work of Jung (1928) must therefore be introduced. His experiments began twenty years ago, and one fragment of a trance has been published in Two Essays on Analytical Psychology. A brief recapitulation of his work is necessary, the more so since it contains important implications in the field of anthropology. Jung's concept of the collective unconscious was assumed in order to interpret dream material of 1909. This material contained images which are found in myths, and images remote from the experiences of the patient. Therefore the "unconscious" was divided by Jung into the personal unconscious which contained "all those psychic contents which are forgotten during the course of life, and all subliminal impressions, and perceptions which have too little energy to reach consciousness, and all psychic contents incompatible with the conscious attitude" (Jung 1928) and the impersonal (collective) unconscious, the contents of which "appertain to a group, nation, or mankind and are not acquired during the life of the individual". That these impersonal contents occurred in the dreams of an individual at a certain moment in a certain situation seemed to indicate that their interpretation would be of value to the patient. Familiarity with myths thus became the first requisite, and subsequent interpretation was aided by comparing one myth with others especially where there was a duplication of symbols and symbolic acts. Quite properly there is and will continue to be a controversy over the interpretation of such material, but no one denies the existence of this imagery in the unconscious of men. When a man with-motion-in-the-hand describes trancing it is difficult to distinguish his meaning from Jung's words:

a vision, which by intense concentration, was perceived on the background of consciousness, a technique that is perfected only after long practice (Jung 1928:246)

He also agrees with C and E that not everyone can succeed, and the "long practice" is similar to the Navaho's apprenticeship. Jung has remarked that if once the resistance to free contact with the unconscious can be overcome, and one can develop the power of sticking to the phantasy, there the play of images can be watched, and the creation of myths takes place. This requires the same concentration which P describes as being necessary for the diagnosis of sickness. Furthermore Jung's material has called forth the following conclusions:

I have to declare that these facts are psychic factors of indisputable effect. They are not the discoveries of an idle mind, but definite psychic events. They obey absolutely definite laws, and have their own law-determined causes and effects, which accounts for the fact that they can be demonstrated just as well among the most varied peoples and races living today as among those of thousands of years ago. As to what these processes consist in I have no theory to offer (Idem.)....

... Diagnosticians unlike the shamans may practice throughout the year but with certain limitations. Since these men and women do not work with masks or other representations of the gods, the use of which is forbidden between the first thunder and the first frost, it is probable that their work is but little curtailed, although they cannot mention the sacred names of the bear, snake, and lightning except in the winter when these latter are "asleep and cannot hear."

During any discussion of diagnosticians, it should be borne in mind that individual Navaho also have "home remedies." If these fail or the element of fear is present, the patient seeks the advice and ministrations of a diagnostician. These minor sicknesses need not involve a trance diagnosis but merely dispensary and outpatient treatment. However much space is here allotted to secondary factors in the Navaho treatment of sickness, it is assumed that only on rare occasions does a patient escape from a shaman or diagnostician without at least one sweat-bath, emetic, or cathartic. These are the more efficacious because Indians are apprehensive of physical ills and are not in the habit of delaying treatment. This comment will be challenged immediately by almost anyone who has talked to a white Reservation doctor or nurse. These latter show unmistakable signs of exasperation with the Indian and the reasons which they give speak for themselves: (1) Indians frequently do not come to a hospital until all efforts of shamans have failed. (2) Indians stop coming for treatment after preliminary improvement. This is especially common with trachoma cases. (3) Indians seriously sick and not improving will often be removed from the hospital by friends and relatives and taken to a shaman. (4) In view of the fact that incision is not practiced by the tribe, it is difficult to persuade an Indian to have an operation.

Sometimes a diagnostician will formulate his own ideas of physiology and how his medicines work which must be most convincing to his patients and enhancing to his reputation. P, a graduate of Haskell, has a theory that sickness is very often in the heart and that it spreads to the head and all parts of the body. It may be in the stomach and may spread to the head. Similarly, he says his medicines will permeate through the body and will cure everything including pneumonia, tuberculosis, gonorrhea, and heart trouble. First he gives an emetic which empties the "stomach and lungs," then he gives a cathartic. He collects his herbs from special places and all but a few he boils and administers internally through the mouth. For burns and sores, he has some moss which he burns and applies to the damaged area after which it is covered with tallow. Sometimes it is the habit to cover sores with the sap of resinous trees. For sprains and lameness certain roots are used; these may be boiled and applied, or they may be chewed by the diagnostician or patient and together with saliva rubbed into the skin. He displayed a carefully wrapped object which looked like a dried root. He said this was his most powerful medicine. He had had it for a long time and gave certain patients a few particles of it boiled in water. It would cure anything. He said it was the penis of a buffalo. Whether it was or not, I could not determine, but several Indians said that a buffalo's penis was known to be "strong medicine."

Even though these medicines may or may not be sung over, their association with other objects in the possession of a diagnostician would make them unusually powerful, and in addition P said he had collected special ones from particular places. The writer does not know whether certain herbs have become standardized remedies and whether an herb used for sore throat must always be collected near a spot struck by lightning. Such prescriptions undoubtedly vary with each diagnostician unlike the rules for gathering ceremonial medicines. Nor was it ascertained how much the shamans trespass upon the diagnosticians' field or short chants and prayers for minor sicknesses. If a patient asked a shaman for medicine to cure a stated illness, no doubt the shaman would give it, but apparently he has no technique for discovering what the illness is or how it was caused. A diagnostician, however, may identify a certain sickness with the malevolence of a certain god, in which case the ceremony would be prescribed in which this god is prominent. It was not determined how many names there are for sicknesses nor the nature of the names. F's letter to her relative said that a man with-motion-in-the-hand had diagnosed their cousin's pain in the side as "air and devil sickness" and had prescribed a Night Chant. Presumably, diagnosticians invent names for sicknesses and probably different gods and spirits can cause the same sickness.

There remain four other functions of diagnosticians; oneiromancy, advice about unusual incidents, provisions for warding off dangers, and help in the recovery of lost possessions.

The first three of these categories may be accompanied by physiological disturbances, which occasionally fall within the conditions defined by Dr. William A. White as "catastrophies" and "disasters."

Diagnosticians are called upon to cure sickness caused by dreams or to prevent sickness predicted by dreams. Indian informants did not hesitate to distinguish good dreams from bad dreams, nor were they reticent about telling their dreams. P said that if the dream is not serious, the individual may pray at dawn in his doorway with or without some special stone before him which has been chanted over for this purpose by some diagnostician. He may pray to the sun-god (whom C considers the "highest god"); or he may pray to a particular god or spirit of some animal made manifest by the dream. If the dream be more serious, he must go to a diagnostician who will use his chants, and minor

rituals, and more powerful objects and prayers. If the dream be still more serious, the diagnostician will advise a ceremony by a shaman. The writer wishes to stress the importance which his informants give to their dreams as factors in their everyday life. A discussion of these dreams cannot be handled within the confines of this report. Suffice it to say that dreams carefully interpreted with related conscious material are indispensable for an understanding of individual Indians.

Another function of the diagnostician is the warding off of dangers. In addition to his necklace and the chamois bag containing special stones and annually renewed pollen which Navaho acquire at a certain time in their protracted initiation, P carried additional bags containing particular stones and pollen. One stone was four inches long, flat, narrow, black, and smooth. The bag was made to fit it. Part of it was supposed to resemble a horse's hoof. This stone had been sung over and protected him from being killed by a man. Some Indians carry an arrowhead for this purpose. Both he and his wife were very much afraid of lightning, in fact once he had nearly been struck. Each had a ceremony held to protect them from lightning and each carried a piece of white shell and a piece of turquoise strung together on a cord with particular knots. This also had been sung over and if a storm came, he could go outside his hogan and the lightning would proceed no further. The different kinds of lightning have often been recorded as well as the belief that when the Thunder-bird shoots his arrow it is straight lightning whereas the Chief Snake makes zigzag lightning. P stated that an object which protects from lightning also protects from snakes and so long as he carried his shell and turquoise a snake might enter his hogan but it would not bite him. Thus most of the stones which are carried are aniconic and are not fashioned or marked in relation to their use.

A diagnostician may also be called in to protect a hogan from lightning. P called my attention to a bunch of mistletoe over his door and twigs from species of trees at the south, west, and north of his hogan under the roof, which were placed there during a chant to prevent lightning. He protects other people's hogans from lightning by chanting, praying, and setting upright in the hogan to the east, south, west, and north an arrowhead or a small stone shaped like a miniature menhir. He then chants and prays. His sets of arrowheads and stones are of four different natural colors. A black arrowhead is placed to the east, a blue one to the south, a yellow one to the west, and on the north side a white one is set up. In the same bag with these stones were more than thirty others of miscellaneous shapes and colors. The innumerable uses which these may serve were not recorded.

Diagnosticians are called in about lost money, horses and sheep, and in fact about lost children. . . .

Rituals and words, spoken or sung, to cure sickness caused by dreams, witches, and the spirits of animals, gods, and dead men have been tenaciously preserved by the Navaho and ably recorded by anthropologists. Further research of these rituals and beliefs lies in the field of racial psychology and involves a study of the conscious and unconscious processes of individuals. Non-academic psychology necessarily remains affiliated with hospitals and it seems probable than an anthropologist will obtain his most dependable information through the investigation of psychopathic cases and organic disorders, because so many of the latter are psychogenic, and because a sick man is invariably less reticent than a man who is not sick. Work in this field seems to fall into three phases: the collection of data, including the investigator's contact with informants for which no university degree can ever prepare a man; the evaluation and interpretation of material which is conditioned by the investigator's understanding of his own psychological processes; and lastly the generalization of conclusions, which is the most difficult phase since it involves the method of successive approximations, which Archimedes aptly called the method of exhaustion. One adequate lead-in for such research, the work of diagnosticians, is outlined in this report.

# 18 Some Social Structural Consequences of Divination as Diagnosis Among the Safwa

*Alan Harwood*

The monograph from which this selection is taken is one of the few field studies that focuses specifically upon the medical system of a culture and views its linkages to the social structure as directly performing ,

Written and specially adapted for this volume by the author from Alan Harwood, 1970, *Witchcraft, Sorcery, and Social Categories Among the Safwa*, Oxford University Press and the International African Institute, with permission of the author and the International African Institute (London).

not only therapeutic functions but social and political functions, not only healing functions for the patient but significant operations on the social networks of which he is a member. When a person suffers a serious ailment his recourse is to share this information with some of his kinsmen and to consult a diviner. The method of diagnosis "assigns a particular cause to the episode from a set of culturally defined categories, each of which implicates dissension in a different kind of social relationship," with a number of possible consequences for the participants in those relationships. Alan Harwood's analysis in the following selection deals with one of these etiological categories, illnesses caused by -*ly*-, one type of the secret power of *itonga*. The act of a diagnosis of -*ly*- brings the illness into the framework of the patrilineal structure, uncovers a dispute or conflict among agnates, and, as a consequence, either preserves or destroys the relationship which is at hazard. The divination also becomes a test of the loyalty of an identified culprit to the solidarity of the patrilineage. In about half the cases presented here the consequence was to resolve the conflict and assuage the feelings of contention among the disputants. When a conflict is no longer kept within the lineage but "goes public," it becomes an open struggle for power between the principals and may aid or frustrate the political ambitions of one or the other. Each party tries to build support for his cause so that others in the community inevitably become involved and polarized around the issue.

Divination as diagnosis among the Safwa then may have among its consequences the strengthening or fissioning of patrilineages. The outcome, says Harwood, "is explainable in terms of ecological, demographic, economic, and political conditions." Obviously, the process of diagnosis of disease among the Safwa, as among many other groups in other selections in this book, moves far beyond the one-to-one dyad of physician and patient that is characteristic of Western medicine. However, it ought to be noted that even in the West, diagnoses of especially disabling ailments inevitably involve others in the social networks of the sufferer, perhaps most severely the already overtaxed nuclear family.

## INTRODUCTION

The Safwa are a Bantu-speaking people who live in the Southern Highlands Region of Tanzania. They have traditionally been swidden cultivators and cattle-keepers, with a primary dependency on eleusine, sorghum, and corn. The major corporate groups in Safwa society are defined patrilineally, and all members of a patrilineal group are believed to be under the protection of the group's ancestors. Illness is conceived as resulting from a weakening of a person's life force, a condition which is primarily caused by discord in human relationships. To discover the etiology of an illness the sufferer and several of his kinsmen consult a diviner who assigns a particular cause to the episode from a set of culturally defined categories, each of which implicates dissension in a different kind of social relationship (for example, among patrilineal kin, among residents of the same community, and among nonkin.) The following selection examines the effects of diagnosing the cause of an illness in terms of one of these categories.

## A FOLK CONCEPT OF DISEASE ETIOLOGY AND ITS SOCIAL CONSEQUENCES

According to Safwa belief, *itonga* is an inherent power to act without being seen. Not all people possess this power, but those who do may use it for the benefit of a group to which they belong, or they may use it selfishly for personal gain. The power of *itonga* may be used in several specific ways to cause illness in others: it may be used to consume their vitals (*-ly-*), to introduce foreign objects into their bodies (*-l dy-*), and to spear them in a mutual battle using this unseen power (*-las-*). Since Safwa believe that illness is caused fundamentally by a disruption in the social relationships of a group to which the sufferer belongs, these different ways of using *itonga* imply dissension within different kinds of groups, all of which are similar, however, in expressing their solidarity in terms of agnatic descent. The following discussion focuses solely on illnesses caused by *-ly-* and analyzes the consequences of introducing this etiological category into interpersonal and intergroup disputes.

If a divination to determine the cause of an illness results in a diagnosis of *-ly-*, those who have participated in the divination are saying in effect that there is someone within the patrilineage of the sufferer who does not cooperate, who is diminishing the personnel of the lineage. Thus a divination of *-ly-* at a séance immediately places the underlying dispute in the context of the patrilineal relationship. From that point, the effects of the divination are either to preserve the relationship or ultimately to sever it.

The major means of attempting a reconciliation is the convocation of a second divination. This occurs when a diviner and his clients agree not only on a diagnosis of *-ly-* but also on the name of the kinsman involved in such opprobrious behavior. If the kinsman is named, then a second divination is arranged and the supposed culprit is invited to attend. He is not told, however, that he is suspected of having inflicted *empongo* on the victim; he is simply informed that his attendance is requested at a divination for a member of his patrilineage.

Since a person is considered obligated to attend a divination only when requested to do so by either his headman or an agnatic kinsman, an agnate's response to this kind of request becomes a test both of his commitment to lineage unity and of the first divination. Thus, if the presumed culprit appears amicably at the divination, it shows that he *is* concerned about the affairs of his patrilineage and, therefore, that the delinquency implied in the first divination was only a temporary lapse. If, however, he either fails to appear or reacts angrily at the divination, the suspicions expressed in the original divination are vindicated.

Should the named kinsman appear at the second divination, one of three outcomes may occur: (1) the disputants may become reconciled, (2) they may henceforward fail to recognize their patrilineal relationship, or (3) they may vie with one another for public support of their position in the dispute. As we show, each of these outcomes can occur only through recognition of the patrilineal ethic of unity, which is introduced into the situation by the diagnosis of *-ly-*.

### Diagnoses Leading to Reconciliation

When patrilineal kinsmen come to a second divination, open discussion of the conflict situation may occur. It is difficult to estimate the actual proportion of these second séances which conclude in harmony, since divinations which implicate a co-member of one's patrilineage are never discussed in public.

Records of divinations kept at my request by two diviners supply our only clue to this proportion. Of the four diagnoses of *-ly-* in this sample, three resulted in a second séance before the same diviner. At the conclusion of the second séance in one of these cases, the protagonists agreed to perform rites to their ancestors to show that they were 'of one heart.' In one of the other two cases a reconciliation was also arranged but without the performance of a special rite. Thus, 50 percent of the diagnosed cases eventuated in ostensible resolution of conflict and mollification of ill feeling.

The following case history also indicates the revitalization of a feeling of 'one heart' after a séance prompted by a diagnosis of *-ly-*.

170

CASE I

There were three brothers in the community of Ipepete—Mamεngε, Empola, and Ndεni. Ndεni confided to me that in the past there had been bad feeling between his two older brothers. The source of this ill will was the division of their father's estate. Mamεngε, as the oldest brother, had been charged with this duty. Since Empola was serving as a conscript in World War II at the time his father died, he felt that he had not been consulted about the disposal of garden land. According to Ndεni, however, Mamεngε had kept the estate intact until Empola's return. From what I could establish, the disagreement centred around two fields in particular.

Mamεngε suffered from coughing spells and consulted a diviner about them. He was told that his brothers were jealous of him. At first he was given a medicine to rub on his face as protection against this, but when the symptoms continued, the diviner concluded that one of the brothers was consuming Mamεngε's vitals (-ly-). The brothers went together to the diviner, and there Empola confessed his anger against his brother. The reasons for the anger were discussed and settlement was reached about the fields. Ndεni claimed that since that time, "We are of one heart."

Thus, perhaps half the diagnoses of -ly- result in the reconciliation of disputing parties today. Moreover, this reconciliation is phrased in terms of a return to one heart, the patrilineal ethic. It is significant that these diagnoses are kept secret: dissension within a patrilineage should not be aired outside it if, in the upshot, the members are of "one heart." Indeed not even the headman need be informed when members of a patrilineage consult a diviner about a possible case of -ly- among them, nor need they inform him of the result of such a divination. It is undoubtedly this pressure toward secrecy which accounts for the infrequence (only one case out of nine) with which instances of -ly- that reached settlement are reported among the cases I gathered in the field.

**Diagnoses Leading to Lineage Fission**

Perhaps the most dramatic result of some diagnoses of -ly- is the avoidance of social contact among patrilineal kinsmen, which leads ultimately to fission of the lineage. Although none of our diviners' cases eventuated in this way, the following case from Ipepete recounts an outcome of this sort.

CASE II

Mwankoshi and Mwangonela were half-brothers from different mothers, who lived around the turn of the century. Although both were headmen, Mwankoshi, being the offspring of the first wife had greater authority than his brother. Mwangonela is said to have been jealous

and began to consume (-ly-) several of Mwankoshi's children. The matter was brought before a diviner and a poison ordeal showed that Mwangonela was guilty. Although he confessed and was thus spared, Mwankoshi burned his compound and those of all his followers. He drove them away, and all contact between the two lineage segments was severed for two generations. After that time a descendant of Mwangonela brought his family back to Ipepete to live, and the lineal bond was re-established.

A slightly more recent case of lineage fission occurred as a result of a dispute between two brothers, Ontewa and Mwanzumba.

CASE III

About 25 years ago there were two full brothers, Ontewa and Mwanzumba, living in Ipepete. Although both brothers reportedly got along well with Shabega, then headman of Ipepete, they quarreled frequently between themselves. The exact cause of the quarrel was difficult to ascertain, but several informants cited jealousy over Ontewa's closer relationship with Shabega as a reason. (This is probably a formula for expressing the cause of a disagreement which concluded in the manner of this one, the true reason having been forgotten by some informants and withheld by others.)

On several occasions when children of Ontewa died, Mwanzumba was held responsible. Friction between the two brothers was intense when one of Shabega's teenage sons died suddenly. A diviner accused Mwanzumba of having consumed (-ly-) him. Ontewa, with the backing of the headman and other elders, placed thorn branches across Mwanzumba's door, a sign that he was no longer welcome in the community. Mwanzumba left with his sons to settle in his mother's natal community.

In this case, Mwanzumba had disregarded several invitations to divinations for Ontewa's children, but it was not until Mwanzumba was charged with the death of the headman's son that a breach between the two brothers occurred formally. It would appear, therefore, that Ontewa needed the backing of the headman and other elders before he could initiate the break with Mwanzumba. Not until Mwanzumba was seen as attacking the community itself by consuming a son of the headman, the symbol of the community, did Ontewa command the support necessary to oust his brother.

In short, the severance of an incorporative (patrilineal) tie was accomplished after a diagnosis of -ly-, but only with community involvement as well. In Case III this involvement was elicited by a divination in which the offending kinsman was made responsible for the death of a member of the headman's family. In Case II community involvement (which was certainly necessary for Mwankoshi to have ousted not only his brother but "all his people" as well, to quote our informants' account) was elicited by the verdict of the poison ordeal. Although there are important differences between these two cases, the fact that the community became involved in both constitutes a striking similarity.

In this respect, therefore, a notable contrast exists between cases of -*ly*- which lead to reconciliation within the lineage and those which lead to fission. On the one hand, cases which lead to reconciliation definitely do not involve the community. (In fact, as we have seen, there are taboos against even speaking of these cases within the community.) On the other hand, cases which result in lineage fission do involve members of the community. Given this contrast, we might expect an interim effect of diagnoses of -*ly*- to be a situation in which the protagonists vie with one another for support within the community. We consider this effect next.

### Diagnoses Leading to Public Tests of Support

Although two instances in the diviners' records led to results of this sort, the following case provides a more detailed example. The genealogies will aid the reader in placing the protagonsits in the case (see Figure 1).

CASE IV

Mpembɛla was a man of *itonga* who had been ostracized from his natal community some time in the latter part of the nineteenth century. He came to Ipepete and was given land to settle there by Old Mwankoshi, then head of a branch of the chiefly lineage. Mwankoshi also gave Mpembɛla a wife, a Bungu girl, who had reputedly been found abandoned on a path after an Ngoni march

through Safwa country. Mpembɛla had a son Mwashitete who sometime later married the daughter of Mwankoshi's assistant. This couple's eldest son was Ntandala, a man of about sixty at the time of my fieldwork.

Mpembɛla's family prospered in Ipepete, and by the time Mwashitete became head of the lineage, they occupied a large stretch of land, called Mabandɛ, at the eastern edge of Onkoshi's territory. Mwashitete acquired many cattle during his lifetime and became a man of considerable renown in Mwanabantu territory. When he died some time in the late 1940's, Ntandala reputedly killed five head of cattle at the funeral ceremonies and interred his father with a bull—an animal usually reserved for burial only with headmen. Henceforth Ntandala began to run his sector of Ipepete like a separate community. He began by using his family fields as a communal field—that is, by holding communal beer drinks for all the people of Mabandɛ. He also began inviting other headmen to the ceremonies in honor of his ancestors, an act which could be interpreted as an assertion of membership in the reigning patrilineage. (It is possible that Mwashitete had preceded his son in some of these kinds of independent activities, although no overt strain in relations between Mpembɛla lineage and Onkoshi lineage occurred until Ntandala's time.)

At the time of Ntandala's push for acceptance as a headman in his own right, the headman of Ipepete and the elder of Onkoshi's lineage was Shabega. A junior branch of the lineage was headed by Lyandile, who was also chief under the British system of administration. Shabega was a traditionalist, whose power and position depended entirely on his status in the lineage and on his ability to carry out the roles of that status. Lyandile, on the other hand, was a dynamic personality who was aware of the political leverage his chiefly office gave him in the traditional system.

Some time in the mid-1940s Shabega's grandson, Ndele, the eldest son of his potential successor, became ill with an infected toe. A diviner said that Ntandala had produced the illness by means of a medicine. This was by no means the first divination implicating Ntandala in

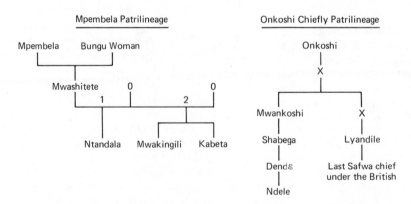

Figure 1.

172

illnesses among Shabega's branch of the lineage. Soon after this divination, Lyandile had Ntandala named to an office (Jumbe) in the British administrative system, but at the same time he curbed Ntandala's pretensions to membership in the chiefly lineage by joining Shabega in the practice of never attending any of Ntandala's ancestor rites. This practice was still maintained at the time of my fieldwork by all members of the Onkoshi minor lineage unless they were also affines of the Jumbe.

Ntandala himself gave me a genealogy in which he made Mpembɛla the son of Old Onkoshi. Many people in Ipepete did not question this interpretation when I asked them about it. To what extent some actually believed it or were simply withholding their beliefs from me, I was unable to determine. Only the last Safwa chief (Lyandile's son and replacement) would tell me openly that the genealogy was false and Ntandala was not a member of the chiefly lineage, although—as I pointed out already—other Onkoshi acted in terms of this fact by not attending Ntandala's ancestor rites.

*Incident 1: The Asthmatic Jumbe.* After Ntandala was appointed Jumbe, his half-brother Mwakingili (who was headman of a subsection of Mabandɛ) was said to have helped him considerably in his work. Ntandala suffered from asthma, and once when he was laid up with an attack, Mwakingili was said to have told people that he would soon take over Ntandala's job. The diviner who was called at that time named Mwakingili as the cause of the disease. The diviner summoned both Mwakingili and his younger brother Kabɛta to drink medicine to stop their half-brother's attacks. Kabɛta appeared, but Mwakingili refused to do so. After that occurrence Ntandala consulted several diviners, including the famous Chikanga in Malawi. All these men named Mwakingili as the culprit, but Mwakingili consistently refused to appear with Ntandala before a diviner. Furthermore, Kabɛta's compliance with Ntandala's request caused ill feeling to arise between the two full-brothers.

*Incident 2: A Mother's Death.* While I was in the field, the mother of Mwakingili and Kabɛta died. She was a very old woman, and informants in Ipepete considered her death to have resulted from old age. Significantly, however, in Mabandɛ an entirely different interpretation of the situation prevailed. About a week after the woman was buried, a rumor began to spread that Mwankingili had consumed (-ly-) his mother. So far as I could determine, the source of the rumor was Ntandala, though I never discovered the exact manner in which he initiated it.

*Incident 3: An Epidemic among Children.* Between mid-October and mid-December 1963 many children in the Magombɛ area died of either measles or chicken pox. In Ipepete alone I recorded six deaths, and many more children were ill. Dendɛ, Shabega's successor as headman of Ipepete, and senior elder of Onkoshi minor lineage after Lyandile's death, called a meeting at the edge of the sacred grove in Ipepete. A large crowd gathered

including all the headmen of the region. Dendɛ conducted the meeting and began by summoning the chiefly ancestors by name and presenting them with the usual list of grievances—the seeds did not germinate, the cows were dry, and women failed to bear children. He then pointed to the fact that many women were walking around with their breasts bared (a sign of mourning for a child), and the headmen present began to discuss the nature of the disease which was sweeping the country. After a brief and inconclusive argument about the exact illness, Dendɛ announced that any woman who knew of tabu sexual activities that were being practiced should report them to the headman.

He then asked each headman in turn if all was well in his community. When it came to Mabandɛ, a half-brother of both Ntandala and Mwakingili related a recent flare-up of the old conflict between his half-siblings. Mwakingili was said to have passed a remark that Ntandala was not a Safwa but a Bungu—a statement clearly designed to impugn his brother's right to either a headmanship or a jumbeship in Safwa territory. Ntandala had called a meeting of the elders of Mabandɛ to hear this charge, but in spite of witnesses' testimony to the contrary, Mwakingili denied ever making this allegation. He again denied the charge at the plenary meeting, and after further inconclusive wrangling, someone suggested that the day's proceedings continue, since this was not a matter which needed to be discussed in front of everyone. (*Enongwa ezyaxaya yakwɛ.* "It is a matter for his compound.")

When Ntaldala's asthma was attributed by divination to -*ly*- and Mwakingili refused to accompany his half-brother to any subsequent divinations, the disagreement between them remained unsettled. On the other hand, it did not lead to an open break between them either. Instead, the dispute became public and was aired periodically over the years—once at the death of Mwakingili's mother, again at a meeting of headmen to pray for the cessation of rain, again at the hearing following the name-calling incident, and still again at the meeting convoked as a result of the epidemic among the children.

This publicity converted the dispute from a private estrangement between brothers into a public test of power between them. Indeed, the hearing which Ntandala called in response to Mwakingili's alleged insult was little more than a demonstration of his own power. By attesting that Mwakingili had uttered the slight, the witnesses publicly proclaimed their alignment with Ntandala.

An additional public display of support occurred several months before the hearing over the insult, when Ntandala held an ancestor ceremony at his parents' graves. This ceremony was marked by the sacrifice of a special bull in order to mollify the ancestors' anger over the improper burial of the son of one of Ntandala's and Mwakingili's half-brothers. The fact that the half-brother sacrificed at Ntandala's rites publicized the friendship and alliance between these two. Many residents of the brothers' community who attended the rites also expressed support for Ntandala by their very presence at this assembly and not at a similar ceremony held by Mwakingili's about a month earlier.

That ceremony, in honor of Mwakingili's and Kabɛta's mother, had been an opportunity for people to show their alignment with Mwakingili. Since he and Kabɛta—who was Ntandala's ally—held separate but simultaneous rites, attendance at one of these rites to the exclusion of the other was an expression of support for the host.

Rather than taking sides publicly with either antagonist, however, many people attended all these ceremonies indiscriminately. For these people, who chose to remain uncommitted to one brother or the other, a knowledge of the dispute was nonetheless essential in enabling them to act appropriately neutral on all of these kinds of occasions.

For Ntandala himself the public dispute was more than a mere test of power with his brother. For him a greater political gain was at stake: his acceptance into the chiefly lineage. So long as this dispute continued to promote factionalism in his home community of Mabandɛ, there was a possibility that the headmen of other neighboring communities might intervene. And, as stated earlier, such intervention would have supported Ntandala's claim to membership in the chiefly lineage, since the only ground upon which headmen of other communities may customarily intervene is common descent.

The early onset of the rainy season in 1963 provided an event which almost brought about this intervention. Since an unexpected deviation from the normal rainfall pattern is believed to be caused by the anger of the chiefly ancestor spirits, and this anger is evoked primarily by wrangling in their homeland, the early rains led the living members of the chiefly lineage to try to stop any disputes in the land. As a result, a meeting of all headmen was convened in the sacred grove at Ipepete in order to stop dissension and thereby hold back the rains.

At this meeting the behavior of those who were "spoiling" the area was discussed at some length. The discussion concluded, however, with the phrase, "It is a matter for their own community (empaŋa)," the very statement which called a halt to discussions of this issue at the public meeting held

several months later in response to the epidemic among the children. This repeated statement by members of the chiefly lineage served two purposes: (1) it helped contain the dispute within the brothers' patrilineage, and (2) by inhibiting involvement of headmen in the quarrel, it frustrated Ntandala's hope of recognition as a member of the chiefly lineage.

In sum, when the dispute became public, it thereby became a focus for power politics. Both Ntandala and Mwakingili held ceremonies which enabled them to demonstrate their backing. In addition, Ntandala exploited the situation to further his personal goal of full acceptance into the chiefly lineage. On the other hand, those not directly involved in the dispute could use the public knowledge of its existence to regulate their own behaviour in terms of the power struggle, taking sides or not as they chose. Since our data, as we observed earlier, show that the community must become involved in an intralineage dispute before fission occurs, both Ntandala and Mwakingili seem to have been building support for such a break. No break occurred during our stay in the field, however, and the efforts of other headmen to contain the dispute within the lineage seem to have been responsible for this.

It is important to note that the ambiguous valuation of the power of *itonga*—the belief that it can be used for both philanthropic and misanthropic ends—is related to its use in these political circumstances, since it allows groups to polarize around their evaluation of the use of this power.

**Summary: The Consequences of Diagnoses of *-ly-***

What these data suggest is that a diagnosis of *-ly-* phrases a dispute squarely in terms of the agnatic status relationship between the antagonists. In other words, a divination of *-ly-* conveys two bits of information—(1) that there is a dispute, and (2) that the protagonists are agnates—rather than just the one bit conveyed by outright discussions of a disagreement. Once this nexus between a dispute and patrilineality has been established, the value of unity—the core concept of the lineal ideology—can be used to help induce settlement of the dispute.

I suggest that this procedure of conflict resolution is necessary because of the vagueness of the norms specifying one's obligations to one's lineal kin. These obligations are expressed in terms of "being of one heart," but the rules specifying the obligations which one must meet in order to comply with this injunction are indefinite. As a result, a particular instance of rule breaking or belligerence may be considered a violation of lineage ethics by some members and not by others. However, by allowing a dispute to become symbolized as a manifestation of *itonga* in the course of a divination, the clients make the connection between a particular dispute and the patrilineal status relationship—in short, they define the activity as a violation of patrilineal ethics.

Once this is done, the culprit becomes subject to the sanctions of the patrilineal status. He must then either demonstrate that he is in fact "of one heart" with his lineage or ultimately deny the patrilineal tie altogether. We have seen that these two alternatives form the opposite poles of response to a diagnosis of *-ly-*, with manipulation for support as the intervening response. Which one of the three responses will actually follow a particular diagnosis of *-ly-* is explainable in terms of ecological, demographic, economic, and political conditions. The concept of *-ly-* and its implication of the patrilineal bond between disputants, however, constitutes the structure within which these various organizational factors are worked out.

# 19 Ndembu Divination and Its Symbolism

## Victor W. Turner

In common with a number of contemporary anthropologists, Victor Turner has been concerned with the functions of symbols in cultural processes, especially various ceremonies (not necessarily segregated as to their "sacredness" or "secularness"). He has made a series of significant contributions to the data and theory of the study of rituals and symbols, which appear in a series of books: *The Drums of Affliction*, from which the present selection has been derived, *The Forest of Symbols* (1967), and *The Ritual Process* (1969), and many papers. For additional data on divination the reader is referred to Turner's (1969) *Ndembu Divination*. In most of his writings, Turner's data and interpretations are so abundant and teeming

Reprinted with abridgments from Victor W. Turner, 1968, *The Drums of Affliction,* Oxford: Clarendon Press and the International African Institute, Chap. II, "Divination and Its Symbolism," pp. 25–51, with permission of the author and the International African Institute (London).

with insights as almost to defy a brief commentary, and a lengthy one is clearly inappropriate here.

In this selection, from which copious illustrative material had to be omitted, Turner shows that precisely because of its sociocultural nature, divination is pregnant with meanings: the actions of all principals, especially the diviner; the events; the paraphernalia of divination; the setting; the very utterances, incantations, and interrogations. The aim of the Ndemu diviner is to uncover the hidden and unknown, especially when these lie at the root of personal and social misfortune. Ndembu divination is not oracular or prophetic, but, as the healing ritual itself, makes known, "albeit in symbolic guise, the unknown and invisible agents of affliction." The patient is not an isolated sufferer but a member of a social and cultural system in which sickness is perceived as the eruption in a single place of conflict and divisiveness in the system. Although, in fact, Ndembu social life is fraught with conflict and fear of conflict and spiritual or human (sorcery, witchcraft) attack, the ideal is just the opposite and the aim of these "redressive rituals" is to expose the sources of social division and redress the balance in social relations. Clearly, then, this model of divination is not only symbolic but structural. The aim of diagnosis and curing is to heal the wounds in the body politic, of which the patient is symbolically an individual expression.

The Ndembu are a matrilineal, virilocal society, now mainly dependent upon agriculture though they formerly depended mainly upon hunting, living in small, constantly shifting, matrilineal villages in Northwestern Zambia.

## INTRODUCTION

To give an adequate explanation of the meaning of ritual symbols, one has first to consider what kinds of circumstances tend to give rise to ritual performances, for these circumstances probably decide what sort of ritual is performed, and the goals of that ritual largely determine the meaning of the symbols used in it. The switchpoint between social crisis and performance of redressive ritual is the divinatory séance or consultation . . . .

Divination has certain affinities with judicial process, for it is vitally concerned with the customs and interests of persons in complex social situations. But it also prepares the way for the more rigidly standardized processes of redressive ritual. It is this mediating function that determines the cognitive and flexible qualities of its symbolism. . . . Divination and redressive ritual are stages in a single process that is peculiarly sensitive to changes, and especially breakages, in the network of existing social relations. Since they are "naturally" so closely involved with the micro-history of contemporary groups and personalities, they must be treated theoretically in conjunction with these. Life-crisis ritual, on the other hand, is less responsive to immediate social pressures and needs, since it is geared to the life-cycles of individuals, and therefore in its theoretical treatment the anthropologist may quite legitimately begin by analysing the cultural structure of these rites. This has many affinities with the social structure, but these are with social regularities which are deeply entrenched in custom, and not with those which are the product of transient alignments of economic and political interests. . . . No recourse is made to divination to find a propitious place and time for life-crisis rites. But all rituals of affliction are preceded by some recourse to divination, however perfunctory, and it is in the divinatory process that quarrels, competition, and alignments among people are brought to light. We should therefore follow the Ndembu in giving precedence, in our analysis, to the symbolism and procedures of divination.

## DIVINATION AND ITS SYMBOLISM

Among Ndembu, the diviner regards his task as the practical one of revealing the causes of misfortune or death. These are almost invariably "mystical" or "non-empirical" in character, although human wishes, desires, and feelings are involved.

The diviners disclose what has happened, and do not foretell future events. Unlike many Southern Bantu diviners, they are seldom oracular or mantic. Furthermore, they do not inaugurate the divinatory process, but wait until clients come to consult them. Modes of divination are regarded as instruments which both detect lies and discover truth, although, since they are operated by fallible men, their verdicts are not always accepted without question. For witches are credited with extraordinary powers of deception, and even great diviners fortify themselves with special medicines to combat the deceits and illusions sent by their secret antagonists to baffle them. One such medicine is used at the first stage of a consultation. A clearing is made in the bush about half a mile from the diviner's village. Two poles are inserted in the ground, and a third placed on them to make a frame resembling goalposts. On this are placed three head-pads (mbung'a), similar to those worn by women when they carry heavy loads. These are made of a special

kind of grass called kaswamang'wadyi. Etymologically, this term is derived from ku-swama, "to hide", and ng'wadyi, "the bare-throated francolin", a bird like a partridge, much prized as a food, that loves to conceal itself in this long fine grass. In hunting cults the grass is used as a symbol for the desired invisibility of the hunter when he stalks game. Here it stands for the witch's attempts to conceal vital matters from the diviner. I translate a text given me by a diviner, explaining the meaning of the head-pad. "The head-pad is a sign to the diviner not to forget anything, for he must not be ignorant of anything. A witch or sorcerer [muloji means both] could use medicine to deceive the diviner [chitahu or mukwakuhong'a], or hide things from him. The head-pad is medicine to prevent this, for it keeps the diviner wide awake, it is a reminder to him. The grass in it is twisted, like the witch's attempts to deceive." Under the frame must pass the diviner's clients, who may unwittingly harbour a sorcerer or witch in their ranks. The medicine may expose him to the diviner.

Another medicine used by diviners, and kept by them in small calabashes (malembu) while they divine, is a nerve from the root of an elephant's tusk. In ritual contexts this is called nsomu. Because it resembles a limp penis, it often has the meaning of masculine impotence. In divination it has the further meaning of a sorcerer, for sorcerers are believed to be able to blast the fertility of their victims. They are also believed to be able to kill them. Nsomu is also a suitable symbol for death, since impotence is regarded as a kind of death. When an impotent man dies, a black line is drawn with charcoal from his navel downwards and over his genitals, indicating that his name, and with it certain vital elements of his personality, must never be inherited by the children of his kin. This is social death. Known sorcerers are treated in the same fashion. . . .

I have cited these texts at length, for two reasons. The first is to demonstrate how readily and explicitly diviners are able to offer interpretations of their symbols. The second is to exhibit an important variation on a theme which pervades all Ndembu ritual, that of "bringing into the open what is hidden or unknown". This variation has the special sense of "exposing deception and secret malice". The main theme of "revealing the hidden" is exemplified in all cults to cure persons afflicted by the shades with disease, reproductive disorders, or bad luck at hunting. The cure is essentially a process of what Ndembu call "making known and visible" (ku-solola or ku-mwekesa), albeit in symbolic guise, the unknown and invisible agents of affliction. This is brought about in various ways. One way is by mentioning the shade's name in prayer and invocation (*ku-tena ijina damukishi*). The belief is that the spirit is aggrieved because it has been forgotten, not only by the victim, but also by many of its other kin. It afflicts its living kinsman, sometimes in his personal capacity, but often in his capacity as representative of a kin-group. If, however, it is mentioned, and hence remembered, by many people, it will cease to afflict and will henceforward benefit its victim, who becomes a sort of living memorial to it. Another way is through representing the shade in some kind of material form, either as a figurine named after it, or as a contraption of branches covered with a blanket whitened with cassava meal. These representations are made at the end of protracted rituals, in sacred sites which only cult-adepts may enter, called *masoli* (from the verb *ku-solola*, "to make visible" or "reveal"). It is said that when the spirit is afflicting its victim, it is concealed in his or her body. This is thought especially to be the case where women suffer from some reproductive disorder. But when the spirit has been adequately represented in symbolic form, and frequently named, it is believed to emerge, reconciled with the victim and his whole kin-group.

The Ndembu term for "symbol" itself contains the implication of a revelatory process. This term is *chinjikijilu*, and is derived from *ku-jikijila*, "to blaze a trail" in the bush. When hunters set out on expeditions into the deep bush (perhaps into thick *Cryptosepalum* forest), they cut marks on trees, and also break and bend over their lower branches to indicate the way back. The blaze or landmark, in other words, leads from unknown, and therefore in Ndembu experience as well as belief, from dangerous territory to known and familiar surroundings, from the lonely bush to the populated village. Ritual symbols have a similar function, for they give a visible form to unknown things; they express in concrete and familiar terms what is hidden and unpredictable. They enable men to domesticate and manipulate wild and wayward forces.

When the diviner confronts witchcraft, he seeks to expose secret deceit and malice, to reveal the identity and the motives of sorcerers and witches. This aim shapes much of the symbolism of divination. Leaving aside the personal acuity of the diviner, the symbols he uses reveal how Ndembu have come to stereotype certain forms of fraudulent and malevolent behaviour. Ndembu have many types of divination. . . . Here I am concerned

with one mode of divination only, since it brings out most clearly the stereotyping of hidden malice, as well as certain other characteristics of divinatory symbolism shortly to be discussed.

This is called by Ndembu *ng'ombu yakusekula*, literally "divination by shaking up or tossing (objects in a basket)". The diviner keeps a set of anything from twenty to thirty objects, of various shapes, sizes, and colours, in a round basket with a lid. When he divines he places these objects in a round flat open basket (*lwalu*), of the type used by women to winnow millet, shakes them, and throws them up so that they form a heap at the far side of the basket. He examines the top three or four objects, individually, in combination, and with reference to their relative height in the heap. . . . His skill as an individual lies in the way in which he adapts his general exegesis of the objects to the given circumstances. For he is usually confronted by a group of kin who wish to find out which particular ancestor, sorcerer, or witch is causing the sickness or misfortune of their relative. Ndembu believe that this group itself may contain sorcerers or witches. In reality, as the diviner well knows, it may contain rival factions, one of which may stand to benefit by the death of the sick person if the latter holds office or is wealthy. If his clients wish him to divine into the cause of a death, the situation is still more serious. In the past, before witchcraft and witch-finding were declared illegal by the British Administration, such consultations took place near the most important village in the neighbourhood cluster of villages where the deceased person lived. Everyone in the neighbourhood was expected to attend, and failure to do so was a cause of suspicion. The diviner had to make a sound appraisal of the balance of power between rival factions interested in the death who were present at the public gathering. If he did not, and gave an unpopular verdict, he was likely to be in some danger himself. Many diviners sought the protection of a chief and performed near his capital village. But I have been told of several diviners who, despite such protection, were speared to death by angry kin of the persons declared to be sorcerers.

The winnowing basket itself stands for the sifting of truth from falsehood. The diviner is believed to be possessed by the spirit of a diviner-ancestor, in a particular manifestation known as *Kayong'u*. *Kayong'u* is also said to be a "man-slayer" (*kambanji*), because people may be slain as a result of a divining decision. It is the *Kayong'u* spirit which causes the diviner to tremble, and thus to shake the basket. Before becoming a diviner he must have been afflicted by this spirit, which causes asthmatic shortness of breath and makes him tremble violently while being washed with medicine. He is treated by a cult-group led by a famous diviner. Many of the symbols of the *Kayong'u* ritual stand for the "sharpness" which he must display as a diviner. These include needles and razors, the former being embedded in the hearts of a sacrificed cock and goat. When the diviner trembles and breathes heavily he is said to be feeling the pricking of the needle, which itself symbolizes the *Kayong'u* spirit, in his heart, lungs, and liver. After he has been treated, the novice-diviner apprentices himself to an established diviner, who teaches him the meanings of the objects in a diviner's basket. The established diviner encourages the novice to divine himself, criticizes his performance, and gives him some of his own equipment. He enlists the aid of a professional wood-carver to make others . . . .

I have information on twenty-eight divinatory symbols. Their total range of meaning embraces the whole sorry story of misfortune, loss, and death in Ndembu life, and of the mean, selfish, revengeful motives believed to be responsible for these afflictions (Junod 1927:571). Since so few objects represent so many things, it is not surprising to find that each of them has many meanings . . . .

The symbolic items are called by Ndembu, *tuponya* (singular: *kaponya*). Some are further designated as *ankishi* (singular: *nkishi*). These are figurines representing generalized human beings in various postures. The root *-kishi* is found in the term for ancestor spirit *mu-kishi*, and in the term for the masks and costumes used at circumcision and funerary rituals, *makishi* (singular: *i-kishi*). The general sense underlying these various meanings seems to be some kind of mystical power associated with human beings, alive or dead. Here I will discuss three figurines or *ankishi*, and seven other divinatory objects or *tuponya*. Both classes have reference to human activity and purpose. Some represent structural features in human life, aspects of the cultural landscape, principles of social organization and social groups and categories, and dominant customs regulating economic, sexual, and social life. Others represent forces or dynamic entities, such as motives, wishes, desires, and feelings. Not infrequently the same symbol expresses both an established custom, and a set of stereotyped disputes and forms of competition that have developed around it. It is roughly true that the human figurines represent social and emotional stereotypes; while many of the other

objects refer specifically to Ndembu structure and culture.

The same *tuponya* are used in different stages of a consultation, and the meaning of each symbolic item may change somewhat at each stage. Rather than follow a consultation through, stage by stage, I will present excerpts from texts about some *tuponya* and analyse those excerpts which exemplify their use at some stages and not at others . . . .

. . . Let us now examine the human figurines or *ankishi*. The most important of these is a group of three, clipped together in a band of horn, representing a man, a woman, and a child. These are called either simply *ankishi*, "figurines" or *Akulumpi*, "the Elders". The prefix *A-* here implies that the figures are invested with some animate quality. They are "Elders" in several senses. In the first place, they are the most important of the *tuponya*, the focal point of reference, so to speak, in the whole set. In the second place, they represent a chief and his kin. The male figurine is compared with *Mwantiyanvwa*, the title of the great Lunda king in the Congo, from whose kingdom the Ndembu, like many other Central African tribes, are said to have migrated about two hundred and fifty to three hundred years ago. If, when the diviner is trying to detect a sorcerer, a piece of red clay in a container of mongoose skin, representing "enmity" or "a grudge", comes persistently to the top of the set with "the Elders", this means that the sorcerer belongs to the close kin of a chief, or might even be a chief himself. In the third place, "the Elders" might represent a headman and his kin, depending upon the question asked. If a thin circlet of iron, called *Lukanu* and representing the bracelet worn among Ndembu only by Senior Chief Kanongesha, repeatedly comes to the top with "the Elders", this means that either Kanongesha or his close kin played an important role in the situation divined into. Or if a lump of white clay (*mpemba* or *mpeza*) were to rise with them when sorcery was being investigated, this would mean that Kanongesha and his kin were innocent. Again, the diviner might himself specify that "the Elders" stood for a particular matrilineage (*ivumu*), perhaps that descended from the dead person's own mother's mother. He might ask "Did the enmity come from this lineage?" If then "the Elders" came to the top three times, associated, for example, with red clay and another object called *Chanzang'ombi*, in the form of a wooden snake with a human face, representing a sorcery-familiar called *ilomba*, this would be proof that a male member of that lineage was the sorcerer, and had killed because he had a grudge against his victim. . . .

. . . What is interesting in terms of social relations is that the man, woman, and child, comprising "the Elders", are not primarily regarded as an elementary family, although they can be specified as such, but as co-members of a matrilineage—not necessarily brother, sister and sister's child, but interlinked in any way the diviner cares to designate. All kinds of groups, relationships, and differences of status can be expressed by this symbol doing all kinds of things. Divinatory symbols are multireferential, and their referents are highly autonomous and readily detachable from one another. Ritual symbols proper are much more highly condensed; their meanings interpenetrate and fuse, giving them greater emotional resonance.

The second figurine we shall consider is called *Chamutang'a*. It represents a man sitting huddled up with chin on hands and elbows on knees. *Chamutang'a* means an irresolute, changeable person . . . .

It is obvious that from one point of view diviners use *Chamutang'a* in their professional interest. They state firmly that, if someone falls ill, people should have speedy recourse to a diviner. Poverty is no excuse. On the other hand, the employment of this symbol asserts certain pervasive social values. People should put the care of their kin before all selfish considerations. Sins of omission in this respect are almost as bad as sins of commission, such as sorcery. Again, people should make up their minds quickly to do their duty; they should not equivocate. . . .

Diviners sometimes use *Chamutang'a* to withdraw from the awkward situation that may arise if they cannot enlist the unanimous agreement of their clients for their judgements. One client may deny the diviner's imputation that he is a sorcerer, others may support him, others, again, may say that they are not certain about it, and yet others may assert that the divination itself was false, perhaps because of the interference of a witch. In such situations, *Chamutang'a* is liable to come uppermost in the basket. The diviner asks *Chamutang'a*: "What have you come here for? Does this mean that my divination is in error?" If it appears two or three times running, the diviner "closes down" the divination (*wajika jing'ombu*), demanding from those who have come to consult him a couple of pieces of cloth for his trouble. The diviner tries to salve his reputation by blaming his clients for the failure, and tells them that the witch in their midst is trying to confuse his verdict. This is one of the sanctions against lack of unanimity in response to a diviner's queries and statements (*nyikunyi*).

The other figurine normally used by diviners is an effigy of a man in the traditional posture of grief with both hands clasped to his head. It is called *Katwambimbi* (from *ku-twa*, "to pound" and *mbimbi*, "weeping"). It means the "one who inaugurates the mourning" when someone dies. *Kutwa* is used here with reference to the position of the two hands on the head, analogous to hands on a pounding pole. The primary sense is "the one who brings news of death" to the relatives of the deceased. . . .

But *Katwambimbi* has another and, if anything, more sinister meaning. In the words of one informant: "*Katwambimbi* is a mischief-maker (*kakobukobu*) who carries tales from one person to another, claiming that each hates and is trying to bewitch the other. If one of them is induced to kill the other by witchcraft or sorcery, *Katwambimbi* is the one who weeps the loudest at the wake, although he is the one who has the greatest guilt. . . ." In Ndembu custom a person divined as a *Katwambimbi* receives the same punishment as a sorcerer or witch. In the past it was death by burning, or ostracism from Ndembu society with confiscation of property; today, banishment from village and neighbourhood. . . .

On the face of it, divinatory symbols seem to reflect explicit human purposes. They are used to enable diviners to discover the causes of misfortune, and to suggest possible remedies. The diviner, as I have said, behaves in an astute and rational way, given his axiomatic beliefs in spirits, mystical forces, and witches. He is not above a certain low cunning at times, as we saw with regard to his manipulation of the figurine *Chamutang'a*. Nevertheless, the bases of his craft are rooted in mystical beliefs, and he is himself a believer. Without belief, I feel that he would not possess insight into Ndembu social life, which is governed by values with which he largely identifies himself. I say "identifies" advisedly, since the diviner himself believes that he harbours in his body the *Kayong'u* shade-manifestation, which, more than any other manifestation, is believed to detect breach of norm, rebellion against, or deviation from, Ndembu moral prescriptions. The shade is using the diviner's sharp wits on behalf of Ndembu society. That is why a diviner must be in a fit moral condition before he undertakes a consultation. For example, he must be sexually continent for some time before and during the period in which he is divining. He must avoid many foods. He must not harbour malice in his heart against anyone, as this would bias his judgment. . . .

The diviner feels that he is not primarily operating on his own behalf, but on behalf of his society. At divinations, the physiological stimuli provided by drummings and singing, the use of archaic formulae in questions and responses, together with the concentration demanded by his divining technique, take him out of his everyday self and heighten his intuitive awareness: he is a man with a vocation. He also measures actual behaviour against ideals. As we have seen, several of the symbols he manipulates owe something of their meaning to values attached to openness, honesty and truthfulness. One of his avowed aims is to make known and intelligible in Ndembu terms what is unknown and unintelligible. Underlying his task is the presumption that unless people bring their grudges and rancours into the open, "into the public eye", these will fester and poison the life of a group. Shades afflict the living with misfortune to bring such hidden struggles sharply to the attention of members of disturbed groups before it is too late. The diviner can then recommend that a cult-association be called in to perform ritual which will not only cure an individual patient, but also heal disturbances in the group. But where animosities have become deep and cankered, they become associated with the lethal power of witchcraft. The malignant individual himself becomes a social canker. At this point it is little use trying to cure the selfish or envious sorcerer or witch. He must be extirpated, rooted out of the group, at whatever cost to those of his kin who love him or depend on him. I am satisfied that some diviners, at any rate, are convinced that they are performing a public duty without fear or favour. It is a grave responsibility to be possessed by the *Kayong'u* shade and become a diviner. For henceforth one is not entirely one's own man. One belongs to society, and to society as a whole, and not to one or other of its structured subgroups.

The diviner is a ratiocinating individual. But the premises from which he deduces consequences may be non-rational ones. He does not try to "go behind" his beliefs in supernatural beings and forces. That is why divinatory objects are better classed with symbols than with signs, although they have some of the attributes of the latter. He treats as self-evident truths what social anthropologists and depth psychologists would try to reduce to rational terms. These scholars, in their professional role at any rate, do not concede that spirits and witches have existence. For most of them these entities are themselves "symbols" for endopsychic or social drives and forces, which they set themselves the task of discovering.

Certain distinctions can be made between divinatory symbolism and the symbolism of rituals of life-crisis and affliction. In the former, the cognitive aspect is much more pronounced; in the latter, the orectic aspect, that concerned with feelings and desires, is clearly dominant. The diviner, granted his premises—which are shared by his consultants—is trying to grasp consciously and bring into the open the secret, and even unconscious, motives and aims of human actors in some situation of social disturbance. In the public ritual of the Ndembu, symbols may be said to stimulate emotions. Both kinds of symbols have multiple meanings, but in ritual symbols proper those *significata* which represent charged phenomena and processes, such as blood, milk, semen, and faeces, are fused and condensed with *significata* which stand for aspects of social virtue, such as matriliny, marriage, chieftainship, etc., or virtues such as generosity, piety towards the ancestors, respect for the elders, manly uprightness, and so on. The emotional, mainly physiological, referents may well lend their qualities to the ethical and normative referents so as to make what is obligatory desirable. They seem, as Sapir wrote, to "send roots down into the unconscious", and, I would add, to bring sap up to the conscious.

But the semantic structure of divinatory symbols shows that the senses possessed by a symbol are not so much "fused" as sharply distinguished. Their semantic structure has "brittle segmentation". I mean by this that a divinatory symbol possesses a series of senses, only one of which is relevant at a time, i.e. at an inspection of a configuration of symbols. An important symbol in a ritual of affliction or of life-crisis is felt to represent *many things at once*; all its senses are simultaneously present. Divinatory symbols may, therefore, be called "analytical", and ritual symbols "synthetical". The former are used to discriminate between items that have become confused and obscure; the latter represent fusions of many apparently disparate items. The brittle segmentation of divinatory symbols may be because the same symbols are used in a series of enquiries, each of which has its one specific aim—such as to discover a relationship between witch and victim, or to find a motive for ensorcelling, or to seek out the precise mode of shade-affliction, and so on. The meaning of each individual symbol is subordinated to the meaning of a configuration of symbols, and each configuration is a means to a clearly defined and conscious end.The system of meanings possessed by the ritual symbol proper derives both from some deep and universal human need or drive and from a universal human norm controlling that drive. A divinatory symbol, on the other hand, helps the diviner to decide what is right and wrong, to establish innocence or guilt in situations of misfortune, and to prescribe well-known remedies. His role falls between that of a judge and that of a ritual expert. But, whereas a judge enquires into conscious motives, a diviner often seeks to discover unconscious impulses behind anti-social behaviour. To discover these he uses intuition as much as reason. He "feels after" the stresses and sore points in relationships, using his configurations of symbolic objects to help him concentrate on detecting the difficulties in configurations of real persons and relationships. Both he and they are governed by the axiomatic norms of Ndembu society. Thus the symbols he uses are not mere economical devices for purposes of reference, i.e. "signs", but have something of the "subliminal" quality of ritual symbols proper. With their aid he can say, for instance, that a shade is "making her granddaughter ill because the people of such-and-such a village are not living well with one another", or that "a man killed his brother by sorcery because he wanted to be headman". With the aid he can prescribe remedial ritual measures. But he cannot diagnose the empirical causes of social "divisiveness" (Beals and Siegel 1966), any more than of sickness or death. The diviner's conscious knowledge and control is limited by supra-conscious social and moral forces and by unconscious biophysical forces. Yet divinatory symbols are as close to "signs" as they are to Jung's "symbols", pregnant with unknown meaning.

## DIVINATION AS A PHASE IN A SOCIAL PROCESS

Divination is a phase in a social process which begins with a person's death or illness, or with reproductive trouble, or with misfortune at hunting. Informal or formal discussion in the kinship or local group of the victim leads to the decision to consult a diviner. The actual consultation or séance, attended by the victim's kin and/or neighbours, is the central episode in the process. It is followed by remedial action according to the diviner's verdict, action which may consist of the

destruction or expulsion of a sorcerer/witch, or of the performance of ritual by cult specialists to propitiate or exorcise particular manifestations of shades, or of the application of medicines according to the diviner's prescription by a leech or medicine man.

Death, disease and misfortune are usually ascribed to tensions in the local kin group, expressed as personal grudges charged with the mystical power of sorcery or witchcraft, or as beliefs in the punitive action of ancestor spirits. Diviners try to elicit from their clients responses which give them clues to the current tensions in their groups of origin. Divination, therefore, becomes a form of social analysis, in the course of which hidden conflicts are revealed so that they may be dealt with by traditional and institutionalized procedures. It is in the light of this function of divination as a mechanism of social redress that we must consider its symbolism, the social composition of its consultative sessions, and its procedures of interrogation.

We must always remember that the standards against which social harmony and disharmony are assessed are those of Ndembu culture and not of Western social science. They are those of a society which, possessing only a rudimentary technology and limited empirical skills and knowledge, consequently has a low degree of control over its material environment. It is a society highly vulnerable to natural disasters, such as disease, infant mortality, and intermittent food shortages. Furthermore, its ethical yardsticks are those of a community composed of small residential groups of close kin. Since kinship guides co-residence and confers rights to succeed to office and inherit property, the major problems of Ndembu society bear on the maintenance of good relations between kin, and on the reduction of competition and rivalry between them. Furthermore, since persons of incompatible temperaments and characters are frequently forced into daily propinquity by kinship norms which enjoin respect and co-operation among them, inter-personal hostilities tend to develop that are forbidden direct expression. Hidden grudges (*yitela*) rankle and grow, as Ndembu are well aware. In the idiom of Ndembu culture these grudges are associated with the mystical power of sorcery/witchcraft.

Ndembu themselves list jealousy, envy, greed, pride, anger, lust, and the desire to steal as causes of discord in group life, and these vices are by no means unfamiliar to us. Nevertheless, these symptoms of a disordered human nature spring from a specific social structure. In their attempts to diminish the disastrous consequences of these "deadly sins" in social life, Ndembu bring into operation institutionalized mechanisms of redress that are ordered towards the maintenance of that social structure. Divination, as we have seen, is one of those mechanisms, and in it we can observe many idiosyncratic features.

In the first place, the diviner clearly knows that he is investigating within a social context of a particular type. He first establishes the location of the Senior Chief's area, then that of the Sub-chief's, then the vicinage, and finally the village of the victim. Each of these political units has its own social characteristics—its factional divisions, its inter-village rivalries, its dominant personalities, its nucleated and dispersed groups of kindred—each possessing a history of settlement or migration. An experienced diviner will be familiar with the contemporary state of these political systems from previous consultations and from the voluminous gossip of wayfarers. Next he finds out the relationship between the victim and those who have come to consult him. He is assisted in this task by his knowledge of the categories of persons who typically make up the personnel of a village: the victim's matrilineal kin, his patrilateral kin, his affines, and unrelated persons. He finds out the victim's relationship to the headman, and he then focuses his attention on the headman's matrilineage, and discovers into how many sub-lineages it may be segmented.

By the time he has finished his interrogation, he has a complete picture of the current structure of the village, and of the position occupied in it by the victim and by those who came to consult him. Since it is common for representatives of each of its important segments, as well as affines of members of its matrilineal nucleus, to visit a diviner in the event of an important man's death, and since these representatives may not make the same responses to key questions, the diviner does not have to look far for indications of structural cleavages in the village. Diviners are also aware that there is a general association between the kind of misfortune about which he is consulted, the sex of the victim, the composition of the group of clients, and the size and structure of the political or residential unit from which they come. Thus only a few close kin or affines will normally consult a diviner about a woman's barrenness or a hunter's bad luck. But a large party, representative of all segments of a Sub-chiefdom, will come to him when a Sub-chief dies. This association does not always hold true,

however, for the death or even illness of a child may sometimes be taken as the occasion to bring into the open the dominant cleavage in a large village if the time is felt to be ripe. But diviners have learnt by experience—their own and their society's, incorporated in divinatory procedure and symbolism— to reduce their social system to a few basic principles and factors, and to juggle with these until they arrive at a decision that accords with the views of the majority of their clients at any given consultation.

They are guided, however, not by an objective analysis of the social structure, but rather by an intuition into what is just and fitting in terms both of Ndembu moral values and an ethical code which would be recognized as valid by all human groups. Just as Africans have been shown to operate in their judicial processes with the universally recognized concept of the "reasonable man" (Gluckman 1955) or "man of sense", so do they operate in their divinatory processes with the universally recognized concept of the "good man" or "moral man", *muntu wamuwahi*. This is the man who bears no grudges, who is without jealousy, envy, pride, anger, covetousness, lust, greed, etc., and who honours his kinship obligations. Such a man is open, he has "a white liver", he has nothing to conceal from anyone, he does not curse his fellows, he respects and remembers his ancestors. The diviner looks for sorcerers and witches among those who do not measure up to this standard of morality. Indeed, he looks for them among the positive transgressors, among those whom his clients admit to be wrongdoers or "slippery customers". In the cases of illness, infertility, and bad luck at hunting, he applies the same measures of the "moral man" to individuals, although he also applies the yardstick of the "moral group", which lives in mutual amity and collectively reveres its ancestors and respects political authorities. But here it would seem he is on the look out not so much for "mortal sins" as for "venial sins", for grudges that have not grown murderous, for offences that may yet be forgiven, for quarrels that have not yet split up a group. . . .

. . . Thus the diviner has to take into account both the specific structure of Ndembu society and a set of moral values and norms. Both these referents are represented in the symbolism of divination. The symbols are mnemonics, reminders of certain general rubrics of Ndembu culture, within which the diviner can classify the specific instance of behaviour that he is considering. Moreover, they have to be of such a nature as to lend themselves to configurational analysis. It is the *constellation* of symbols rather than the individual symbol which forms the typical unit of interpretation. A symbol may appear as a substantive, and in this role it may possess, say, half a dozen basic senses. By noting the reactions of the clients and attenders, the diviner can make a guess, or "formulate a hypothesis", which will enable him to establish the particular sense of the substantive symbol: he can then allocate senses to the modifiers. Here the vagueness and flexibility of the series of referents of each symbol leave him free to make a detailed interpretation of the configuration of symbols corresponding to the diagnosis he is making of the state of relationships between his clients and the deceased, and between the living kin concerned in the matter. And once he has established a *chidimbu*, a definite point of divination, and obtained agreement on its veracity or likelihood, he has a point of departure for further enquiry, something firm to go on. He may then deduce logical consequences from the *chidimbu*, regarded as a set of premises. Furthermore, he has established a certain psychological ascendancy over his audience, so that they tend to become less guarded in their replies, for with growing credulity in his divinatory powers they become more eager to give him the hard data he requires. I believe that this is one of the reasons why a basket-diviner tries to find the name of the deceased quite early in the seance. Diviners, as we have seen, have learnt that the vast majority of Ndembu names can be classified under relatively few main heads—"water", "hoofed animals", "chieftainship", etc., and after the manner of the English party game, "Twenty Questions", they can quickly proceed from the general to the particular. In a society not specially remarkable for its power of abstract thinking, the diviner's ability to do this must appear little short of miraculous. When the diviner names the deceased, therefore, he has won the credulity of his audience to such an extent that he can elicit key information without much difficulty. In other words, the logician is felt to be a magician.

It may be said in conclusion that the diviner occupies a central position with reference to several fields of social and cultural relationships. He acts as a mechanism of redress and social adjustment in the field of local descent groups, since he locates areas and points of tension in their contemporary structures. Furthermore, he exonerates or accuses individuals in those groups in terms of a system of moral norms. Since he operates in emotionally charged situations, such norms are restated in a striking and memorable fashion. Thus he may be said to play a vital role in upholding tribal morality. Moral law is most vividly made known through its breach. Finally, the diviner's role is pivotal to the system of rituals of affliction and anti-witchcraft/sorcery rituals, since he decides what kind of ritual should be performed in a given instance, when it should be performed, and sometimes who should perform it. Since diviners are consulted on many occasions, it is clear that their role as upholders of tribal morality and rectifiers of disturbed social relationships—both structural and contingent—is a vital one in a society without centralized political institutions.

# 20 The Diagnosis of Disease Among the Subanun of Mindanao

## *Charles O. Frake*

This paper has achieved something of the status of a minor classic in the decade and a half since its original publication, if one may judge from the frequency of its citation and selection for anthologies. It was one of the early studies in what has come to be called *ethnoscience* or the "new ethnography" or, when the focus is mainly on the indigenous meaning of the material under observation, *ethnosemantics*. This approach assumes that culture consists of, among other things, shared cognitive consensuses about the nature of the universe in which a society finds itself, or, as Sturtevant (1964) phrases it, ". . . an important aspect of culture is made up of the principles by which a people classify their universe." As Sturtevant goes on to say, this is hardly a new point of view in anthropology, but what ethnoscience attempts to do is provide a methodology and a set of models for more systematically discovering such principles from the perspective of the native, as uncontaminated as possible by the cultural constraints and ethnocentric categories of the observer. It makes no sense, say the ethnosemanticists, to impose external or "objective" categories of meaning and function upon the data of an observed society since this may not be at all the way the group structures its world. At the very least, the traditional "etic" approach of anthropology will distort the picture of the culture since it will not be consonant with the way the people themselves

Reprinted with abridgments from Charles O. Frake, 1961, "The Diagnosis of Disease Among the Subanun of Mindanao," *American Anthropologist, 63*: 113–132, with permission of the author and the American Anthropological Association.

perceive, structure, divide, and articulate their universe. These cognitions may only be elicited carefully through special methods and techniques that have been spelled out in a series of papers (Sturtevant 1964, Frake 1962, Spradley 1972), utilizing a number of organizational principles and categories such as semantic domains, terminological systems, levels of contrast, and so on. (An interesting question might be the extent to which these very principles are artifacts or elements of the culture of the ethnoscientist, or the way *he* structures the way people classify the universe.)

Whatever one thinks of ethnoscience—and ethnologists have tended to become polarized in regard to their position on it—Frake's paper is a contribution to our knowledge about the diagnosis and classification of disease in one Southeast Asian culture. Unlike the previous papers in this book, Frake sees diagnosis not so much as a sociocultural but as a cognitive process. As he puts it, "Diagnosis—the decision of what 'name' to apply to an instance of 'being sick,'—is a pivotal cognitive step in the selection of culturally appropriate responses to illness by the Subanun." The knowledge one thus obtains clearly yields a dimension of ethnographic knowledge that would not be as readily or fully available to us by using the more traditional datacollecting methods of ethnologists. Still, such a study may tend selectively to ignore systems of interaction and transaction that are the very marrow of a social structure. As Fried (1968:82) has stated, "Indeed the result of such a formulation is to raise the question, what is reality? Specifically, is reality the environment or is it the perception of the environment?" As the reader will already know from my comments on Glick's paper in Chapter 5, I would favor ideally a combined emic-etic approach to the study of medical systems. The ethnosemanticists have made their impact, even upon their critics, and I presume that in the future, as the controversies dissipate, field ethnographers will want to use the best of both approaches.

Although my original field work among the Eastern Subanun, a pagan people of the southern Philippines, was focused on a study of social structure, I found it exceedingly difficult to participate in ordinary conversations, or even elicit information within the setting of such conversations, without having mastered the use of terminologies in several fields, notably folk botany and folk medicine, in which I initially had only marginal interest. Effective use of Subanun botanical and medical terminologies required more knowledge of verbal behavior than linguists typically include in their conception of a structural description. To generate utterances which were grammatical (Chomsky 1957:13–17) but not necessarily meaningful or congruent (Joos 1958) did not suffice. Yet descriptive linguistics provides no

methods for deriving rules that generate statements which are semantically as well as grammatically acceptable. Having acquired only an unsystematic and intuitive "feel" for the use of certain portions of the Subanun lexicon during a first field study, I attempted during a second study a more rigorous search for meanings. This investigation became a major focus of my field work. Presented here is a partial analysis of one of the less numerous terminologies: 186 'disease names.' (Single quotation marks enclose *glosses*, English labels which substitute for, *but do not define*, Subanun terms.)

## THE SUBANUN

Some 50,000 Eastern Subanun inhabit the eastern portion of Zamboanga Peninsula, a 130 milelong extension of the island of Mindanao in the Philippines. Most of this population practices swidden farming in the mountainous interior of the peninsula, leaving the coasts to Christian immigrants of recent decades from the Bisayan Islands to the north. Prior to this century the coasts were controlled, and sporadically occupied, by Philippine Moslems, who established an exploitative hegemony over the pagan Subanun in certain locales (Christie 1909; Frake 1957b).

. . . All Subanun are full-time farmers. Special statuses are few in number, filled by achievement rather than ascription, restricted in domain, and limited in economic rewards. The status of legal authority has been discussed elsewhere (Frake 1957a). In the sphere of making decisions about disease, differences in individual skill and knowledge receive recognition, but there is no formal status of diagnostician or even, by Subanun conception, of curer. Everyone is his own 'herbalist' (*memuluy*). There are religious specialists, 'mediums' (*belian*), whose job it is to maintain communications with the very important supernatural constituents of the Subanun universe. Mediums hold curing ceremonies, but the gods effect the cure. They make possible verbal communication with the supernaturals, but again the information received comes from the gods. The medium is but a channel for the divine message.

A consideration of disease etiology, together with etiologically derived therapy, would require extended discussion of Subanun relations with the supernatural world. In limiting ourselves to diagnosis, on the other hand, we can largely ignore information derived from very noisy, supernaturally produced signals.

## DISEASE CONCEPTS

"Am I sick?" "What kind of disease do I have?" "What are my chances?" "What caused this disease?" "Why did it happen to me (of all people)?" Illness evokes questions such as these among patients the world over. Every culture provides a set of significant questions, potential answers, and procedures for arriving at answers. The cultural answers to these questions are *concepts* of disease. The information necessary to arrive at a specific answer and eliminate others is the *meaning* of a disease concept.

The Subanun patient, no matter how minor his illness, rarely depends upon introspection to answer these questions. He solicits the readily proffered judgment and advice of kin, neighbors, friends, specialists, deities, and ethnographers. Sickness comprises the third most frequent topic of casual conversation (after litigation and folk botany) among Subanun of my acquaintance, and it furnishes the overwhelmingly predominant subject of formal interviews with the supernaturals.

Because disease is not only suffered and treated, but also talked about, disease concepts are verbally labelled and readily communicable. Their continual exposure to discussions of sickness facilitates the learning of disease concepts by all Subanun. Subanun medical lore and medical jargon are not esoteric subjects; even a child can distinguish *buni* from *buyayag*—two fungous skin infections not, to my knowledge, differentiated by Western medical science—and state the reasons for his decision.

This corpus of continually emitted and readily elicitable verbal behavior about disease provides our evidence for the existence and meaning of culturally defined disease concepts. We begin with actual disease cases—instances of 'being sick' (*miglaru*) by Subanun identification. We note the kinds of questions *the Subanun ask* about these cases, we record the alternative (or *contrasting*) replies to each kind of question, and then we seek to differentiate the factors by which a Subanun decides one reply, rather than an alternative, applies in a particular situation.

Among the questions evoked by a disease case, there invariably appears one of a set of utterances which demands a 'disease name' (*ŋalan mesait en*) in response. Answering a question with a 'disease name' is *diagnosis*. Subanun diagnosis is the procedure of judging similarities and differences among instances of 'being sick', placing new instances into culturally defined and linguistically labelled categories. Diagnostic decisions pertain to

the selection of 'medicinal' (*kebuluŋan*) therapy, to prognosis, and to the assumption of an appropriate sick role by the patient. They do not answer, nor depend upon, the crucial etiological questions that guide the search for 'ritual' (*kanu*) therapy in severe and refractory cases. The Subanun thus discriminate among the various constellations of disease symptoms and react differentially to them. They diagnose *kinds* of disease.

## DISEASE NAMES

The fundamental unit of Subanun diagnosis is the *diagnostic category* (or "disease") labelled by a 'disease name.' Whereas an *illness* is a single instance of 'being sick,' a diagnostic category is a conceptual entity which classifies particular illnesses, symptomatic or pathogenic components of illness, or stages of illness. The course of an illness through time and its symptomatic components at any one time do not always fit into a single diagnostic category. Consequently, a single illness may successively or simultaneously require designation by several disease names.

Although not all illnesses can be diagnosed by a single disease name, every disease name can diagnose a single illness. Disease names thus differ from designations of kinds of symptoms, such as 'itch' (*matel*), or kinds of pathogenic agents, such as 'plant floss' (*glaŋis*), which do not function as diagnostic labels for illnesses.

The question "What kind of illness is that?" (*dita? gleruun ai run ma iin*) will always elicit a diagnostic description. Actually, however, a Subanun rarely states this question explicitly; rather he implies it when making an assertion such as "I feel sick" (what do you think is wrong with me?); "You look sick" (what is the matter with you?); "I hear he's sick" (do you know what he's got?). When accompanied by the proper intonation and inserted particles to express worried concern, such utterances invariably stimulate diagnostic discussions resulting in a consensual linguistic description of a particular illness.

If none of the linguistic components of a description of an illness can by itself describe a disease case, then the description as a whole constitutes a disease name, labelling a single diagnostic category. Thus the description *mesait gulu* 'headache' labels a single diagnostic category, for neither *mesait* 'pain' nor *gulu* 'head' can alone diagnose an illness. On the other hand, the description *mesait gulu bu? mesait tian* 'headache and stomach ache' constitutes two diagnostic categories because each component can itself serve as a description of an illness. A single disease name is a *minimal* utterance that can answer the query "What kind of illness is that?"

At the most specific level of contrast (see below), we have recorded 186 human-disease names (apart from referential synonyms), and the productivity of Subanun disease terminology permits the formation of an indefinite number of additional names. For example, we never recorded *mesait kuleŋ kay* 'little-finger pain' as a disease name, but should a Subanun find occasion to communicate such a concept he could unambiguously do so by constructing this label.

Standard descriptive phrases of the productive (polylexemic) type, such as *mesait tian* 'stomach ache' and *meŋebag gatay* 'swollen liver,' label a number of common ailments. A few other disease names, which one might call "suggestive" rather than "descriptive," have constitutents not productive in the formation of new disease names: for example, the derivative *penabud* 'splotchy itch' < *sabud* 'to scatter, as chicken feed.' There remain 132 diagnostic categories which possess unique, single-word labels. The Subanun must consequently rote learn unique and distinctive labels for the vast majority of his diseases, a situation paralleled even more markedly in the botanical lexicon of well over one thousand items. The fact that all Subanun do, in fact, learn to use such a copious vocabulary of disease and plant terms with great facility reflects the prominent place of these terminologies in daily conversation.

## LEVELS OF CONTRAST

In a given diagnostic situation, a Subanun must select one disease name out of a set of contrasting alternatives as appropriately categorizing a given set of symptoms. Before considering his criteria of selection, we must determine which disease categories, in fact, contrast with each other. Two disease names *contrast* if only one can correctly diagnose a particular set of symptoms. (We consider later the question of disagreement about "correctness.") A particular illness may require the diagnoses of more than one set of symptoms for complete description, as with the case of 'being sick' with both a 'headache' and a 'stomach ache.' In such cases the linguistic construction with 'and' (*bu?*) makes it clear that the illness comprises a conjunction of two contrasting diagnostic categories. With reference to the set of symptoms of pains in the head, only one of the contrasting responses is applicable. Any difficulties caused by conjunctive descriptions of illnesses can be obviated by taking evidence for contrast only from illnesses described by a single disease name.

When the same set of symptoms elicits different single-disease-name responses, and informants consider each response to be correct, two things may be responsible. The disease names may be referential synonyms; i.e., the categories they designate are mutually inclusive or equivalent. This happens when, for example, the terms are dialect variants or variants appropriate to different kinds of discourse, such as casual as opposed to formal speech. The second possibility, and the one that concerns us here, is that one category totally includes another; it is superordinate and operates at a less specific *level of contrast*. . . .

A *taxonomic hierarchy* comprises different sets of contrasting categories at successive levels, the categories at any one level being included in a category at the next higher level. Taxonomies divide phenomena into two dimensions: a horizontal one of discrimination (poodle, collie, terrier) and a vertical one of generalization (poodle, dog, animal).

The importance of recognizing levels of contrast in Subanun disease nomenclature first became apparent when, early in the field work, I had an infectious swelling on my leg. I asked all visitors for the name of my ailment and received a variety of different answers (all single disease names) from different people or even from the same people on different occasions. Subanun disease naming seemed to be an inconsistent and unpredictable jumble. Further interrogation, together with closer attention to the socio-linguistic contexts of responses, soon made it clear that all respondents were right; they were just talking at different levels of contrast. Some—especially those who wished to avoid a detailed medical discussion of my ills in favor of another subject—were simply telling me I had a 'skin disease' (*nuka*) and not another kind of external disease. Others were informing me that I had an 'inflammation' (*meŋebag*) and not some other 'skin disease.' Still others—habitual taxonomic hair-splitters and those who had therapeutic recommendations in mind—were diagnosing the case as 'inflamed quasi-bite' (*pagid*) and not some other kind of 'inflammation.'

Figure 1 diagrams the taxonomic structure of a portion of the twenty-nine specific 'skin disease' (*nuka*) categories. Superordinate categories stand above their subordinates. A given category

| samad 'wound' | nuka 'skin disease' | | | | | | | | | | | | |
|---|---|---|---|---|---|---|---|---|---|---|---|---|---|
| | | meṅebag 'inflammation' | | | beldut 'sore' | | | | | | buni 'ringworm' | | |
| | | | | | telemaw 'distal ulcer' | | baga? 'proximal ulcer' | | | | | | |
| pugu 'rash' | nuka 'eruption' | pagid 'inflamed quasi bite' | bekukaŋ 'ulcerated inflammation' | meṅebag 'inflamed wound' | telemaw glai 'shallow distal ulcer' | telemaw bligun 'deep distal ulcer' | baga? 'shallow proximal ulcer' | begwak 'deep proximal ulcer' | beldut 'simple sore' | selimbunut 'spreading sore' | buyayag 'exposed ringworm' | buni 'hidden ringworm' | bugais 'spreading itch' |

**Figure 1.** Levels of contrast in "skin disease" terminology.

contrasts with another category at the level at which the two share an upper horizontal boundary not crossed by a vertical boundary. Any case, for example, diagnosed as *telemaw glai* 'shallow distal ulcer' can also be labelled *telemaw* 'distal ulcer,' *beldut* 'sore,' or *nuka* 'skin disease' depending on the contrastive context. If, pointing to a 'shallow distal ulcer,' one asks:

1. Is it a *telemaw glibun* ('deep distal ulcer')?
2. Is it a *baga?* ('proximal ulcer')?
3. Is it a *meṅebag* ('inflammation')?
4. Is it a *samad* ('wound')?

The predictable responses are respectively:

1. No, it's a *telemaw glai* ('shallow distal ulcer')
2. No, it's a *telemaw* ('distal ulcer')
3. No, it's a *beldut* ('sore')
4. No, it's a *nuka* ('skin disease').

The clearest examples of different levels of contrast appear when a disease category subdivides into "varieties." Systemic conditions producing discolored urine, for example, known generally as *glegbay,* have 'red' (*glegbay gempula*) and 'white' (*glegbay gemputi?*) subcategories. The 'distal ulcer' *telemaw* subdivides into *telemaw glai* 'male (i.e., shallow) ulcer' and *telemaw glibun* 'female (i.e., deep) ulcer.' Although in these examples, subordinate levels of contrast are indicated by attaching attributes to superordinate disease names, such

linguistic constructions are not necessarily evidence of inclusion. Thus *beldut pesui* 'sty,' literally, 'chick sore,' is not a kind of *beldut* 'sore' but a kind of 'eye disease' (*mesait mata*). It is the way linguistic labels are applied to phenomena and not the linguistic structure of those labels that points to levels of contrast.

As a matter of fact, when we systematically investigate the contrasts of each Subanun disease term, we find a number of cases in which the same linguistic form appears at different levels of contrast. The term *nuka* 'skin disease,' for example, not only denotes a general category of ailments which includes conditions like *baga?* 'ulcer,' but it also denotes a specific kind of skin condition, a mild 'eruption' that contrasts with *baga?* (see Figure 1). In all such cases, if the context (especially the eliciting utterance) does not make the level of contrast clear, respondents can indicate the more specific of two levels by means of optional particles: e.g., *tantu nuka* 'real *nuka*,' i.e. 'eruption', not *any* 'skin disease.'

The use of the same linguistic form at different levels of contrast, while a source of confusion until one attends to the total context in which a term is used, should not surprise us. It is common enough in English. The word *man,* for example, designates at one level a category contrasting with nonhuman organisms. At a more specific level, *man* designates a subcategory of human organisms contrasting with *woman*. Subordinate to this we find the contrast: *man* (adult male)—*boy*. *Man* can even appear at a still more specific level to designate a kind of adult male human, as in Kipling's ". . . you'll be a man, my son."

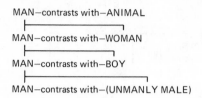

```
MAN—contrasts with—ANIMAL
   |————————————|
MAN—contrasts with—WOMAN
   |————————————|
MAN—contrasts with—BOY
   |————————————————|
MAN—contrasts with—(UNMANLY MALE)
```

This use of single forms at several levels of contrast seems particularly characteristic of Subanun disease terminology. It appears elsewhere as well, in botanical nomenclature and kinship terminology for instance, but not so extensively. The reasons for its use in disease terminology become, in part, explicable when we consider the use of disease names to designate sequential stages of illness.

The changing and unpredictable course of disease symptoms considerably complicates diagnosis. Of course other phenomena also change. A plant, passing from seedling to mature tree, changes radically in appearance. But a seedling of one kind invariably produces a mature plant of the same kind. A papaya seedling never grows into a mango tree. Consequently, the members of a plant category can be identified at any stage of growth,

and terminological distinctions of growth stages do not affect classifications of kinds of plants. Given an illness at a particular stage of development, on the other hand, its symptoms may proceed along a variety of different courses or it may heal altogether. Just as one illness sometimes requires several disease names for complete description at any one time, so its course over time may pass through several distinct diagnostic categories.

Every disease name designates a potential *terminal* stage: a stage of 'being sick' immediately preceding 'cure' (or 'recuperation') or 'death.' But some disease stages, potentially terminal, may also be prodromal stages of other terminal diagnostic categories. This situation occurs especially among the skin diseases. Each sequential stage leading to an ulcer or an itchy skin disease is, in itself, a potential terminal stage designated by a disease name. A case of *nuka* 'eruption,' for example, sometimes heals without complication; at other times it eventually develops into one of 23 more serious diseases. Consequently, *nuka* not only designates a terminal disease category but also a stage of development in a variety of other diseases.

Figure 2 shows that *nuka* is the pivotal stage in the development of the majority of 'skin diseases.' And it is this term that also serves as a general designation for 'skin diseases,' including some for which *nuka* 'eruption' is not a prodrome.

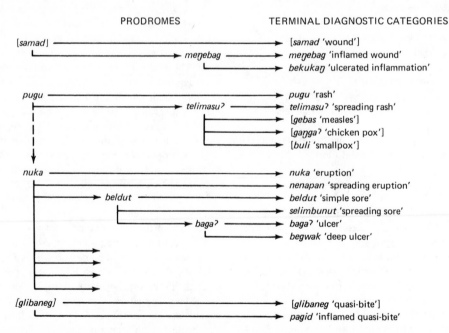

**Figure 2.** Skin disease stages. Only a few of the diseases arising from *nuka* "eruption" are shown. Diseases enclosed in brackets are not classifiable as *nuka* "skin disease."

The term *nuka* thus has three uses:

1. As a general designation for 'skin disease,' applicable to any skin disease at any stage of development;
2. To designate a prior stage of some, but not all, 'skin diseases';
3. To label a terminal diagnostic category, 'eruption,' which contrasts with other 'skin-disease' categories.

The reader will find further examples of multiple semantic uses of single linguistic forms by comparing Figures 1 and 2.

Subanun disease terminology well illustrates the proviso, often stated but rarely followed through in semantic analysis, that the meaning of a linguistic form is a function of the total situation, linguistic and nonlinguistic, in which the form is used. Essentially it is a matter of determining with what a term contrasts in a particular situation. When someone says, "This is an *x*," what is he saying it is *not*? (cf. Kelly 1955:59–64).

Figures 1 and 2 reveal a partial relation between levels of contrast and stages of development in 'skin disease' terminology. Among 'skin disease,' where the course of development *through different diagnostic categories* is most complex, the segregation of different levels of contrast is more elaborate than elsewhere in the disease taxonomy. But the terminological complexity of skin disease development does not suffice to explain why this area of the disease vocabulary exhibits more levels of contrast than other areas. A similar variability of number of levels in different segments of a taxonomy, not correlated with the designation of developmental stages, also occurs in botanical and zoological nomenclature.

To explain why some areas of a folk taxonomy subdivide into a greater number of superordinate-subordinate levels than others, we advance the following hypothesis: the greater the number of distinct social contexts in which information about a particular phenomenon must be communicated, the greater the number of different levels of contrast into which that phenomenon is categorized. Skin diseases, for example, enter into a wide variety of social contexts, apart from the therapeutically oriented discussions. They can influence bride-price calculations. Here, the concern is over the degree of disfigurement and the contagiousness of the disease. They can be used to justify, perhaps to one's spouse, a failure to perform an expected task. Here the disabling properties of the disease must be communicated. Skin disease terms figure prominently in competitive joking and maligning, thus entering into special kinds of discourse such as drinking songs and verse. In many of these situations it is imperative to speak at just the level of generality that specifies the pertinent information but leaves other, possibly embarrassing, information ambiguous.

The same hypothesis should hold cross-culturally. If the botanical taxonomy of tribe A has more levels of contrast than that of tribe B, it means that the members of tribe A communicate botanical information in a wider variety of socio-cultural settings. It does not mean that people in tribe A have greater powers of "abstract thinking." As a matter of fact it says nothing about general differences in cognition, for when it comes to fish, tribe B may reveal the greater number of levels of contrast.

Folk taxonomies are cultural phenomena. Their structural variation within and between cultures must be explained by the cultural uses to which a taxonomy is put, and not by appeal to differences in the cognitive powers of individual minds (cf. Brown 1958:284–285).

## DIAGNOSTIC CRITERIA

A 'disease name,' it will be recalled, is a minimal, congruent (i.e., meaningful) answer to the question, "What kind of illness is that? (*dita? gleruun ai run ma iin*)." Alternatively, it is a congruent insertion in the frame, "The name of (his) disease is _____. (*ŋalan en ig mesait en _____*)." Since different *illnesses,* that is, different instances of 'being sick' (*miglaru*), may elicit the same disease-name response, a disease name labels a class of illnesses: a *diagnostic category....*

Our choice of procedures for arriving at meanings of disease names is, in part, a function of the kind of category such names label, and, in part, of the kind of field data we succeeded in obtaining about diagnostic behavior.

Distinctive-feature analysis is ruled out on both counts. The preliminary denotative definitions would require a listing of illnesses assigned to each disease category in recorded diagnoses. The only meaningful etic units available for such a list are the diagnostic categories of Western medicine. Practical and methodological problems prevent their use. We had neither facilities nor personnel to make competent Western diagnoses of all disease cases

189

we observed. Yet, as useful as such information would be for many other purposes, it would, in fact, prove of little help in defining Subanun diagnostic categories. For one thing, too few illnesses actually occurred during our stay in the field to sample adequately a sufficient proportion of Subanun diagnostic categories. Moreover, even if one could match each Subanun diagnostic category with a series of Western diagnoses, the latter would still provide very deficient etic types. We cannot assume, as we can when working with phone types or kin types, that every Western diagnostic category will be totally included by some Subanun category. Every case diagnosed by Western criteria as tuberculosis will not receive the same Subanun diagnosis. Furthermore, a Subanun category such as *peglikebuun* 'chronic cough,' which sometimes matches with tuberculosis, will not always do so. The criteria and cues of the two diagnostic systems are too disparate for one-to-one or one-to-many matching. The problems presented to the analyst by this overlapping of categories in the two systems are compounded by the superabundance of information encoded in a Western diagnostic category. Knowing only that Subanun disease $X$ partially matched Western diagnostic categories $a, b, c,$ and that Subanun disease $Y$ partially matched Western categories $d$ and $e$, one could not easily extract from medical knowledge about $a, b, c, d,$ and $e$ distinctive features defining the contrast between $X$ and $Y$. For all of these reasons, distinctive-feature analysis from lists of matched native and scientific names is not feasible for folk taxonomies of disease nor, for that matter, of plants, animals, and most other natural phenomena as well.

Inadequacies of our data largely prevent confident definition of Subanun diagnostic categories by distinctive stimulus attributes, or cues, of illnesses. The discovery of what cue discriminations informants are making when contrasting one disease with another is exceedingly difficult. Many apparently pertinent cues, such as the ones that enable a Subanun patient to distinguish 'headache' (*mesait gulu*) from 'migraine' (*tampiak*) are known only by verbal descriptions. A disease "entity" such as 'headache' is not something that can be pointed to, nor can exemplars of diseases ordinarily be brought together for visual comparison and contrast as can, say, two plants. Moreover, situational features other than stimulus attributes of the illness bear on the final diagnostic decision. The same degree of pain, if objectively measured, could probably lead to a diagnosis of either 'headache' or 'migraine' depending on current social or ecological role demands on the patient. Nevertheless, very few diagnostic decisions are made by the Subanun without some apparent appeal to stimulus properties of illness; and in the majority of diagnoses these are the overriding considerations.

It is difficult, then, to define Subanun diagnostic categories in terms of analytic or perceptual attributes of their denotata. On the other hand, these very difficulties facilitate recognition of diagnostic criteria: explicit defining attributes of disease categories. Since one cannot point to a disease entity and say "That's a such and such," as one can with a plant specimen, and since no one individual ever personally experiences but a fraction of the total number of diseases he can, in fact, differentiate, the Subanun themselves must learn to diagnose diseases through verbal description of their significant attributes. It is thus relatively easy for a Subanun to describe precisely what makes one disease different from another. He can tell us, for example, that the ulcer *begwak* produces a marked cavity, unlike the ulcer *baga*? He can describe the difference in appearance between *glepap* 'plague itch' and *penabud* 'splotchy itch,' the difference in locale between the 'ringworms' *buni* and *buyayag,* the difference in pathogenesis between *meŋebag,* an 'inflamed wound,' and *beldut,* a spontaneous 'sore.' This not to say that the evaluation of the cues of a particular illness as exemplars of diagnostic criteria is always easy or consistent. Informants operating with identical diagnostic concepts may disagree about the application of these concepts in a particular case, but they rarely disagree in their verbal definitions of the concepts themselves.

The procedures for eliciting and analyzing diagnostic criteria parallel those used to determine the system of nomenclature: we collect contrasting answers to the questions the Subanun ask when diagnosing disease. By asking informants to describe differences between diseases, by asking why particular illnesses are diagnosed as such and such and not something else, by following discussions among the Subanun themselves when diagnosing cases, and by noting corrections made of our own diagnostic efforts, we can isolate a limited number of diagnostic questions and criterial answers.

A classification of Subanun diagnostic criteria follows from (1) the questions which elicit them and (2) the status of the answers as diagnostic labels.

1. By eliciting question
   1.1 Pathogenic criteria.

1.2. Prodromal criteria.
1.3 Symptomatic criteria.
1.4. Etiological criteria.
2. By status of the answer as a diagnostic label
   2.1 Elementary criteria.
   2.2. Complex criteria.

1.1. *Pathogenic criteria* are diagnostically significant responses to questions of 'pathogenesis' (*meksamet*), which is different from '*etiology*' (*melabet*). 'Pathogenesis' refers to the agent or mechanism that produces or aggravates an illness, 'etiology' to the circumstances that lead a particular patient to contract an illness. Thirty-four elementary diagnostic categories require pathogenic information for diagnosis. Examples are 'wound' (*samad*), 'burn' (*pasu?*), 'intestinal worm' (*bulilaŋ*), 'skin worm' (*tayeb*), 'pinworm' (*glelugay*), 'exposure sickness' (*pasemu*). In such cases, where the identification of a pathogen is criterial to diagnosis, the association between the pathogen and the illness is relatively obvious both to the investigator and to his informants.

In addition, the Subanun posit the existence of many pathogens—such as 'plant floss' (*glaŋis*), 'microscopic mites' (*kamu*), 'intrusive objects' (*meneled*), 'symbolic acts' (*pelii*), 'stress' (*pegendekan*), 'soul loss' (*panaw i gimuud*)—which are not diagnostically criterial. These noncriterial pathogens, whose presence generally must be determined independently of diagnosis, provide clues in the search for etiological circumstances and serve as guides to prophylactic measures. But standard, named pathogens, whether criterial or not, have a limited range of pertinence. In the cognitive decisions occasioned by an illness, pathogenic mechanisms are significant only when they are necessary appurtenances to diagnosis or to etiological explanations. Otherwise they are of little interest. Like Western physicians, the Subanun do not know the pathogenic agents of many of their diseases, but, unlike the former, the Subanun consider this lack of knowledge to be of trivial rather than of crucial therapeutic significance. Consequently a large number of Subanun diseases lack standard pathogenic explanations, and many disease cases go by without any effort (except by the ethnographer) to elicit them from consultants or supernaturals.

1.2. *Prodromal criteria* are diagnostically significant responses to questions of the origin or 'prodrome' (*puunan en*) of a given illness, the 'prodrome' always referring to a prior and diagnostically distinct condition. A *derivative* disease is one whose diagnosis depends on its having a specified prodrome. When referring to a derivative disease, a query about its prodrome *must be* answered by another disease name, previously applicable to the illness. A *spontaneous* disease, in contrast, is one for which the response to a query about prodromes *can be* 'there is no prodrome' (*nda? ig puunan en*).

Figure 2 shows a number of illnesses whose diagnoses depend on their having passed through specific other stages. One cannot have *begwak* 'deep ulcer', unless one has previously, as part of the same 'illness,' had *nuka* 'eruption,' *beldut* 'sore,' and *baga?* 'ulcer,' in that order. 'Eruption' (*nuka*), on the other hand, need have no prodrome, though it sometimes begins as 'rash' (*pugu*). The latter disease is always spontaneous.

For any derivative disease, a given prodrome is a necessary but not a sufficient diagnostic criterion. If the evidence of other criteria overwhelmingly points to a contrary diagnosis, one must conclude—since the criteriality of the prodrome cannot be discounted—that the previous diagnosis, or current information about it, is erroneous. Thus an informant insisted that an inflammation on my leg was an inflamed insect bite (*pagid*) rather than an inflamed wound (*tantu meŋebag*), even though I had told him I thought it originated as a 'minor cut.' I simply, according to him, had not noticed the prodromal bite. In such cases the existence of the prodrome is deduced from its criteriality to a diagnosis actually arrived at on other grounds. Our data would have been much improved had we earlier recognized the importance of these *ex post facto* classificatory decisions as evidence of criteriality.

1.3. *Symptomatic criteria* are diagnostically significant responses to a variety of questions about the attributes of an illness currently perceptible to patient or observer. These are the most frequent, wide-ranging, and complex of diagnostic criteria. Our data are not, in fact, complete enough to list, or even to enumerate, all the questions, with all their contrasting responses, necessary to define in explicit Subanun terms the symptomatic differences among all disease categories. Moreover, we can present here, in analyzed form, only a small proportion of the data we do have.

To exemplify symptomatic criteria we shall discuss several major questions that occur repeatedly in the diagnosis of a variety of illnesses; then we shall illustrate how these and other criterial contrasts intersect to define a segment of skin-disease terminology.

191

Specifications of locale along several dimensions provide fundamental criteria of Subanun diagnosis, closely relating to selection of appropriate therapeutic measures, to prognostic judgment, and to the evaluation of the disabling potential of an illness. First of all, disease symptoms can be located along a dimension of depth or penetration with two basic contrasts: 'external' (*dibabaw*) and 'internal' (*dialem*), depending on the presence or absence of visible lesions on the surface of the body. An external disease may penetrate to produce internal symptoms as well as external lesions, in which case the disease has 'sunk' (*milegdaŋ*). Rarely, a disease may penetrate to the other side of the body producing 'balancing' (*mitimpaŋ*) or 'pierced' (*milapus*) lesions. Penetration is prognostic of seriousness; the therapy of a number of skin diseases aims at preventing 'sinking.'

Those diseases which may be pinpointed anatomically (in Subanun terms, of course) are *localized* diseases. Should an initially localized condition begin to spread to adjacent areas within the same penetration level, then it will often fall into a new and distinct disease category. The distinction between circumscribed and spreading conditions pertains especially to external lesions. If a 'sore' (*beldut*) becomes multilesional (*misarak*), it is no longer *beldut*, but *selimbunut* 'spreading sore.' Other diseases for which spreading is an important diagnostic criterion are 'spreading rash' (*telimasu?*), 'spreading eruption' (*nenapan*), 'yaws' (*buketaw*), and 'spreading itch' (*bugais*). The Subanun describe an external condition that covers all or most of the body surface as *mipugus* or *miluup,* the latter term also designating a completely dibbled rice field.

Degree of penetration and spreading correlate closely with prognostic severity, hence their diagnostic importance. Distinctions of specific locales seem to reflect in part the disabling potential of a disease. Thus, lesions on the hands and feet often receive different designations from similar lesions elsewhere on the body; compare *baga?* 'proximal ulcer' with *telemaw* 'distal ulcer.' Among itchy skin diseases which seldom cause severe discomfort, distinctions of locale correspond with unsightliness. Thus the Subanun, who regard these diseases as extremely disfiguring, distinguish lesions hidden by clothing from those visible on a clothed body: compare *buni* 'hidden ringworm' with *buyayag* 'exposed ringworm.'

Specifications of interior locales usually refer to the area below an external reference point: the 'head,' 'chest,' 'xiphoid,' 'side,' 'waist,' 'abdomen,' and so on. The only internal organs commonly named as disease locales are the 'liver' and the 'spleen.' The liver in Subanun anatomical conceptions is somewhat akin to the heart in popular Western notions. (We recorded no Subanun diseases attributed to the heart.) The choice of the spleen as a disease locale seems to represent an instance of Subanun medical acumen. The term for spleen, *nalip* (identified during dissections of pigs), names a disease characterized by externally visible or palpable swelling attributed to this organ. The Subanun regard *nalip* as a complication of actual or latent malaria (*taig*). In Western medicine, an enlarged spleen (splenomegaly) may indicate malaria infection (Shattuck 1951:50).

Most peoples probably single out disorders of sensation as one of the most pertinent characteristics of diseases: witness our own stock query, "How are you feeling?" The Subanun ask "Does it hurt?" (*mesait ma*). The contrasting replies to this question are, first, an affirmative, "Yes, it hurts"; second, a denial of pain followed by a specification of a contrasting, nonpainful, but still abnormal sensation, "No, it doesn't hurt; it itches"; and, third, a blanket negation implying no abnormal sensation. Thus the Subanun labels a number of contrasting types of sensation and uses them to characterize and differentiate diseases.

The contrast between 'pain' (*mesait* or *megeel*) and 'itch' or 'irritation' (*matel*) has special relevance to skin lesions. 'Sores' 'hurt', whereas scaly lesions 'itch.' But should a sore-like lesion both 'itch' and at the same time multiply and spread, a distinctive and serious disease is indicated: *buketaw* 'yaws.' The type of sensation also indicates possible pathogenic agents. Pain usually follows some kind of trauma so if the patient has suffered no obvious injury, the supernaturals have very likely inflicted an invisible wound. Itchiness signals the presence of an irritating agent, often *glaŋis* 'plant floss.'

Once a condition has been labelled 'painful' in contrast to other possibilities, the kind of pain can be specified at a subordinate level of contrast. However, the Subanun make such specifications more in contexts of complaining about discomfort than in diagnosing. Consequently the terms descriptive of pain are often chosen for their rhetorical rather than denotative value. Such terms resemble English metaphors: 'burning,' 'piercing,' 'splitting,' 'throbbing.'

There are, or course, many other sensations criterial to diagnosis and a long list of diagnostic questions referring to appearances and to bodily functions. Rather than attempting to discuss each

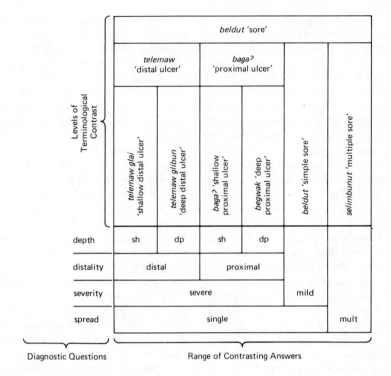

**Figure 3.** Criterial contrasts differentiating the "sores."

of these, it will be of greater methodological advantage to illustrate how a series of questions with their contrasting answers defines one small segment of the disease terminology. Figure 3 diagrams the criterial definitions of the types of 'sores' (*beldut*) distinguished by the Subanun (cf. Figure 1). The 'sores' contrast with 'inflammations' (*meɲebag*) in having the prodrome *nuka* 'eruption'. 'Inflammations' and 'sores,' on the other hand, fall together in contrast to many other skin diseases in being 'painful' (*mesait*) rather than 'itchy' (*matel*). Answers to questions of spread, severity, distality (hands and feet versus rest of body), and depth differentiate all the sores.

Depth, and especially severity, are not sharply defined by distinctive cues. In the case of 'sores,' size, persistence, and a variety of specific symptoms may point to severity: suppuration (*dun ig mata nen*), opening (*miterak*), hot sensation (*minit*), throbbing pain (*kendutendut*), intermittent burning pain (*metik*). Although not explicitly stated, judgment of severity is, in fact, partially a function of social-role contingencies. Do the patient and his consultants wish to emphasize the former's crippling disability, which prevents him from discharging an expected obligation? Or do they wish to communicate that the patient's lesion is not serious enough to interfere with his duties? Diagnosis is not an automatic response to pathological stimuli; it is a social activity whose results hinge in part on role-playing strategies.

1.4. *Etiological criteria* are diagnostically significant responses to questions of 'etiology'; how did the patient 'encounter' (*melabet*) his illness? These questions ask "Why did it happen to me?" rather than "What causes this kind of disease?" Diagnostic knowledge of the kind of disease does not give knowledge of 'etiology' in this sense. Confident determination of etiological circumstances requires communication by divination or séance with the supernaturals. Since this kind of communication tends to be costly, patients reserve etiological searching for cases when ordinary 'medicinal' (*kebuluŋan*) treatments predicated on diagnosis have not met with success. Etiological determination generally enables the patient to undertake propitiatory rituals (*kanu*) with therapeutic value. But some etiological circumstances, notably those involving human agency, cannot be counteracted by propitiations to supernaturals. These cases require treatment with specially acquired 'medicines' such as 'charms' (*pegbeliŋen*), 'amulets' (*buluŋ penapu*), 'potions' (*gaplas*), and 'antidotes' (*tekuli?*). When illnesses have a medicinally treatable etiology, the disease is then *named* for the etiological circumstance regardless of previous symptomatic diagnosis. There are seven such diseases, only two of which were recorded as diagnoses during my two years in the field: *mibuyag* 'bewitched' and *pigbuluŋan* 'poisoned.'

In view of other descriptions of primitive medicine, the surprising fact about Subanun diagnosis is that in naming all but seven of the 186 human disease categories, diagnostic questions refer directly to the empirical evidence of the disease itself and its history. The exceptional cases result from these few etiological circumstances whose determination by divination or séance necessitates renaming the illness they caused. Otherwise the results of etiological determinations do not affect previously determined empirical diagnoses. A deity may have to inform a Subanun how and why he got sick, but the symptoms themselves normally provide the information to name the disease, and by naming it, the Subanun is well on the road to prognosis and preliminary therapy.

2.1. *Elementary criteria* are those whose linguistic expression is not a disease name. 'Pain' (*mesait*) is an elementary criterion because *mesait* by itself, cannot function as a disease name.

2.2. *Complex criteria* are themselves diagnostic categories labelled by a disease name. 'Malaria' (*taig*), for example, is diagnosed by the presence of the *disease* 'fever' (*panas*) plus the elementary criterion of 'periodic chills' (*seleŋaun*). The disease 'fever' (*panas*) is, in turn, diagnosed by the presence of the disease 'malaise' (*mesait glawas*) plus elementary criterion of 'feeling feverish' (*mpanas*). Earlier we noted that some illnesses require a simultaneous conjunctive description by more than one disease name, e.g., 'stomach ache and headache.' A few conjunctive combinations diagnose distinct disease categories. The diseases 'stomach ache' (*mesait tian*), 'difficult breathing' (*bektus*), and 'chest pains' (*mesait gagdeb*) function as complex criteria in the diagnosis of *ba?us*, a systemic disease for which we have devised no satisfactory gloss.

## THE SIGNIFICANCE OF DIAGNOSIS

The diagnostic criteria distinguishing one Subanun disease from another, in their explicit verbal formulation by informants, define conceptually distinct, mutually exclusive categories at each level of contrast. Informants rarely disagree in their verbal descriptions of what makes one disease different from another. This does not mean, however, that they are equally consistent in their naming of actual disease cases. Two informants may agree that the ulcers *baga?* and *begwak* differ in degree of penetration, yet disagree on whether a particular ulcer they are examining exhibits sufficient depth to exemplify *begwak*. The "real" world of disease presents a continuum of symptomatic variation which does not always fit neatly into conceptual pigeonholes. Consequently the diagnosis of a particular condition may evoke considerable debate: one reason a patient normally solicits diagnostic advice from a variety of people. But the debate does not concern the definition of a diagnostic category, for that is clear and well known; it concerns the exemplariness of a particular set of symptoms to the definition (cf. Goodenough 1956:215).

Conceptually the disease world, like the plant world, exhaustively divides into a set of mutually exclusive categories. Ideally every illness either fits into one category or is describable as a conjunction of several categories. Subanun may debate, or not know, the placement of a particular case, but to their minds that reflects a deficiency in their individual knowledge, not a deficiency in the classificatory system. As long as he accepts it as part of his habitat and not 'foreign,' a Subanun, when confronted with an illness, a plant, or an animal, may say he does not know the name. He will never say there is no name. The conceptual exhaustiveness of the Subanun classification of natural phenomena contrasts with the reported situation among many other peoples.

Diagnosis—the decision of what 'name' to apply to an instance of 'being sick'—is a pivotal cognitive step in the selection of culturally appropriate responses to illness by the Subanun. It bears directly on the selection of ordinary, botanically-derived, medicinal remedies from 724 recorded alternatives. The results of this selection, in turn, influence efforts to reach prognostic and etiological decisions, which, in their turn, govern the possible therapeutic need for a variant of one of 61 basic, named types of propitiatory offerings. All of these decisions and resulting actions can have far-reaching social and economic consequences.

In this paper we have presented some methodological devices which we feel are effective in delimiting the basis for decisions underlying terminological systems. Unfortunately, while in the field we did not reach even the methodological sophistication of this article. Consequently, our data have proved deficient at a number of critical points.

# VI

## Sorcery and Witchcraft in Sickness and in Health

### Malign and Benign Methods of Causing and Curing Illness

Sorcery and witchcraft have a time-honored past in anthropology. No ethnography would be complete without a discussion devoted to these phenomena in those societies in which they exist—which appear to be the majority. And yet, as I note in my introduction to Section XIII, the concepts of sorcery and witchcraft and their corollaries, sorcerer and witch, are often confused and ambiguous in the literature. It is not always possible to know which phenomenon is being described or if the confounding of terms and related data is the consequence of the ethnologist's inability to distinguish between them himself, of his inability to elicit distinctions from informants, of ambiguity inherent in the local belief system, or of unconscious ethnocentric bias on the part of the ethnographer. Sometimes the two terms are quite deliberately equated, as by I. M. Lewis (1971), which, of course, renders their use in the same report meaningless. The first anthropologist to make clear and consistent distinctions between sorcery and witchcraft was E. E. Evans-Pritchard (1937), who in doing so performed a valuable service, even if, as Marwick (1970:12) asserts, this was because ''...an African tribe, the Azande, are more precise in their categories of the supernatural than we are; and Evans-Pritchard, the anthropologist who studied them and wrote what has become a classic in this field, found the existence in English of these two words a useful means of translating the distinction that his informants perceived.'' Even in relatively recent reports, however, one encounters some of the ancient ambiguities.

Following Evans-Pritchard, it will be helpful to restrict the meaning of sorcery to the power to manipulate and alter natural and supernatural events with the proper magical knowledge and performance of ritual. I depart from Evans-Pritchard in that he confines sorcery to "bad" magic ("magic that is illicit or considered immoral") whereas I would insist that the sorcerer can, and in many instances does, use his abilities for "good" as well as "bad" ends. Additionally, the sorcerer acquires his powers through apprenticeship, purchase, theft, and in other ways (see my introduction to Section XIII), but is required to have no special attributes beyond the intelligence to utilize his capabilities. In other words, anyone theoretically could be a sorcerer in most societies where sorcery is practiced, but this contrasts with the "requirements" for being a witch.

Still following Evans-Pritchard, I see witchcraft as the possession of an *inherited* power (in the case of some peoples, such as the Azande, physiologically inherited and, in the Azande case, transmitted patrilineally), used only for evil ends (though a few societies presumably have "good" witches, too). As Marwick (1970:12–13) notes, the sorcerer depends upon magic to implement his power, whereas the witch's power derives from his/her mystical inheritance and not from magic. Marwick goes on:

> There are other differences between them. As to motive, witches are considered to be slaves of aberration and addiction, and, thus conceived, are weird, sometimes tragic, figures. Sorcerers, on the other hand, are considered to be ordinary people driven to understandable, even if disapproved, urges, such as malice, envy or revenge, which are part of everyone's experience.

As Kluckhohn (1962) demonstrated so incisively in his study of Navaho witchcraft, the witch is an outcast and a deviant, an outsider in his/her own society. From this, and from Marwick's suggestive contrasts, it would follow that the witch embodies all the feared, despised, negative aspects of a culture and thus provides a negative role and behavior model; the sorcerer embodies rather more common antisocial urges and is a perhaps more ambiguous negative model, and insofar as he uses his powers for benign ends, a positive model as well. The witch is thus unrelievedly evil, the sorcerer combines evil with good and is much closer to the total community.

Sorcery and witchcraft, and the latter's offspring, the evil eye, interest us here because they enter the realm of medical anthropology through their role in causing illness and in the role of sorcerers in curing illness as well (sometimes the very same illness the sorcerer may have caused). We have already encountered this aspect of sorcery and witchcraft in some of the preceding papers, especially in Sections IV and V, and in the studies in this section they are the focus of attention. As we discover, the interest of anthropologists in these phenomena does not end with their role in magic, in the supernatural, in the social roles of witch and sorcerer, and in the part they play in the medical system, but extends to their role generally in the social system. At the macrocosmic level, witchcraft and sorcery frequently are seen as symptomatic of the strains and conflicts besetting social networks, and the divination process, as we learned in the last section, uncovers not simply illness or misfortune of individuals but, by implication, of social groupings.

Similarly, the therapeutic process (including diagnosis, prognosis, treatment, and cure) assists in assuaging not only the illness of the individual and reintegrating him into his social system but also works to repair the tears in the fabric of social structure and thus to reintegrate the system that was temporarily disrupted by the eruption of the evil act and its consequence. However, this is essentially an equilibrium theory which, although helping to explain the integrative functions of witchcraft and sorcery (and in an equilibrium theory all events in a system must "contribute" toward that system's operation no matter how destructive they may seem), does not explain sufficiently the disruptive consequences of these events. As the papers in this section and elsewhere show, the effects, in fact, may be quite destructive and may require the effective use of countervailing powers to stave off the terrorization of the whole society. This is well demonstrated in a brief study (Cardozo 1970) of McCarthyism as a variant of witchcraft in the United States of the early 1950's. As with all instruments of social control, sorcery and witchcraft may serve important social functions, but must themselves, in turn, be socially controlled else they run rampant and control the social system they supposedly serve.

196

As Robin Horton (1970:342–368) has suggested in an ingenious essay on "African Traditional Thought and Western Science," witchcraft and sorcery, like religion, serve important philosophical and metaphysical functions for their practitioners, functions that are analogous in many ways to those served by Western science to its practitioners. For example, both represent a similar universally human quest: "The quest for explanatory theory is basically a quest for unity underlying apparent diversity; for simplicity underlying apparent complexity; for order underlying apparent disorder; for regularity underlying apparent irregularity...." Horton shows that anthropological fieldwork has given the lie to the myth that whereas science provides such unity, simplicity, order, and regularity, religion with its "unruly complexity and caprice of the world of gods and spirits" does not. Horton also suggests that "theory places things in a causal context wider than that provided by common sense," and this is what happens in the case of witchcraft or sorcery as the explanation for sickness. Referring to the Kalabari of the Niger Delta, he shows that most diseases are first treated with herbals and other specifics in a purely secular, "natural," and unreligious way, whether by domestic agents or a curer.

Sometimes, however, the sickness does not respond to treatment, and it becomes evident that the herbal specific used does not provide the whole answer. The native doctor may rediagnose and try another specific. But if this produces no result the suspicion will arise that "there is something else in this sickness." In other words, the perspective provided by common sense is too limited. It is at this stage that a diviner is likely to be called in (it may be the native doctor who started the treatment). Using ideas about various spiritual agencies, he will relate the sickness to a wider range of circumstances—often to disturbances in the sick man's general social life.

Again, a person may have a sickness which, though mild, occurs together with an obvious crisis in his field of social relations. This conjunction suggests at the outset that it may not be appropriate to look at the illness from the limited perspective of common sense. And in such circumstances, the expert called in is likely to refer at once to certain spiritual agencies in terms of which he links the sickness to a wider context of events. What we are describing here is generally referred to as a jump from common sense to mystical thinking. But, as we have seen, it is also, more significantly, a jump from common sense to theory. And here, as in Europe, the jump occurs at the point where the limited causal vision of common sense curtails its usefulness in dealing with the situation on hand.

The subjects of sorcery and witchcraft are immense indeed, and I cannot further discuss them here. There are many excellent monographs and anthologies on these subjects. A superb anthology will be found in the recently published collection edited by Max Marwick (1970). In addition to Kiev (1964) and Middleton (1967), whom I have noted in the introductory chapter, I would recommend Middleton and Winter (1963), among others. In this section I have used only works that are oriented around the occurrence of illness and healing in a community. Many fine papers dealing with sorcery and witchcraft that are not so oriented had to be excluded.

# 21 Sorcery and Sickness in Dobu

## Reo F. Fortune

In his introduction to Reo Fortune's classic ethnographic study of sorcery and social organization, *Sorcerers of Dobu*, Malinowski called the chapter from which the present selection is taken, "The most spectacular chapter of the book, and the one which will attract not only the anthropologist but a wider public...." The monograph is a solid contribution not only to our understanding of sorcery and social organization but to the ethnography of the Papuan island-dwelling peoples as well. Much of the abundant case material is regretfully omitted here but the reader is urged to consult this fine work in the original. There, and partially in the excerpts reprinted in the present selection, one may observe the careful attention paid not only to the detail of the forms and functions of sorcery but also how they are interrelated with the medical system, with the social structure, and with the economic system. We see that attitudes toward sickness are correlated with attitudes toward members of one's family and other kin, with the world-view of these Pacific islanders, and with the ecological situation to which they must adapt. The reader is introduced to the theories of disease and of sorcery, and of how these theories are transmitted professionally in the sorcerer-apprentice transaction. The key role of the diviner is analyzed in considerable detail; Fortune sees him as the agent of Dobuan justice and equity. In this highly competitive, profoundly suspicious culture, where in effect a kind of Hobbesian amalgam of fear, hostility, jealousy, and distrust rule the passions, where the greatly valued behaviors and achievements are also the most dangerous, sorcery and its concomitant, disease, exist side by side in a hazardous game of life.

## I  DISEASE INFLICTION

...In Dobu not only is personality immanent in yams, and also present in various supernatural persons who are under the control of men wishing to grow yams, but disease, sickness, and death are ascribed to persons, as in the dogma found in our

Reprinted with abridgments from Reo F. Fortune, 1963, *Sorcerers of Dobu: The Social Anthropology of the Dobu Islanders of the Western Pacific*, New York: E. P. Dutton & Co., Inc., Chap. III, "The Black Art," pp. 133–177, with permission of the author, E. P. Dutton & Co., Inc. (Copyright 1932; renewal © 1959 by Reo Franklin Fortune), and Routledge and Kegan Paul, Ltd. (London).

own society in the religion that was largely formulated out of the older attitudes by Mrs. Eddy. Here, again, the importance is laid upon living persons who manipulate the supernaturals for their own ends.

In our discussion of social organization in Dobu we have examined the relationships between living persons in the area. Since personality is carried over into the garden, and into the creating and curing of disease and serious illness, we must expect that Dobuan thought and practice about gardening and about medicine will follow the tenor of personal relationships in Dobu. In gardening we have seen this to be true. It is no exaggeration to say that the Dobuan attitude towards garden yams is in some important respects similar to the attitude of the Dobuan man towards his wife. The wife like yams is spoken of as property. Just as it is considered good form to try to "steal" other men's wives whenever possible, so in gardening the current view is that every man should try to entice the yams, greatly desired personal beings in metamorphosed form, from other persons' gardens. Just as a man keeps close watch upon his wife to ensure her fidelity as far as is possible, so also a Dobuan native keeps close watch upon the garden. It is impossible to induce a native to leave his or her garden unattended. The garden must literally be brooded over, with constant repetition of magic nearly all the year. I have given the main charms for the garden but not the number of times each charm must be repeated. The *kasiara* charm for keeping the yams steadfast in the garden is not used too early in the growing season, or it is said the yams will be rebellious at the too early curtailment of their night prowling liberties, and refuse to grow. But once the *kasiara* charm is used it is repeated often as the garden owner becomes nervous about the *sone*, the charms used to alienate the yams from the garden by other men. Towards the last months of the garden season especially the use of the *sone* on other persons' gardens and the use of protective charms on one's own garden multiplies. Jealousy towards everyone else intensifies. The whole atmosphere is most closely related to the jealous watch over each other of man and wife. The attitudes of man and wife are themselves related not only to the social structure, but also to the magical world view....

A reputation in Dobu is built upon successful magic. He whose yam crops are good, whose success in obtaining favours from the other sex is conspicuous, whose health has been better than the health of his enemies, will become known. The magician who practises his art for payment has inherited a traditional magical "good-will", or "practice". But amongst such magicians some will stand out as having been more socially successful than others. Social success is desired by everyone. In personal relationships it consists in having seduced many women, in having been a great adulterer. Good gardening is phrased in equivalent terms. Since yams are personal beings the best gardeners are those who have seduced yams most successfully from the majority of poorer gardeners. Since health and ill-health are due to the personal activities of human persons only, the healthy person is he who has powerful magic, the sick or deformed or dying person is he who has weak magic. It is assumed throughout that social success is necessarily gained at the expense of others. The healthy person is he who has defended himself from the black art of others in his pursuit of social success at the expense of others. The sick, deformed, and dying are those whose magic has not been as strong as that of those others who have felt themselves injured by their social climbing.

In this society it is not possible to say that the attitudes of the social organization are created by the attitudes of the magical outlook, or that the attitudes of the magical outlook are created by the attitudes of the social organization. It is, however, possible to show a unity of feeling throughout. Jealousy of possession is the keynote to the culture. In social organization this jealousy is found in a conflict between the kin and the marital groupings. In gardening this jealousy obtains between gardeners. All illness and disease and death are attributed to jealousy, and provoke recrimination. It is also possible to show that poverty and a great pressure of population upon land accords well with the prevalent tone of jealousy of possession. But here again it is not possible to say whether poverty has created the jealousy or vice versa. Either point of view could be put forward. Accordance is all that can be demonstrated, and in truth it is probable that the more accordance there is in the elements of a culture the stronger an intensification of the mutually agreeable elements will result. They will react upon one another.

In Dobu the race is conceived as going to the strong. For the permanently deformed or permanently sickly there is little or no sympathy. At first the ethnologist is greatly surprised at the use of the words he takes to mean good and bad. "Here comes a bad man" says one's canoe paddler with great emphasis on the "bad" as another canoe comes up. The ethnologist looks with interest,

thinking to find a moral reprobate. But no—it is a miserably deformed person. After this type of incident happens many times it is realized that to be a bad person is to be a deformed or incurably sick person. To be a good person is what we mean when we say to have a good person. Such a man is good irrespective of his morality. If he is an accomplished adulterer and a successful thief, who has won all the conflicts that arose from these activities, then he is not merely good, but very good. Deformed and incurably sick persons are those who have not won in the conflicts (of sorcery) that arose from the anti-social acts which all those not deformed or sickly pride themselves on having accomplished without bodily hurt from hostile sorcery....

Introduced diseases such as measles (which kills natives), tuberculosis, influenza, dysentery, are recognized by the natives as being of introduced origin. Tauwau is the mythological creator of the white race and of European artefacts. Tauwau placed a devil of his, a supernatural being, in the hot springs of Dede in Bwaioa. When this supernatural being emerges from the hot springs a wave of introduced epidemic disease strikes the country. Any white man may be referred to as a *tauwau*, a bearer of introduced diseases, as the typical feeling behind the term necessitates its correct translation. I never heard the theory, however, that this devil is made to work by white sorcery. As far as I could tell the Tauwau devil is supposed to work independently—but I did not see any time of introduced epidemic. There was measles killing many in the Trobriands, but I did not know the Trobrianders well enough to ascertain their feeling. Dr. Malinowski refers to the *tauwau* as *tauva'u* (Malinowski 1922:76). The Dobuan character is notably more outspoken in unpleasant matters than the Trobriand— and I have a more outspoken account of the term.

Disease and modes of death that are indigenous are well known and catalogued by the native. Their production and infliction upon near neighbours is one of the customary occupations of the people. Underneath the surface of native life there is a constant silent war, a small circle of close kindred alone placing trust in one another. The whole life of the people is strongly coloured by a thorough absence of trust in neighbours and the practice of treachery beneath a show of friendliness. Every person goes in fear of the secret war, and on frequent occasion the fear breaks through the surface.

A man imitating the effects of a cruel disease with obvious enjoyment in his believed power of inflicting it on his neighbour, telling with éclat how his incantation may be placed on a pregnant woman and how it will kill the child within her, and bring about her end in torture, imitating her struggles and her groans in convulsion on the ground, or shrieking in convulsion as he illustrates the agonies of a disease that eats away the skin and leaves a deformity of such a red mass of streaming and streaked jelly where was once a human face, as I saw at least twice, and could scarcely look at as the man tried to turn his head away, is a vile enough object. This debonair and faithful imitation of the worst effects of disease or death is the ordinary procedure adopted in the teaching of black magic. It illustrates what can be done with the incantation; it is done with fidelity, and with a satisfied conviction of the power to produce such effects and of having produced them on previous occasions. The natives followed their customary procedure in giving me secret knowledge. Thus a man giving me a simple for curing a disease would always chew and swallow some of it in my sight, and call my attention to his doing it. The fact behind this is that treacherous poisoning is a common enough custom. A native will never accept food except from a few people that he knows and trusts, people who accept his food....

My medicine man had a very good "bed-side manner", as I found when I summoned in his curing incantation for a fever that I had. He actually did exert considerable compelling power over me in the way of a will to feel better. So in teaching me incantations for killing he communicated a thoroughly villainous atmosphere with equal pride in his power and with some inevitable contagion of feeling, for anything to the contrary had to be dissembled on my part.

Every disease is held to be caused by a *tabu*. *Tabu* denotes an incantation, expressing black hatred in an extremely ugly form, which has the power of inflicting disease. Each disease has its own *tabu* or incantation. Every man and woman knows from one to five *tabus*—I made a census of *tabus* and their possessors in Tewara—how they are distributed and held is common knowledge....

The *tabus* are commonly used to protect private property in trees situated away from the village. They are also used, however, in the ordinary course of private feuds. The use of the disease-causing incantations on the *didila*, a dry coconut palm frond tied about a protected tree as a sign of its giving abode to a malevolent charm, creates some resemblance between the Dobuan *tabu* and the Samoan hieroglyphic *tapui* (Mead 1930).

The names of the great majority of the *tabus* are the names of certain shell-fish, insects, birds, and animals with the prefix *lo*. A few are the names of trees with the prefix *lo*; and there are a few further *tabus* outside these categories. The prefix *lo* is used elsewhere in terminology—thus *lo-mwali* is to obtain *mwali* or armshells, *lo-bagura* is to get food from *bagura*, the garden. By equivalence *lo-binama* is to get *binama*, the hornbill, *lo-moata* is to get *moata*, the snake. To get the hornbill is to get gangosa, to get the snake is to get paralysis....

First we may consider the native attitude to an incantation.... The attitude is essentially one of great fear. My informant insisted in giving me the charm that no word of it could be uttered anywhere near an inhabited place. It had to be uttered on a far and desolate shore as I have said above. We had to cleanse ourselves in the sea after its ritual, and we had to refrain from going near the village for hours afterwards. I had to cease using my informant's name. Thereafter I observed this prohibition carefully, calling him *igu esoi*, "my partner of a day long sojourn apart," whenever I called to him or referred to him to others.

"Do not say that name idly" several men cautioned me, I having used the term *lobinama* in my house in speech with them. "If we crack a twig, it hears, if we whisper, it hears"....

The charm is uttered into an object—the *didila* or *didina* (the term changing according as the dry coconut frond is bound on to a betel nut or a coconut palm). It may also be uttered into a creeper twined across a track, or any other object. The pronouncer of the incantations chews ginger, stands three or four feet away from the object charmed and utters the charm in short staccato phrases with a vicious spitting of ginger on to the object charmed, punctuating each phrase (roughly as I have phrased it), and taking care that his shadow falls behind and not in front of him....

The term for catching a *tabu*, a disease, is *enunulatui*. Charms such as these cause all disease, and conversely wherever a diseased person is found there are accounts of his or her success with the other sex, or success in trade, or success in the garden—in which case an envious and more backward rival has intervened as is the custom; or the diseased person may have stolen from a tree protected by a *tabu*. Again, a man will put a *tabu* on a woman who has refused his advances, improper or otherwise.

My personal boy contracted *lomague* while on the sea. He got *mague*—a shell-fish, the sting of which kills—a child was killed so in my vicinity in Basima. In other words he had a swelling in his arm due to exposure to the sun (the heat beating down on the open canoe) and paddling. He was in some fear—the *mague* had entered his arm, not a shell-fish in material form, but its double of the *tabu*. He had counter incantation performed. He then had his arm ligatured tightly near the arm-pit. This was to prevent "it" from entering his body. If "it" entered beyond the arm-pit he was a dead man....

The following are some of the names of other diseases—

*tabu* and names at the beginning of his exorcism the names of the *tabus* which he knows the owner of the tree possesses, as well as the name of his own *tabu*. In treating sickness every care is taken to obtain the exorcism proper to the disease. Here, however, the superimposing of a second *tabu* is evidently thought to make a difference. At the same time I do not believe that *putautaona* is very consistently practised. In point of fact there is usually tremendous respect for and fear of any *tabu* protected tree. I was told of definite cases of *putautaona* and stealing from a *tabu* protected tree; but they occurred in time of famine and drought when the poorer

| Native name | Disease | Demon involved |
|---|---|---|
| *Lobwebwai* | Cerebral malaria and meningitis | The white-headed Osprey. |
| *Logumo* | Inflammation of the gums | The paper wasp. |
| *Lokwalawa* | Intestinal trouble | The shark. |
| *Logaga* | Toothache | A small flying sea-water insect. |
| *Loiaio* | Elephantiasis | A swollen-looking shell. |
| *Lomagawau* | Intestinal "eating out" | A small eagle that lives on snakes exclusively. |
| *Losakasakalulu* | Goose-flesh | Porcupine fish. |
| *Losakwara* | Wasting in hookworm | Sakwara is a tree, the leaves of which wilt with remarkable rapidity when plucked. |

... The Doubles may be exorcized out of the charmed object by the man who summons them; only he who knows the incantation to summon a zoological or a botanical Double knows also the incantation to exorcize it. As each *tabu* is a separate incantation so also each exorcism is a separate incantation, and a *tabu* and its exorcism go together, never apart. The exorcizing spells are termed *lolas*. Different families own their different *tabus* and *lolases*—so it is possible to protect private property. There is not too much overlapping in their possession in a community. In order to get at his own private tree a man must first exorcize the charm he has put upon it. The exorcisms are also used to cure disease. Women take watergourds to a person who knows the *tabu* and exorcism of the disease from which one of their kin is suffering, the person breathes the exorcism into the water, and the women return to bathe the invalid with it. This procedure is often to be seen.

The exorcism for gangosa is a repeated injunction to the spirit to fly away. "They fly away, they go, they fly away quickly." The plural "they" is due to *putautaona*. *Putautaona* is said to occur when one man coming on another man's property protected by the sign of the *tabu* is not deterred thereby. He superimposes his own *tabu* on the owner's *tabu*. He then uses the exorcism of his own

persons, who had few or no trees, were driven by urgent necessity, careless of risk. *Putautaona* is, however, typical of the "try it out" competitive feeling about magic.

After the thief has put his own disease on the tree, on top of the different disease put on originally by the owner, and used the exorcism for his own disease, modified by the addition of the names of the tree owner's disease charms, he (or she) climbs the tree and steals. Then after stealing the thief reimposes his or her own disease spell without exorcism, as it is believed that a *didila* or a *didina*, the dried coconut frond tied about the tree trunk, will slip to the ground if it is left untenanted by a disease. Hence the rightful owner of a tree, in exorcizing his own disease charm, names other disease charms also and uses the plural form—a precaution against stealing having occurred.

Here we see that the strong thieving tendency of the natives sometimes breaks through their own very great fear of sorcery, and makes a subversion of magical dogma in doing so. The dogma is most strongly stated that only the exorcism proper to gangosa will drive out the effects of the gangosa spell when they are contracted, only the exorcism proper to tertiary yaws will drive out the effects of the tertiary yaws spell when they are contracted, and so on. A person afflicted with gangosa is never treated with the exorcism for tertiary yaws or vice versa. But in stealing, a tree affected with gangosa may be exorcized with the exorcism for tertiary yaws or some other disease, the exorcism being modified by the addition of supplementary references to other diseases than that for which it is the true and traditional exorcism as used invariably in treating actual cases of disease....

The exorcism of paralysis commands the *lomwata* to fly away (a flying snake, this Double) and finally, after much repetition of verbs of flight, helps its exit by reference to small shell-fish that scatter from the rocks at a man's approach and by reference to the eggs of two seashore birds, *Yodudu* and *Legiagia*, eggs which no native has ever succeeded in finding. The Double is referred to as *makamakaiau*, the word for spirit used of the spirit of the human dead.

The exorcism for tertiary yaws is similar in its tenor. I learnt no new thing from it after carefully working it out. So much as we have learnt is the etiology and treatment of indigenous disease. I have considered it somewhat exclusively from the point of view of tree protection. When the charms are used in feuds the customary procedure is to breathe the spell into a bush creeper about the track that the intended victim is known to be ascending. The sorcerer then retreats into hiding nearby to assure himself of his victim coming into bodily contact with the creeper. After such contact has been made the sorcerer takes the creeper with him, keeps it in his hut, and ultimately burns it over a fire.

When the exorcism is breathed into water with which an afflicted person is to be bathed for curing, there is no striking of stray stones and sticks lying near with a tapping stick wielded by the exorcist. The exorcist as already stated does not usually approach his patient. Water gourds are carried to him. He breathes the charm into the water in the gourd, closes up the gourd and gives it to the patient's kinswoman, who has come to him. She returns and bathes the patient with the water. In all manner of its operation the spell is given a local habitation with which the person to be afflicted by it must come into bodily contact. All the disease spells, it is believed, lead inevitably to death, unless the diseased patient is treated with the correct exorcism. This exorcism may recover the patient entirely. Often it only prevents death, not deformity. Since many of the indigenous diseases cause deformity rather than death, the curative exorcisms are automatically credited with more power than they deserve.

## II  TEACHER AND PUPIL

In discussing further the relationship between teacher of spells of the black art and learner we shall not confine ourselves to the *tabu* spells. Here the teacher is the mother's brother of the learner.... In other spells of the black art, which we are now approaching, with very few exceptions the teacher is either the father, the mother's brother, or older Boundary Man cross-cousin of the learner. Without seniority, Boundary Man would hardly have a knowledge superior to that of his Owner cross-cousin.

Any spell of black magic, the *tabus* included, is taught in several sessions. The greatest care is taken that the spell is learnt word perfect. The pupil strengthens his memory by a charm to assure learning correctly. This charm is done with a process known as *tolu*. Four holes are scooped close to one another in a straight inland-seaward line on a slope. When water is found in the most inland hole some of it is used for drinking, a spell being uttered during the drinking. This spell is directed towards clearing the stomach of digested and partly digested food. Then a channel is made from this hole to the next seaward one so that water flows down it. Water from this hole is used for drinking, the drinker muttering a spell designed to ensure removing the blood from his stomach as he drinks. The process is repeated and at the next hole the spell is designed to remove water from the stomach. The process repeated again leads to the last most seaward hole, where the spell used is designed to make certain that the stomach is now absolutely empty (despite the last draughts of water, which are, of course, not considered in a sacred performance). The stomach is now in a receptive condition to hold magic. As in the Trobriands it is the seat of memory.

Once the pupil has declared himself satisfied that he knows the incantation perfectly he must undergo a most serious ordeal. The teacher must place the spell on an object and bring it into contact with his pupil's body. If the pupil has learned the spell and the exorcism word-perfect this attempt at infection cannot succeed; for his magic is the same as, and equal in power to, that which is used against him. If this is the case the pupil's magic is believed to be the complete and perfect prophylactic. But if the pupil does not retain his firm memory of the spell and excorcism then his magic is inferior, will not resist the attack, and the unfortunate pupil will contract the disease. Some youths are afraid of learning sorcery, but the great majority realize that it should be done, and face the ordeal bravely.

The next step is a further obligatory test. The pupil who, as is usual, has survived the ordeal, must now "try out" the spell on someone else, someone not too closely related to him. Theoretically it should be the first person he encounters, but actually one man told me that it was customary to avoid encountering close relatives and friends until the test had been made. It is singular that, despite this emphasis on testing, "trying out," of hocus pocus, nevertheless every native swears that the hocus pocus is powerful, and lively fears, quarrels, secret vendettas, and sometimes undisguised murders flow from the belief in its strong efficacy. The concept of proof is not sufficiently stringent. Once in a while a man uses a spell on another and the other happens to sicken shortly after. Meanwhile, when the owner of the spell teaches it to another he always says: "I used it on one man; the day after, it took effect, and he died immediately." A statement that is a lie is used always in warranting the efficacy of the spell. It is a social lie, socially always used in the circumstances, a manner of lie that descends from father to son or from mother's brother to sister's son quite irrespective of the actual experience of any one generation in the use of the spell; and quite surely the faith in the force of magic is such that it is really a faith which is impervious to individual experience, or individual conceptions of proof in ordinary secular affairs. The fact that magic can enjoin an obligatory test case such as that incumbent upon the young learner of sorcery, and yet have the faith in it undimmed by such testing, is curious. And yet again it is not so curious. For sickness, disease, and death are common enough. No other explanation of them than the sorcery and witchcraft used by living persons near by, for they must be near by, exists. The neophyte whose own test of his own spell yields a negative result will not betray any feeling of inferiority over it, except by boasting beyond the limits of reason, as is commonly done in teaching the spell again.

I do not know if failure is ever even self-admitted. If so it would be the last secret of the Dobuan soul, and in view of the obvious success of others as measured by the sicknesses and deaths that occur, the mainspring of fear. What is certain is that fear far beyond reason is actually present.

Testing out of magic is not confined to black magic, as we have seen. It is the first step invariably. The testing of the pupil by the teacher is the individual departure.

## III  WITCHCRAFT AND SORCERY

Death is caused by witchcraft, sorcery, poisoning, suicide, or by actual assault. There is no concept of accident. Falling from coconut palms or other trees is due to witchcraft; similarly of other accidents....

Witchcraft is the woman's prerogative, sorcery the man's. A witch does all of her work in spirit form while her body sleeps, but only at the bidding of the fully conscious and fully awake woman and as the result of her spells, it is said. Not only is all that we term accident as opposed to sickness ascribed exclusively to witchcraft, but a particular way of causing illness and death is the monopoly of women. This method is that of spirit abstraction from the victim.

The man, as sorcerer, has the monopoly of causing sickness and death by using spells on the personal leavings of the victim. When the diviner of the person responsible for an illness beards a witch he says: "Restore $X$'s spirit to him"; when he beards a man he says: "Produce $X$'s personal leavings that you have in your house." Such personal leavings may be remains of food, excreta, footprints in sand, body dirt, or a bush creeper with a malevolent charm first breathed into it which the sorcerer watched his victim brush against and which he subsequently took to his house to treat further.

Moving among the men mainly I soon became aware of a convention. Death is always referred to the *werebana*. That village is weeds and grass, that island is uninhabited now—the flying witches. Yet these same men in reality feared sorcery as much as witchcraft, all had their killing powers, and little by little I heard of what they had done with them. By convention only, death is referred to the women's activities. Underneath the convention was the knowledge that men themselves had a great hand in it—only this is not referred to by men, except in great confidence that usually betrays itself first in a panic and is pressed home from the panic by the field worker. The sorcery of other places is referred to freely—the sorcerers there, the danger of poison in the food offered one.

The women do not seem to have enough solidarity to turn the tables and to blame all death upon the *barau*, the male practitioner, as they might. Instead, they voice the general convention—the flying witches are responsible. The diviner takes no notice of this convention of speech. He is as likely to divine a sorcerer as a witch in any concrete case of illness.

The women, however, have a counter convention established. No woman will admit to a man that she knows a witchcraft spell. The men have the benefit of a general alibi. But a man will admit to his wife that he knows death-dealing spells, whereas she will not reciprocate. The women have the benefit of an individual alibi. The diviner, and all persons discarding courtesy of speech, take no more account of the women's alibi than of the men's. Courtesy of speech in direct conversation matters greatly in Dobu. If *A* tells *B* that *B*'s greatest friend is vile, *B* replies: "Yes, he is vile." *B* may take secret measures to revenge himself on *A*, but in conversation there is never any controversy in such a matter.

The Dobuan men are quite certain that the women of the Trobriands do not practise witchcraft spells, as they are equally certain that their own women do so practise. Accordingly the men of Dobu feel safer in the Trobriands among a strange people of a strange speech than they do in their own homes—in direct and striking contrast to their greater fear in the Amphletts and in parts of Fergusson Island than in their own homes, and in contrast also to their greater fear in other Dobuan districts than in their home districts. I saw this most clearly for myself; there was no doubt about their attitudes—considerable fear at home, sharpened greatly in all strange places, but blunted in the Trobriands. Whether this great certainty of feeling is founded on a solid fact that women in Dobu do practise witchcraft spells, or merely on acceptance of the Trobriand freedom from Dobuan-like fears, I should be loath to say. I have worked with the men intimately and I know that the diviner's discarding of the convention clearing the male sex is correct. I know the men complain about the lying they believe there is in the women's convention. But only a woman working with women could tell what the facts are—whether they are really innocent or whether they are putting up a convention counter to the men's. Personally I suspect the latter. The women certainly own *tabus*. A few men say themselves that they penetrated beneath the women's convention and actually got witchcraft spells from women by threatening them with violence. Such men are few, and may be telling the truth or not. The probability is that women do own spells, however. The witch charged as a witch by the diviner summoned to a sick person does not deny witchcraft any more often than a sorcerer in a similar position denies sorcery. Such denials are few in all, for a reason that we shall discuss later. It would be unreasonable that women should suffer

so without benefit when spells may be so easily made from the natural expression of hate....

Because of danger from witch or sorcerer it is not advisable to go alone. Frequently in broad daylight I was warned not to do it. "You go alone" in surprise and in dissuasion. In strange places they looked after me well.... The night is a little more feared than the day because it is the time for sleep when the spirits of the sleepers go abroad in the pursuit of the black art. Most of the black art of the daytime is done in the flesh. But fear of the night work is only slightly greater than fear of the day work.

The situation created by witchcraft beliefs in marriage we have already treated. The members of village *x* may refer freely to their fear of certain women of village *y*, until inter-marriage takes place. Then comment is forced underground, as it is a great insult to "call witchcraft" within a husband's range of gaining report of comment upon his close relatives in law or upon his wife. All men have a nervousness of their wives' complicity, and a fear of mothers-in-law. Only the most reckless will say privily of another man: "It would appear that last night he slept with his wife—but did he sleep with his wife? Or was she far away? With an empty skin at his side he slept."

I may add that as well as witches who are mortal women (*werebana*) there are also sea witches (*gelaboi*) who have no present human embodiment.

## IV    METHODS OF DIVINATION

Divining is usually done by water-gazing or crystal-gazing. In the former case water is put into a wooden bowl and hibiscus flowers thrown on the water. The diviner charms: "the water is water no longer." He cuts the water-in-changed-nature open. At the bottom of the cut he sees the spirit of the witch who has abstracted the spirit of his patient and who now has it concealed or the spirit of the sorcerer who has the *sumwana*, body leavings of the patient and now has them concealed. Volcanic crystals may be used instead of water.

Spirit abstraction by a *gelaboi* may be indicated by the patient making delirious or semi-delirious statements about canoes at sea, canoes used by the spiritual *gelaboi*. Great attention is paid to the patient's ravings if there are any.

If the patient runs about in delirium then again his *sumwana* has been taken by a sorcerer. The sorcerer in such case has bound up the *sumwana*, winding it about in some receptacle with bush creeper. This winding is compared to the way in which the tree opossum, Cuscus, winds its tail around branches and darts about apparently aimlessly. The sorcerer's winding of *sumwana* has made the patient run about like the opossum.

The diviner may bend forward the middle finger of the patient, grasping it tightly at the first joint. If the tip of the finger does not flush then spirit abstraction by a witch has occurred. If it does flush then the patient's *sumwana* has been taken by a sorcerer.

Again the diviner may tell by the body odour of the patient the sex of the person responsible. None could define how this was done.

These measures of noting the symptoms of delirium, or of trying the finger bending or the smelling tests, precede the water or crystal gazing which finally determines the exact identity of the person responsible for the illness. The attention paid to delirium narrows down the circle of people within which the diviner's judgment may operate, but the other two tests leave him free by their nebulousness. Flushing or no flushing in the finger bent is rarely so obvious as to rule out subjective appraisal of the results, a subjective factor that is even more obvious in the smelling test.

Unless the agent revealed is a *gelaboi*, a *yatala* or, as it is also called, a *bwokumatana* follows. The diviner summons the village, a member of which he has "seen" in his water-gazing. The person divined is charged with the deed by the diviner. Then follows a promise of cessation of enmity and of active black magic by the witch or the sorcerer charged, provided her or his just complaint against the patient is remedied by the patient immediately. The patient pays the black magician and the diviner, and recovers—unless unremedied grudges undivined as yet still exist elsewhere.

After a death the kin of the dead divine whose grudge killed their kinsman by watching the corpse as the mourners file by one by one as is the custom. When the guilty person passes the corpse it is believed to twitch in one place or another. So strong is this belief that twitches are probably often fancied. In any case common fact is often relied on rather than the pure magic of divination. If one man has sought out another's company too much and for no reason that appears customary, and the latter dies, suspicion falls on his unexplained companion. False friendship is suspected. I heard from three different sources: "If we wish to kill a man we approach him, we eat, drink, sleep, work,

and rest with him, it may be for several moons, and we wait our time; we *kawagosiana*, call him friend." It will be recalled that the black art is believed to be ineffective at a distance as it is conducted by men. Men have to work in the flesh. Even witches are believed to confine their work to within the locality to which they belong.

It is realized by the Dobuan that relationship considerations debar certain persons who might be responsible for the death from mourning, so that divination by the corpse is not perfect. As well as consideration of unreasonable companionship there is consideration of possible grudges left unhealed. Then again the possibility of poison in food eaten is canvassed. I have heard these considerations being turned over in the heat that followed the sudden death of a father and child together without marks of violence. Every meal for several days back was considered in detail. So also of companions of the pair, and old hostilities. It was all done in my presence in about ten minutes, provoked by the sudden reception of the news by two men related to the dead.

Divination in Dobu is practised by everyone without magic, and by a special class with more authority and with magic.

## V   THE DIVINER AT WORK

Alo's second wife of the Brown Eagle village died. Alo performed the mourning observances for a year, and shortly after his mourning was done and he returned to his own Green Parrot village, he fell seriously ill.

Bwai of the place Bwaioa, two days' journey away, was summoned, as diviner. Bwai duly performed the water-gazing divinatory rite, and saw at the bottom of the wooden dish Alo's recently deceased wife's mother. He pointed out that Alo had failed to give her her due of bananas (in an obligatory gift to his mother-in-law incumbent on the widower a year after the death of his wife). Bwai had probably made discreet inquiries before doing his divining, as the sequel proved. No objection to his divination was offered. A summons for the *bwokumatana* or *yatala* went out to the Brown Eagle people. They filed past Alo one by one, each protesting innocence. When Alo's late wife's mother came she was given no time to protest. Bwai accused her of witchcraft from the evidence of his water-divining, and asked her if Alo had not a bad debt to her which he had been obdurate in paying. She admitted that Alo had declined to pay her her just due, and she admitted anger and witchcraft against him. She assured Alo that he would not die, at least by her witchcraft, if the bananas were paid her at once. She would restore his spirit to him the moment the bananas were received by her. He would not die while she lived. But if she herself died, he would also be likely to die at the same time (with a veiled threat and a shrewd warning against his undertaking future sorcery reprisals against her).

Alo's kin pointed out forcibly to the witch mother-in-law and her kin that not so long ago the witch's daughter had died. They had felled a sago tree, worked it, cooked the sago and brought it to the witch and her kin for their eating. If Alo were to die now, the return gift would be due. The witch and her kin would have to fell a sago tree, work and cook sago for them to eat. The diviner had put the entire matter on a sound business footing. Alo rapidly put on several stone in weight and recovered. I did not see the affair. The above is Alo's account of it.

When the diviner makes a just charge, as that which Bwai made in the case of Alo bewitched by his late wife's mother, there is little thought of sorcery or witchcraft reprisals being made by the sick person on recovery. It is held that the black art has been practised fairly, its justice has been made public, justice has been appeased, and the affair is over. If the sick person does not recover, but dies, his death is not attributed to the anger of a witch who has been publicly exposed and publicly appeased and placated, but to someone else who up till death supervened was undetected and un-placated. . . .

Just as we have seen the *tabus*, spells to cause disease, used most typically in the protection of private property in trees, so now we see witchcraft used most typically to enforce economic obligations. *Tabus* and witchcraft and sorcery may also be used in feuds. That I shall discuss in more detail later. Meanwhile it should be appreciated that there is a very strong legal background to the use of the black art. The natives understand how our own legal system is imposed with the help of rifles perfectly. They say typically: "You have your rifles—we have *tabu*, witchcraft, and sorcery, our weapons." Behind this statement is the knowledge that the native weapons are used to maintain native law, as well as in private feuds—a thing that I knew, as also my informants. "If we are caught using our weapons to maintain our just rights by the white Government it gaols us. . . ."

## VII    CONSIDERING THE DIVINER

I shall consider the diviner first from the point of view of justice. I do not pretend that sorcery cannot be used unjustly. But I do most certainly insist that the diviner's craft is one in which native justice must be paid scrupulous regard, and in which scrupulous regard to such justice is paid. The diviner who did not ply his divining within just bounds would have had a short life in the old days. Now he has still the benefit of this good tradition, and as sorcery still goes on undiminished, he still believes that he is under the check of his fellows.

Consider theoretically that Bwai, the diviner from Bwaioa, had selected his witch unwisely in the case of Alo's illness. I have heard that in rare cases an unsatisfactory divining has occurred. Then the person unjustly accused of causing the illness and his or her relatives violently oppose the diviner—"their minds towards throat cutting", as one informant phrased the situation.

Or the diviner might be conceived to make the other possible mistake of accusing a person such as Hill Man, a person in the wrong to whom no just propitiation could be made, between whom and his victim no reconciliation could be effected.

I have only three good accounts of divining; but it is worthy of notice that Bwai made no mistake and acted rather shrewdly; and that further a large fee (by native standards) is always given the diviner. An advance on the fee was sent out to summon a diviner by the relatives of $X$, the victim of Hill Man, but no diviner would touch it. (This all occurred well before I knew of the case and had no possible connection with me or with any other white influence.)

The diviners are not fanatics gazing altogether too religiously, or fee seekers gazing altogether too arbitrarily into a bowl of water or into a volcanic crystal. They apparently know all that is necessary to make their work socially acceptable. In other words they administer native justice as well as is possible in terms of the fact that illness alone brings investigation to the fore.

My third account of divining does not belie these conclusions in the slightest. Two weeks after one of the Bobo-Emu duels (between abandoned wife and new wife of Alo) Bobo fell very ill and her flesh wasted on her bones until it looked almost like a hide hanging loosely on a frame. The diviner was called in and did his divining unbeknown to me until afterwards. Bobo owed no one debts. She was now divorced, her mother and her children were living, her father long dead. Neither marriage exchanges of property, nor exchanges following a death were in point. In Dobu economic exchanges are not very frequent and the diviner cannot very often select unpaid debts as the cause of illness. In Manus of the Admiralties economic exchanges are due constantly, owing to a tremendous elaboration of exchange, so that the diviner is seldom at a loss. Bobo's only enemies were Alo, her deserting husband, and Emu, her successor in his house. It is considered right and reasonable that Bobo and Emu should fight with stones and knives under such circumstances. Consequently the diviner did not select Emu as the witch responsible. Alo was somewhat uneasy about the issue of the divination. He questioned Bobo's village sisters closely and tried to "pump" the small children of the village for hours.

The diviner, it appeared, had fallen back on a non-human explanation. The witch responsible was a sea witch, a *gelaboi*, the type that has no human embodiment. After securing this result from water-gazing, the diviner performed a circular dance with its magical song designed to get the abstracted spirit of his patient back from the *gelaboi*. The diviner is always summoned in from another locality than that of the patient, in order to secure impartiality and his own subsequent safety. In consequence I did not obtain the ritual used. ...

I do not believe that the diviner touches a case after death has supervened, in order to divine the direction vendetta should take. The diviner is a well known and generally respected practitioner. The profession could hardly survive if it took up proceedings that placed it in the greatest danger. There is no disguising of the diviner, such as that which is said in West Africa to conceal his identity, and allow post mortem divination by him compatible with his personal safety.

Moreover means of divination after a death are used by non-professionals, by the near kin of the dead for the purpose of vendetta. The magic in divination is decidedly secondary to the amount of private judgment displayed in it. Where there is the fire of sorcery or witchcraft there has been very often the smoke of quarrel. In Dobu granted the quarrel the subsequent black magic is practically assured. Everyone knows gossip of local dissensions. There is no strife over small points in such an atmosphere. In all small matters there is an over great show of cordial agreement, the sincerity of which is a sincere appreciation of the sorcery milieu rather than anything else.

## VIII   THE SORCERER IN ACTION

I find in my notes one instance of some play with the sorcery of *sumwana*, personal leavings. This, however, is not at all a gruesome story. Aines and Peter were one day far from home, and outside their own locality, cutting *sakwara* sticks for house building. They killed the domestic pig of Luilo, under the impression that it was wild bush pig. Discovering their mistake they concealed the dead pig in the bush and went home quickly hoping to escape discovery. Luilo hunted for his pig and finally found it when it was partially decomposed. Meanwhile he had ascertained that the only outsiders who had been about the locality had been Aines and Peter. On finding his pig with tell-tale spear wounds near cut *sakwara* trees, he set out to watch Aines and Peter. He collected sand fresh with their foot-prints. He then went to Aines and Peter and demanded pay for his pig—or he would work the *sunwana* sorcery on their sand tracks. Aines and Peter paid up, a handsome recompense.

Such men are not men acting contrary to native ideas of justice. But because the braver man acting with justice and openly, is open, he is the sorcerer that Administration usually hears about, secures, and is likely to imprison—for exactly the wrong type of sorcery. The anti-social type of sorcerer is just the kind where neither openness by the sorcerer, before acting or after acting, nor the work of the diviner, is possible. Owing to native antagonism to Administration interfering with sorcery there is surprisingly little betrayal, however. This is in part resentment of overlordship, in part, prospective fear of the sorcerer returning from prison after his term with what everyone would regard as a just score to settle. ...

The fear of being poisoned dominates native life. Food or tobacco is not accepted except within a small circle. The woman of the house when cooking does not leave the pot and go away for as long as a half minute even. The antithesis "The Boyowans (Trobriands) use *soki*; here we who know the secret use *budobudo*" was merely an expression of the moment. For at a later time Christopher told me that he had caught a *soki* fish, and had it now concealed in a private hiding place in the bush. It is a globe fish with a gall which contains a swift and fatal poison. Despite the fear of accepting food or drink, poisoned, from false friends, mistakes are sometimes made.

To act in a proud or in any way overbearing manner is regarded as a great crime in Dobu. It is resented most keenly. ...

## IX   AN EVALUATION OF CLAIMS

It is apparent that we must pause to consider how effective the black art of Dobu actually is in attaining its objects. It must be remembered that magic is an element of social prestige. The magician will inevitably claim results when he sells a spell or a magical technique for payment or when he hands it down to his heir. The rainmaker will tell of droughts broken, the gardener will tell of great harvests. The sorcerer in handing on a *tabu* will tell of persons who contracted a disease from his *tabu*. Such beliefs are patently false. Whatever else suggestion may do I have heard no evidence that it can produce yaws or gangosa or elephantiasis, the objects of the *tabus*.

Now sorcery in general is but a part of the magical complex, and subject to the same limitations. Let us examine first the alleged poison used by Christopher, the sap of the tree *budobudo*. I secured specimens which were identified by Kew Botanical Gardens, through the courtesy of the Botany Department of the University of Sydney, Australia, as *Cerebera odollam*, Hamilt. *Cerebera odollam* has been analysed by M. Greshoff....

It is evident that the milky sap of *budobudo*, believed to be a poison by Christopher is not poisonous. Hence his account of how he killed a child with it cannot be accepted. In the same way his claimed killing of two men by magical spells cannot be accepted. The statement that all three died the day after he proceeded against them is obviously a lie of prestige. (Even in the case of Hill Man's sorcery where Hill Man met his victim face to face in the bush, and the thing was not done from concealment as in Christopher's two spell bindings, the victim, apparently suffering from suggestion, had been two weeks indisposed when I encountered him.) Doubtless natural deaths occurred in three cases of those that Christopher had proceeded against magically beforehand, possibly months beforehand.

Certain poisons are known to everyone. Derris, a vegetable poison in the roots of a tall liana, is used publicly for stupefying fish. The gall of a globe fish called *soki* is a poison more deadly than *tuva*. These two poisons are known to everyone. But apart from these two there are many simples believed to be poisonous that are family secrets, just as spells are. *Budobudo*, told to me by Christopher in the last material quoted, is just such a family secret.

Such secrets are not obtained easily by the white man. The native usually gives a facile lie or preserves silence on the matter. The literature on the area has no instance of such clear truth-telling in it, as Christopher gave to me. I think it is clear that he did give me a traditional secret simple without reticence or lying. *Cerbera odollam*, Hamilt., clearly is a tree that produces a poison traditionally recognized as such in southern Asia by the natives. In Dobu, at least in Christopher's case, knowledge of its properties has not been handed down quite faithfully. It is apparently one case of the loss of a useful art, the sap being now believed to be a poison. From this incident, however, I may demonstrate that Christopher probably told me the truth in his other accounts of the black art with only the customary lies of prestige.

After my initiation into the black art as it is practised in Dobu, I pin my faith to the kind of sorcery Hill Man used on *X*, and Christopher's wife's mother's brother in company with Christopher used on the gardener. In this type of sorcery (for the further proof of which see Appendix II), the sorcerer fronts his victim, who actually knows for certain that trouble has come upon him. I refer to the method by which the victim's internal organs are removed [*sic*] by the sorcerer in person, and in full fleshy person).

For the rest, witchcraft, sorcery upon body leavings, *tabus*, and the secret poisons are for the most part ineffective psychologically. For the most part their use in feuds is most secret.

In a few cases threats before execution occur. Unwelcome conduct may be taken as the equivalent of a specific threat. In such cases of known trouble impending both parties must live at a very high tension. The victim does not know of the sorcerer's intention unless by threat or threatening behaviour in advance. There is no pattern of anonymous message after execution; complete anonymity is sedulously preserved in most cases. There is no belief that the diviner is necessarily right and that one must be found out if one is successful.

If a threat of execution can be averted by payment, such payment is usually made, as Aines and Peter paid Luilo about double the value of his slaughtered pig.

## X   GENERAL ATTITUDES

To sum up, the black art is used not only for collecting bad debts and enforcing economic obligation, in vendetta to avenge one's own sickness or one's kinsman's death, to wipe out any serious insult offered to one, and for the sake of "trying it out" to see how it works. It is also used generally "to cast down the mighty from their seat". There is great resentment of any conspicuously successful man in Dobu. There is respect for old age and for primogeniture, but nothing except anger for any differences in success due to ability.

The black art is used against an over successful gardener, since he is believed to have stolen other person's yams from their gardens by magic. The black art is used against rivals who interfere with one's own success in overseas exchange, where armshells are exchanged for necklaces; a long time elapses between gift and counter gift, giving a rival a chance to cut in. Such cutting in is not rare as we shall see later. There is real competition here since the most prized valuables are not numerous enough for every one to handle them. Even a man who has too many domestic pigs is in danger—his greater wealth is regarded as an affront.

The desirable man in Dobu is he who has been more successful than his fellows in gardening, overseas exchange of valuables, in the pigs he has and even more importantly in the number of women he has seduced (this last is of course a case of real competition). It is interesting to note how our distinction between real competition where one man's gain is another's loss, and rivalry where all may gain, but not at one another's expense, is not made in Dobu. All matters of economics fall under the real competition concept. But with all this success the desirable man must be sound in body and in health. In other words the desirable man is he who has sought and gained the dangerous values unhurt by the black art of his rivals, who have used their sorcery against his success. He is the *tai bobo'ana*, the desirable man.

A man who is not conspicuously successful, but who has a sound body is neither *bobo'ana* nor *tokumali*. And in the rare cases where a deformed person remains socially successful Dobuans hesitate to use the term *tokumali*, which applies to nearly all hurt persons.

By means of a theory which makes the most prized social values so dangerous it is possible to explain a great many cases of disease and death. We have here a good blanket explanation for the misfortunes of men.

The diseased or deformed man in Dobu normally falls back in the scale. He is not a success with women, or with overseas exchanges; whether from infirmity or from fear of further disaster or from both, his economic status is normally low.

The diviner does not use this diagnosis of disease or deformity or death in his divining, probably because there is no just reason why a too rich man should give away some of his wealth to the one particular rival only whom the diviner might select as causing illness. This diagnosis is popular, not professional.

The concepts good and bad in the purely moral sense do not exist in Dobu. If it were said: "He did not mourn his wife, he is a *tai tokumali*," what would this mean? For a cripple, a person with tertiary yaws, with gangosa or what not *tokumali* is practically always used, irrespective of whether that person is now conforming to the Dobuan code of what is safe conduct or not. Some serious departure from pleasing others in the past life of the cripple is assumed—hence his physical trouble. The exact departure can almost always be named. So if a man who did not mourn his wife were called *tokumali* there would be implicit in the term, some anticipation of proceedings against him that might be expected to damage his health.

In point of fact I have never heard that sorcery proceedings are actually taken against the non-conformist widower by his late wife's relatives. They are incensed and taunt him if they meet him. They remark on him disparagingly to everyone. He gets a bad name. But that is all. Consonantly it is never said "he did not mourn his wife; he is a *tai tokumali*". *Tokumali* is too strong a term here.

I may remark that the translator of the Bible into Dobuan, the Rev. W. E. Bromilow, D.D., has made *bobo'ana* and *tokumali* the equivalents of moral good and bad. There is a real difficulty here, as the Dobuan categories are not closely related to our own. Such translation is linguistically unsound, but there is nothing else that could have been done than to try to change the meaning of the terms. This is not impossible provided that the true native use of the terms is specifically guarded against. The fact that the *tokumali* do not get into the Dobuan spirit land adds a fine touch of trouble after death as well as trouble during mortality. But the attitude towards the deformed and the diseased in Dobu is hardly Christian....

# 22 Paiute Sorcery: Sickness and Social Control

## Beatrice Blyth Whiting

In her monograph of Paiute sorcery, Beatrice Whiting set out "to present a descriptive analysis of the way in which social control operates among the Harney Valley Paiutes;... to formulate hypotheses concerning correlations between certain conditions and types of social control; and... to test these hypotheses cross-culturally." She assumed that in any society people must cooperate peacefully with one another, compromise their differences to avoid conflict, learn or be compelled to learn such cooperation, and be punished when their antisocial behavior causes conflict. The objective of mechanisms of social control, of which, in small, egalitarian, band-sized, acephalous societies sorcery is a major institutional type, is to motivate and compel an individual to learn and to use conforming behavior. The Paiute possess the first five of the six types of social control noted by Whiting (internalized conscience, public opinion, reciprocal obligations, religious punishment, retaliation [feuding], and institutionalized legal authorities). Two of the major causes of illness are sorcery and ghosts. Critical to the Paiute medical and religious system is the concept of power and a major means of attaining it is through sorcery. In the present selection, in which a wealth of ethnographic data had to be excluded, we learn about the Paiute notion of special power, how it is obtained and used, and how it relates to the local theory of disease, diagnosis, and therapy. Central to this system is the role of the sorcerer and of the healer who is capable of combatting the ill effects of the sorcerer's deeds. And we see how fear of sorcery acts as a social control, and fear of sorcery accusation, since it stimulates swift and violent retribution, also acts as a means of discouraging antisocial actions.

On the basis of her study, Whiting suggested that there were two major forms of social control: *coordinate* (essentially peer control in equalitarian social systems) and *superordinate* (essentially control by authority figures or groups through "birth, talent, or popular election"). Since she found a marked emphasis on sorcery and coordinate control among the Paiute, she believed that these should be correlated and that superordinate control and de-emphasis on sorcery (or lack of it) should also be correlated. Her

Reprinted with abridgments from Beatrice Blyth Whiting, 1950, *Paiute Sorcery*, Viking Fund Publication in Anthropology No. 15, pp. 27–66 (chapters entitled: "The Concept of Supernatural Power," "The Theory of Disease," "Therapy," "The Problem of Diagnosis," "The Sorcerer"), with permission of the author and the Wenner-Gren Foundation for Anthropological Research, Inc., New York (Copyright 1950).

hypothesis was tested (in a portion of the monograph not reproduced herein) on a sample of 50 tribes in the major culture areas taken from the Human Relations Area Files and found to hold, although the associations among these variables are not absolute. Subsequently Richard Lieban (1960, 1962) added an additional possibility, namely, of sorcery being relatively strong in a society where the means of social control were structurally superordinate but inadequately implemented. In the agricultural municipality of Sibulan in the central Philippines, Lieban found that though people were not "obsessed with sorcery," it plays an important role in their lives, not only as a significant cause of serious illness, but as a means of social control where uncertainty regarding land titles and ineffective governmental methods for dealing with this problem lead to constant conflict over real property. Sometimes these disputes are settled by violent means, sometimes through sorcery. As Lieban demonstrates, in Sibulan sorcery is an expression not simply of vengeance but of justice. Before a sorcerer accepts a case, his client must appear to have a morally sound basis for wanting to inflict illness or other retribution upon a potential victim. The same sorcerer who causes an illness may be called upon to cure it, but "the contrastive roles of sorcerer and healer may be assimilated by scheduling each for the appropriate occasion, whether that of service for health or service for 'justice.'"

## THE CONCEPT OF SUPERNATURAL POWER

The role of sorcery in social control can be understood only in terms of the concept of supernatural power. There are three main types of such power recognized by the Harney Valley Paiute: *pu.ha*, doctoring power; *madaiya*, other types of good power; and *pu ha.ba*, sorcery power. All of these are thought to be bestowed on individuals by spirit helpers. In general, those individuals who have certain special talents are said to possess good power, while those who are thought to be "bad actors" are said to have sorcery power.

In general, the types of good power bestowed upon individuals by their supernatural friends are useful in meeting those problems posed by the environment for which no satisfactory realistic solutions are provided by Paiute culture. The doctors, the men who have *pu.ha*, are the only people who can diagnose and cure disease. Their ability to do this is completely dependent upon their spirit helpers, who are invoked by them to discover the cause of the illness and to effect a cure. In addition to the doctors, there are individuals who, by virtue of their power, are able to practice certain minor therapeutic techniques. Some treat local aches and pains by letting blood; others specialize in treating trachoma, a very common malady, by scraping the inflamed eyelids with rye grass.

Some of the unsolved problems were posed in the old days by dangers from rattlesnakes and bears. Moccasins were poor protection, and many Paiutes were bitten by rattlers. Most people are still extremely cautious even when they are protected by heavy shoes, and women carry sticks with them when walking in the sagebrush. Some individuals, however, do not fear rattlesnakes; in fact, it is said that they are on friendly terms with them and even pick them up in their hands and talk to them. Some of these people can cure bites and influence the snakes not to attack their friends. In the old days some men had power over bears. They were envied because they dared to hunt them and as a result procured skins which made more satisfactory blankets than those of rabbit skin. It is reported that these men went into caves and killed the bears with sticks.

In former times some men had antelope power, and they led the communal drives. They were said to be able to discover the antelope, to decide where the corral should be built, and to lure the animals into it. They could tire them magically so that they could be easily killed. The antelope power of one man manifested itself in an ability to run fast. He was able to kill mountain sheep with his feet and hands. Two women also had antelope power and were swift runners. They seem, however, to have used their power merely to win foot races.

The firearms used by the whites against the Paiutes in the latter half of the nineteenth century were another problem which the Paiutes had to face. Against bullets, their bows and arrows were of little use. To most men it seemed suicidal to fight against such odds, but some men had supernatural power which made them bullet proof. Since bullets could not hurt them, they were able to hold off companies of soldiers while the women and children escaped. They inspired the other men and led them in raids against the whites. Women also had this type of power and could be killed only by stoning.

Some individuals had love power, by which they could make anyone succumb to their charms. It was employed primarily by old men and women to win young lovers.

Those persons who had "bad power," i.e., sorcery power, could use it to hurt others. They could make sick or kill any person they did not like. They were often referred to as "people eaters...."

The spirit appears to the individual in recurrent dreams and bestows power upon him. The dreams are thought to come unsolicited. In them the person meets his spirit helper, e.g., a chicken hawk, waterbaby, or gun, and is instructed in the nature of the power he is to have. The spirit usually tells him to carry some object at all times and to bathe on certain occasions. He teaches him a song and, if he is to be a doctor, some dances. The dream recurs until the individual becomes familiar with the instructions. Thereafter unless he carries them out in every detail, he will either lose his power or sicken and perhaps die....

Obviously what actually takes place is somewhat different from the above theory. From analyzing the case material gathered, in actuality the acquisition of power seems to work in one of three ways. A doctor's son sees his father practice and purposefully or unintentionally learns the different dances, songs, and techniques. The father instills in his son the desire to be a doctor and convinces him that he will dream. He tells him what type of dreams to expect and warns him to remember them and to follow the instructions he receives, lest he incur the anger of the spirit who is trying to befriend him and become ill. There is constant parental pressure to dream and to remember the dream, and this pressure is backed up by the community. A person with power is revered. Furthermore, a doctor, blood-letter, or special technician can expect to gain both prestige and material benefit from his power.

Another way in which the acquisition of power takes place may be seen in the case of Louise M., a girl of about sixteen. Louise was very deft at blood-letting. Her father had had power and she had watched him let blood from the time she was a small child. Although there were other children in the family, Louise was the most interested. After her father's death, she volunteered one day to treat her sister who was complaining of an ache in her arm. Gaining confidence she started to practice on others and soon won a good reputation. ...

A third indication of power which is recognized by the family and community is nervousness or sickliness. If a child has nightmares, is restless in his sleep and unduly nervous in his waking hours, the family is apt to attribute the aberrant behavior to the fact that the child is acquiring power. If a child is constantly sick, the family and doctor will suspect that the sickness is caused by the failure of the child to recognize power dreams. The doctor and the family will then encourage the child to remember and recount any recurrent dreams and they will interpret them in terms of power.

Theoretically, no one should reveal the fact that he has power nor tell his dreams. To do so would antagonize the spirit and result in the loss of power. Actually there is constant gossiping and speculation in the community as to who is gifted. Furthermore, it gives prestige to have power and some proud parents cannot resist hinting at the peculiar gifts of their children. Children, on the other hand, get their instructions in power from their family and naturally turn to them for guidance.

The above discussion would lead one to expect a great similarity in the type of power found in family lines. Such is indeed the case. There is not only pressure within the family for children to acquire power similar to that of their parents but there is a tendency for the community in general to expect them to have the same type of power. The result is what appears to be the inheritance of power although theoretically it cannot be procured except in dreams....

On the other hand, not all people have power and there are distinct disadvantages to seeking and acquiring it. In the first place, a person must behave well if he is to be befriended by a spirit. He must be a respected and conventional member of the community. Secondly, power is a tremendous responsibility. A person who has acquired a reputation is expected to live up to it. Thirdly, power is dangerous. Failure to obey commands and instructions will lead to sickness and even death.

It is natural that an individual should be placed in some conflict in deciding whether or not he really wants power. The predominance of power in family lines would seem to indicate that in general the pressures are strongest on children who have parents who are gifted and can teach them the special techniques and rituals.

The importance of the concept of power in Paiute life can only be understood when one turns to other aspects of the culture. The complex beliefs and practices directly concerned with sickness and indirectly related to social control will be shown to be closely integrated with this concept.

## THE THEORY OF DISEASE

The Harney Valley Paiute recognize four main causes of disease. First, a man may be sorcerized; that is, he may be killed or made sick by a man who possesses bad power. Second, a man may be killed or made sick by his own spirit helper by refusing to recognize it or obey its commands in every detail. These two theories of causation are directly related to the concept of power. Third, a man may be "ghosted," i.e., he may be attacked by a ghost and his breath stolen. Fourth, sickness may result from the deterioration of his blood.

The most dreaded illness is that caused by sorcery. According to native belief, a person with bad power can kill an individual by thinking mean thoughts about him and wishing him dead. The bad power travels by means of the thought into the body of the victim. The sorcerer may do this willfully or unwittingly, depending on whether his bad thoughts are conscious or unconscious. In some cases of comtemplated murder, the sorcerer throws his power into his enemy by striking him with a small stick or rock. A sorcerer may also cause sickness by dreaming that he kills his enemy or tells him to die. Although the victim usually does not know who has caused his illness, sometimes he may dream of something related to his enemy's power, which will give him a clue as to the identity of the sorcerer....

The second common cause of sickness is one's own power, for it is believed that if a person fails to obey his spirit helper he will become ill. To avoid such sickness one must perform in every detail the rituals taught by the spirit helper....

Mrs. Porter and her husband became ill several times because they refused to use their bad power. In order to cure themselves they were forced to sorcerize others. As will be seen later, many young people became ill as a result of not recognizing power dreams.

A second way in which one's own power can cause sickness is closely related to the first. If a person loses paraphernalia given to him by his spirit, he will sicken and die....

The loss of power through theft is a third way in which one's own power may be indirectly responsible for sickness. Hany Egan had power in horses which made it possible for him to escape from enemies when he rode. Oites stole his power, "taking it out of his forehead," and Hany became delirious because "when one's power goes the breath goes with it." Old Winimucca treated Hany and made Oites suck the stolen power off the back of his own hand and then return it by sucking Hany's forehead.

There is a fourth way in which a person with power can hurt himself. A parent may unintentionally kill his own children. If a parent who has bad power or is beginning to get bad power dreams about his child, it is believed that the child will die. The implications of this belief will be discussed later.

The third major cause of illness is ghosts. According to Paiute belief, when a man dies, his breath leaves his body and travels up the Milky Way into the sky. It is not clear whether it is the breath alone or other attributes of the person as well which become the ghost, but the ghosts live together in the sky. They attempt to capture the breaths of their relatives so as to have company. They come in the daytime or at night in whirl-winds and snatch the breath of their loved one and carry it off. The victim becomes unconscious or delirious, and, unless a doctor can recapture the breath and restore it to the body, the person will die.

It is believed that if a person thinks of a dead relative or friend, the ghost will come after him and he will become sick. A person must forget the dead, particularly those who have been dear to him, if he wishes to remain among the living. The sick must be particularly careful as they are the most vulnerable—since ghosts are apt to come to their homes because it is easy to capture their breaths.

If a person dreams of a ghost and if the ghost touches him, or if he dreams about someone who is dead, the ghost is said to take away his thought. This is similar to taking away the breath and the dreamer becomes ill....

## THERAPY

The Paiutes believe that only a doctor can diagnose and cure major diseases. Faced with illness, a person and his relatives depend upon these specialists. In this chapter I will present the formal relations between doctor and patient and a brief summary of the technique of therapy.

When a person becomes ill, he may do one of a number of things depending on the nature of his ailment. If his symptoms are mild, he may try pharmacological treatment, brewing for himself an herb tea or making an herb poultice to be applied externally; or he may resort to private rituals. On arising in the morning, he may pray to the sun. Standing, facing the east, he appeals to "our father sun" as he splashes cold water on his face. Or he may visit the sweat house and pray to the sun. For headaches or aches in other parts of his body, he may try blood-letting, paying some member of the

community, skilled in this practice, to perform the operation.

If the pain continues for more than a day or two and increases in intensity, if new symptoms appear, or if there is high fever, delirium, unconsciousness, or protracted vomiting, the individual turns to the doctor for aid. The sick person's immediate family and any close relatives who live nearby discuss the situation, and, if they decide that action should be taken, they see that enough money is collected and summon a doctor. Although the majority of shamanistic rites take place after sundown, it is customary to summon the doctor before sunrise of the day on which he is to work. The doctor's fees do not seem to vary from year to year or with the nature of the illness, so there is no necessity of inquiring as to cost. The relatives know beforehand how much money is needed and know that no doctor will give credit. In every case a doctor is instructed by his supernatural guide not to work unless he first collects his fees. Should he fail to do so, he runs the risk of becoming ill.

In the old days the charge for doctoring was usually a hide: a fawn skin for a child, a doe skin for a woman, and a buck skin for a man. Each doctor dictated the manner in which the hide was to be presented, some requiring that it be put on a pole behind the doctor's house, others that it be placed in the rafters. Nowadays, when money is used, the charge varies from three to five dollars a night and must be paid in silver which is placed in a cup of water until the doctoring is completed. If a woman is ill, it is customary for some woman relative to take the money to the doctor; if a man, a male relative. Occasionally when a doctor is on some case, he will treat the minor or chronic ills of other persons for a reduced rate, charging only one dollar for such service.

The choice of doctors is limited. In the old days, when the camp groups were scattered, it was usually necessary to send someone in search of a doctor and there was little opportunity for choice if the matter was pressing. Today, when the community is localized and there are two doctors, the family will choose the one they trust most—the one who has been most successful in treating the family. If the disease is unusual, however, and one in which the other doctor is reputed to be particularly versed, they may summon him instead of the family doctor. For example, some doctors have a reputation for being particularly adept at working on unconscious people. If the symptoms have lingered for a long time and doctorings have not been successful, the family may postpone further treatment until they can get some visiting doctor from another locality or band.

The doctor, after he has been summoned and paid according to his specifications, sets a time and a place for the doctoring. In the old days, it seems to have been customary to construct a special house for the ceremony. If the weather was clement, a sagebrush enclosure sufficed; when this was impractical, a thule or cloth house was set up. Nowadays, the doctorings are held in the ordinary wooden dwellings, usually the home of the patient. A stove replaces the old fireplace which was located in the center of the dwelling. Formerly, the patient was placed on one side of the door and the spectators sat in a circle inside and close to the walls of the house, leaving the central space around the fireplace clear. In so far as it is possible, the same arrangement is attempted in the frame house, although the position of the stove usually necessitates a slightly different organization.

Doctorings usually take place soon after sundown and last late into the night, sometimes until dawn. There were a few exceptions to this recorded. In one instance the doctoring took place in the day time because the patients were drunk in the evening when the doctor had said he would work, and, since he was leaving Burns the following evening, he agreed to work in the morning.

It is considered important to have a large company present for each doctoring. All adults, except pregnant or menstruating women, are permitted to attend. It is claimed that such women cause the patient to sweat, and, when they attend the meetings despite the taboo, they are thought to cause some doctors to become hoarse and have difficulty in speaking. Children are not allowed. In the old days when the camp groups were small, every one in the community who was able usually attended; but now, when the community is much larger, the people who participate seem to be limited to the members of the patient's family and clique....

The procedure differs somewhat from doctor to doctor but the underlying pattern is always the same. The doctor appeals to his spirit helpers by singing and praying and asks them to aid him in diagnosing and curing the disease. The men and women of the audience join in the songs after they become familiar with them. It is thought that they help influence the doctor's powers. A man, who is known as the repeater, leads the spectators in the singing and interprets the doctor's orders concerning procedure.

Sometimes the doctor asks his power to show itself in some way, so that he and the spectators may know of its presence. For example, a doctor with power in clouds might ask them to make known their presence by sending rain, or another might ask the lightning and thunder to come. Some doctors perform tricks to demonstrate the presence of their power. One doctor walked on live coals. Another was reported to have cooled a red hot stove with his body. As he danced around the stove, occasionally leaning his body against it, he told the people that if the stove cooled it was a sign that his power would cure the sick man.

The appeal to the power is always accompanied by vigorous dancing. While singing and between songs the doctor dances around the fire, pausing now and then to rest and smoke his pipe, which is passed among the spectators at other times. A few doctors have assistants who dance with them.

Water is often sprinkled around the room at some time during the ceremony. I do not know the explanation for this except that water is recognized as a purifying agent and is spoken as being like the human breath.

Sucking is part of nearly every ceremony. The doctor often sucks out some foreign object and thus effects a cure. He spits the object out of his mouth and shows it to the people. He then mixes it with dirt in his hands, rubs his hands together, and the object disappears. Sometimes he vomits the object into a pan of earth to make it disappear. In the case of the bullfrogs, the doctor sucks them from the patient's body and then drives them out of the house.

This is the basic pattern which varies according to the special rituals of the doctor and the nature of the disease which is being treated. It is difficult to say just which part of the ceremony is for the purpose of diagnosis and which for curing. As in other aspects of the culture, the Paiutes did not make general statements and I was forced to deduce the theories from an analysis of the reports of the treatment of concrete cases. For example, sucking is sometimes for the purpose of diagnosis, sometimes part of the cure, and sometimes for both....

Sometimes the "laying on of hands" or the touching of the patient's body with a feather seems to be directly related to diagnosis, at other times to curing. Although the singing and appeal to the power seem to be most often solely for diagnosis, in one case it was stated that the doctor's songs drew the bad power from the patient's body.

It is possible to deduce several generalizations concerning the method of curing certain diseases. When the doctor decides that an illness is caused by sorcery, he does one of three things. He may discover the identity of the sorcerer, and persuade him to repent and to call off his power by bathing and praying to the sun; or he may suck the diseased object sent by the sorcerer out of the patient's body and cure him without the aid of the sorcerer; or he may exorcise the bad power by song alone without sucking, or by both singing and sucking.

When the disease is found to be caused by the patient's own power several things may be done. The doctor may take the power away from the patient either by sucking it out or in some other way, thus permanently removing the power; or he may take the power out, "fix it up" and restore it to the patient. If the doctor finds that the patient has failed to obey the power, he determines the unheeded orders and instructs the patient to carry them out in the future. If it is found that the patient is suffering because of the loss of his power through theft, the doctor can discover the thief and see that the power is returned. Lastly, if the patient is suffering because he has lost part of his para-phernalia, the doctor can, with the aid of his own power, find the lost object, or he can make a copy of it for the patient.

When the diagnosis is ghost sickness, as a general rule the doctor does not suck. He identifies the ghost who is trying to steal the patient's breath and attempts to drive it away with his power songs, or he prescribes rituals, such as sprinkling ashes around the house or putting bunches of wild rose by the door, to keep the ghost away in the future. If the ghost has already made off with the patient's breath, the doctor can cure him only by pursuing the breath. A doctor who specializes in breath-catching has a formalized procedure. He dances until his breath begins to leave him, then he either falls or lies down beside the patient. Often he has his assistants cover both him and the patient with the same blanket. According to native theory, the doctor is like a dead man when his breath goes up the Milky Way after the patient's breath. His voice travels with his breath and reports his experiences as he wanders around searching, and the audience can hear him talking to the patient's breath when he finally finds it. Then the two breaths return to earth and to the bodies which have been lying rigid. Often the assistants have to lift the bodies to aid them back to life.

When the ghost sickness is caused by bad dreams, cures are sometimes effected by finding out the content of the patient's dream. In some cases when the patient has fainted or is "out of his mind," the doctor sprinkles water on him. One informant explained that a doctor did this only when he caught the ghost sickness before it was "in the blood...."

## THE PROBLEM OF DIAGNOSIS

As has been shown, there are four major causes of illness recognized by the Paiutes and diagnosed by the doctors. It is formally stated that the doctor decides with the help of his power which type of disease is responsible for the condition of a patient. When asked, informants said that there was no way of diagnosing from symptoms and that no layman could predict what a doctor's power would tell him. They refused to recognize the fact that often the relatives and the community as a whole have definite ideas as to the nature of the disease before they ever summon a doctor. They refused to recognize that doctors do not choose at random from the possible explanations, and that their choice is usually in accord with, and influenced by, public opinion.

I have attempted to discover the unformalized criteria which both the laymen and doctors use in diagnosing disease. Cases which were complete enough to give an analyzable segment of the social events preceding the sickness were selected for study and it was found that there were similarities in the life events, in the ages, and in the circumstances surrounding the onset of sickness of people who were said to suffer from the same diseases.

A study of the cases where the patient's own power was given as the cause of illness suggests that this diagnosis is given when some of the following conditions are present: when the patient is young; when one of the patient's parents or close relatives has power; when the patient is known or rumored to have power or when he can remember recurrent dreams; when the patient has special talents which he does or does not use; or when some major affliction, such as blindness, occurs when the patient is still young....

The stealing of breath by ghosts, the second explanation for sickness, is usually diagnosed when the patient reports that he feels faint or when he is unconscious or delirious. These symptoms are believed to indicate loss of breath. This diagnosis is also made when people are elderly. The reason given is that aged patients have many friends and relatives in the land of the dead who desire their company and therefore steal their breaths. It is thought to be dangerous to think of deceased persons, for this may have the effect of summoning them. Finally, the doctor is likely to diagnose "ghosting" if the patient reports bad dreams, particularly if they are about dead people. . . .

In general, sorcery is diagnosed if there is a feud in the camp and the person who is sick is either one of the parties involved in the dispute or is related to one of the parties, or if it is known that the sick person has either antagonized someone or been antagonized by someone. The person accused of sorcery, if he is not clearly indicated by the nature of the feud in which the patient or his relatives are involved, is usually a law breaker or someone who is generally unpopular; such a person is accused on general reputation rather than for any specific behavior at the time. A further condition which may be correlated with the diagnosis of sorcery is sudden death not preceded by a definite period of illness or obvious degeneration due to old age. As we have seen, ailments and disabilities which develop slowly and linger on are most frequently explained as caused by one's own power; while death in old age is attributed to ghosts. . . .

Thus it is evident that the doctor's diagnosis of disease is not fortuitous. In determining the cause of disease, both he and other people interested in the case draw upon all the facts they know concerning the patient and the incidents preceding his illness. In diagnosing the disease, the doctor and the community pass a certain type of judgment on the patient and often they also judge other members of the society. Thus when they determine the cause as failure to obey one's own power, the censure is on the patient's own action; in ghost sickness, the blame may be laid on the deceased's relatives or on the patient for thinking of them. In the case of sorcery, the blame is placed on someone else. These facts begin to shed light on the importance of the concept of power and the theory of disease and therapy and suggest how these beliefs function in social control.

## THE SORCERER

As following chapters will show, one of the main mechanisms of social control in Harney Valley is retaliation. Family solidarity manifests itself by aiding its wronged members to retaliate and by defending them against unfair retaliation from others. The second important mechanism of control is the fear of being accused of sorcery. This fear acts as a check on retaliation, as an indirect means of retaliation, and as an independent deterrent to anti-social behavior. A person who becomes known as a sorcerer runs the risk of having to face action by the entire community and cannot expect even his own relatives to come to his defense. The important problem, therefore, if social control in this society is to be understood, is to determine how a person comes to be known as a sorcerer.

From the preceding chapters it is evident that the presence of power in an individual is usually made known to the community either by individual excellency or deficiency in some pursuit, or by the doctor's diagnosis in the event of disease. The concept of power is, therefore, not only an explanation for disease, but also an explanation for all behavior which differs from the norm. A man who is especially attractive to women is rumored to have love power, a man who is an exceptionally good hunter is said to have power in hunting, a man who is very brave and a good fighter or a good shot is said to have bullet power. In a similar way, behavior which is unacceptable is attributed to the possession of bad power. Anyone who frequently loses his temper, who criticizes others in their presence, who is solitary and unsociable, who does not look others straight in the eye, is said to be "mean" and is apt to be accused of having sorcery power.

The presence of power to doctor is most clearly discernible because its possessor employs it in public and thus must make known his gifts and convince people of their validity. All other people are supposed to keep their endowment secret lest they antagonize the spirit that befriends them. It has been shown that usually an individual is not aware that he had good power until either the pressure of his immediate family, the pressure of community gossip, or the diagnosis of the doctor brings to his consciousness dream experiences which are attributed to encounters with spirit helpers. These pressures are especially strong when the family, parents, grandparents, or other close relatives, have had power.

With respect to bad power the situation is somewhat different. In general no one admits to being a sorcerer unless by so doing he can save himself from punishment. For example, if the doctor, backed by the community, accuses a person of having made someone ill, and if it seems evident that action will be taken against him, the safest thing to do may be to admit guilt, repent, and bathe so that the victim will recover. If a person is so terrified by the accusation that he flees from the band or stays away from all the relatives of the sick person, his action is taken as proof of his guilt.

It will be remembered that a person who has bad power is believed to be able to make others sick by thinking evil thoughts about them. He may use his power intentionally or unintentionally. If he uses it intentionally he may do it in one of the following ways: he may think aggressive thoughts about the victim; he may tell his victim to expect sickness and death; he may throw his power into his victim by hitting him with a stick or stone; or he may put his power in his victim's food, either directly or by biting something which the victim is going to eat. Any one of these things may be done to one of the victim's relatives, rather than to the victim himself. It is believed that the latter procedure will hurt the intended victim even more than injuring him directly.

When a sorcerer is angry, he may unintentionally kill someone in one of the following ways: he may think bad thoughts about the individual without being aware of his thoughts; in a fit of temper, he may express aggressive wishes about an individual without the intention of injuring him; or he may dream bad dreams about an individual. In the latter case, the victim may have dreams in which the sorcerer's power appears....

From the .... cases one can make the following generalizations as to how a person comes to be known as a sorcerer. First, one is accused of meanness and having bad thoughts. This type of behavior is recognized by the community as often resulting from being brought up by mean parents, so that the children of men or women already considered sorcerers or potential sorcerers are most closely scrutinized. Any mean behavior on their part is apt to be taken more seriously than comparable behavior on the part of others. Any behavior which is unfriendly, critical, or excessively aggressive is considered mean. Any behavior which antagonizes other members of the community is defined as aggressive.

The second most important factor in the genesis of a reputation for sorcery is gossip. It is almost impossible to find a single individual in any community who has not been accused by someone at one time or another. But single accusations do not make one a sorcerer. Until the gossip has spread and been accepted by a large group it is not dangerous. A person who has many relatives and friends who will stand behind him and deny such gossip is much safer than a person who has few

close relatives or has few friends. The groups within a community are based on family ties; but inasmuch as almost all the people in Burns were related in varying degrees, kinship is not the sole basis for cooperation. One's relations with more remote relatives depends on one's behavior, and kinship bonds are no insurance against accusations. The more people one antagonizes, the greater the danger of malicious gossip being spread. Tom T. antagonized half of the community at Burns by taking a very aggressive stand on the political issues, and by threatening those who disagreed with the policies he supported. Betty and Anne antagonized almost all the women by philandering with their husbands. The Porters reacted with disproportionate aggression against many different people, each of whom were supported by a group of close relatives and friends.

Given these two factors, the third important element is circumstantial evidence. A reputation for meanness and gossip cannot make a person a sorcerer unless some event occurs in which the person is involved to such an extent that it is possible to blame him. The death of Polly in the Porter-Simms case is a good example. There was a feud between the Simms and Porters. The Porters threatened the Simms and then one of the latter's close relatives died. This in itself could be used against the Porters. Even more evidence was brought to bear against them when it was remembered that Polly was standing by Jane Simms at the funeral of the Porter boy. In the same way Tom T.'s attempt to keep Pedro from moving to the new camp before Pedro's death was damning evidence. As one's reputation gets worse, the circumstantial evidence necessary for incrimination becomes more and more flimsy.

The fourth factor of great importance is the sanction of the doctor. It has been seen in a previous chapter that a doctor does not risk incriminating a person by pointing him out as the sorcerer until he is sure that he has the support of a large part of the community. When he does accuse a person of sorcery, it is an official seal and a very serious matter. By giving his sanction to the gossip and accusations which have been circulating about a person, he also gives social sanction to retaliation against this person.

The fifth factor of importance is the action of the person when the doctor puts the stamp of incrimination on him. If the individual reacts with strong fear and either avoids the relatives of the sorcerized person or flees from the community, he is considered to have confessed his guilt. If the situation is very tense and a man has many enemies, this is obviously the safest thing to do. Another course of action is to confess guilt, plead unwitting sorcery and bathe and call off one's supposed power. It is probable that this course of action is dangerous unless the person is just beginning to get a reputation for sorcery and unless the patient is likely to recover. The third course of action is to go about one's life as before, hoping that retaliation will not occur and that the reputation can be lived down. Nowadays, when the government forbids the murder of sorcerers, social ostracism and flight often follow the accusation of sorcery by a doctor. From the accounts, however, it would appear that in the old days in many cases the accused was killed by the community before he could flee.

Lastly, once a person has a reputation for sorcery he becomes a scapegoat and is likely to be blamed for offenses when no one knows who committed them.

In broad outline, then, we can see how the concept of sorcery works in social control. The important threat is that of ostracism or mob action. This punishment comes when the majority of the community and a doctor agree that a person is guilty of sorcery. The majority of the community will only agree to this if the individual has frequently behaved in such a way as to antagonize them. The behavior which annoys them may range from minor aggressive acts, such as speaking impolitely, to more serious offenses such as threatening others, adultery, destroying property, etc. Thus the fear of being accused of sorcery acts as a check on a great variety of anti-social behavior.

# 23 The Evil Eye Belief Among the Amhara of Ethiopia

## *Ronald A. Reminick*

In his much-quoted monograph on the "theories" of disease, Clements (1932) does not mention the evil eye. Sigerist (1951), though he quotes from Clements unquestioningly, does discuss the evil eye belief in

Reprinted with abridgments from Ronald A. Reminick, 1974, "The Evil Eye Belief Among the Amhara of Ethiopia," *Ethnology*, *13*:279–291, with permission of the author and *Ethnology: An International Journal of Cultural and Social Anthropology.*

several passages, but Alland (1970:138–149) in his very useful classification of the causes of illness does not mention the evil eye at all. This study by Ronald Reminick is one of the few by anthropologists that deal with this concept, which may be considered to be a subclass of witchcraft beliefs. Among the Amhara people whom Reminick studied, land ownership and personal loyalty are of paramount importance. Sibling conflicts over land inheritance and ownership are frequent, and the landowning (or desiring) Amhara perceive themselves as a nobility interacting out of economic necessity with a class of highly skilled craftsmen, the *buda*. The latter are landless, considered to be outsiders not equal to the superordinate Amhara, and possessed of the evil eye. The occupation of skilled potter, weaver, or ironsmith is the diagnostic trait of possession of the evil eye and not a physical characteristic as in other areas having this belief. The evil eye inflicts illness when the victim is in a state of worry or tension so the *rega* (noble Amhara) try to maintain their composure and not appear to be too handsome, accomplished, or prosperous. The *buda* have the compulsion to exercise their evil power as a way of gaining equality with those who have land and superior power and status.

As Reminick says, "The dominant theme expressed in the Amhara evil eye belief system is one which is shared by possibly all those societies that maintain a belief in the evil eye: the fear of being envied and the interpretation of certain misfortunes as the consequences of another's envy." In a society with limited resources (there are, of course, limits in *all* societies, so this phrase is used relatively), and where there is a class of haves and have-nots, "it is the relative differences between two parties that triggers the omnipresently latent envy into overt expression." In the absence of a mediating *external* authority between the Amhara and the *buda* people, the latter pose a threat to the former by their very difference and relative deprivation. The evil eye symbolizes the social and economic conflicts that are latent within the Amhara and between them and the *buda*.

Variations of the belief in the evil eye are known throughout much of the world, yet surprisingly little attention has been given to explaining the dynamics of this aspect of culture (cf. Spooner 1970; Foster 1972; Douglas 1970). The Amhara of Ethiopia hold to this belief. Data for this study were gathered among the Mänze Amhara of the central highlands of Shoa Province, Ethiopia. Their habitat is a rolling plateau ranging in altitude from 9,500 to 13,000 feet. The seasons vary from temperate and dry to wet and cold. The Amhara are settled agriculturists raising primarily barley, wheat, and a variety of beans and importing teff grain, cotton, and spices from the lower and warmer regions in the gorges and valleys nearby.

Amhara technology is simple, involving the bull-drawn plow, crop rotation, soil furrowing for drainage, and some irrigation where streams are accessible. The soil is rich enough to maintain three harvests annually. Other important technological items include the sickle, loom, and the walking and fighting stick for the men; the spindle, large clay water jug, grindstone, and cooking utensils for the women. The most highly prized item of technology is the rifle, which symbolizes the proud warrior traditions of the Amhara and a man's duty to defend his inherited land.

The homestead is the primary domain of authority within the larger political structure. The homestead varies in size from that of a nuclear family to a large hamlet consisting of several related families and their servants, tenants, and former slaves. The system of authority can be characterized in terms of Weber's patriarchalism, where a group is organized on the basis of kinship and economics with authority exercised by a particular person controlling the resources upon which the group depends (Weber 1948:346 ff). Obedience and loyalty are owed to the person rather than to the role or the rule, and this person rules only by the consent of the group members who stand to gain a portion of their patriarch's wealth as a legacy upon his death. This institution of patriarchal authority is reinforced by a cultural emphasis on male qualities of aggressiveness oriented around the acquisition and defense of land. Land is the fundamental requirement of the patriarchal system, for without it a man cannot fulfill his basic role of supporting his dependents and providing a legacy for his children as a reward for their loyalty and service. But land is a scarce resource, and there are often more claims to land than can be supported. Thus, closest siblings may unite against a more distant relative to maintain land among themselves or siblings may compete for scarce land among themselves, becoming bitter enemies and dividing the kinship or domestic group.

The Amhara peasant's supernatural world includes both Christian and pagan elements. Although Monophysite Christianity is the legitimate religion of the Amhara people, who in fact define their tribal identity largely in terms of their Christian God, the pagan or "nonlegitimate" systems of belief also play an important role in the everyday routine of the peasant's social and cultural life. There are essentially four separate realms of supernatural beliefs. First, there is the dominant Monophysite Christian religion involving the Almighty God, the Devil, and the saints and angels in Heaven. Second, there are the zar and the adbar spirits, "protectors" who exact tribute in return for physical and emotional security and who deal out punishments for failure to recognize them through the practice of the appropriate rituals. Third is the belief in the buda, a class of people who possess the evil eye, and who exert a deadly power over the descendants of God's "chosen children." The fourth category of beliefs includes the čiraq and satan, ghouls and devils that prowl the countryside, creating danger to unsuspecting persons who cross their path.

## THE STATUS OF THE EVIL EYE PEOPLE

In contrast to much of sub-Saharan Africa, evil power is not attributed to a person occupying a status at a point of social disjunction within the structure of social relations. Rather, those people who are believed to have a dangerous power are not a part of Amhara society. The buda or evil eye people are a completely separate category of population of different ethnic origin, with a rather minimum amount of interaction with the Amhara people. The buda own no land and therefore work in handicrafts, making pots from clay, fashioning tools from iron, and weaving cloth from hand-spun cotton and sheep's hair. They are known generally as ṭayb. The term is derived from the noun ṭebib which means "craftsman." It is also associated with an idea which means "to be wise" or "to be very clever." The terms ṭayb and buda are synonymous. To be buda is to have the evil eye. The term "evil eye" is also known as ayn og and sometimes kifu ayn. It designates the power to curse and destroy and reincarnate, harnessing the labor of the dead for one's own words.

The beautiful craftsmanship of the buda's work is one sign of his status. The finely made, well-proportioned water pots with their black finish are unmatched by any Amhara peasant who would deign to make one in the first place. Fashioning tools from iron takes considerably more skill and is not practiced by anyone but the ṭayb people. Although weaving is associated with the ṭayb people, many Mänze peasants have also taken up the skill, not as a trade but to accumulate needed cash. Yet the peasants say the ṭayb know a special form of weaving that the Amhara cannot learn. There is, though, a critical distinction made by the Amhara peasant that frees him from the stigma of the craft, *viz.*, that he did not inherit the trade from his father.

There are, then, two major social categories. The *rega* are those people whose ancestry are *nişu atint*, of "clean bone," unblemished by social stigma or bodily catastrophe, such as leprosy. They are the "noble people," Most Amhara trace their lineages to a near relative or ancestor who had wealth and status and who was patron of many who worked the land of their estates. A *rega* person is known by his community; his relatives and ancestors are known, and hence he cannot be suspected of being "impure." The *buda* person, on the other hand, is one who has inherited through his line the lower status. One may inherit status through either the mother's or the father's line, or both. One cannot avoid the status of *buda*. It is his destiny to be born into the tradition.

Anyone whose ancestry or kin are unknown may be suspect. If one is suspected of being *buda*, he may be liable to accusation by a family that fears that he "attacked" or "ate" or "stabbed" one of their members. Accusation must be carried out on one's own without the sanction of the courts. If one marries a person whose family is unknown, and it is later learned that the relatives were of *buda* status, the *rega* spouse will be forced to effect a divorce and another spouse of "clean bone" will then be found as a substitute. Sometimes the spouse who is *buda* will be driven from the community, or more rarely killed, for attempting to taint a family's line.

There is no sure way to recognize a *buda*, for their physical qualities may not differ discernibly from other people. They may be thinner than usual, because their blood is believed to be thinner than a normal Amhara person's blood. They may have an eye deformity or suffer discharge of tears or pus from their eyes. They may tend to look sidewise at people, or they may have very light skin, or they may be believed to have an ashen substance in their mouths and be unable to spit saliva. But these qualities are not, in themselves, sufficient to arouse suspicion. There are other more convincing characteristics, such as occupation. If a stranger comes to town and is overly friendly, suspicion may be aroused that he is too eager to befriend others, and hence, possibly over-anxious about concealing his true identity. The relations of *buda* people with *rega* people are in *status quo*, being neither overly peaceful nor overly combative. They mix with each other easily, as in court, in the shops, and in market places without repercussions, as long as their social relations are on a superficial basis.

## THE ATTACK OF THE EVIL EYE

The real threat of the *buda* people to the *rega* people is the ever-present possibility of attack. Most people are fearful of even mentioning the *buda*, especially at night, because if they are overheard by a *buda* he will become angry and one of the family may be "eaten," thereby causing sickness or death. A person is most vulnerable to being "eaten" when the *buda* sees fear, worry, or anxiety in his potential victim. Therefore, it helps to maintain one's composure when in the presence of a *buda*, acting naturally as if the *buda* did not matter at all. The peasant who is especially good looking or whose child is considered beautiful, or someone who does something extraordinary, may fear the attack of the evil eye because of the envy believed to be kindled in the *buda*. The attack is not limited to human beings. The evil eye can attack any living object. When a person is "eaten" he may know immediately that he has been attacked, for the consequences may occur at the same time as the strike. But the symptoms can just as easily be delayed for a few hours, a day, or a week, rarely longer. If a *buda* has planned an attack on some victim, but this victim suddenly falls ill before the strike is to be made, then the *buda* may merely wait patiently to see the outcome of the patient's illness. If the person recovers, the *buda* may then attack. If he dies, the *buda* will then attend to the activity that involves *buda* people with the dead. It is believed that when one is feeling ill the body is more vulnerable than ever to an attack by the evil eye.

The process of attack may occur in one of several different manners. Because of the power of the evil eye, *buda* people can change into hyenas and roam the countryside at night. It is convenient for a *buda* to attack a victim in this form in order to conceal his human identity. The Amhara attach great salience to the hyena, partly because they believe in both the natural and the supernatural forms of this animal. If the *buda*, in seeking out a victim, assumes the form of the hyena, the transformation takes place by his first taking off the hair and then rolling in the ashes of the hearth. Once transformed into a hyena, he then searches for a victim, and on finding one, fixes the unfortunate person with an evil gaze, returns home, rolls in the ashes to turn back into human form, and waits for the victim to die. The second method of attack involves the evil eye person finding a victim, twisting the root of a certain plant and forming a loop with this root as if one were tying a knot. The loop is then drawn smaller very slowly, and while this is being done, the victim dies. After the victim is buried, the *buda* squats by the graveside and slowly loosens the knot while shouting to the corpse to arise. The body is exhumed and the grave is then closed up again by retightening the knot. The third method of attack involves giving the evil eye gaze to the victim and then waiting for his death. After burial the body is exhumed by carrying two round, thin, lentil-pancake breads to the grave, one lying flat and the other folded twice. Unfolding the one bread opens the grave and brings out the body. Folding up the other recloses the grave.

The people most liable to attack are those who have a bit more wealth than the average person, who are handsome, and who are proud of their beautiful children. Those who become especially liable to attack are those who become too familiar with the *buda* person, which heightens one's chances of succumbing to the gaze of the evil eye. One comes into physical proximity with *buda* people in daily affairs, but social distance is usually maintained. A likely danger to the *rega* people is the presence of a beautiful *buda* woman or handsome *buda* man. A *rega* who sleeps with a *buda* will grow thinner and thinner because the eye of the *buda* will suck the blood out of the victim, causing the victim to lose his or her appetite and to become weak and helpless. When a *rega* is attracted to a *buda* and the *buda* wishes to draw the *rega* nearer, the *buda* will wait for a moment of privacy and then will utter to the *rega* something about seeing the genitals revealed through the *rega's* clothes. This will fill the *rega* with excitement and then the *rega* will "fall with" the *buda* lover. The warm affectionate relationship can be maintained without serious danger; but when there is a quarrel, the *rega*, already weakened by the blood given up to the *buda*, will be "eaten" and become seriously ill.

However the attack is effectuated and however the corpse is taken from the grave, the ultimate goal of the *buda* is to use the victim as a slave. After being exhumed, the corpse is taken to the house of the *buda* where it is brought back to life in order to serve the *buda*. But the slave is mute, unable to utter a single sound. The *buda* owns two switches. One switch is used to turn the slave into a pot when visitors come; and then when the outsiders have left, a rap on the pot with the other switch transforms the pot into a slave again. In this way outside interference is prevented. When the slave is treated cruelly, it will shed silent tears, desperately trying to weep. (It is interesting to note that to be silent in the presence of one's superiors and to suffer indignities in silence is the obligation of

children and the traits attributed to the despised dog.) The slave of the *buda* does not go on indefinitely in its risen state. After seven years the body begins to disintegrate, finally turning into ashes and leaving the *buda* without a "helper."

The *buda's* distinctive activities are not fully intentional. The *buda* has within his body a quality or power known as *qalb*. *Qalb* is a subtle, internal, unconscious desire to perform those activities which make the *buda* so notorious. In the *buda's* daily interactions with the *rega* people of the community, there is really little difference between the two groups, both sharing feelings of love and hate, envy and covetousness, anger and aggression. But the *buda* has this additional power gained from the association with the devil that creates an illegitimate advantage over those of higher status and greater legitimate advantage. The *buda*, by his very nature, must "eat" others. He does this in order to better his chances for gaining opportunities and achieving success in his daily life among the *rega* people. He uses his power, then, to make himself equal with others who have more land, more "helpers" such as tenants, servants, and former slaves, and thus he attempts to acquire those objects, persons, and services that he covets among the *rega* Amhara people. There is a difference of opinion as to whether or not the *buda* himself can be the object and victim of evil eye attack. Some Amhara say that just as the *rega* fight among themselves for the wealth of the lineage, so the *buda* people fight and attack each other with the evil eye for more equal shares of wealth. But other Amhara say that this is not true; that the *buda* people have much more to gain from the *rega*, and furthermore, know how to protect themselves from each other's attack.

## PRECAUTIONS AGAINST EVIL EYE ATTACK

Since amorous relations with *buda* are not condoned by the Amhara, especially by the clergy, the priests teach that one's only protection against a *buda* lover is to crawl to church on one's hands and knees for seven days, the priest's intent being to frustrate the beginnings of such a relationship. Parents who fear their child is weak and vulnerable to the influence of the evil eye may, on the advice of a *däbtärä* (lower order clergyman), adopt the custom of addressing their child in the gender opposite to the child's actual sex. The custom of shaving the heads of children, leaving only a tuft of hair over the former fontanelle of the boys and a ring of hair around the heads of the girls, provides protection against minor attacks of lice, most often considered initiated by an envious *buda*. If an Amhara is worried about a child's imminent danger from an evil glance, a light, rapid spitting into the child's face provides a short-term protection. Compliments are always suspect if not accompanied with the invocation, "Let God protect you from the evil eye!" And at feasts all must be served equally lest someone deprived becomes envious and curses the food, making the participants sick.

Another precaution taken by the Amhara peasant against the possibility of attack is to be silent and guarded. When one expresses his emotions too freely and becomes too outgoing with others, he places himself in a position of vulnerability to the evil eye. This disposition is fairly generalized. When one is seen laughing and joking freely with others it is usually with close and trusted friends and relatives. At most other times the peasant presents a facade of stolidity and silence. In this way one does not attract the attention of an envious *buda*, who may resent persons enjoying themselves while he is not invited to share in the mirth. The custom of hiding one's face behind the large soft cloak, concealing especially the mouth and the nose, is one common way to avoid the penetration of the evil eye.

If a person succumbs to the attack of the evil eye, the family of the deceased may intercede and prevent the *buda* from wresting the corpse from its grave. A member of the family must watch the grave for forty days and forty nights (some say twelve days and twelve nights) after the body has been interred, allowing sufficient time to elapse so that the body will be adequately decomposed and thereby deprive the *buda* of a body to possess. If the grave is watched the *buda* will not come. In this way the family saves their relative from seven years of slavery.

## DIAGNOSIS AND CURES FOR THE EVIL EYE ATTACK

Diagnosis of the symptoms and subsequent treatment may be carried out in one of four ways. In the first method, if the family is poor and they know a *däbtärä* of the local church, they may take the patient to him. For a modest fee, he performs a rite over holy water, praying and pronouncing words in the ancient language of Giiz used in the Christian religious ceremonies. The patient then drinks the holy water and breathes in the smoke of a burning root. The *däbtärä* may find the diagnostic answer in his magic star book, while the holy water and inhaled smoke may effect a cure.

A second alternative is to bring the patient to a wizard, one who has powers gained through agents of the devil, to communicate with the *zar* spirits and to effect cures for many kinds of illness. First, a silver bracelet is placed on the patient's left wrist. The wizard then goes into a trance, seeking possession by a devil who may reveal the appropriate cure for the illness. In seeking out the attacker, a very hot fire is made in the hearth and a piece of metal, a sickle or knife blade, is put into the flames and heated until glowing. The hot metal is applied to the patient's face, making a small pattern of burns. As the wounds heal, the scars will become transferred onto the face of the attacker in the same place and with the same pattern. The family must then seek out the guilty party.

A third method does not involve the use of specialists outside of an elder member of the family who knows the procedures and whose age gives him a bit better judgment. When a person begins biting his lip it is the first sign that he has been attacked by the evil eye, although this symptom does not always appear. If relatives are around they will first tie the victim's left thumb with string. Then the victim will be made to breathe the smoke from the dung fire. After taking in sufficient dung smoke, the victim gains the power to speak in the spirit and voice of his attacker. The victim begins recounting the chain of events of his attacker that led to the confrontation and the attack. Then the relatives ask the possessed victim what form of compensation should be given to counteract the attack. The victim, speaking in the voice of the attacker, demands some filthy matter such as beer dregs, ashes, a dead rat, or human or animal excrement. The victim eats this and soon cries, "I've left him! I've left my victim!" or something of this order. Then the family knows that the devil has left the body, and the stricken person may now recover. The cure involves active vocal participation. If the victim cannot speak, he will surely die.

The fourth method of diagnosis and counteraction involves the evil eye person in a more direct, mundane way. When the victim is attacked and he begins to bite his lip and to act strangely, he may appear to go into a daze and begin to jump and shout "in tongues." At this point, a relative must try to get the victim to utter the name of his attacker. If he does not, the family may tie a rope to the victim and then have the victim lead the relatives to the house of his attacker. If neither of these tactics are successful, they may have one other indication. If the victim begins crying suddenly, it is a sign that the attacker is in close proximity and that the relatives must only scout the area and seize the *buda* person they come across. If the suspect is found, he is brought to the bedside of the victim, by gunpoint if need be. The relatives take a lock of hair and a bit of clothing from the *buda*, preferably without his knowledge, and then the *buda* is made to spit on the victim and walk over him. A fire is built with the hair and cloth and the victim then breathes in the smoke. He continues inhaling the smoke until he cries, in the voice of the spirit, that the illness has left his body.

No matter what the method, if the *buda* gives up his victim there will be no reprisals by the victim's family. If the victim dies, the *buda* may be ejected from the community or killed.

## THE MYTHOLOGY OF THE ORIGIN OF THE BUDA PEOPLE

According to the Amhara, the beginnings of *buda* status go back to Creation. It is said that Eve had thirty children, and one day God asked Eve to show Him her children. Eve became suspicious and apprehensive and hid fifteen of them from the sight of God. God knew her act of disobedience and declared the fifteen children she showed God as His chosen children and cursed the fifteen she hid, declaring that they go henceforth into the world as devils and wretched creatures of the earth. Now some of the children complained and begged God's mercy. God heard them and, being merciful, made some of them foxes, jackals, rabbits, etc., so that they might exist as Earth's creatures in a dignified manner. Some of the hidden children he left human, but sent them away with the curse of being agents of the devil. These human counterparts of the devil are the ancestors of the *buda* people. There occurs a pleat in time and the story takes up its theme again when Christ was baptized at age thirty. As told by an old Amhara peasant farmer:

The angry devils, envious of God's favoring Christ while they suffered God's curse, tried to kill Christ. But Christ ran and fled his enemies. He hid in the crevice of a great cliff, sharing it with the giant *gabalo* lizard. While hidden, many children were killed by the devils in their search for "God's child," but they were unsuccessful in finding Christ. All the animals were asked to betray the whereabouts of Christ, but they refused and they were

beaten and tortured to no avail. But the lizard waved his head from side to side showing Christ's pursuers where he hid. Christ saw this and cursed the lizard so that to this day this lizard still sways his head so. No one could get Christ down out of the crevice in the cliff. They tried with ropes and ladders to no avail. Then, the clever *buda* people made giant tongs of wood and plucked Jesus Christ out of the crevice. The blacksmiths made the nails and the carpenters made the cross and while Christ hung on the cross he cursed those people whose skills made it possible to crucify him.

Some Amhara claim that the devil is the sole source of *buda* qualities and power. Others say the origin of *buda* existence is different from the source of their power. Although their existence is associated with the devil, their power comes from a different source only questionably related to the devil. Although there are several versions of the myth, the following example narrated by an adolescent Amhara student is typical:

The source of *buda* power is an ancient man who has immortality. He has no arms and no legs. He is like a lump of flesh and just sits at a place called Yerimma which is a cave of extremely great depth. He is, indeed, endowed with supernatural powers. Each year the *buda* people make their annual visit to this lump of man with their small children who are just learning to walk and to talk. This ancient man can distinguish between the *rega* who may come and the *buda* themselves. He rejects the former and accepts the latter. The ancient man then teaches the *buda* children all the "arts" to the *buda* trade and then presents the child with the leaf from an *iṣ* plant (also used by devils to make themselves invisible so as to avoid being eaten by the hyena). And every year each *buda* must make a sacrifice to this ancient man of one human being. The sacrifice is like a tax, and if the *buda* cannot find a suitable victim by the time the sacrifice is due, he must sacrifice his own child.

## INTERPRETATION

There are essentially three analytically separable levels of behavior upon which to focus. First, there is the overt and manifest level of verbal behavior that expresses the configuration of ideas and feelings recognized as the evil eye belief system. This level of behavior is explicated through ethnographic description. Second, there is the analysis of values and psychological pre-dispositions, areas of positive attraction, indifference, anger, and fear or dread. The symbols in the cultural configurations, as expressed through the narratives of the Amhara, point out these areas of emotional salience and foci of concern. Through a symbolic analysis particular kinds of themes become evident. Some of these themes are based in the manifest functions of the belief, while others point to covert symbolic and latent functions of the belief system. Third, there is the social context that the symbols express and the social context of the actual behavior that expresses the evil eye belief.

With this approach it is possible to examine "the relationship between explicit cultural forms (symbols) and underlying cultural orientations" (Ortner 1973:49), where these symbolic forms provide the vehicle for the analysis of the relationships between underlying cultural orientations and observable patterns of sociocultural behavior. Foster (1972:166) offers a caveat that must be taken into consideration when analyzing the motivational significance of a particular belief or custom, which is, that original motives often disappear with the institutionalization of the belief or custom, and in its place, habit becomes the primary source for the reinforcement of the pattern. Also Kennedy (1969) argues against the more familiar teleological functional interpretations offered by social anthropologists when he proposes that these institutionalized beliefs and customs may themselves be the source of fears, or pathological responses to situations that present no real threat and could conceivably be defined in more innocuous terms. In his discussion of witchcraft belief, Kennedy (1969:177) states:

...witchcraft systems are forms of institutionalized patterns of psychopathology which tend to be pathogenic and which create built-in self-perpetuating stress systems... (and) tend to regularly generate the hate and aggression which they allegedly function to relieve.

Including the evil eye belief within the purview of the problem of witchcraft is not without justification, for, although there are quite noticeable differences, the similarities demand some scrutiny. Spooner (1970:311) notes how well known the evil eye belief is to us all, yet how little attention has been given to it by ethnographers:

...the concept of the Evil Eye is reported throughout Europe, the Middle East, and North Africa, and in so many cultures elsewhere that it may be regarded as a universal phenomenon. Further, it is reported in circumstances which show it to be undoubtedly of the same order of phenomena as witchcraft.

Douglas, in agreement with Spooner, identifies the evil eye belief as a special case of witchcraft belief which becomes expressed at critical social

disjunctions between persons who hold structurally generated enmity toward each other. Her definition (Douglas 1970:xxx) of a witch can be generalized to the Amhara's conception of the *buda*:

The witch is an attacker and deceiver. He uses what is impure and potent to harm what is pure and helpless. The symbols of what we recognize across the globe as witchcraft all build on the theme of vulnerable internal goodness attacked by external power.

Douglas fits the evil eye belief into a typology she develops from the cases written up in the volume she edited. She (Douglas 1970:xxvii) proposes two general categories of witches: (a) the witch as outsider, and (b) the witch as internal enemy. Each of these categories has subtypes. The outsider type can be either (1) a witch not identified or punished, or (2) a witch expelled from the community. In this outsider type, the primary function of accusation is to redefine the boundaries of social solidarity. The witch as internal enemy appears in the more complexly organized societies, where two or more factions are involved within the community. The body of the victim is usually symbolized in the image of the betrayed community, where the internal strength is sapped or polluted by one in very close contact with the other members of the community. Where the witch is conceived as an internal enemy, the witch can be identified (1) as a member of a rival faction, where the function of the accusation is to redefine faction boundaries or the faction hierarchy; (2) as a dangerous deviant, where the function of the accusation is to control the deviant in the name of community values, or (3) as an internal enemy with outside liaisons, where the function of accusation is to promote factional rivalry, split the community, and/or redefine the hierarchy. Given this typology, Douglas (1970:xxx) then suggests an hypothesis for further testing:

...when the source of witchcraft power is thought to come from inside the witch, particularly from an area beyond conscious control, the social situation will correspond to type 3 above, where the witch is seen as an internal enemy, not as a member of a rival faction.

In the Amhara case, we can recognize similar qualities between the witch defined by Douglas and the *buda* as conceived by the Amhara peasant. However, the correspondence that Douglas suggests is not borne out in the Amhara case. The *buda* with internal and somewhat uncontrollable powers is not conceived of as a person internal to the

Amhara group. The Amhara conceive of the *buda* as an outsider who nevertheless lives, geographically but not integrally, within the social networks of the Amhara people. Thus, the *buda* does not quite fit into any of the categories that Douglas has proposed. This exception to her typology suggests that much wider comparison is still necessary.

The dominant theme expressed in the Amhara evil eye belief system is one which is shared by possibly all those societies that maintain a belief in the evil eye: the fear of being envied and the interpretation of certain misfortunes as the consequences of another's envy. In Spooner's (1970:314) discussion of the evil eye belief in the Middle East, this theme is especially salient:

> ...the concept of the Evil Eye appears to be an institutionalized psychological idiom for the... personification of misfortune,... insofar as misfortune, or the fear of it, may relate to the fear of outsiders and their envy.

In his careful analysis of the concept of envy Foster (1972:167) defines envy as the act of looking maliciously upon someone; looking askance at; casting an evil eye upon; feeling displeasure and/or ill-will in relation to the superiority of another person. Foster (1972:168) states that envy, along with the closely associated feeling of jealousy, "involves a dyad... whose relationship is mediated, or structured, by an intervening property or object." Thus, a jealous person is jealous of what he possesses and fears he might lose, while an envious person does not envy the thing, but rather envies the person who has it. Foster considers the predisposition to envy to be most apparent in peasant societies, or in what he calls "deprivation societies" of scarce resources where people hold to the "image of limited good" and where social interaction and transaction is defined and perceived as a "zero-sum" game, and where one's advantage derives from the other's loss. Foster (1972:169) maintains that in those societies where the "zero-sum" game is the definition of the situation, it is the relative differences between two parties that triggers the omnipresently latent envy into overt expression. He further notes that in primitive and peasant societies, food, children and health, those things most vital for the survival of the family, rank at the top as objects of envy. Cattle and crops have some, but lesser, salience.

Congruent with sub-Saharan witchcraft belief in the context of well-defined and enforced rules and norms, envy and its consequences are mitigated to a considerable degree, primarily because both the structures of the family and of the class/caste system involve cultural definitions stipulating that the relationships between status classes or between the generations are noncompetitive. Foster (1972:171) maintains that the function of this kind of definition is to eliminate or mitigate rivalry between persons in different categories of status or between persons in different social classes, thereby lubricating interclass and interpersonal transactions. Among the Amhara, the principle of patriarchal domination maintains order in domestic and political groups. The absence of the patriarch or of a mediating superior authority generates, or is believed to generate, anarchy within a group having no mediating authority among equals. Although this principle holds among the Amhara, the *buda* people are of non-Amhara tribal identity, and hence can only pose a threat to the Amhara by virtue of their being different. This difference, I maintain, is symbolic of what the Amhara detest, fear, or dread.

The *buda* people are "strangers" to the land of the Amhara. Originating from a different region, they are landless and make a living with their manual skills of smithing, tanning, weaving, and pottery-making. *Buda* status contrasts with *rega* or "nobility" status. Both statuses are inherited consanguineally on a bilateral basis. The origin myth of the *buda* people expresses the basic themes found in the belief system in general and in certain actual social situations: envy and conflict between siblings who are treated differentially by a superior authority. In the myth, envy and conflict are generated by the curse of God for the sins of the mother Eve. Added to this is God's favoring of His child, Christ, the "chosen" son of God. The story of the envious siblings' hunting down of Christ in order to attain equality among siblings has a strong parallel in real-life situations where a father favors one child with the lion's share of land, creating sibling conflict over the equalization of their rights to their father's land. The myth and the belief have it that the *buda* people inherit their *qalb*, a power gained from the devil which gives them the uncontrollable drive to "eat" the *rega* people, who happen to be the Amhara, to cause their death and to bring them back to life as slaves. It is a conception that expresses a dominant theme of envious status inferiors using illegitimate means to gain an advantage over status superiors who possess a legitimate means of domination.

The *buda* belief suggests that the *buda* are the symbolic expression of the latent consequences of unmediated equal status relationships between men and between a man and a woman. Without pyramidal control mechanisms, this form of relationship generates the anxiety of unstable and unpredictable consequences between two dependent and self-oriented egos, the ultimate consequences of which are symbolized in the logically extended extreme of domination—the relationship of master and slave. The function of the evil eye belief in maintaining the social system can be teleologically interpreted as the displacement of a threat and its projection onto an outgroup. The threat of equal status rivalry between kin and siblings outside of well-defined situations is projected onto the *buda* people, thereby preserving the internal solidarity (what there is of it) of the Amhara people. *Buda* belief appears to be a function of a power superiority among status equals based on the model of the eldest son as the object of envy by his less fortunate younger siblings, for it is the eldest son, in Mänze, who normally is the favored one and who inherits the lion's share of the father's land.

Belief in the evil eye among the Mänze Amhara, then, has a projective function which, through the transformation from personality trait to cultural configuration, becomes manifest as a form of domination anxiety expressed through culturally legitimated ideas of reference. This projective process is by no means complete, for it is known that the most serious concerns of the Amhara involve sibling and other kin conflicts over unequal usufructory rights to land. The landless *buda*, who is dependent upon others for his livelihood, is the symbolic reflection of the threat of becoming landless and without authority, *ergo*, without identity, because of the ambitions of a more powerful relative or the father's curse of disinheritance.

# 24 Witchcraft as Negative Charisma

## Paul R. Turner

Anthropological literature abounds with accounts of witchcraft seen as a means of social control and as the force by which the social equilibrium is re-established

Reprinted from Paul R. Turner, 1970, "Witchcraft as Negative Charisma," *Ethnology*, 9: 366–372, with permission of the author and *Ethnology: An International Journal of Cultural and Social Anthropology*.

when conflict shakes the social networks. Since witchcraft accusations may be leveled not only at cultural misfits and downwardly mobile persons as Kluckhohn (1962) discovered, but at those in positions of power as well, Paul Turner in this brief article asks under what circumstances such a person's behavior will inspire the dreaded indictment. In this Chontal village in Oaxaca, Mexico, it is believed that illness or other misfortunes may be caused by spiritual or human agencies, the latter being people with superhuman power to cause harm, most especially witches. Here an individual who had attained the highest statuses in the community is accused of witchcraft and executed by a hired gun employed by the father of the presumed victim. The ethnologist is able to elicit testimony concerning the ways in which a witch is identified, the most important being the making of witchcraft statements. Says Turner, "These are dangerous statements to make in a disease-ridden society where people are especially subject to sudden illness and death. In this context, threatening talk and sickness reinforce each other because witchcraft talk without sickness would soon lose its significance, and sickness without threatening talk would only be puzzling."

Most witchcraft studies to date have been what Victor Turner (1964) calls taxonomic rather than dynamic descriptions. They have been static descriptions, using a traditional structural-functional approach, that have failed to explain the practice of witchcraft. This failure has been due in part to an excessive concern with social variables and with little or no mention of psychological variables. Thus we are told that witchcraft acts to maintain the individual in equilibrium with his neighbors (Wolf 1967: 512), but no reason is given as to why anyone would disrupt that equilibrium. Previous studies have also failed to provide enough of the context in which witchcraft is practiced. We are thus told which persons are likely to be accused of witchcraft (Marwick 1967) but not the circumstances that actually trigger such an accusation. This paper will attempt to provide a dynamic description of a witchcraft incident among the Highland Chontal Indians of Oaxaca, Mexico, by both supplying the necessary context in which the act took place as well as the motivation of the alleged witch.

The data come from the village of Santiago, one of nineteen Chontal villages located in the southeastern part of the state of Oaxaca. These villages are about a day's journey by foot from the Pan-American highway and are linked to each other by mountain trails. The average population of the villages is 500 people, and they fit rather closely the concept of the typical corporate peasant community developed by Wolf (1967:505–513).

The people of Santiago speak a language that is considered to belong to the Hokan family of languages. They also speak Spanish, but no one in the village is completely fluent in Spanish and only a few can read it with any degree of comprehension. However, Spanish has been the language used in the relatively few contacts that the villagers have had with outsiders. Because of their limited knowledge of Spanish, the Chontal have only vaguely understood some of the ideas and concepts that priests and school teachers from the larger Mexican society have tried to convey to them. After more than 400 years since the conquest of Mexico, the belief system of these people still contains concepts that were held in pre-conquest times.

This belief system describes a world controlled by personal and visible beings rather than by impersonal forces. The pantheon of gods includes such celestial beings as the sun and moon and such earthly animals as foxes and snakes. Each of these gods has power, and the appropriate ones must be appeased before certain events are undertaken. Such events include the birth of a child, marriage, building a house, oven, or sugar-cane press, raising livestock, planting and harvesting a field, and holding an important office in the civil-religious hierarchy. Each event has its appropriate ritual, that is performed in secret following a written formula that involves the counting out of hundreds of pitch-pine sticks. This must be done secretly because the younger men do not know the difference between a witchcraft ritual and a beneficial one. Only a few men in their forties or older own the written formulas, and they either use them for their own needs or sell their services to others who are willing to pay a fee of a week's wages or more. The performer of the ritual abstains from smoking, drinking, and sexual intercourse just before carrying out the act, but the beneficiary must be ritually clean for a longer period of time. This period may be as long as a year for the president of the village, who may not have sexual intercourse during his term of office. Failure to placate a god properly is believed to result in misfortune to the negligent one—usually in the form of sickness to him, his family, or his animals which is often fatal.

Sickness can also be caused by soul-loss due to fright. The soul is believed to have such a precarious relationship to the body that any startling event can cause some of the soul to leave the body. This displaced soul substance or power is seized by the earth at the location where the person was frightened. The sick person can only be restored to health by someone, usually a native curer, performing a healing ceremony, which involves entreating the earth to release the sick person's soul so that it may re-enter the body of its owner.

Not only is the earth inhabited by powerful beings who can make a person sick, but some men are also thought to have this power. People believe that years ago the old men were particularly powerful. So powerful were they thought to be that if a younger person met one of them on the trail without addressing him respectfully and bowing, the younger person would stumble, fall, and die as he passed. One old man in particular was so powerful that everyone in the village notified him before doing anything of importance. If they failed to notify him they believed that they would become sick and die. He was called the "dangerous man," and no one in Santiago today is comparable to him. Old people are not feared as they once were, but they still are accused of making others sick and causing their deaths.

Old men are the most respected and powerful individuals in the social system of the Chontal. Their status is based on sex and age, but there is relatively little difference between one old man and another. Almost all of them have held the same offices in the civil-religious hierarchy and own about the same amount of material possessions.

No one can accumulate much wealth in Santiago because of the low subsistence level of the economy, which is based on milpa farming of marginal land on the sides of mountains. A number of factors, such as lack of rain, insect infestation, and strong winds, combine effectively to prevent anyone from having a surplus of corn to sell.

Corn is the main part of the low-protein, vitamin-deficient diet that these people eat and that lowers their resistance to disease. They do not understand how people become infested with parasites nor how disease germs are spread, so they are unconcerned with matters of sanitation. Not only do difficult-to-control virus epidemics sweep through the village, but more easily prevented diseases, such as paratyphoid, amoebic dysentery, and worm infestation, also affect large numbers of people. I kept a record of the medical cases for the first six months of 1963 and found that over half of the people of Santiago came to me for treatment in that period of time. Their symptoms divide into two categories that account for most of the cases:

fever, chills, cough, and headache for half of the patients; stomach distress, vomiting, and diarrhea for the other half. These are symptoms of serious diseases that can result in death if medical treatment is not available. The incidence of these diseases is more than four times greater among the Chontal than among American Indian groups for which we have records covering the same period of time (U.S. Department of Health, Education, and Welfare 1967:14).

Adequate medical treatment is usually not available in the village nor sought elsewhere because the Chontal does not understand the modern concept of disease. He has a different set of cultural values that makes it difficult for him to participate in a doctor-patient relationship. Even his own language is a hindrance because it does not provide him with the vocabulary that he needs to describe his symptoms to a Spanish-speaking doctor. When a Chontal does seek outside medical help, he usually goes to the cultural equivalent of his own native curer and not to a medical doctor.

In those instances when he does go to a doctor, it is often too late for treatment. This was the case with N, a man from Santiago who died last year. N took sick when he was still president of the village, and he thought that his illness might have been caused by his failure to perform the appropriate ritual when the church was built. He called the elders of the village to his home and asked them to perform the ritual to see if that would result in his being restored to health. The elders did as he requested, but his condition continued to get worse. Some friends then persuaded him to go to the hospital in Oaxaca for treatment. On the way they stopped in Tlacolula and consulted a curer, who told N that he had either a rock, a piece of beef or pork, or a dog's head in his stomach and that he would not recover. They also saw a doctor there, who diagnosed N's illness as a bad tumor. They went on to Oaxaca and stayed in the house of a friend who was related to N. Another curer was consulted, and he told N that he would not recover. A young doctor who lived nearby gave N an injection for his pain and told him that he needed to go to the hospital for an operation. N was taken to the hospital for X-rays, and he stayed there for about four weeks; but no surgery was performed. He was then released from the hospital and died in Oaxaca shortly thereafter.

This man evidently died from cancer that was not detected until it was too late for treatment. Although that explanation might satisfy a person with some knowledge of modern medicine, it does not satisfy a Chontal. The kind of an explanation that makes sense to him is one framed in terms of witchcraft. Hence, despite the doctor's diagnosis, the people of Santiago are convinced that N was a victim of witchcraft. N himself blamed a compadre of his for making him sick, even though the compadre never made any statements that could be interpreted as witchcraft threats. A close friend of N blamed a man from a neighboring village for the witchcraft act. This man burned some of N's sugar cane by mistake and had to pay a fine. When he heard of N's sickness, he made a statement that was considered to have witchcraft implications. Such statements are taken seriously by the Chontal, who believe that there is a connection between threatening talk and sickness.

As recently as 1966 a man whom I had known over a period of eight years was killed for making witchcraft statements. The alleged witch, R, was a man in his fifties who had strong likes and dislikes that he freely expressed. He had advanced through every office in the village until he was elected president and later became a member of the socially respected elders. He was not a social misfit in any sense, and I was shocked to read in a letter that he had been killed. I visited Santiago several months later and was told the following account. R had a mother-in-law who raised turkeys, and one of them wandered into her neighbor's kitchen and began to eat some corn. The neighbor's daughter threw a stick at the turkey and inadvertently killed it. She hid it in a ditch, and, when R's mother-in-law asked the girl about the missing turkey, she claimed that she knew nothing about it. The old woman soon found the dead turkey and confronted the girl with it. R's mother-in-law said that something bad would happen because of this, and the girl's father, L, replied that if anything did happen, he would know who had caused it.

Shortly afterward, L's burro died suddenly, and his daughter became ill and soon passed away. R's mother-in-law claimed that the girl died because she was the one who had secretly killed her turkey. L blamed the old woman for having his daughter killed through the witchcraft of her son-in-law, and he went to the village authorities and asked them to intervene. They refused, and the matter seemed to be settled. Then, however, L's wife took sick and died. At this point, R and his wife made a trip to a valley town and returned saying that he had ordered a Mass said so that L and all he had might be destroyed. The village authorities arrested R and his wife and made them pay a fine of 300 pesos, even though R claimed to know nothing about witchcraft. R made his wife pay the fine because he said it was her mother's turkey that had started all the trouble. In retaliation, R's wife began to tell people that her husband actually was a witch. Three months later he was ambushed late at night and shot by a gunman whom L had hired. When I asked five men from this village to tell me in private conversations whether they thought R was a witch or not, they gave me the following accounts.

## ACCOUNT 1

They say he is a witch because he made a candle out of a cup of oil with a wick of cotton and grass and put it in the church to burn. When it began to burn low, it sputtered and flamed like a match when it is lit. When people saw it, they recognized it as the work of a witch. The officials took it and began looking for the one who did it. R came one day and asked them if they had seen what had happened to his cup, so they knew who had put it there.

Then, too, people from the village of San Pedro tell us that R knew how to practice witchcraft because he was telling them how to do it. Not only was he telling them, but he made witchcraft books and sold them to people from that village.

Then when I wanted to leave the religion of the village, he said that if I did I would be dead in a year. My brother-in-law told me that if I would say the word, he would kill R for what he had said.

## ACCOUNT 2

Half of his life was good and half was bad. He was bad like his father, who had such a severe case of skin disease that it bled. People say that R was a witch, but I do not know. They said that he had a witchcraft book bound in some kind of hide.

He once told his daughter, after he had some mescal to drink, that he was responsible for the sickness of his stepson's wife, and if she did not respect him as she should she would die. His daughter told someone else, who finally told the stepson, who agreed that his stepfather was a witch. My wife took two pieces of bone out of the sick woman's urinary tract, and she got well. Now, how could those bones have gotten in there if R had not placed them there through witchcraft?

## ACCOUNT 3

They say that he was a witch, but I do not know. What is a witch like? They might know what a witch is like, but I do not, and it is not right to kill your fellow man.

## ACCOUNT 4

They say he was a witch because he taught others the old customs, and he had his witchcraft book. I do not know whether he was a witch or not.

## ACCOUNT 5

Who knows whether he was a witch or not? But my son had already made plans to marry when R said something bad. I didn't think much about it at the time, but when my son took sick right afterwards and died in seventeen days, I realized that R was a witch.

He also got mad and said bad things because I gave my son-in-law a horse. Later the horse died because of R and his witchcraft.

Then, when I was president, his father would not do his share of the communal work. When we tried to force him to work, R told us to leave his father alone because he was a witch. I asked the Alcade what we should do, and he said to leave the old man alone if he claimed to be a witch.

In three of the above accounts R is accused of making witchcraft statements. These are dangerous statements to make in a disease-ridden society where people are especially subject to sudden illness and death. In this context, threatening talk and sickness reinforce each other because witchcraft talk without sickness would soon lose its significance, and sickness without threatening talk would only be puzzling. R had used threatening statements down through the years to coerce others into doing what he wanted them to do. Enough of these statements had been followed by the sickness and death to his victims that a consensus of opinion began to form against him. He would probably never have been killed, though, if L's burro, daughter, and wife had not died in rapid succession after the turkey incident. The clustering of these events was convincing evidence to L that he was a victim of witchcraft and that he had to take immediate action before he was completely destroyed.

Probably no anthropologist has ever witnessed the actual practice of witchcraft. Indeed, few Chontal have witnessed it either. What they consider to be the practice of witchcraft is the threatening statement accompanied by misfortune. Not only is R's case an example of this, but it is a recurring element in the following accounts told me by a man in his fifties who was asked to describe all the witches he had ever known.

## ACCOUNT 6

There was a man named C who used to kill people by using pitch-pine sticks and copal (tree resin).

Question: How did people know about it?

Answer: That's what he told people.

Question: What happened to C?

Answer: He died a natural death. A long time ago there used to be lots of witches, and they didn't kill them like they do now. Today people are not afraid of witches, so they kill them.

## Account 7

A witch by the name of M would begin to talk after drinking just a little bit of mescal.

Question: What did he say?

Answer: He'd say that he knew lots of things. He claimed that whoever said bad words to him or got into a fight with him would suffer. But he didn't scare people. One time late at night they went to kill him with a machete. They caught him by surprise and hit him in the head and neck but they didn't kill him. He told the town officials about it and then notified the district judge. The ones who had attacked him were arrested and paid a big fine. He got over his wounds and died a natural death.

## Account 8

Another witch was named D, but he was just a young man about 25 years old.

Question: What did he do?

Answer: He caused small children to die. He also caused the death of women who would not make love with him. He would get mad it they refused to have intercourse with him. Then when the woman got sick, he would say that it was too bad that she had refused him and had to suffer. Finally a group of young men took their rifles and machetes along with them and went to his ranch. There they killed him and his wife.

## Account 9

The brother of D was also a witch. His name was F, and he always performed the rituals before he did anything. One day he beat his wife, and she had a relative who told people all about the rituals he performed and how he was the cause of little children's deaths. Soon afterwards some people ambushed him on the road and shot him. He lived through it, though, and later moved to another village. But he still continued in his old ways and got mad at a woman who let her chickens wander into his house. She wouldn't listen to him, so he told her that something bad was going to happen. It wasn't long until she died in childbirth and her husband blamed F for her death and shot him.

Since the use of threatening talk casts suspicion on a person, the question should be asked why anyone would take this risk. However, the risk involved is not as great as it might appear because the statements are almost always ambiguous and can be interpreted in different ways. There must probably always be an element of ambiguity in witchcraft for it to be operative in any culture. If witches could be easily identified among the Chontal, they would be eliminated before they could cause any anxiety. But no Chontal openly admits being a witch, and any of them, when angry, can make a statement which may have witchcraft implications. Accusations of being a witch are sometimes hurled back and forth when people are angry with each other. The Chontal make allowance for this kind of verbal abuse with a saying, "The tongue is not heavy," which means that it is easy to say something that the speaker may later regret.

There is a certain amount of risk in making a threatening statement, but this seems unavoidable. Witchcraft among these people involves one person coercing others, and this is only possible when the one practicing witchcraft is known. The motivation of R as well as of the other accused witches mentioned above, seems to be a desire to exercise power over others. In the process they must expose themselves, at least in part. They have what Aberle (1966:226) has called negative charisma in the sense that they are disvalued but have unusual influence over others. If "...it is through the unpredictable and uncontrollable that man most experiences power" (Aberle 1966:221), then witches have almost unlimited power. They not only predict life's most crucial uncertainty, death, but are believed actively to cause it.

# VII
## Public Health and Preventive Medicine

### Prevention of Illness and Social Control

The prevention of illness and the containment of disease are part of every medical system. But much more is involved than questions of sanitation and private and public cleanliness and robustness. For notions of contagion are bound up with religion and world view and with perceptions of the powers and intentions of one's neighbors and friends, not to mention strangers. Though intent may not be subject to control or change, behavior to some extent is, and, therefore, the medical system, especially with regard to contagion and sanitation, is directly hooked into local systems of social organization and social control. In the ultimate sense, public health as a separate field of study and practice is in fact the attempt by a society to control the behavior of its members for what the reigning groups and belief systems define as the welfare of the community as a whole. In preindustrial societies this usually includes also the control, or at least the effort to influence, the spiritual and cosmic forces that may attack the health and well-being of any mortal.

In some instances these societies evolve pragmatic means of sanitation that, whatever the intended religious or magical purpose, may in fact function to protect health and ward off disease. That is, through a long process of trial-and-error a society learns to invent at least some measures that will aid its quest for health and freedom from sickness. But empirical devices are not to be fully depended upon and appeal to spiritual beings must also be effected through ritual, prescribed ways of behaving and not behaving, and the use of fetishes, amulets, and talismans to ward off all forms of evil that may bring disease or other misfortune (Sigerist 1951:143–146).

Malevolent beings not only may be superhuman but human as well, and so the maintenance of health and control of disease also include systems of sorcery and countersorcery. Furthermore, in the sense that preindustrial societies place heavy emphasis upon individual responsibility and culpability in regard to one's own behavior, the maintenance of health requires the observance of a usually complex system of taboos, and for many illnesses it will be assumed that the individual is himself the culprit because he has transgressed a social, spiritual, or moral law.

As the papers in this and other sections show, such beliefs and practices, to be comprehended, must be seen within the context of the social structure, religion, and other institutions and processes of a society. Recently, especially with the surge of interest by anthropologists in the functions and significance of symbolic behavior, this topic has undergone rather interesting analysis and theoretical discussion. One such study, *Purity and Danger: An Analysis of Concepts of Pollution and Taboo* by Mary Douglas (1970), provides some fascinating insights and hypotheses. Needless to say, this aspect of what has come to be called symbolic anthropology·is of direct significance to medical anthropology.

In an essay that is too intensively organized and lengthy to be anthologized, Charles Hughes' (1963) "Public Health in Non-Literate Societies" makes a signal contribution to this area of study by drawing the topics of public health and preventive medicine into the purview of anthropology. Hughes finds that in a basic sense all health is public, that is, that no person is ever isolated completely from society so that his health necessarily is a cause of concern to others, and each ailing person, no matter how rare his disease, is a member of a class of persons suffering from the same disability. His review of the cross-cultural data impels Hughes (1963:166–174) to make four generalizations:

1. In any society, practices relevant to public health are generally neither wholly "magical" nor wholly "empirical" or scientific; they are a mixture of both orientations, and often may simply be habitual. . . .
2. The relations between the state of public health of any group and its way of life are reciprocal. . . .
3. In "primitive" societies the health of the public is a continual and encompassing concern of the entire group, which recognizes few bounds in protecting itself from disease or the threat of disease. . . .
4. A people's health is a function of a total life situation.

Hughes believes that the behaviors of preindustrial societies that have a direct bearing on the health of the community may be subsumed under the following categories: magico-religious prevention, empirical prevention; personal hygiene; clothing and adornment; physical culture; cosmetic and nutritional practices; occupational health, housing, and settlement patterns; handling of contagion, and other health-relevant practices. These propositions are profusely illustrated with ethnographic data and the reader is urged to consult the original of this important work.

Alland (1970:128–133) takes a rather dim view of preventive medicine in preindustrial societies, but though he feels it is not very systematic or effective, he nevertheless states that ". . . Much (certainly not all) of what appears to be irrational behavior will turn out to fit the prevailing ecological conditions and demonstrate that much of behavior is either health-oriented or produces maximization [of resources] in some other way." Alland even goes on to conclude that ". . . The most effective behaviors in relation to disease actually fall under the rubric of preventive medicine as it has been defined here rather than under native medical theory of disease, treatment, or disease prevention." But this is because Alland would probably define medical system more narrowly than I would. In other words, I would contend that in whatever segment of culture certain measures may result in the improvement of health and avoidance or control of disease, these should be included as parts of the system of public health and preventive medicine, and, therefore, as a part of the medical system. That such measures may also be seen as religious, economic, political, and so on in no way gainsays this point.

# 25 The Role of Beliefs and Customs in Sanitation Programs

## Benjamin D. Paul

Although health professionals see health as a value of the highest priority and public health and sanitation measures are viewed as the most important obligation of a community to its citizens, health is not a value of equal priority among the people of a society or the power structure that governs them. In this paper Benjamin Paul indicates why public health workers—in this case sanitation engineers, but the same lessons apply to all health workers—must "case" the culture of the community with which they intend to deal. As in the assessment of Paul's theoretical contributions to medical anthropology in the earlier paper by Wellin, Paul treats culture as a system of interlinked beliefs and customs. Introducing sanitation programs is an exercise in culture change, and Paul shows why the health worker must identify and understand the linkages of that sector of a culture he or she wishes to change instead of simply presuming that the people should be able to grasp the "rationality" of the beliefs and practices being introduced. As Paul says in his casebook of public reactions to health programs (Paul 1955),

> If you wish to help a community improve its health, you must learn to think like the people of that community. Before asking a group of people to assume new health habits, it is wise to ascertain the existing habits, how these habits are linked to one another, what functions they perform, and what they mean to those who practice them.

Polgar (1963) describes four fallacies that commonly afflict public health programs: (1) the fallacy of the empty vessels (the subject populations do not have established health customs and are empty vessels waiting to be filled with whatever health program is being advocated); (2) the fallacy of the separate capsule (health beliefs and practices comprise a bounded, separate capsule of behavior and cognition apart from the remainder of culture); (3) the fallacy of the single pyramid (the communication structure of a society is organized within the social units as a single pyramid so that information and behaviors poured in at the top will trickle down to all levels); and (4) the fallacy of the interchangeable faces (all clients are alike). All of these errors derive from a lack of

Reprinted from Benjamin D. Paul, 1958, "The Role of Beliefs and Customs in Sanitation Programs," *American Journal of Public Health*, 48: 1502–1506, with permission of the author and the American Public Health Association.

understanding of the nature of culture and social organization and their involvement in public health practices. Incidentally, the high valuation placed on health not only is not necessarily shared by the members of another society but may not be shared by members of the health worker's own society, either. Here I differ a bit from Paul's statement in this paper: "An engineer can construct health facilities in his home area without worrying too much about the cultural characteristics of the people who will use the facilities." Members of our own society still place the pleasures of smoking, eating, easy living, and many other practices far above their valuation of health. The billions of dollars spent on advertising demonstrate that most Americans have to be persuaded to be concerned about their health (or have their anxiety level needlessly raised over what may not really be a critical health problem at all).

Man is a biological and social animal; he is also a cultural animal. He is cultural in that he runs his life and regulates his society not by blind instincts or detached reason alone, but rather by a set of ideas and skills transmitted socially from one generation to the next and held in common by the members of his particular social group. Culture is a blueprint for social living. Man resides in a double environment—an outer layer of climate, terrain and resources, and an inner layer of culture that mediates between man and the world around him. By applying knowledge which comes to him as part of his cultural heritage, man transforms his physical environment to enhance his comfort and improve his health. He also interprets his environment, assigning significance and value to its various features in accordance with the dictates of his particular culture. Among other things, culture acts as a selective device for perceiving and understanding the outer world. Since cultures vary from group to group, interpretations of the physical environment vary correspondingly.

Ordinarily people are unaware that culture influences their thoughts and acts. They assume their way is *the* way or the "natural" way. Interacting with others in their own society who share their cultural assumptions, they can ignore culture as a determinant of behavior; as a common denominator, it seems to cancel out. An engineer can construct health facilities in his home area without worrying too much about the cultural characteristics of the people who will use the facilities. Sharing their habits and beliefs, he has in effect taken them into account. But in another country with another culture, his assumptions and those of the residents may not match so well. In parts of Latin America maternity patients of moderate means expect a private hospital room with an adjoining alcove to accommodate a servant or kinswoman who comes along to attend the patient around the clock. In parts of rural India the hospital should be built with a series of separate cooking stalls where the patient's family can prepare the meals, in view of cultural prohibitions against the handling of food by members of other castes. And of course the effect of cultural differences looms even larger where sanitation has to be built directly into the habit systems of people, rather than into structures and plants that serve the people.

Anyone familiar with the operation of technical assistance programs knows about the kind of behavioral differences I have mentioned. Unfortunately, however, it is easy to misconstrue these observed differences. Three kinds of misinterpretation are common. The first is to suppose that "they" have more odd beliefs and habits, while we have less of them. We tend to see them as captives of blind custom and ourselves as relatively free from cultural peculiarities. The fact is that all men are creatures of their culture with its inevitable admixture of rational and nonrational elements. Cultures differ and rates of cultural change differ, but peoples do not differ appreciably in the degree to which their actions are influenced by their respective cultures. We are quick to apply the term "superstition" or the epithet "uncouth custom" to the other fellow's manner of thinking or behaving. We may be repelled by the custom of eating domesticated dogs and yet impatient with people who would rather go hungry than eat their cattle. Americans take offense at the odor of night soil in the settlements of Korea and other parts of eastern Asia; a Korean gentleman on his first visit to New York was asked by a friend how he liked the great city, whereupon he replied: "Oh, very well, but the smells are so bad!" (Moose 1911). Measured by the standards of one culture the manifestations of another are bound to appear more or less arbitrary or bizarre. We need to realize that we have culture, too, and that our ways can seem as peculiar to others as theirs do to us.

Even allowing that our behavior as well as theirs bears the stamp of cultural conditioning, a second facile assumption is that our ways and ideas are more advanced than theirs, that they have yet to catch up with us. The trouble with this assumption is that it represents a partial truth: Some aspects of culture, notably scientific knowledge and technical skills, are indeed subject to measurement and

relative ranking. But knowledge is not wisdom, and many aspects of culture, including language, esthetics, moral codes, and religious values, lie beyond objective rating for want of a culture-free standard of measurement. It is a mistake and an insult to imply, as we inadvertently do at times, that because some areas of the world are technically underdeveloped their people or their cultures are in general underdeveloped.

A third and particularly common shortcoming in our understanding of cultural differences is a tendency to view customs and beliefs as isolated elements rather than as parts of a system or pattern. The linkages between the parts of culture may be loose or tight and the connections are not always apparent upon first inspection, but it frequently turns out that people cling to a particular practice or belief not merely because it is familiar and traditional but because it is linked to other elements of the culture. Conversely, a change effected in one area of the culture may bring with it unexpected changes in other areas or may result in awkward dislocations, as the following illustration will indicate.

On the island of Palau in the western Pacific the pattern of living calls for frequent and large gatherings of people to celebrate or solemnize certain social events. In the old days. Palauan houses were large enough to hold many people. There were no partitions, and it was possible for each man attending a feast to receive his food in the order of rank and to sit in such a way as not to cause offense by turning his back on anyone. Since the last war, most Palauans live in small two-or three-room houses built in the Japanese or American style. They try to maintain the old customs but they have their troubles. Visitors overcrowd the small house and sit packed together on the floor. They must suffer the insult of having to look at a neighbor's back and must take their food in any order they can. The Palauans are incessant betel chewers—and spitters. The old houses had several doors and numerous floor cracks to accommodate this habit. The new buildings, especially the Quonset huts now being created for chiefs' dwellings and council chambers, have caused a minor crisis. The two Quonset doors are premium locations; knotholes in the plywood floors are too scarce to provide relief for the majority of chewers. Tin cans are coming in as spittoons, but these are in scarce supply (Barnett 1951:91).

Housing customs and hospitality customs, once closely linked in Palau, are now in strained relationship. It should be stated parenthetically that social or cultural strains are not necessarily good or bad in themselves; depending on the case, they can lead to increased cultural disorganization or to an eventual reorganization of the sociocultural system on a new basis.

In some instances people strive to prevent cultural strain by resisting environmental and sanitary improvements. In rural India, fecal contamination of food and water by direct contact or contact through flies and rodents constitutes a difficult problem. The source of the trouble is the custom of defecating in the open fields. Use of latrines would go far toward solving the problem. Public health engineers and others working in India have devised special types of latrine adapted to the local squatting posture and designed to meet varied soil, climatic, and water supply conditions. Numerous latrines have in fact been installed, but follow-up studies reveal that only a small proportion are used regularly. Women in particular tend to avoid the latrines. Every morning and afternoon women go in groups to the field, not only to relieve themselves but also to take time off from busy domestic routines, to gossip and exchange advice about husbands and mothers-in-law, and to bathe with water from tanks located in the field. The linked habits of going to the fields for social gatherings and for toilet and bathing activities meet a strongly felt need for community living and relaxation from daily toil. In the women's view, defecation customs are usefully linked to other customs. In the view of sanitation specialists these customs are harmfully linked to a cycle of contamination and intestinal disease. To disrupt the contamination cycle the women are urged to use the new latrines. They shy away from following this advice, partly because doing so would disrupt an ensemble of customs they prefer to keep intact, and partly because their culture has given them little basis for comprehending the connection between feces and enteric diseases.

I began by saying that culture mediates between man and his material environment. In an article analyzing the outcome of a rural sanitation program in a small Peruvian town, the author explains how perceptions of so common an environmental element as water are culturally screened:

A trained health worker can perceive "contamination" in water because his perceptions are linked to certain scientific understandings which permit him to view water in a specially conditioned way. The Peruvian townsman also views water in a specially conditioned way. Between

him and the water he observes, his culture "filters out" bacteria and "filters in" cold, hot or other qualities that are as meaningful to him as they are meaningless to the outsider.

An important part of the local culture is a complex system of hot and cold distinctions. Many things in nature, including foods, liquids, medicines, body states, and illnesses are classified as essentially "hot" or "cold" or something in between, irrespective of actual temperature. Sick people should avoid foods that are very cold, such as pork. "Raw" water is cold and fit for well persons; "cooked" water is hot and fit for the sick. The times of day when water can be boiled are hedged in by limitations of time and fuel and further restricted by "hot" and "cold" considerations. Water is consumed mainly around noon. Water boiled later in the day and standing overnight becomes dangerously "cold" and must be reboiled in the morning. So it is useless to boil it at any time other than the morning in the first place. The patient efforts of a local hygiene worker to persuade housewives to decontaminate their drinking water by boiling it met with only limited success in the face of these cultural convictions (Wellin 1955).

It is interesting to note that the hot-cold idea system now widely current in Latin America apparently goes back many centuries to the humoral theory of disease expounded by Hippocrates and Galen and transmitted by Arabs to Spain and by Spaniards to the New World, where it retained a place in formal medical teaching until the 18th century (Foster 1953). Folk theories of medicine in contemporary rural India and in other parts of Asia indicate that the humoral theory spread in that direction, too, if indeed it did not have its origin somewhere in Asia. In the course of its travels the humoral theory underwent modification, so that its present form in Asia is not identical to the one in Latin America. It is remarkable that cultural complexes such as the hot-cold idea system should persist, however altered, through such long periods of time.

Objectively viewed, the cosmos and all its contents are morally neutral; nothing is good or bad in itself; it simply is. But man clothes his cosmos in a moral cloak. He evaluates it, holding some things to be good and others evil. Values, the fundamental bases for choosing between alternative courses of action, are a central part of any group's culture. Values differ, but these differences are less apparent than differences in language, dress, posture, rules of etiquette, or other overt features of the culture. Because values usually remain below the level of awareness, we are particularly apt to impose our own values upon others on the innocent assumption that we are merely helping them achieve better health.

Members of our own middle class tend to make a virtue of tidiness, apart from its possible bearing on sanitation. Cleanliness is both a health measure and a cultural value. This distinction can be appreciated if we glance back through history to see the shifting value assigned to bathing and cleanliness from the time of the ancient Greeks. Such a review also illustrates the connectedness of the parts of culture (Kroeber 1948:600–602; Sigerist 1941:69–72; Varron 1939–1940: 213–214).

Although they built no great baths, the Greeks valued athletic sports and despised the Persians for their false modesty in keeping the body covered. The Romans, taking over much of the Greek cult of the body, constructed enormous public baths where men of leisure spent hours daily. The early Christians set themselves against the established pagan religion and also against many of the attitudes and amenites inherent in Roman culture. Baths were construed as instruments of paganism and vice, as devices for softening the body rather than saving the soul. Before long, even minimum cleanliness by current standards was seen as the road to ruin. The ascetic saint was indifferent to filth; attention to personal cleanliness, especially on the part of a man, incurred the suspicion that one might not be too good a Christian.

Bathing occupied an important place, however, in the lives of Europeans during medieval times. As the vessel of the soul, the body needed to be preserved. The monastery of the early Middle Ages had its bathroom for friars and pilgrims. By the 13th century, public bathhouses had come into use in the cities, providing both steam and water baths along with haircuts and minor surgery. But the presence of food and drink, girls and music increasingly converted the bathhouses into places of amusement and eventually earned the opposition of the clergy. Moreover, the bathhouses became centers of infection when syphilis began to plague Europe at the end of the 15th century. Municipal bathing disappeared from the urban scene, private houses lacked baths, and the entire custom of bathing was condemned for reasons of morality and health.

Interest in bodily cleanliness was revived in the 18th century with the growth of enlightenment, the increase in comforts, the refinement of social manners, and the rise of the bourgeoisie. The lead in this direction was taken in countries where the new wealthy middle class became especially influential; hence the scrubbing of Dutch doorsteps and the proverbial Englishman with his portable bath. Today, in the United States, prosperity, democracy, and frequency of bathing have become linked values. Americans say that cleanliness is next to godliness, an indication that bathing and cleanliness are affect-laden values in contemporary middle-class culture as well as a means to better health. Yet even in the United States bathing is neither as old nor as general as people now assume. Ackerknecht reminds us that President Fillmore was as much attacked for buying a bathtub for the White House in 1851 as was Harry Truman in our time for his balcony.

We might have more success in exporting our technical means for improving the world's health if we could manage to divest these means of the values and other cultural trappings that accompany their use in the American scene. It might then be easier to fit our technical means into foreign cultural contexts. To do this we need to become skilled in perceiving our own cultural contours and those of the country we strive to help. This is one of the reasons why instruction in cultural anthropology and other social sciences is rapidly being introduced into schools of public health.

# 26 Social and Cultural Implications of Food and Food Habits

## *John Cassel*

This chapter illustrates, through a descriptive analysis of a program for changing health practices among Zulu peoples in South Africa, many of the concepts and principles described in the preceding paper by Paul and in my introduction to this section. John Cassel, a public health physician and epidemiologist, exhibits a fine appreciation for the contributions to be made by social science knowledge to public health problems and by the use of social scientists on teams dealing with these problems and attempting to introduce cultural

Reprinted with abridgments from John Cassel, 1957, "Social and Cultural Implications of Food and Food Habits," *American Journal of Public Health*, 47:732–740, with permission of the author and the American Public Health Association.

changes. This paper is concerned only with food but similar experiences have been found in attempting to change other categories of cultural practices and values. (See the case studies in Paul [1955] in which much of the present paper first appeared in extended form.) Without in any way underestimating the factor of poverty in the malnutrition and undernutrition of these Bantu people, it is nevertheless clear that ingrained food customs (or "habits" as the author says, though I would reserve this term for individual practices, not group ones), as well as many other attitudes tightly wrapped in deeply held beliefs, some ancient and some, as the reader will see, only thought by the people to be of long tradition, obtruded in the path of healthful nutrition. The success of the program ultimately is reflected in the changes that took place after a dozen years in infant mortality and the near disappearance of pellagra and kwashiorkor.

. . . It is no coincidence that one of the major areas of interest common to both the health professions and the social sciences should center round the topic of food. From the dawn of medical history the role of food in health and disease has been under investigation by health workers, and its significance increases as further advances in nutritional knowledge are made. For social scientists a study of food ways and the system of attitudes, beliefs, and practices surrounding food may constitute an important technic in unraveling the complexities of the over-all culture pattern of a community (Du Bois 1941). Health workers are, in addition, now learning that food habits are among the oldest and most deeply entrenched aspects of many cultures, and cannot therefore be easily changed, or if changed, can produce a further series of unexpected and often unwelcome reactions. . . .

This paper is an attempt to illustrate by means of a case study some of these social and cultural factors of significance in programs designed to change food habits; an attempt will be made to derive certain general principles from this illustration; and finally some of the specific contributions that social scientists could make in such programs will be indicated.

Before considering these factors, however, it is desirable to elaborate somewhat on the degree to which we as health workers are "culture bound." The type of training the majority of us receive makes it difficult for us to see any merit in points of view or patterns of behavior different from our own. Food patterns for example which differ from our concepts of "good" practices are automatically labeled "bad." Attitudes and beliefs differing from ours are regarded as "illogical," "misinformed" or

"wrong." The people who hold these different concepts are regarded as "ignorant" or perhaps "superstitious," "childlike" or plain "stupid."

Unfortunately there are still too many of us who are convinced that our own particular set of beliefs, attitudes, and practices is the only correct way of life and one that should be emulated by people of all cultures and all social classes. Such a philosophy on our part presumes that only we as professional health workers know what is good for all people. Furthermore it is frequently our fond belief that our nutritional education is being executed in a "knowledge vacuum" (to use the words of Edward Wellin 1955) as far as the recipients are concerned; that because the population we are serving knows nothing of our nutritional concepts, they therefore have no concepts whatever about nutrition. It is evident that documentation of the relevance of social and cultural factors to health programs is unlikely to lead to any effective application of these concepts as long as such attitudes are maintained by the majority of health workers.

## THE CASE STUDY

In 1940 the Pholela Health Centre was established on a "native reserve" in the Union of South Africa. Health conditions among the Zulu tribesmen to be served by this center were extremely poor. The crude mortality rate was 38 per 1,000 population and the infant mortality rate 276 per 1,000 live births. Poor environmental sanitation and communicable disease represented two major health problems, but of greater significance, perhaps, was the extensive malnutrition that existed. Eighty percent of the people exhibited marked stigmata of this malnutrition and evidence of gross nutritional failure in the form of pellagra or kwashiorkor was common.

The Pholela Health Centre, charged with the responsibility of providing comprehensive medical care and health services to the population, was organized on the basis of a number of multidisciplined teams. Each team, consisting of a family physician, a family nurse, and a community health educator (health assistant), was responsible for the health of a number of families living in a defined geographical area. The major health problems of the area were defined by the teams and broadly classified into "unfelt" and "felt" needs. Health programs to meet these needs were then initiated on two planes in which the promotive-preventive and curative aspects of the services could be integrated.

Basically the function of the health assistants was to develop community health education programs whereby the "unfelt" needs could be made apparent to the community, and members of the community stimulated to change aspects of their way of life to meet these needs. Simultaneously curative and preventive services to individuals within their family units was the responsibility of the doctor and nurse on the team. Each individual was offered complete periodic health examinations, followed by a family conference to discuss the health problems of that family, and any illness in any family member would similarly be treated by his family doctor and nurse. At the clinical sessions the community health education programs were reinforced in the specific advice given the individual patients.

The case study to be presented here is a description of one program which was designed to change the food habits of mothers and infants. Dietary surveys revealed that the existing diet consisted principally of a single staple, corn, prepared in numerous ways, supplemented by dried beans, negligible amounts of milk and occasionally meat and wild greens. Potatoes and pumpkins were eaten seasonally, and millet (sorghum) was fermented to brew beer which was consumed in large quantities. Whenever funds allowed, sugar and white bread were also bought. Even though this was a rural agricultural community, poor farming methods and poverty of the soil made it impossible for the vast majority of the people to raise adequate food supplies. Consequently a large percentage of the food consisted of refined corn meal purchased with money sent home by the migrant laborers. Furthermore, during the best month of the year, if all the milk had been equally distributed, only one-twentieth pint per head per day would have been available. Having determined the existing food patterns an analysis was then made of the major factors responsible for the inadequacy of the diet. These included the extreme poverty of the people, the extensive soil erosion, certain traditions as to which foods were customary, and inefficient use of available resources. In addition prevailing cooking methods frequently destroyed a large fraction of what nutrients were present.

As anticipated, early attempts at group meetings and home visits to demonstrate the causal relationship between a poor diet and a low standard of health encountered considerable skepticism. People maintained that their diet had always been the diet of their people. On this same diet, they maintained, their ancestors had been virile and healthy and consequently there could be no possible relationship between the present diet and ill health.

It was difficult to refute this point without having any reliable information about the health of their ancestors.

A search of the available literature, however, revealed that the present diet had not always been the traditional diet of the Zulus and other Bantu-speaking tribes. Prior to the arrival of the whites, the indigenous cereal had been millet, corn having been brought into the country by the early white settlers. Because of its greater yield, corn had gradually supplanted millet as the staple cereal, millet being reserved solely for brewing. Furthermore, historically the Zulus were a roving pastoral people owning large herds of cattle; milk and meat had played a prominent part in their diet. So important was milk as an article of food that no meal was considered complete unless milk was included. The relatively fertile nature of the land at that time and the extensive wild game resulted in further additions of meat to the diet and a plentiful supply of wild greens. Roots and berries gathered from the forests were also extensively used.

These facts were presented to the community at the regular small group meetings initiated by the health assistants and discussion invited. In particular, confirmation was sought from the older members of the tribe, and in most instances such confirmation was received. This endorsement by the prestigeful and usually most conservative segment of the population insured that interest in the topic of food would remain high. Realization that the modern diet was not as traditional as had been supposed assisted in reducing resistance to the changes that were later advocated.

At subsequent meetings concepts of digestion and the functions of different foodstuffs were discussed. It was widely, though not universally, held that in some manner food entered the blood stream, but what happened to it thereafter was unspecified. Greatest interest was aroused by considering how a fetus was nourished in utero; discussion on this point would sometimes continue for hours. Many women were of the opinion that there must be a breast in the uterus from which the fetus suckled, but others indicated that calves in utero must be receiving nourishment in the same way, and no one had ever seen a breast in a cow's uterus. Some women maintained that the fetus was nourished by the placenta as the Zulu term for placenta literally means "the nurse." But when challenged, they were unable to explain how the placenta could feed the baby.

The result of these and similar discussions was to arouse a desire for further knowledge. When the functions of the placenta and umbilical cord were explained by use of posters and models, the interpretation was readily accepted. Over a period of time the concept that body tissues were nourished by the food via the bloodstream became generally agreed upon.

As the concepts about the digestion and absorption of food began to change, it was possible to direct discussion to the function of different types of food. The view generally held was that all food had only one function, to fill the stomach and relieve hunger. This view was challenged, however, by a number of people who maintained that certain foods gave strength and others were fattening—fat being a bodily attribute much valued in this community.

Gradually it became more generally accepted that different foods had different functions, particularly in regard to infant health and nutrition. In attempts to improve infant nutrition, and in view of the existing resources, it appeared that green vegetables, eggs, and milk were the foods on which greatest emphasis should be laid.

## INTRODUCTION OF GREEN VEGETABLES

Even though green vegetables had rarely formed part of the diet, and then only in a few families, their introduction for a number of reasons appeared to be a promising first step. Wild greens gathered from the forests had always been eaten and were enjoyed, but due to soil erosion these were becoming increasingly difficult to find. There were no very strong feelings or set of beliefs about green vegetables. The climate was suitable for their cultivation and each home had adequate space for use as a garden. Thus no marked objections to green vegetables was anticipated, their similarity to wild greens could be usefully exploited, and resources, at present unused, could be brought into use to make the vegetables available. In view of these circumstances the procedures that appeared to be necessary consisted of attempts to:

1. Increase the motivation of the people to eat vegetables—These included emphasis on their nutritional value in terms of concepts previously discussed; relating their taste to that of familiar wild greens; and emphasis on the financial savings that could be made by replacing part of the purchased food by home-grown

vegetables. These views were presented at the group discussions held in the homes of the people and reinforced at the clinical sessions, particularly the prenatal and mother and baby sessions.

2. Demonstrate the means by which these vegetables could be obtained by the families—A demonstration vegetable garden was developed at the Health Centre where members of the staff could themselves gain practical gardening experience and where the families could have the methods of growing vegetables demonstrated. Vegetables from this garden were made available to certain families on prescription. The more cooperative families were assisted in starting their own gardens and as the number increased a seed-buying cooperative was initiated. Over the years a small market was established where families could sell their surplus produce, and annual garden competitions and an annual agricultural show were organized. As members of the Health Centre staff, particularly the health assistants, became more proficient gardeners themselves they were able to give practical advice and assistance to any of their families who desired it.

3. Demonstrate the palatability of the vegetables and the best means of incorporating them into the diet without destroying their nutrient values—Cooking demonstrations were organized both at the discussion groups and for the waiting patients at the Health Centre sessions. As far as possible, traditional means of preparing food were adhered to. Over the years different recipes were introduced and women from the area who were successfully incorporating vegetables into their families' diets were encouraged to organize these demonstrations.

The response of the community to these programs was satisfactory. In 1941 the first garden survey revealed that only 3 per cent of the homes had any form of vegetable garden, and that a total of five varieties of vegetables were growing. By 1951, 80 percent of the homes had gardens and were growing more than 25 varieties of vegetables. This response was all the more gratifying as the size of the area served had been increased sixfold over the course of the 10-year period, so that some families had had only relatively recent contact with the program.

## INCREASING EGG CONSUMPTION

The attempts to increase the consumption of eggs encountered somewhat greater resistance than did the vegetable program. Surveys revealed that over 95 percent of the families had poultry, and that eggs were relatively plentiful at certain seasons of the year. Eggs were infrequently eaten, however, but in contrast to vegetables, very definite views were held about them. It was considered un-economical to eat an egg that would later hatch and become a chicken; egg eating was regarded as a sign of greed; and finally eggs were thought by some people to make girls licentious.

After prolonged staff meetings the consensus of team opinion was that none of these beliefs had any deep emotional associations and that probably the concept of it being poor economy to eat eggs was the most important of the factors preventing further use being made of eggs. The program based on this analysis therefore was patterned on the same general lines as the vegetable program. Technics for improving the egg yield whereby eggs could both be eaten and leave sufficient for breeding were discussed; the nutritional value and palatability of eggs were stressed both in the community education programs and for each specific patient at the prenatal and mother and baby sessions; and various methods for in-corporating eggs into the diet without any marked modification of prevailing recipes were demon-strated. The fact that certain adverse views were held about eggs was of importance, however. Even though these views were not strongly held they indicated that relatively greater effort would be required to motivate the community to use eggs.

As might have been anticipated, therefore, response to this program was slower than to the vegetable garden program. In the course of 12 years however the technics proved relatively successful, and the consumption of eggs, particularly in infant diets, steadily increased. Furthermore, toward the later years of the program, families began to put excess eggs on the local market and found purchasers among their neighbors, a phenomenon totally foreign to this community.

## THE MILK PROGRAM

Increasing milk consumption proved to be a considerably more difficult and complex problem. Not only was the supply extremely limited, but frequently the available milk was not being consumed. In particular, women took no milk whatsoever, and this became a matter of some concern to the Health Centre in regard to expectant and lactating mothers. Investigation disclosed that milk drinking was associated with very deep-seated beliefs and customs. Only members of the kin group of the head of a household could use milk produced by that man's cattle. This restriction applied equally to men, women, and children, so

that no family could supplement its milk supply from another family outside the kin group, but the situation was more complex in the case of women.

During her menses or when pregnant, a woman was thought to exert an evil influence on cattle and was not allowed to pass near the cattle enclosure or partake of any milk. This applied even in her own home. Since it was usually impossible for men to know when a woman was menstruating, it was customary to exclude milk from the diet of the majority of girls once they had passed puberty. When a woman married and went to live with her husband's family group she fell under a double restriction. Not only was she a woman, but she was now in the home of a different kin group. Consequently, of all people in the community, married women were most rigidly excluded from partaking of milk. Under two conditions only might she have milk. If her father presented her with her own cow at the time of her marriage she could use milk from that cow, or if her husband performed a special ceremony involving the slaying of a goat, she would be free to use any milk in his home. Because of the general poverty of the area neither of these two procedures was common although several decades ago they were not uncommon in certain families.

The reasons for these customs were lost in the mists of antiquity, not even the oldest people in this community being able to explain them. "This is our custom, and this is how it has always been" was the only explanation offered. In all probability the customs are closely related to native religious beliefs centered around ancestors. Even today when some 60 percent of the community are Christians, ancestors play a very important part, protecting a person from all manner of misfortune and ill health. The link between a man and his ancestors is his cattle, and ceremonies of propitiation involve the slaying of cattle. Accordingly, anything that might have an evil influence on the cattle would endanger the relationship between a man and his ancestors. In addition, a married woman continues to have her own set of ancestors derived from her family and may not interfere in any way with her husband's.

The degree to which concepts concerning milk were enmeshed in the over-all cultural pattern made it obvious that the general approach used for increasing vegetable and egg consumption would be of little avail. Considerable motivation for drinking milk already existed in the community, and attempts to increase this motivation would be unlikely to change existing practices. Attempts were nevertheless made on several occasions to change these practices by stressing the importance of milk as an ideal food for lactating and expectant mothers, but were futile.

Analysis of the underlying beliefs indicated clearly that the barrier to greater milk consumption lay in the link between milk and the specific cattle from which it came. If milk from cows which did not belong to any member of the tribe or any other related groups could be introduced into the community, presumably the barrier would be overcome. The most practical method of accomplishing this was to make powdered milk available. Accordingly, supplies of powdered milk were obtained by the Health Centre and offered to families on prescription. No secret was made of the fact that this powder was a form of milk, but it was stressed that this milk did not originate from cows belonging to any of the Bantu people.

From the inception of this program it was clear that no stigma was attached to the use of the powdered milk. Even the most orthodox of mothers-in-law or husbands had no objection to this powder being used by the young women of their families. The only barrier that remained was that it was an unfamiliar food stuff with a strange taste. To overcome this, the familiar formula —increase the motivation, help make the product easily available and demonstrate methods for incorporation into the diet—proved all that was necessary. The application of these technics produced a demand for the powdered milk that, over the years, steadily outgrew the Health Centre supply. Families were then encouraged to budget their slender incomes to allow for its purchase from the local stores. By 1954 it became apparent that in some families the demand for milk had become too great to be met from either of these two sources. To the gratification of the Health Centre staff permission was given in a number of the more educated families for women to consume milk from the family cows without any marked reaction from the rest of the community.

Some of the results of the Health Centre's programs are of interest. In the course of 12 years the infant mortality rate dropped from 276 to 96, pellagra and kwashiorkor all but disappeared from this area and the average weight of the babies at one year had increased by two pounds. This trend, as far as was known, was not occurring elsewhere in the country, and in fact in neighboring areas where the Health Centre provided only medical care but no community health education program, no such changes were discernible.

## SOME GENERAL PRINCIPLES

From this illustration it is now possible to derive some guiding principles indicating the significance of social and cultural factors to health programs in general.

The first is self-evident. Health workers should have an intimate detailed knowledge of the people's beliefs, attitudes, knowledge and behavior before attempting to introduce any innovation into an area. While this principle is frequently violated in practice it is certainly no new concept in public health. What is not so well recognized however is that the intimate knowledge of these factors is but the initial step in the evaluation of cultural factors.

The second principle, which is usually more difficult to apply, is that the psychologic and social functions of these practices, beliefs, and attitudes need to be evaluated. As stated by Benjamin Paul (1955), "It is relatively easy to perceive that others have different customs and beliefs, especially if they are 'odd' or 'curious'. It is generally more difficult to perceive the pattern or system into which these customs or beliefs fit." It is in this area of determining the pattern or system into which these customs or beliefs fit that social scientists can probably make their greatest contribution to health programs. This is the knowledge that will help determine why certain practices obtain, help predict how difficult it will be to change them, and give indications of the technics that can be expected to be most helpful.

A third principle that should be emphasized was unfortunately not well illustrated in the example but is of fundamental importance in the United States. It should be appreciated that while it is permissible for some purposes to consider an overall "American Culture," numerous distinct subcultures exist, sometimes even within a single county. These subcultural groups must be carefully defined, as programs based on premises, true for one group, will not necessarily be successful in a neighboring group. This also is an area in which we as health workers can receive invaluable assistance from social scientists.

There are a number of very interesting illustrations of the importance of these subcultural groupings in regard to food habits in the United States, of which only two will be mentioned. Margaret Cussler and Mary de Give (1952) differentiate five major subcultural groupings in the South: white owners, white sharecroppers, Negro owners, Negro sharecroppers and wage laborers. To a greater or lesser degree each of these groups had different attitudes, beliefs, knowledge, and practices in regard to food, and for different reasons. John Bennet, Harvey Smith, and Herbert Passin (1942) have distinguished in the southern part of Illinois eight separate and distinct subcultural groups, each with its own set of attitudes toward food. Interestingly enough, none of these attitudes were based on a knowledge or interest in the nutritional value of the foods.

Many nutrition programs today are designed for application to the total area under the jurisdiction of the nutritionist—an area that is often very large. The underlying premise would be that this total area—region, state, district, or even county—has a completely homogenous culture. Greater concentration of a nutritionist's time in a carefully defined subcultural group with the development of programs specifically designed for that group would eventually be more efficient in effecting permanent changes in food habits.

There are a number of other social and cultural factors, some of which have been implied in the case study and which, though important, have not been emphasized. These include a determination of the leadership patterns within a community, a definition of the decision makers in a family or larger institution, and determination of the status of various groups within the community and the status of the health worker in comparison to these groups. The importance of these factors has been well recognized by health workers in planning and executing programs and requires little further emphasis here. In this connection it is of interest to note however that several investigators (Cussler and De Give 1952; Lewin 1952) report that in the majority of American homes all major food decisions are made by the housewife. Concentration of the nutritional education on the housewife alone therefore would probably be more beneficial than attempts to educate the total community in many subcultures in the United States.

A further area in which profitable collaboration between social science and health could occur is concerned with the prediction of the long-range effects of any program. Following a program two interrelated series of questions would be of interest to all health workers. Are there likely to be any unanticipated repercussions of the program and, secondly, how permanent can the changes introduced be expected to be?

The answers to these questions will be largely determined by the degree to which the innovations are absorbed into the cultural framework and the impact they have on other facets of the culture. For example, in our illustration the effect of the acceptance of new dietary patterns by the Zulu women might conceivably eventually threaten the status of males as decision makers in that society. Similarly permission given to women to take milk might eventually be one of the factors changing the intensity of religious beliefs.

By indicating the possible effects on other segments of the culture, and by determining the degree to which the concepts embodied by the new program have been absorbed into the existing cultural framework, social scientists would have a significant contribution to make in sensitizing health workers to the possible long-range effects of their programs.

The concluding consideration is the degree to which we as health workers are "culture bound." Unless we can avoid cultural bias or ethnocentricity in our dealing with people, much of the crucial data will not even be made available to us by members of the community. Even should we be fortunate enough to have access to some of these facts, our analysis of the situation will continually be distorted through imposition of our own culturally determined system of values onto the behavior of others. In this regard social scientists can perhaps help us to become somewhat less "culture bound," but fundamentally for many of us this requires a major reorientation of our own philosophy which only we ourselves can achieve.

# 27 Ritual Purity and Pollution in Relation to Domestic Sanitation

## R. S. Khare

The subject of cultural beliefs in ritual cleanness and uncleanness is one that has long occupied the attention of anthropologists, at least since the time of Sir James Frazer, Edward Tylor, and Hutton Webster. The topic is also dear to the hearts of theologians and students of comparative religion. The relation between the concepts and practices of ritual purity and those of

Reprinted with abridgments from R. S. Khare, 1962, "Ritual Purity and Pollution in Relation to Domestic Sanitation," *The Eastern Anthropologist, 15*:125–139, with permission of the author and the Ethnographic and Folk Culture Society (Lucknow, India) and *The Eastern Anthropologist.*

a pragmatically hygienic nature are not always clearly spelled out in ethnographies or in studies of religions. And theologians not infrequently attempt to "prove" that the original purpose of many ritual practices and taboos was actually health-directed, often thousands of years after such concepts first appeared. In many anthropological accounts, moreover, little effort may be made to link the two, in either an emic or etic sense. This study strives to do just that, drawing upon the data of the complex religious system of Hinduism in a Northern Indian village. This is, in R. S. Khare's phrase, "an anthropological inquiry on domestic sanitation."

We see that whereas the extermination of the sources of disease—germs and insect pests—may be uppermost on the agenda of public health experts, they are not part of the villager's notion of cleanliness (or of preventive medicine). Nevertheless, although in some instances practices of ritual purification are irrelevant to health, and some practices of cleanliness are, in some instances, irrelevant to ritual purification, there are many instances and areas where they overlap, and as Khare shows, promote and reinforce each other. Even practices that are presumably secular and with a specifically hygienic intent may in time become ritualized. Khare shows that pollution varies by gradations in different sectors of life and of the domestic household, and that the same act or object may be variously polluting depending upon circumstance, actors, and so on. Thus, the system differently affects members of the several castes, with a claim of greater purity as one ascends the caste ladder though not in a simple fashion. Finally, Khare discusses some of the changes taking place under "modernization" and presents a three-stage model of modifications occurring in practices and ideas relating to ritual purity and pollution, both in terms of modernization and of Sanskritization. Khare urges public health workers to attempt to keep this process in mind when instituting changes in health and sanitation policies and behaviors. As he points out in a concluding passage not included in this abridgment, both the public health system and the traditional one of ritual purity promote health and have several points of overlap and potential linkage or transference, and the public health worker can utilize this knowledge to increase communication, efficiency, and understanding between himself and the villager.

# I

The present paper seeks to establish that a relationship exists between the ritual state of purity and pollution and the physical states of cleanliness and uncleanliness in domestic surroundings. This relationship, it is assumed, will help in clarifying the role played by *Chhoot-Pak* concepts in domestic sanitation, and may also be helpful in

pointing out its importance in orienting Action Programmes on environmental sanitation in rural India. This paper attempts to point out the nature of ritual purity and pollution involved in the domestic activities and also underlines the importance of studying it with public health aims in view. The data for this study were collected during 1958–1960 in a peasant village, namely Gopalpur, in Uttar Pradesh.

# II

. . . It is a multi-caste village with a population of 572 people. Among the "twice-born" there are only Brahmins and Kayasthas. The other prominent castes are: the Ahir, the Kurmi, the Pasi and the Barhai. The numerically dominant castes of the village, viz. the Kurmi, the Pasi and the Ahir, are sanskritizing as well as modernizing themselves. They are observing rules of ritual purity and impurity, on the one hand, and taking to modern practices, on the other.

# III

In Gopalpur, as in the whole of Northern India, several words, such as, *Pavitra-Apavitra*, *Suddha-Asuddha*, and *Chhoot-Pak* are used to denote the ritual states of purity and impurity. Similarly, the words *Saaf-Ganda* are used to refer to physical states of cleanliness and dirtiness.

Ritual purity and physical cleanliness are two things: one refers to the ritual or religious state and the other to the physical state. The terms, *Chhoot-Pak*, are used in two senses: one, in which they refer to situational purity-impurity of an individual "at a given moment in relation to other individuals, as determined by events occurring in his family or in his own life", and the other in which they refer to the place of a caste group in the ritual hierarchy of caste system (Dumont and Pocock 1959). Human beings suffer ritual impurity through *natural happenings* (birth, death, menstruation, etc.), association with *material objects* (human skin, excreta, menstrual blood, spittle, reproductive fluids, etc.), and *human beings* (untouchables, Mahabrahmins, etc.). Human beings also suffer from ritual impurity owing to the internal or intrinsic nature of individual selves—the *Suddha-Asuddha Atman* (pious and impious soul).

Ritual impurity calls for remedial actions on two planes: of relations with materials or men, and of relations with the soul. These concepts of ritual purity and impurity (*Chhoot-Pak*) give meaning to individual as well as group conduct. As exemplified below, in the case of homesteads in Gopalpur these concepts thoroughly control the pattern of behaviour of an individual within the domestic group. These elaborate ideas are ultimately based on social inoculation, especially in childhood.

Here we are primarily concerned with the relations that various beliefs and practices of ritual purity and impurity have with physical cleanliness. Though the activities concerned with ritual purity and impurity are oriented towards the patterning of human behaviour in relation to a non-empirical referent—the welfare of the soul, and the religious piousness—they also have a physical dimension which consists in employing certain operations resulting in the removal of dirt and filth, disposal of refuse, use of air, water, and the sun as cleaning agents, and avoidance of contact with dirty objects. Although these activities result in both ritual purification as well as physical cleanliness, the villagers often give much less importance to the latter than to the former, so much so indeed that a casual observer may come to conclude that the people are surprisingly unconscious of the physical aspect of the situation; almost as if they did not understand it. On certain other occasions, for example, a sacrifice, the people resort to physical cleaning of person, place or thing as a preliminary measure for leading up to the requisite state of ritual purity. It is due to these implicit or explicit hygienic dimensions in the concepts of ritual purity and impurity that they are relevant to an anthropological inquiry on domestic sanitation.

Ritual impurity may be of several kinds: it may be external or internal, temporary or permanent, voluntary or involuntary. The internal impurity is more serious than the external: the intensity of impurity through impure food and water will be greater than a physical (external) contact with a lower caste man. Dumont and Pocock (1959) analyse the severity of pollution in the latter case as attributable to "the notion of appropriation of the object; when a man uses an object it becomes a part of him, participates in him" (. . . .). "And the point is that appropriation precedes absorption". "In the kitchen, cooking may be taken to imply a complete appropriation of the food by the household" (p. 37). The temporary pollution, which is more significant for domestic sanitation, is "situational, it is a function of the relations between an individual and the commensal, endogamous and local groups of which he or she is a member", while the permanent pollution "is a function of the relations between commensal and endogamous groups, between men and phenomena of the natural world, and among these phenomena themselves" (Srinivas 1952). The voluntary pollution is acquired through wrong behaviour, such as touching of excreta, taking water from a low caste-man, etc., while the involuntary pollution is the result of natural crisis over which man has no apparent control; for example, defecation, menstruation, birth, death, etc.

In an Indian village, the values of ritual purity and impurity form an important part of the *Karma* (action) and the *Dharma* (religion) of an individual; they help in attaining the *summum bonnum* of one's life. Pollution from various evitable and inevitable sources is expunged as readily as possible so that one may live in a state of ritual purity—a condition favourable for "upward spiral of soul". According to Srinivas (1952), ritual purity, normal ritual status, and ritual impurity form a hierarchy. The normal ritual status, "or neutral state" is enjoyed by the person most of the time. The deviations from it towards purity and impurity are mostly temporary.

For our purpose, the word "cleanliness" may be used in the sense of habitual actions designed to free a person, place or thing from unclean matter that soils, anything which is out of place, or worthless. This definition of cleanliness is based upon the *Oxford English Dictionary,* and it avoids various specialised notions of the public health expert in order to fit in with the villagers' notion of cleanliness. The killing of germs, insects, and pests, as they are vectors of all sorts of diseases, forms the major part of the expert's notion of cleanliness, but this has scarcely any place in the villager's notion.

The villagers use the word "*Ganda*" for: (a) the unclean state of persons, places, and things which need to be washed, cleaned, removed or replaced, and (b) the actions or habits which tend to create unclean state or disorderliness. The words "*Ganda*" and "*Gandgi*" as used by the villagers are therefore something more than "*dirty*" and "*dirtiness*" of the English language. Hands in the cooking activities become dirty (*Ganda*) when they are soiled by ashes, earth, flour, etc., and have to be washed to be clean again. Similarly, once the cooking and the eating in the kitchen is over, everything in the kitchen contributes to the "dirtiness" (*Gandgi*) of the kitchen and is required to be removed, washed and cleaned before the commencement of next cooking. Not only this, actions leading to disorderliness, such as throwing

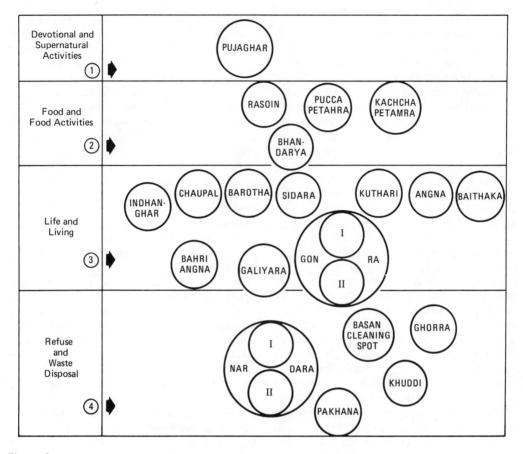

**Figure 1.**

of clothes on the floor, scattering of grain and scraps of vegetables in the courtyard or verandah make the place dirty. In a room if various articles, such as, clothes, utensils, provisions, baskets, etc., are out of their *proper* places (these are largely subject to a cultural definition) and are scattered in the room, they contribute to the "dirtiness" of the room. The habits or actions leading to such a state are called *gandi-adat* (unclean habits). Those habits, which in the villager's opinion help create dirty or unclean state, evoke disapproval. There can also be *ganda-kaam* ("dirty", obscene, indecent or unbecoming act) which may not have any relation with physical uncleanliness, as for example, the violation of a commensal or a sexual taboo.

In the domestic life of a villager, the difference between physical cleanliness and ritual purity is striking in some situations, while in certain others the two overlap and become coterminus. Sometimes the values of cleanliness and ritual purity are clearly identified without harming the role various

practices of ritual purity play in promoting sanitation. The following situations may be recognized in this respect.

**A. Dichotomous Situations**

Within a homestead, certain places and things are dirty but not polluting, or certain things are dirty and polluting but the members of the household do not come into frequent contact with these, and pollution through them can therefore be easily avoided. The examples of the first category are cob-webs in the place of worship, vegetable peels, and scrap-heap within the kitchen, rodent excreta in flour, mud, and tiny worms in the drinking water, and flies. The examples of the second category are: drains, sewage, soakpits and ditches. These places are polluting as well as dirty. They can be cleaned but cannot be freed from the pollution which they permanently carry. A drain is a polluting object, howsoever clean it may be. Whenever contacted, it will make a person ritually impure.

The dichotomous situations can be of several types from the points of view of cleanliness: first, in which the purificatory steps also help promote cleanliness; second, in which the purificatory steps become irrelevant to it. In a third case, physical cleaning may be resorted to for its own sake. Let us take examples. The removal of scrap-heaps, vegetable peels and leavings of food from the kitchen, the disposal of ashes, and the plastering of hearth and floor with mud-paste are villager's essential purificatory steps which remove the ritual impurity of the kitchen and make it fit for the next cooking. These very steps promote the removal of dirt, ashes, filth and useless matter from the spot and accomplish cleanliness. But I wrote earlier that the notion of ritual purity is always a primary concern in the kitchen because the slightest ritual impurity in cooking or taking food immediately causes internal pollution—a state which should be scrupulously avoided. Permanent pollution can be caused in the household group due to such natural phenomena as, birth, death, and menstruation. In all these examples, the ritual impurity cannot be expunged at once. It takes its specified period of time before it can completely be expunged. But, it must, however, be noted that the severity of pollution decreases as the time that elapses after the polluting act. The impurity is also successively diminished (Dumont and Pocock 1959), as several intermediate purificatory steps are undertaken. For example, in birth-pollution, several *Nahans* (baths) successively diminish impurity of the mother and the child, and these allow them to return gradually to the normal state. These *Nahans* are essentially purificatory steps, but they also insure physical cleanliness. The room where the child is born (*Saur*) is thoroughly swept, washed, and plastered on the days of these *Nahans*; the bedsteads are washed with water; the beds are changed; and the clothes on the persons of the mother and the child are changed after they have undertaken the ritual baths. These baths are preceded by rubbing and massaging the bodies of the mother and the child with oil and/or *ubtan-paste* (a paste of flour in water and oil). The *saur* (nursery) is finally fumigated with double ends in view; that it cleans the atmosphere, and that it protects the mother (*Jachcha*) and the child (*Bachcha*) from evil spirits. Such *Nahans* are three in number and each of them marks a "stage" in the diminution of impurity.

Similarly, menstrual blood is not only polluting but also dirty and repelling. The purificatory rites on the third day, are preceded by several cleaning steps. The period of pollution extends as long as the blood does not stop flowing completely. However, in practice, after the first ritual bath, women begin doing limited domestic work, such as, peeling and scraping of vegetables, but not cooking them.

Not only in the removal of impurity, but also in raising the ritual purity of a person, place or thing, physical cleaning is resorted to. An apartment for normal living, is swept and washed afresh for making it fit for any ritual ceremony or for any religious festival. The *Satya-Narain-Katha* cannot be performed without cleaning an apartment which is considered fit for normal life. In any religious sacrifice (*Havana,* or *Yajna*), such purificatory steps as the repeated plastering of floor with cowdung paste, repeated baths of the participating individuals, not only elevate them to the required level of ritual purity, but also promote cleanliness on the occasion.

In the above examples, the notions of ritual purity and impurity are dominant, and are the main concern on these occasions. The dichotomy between the ideas of physical cleanliness and ritual purity is marked. Yet, the purificatory steps involved on all these occasions promote sanitation or physical cleanliness. It can, therefore, be observed that the dichotomy need *not* necessarily preclude sanitation. In all the above cases, the practices of physical cleanliness ultimately help in expunging or diminishing pollution or raising the level of ritual purity. On such occasions the villager's view of cleanliness is "ritualised"; the steps of physical cleanliness find their full meaning and expression only in the context of ritual states. A place swept with a broom is clean but ritually impure, and hence as such it is unsuitable for worship, unless it is washed by water or cowdung paste. If one soils his feet with a polluting object like human excreta which is dirty as well as polluting, a wash with mud and soap may "clean" the feet but cannot "purify" the person, unless bath has been taken. In such examples, the practices of physical cleanliness are stepping stones, are a means to the end of acquiring ritual purity.

In the kitchen, even when cooking, the washing of hands and feet may be done with three purposes—for cleaning, or for ritual purity, or for both. One washes one's hands when they are soiled with, for example, flour. The aims of washing hands may be many: sometimes purely for cleanliness; and at other moments it may be necessary to wash them for ritual purity, for example, the hands require washing before serving the cooked vegetable kept "outside" the *Kachcha*-kitchen because the "contact" of a speck of wet flour (*atta*) with vegetable will render the whole vegetable impure and will no longer be fit for consumption as Pucca food. In a third situation, while finishing the cooking activity, the hands are washed with water so as to remove the *atta* (flour) which is dirty as well as impure.

Under certain circumstances, the purificatory steps become irrelevant to physical cleanliness. Here the dichotomy becomes still more marked, and there is relatively more emphasis on ritual states. Water in a jug (*Lota*) may be clean but not pure on account of the impure state or nature of the receptacle. For a Brahmin, an earthen vessel is greatly polluting if it has been touched by a low caste individual. A brass or bronze utensil, which has been used for drinking and has not been rinsed, is impure and the water kept in it will also be consequently impure. The level of ritual purity of the container directly affects the ritual level of the thing contained in it. Similar is the case of *Dhoti* (loincloth), which is clean after it has been washed by *Dhobi*, but not pure (this example has been taken by Srinivas 1952, as well as Dumont and Pocock 1959, to elucidate the difference between ritual and physical states). Taking of *Panchgavya* is another example; it is extremely beneficial mixture for ritual purity (See, Dubois, 1906) and is a purificatory step of the highest order in Hindu religion, nevertheless it has a negative value with regard to physical cleanliness. It is, by physical standards, even a "dirty" preparation. Ceremonial *achman* (a purificatory step, usually before worship, in which a few drops of water are poured on the flattened palm and sipped three times), the sprinkling of *ganga-jal* (water of the Ganges) over a person, place or thing, and the differentiation between the *Kachcha* and *Pucca* foods, are some more examples which are symbolic of ritual states and may help raise the level of ritual purity. But they do not lead to physical cleanliness. The latter is rather put out of question or precluded in such cases.

In the third case, physical cleanliness is practised for its own sake in the normal life and even on those occasions in which the dichotomy is quite marked. Even the most backward people have notions of physical cleanliness and dirtiness, and they differentiate between what is clean and what is unclean. They have a set of practices designed to keep up the cleanliness. In normal living, cleanliness is valued, the cleaning practices, such as, washing of hands and feet, bathing when dirty, perspiring or feeling hot, sweeping of floors, and arranging articles in various apartments are

followed by all the villagers according to their awareness and the emphasis laid by them on such activities. While worshipping a deity or cooking in the kitchen, cleaning steps are undertaken alongside the ritual practices of purity and impurity. It is a general habit to wash hands, whenever handling anything that soils. Those who work with mud in the fields, take bath to "clean" themselves when the work is over. In Gopalpur, as mostly in the whole of Northern India, a bath may serve a double purpose: first, that of removing dirt and second, that of either making the person ritually pure, or ending the impure state (Srinivas 1952:83; See also Dumont and Pocock 1959:17). In practice, a ritual bath is not characterised by any special feature; no *mantras* are chanted on the occasion.

The presence of rodent excreta in the flour, and mud and tiny water worms are dirty but not polluting. As far as they can, people remove the physical impurity from the water by sieving, decanting and picking, etc. Similar is the case with flies. These are dirty, but not ritually impure. If they settle on food, or on the person, it makes the object *dirty* but does not *pollute* it. If there is a fly in milk, or in a curry-bowl, most of the villagers throw the fly away as soon as they notice it and make use of the milk and curry. Such notions of cleanliness have become a part of the life of the villager and health educators would do well to attend them in right earnest.

### B.  Overlapping Situations

In those places where the values of ritual purity and physical cleanliness overlap, the ways of acquiring one also lead to the promotion of the other. The natural functions of the body are a great source of pollution; they are also dirty; for example, faeces, menstrual blood, spittle, hair, nail clippings, reproductive fluids, etc. These things are dirty as well as polluting, and therefore, those purificatory steps which are resorted to are also the steps for physical cleanliness. On all occasions, the contact with the above noted things is polluting, and in order to remove the pollution, one has either to take a bath or at least wash the affected part of the body. In such circumstances, the pollution as well as dirtiness are removed by one and the same method; the values of physical cleanliness and ritual purity, both are emphasised. In the above, such actions as: washings, ablutions, baths, removal of clothes, sweeping and plastering are the usual steps which purify as well as clean a person, place or thing. In domestic life, the occurrence of temporary and external pollution is inevitable as well as more frequent (the casual permanent pollution due to birth, death and menstruation, has already been dealt with earlier). Since the household group is composed of those only members who belong to one endogamous and commensal group, the permanent ritual impurity from that source within the homestead is ruled out. Also in the house some places like drains, which carry permanent pollution, cannot be purified but only cleaned by such methods as flushing and scavenging.

## IV

The degree of pollution is different in different apartments of the homestead. Thus the cleaning of the place of worship, the kitchen, the upper and lower portions of the courtyard (usually having drains, etc.), the drawing room, the compound and the cattleshed do not involve the equal degree of pollution.

This scale of ritual purity and pollution for various apartments of a homestead in North India offers sufficient support to the observation that physical cleanliness is practised mostly according to the main cultural theme of ritual purity and pollution. In the villager's opinion, ritual purity and physical cleanliness are two words necessarily implying each other, especially in domestic life.

Division of a homestead into various levels of ritual purity (see the Diagram) promotes as well as prevents sanitation. This is largely dependent upon: (a) the occasion, and (b) the strictness with which elaborate practices of ritual purity and pollution are observed in a household. In lower castes, for example, the Pasis (*Shakta* group) and the Chamars, it was observed that while their women were engaged in cooking food, they did not hesitate to touch broom, and, if necessary, even clean the courtyard or the verandah (but not the drains). This is never found with the women of the Kayasthas and the Brahmins. Once the women have taken bath, they do not engage in domestic cleaning; they usually do worship, or cooking or any other activity which cannot harm their normal ritual status. The cleaning of polluted places, if still undone, is postponed either to the evening or to the next morning.

Varying with situations, men, materials, places, and actions are all endowed with a certain kind and degree of ritual impurity in the Indian village. Accordingly, the associated cleaning activities are also polluting, and this pollution also requires to be

expunged by following appropriate practices of regaining ritual purity.

...Individual as well as group differences in opinion and practice are always possible. For some Kayastha individuals, cleaning of cattle shed must be followed by a purificatory bath. For others, it is not so.

Broom is a polluting object and therefore touching of broom is also polluting. The degree of pollution that the broom carries is dependent upon the apartment which is cleansed with it. Thus, a broom used for clearing a courtyard, a verandah, and a room will be ritually more polluting than the one used for cleaning a kitchen or a place of worship. In terms of the diagram on the level of ritual purity in a homestead, the pollution carried by a broom increases from the 1st to the 4th level. Therefore, a broom used for the apartments of the 1st level is fit to be used for all others. In practice, as the broom gets worn out and old, it is employed for cleaning the apartments of 2nd or 3rd, or 4th level.

Only a new broom and unused broom (*bina barti jharoo*) is ritually fit for use at the 1st level. No broom which has even once been used at 2nd or 3rd, or 4th level, remains fit for the first level. In other words, 1st level cannot receive a broom used at 2nd, 3rd, or 4th level, while the 4th level can receive all brooms used in the homestead.

Touching of a broom is as much polluting as cleaning an apartment with it. Hence a touch with the broom is avoided especially when engaged in worshipping or cooking food, and if touched, appropriate purificatory steps should be undertaken, depending upon the ritual level at which the broom was used.

## V

As cultures change, for whatever reason, people learn new things. The adults adopt new ways, "take them by and by under their moral umbrella by usage, and recommend them to the younger generations" (Dollard, 1945). Today in Gopalpur, the concepts of ritual purity and pollution are no exceptions to this remark. New learning situations are created in the village day by day. In Gopalpur, some people like Kayasthas are fast undergoing modernization and westernization. There are others like Kurmi, Ahir and Pasi who are undergoing sanskritization as well as modernization. Such a dynamics of the two processes of culture change is also operating on the concepts of ritual purity and pollution. Within one social group, a caste or a sub-caste, the two standards, one sanskritic and the other modern are acquired together. Youths are claiming whatever is modern; while the old people, especially of lower castes, are increasingly observing details of ritual purity in the rules of commensalism, and in the activities of kitchen. Even within one household, the dual standards are applied today. A few educated Kayastha youths would not think it "clean" to squat in the kitchen-yard for taking food. Instead, they would like to sit on chairs and place the food on a table, while old people think it to be ritually polluting. But old people do not quarrel with youths on this matter, they are allowed to go their own way. Today, those people in Gopalpur who got one or the other apartment of their house sprayed with D.D.T. do not think that this spray is ritually polluting for those apartments. Still no body would like a place of worship, a kitchen, a pantry to be sprayed with D.D.T. because the ritual purity of these places will be affected. D.D.T. is a polluting substance for these places, a harmless and even useful substance for living verandahs, rooms, scullery, etc., and an "essential" thing, according to some Kayasthas and Kurmis, for the drains and ditches, refuse dumps which are the seats of flies and mosquitoes.

There is another example: thirty households of Gopalpur were sprayed with D.D.T. in the summer of 1959 because the youths of the house pressed their elders for it. Youths compete for such new "acquisitions". With the youths of the hamlet of Gopalpur, the spray of D.D.T. became an issue of social prestige—if Kurmi youths got it done, why should the Pasi youths lag behind. It is an important tendency where the old ways are less valued in the face of a *new* practice. The polluting dimensions of such things as D.D.T. gradually shrink and may even be lost with time.

The value of cleanliness is always culturally defined and changing with time; it may on occasions correspond to the modern notions of cleanliness owing to the vigorous emphasis on modernism. For example, among the Kayasthas of Gopalpur, the use of soap is generally not ritually polluting: it cleans the body as well as it does no harm to the normal ritual purity attained by a bath. For Kayasthas, the soap is no longer an item of polluting value. They use soap in bathing and then go for daily worship.

Formerly, (See also Dubois 1906) people did not eat tomato and carrot, because these had a "foreign" origin and were treated as non-vegetarian (ritually polluting) diet. Today, nobody

avoids eating them. They are eaten by the people of upper and lower castes alike. Similarly, leather shoes were formerly thought of as polluting, so much so that they were always kept outside the main domestic building. Feet were washed regularly before one entered the inner courtyard. At present, except the kitchen and the place of worship, people enter all apartments with shoes on without any harm to the normal ritual status of various apartments. In the past, villagers avoided drinking water from water-taps and hand pumps in the cities because both of these employed washers made of leather. Today hand pumps are greatly in vogue in the villages and the villagers prefer them over wells. To satisfy themselves the more strict persons would first rub the cock with muds and wash it and then take the water from it for worshipping and drinking purposes. In Gopalpur, however, there is no water pump but the people of the village, whenever they visit the cities, have experienced such difficulties. Today, no villager objects to the dropping of potassium permanganate (red medicine, *lal dawa*) in a well which has dirty and smelling water.

In Gopalpur the Kayasthas and a section of the Kurmis and the Ahirs represent the trend of modernization, while the Pasis, a section of the Ahirs, and the Brahmins represent the trend of sanskritization. Brahmins of the village are still the fountainheads of sanskritic tradition for the low and the artisan caste people. In the areas of ritual purity and pollution the change is occurring in the following stages:

## Stage I

This stage is characterized by dropping out of the details of practices connected with ritual purity and pollution. The *Chhoot-Pak* complex in the kitchen is becoming less rigid with use, still the majority of them do not disregard it completely. At present, the youth do not mind taking food (*Kachcha*) outside the kitchen-yard; however, they may not wash hands and feet prior to taking *Kachcha* food. The woman who is preparing food in the kitchen does not think herself as polluted by touching and feeding her child, yet she may avoid touching cots, beds, clothes, brooms, etc.

## Stage II

This stage consists in practising the "atrophied" version of ritual purity *along with* occasional resort to the modern methods of cleanliness. We may take as examples: the use of soap, the wearing of leather-band wrist-watches and leather shoes by

249

the people. While even going for worship, the nephew of the village priest thinks that mere washing of hands and feet does away with the "pollution" acquired through wearing leather. Generally, the people use double standards for observing *Chhoot-Pak*: one for intra-domestic life and the other for extra-domestic one. *Chhoot-Pak* can be maintained only in the former case, while in the extra-domestic life one has to be less rigid. adaptive and tolerant. The example of this trend can be found among the Ahirs of Rampur who claim to sanskritize fastest. Normally, they observe the commensal taboos rigidly while within the village. But when they go to sell milk in the city of Lucknow, they have to eat, out of necessity, at various way-side shops and restaurants. Among the Ahir youths, the laxity of behaviour in observing the roles of pollution is widely manifest outside and is finding its way into domestic life. This is affecting the socialisation of children in the family. They are acquiring what the villagers themselves call "*newlight*" (*nai roshani*).

**Stage III**

It consists in dropping out the old practices of purity and pollution without systematic replacement by the new ones. This stage is not well represented in Gopalpur. The educated "elite" of the village dropped several practices of *Chhoot-Pak* as "superstition", but did not replace it with, for example, sanitary practices. A gap which has thus been caused by the process of culture change may be used with advantage by health educators. Such people (only Kayasthas) know a good deal about the *Chhoot-Pak*, as well as the principles of sanitation, but they have not been geared to action to reorganise their existing system of practices. They need to be won round to the hygienic ideas. Such a section of the population may be easily amenable to health education, if it is given properly. . . .

# VIII

## Anatomy, Surgery, and the Medical Knowledge of Preindustrial Peoples

### The Use of Surgery and the Limits of Medical Knowledge in Preindustrial Society

In an early paper in the *Bulletin of the History of Medicine*, Erwin Ackerknecht (1946) states that the general scope of "primitive" surgery could be summarized about as follows: All "primitive" tribes use some form of treatment of wounds, fractures, and dislocations, and most use medicines in these treatments as well as bone-setting, massage, bleeding, and incisions. "More complicated operations, such as amputation and excision, are extremely rare," says Ackerknecht, and he terms surgery among preindustrial peoples as "poor" in quality, when it is done at all. He admits that there are some exceptions in another paper (Ackerknecht 1947a), but cannot account for them and attributes their presumed "poor" surgery to a lack of anatomical knowledge and physiology and an underdevelopment of technological and scientific knowledge and organization. Ackerknecht also believes that the presumed dependence of such peoples upon "supernatural" causation is a deterrent to the development of better surgery and of the requisite biological and technological knowledge. Ackerknecht's statements have been strongly influential among medical anthropologists and others; for example, Sigerist (1951) and Alland (1970) agree with his position.

Clearly this problem necessarily brings into consideration some attention to the extent and limits of medical knowledge in preindustrial societies. Generally, it has been asserted that the basis of medical comprehension among "primitive" peoples has been essentially magico-religious and, therefore, the focus of diagnosis and treatment was mainly on symptoms. (Whether magic, science, and religion can be sufficiently separated from each other is itself an important question, but one I cannot discuss here. But see my remarks in the introduction to this book.) Indeed, such scholars aver that the symptoms of disease may themselves be ignored in order, according to the indigenous disease theory, to treat the patient for such "supernaturally" induced causes of illness as spirit or object intrusion, sorcery or bewitchment, soul loss or possession.

Certainly it has been scarcely 200 years that the bases of scientific medicine were laid down in Western cultures, a system based on the systematic study of anatomical and physiological function, the germ theory (Sigerist 1951:206ff), the denial of spiritual or humoral causation, complex industrial technology and social

251

organization, and the development of the scientific ethos. Generally, there is broad agreement, reinforced by the position of Ackerknecht and others, that healers in nonliterate societies had little actual knowledge of physiology, anatomy, or chemistry, and that their surgery was largely absent or, where it existed, with rare exceptions was ineffective and probably dangerous for the patient.

Countering these views are the arguments of a few anthropologists such as Laughlin (1961, 1963; Marsh and Laughlin 1956) who contend that probably more preindustrial societies than we are aware of developed a rather extensive familiarity with anatomy and physiology and in many instances their healers were able to perform operations skillfully and efficaciously. The hypotheses and findings put forth in the essay by Laughlin in this section are further developed in another excellent paper (Laughlin 1963), "Primitive Theory of Medicine: Empirical Knowledge."

The evidence of learning among preindustrial peoples that bears on medical knowledge is particularly impressive in the area of the use of botanical and other substances as medicaments. Thus, Bryant (1970) describes in detail 240 medicinal plants used by Zulu curers in South Africa and estimates that they made use of at least 700 botanical substances in their medical system. Vogel (1970), a historian, has published a brilliant study of American Indian medicine in which he concludes that North and South American Indians have used hundreds, perhaps thousands, of herbals and various materials and compounds for the treatment of disease and "well over two hundred of their drugs . . . have been included in the official drug compendia of the United States" (Vogel 1970: 262). Vogel substantiates these in detail in a 200 page appendix. His findings lead him to state:

> While the aboriginal uses of these drugs were frequently incorrect in the judgment of modern science, the examples of efficacious usage which have been cited constitute an imposing monument to the original Americans. There can be no doubt that by trial-and-error methods they arrived at an understanding of the properties and effects of many useful botanical medicines. Moreover, independently of Old World influence, they discovered some useful medical inventions and procedures. The surgical use of rubber and cotton, the bulbed syringe for enemata and medical injections, the Credé method of manipulation in parturition, and the use of anesthetics and antiseptics have all been credited to American Indians (Vogel 1970: 262–263).

Even though some reports undoubtedly were exaggerated, Vogel believes that

> Accounts of successful treatments or cures by Indian doctors of such external afflictions as snake and insect bites, burns and scalds, wounds of all sorts, fractures, dislocations and bruises have been frequent enough in early accounts of credible persons. They have earned for Indian healers varying degrees of approbation from medical men who either observed their practice personally or had learned of it by other means (Ibid.: 264)

Vogel and other writers have suggested that American Indian medicine was at least equal, and probably superior in many respects, to that of sixteenth- and seventeenth-century Europe, and was widely used there as well as in the Americas (see also Scully 1970). Anthropologists working in recent years on research into curers who use hallucinogenic drugs (for example, Dobkin de Rios 1972; Harner 1973) have suggested that a full understanding of the properties and uses of these drugs as well as the actual functions they play in healing required at least some botanical, chemical, and even physiological knowledge.

Recently an article in *Science* (Brown 1975) suggested that given the environments in which they lived and the uses to which they put their knowledge, the empirical and systematic learning and discoveries of Native Americans in science, engineering, and medicine probably were far in excess of that possessed by the sixteenth-century European immigrants to the lands which had been

252

forcibly, cruelly, and corruptly wrested from these "savages." As the author suggests,

One would not argue that the traditional Native American cultures were or are science-based cultures, nor that the people living in them understood the scientific basis for their daily practices, any more than the average U.S. farmer understands the process by which fertilizer increases yields or the reasons why hybridization can combat disease. The impressive knowledge of the Native American peoples about a wide variety of natural phenomena is not, however, accidental, nor has its acquisition been haphazard. It is based on generations of systematic inquiry. It is the accumulation and transmittal of repeated observations, experiments, and conclusions. Some of the elements of the scientific method were inherent in their processes. Native Americans have understood, beyond the obvious, many of the relationships among different types of substances. With respect to plant taxonomy, for instance, some Native Latin Americans knew the pharmacological uses of what is now known to be vitamin C, and they knew that it could be found in certain barks, other leafy plants, and mosses that are totally different from each other in outward appearances and specific environments in which they grow. Repeated use of the plants led to the development of a chemo-taxonomy. The Native Americans had recognized, quite accurately, the similarity of substance—which can now be verified by gas chromatography (Brown 1975:38).

In January, 1975, the Council and Board of the American Association for the Advancement of Science passed this resolution: "Be it resolved that the Council of the Association (a) formally recognize the contributions made by Native Americans in their own traditions of inquiry to the various fields of science, engineering, and medicine, and (b) encourage and support the growth of natural and social science programs in which traditional Native American approaches and contributions to science, engineering, and medicine are the subject of serious study and research." Without overstating the case, I believe that it will also be possible to make similar statements about other indigenous peoples of the world whose intellectual, humane, and aesthetic accomplishments frequently have been swamped in the tides of colonialist military-economic domination that engulfed so many of their cultures. Perhaps it ought to be recalled that for hundreds of years European anatomy was learned from nonhuman animals and resulted in often grotesque distortions of knowledge, that anatomy became a science against the religious and political resistance of most European societies and for long had to be practiced clandestinely on exhumed corpses stolen from graveyards, and that the requisite achievements in antisepsis, asepsis, bacteriology, anesthesiology, and all the other kinds of knowledge and techniques so necessary for successful surgery are of relatively recent origin. My own wonder, in viewing the extent of medical knowledge among preindustrial societies, is not that they knew so little but that they knew so much.

# 28 Acquisition of Anatomical Knowledge by Ancient Man

## *William S. Laughlin*

In one of the papers by Ackerknecht (1946, 1947a) cited in the introduction to this section, he concludes that "Primitive surgery is indeed poor in scope and quality," and "The anatomical knowledge of most primitives is notoriously bad." He suggests that logically there are four possible explanations: these societies had no need for surgery, they lacked technical skill, they lacked requisite knowledge, and/or "other elements of their socio-mental make-up have been unfavorable to the development of surgery...." The first two explanations he easily dismisses, but Ackerknecht believes that the anatomical knowledge of "primitive" people was rudimentary and this can be attributed to their overal magical, supernatural orientation. Ackerknecht makes an important distinction between magico-religious and irrational beliefs, stating that they are not synonymous and that the beliefs under discussion are logical within the cognitive systems within which they are formulated, even though they are magical and spiritual in nature. Nevertheless Ackerknecht is hard put to explain the exceptions to his generalizations, for example, the Masai of East Africa, whom he calls "primitive master surgeons."

In this paper William S. Laughlin, a biological anthropologist, responds to Ackerknecht's negative, gloomy assessment of anatomical knowledge among preindustrial peoples. Laughlin is not content merely to counter Ackerknecht's dismal conclusions, but presents a brilliant essay on the limits of knowledge (which he finds much wider and deeper than Ackerknecht) in nonliterate societies. But moving beyond even this demonstration, he utilizes an evolutionary framework within which to show adaptive continuities between contemporary peoples, especially hunter-gatherers, and their earlier hominid progenitors. Laughlin illustrates his arguments with data from his own research among Aleutian Islanders in the Bering Sea and from related Siberian groups, particularly the Tungus. Perhaps most significant of all, Laughlin not only makes an impressive case (although it can be debated at several points) for relatively well-developed *organized* anatomical and other knowledge

Reprinted with abridgments from William S. Laughlin, 1961, "Acquisition of Anatomical Knowledge by Ancient Man," in *Social Life of Early Man*, ed. Sherwood Washburn, Viking Fund Publication in Anthropology No. 31, pp. 150–175, with permission of the author and Wenner-Gren Foundation for Anthropological Research, Inc., New York (Copyright © 1961).

among at least some "primitive" people and for the probability that such knowledge existed as far back as the Pleistocene but he also demonstrates the *limits of anthropological knowledge* of this and other crucial aspects of the intellectual repertory of the supposedly "backward" peoples. Large portions of his material have been omitted for reasons of space, but the reader is referred to an earlier paper (Marsh and Laughlin 1956), a later paper (Laughlin 1963), and to the original version of the present one. In a recent publication dealing with the Noatak Eskimo, Lucier, VanStone, and Keats (1971) carry further some of Laughlin's notions and present another persuasive response to Ackerknecht and others who share his view.

I cannot forbear a point that seems to have escaped the attention of both Ackerknecht and Laughlin, namely, that the conservatism with which most preindustrial societies regarded surgery may have indeed been adaptive. Normally surgery in most instances in Western medicine is—or should be—a treatment of last resort. Problems of surgical shock, anesthesia, dangers of infection in the hospital, and so on, are exceedingly difficult to solve. For example, the threat of staphylococcus infections in hospitals is still not under complete control. And it is doubtful if surgery was resorted to mainly to enrich the operators, as seems to happen at times in Western society. Recently the Massachusetts Commissioner of Welfare stated that many hospital staffs have performed unnecessary surgery on welfare patients to increase income from Medicaid payments. Other have estimated that much "routine" surgery, especially that performed on women, may be essentially unnecessary and perhaps even counter-productive.

...The acquisition of anatomical knowledge, including treatment of pathology, birth practices, and observations on the effects of close inbreeding, is of interest not only because of its priority in the intellectual history of man and its evolutionary function but also for the light it throws on systems of organization. The anatomical knowledge of many peoples—here the example provided by the Aleutian Islanders will be used—does not consist merely of an elaboration of words for an area of cultural interest. It is a commonplace fact that people enlarge their lexicon in those areas with which they are concerned, thus the Lapps have a truly enormous number of words for reindeer, the Hottentots and Nuer for cattle, and the Arabs for camels. More important is the use of genuinely technical terms, systemization of the observations, discreteness of the observations, their extension beyond the superficial, and verification by actual and intentional dissection for the purpose of learning about the structures....

The possibility of extending inferences back to the beginning of the Pleistocene is considerably enhanced by the presence of certain elements that have remained relatively constant. First among these must be listed the constancy or uniformity of animal morphology and physiology during the Pleistocene and, by the same token, animal behavior. Second is the indubitable requirement that humans adapt to the behavior of animals, both to secure the animals for food and fabricational purposes and to preserve themselves from the animals. The third constant element is the essentially carnivorous behavior of humans. A fourth consideration is the existence of many retentions in human behavior from prehuman days. Humans did not become human and then learn how to hunt other animals but already were hunters and simply altered their methods of hunting in conjunction with the acquisition of ideas that permitted the use of tools and, later, their manufacture....

Recognition of blood must surely be numbered among the first conscious thoughts to flicker across the mind of ancient man. Primary distinctions between liquids and solids are, after all, made by animals because of the simple necessity of drinking one and chewing the other. Ancient man simply rationalized existing behavior toward blood and many other animal substances. Similarly, humans did not discover the difference between marrow and bone, or brain and flesh, but rather they elaborated a variety of new ways of utilizing these substances. Many animals are quite specific in their tastes and select only a particular organ to eat (Washburn 1957).

Whether a stranded whale discovered on a beach is regarded as a fortunate supply of food or as an embarrassing object to be towed out to sea or buried depends now on cultural systems that provide an interpretation. Diarrhea produced by eating the toothed whale was likely the same intestinal reaction in ancient man as it is in contemporary peoples. Ancient man, like other animals and contemporary peoples in search of food, undoubtedly regarded stranded sea mammals and carcasses of dead animals as the dietary gratuities that they are. With reference to the morphology and related attributes, then, the animals upon which man and his ancestors fed have changed considerably less during the Pleistocene than have the uses to which they have been put.

...The pertinent effect here is the constant concern of man with the morphology of the animals he hunted. In order to hunt effectively, a large amount of information concerning the animals was required. In order to capture and kill the animals and secure maximum use of them, a detailed knowledge of their anatomy was decidedly advantageous. That we should find extensive anatomical knowledge among people who are constantly hunting and butchering mammals is quite understandable. That such knowledge should be as extensive and intensive as it is among the Aleuts and that it should be organized along comparative and experimental lines is understandable in retrospect, but it could have been neither predicted from a knowledge of their economy nor reconstructed from artifactual and osseous remains.

A brief survey of anatomical knowledge among the Aleutian Islanders, and their sources of such knowledge, may provide useful comparative information for projection into the past. The Eskimos and Aleuts have been frequently used as contemporary models of life in the Mesolithic and Upper Paleolithic....

## DEVELOPMENT OF HUMAN ANATOMICAL KNOWLEDGE IN THE ALEUTIAN ISLANDS

The Aleutian Islanders are unique among all the preliterate populations of the world for their active interest in and extensive knowledge of human anatomy. Early observers, such as Count F. P. Lutke (1835–36) and the Reverend I. Veniaminov noted and documented this unusual development. The observation of Veniaminov is especially pertinent:

In the Aleut language there are and formerly were words referring to Anatomy. I do not have in mind such ones as *heart, liver, intestines* and so forth, but those which are of some higher understanding, such as tugix, a large blood-carrying vessel, cugudagil'uk, cunumguday, sigidaq, and so forth, which I, through downright ignorance of anatomical language, am unable to translate. Such words, apparently, were composed from what the Aleuts before the arrival of the Russians had been studying through the examination of the innards of a person, either of one killed in combat or of a deceased serf, expressly for the science of doctoring [Veniaminov, *Essay of a Grammar of the Aleut-Fox Language*, Foreword, p. v (trans. Gordon H. Marsh from the original Russian].

It speaks highly of the intellectual candor and honesty of this Russian Orthodox priest that he recognized an important area that he was unable to investigate, and his observation immediately suggests that similar developments among other peoples may suffer from lack of investigation. The successful attempt of the Aleuts at a rational practice of medicine and physical culture and their skilful practice of dry mummification are further supported by the practice of true comparative anatomy—a practice aided by their use of the sea otter, by a generous amount of daily dissection of the mammals on which they lived, and, above all, by a well-developed empiricism, which facilitated the transference of their knowledge of animal anatomy to that of humans.

Our method of studying the Aleut knowledge of anatomy quickly revealed the fact that they could identify an organ or part of an organ as well as provide a name for it. Dr. Victor B. Scheffer of the United States Fish and Wildlife Service kindly placed an abandoned fur seal pup at the disposal of an Aleut, who dissected it for us, picking up each part, ureter or pancreas, with forceps and giving us the appropriate name at the same time. We attended the butchering of several animals. When we provided the Aleuts with a human skeleton, they obliged us with lectures in basic osteology, noting that the human mandible was composed of two parts in the immature person and that, unlike the seal's, it fused into a single bone. Aleut and Eskimo are ideal languages for mammalian anatomy because they have a dual ending. Thus, when one-half of the mandible is under discussion, the singular ending is employed; and when the entire mandible or both os coxae are under discussion, the dual ending is employed.

## METHOD OF DESCRIPTION

It is of major interest that all the terms in their anatomical description are contained within a single language. In contrast, our anatomical vocabularies are based extensively on Latin and Greek words and on terms fabricated from combinations of them. Many of the terms that we consider technical are considered so because of the foreign linguistic elements of which they are composed; they are often merely descriptive rather than specific.

Within the Aleut language are many specific terms for external and internal topography. These may be classed into monosyllabic, disyllabic, and polysyllabic words. Many terms have a derived origin. Such words are "tooth" (literally "biter"),

"nose" (literally "breather"), "ear" (literally "hearer"), and "trachea" (literally "place of sound"). Diminutive suffixes appear in the words for the uvula, little finger, little toe, whorl of hair/dermatoglyph. The word for the uvula is, interestingly, initiated with a uvular sound in all three dialects of Aleut.

Descriptive expressions of two or more words represent a large part of the vocabulary: the socket for the eye is, literally "customary hole/bed of the eye"; the two mental foramina (literally "both customary holes of the blood vessels of the jaw"), the bicipital tendon (literally, "tendon on the inside of the bend of the arm").

The detail of their anatomical classification is demonstrated by their nomenclature for musculature. Muscles fall into three categories: muscles with large bunched bellies, such as the *biceps brachii*; flat muscles, such as the pectorals; and long stringy muscles, such as the sartorii.

It is of interest that the Aleut frequently use anatomical analogies to describe anatomical features. Thus the first posterior sacral foramina are termed the "eyes" of the sacrum. These were important sites for acupuncture. The septum of the nose is also known as the "little man of the nose," the tragus is the "post" or "little man of the ear," and the root of the molar tooth is, naturally, a "leg."

Concerned with bone, they distinguish "bone in general," "soft, cancellous or interior bone," "hard bone or ivory." Marrow is, of course, distinguished

Sample Glossary of Human Anatomical Terms
(From Marsh and Laughlin, 1956, pp. 58–76)

| English | Literal Translation |
|---|---|
| Tragus | Post/little man of the ear |
| Root of molar | Leg of the tooth |
| Pericardium | Sac of the heart |
| Pyloric end of stomach | Umbilicus of the stomach the stomach its curl |
| Spleen | Backpack of the stomach |
| First posterior sacral foramina | Both eyes of the sacrum |
| Thenar eminence | Place of stoneflaking |
| Moon of the thumb | Moon of the thumb |
| Pulse/artery | None |
| Vein | Blue thing (on back of hand, etc.) |
| Sesamoid bone | The muscle-itself-its having kinked |
| Caul | Kamleyka (waterproof parka) of the baby |

from brain and spinal cord. Nerves are distinguished from tendons, and blood flowing from the heart is distinguished from blood returning to the heart. It is within the realm of possibility, though no longer capable of demonstration, that the Aleuts had discovered the principle of circulation of the blood. Until the seventeenth century in England a majority of medical scientists believed in the existence of perforations in the septum of the heart (Galen's septum perforations), which permitted blood to flow from one side to the other. The Aleuts had such frequent recourse to dissection that we may safely say that they would never have believed in the existence of holes in a septum that they could see was intact.

The Aleuts and the Eskimos are able to state position very precisely. This is done by means of demonstratives and postpositions, so that position, relative position, relative level, invisible position (invisible to the speaker), down on the water, upward on the land and toward the interior, and enclosure or house position (the one farthest back or nearest the entrance, etc.) can be deftly depicted. This habitual concern with position is expressed in internal anatomy as easily as in external geography.

## SOURCES OF ALEUT ANATOMICAL KNOWLEDGE

The sources of Aleut anatomical knowledge may be partitioned into categories that are also suitable for comparative purposes. Consequently, they are arranged in descending order of ubiquity: (1) study of anatomical structures, (2) rational medicine and physical culture, (3) dissection of human bodies, (4) true comparative anatomy, employing especially the sea otter, and (5) making of dried mummies.

First, subsisting almost exclusively on fish, meat,

| | |
|---|---|
| 1. Pericardium | Water bags, containers |
| 2. Intestines | Shirt (kamleyka) rain parkas, pouches, bags, insulation on harpoon and spear lashings, etc. |
| 3. Oesophagus | Leggings of boots, parka, and pants and leggings of water boots |
| 4. Stomach | Floats, food storage containers |
| 5. Tongue (whale) | Rain parka, using skin of whale's tongue |
| 6. Caul (of humans) | Carried as protective charm |
| 7. Bladder | Floats |

and fowl, they acquired from the butchering of these animals the kind of familiarity with animal structures that all hunting peoples achieve. And this may be extended back to ancient man. However, here as elsewhere in their culture, they practiced their disciplined art of observation more extensively than did most preliterate people. This much is shared with Eskimos. "However, as a branch of the Eskimo-Aleut stock—a stock whose culture emphasizes a pragmatic orientation to its environment and a concentration on structural details of practical importance—they extended more minutely their observation and utilization of animals' tissues than, for example, most of the Indian tribes of North America" (Marsh and Laughlin 1956:40). Even an abbreviated list of the uses of internal tissues indicates the great fabricational use that they made of tissues that in many or most parts of the world are discarded.

A large glossary would be required to itemize the medical, magical, and religious uses of internal organs and tissues. Marrow was used for paint base, eyeballs and blood for glue, ink sac of octopus for black pigment.

Second, they generalized from animal morphology and behavior to human, making use of their habits of observation and experimentation, and used these observed similarities in their practice of medicine, hygiene, and physical culture. They note that the blood of the hair seal is much darker than that of other sea mammals and they infer that this is because he "sleeps too much." They appear to be aware of the effects of oxygenating blood and have, further, the opportunity to observe this in themselves in their recourse to annual blood-letting. Sick animals eat and drink very little, and so the Aleuts emulate them. A vast majority of medical treatments include resting and fasting for several days. A former headman of a village on Kagamil Island was famous for the training he gave his boys. They ran up and down the steep hill by the village carrying large stones. He would listen to their heartbeat to see whether they remained in sufficiently good condition to perform these exercises without undue exertion....

Third, the Aleuts dissected the dead to find out why they died and also to become more familiar with the internal anatomy of humans. A number of early Russian observers call attention to this practice, as recorded by Veniaminov in *Notes on the Islands of the Unalaska Division.*

The Aleut medicine men in former times were famed for their knowledge. In order to more properly learn the internal parts of man, and especially those parts on which they used to perform operations, they used to open dead serfs, or killed enemies. Even I had the chance to see several old Russians who had been treated by Aleut doctors who had lauded them to the limit [Veniaminov (trans.), in Hrdlička 1945:176].

The last person to witness such a dissection was an old woman, over ninety, who died at Nikolski, Umnak, in the 1930's. As a woman doctor she was permitted to attend post mortems but not to dissect.

Fourth, comparative anatomy was deliberately practiced on the sea otter. This animal was chosen because of his morphological and behavioral similarities to humans. The behavioral similarities are fairly well described in the literature, though not as accurately as is known to the Aleuts. Their use of rocks has been frequently referred to and their human-like behavior has been noted by a wide variety of observers. The sea otter has succeeded in freeing his hands by supporting his body in water and swimming on his back, an interesting evolutionary substitute for erect posture in terrestrial mammals. It is in this position that he uses a rock for an anvil, upon which he crushes shellfish. It is this characteristic that is represented by the cleft bow of the Aleutian kayak.

In addition to its behavioral characteristics, the sea otter has a number of points of morphological similarity to man, and, compared with other sea mammals, it is the most similar. The retention of a pronating and supinating forearm in contrast to the flippers of seals; flat grinding molars; femur, tibia, and fibula of marked similarity to man's; and the tendency toward white hair in the aged further provide a logical basis for use of the sea otter in the study of anatomy and for the conception that it is descended from man. The comparative dissection of sea otters survived beyond the dissection of humans. The last dissection was made in 1911, at which time the killing of sea otters was outlawed by the United States government.

Fifth, the manufacture of dry mummies of selected individuals and families, especially in the Eastern Aleutians, was a notable source of information as well as an application of knowledge. Often the viscera were removed through an incision in the perineal region or in the abdomen or upper thorax. The interior was then stuffed with dried grass or moss and the exterior was wiped and dried at intervals. After some months the body was flexed and encased in grass mats and sealskin bags, bound, and then placed in a case or under a rock overhang. The bodies might be disposed on wood racks, suspended in cradles, or simply placed on the floor of the cave, where they were preserved from moisture. The distribution of mummification, the associated artifacts, and the condition of the mummies indicate that this practice was a comparatively recent development, perhaps of only a few hundred years' antiquity prior to the eighteenth-century arrival of the Russians. It was probably introduced by the Neo-Aleuts....

## APPLICATION OF ANATOMICAL INFORMATION

Acupuncture, blood-letting, and massage are the three most common applications of anatomical knowledge, in addition to the various skills employed in delivering babies. Acupuncture was performed both at fixed sites on the body, such as "the two eyes of the sacrum" previously cited, and at various places indicated by the particular illness. The Aleut practice of acupuncture differs from the Chinese in being less elaborate and less rigidly prescribed. Two techniques are distinguishable. In the first, two dots are marked on the skin, a fold of skin between the two dots is raised, and the lancet is then run through the fold of skin from one dot to the other. Even the scalp was raised in this fashion for piercing. The second technique was more hazardous, for it consisted of thrusting the lancet straight into the body.

Closely related to acupuncture is the regular blood-letting, employed once a year on many men, seldom on women. The blood may be let either at the angles from the long saphenous vein (*kitam namii*), where it passes in front of the medial malleolous, or at the elbow from the cubital or basilic vein. The blood is let in the same month of each year but never from the same vein in two successive years. Some persons let their own blood. Sucking was also employed.

Massage is extensively employed and is a specialty of female practitioners; it is used especially during pregnancy and childbirth, being given at regular monthly intervals during pregnancy and after the delivery to place the organs back in their proper positions. One objective was to prevent the baby from getting too large. The last female doctor to witness a human dissection was noted for the effectiveness of her massage and of her palpation in locating disorders. Though her fingers had become crooked and flexed with arthritis, she straightened them by binding them to wood sticks and thus continued her practice until her death.

Surgery was employed, but few references remain. Suturing with sinew was apparently common. More serious operations were performed while the patient was kept warm in the sweat bath. Application of herbal hot packs to sore points was also done in the sweat bath....

## PROJECTIONS OF ANATOMICAL ORIENTATION

Generically there are two principal kinds of projection of anatomical orientation: conceiving inanimate objects in anatomical form and applying the same basic stem to diverse objects, which are thus viewed as sharing a common attribute and as representing characteristics similar to those of animals.

In their material culture many objects receive anatomical designations. The parts of the throwing board are so named: the little ivory pin that engages the butt of the harpoon or spear is termed the "ziphisternum"; the flat surface above the pin is the "forehead of the throwing board"; the ridge along the underside of the back is the "hump of the throwing board"; and the concavity, also on the underside, that is hollowed to accommodate the thenar eminence is named the "thenar of the throwing board." This side of the throwing board is painted black to represent the fur of an animal, and the other side is painted red to represent blood....

Occasional anatomical terms appear with high frequency. The name for the funnel-shaped entrance to the impounding pool of the fish weir is "penis of the creek/fish-weir." The bifurcated base of the single-piece harpoon socket is known as the "legs" of the socket, using, of course, a dual ending. The small hole in the parka for the ends of the drawstring, also that at the waist of the pants, is termed "its biters." These are the places where the drawstrings are secured, and the analogy with teeth is of a very common type.

Personal names, traditional tales and games and riddles are lavishly endowed with anatomical themes. A man with short arms and long trunk is named "hair seal" for his external resemblance to the seal. Dismemberment is extended to hawks and owls and occurs frequently in stories. Cannibalism is very common in the stories, taking on clever forms—a man, for example, brings home animal entrails for his wife, and she later discovers that she has been eating her relatives....

If we take those words that share a common stem, we find a cogent relation for seemingly diverse things. The words for (1) blowhole of the whale, (2) intestines, (3) daylight, (4) brachioradialis muscle of the forearm, (5) breath, and (6) holy spirit (a word constructed since the arrival of Christianity) all share a common stem. If we bear in mind the Aleut belief in a breath soul and the identification of breath soul and daylight, the blowhole of the whale is the place where the breath can be seen to emanate; the intestines are the seat of the soul; the arm loses its life when it is paralyzed in fighting by a blow on brachioradialis; and the holy spirit is an especially large light.

In retrospect, it is seen that the Aleutian Islanders have elaborated a culture saturated with anatomical themes and concepts. There is no segment of the culture that is not so structured. It is pertinent to ask two questions: How much of this orientation and elaboration could be inferred from the material remains available in an archeological record? and What led to this development among the Aleuts (the Koniags of Kodiak Islands probably had much the same development) but not among other Eskimo groups, even those with much the same ecological base and material culture?

## SOURCES OF ANATOMICAL INFORMATION AMONG THE TUNGUS

Mummification involving evisceration and the use of a particular animal for comparative anatomical dissection are two distinctive features of the Aleuts in contrast to other Eskimo groups. Either autopsy of the dead or mummification is not uncommon in the Bering Sea region and, of course, in other areas around the world.

The Chukchee practiced a form of autopsy in which one man, the "fortifier," exposed the internal organs and announced the "probable reason" of death on the appearance of the liver and heart (Bogoras 1909:527–28). Similarly, "The Reindeer Koryak of the Palpal Ridge dissect bodies before burning them, in order to find out what ailed them" (Jochelson 1908:113). The Yukaghir cut the flesh from the bones of the deceased shamans, dried them in the sun, and distributed them to the relatives of the shaman. The skull was placed on a manikin, which was used for divination and other purposes. The likelihood that a more typical autopsy was also practiced is indicated in an account of a traditional tale in which, following the death of an older brother: "according to custom, his body was dissected to learn the cause of death, and, according to the tradition, his heart was found to be torn in two" (Jochelson 1910:221, 79). The Ainu are credited with a rather ingenious system of evisceration for mummification, namely, removal of the intestines through the anus (Montandon 1937:150). Mortuary customs involving the use of parts of the dead, skull cults, etc., have been reported for every major area of the world (MacLeod 1925; Kroeber 1948:300–304) as well as for the Bering Sea and North Pacific area, and they obviously constitute a rather ubiquitous source of information. . . .

One of the richest sources, based on direct observations made over a long period of time under eminently suitable conditions, is that of the anatomical knowledge of the Tungus, by Shiro-kogoroff (1935:73–76 *et passim*). Here, as with the Aleuts, we may see the part played by anatomy in the daily life of these hunters and reindeer-breeders. At least five major points stand out in clear relief: (1) the Tungus are anatomists and not simply butchers; (2) variations, similarities and dissimilarities, and homologies and analogies are carefully studied; (3) animals are caught and kept for the purpose of study; (4) surgery involving tissue transplantation is conducted; (5) sophisti-cated observations permitting the recognition of microorganisms are made; and (6) (the basic point) these practices are all part of a necessary method of adaptation for survival.

Shirokogoroff speaks directly to the point in documenting the anatomical preoccupations of the Tungus:

When killing a new animal a Tungus is first of all interested in finding the anatomical peculiarities of this animal. Indeed, it is very essential, for he must skin and sometimes dissect the animal without breaking the skin and bones. Here the Tungus appears before us as an anatomist. As a matter of fact, the skinning and dressing of the animals is one of the essential elements of the Tungus education. The man who does not know how to do it, will not be able to carry out this industry. A fact may help us to understand the Tungus attitude in this matter. A man amongst the Birarcen did not know that the articulation of ribs of the bear is not like that in some cervines with which he was familiar. In fact, when the breast bone is taken off the ribs in cervines must be turned outside, while in the bear they must be pressed inside. He did try to dissect the animal and he could not do it. Then he tried to break the chest with a heavy piece of wood. This did not solve the problem, but the meat was reduced to pieces, and thus could not be transported and used. This man's name was always repeated as an instance which must not be followed. Everybody laughed at him. However, the Tungus is not only a butcher, he is an

anatomist. He is interested in the comparative study of bones and soft parts of the body and he comes to form a good idea as to the anatomical similarities and dissimil-arities in animals and even man. Let us remark that the occasions of studying human anatomy present themselves rather often, especially, in former days, for the Tungus at least those of Manchuria did interfere in the traumatic cases and they did practise the cleaning of bones after a certain period after death and thus could and must know the skeleton, also soft parts of the body (Shirokogoroff 1935:73).

The Tungus compare the analogous and hom-ologous bones of different animals and may use the same word for the same articulation even though it occurs in a different position. They have noted that the bat has long arms, like man, and is not a bird.

Of considerable importance is the practice of capturing animals for observation of their behavior and anatomy. One example is cited of a group of Tungus who searched for a bird that was reported to dive into holes in the ice and to emerge from other holes. Finally catching such a bird, they attached a string to it in order to facilitate their observations of how it dived, what it ate, etc. Finally, they killed and anatomized it, examining the skin especially for insects.

Closely related is the practice of keeping the young of various animals, especially those with which they want more familiarity, though they may rationalize this by explaining that the animals are kept for the amusement of children. The adults spend their time observing them, and it is clear that here lies a possible preliminary step in the domestication of animals.

Sinew from the leg of a partridge is used to splice the severed sinews in the hand of a man, and the separated ends are joined with a long hair (Shirokogoroff:95).

They infer the idea of microörganisms from the observation of worms in wounds, as they gradually grow large enough to be visible to the naked eye. They infer that there are very small worms that cannot be seen and that various diseases may be caused by these.

Throughout their observations is the recurring argument to men. Hair and skin are subject to change. Though taking a long time in man, it occurs most rapidly in snakes. Going beyond the changes within an individual in his life span, they infer that man was formerly hairy but lost his hair as a consequent of using salt and must therefore use clothing. Interestingly, they credit salt and hot food for the loss of formerly good olfactory functions in man. Like the Aleuts, they are not in the least hostile to the idea of evolution....

Shirokogoroff itemized four conditions that affect the relative familiarity of man with the various animals: (1) they may pay more attention to animals on which they are living (and within this we should note that, as with the Aleuts, where certain tissues are used for fabricational purposes, they are well known, thus the Tungus have names for some of the most important tendons because they are used for thread); (2) not all animals allow man to approach them closely; (3) the number of animals is different for different species; and (4) the animals behave differently toward man, and those that are dangerous attract more attention.

The ideas of the Tungus, like those of the Aleuts, are well elaborated in the general idea of functional and gross anatomy and in behavior. They admit that these animals have certain territories. Recognizing the ownership of territory, then, requires various specialized behavior on the part of the human. Depending on whether the animal is considered very intelligent and whether he can understand human speech, they placate or frighten him upon entering his territory. "Yet, when a Tungus speaks to the tiger, he leaves his gun down, etc. and does not believe the tiger to be a being endowed with supernatural power. He hopes to be understood but if he fails he has to fight.... It is different with the bear which cannot understand speech" (Shirokogoroff: 79).

A final observation consists in a similarity between European and Tungus anatomists. The Tungus seem to have imported a number of terms from Mongol, sometimes preserving their own as well. This is analogous to the substitution or addition of Latin anatomical terms for Anglo-Saxon terms.

## FACTORS IN THE UNDERESTIMATION OF PRIMITIVE KNOWLEDGE

The consistent underestimation of primitives' knowledge is a notorious and unfortunate fact, though the reasons are not difficult to assay. Apparently without exception, every fieldworker who has included such an investigation in his schedule has remarked that he was unable to exhaust the native's knowledge because of too little time or because he himself lacked the necessary knowledge to record those things that the native informant wished to tell or show him. We have already seen Veniaminov's candid admission that

he did not possess sufficient anatomical information to record what the Aleuts knew. Shirokogoroff notes: "I have carried this experiment with many Tungus in order to find how far they are familiar with the small bones and for gathering data for my dictionary. Indeed, I was unable to exhaust this branch of their knowledge as it was impossible to do with all the plants and animals, known to the Tungus" (p. 74). Dr. Cooper notes that after a Cree hunter explained to him in considerable detail the shape, position, and functions of the four parts of the caribou stomach, "I had to look up the point when I got back home to my books. He was right" (Cooper 1935: 361). Dr. Steggerda recorded the names of 441 plants and animals known to one Maya Indian and observed that the Indian could doubtless have enumerated at least one-third more animals and plants had time permitted working longer (Steggerda, *Proc. Eighth Amer. Sci. Cong.*: 91). Such statements can be multiplied many times over by recourse to reports of field investigators. They are notoriously absent in secondary works.

Failure to speak the language, or at least to record in the native's language, is a serious barrier. This failure leads to inaccuracy and often blunts the interest of the native. It precludes any chance of examining the system of organization in detail and omits a practical test of what the native actually does know. It may also lead to obscure discussions of whether the native was "aware" of the true meaning of physiological paternity and so dissolve into semasiological ambiguities. Additionally, the interesting speculations and discussions concerning the identification of parts and their functions, which so often form a part of the conversation of natives, are lost. In this respect it is interesting to see how Chamisso overcame the linguistic problem in his study of the Aleut knowledge of whales. He asked the Aleuts to carve wooden models of each of the whales known to them. As a consequence he was able to place on record a study of whales that has never been duplicated (Chamisso 1824). The disposition of this study (published in Latin) provides an example of intellectual embalming, and the author will probably continue to remain better known for his authorship of *Peter Schlemihl*.

Lack of training in the natural sciences not only may disqualify an observer but also may lead to imputations of magic where none in fact exists. Even the use of divination may have a very valuable function in randomizing the choice of hunting routes selected by the hunter and thus maximizing the likelihood of meeting game that has come to know the hunter's habits over a period of time. Arctic Eskimos avoid eating the liver of polar bear for the very good reason that it makes them sick. Whether this is called hypervitaminosis or magic will depend upon the knowledge of the investigator. After all, few Europeans have seen a vitamin, much less a hypervitamin. Most investigators have not hunted for a living, and many have not dressed out anything larger than a rabbit or pheasant. As Shirokogoroff points out, "hunting stories" have become synonymous with imagination of not ill-natured liars in our society. "It shows only one thing, that the life of cities does not impose knowledge and accuracy regarding wild animals" (p. 77).

Another source of underestimation lies in the fact that much knowledge is secret. It may be confined to members of a guild or union and transmitted only in schools and between members, as in the Poro (Harley 1941:123). In addition, the complex of practices that involves such knowledge may have been suppressed for political or religious reasons. Suppression of shamanism in the Aleutian Islands and in Greenland has undoubtedly removed much information from the reach of even assiduous investigators.

Where an important animal, such as the sea otter used for comparative anatomy by the Aleuts, is protected by federal law, the practice of comparative anatomy must suffer accordingly. Thus conservation measures have affected the continuation of anatomical knowledge in many places in the world. Removal of Indians to reservations, where they can no longer practice their traditional economy effectively, eliminates maintenance and transmission of the anatomical knowledge previously essential to their survival. The discouragement of cannibalism and head-hunting similarly interferes with a basic source of information.

The supply of informed observers, anthropologists, zoologists, botanists, etc., was unfortunately in short supply at the time Europeans first made contact with many remote people. At present there is a more ample supply of observers, but the supply of subjects has diminished. In addition, there are many current fads of research that place more stress on feelings and attitudes of natives and less on their abilities, achievements, and adaptations to local circumstances (Linne 1957; Kroeber 1957).

Other factors that have led to the underestimation of the knowledge of primitive peoples are the short periods of time that are spent in the field with the people and a belief in the inability of natives to accumulate knowledge in the same way

Europeans do. Harley's expression of this fact, phrased for studies of native medical practice, is precisely to the point.

The best accounts of native medical practice are from men who have spent years of actual residence among the natives, either as missionaries or as government officials. This is especially true where anthropological training was part of their equipment for life among people of so different a culture. Those who have gone to Africa primarily as anthropologists have either lacked medical training or failed to stay long enough to penetrate the secrets of the native leech Harley 1941:xiii.

## UNRECONSTRUCTABLE ASPECTS

Two categories of information that are unreconstructable deserve mention, for in themselves they are important and also indicate other things that are beyond recall. The first of these, consisting of the words, meanings, relations, and intellectual organization thereof, is largely if not totally beyond apprehension. The second of these categories consists of those artifacts or devices that depend upon transformation states. One of these, the baleen or bone blade used to puncture the intestines of the polar bear, is an item that cannot be appreciated from any archeological record. Arctic Eskimos place a blade of baleen or thin bone into a ball of blubber or fat, having folded the blade into an S shape, and freeze the blade and fat. After being swallowed by the bear, the fat thaws out and the blade unfolds, thus piercing the intestines and other internal tissues. Other examples of the use of transformation states consist of the manufacture of whole sleds of frozen flesh, and runners of frozen mud and water. A change in temperature may eliminate an entire trait—disastrous for the archeologist and for the traveling Eskimo....

One more category, that of diseases and fractures, was undoubtedly crucial in the life of early man, as it still is for both modern man and his primate relatives. Attention to parasites, diseases with visible manifestations, and fractures constitute a source of anatomical information....

## THE ARGUMENT FROM CONTEMPORARY DISTRIBUTION

Acceptance of the general proposition that traits with wide distribution are older than those with a more limited distribution permits us to infer great antiquity for practices connected with childbirth and menstruation. Equally or more interesting is the similarity of attitudes and beliefs concerning these found in widely separated and unrelated areas around the world. In his study of "Primitive Obstetrics" Professor Spencer called attention to similarity of such beliefs: "But since the human frame is everywhere subject to the same laws, it follows that many widely scattered and culturally divergent groups may arrive at similar conclusions with respect to birth and so develop quite similar ceremonial attitudes" (Spencer 1950:1158–59).

The fact that trephining is found in widely separated areas (Peru, Denmark, Algeria, and Oceania) constitutes good evidence that some independent invention is involved (Popham 1954; Stewart 1958). The same problem and the same morphology have been combined with a similar conclusion and technique. Thus it is not simply the ubiquity of anatomical practices among primitive peoples but the development of analogous attitudes, beliefs, and practices, based on a demonstrably similar morphology, that suggests the likelihood that such practices occurred very early in human history. The basic ways of eviscerating a mammal are considerably more limited than are the grammars that are used to describe such an activity.

Caesarean operations are comparatively rare in their distribution, but the idea of assisting women at childbirth is universal. Autopsy of the dead is comparatively rare, but attention of some sort to the dead is universal.

Referring to the use of contemporary distributions I would suggest that Boas overlooks anatomical knowledge in claiming that astronomical observations are most widely distributed. His remarks are pertinent:

Man has not only utilized his experience in handling materials but has also, at an early time, learned to observe nature in such a manner as to utilize his experiences in regulating his activities. Astronomical and meteorological observations and those relating to the tides are probably most widely found [Boas 1938:274].

Since the occurrence of animals with the seasons, and their morphological variations are carefully noted, these two bodies of observations have an equally long history and widespread distribution....

## SUMMARY

Contemporary evidence and inferences from archeological and paleontological evidence all indicate that man recognized his affinity with other animals from earliest times. Ancient man appears to have been a hunter, and a big-game hunter where big game was available. *Zinjanthropus boisei* appears to have eaten not only small mammals, birds, and reptiles but also the immature specimens of giant pigs (Leakey 1959). The extent to which he was carnivorous must be inferred from the broken bones in his living sites and, later, from the presence of tools. It is likely that his protohominid forebears were carnivorous in many of their habits and that many of man's habits were retained from this kind of ancestry and then elaborated. Ancient man was a carnivore who had to hunt in order to eat and in order to utilize animal products for fabricational purposes as well as for food. Knowledge of anatomy has thus been of immediate value in making a living.

The body size of the protohominids, together with simple instrumentation, and pack hunting, is sufficient to enable them to kill all terrestrial animals, including man. The simplicity of implements that can be used to kill large herbivores and carnivores is remarkable. Selection of suitable stones, superseded by worked stone tools, clubs, and pointed shafts, is quite adequate to secure all kinds of animals by an animal who makes relatively acute observations. The elaboration of his knowledge of anatomy was facilitated by the constancy of animal morphology, physiology, and behavior during the Pleistocene. In addition, man had the advantage of being able to transfer observations based on his own structure to that of most of the animals he hunted and, similarly, to argue from the animals back to his own condition. Universal situations, such as childbirth, pathologies, growth and death, in addition to the same kind of sensory apparatus, provides sources of information that were applicable to both the observers and the observed.

The extent and the system of organization of such knowledge, revealed in such contemporary groups as the Aleutian Islanders and contiguous Eskimos, cannot be reconstructed from archeological evidence. Though varying greatly around the world, the anatomical information possessed by most peoples has probably been consistently underestimated. Rational medicine and physical culture, true comparative anatomy, dissection of the deceased for information, and mummification have appeared in many places and have collectively occurred with a single grouping of people whose life bears many similarities to that of Paleolithic man, that is, the Aleutian Islanders. The ubiquity

263

of such occurrences, separately and collectively, plus the immediate practical value of such practices, permit us to infer the value and likelihood of such underlying anatomical knowledge with the first appearance of hunting. Further, it can be inferred that anatomical knowledge was prior to other categories of learning in humans and that such observations provided the basis for the design of tools, beginning with the first club, knife, and spear. The organization of the mammalian body provides a basis for intellectual organization, and anatomical analogies and reasoning are found in all cultures. The ancient Greek maxim that "man is the measure of all things" is literally true. Units of measurement based on dimensions of the body (cubit, ell, fistmele, fathom, hand) are universally distributed. It is suggested that while learning to learn, ancient man was learning anatomy.

# 29  Changing Folk Beliefs and the Relativity of Empirical Knowledge

*Charles John Erasmus*

Despite the use in this paper of such anachronisms as "backward" and "retarded" in referring to non-Western peoples, this paper retains a significant contribution to medical anthropology. Charles Erasmus asks whether the thought processes of such people are different from those of Western society, their knowledge and beliefs less empirical and grounded simply and unrelievedly in magic and superstition, and whether Western scientific thinking is necessarily superior to its presumed opposite. Using data from several Latin American communities, Erasmus explores these questions through an investigation of the clash and interplay of the so-called folk system of medicine with that of modern science. He finds that despite an often ready acceptance of Western medicine these South American populations do not necessarily accept the accompanying "scientific" explanation, and that indeed for many illnesses, despite the availability of modern medicine, they prefer native medicines and healing. Erasmus' investigations uncover a kind of

Reprinted with abridgments from Charles John Erasmus, 1952, "Changing Folk Beliefs and the Relativity of Empirical Knowledge," *Southwestern Journal of Anthropology*, 8:411–428, with permission of the author and the *Journal of Anthropological Research*.

system and logic in the thinking that characterizes the native medical system that has its own internal rationality and that indeed "makes sense" as well as scientific medicine does to its believers. Erasmus suggests that the nature of inductive inference that underlies systems of explanation in the final analysis comes down to "a matter of experience and not of reason," and that all systems of thought rest on increments of probable rather than absolute knowledge. In all belief systems, says Erasmus, there is a reliance on what the philosopher of science, Hans Reichenbach, called "posits," that is, "...a statement which we treat as true although we do not know whether it is so." All systems, then, tend to choose those posits that are more likely to be true since "posits are the instruments of action," and the objective of knowledge is action. Erasmus then shows how the folk medical systems he observes seem to operate, as do the scientific, in just this fashion. Knowledge is thus always empirically relative and always functions within the boundaries of certain limitations and variations. Whether the folk or scientific system is "better" then depends upon whether one is making a value judgment, but this has little to do with the inherent inferiority or superiority of either system. As this author concludes,

> We can speak of an evolution from magic to science that is culturally relative. The relativity of this evolution depends upon the fact that the probability of knowledge is itself relative to the limitations inherent in a given cultural situation, and at no point in a progression is it "better" except as measured by the value system of an observer at that point.

...We are generally inclined to think of backward peoples as being more concerned with the supernatural and with magic than ourselves, a circumstance which led Levy-Bruhl, for instance, to consider primitive man to be pre-logical in his thinking. Recently, in his search for an "objective" criterion of progress (which he defines as the "advance to something better"), Kroeber has suggested that the advancement of a culture can be determined by the degree to which it has disengaged itself from reliance on magic and superstition. Retarded peoples, he says, place greater emphasis on phenomena that have only mental or subjective existence and thereby tend to reward certain types of psychotic and neurotic behavior that more advanced groups would consider pathological (Kroeber 1948:296–300).

More recently, Tax has said that although primitives reach conclusions through the same logical processes that we do, they reason from premises which differ from ours according to their "content of cultural experience." He therefore proposes a cross-cultural distinction between "knowledge" and "ignorance" by defining knowledge as "any item of information that is derived from the scientific interrelating of sense-perceived phenomena" and which accumulates through increased intercultural contacts, literacy, improved technology, increased division of labor, and the greater secularization of society. Furthermore, he equates "rational thinking" with "knowledge of the world of nature and of man" provided by the "scientific method" while "irrational thinking" he equates with "ignorance," the state in which mankind began (Tax 1950). Pointing out that "experimental verification" at best yields only "a statement of probability based on a correlation," Rowe accuses Tax of setting up universal cultural values on an ethnocentric basis, of assuming "absolute truth" and of suggesting a unilinear evolution of knowledge whose furthest development to date is represented by our own culture (Rowe 1950).

To what extent can we truthfully say that backward peoples think differently from ourselves, that their knowledge and beliefs are less empirical, that a transition from magic to science represents progress or that an evolutionary concept of knowledge must be unilinear and ethnocentric? In the pages which follow we shall endeavor to throw more light on these questions through a study of folk vs. modern medicine in Ecuador. Special attention will be given to situations where folk practices and beliefs are being challenged by their modern counterparts, for the type of acceptances and resistances we encounter in these situations can help us to evaluate whatever differences may exist between folk and modern thought. . . .

## FOLK MEDICINE

Beginning with the folk concepts of disease etiology, we may consider first those illnesses attributed to contagion, although the folk concept of contagion is different from the modern one. The major folk explanation is concerned with the fear of bad body humor. This is most commonly described as due to lack of personal cleanliness. It is a substance which exudes with perspiration, and if one does not bathe frequently it may re-enter the pores and infect the blood. Not only is it a source of auto-infection, but it may also be passed between persons. Thus it may cause such ailments as skin diseases, infected wounds, and syphilis. Close contact, sexual relations, or seats still warm from a previous occupant are means by which it may pass from one individual to another.

Next we may consider those folk illnesses attributed to "mechanical" etiologies. By mechanical we refer to such things as temperature change, harmful foods, fatigue, and body blows. Of all the mechanical causes those concerning temperature are probably the most important for the folk. Exposure to cold air when overheated is considered very dangerous, and being caught in a thunder shower when working in the fields or drinking cold water when perspiring are other variants. Symptoms may include dysentery, menstrual and postnatal cramps, pneumonia, urinary difficulties, rheumatism, measles, partial paralysis, and malaria. Body heat may cause skin diseases, and heat generated in the body by coughing may lead to angina. Certain foods are dangerous by reason of their "heaviness," "sourness," "acidity," or inherent "coldness." Some foods stick to the stomach and others lead to an overabundance of body bile which is related to liver trouble. Any cooked food which is left to stand acquires a quality of coldness which is especially feared. Fatigue from hard work and insufficient food lead to "liver" and "kidney" ailments as well as skin infections and "inflamed uterus." Body blows can cause meningitis and tumors. Diarrhea with fever is said invariably to accompany the process of teething. For some informants, diarrhea at this age is simply a kind of "natural" consequence. Others give a psychological explanation. They say that because the child is irritated he develops "anger" sickness.

There are several illnesses that the folk ascribe to psychological causes. Among these is anger sickness due to quarrels, jealousy, etc. This may result in such symptoms as vomiting, diarrhea, fever, inability to walk, depression, "fits," and "palpitation of the stomach." An unfilled desire such as a sexual desire, a food craving of a pregnant woman, or the desire of a small child to possess a toy or candy may result in a variety of maladies. "Fits," syphilis, and urinary difficulties are examples. Sadness due to a personal loss (loss of a loved one, money, property, etc.) may also cause "fits" as well as palpitation of the heart, fever, lack of appetite, severe headaches, loss of consciousness, etc.

Among the supernatural ailments fright and malevolent air are the two most frequent causes and the victims are predominantly children. The stimulus for a fright may be anything as natural as a sudden fall or as supernatural as an encounter with a ghost or a spirit. For many individuals there seems to be a definite feeling that the fright produces soul-loss. Malevolent air may be contracted by a small child if he is taken to a cemetery, too close to a corpse, to solitary places in the mountains, down into mountain canyons, or is exposed to a rainbow or night air. Another prevalent childhood illness, especially among pretty children, is that due to evil eye, the malevolent glance of certain adults who have "electrical" or "strong" eyes. For adults witchcraft is the primary supernatural cause of illness. The methods of the witch include magical poisoning of the victim's food and imitative magic using dolls to represent the victim. Symptoms of all ailments having supernatural etiologies are so generalized that they could point to almost any malady in a modern classification. However, among those listed for children, informants always included fever, vomiting, and diarrhea.

The pains frequently experienced by women after parturition are also attributed to supernatural causes, for they are considered likely to occur if the placenta is discarded in such a way that it comes in contact with water or cold air or is eaten by dogs. The placenta should be buried in a dry, safe place such as the ground beneath the kitchen hearth. . . .

Very often diagnosis is made by reflecting over preceding events. Was the sick person recently exposed to a sudden change of temperature? Did he enter a canyon where there might have been spirits? Did he make an enemy who might have had him bewitched? Professional curers diagnose largely by magical means such as measurement of the patient with red ribbons (Esmeraldas), cracking the patient's back, or throwing corn grains in the embers of a fire. Some of these magical methods of diagnosis are curative as well.

The predominating type of folk remedy consists of herbal solutions and broths, the cathartics being the most popular of all. Calmative herbal broths employed for stopping diarrhea and vomiting as well as sudorific herbal broths are, like the cathartics, usually taken orally while others are administered in the form of enemas and vaginal douches. Among the external remedies, herbal poultices are very often used. On the supernatural side, cupping may be employed to extract malevolent air. But the most popular remedy for ailments with supernatural etiologies is that of "cleaning" the patient with special plants, eggs, or guinea pigs. The "cleaning" process consists of slowly rubbing the remedy over the patient's body until the illness is drawn into it. Religion also plays an important part in curing in the form of vows to saints or praying "Our Father" and Credos in magical sets of three, etc.

In a sense, every adult is a medical specialist. The folk share a common knowledge concerning the diagnosis, classification, and treatment of symptoms and are most likely to consult a curer only when their own household remedies fail. If a supernatural cause is suspected, however, only the curer is considered capable of properly administering the "cleaning" treatment.

An attempt was made to gauge the incidence of folk illnesses and the extent to which folk remedies are used by observing purchases of herbs for a period of several days at the central public market in Quito. These remedies were sought for practically every kind of malady imaginable, but a few illnesses had a considerably higher incidence than others. The six illnesses of highest incidence were malevolent air (nearly all children), "cough" (children), fright sickness (children), menstrual difficulties (mostly cases of retarded flow, and the cathartics purchased may well have abortive effects), urinary difficulties (mostly adults with symptoms of blood and pain), and bewitchment (all adults). If the period at which the investigation was made is representative of yearly conditions, at least 180,000 purchases are made each year at this one market alone, a figure almost as great as that of the population of Quito. One fifth of all the purchases were for supernatural ailments and consisted of herbs with magical "cleaning" properties.

## CHANGE AND CONFLICT

Some general knowledge of the modern concept of microbial infection was found to exist in all locales where studies were made. However, even though school children in particular were often capable of giving good explanations of modern concepts of disease etiology, they were also capable of giving just as good explanations of the traditional concepts. . . .

Interview material showed that in general the illnesses with supernatural etiologies are treated by folk specialists, while others such as infected wounds, measles, anger sickness, and skin infections are treated at home. However, even such folk specialists as curers and professional herbalists will agree that the doctor is the one best qualified to treat such ailments as diphtheria, tuberculosis, venereal disease, and appendicitis. In many cases the informant will admit that he goes to the doctor only when his own remedies or those of the curer have failed. Judging from the symptoms given for many of the folk etiologies, it would seem that even though the folk have more confidence in the doctor as a medical practitioner for many maladies with modern names, they do not always classify their symptoms according to those names until the doctor has been consulted at an advanced stage.

In another set of tests conducted in a Quito grammar school, the children were given a list of twenty-two illnesses and asked to check the ones they would treat at home, those they would have treated by folk curers, and those they would have treated by a doctor. The list included folk and modern illnesses and in no case was there a 100 percent response in favor of any particular means of treatment. Responses in favor of the doctor ranged from 96 percent in the case of tuberculosis to only 2 percent in the case of fright sickness. All the supernatural ailments as well as such maladies as skin infections, infected wounds, and diarrhea fell among those for which more than 50 percent of the subjects would seek a curer or treat at home. For ailments such as bronchitis, typhoid, paralysis, whooping cough, and malaria more than 50 percent preferred the doctor. The same children were also given a list of causes and asked to match them with these illnesses. The most frequently indicated cause of illness was microbes, which gained its weight from those diseases on the list bearing modern names. In all, however, it accounted for only 19 percent of the total number of responses. Folk causes were predominantly given for illness treated at home or by a curer. The most significant fact was that even in the case of those illnesses for which medical treatment was favored, supernatural causes were in some cases predominant.

From a consideration of our data so far, it would appear that the folk look up to the doctor for his ability to cure serious illnesses for which their own remedies are less likely to be efficacious, independently of whether or not they understand or believe in his explanation of causes. Their acceptance of the doctor rests primarily upon empirical observation and experience. To test this further, we will now compare the results of investigations at Esmeraldas and Tulcán. In the Negro coastal area about Esmeraldas, yaws was a prevalent disease until an extensive campaign of injecting penicillin was inaugurated. Doctors who served in the campaign encountered considerable public resistance at first. By the time of my visit, however, yaws had been pretty well brought under control,

and if there ever had been any resistance to the program it was certainly no longer in evidence. Although investigations in Esmeraldas showed a strong adherence to folk medical beliefs and treatment, house to house interviews disclosed nothing but praise for the yaws campaign and a complete conviction that yaws was a disease which the doctor alone was capable of curing. This attitude was shared even by local curers. As some informants expressed it, you cannot deny what you see with your own eyes.

The situation in the highland town of Tulcán was somewhat different. A water purification system has just been installed and house to house visits revealed that while the folk were very much in favor of the purified water, their reasons had nothing to do with disease prevention. Previously they had had to let their water stand in buckets until the dirt settled; now it was possible to use it directly from the public taps. For the most part, however, they did not believe that the former water had caused them any harm. Interviews with informants and a native curer disclosed that the symptoms of intestinal infection were being attributed to malevolent air and fright sickness and were being treated by magical means.

The data from Esmeraldas and Tulcán give further indication that the acceptance of the doctor is based primarily on empirical knowledge and observation. The campaign at Esmeraldas was curative with spectacular and observable results. At Tulcán, on the other hand, the program was one of preventive medicine based on modern concepts of disease etiology that were not as easy to grasp on a purely empirical basis. Perhaps a noticeable change in the incidence of certain syndromes at Tulcán will lead the folk to an empirical judgment in favor of modern preventive medicine. But it seems just as likely that their failure to grasp the modern concepts of disease etiology will result in the contamination of food and water through other means, thus preventing any noticeable change in the incidence of syndromes. . . .

As far as tradition is concerned, we may say that the folk beliefs in themselves are offering no resistance to modern medical practices in so far as those practices may be judged by the folk on an empirical basis. Preventive medicine, however, is being resisted because its comprehension is largely at a theoretical level that does not readily lend itself to empirical observation. Let us now consider the effect produced on the folk beliefs by higher education and special theoretical training.

A test on medical beliefs was given to fifty-five nurses' aids at the maternity hospital Isidro Ayora and an equal number of student nurses at the national school of nursing. While the nurses' aids had had only grammar school education, the student nurses were all high school graduates.

By comparing, first, the responses of the nurses' aids (who had had little additional theoretical training) with interview material and the tests of grammar school children, it is possible to make some estimate of the extent to which hospital life has affected their beliefs. In doing so we find that the only clear distinction pertains to the more supernatural ideas. Causes such as witchcraft and improper disposal of the placenta, preventive measures such as red ribbons and religious medals, and such treatments as "cleaning" and praying were no longer important to them. However, while beginning nursing students, with the advantage of a high school education, were much more inclined to affirm their disbelief on these questions, many of the nurses' aids refused to answer them. Third-year nurses showed the most remarkable change, for over seventy-five percent stated disbelief. Third-year nurses also distinguished themselves from all the rest by a forty-five to sixty-one percent greater frequency of stated disbelief concerning postnatal food taboos, "natural" diarrhea as an accompaniment of teething, fright sickness, malevolent air, and sickness due to desire. The most persistent beliefs among all groups were those concerning anger and sadness, body humors, body biles, temperature changes, and the preventive and curative use of laxatives. (Among the better educated groups very innocent symptoms were attributed to the two psychological etiologies, anger and sadness.)

When one considers that none of the subjects had ever had any course which directly discussed and attacked their folk beliefs, the results indicate the extent to which they themselves have reconciled the old and the new. When asked what they thought accounted for their greater degree of disbelief in folk concepts, the third-year nurses attributed the change to a course in obstetrics that the second-year nurses had only just begun. General education as well as specialized work which brings the person in contact with modern practices correlates with greater disbelief in the more supernatural and magical concepts. Contact with modern practices does not, however, have as marked an effect on changing those beliefs concerning cause and prevention that we have called "mechanical" as do more advanced theoretical explanations. Those beliefs that are most persistent under any circumstances are those whose psychological or mechanical explanations most closely approximate the modern.

The marked influence of high theoretical training may well correlate with greater relegation of authority to the modern specialist. In response to a question that asked the subjects to state what they would do in case a mother in a maternity hospital requested a postnatal laxative, the third-year nurses were far more apt to leave the decision to the doctor, while the nurses' aids were inclined to agree with the patient and accept the responsibility for administering it. In general, the folk seem much more prone to consider themselves self-sufficient in medical treatment and diagnosis than the average North American. Where the North American may become nervous at the slightest symptom and run to a doctor, the folk immediately classify or diagnose the symptoms according to their own extensive body of knowledge and beliefs and attempt to cure them by themselves. In the grammar school class that was asked to designate which illnesses could be cured at home and which by a curer or doctor, the boys showed a greater dependence on the specialist whether he be a curer or a doctor while the girls had more faith in the home remedies they had learned from their mothers.

Social factors are also important in the process of acculturation from folk to modern medicine. Among white collar and professional classes in Quito a feeling exists that only people of inferior status use herbal remedies and go to folk curers. The "better" people are supposed to rely on drugstore remedies and doctors. A test given to one hundred boys in a public school attended by children of the white collar class showed a much greater reliance on the drugstore and the doctor than the children of the poorer districts. However, in their concepts of disease etiology the two groups were much more closely allied. It would seem that the acceptance of the doctor and his remedies is related in some degree to prestige, independently of an understanding of modern etiology.

In Bogotá, Colombia, where the author has made similar investigations, social factors play an important part in public resistance to free health centers. Although the folk beliefs themselves do not appear as strong nor as well organized as in Quito, there is greater hostility toward modern medicine in the poorer districts. Colombia has been affected by a tremendous urbanization movement that has disrupted the old class system. "Good family" is not the important social criterion it was formerly, while acquired economic status is becoming more and more important. The cities have been flooded by rural immigrants who no longer classify themselves or one another according to a traditional system. As a result of the competition to rise socially, individuals with some small position of authority press their weight on others to force a recognition of the status they wish to have associated with that authority. Thus, the nurses and doctors employed in the government health centers are often overbearing in their treatment of the public. In resentment, the Bogotá folk freely voice their hostility toward modern medicine. Common household items are books on folk remedies written with overtones of spiritualism by nationally famous curers.

The social factors are related to economic ones. If the "better" people in Quito rely more on the doctor despite a persistence of folk beliefs among them, this is not only due to the doctor's prestige but to the fact that they are in a better position to afford him. Where modern medical therapy is free, attendance is often greater than the traffic will bear. To judge from their appearance, the great majority of the people who frequented the herbalists at the public market undoubtedly belonged to the lowest economic groups in Quito.

## CONCLUSIONS

First, let us consider the problem of whether the folk can be said to think differently from ourselves or whether their knowledge is less empirical. In treating this problem we shall make use of concepts employed by Hans Reichenbach (1950) in his *The Rise of Scientific Philosophy*. Dr Reichenbach states that the essence of knowledge is generalization and that correct generalization is dependent upon the separation of relevant from irrelevant factors. By "relevant" he means that "... which must be mentioned for the generalization to be valid." Further, he considers generalization to be "... the very nature of explanation" which is sometimes achieved "... by assuming some fact that is not or cannot be observed." He gives as an example the casual explanation whereby the barking of a dog is attributed to the presence of a stranger in the vicinity of the house, an unobserved fact which is "... explanatory only because it shows the observed fact to be the manifestation of a general law that dogs bark when strangers approach...." Such inductive inference, he claims,

goes beyond a mere summary of previous observations and becomes an instrument for predictive knowledge. But we can never be sure that dogs will always bark at strangers. In this vein, Dr Reichenbach says, "The study of inductive inference belongs in the theory of probability, since observational facts can make a theory only probable but will never make it absolutely certain." Thus, in place of absolute knowledge he speaks of "probable knowledge," a term he does not find self-contradictory because it is based on "frequency interpretation" in which "degree of probability is *a matter of experience* and *not of reason*." From here we may proceed to his concept of a *posit*, "...a statement which we treat as true although we do not know whether it is so." Yet, "we try to select our posits in such a way that they will be true as often as possible." The reason we try is "... because we want to act—and he who wants to act cannot wait until the future has become observational knowledge.... Posits are the instruments of action where truth is not available; the justification of induction is that it is the best instrument of action known to us."

To what extent is folk belief and knowledge a result of induction or "frequency interpretation"? The material resulting from our study of changing folk beliefs in Ecuador has indicated that for the most part the changes are transpiring on just that basis. In the field of therapy, modern medicine is making demonstrations on such a scale that the folk can readily establish *posits* for future behavior in favor of modern therapeutic methods. Resistance is primarily directed at modern preventive medicine in which the generalizations and explanations involved result from frequency interpretations that are not possible under situations of casual empiricism but are dependent upon the observations of trained investigators. The communication of this type of frequency interpretation to non-investigators takes place most easily under situations of special training as we saw from our testing of nursing students.

If we consider the folk beliefs alone without reference to change, it is possible to encounter many generalizations resulting from frequency interpretations, in other words, correlations made between repetitive phenomena. The concept of bad body humor, for example, is very close to our own explanation of contagion. It involves an inductive inference based on past observations of a correlation between the onset of disease and certain situations in which contagion is likely. The explanation also assumes something that is not observable, a substance called bad body humor. However, it leads to predictions of situations in which disease can be contracted or avoided. Bodily cleanliness, for example, is a predictable preventive measure that still holds good under modern explanations of contagion although the prediction that disease may be contracted from a warm bus seat does not. The entire concept of bad body humor is a type of probable knowledge involving posits that definitely aid the folk to take action even though some of its posits are far less probable than others.

According to folk belief, cooked food that has been left to stand may acquire a dangerous quality of "coldness." Symptoms resulting from eating such food sound remarkably like those of botulism or enterotoxin-producing staphylococci. The folk have made a correlation between illness and cooked food that has been left to stand, and their prediction that illness can be avoided by re-cooking the food and thus removing the "coldness" is valid to the extent that in practice it would lead to a detoxication of the poison. But we must note that the preventive measures of cleanliness and storage that would also help to prevent food poisoning are irrelevant to the folk in view of their theory of "coldness." However, unlike bad body humors, the "coldness' of cooked food that has been left to stand is a part of folk observation. Since food infected by staphylococci or spores of *C. botulinum* does not necessarily change in taste or smell, the modern explanation is beyond the limitations of folk experience. Therefore, we see how the validity of an inductive generalization or correlation may be independent of the validity of its *causal* explanation: a condition that is common knowledge to any statistician and the principal reason why the modern scientist has come to think in terms of probability rather than causality. The modern refinement of this folk explanation has resulted from the frequency interpretations of trained laboratory investigators who have simply *increased* the posits by which we govern our actions to avoid food poisoning.

The folk have also drawn a correlation between the symptoms of intestinal infection and the teething stage in the child's development. In this case the explanations add so little that no prediction is possible except that the sickness is inevitable. Since we know that teething children are more apt to insert objects into their mouths and thereby increase the possibility of intestinal infection (under conditions of folk life almost any object on the dirty floor), the folk correlation or

generalization is both relevant and valid. However, it is a very simple empirical correlation. The correlation between the symptomatology and the many diverse activities of the teething child that would be necessary to provide a modern generalization is so complex as to make its empirical observation very difficult on a casual basis.

Let us now consider the supernatural type of explanation. Using a completely hypothetical example, we may take the case of a group of mothers who cross a canyon and stop to give their children a drink of water from the polluted stream flowing through it. Later, when the children show symptoms of intestinal infection frequently classified by the folk as malevolent air, the mothers may make a correlation between the illness and the trip through the canyon. Their correlation may be partly correct despite the irrelevance of their belief in spirits or the fact that they overlooked the relevancy of the stream. We cannot, however, use this hypothetical example as an argument that some empirical correlation invariably underlies all folk beliefs. But, as the testing of the nursing students and nurses' aids would seem to indicate, situations providing greater opportunities for understanding modern frequency interpretations are more detrimental to the supernatural explanations and practices than those for which it is easier to discover some underlying empiricism.

On the side of magical treatment, it is hard to see exactly how empiricism enters into the picture at all when a curer attempts to remedy an illness with "cleaning" herbs or guinea pigs. However, we must consider the fact that not all illnesses are fatal. On the average, success is in favor of the curer. This is not so true in the case of modern classifications of illnesses by which we can appraise the relative danger of syndromes with greater exactness. But the symptoms which the folk ascribe to many of their classificatory terms and etiologies are so highly generalized that they may include both fatal and innocent maladies. As long as the law of averages works in favor of the curer, his results are an empirical demonstration that his methods, as well as the theories and explanations on which they are based, are in general valid though not infallible. Our own reasoning may work along similar lines. Recently a well-known professor of medicine from an American university admitted to me that had he been treating himself with one of the modern "miracle" drugs he would probably have credited it with his recovery from a cold that had unexpectedly disappeared without any treatment whatsoever.

In many cases of "supernatural" illnesses the etiology may be psychological. The kinds of partial paralysis that some informants gave as the symptoms suffered by close relatives who had been bewitched as well as their claims that doctors were unable to find a cause, much less a cure for these cases, sounded very much like descriptions of psychosomatic conditions. Furthermore, curers succeeded in relieving the symptoms in a single magical treatment. Again, this constituted a definite demonstration to the informants that the cure was a proof of the correct diagnosis of the cause as well as the efficacy of the treatment. The similarity between these cases and those of psychological or religious practitioners in our own society almost tempts a comparison. A large part of the influence of psychoanalytic dogma on the social sciences is undeniably due to a logic that accepts a cure as "scientific" proof of the theoretical postulates underlying the method of treatment. This writer wonders if "magic" in its broadest sense can ever be completely divorced from "science." Both provide posits for future action, both may include irrelevant correlations, and both may be based on probable knowledge resulting from frequency interpretations. However, the experiences of the folk cannot provide them with the type of quantity of frequency interpretations that can be derived from laboratory experiences.

If it has been difficult to find any difference in kind between the thinking of backward and "civilized" peoples, to what extent are we justified in claiming a greater dependence on magic and supernatural explanations among the more backward? We feel that this question can best be answered by making use of the distinction between esoteric and exoteric population components. Few persons in the exoteric component of modern society attempt to recapitulate the discoveries of such men as Pasteur and Koch, much less view a microbe through a microscope. They accept the authorities belonging to our esoteric component who claim that microbes cause certain maladies that may therefore be prevented or cured in a certain way. During experimental health lectures given to a group of school children in Quito, the children were questioned about spirits and ghosts. None had ever seen one, but certain authorities such as curers or professional herbalists had. Thus it would appear that the greater dependence on magic and supernatural explanations among backward populations is due principally to differences between their esoteric components and ours. How can we explain this difference between the esoteric

components of backward and modern populations?

The answer to our question seems obvious enough. Due to technological advances a far greater proportion of individuals in our society have been freed from direct food pursuits to enter many fields of specialization. Our technological system is therefore capable of supporting an esoteric component within our population that can devote full time to checking our casual empiricism, to expanding our frequency interpretations, and to providing us with a knowledge that is much more probable in comparison with that of backward peoples. This becomes clearer when we consider the fact that even the folk curer is usually only a part-time specialist. The author knows of young doctors who attempted to practice in rural areas and were forced to leave because even what few payments they received for their services were generally payments in produce. It is not difficult to understand why the type of "pure" research which is not even directly related to immediate needs is dependent upon a very complex technological system as compared to that of the folk. Nor is it difficult to understand why a society that cannot extend its opportunities for frequency interpretation beyond the casual empiricism offered by every-day situations will focus its interests in such a way as to reward its esoteric component for posits that appear to have a strong supernatural basis from a modern point of view. In this way, "backward" groups may come to reward certain types of individual behavior that might be regarded as pathological when occurring among members of our society. Therefore, the difference between what we tend to think of as two extremes, magic and science, is related in large part to the limitations placed upon the esoteric component of a given population by the technological system.

The final problems mentioned in our introduction are concerned with concepts of progress and evolution. The major objections to the word "evolution" among present-day cultural anthropologists are related to the fact that early anthropologists explained all parallels between cultures as due to a unilinear type of progression, and because they reconstructed culture history by assuming that what was different from Western civilization was inferior and therefore older. Subsequent studies have not only demonstrated differential development but the cultural relativity of values. Objection has also been raised against evolutionary schemes because they did not seem as applicable to non-material aspects of culture as to those that were strictly technological. Yet, if we consider the work of three modern neo-evolutionists, we find we can apply their concepts to such a "non-material" subject matter as magic and science without repeating the mistakes of the earlier evolutionists. Leslie White (1949) has seen a progression in culture based on the energy harnessed per capita per year. His evolutionism is primarily technological. While not an avowed cultural evolutionist, Carleton Coon (1948) has scaled cultures by levels of complexity on what he calls a quantitative basis. His quantification rests upon the complexity of institutions, the number of institutions to which the average individual belongs, the amount of trade, and the degree of specialization. George P. Murdock (1949), who is more concerned with accounting for similarities between cultures than with systems of progression, explains the development of parallel social systems as due to limitations in the number of variations possible.

By combining the three perspectives above we may arrive at a tentative hypothesis. The amount of energy harnessed per capita per year by the technological system of a society places limitations on the size and the type of its esoteric population component as well as limitations on the range of experience available to that component as a basis for frequency interpretations. This in turn limits the range of a society's probable knowledge and the degree to which its participants can estimate the probability of their predictions. Such limitations do not determine precise historical sequences nor precise regional variations. Within the limitations are such allowable variations as were treated in our comparison of social factors in Quito and Bogotá. Nor does this specialization necessarily imply any change from "worse" to "better." On the contrary, we can speak of an evolution from magic to science that is culturally relative. The relativity of this evolution depends upon the fact that the probability of knowledge is itself relative to the limitations inherent in a given cultural situation, and at no point in a progression is it "better" except as measured by the value system of an observer at that particular point.

Returning now to the disagreement between Tax and Rowe, we find that the conclusions of this paper are in accord with Tax's main thesis. The principal differences between the positions of Tax and the present paper are that we have made no qualitative dichotomy between "knowledge" and "ignorance," have suggested a quantitative difference in degrees of probable knowledge and have employed Reichenbach's distinction between probable knowledge and reason. Except for Tax's failure to stress the difference between rationalism and empiricism, we find nothing in his paper that would justify Rowe's criticism that he was assuming absolute truth and using universal and ethnocentric values. According to Rowe, all ethnographers are faced with "... the great dilemma of cultural anthropology: the dilemma of cultural objectivity." Thus, the anthropologist who is striving to be objective, that is, to keep his own cultural values out of his comparisons, has but "two obvious choices": (1) "... to accept, in so far as possible, the cultural values of the culture being studied..." or (2) "... to attempt to set up universal values which we can then apply to all cultures." Rowe admittedly prefers the first choice and ascribes the second to Tax. However, if each culture must be appraised separately in relation to its own "values," cross-cultural comparisons are doomed to rationalistic rather than empirical treatment and cultural anthropology to an anecdotal preoccupation with the minutiae of differences. Is there really no other choice than the two Rowe offers? Is there no other way of guarding against value judgments than to adopt a different set of values?

In Ecuador, the magical treatment of illnesses reaches its greatest incidence among children below the age of five, who, like the old, are considered to be weaker and more susceptible to supernatural causes. However, the illnesses from which these children actually suffer are not a peculiar figment of this culture; they are the same which may afflict children anywhere. The death rate of this age group, furthermore, is over fifty percent of the recorded yearly deaths in Ecuador as compared to a figure of less than ten percent in the United States. Given these two societies, each of which is endeavoring to apply its knowledge to the prevention and cure of the same illnesses, it is perfectly legitimate to state that the knowledge of the great majority of Ecuadorians with respect to childhood illnesses is *less probable* than the knowledge of North Americans. To claim their knowledge is "inferior" would depend on whether or not we consider a lower infantile death rate as "better." But the second proposition is not necessarily a corollary of the first. The first is concerned with the observation of human behavior, the second with a value judgment about that behavior.

# 30  On the Specificity of Folk Illnesses

## Horacio Fabrega, Jr.

This chapter is a partial report on a larger study by Horacio Fabrega, Jr., a physician, and an anthropologist (Fabrega and Silver 1973), of illness and curing in the Mayan community of Zinacantan. The final report is, in my estimation, one of the finest examples of careful, systematic, and imaginative analysis of a medical system, and, in particular, the institution of the healer, in all the literature of medical anthropology. This paper is addressed to the question of what relationship exists between native terms dealing with illness and the actual manifestation of bodily states and behaviors. Interestingly, no statistically significant differences are found between Zinacantecan healers and laymen, which leads Fabrega to conclude that these healers and laymen are similar both in associating specific signs and symptoms with specific illnesses, and in associating disturbances and folk illnesses. These findings "support the impression that knowledge involving features of illness in Zinacantan is widely shared among the male members of the culture." Therefore, it is not their special knowledge that validates the position of healers in Zinacantecan society but "their ascribed powers and capacities, which, at the sociocultural level, are the result of such factors as revelation, presumed natural endowment, and the processes of recruitment and socialization that bear directly on their training."

When the responses of both groups of subjects were combined "it was noted that Zinacantecos linked a relatively large number of disturbances with almost all of the illnesses." Thus, although the model of illness in this Mayan community seems to fling a broad net over somatic and behavioral factors, so that "The majority of these symptoms, when analyzed from a scientific perspective, are general and nonspecific," this folk theory of sickness is not as vague as it may seem. Indeed, it seems to me reminiscent of the General Adaptation Syndrome so cogently argued by Hans Selye (1956), described in my introduction to Section X. In another paper on other facets of this same problem, Fabrega and Silver (1970) found that healers and nonhealers did not differ significantly in most features of their socioeconomic backgrounds, but that the healers were rather less acculturated to the dominant Ladino ways, that is, their involvement in Ladino culture was less than that of nonhealers and they possessed an expectedly greater identification

Reprinted from Horacio Fabrega, Jr., 1970, "On the Specificity of Folk Illnesses," *Southwestern Journal of Anthropology*, 26 : 304–314, with permission of the author and the *Journal of Anthropological Research*.

with indigenous Zinacantecan values. See also Fabrega (1971) for an additional study of Zinacantecan medical knowledge.

## INTRODUCTION

That sociocultural units have as part of their culture a relatively elaborate body of knowledge dealing with medical phenomena is commonly known. Previous studies in medicine and behavioral science have repeatedly verified this by describing the various features that comprise folk or primitive medical systems (Rubel 1960; Fabrega and Metzger 1968; Adams 1952). In these descriptions, treatment practices have received a great deal of attention, and the development of illness has been ascribed to the violation of social and religious rules. Exotic and "peculiar" features or symptoms of illness which may or may not be intraculturally significant, however, often appear to receive more attention than the basic question of the bodily and/or behavioral elements that comprise the general model of illness in the culture (Yap 1951). In addition, although certain natively differentiated illnesses have been described with some fidelity, the problem of the distinctness and invariance of their content in the culture has not been probed in a controlled manner (Rubel 1964). The result is that while much is known about the striking ways in which culture can shape illness manifestations, the underlying and related issues of how illness is modeled and how distinctly this model and its component parts are reflected in the minds of representative members of the culture have not been carefully explored. The principal aim of this study is to evaluate the degree of clarity and specificity with which native subjects interpret illness. The empirical procedure centers on the determination of the extent to which subjects differentiate between various symptoms, signs, and the clustering of these in syndromes.

A related objective of the paper is the examination of the extent to which conceptions of illness are specific or special to folk medical practitioners. In the past, the practitioner has been investigated principally from the standpoint of his contribution to the healing processes associated with curing ceremonies. It has been assumed that the social and psychological forces mobilized in these ceremonies stem entirely from the persuasive manner in which the practitioner exercises his role functions (Frank 1961; Murphy 1964; Fuchs 1964). Whether the performer validates his social position by commanding and using a special body of medically relevent information is not clear. It is known, for example, that non-practitioners who are co-members of the cultural group are acquainted with the various native illness terms. Frequently, they are able to list the symptoms of specific "folk illnesses," their general implications, and the type of treatment usually prescribed. In this sense, knowledge about health and illness can be said to be generally shared within the culture. It is possible, however, that practitioners' knowledge of medical phenomena will be found to differ from that of non-practitioners if precise discovery procedures are utilized; this problem will be considered in the course of the study.

As background it is desirable to point out the utility of separating the concept of disease from that of illness. Disease refers to bodily events and processes conceptualized in terms of a scientific framework; while illness designates the sociocturally structured behaviors and interpretations of persons which are a response to these processes (Mechanic 1962; Feinstein 1967). Previous studies involving folk or primitive medicine have not always distinguished between these concepts. This is reflected by the fact that global and essentially socio-behavioral dimensions (e.g., nervousness, absence of well being, or sleep disturbances) are usually singled out as being necessary concomitants of illness. Students of folk medicine have rarely singled out particular dysfunctions with a direct physiological basis (such as vomiting or excessive urination) as elements of native constructs of illness states. In the light of these observations it may be said that the preoccupation with the role of culture in relation to psychiatric syndromes is both a cause and a consequence of the investigator's tendency to avoid dealing with bodily events and processes.

## RESEARCH SETTING

The study was conducted in the municipio of Zinacantan in Chiapas, Mexico. Zinacantan is a community of some 8,000 Maya Indians located near the Ladino (non-Indian, Spanish speaking) city of San Cristobel de las Casas. Their language is Tzotzil, one of several Maya dialects spoken in the Chiapas highlands. Although Zinacantan shares Maya cultural traditions with surrounding municipios, it is distinguished from its neighbors by an exclusive communal religious system and by a distinctive mode of dress (Vogt 1966; Cancian 1965).

Zinacantecos, like members of other sociocultural units, deal with conditions of impaired well-being in accordance with established rules and patterns. To them, illness belongs to a class of events that we can roughly translate as representing crises or misfortunes. These events all pose a threat to the individual and to his group. In Zinacantan, as in other Maya groups, there is an elaborate body of knowledge about illness. This medical knowledge consists of criteria for differentiating among illnesses, ideas of causation, rules of conduct with regard to obtaining relief or cure, and behavioral prescriptions designed to promote healing and avoid future illness (Silver 1966).

## PROCEDURE AND METHODS

Two bilingual Zinacantecos who served as principal informants enlisted the cooperation of 30 male h'iloletik, who are the most numerous and important medical practitioners in Zinacantan. For comparison, 30 non-h'iloletik males were selected. Several representative hamlets were used and within each hamlet an attempt was made to choose all those males who were practicing h'iloletik. Non-h'iloletik were obtained employing a similar procedure, except that proportionately fewer of the eligible males were selected from each hamlet. Only adult non-h'iloletik who resided in separate households were used in order to avoid sampling persons with very similar medical experiences.

Each subject was asked a series of questions in the Tzotzil dialect which dealt with medical issues. The questions included 18 Tzotzil terms, each of which defined an illness condition in Zinacantan, and 24 items which referred to behavioral events and to disturbances in bodily processes and functions. These items were chosen after informants had indicated that they represented meaningful units of Zinacanteco discourse regarding behavior and bodily concerns. The subject was asked whether each of the 24 potential illness manifestations constituted an element of each of the various illness terms.

The information utilized in this study is represented in matrix form in Table 1. The rows in this matrix are elements representing bodily events and disturbances, as well as behavioral manifestations, which could be termed potential symptoms and signs presented in meaningful units of Zinacantecan discourse. Each column in the matrix represents a Zinacantecan illness term. We selected

**Table 1**

Matrix Showing Association of Bodily Disturbances with Folk Illness Terms

| Bodily Disturbances | k'elel A | ta skuenta B | sarampio C | taxk'ásrinyon D | sim nak'al E | tup'em sat F | komel ta balamil G | takicamel H | cuvah I | sak óbal J | sik k'ok' K | pumel L | mahbenal M | mévinik N | ip hsekubtik O | k'ux holol P | makel Q | hik'ik'ul óbal R |
|---|---|---|---|---|---|---|---|---|---|---|---|---|---|---|---|---|---|---|
| 1 sleepiness | | | | | | † | | | | | | | | | | | | |
| 2 excessive urination | | | † | | | | | | | | | | | | | | | |
| 3 difficulty in hearing | | | | | | | | † | | | | | | | | | | |
| 4 stomach (abdominal) distension | | | | | | | | | | | | | | | | | † | |
| 5 lack of appetite | | | | * | * | * | | | * | | * | | | | | * | | * |
| 6 chills | | * | * | * | | * | * | | * | | * | | | | | | * | * |
| 7 pain while defecating | | | | * | | | | | | | | | | | | | | |
| 8 headache | * | * | * | * | * | | * | * | * | * | * | * | * | * | * | | | * |
| 9 leg pain | | * | * | * | | * | * | | * | | * | | * | | | | | |
| 10 throat pain | | | | | * | | | * | * | * | * | | * | | | | | * |
| 11 crying and sadness | * | | * | * | * | * | * | * | * | * | * | * | * | | | * | | * |
| 12 weakness | * | * | * | * | * | * | * | * | * | * | * | * | * | | | * | | * |
| 13 blood in stool | | | | | | * | | | | | | | | | | | | |
| 14 blood in urine | | | | † | | | | | | | | | | | | | | |
| 15 pruritus (with/without skin eruption) | | | | | | | | | | * | | | | | | | | * |
| 16 chest pain | * | * | * | * | * | * | * | * | * | * | * | * | * | * | * | * | | * |
| 17 quarrelsomeness or excessive hostility | | | | | | | | | * | | | | | | | | | |
| 18 impaired vision | | | | | | | * | | | | | | | | | | | |
| 19 vomiting | * | * | * | * | | | * | * | * | * | * | * | * | * | | | | * |
| 20 coughing | * | * | * | * | | | * | * | * | * | * | * | * | | | | * | * |
| 21 feverishness | * | | * | | | | * | | | * | | * | | | | * | | * |
| 22 pain while urinating | | | | | | | | | | | | | | † | | | | |
| 23 stomach (abdominal) pain | * | | | * | | | * | * | * | | * | | * | | | * | | |
| 24 arm pain | * | * | * | * | | | * | | | * | | * | | | | | | |

* Eighty percent or more of the respondents linked disturbance with illness term.

† Illness term to which respondents most frequently linked disturbance where no strong consensus was noted (i.e., no term was linked to disturbance by at least 80 percent of respondents).

terms that were diversified; that is, they referred to many different bodily abnormalities, as well as to notions of morality, and social processes. The terms, we believe, represent a cross section of Zinacantecan folk illnesses.

The first part of the study involves comparing the responses of *h'iloletik* with those of non-*h'iloletik*. The chi-square test was used to assess differences in the proportion of each group which associated a particular sign or symptom with a particular illness. The responses of both groups were then combined and the manner in which the subjects associated illnesses and their manifestations was examined. In particular, whenever 80 percent or more of the 60 subjects linked a particular disturbance with a folk illness, we assumed that the linkage represented a typical or meaningful one in Zinacantan. Consequently, whenever reference is made in the discussion to the components of Zinacantecan illnesses, it should be clear that this is based on an association of 80 percent or more of the subjects' judgments.

## RESULTS

### H'iloletik/non-H'iloletik Differences

The proportion of individuals of each group which associated each of the symptoms and signs with the various illnesses was compared by means of the chi-square test (18 × 24, or 432 comparisons). Only in one instance was the value obtained statistically significant, and this result can certainly represent chance fluctuation. We conclude that there is no evidence to indicate that the groups differ in their association of discrete symptoms and signs with discrete illnesses.

We next attempted to determine whether the subjects of either of the two groups tended to more consistently be in agreement about the various disturbance-illness linkages. First, focusing on the individual disturbances (i.e., rows), we noted whether one group more frequently had a larger proportion of its members linking that disturbance with the various illnesses. This procedure was repeated using illness terms (i.e., columns) as units of analysis in order to determine whether one of the groups tended to have a larger proportion of its members link the various disturbances with each illness term. No consistent patterns emerged from these two analytic procedures. We concluded, then, that there are no consistent differences in the way h'iloletik and non-h'iloletik associated disturbances with the folk illnesses.

### General Zinacantecan View of Illness

The responses of both groups of subjects were combined for this portion of the analysis; the results are presented in Table 1. The symbols in the table indicate the degree of consensus among respondents with respect to the association of bodily disturbances and illness terms: an asterisk indicates an agreement of at least 80 percent, the dagger designates the most frequent association where an 80 percent or greater consensus was not obtained, and the blank space represents lack of consensus.

Concentration on the rows of the matrix makes it possible to determine whether an illness manifestation is considered to be aligned with a particular Tzotzil term or with many terms. For example, elements 8, 11, 12, 16, 19, and 20 are each regarded by more than 80 percent of the sample to be correlates of most of the 18 folk illnesses. These elements, thus, can be regarded as relatively undifferentiated Zinacantecan units of illness. If we assume that the 18 terms are representative of illness conditions in Zinacantan, this cluster of elements can be said to bear a strong association to the general conception of illness. The content of some of these elements, in fact, refers to what in scientific medicine are regarded as general and/or systemic manifestations of disease (i.e., weakness, headache), whereas others (e.g., vomiting and coughing) represent salient manifestations of gastrointestinal and respiratory disease respectively. The element "crying and sadness" in the 11th row reflects the fact that in Zinacantan there is a strong affective or emotional dimension to the condition of impaired health.

Elements 5, 6, 9, 10, 21, 23, and 24 are illness manifestations exhibiting a high degree of generality, though not as great as those mentioned above. Given the relatively high association that these elements have with Zinacantecan illness, they also appear to be constituent parts of the general conception of illness. Four of these (9, 10, 23, 24) refer to pain localized in different parts of the body. It would appear that in Zinacantan, pain, even though explicitly referred to a segment of the body, is a relatively general and undifferentiated construct that may be associated with a large subset of illness conditions. Many "illnesses," in other words, can include pain, which can be referred to many parts of the body; there does not appear to be a unique medical significance to explicitly localized pain. Elements 6 and 21 refer to chills and feverishness. In the Western scientific medical system these symptoms are believed to be typical accompaniments of infectious processes, and the fact that subjects linked them to a number of illness terms suggests that many Zinacantecan definitions of illness comprehend these processes. Element number 5 (lack of appetite) is also a frequent correlate of infectious processes, and in addition can be regarded as a general and relatively nonspecific symptom of illness.

Subjects infrequently demonstrated consensus regarding association of the remaining elements with Zinacantecan illnesses. These symptoms and signs evidently are not regarded as general accompaniments of illnesses: some (7, 13, 15, 17, and 18) have distinct and narrow linkages with particular illnesses; others (4, 14, and 22) have no generally agreed upon relationship with any illness. It may be that these latter bodily manifestations are infrequently encountered or reported in Zinacantan.

The information presented in the preceding paragraphs can be summarized by using the columns of the matrix (i.e., Zinacantecan illness terms) as units of comparison. It will be seen that subjects tend to link a relatively large proportion of the disturbances with most of the illnesses. Sixteen of the 18 illness terms, for example, are associated with between seven and 13 disturbances. Terms F ("spot in the eye from staring at the moon") and I ("madness"), because they are associated with only three and four disturbances, respectively, are among the relatively rare exceptions. Assuming that the terms are representative of all illness terms in Zinacantan, the folk model of illness that emerges includes generalized pain, evidence of debility, toxicity, infection, and depressed emotional tone, which are highly visible manifestations of system dysfunction.

## DISCUSSION

It must be emphasized that the procedure of this study does not deal directly with the question of the *actual* physical or bodily correlates (i.e., symptoms and signs) of specific folk illnesses. To investigate this question it is necessary to sample the knowledge of persons who have actually been diagnosed as having each of the particular illnesses. What is more, such sampling should be undertaken with explicit instructions that the subject use the particular illness episode as the unit of reference. The procedure used in the current study, instead, inquires about the *general* knowledge of the subject. This knowledge is probably composed of direct experiences with some of the illnesses, indirect experiences through exposure to friends and relatives who have been ill, and the general knowledge held in Zinacantan about illness which individuals learn during the process of enculturation. Compared to the goal of determining the actual bodily correlates of folk illnesses, our study should be viewed as investigating the question of the relationship that Zinacantecos establish between specific bodily disturbances and natively construed states of illness.

Evidence that the responses of *h'iloletik* and non-*h'iloletik* are similar, in general, support the impression that knowledge involving features of illness in Zinacantan is widely shared among the male members of the culture. There appeared to be no conceptual discontinuity across the groups; the group proportion differences that resulted are explainable on the basis of chance fluctuation. Our search for a representative list of illness terms, as well as for a meaningful subset of bodily disturbances, leads us to believe that we have isolated a relevant portion of the fundamental medical concepts in Zinacantan.

The implications of these results seem to be that *h'iloletik* as a group do not validate their social position in Zinacantan by controlling shared specialized knowledge about illness. Their validity as healers and their ability to exercise sanctions appear inherent in their ascribed powers and capacities which, at the sociocultural level, are the result of factors such as revelation, presumed natural endowment, and the processes of recruitment and socialization that bear directly on their training.

The role of personality factors in the process of shamanistic curing must also be considered. When the psychological characteristics of *h'iloletik* and non-*h'iloletik* were compared by means of a projective test, several differences were noted which suggest that personality factors may be important (Fabrega and Silver 1970). Further, research in progress is aimed at specifying whether the relatively uniform understandings about illness which obtain among adult Zinacantecos exist when other facets of medical knowledge are probed.

When the responses of the two groups were combined it was noted that Zinacantecos linked a relatively large number of disturbances with almost all of the illnesses. In general, widespread bodily pain, non-specific "systemic" symptoms such as weakness and loss of appetite, references to bodily events suggestive of infectious processes, highly visible bodily disturbances (e.g., vomiting), and depressed emotional tone were associated with many illnesses. With regard to sensori-motor and behavioral concerns, then, these elements appear to comprise the Zinacantecan model of illness. The critical features of folk illnesses may refer to the social and moral characteristics of the person who is ill, as others have suggested. Nevertheless, in Zinacantan it appears that the label of illness is associated with a fairly general model comprised of bodily and behavioral elements.

The results can be interpreted from a different standpoint, namely from one that emphasizes the semantic profile of folk illness terms. It is tempting to conclude that folk illnesses in Zinacantan, although labeled by separate terms and characterized by diverse semantic dimensions (e.g., notions of cause, severity, etc.) share a body of meaning in that a large proportion of them are viewed as being composed of a distinct cluster of bodily manifestations. The majority of these symptoms, when analyzed from a scientific perspective, are general and nonspecific. It should be remembered, however, that a few malfunctions had a distinct

277

association with specific illnesses. Similarly, careful inspection of Table 1 shows that only four of the 18 terms (C and M; L and N) have an identical disturbance profile. These observations argue for some specificity of meaning at the level of bodily disturbances.

Our contention is that the concept of a folk illness has utility if its denotative meaning in a cultural group has some degree of specificity; that is, if it designates something that members of the culture agree upon. We conclude tentatively that members of a cultural group reliably label events of ill health, provided it is understood that to a subset of subjects, illness terms are likely to have contrasting and shifting referents. This is but to imply that the native classification of medical knowledge is complex. What determines the actual complexity of the classification is that the referents of this knowledge involve behavior (which is fluid), verbalizations about subtle intra-organismic sensations, and natively structured moral and existential premises. The units of this knowledge system, thus, are often vague and rarely mutually exclusive.

In this paper we have taken folk illness *specificity* to mean that certain native illness terms that have currency in a culture have a unique meaning, composed of a set of distinct semantic identities. We grant that the semantic identities relevant to the domain of illness are not necessarily mutually exclusive, nor partitioned in a dichotomous fashion; their profiles must be exhaustively mapped in relation to themselves and to other domains in order to specify their values with respect to a particular illness. This research, then, is an exploratory attempt to evaluate in a controlled fashion the relationship between culture and illness manifestations. We began with a large cluster of known illness symptoms and searched for a subset to these that has saliency as well as equivalent units of meaning (i.e., referred to clearly specified bodily and behavioral disturbances) in Zinacantan. We cannot exclude the possibility that we may have overlooked key Tzotzil terms referring to culturally specific behavioral events or bodily perceptions that are criterial for the application of folk illness terms.

# 31 Pollution and Paradigms

## R. G. Willis

The author of this paper raises an old question: To what extent may we draw a line between scientific and nonscientific systems of medicine and, by extension, scientific and nonscientific versions of any system of human knowledge? R. G. Willis addresses this question by testing to see whether Kuhn's notion of "scientific paradigm" is applicable to the medical system of a nonliterate agricultural people of Africa, the Fipa of Tanzania. His ethnographic data reveal two models existing in complementarity for explaining the etiology of sickness: the "lay" or "folk" theory, and the "doctor" or professional theory.

Both models are based upon views of the person and his body in Fipa environment-society. The doctor theory sees the self as the center of a series of social relationships in family, kin groups, village, and society, as in fact emerging from these relationships. Injuries to these interpersonal bonds, and, therefore, to the self—the causes of illness—come from ancestral and territorial spirits and sorcerers. This model of the person both explains the cause of illness and guides its cure. The folk theory views illness as being caused essentially by sorcerers' contaminating food and drink through poisoning as a result of jealousy and resentment of the victim. As Willis phrases it, the "folk theory sees sickness as the manifestation of a kind of injurious communication between human beings. The theory is understandable as the logical complement, the polluting and polluted obverse, of the Fipa perception of the self as emerging from a continuing process of constructive interaction with others." The more complex model or paradigm of the doctors structures the body, as the phenomenological expression of the person, "as strategically located at the intersection of the social and natural worlds and as homologous in structure and process with the macrocosmic structure and process by which human society relates to wild nature; the body thus forms a kind of cosmological map," and the model provides the healers with "a conceptual framework within which to diagnose and treat illness."

Willis shows the similarities and differences of the Fipa and Western professional medical paradigms. The former seems closely and logically interrelated to the total sociological and cosmological situation, the latter much less so. Thus, the "superiority" of the Tanzanian or Western system of medical knowledge becomes quite relative to a host of philosophical and even practical questions, and not nearly so apparent as

Reprinted with abridgments from R. G. Willis, 1972, "Pollution and Paradigms," *Man*, 7:369–378, with permission of the author and the Royal Anthropological Institute of Great Britain and Ireland.

practitioners of Western medicine and philosophy might hastily suppose. Of relevance for further anthropological study of such phenomena is the question of cross-cultural comparisons. Watson and Nelson (1967) have suggested a model for standardizing cross-cultural analyses of body-environment transactions.

As S. B. Barnes (1969) remarks, the work of Evans-Pritchard, Lévi-Strauss and Horton has combined to narrow the gap between "primitive" and "scientific" thought as this difference has been defined by Frazer and Lévy-Bruhl. Barnes himself adduces T. S. Kuhn's *Structure of scientific revolutions* (1962) as evidence that scientists are in fact more "primitive" in their thinking than their public self-image allows—thus narrowing the gap still further. In the present article I approach the general question of the primitive/scientific relation, or disjunction, by seeing how far Kuhn's concept of the "scientific paradigm" is appropriate to indigenous theories of causation of disease among what is still substantially a non-literate society, that of the Fipa of south-west Tanzania.

Putting the question in this way reveals that there are two identifiable indigenous models of sickness causation among the Fipa, who are primarily agriculturalists and number about 90,000. The first model is general among the ordinary people, and I propose to call it the "lay" or "folk" theory. The second model is peculiar to a small category of specialists, numbering perhaps 500, who are called *asiŋaanga* (*s., siŋaanga*), or "doctors". These are men who have acquired the craft of indigenous medicine through years of apprenticeship to an acknowledged master (Barnes 1969). It is the model of sickness causation they hold which, as I hope to show, deserves to be called a "paradigm" in the sense of Kuhn's definition of "universally recognized scientific achievements that for a time provide model problems and solutions to a community of practitioners" (1962: viii).

## "LAY" AND "SCIENTIFIC" THEORIES

Fipa live in compact settlements with an average population of 250 inhabitants. The *unnsi* ("village") is the basic land-holding corporate group. There is no lineage system, and descent is of minor importance as an organising principle. "Lay" Fipa generally explain sickness as resulting from the wilful contamination of food and drink, and particularly the latter, by a sinister and usually anonymous minority of their fellows in village

society. Fipa refer to these anti-social beings as *aloosi* (*s., unndoosi*), "sorcerers". The sorcerer is conceived as being animated by an emotion of jealous resentment called *usuwa*, which prompts him to introduce a noxious ingredient which may be called by the ethically neutral term *ileembo*, "medicine", but to which the English term "poison" is now often applied. When, typically through the medium of millet beer, this noxious substance is ingested by its intended victim, sickness follows. Such is the causal model which ordinary Fipa propose to explain sickness. Although quite simple, the theory is by no means self-evident. It posits a linked chain of hidden events, starting with the occurrence of *usuwa* in the heart of the sorcerer, continuing with his secret administration of injurious "medicine", and culminating in the concealed operation of the same "medicine" within the body of the victim. The lay theory can be understood as the polluting and polluted obverse of the dominant Fipa value of sociability (*ufukusu*), which requires people to come together as frequently as possible in agreeably communicating groups. Consumption of millet beer (*isuute*) is a virtually inseparable part of this communal activity. Fipa protect themselves as best they can from the hazards supposedly involved in what for them is more or less obligatory social intercourse by the use of protective "medicines" and by the custom according to which anyone offering millet beer to a guest has first to take a sip himself. Nevertheless the artful sorcerer can sometimes penetrate this defensive screen. What he essentially does, as ordinary Fipa see it, is to use the same medium of social interaction through which man creates and re-creates himself to deliver a contrary, life-destroying message.

The model or paradigm proposed by the Fipa doctors elaborates this layman's theory in various ways. Its central constituent is a theory of the person (*unntu*) who is seen as a centre from which radiate several "paths" (Fipa: *insila*; Swahili: *injia*). The "paths" are identified with the various modes of social relationship experienced by men and women in Fipa society. These modes are those of common descent, co-residence and a mode which contains and transcends both descent and shared attachment to a specific village—the relation uniting man to his fellow. The primacy of the latter mode, the most abstract but also the most immediate of all social bonds, is a consequence of the Fipa concept of the self, which is seen as an original construction which emerges out of communication between the self and others. A disturbance of any of these modal social relationships manifests itself, according to the "scientific" paradigm, as an intrusion into the person of injurious forces which are called *imisimu* (ancestral spirits) in the case of relations of common descent, *imyaao nkaandawa* (territorial spirits) in the case of relations of co-residence, and *uloosi* (sorcery) in the case of disturbance of a basic relationship between the self and an interacting other.

This is the point at which the two models of causation, "folk" and "scientific", are connected, inasmuch as the 'folk' theory reduces to its common denominator, in the concept of *uloosi*, sorcery, the complex differentia of the doctors' paradigm. The latter is, however, much more than just a model of the person as constituted by a set of modal social relationships. It is also a guide to therapeutic practice, and the full significance of the "scientific" paradigm emerges only in this operational context.

## THE BODY AS A MODEL OF THE COSMOS

The doctors' interpretation and response to sickness in their patients is moulded by their perception of the human body (*umwiili*) as a locus of intersection of the life-process of human society and the world of wild nature. It is in and through the body, the visible, phenomenal aspect of the person, that force is applied by the doctors, acting on behalf of their patients and clients, with the object of achieving some desirable change in the social and natural environment.

Not only is the body such a strategic locus, it also parallels, as both structure and process, the macrocosmic order, so constituting a kind of cosmological map. For in Fipa cosmology, the cosmic life-process consists in the interaction of human society and wild nature. Human society has a dominant and central position in this relation, controlling and exploiting the (in theory) unlimited domain of external nature. In the body-structure, the upper part of the trunk, and most particularly the head (*unntwe*) is identified with the dominant, intellectual force which in Fipa cosmology is the characteristic of human society in relation to wild nature. In opposition to the head and upper trunk the lower abdomen and genital region, together called *unnsana*, "loins", form a morally inferior area which is nevertheless the site of enormously powerful forces which it is the proper purpose of

the intellect to control and rationally to exploit. The heart (*umwecso*) occupies a medial position between head and loins, belonging ambiguously to both structurally opposed regions. As in modern Western culture, the heart is conceived as the seat of emotion. But its contents are in substantial measure inaccessible to the intellect: "What is in the heart, only the heart knows", says a proverb ("*Ica umu mweeso, caamanyile umweeso unnkola*"). Nevertheless the heart of a person whose social relations are in a healthy state is conceived by Fipa as "white" or "clear"—the colour associated with the intellect (cf. Willis 1967: 526), whereas the heart of the sorcerer is "black"—the colour associated in Fipa symbolism with the lower body. The point is that the heart, like the lower body, should properly be under the control of the intellect, even though its contents are never entirely brought into the light of consciousness.

A number of verbal correspondences link the lower body, particularly the lower abdomen and genitals, with the wild bush. One of the general terms for the latter, used of the political administration of a defined territory, is *icikaandawa* (the same root occurs in *umweene nkaandawa*, district governor, and *imyaao ukaandawa*, the divinities of the bush): in its plural form, *ifikaandawa*, this word is also employed by Fipa, albeit in a slang usage, to denote the male and female genitalia. A common euphemism for the penis (*ulufono*) is *imbea*, a burrowing bush rat; and the vagina (*innyo*) is similarly referred to as *ikoyo*, bush mouse. It is probably also significant that the word *insiinda*, anus, also means "tail"—an attribute of, in relation to man, inferior bush-dwelling animals; and that fertility medicine, which is thought of as penetrating the vagina and womb, is called *ituunko*, "mole".

These general ideas, which belong to the common stock of Fipa consciousness, are articulated by the doctors into the explicit paradigm of the body as both a strategic component of the cosmos and a structurally homologous model of that totality. The intellect, identified with the head, occupies the same central and dominant position in relation to the lower body as human society, identified with the village, *unnsi*, occupies in relation to the surrounding bush. Because the body is linked to the cosmos through the "paths" of social relationships (the whole—body and relationships—constituting the person, *unntu*), action on and in the body is also action on and in the cosmos. And the direction of that action, the therapeutic intention, is guided for the doctors by their perception of the body as a mirror of the cosmic structure and process.

## OPERATING ON THE BODY TO CONTROL THE COSMOS

In treatment, the doctor employs substances called *amaleembo* ('medicines') which are sub-divided into two categories. There are primary ingredients, which are normally collected *ad hoc* from the bush to suit the needs of particular patients: these ingredients are called *ifiti fikola*, literally "the pieces of wood in themselves"; and secondary ingredients, which are held to act by heightening and reinforcing the object intended by the doctor's use of the primary materials. These secondary ingredients are called *ifisiimba*, "latent things", or *ifingila*, "*things that enter in*". The doctor keeps a permanent stock of them in a special bag called *intaangala*.

During fieldwork, I was fortunate in making the acquaintance of a well known indigenous doctor living in central Ufipa, Matiya Isaamba Msangawale. *Siŋaanga* Matiya was kind enough to allow me to observe him during a number of consultations with patients, commenting afterwards on each case and explaining the manner and purpose of the treatment adopted by him. During some of these consultations, as described below, Matiya went into what appeared to be a trance state, characterised by initial heavy breathing and yawning, and continuing with violent trembling and convulsive movements of the whole body, accompanied by strange cries and the utterance of gibberish words. This anomalous behaviour was, however, invariably interspersed with intelligible questions addressed to his patient, bearing on his or her social relationships. The apparent trance state might last for up to twenty minutes, and its conclusion was always signalled by Matiya's utterance of the word "*Katiluumi!*" ("Farewell").

CASE 1

Two women, apparently in their early or middle twenties, said to be sisters. According to Matiya they were suffering from a condition he called *zunguluka*, which is a Fipa corruption of the Swahili verb *zunguka*, "to go round and round". His description implied not merely physical "dizziness", but a state of psychological disorientation. They were also said to be suffering from insomnia.

After going into an apparent trance state, Matiya told me that the trouble of both patients was caused by the posthumous resentment of their dead mother, because they had rejected her wish that they become sorcerers

(*aloosi*). At night her spirit would whisper into their ears. The treatment, Matiya said, would consist in introducing into the patients' bodies a preparation in which the primary ingredient was a portion of a swallow's nest (*icisaaso ci ndyeelela*).

As usual in treatment involving diagnosis by reference to disturbance of social relationships, or "paths", the therapeutic intention is expressed in the symbolic meaning of the "medicine" selected by the doctor. The Fipa name for "swallow", *indyeelela*, means, "what goes round and round" (from the verb *ukuleela*, "to go round and round", "wander aimlessly")—a reference to the bird's characteristic circling flight. In contrast the nest, *icisaaso*, represents centrality and fixity—the desired and proper position of dominance of the controlling intellect in relation to the whole person. The nest is also, as a deliberate construction, representative of what Fipa conceive as the nature of the self.

The preparation and administration of the "medicine" further underlines the intention symbolised in its selection. The ingredients—primary and secondary "medicines" now mixed together—are placed on a fragment of pottery and burnt to ashes over a fire. That is, the ingredients are subjected to a deliberate transformational process. This process is adopted with all ingredients which, as in the present case, are introduced into the patient's body through incisions in the skin. Ingredients used to make decoctions and potions are first boiled.

Having thus prepared the "medicine", Matiya introduced it into incisions (*innkalo*) made in the bodies of his two patients, in the following manner and order: on the forehead (*apa ceeni*); in the back of the neck (*apa ngaalo*); over the diaphragm (*apa kameme*); and in the centre of the spine (*apa ntiindi*). This procedure could be interpreted as establishing a kind of grid directing power from the properly superior head, down through the body.

CASE 2

A woman aged about thirty complained of persistent abdominal pains. She was said to have been treated unsuccessfully for this condition at the Government hospital in Ufipa. Matiya diagnosed her disorder as caused by the sorcery of a man whose erotic advances she had spurned, and who was consequently animated by an intense feeling of jealous resentment (*usuwa*) towards her. Matiya gave her certain medicines (I did not discover their nature), which she drank in a decoction. Soon afterwards I heard that her abdominal pains had ceased.

CASE 3

A youth of about eighteen years, said to be suffering from "sleeping sickness" (the English expression was used). He too reported being unsuccessfully treated at two Government hospitals in Tanzania, in distant Mwanza and Kigoma. Now he had come home to seek again for a cure. When I talked to him this young man appeared to have great difficulty in bringing out his words, while his eyes seemed to be focused at some distance behind me. His movements were slow. Matiya's diagnosis was that his patient was suffering from the action of ancestral spirits, *imisimu,* which had invaded his heart.

Treatment, Matiya said, would consist of rubbing the heart's blood of a freshly killed lizard (*insyoondooli*) into incisions made on top of the patient's head, over the diaphragm and on his back. The patient's face and upper body were to be asperged with a lotion made from shaking some pieces of pinkish wood together with fragments of dog's bone in a bottle of water. This treatment was to take place in the bush and after the washing with the lotion the bottle would be smashed and left on the ground. . . .

On their return after treatment Matiya gave his patient some dark sticky fluid, wrapped in a strip of banana fibre. This fluid was made from mixing oil with ashes produced from burning a selection from the doctor's stock of secondary "medicines". This preparation was to be rubbed into the existing incisions on the patient's return home (he lived about fifteen miles away).

CASE 4

A woman of about thirty suffering from barrenness (*umuumba*). Matiya again went into a trance, and I gathered that he was questioning her about her relations with men other than her husband. Afterwards he recommended to her what he described as a "cleansing" medicine to be followed by a fertility "medicine" of which the primary ingredients were a portion of the uterus of a hen and the roots of a shrub called *inakaloondo,* "the seeker".

## CLASSIFICATION OF SICKNESS

In observing Matiya dealing with his patients and in discussing sickness in general with him and with other Fipa doctors, it became clear that the "scientific paradigm" which defines the nature and structure of the person and the significance of the body also determines the way in which Fipa medicine classifies sickness, on a scale running from the negligible or mild, to the mortal. What Fipa consider to be relatively mild sickness is illustrated in the following three cases, in which Matiya did not consider it necessary to uncover "deep" causes by going into trance, but administered treatment immediately.

CASE 5

A woman aged about thirty-five complained of persistent pains in the arms. Matiya gave her a amall quantity of medicine, instructing her to introduce it in incisions to be made (presumably by a friend) on her forehead, between index finger and thumb of both hands, and between big and first toes of each foot. He also gave her the same dark fluid as in Case 3, this time with the instruction that it should be rubbed into the arms.

CASE 6

A man of middle-age, said to be suffering from swelling of the testicles, a condition called *inyaanga.* The treatment consisted of administration of "medicine" through incisions made on the forehead and chest, drinking an infusion made from the primary ingredients (roots and twigs) of the "medicine" and fumigation—sitting under a blanket, inhaling the smoke produced by burning some of the twigs constituting the primary ingredients of the "medicine".

CASE 7

A man, again of middle-age, suffering from ulceration of the lower leg. Matiya prepared a poultice, made of oil mixed with various "medicines", spread it on a banana leaf and bound it over the ulcer.

At other times Matiya told me of what he evidently considered were standard remedies for various disorders. Thus pneumonia (*impiinsi*) was treated by administering to the patient a decoction made from the roots of a thornbush called *unnsikisi*; epilepsy (*icisooce*) was curable by administration of a medicine made from a small bird of the bush called *impeempe*; gonorrhea (*insaankulwa*) is treated with an infusion made from a plant called *iliika*; syphilis (*amasapu*) is treated with an infusion made from the roots of a tree called *ipupwa*; sore eyes (probably conjunctivitis) are treated with the sap of a tree with large heart-shaped leaves, called *iteketela.*

These examples show that Fipa medicine considers sickness to be "serious", in the sense of providing *a priori* evidence of the invasion or "pollution" of the person through disturbance of one or more of his modal social relationships, when the symptoms fulfil the following criteria:

1. They affect the middle and lower trunk, including the heart;
2. They are felt to be "inside" the body;
3. They are persistent.

Where all these criteria are not met Fipa medicine tends to treat the disorder as relatively insignificant. Thus epilepsy, venereal disease and pneumonia fall into this class, together with rheumatism, arthritis and skin disease. The essence of this classificatory scheme is distilled in a proverb,

'He with skin trouble, let him work, but he who has a swelling, is sick" (*Uwa upele, akalime; uwa ipute, alwiile*').

But the most dangerous form of sickness, and one that is held to be inevitably fatal unless properly treated, results from clandestine adultery. The polluted condition, called *incila*, is held to be transmitted through social contact with a person who has recently had secret, adulterous sexual relations. The most vulnerable are husbands and wives who, unknowingly, have social contact with their partners' lovers. An infant's parent who commits adultery before its "coming out" ceremony (*ukuseend' umwaana*)—which normally occurs several months after birth—will, it is held, transmit *incila* to his or her child.

A peculiarity of *incila* is that it has no identifiable objective symptoms, although it is supposed to worsen an existing malady. According to Fipa the sufferer from *incila* experiences an overwhelming sense of oppression, as though a great weight were pressing down on him. The reported symptoms suggest severe mental depression. A curiosity of *incila* is that Fipa define it in such a way as virtually to exclude empirical identification of the condition. It cannot be recognised externally, and the putative sufferer's "polluted" state is caused by his very lack of awareness that he is in that state. During nearly two years in Ufipa, I did not encounter anyone who was positively described, by himself or others, as suffering from *incila*.

*Incila* thus appears from the anthropologist's point of view to be a purely theoretical disorder which exists as a concept simply to satisfy the internal logic of the "scientific paradigm" of sickness causation. Given the functional interdependence posited in that paradigm between the human body as structure and process and the cosmic structure and process, it is understandable that the worst sickness is caused by a combination of the sufferer's lack of intellectual control over his most intimate social relationship, that with a conjugal partner, with the idea of uncontrolled sexual energy. This conjunction is conceptualised by Fipa as a direct attack on the centre of the sufferer's being, his intellect. Hence the gravity of this notional condition, and its putatively fatal outcome, unless promptly and adequately treated.

## THE MEANING OF HANDS

But man is also able to take active measures to transform his world. Indeed, as Fipa see it, it is

through such action that he constitutes himself as a person. The significance Fipa symbolism and medicine attach to the human hands (*amakasa*) reflects a perception that these organs are the means by which consciously meditated intentions are realised in a transformation of the natural environment. Through their social *praxis*, mediated through the hands, human beings transform nature and in so doing create their society and culture. And since the human body is seen as not only an integral part of the cosmos, but also as its image, as both structure and process, it is understandable that Fipa see the consciously controlled use of sex as analogous to the social transformation of nature. The highest symbolic value, therefore, attaches to acts of ritual masturbation:

The night before beginning cultivation, the man is obliged to have sexual intercourse with his wife. After the act, he must spend a long time touching and manipulating his genitalia and those of his wife, so that his hands become thoroughly impregnated with the odour of those parts. The next morning, without washing his hands, he must touch the seeds he is going to sow in his fields, afterwards rubbing them with a specially prepared "medicine".

The husband then tells his wife to bring him a winnowing tray containing the "medicine", a wooden spoon and the seeds. He strips naked and sits down, placing the tray between his legs so that his penis rests on the edge of the tray and, if possible, touches the seeds. He shuts his eyes. Then rubs the "medicine", which is mixed in a ball of millet porridge, over his penis, which becomes erect. In this way, so informants say, the future crops will grow and become big, like the man's sexual organ (Robert 1930).

A similar symbolic intent is evident in the custom by which an ironsmith, on the day he begins work on a new kiln, eats a meal of millet porridge prepared by his wife with hands unwashed after sexual intercourse and masturbation the previous night; and in the similar ritual acts performed by the married woman, usually the mother or father's sister of the bride, who is charged with preparing the ceremonial millet beer for a wedding feast (Robert 1949; 70). Fipa refer to such rituals as performed "through or 'with' the hands" ('*uku makasa*'; Swahili, '*kwa mikono*').

Consciously controlled sex is also seen as being able to obliterate or cleanse the pollution called *amafo* which affects the survivor of a marriage on the death of his or her conjugal partner. *Amafo* isolates the sufferer from his fellows, who avoid him out of fear of participating in his pollution; but like *incila*, it has no recognisable physical symptoms. *Amafo* can, however, be removed by an act of ritual copulation. A man whose wife dies is entitled to call upon his parents-in-law to provide him with a woman for this purpose, so that he can rid himself of pollution. If no such woman is available, the parents-in-law should provide him with money so that he can obtain this service elsewhere (Robert 1930:50).

Similarly, a man who inherits a widow has the duty of copulating with her as soon as possible, to cleanse her *amafo*. If the dead man was a polygynist the heir has to copulate with them all in turn, in order of seniority. In all cases the act has to be strictly controlled. Manual stimulation is employed to induce a quick erection, after which the heir is obliged to restrain ejaculation until copulation with the most junior of the dead man's wives. If he succeeds in this test an official observer chosen by the kin group (*uluko*) makes the news known to those waiting outside by shouting "The dead one is finished!" ('*Imfwa yaasila!*")—if he fails, either by inability to produce an erection or through premature ejaculation, the observer shouts "The dead one refuses!" ('*Imfwa yaakaana!*'). In this case the heir is considered unfit to inherit the widows, and another heir has to be chosen by the kin group and submitted to the same test (Robert 1930). Until the test of controlled copulation has been successfully passed, the widow or widows remain polluted with *amafo*, and barred from entertaining social relations.

## CONCLUSIONS

A main purpose of this article has been to identify and relate to one another two theories of causation of sickness which are current in Fipa society. The first, or "folk" theory, sees sickness as the manifestation of a kind of injurious communication between human beings. The theory is understandable as the logical complement, the polluting and polluted obverse, of the Fipa perception of the self as emerging from a continuing process of constructive interaction with others. The second theory is associated with the indigenously educated elite of Fipa society, the *asiŋaanga* or "doctors". The doctors operate with a paradigmatic model of the person (*unntu*) as including in his being constituent modes of social relationship called "paths". It is through or along these "paths" that sickness is conceived as invading the body (*umwiili*), which is the visible, phenomenal aspect of the person. The body is also conceived in

the doctors' paradigm as strategically located at the intersection of the social and natural worlds and as homologous in structure and process with the macro-cosmic structure and process by which human society relates to wild nature; the body thus forms a kind of cosmological map. In this scheme the intellect, identified primarily with the head, is seen as occupying the same central and dominating relation to the forces of the lower body as human society in relation to the surrounding bush. This paradigm of the body and the person provides the doctors with a conceptual framework within which to diagnose and treat sickness, and a number of cases are described which illustrate their concepts and therapeutic practice.

Application of the doctors' paradigm to the diagnosis and treatment of sickness also produces a classificatory scheme according to which bodily disorders are evaluated on a scale ranging from negligible or mild, through serious, to dangerous. The latter category refers to the concept of mortal pollution called *incila*, which is held to result from a combination of a sufferer's lack of conscious control over his intimate social relations with the idea of uncontrolled sexuality. This entirely notional category of pollution, as it appears to be, is explained as a necessary theoretical consequence of the Fipa cosmological system, in which intellect is properly in a relation of dominance and control over the forces of the lower body.

The underlying structure of Fipa cosmological assumptions also explains the peculiar significance invested in the hands, as mediators of the intellect's transformational intentions towards both external nature and the forces of the lower body, in certain ritual contexts involving masturbation and the consciously controlled use of sex. The latter is seen by Fipa as able to cleanse the pollution called *amafo* which results from the death of a sexual partner.

The present article is also intended as a small contribution to the long and continuing debate on the respective characteristics of "scientific" and "primitive" thought. By attempting to apply Kuhn's seminal concept of "scientific paradigm" to the organised thought and professional practice of an indigenously educated minority in a small-scale, non-Western society I hope to have shed some light on the general nature of the "scientific" enterprise. It goes without saying that I regard the Fipa doctors' "paradigm" as the joint product of a number of real, albeit anonymous, human beings, rather than as an emanation of some hypostasised "collective consciousness" or "folk memory". In this context it is also pertinent to refer to Kuhn's interesting remarks on the difficulty of establishing precisely who were the originators of some of the most crucial innovations in Western science (1962:136–43).

But the comparison I have here made between Fipa and Western thought also reveals significant structural differences. In Ufipa, the lay theory of sickness causation—what Barnes (1969:100) calls a "social paradigm"—is a condensed and simplified version of the doctors' paradigm; and both "scientific" and "social" paradigms are built on a set of shared assumptions about humanity and the universe which permeate the thought and emotions of laymen and doctors alike. In modern Western societies, however, it appears to be the case that scientific paradigms (for example, in physics) can exist in flat contradiction of corresponding social paradigms and there is an absence of shared cosmological assumptions which might serve to integrate these disparate areas of knowledge and experience.

These different characteristics can be correlated with the different degree of labour specialisation in Fipa and Western society. *Asiŋaanga* form a distinctive social category, generally enjoying high prestige and frequently a substantially higher standard of living than their fellows in village society; nevertheless they remain only part-time specialists, being cultivators who practise their craft after labour in the fields and during the dry season period of reduced agricultural activity. As social persons they are fully integrated into the network of rights and obligations which embraces all adult members of Fipa society. Their position is in marked contrast with that of most professional "intellectuals" in Western society. Of the Fipa Gramsci's comment (1971:9) applies with particular force:

All men are intellectuals, one could therefore say:
but not all men have in society
the function of intellectuals.

# IX
## Obstetrics and Population Control

## Reproduction, Childbirth, and Population Limitation in Preindustrial Societies

All cultures have evolved some system of explanation regarding conception, pregnancy, and childbirth and all have developed sets of beliefs and techniques for dealing with these mammalian and human processes. Thus, all cultures have a gynecology, embryology, and obstetrics, and, insofar as all use systems of child care and treatment, a pediatrics (Deruisseau 1940, Ford 1964, Montagu 1949, Spencer 1949. See also Cianfrani 1960, Himes 1970, Oppenheimer 1967). Each of these arts and sciences is predicated upon the statuses and roles of mother, father, child, and those members of their social networks most intimately related to them. Gynecological, embryological, obstetrical, and pediatric values, traditions, and practices are framed within a cosmology and world-view of a people and their place in the universe, and within a particular type of social system.

The gynecology is based often upon a limited knowledge of anatomical structure and physiological function (but see Section VIII in this volume). It is my assumption that of especial importance in the fate and vicissitudes of mother, child, and father in these events is the relative ascribed place and power of female and male in the social structure.

Embryologies include origin myths, theories of impregnation and conception, and theories of foetal growth and development (Montagu 1949) and spiritual forces play a large, often decisive role in all these processes as well as in the birth process itself. All societies have been able to connect the act of sexual intercourse to the onset of pregnancy, the two possible exceptions being among some Australian aborigines and the famous Trobriand Islanders of Melanesia who were so thoroughly investigated by Malinowski. In these two areas the fact of paternity is reportedly unknown and conception is assumed to take place through impregnation of the mother by "baby spirits." (Malinowski's statements have aroused great controversy and disbelief; the arguments are nicely reviewed by Himes 1970: 29–36.) Although as a myth this belief is held in many parts of the world including the folk societies of the West (Spencer 1949), specific paternity nevertheless is usually established; in other words, spiritual *and* biological insemination are believed to occur.

The pregnant woman is often subject to an extensive set of taboos that may include her diet, activities, social relations, and sexual contacts. Fathers are also frequently prohibited from performing certain actions, eating certain foods, participating in sexual intercourse during certain periods, and so on. Activities of both parents as well as the designs or whims of the gods can influence the fate of embryo and mother. Pregnancy taboos are usually directed toward the well-being of mother, father, child, and social group, and generally are concerned with making parturition easy and painless. However, despite many misconceptions that still linger in Western thinking, childbirth is probably not less painful for the mother in preindustrial society than in industrial society—and sometimes it is quite severe (Freedman and Ferguson 1950). It is my own hypothesis that the experiencing of obstetrical pain in any society is, among other things, heavily conditioned by the relative social status and power of women.

In most non-Western preindustrial societies all the processes concerned with reproduction at first glance do not seem to be closely associated with the medical system, indeed in many cases scarcely at all. They are taken, as other expected events in life, as natural and part of living. There are, however, some exceptions, and when difficult births occur a medical personage of some sort may be called in, usually as an act of desperation. Furthermore, in the broad anthropological sense in which I have defined medical systems (see my introduction to Sections I and IV) all actions concerned with reproducing life, bringing it into being and protecting the mother and—if possible—the infant must be seen as being part of the medical system. Furthermore, insofar as the carrying capacity of a society's environmental niche is directly affected by population size (Alland 1970: 36 passim) as well as the techniques for preserving health and combatting disease, what the society does to control the magnitude and density of its population bears critically upon the potential for success of the medical system.

Almost all human cultures have devised some methods for controlling population growth, including contraceptive techniques, abortions, infanticide, and so (Devereux 1967). Where population growth seems very high by Western middle-class standards, generally there are cultural and social obstacles to family planning, or perhaps more accurately small family planning (Newman 1970, 1972). A society's technology for exploiting the food potential of its environment bears directly upon the size of population the environment will support. And, of course, the medical system's capabilities are of vital importance in determining the longevity of those individuals surviving beyond the birth process.

# 32 Embryology and Obstetrics in Preindustrial Societies

## Robert F. Spencer

Ethnographic coverage of the behavior and ideas concerning reproduction and childbirth in non-Western and preindustrial societies has generally tended to be spotty and incomplete. Even from the purely descriptive point of view there are not enough fully informative ethnographic accounts. There are a few exceptions, as in the fine ethnography, *Both Sides of the Buka Passage* (Blackwood 1935: the author, not surprisingly, was a female anthropologist), or in a monograph dealing with the topic in a major ethnographic region, *Southeast Asian Birth Customs* (Hart et al. 1965). Few anthropological journal articles of relevance exist, though again there are exeptions, for example, "Reproduction in Truk" by the late anthropologist Ann Fischer (1963). This report of one of the Caroline Islands in the South Pacific is useful because the materials are clearly and systematically organized and because Dr. Fischer had the data to take the reader into a number of areas frequently scanted in ethnographies. These include the desire for children, fertility factors, "illegitimacy," abortion, infanticide, sexual and reproductive practices, and the obstetrical process itself. She also considers certain theoretical problems in handling such data. (I have placed quotation marks around "illegitimacy" because anthropologists and other behavioral scientists frequently tend to use it ethnocentrically. The occurrence of birth out of wedlock does not mean universally that the child is considered illegitimate. Only if there is evidence that the people themselves so define such a child would this designation hold. Where such practices so easy and widespread adoption obtain, as on Truk and in many other places [for example, for Puerto Rico see Landy 1965], we may assume that extra-marital birth will have few harmful consequences for the child.)

Clellan Ford (1945) attempted three decades ago to derive certain broad principles of reproduction and childbirth behavior through a comparative investigation of a worldwide sample of societies, using what was then called the Cross-Cultural Survey and later came to be known as the Human Relations Area Files. Another noteworthy early attempt at representativeness, if not comprehensiveness, is a series of

Reprinted with abridgments from Robert F. Spencer, 1949–1950, "Primitive Obstetrics" (including "Introduction to Primitive Obstetrics," "Pregnancy Among Primitive Peoples," "Childbirth Among Primitive Peoples," and "Primitive Obstetrics and Surgery"), *Ciba Symposia*, *11*:1158–1188, with permission of the author, Ciba-Geigy Corporation, and the Ciba Collection of Medical Illustrations.

papers appearing in one issue of the now extinct *Ciba Symposia* by the anthropologist Robert F. Spencer, the whole of which was entitled "Primitive Obstetrics." Though the study was done a quarter-century ago, it remains a useful introduction to the topic. We present here a drastically shortened version, and the reader will wish to consult the original fully to savor the richness of the ethnographic data the author uses. Spencer endeavors to organize the data scattered in many places into a relatively systematic, coherent set of propositions regarding the ways in which "primitive" peoples organized their embryology and obstetrics, and indeed, by his very choice of such Western medical labels, to rescue the material from the limbo of exotica in order that it can be seen as having, however mystically enshrouded, a pragmatic rationale. His treatment is noteworthy for its time in that he consciously attempts to view the data in a nonracist, nonpejorative, way. A quotation from Spencer's introduction indicates his thoroughly contemporary approach:

> The so-called "savage" is not child-like in his thinking; he meets the problems of his environment in terms of the cultural heritage which his group has provided him. A recent definition of the term "primitive" passes no value judgment but conceives itself as descriptive of those cultures which possess a more limited array of artifacts and which are thus technologically handicapped. Material complexity is in no way related to social development; it is accordingly difficult to categorize in terms of higher or lower development of the social, familial, political, or religious. By the same token one cannot speak of "primitive culture" or "primitive society," as though the non-civilized peoples of the world shared a common cultural heritage.

Nothing done by anthropologists begins to approach the scope of the Ford and Spencer studies. However, a stimulating recent paper by Lucille F. Newman (1972), "The Anthropology of Birth," though using data mainly from the United States, Japan, and India, provides a number of cogent theoretical and conceptual points on the topic and helps frame problems in this important area for future research by medical anthropologists.

## PREGNANCY AMONG PRIMITIVE PEOPLES

. . . The various cultures of the world, primitive as well as civilized, are sufficiently acquainted with the facts of biology to relate the pregnancy of a given woman to the act of sexual intercourse. It is of course true that native lore regarding the physiological processes of gestation is highly variable from area to area in the world. In only two culture areas of the world is there apparently a denial of the facts of physical paternity. Various tribes in Australia, together with the native inhabitants of the Trobriand Islands, an archipelago to the northeast of New Guinea, are reportedly ignorant of the causal connection between coitus and pregnancy. Somewhat similar beliefs prevailed before European contact in both these areas. These were to the effect that spirits of various kinds, including "baby spirits," might enter the body of a woman. Among the Arunta, for example, a group in Central Australia, spirit children were believed to have been placed in pools by a mythical being. Such spirits wandered about the countryside and, according to native belief, infested certain special places. The aboriginal peoples describe these spirits as resembling little red frogs or as tiny *homunculi*, the size of a walnut. While descriptions from the Australian continent are somewhat variable, it is agreed that when such a spirit child enters the body of a woman conception occurs....

The late ethnologist, Professor Malinowski, offers a similar description of beliefs relating to conception among the peoples of the Trobriand Islands. Here the spirit child is placed in the body of the woman through the head, according to some informants, or, in the view of others, through the genitalia. The woman who conceives often dreams of the spirit agent and in most cases is able to name the being who is responsible. Reincarnation is also known, and there is the rather vague belief that the spirit derives substance, and grows in the menstrual blood.

These two rather unique views regarding conception, occurring as they do in areas which do not appear to be culturally connected, have been the subject of considerable debate. The evidence in favor of accepting the disavowal on the part of these groups of knowledge of physical paternity seems convincing and has been considered critically by Ashley-Montagu in his book, *Coming into Being Among the Australian Aborigines*. In both the Trobriands and Australia, sexual intercourse is held to be a necessary adjunct of child-bearing but in no sense is it regarded as the cause. An argument which has been advanced in favor of accepting the native views of these areas as authentic is the biological fact that not every sexual union results in offspring. Equally important, however, is the fact that these cultures have interested themselves in explaining the origin of children from the spiritual rather than from the physical point of view. The preoccupations and the interest of the two cultures channel the beliefs of their members. In further support of the Australian and Trobriand view,

Malinowski comments that despite considerable sexual license, illegitimate births are most rare. The same point has been made by others with respect to Australia. Early marriage, coupled with facts on adolescent sterility which have recently been adduced by Ashley-Montagu, would appear to lend support to native theory in these societies....

Some primitive groups, while they recognize that coitus is the normal cause of pregnancy, entertain the notion that women may conceive in other ways. The South African Hottentot, for example, have a myth telling of a woman who became pregnant by eating a certain kind of grass. In a number of other societies food taboos have arisen based on much the same theory. In India, various of the cults devoted to the worship of Siva, a patron of fertility, ascribe to the phallic symbol, the *lingam*, procreative powers. The mythology of the Bontoc Igorot of the Philippine Islands is so ridden with magical tales that magical conceptions are not regarded as improbable. If the menstrual discharge is washed downstream it may be used by spirits to create heroes of great power. In myths, the frog motif is popular; the frog, lapping up the spittle of a hero, is impregnated and gives birth to an attractive and talented child.

But other societies all over the world apparently recognize only the connection between coitus and conception. Depending upon cultural convention, interpretation or myth, the role of each principal in a childbirth situation may or may not be clearly defined. A theory which is not without a certain logic and which obtains credence in a number of unrelated societies holds that the fetus is formed from semen and menstrual blood. In Dobu, an island in the same general area as the Trobriands, there is apparently no reflection of the ignorance of physiological paternity. Semen is believed to be voided coconut milk which mixes with the coagulates of the menstrual blood, thus forming the fetus. The Dobuans, aware of the theory current in the Trobriands, speak of the natives of the latter area as "liars." Variations of this belief appear in other sections of the world. The Azande, a tribal group in Central Africa, hold the fetus to be formed from semen and vaginal mucus. As the child develops in the womb it derives nourishment from semen and blood. Some societies place a taboo on sexual intercourse during pregnancy. Not so the Azande who believe that the emissions of the father provide nourishment for the fetus. The East African Bavenda believe that all the white elements of the child's body, teeth, bones and so forth come from the father, while the red elements, blood, skin and the like, are the gift of the mother. The Ashanti of West Africa relate the soul to the father and the body to the mother. Variations of such beliefs appear among the Hopi Indians of Arizona, in Madagascar, and in Tibet....

Ethnographic accounts offering descriptions of the majority of the cultures of the world are not generally helpful in explaining the ways in which the various primitive groups determine when conception occurs and pregnancy begins. As nearly as can be ascertained, cessation of the menses is symptomatic of pregnancy in the belief and according to the observation of nearly every society. To choose an example from Africa: the Loma and Gbunde of Liberia take the view that conception may follow immediately upon menstruation. Thereafter the disruption of menstrual regularity is regarded as proof of pregnancy. But some other societies utilize other symptoms as indications. Various scattered groups over the world look for changes in the breasts as well as cessation of the menses. Morning sickness is considered as evidence of pregnancy by some primitive groups, although Margaret Mead, writing of the Arapesh in the mountains of New Guinea, mentions that nausea in conjunction with pregnancy is unknown. It is also interesting to note that a number of disconnected groups ascribe loss of appetite and laziness to a pregnant women. Those various tribal groups who, through a process of observation, have come to note the definite period of time involved in gestation, generally reckon an approximate nine months between the birth and the first interruption of the menstrual cycle.

*Telegony* is the term generally used to refer to the concept that a male may exert a physical influence, after one mating with a given female, on offspring which she may later produce by other sires. This belief, in fact, is not unknown in our own society. Now and again one encounters survivals of this formerly rather popular folk notion. In the main, the concept is rarely applied to humans in our culture, although the breeders of various kinds of animals may stoutly maintain that dogs, cats, horses, and the like can be so influenced by the mother's previous matings. This view is not generally found among primitives, although there are suggestions of variations of it. Among some of the African groups, should a woman commit adultery during pregnancy, both she and the child may be affected. The West African Ashanti demand abortion in such a case while others demand confession so that medicinal prevention

may be offered to avert any danger. Nor is this concept limited to Africa; it has also been noted at Hopi in Arizona and in Assam. In each case, however, the attitudes toward the pregnant adulteress are variable. The Navaho believe that if a woman at the time of conception has intercourse with more than one man she will give birth to twins.

But the term telegony is also used in a slightly different sense. Here it may refer to the ways in which the pre-natal experiences of the mother work an influence on the child. A number of societies take the view that a woman is able to influence the looks, health, character, and the like of her unborn child. Nor has our culture succeeded in ridding itself of such superstitions. Witness, for example, the not uncommon belief that birthmarks, other physical or even mental peculiarities, may be dependent on pre-natal happenings. Various kinds of food taboos have been instituted by different societies in accord with this theory. In the Torres Straits Islands, for example, should a pregnant woman eat certain types of fish, the baby at birth might show some of the physical characteristics of these fish. In the same area, the child with a dark complexion reflects its mother's laziness since she is then proven to have avoided the trouble of roasting a type of earth customarily eaten by pregnant women....

Birth magic is usually designed to insure the well-being of both mother and child. It generally takes a sympathetic form in that the pregnant woman is cautioned to avoid all acts, foods, and the like which suggest the ways in which easy delivery might be prevented or the health of either the mother or child in some way endangered. Thus among the Yukaghir of Northeastern Siberia the pregnant woman may not eat the fat of any animal nor the fish from which glue is obtained. Here the reasoning is that such food works against an easy and successful delivery. Similarly, among the Arapesh of New Guinea no pregnant woman may eat bandicoot lest she die in hard labor. This is a magical transfer based on the observation that the bandicoot burrows deep into the ground. By the same reasoning, no Arapesh woman may eat frog, lest her child be born too suddenly, and it is also believed that the child will be born too soon if the woman eats eel.

But not every society has such taboos against the eating of certain foods. Now and again a culture may evolve the concept that the dietary desires of the pregnant woman should be met. In the Andaman Islands, for example, while there are some proscribed foods, there is the recognition that a woman may desire a great variety of food during the course of her pregnancy....

The concept of telegony is further operative in a number of societies in that the infant may be influenced by what its mother has seen or experienced during the course of her pregnancy. The Mohave, Maricopa, Pima, and numerous other Indian tribes of Arizona place a prohibition on the viewing by a pregnant woman of all "ugly" things. Thus in these societies she may not look at dead or maimed things, into a grave, or at certain animals. The Maricopa pregnant woman could not touch snakes, lest the child be born crippled, seemingly lacking bones. Violation of such prohibitions might mean a stillbirth or a crippled child. In Ashanti no pregnant woman dares look at a monkey or at a badly executed carving "lest she give birth to a child like it." On the other hand, she may carry an attractively carved figure, the presence of which will insure the good looks of her offspring....

The mystical relationship between the husband and his wife is stressed by many societies when the latter is pregnant. Not only may the husband work magic or perform acts designed to facilitate his wife's delivery but he may also, by his actions, have some effect on the unborn child. Many cultures prohibit the taking of life by the husband of a pregnant woman. This means that he may not hunt or go to war. The Australian Arunta, despite their philosophy of conception, have instituted a prohibition against the hunting of large game by a pregnant woman's husband lest the woman have a difficult confinement. Here the attentions appear to be directed primarily in favor of the woman rather than of the child. The Hopi Indians demand that the prospective father avoid the taking of any kind of life. If he were to do so, it is believed that the child might be born dead or deformed in some way....

Most of the various cultures of the world have some further attitude towards the relations of husband and wife during pregnancy. This may take the form of prohibitions with regard to both social and sexual intercourse. Some societies take the view that coitus during pregnancy may be harmful to the fetus especially in the latter months of pregnancy. There seems to be considerable variability among the peoples of the world as to the periods in pregnancy during which coitus is taboo. The Murngin of Northern Australia, for example, are described as regarding the sex act as potentially harmful to the unborn child. In this society, while the reasoning is clear, continence is not usually followed in practice. The Masai of East Africa believe that coitus with a pregnant woman causes an inevitable miscarriage. In the event that a man causes his wife to lose a child in this way, he is subject to the vengeance of the women of the community who may seize and flog him and run off with his cattle, his most prized possession. Certain of the New Guinea tribes, among many others, forbid coitus during pregnancy and take the view that the parents must enter into a somewhat formal and mystical relationship, their various acts and behavior patterns being prescribed by custom....

The Chinese belief suggests another rather widespread view which attaches itself to the person of the pregnant woman. This is the fact of her uncleanness, the view held by many societies that she may attract various malefic influences both personal and impersonal. Of interest in this respect is the remarkable association between menstruation, in many areas a cause of pollution, and pregnancy. Often the same attitudes prevail. Indeed, the woman in giving birth to a child may be forced to seek the seclusion of the hut reserved for menstruating women. The harmful influences which emanate from the menstruant and the *enceinté* are conceived to be of the same kind by many scattered societies. Some of the tribes of the Amazon drainage area hold that if either the pregnant woman or the menstruant eats game caught by hounds, the dogs will never be able to hunt again. By the same token she may hinder the success of the hunter....

Somewhat uniform also are the rules governing the behavior of the husband of a pregnant woman. Some groups forbid him to hunt, other tribes place a prohibition on the hunting by the husband during or after the confinement. Violation of these taboos necessitates special ceremonials to right the wrong, such ritual often being entrusted to the shaman.

The complexities and variabilities in human thought in a childbirth situation appear in nearly every society to have as their aim the protection of the principals involved. A secondary view seems to be very largely the protection of the community arising from the concept that a pregnant woman occupies an unusual status. The presence of so many analogous attitudes and beliefs in unrelated and scattered cultures over the world would seem to reflect observations of a similar physiological situation and a transfer to such situations of practices and concepts drawn from the culturally determined content in each society of magic ritual and religious emotion.

# CHILDBIRTH AMONG PRIMITIVE PEOPLES

One might think that the child born into a society of lower technological advancement, without the benefits of asepsis or of scientific obstetrical knowledge, might have considerably less chance of survival than the infant born in the modern hospital. But, in general, this does not seem to be the case. Because in so many societies the parturient woman is isolated, her child, if the birth is normal, need not be exposed to many of the dangers of infection. Since the assistants at a birth in most primitive societies rarely attend more than one woman at once, the possibilities of the contagion of one patient by another through a midwife are minimized. Stillbirths and the infection or susceptibility to disease of both the mother and child are, of course, more frequent in areas where a teeming population is in constant conflict as a result of an undependable food supply. China and India offer a case in point. In the former area, indeed, infanticide is a reflection of economic necessity. But in areas where the communities are relatively small, where a fairly normal balance exists between population and food supply, the mother is assured of her nutritional complement. In such societies infant mortality, infection, and childbed diseases appear to be kept at a minimum. Among many peoples, however, abnormal births create a problem for which there is often no solution.

One popular fallacy with regard to childbirth among ethnic groups other than the Northern European is deserving of mention and refutation. This is the belief that the women of other races and from different cultures have a much easier confinement. Women in primitive society reputedly have a much shorter period of labor, are subject to less pain, and may often resume their daily tasks almost immediately following parturition. Ploss and Bartels, in their memorable work, *Das Weib*, categorically deny that a confinement is any easier for the woman in a primitive society than it is in our own. But this does not solve the problem; a number of accurate observers have noted the apparent ease with which the women in some societies deliver their children. In this respect an important point that is often forgotten is the demands of the cultural background. The individual society determines the behavior of the parturient woman just as much as it does the patterns of religion or of social organization. In the villages of modern Japan, for example, birth is a highly secret affair. A woman in childbirth, living as she does in a flimsy dwelling in close proximity to her neighbors, avoids at all costs crying out during her labor or delivery, or letting her agonies be known in any way. Social disapproval and considerable embarrassment await the woman who violates these *mores*. In such a case the untutored observer might easily note that delivery for the Japanese peasant woman was exceptionally easy....

Birth, in most societies, lies completely in the domain of the women. Assistants at a birth are generally women. Only in a very few societies, our own included, may a man have a function at a childbirth situation. Male help may be called upon in various scattered cultures if the delivery proves to be an exceptionally difficult one. Thus the Tarahumare, an Indian tribe in Chihuahua in Northern Mexico, generally make use of a midwife to assist at a delivery. In this tribe, however, the husband of a woman in labor reserves the services of a shaman who stands ready to be called only if a prolonged labor demands it. The same is essentially true of the Mexican Huichol. Here the shaman is ready to offer his magical aid to any woman at birth if difficulties arise, but it is of interest to note that the Huichol shaman generally attends his own wife at the critical time of childbirth....

...But the prohibition may be subject to further rationalization. Among the Arapesh of New Guinea the food-getting functions of the man, surrounded with much ceremony and magic, are considered an antithesis of the physiological functions of the woman. For this reason, no man is present at a birth, a taboo which applies particularly to the father. Rather general in Australia is the same concept; childbirth lies so strictly within the woman's province that ordinarily no reference is made in the presence of men to the menstrual blood, the placenta, or the lochia. In both of these areas a woman retires from the group at childbirth. But in other cultures, as for example, among the Philippine Ifugao, the husband may be at hand to aid his wife during her labor. Among some of the Siouan tribes of the North American Plains the parturient woman may stand erect clinging to the shoulders of either her husband or some other male relative. Such instances are by far the exception; the general view is the barring of men from the scene of the birth. One marked difference appears in Samoa, however. Here the woman generally goes to her parents' home, especially if she is about to bear her first child, and delivers it before a number of interested spectators of all ages and both sexes.

In most primitive societies preparations for the delivery are made with the onset of labor pains. In keeping with the concept of seclusion of menstruating and parturient women which appears in so many scattered societies, the woman in labor generally retires with her assistants. Very frequently, as in the Samoan case mentioned above, the woman goes to her own parents' home for delivery. The West African Ashanti, for example, have this custom. Here, should anything be wrong with the newborn child, the secret is not divulged to the family of the husband and ridicule is avoided....

...Few of the primitive societies of the world allow a birth to take place without some experienced person in attendance. Some cultures have elevated the midwife to a professional status, allowing payment for her services in terms of whatever the group regards as valuable. But as often as not, help is sought from a female relative or from some older woman who has had experience in assisting at a birth or who has borne children of her own. Even if a woman needs no immediate assistance at delivery, there is generally help at hand should she require it. In the Kgatla tribe in South Africa, the woman in labor retires alone to her hut. Normally she delivers herself, although her mother or some older woman of her family remains outside prepared to enter if needed. In the Trobriands the mother of the parturient generally acts as midwife. The Todas of the Nilgiri Hills in Southern India require that woman be attended by a midwife and also by her husband. During delivery, the Toda woman clings to her husband, or to one of them, since the Todas are polyandrous. The husband may offer magical aid or prayers in case of a prolonged labor. The shaman, priest or religious dignitary may, among some groups, aid the midwife in cases of difficult delivery.

The various societies of the world offer an astounding number of differences in their birth practices. Not only is there great variability in regard to the position and posture of the woman at delivery, but there are also those differences which the individual society has developed in ceremonial, attitude, and medical treatment. For this reason, it seems advisable to consider in some detail the birth customs of one or two typical peoples....

While there are, as in every culture area of the world, numerous local differences, the tribes of Australia generally required that the parturient woman retire from the group. Assisted by her mother and by some other old female relative, one of whom acted as a midwife, the woman delivered her child either in a temporary shelter or simply in the "bush." The midwife's function was not well defined; the birth was allowed to proceed naturally and without any manipulation. Rather was the rôle of the attending women a ceremonial one. With some frequency throughout Australia songs were sung during labor by the women in attendance. These were designed to facilitate delivery and to prevent hemorrhage. In Central Australia, as among the Aranda and other groups, the husband of the woman in labor had a special task to perform. If the labor were prolonged, he stripped off all adornment, emptied his pouch or bag of all its contents, and walked slowly past the place of birth in an effort to induce the child to follow him. Until the delivery of the placenta the child was not touched. Then the mother herself cut the umbilical cord usually with a stone knife, and with great care secretly buried or burned the afterbirth lest it be used to work evil magic against herself or the child. It may be mentioned parenthetically that a mystical or magical notion often attaches itself to the afterbirth and to the umbilical cord; many cultures regard this as a kind of double of the child. It must be disposed of with exact care in order to avert evil. The Aranda woman made a necklace of the dried remainder of the navel cord which the child wore as an amulet against illness.

In the New Guinea area, where there are found such peoples as the Arapesh, the Kwoma, and the Tchambuli, among others, similar customs prevail. Somewhat analogous practices are encountered in the adjacent Trobriands and in Dobu. Among these groups, the pregnant woman, as soon as she feels the first pangs of labor, retires with her attendants either into a house from which men have been excluded, or, as among the Arapesh, where the blood of birth, like menstrual blood, is considered highly dangerous, away from the village entirely. The woman seats herself on a mat, her attendants bearing down heavily on her shoulders and abdomen. Birth is allowed to proceed naturally, the child remaining untouched until it is completely expelled. Nor is the cord cut until the placenta is delivered. This task falls to an attendant, usually the mother of the parturient, who may cut the cord with a bamboo knife. The Kwoma demand that the placenta be carefully buried for fear of sorcery which someone may work against the child. In the Trobriand area, the umbilical cord and the placenta are buried in a yam plot, on the supposition that the child will then be a good gardener. In some of the societies in question, the father is placed in a somewhat delicate position.

The Arapesh and Kwoma, for example, feel that man must undergo purificatory ceremonies, just as he does earlier when he is subjected to the initiation rite or when he slays an enemy for the first time in battle. He cannot touch tobacco with his hands, nor may he scratch himself except with a special stick. He must remain secluded for five days and is only released from these restrictions when he has undergone a series of special rites under the tutelage of another man who is already a father. This custom suggests both the change of status which accompanies parenthood and the custom known as the *couvade*, a practice discussed below....

A somewhat different situation occurred in the Marquesas in the Polynesian area. Here, during the latter stages of pregnancy, the head of the house remained nearby to ward off evil influences, malignant forces always being drawn to a woman in labor. A special hut was erected for the birth near the usual dwelling. The Marquesans believed that if a birth took place in a usual house it became defiled and had to be burned. Marquesan society permitted no midwives; so strong was the belief in malevolent spirits that no woman would approach a parturient. Women customarily delivered themselves although the father might aid, pressing down on the uterus or on the shoulders. The mother herself cut the umbilical cord, either by biting it or working it with her fingers until it separated. The placenta was taken by the father and buried in a wet place, since it was believed that the child would be ill if it were buried in a dry location. Mother and child then plunged into an icy stream. Immediately upon her return she had intercourse with her husband, an act believed to have some medical efficacy since the uterus and other organs were thus returned to their proper positions. This was also done in cases of prolonged menstruation even though the menstrual blood and the lochia were considered defiling....

Turning to Western and Central Asia, certain parallels in birth customs are noted between groups such as the Kirghiz-Kazak of the steppe regions, various other of the Turkic-speaking groups, and the Bedouin peoples of Arabia. The common economic base of pastoral nomadism and the nominal adherence to Islam found throughout the area are probably effective in part in bringing about these apparent similarities. The Kazak. woman works until labor begins, then retires with female relatives to a tent. If delivery is difficult, the woman's body is pressed, exorcistic songs are sung, and the woman's hand may be held over a fire to

cause spasms to force the fetus. If this fails, the woman drinks a potion of water mixed with the sand from a grave. The afterbirth and umbilical cord are buried and the woman resumes her work within two or three days after confinement. Among these people, as among the Rwala Bedouins of Northern Arabia, the impurity of a woman at birth is somewhat minimized. Nor does the father apparently have any duties or taboos to observe. Among the Rwala, Musil mentions the case of a woman who delivered herself while mounted astride a camel when the group was on the march. Such a case is apparently not unusual. The Rwala apparently fear a woman who has miscarried or whose child has been born dead....

...In the ancient civilization of the Aztecs which, because of its high material attainments, hardly deserves to be ranked with the primitive cultures of the world, there are some customs connected with birth which are deserving of mention. The Aztecs regarded motherhood as a feminine equivalent of war. The newborn child was compared with a war captive. Should a woman die, she was treated with honor just as a warrior slain in battle. The midwife, at the moment of birth, raised the national battlecry and announced that a captive had been taken. It was the midwife who prepared the ritual steam bath for the mother. The midwife also acted as ceremonial sponsor for the child. During pregnancy, both the prospective mother and the father were under certain food taboos.

In the Inca civilization of Peru, births were reported to the state and a census kept. The Peruvian women delivered their children without assistance, as nearly as can be determined from the early accounts. The umbilical cord was carefully preserved and the child was allowed to chew on it when ill....

Much has been written concerning the custom of the couvade. It is not to be implied that the complex is limited to South America, but it does appear on that continent with some elaboration. The custom may be best defined in the words of an observer: among the Arawak Indians of Guiana: "On the birth of a child the ancient Indian etiquette requires the father to take to his hammock, where he remains for some days as if *he* were sick, and receives the congratulations and condolences of his friends. An instance of this custom came under my own (Rev. W. H. Brett: *The Indian Tribes of Guiana*) observation; where the man, in robust health and excellent condition, without a single body ailment, was lying in his hammock in a most provoking manner; and carefully and respectfully attended by the women, while the mother of the newborn infant was cooking—none apparently regarding her." Among the Canella of Northeastern Brazil both parents remain rigidly secluded for a time, eating no meat and abstaining from their usual chores lest the child in some way be injured. This restriction applies not only to the husband of the parturient, but also to any paramours she may have had during her pregnancy. Among the Ona and Yaghan, in bleak Tierra del Fuego, the father takes his wife's place on the confinement bed while the wife resumes her normal tasks. The Witoto husband, during his period of confinement, could not touch his weapons, and was limited as to diet. Among some of the tribes of South America, the couvade was particularly onerous. Not only the "lying-in" period for a man, but the dietary restrictions, especially as against meat, might last for a long period of time.

The custom of the couvade is a highly variable one from area to area. It might be supposed that any group which places restrictions on the activities of the father practises some aspect of it. . . .

Information on unusual births among primitive peoples is rather scanty. One point in this connection may be noted. This is the attitude regarding twins so prevalent among primitive peoples. Some groups welcome multiple births but others fear them. The Mohave Indians of the Colorado River area held that twins came from the sky and had great clairvoyant powers. In a sense, the Mohave considered twins unreal, since their relatives were in the sky and they had "only come to visit." In many societies twins are killed at birth, or one of twins may be abandoned or strangled. Sometimes, if twins are brother and sister, it is considered that they have violated the incest taboo in their intimate position in the womb. Such slaying of one or both twins may occur in all parts of the world. Some societies, however, such as the African Baganda, welcome twins and have a special fraternal organization to which the fathers of twins belong.

If children are born deformed, if there is a stillbirth, or if the child is a monstrosity, most primitives believe that the ritual prohibitions surrounding birth and pregnancy have in some way been violated.

As one compares the birth customs of the peoples of the world with those which have evolved for pregnancy, it appears that the latter are more elaborate. Most peoples prepare for the event of birth by a series of prescribed or prohibited acts. If these are observed with care, the delivery itself should proceed without difficulty. Birth magic is often counter-active—it is designed to relieve difficulty. The rituals and ceremonies, the customs which follow the birth work for the well-being of the newborn child. Once the infant has been born, it is a potentially useful member of the given society and its welfare must be assured.

## PRIMITIVE OBSTETRICS AND SURGERY

The various primitive societies of the world in seeking to solve the problems which parturition creates, only rarely resort to surgery of any kind. The failure of the processes of normal birth often leads to a magical rather than to a practical solution. Since the inefficacy of magic may be subject to easy rationalization—explanations in terms of failure to perform rituals properly, breach of taboo, or the like, the importance of the supernatural may be perpetuated. As has been noted, most societies employ some kind of assistant at a birth. The midwife, though she may have at her disposal any number of techniques to facilitate delivery, is dependent upon the background with which her culture has provided her. Almost never does she perform surgery. Indeed, many societies do not include in the functions of the midwife the cutting of the navel cord, a task which the mother, the grandmother, or some other relative may perform. In the few societies which permit obstetrical surgery, the knife is generally wielded by men.

It is thus to be emphasized that surgery as such, in the contemporary sense, is unusual among primitive peoples. Some tribes have learned the art of manipulation in order to induce the birth. Some of these in fact carry out this practice to what by our standards is a most brutal extreme. But other groups allow a birth to take its normal course and, as in the Trobriands, are most hesitant to attempt manipulation of the fetus. The Trobriand area offers a good example of dependence on magic. Here a difficult labor is ascribed to evil magic which chills the uterus. The only way in which this may be averted is to summon a person who knows the counteractive spells. These are recited over the leaves of a plant known to native lore and the body of the woman is rubbed with them. Or such leaves are set on the head of the woman and thumped with the fist in the effort to drive the fetus from the body. Should such magic fail, there is a timid and inexpert attempt to manipulate the child. The same magic is used should the Trobriand woman fail to expel the afterbirth. In this case, however, one method is used with perhaps questionable results. Spells are recited over a stone which is tied to the mother's end of the navel cord. She is then made to stand. Malinowski says, "If that does not help, they are at their wit's end, and the woman is doomed, as they do not know how to extract the afterbirth by manipulation."...

In many cultures the rise of complications in delivery often calls forth both impractical and brutal methods to facilitate birth. In some of the groups in the Philippines a delayed delivery involved a complex remedy. The parturient woman lay on the floor and a cloth was passed around her body so as to bring pressure on the fundus of the uterus. Two persons sat on each side of the woman holding the ends of the cloth and pressing their bare feet against her abdomen. As she gave evidence of labor pains, the cloth was pulled tight and the feet were pressed into her body. A fifth attendant stood by ready to grasp any part of the child that appeared. The child was seized and vigorously drawn forth regardless of consequences. Should this forceful method fail, still further punishment awaited the unfortunate woman. A description from the Visayan of the Central Philippines suggests the former use of a long plank which was placed across the abdomen. The assistants, in a kind of teeter-totter, worked pressure against the patient's body. It is said that this method was usually effective except in breech presentations. In such cases, the assistant, usually a man, made an attempt to turn the fetus. Under such vigorous treatment it was virtually impossible for the mother or the child to escape injury.

The same Philippine groups promoted the expulsion of the placenta in much the same way. If the process was delayed the umbilical cord was seized by an assistant and jerked. The traction is said to have been so violent as to tear away portions of the placenta, leaving others in the uterus as a dangerous or fatal source of infection. C. S. Ford has reached the conclusion that fatalities resulting from treatment of this kind may, in many cultures, have been effective in curtailing any explorations into the field of surgery. The Central Philippine instance cited above is such a rarity that even its authenticity may be subject to some doubt. Some societies, it is true, do permit the midwife to tug gently on the cord should the placenta be delayed. Further tampering is only occasionally allowed by the many primitive societies of the world....

For all primitive peoples prolonged labor or the failure of the placenta to appear offer great difficulties. Since obstetrical surgery is apparently a rarity it follows that other methods must be utilized. Massage, as has been indicated, is known to a good many cultures and it would seem that there are few societies without their quota of skilled natives. While it is true that midwifery may be surrounded by magic, sorcery alone may be employed when other methods are exhausted. The skill of the primitive obstetrician may be clearly seen among the Atjeh of Northern Sumatra and among the peoples of the neighboring island of Nias. In both of these societies, and indeed, in Indonesia generally, the midwives, possessing considerable practical skill, attempt to determine the position of the fetus. Should this be unfavorable to an easy delivery, the patient's body is massaged and at birth an attempt is made to turn the fetus....

...A question of interest arises when the surgical means devised by various primitive peoples to facilitate delivery are considered. Such a concept as that of the Caesarean operation is very rare but does occur in a few primitive societies. The fullest description of this operation comes from the Baganda of Uganda where, in 1876, it was witnessed by the explorer and physician, Felkin. The patient, a woman of twenty, bearing her first child, was placed on an inclined table. She was in a semi-intoxicated state, having been liberally plied with banana wine or beer. The surgeon and his assistants were clustered about her and muttered incantations over the patient and the knife. As the operation began, the surgeon uttered a shrill cry which was taken up by a crowd of spectators clustered about the hut. In a single incision, commencing just above the pubis and ending a bit below the navel, the abdominal wall and part of the uterine wall were laid open. An assistant touched the bleeding parts with a hot iron. A second incision opened the uterine wall. As this was done, an assistant held the incision open with both hands. The child was quickly removed, the cord cut, while the surgeon went to work to extract the placenta. In so doing, he kept firm hold of the uterus, retaining his hold until the organ was contracted. The patient, after undergoing further applications of the hot iron to prevent hemorrhage, was turned gently to her side to allow the escape of the fluids in the abdominal cavity. The edges of the peritoneum were then brought together and the abdominal wall was sutured. Seven brightly polished iron nails were used, placed like acupressure needles, and bound together with a string made from bark-cloth. Over this was placed a paste made from two different roots chewed and spit into a bowl. This was covered with a warm banana leaf and a bandage of native cloth. The patient showed pain at the insertion of the needles but was apparently quite comfortable after the operation. Felkin remarks that her pulse and temperature remained virtually normal. Between the third and sixth days the pins were gradually removed and the paste and bandage replaced. In eleven days the wound was entirely healed and the patient, with normal uterine discharge, was quite comfortable. The child was also apparently healthy.

So complex and successful an operation as the Caesarean has not been described for other primitive peoples in such detail. The Baganda instance, although the literature reveals only the above description, would appear to be not uncommon practice. An early account mentions that West Indian slave women might perform the operation on themselves. If this statement is true, the concept may again have been imported from Negro Africa. There are a number of peoples who possess myths of such operations. The Maori of New Zealand, for example, connect the Caesarean operation with a god. In the Maori myth, as well as a similar one which appears in New Guinea, the operation is always fatal to the mother....

When a delayed and difficult birth occurs among the various primitive peoples, the society is often confronted with the choice of permitting either the mother or the child to live. It may be generally stated that the decision is generally in favor of the mother. One reason for this is the view held by a great many cultures that the child is really not human, not a member of the community. Often it is not until initiation of some kind, such as the name giving, that the newborn child is regarded as part of the group. Hence an aborted fetus, a miscarriage, or a stillbirth usually require no special treatment of the fetus. Without funeral ceremony, it may be simply thrown aside. But when a birth is delayed and where the advantages of the Caesarean technique are unknown, it may become necessary to eject the fetus to permit the sparing of the life of the mother. Accordingly, a number of cultures have developed the concept of perforating and dissecting the fetus and removing it piecemeal. In ancient India, if the head of the fetus could be reached, embryotomy might be practised by pushing through the top of the skull with a hook. The mother was then subjected to a long period of medical care, including special diet. A number of the peoples of the ancient world, the Greeks, the

post-Christian Jews, and others had developed techniques of embryotomy....

All peoples are confronted with the necessity of separating the newly born child from the placenta. Hence each culture has had to develop some means of cutting the umbilical cord. The ways in which this is done are generally dependent upon any number of beliefs and attitudes towards the placenta and its relation to the child. Birth magic is often used not only to facilitate the delivery of the child itself but of the placenta as well. The careful disposal of the placenta, as well as the attitude which appears in some societies regarding the umbilical cord, indicate that many peoples exercise considerable caution in separating the navel string. Unless this is done properly, the child may in some way be caused to suffer. Only rarely among the primitive peoples of the world is the cord cut according to individual preference; much more frequent is the culturally prescribed method of severing the string and a traditional disposal of the afterbirth....

There is one aspect of the birth process which is deserving of mention and discussion as a highly significant point in the obstetrical practices of primitives. This is the question of abortion, around which, from society to society, some highly ambivalent attitudes circulate. Some societies, like our own, are highly opposed to feticide, but others condone and sanction it and have developed ways in which a woman may, with social approval, rid herself of an unwanted child. Nor, in such cases, is there a necessary connection with infanticide; it seems more often the case that those societies which permit abortion welcome children when they arrive....

In most cultures there has arisen a positive attitude toward the process of abortion. Since by this means the society is being deprived of a potentially useful member, some form of opposition may be said to exist. When it does occur with societal sanction there is generally a reason why approval is forthcoming. Among the Murngin of Northern Australia, for example, abortion is permitted if a woman conceives following a birth. Here is clearly an economic case; the life of the Murngin is such that extra children create a serious burden. Where abortion is forbidden, there may again be a ceremonial sanction. Among some of the African Bantu a woman who has procured an abortion can kill a man by lying on him. She can also endanger cattle and crops. The North African Kabyle formerly demanded the death penalty for a married woman who procured a miscarriage on the ground that she was depriving her husband of his rights to fatherhood.

Abortion in the cultures of the primitive peoples may reach considerable proportions of brutality. There is generally the dependence of drugs of some sort coupled with various mechanical measures. The South African Hottentot have several means of producing abortion. Decoctions of rabbit urine or of thorns may be used and there is also the custom of binding the abdomen tightly. More primitive are the practices of some of the Papuan groups where a woman may leap from a high place in order to promote a miscarriage. Abortion and infanticide do appear together among the Eskimo groups. Such mechanical means as pummeling the abdomen have been noted in many parts of the world. Some of the Ge tribes of the forest regions of South America bury the patient in hot sand and beat upon the sand with clubs over the woman's abdomen. In the Torres Straits region a woman desiring an abortion may climb a tree, bumping her stomach as she climbs up and down. In the Gilbert Islands a cord was wound about the body and beaten.

Whatever the reasons for the practice of abortion by a given group, it is clear that the primitive society has at hand virtually no means by which the success of the procedure can be assured. It is of interest to note that while obstetrical surgery as such is a rarity, abortions are much more widely known. It may be that abortion, performed voluntarily, may be further removed from the realm of magic than the natural process of birth. Individuals are willing to undergo pain and hardship to escape the burden of child-bearing but once the child is on its way the society appears less willing to subject one useful member and one potentially so to methods which can at best have been proved only relatively successful. The limitations on both surgery and abortion would seem to reflect this view rather universally.

# 33 The Limitation of Human Population: A Natural History

*Don E. Dumond*

The outcome of the reproductive process in human groups holds a key to the biological survival of the group, and to its genetic composition for as long as it is a viable society. Among the many factors that directly affect reproduction are the rates of disease and the efficacy of the society's medical system. Indeed, from one point of view the medical system may be seen as one basic device by which a society ensures its survival. The demographic patterns of the various types of human societies are of profound interest to anthropologists, and medical anthropology will have its contributions to make to human demography. In this chapter, Don Dumond brings to bear upon the question of present and future demographic trends our knowledge of past societies, and, in particular, the earliest mode of human group adaptation, hunting-gathering cultures. Dumond takes the conjunction of data from several disciplines to make his case: that the strong emphasis on the nuclear family as the basic social-economic unit of industrial society seems to signify a return to the importance it possessed in the earliest stages of human evolution, and that decisions regarding population control were made volitionally by the nuclear family in the ancient past no less than in the present—and this is a prerequisite for effective population limitation in the future. Dumond even suggests that the downturn in mortality and increase in fertility may have slightly predated the industrial and medical revolutions. Whether one accepts Dumond's intriguing hypotheses as reasonable, they are provocative of a new way of looking at the data of demography and of those aspects of medical anthropology that relate to it. Independent agreement with Dumond's hypotheses is found in another recent paper by a social demographer (Peterson 1975) in a critique of prehistoric demographic research. See also Chapter 8 by Cockburn and Chapter 9 by Dunn in this volume.

In demographic circles it has been commonly asserted that the long-term evolution of man was possible only because his high natural fertility permitted him to overcome the effects of an exceptionally heavy premodern mortality—mortality amounting to a loss before the age of reproduction of as much as 50 percent of all individuals born

Reprinted with abridgments from Don E. Dumond, 1975, "The Limitation of Human Population: A Natural History," *Science, 187*:713–721, with permission of the author and the American Association for the Advancement of Science. Copyright © 1975 by the American Association for the Advancement of Science.

(Davis 1955, Peterson 1969, Durand 1967, 1972).

A corollary of this same viewpoint is the conclusion that the direction and degree of change in human population size has been governed in preindustrial eras solely by mortality. It is this preconception that has been largely responsible for "transition theory," which holds that the so-called demographic transition of modern times is the result of a new response toward reduction of growth induced by the rising standards of living and health that have followed upon the industrial and medical revolutions (Freedman 1961–62).

Recent years have seen attempts to modify these opinions, however, on the part of historical demographers [for example (Carlsson 1966, Glass 1972, Wrigley 1968, Demeny 1968, 1969)], anthropologists [for example (Birdsell 1968, Nag 1962, 1973, Polgar 1971, 1972)], and others (Neel 1970), who base their views upon various data from their respective disciplines. Unfortunately, discussion of the question is hampered on the one hand by the difficulty of constructing adequate demographic arguments from evidence of populations long dead (Brothwell 1971, Angel 1972), and on the other by the fact that acceptable studies of hunter-gatherers or nonindustrial agricultural peoples are limited by the scarcity of such peoples still available for study whose lives have not already been drastically changed by the modern world. Nevertheless, my aim in this article is to recapitulate some of this evidence, and to argue from it not only that the recent reduction in population growth in industrial countries is not a new response but that it is the modern equivalent of a pattern of behavior that has characterized most of mankind over the past million years.

## NATALITY AND NATURAL SELECTION

Biological evolution of any population may be viewed as proceeding by means of an overproduction of young, a portion of which are then forced to die by factors essentially external to the population—predation, parasitism, and the like—or are forced either to emigrate or to die by competition with other population members for scarce resources. The survivors reproduce, and population-wide frequencies of advantageous and disadvantageous characteristics are changed. The most grossly density-dependent factor, overcrowding in relation to resources, leads not only to the outright death of some of the younger individuals who are eliminated in competition, but commonly

leads also to a general decline in fertility, apparently as the direct result of a slightly lowered level of nutrition that is otherwise not sufficient to seriously inhibit normal biological functions or behavior. Thus the total size of the population is limited both through reduction in natality and in deaths heaviest in the relatively young, while adult members of the population tend to remain in at least moderate health (Birdsell 1968:7, Slobodkin 1961).

Both the overproduction of young and the damping of fertility by slightly lowered nutrition provide the potential for a sharp population increase in the event of an increase in resources. It is this that permits rapid expansion of a species to fill a newly opened niche to which it is suited, and it is this that is absolutely necessary to any successful organism, in order to provide for recovery from the occasional nonroutine demographic catastrophies to which all natural populations are potentially subject.

What if a set of expectations based upon the foregoing is translated to the human societies that must be the closest modern equivalents of those of early men? It is true enough that a substantial number of the children in these societies die before the age of reproduction—at least a third of those born, in most cases (Weiss 1973:49)—largely as a result of disease, that is, parasitism. But while natural predation may be present in some situations, it is not a significant check to any known population; and although men fight one another with relative regularity, so that even unorganized and desultory combat might be argued to provide some selective pressure, it seems clear that such fighting has never consistently provided as much pressure as have childhood diseases. One of these elements, then, is uniformly significant, the other only indifferently so; together they may be considered the routine external selective factors.

But a serious reservation must be entered in respect to the dependent factor of the lethal intrapopulation competition for resources. In the first place, no examples are at hand of any hunting-gathering people whose population has routinely suffered year-by-year inroads by starvation; rather, their population sizes seem to have been consistently and significantly less than those that could be supported in normal years within the areas in which they reside and by the technologies which they apply. In the second place, the food-sharing propensities of humans and their tendency to imbue close relationships with affective content combine so that when starvation does threaten, it is the entire population, not simply younger and weaker individuals, who experience deterioration. For hunting humans, then, any consistent production of young substantially beyond that necessary to maintain a stationary population must serve in the long run not as a selective advantage, but rather as a serious hazard.

Nevertheless, it can be shown that human populations commonly are fecund enough to permit rapid growth in circumstances of especially favorable resources. Examples are legion: recovery from the effects of epidemics that have resulted in underpopulation, the rapid filling of newly colonized areas, and so on; and it has been suggested that the natural fecundity of human populations is sufficient to permit them to more than double in size in a single generation despite normal mortality (Birdsell 1957, Dumond 1965).

The model that must be adopted for early humanity, therefore, is one in which natality is in approximate balance, with mortality from natural and routine external causes, in which the stable population is of a size well within the normal carrying capacity of the region, and yet in which a margin of fecundity—unrealized fertility—somehow exists as a necessary safety mechanism.

## SOME VITAL PROCESSES AMONG NOMADIC HUNTERS

Indications are that the general state of health among modern hunting-gathering peoples not under close contact with the urban world is relatively good (Neel, 1970, Dunn 1968). Unfortunately, only in few cases is it possible to obtain adequate data regarding mortality, particularly that in infancy and childhood. One survey of available literature suggests that survival of more than half the population to age 15 is generally to be expected among untouched peoples (Weiss 1973: Tab. 7).

Especially telling is the carefully collected demographic information from a population of !Kung Bushmen of the Dobe area in Botswana. Studies of 165 women, in which their probable ages, their childbirth histories, and the probable ages at death of their parents were determined, led to the conclusion that the expectancy of life at birth was on the order of 32.5 years, with 60 percent of all born surviving to age 15 (Howell 1968).

Although low by modern health standards, these rates are high enough that had they been accompanied by natality at the level common in many developing nations, there would have been a Dobe !Kung population explosion of remarkable proportions, and for which there is no evidence. Rather, the average completed fertility—that is, the mean number of children born to women who survived to the end of the childbearing period at age 45 to 50 years, was no more than about five even before the increased outside contact of the past few years, a figure just sufficient to produce a stationary or very slowly growing population.

Evidence of similar population balance is available from other recent hunting-gathering societies (Birdsell 1968, Woodburn 1968: 244), and additional sources bear witness to a customary low natality among seasonally nomadic hunters (Carr-Saunders 1922, Krzwicki 1934). Furthermore, there seems to be every indication that the population levels are well below the maximum limit imposed by resources routinely available. Indeed, food is plentiful enough that among peoples such as these it has been suggested that social factors are more important in the control of population size and distribution than are resources (Woodburn 1968, Lee 1968).

These known examples do not serve to contradict the contention that before the modern era the balance between human survival and extinction has been a delicate one; for although mortality may seldom have been astronomical, natality has generally been only sufficient to provide for replacement. Contradiction is provided, however, in the factor that apparently contributes most strongly to that modest natality: the spacing of births, necessary both to accommodate activities normal to hunting-gathering peoples, and to provide for the nutrition of the very young, as will be explained.

The realization of the existence of such a need among hunters was articulated more than 50 years ago in consideration of reports dating about as much earlier (Carr-Saunders 1922, Krzwicki 1934). In one of its most specific formulations, it is said that the simple inability of a mother to carry more than a single child together with her normal baggage, and her inability to nurse more than one child at a time, imposing a minimum limit of 3 years between offspring (Birdsell 1968). Other evidence suggests the birth interval among nomadic hunting peoples is more commonly around 4 years (Deevey 1968, Sussman 1972, Hassan 1973).

One student of the problem has calculated the difference in work that would be assumed by a Dobe !Kung mother under various birth intervals,

**Table 1**  Effect of Birth Interval on Amount of Work Performed by Dobe !Kung Mothers Over a 10-year Period. [Constructed from Lee's data (1972, tables 14.4 and 14.5)]

| Work details | Birth interval in years | | | |
|---|---|---|---|---|
|  | 2 | 3 | 4 | 5 |
| Number of offspring after 10-year period | 5 | 4 | 3 | 2 |
| Number of years spent transporting two children | 8 | 3 | 0 | 0 |
| Number of years spent transporting fewer than two children | 2 | 7 | 10 | 10 |
| Average baby weight transported per year (kilogram) | 17.0 | 12.2 | 9.2 | 7.8 |
| Average baby weight (kilogram) times average distance traveled (kilometer) | 32,064 | 22,824 | 17,808 | 14,256 |

with the results summarized in Table 1. When one bears in mind that each woman travels an average of 4200 kilometers per year carrying her baggage and young children, the differences in labor expenditure are substantial (Lee 1972). Furthermore, the extra labor required for the provision of food for the young does not end when the child begins to walk for himself.

A probably equally compelling need for birth spacing is presented by the relative unavailability to hunting-gathering peoples of foods soft enough to permit weaning of infants at ages under about 2.5 to 3 years (Krzwicki 1934:127, Lee 1972). It should be stressed that this inability to care for more than a single infant at a time is not based simply upon observer's inference, but has been clearly articulated by the people themselves in case after case (for example, Howell 1968, Krzwicki 1934, Marshall 1970).

But given the recognized need for and presence of a relatively long interval between births, the mechanisms that actually effect it are not entirely clear. People of many societies practice postpartum sexual abstinence for a period of significant duration. In a number of cases these periods may in fact last as long as 2 years and more, although the great majority are of 1 year or less (Saucier 1972)—sufficient to result in birth spacing of no more than about 2 years. Although induced abortion has been shown to be well-nigh universal (Devereux 1967), it need not be thought to account consistently for the interval: among the Dobe !Kung, for instance, fetal wastage is reportedly too moderate to indicate a systematic practice of induced abortion (Howell 1968). One suggestion is that among these last people the lactation of 2.5 to 3.5 years serves to suppress ovulation, although it is admitted that evidence for any clear and complete suppressive effect of ovulation in human populations is most ambiguous (Lea 1972).

Among some hunting-gathering groups, evidence suggests that the rate of infanticide has been substantial (Nag 1973, with references therein); in particular, data concerning aboriginal Australians have been said to indicate its practice in between 15 and 50 percent of all births (Birdsell 1968, Krzwicki 1934). Infanticide was admitted by Dobe !Kung women in cases in which births followed too closely upon one another, although specific instances noted constituted little more than 1 percent of births (Howell 1968); it was, however, a topic treated with some secrecy, with men apparently suspecting women of practicing it more often than admitted (Spooner 1972:371). Some reports from other !Kung suggest it was probably not uncommon (Marshall 1970).

Whatever the means or combination of means employed by hunting-gathering peoples to effect the necessary child spacing, the evidence discussed seems to point to a situation very like the model referred to above: The total population of successful hunters is well within the bounds of available resources and remains at a near-stationary level, yet there is a margin of fecundity above the level of surviving births; this margin is held under control by conscious and personally applied mechanisms adopted to effect birth spacing.

If it can be presumed that the mobility- and baby-food-induced limitation upon the natality of relatively modern hunting-gathering peoples also applies to their Pleistocene counterparts, it will allow the projection of some fertility rates reasonable for earlier periods of human development. A series of hypothetical schedules of age-specific fertility rates is provided in Table 2, together with the actual rates for the Dobe !Kung.

## NATALITY AND CHILD TRANSPORT

Before I turn to early humans, I shall consider briefly some studies of monkeys and apes, although accurate demographic data collected under completely natural conditions are seldom available. In terms of their mobility, these forms are somewhat similar to human hunters, although moving according to different rhythms.

One study of baboons, based unfortunately on a very small sample, suggests that 40 percent of the offspring survive to the age of reproduction, and that young are born at the annual rate of about 550 per 1000 females of all ages—that is, at least as frequently as every second year for sexually more active females (Altmann and Altmann 1970). Gestation requires about 6 months, and nursing and transport of the young by the mother occupy 11 to 15 months (Hall and DeVore 1968), when she comes into estrus again and breeds.

Mountain gorillas have been reported to have a birth rate of about 250 per year per 1000 females, with intervals between young varying between 3.5 and 4.5 years. The infant is carried by the mother for about 3 years. About 40 to 50 percent survive to the age of sexual receptivity at 6 or 7 years. The chimpanzee is similar, with birth intervals somewhere between 3 and more than 4.5 years (McKinley 1971, Schaller, 1963).

In all of these cases, which may be taken to represent higher nonhominid primates generally, the mother physically transports her infant during much of the period of nursing; at the end of the period, care of the juvenile by the mother either ends entirely or is substantially reduced. Thus she is not faced with the problem of transporting more than a single infant at a time, and she is not faced with a continuing problem of the provision and preparation of food for her young. Birth spacing is, of course, under involuntary hormonal control (Simonds 1974).

For the early hominids even less information is available. It is thought that even before the advent of the Pleistocene, forms such as *Australopithecus*, now sometimes referred to as *Homo africanus*, had shifted to an omnivorous diet (Robinson 1963), implying a pattern of subsistence and movement closer to that of known hunters and gatherers than to that of ground-dwelling monkeys and apes.

Estimates of age at death of slightly more than 300 *Australopithecus* individuals—a sample within which, unfortunately, infant specimens are almost certainly underrepresented—average 18 to 23 years (McKinley 1971, Mann 1968). In one manipulation of the data, McKinley (1971) assumed an age of 11 for sexual maturation, and a period of about 6 years for infant dependency; a comparison of these figures with the data available on survivorship, corrected as nearly as possible to account for missing infant mortality, suggested to McKinley a birth interval of 3 to 5 years, significantly less than the probable period of total infant care (Ibid.), but one that would accord with a time of infant transport. The length of the fertile period is, of

Table 2   Annual Age-Specific Natality Rates (per 1000 married women). Schedule 4 is presumed to represent the highest natality feasible for relatively nomadic hunters. For simplicity, figures for births expectable to females over age 44 are here combined with those of age 40 to 44 years.

| Age (years) | Hypothetical schedules | | | | | | Dobe !Kung† (actual figures) |
|---|---|---|---|---|---|---|---|
|  | 1* | 2 | 3 | 4 | 5 | 6 |  |
| 15 to 19 | 300 | 250 | 200 | 200 | 150 | 100 | 46.5 |
| 20 to 24 | 400 | 350 | 350 | 300 | 300 | 250 | 260.5 |
| 25 to 29 | 500 | 400 | 350 | 300 | 250 | 250 | 205 |
| 30 to 34 | 400 | 350 | 300 | 250 | 200 | 200 | 174 |
| 35 to 39 | 350 | 250 | 250 | 200 | 150 | 150 | 120 |
| 40 to 44 | 250 | 200 | 150 | 150 | 100 | 50 | 64 |
| Average completed fertility among mothers over age 44 | 11 | 9 | 8 | 7 | 6 | 5 | 4.35 |

* Schedule 1 is based on data from 20th-century Hutterites, who are among the most fecund people known (Henry 1961, Eaton and Mayer 1953). †Modern, !Kung Bushman figures are from Howell (1968); their completed fertility before they had contact with Europeans is thought by Howell to have been about 5, so that their precontact natality may be assumed to be roughly approximated by schedule 6.

course, not known. The degree to which natality was under the control of an estrus cycle damped by nursing and child care is also unknown, but in view of some essentially human physical developmental progressions, such as in the teeth (Mann 1968), it is not farfetched to think that involuntary hormonal control of breeding was giving way at this time.

With the advent of the Middle Pleistocene and the hominids once referred to the genera *Sinanthropus* and *Pithecanthropus*, now more often termed *Homo erectus*, the developmental scene is clearer. The substantially modern postcranial skeleton seems to imply a development to maturity not significantly different from that of *H. sapiens*; a similar inference has been drawn from a consideration of the complex matter of cranial suture closure (Acsadi and Nemeskeri 1970). Such food refuse as is available, together with instances of the use of fire, suggests strongly that the pattern of subsistence, hence of seasonally nomadic movement and of infant transport, was essentially that of more modern hunting-gathering peoples. It therefore seems probable that the period of fertility and the reproductive system in general was substantially that of *H. sapiens*.

## A NATURAL HISTORY OF HUMAN VITAL PROCESSES

Ideally, evidence of mortality can be derived directly from skeletal remains. Yet practically speaking, even with large samples there are problems of deciding the extent to which a valid contemporary population is represented (Angel 1972). Misrepresentation of infant deaths is especially frequent (Vallois 1960), both because of differential survival of bones and because of different disposal measures practiced for corpses of adults or subadults and for those of small children. Valid age and sex determination can also be problems.

Despite these limitations, however, some samples are available that can be used in a tentative way. With the mortality suggested by these, and with some idea of the overall rates of world population growth before the industrial revolution (Durand 1967, Polgar 1971), it is possible to estimate the level of natality necessary to provide at least minimally for such an increase.

A recent study by Acsadi and Nemeskeri (Acsadi and Nemeskeri 1970) has focused in particular upon the history and prehistory of mortality, and offers the unusual advantages that comparable and systematic methods of age determination were used in assessing most of the populations, and that relatively detailed life tables were generated from the data.

Based on the life tables, some relevant survivorship schedules are plotted as curves in Figure 1. Curve A is based ultimately upon fragments of 22 individuals of *H. erectus*, of the subspecies formerly assigned to the genus *Sinanthropus*, which were recovered in excavations at the Chinese cave of Choukoutien, and probably date from the Middle Pleistocene (Acsadi and Nemeskeri 1970).

Curve B is based on the remains of more than 200 individuals recovered from the caves of Taforalt and Afalou in the Maghreb region of Morocco and Algeria, dating from the end of the Paleolithic or the beginning of the Mesolithic, at the end of the Pleistocene (Acsadi and Nemeskeri 1970). It would almost certainly be a mistake to assume this schedule to represent a typical nomadic hunting population, however, for the sample derives from the very period in which increased sedentation is demonstrated in the archeological record. Indeed, the systematic disposal of dead in a single location must of itself indicate a measure of residence stability, so that any cemetery must be suspected either of deriving from relatively sedentary folk or of providing only a haphazard mortality sample. The caution must apply also to the remains from Choukoutien, as well as to those from certain other series that are not dealt with directly here (Snow 1948, Johnston and Snow 1961). This problem of sampling the mortality of prehistoric hunters will be returned to.

Curves C and D are derived from the highest and lowest of the age-specific mortality rates from substantial series of skeletons of European agricultural peoples (Ascadi and Nemeskeri 1970). A number of other rates were eliminated from consideration here, simply because the collections on which they were based included no figures for deaths in early childhood. Indeed, even curve D may be suspect in that regard (Brothwell 1971, Angel 1972). In all curves, pooled data for both sexes is used, both for consistency, since separate information for the sexes is not available in all cases, and because it seems safer in view of the difficulty of accurately sexing immature skeletons and of the apparent tendency to wrongly identify the sex of even a proportion of older ones (Weiss 1973).

Table 3 presents estimates of the net reproductive rate (that is, the proportion of itself that one generation of females will produce) within a

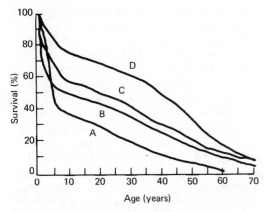

**Figure 1.** Survivorship derived from skeletal evidence, both sexes, constructed from the data of Acsadi and Nemeskeri (1970). (A) Sinanthropus (Ibid., Table 49); life expectancy at birth, 13 years. (B) Maghreb type derived from remains of late Paleolithic or early Mesolithic populations at Taforalt and Afalou (Ibid., Table 104); life expectancy at birth, 21 years. (C) Agriculturalists, composite data from 1st- to 4th-century Roman era population and 9th-century Frankish population (Ibid., Tables 121, 127); life expectancy at birth, 25 years. (D) Agriculturalists of the late Roman era (Ibid., Table 124); life expectancy at birth, 35 years.

stable population in which the females conform to the mortality curves of Figure 1, and to the natality rates of the separate hypothetical schedules of Table 2. For simplicity, an equal sex ratio is assumed. In succeeding sections I will trace the history of vital processes through several stages of human culture.

## EARLY HUNTERS

The world population of 10,000 years ago—the end of the Pleistocene and the practical beginning

of the era of more sedentary human living patterns—has been estimated at from about 3 to 5 million, the culmination of a long-term rate of increase averaging from 0.0007 to 0.0015 percent per year, and spanning 1 to 2 million years (Durand 1967, Hassan 1973). In the present discussion, a rate of increase sufficient to achieve this long-term result is taken to be represented by any net reproductive rate over 1.0.

Table 3 indicates that a population with a stable mortality of type A (Sinanthropus) and a stable natality such as that of the rates in schedule 4 (the highest probably feasible for hunting-gathering peoples if the assumptions regarding child spacing are correct) would replace only about two-thirds of its female population each generation. A population with such mortality among females could replace itself fully only with fertility approaching that of schedule 1, which is based on modern figures that are the highest ever recorded for a group of humans. It is therefore possible to conclude that the small Choukoutien skeletal collection almost certainly does not constitute a valid sample of *H. erectus* mortality (Acsadi and Nemeskeri 1970).

On the other hand, a population with mortality of type B (Maghreb) could maintain itself with a fertility similar to that of schedule 5. And a population with mortality similar to that of Dobe !Kung, which falls between C and D, much closer to the latter, would experience with the same natality a significant population increase, an increase which surely could not have been accommodated for any substantial period of time under stable hunting-gathering conditions.

What seems to be a weakness of the model developed here is that it presumes substantially all of the females of the population to be married at a very young age. However, it is clear from the anthropological literature that in nomadic hunting-gathering societies virtually all nubile

**Table 3** Net Reproductive Rates Calculated from Natality Shown in Table 2 and Mortality Shown in Fig. 1. It is assumed that sex ratios are equal and that all women are always married.

| | Natality schedules (Table 2) | | | | | | |
|---|---|---|---|---|---|---|---|
| Mortality (Fig. 1) | 1 | 2 | 3 | 4 | 5 | 6 | Dobe !Kung |
| A (Sinanthropus) | 1.05 | 0.87 | 0.78 | 0.69 | 0.58 | 0.50 | 0.43 |
| B (Maghreb type) | 1.89 | 1.56 | 1.39 | 1.21 | 1.02 | 0.88 | 0.76 |
| C (Agriculturalists) | 2.25 | 1.86 | 1.65 | 1.45 | 1.21 | 1.05 | 0.91 |
| D (Agriculturalists) | 2.81 | 2.70 | 2.41 | 2.11 | 1.75 | 1.52 | 1.31 |

females are married (with nubility frequently arriving before puberty), creating thereby the most important economic unit as well as the reproductive one.

Through the recognition of real kinship bonds, or through various more or less fictive kinlike ties, any such nuclear family is then presented a wide choice among other families with whom legitimately to affiliate and draw assistance in the face of fluctuating resources; despite any number of these affiliations, however, it remains a relatively autonomous unit (Krzwicki 1934, Service 1966, Steward 1955). Put another way, responsibility for the day-to-day business of maintaining life falls squarely upon the small family, parents and their children, hence the repercussions of overprocreation are felt immediately and inescapably by the procreators themselves; each couple is responsible for its own progeny.

As noted earlier, it has been suggested with some empirical support that humans have commonly been fecund enough that, when presented with unoccupied, favorable territory, they have been capable of doubling their population in a single generation—that is, of achieving a net reproductive rate of·2.0. From Table 3 it is evident that populations with mortality no heavier than that of type C, normally balanced by fertility equivalent to that of type 6, could without shortening birth intervals below about 3 years succeed in achieving a population growth at the rate of 50 percent per generation, if their natality were allowed to increase to that of schedule 4. As mentioned, this level is probably the highest ordinarily feasible for nomadic hunters (Neel, et al. 1964). Furthermore, if either mortality or the need for mobility were temporarily lessened for such people by an entry into new, rich surroundings, even more rapid growth (whether at the rate of 2.0 is not so certain) would be possible.

In short, an early hunting population with mortality no more stringent than that of type C might be expected to maintain itself and to possess at least a modest margin of unrealized fecundity, even if the need for child spacing is taken into account. In view of the data on the !Kung Bushmen, survivorship among most early hunters may have been substantially better than that of type C, providing an even greater margin of fecundity to be held in check by simple, consciously applied controls.

It is unfortunate and somewhat embarrassing that we have no convincingly complete sample of the mortality of any fossil population of hunter-gatherers. It would be foolish to argue that mortality as low as that of the single example of the Dobe !Kung was consistent either among modern hunters or their Pleistocene forebears. On the other hand, if the requirement for mobility and the resultant reduction in natality have been consistent and real, the relationships between natality and mortality that are summarized in Table 3 seem to hint that mortality was effectively no higher under conditions of hunting than under those of a more sedentary life, including agriculture. Indeed a probable increase in the level of parasitism in sedentary agricultural societies (to be mentioned shortly) may mean that the mortality rates of hunters were more often significantly lower.

## PREINDUSTRIAL AGRICULTURALISTS

It has been estimated that between about 8000 B.C. and A.D. 1750 the population of the world increased some 160 times, to around 800 million. To do this it doubled itself less often than once each 1000 years, achieving an average yearly growth rate of less than 0.1 percent (Durand 1967). Approximately this rate has been estimated for the Near East during the Neolithic (Carneiro and Hilse 1966); it is less than the rate of growth that is indicated in major countries after the beginning of the Christian era, which may over the long run have amounted to between 0.15 and 0.4 percent per year (Polgar 1972, Dumond 1965). Although these overall rates of growth are small when compared with some of those to be encountered in the modern world, they are drastically above that of the Pleistocene.

Several arguments have recently been made to the effect that sedentism itself is sufficient to promote population growth, simply by relaxing the need for movement and child transport (Sussman 1972, Lee 1972, Dumond 1972). Certainly it is with the Mesolithic era that the growth of settled villages can be generally observed. Then and later, efficient strategies of collecting seeds or coastal products are known to have been successfully employed by people with relatively high population densities. In some places what have been claimed to be true urban population agglomerations may even have been supported in this way (Kenyon 1960, Lanning 1967); yet in most favorable locations agriculture apparently followed shortly after the development of intensive collecting economies such as those that characterized the Mesolithic.

Whether one adopts a populationist notion of

the causes of agricultural development (Spooner 1972, Boserup 1965), or a more traditional or "neo-Malthusian" approach in which innovation in agriculture is conceived as bringing on population increase (Hassan 1973, Childe 1936), or one that is somewhere between the two (Dumond 1965, 1972), there seems to be no argument against the proposition that overall population growth and agriculture as a way of life have gone hand in hand. And with them have come increasingly ramified and exclusive family systems, possessed of increasingly complicated property arrangements and inheritance practices. These larger kin groups take over control from the nuclear family as the basic economic unit of society. Marriage becomes a union of these greater families, implying new adjustments of property rights. The management of power becomes a problem, specialists in its management appear. Classes emerge. An elaboration of religion, at times involving ancestral cults that extend kinship concepts outside the realm of the living, may provide a sacred rationale for a plentiful issue.

Certain prominent results of this changed way of life would seem to militate against population increase. In most agricultural societies there are a significant number of individuals of both sexes who never marry. The degree to which this is the case varies greatly from society to society, and no attempt at exhaustive review need be made. But, as an extreme example, the common Medieval European practice of impartible inheritance of land tended to accompany the development of the so-called "stem" family, in which only the heir to the property achieved sanction to marry and reproduce, while younger siblings remained unattached and unpropagating; in some cases fully half the nubile females were reportedly so removed from reproduction. Where lands have been divided among siblings, on the other hand, marriage has been less restricted, with fewer than one-fifth, and sometimes almost none, of the females remaining unmarried (Wrigley 1969, Birdsell 1957, Krzwicki 1934, Davis and Blake 1956). When marriages and attendant property settlements are negotiated by families there also frequently has resulted delay in marriage for those who do achieve it—this being a condition that will lower overall natality, of course, inasmuch as the total number of children produced is in approximately linear relationship to the age of females at marriage, when that age is between 20 and 35 (Henry 1961).

Nevertheless, it is almost a truism that agricultural endeavor has commonly tended to encourage high natality, because additional offspring are thought to be economic benefits (Krzwicki 1934, Nag 1972). Some students suggest that this tendency may be further increased where there are certain kinds of taxes levied by central governments—colonial or otherwise—making the perceived economic advantage of another offspring sufficiently attractive that it outweighs even a noticeable resultant depression of family living (Nag 1972, Geertz 1963). Furthermore, the existence of the more complex and economically dominant extended family, often reflected in an expanded, supranuclear family residence unit, tends to remove parents from direct responsibility for both the economic and the affective support of their own progeny, hence from direct and immediate experience of consequences of any excess in procreation. Whatever the factors most at work in specific cases, among married women the rate of natality increases, so that the average interval between births in preindustrial agricultural societies often approaches, if it seldom quite achieves, the low figure of 2 years (Wrigley 1969, Henry 1961, Whiting 1968:249).

Mortality is often suggested to have declined somewhat with the beginnings of agriculture, with the decline responsible for much of the estimated increase in the rate of overall population growth (Durand 1967, 1972, Acsadi and Nemeskeri 1970); such a suggestion has nevertheless been questioned by others (Polgar 1972). And although the survival curves of Figure 1 may seem to support it, the evidence for a decline in mortality is in fact sketchy, simply because valid evidence of mortality among hunting-gathering peoples is so difficult to come by. The level of disease must have increased with sedentary living and the accompanying crowding of population, and disease-caused mortality, at least, must have risen significantly. In preindustrial cities it was apparently especially high (Polgar 1964). For present purposes it seems more acceptable to conclude that mortality remained at least as heavy as it had been during earlier less sedentary millennia.

Meanwhile, any increase in natality, perhaps up to as high as schedule 3 in the long run, could provide for substantial population growth even though the age at marriage was raised, and even though a significant portion of females might be withdrawn from reproduction through failure to wed.

Despite the probability that agriculture as a way of life tends to promote the production of children as economic assets, it cannot be really surprising to find it shown by historical demographers that many populations of this sort purposefully limited their production of children before they ever felt the effects of the revolution in medical technology (Demeny 1968, Wrigley 1969). They must have done so, for in spite of the inhibiting social factors mentioned earlier, population increase throughout the era of preindustrial agriculture would otherwise certainly have exceeded the relatively modest overall rate it in fact achieved.

## AFTER THE REVOLUTIONS

The situation occasioned by the industrial and medical revolutions is familiar to all of us, and will be touched upon only lightly. In those countries participating directly in the industrial revolution, a sudden burgeoning of population was responded to by a drastic drop in natality, in what has been called the "demographic transition." The original view, that the population increase had been brought on by a sharp decline in mortality, seems to be modified now by knowledge that the actual population rise was triggered by an increase in fertility shortly before or contemporaneously with the advent of the industrial revolution, and significantly before any real decline of mortality through medical advances (Freedman 1961–62, Wrigley 1969; Compare with McKeown et al. 1972, Razzell 1974). Even as mortality was being drastically reduced by the medical extensions of the new technology, a marked downturn in natality occurred, the result of individual choices exercised regarding marriage and childbirth, the latter assisted by technological applications. Sociological explanations of the fertility decline include the point that the major functions of the old extended family were shifted to other specialized institutions, and that the decrease in mortality called for the production of fewer total offspring in order to provide a desired level of issue (Freedman 1961–1962).

While this may be true, I prefer to place emphasis on the return to primary importance of the nuclear family, with a renewal of its former status as the basic economic, affective, and residence unit (e.g. T. Parsons 1955). Except for the absence of any immediate need for the modern human mother to transport her offspring several thousand kilometers per year on her back or her hip, the position of the nuclear family within industrial society is remarkably similar to its position in societies of nomadic hunters and gatherers: as an autonomous unit it assumes direct responsibility for its own progeny.

Given the success with which human hunting populations regulated themselves for so long and in such nice balance with available resources, it should not be at all surprising on the one hand that the relatively high fertility of agricultural society was capable of being reduced substantially and rapidly to cope with the new needs of industrialization, and on the other that Western prosperity in the mid-20th century was often accompanied by a marked rise in natality.

The recent general rise in population in the industrially undeveloped countries is a rise that *has* clearly been brought about by extensions of the revolution in medical technology and has not been accompanied by a redefinition of economy and social life around the independent nuclear family. The presumed advantages of offspring to agricultural peoples have continued within the general perception, and total numbers have swelled sharply with the new and improved level of survivorship. Increased communication and cooperation between modern and increasingly compassionate nation states have even, by leading to massive programs of international assistance and relief, decreased the punitive effect on individual procreators of their own steadily declining resources. Even should old, tried measures of abortion, infanticide, and the like be resorted to, the limits of their efficacy have been overshot. Where these measures may have been adequate for a population faced with a normal mortality of a third of all offspring in the first 15 years of life, they are not adequate at all for populations faced with child mortality a fifth of that. Furthermore, the imposition of official value systems of Western industrial nations have often caused the use of some of these older and once-practical measures of population limitation to be held criminal or at least thoroughly unacceptable.

This is the dilemma that is so often decried in articles like this one, where a resolution is both groped for and argued.

## SUMMARY AND CONCLUSIONS

In this article I have suggested that overproduction of offspring by early human populations would have tended to work to the selective disadvantage of the entire society, but that, nevertheless, a permanently successful society requires some margin of unrealized fecundity with which to respond to any catastrophic decreases in size. If this is true, without involuntary hormonal control of breeding and in the absence of a clearly effective damping of ovulation by lengthy lactation, it must also be true that people of successful societies have always limited their natality below the level of their reasonably achievable fecundity.

Among early hunters, the strongest motive for keeping this margin of possible births unrealized apparently lay in the need experienced within each nuclear family to space births in order to permit the mother to perform the tasks expected of her. This motive probably existed throughout the Pleistocene, and would have resulted in relatively consistent efforts by individuals to space their offspring.

With the advent of sedentary life, this motive for child spacing was considerably weakened. Residence in extended families tended to remove parents from direct economic and affective responsibility for their own issue. Among agriculturalists, in particular, children have generally been considered an economic advantage, and this has encouraged some increase in fertility rates, although natality has at the same time been inhibited by a rise in age and a reduction of the proportion of the women who married. Under conditions of centralized rule, social stratification, and colonialism, demands of rulers for taxes and rents may often have served to promote a further labor intensification and population increase. But seldom, if ever, has natality approached the maximum possible.

In these preindustrial cases, the rate of natural mortality was sufficiently high to have made the margin between tolerable and intolerable births relatively small, so that the number of births to be aborted or offspring to be disposed of by any single female were relatively few, whatever her motivation. Although it may be technically correct to say that mortality served as the chief controlling factor of population dynamics—simply because natural deaths before or during the period of reproduction took away a far greater proportion of the population than was prevented or removed by conscious population limitation measures—it seems more meaningful to argue that the significant margin of control lay in voluntary measures.

Furthermore, and despite some arguments to the contrary, the evidence provides no clear support for any general decline in human mortality before the industrial and medical revolutions. I suggest rather that there was no consistent decline until around A.D. 1900; that earlier population fluctuations were the result of fluctuations in natality at least as often as they were of short-run variations in mortality; and that a regular component in the natality rates was voluntary intent. Thus it is unreasonable to argue as has been done that human beings, alone among living organisms, have failed to develop any density-dependent mechanisms of population control (Boughey 1973). Rather, their primary density-dependent mechanism is the most flexible there is, the only device flexible enough to suit the needs of the enormous variety of societies of humans, and a device that is consequently subject to considerable short-run aberration—that is, self-consciousness and volition.

Decisions regarding population limitation have been highly personal ones made by individuals not so much upon the basis of broader long-range subsistence questions or of community policy as upon considerations regarding the amount of short-run effort they are able and willing to invest in each child. It is no doubt fair to say that there have always been families larger than average, willingly produced by parents who accept the added burden. In the modern industrial world, despite the evident current fad for zero population growth as an abstract ideal, the most cogent consideration will undoubtedly continue to be whether the production of another offspring is worth the investment of time and money for the care and education that is now demanded for full social membership. Thus the position of the potential parent is directly analogous to that of the adult in a hunting-gathering society, in which the question is whether the child is worth the extra labor in transport and the preparation of food, or the risk of depriving a sibling of milk. In both, the cost of children to parents is high. And in either case the decision is a personal one that may be expected to vary somewhat between individuals, regardless of the similarity of their particular histories or of their cultural surroundings.

Although a similar choice is made in modern agricultural societies and in developing countries, the limits of the decisions are different simply because the cost of children to their immediate parents is still low: portability is not a factor, neither is education, and the general decline in living is spread among everyone. The choice may be expected to change significantly only as the direct cost to each parent of each child—in effort, in money, or in anguish—rises.

This is an argument that a change in values and social organization is the key to a change in the present upward population trend, but it is by no means an argument that improved birth control technology is not similarly important (Davis 1967, Polgar 1972). For modern mortality reducing measures have vastly increased the numbers of family limitation decisions that must be made; to assist in this, improved technology is indispensable.

There has been a tendency for demographers to assume that all preindustrial peoples have possessed values similar to those of modern, predominantly agricultural, underdeveloped nations, with high fertility and high mortality. I have tried here to argue briefly that this has not been the case,

that, indeed, the outlook of humans for most of their career as a species has been rather different, and that their behavior in industrial nations has been more like a return to that of our earlier evolutionary history, than a uniquely new development.

In most cases where growth of population has occurred, it has been both recognized and tolerated. The modern growth of population will be slowed permanently only to the extent that in the judgment of each individual, whatever his background, extra children are worth less than they will cost in time, in effort, in money, in emotion—or in the threat that is posed by their very existence.

# X
# Pain, Stress, and Death

## Pain, Stress, Death, Cultural Conditioning, and Environmental Pressures

Stress and pain exist in all societies and, in a very basic sense, are part of the human condition. What is important for people is what kinds of responses to pain and stress they learn to make as a result of growing up in a particular environment and culture. Whether the response is adaptive may decide the ultimate fate of the individual and the group. The only societies without stress exist as wished-for utopias or as the smoothly functioning, effortless, nearly passionless social orders constructed for our entertainment by writers of science-fiction. Disease and illness are usually exemplified by pain of some kind and may be considered as responses to stress, whether the stress results from attacks of micro-organisms or human or spiritual agencies. Stress may be grouped broadly into two categories: *acute* stress of relatively brief duration and with relatively clear concomitants and resultants, and *insidious* stress of rather longer duration (weeks, months, years, a lifetime) having long-range, cumulative but less clearly certain effects on the organism. Humans may experience stress from almost any aspect of their environment, culture, social organization, or organisms.

In the field of psychosomatic medicine it is accepted that many pathological responses may involve, for instance, the endocrine system, one or more organ systems, the circulatory, respiratory, or gastrointestinal system, and all may have had their origins either in acute or insidious stress. Not infrequently in the case of insidious stress the individual is not aware of why he is stressed, or that he is suffering its effects over prolonged periods. Dramatic proofs of these kinds of effects have been demonstrated in many clinical and laboratory studies where experimentally induced stress will initiate anxiety (not always consciously) in the human or other animal and stimulate what Harold Wolff called a "protective-adaptive" response because it activates latent feelings and fears that were themselves developed through coping with long-term stress processes.

In a normal state everyone is subjected to stress processes and, when it is working effectively, the General Adaptation Syndrome, as Hans Selye (1956) has labeled his broad concept, mobilizes the defenses of the body to deal with local or long-term stress. The manifestation of this defensive mobilization may be disease, but in this context disease is seen as itself an adaptive mechanism, and a healthy organism "lives through" this kind of adaptive response, becoming its master instead of its victim. In a physically or psychologically unhealthy (that is, inadequately prepared) organism, however, the normally adaptive response of disease itself becomes dominant and the body or mind succumbs to its attack. As Wolff, Selye, Cannon, Cobb, and many others have demonstrated, infectious and chronic diseases frequently, perhaps usually, have social, cultural, and psychological components. Thus, in the case of tuberculosis, as René Dubos has demonstrated cogently, the forces of stress at work that are responsible for the particular incidence of the disease in any one population and period may be seen—in fact may only be understood—on the levels of history, geography, economics, social structure, and culture (see Chapter 2 in Section I). Dubos has suggested that everyone probably harbors the tubercle bacillus but that only some become diseased, those whose resistance has been lowered by stressful conditions of life.

The delicate hormonal-neural steady state that enables the organism to survive and enjoy life may be upset by any of a number of stimuli, internal and external, ranging from the assault of a micro-organism to the loss of a job or loved one or unresolved problems of love and identity. As Selye's work has indicated, in terms of disease, stress may be considered a specific syndrome that is nonspecifically induced, and that usually provokes a nonspecific reaction. He tells us: ". . . Only a few signs and symptoms are actually characteristic of any one disease; most of the disturbances are apparently common to many, or perhaps even to all, diseases" (1956:15) and, therefore, in their early stages most diseases are not easy to distinguish. Selye has also demonstrated that when the organism is under *general* stress, many inflammations that ordinarily would occur in *local* areas do not occur since the adaptive response is massive and total, and thus, interestingly, local response is inhibited. This knowledge was the empirical, though little understood, basis for such early forms of treatment as induced fever to treat syphilis. Thus, too, the well-documented observation that soldiers in the heat of combat are unaware of minor, or often serious wounds, but the further observation that, as exposure to death or injury is prolonged, intense concentration on the body's safety occurs and hypochondriacal attention will be paid to small or even imagined hurts. (This latter observation makes it clear that the nature and effects of prolonged stress are quite different from those of sudden and intense stress).

In addition to insidious stress that affects the individual and family, one may also consider slow cumulative stress that affects larger social units. Here the level of analysis is necessarily cultural, social, and for some problems historical and economic, though, of course, the consequences may be measured either by social or psychological (that is, personal) indexes. It is perhaps worth keeping in mind that humans may be affected not only by actual dangers but also by symbols of dangers actually experienced or imagined, as Wolff, Freud, and others have pointed out. Furthermore, an individual or his group may be affected by symbols of the stressful experience of others, but which they have not ever themselves experienced. Only the people of Hiroshima and Nagasaki experienced the effects of the atomic bomb, but the world has lived in its mushroom shadow ever since.

In the chapters that follow we consider a number of questions relevant to our subject. The first one examines ethnographic and experimental evidence (though not all in either category) that bear on the experience of pain. Here the question for medical anthropology is, to put it in Zborowski's (1952, 1969) phrasing, what are the cultural components of responses to pain? How is pain experienced in various cultural groups? In the next paper we find that the stresses resulting from nutritional deficiencies may be the cause of many kinds of diseases, although I would suggest a good many more cultural and social factors are probably at work as intervening variables in the etiological chain. But the paper is important for its ecological perspective and because it brings a huge mass of data on this question into focus. It ought to be read as well in conjunction with the papers in Sections II and III. Finally we encounter the interesting phenomenon of magical death, one that we may place under acute stress. What such studies tell us is that stress may not only physically damage the human organism in many ways but that under specified social-cultural conditions it may inflict psychic pain, anxiety, and fear so difficult to bear that the victim seems to have no recourse except death itself. This kind of culturally induced stress succeeds in forcing the person to cooperate in his own extinction.

In Section XI we shall encounter several studies that deal with still another corollary and consequent of social-cultural stress: intense emotional states that accompany behavioral disturbances, how these arise under various social-cultural-historical conditions, and how they are coped with in various cultures and social systems.

# 34 Cultural Factors and the Response to Pain

## B. Berthold Wolff and Sarah Langley

The sensation of pain is a universal human experience. It has been suggested that even embryos seem to respond aversively to noxious stimuli. Perhaps the only exception to the human experiencing of pain are those rare individuals who either genetically or congenitally come into the world possessing nerve-endings insensitive to hurtful insults and injuries. But, we may ask, given the overwhelming, at times over determining influence of culture, are there differences in response to pain not only on an individual level (this seems to be clearly established), but on the basis of inculcation with the world view, values, and perceptual screen supplied by virtue of membership in a particular cultural group? Until recent years the evidence from anthropology was fragmentary on this point, with at least some ethnologists succumbing to the notion of some missionaries, travelers, and other laymen (and even some medically trained persons) that "primitive" peoples tend to be less sensitive to pain than "civilized" ones. The facts, if carefully assessed, turn out differently. Indeed, whether a people are more or less sensitive to pain—or express a pained response—depends, among other factors, on whether their culture values or disvalues the display of emotional expression and response to injury. Thus, if women in a particular society do not *seem* to be experiencing obstetrical pain, it could mean that their culture places a premium on the

appearance of stoicism and forbearance under travail (see Section IX).

The much anthologized paper by Zborowski (1952) "Cultural Components in Response to Pain," and his later publication of the complete report (Zborowski 1969) seemed to demonstrate dramatic differences in response to pain according to whether the subject is of Italian, Jewish, Irish, or "Old American" ethnicity. The present review of relevant studies by B. Berthold Wolff and Sarah Langley qualify Zborowski's findings somewhat, present other observational and experimental data, and conclude in their abstract (not included herein) of the original version of the paper as follows:

The few existing experimental studies yield equivocal results as to the significance of such factors [as ethnicity] and suffer from anthropological naivete. On the other hand, only one anthropological report dealing specifically with this problem was found [Zborowski's], but it lacks experimental control of pain. Consequently, the question as to whether or not there are basic differences between ethnocultural groups in response to pain remains unanswered. However, there is some experimental evidence that attitudinal factors do influence the response to pain within cultural groups. There is need for the cultural anthropologist to combine forces with the medical investigator in order to add to our knowledge about the pain response.

This study appeared one year before Zborowski published his complete report. My own feeling, as an anthropologist, is that Zborowski's study is anthropologically (if not experimentally) sound. However, one of my students in medical anthropology recently surveyed the experimental and other evidence since 1967 and concluded that the more recent material "does not suggest any contradictions or amendments to Wolff and Langley's conclusion" (Bennett 1975:8).

Reprinted with abridgments from B. Berthold Wolff and Sarah Langley, 1968, "Cultural Factors and the Response to Pain: A Review," *American Anthropologist*, 70:494–501, with permission of the authors and the American Anthropological Association.

The response to pain is certainly an important component of human behavior and thus deserves study by anthropologists. It is, therefore, with distinct disappointment that one searches the literature for material on the influence of culture on the form of response to pain. Tangential references to pain are often found in anthropological studies, but there appears to be a dearth of published reports specifically concerned with cultural factors and the human pain response.

Pain is the most common symptom of disease or injury as well as the most frequent aversive stimulus for manipulation of behavior. Physicians are concerned with the alleviation of pain, while educators, psychologists, and sociologists have studied the deterrent effects of pain in child development, on adult behavior, and in penology. Furthermore, aversive and noxious stimuli, especially electric shock, are administered almost routinely in most experimental psychological laboratories, although it is curious that usually the resultant pain sensation is not directly studied.

In medicine and physiology, philosophical theories of pain have existed for thousands of years and are still met in hedonistic attitudes and in psychoanalysis. Systematic scientific studies of pain probably did not begin until Schiff in 1858 made the definitive formulation that pain deserves to be placed in a sensory category of its own, later confirmed by Funke (1879). A great impetus for the study of pain was the discovery of pain sensitive points in the skin by Blix (1884) and Goldscheider (1884). Since then neuroanatomists and neurophysiologists have been actively engaged in pain research. However, their investigations have been focused on somatic rather than behavioral aspects of pain. Apart from nonexperimental theorizing by philosophers and psychoanalysts, usually utilizing some variation of the hedonistic pleasure-pain principle, there have been few experimental behavioral studies of pain until comparatively recently. Modern systematic behavioral studies commenced with the work of Hardy, Wolff, and Goodell (1940, 1952). Their work utilized psychophysical principles, but they were not primarily concerned with the study of cultural and psychological factors on pain sensation and reaction. Beecher (1959) strongly criticized Hardy, Wolff, and Goodell as he considered that they did not take into account the psychological aspects and subjective nature of pain.

Beecher has played a very important role in modern American clinical pharmacology by repeatedly emphasizing the importance of double-blind procedures and use of placebo in the study of analgesic drugs (1959). Clinical pharmacologists are thus well aware of placebo effects in analgesic assays. Nevertheless, current pharmacological studies on the whole fail to take cognizance of cultural and psychosocial effects, such as the patient's cultural group membership, socioeconomic class and expectation of treatment (Wolff 1967).

The research investigator is more concerned with the physical nature and somatic basis of pain than with psychosocial and cultural components. The practicing physician, on the other hand, tends to be aware of psychosocial and cultural components in the human pain response; his clinical observations have made him realize that there are ethnic and cultural differences in patients' responses to pain. However, the paucity of adequately controlled experimental studies in this area is remarkable. In fact, with few exceptions, our knowledge of cultural and psychosocial differences in the human pain response is based on empirical rather than experimental evidence.

The Pain Group of the Department of Medicine of New York University Medical Center has been investigating behavioral mechanisms of human pain for some years. Initially, the group developed objective psychophysical techniques for measuring cutaneous and deep somatic pain (Wolff and Jarvik 1964, 1965), and for evaluating analgesic drugs (Wolff, Kantor, Jarvik, and Laska 1966). More recently the group has studied the effects of certain psychological variables, such as suggestion, upon pain (Wolff, Krasnegor, and Farr 1965; Wolff and Horland 1967). An impressive fact, emerging from investigations involving a large number of healthy individuals and patients with arthritis, has been the difference in the pain response due to ethnocultural factors. This difference resembled that observed by clinicians among patients in pain. A review of publications dealing with the effect of cultural variables on pain was, therefore, begun. Initially, this review focused on experimental studies published in scientific journals within the general areas of medicine, physiology, and psychology. We were astonished to observe that in the field of experimental algesimetry there is almost a complete lack of published papers discussing cultural factors. Thus, the literature search was extended to the field of anthropology, but here the yield was even poorer. Consequently, we decided to assemble the few isolated published experimental studies into this review paper. Our purpose is twofold; namely, to inform other investigators of the current status of work in this area, and, more hopefully, to stimulate interest among anthropologists in the experimental study of human pain.

Chapman (1944) and Chapman and Jones (1944) compared the pain responses of 18 Southern Negroes with those of 18 Americans of North European ancestry (not otherwise specified), matched for age and sex, employing the Hardy, Wolff, Goodell (1940) radiant heat technique with stimulation of the forehead. They found that Negroes had a lower pain perception threshold (i.e., point at which pain begins) than the North Europeans, indicating that they are more sensitive to pain. Even more interesting was their finding that Negroes had a much lower pain reaction threshold (i.e., point at which the subject winces and tends to withdraw) than the North Europeans. Thus Negroes were able to tolerate much less pain and the range between their perception and reaction thresholds was much smaller than that for the North Europeans. Chapman and Jones in the same study investigated the role of skin pigmentation and concluded that the difference in pain responses between Negroes and North Europeans was unlikely to be due to pigmentation. These investigators also studied 30 Russian Jewish and Italian subjects (not specified in what proportion) and found that they tended to have pain perception and reaction thresholds similar to those of the Negroes, being much lower than those of the North Europeans. The Negroes, however, did not complain, while the subjects of Mediterranean ancestry complained loudly at pain reaction threshold. Chapman and Jones's overall conclusion was that differences exist in pain sensitivity and pain tolerance due to ethnic factors.

Meehan, Stoll, and Hardy (1954) compared 26 Alaskan Indians from Fort Yukon, 37 Eskimos from the Endicott Mountains and 32 whites from the Ladd Air Force Base. They also used the Hardy, Wolff, and Goodell radiant heat technique, but stimulated the back of the hand, instead of the forehead, measuring only the pricking pain threshold (i.e., point at which a pricking sensation is first noticed). They found that the whites and the Indians had similar, but the Eskimos higher, pain thresholds. However, after applying a conversion formula to correct for skin temperature, they found that the whites had the highest and the Eskimos the lowest pain thresholds, but these differences were not statistically significant. Meehan et al., in another study, used a modification of the radiant heat technique and with it compared four whites to 16 Eskimos. Once again they found the differences

in pain threshold after temperature correction to be insignificant. They concluded, therefore, that there were no significant differences in pain threshold between these three ethnic groups.

In a recent study in England, Merskey and Spear (1964) compared the pain reactions of 28 white and of 11 Afro-Asian male medical students. They used the pressure algometer, a simple mechanical device for experimental pain induction by pressure, which is placed against a hard, bony surface, such as the shin or forehead. Pressure is gradually exerted until the required pain responses have occurred. They found that there were no significant differences between the white and Afro-Asian students in the verbal report of pain (i.e., pain threshold), the pain reaction point (i.e., when the subject stated that it hurt a lot), and the reaction interval (i.e., the difference between the verbal report to pain and the pain reaction point). Merskey and Spear concluded that there were no significant differences in the pain response between white and colored medical students of the same sex.

Sternbach and Tursky (1965) studied pain and skin potential responses to electric shock in 60 housewives, divided into four ethnic groups of 15 women each. "Yankees" were Protestants of British descent whose parents and grandparents were born in this country, most were from old New England families. All other groups consisted of women whose parents came to the U.S. as immigrants. The Irish and Italian groups were Roman Catholic, and the latter came mainly from Southern Italy and Sicily. The Jews were either Orthodox or Conservative and the majority came from Eastern European countries. There were no significant differences between groups for a variety of physical variables, such as age, height–weight ratio, etc. All groups fell into the same social "middle class" on the Hollingshead scale (i.e., class III), but the difference between Hollingshead scores of "Yankees" and Jews, on the one hand, and Irish and Italian, on the other, was significant at the 5 percent level. Each subject participated in an interview during which relevant personal information was collected. Several weeks later each woman returned to the laboratory for measurements of her pain responses and autonomic reactivity. Electrical stimulation was administered to the dorsal surface of the left forearm from a constant current source, and skin potentials were recorded from the right palm. Sternbach and Tursky found consistent differences among the groups, both at pain threshold and pain tolerance levels, but these reached significance only at pain

315

tolerance. Italian women differed significantly both from "Yankee' and from Jewish women. At pain tolerance levels, the "Yankees" had the highest mean scores, followed by the Jews and then the Irish, with the Italians producing the lowest mean scores. There were no significant differences between the groups in stimulus magnitude estimation, but "Yankees" produced a significantly more rapid and greater decrease in skin potential than the other three groups. Sternbach and Tursky concluded that attitudinal differences among these four subcultures accounted for the psychophysical and autonomic differences. "Yankees" tended to have a matter-of-fact attitude toward pain, while the Italians showed a present-time-orientation in respect to pain and thus focused on the immediacy of the pain. The Jewish housewives, being future-oriented, were not dismayed by the experimental pain and thus tended to resemble the "Yankee" and Irish groups, the latter being undemonstrative with respect to pain. Sternbach and Tursky utilized Zborowski's (1952) hypothesis to arrive at their conclusions. Zborowski's study will be discussed later.

Lambert, Libman, and Poser (1960) studied the effects of religious affiliation rather than of ethnic group on pain tolerance. They used the Hollander (1939) technique, which induces pressure pain by means of a blood pressure cuff into which hard rubber blocks have been sewn. This cuff is placed around the forearm and gradually inflated. The resulting pain responses are measured as pressure in millimeters of mercury. Lambert et al. used 80 female students, 40 Jewish and 40 Protestant, between 18 and 23 years of age. Each group was subdivided into an experimental and a control subgroup of 20 subjects each and given two administrations of the pain-inducing technique. In the first administration, which served as a base with similar experimental conditions for all groups, it was found that the mean pain tolerance scores for the Jewish groups were somewhat, but not significantly, lower than those for the Protestant groups. In the second, the experimental Jewish subgroup was informed that Jews could not tolerate pain as well as Protestants, while the experimental Protestant subgroup was told that Protestants could not tolerate as much pain as Jews. The original instructtions were repeated for the two control subgroups. It was found that on the second trial the experimental Jewish subgroup significantly increased its mean pain tolerance, whereas neither the Jewish controls nor the two Protestant subgroups showed significant changes

in their pain tolerance. Lambert et al. interpreted these results as indicating that Jews try to become more like the majority group when they are made aware of differences, whereas this is not true of Protestant groups.

In a second study, Lambert et al. used 160 female undergraduate students (80 Jews and 80 Protestants), and two experimenters, one of whom was obviously Jewish and the other obviously Protestant. The subjects were divided into three subgroups of 30, 30, and 20 respectively with the latter serving as controls. The first experimental subgroup was told that Jews (or Christians) could take less pain than Christians (or Jews), whereas the second experimental subgroup was told that Jews (or Christians) could take more pain than Christians (or Jews). The authors used the term "Christian" to emphasize a distinction between Jews and Christians that did not appear to have been present in their study when they used the term "Protestant."

Lambert et al. again found no significant differences between all six subgroups on the first trial. On the second trial the experimental Jewish subgroup, which had been told that Jews take less pain than Christians, again increased its pain tolerance significantly. However, the second experimental Jewish subgroup, previously informed that Jews take more pain than Christians, did not significantly increase its mean pain tolerance. On the other hand, both experimental Protestant subgroups (i.e., those told that Christians take less and those told that Christians take more pain than Jews) significantly increased their mean pain tolerance. The two control subgroups showed no significant changes between first and second trials.

The researchers concluded that Jews tend to increase their pain tolerance when told that Jews take less pain than non-Jews (i.e., the majority group), but are quite satisfied with the *status quo* when told that Jews can take more pain. On the other hand, when a religious difference is made explicit to Protestants they strive to increase their pain tolerance, even if they "know" that supposedly they can take more pain to start with. These results suggest that even if there are no basic ethnic differences in terms of pain response between groups, cultural factors, such as those relating to religious affiliation if made explicit, can impose a differential pain response pattern between Jewish and Protestant groups of the same sex, education, and socio-economic status.

Poser (1963) extended these studies, using a total of 88 subjects, divided into Jewish and Roman

Catholic groups. The Jews were subdivided into 22 Jewish students born in Canada and 22 Jewish immigrants, and the Catholics were similarly classified into two subgroups, each with 22 subjects. He also used a Jewish and a Roman Catholic experimenter and employed the Hollander technique. Poser's measure of pain tolerance this time was the difference between pain tolerance and pain threshold, which Wolff (1964) terms "pain sensitivity range" (PSR). With a Jewish experimenter the Jewish students had a significantly lower mean PSR than the Roman Catholic students. Similarly, the Jewish immigrants had a significantly lower mean PSR than the Roman Catholic immigrants. However, with a Roman Catholic experimenter, there was no significant difference between Jewish and Roman Catholic immigrants, the former having a lower mean PSR. Furthermore, the effect of a Jewish experimenter as compared to a Roman Catholic experimenter was significant only for the Jewish students. An analysis of variance indicated the ethnic origin of the subject to be a very significant factor with the ethnic origin of the experimenter being a significant second factor. However, citizenship and interactions were found to be nonsignificant. Poser concluded that there were cultural differences that are much more marked for immigrant groups than for native Canadians who were able to follow the behavior pattern of the majority group if made aware either explicitly or implicitly of ethnic differences.

These few studies appear to be the only published reports in which experimenters skilled in the application of experimental pain-inducing techniques specifically investigated the possible effect of ethnic or cultural factors on the pain response. It appears to be quite clear from the studies by Lambert, Libman and Poser (1960), Poser (1960) and Sternbach and Tursky (1965) that cultural factors in terms of attitudinal variables, whether explicit or implicit, do indeed exert significant influences on pain perception.

However, the results from the other studies reported here are inconclusive from an ethnocultural standpoint. The early study of Chapman and Jones (1944) does indicate ethnic group differences in the pain response between Southern Negroes and Americans of North European stock, but Meehan, Stoll, and Hardy (1954) obtained no significant differences between Alaskan Indians, Eskimos and whites. Since both groups of investigators used the radiant heat technique, their different findings can not be attributed to differences in method. However, Meehan et al. corrected their data for skin temperature, while Chapman and Jones did not. It is thus possible that had the latter also corrected for skin temperature, they might not have found significant differences. In any case, these two teams of investigators used different ethnic groups, and consequently their results would not be comparable even if skin temperature corrections had been applied to all data. It is thus not possible to draw any conclusion as to whether or not ethnic differences in pain response are detectable with the radiant heat method. Merskey and Spear (1964), using a completely different pain-inducing technique, found no significant differences in pain threshold and pain tolerance between the white and Afro-Asian medical students. Their study is important as they controlled for socioeducational level.

Care must be taken in evaluating these experimental results. Merskey and Spear's study is experimentally sound, but unfortunately they were able to compare only a very small number of subjects from an ethnocultural standpoint. Similarly, Chapman and Jones, in order to match Negroes and Northern Europeans for sex and age, had to reduce the number to 18 each, although they started with a total of 200 subjects, consisting of 130 Northern Europeans, 25 American Negroes, 15 Ukrainians, and a miscellaneous group of 30 Jews and persons of Mediterranean ancestry. Furthermore, the fact that Chapman and Jones did not correct their results for skin temperature poses another problem. There is a possibility that skin temperature varies among ethnoracial groups. If so, pain responses obtained with a thermal method, such as the radiant heat technique, should be corrected for temperature. Johnson and Corah (1963) obtained significant differences in basal skin resistance between 120 white and 54 Negro children as well as between 21 Negro and 21 white adults. This suggests that there may be basic differences for certain physiological skin variables between different groups.

Meehan, Stoll, and Hardy used a sophisticated formula for correcting skin temperature, yet their experimental conditions were completely different for their three ethnic groups as they themselves point out. The Eskimos were tested as a whole group in a tent at a temperature of $5°C$ with distraction to the subjects due to noise and conversation. Furthermore, an interpreter had to be used and it is not certain if the Eskimos fully understood the instructions. The Alaskan Indians, some of whom also required an interpreter, were

317

tested individually in a heated room. The white control subjects were tested in small groups of four and five in a heated room. Thus, from a strictly scientific point of view these results are not directly comparable, thus making generalizations risky.

Similarly, from the standpoint of the anthropologist, the validity of Meehan, Stoll, and Hardy's study is doubtful, as there was a distinct possibility that the white group was mixed in cultural background. The implied equation of race and culture, while doubtless unintentional, is, of course, invalid (Boas 1940; Benedict 1940). Their results indicated no significant differences in temperature-corrected pain thresholds for Indians, Eskimos, and whites; and they concluded that behavioral differences among these three groups are culture-bound.

Therefore, none of these experimental pain studies allows a definitive conclusion as to whether or not there exist basic differences in pain response among ethnic groups. On the other hand, there is strong experimental evidence that attitudinal factors tend to influence the pain response of different cultural groups.

The paucity of published studies in anthropology dealing specifically with pain has been mentioned previously. Apart from the many indirect and tangential references, Zborowski's (1952) study appears to be the only one in anthropology pertinent to the theme of this review. Zborowski distinguished between self-inflicted, other-inflicted, and spontaneous pain. He defined self-inflicted pain as deliberately self-inflicted, such as self-mutilation, whereas other-inflicted pain is that incurred in culturally accepted and expected activities, such as fights, sports, war, etc. Spontaneous pain denotes that resulting from disease or injury.

It would seem that Zborowski created conceptual and semantic difficulties for himself by attempting to distinguish between "pain" as a basically physiological phenomenon and the "pain experience," which has emotional components. This distinction between the physiological and psychological components of pain has been made frequently (e.g., Beecher, 1959), possibly because there is still no generally acceptable all-inclusive scientific definition of pain (Lewis 1942; Beecher 1959). However, it appears to us that conceptually pain sensation and pain experience are at different connotative levels. The pain experience is a higher order concept than pain sensation and would seem to include the latter. Semantically, it would have been more meaningful to use the terms pain sensation and pain reaction instead of pain and pain experience. It is unfortunate that there exists no general terminology for pain, thus frequently leading to confusion in the literature, especially when different studies are compared (Wolff 1964). We would like to suggest that, in any case, it is not too rewarding for the behavioral scientist to attempt to differentiate between physiological and psychological components of pain, but to recognize that both components contribute to pain, pain reaction, pain experience, or whatever terms are used. It is, of course, very true that pain response parameters differ in their loadings of physiological and psychological components (e.g., Gelfand 1964). The behavioral scientist should concern himself with evaluating the effects of affective, autonomic, cognitive, cultural, psychosocial, and similar factors on the pain response and thereby add to our understanding of pain.

Zborowski (1952) studied clinical pain qualitatively in 103 subjects (87 hospitalized patients and 16 of their healthy relatives or friends), but restricted his main comparisons to 26 "Old Americans," 24 Italians and 31 Jews. Zborowski indicated that the hospital staff tended to uphold the "Old American" tradition in which pain is reported but few emotional side reactions are permitted. Hospital staff members stated that both Italians and Jews tended to overreact to pain, to be emotional about pain, and to complain excessively. Zborowski disagreed with this rather simple description of pain response in Italians and Jews. He found that Italians tend to call for immediate relief of pain by any means, such as drugs, and are happy when pain is alleviated. On the other hand, whereas Jews also seek relief of pain, they are skeptical or suspicious of the future and tend to keep complaining even after their pain has been diminished. Zborowski concluded, therefore, that Italians are present-oriented, and when in pain demonstrate present-oriented apprehension. Jews are future-oriented, and when in pain present future-oriented anxiety. "Old Americans" are also future-oriented but, unlike Jews, tend to be rather optimistic. When in pain, the "Old Americans" tend to withdraw socially, while both Jews and Italians prefer the social company of their relatives. Zborowski drew the following two conclusions: (1) similar reactions to pain demonstrated by members of different ethnocultural groups do not necessarily reflect similar attitudes to pain, and (2) reactive patterns similar in terms of their manifestations may have different functions in various cultures.

Zborowski's concern was less with recording differences in overt behavior among his groups than in preparing an analysis of the traits in each culture that contribute to the observed patterns. His approach is thus basically functional, paralleling that of Linton (1945) in the area of mental disorders, as is reflected in the latter's conclusion that similar patterns do not necessarily have the same function.

Opler (1961), expanding on Zborowski's findings, suggested that the excessive response to pain by Italian patients, male and female, may be due at least in part to a general preoccupation with bodily function and body image. He concluded that, by contrast, the stoicism of the Irish may stem in part from a tendency to pride themselves on disregarding the physical self.

In comparing well-matched male schizophrenic patient groups, Opler (1959) found that while the Irish are inclined to be nondisruptive, docile, given to fantasy and well-organized delusional systems, the Italian group tended to be more overtly emotional, unpredictable, and even assaultive.

It would appear from these studies that the response to pain for a given cultural group, such as the Italian, is similar irrespective of the underlying disease. Therefore, any attempt to delineate cultural factors in the pain response should be made within the wider context of cultural attitudes toward sickness and health. It is possible that religious attitudes, insofar as they influence the perception of the physical self, may also color the pain response. . . .

An effort was made to see if additional ethnographic material could be found. A missionary priest (Morice 1901:20–21), writing of the Déné, an Athabascan tribe of inland Alaska, stated that these people could tolerate extreme pain calmly and remarkably well for brief periods, provided it was accompanied by the hope of fast relief or recovery. He added, however, that prolonged discomfort was very poorly tolerated. An informant of ours, a registered nurse with a background of ten years practice among the Alaskan Eskimos, gives parallel information for this group, stating that when a favorable outcome is anticipated, pain is well tolerated, but that when the prognosis of the disease or injury is unknown, tolerance is notably poor. This supports the suggestion of Meehan, Stoll, and Hardy (1954) that the slightly lower temperature-corrected pain threshold obtained for the Eskimo was probably due to lack of understanding by them of the testing procedure.

An attempt has been made to show that although there is a wealth of anthropological material in which pain is discussed, there is nevertheless a paucity of studies in which the pain response and cultural factors are directly and experimentally controlled. The few experimental pain studies that do exist suffer from anthropological naiveté, while the anthropological reports lack experimental control of pain.

It is not being suggested that medical scientists become experts in cultural anthropology. What is being suggested is that the techniques of cultural anthropology can profitably be applied by those who would understand such aspects of human behavior as response to pain. Some knowledge of a patient's cultural matrix can, in all probability, provide the researcher with insight into the general form of that individual's behavior. In short, it can have both predictive and interpretive value. There is thus a need for the cultural anthropologist to combine forces with the medical scientist in order to add to our knowledge about the human pain response.

# 35 Ecology and Nutritional Stress

## *Marshall T. Newman*

The kinds of stress that cause immediate pain in humans generally tend to be of short duration, except perhaps for the sometimes slowly mounting stress produced by a lengthy but fatal illness such as terminal cancer. Other stresses are of a longer duration, cumulating over what may be several years, perhaps even most of a lifetime, and include the chronic diseases but also other factors such as malnutrition or undernutrition as well as other environmental effects. In this paper a biological anthropologist, Marshall Newman, reviews some factors that make for ecological situations that produce, or combine with, nutritional deficiencies either to result in certain diseases directly because of such deficiencies and/or to undermine the resistance of the human organism to a whole host of diseases. Indeed, there is now evidence that malnutrition may lead to brain damage and cause a lowering of intelligence, as well as possibly causing other disturbances in children of poverty-stricken

Reprinted from Marshall T. Newman, 1962, "Ecology and Nutritional Stress in Man," *American Anthropologist*, *64*:22–34, with permission of the author and the American Anthropological Association.

families. In some cases, the equation may be more complicated than it seems in Newman's article. For example, when Newman asserts that "...the areas of undernutrition and malnutrition closely coincide with the tropical and warmer temperature regions of backward food producing technologies," the missing factor in the ecology-nutrition-disease calculus could well be not so much the consequents of tropical or warm temperate climate directly but their combination with an exploitative situation where the foods produced by a people are consumed by others. In other words, there may be a correlation between these climates and imperialist domination, so that the amount and nutritional quality of food produced is not a measure of the amount and quality of food consumed by the food-producers, since they are drained off by economically more powerful forces. Thus, although agreeing with Newman that "nutritional stress in man has very strong ecological and cultural correlates," one should probably add political and historical correlates as well.

Beyond the quite considerable metabolic tolerance of man to dietary inadequacies lie extreme conditions of nutritional stress where health and physical status may be affected from prenatal life onward. Through either starvation or acute shortage of essential nutrients, severe nutritional stress may result in death, especially in the young. When less severe, it retards physical development, reduces vitality, and increases susceptibility to most infectious diseases. Nutritional stresses in man are clearly a reflection of his ecology, culture, and biology. The ecological factors of particular importance in this regard are the direct effect of climate upon dietary needs, the disease environment that must be endured, and the food producing potential of the living area. Cultural factors are reflected principally in food producing technologies, food preparation, differential distribution to the people, and food habits. Biological factors of major import are population dynamics and the degree of acclimatization and adaptation to stress conditions. All these factors focus upon man's food intake, which in fair measure determine who thrives and propagates and who does not in this rapidly changing world.

## CLIMATE AND NUTRITIONAL REQUIREMENTS

Quite apart from matters of food supply, the climate where humans reside has a direct bearing on their nutritional requirements. In cold climates, as Mitchell and Edman (1951:17–20) have shown,

caloric needs are increased to help keep the body warm and allow for extra energy expenditures such as imposed by the hobbling effect of heavy clothing. In man there is a linear increase of resting metabolic rates below the critical level 78°–81°F. air temperature, although this is partly mitigated by well-designed clothing and built-in biological adaptations. There is, nevertheless, a highly significant average increase in basal metabolic rates with decreasing ambient temperatures, as Roberts (1952:174) has shown. In addition to enhanced caloric needs in cold climates, an increase in fat intake is also advantageous in helping preserve body temperatures at tolerable levels. The clinical consequences of inadequate fat intake in the Arctic is the sort of "rabbit hunger" described by Stefansson (1956:31).

Vitamin-wise there is incomplete evidence, drawn partly from animal experiments, that cold climates slightly decrease the need for niacin and increase it for ascorbic acid (Mitchell and Edman 1951:32–33; Dugal and Fortier 1952:146). Increased requirements for dietary Vitamin D also characterize cold climate living, since clothing and cloudy skies reduce the amount of ultraviolet radiation received by the body.

Caloric needs decrease in warm climates, partly because of the smaller body mass that must be sustained and partly because extra dietary calories are not needed for body heating. There is, however, a slight increase in protein needs in the heat, possibly 5–10 gm. per day (Mitchell and Edman 1951:94). This may be wholly cancelled by smaller body mass and by other adjustments to a hypoprotein intake. There are usually small vitamin losses through sweating in hot climate people, but these losses are most inconsequential except in the face of decidedly low intake for a particular vitamin. There is, of course, an increase in water needs and a great increase in salt requirements, although fully adapted or acclimated peoples possess special physiological mechanisms fostering water and salt economy. Increased sweat and fecal losses in hot climate peoples also call for increased iron and, less certainly, calcium needs. Increased fat intakes in hot dry climates and other areas of marked atmospheric aridity may also be indicated.

## NUTRITION AND DISEASE

The bearing of disease upon nutritional status is summed up in the historic relationship of famine and pestilence. The diet-and-disease experiments on man and other animals clearly show that inadequate food intake increases the frequency and severity of most infections (Scrimshaw et al. 1959). There are only a few diseases such as malaria where inadequate diets serve some alleviative function (Scrimshaw et al. 1959:380–82). As Allison (n.d.) has indicated, malarial parasites do not thrive in human systems when hemoglobin levels are low because of grossly inadequate iron intake. Yet in such deficient hosts even a low parasite count may result in active malaria. But since dietary deficiencies are synergistic to many diseases in man, the actual cause of death in a poorly nourished individual may be in doubt. Unless special studies are made of the usual mortality records, credit is often given to some respiratory or gastroenteric disease that may in fact have only administered the coup de grâce.

## AGRICULTURE AND FOOD PRODUCING POTENTIALS

The food producing potential of a living area depends basically upon the fertility of its soils, whether used for cultivation or pasturage. Soil fertility depends upon the available macro-and micro-nutrient elements and their interbalances, interacting with the climatic factors of rainfall, temperature, and their seasonal qualities. It is quite impossible to make broad generalizations by world zone on soil fertility. Large-scale detailed maps are needed to show nutritionally meaningful differences in soils. Phillips (1960) was only able to reduce the soils of subsaharan Africa to some 40 type-regions on the basis of climate and vegetation associations. Each type-region has its own particular problem in agricultural technology.

In general, however, the vast tropical zone within the 64°F. coldest month isotherm and the <30″ annual rainfall isohyet has the poorest agricultural soils. Due to extensive leaching by heavy rainfall the tropics has many areas of very poor soils, although some more fortunate areas have very fertile soils. The best agricultural lands, on the other hand, are in the middle latitudes of temperate climate. In this broad zone the soils of only moderate development by a medium and seasonally well-distributed rainfall are superior. Other temperate zone soils are less satisfactory, being either drought-prone as in the mineral-rich prairie areas or overdeveloped as in the formerly heavily forested areas. Drought-prone areas are susceptible to crop failure and famine; areas of overdeveloped soils have problems akin to those in the extremely leached tropical soils.

It seems likely that within the broad framework of agricultural land use, proper solutions of the technological problems are more important to human welfare than soil fertility per se. In terms of technology, many of the New World and African cultivators in the tropics practice the extensive methods of shifting agriculture that exploit but a small portion of the arable land. These practices have low output in terms of harvest per unit area and low productivity viewed as yield per man-day. As Gourou (1956:343) indicates, these techniques limit slash-and-burn cultivators to the poorer lands such as the lighter soils of terraces and plateaus. Although he urges use of the swampy and heavy soils of the valley bottoms, they may have been avoided by shifting cultivators for epidemiological as well as technological reasons. In contrast, the Asian cultivators in the tropics use intensive methods on even the poorest soils and achieve a quite high proportion of land use, a high output, but a low productivity that is prodigal of human labor. Many of the temperate zone countries cultivate a high 40 to 60 percent of their total arable land, much more than in most of the tropics. Output is mostly high as well. Excepting the special hand techniques such as required in wet rice culture, productivity in the temperate zone is only high where advanced mechanized technologies are used.

## NUTRITION AND HUMAN ADAPTATION

It is clear that the bulk of the world's population today is principally dependent upon agriculture for its sustenance, and that this dependence came only with the Neolithic Revolution less than 8,000 years ago. Thus, agricultural man anywhere has had only 150 to 400 generations to adapt himself to new dietaries, principally the grain and root crops that now support the world. Moreover, man has also been faced with adapting to different varieties of the same crop that have quite distinct nutritional properties and, indeed, have their own evolution. In this regard, Scrimshaw (1953) has emphasized that the variation is great enough in corn consumed in Central America to have important nutritional consequences. Increased yield and disease resistance in these corns may do damage to protein and oil content, and the amount of protein may bear no direct relationship to the content of tryptophan, methionine, and lysine.

In the long evolutionary view, 150 to 400 generations have been insufficient time for man wholly to adapt himself to new and changing foods. The degree of adaptation to shortages of different nutrients may vary considerably in human populations. Some of these differences may be regional and could reflect the length of time that adaptations to specific nutrient deficiencies have been necessary. For example, there is a possibility that the generally salutary adaptations of Negro Africans to low calcium and ascorbic acid intake (Scientific Council for Africa 1956:79) reflect a longer evolution than do their manifest and clinically expressed difficulties with protein and niacin shortages. The study of human responses to changing dietaries engendered by ecological and technological alterations is, in my opinion, equal in importance to researches on man's reactions to changing disease environments. Adjustments to dietary and disease hazards, themselves closely related, are rarely adequate over the present-day world except with the intervention of advanced food technologies and costly public health services. Neither biological nor cultural evolution have fully kept pace with rapidly shifting total environments. Yet in the fairly immediate past, the major racial blocks of mankind—Whites, Mongoloids, and Negroes—achieved salutary enough adaptations to their separate and distinct environments to undergo population explosions (cf. Hulse 1955:190).

## NUTRITION AND POPULATION

In terms of the numbers of mankind, the world areas where intensive agricultural technologies are practiced are also the areas of the greatest population densities. Indeed, man's reproductive success can be seen to be pressing his food supply in almost all populous areas of the world. Food surpluses are a rarity among nations. Population increases move at such a rate that strong outmovement, such as from Italy to the United States around the turn of the century, only offers temporary relief before the gap is closed again. It would appear that man's biological success vis-à-vis reproduction is fully sufficient to strain his food resources and thus create a nutritional stress situation. As Spengler (1960:1499) recently put it, "Much of Asia, Africa, and Latin America— perhaps two-thirds of the world's population—is

caught in a Malthusian trap, in a quasi-stable equilibrium system in which forces making for increase in income evoke counter-balancing income-depressing forces, among them a high rate of population growth."

## UNDERNUTRITION IN MAN

It is the nutritional consequences of this stress situation that are to be examined here. The observable aspects of nutritional stress lie in diet-connected mortality and morbidity rates, and in the residues of the latter. These residues are most readily observable in the altered growth and maturation rates of the children surviving these dietary crises, their disease susceptibilities, and in the vitality of the adults.

On a gross world basis the American Geographical Society (1953) maps show that the areas of undernutrition and malnutrition closely coincide with the tropical and warmer temperate regions of backward food producing technologies. Undernutrition in a hypocaloric sense and malnutrition in terms of vitamin and mineral deficiencies usually go along together, aiding and abetting each other, as it were, in creating human misery. The effects of famine and qualitative deficiencies in diet are therefore hard to separate. Where famine strikes, as in war disasters, the civilian mortality is quite selective, bearing down as it does on the very young and the old as well as the lower socioeconomic strata. The effect of severe maternal undernutrition on the developing fetus is buffered to a considerable extent by a sort of homeostasis. In experiments where maternal nutrition has been carefully measured, intakes were never low enough to influence significantly the condition of the newborn. In the less well controlled war-time food crises, striking diminutions in birth size have been observed. For example, the undernutrition in northwest Holland during the war winter of 1944–45 was severe enough to interfere with the prenatal growth of infants born during that period (Smith 1954). Congenital malformations, which appear irregularly in normal times, were so slightly increased as to be inconclusive in the few conceptions occurring at the worst stage of the undernutrition. With this degree of famine the frequent intervention of amenorrhea, as a protective device, makes it virtually impossible to collect useful data on fetal anomalies.

When severely undernourished women go into labor, it may be prolonged by as much as five hours. This constitutes a well recognized hazard for both mother and newborn. Very poor nutrition can also affect lactation and cause sharp rises in infant mortality. This is especially the case in societies having no ready milk substitutes and no inter-family cooperation in wet nursing. Such was the case among Okinawans after the 1945 invasion of their island (see Emory 1946:616).

There is a vast literature on the influence of dietary deprivations on child growth. One of the most interesting of these reports concerns Howe and Schiller's (1952) unique 40-year record spanning the two World Wars for statures and weights of school children in Stuttgart, Germany. These cross-sectionally presented data show extreme sensitivity to economic conditions bearing upon nutritional status. Thus, there were dips in the stature and weight curves during World War I, the 1922–23 inflation, the 1932 unemployment crisis, World War II, and the 1946–47 food shortage due to drought. For these German children, as well as those from Belgium, France, England, and Japan, Howe (n.d.) believes that, unless the undernutrition is of long duration, growth simply slows down and, as it were, waits for better times. When they arrive, growth takes place with unusual rapidity until the bulk of the children approach their genetically-determined growth tracks, along which they proceed as before. Viewing Howe's thesis critically, one significant consequence of a belated re-cuperative cycle lies in the timing of growth and its allometric effect upon somatotype. Another consequence of chronic undernutrition is reduced resistance to disease. Both consequences are well illustrated in Lewit's (1947) study of 4,000 Czech children at the end of World War II. In these children the pre-pubertal growth spurt in leg length was stated to be greater than the trunk height increases, resulting in a thin ectomorphic body build with weak musculature. Some 10 to 15 percent of the children were tested as tuberculin-positive, with the percentage increasing in each succeeding age-grade. Telltale enlargement of cervical glands was found in almost every child.

Another consequence of chronic undernutrition is the delay in skeletal maturation, which not only involves belated appearance of ossification centers and their slow subsequent development, but also a noteworthy increase in osseous anomalies (Snodgrasse et al. 1955; Dreizen et al. 1958). Studies thus far on non-Western children show them to average one to four years behind Greulich-Pyle (1959) and other standards for skeletal maturation, and for the gap to widen with increasing age. And there may

also be, as Keys (1950:372) has suggested, far more critical residues of undernutrition and malnutrition expressed in lowered work capacities, reduced disease resistance, and various psychological traumata.

The classic study on the effect of famine upon physique was done by Ivanovsky (1923) during the long starvation period in post-Revolutionary Russia. In 16 populations of varying ethnic origins within the Soviet, adult statures decreased on average 3.8–6.6 cm. in men, 3.6–4.8 cm. in women, on a longitudinal basis. Weight losses of 30 percent occurred in a great number, and other bodily measures showed gross decreases. Organic and psychological traumata were common. A milder laboratory version of Ivanovsky's study was carried out on 34 U.S. White volunteers who were put on a semi-starvation diet for 24 weeks (Lasker 1947). They averaged a 24 percent weight loss and showed a 66 percent increase in ecto-morphy.

The biological and psychological effects of seasonal shortages in food supply constitute another aspect of undernutrition. The effect of the "hungry months" from January to March upon social interactions is one of Richard's (1939) principal cultural themes for the Bemba of northeastern Rhodesia. Brock and Autret (1952:48) indicate that seasonal fluctuations in food supply are marked in subsaharan Africa, and the birth weights of infants are significantly less there during the "hungry months." Vitamin-deficiency states and kwashiorkor are also more prevalent during these lean times. These lean times occur elsewhere in the world. For the Vicos Quechua in the northern Peruvian Sierra, the rainy season from December to February or March includes a period of food shortages for families without emergency stores. Kuczynski-Godard (1945:35–38) indicates that among the Aymará of Ichu the diet is particularly low in energy producing foods at just the time that the hardest harvesting labor is needed.

## MALNUTRITION IN MAN

To a considerable extent the nutritional deficiency diseases are distributed by climate zones, are often worse at certain seasons, and are sometimes related to specific food crops. When these deficiency diseases reach epidemic proportions, they appear to represent the worst lags in man's adaptation to his nutritional environment.

Rickets and osteomalacia are typically the nutritional deficiency diseases of cold climates. In the higher latitudes with more cloud cover, ultraviolet radiation is reduced, especially in the winter. In the United States wintertime, the percentage of total possible sunshine varies from 20 to 40 percent around the Great Lakes and the Pacific Northwest to 70 to 90 percent in the Southwest. Moreover, use of heavy clothing as a protection against cold blocks out most of the solar radiation reaching near-ground level. Bodily absorption of ultraviolet radiation makes possible the production of irradiated ergosterol which goes through a series of reactions to form vitamin D (Clark 1953:23). But where solar radiation is slight and blocked off, dietary vitamin D must take its place or deficiency diseases will result. It is in the dietarily acculturated cold climate peoples that rickets and osteomalacia are the greatest problems. Among the Labrador Eskimo who have largely abandoned their native dietary, rickets, scurvy, and combinations of these two deficiency diseases are said to be universal (Anonymous 1943:207). In Swedish Lapps who had also shifted their diet, almost one-half of the children had rickets. The severity of rickets was notably greater during the winter. Rickets and osteomalacia are also prevalent in the poorest socio-economic classes in the colder urbanized areas where intake of the so-called protective foods is very low. Neither rickets nor osteomalacia are likely to be killers of the very young, but they retard and deform and in so doing affect work capacity and disease resistance.

The present world distribution of scurvy shows no strong distributional patterning. Two centuries or more ago, however, it was a wide-spread disease throughout the northern part of the Western world and in other regions where antiscorbutic vitamin C was largely omitted from the dietary. Thus, we may think of scurvy as a wind sailor's disease and associate its ravages with Stefansson's (1956) "Pemmican War" between the Hudson Bay and the Northwest Companies. But scurvy used to be so common during the English winter months that it was known as the "London Disease." Lack of fruits and lightly cooked vegetables in the diets of all people at that time rendered all socio-economic classes scurvy-prone. Infantile scurvy can be a real killer, and very low vitamin C intake at any age can bring on the classic symptoms of joint pain, hemorrhage, gum softening, and tooth loss.

The iodine deficiency disease of goiter has an interrupted distribution in the mountainous parts of the world as well as the northern continental segment of North America (Amer. Geog. Soc., 1953:map 1). While more unsightly than serious in moderate form, strong iodine deficiencies in combination with other shortages can lead to severe degenerative syndromes such as D. C. Gajdusek (personal communication) found in the Mulia of the Central Highlands of Netherlands New Guinea.

Pellagra, due principally to niacin deficiency, is much more prevalent in the world's temperate zones than elsewhere and is more severe during the warmer months' maxima of solar radiation (Gillman and Gillman 1951:33). Moreover, pellagra is likely to be endemic in those areas where maize is a principal food crop, although the nature of this association is in some dispute (Gillman and Gillman 1951:40–41). Pellagra reached epidemic proportions during the 19th century in European countries such as France, Italy, and Rumania. After ameliorative measures reduced its morbidity and mortality rates in Europe, pellagra became the scourge of the southern part of the United States. Between 1890 and 1909, some 22 percent of those afflicted with pellagra in the South did not survive (Thompson-McFadden Pellagra Commission 1913), and since that time the death rate has risen to 40 to 60 percent during epidemics. After an intensive campaign of agrarian and industrial reforms in the Southern States, pellagra became a much less serious public health problem. But in South Africa Gillman and Gillman (1951:64) tell us that the steep increase in pellagra "...is a reflection of the economic deterioration of the African. While at the moment [over 10 years ago] the disease in South Africa is not virulent, the history of pellagra in other countries has shown that the mortality rate can become very great, claiming as much as 60 percent of the afflicted." Pellagra is quite variable in the forms it takes, but often involves severe dermatoses, hepatic derangements, and severe alimentary and neurological disorders. It is a killer at all ages, from prenatal life onward. The growth and maturational disturbances and loss of vitality residual in the survivors is such that Africans recruited from pellagroid areas for work in the mines are said to be routinely "fed up" before they are expected to do the full day's work required of them.

What pellagra is to the maize consumers, so is beri-beri to the eaters of rice. The thiamine deficiency associated with diets based largely upon milled rice is the undeniable cause of beri-beri. Accordingly, this deficiency disease is largely restricted to Southeast Asia, but it is also present to some extent in Venezuela, the Minas Gerais area of Brazil, the former Cameroons, and Madagascar (Amer. Geogr. Soc. 1953). Beri-beri takes various forms in which a polyneuritis strongly affecting the lower extremities is an almost constant feature. This is "dry" beri-beri. "Wet" beri-beri also involves edema and the collecting of fluid in the body cavities. "Cardiac" beri-beri has the obvious association with heart failure. Infantile beri-beri can be a real killer. This used to be the case among lower class Burmese in Mandalay, where food restrictions imposed upon pregnant and lactating women and upon their ailing offspring caused high mortality in the latter (D. C. Sharma, personal communication). The East Indians and Chinese then resident in Mandalay imposed no such deprivations of thiamine-rich foods and had little infantile beri-beri. This is but one of the many instances where nutritional stresses are both class-structured and culture-conditioned.

The protein deficiency syndrome known as kwashiorkor has a broad distributional sweep of the lower latitudes from Mexico south to many parts of northern South America, throughout subsaharan Africa except for the cattle-raising eastern portion, and in India and much of China. Notably these are the countries of low agricultural productivity in terms of yield per man-day. Kwashiorkor, which means "knee-baby," is most serious in infants and younger children but also leaves perceptible residues in older children and adults who survive. The trouble may start with a poor prenatal and immediately postnatal nutritional environment. In Central America, Scrimshaw et al. (1957) found that partial starvation during the first year of life from insufficient maternal milk is more likely to result in marasmus (progressive wasting of the body) than kwashiorkor. For most children, however, the critical time for onset of kwashiorkor is toward the end of the first year when maternal milk fails to supply enough protein, and supplementary foods—if given at all—are principally carbohydrates. The clinical changes involved in active kwashiorkor include grossly retarded growth and maturation, apathy and anorexia, edema, depigmentation and other changes in the hair (hence "red boy"), diarrhea, and anemia. According to researches cited by Brock and Autret (1952:56–58) for subsaharan Africa, protein requirements per given caloric intake are perceptibly higher in children under five years of age than they are later on in life. The progressive decline in body weight for large numbers of Kampala infants and children, as viewed cross-sectionally in comparison with European standards, is but one of the observable symptoms of kwashiorkor in that area.

The mortality rate attributable to kwashiorkor is impossible to determine without special studies. Such studies were made, however, by Scrimshaw and his colleagues (1957) in four Guatemalan towns totaling 7,000 in population. In Guatemala as a whole the leading cause of death in children is listed as "gastroenteritis and diarrheal disease," yet a careful study of the four towns indicated that at least one-quarter of all deaths under five years of age was due to kwashiorkor or some other nutritional deficiency. Excepting the first year of life, at least half the deaths in one- to four-year-olds appeared to be a direct consequence of malnutrition. These death rates are highly class-structured in Guatemala and are race-conditioned as well, since the lowest socioeconomic class and the most Indian are usually one and the same.

Even when protein deficiencies were not strongly expressed clinically, Scrimshaw et al. (1957) felt that the poorly nourished Guatemalan children were an easier prey to other diseases and might die as a direct consequence of pneumonia, measles, whooping cough, infectious diarrhea, or tuberculosis. Moreover, extra stresses of any kind could result in the expression of frank clinical symptoms of kwashiorkor. Thus, if a child developed a heavy parasite load, it might lapse into severe kwashiorkor.

In subsaharan Africa, Brock and Autret (1952:24) report that mortality among kwashiorkor sufferers was high, especially in cases with edema. Until the advent of modern treatment the reported mortality rate never went below 30 percent. In the absence of such treatment, death was a 100 percent certainty in kwashiorkor-afflicted Congolese children. Closely associated with kwashiorkor in Africa are apparently irreversible fatty changes in the liver, hence the frequently used synonym of "fatty liver disease." There is a strong seasonal association of kwashiorkor outbreaks in Africa with the "hungry months."

Mention must be made of other nutritional deficiency diseases of less dramatic but nevertheless significant stress in man. There are the pro-vitamin A and vitamin A deficiencies associated with retarded growth rates in experimental animals and perhaps man (Clark 1953:12–13), as well as with dermal hyperkeratosis and impaired night vision. Ariboflavinosis is also associated with skin and visual disturbances. Then there are the various minerals that are often deficient in the soils or in the diets selected from them. Of the so-called macronutrients, calcium and phosphorus appear to be the most important to human welfare, but in part this is because they have been the best studied. Marett (1936:226–27) claims a strong ecological correlation between tropical rainforests and soils deficient in calcium and phosphorus and hypothecated that pygmy body size represented an advantageous economy in these macronutrient elements. There is fair evidence that other human populations have successfully adapted themselves to low calcium intakes by slow growth and maturation and small adult body size (Nichols and Nimalasuriya 1939; Schraer and Newman 1958). In the micronutrient group—iron, copper, zinc, and manganese—iron-deficiency anemias are widespread in man and have clear ecological and epidemiological correlates. One rather curious ecological association in Alaska Eskimos is the widespread but usually mild anemia (Scott et al. 1955) with heavy consumption of fish (Margaret Lantis, personal communication). Comparable anemias are not found in the caribou and sea mammal hunters.

## CONCLUSIONS

Undernutrition and malnutrition often go together in man to provide gross and general stressing of a nutritional nature. Qualitative deficiencies are often multiple because of the metabolic interactions of the various nutrients. Where deficiency diseases principally attributable to a single nutrient are apparent, these diseases have strong ecological associations—rickets and osteomalacia with cold climates; scurvy and pellagra with, respectively, the more northerly and more southerly portions of the world's temperate zones; and beri-beri and kwashiorkor with warmer temperate and hot climates. Moreover, pellagra is associated in some way with maize cultivation, while beri-beri has a more direct relationship to heavy dietary use of milled rice. Most of these deficiency diseases have strong seasonal associations—rickets, osteomalacia, and scurvy with the winter months, pellagra with the summer months, and kwashiorkor with the "hungry months" whenever they occur.

Mortality attributable to dietary shortages is therefore frequently differential in its effect upon human populations, by region, socio-economic

class, and age-grade. So are the biological and psychological residues in those who survive these diseases. In terms of mortality and morbidity rates, the greatest nutritional stresses are present in the underdeveloped countries of the world, especially where agricultural output and/or productivity are low. These are principally the countries of the tropics and warmer temperate zone, where the vectors of disease seem to be most strongly entrenched. Disease often goes along with poor nutrition, and the two are largely synergistic in relationship.

In terms of the histories of diseases, the underdeveloped countries are currently plagued by many of the nutritional deficiency and other diseases common less than several centuries ago in the more advanced countries. As Gordon's (1952:49) data suggest, the technologically more advanced countries have proceeded apace to develop new mortality patterns, with the degenerative diseases such as atherosclerosis and cancer now high on the list of killers. Atherosclerosis, for example, has a quite clear association with high intake of saturated fat and with reduced physical exercise, and hence has very obvious ecological and cultural connotations.

As a whole, then, nutritional stress in man has very strong ecological and cultural correlates. It should be equally apparent that the nutritional stresses that play such a potent role in human malaise must also impose their stamp upon the forms and functions of many aspects of man's culture as well.

AUTHOR'S POSTSCRIPT, 1975:

The 14 years transpired since this article was written seem not to have dimmed the validity of the conceptual and substantive data therein. It was generally prophetic of the famine in many parts of the Third World today, which Annie and Paul Ehrlich cover in their "Starvation: 1975," (*Penthouse*, July 1975). More detail on these and other nutritional matters are available in my paper "Nutritional Adaptations in Man," (pp. 210–259 in Albert Damon, ed., *Physiological Anthropology*, New York: Oxford University Press, 1975). Had the research then been done, I would have included the increased nutritional needs under heavy workloads in hot climates, the moderate but significant correlations of physical growth with mental and emotional growth under conditions of mild-to-moderate protein deficiency, and the problems of iron and zinc assimilation from an all plant food diet.

# 36 Voodoo Death: New Thoughts on an Old Explanation

## Barbara W. Lex

A phenomenon that has long intrigued anthropologists, explorers, and other observers of non-Western peoples is that of so-called "voodoo" death, or, as I prefer to call it, *magical death*; indeed an even more appropriate term might be *sociocultural death*. In the accounts of such events there are many variations but most observers seem to agree that it is an actual and not a faked occurrence and that once the process is set in motion, usually by a supposed religious or social transgression that results in the transgressor's being marked out for death by a sorcerer acting on behalf of society through a ritual of accusation and condemnation, then death occurs within a brief span, usually 24 to 48 hours. The classic statement on the phenomenon is that of the famed physiologist, Walter B. Cannon (1942) in a paper in the *American Anthropologist*. Having investigated the literature and polled through questionnaire large numbers of medically qualified observers in many parts of the world, Cannon was convinced that the phenomenon could be explained in terms of his "flight or fight" hypothesis. An animal or human facing mortal threat is mobilized physiologically and endocrinologically to react either through attacking the threatening stimulus or fleeing from it. He was impressed with what he assumed were the "superstitions" of "primitives," and their high suggestibility in threatening situations. Under threat and intense stress the sympathetic nervous system liberates sugar from the liver, accelerates the heart, contracts certain blood vessels, discharges adrenalin, and dilates the bronchioles. This state prepares the organism for survival through flight or fight. But if the animal becomes completely immobilized and is unable to do either, the result is dire. Without repeating the whole explanation here, suffice it to say that Cannon believed that voodoo death was really caused by overexcitation of the sympathico-adrenal system without consequent action.

Sometime later a psychophysiologist, Richter (1957), observing the behavior of experimental rats forced to swim in a jar until they drowned, concluded that voodoo death, contrary to Cannon's view, was a situation demanding neither flight nor fight as in fear and rage, but the acceptance of hopelessness, of literally giving up the will to live, and the physiological involvement was of the parasympathetic rather than sympathetic nervous system. More recently, Lester (1972) believes a psychological explanation is more probable, and that basically magical death is mainly the result of susceptibility to suggestion while in a highly vulnerable state. Clune (1973) suggests poisoning, but without any evidence, and this explanation was originally rejected by Cannon.

In this essay, Barbara Lex suggests an alternative explanation in physiological terms, that of "tuning" of the human nervous system. Here she explains how tuning works and she concludes that, in addition to helping to explain psychosomatic disturbances, it affords a likely explanation of voodoo death. Responses to sympathetic nervous activity are ergotrophic, to parasympathetic activity they are trophotropic, and—something neither Cannon, Richter, nor others have shown, the two systems work together in mutual equilibrium. Lex's explanation is ingeniously put together, and offers a whole new field of thinking for medical anthropologists interested in the occurrence of magical death and human reactions to stress. What can be said here is that the psychic pain of extreme stress may, under some cultural conditions, result in massive somatic damage up to and including death. The reader is referred to Yap's formulations on "culture-reactive" syndromes in Chapter 38.

Discussion of the etiology of voodoo death has been recently revived in the pages of the *American Anthropologist*. Lester (1972) endorses a psychological explanation, that of suggestion, while Clune (1973) favors a pharmacological explanation, that of poison. Both authors give little credence to physiological processes as causal factors in cases of voodoo death. However, in 1957 Richter, a physiologist, identified voodoo death as a human manifestation of vagus death resultant from overstimulation of the parasympathetic nervous system. His paper supplants the earlier work of Cannon (1942), in which the physiological cause of voodoo death was attributed to hyperreactivity of the sympathetic nervous system. Revival of the question indicates that ethnographers either lack knowledge of autonomic nervous system functioning or disavow the significance of the autonomic nervous system in human behavior.

## NEUROPHYSIOLOGICAL EVIDENCE

Although Chapple (1970), an anthropologist, has amply documented the importance of the autonomic nervous system in human behavior,

Reprinted with abridgments and with changes by the author from Barbara W. Lex, 1974, "Voodoo Death: New Thoughts on an Old Explanation," *American Anthropologist*, 76:818–823, with permission of the author and the American Anthropological Association.

manifested, in his terms, in "emotional-interaction patterns," the broad implications of his work have been little recognized in anthropological approaches to religion and magic. A brief, necessarily simplified overview of structure and function in the human nervous system provides a basis for further discussion.

Fundamental to an understanding of the autonomic nervous system is the property of mutual antagonism in the reciprocal excitation of subdivisions known respectively as sympathetic and parasympathetic. As a major system maintaining bodily homeostasis, the autonomic nervous system rapidly responds to intra-and extrasomatic stimuli, promoting appropriate reactions in innervated organs and in the skeletal muscles as well as influencing excitation in the cerebral cortex. In response to ordinary stimuli autonomic fluctuations are almost imperceptible; but exposure to more intense stimulation, such as cold or an unexpected sound, results in a greater degree of sympathetic reaction, while parasympathetic arousal accounts for reaction to the smell of food or to stroking of the skin, to cite some simple examples. Up to certain thresholds, which vary slightly from person to person because of individual differences produced by both inheritance and learning, increased discharge in one division is accompanied by inhibition of the other. Crossing that threshold, however, results in sensitization or "tuning," to use a neurophysiologist's term.

Cannon, a pioneer of modern neurophysiology who initiated the neurophysiological discussion of voodoo death in 1942, had earlier (1929) explained response in the sympathetic nervous system in terms of preparation for emergency situations. His findings established that in "fight or flight" contexts some arteries relax while others contract, diverting blood from the viscera to the striated muscles; blood pressure and heart rate rise accordingly; the pupils dilate; perspiration increases body cooling; the bronchioles to the lungs dilate, providing more oxygen; and digestion, maintained by the parasympathetic nervous system, is inhibited. Briefly stated, the sensitized sympathetic nervous system mobilizes the individual by arming muscle structures and at the same time halting or reducing activity in body organs not immediately necessary for combat or escape.

In contradistinction, parasympathetic nervous system activation, which inhibits sympathetic reactivity, is characterized by slowed respiration and heart rate, pupillary constriction, reduced blood pressure, and diversion of the blood from the striated muscles to the viscera. These conditions usually prevail during sleep, digestion, grooming, and other pleasurable states. More importantly, after high sympathetic discharge, parasympathetic compensation inevitably follows.

Through a series of experiments with rats, Richter (1957) analyzed the phenomenon of sudden death and extended his findings to the topic of voodoo death by pointing out that such events were best explained as the result of parasympathetic hyperreactivity, or vagus death. The vagus nerve is one major component of the parasympathetic nervous system, but in his discussions Richter omitted two important points. First, the mutually antagonistic interplay of sympathetic and parasympathetic functions which occurs in ordinary life is not clearly spelt out for readers, including anthropologists, unacquainted with human neurophysiology. Cannon's emphasis on "fight or flight" and the emotions of fear and anger, although generally known, obscures the more usual contribution of the sympathetic nervous system in alert, wakeful response to stimuli. Moreover, investigation of the sympathetic nervous system has received more attention than that devoted to examination of parasympathetic functioning. Second, although Richter noted that a stress response characterized by accelerated heart rate often preceded the decelerated heart rate, slowed respiration, and decreased body temperature which ultimately precipitated the demise of the rats in his experiments, he did not explicitly state that this response is parasympathetic overcompensation evoked by an initial condition of intense sympathetic excitation. For readers unacquainted with the reciprocal action of the two subdivisions of the autonomic nervous system, in Richter's paper the role of the parasympathetic nervous system in exhaustion is neither identified nor described.

Lester (1972), an anthropologist, has faulted the work of Cannon and of Richter as limited and based only on animal research. Dismissing both Cannon's and Richter's physiological explanations as possible but undemonstrable, he instead proposes a psychological explanation, that of "death by suggestion." In this context "suggestion" is a reductive assertion unless the process denoted by this term is subjected to scrutiny and clearly defined. Furthermore, Lester implies than mental processes alone determine psychological states. This is an overly truncated perspective that imposes a false separation between "mind" and "body."

Cognitive activity is highly influenced by an individual's physiological state. Therefore, the frequency, intensity, and duration of excitation prevailing in the central, motor, and autonomic nervous systems should be identified for any given state.

In the 16 years intervening between publication of Richter's article and the present writing much painstaking research in neurophysiology has uncovered the impact of tuning on the human nervous system. However, most neurophysiologists and psychophysiologists not only lack the cross-cultural orientation which would prompt research on topics of specific interest to anthropologists but also maintain a laboratory research orientation which effectively precludes investigation of non-Western subjects. Their attitude of skepticism toward voodoo death is exemplified by Barber (1961). Recently, however, some interest in certain cultural practices, such as Zen or Yoga meditation, has begun to generate neurophysiological and psychophysiological research which examines behavior not ordinarily found in Western subjects. Findings derived from animal research and from studies of experimental neuroses in man also have been applied to clinical observation of human psychosomatic disorders (Gellhorn and Kiely 1973), thereby negating Lester's criticism of Cannon and Richter. Significantly, nervous system tuning, which is explored as follows, is fundamental to cause and cure in psychosomatic disorders as well as to the physiological component of meditation practices (Gellhorn and Kiely 1972), and also provides an explanation for the mechanisms operating in voodoo death (Gellhorn 1970:79).

## TUNING THE NERVOUS SYSTEM

Gellhorn and his colleagues have devoted lengthy, systematic research to the study of the nervous system in animals and man. Referring to "sensitization or facilitation in particular centers" (Gellhorn and Loofbourrow 1963:91), tuning may be accomplished by direct stimulation of either the sympathetic or parasympathetic subdivisions of the autonomic nervous system, by use of certain drugs which excite or block one or the other subdivision, or by types of mental activity. Through interconnections in the hypothalamus reticular formation, and limbic system—all subcortical structures—each subdivision is linked to the brain and to the skeletal muscles (Kiely 1974:518). Generally, only under special circumstances, such as in laboratory experiments or in pathological conditions, are somatic responses separable from autonomic functions (Lacey 1967). Hence, integration of two reciprocally balanced systems, termed *ergotropic* and *trophotropic*, is emphasized (Kiely 1974:518). Ergotropic response consists of augmented sympathetic discharges, increased muscle tone, and a state of excitation in the cerebral cortex manifested as desynchronized (alert) rhythms. The trophotropic pattern is constituted of heightened parasympathetic discharges, relaxed skeletal muscles, and synchronized (resting) cortical rhythms (Gellhorn and Kiely 1972). In addition, each system promotes circulation or release of distinctive neurochemicals (Kiely 1974:518).

Three stages of nervous system tuning are recognized (Gellhorn and Kiely 1973:238). In the first stage response in one system increases while at the same time reactivity in the other system diminishes. If augmented reactivity of the sensitized system continues past a certain threshold, as in the case of sudden or sustained stimulation, not only is inhibition of the nonsensitized system complete but also there occurs a condition wherein stimuli which usually elicit response in the nonsensitized system instead evoke a response in the sensitized system. The second stage is said to be characterized by *reversal phenomena*. Continued stimulation can lead to a third stage, in which reciprocal relationships fail entirely and simultaneous excitations result. Chronic heightened activation of both systems is maladaptive, disrupting homeostasis, and characteristic results are experimental or clinical neuroses, psychosomatic disorders, or psychoses (Gellhorn and Kiely 1973:238–239).

However, simultaneous excitations of both systems, termed *mixed discharges,* also characterize Zen, Yoga, and Transcendental Meditation as well as Zen ecstasy (Gellhorn and Kiely 1972), suggesting that the specific anatomical location of neural excitation as well as cultural explanations of individual experience are both important in the etiology of disorders resultant from stage three tuning. This also explains why classification of emotions into those involving only one or the other system is not a workable solution to the problem of identifying the autonomic component of human behavior. As Gellhorn points out (1970:70–71), distinctions of pleasant from unpleasant states provide no assistance for analysis of the more intense emotions, such as anxiety, in which both the ergotropic and trophotropic systems are excited.

329

Instead, he suggests striated muscle tone as a better diagnostic for classification purposes, and indicates that cognitive factors and muscle tone may be mutually reinforcing.

Furthermore, activation of these reciprocally interconnected systems beyond certain thresholds retards or prohibits logical reasoning. Although under ordinary circumstances the sympathetic nervous system contributes to alertness, intense ergotropic excitement usually results in a restorative, life-conserving trophotropic phase of "let down" or compensation. Thus, in resting phases, with the exception of rapid-eye-movement, or "paradoxical," sleep, sympathetic reactivity is relatively low and regular. In the second stage of tuning, activation of the tuned system exceeds the threshold of analytical judgment, for in conditions of heightened activity in either system, incoming stimuli have little impact beyond further arousal of the tuned system. Further, in the third stage mixed discharges accordingly produce mixed cortical response—resting *and* alert rhythms appear—and the complexly excited state of the individual precludes the clear thinking typical of information processing in ordinary homeostasis. Hence, a tuned individual is by definition uncritical and therefore ripe for the suggestion that he or she will die by magical means.

If an individual in stage two tuning perceives this situation as personal helplessness and hopelessness, as Lester indicates, contrary information only reinforces and intensifies that person's depressed state. The heightened trophotropic response to stress—exhaustion—characterizes the frightened person who gives up. The stage is then set for acute trophotropic discharge and voodoo, or vagus, death. Although mild trophotropic response is usually pleasurable, as in a mouthwatering reaction to one's favorite food, more intense trophotropic activation in stage three tuning can promote symptoms which prevent ingestion of nourishment: heartburn, ulcers, nausea, vomiting, and diarrhea. Treated as socially dead, "boned" or "voodooed" persons refuse proferred food and water simply because they at the very least experience anorexia (appetite loss), which accompanies heightened trophotropic activity, and, more likely, their sensitized bodies are unable to tolerate ingestion of food or fluid. Apathy, fatigue, and anorexia are symptoms of depression, another but less acute (stage two) example of tuning in the trophotropic system (Gellhorn and Kiely 1973:148). Furthermore, individuals already in ill health, whom Barber (1961) indicates as those most likely to succumb to death via witchcraft, have been under stress, and therefore are in a state of lassitude which can be aggravated by witchcraft.

Chapple (1970:317) has demonstrated that one important function of ritual is the establishment of autonomic synchrony, whereby participants, through various sanctioned means, experience a certain emotion. Likening the process by which synchrony is achieved to that of abreaction, which can be defined as "a process of reviving the memory of a repressed unpleasant experience and expressing in speech and action the emotions related to it, thereby relieving the personality of its influence" (Gellhorn and Loofbourrow 1963:297), Chapple explains the relationship between rites of passage or rites of intensification and autonomic synchrony:

It seems quite evident, but little studied systematically, that the rites have evolved, in part at least, as structured means through which equilibrium—in all its complex emotional-interaction patterns is reestablished ... rites of passage in many societies enable individuals to abreact ... in so doing, they discharge the emotional tensions [of] the sympathetic nervous system (1970:317).

Therefore, a similar case can be made for the role of nervous system tuning in curing rituals. Many psychosomatic illnesses, from a neurobiological perspective, are produced by mixed discharges resultant from stage three tuning engendered by stressful life circumstances. Curing rituals manipulate the human nervous system, in whole or in part, in order to regain homeostasis, thus alleviating the dysfunctional symptoms which accompany mixed discharges.

Diagnosticians who prescribe specific rituals and substances for the ill must have a good working knowledge of potential fluctuations in autonomic functioning. Hence, in the case of the shaman or the medicine society member, apprenticeship is usually served through personal illness, resulting in empathy as well as an augmented ability to recognize symptoms and to ascertain the possible etiology of disorders. Indeed, ritual therapies of Iroquois medicine societies reflect considerable insight into neurophysiological dynamics. Ministrations of the False Face Society, for example, are appropriate for disorders or injuries involving the flow of blood, dysplasias, and dreams or hallucinations of the False Faces themselves. In traditional Iroquois belief such events require False Face curing rituals, and once treated, the individual becomes a member of that medicine society and participates in the treatment of others.

330

It should not be assumed that knowledge about body functions, as well as about their disorders and cures, is to be found only within the practice of Western medicine. To illustrate, an informed and careful observer can discover trophotropic activation in weeping, dizziness, weakness, profuse salivation, nausea, frequent elimination of wastes, and pupillary constriction. Similarly, ergotropic activation is exhibited in profuse sweating, constipation, muscular rigidity, dry mouth, and pupillary dilation. Mixed discharges are evinced by the simultaneous presence of symptoms characteristic of both tropic systems. Having discerned the nature and degree of tuning involved in a particular disorder, appropriate therapeutic measures can be taken. More importantly, the means to alleviate disorders also should provide the knowledge to cause illness. In other words, practical knowledge of human autonomic functions and emotions permits manipulations which can result in dysfunction, if not death. Thus, knowledge necessary for cure also provides information about how to diminish vital functioning below a critical threshold. Rather than sly poisoning (Clune 1973) or the vague notion of suggestion (Lester 1972), the physiological conditions of nervous system tuning adequately explain the phenomenon of voodoo death.

## CONCLUSIONS

Suggestion is indeed at work in voodoo death cases, but suggestion must be understood as one aspect of the complex emotional-interaction forms characteristic of human biology. In this view the hitherto mysterious, arcane nature of voodoo death is supplanted by a physiologically based interpretation. Suggestion in this context is accomplished by the practitioner's manipulation of the ergotropic-trophotropic system through the victim's cognitive apprehension of the meaning of witchcraft. The extreme fright experienced by the individual who has been thus singled out can be as fatal as a dose of poison.

Empirical testing of this explanation should be neither difficult nor require sophisticated laboratory apparatus. Pupillary constriction, easily observable and indicative of parasympathetic dominance (or conversely, sympathetic inhibition), provides one ready diagnostic for fieldworkers, whereas the amount of saliva and of perspiration as well as degree of muscle tonicity and skin pallor in an individual are also discernible without complicated instruments. Fieldworkers contemplating research in societies where voodoo deaths are possible occurrences should familiarize themselves with the visible effects of nervous system tuning and carefully note observable physiological responses in such cases.

NOTE

Research on human neurobiology, a portion of which is reported in this paper, was supported by the Faculty Research Fellowship Fund of Western Michigan University and permitted observation and consultation at the Langley Porter Neuropsychiatric Institute, San Francisco, California, in 1973. Fieldwork of Iroquois medicine societies was assisted by a grant from the Phillips Fund of the American Philosophical Society in 1966. I wish to thank Robert F. Maher for his comments and suggestions, but of course the final responsibility for assertions in this paper are mine.

331

# XI
# Emotional States and Cultural Constraints

## The Cultural Shaping of Behavioral Disorders

In a passage in Chapter 1 of this book, Richard Lieban acknowledges that cultural psychiatry and psychological anthropology are part of medical anthropology, but since they are covered in other chapters in the handbook in which Lieban's essay on medical anthropology appears, he does not include these topics. However, in his brief historical overview Lieban does not acknowledge the role played by these subfields of anthropological inquiry in the making of what we now term medical anthropology. Although I am in complete agreement with those historical antecedents included in Lieban's essay, it is my belief that a large part of the impetus for the development of medical anthropology derived from the original interest of many anthropologists in the relations between the individual and culture, that is, "culture-and-personality" studies or, more frequently now, psychological anthropology. Pursuit of the problems in this subdiscipline of anthropology led many of us to raise some basic questions regarding human behavior. We revisit a few of these problems in this section in order to point up their relevance for psychological and psychiatric anthropology, and thus for medical anthropology.

Human reactions to stress, as we observed in the preceding papers, may take many forms. Among the responses to what I termed in that section insidious, or long-term, stress is the assumption of emotional states of intense excitability and activity, or of extreme passivity and withdrawal. These states usually involve some degree of alienation from the values that form the prevailing ethos or exaggeratedly implement current values and norms in obsessive and compulsive actions. Such behaviors may be seen as undercompensation or overcompensation of the dominant norms and value-orientations of the culture, or as the underplaying or overplaying of the conventional statuses and roles that comprise the social structure.

Although the cultural relativity of Ruth Benedict's (1934a) classical position on abnormality cannot be denied—that some cultures highly value behaviors that are despised and proscribed in others—there are universal boundaries outside of which asocial, antisocial, and socially disruptive behaviors cannot extend without threatening the foundations of any human social order. *Homo Sapiens* is one of the most elastic species in the animal kingdom in terms of the remarkable range of ecological and demographic conditions to which it has adapted, but even so there are limits, just as there are limits internally, to the amount of disruption and difference that any human group may accept and still retain its integrity. So without exception, every society circumscribes to some degree the behavior and activities of its members. And every society has a conception of the acceptable, normal, and "natural," and of the unacceptable, abnormal and "unnatural," roughly coterminous with its notions of good and bad (or evil) (Benedict 1934b).

But to aver that human behavior occurs always in a cultural milieu and that the judgment of that behavior is always culturally relative may still beg the even more basic question: Can we speak of some aspects of behavior as normal or abnormal in a panhuman sense, that is, species-specific? Can we also speak of some aspects of behavior that vary according to history and society, that is, culture-specific? A number of excellent books deal with this question in detail (for example, Barnouw 1974; Haring 1956; Honigmann 1967; Hsu 1972; Hunt 1967; Kaplan 1961; Kiev 1964; Kluckhohn, Murray, and Schneider 1953; LeVine 1973; Linton 1945; Opler 1967; Plog and Edgerton 1969; Wallace 1970). Ultimately the question may be unanswerable, since almost every facet of human behavior seems to be either modifiable or impressively influenced by cultural factors. Modes of breathing, functions of the various organ systems, and even what has been assumed until recent decades to be purely autonomic physiological activities are now believed, as a result of ingenious experimentation, to be conditionable by social, cultural, and psychological factors or by an act of conscious will of the individual. But at least one variant of this question remains to intrigue medical anthropologists: Are the psychoses of Western psychiatric experience and nosology universal and transcultural, or are they strongly shaped by cultural pressures and conditioning? Because the very act of labeling behaviors tends to preordain the answers to such questions, I have headed this section with the terms *emotional states* and *behavioral disorders* because they seem to me less culture-bound than psychoses, neuroses, and the like. I would agree with Edgerton in his paper on East African conceptions of psychoses that the attempt to answer this problem now is probably premature. A good deal more systematic data will have to be gathered first.

Another related question is, are there clusters of behaviors displayed by seriously disturbed persons that are characteristic of particular cultures, in fact so peculiar to them that we may speak of them as cultural or ethnic psychoses or neuroses? The paper by Yap deals with this problem, attempting to classify certain behavior clusters that have appeared in the anthropological and psychiatric literature and to place them in proper perspective both for clinical recognition and for systematic anthropological research. Recently Robert LeVine (1973:29–37) has provided new insight and help in this area by suggesting that the term *rare-zero differentials* may be applied to these behaviors. LeVine attempts to study such problems in an ecological, evolutionary fashion and to use the concept of populations and the methods of epidemiology. He says, "Some traits thought of as characteristic of a given population are actually rare within it but are totally absent in the populations with which it is being compared." He notes such culture-reactive syndromes (to use Yap's terminology) as *pibloktoq, windigo, latah,* and *amok*, and suggests that "All of these conditions are rare in the populations mentioned but are believed to be absent elsewhere; insofar as they are truly absent in other populations, they represent genuine rare-zero differentials." However, LeVine extends this notion well beyond emotional states to art, religion, politics, and, in fact, to all aspects of human life: "Any individual pattern of social responses that is recurrent in a population, limited to a minority of individuals within it, and absent in compared populations falls into the category of rare-zero differential." One could ask, nevertheless, how LeVine would deal with a culture-reactive syndrome like *susto* (see Chapters 12, 38, and 45 by Rubel, Yap, and Uzzell in this volume), which is characteristic of many Hispanic-American societies and seems relatively high in incidence as well, but absent from compared populations. LeVine discusses this possibility but the question is one requiring a good deal more inquiry. In any event, LeVine's notion of rare-zero differential seems to lend some clarity to the kind of phenomena that interest Yap and others.

The questions of just how culture shapes individual personality and how psychopathological states may be understood within the context of the culture and predominant personality type of a society are explored by Parker in his paper on the Eskimo. For comparison, Parker uses the southern neighbors of the Eskimo, the Ojibwa. An understanding both of the etiology and the nature of emotional disturbance in a society is greatly aided by describing these states carefully and placing them within the context of the culture, social organization, and patterns of socialization in which they occur.

How do non-Western, preindustrial peoples themselves perceive and structure the behavioral disorders that they experience and confront? Edgerton tackles this problem with admirable methodological rigor in his study of the way in which the people of four East African societies conceive and deal with serious emotional disorders among their members. Edgerton comes up with some rather surprising findings of enormous significance for the questions raised herein.

In the case of an institutionalized, culture-reactive syndrome of broad incidence, such as possession, how is this state perceived, structured, and defined, and how is the role of a possessed individual fulfilled in a society? What are some of the psychological and social implications of such a phenomenon and what are its links to the social system and culture? These questions are explored in the study of possession among the Sidamo, an Ethiopian people, by John and Irene Hamer, who use a wealth of ethnographic and case data.

The methods of coping with the stresses of life and the emotional disorders that sometimes erupt as a result are of great interest not only to medical anthropology but to clinical psychiatry and psychology as well. Kiev (1964) devoted a volume of studies to what he called in his subtitle "primitive psychiatry today," that is, under conditions of culture change. Among preindustrial peoples therapeutic methods are closely associated with their spiritual and ceremonial life, and indeed are part and parcel of that life. John Kennedy's study of the *zar* cult among Nubians in Egypt addresses such questions as what kinds of emotional problems and states are properly within the domain of native psychotherapies, how do they enable the patient to cope more adequately with the stresses that beset him, how are these therapeutic techniques related to their cultures and social structures, and under what conditions are they resorted to?

Finally, moving beyond the rare-zero differentials, one must ask an even more fundamental question: how are various emotional syndromes distributed in populations? That is, what is the epidemiology of behavioral disorders in a society? One such study attempting to learn of the incidence of emotional disorders in an aboriginal population (if one can any longer be so termed) is the study by Kidson and Jones of psychiatric disorders among Australian aborigines. Studies of this kind are all too rare, and although certain questions may be raised about the methodology (see my introduction to the study), they are nevertheless most welcome in moving toward broader epidemiological knowledge of behavioral disorders in preindustrial societies.

# 37 Psychiatric Disorders Among Aborigines of the Australian Western Desert

*Malcolm A. Kidson and Ivor H. Jones*

Opler (1967) holds that prevalence and incidence studies of emotional disorders of populations may be useful for knowledge of rates of such disorders and for planning and public health, but they are "useless etiologically." Insofar as social and cultural factors are involved in etiology, I should think that a knowledge of the distribution of particular disturbances in a population could provide if not keys then clues to the etiology of those disorders. Be that as it may, in the present study of the prevalence of psychiatric disorders among Australian aborigines, Kidson and Jones do attempt some etiologic speculations. I would suggest that these speculations are of limited usefulness if not accompanied, as they are not here, by detailed case materials on individuals. It is also difficult to know if these data represent "true" prevalences, since the method of survey was to ask information from individuals about *other* individuals. Since only the most florid symptomatology apparently was used in arriving at a diagnosis, my own guess is that, except perhaps for the childhood disorders (for reasons offered by the authors in the paper), the figures for adult disorders given here may be underestimates. Prevalence studies are usually based on cases which come in for some sort of official mode of treatment (clinics, hospitals, practitioners), and themselves, therefore, do not represent untreated cases in the population) whereas the present data are also skewed but in a different direction.

Nevertheless, the findings are interesting in themselves, since in this relatively unacculturated population of aborigines we find that although so-called functional psychoses, personality disorders, and organically based disturbances are present, "classical neuroses, psychosomatic illness, and suicide were not detected." It is interesting to discover that despite what must be the severe stresses of living a reservation-type existence and coping with the impact of the Australo-European culture, the rate of emotional disturbance among these aboriginals is remarkably low by comparison with that for an Australian country town, and also for a more acculturated group of eastern Aranda. Even under these disadvantageous conditions of life

Reprinted with abridgments from Malcolm A. Kidson and Ivor H. Jones, 1968, "Psychiatric Disorders Among Aborigines of the Australian Western Desert," *Archives of General Psychiatry*, *19*: 413–417, October, with permission of the authors and the American Medical Association. Copyright © 1968 by the American Medical Association.

apparently there are still sufficient supports within the culture of the people of the Warburton Ranges to sustain most of them in a reasonably integrative fashion. Naturally, the full meaning of these findings must await more detailed reports and, hopefully, case histories.

The Australian aborigines are a unique people who provide one of the few remaining examples of a "primitive" society in the evolutionary sense employed by Parsons (Parsons 1966). This situation however will not persist as contact with modern Australian society is exposing more and more aborigines to different concepts of economy, intrafamilial and extrafamilial relationship, political organization, religion, and land ownership. Psychiatric investigation of these people is warranted because of the theoretical interests aroused by their rare culture and also because of the apparent increase in morbidity. In remote parts of central Australia traditional communities still exist where "modern" influences are not great. The present paper reports an investigation of psychiatric disorders in such a community. This work forms part of a comparative study of psychiatric disability of aborigines in remote and urban environments. A previous investigation suggests that the existing patterns are similar to those of western society but that neuroses, psychosomatic conditions, and suicides are rare (Kidson 1967). The investigation reported here provides additional basic data.

This paper describes a survey of psychiatric disorders, which we carried out in August 1967, among western desert aborigines who were at that time encamped at the Warburton Ranges Mission in the Great Victoria Desert of Western Australia. This settlement was established in 1934 and its aboriginal population increased over the years as more and more nomads deserted their traditional territories for an easier and less precarious life. In 1967 the population was 441 persons. Their age and sex distribution is indicated in Table 1.

In earlier times aborigines living in the area were nomadic hunters and food gatherers who traveled from place to place by foot carrying a few weapons and building flimsy shelters for their overnight stops. Group numbers increased for important social-religious ceremonies and decreased in times of drought. Their physical environment was an arid semidesert of plains, sand ridges, and low hills sparsely covered by low trees, desert scrub and grasses. Extremes of climate were experienced and clothes were not worn. Detailed accounts of the

**Table 1** Age and Sex Distribution of Aboriginal Population

|          | Males | Females | Total |
|----------|-------|---------|-------|
| Children | 105   | 103     | 208   |
| Adults   | 108   | 125     | 233   |
| Total    | 213   | 228     | 441   |

culture, social structure, and environment have been given by Berndt (1966), Strehlow (1965), and Berndt and Berndt (1964).

Now there are only a few aborigines in the area who have not made contacts with Europeans, and in most instances contact has been considerable. However the strength and importance of traditional culture remains great. The findings presented here are compared with those of a previous and methodologically similar survey (Kidson 1967) of psychiatric disorders occurring among the Walbiri, a tradition-orientated and culturally similar community in central Australia. Prevalence figures are presented for each community separately and for a total or combined population of 1,091 persons. There are perhaps 40,000 full-blood aborigines in Australia.

## METHOD

Information was sought from both European and aboriginal residents at the settlement. Europeans were asked for information about individuals who at some time during their lives had displayed abnormal or unusual behavior or criminal conduct. Information was similarly sought from paid aboriginal informants who were engaged by the investigators as interpretors. Case

**Table 2** Neuropsychiatric Disorders Among Children at Warburton Ranges

|                                            | No. Cases |
|--------------------------------------------|-----------|
| Behavior disorders                         |           |
|   Impulsive aggressiveness       | 2         |
|   Delinquency—stealing           | 1         |
|   Intellectual handicap due to blindness | 1 |
| Organic disorders                          |           |
|   Febrile convulsions only       | 1         |
|   Encephalocoele (excised) with  |           |
|     intellectual handicap | 1      |
| Other                                      |           |
|   Intellectual handicap          | 1         |

records were made out for all individuals so reported and further information about them specifically was sought from Europeans, relatives, and from other aborigines. Hospital records of reported cases were checked. Subjects were interviewed by one or other of the investigators and physical examinations were performed when appropriate. The criteria of inclusion of cases were that subjects should be residing at the Warburton Ranges settlement and that reports of abnormal behavior should be sufficient in quantity and quality to indicate, in the investigators' opinion, a psychiatric disorder.

## FINDINGS

Subjects showing evidence of psychiatric disability have been grouped into one or two age categories. All persons aged 16 years or less were listed as children and all persons over 16 as adults. Aged persons or "pensioners" were included in the adult category but also they were considered separately. Estimation of age in the latter group is not accurate and may vary by as much as ±10 years.

**Table 3** Frequency of Psychiatric Disorders

| Diagnosis | Warburton Ranges n = 541 | | Walbiri n = 650 | | Total n = 1091 | |
|-----------|------|------|------|------|------|------|
|           | No.  | %    | No.  | %    | No.  | %    |
| Schizophrenia | 1 | 0.23 | 4 | 0.62 | 5 | 0.46 |
| Affective psychoses | 2 | 0.45 | 1 | 0.15 | 3 | 0.28 |
| Organic disorders | 4 | 0.90 | 9 | 1.39 | 13 | 1.19 |
| Personality disorders | 3 | 0.68 | 5 | 0.77 | 8 | 0.73 |
| Depression | 3 | 0.68 | 2 | 0.31 | 5 | 0.46 |
| Mental subnormality | 1 | 0.23 | 2 | 0.31 | 3 | 0.28 |
| Possession syndrome | 2 | 0.45 | 1 | 0.15 | 3 | 0.28 |
| Behavior disorders of childhood | 4 | 0.90 | 5 | 0.77 | 9 | 0.83 |
| Hypochondriasis | 6 | 1.36 | 1 | 0.15 | 7 | 0.63 |
| Situational reactions | 2 | 0.45 | 0 | | 2 | 0.18 |
| Other and uncertain | 2 | 0.45 | 5 | 0.77 | 7 | 0.64 |
| Total | 30 | 6.78 | 35 | 5.39 | 65 | 5.95 |

337

*1. Children.* There were six boys and one girl or 3.4 percent of a total of 208 children who showed evidence of a significant neuropsychiatric disorder. Minor behavioral problems were not included. Diagnosis according to the predominant abnormality or behavior disorder are listed in Table 2.

*2. Adults.* Of a total adult population of 233 persons 15 men and 8 women or 9.9 percent had at some time in their lives suffered from a significant psychiatric disorder. The comparative Walbiri figure was 7.9 percent. The diagnostic breakdown of cases, based upon the international classification of diseases (W.H.O. 1965), is presented in Table 3 for both adults and children along with Walbiri findings and also the combined figures for both communities.

A more detailed examination of each diagnostic category will be made later.

*3. Aged Persons.* The aged persons or "pensioner" category at the Warburton Ranges is comprised of men whose ages were estimated to exceed 65 years and women who exceeded 60 years. Ten men and 19 women received a retirement pension. Of five aged persons nominated by informants three were considered by the investigators to have suffered at some time in their lives from a significant psychiatric disorder, one a senile confusional state following dental extractions, another a long standing personality disorder, and the third man though clearly abnormal could not be placed in any of the categories. Thus, 10.2 percent of this aged group were psychiatrically disabled. This finding is consistent with the Walbiri rate of 8.7 percent and with findings of Western society (USDHEW 1959) that the greatest frequency of psychiatric illness is among aged persons.

## COMMENT

The frequency of all psychiatric disorders occurring among this western desert group of aborigines was 6.8 percent compared with 5.4 percent for the Walbiri in central Australia. A figure of 6.0 percent for both groups combined probably indicates with fair accuracy the amount of significant psychiatric disability in tradition-orientated aboriginal communities in central Australia. A comparison of this finding with the reported prevalence rates from other parts of the world is made difficult because of the enormous scope for variability which such factors as data collection, criteria of inclusion of cases, and diagnoses allow. (Dohrenwend and Dohrenwend 1965). However the aboriginal figure is considerably smaller than findings for western societies which often exceed 25 percent (Leighton 1956, Helgason 1964), and for an Australian country town (Krupinski 1967), but is larger than the rate of 1 percent reported by Lin for Formosan Chinese (Lin 1953). Within Australia a comparison can also be made with the findings of Cawte (1965) who reports that 10 percent of an aboriginal community of 120 persons of the eastern Aranda group had suffered from a serious mental disorder in the five years which preceded his visit. The social structure and culture of this community were fragmentary. It seems likely that rapid sociocultural disintegration is a factor of major importance accounting for the high prevalence of severe psychiatric illness among the eastern Aranda compared with western desert people and Walbiri.

It has become folklore that "primitive" people are less subjected to the stresses of life than the members of modern communities and in consequence are less prone to the psychiatric ills of Western society. This view can be strongly challenged on the grounds that a "primitive" society is in fact not stress free but that its tensions are coped with in different ways. This certainly seems to be the case in aboriginal society where high levels of emotional tension are coped with by direct expression and by projection of hostile impulses. Hostile feelings are expressed vehemently often by ritualized combative display or by actual combat which among men leads to spearing and among women to clubbing. These patterns are learned from an early age by instruction, observation, and interaction. This major difference in the mode of handling an important instinctual drive may provide an explanation of the low incidence of some neuroses and of psychosomatic disorders. No syndromes clearly resembling classical Western neuroses—anxiety states, phobic states, or obsessive compulsive states, were detected. No special factors were found which would explain why they should not come to notice. It therefore seems likely that these disorders do not occur. No instances of suicide or attempted suicide were detected. Informants knew of no such occurrences. The absence of suicide can perhaps be explained as a consequence of strong fears of death and also because of the tendency to act out and project hostile impulses. Other people and other things are blamed for personal misfortunes and illness. Transcultural investigations of this sort do therefore provide evidence of sociocultural and personality interactions relevant to the genesis of these disorders. Further studies are of course required to substantiate these suggestions and they must be done soon; it is likely that only a few years remain during which substantial groups of aborigines relatively unaffected by Western culture remain in existence.

A number of subjects were seen whose main complaints were of chronic somatic symptoms. These subjects appeared to be quite preoccupied with bodily sensations and they believed that they were ill though to the best of our knowledge no physical illness existed. They attended the settlement clinic frequently for medicines. This hypochondriacal syndrome was detected in 1.4 percent of people at the Warburton Ranges and in 0.2 percent of the Walbiri. In traditional times "primitive" Aborigines sought "treatment" from native practitioners for somatically experienced "illness." In "modern" society hypochondriasis is sometimes considered (W.H.O. 1965, Kenyon 1966) a neurotic disorder therefore based on conflict and repression. If this is so one might expect that aborigines in transition, that is, moving from an environment of freer expression of instinctual drive to one of increased restraint and repression, would be likely to express with increasing frequency their neurotic symptoms in a hypochondriacal way. It is hoped that comparative figures from an urban community will be obtained later which will show whether this in fact happens.

Possession syndromes may be viewed as either primary or secondary phenomena. A "primary possession" syndrome is here regarded as a reaction to sorcery or to the belief that injury by supernatural means had occurred and a "secondary possession" syndrome as a reaction to physical or mental illness which is interpreted by the sick person as the manifestation of object incorporation or loss of vital material. Cases recorded here were probably of the primary variety. They were characterized by a reactive syndrome of withdrawal, inactivity, food refusal, and by expectations of death if a cure could not be effected by a native doctor. This reaction had wide social implications. The prevalence of such disorders at the Warburton Ranges was 0.5 percent and the total prevalence for both communities was 0.3 percent. Secondary syndromes were placed in appropriate diagnostic categories.

One probable case of schizophrenia was located at the Warburton Ranges. Among the Walbiri four likely schizophrenics were found. These numbers are small and the difference is unlikely to be significant. The overall frequency of schizophrenia

in the combined population is 0.5 percent. Variations in the prevalence of schizophrenia from group to group and from society to society are, according to Kallman, surprisingly limited and the general expectancy of the disorder is close to 1 percent (Kallman 1959). The finding here of 0.5 percent is consistent with this general expectancy but contrasts with Cawte's eastern Aranda group where the frequency of schizophrenia was in excess of 3 percent. Perhaps this difference is accounted for by the social disorganization and cultural disintegration which had progressed to an extreme degree among eastern Aranda people. The two groups are probably genetically similar.

Affective psychoses occur among desert aborigines. Two subjects, one with a cyclic manic depressive state and one with symptoms rather suggestive of endogenous depression, were located at the Warburton Ranges. A further case of affective psychosis was found among the Walbiri making the frequency of severe affective disorders 0.3 percent. The "depression" category in Table 3 refers to likely depressive illness which does not resemble the clinical syndrome of endogenous depression. Three cases were located at the Warburton Ranges and a further two among the Walbiri. The overall prevalence for affective disorders was 0.7 percent. Guilt and self-recrimination did not seem to be a feature of depressive illness in this people.

Organic disorders were found both at the Warburton Ranges and among Walbiri to be a common group of detected psychiatric syndromes and occurred in 1.2 percent of the combined populations. This group has been further analyzed in Table 4. There the "other" category refers to individuals who had either congenital or acquired brain disorders other than acute or chronic brain syndromes. The epileptic group in Table 4 showed no evidence of psychiatric disability. Dementia certainly occurs in central Australia and its

**Table 4** Organic Psychiatric Syndromes

|  | War-<br>burton | Walbiri | Total | %<br>Frequency |
|---|---|---|---|---|
| Acute brain<br>syndrome | 1 | 1 | 2 | 0.18 |
| Chronic brain<br>syndrome | 1 | 5 | 6 | 0.55 |
| Other | 1 | 2 | 3 | 0.28 |
| Epilepsy only | 1 | 1 | 2 | 0.18 |
| Total | 4 | 9 | 13 | 1.19 |

presence in traditional communities can be ascertained from aboriginal informants. This disorder occurred in 0.6 percent of the combined population. Traumatic brain injuries and epileptic sequelae would probably be much more frequent among women if the aboriginal skull was less thick at the vertex (Elkin 1964) where blows are actually delivered and with alarming force.

The "behavior disorders of childhood" diagnosis was used to describe disturbed children in whom an organic etiology was not indicated. Quite obviously the stated frequency of such disorders depends largely upon the criterion of their inclusion. In the present survey information about cases was obtained mainly from European school teachers and only "seriously" disturbed children were included. Aboriginal informants were reluctant to admit to strangers that their children had faults or created management problems unless these were gross. Lesser disorders were therefore probably not detected. Cases are listed in Table 2. Situational or abnormal reactive states were diagnosed when individuals who had shown no evidence of significant premorbid personality disorder developed an excessive or abnormal nonpsychotic reaction to an actual environmental stress. The prevalence of such disorders at Warburton was 0.5 percent. Personality disorders have been defined in a previous paper (Kidson 1967). They occurred among 0.7 percent of Warburton residents and in 0.8 percent of Walbiri. No evidence of homosexuality was obtained. It seems very unlikely that homosexual acts occur between men or that homosexuality forms any appreciable part of ceremonial behavior (Jones 1968). It is doubtful if anyone in this society with homosexual orientation would be permitted to disregard or avoid the normal obligations of initiation marriage and kinship.

## SUMMARY

This paper describes a survey of psychiatric disorders among a tradition-orientated community of aborigines in the Australian western desert. The prevalence of a wide range of psychiatric disorders is presented. Findings are combined with those of a previous and methodologically similar study and then are representative of 2.5 percent of the total estimated full-blood Aboriginal population. Functional psychoses, personality disorders, organic psychiatric syndromes, and an exotic "possession" syndrome were found in this people but classical neuroses, psychosomatic illness, and suicide were not detected. An attempt was made to explain some of these findings.

# 38 The Culture-Bound Reactive Syndromes

## Pow Meng Yap

The so-called ethnic psychoses have been of interest to anthropologists and psychiatrists for a long time. One of the first attempts by a psychiatrist to "make sense" of the phenomena and at the same time cast them within the nosological systems of Western psychiatry was that of Pow Meng Yap, who observed some of them firsthand in his clinical practice in Hong Kong. Yap published papers (Yap 1951) that were widely used and quoted. Other psychiatrists, for example, A. A. Brill (1912), an early translator of Freud into English, wrote on *pibloktoq* or arctic hysteria among Polar Eskimos, and accounts of hyperdramatic, "bizarre" behaviors among non-Western peoples appeared in the accounts of Western travelers long ago. David Aberle (1952) wrote on arctic hysteria and latah at the time of Yap's early papers, and Gussow (1960, 1963), Wallace (1972), and many other anthropologists have studied extreme behavioral reactions among nonliterate peoples. A comprehensive review and new synthesis has recently appeared by Foulks (1972). Opler (1967) notes a formidable list of psychiatrists who have been interested in these exotic behavioral disturbances since the time of Freud and Jung.

In this paper, the late Dr. Yap further classifies and defines the criteria for recognizing these "culture-bound reactive syndromes," a term that I find preferable to earlier ones (for example, ethnic psychoses). Whether the reader will agree with such classifications or with Yap's attempts to decide what disturbances properly do and do not belong within the diagnostic systems of Western psychiatry (and even as Yap admits, there is not full and common agreement within Western psychiatry on how to deal with these behaviors in non-Western societies), the paper nevertheless is useful in attempting to deal systematically with these emotional states and in recognizing strongly the essential need to consider social and cultural factors in investigating them. The reader should recall my remarks in the introduction to this section,

Reprinted with abridgments from Pow Meng Yap, 1969, "The Culture-Bound Reactive Syndromes," in William Caudill and Tsung-Yi Lin, eds., *Mental Health Research in Asia and the Pacific*, Honolulu: East-West Center Press, with permission of Virginia Chang, the East-West Center Press, and the University of Hawaii Press.

especially regarding LeVine's notion of rare-zero differential, to place these behavioral syndromes into ecological-demographic perspective. Also relevant are Lex (Chapter 36); my introduction to Section X, Rubel's study (Chapter 12) of *susto*, and the chapters by Parker, Kennedy, and the Hamers in this section.

Inquiry into the problems of comparative psychiatry and systematic examination of *latah*, the possession syndrome, *koro*, and the hypereridic state indicate that the so-called exotic psychoses can be classified properly under the rubric of the "psychogenic psychoses" as described by Faergeman (1963) and others before him. In 1962 I suggested that the term "atypical, culture-bound psychogenic psychosis" be adopted to embrace these conditions. For general purposes I would retain the adjective "atypical" because each of these psychoses is relatively unfamiliar even in its own cultural milieu, but I would now substitute "reactive" for "psychogenic," in spite of its more narrow connotation, and "syndrome" for the more controversial "psychosis."

## THE NEED FOR NOSOLOGY AND STANDARD NOMENCLATURE

The need for a generally accepted nomenclature and classification of mental illness is nowhere more urgent than in transcultural psychiatry (Yap 1962). Rigidity in basic nomenclature has its value, but if classification of mental illness is to fulfill its function we must temper inflexibility by the demand for assimilating new observations. On the one hand, common disease concepts are needed for purposes of communication; on the other, a need exists to integrate new knowledge into old or, conversely, to allow application of accumulated knowledge to fresh clinical problems. It is possible for excessive insistence on the simple communicative function of nosological systems to blind us to unusual phenomena, hampering further investigation of them. The interpretative function of nosological classification needs emphasis, although it varies according to the nature of the axis employed for differentiating one disorder from another. The more etiologically fundamental the axis, the narrower is the possible range for its use when studying puzzling new conditions. The more symptomatically conceived the disease category, the less valuable it is in helping to define and trace the causes of unfamiliar illness, for measurements of variables in a broad and necessarily heterogeneous group will not appear to be significant, although they are significant for a smaller homogeneous one. For example, the frequency of positive urine tests in phenylketonuric amentia is not statistically significant when a random sample of children is examined rather than a narrowly defined clinical group of retarded children. . . .

The term "reactive" (which is not to be confused with "exogenous") means that an abnormal reaction has been produced by an external traumatic shock of great severity in a mechanical manner or has been brought into open expression in a predisposed subject by an external, experimental stress. Since most cases of psychogenic psychosis are of the latter type, the term "reactive," when applied to them, must be understood in that sense. In practice, it is not possible to relate the response to the stress without further taking into account the direct effect of sociocultural factors in patterning affective and behavioral responses to pernicious stimuli. . . .

## JUSTIFICATION FOR THE CLASS OF "REACTIVE PSYCHOSIS"

. . . A standard objection to the concept of reactive psychosis is that it fails to do justice to the multifactorial nature of mental disease. The objection can be resolved into the assertion that experiential factors are much less important in causing mental disorder than are somatic factors. The basic reason for such an attitude is the difficulty in identifying causally significant, traumatic psychological factors. It is trite to point to the rarity of cases fulfilling Jaspers' (1962) criteria for reactivity—criteria such as a meaningful relation between the precipitating cause and the content of illness and a parallel time relation between the two. It also is arbitrary to attribute acute brain syndromes to physical lesions. The fundamental difficulty in discussing psychogenesis lies in applying the idea of causality to mental phenomena, when the subject-predicate grammar of the Aryan type of language constrains us to think of mind as a *substance*, but one without position and spatial extension (Northrop 1963).

The multifactorial approach is appropriate to the complexity of the problem, but it should not be allowed to disguise what is really reductionism. It would be self-deceiving to accept only a primary neurophysiological lesion, relegating all other factors to vague epiphenomena, and not bothering to enumerate, much less demonstrate, them or to test hypotheses implicating them. When confronted with a patient, serious scientists are responsible for evaluating significant etiological factors and assigning them some order of importance: which factors are necessary but not sufficient, and which factors perhaps are sufficient by themselves? To regard a case as reactive does not exclude appreciation of constitutional factors, which are after all partly the result of earlier psychic experience, but emphasizes the outstanding importance of experiential factors, which may sometimes, if severe, be sufficient in themselves to bring about illness.

The restriction of the term "disease" to mean only the structural alterations caused by physical lesions is unacceptable. Not only are organic disorders like asthma, tetany, migraine, and essential hypertension defined in terms of functional symptoms, but so also are the functional psychoses—manic-depressive insanity and schizophrenia—and the psychoneuroses. If one is persuaded by Slater (1965) to deny hysteria the status of a disease because it is a purely psychological disorder without genuine physical symptoms, the same reasoning must be extended to the functional psychoses and the other psychoneuroses. Roth (1963) has pointed out the illogic of attempts to separate medical and behavioral parts of medicine because all functional psychiatric syndromes, when defined in terms of symptoms and signs, include a minority of cases associated with organic disease in a causally significant way, e.g., schizophrenia in rare cases with amphetamine intoxication, and depression in the aged sometimes with physical disease. . . .

## THE POSITION OF THE "EXOTIC SYNDROMES"

Arieti and Meth (1959), Ellenberger (1965), and Kiev (1965) have given accounts of the "exotic syndromes." Arieti and Meth suggested that they are unclassifiable. On the contrary, it is my belief that systematic analysis places the "exotic syndromes" within the psychogenic psychoses grouping, although patients may not always be disturbed enough in the sense discussed earlier to merit being called "psychotic." These syndromes are culture-bound in that certain systems of implicit values, social structure, and obviously shared beliefs produce unusual forms of psychopathology that are confined to special areas. Social and cultural factors bring about special forms of mental illness, although these are only atypical variations of generally distributed psychogenic disorders. It is necessary to avoid overgeneralizing about the relation between culture and mental disorder from the material available. In theory, there are almost a dozen ways in which this relation can be spelled out (Murphy and Leighton 1965). Van der Kroef (1958) has made an elaborate attempt to explain *latah* and *amok* in terms of the Indonesian ethos, relying heavily on Jung, and Wallace (1961) has propounded an ecological theory of mental disorders which he calls "bio-cultural," with special reference to Eskimo *piblokto*. It does not appear that any one schema, however, can do justice to all the facts. For the whole group of culture-bound reactive syndromes, diverse links are traceable between illness and its sociocultural background, although the subject is not considered systematically in this chapter.

It is mistaken to suppose that all these syndromes are rare. Psychogenic death from extreme terror in its complete form (so-called thanatomania) may be rare and of scientific interest only as an example of the utmost limits of psychophysiological derangement, but *amok*, *latah*, "malignant anxiety," and to a less extent *koro* are not uncommon. Indeed, the psychiatrist in his ordinary practice is faced with the inescapable problem of diagnosing and classifying such cases for which he has no guide, since these disorders are treated in textbooks only as remote medical curiosities. Certainly, they are at the very least of the same order of frequency as cases of sexual deviation. Schmidt (1964) stated that in Sarawak *amok* is only one of many "short-lived explosive psychoses" and that *latah* is still common. Sangsingkeo (personal communication) has found *latah* common in Thailand. Both Maguigad (1964) and Zaguirre (1957) reported that *amok* is frequent in the Philippines; in fact, the latter recorded that it has become more common since World War II. As for the undifferentiated syndrome of panic that Lambo (1962) has called "malignant anxiety," all workers in Africa agree on its frequency. Lambo was able within a period of six years to gather 98 cases of persons so afflicted charged with offenses involving capital punishment.

Many cases of the "exotic syndromes" may not come to the attention of the clinician because they are not severe, or, as best exemplified in the very wide-spread possession syndrome, the reactions may be exploited socially so that doubt arises over their medical abnormality. Possession may be valued in various religious contexts and in spiritualistic mediumship. *Amok*-like behavior has in the Philippines found expression in ritually supported *jurmentado*, and it appears that Philippine law enforcement agencies tend to be lenient toward homicidal violence. The reactions, however, may become quite uncontrolled on the part of the subject so that he commits serious antisocial acts. Medico-legal issues arise, and psychiatric expertise, if only in differential diagnosis, is called for. For this reason, Lambo has stressed the forensic importance of malignant anxiety in Africa, and an early paper by Lloyd-Still (1940) gave case histories illustrating the forensic significance of *latah* in Burma. In Burma according to Hazel Weidman (personal communication), *amok*-like behavior can arise out of the startle reaction. The criminological aspects of *amok*, which need hardly be elaborated, have been dealt with by Zaguirre (1957). The reality of psychogenic death in Africa sometimes becomes a practical issue in death inquiries (Lambo 1962).

The successful exploitation of some minor or moderate examples of a number of these reactions by both the patients themselves and society should not obscure the fact that the fully developed forms exhibit abstruse and psychiatrically technical

phenomena, e.g., depersonalization, dissociation, hypereridism, echo-reactions, command automatism, and psychophysiological changes. The fact that illness is capitalized upon by society is not an argument *per se* against its abnormality; similar exploitation of physical diseases occurs, for instance, exhibiting midgets, giants, and Siamese twins in circuses, using deformed children for beggary, or training the blind for mediumship (as happens in certain parts of northern Japan).

It should not be overlooked that characteristically developed forms of these reactions are regarded by their own societies as abnormal, although, as far as possession is concerned, the abnormal may not always be clearly distinguished from the preternormal and numinous, so that the social response is ambiguous. Devereux (1963) has suggested that in folk cultures patients who consider themselves unfit in one way or another seek to define themselves in terms of some socially supported model of insane behavior in order to obtain certain satisfactions associated with the sick role and to avoid being treated as criminals. Such a formulation is overgeneralized, ignores the fact that cultural patterning of abnormal behavior must

**Table 1**　Atypical and Typical Syndromes of Reactive Psychoses

| Atypical "Exotic Syndrome" | Typical Prototype |
|---|---|
| *Primary Fear Reactions*<br>　Malignant anxiety | Undifferentiated states of acute anxiety and panic with varying degrees of egodisorganization |
| *Latah* reaction, including *mali-mali, mir-yachit, imu, bah-tschi, young-dah-hte;* "jumping" | States of hypersuggestibility with echo-reactions following psychogenic shock, commonly with other predisposing causes, e.g., toxic-exhaustive; "startle neurosis" |
| *Susto*, including *espanto* | Traumatic anxiety-depressive states with psychophysiological changes |
| Psychogenic "magical" death or "thanatomania" | Severe psychophysiological disorganization with surgical shock from terror in catastrophic situations |
| *Hypereridic Rage Reaction*<br>　Amok (including *negi-negi?*) | Acute psychopathic reaction issuing from states of morbid hostility in predisposed personalities |
| *Specific, Culturally Imposed Nosophobia*<br>　Koro | Depersonalization states associated with severe anxiety, arising from unrealistic fears, e.g., "venereophobia" |
| *Trance Dissociation*<br>　Possession syndrome, including *windigo* psychosis, *hsieh-ping* | Possession states, with varying degrees of social sanctioning, often poorly delimited and beyond patient's control |

take place on the basis of individual psychological or psychiatric dysfunction, overestimates the degree of self-control in the patient, and also exaggerates the freedom of choice open to him in expressing his disabilities. Moreover, Devereux wrongly sees all mental illness as merely psychogenic, as does Szasz (1961). The insight of the ethnologist needs to be balanced by the perception of the clinician interested in the structural analysis of mental disease.

There are typical and atypical forms of the reactive psychoses everywhere, the atypical forms appearing in puzzling ways because of specific cultural forms and social structure. Atypical culture-bound variations of psychogenic reactions in European and American countries include homosexual-panic; depression, which Hutterites call *anfectung* and regard as surrender to Satanic design; mass excitement, sometimes accompanied by fainting of female adolescents at the sight of popular male idols; and perhaps also school-phobia and anorexia nervosa. These reactions have not been dignified as basic syndromes in themselves, partly because they are not common to all cultures and partly because the conceptual apparatus of psychiatry has not been applied to their fundamental analysis. The same cannot be said of the "exotic syndromes" in general. Table 1 attempts to draw parallels between these and related conditions that are typical and generally distributed, the aim being to expound the basic psychopathological nature of the "exotic syndromes." Certain conditions, e.g., the *piblokto* of the Arctic, the *banga* of the Congo, and the *misala* of Malawi, are not included because they are only vague generic terms for mental illness or denote only ordinary, unspecialized hysterical reactions. Such terms should not be allowed to creep into the

psychiatric literature. One of the purposes of this paper is to prevent their proliferation.

Psychopathologically, it is possible to distribute the less familiar atypical reactive syndromes into the four groups indicated. In the unlikely event that new conditions are discovered, they also probably could be accommodated in these groupings. The culture-bound fear reactions occupy a prominent place, a factor which cannot be surprising, for fear, even more than rage, has the power to impair ego functioning and ultimately bring about a level of mental functioning that is nondiscriminative, impulsive, and thus rudimentary. At this level, cultural forces can build up distinct and unique patterns of abnormal behavior. Kretschmer (1934) called mental functioning on this plane "hypobulic-hyponoic" or "primitive" in contrast to individual personality reactions of a less regressive kind; he also stressed the ease with which hysterical reactions grew out of them. Furthermore, it is not surprising that specialized primary fear reactions (as opposed to the culturally inculcated phobias) are found in simple folk societies, for being technically backward such peoples have inadequate mastery over their environment and live in a psychological world hostile beyond the comprehension of metropolitan man.

## CLASSIFICATION OF REACTIVE PSYCHOSES BY SYNDROME

A formal ordering of the reactive psychoses within an acceptable and relevant nosological scheme is needed for clinical, didactic, forensic, and administrative purposes. A widely used classification is that of Schneider (1959), which has

**Table 2** Tentative Classification of Atypical Culture-bound Reaction Syndromes

| | |
|---|---|
| 1. Paranoid syndrome | |
| 2. Emotional syndrome | 2.1 Depersonalization state: *koro* |
| | 2.2 Fear-induced depressive state: *susto* |
| 3. Syndrome of disordered consciousness | 3.1 Impaired consciousness: *latah* reaction |
| | 3.2 Turbid states: malignant anxiety, *amok*, *negi-negi* |
| | 3.3 Dissociated consciousness: certain types of possession syndrome, *hsieh-ping, windigo* psychosis |

Note: It may be possible with further information to add to the three main headings a meaningful fourth: Extreme and irreversible psychophysiological disorganization from terror: psychogenic death.

been adopted by Stromgren and Faergeman. It subdivides the generic grouping of psychogenic (reactive) psychosis into paranoid and emotional syndromes, and disorders of consciousness. The suggestion is tentatively offered that the culture-bound syndromes can be fitted usefully into the classification shown in Table 2. *Latah*, *amok*, and the possession state involve disturbances of consciousness, as does severe malignant anxiety. *Koro* and *susto* belong rather more to the emotional syndrome, although an intense reaction may be accompanied by clouding in the case of *koro*, and perhaps also in *susto*. Possession, *koro*, and *susto* implicate delusional beliefs, but only in a special sense, since the social consensus in the patients' subcultures buttresses these beliefs. Psychogenic death is prefaced by such unusual behavior and involves such extreme psychosomatic reactions that at present it also can be considered psychotic.

As any other classification, Table 2 is unduly neat and precise. It is based on clinical symptoms, but it cannot take into account minor variants and mixed pictures in differentiating one form from another. As a classification it is, in our present state of knowledge, zealously comprehensive, but it is offered mainly to provoke thinking and discussion. The various syndromes require further elaboration.

*Koro*. This is a culture-conditioned acute depersonalization syndrome, with localized depersonalization confined to the penis, occurring in the context of a panic state with fears of impending death (Yap 1965a; Rin 1965; Gwee 1963). It is encountered in Hong Kong and Southeast Asia where the belief in a mortal *koro* illness with penile shrinking intensifies ordinary guilt and anxiety over real or fancied sexual excess, especially autoerotic activity, and also determines specifically the unique presenting symptom in a psychologically comprehensible way. Cultural forms therefore can be pathogenic as well as pathoplastic. Immaturity of personality, an anxious temperament, and cold are contributing factors; sudden fright can precipitate an attack.

It occurs in all degrees of severity, leading rarely to clouding of consciousness with extreme panic. It is never welcome and always feared; consequently *koro* is never exploited for social ends. The institution of polygamy in one form or another, with its demands for adequate male sexual performance, may be a precondition for its occurrence in any society, as is the tradition of ancestor veneration with its emphasis on maintaining the family line.

Comparable abnormally intense fear reactions induced by socially supported beliefs have been described among the Saulteaux, who learn to be unrealistically frightened of certain snakes and caterpillars (Hallowell 1934). These specifically imposed and pathological fears have to be distinguished from abnormal primary fear reactions.

*Susto, Including Espanto*. This illness, which occurs in the people of the Andean highlands, is usually brought on by fright, e.g., from a fall, a thunderclap, or meeting a ferocious animal. It affects mainly children and adolescents, but no age group is immune. The symptoms are insomnia, asthenia, apathy, loss of appetite and weight, depression, and anxiety with its physiological accompaniments. It is treated by indigenous ritualistic psychotherapy (Sal y Rosas, personal communication; Leon 1965; Rubel 1964)....

*Susto*, although it is precipitated by fright as is *latah*, presents a dissimilar picture. The crucial part that cultural conditioning plays in determining responses to fear is plain.

*Latah*. I have used this one term to cover a number of different terms which describe the same reaction in widely separated countries (North Africa, Southeast Asia, Siberia, Hokkaido, North America) in order to emphasize the psychodynamics of the reaction (Yap 1952). *Latah* is identical with the "jumping" of Maine, to which Stevens (1965) has devoted a recent paper. Thorne (1944), without being aware of *latah* or "jumping," described in white American draftees what he called "startle neurosis," in which a sudden stimulus such as a slap or putting the finger in the gluteal fold ("goosing") produces acute distress with trembling, jumping, or whirling around. This reaction could be provoked repeatedly in the same subject to the point of exhaustion.

*Latah* is based on a variant of Kretschmer's "primitive reactions," and exhibits hypersuggestibility, automatic obedience, coprolalia, and echolalia. It is very much like the traumatic neuroses described by Kardiner (1959) in that it sometimes becomes progressively more severe, with permanent psychic changes attributable to a reduction of the adaptive powers of the ego, leading to social incapacity. The part that organic factors play in determining such a course is not clear. The *latah* subject is unable to cope with sudden stress, or shock, which may in itself be quite ordinary, and reacts to it with severe ego-disorganization and anxiety. Many cases develop after an acute traumatic experience, although the experience may in some be traumatic only because of idiosyncratic fears, e.g., of certain worms and animals. The reaction may be precipitated even by mention of the feared objects, or—of great psychopathological interest—by tickling.

As a rule, *latah* patients are nervous and yielding; Aberle (1952) attempted to interpret this fact in terms of ambivalence toward submission, arising from "an unconscious connection between submission and a dreaded and desired passive sexual experience akin to being attacked." It is true that most patients are females and moveover females of low social class. Cross-culturally, an explanation in terms of class may be apposite, though it would not exclude psychodynamic formulations. Carluccio, Sours, and Kolb (1964) have sought to explain echo-reactions as mocking behavior, as well as on the basis of identification with the aggressor. I have interpreted *latah* in terms of gestalt field concepts and pointed out that echo-reactions are the simplest responses a psychologically disorganized subject can exhibit when placed in a demanding situation, since the figural stability and dominance of the impaired ego is overcome by the valences that bind it to the behavioral field (Yap 1952). In technologically backward societies, the sense of hazard is so diffuse and pervasive that it is not practicable to develop a definite psychological set toward distinguishable dangerous objects in the environment; consequently powers of mastery are ill-developed and the ego weak. The *latah* reaction provides a clear example of impairment of consciousness produced by purely psychological factors and is thus important for general psychopathology.

*Latah*, like other (including somatic) diseases, is not regarded as abnormal unless it is of a certain degree; infrequently, severe cases involve homicidal complications, requiring expert diagnosis (Lloyd-Still 1940).

*Malignant Anxiety.* This is the name given by Lambo (1962) to a common African syndrome of chronic anxiety without latent or manifest psychosis of separate etiology. It runs a progressive and socially crippling course but does not end in schizophrenic or organic deterioration. It is marked by tension and hostility, which in men (who more often show it) may lead to homicide, and in women to suicide. The patients often have markedly sensitive, moody, restless, and egotistic personalities and are usually preoccupied by fear of bewitchment. The bouts of intense anxiety with confused excitement not followed by amnesia cannot be explained on the basis of cerebral dysrythmia or hypoglycaemia. Lambo examined 29 patients and mentioned the occurrence of three major epidemics of this disorder. French workers in Africa also have described it and remarked on its frequency (Yap 1962).

Malignant anxiety can be regarded as a clinically undifferentiated form of the hypereridic state, in which hostility accumulates in the patient without conversion into depression or psychoneurotic symptoms and may ultimately issue in destructive behavior either against himself or others, or, since ego-disorganization occurs, against both at the same time. The direction which aggression takes depends on a number of personality and environmental factors; when a culture prescribes a certain mode of aggressiveness against others following frustration, malignant anxiety can give the appearance of *amok*.

*Amok.* I have defined *amok* as a strictly psychogenic reaction based on hypereridism (Yap 1958b). It therefore is to be placed alongside the acute psychopathic reactions described in constitutionally predisposed or intellectually subnormal persons under stress, familiar to psychiatrists everywhere; and should not be confused with apparently similar behavior caused by schizophrenia, epilepsy, or acute brain lesions resulting from toxic, exhaustive, or infective causes....

*Amok* is associated with dazing or clouding of the sensorium and subsequent amnesia, preceded by frustration. Too much weight should not be given to the element of learning involved in this reaction. The argument that all psychoneurotic behavior is due to maladaptive learning is no longer novel, and does not affect clinical diagnosis. *Amok* is definitely maladaptive and deviant and requires medical attention, as Zaguirre's material so well illustrates. No doubt many attacks are aborted because prompt measures are taken; the patients are kept in custody after their initial violence has been curbed but are not changed (Sechrest, personal communication). The report that the incidence in Java fell after *amok* runners were captured alive and jailed need mean no more, even if true, than that social measures can change the pattern and therefore the incidence of psychogenic reactions. It is not an argument against the abnormality of *amok*. Because of certain cultural forms, people in areas where *amok* occurs tend to develop a low frustration tolerance to interpersonal stress, reacting to such stress with blind rage. Such rage, however, is regarded as abnormal in its own milieu, and only a small minority exhibit this extreme reaction. It is mainly because of the significant cultural influence in the patterning of this reaction that the ordinary label of "acute psychopathic reaction" is not appropriate to it.

A psychogenic *amok*-like reaction occurring in Puerto Rico has been described by Rothenberg (1964) under the name of "Puerto-Rican syndrome" or *mal de pelea*. It is desirable to analyze such conditions going under their native designations in relation to the better-known *amok*. Rothenberg pointed out that in the local language the word "nervous" also means "angry."

*Negi-Negi.* This condition in the New Guinea Highlands has been reported upon recently by Langness (1965). He quoted the field and clinical observations of Sinclair (1957), who used the term "acute hysterical psychotic state." A similar condition in Papua under the name of *lulu* affects only males and takes the form of aggressive behavior which may be homicidal. Usually it is associated with the death of a relative, but the essentially involved frustration and hostile tension arising from it suggests a relation to *amok*. It is accompanied by fears of the departed and, as might be expected, is thought to be caused by spirit possession. More information is needed about this disorder. Although glossolalia is absent, perhaps it lies closer to the trance possession states than to *amok*.

*Trance (Possession) States.* It is useful to follow the example of Bourguignon and Haas (1965) and Bourguignon and Pettay (1964, 1965) and make a distinction between trance states and states of possession. I mean by trance any state of dissociated consciousness, psychologically induced and reversible, which is not associated with primary schizophrenic symptoms. From a certain point of view, dissociated consciousness also may be said to be narrowed or restricted. Automatism may appear in thematic speech and semipurposive behavior out of keeping with the subject's normal personality. Trance may be viewed in different cultures or subcultures as a mystical state, a disease per se, soul loss, or possession either by a feared or a benign spirit. Possession by benign spirits and, to a lesser extent, possession by evil spirits may not be considered within the field of medicine, but even when it occurs in a religious context the trance behavior may become so extravagant and uncontrolled that the subject is taken to a psychiatrist. It is true that in folk societies the medical and priestly functions of the shaman are not clearly separated, reflecting the uncertainty with which such reactions are regarded by the group. In terms of the modern psychiatrist's professional orientation, however,

most instances of possession must be defined as abnormal. I have analyzed a series of patients who were brought to the psychiatric clinic because of spontaneous possession or possession with behavior so excessive that relatives and neighbors could not reconcile it with accepted spiritualistic cults or professional mediumship (Yap 1960). As a rule, in such patients there is some degree of clouding and incoherence, but often it is possible to discern a thematic content in the symptoms, understandable in the light of the patient's real difficulties.

Because of differing social attitudes toward trance and because of the need for diagnosis differentiating trance, especially trance possession, from other illnesses, a clearcut definition of possession is necessary. I have offered the following basic definition (Yap 1960), which utilizes a fundamental concept of G. H. Mead and H. S. Sullivan, to identify the condition even in little-known and disparate cultures:

It is a condition where problem-solving processes result in an unusual dramatization of the "me" part of the Self, that aspect being constituted by previous partial identification with another personality, believed to be of transcendental nature, whose relationship to the subject is not tested in reality but is elaborated in fantasy. The nature of the possessing personality can be psychologically understood in the light of the subject's own personality needs; his life situation; the personality characteristics either historical or symbolical of the possessing agent; and the subject's cultural background, which determines the normality or otherwise of such a condition.

*Windigo.* This psychosis, called *witigo, witiko,* and so on, is another example of a culturally patterned possession syndrome, occurring among the Indians of northeast Canada. The most systematic account of it is that by Teicher (1960), but Parker (1960) has offered the most painstaking discussion of its relation to sociocultural and psychological factors. *Windigo* always is regarded as undesirable, deviant behavior which can culminate in homicide through cannibalism. The patient shows prodromal depression and anxiety before becoming possessed by the *windigo*, a giant monster with a skeleton and heart of ice feeding on human beings. The intrusion of this spirit sometimes cannot be resisted; subjects in the prodromal stage even may ask to be killed themselves. A *windigo* patient is treated first by shamanistic techniques, but once he becomes cannibalistic he is put to death. Experience with and fears of winter famine make the thematic content of this disorder comprehensible, but they cannot explain the clinical form it takes.

A further example of the possession syndrome goes under the name of *hsieh-ping* in Taiwan; it has no remarkable features (C. C. Hsu, personal communication) and appears to be similar to syndromes I have studied in Hong Kong. The introduction of this term into the literature was fortuitous and is a reminder that we must be on guard against a meaningless terminological explosion in comparative psychiatry.

*Psychogenic "Magical" Death.* The existence of this condition,—bearing also the deceptive name of "thanatomania"—must remain scrupulously *sub judice*, yet it is of outstanding importance for psychosomatic medicine. Cannon (1942) urged observers to give serious attention to it and even outlined simple clinical examinations for use in the field to test his hypothesis of the cause of death. Cannon's hypothesis is that grossly excessive sympathetic activity causes vasoconstriction in the visceral blood vessels and consequent damage through anoxemia to the capillary endothelium, leading to loss of blood plasma and blood volume, ultimately resulting in a fatal fall in blood pressure. He compared this process to the death of a decorticated cat from sympathetic overexcitement when the sympathetic system was intact. He also drew attention to deaths of men suffering from surgical shock, who are caught in a vicious circle of progressive hypotension, and pointed out that the relevance of psychological factors in this condition have long been recognized. Cannon's "emergency reaction" has its modern parallel in the "alarm reaction" of Selye; but facts accumulated in the study of the latter have yet to be applied to the subject here. Richter (1957), based on evidence from a study of sudden deaths provoked in laboratory rats, has suggested that excessive parasympathetic stimulation may be involved, but whatever the mechanism of death it is probable that an uncontrolled and unbalanced autonomic response based on terror is implicated (*see also* Barnett 1964). Whether a cataleptic reaction similar to "decerebrate rigidity" arising from vascular, physiological decortication of the brain also takes place is a matter for speculation. Examples of stuporous conditions with shock occurring in war, accident, and disaster have been reported by many writers. In such cases, loss of fluid intake could have aggravated shock fatally. It is reported that patients succumbing to "voodoo death" are so convinced that they are about to die

that they no longer eat or drink, but death comes too rapidly to be due to dehydration. In rural Hawaii, belief in the potency of Kahuna sorcery is still so strong that a case was reported recently of a child allowed to die of illness without the parents' attempting to seek medical treatment (Johnson 1964).

Psychogenic death has been described in Polynesia, Australia ("boning"), and Africa. Lambo (1962) mentioned that African patients with malignant anxiety from fear of bewitchment may die unless indigenous psychotherapy is instituted. Cannon quoted reports of such patients, including several by medical men in the field; some of these reports stated that breaking of the spell by the same or another witch doctor led to sudden recovery. These examples seem to exclude the possibility of poisoning; in any case, a knowledge of powerful but subtle poisons or of their antidotes is not likely in most of the tribes where psychogenic death has been reported. This subject also has been surveyed by Ellenberger (1951). Needed now are alertness to the problem on the part of ethnologists and medical field workers, proper facilities for observation, and additional concrete findings which can stand up to criticism. It is relevant to draw attention to the *British Medical Journal* of November and December, 1965, wherein a number of clinicians in Britain gave admittedly anecdotal accounts of cases in which psychogenic factors appeared to be decisive in the deaths of patients seen in their ordinary practice. Psychogenic death, however, is more probable among primitives who can be plunged into unrestrained terror as a result of the absolute conviction that they are being killed by magical means than it is among others; even among them, it is likely that the psychophysiological reactions can appear in varying degrees of severity short of death. If this relativistic point of view is adopted, the condition becomes one of great interest to the student of medical psychology.

## FURTHER RESEARCH

The principal aim of this chapter is to show that it is possible to place the "exotic syndromes" in the context of present-day clinical psychiatry. Once this idea is accepted, the way is open to the use of various tested clinical research techniques to explore the nature of these syndromes, much as the reactive psychoses have been studied in psychiatrically developed countries. Undoubtedly modifications in tool and method will have to be made. It is important that first steps be taken in an effective direction. Detailed and systematic nosographic effort, as we have seen, is still required; attempts should be made to distinguish essential from accessory symptoms, to tease out possible associations with other psychiatric and somatic illnesses, and to trace the natural history of each disorder in its elementary psychogenic form. From such studies, a consistent definition of each disorder in terms of modal symptomatology, and eventually, psychopathology, can be arrived at and provide a firm basis for further clinical research.

Much can be expected from the expert application of epidemiological techniques in this area, although it always will be necessary to find or to produce collateral demographic and socioeconomic control data in order to evaluate the significance of variations in incidence among different groups. Where social and cultural variables are difficult to interpret, they can be illuminated by life-history studies, which enrich and stimulate epidemiological research.

The skills and insight of the anthropologist are needed to help identify role and value conflicts and to analyze the belief systems at their basis. Personality formation as it is related to early training still merits attention, although interest in later life experiences should be given more careful scrutiny. It is necessary to find out why certain specific ego-defenses are employed rather than others more commonly encountered in ordinary clinical practice. Another approach would be to inquire how cultures specially organize biologically founded emotional responses, particularly the fear and rage responses, into unusual patterns that can become deviant even within their own cultures. Interesting data may be accumulated to enlarge understanding of ego development and, of crucial importance, ego strength.

Sophisticated inquiries of this kind can be expected to add a new dimension to classical controversies associated with such names as Bonhoeffer, Kleist, and Stertz over (1) the determination of clinical symptomatology by trauma; (2) whether there is a specific link between reaction and trauma; and (3) the extent to which fundamental human reaction forms as well as individual constitutional and personality predispositions determine responses to trauma. It seems, for example, that culture can induce highly nonadaptive, abnormal reactions to ordinary trauma which otherwise occur only after massive calamity. It appears also that symptoms normally associated with the acute brain syndrome can be produced by psychogenic, nonphysical factors, given the requisite cultural background. Indeed, it might be queried whether examples exist of specific psychological stress or trauma directly bringing about singularly abnormal behavior. Quite apart from practical gains, the identification of the "exotic syndromes" as atypical culture-bound variants of reactive psychosis thus raises a number of interesting questions for research, questions that touch on some of the basic problems of psychiatry.

# 39 Eskimo Psychopathology in the Context of Eskimo Personality and Culture

## *Seymour Parker*

For many reasons the peoples of the frozen Arctic lands have long held intense interest for anthropologists, medical scientists, explorers, and others. Their amazing physical and cultural adaptations to an extreme ecological situation never cease to fascinate the ethnologist no less than the physiologist. But although Eskimos are frequently described in cheerful, happy terms (for example, one recent study of Eskimo family life was called *Never in Anger* [Briggs 1970]), they seem to be no freer of severe emotional disturbance than any other human group. One prevalent form of behavioral aberration, dramatic in form and consequences, is "arctic hysteria" or *pibloktoq*, which, as Seymour Parker shows in this paper, has been described frequently, with much speculation about its etiology. In an attempt to understand the roots of this and other forms of emotional disorder among the Eskimo, Parker presents a number of factual and speculative propositions about Eskimo culture and personality, and compares the Eskimo at several points with their neighbors in northeastern Canada, the Ojibwa Indians, another group for which the ethnography is relatively well known. In the process we find some important links between cultural pressures and values on the one hand, and extreme behavioral deviance on the other. In addition to the studies noted by Parker, the reader would benefit from papers by Gussow (1960, 1963), Wallace (1972), and an exhaustive survey and synthesis of the literature by Foulks (1972).

Reprinted with abridgments from Seymour Parker, 1962, "Eskimo Psychopathology in the Context of Eskimo Personality and Culture," *American Anthropologist*, *64*:76–96, with permission of the author and the American Anthropological Association.

## 1. INTRODUCTION

...The literature on the Eskimos indicated that the psychiatric symptoms reported for them were very different from those of the Ojibwa. This seemed to be related to marked differences in the cultural beliefs, societal organization, and personality development in these groups. It was decided to report on the Eskimo data, with incidental comparisons to the Ojibwa. Material from the latter group will be offered only in order to bring into sharp relief the discussion and analysis of Eskimo society.

The purpose of this paper is to contribute to an understanding of the dynamics underlying the relationship between psychiatric symptoms and the socio-cultural environment. Symptoms will be viewed not simply as a reflection of socio-environmental pressures, but as they function in the personality and social systems in which they appear....

...Evidence will be presented in later sections of this paper to support the assumption of a considerable degree of homogeneity in the specific areas of early socialization experiences and personality characteristics. In regard to the time period under consideration, material will be drawn, as far as possible, from traditional Eskimo society before it was appreciably changed by contact with "Western" civilization.

## 2. PSYCHOPATHOLOGICAL SYMPTOMS AMONG THE ESKIMOS OF GREENLAND AND NORTH AMERICA

The rather scant and uneven literature in cross-cultural (or transcultural) psychiatry suggests that the range of psychopathological symptoms in all societies is fairly similar. However, it is probable that the relative prevalence of specific types of psychopathological symptoms differ from society to society. The reports on the Ojibwa Indians indicate that, aside from the very bizarre concern (at the overt and covert levels) with cannibalism, the most frequent psychopathological symptoms are morbid depressions, anorexia, and obsessive and paranoid ideation (Hallowell 1934; Landes 1938a; Cooper 1934). On the other hand, reports either of classical depressive or violent acting-out psychopathological behavior have been relatively rare for the Eskimos. By far the most frequent symptoms noted by different observers have been convulsive hysterical attacks and, less frequently,

conversion symptoms. Among the early reports on Eskimo mental disorders were those of W. H. Dall (1870:171–72) on an Alaskan group and Whitney's (1911:67) observations on the Polar Eskimos. They noted a form of mental illness in which the patient fell into a convulsive fit or engaged in other forms of histrionic behavior. Aggressive behavior was not part of the syndrome. This condition was often epidemic, and many natives were afflicted during a short period of time. The explorer Peary (1910:166) was also struck with a somewhat similar type of affliction among the Polar Eskimos known as *piblokto*. Peary commented on the commonness of the condition and observed that it frequently afflicted females who were brooding over absent or dead relatives or who had "a fear of the future." Among the symptoms noted by Peary were screaming, sobbing, wild gesticulations, and running out on the ice naked. The attack usually ended in a fit of weeping, and when the patient quieted down her eyes were usually bloodshot, her pulse high, and bodily tremors were evident for about an hour afterward. The noted psychoanalyst, A. A. Brill, who had access to the notes of the arctic explorer, Macmillan, regarded the condition as an hysterical manifestation and pointed out that it was common in women and that intent to harm the self or others was not part of the symptomatology (Brill 1912).

In 1905, A. Bertelsen, a Danish physician, presented an analysis of 60 case histories of a hysterical condition among the Eskimos of Greenland that he refers to as "kayak fright" (Bertelsen 1905a, 1905b). The common symptoms afflicting these young to middle-aged male hunters were sudden dizziness, excessive palpitation of the heart, excessive sweating, and varying degress of "hysterical paralysis." The situations in which the attacks usually occurred involved some objective danger to the individual (i.e., hunting on a mountain height or at sea). Patients reported that in these situations they suddenly experienced an overwhelming fear that they had been abandoned—as if they were completely "on their own" without any possibility of being aided by others. They also reported a strong desire to be helped by other people and when they felt that this help was forthcoming their symptoms abated. The life histories indicated that, outside of the immediate period preceding the attack, depression and melancholia were not usual. Also, there was little evidence either of hostile or paranoid ideation, or fantasies of violent acting-out against others. Bertelsen, based on his own long clinical experience with the Eskimos of

Greenland, stated that hysterical symptoms involving degrees of convulsive behavior and paralysis are fairly common among these people.

These findings were confirmed in a recent medical study of the health of the Eskimos of North Greenland (Ehrstrom 1951). This study reported that hysteria and other "primitive reactions" such as kayak fright were well-known and were associated with such general Eskimo characteristics as impulsiveness, suggestibility, and "instability." The author of this study made the interesting observation that Eskimos who had had greater contact with Western civilization tended to have more psychophysiological reactions, while those who were relatively unacculturated were more likely to manifest hysterical behavior (i.e., convulsive excitements and fits of trembling) uncomplicated by somatic reactions. If this is true, then one can speculate that simple hysterical behavior was more common among the Eskimos in the past, and that psychophysiological symptoms are becoming increasingly prevalent.

Anthropologists who have lived with the Eskimos also comment on the hysterical nature of their psychiatric maladies. Birket-Smith (1935:55) states that a trifling incident will often turn Eskimos (especially women) quite crazy, and they will be "seized by a psychic cramp during which time they engage in meaningless jabber and break things within reach." He, too, makes the point that these disturbances are rarely accompanied by attempts to do harm to others. Diamond Jenness notes that "hysteria is peculiarly common around the Polar Basin; the long winter darkness and the loneliness and silence of the hunter's life make the Arctic people more susceptible to this disorder than the rest of the human race" (Jenness 1959:52). Although cannibalism has rarely been associated with the mental disorders of the Eskimos, there have been occasional reports of such behavior during disturbed states (Weyer 1932:118).

## 3. SPECULATIONS CONCERNING FACTORS ASSOCIATED WITH HYSTERIA AMONG THE ESKIMOS AND IN OTHER SOCIETIES

In the attempt to explain hysteria among the Eskimos, Weyer (1932:386) and Jenness (1959:52) emphasize such things as the prolonged darkness of the arctic, severe climate, and the long periods of silence in the hunter's life. Novakovsky (1924) concurs with this opinion. However, this geographic-environmental explanation is rejected by Ackerknecht (1948), Aberle (1952), and Yap (1951). They note that hysterical disorders are also to be found among peoples in different climates and geographical environments. The fact that the Ojibwa Indians, who also experience severe climate and long periods of isolation, usually manifest very different psychopatholgoical symptoms (i.e., depression and paranoid ideation) also leads one to question the simple environmental explanation. Finally, Ehrstrom's findings (cited above), that hysterical symptoms seem to give way to psychophysiological complaints among the more acculturated Eskimos, indicates that the climatic explanation is inadequate. Peary (1910:166) and Macmillan (Brill 1912) felt that the reaction took place in women who were abused or rebuffed by their husbands, or perceived themselves to be abused. Brill (1912) after examining the field notes of Macmillan concludes that the common factor in all the reported cases is an ungratified desire for affection and tenderness (Brill 1912)....

A survey of reports on the distribution of hysterical behavior indicates that it appears to be more common in nonliterate societies than in Western groups (Benedict and Jacks 1954; Yap 1952; Carothers 1959), in females compared to males (Abse 1959; Chodoff and Lyons 1958), among rural dwellers (Abse 1959), members of the lower socio-economic group (Yap 1960), and in some minority ethnic groups (i.e., Mediterraneans and Negroes) in the United States (Schilder 1938; Fitzgerald 1948). Although the picture is by no means clear, the epidemiological evidence suggests the possibility that hysteria (as against depression) may prevail in groups where there is a relatively greater degree of dependency need satisfaction and less stress on early independence and individual achievement striving. In any case, the evidence gives little support to the over-socialized and severe super-ego theory of hysteria....

The literature has been surveyed for the purpose of suggesting ideas that provide a focus for the discussion of Eskimo society and personality. The summary points listed below stand out as worthy of attention. They are not to be regarded as definite hypotheses to be tested in subsequent sections but rather as general ideas that will be explored by means of ethnographic data.

Hysterical behavior tends to prevail in societies:

a) Where early socialization experiences are not severe and involve minimal repression of dependency needs and sexual drives. In such societies, where there is relatively high gratification of dependency needs, the modal super-ego structure will not be severe or rigid.

b) Where there is an emphasis on communalistic values, a relatively great amount of face-to-face cooperative patterns, and high expectations of mutual aid.

c) Where the female role involves considerable disadvantages and lower self-esteem compared to the role of the male.

d) Where the religious system involves beliefs in supernatural possession, and where "hysterical-like" behavior models are provided in the institutionalized religious practices.

With this background presentation, we can now turn to an examinaton of Eskimo culture, society, and personality.

## 4. CHILD-REARING PRACTICES AND THE EARLY SOCIALIZATION OF THE ESKIMO

Observers of the Eskimos are unanimous in their opinion that the Eskimo child is usually welcomed in the home and treated with affection and tenderness by its parents. These findings are reported from different Eskimo regions (Birket-Smith 1935:57; Hrdlička 1941; Jenness 1922:169; Holm 1914; Honigmann and Honigmann 1959). During infancy and childhood little distinction is made in the treatment of a boy and a girl (Honigmann and Honigmann 1959). Youngsters are usually nursed till they are about three or four years old (Holm 1914; Jenness 1922:165; Jenness 1959:208) and are carried close to the body of the mother as she performs her daily chores (Hrdlička 1941; Jenness 1959:208; Jenness 1922:169). Not only are they nursed till a relatively late age, but they are also immediately given the breast whenever they feel uncomfortable and begin to fret (Honigmann and Honigmann 1959). Children are seldom severely punished or subjected to harsh discipline (Honigmann and Honigmann 1959; Holm 1914) and are rarely frightened with stories about dangerous monsters and "bogeymen" (Honigmann and Honigmann 1959). The generally permissive atmosphere in which the child is raised also extends to the area of toilet training (Honigmann and Honigmann 1959). However, it is not possible to generalize here due to the scarcity of literature on this subject. In general, "the education of the child is not a process in which the young person learns demands that are beyond his tastes or capacities to perform" (Honigmann and Honigmann 1959). From the foregoing descriptions it appears that the normal dependency needs (i.e., need for support, help, affection, and protection) of the child are met with a high degree of gratification.

Children are prepared for their mature roles gradually, mainly by such mechanisms as affection and group pressure. Even at an early age, the larger social community is important as a motivating and a disciplinary influence (Hrdlička 1941; Jenness 1922:169). Some observers attribute this pattern of tender child care to the widespread Eskimo belief that the child is the repository of the soul of a recently departed member of the family (Birket-Smith 1935:154). Because of this, the child commands a singular respect (Weyer 1932:133; Ehrstrom 1951; Honigmann 1954:301; Ackerknecht 1948). Stefansson (1914:358) attributes to the Eskimos the belief that if the child is not treated kindly the "soul-nappan" will either become very unhappy or will leave his body. In any case, this will result in sickness or death. The beliefs of the Ojibwa concerning the nature of the newborn child present an interesting contrast. They believe that the child is born "empty" and is very vulnerable to various evil powers and misfortunes. Thus, it is felt that youngsters must be disciplined severely at an early age in order quickly to overcome this potentially dangerous void.

When the Eskimo child reaches the age of about 11 or 12 and has acquired strength and experience, he is no longer considered to be vulnerable to the loss of his "soul." Accordingly, at this time parents become firmer in disciplining him. The severe and rigorous conditions of Eskimo life impose the need to train youngsters to be efficient and independent in the various economic and domestic arts. However, independence training is graduated accordingly to the capacities of the growing individuals. Boys do not generally participate in full-scale hunting activities till they are in their mid-teens (Hrdlička 1941). It appears that girls are required to take on some of the adult responsibilities at an earlier age than are boys (Hrdlička 1941; Lantis 1946:226). Youngsters are aware that they have a claim on the assistance of others in the community in the event of food scarcity or other crisis situations (Honigmann 1954:269).

The socialization practices discussed thus far probably involve but a minimal need for repression of dependency desires. Does this relatively low degree of frustration also apply to the disciplines affecting the sexual development of the individual? Observers of Eskimo society generally attest to the considerable sexual freedom and lack of restraint among these people (Holm 1914). . . .

Although Eskimos are hunters and often face starvation, they, unlike the Ojibwa Indians, have not generally institutionalized severe and painful ritual fasting for young men. The Ojibwa subject the male child, before the age of 10, to graduated periods of food denial, and finally at the onset of puberty he is required to undergo a torturous period of fasting alone in the frozen forest. In the rare instances where fasting has been reported for the Eskimos (Lantis 1946:227), the young man is about 19 or 20 years of age and engages in a brief fast in his own home in the company of his mother, who shares this ritual with him. Finally, the different purposes of the ritual casts further light on the aims of socialization in these two societies. The Eskimo fasts during a period of community festivity, *after* the completion of a successful hunt and community recognition of his adult status. The young Ojibwa boy deliberately seeks pain in order to have a vision that will provide him with power in his later life. This is but the beginning of a series of vision-seeking experiences through which he must constantly test his power and prove himself. Rasmussen (1932:27) observes that among the Copper Eskimos it is only a shaman, or a child destined to become a shaman, who goes out into the cold to seek power visions. Masochistic devices that prepare the individual for extreme individualistic self-reliance are, for the most part, foreign to these people. It may be that self-inflicted pain is indicative of deviance in one society (i.e., Eskimo) and of normality in the other (i.e., Ojibwa).

## 5. SOME ASPECTS OF SOCIAL AND ECONOMIC LIFE AMONG THE ESKIMOS

The habitation arrangements of the Eskimos vary considerably from group to group and from season to season. They are usually dependent upon the nature of the food supply of the group. Weyer (1932:204 ff), in reviewing the literature on this subject, observes that favorable hunting opportunities attract families of Eskimos to certain sites where nodes of population are formed. He estimates the usual Eskimo villages as ranging in population from 100 to 300 persons. A village of 200 is considered to be a fairly large settlement. It is safe to say that most Eskimos live together in villages for varying periods during the year. They band together in villages during the winter months when their food supply is most precarious—in this way they can depend on each other for help in periods of scarcity and insecurity. This is in sharp contrast to the Ojibwa, who (usually) live in isolated dwelling units during the winter when the danger of starvation is greatest. Village endogamy among the Eskimo also encourages high expectations of mutual aid, since many of the villagers are related by consanguine or conjugal ties (Ackerknecht 1948).

A feature of Eskimo village housing that has been frequently noted is the tendency for the dwellings to be "huddled" together. In describing the Copper Eskimos, Jenness states that "food had been common to all, and their snow houses had adjoined each other so closely that the families seemed absorbed in the group" (Jenness 1959:137). In addition, they cluster together so that evil spirits may not harm them when they wander at night from one snow hut to another (Jenness 1959:75). . . .

The strong cooperative and communal values of the Eskimos (Hughes 1958) becomes apparent in an analysis of their economic practices and beliefs. Although there are local variations, Eskimos are prone to share their resources and depend heavily on the community. Weyer (1932:189) derives the "communalistic" values of the Eskimos from the demands imposed upon them by their physical environment and concomitant food-gathering techniques, such as cooperative hunting from kayaks (Weyer 1932:144) or the organized caribou drive and hunting for whales (Weyer 1932:143). Whatever the reason, it is interesting to note that the economic behavior of these people certainly differs from the very individualistic practices and values of their Ojibwa neighbors, who also face severe survival problems.

The notion of private property in such things as storage houses and hunting grounds in not usually found among the Eskimos (Birket-Smith 1935:148; Jenness 1922:91; Weyer 1932:173). Kroeber (1899:301) states: "Among the Polar Eskimos there is a community of food as of dwellings, only clothing and implements and utensils being personal property." Observers of the Eskimos have attested to their propensity to share food resources, especially in time of scarcity (Jenness 1922:87, 90, 114). As long as some members of the community have little to eat, the others are obligated to share their resources (Holm 1914; Birket-Smith 1935:148–49). . . .

The communalistic emphasis becomes more apparent from an examination of the values implicit in some of Eskimo ritualistic practices. The lone Eskimo hunter of Baffin Land and Hudson Bay is sometimes not permitted to eat his catch until he finds company (Boas 1907:150). Among the Unalit of Alaska, the first large game killed by a young hunter is divided and consumed by the villagers "without leaving a particle for the young hunter" (Nelson 1899:307). . . .

Because of the communal ownership of land and hunting territories, and mores concerning sharing, the Eskimos have developed a society where there is extremely little emphasis on social class position or even individual rank (Birket-Smith 1935:147; Weyer 1932:208). Eskimo villages have a headman who is supposed to have superior ability and good judgment. There is no office of chieftain in its ordinary sense—"leadership exists only in a very elementary and restricted form" (Weyer 1932:209). Although the existing prestige system is based mainly on hunting accomplishment (Lantis 1946:36), each individual feels that he has the same rights and privileges as every other man in the community (Jenness 1922:93–94). If an individual succeeds in amassing food and other forms of property that he does not share with others, he becomes a target for negative social sanctions and even physical violence. The familistic nature of some Eskimo communities is underlined by a tendency in certain groups to use kinship terminology among unrelated individuals. This serves "to cement the local group together." (Willmott 1960).

## 6. RELIGIOUS PRACTICE AND BELIEFS AMONG THE ESKIMOS

In discussing the religious practices and beliefs of the Eskimos the assumption will be made that the religious institutions of a people are partly a projective system that reflects the socializing disciplines (both in childhood *and* adulthood) to which it has been subjected. This does not imply that religious beliefs and practices can be conceptualized as mere passive factors in the life of a people. There is ample evidence that they have active functional implications for the social system as well as for the psychological behavior of individuals. . . .

It was hypothesized that hysterical symptoms tend to prevail in a society where there is a relatively high satisfaction of dependency needs. In the preceding sections it was concluded that at all phases of the Eskimo life cycle the individual experiences a relatively high degree of dependency satisfaction and learns to need and expect a relatively high degree of nurturance and aid from others. This relative lack of dependency need frustration is in sharp contrast to the situation in Ojibwa society, where there exists a very early and severe frustration of dependency needs. This experience prepares the (Ojibwa) individual for an adulthood of overt strong individualism and self-reliance, and a heritage of covert unresolved and unsatisfied dependency cravings (Parker 1960). On this basis we would expect to find considerable differences in the ways in which these two societies deal with the supernatural. More specifically, we would expect that the relationship of the Ojibwa individual to his gods would be characterized by more dependence and a consequent greater attribution of omnipotence. The distinction sometimes made between magic (as a ritualistic manipulation of supernatural forces to insure certain results) and religious prayer (as a means of humbling oneself and begging for supernatural aid) is a convenient device to "test" the above idea. Although the two techniques are inevitably intermeshed in any actual religious system, societies can be placed on a continuum between these two ideal concepts. . . .

Although magical practices are by no means absent among the Ojibwa, there is ample evidence that the dominant mode of relating to the supernatural involves extreme dependence, prayer, and begging for pity. Cooper (1933b) observes that magic (in the sense of ritual *control* over the supernatural) is not developed to any degree among these people. Hallowell (1950) notes that the blessing of the gods "could not be compelled, but bestowed because of the superhuman entities took 'pity' upon the suppliant." In the Ojibwa language to "pity" another is to adopt him and to care for him as a parent or grandparent cares for a child (Landes 1938b). So complete is the Ojibwa's dependence on the supernatural that he attributes all of his successes, failures, and capabilities to supernatural intervention. In a discussion of this point, Hallowell (1954) observes that the fundamental relationship of the Ojibwa to the supernatural "is one of dependence and is the root of their deep motivational orientation toward these powerful beings." In discussing some general characteristics of the Eskimo's mode of dealing with the supernatural, Birket-Smith notes:

They are not prayers addressed to any particular deity; the happy result is due to the power of the wish itself and the manner in which it is expressed.... On the whole the Eskimos endeavor more to exercise magical *control* over nature and the supernatural than to seek favor of the power (Birket-Smith 1935:170).

Somewhat similar statements concerning this aspect of Eskimo religion are given by Weyer (1932:317, 319, 321), Ray (1885:43), Lantis (1946:205), and Jenness (1922:229). Although such magical practices appear to predominate, it would certainly be untrue to state that religious prayer and propitiation are unknown among these people. Sedna, who is a common chief deity of many Eskimo groups, is frequently the object of great veneration and prayers for aid. However, even her power is conditional upon other circumstances and she is by no means omnipotent....

Kardiner (1939:440, 444) relates masochistic features in the personality to an early frustration and repression of some basic need by a socializing agent. He also maintains that a severe frustration of dependency needs results in projecting omnipotence onto an agency outside of the self. Consequently, the hostility resulting from this and subsequent frustrations (by those in authority) cannot be expressed directly by the dependent person. This would threaten his security system. Such a person is likely to resort to masochistic techniques (i.e., humbling, belittling, and harming himself) in order to placate or manipulate authority figures. If this reasoning is valid, one would expect the Ojibwa to manifest a plethora of masochistic techniques in their religious system relative to the Eskimos. This expectation is borne out by an examination of the ethnographic data. Among the Ojibwa the main way of gaining supernatural favors is by self-induced starvation, isolation, and other forms of denial. Even the young child is required to suffer so that the gods will "pity" him and grant him power. The child is besieged by his parents to go without food in order "that you may learn what to do with your life" (Landes 1938b:3). These practices have been institutionalized and pervade Ojibwa rituals. In contrast to this, the Eskimo ritual fast (when present) is extremely mild. Food denial is not used as a socializing technique in childhood. Lantis notes that among the Nunivak Eskimos of Alaska ceremonialism does not contain any harsh self-punishment—" The medicine man did not have to torture himself before the spirits come to him. He did not purify himself by fasting, bathing, or

whipping himself, did not mutilate himself, or go into solitude" (Lantis 1946:200). Among the Copper Eskimos the diagnosis of an illness in itself is usually considered sufficient to arrest the evil....

...Among the Ojibwa, serious illness or failure of food supply is believed to result from a violation of a taboo by the patient or, occasionally, by one of his parents. A common alternative explanation is malevolent sorcery. I found no instances in the literature to suggest that the individual can be exposed to illness or starvation (or other misfortunes) because of violation of a taboo by an unrelated person(s) in the larger community. Similarly, the larger community is not afflicted with misfortune because of the misdeeds of one of its members, nor is there any requirement for communal atonement for the sins of an individual. The situation is not quite the same among the Eskimos. Weyer, in his summary of Eskimo religion, states:

The beliefs that one who has transgressed taboo is a menace to others engenders the conviction that a solemn duty rests on every member of an Eskimo community to confess his offenses.... Divine retribution following disregard of taboos falls upon the community as well as upon the offender (Weyer 1932:377–78).

An entire village may be exposed to starvation because one woman has kept her miscarriage a secret or transgressed another rule (Boas 1907:121, 128). Communal ritual atonement for the transgressions of individuals are not uncommon (Ackerknecht 1948). In Eskimo religion the concept of collective guilt, punishment, and atonement exists side by side with the more individualistic ideas of sin and punishment.

It was hypothesized that hysterical behavior would tend to be relatively frequent in a society where there were high expectations of mutual aid and nurturance. The reasons used by the group to explain misfortune will have implications for its ability, or inability, to depend on the social environment for aid and support. In crisis situations, the belief system of the Eskimo makes them more prone than the Ojibwa to depend on others for help. For the Ojibwa "impersonal forces are never the causes of events. Somebody is always responsible" (Hallowell 1954). Illness and lack of success in hunting cause great anxiety among the Ojibwa, not only because of the obvious danger to the physical self, but also because it is often regarded as a direct personal attack on the self by an enemy (not infrequently a member of one's family) by means of malevolent witchcraft (Hallowell 1954). The writings of Hallowell and Landes attest to the considerable prevalence of witchcraft in this society. Personal misfortune also frequently signifies to the individual that others have more power than he. It thus appears that these beliefs of the Ojibwa seriously interfere with their expectations of support and sympathy from their social environment. Misfortune means rejection and/or a loss of esteem. . . .

The relative frequency with which personal or communal misfortunes are attributed to supernatural forces or an impersonal fate (Honigmann and Honigmann 1959) serves to deflect hostility from the social environment. Thus, in crisis situations the Ojibwa are likely to feel rejected by, and hostile toward, others and also to experience a loss of self-esteem. The Eskimos, on the other hand, are prone to project hostility elsewhere and to band together with their fellows to cope with the situation. "Membership in the community confers, in a sense, insurance for the individual and for the family" (Weyer 1932:189).

Finally, another aspect of the religious practices among the Eskimos has relevance for an understanding of hysterical symptoms. During the cold winter nights Eskimos frequently crowd together in one of the snow huts to watch the hysterical-like behavior of the shaman who is believed to be possessed by a foreign spirit with whom he is doing battle. This histrionic exhibition is contagious and the awestruck onlookers are often thrown into a similar state of ecstasy (Weyer 1932:437). Thus, the Eskimos frequently witness and partake in socially sanctioned (phenotypical) hysterical-like behavior designed to achieve various gratifications, control supernatural forces, and alleviate misfortune. Such experiences could provide a model for pathological behavioral reactions to personal psychological crises. However, as frequently noted by students of social psychology, the concept of imitation is, by itself, inadequate to explain behavior. Imitation of specific role behavior is initiated by experienced needs and guided by goals (Krech and Crutchfield 1948:31–32). . . .

the male. Macmillan observed that Eskimo women afflicted with piblokto were either really abused by their husbands or perceived themselves to be abused (Brill 1912). Holm (1914) reports that among the Ammassalik Eskimos the position of the woman is hardly better than that of servants. He goes on to say that wives dread to incur the displeasure of their husbands and may suffer severe physical punishment if they do not succeed. Husbands often, for the sake of personal gain or pleasure, exact the "strangest compliances" from their wives, to which the women patiently submit. In addition, the wife and children may be deserted by the husband in times of scarcity, while the latter is living on the hospitality of others (Holm 1914; Lantis 1946:160). In traditional Eskimo society, a woman has little or nothing to say about whom she marries. She may even be taken by force against the will of her family (Holm 1914). During marriage it is not unusual for an Eskimo husband to exchange wives for varying periods or to permit another man to have sexual access to his wife. This may be done with or without the consent of the woman involved (Mirsky 1937). A woman may be severely punished by her husband for having extramarital sexual relations, not because the act in itself is a moral transgression or indicates unfaithfulness, but because he has not given her permission for this behavior. The sexual potential of the wife is considered almost as a property right of the male (Birket-Smith 1935:145) and is indicative of his superior position (Ackerknecht 1948). The Nunivak Eskimos consider a woman unclean (and potentially dangerous) right after childbirth and impose various taboos on her (Lantis 1946:224). . . .

Although women in Eskimo society experience a high degree of dependency need satisfaction during their early socialization, the literature suggests that during their adult years they may be more subject than men to situations that could be perceived by them as "love deprivation" and frustration. It certainly appears that in traditional Eskimo life, the woman's role carried with it more disabilities and less prestige than that of the man.

## 7. PSYCHOLOGICAL DEPRIVATION IN THE FEMALE ROLE

. . . The adult female role among the Eskimos will be examined to see if it has greater potential for frustration and feelings of deprivation than that of

## 8. GENERAL OBSERVATIONS ON ESKIMO PERSONALITY

This paper has been oriented around the idea that prevalent pathological symptoms in any group can best be understood within the context of its sociocultural environment and the normal personality patterns of its members. Is it possible to generalize about "the Eskimo personality"? The literature indicates that there is considerable consensus regarding personality differences between the Eskimos and their Indian neighbors. Both Kroeber (1948:599) and Jenness (1922:233) feel that the Eskimos show a marked contrast with the "stoicism" and "inhibition" that generally characterizes American Indian personality. In comparisons of the Eskimo and the Indians of the northern forest (i.e., Ojibwa, Cree, etc.), the latter have been described by the Honigmanns (1959) and by Birket-Smith (1935:54) as sullen, reticent, aloof, and restricted. The writings of Hallowell (1946) and Landes (1937b) picture the Ojibwa as being sullen, hostile, scheming, introverted, boastful, hypersensitive to criticism or insults, having exaggerated pride, and prone to nurse a grudge for extended periods. On the other hand, the Eskimo has been generally described as cheerful, jovial, modest, spontaneous and open in human relationships, empathetic, carefree, emotionally demonstrative, and extroverted (Dall 1870:396; Ehrstrom 1951; Jenness 1922:233ff; Ackerknecht 1948; Weyer 1932:2,237,253; Lantis 1959; Peary 1910:46,67; Rasmussen 1932:18).

Some of the research on the etiology of depression (Rado 1928: 1951) warrants the hypothesis that in groups where depressive symptoms prevail, hostility will tend to be directed toward the self rather than be spontaneously expressed in social relations. Although the Eskimos have been generally characterized as emotionally spontaneous, the precarious conditions of existence, plus their cooperative arrangements, require control over expressions of hostility and anger (Honigmann and Honigmann 1959; Sherman 1956:142; Lantis 1959). This is also true of the Ojibwa, who are similarly faced with a precarious food supply. How do these people deal with their hostility? Among the Ojibwa, feelings of hostility tend to remain covert or are expressed obliquely by means of malevolent sorcery and gossip (Hallowell 1946). No institutionalized means exist in this society that permit a direct and cathartic expression of hostile feelings toward other group members. The widespread Eskimo institution of the "drum song" provides a mechanism par excellence for just such a direct and cathartic expression of hostility. Observers have been impressed with the fact that the two aggrieved individuals show few signs of ill feelings toward each other directly after hurling verbal insults (and sometimes dog dung) at each other, or

even exchanging blows (Boas 1907:116; Ackerknecht 1948; Weyer 1932:219,226–27; Sherman 1956:142; Mirsky 1937). Such evidence suggests that Eskimos have less need than their Ojibwa neighbors to repress feelings of hostility and may therefore be less prone to turn such feelings onto the self.

It was noted above that hysterical-like behavior is manifested in some of the religious rituals of the Eskimos. The considerable responsiveness and empathetic ability of the Eskimos (Lantis 1946:251; Honigmann and Honigmann 1959) probably accounts for the reported contagious "fits" of laughter or weeping among these people (Jenness 1922:233; Birket-Smith 1935:56). Such (normal) labile and spontaneous personality traits have been associated with a tendency toward hysterical behavior.

The Honigmanns observe that the Eskimo mother quickly resorts to appeasement techniques of various sorts (e.g., "a brief session at the breast, distraction by pointing out some interesting feature in the environment, or a ride upon mother's or sister's back") as soon as her baby shows the first signs of discomfort. Thus, the child integrates the idea that his fretting will bring a quick and comforting response from his environment. "Accustomed to being appeased, the child becomes an adult who is able to appease and expects appeasement" (Honigmann and Honigmann 1959). This very interesting description of the Great Whale River Eskimos is related to the idea that the hysterical-prone individual has not learned techniques of delaying satisfactions and expects that his overt signs of tension and anxiety will immediately attract the attention of his social environment and bring nurturance and comfort. However, he uses basic techniques of human relations, learned through socialization experiences, inappropriately.

## SUMMARY AND CONCLUSIONS

I have tried to show some of the socio-cultural and personality factors associated with psychopathological symptoms. The Eskimos, who are characterized by a tendency toward hysterical behavior, experience a relatively permissive early childhood in which there is minimal frustration of the needs for dependency and affection. It is probable that most Eskimo children learn that they can depend on others for nurturance, and the prompt satisfaction of their needs. There is little emphasis on denial, deprivation, or masochistic techniques as mechanisms of gaining security. The cooperative social organization and communalistic value system of the Eskimos perpetuate the tacit assumption that their social environment is essentially nurturant, and that their needs would be satisfied by merely calling attention to them. This assumption about a basically nurturant social environment is particularly operative during periods of crisis. In addition, the institutionalized religious practices of the Eskimos provide socially sanctioned outlets for hostility and role models for hysterical-like behavior. Finally, the prevalence of hysterical behavior in women seems to be related to a (nearly universal) societal sanction for greater dependency need satisfaction in female socialization, combined with some relative deprivations and disabilities attached to the role of the Eskimo women.

There has been no implication in this analysis that the Eskimos have (neurotic) "dependent" personalities. On the contrary, they are trained for individual competence. However, their socialization for such capacities involves little frustration (and, in fact, high gratification) of normal dependency needs, compared to the Ojibwa. This would imply that there is little repression of such needs, and, thus, little conflict involved in their overt expression.

This paper obviously does not explain why particular individuals are subject to psychopathological hysterical symptoms. However, it does provide an understanding of why, when psychopathogenic factors are present, the resulting condition is more likely to result in hysterical excitement than in depressive and paranoid symptoms. The contrast provided by the Ojibwa Indians was designed to provide further clarification of this point. Because of the individualistic emphasis of Ojibwa society and the early and severe frustration of dependency needs, the Ojibwa not only fails to integrate an expectation of aid and nurturance from his social environment, but he is actually prone to interpret his misfortune and deprivation as resulting from hostile rejection by those around him. Such factors are more likely to lead to a loss of self-esteem and/or hostility toward others. Figuratively (and teleologically) speaking, the "function" of the Eskimo's symptoms is to call attention to his plight and to place himself in the "bosom" of the group. In contrast to this, the Ojibwa's symptoms represent an attempt to obliterate the self and/or significant others in his social environment. This study indicates that the psycho-

pathological process (whatever its somatic causes or concomitants) is part of culture and should be understood in this context. In a sense, the symptom "fits" the situation.

# 40 Conceptions of Psychosis in Four East African Societies

## Robert B. Edgerton

This exceptionally well-designed and executed study addresses itself to a critical need in psychiatric anthropology as a subfield of medical anthropology: How do members of non-Western societies perceive, conceptualize, and respond to illness, in this instance, severe emotional disorder, or in Western nomenclature, psychosis? I know of no other study of non-Western, nonliterate societies that has been done so systematically, using probability sampling techniques, carefully constructed and implemented interviews under standardized conditions, and projective tests, all within the context of a larger ethnographic survey of these cultures. Robert Edgerton writes of the need for such studies for Africa, but ones as carefully operationalized as this are needed for *all* culture areas.

Edgerton found not only that in all four societies there are native linguistic equivalents of the Western notion of psychosis (a point that has previously been denied by some anthropologists, not only for East Africa, but generally for most nonliterate cultures), but that there are many and varied reasons given for the cause of severe emotional disturbances. Thus, Edgerton discovered that these disturbances are not often attributed to witchcraft (a finding certainly at variance with studies of other cultures); that all four societies, despite internal differences, generally shared a broad area of agreement about the actual behaviors that they presume cause a person to become psychotic; that these are not greatly different from Western psychiatric nosological criteria for psychosis; and many other remarkable findings. These native etiological theories are also discussed within their ethnographic, social, and therapeutic contexts (treatment regimens, for example, seem to be a function of whether the native theory is prognostically optimistic or pessimistic).

Finally, Edgerton raises the question of the light shed by this study on the question that seems to divide medical anthropologists and psychiatrists: Is psychosis basically the same universally or is it shaped funda-

Reprinted with abridgments from Robert B. Edgerton, 1966, "Conceptions of Psychosis in Four East African Societies," *American Anthropologist*, 68:408–425, with permission of the author and the American Anthropological Association.

mentally by cultural determinants? Edgerton suggests that his findings could support either view and believes that the problem cannot be reasonably solved until we have much more research, preferably of the caliber of that done by Edgerton and the Culture and Ecology in East Africa Project of which it was a part.

...For psychiatry as well as for anthropology we need to know how Africans perceive, define and respond to mental disorder in their own perceptual-conceptual terms, for without such research in native phenomenological systems, we do not know whether, or to what extent, the nosologies of Western psychiatry may distort African social and cultural reality.

This paper will examine conceptions of psychosis in nonliterate African populations—specifically, it will report the results of a survey with over 500 persons sampled from four East African tribes.

## PROCEDURE

...The four tribes studied were the Sebei of southeast Uganda, the Pokot (or Suk) of northwest Kenya, the Kamba of south central Kenya, and the Hehe of southwest Tanganyika. The distance from the Sebei in the north to the Hehe in the south is over 600 miles by air and 1,000 miles by road. Each of the four tribes is engaged in a varied economy ranging within each tribe from a heavy emphasis upon pastoralism (principally the herding of cattle) to an almost exclusive concern with agriculture. The Hehe and Kamba speak related Bantu languages whereas the Sebei and Pokot speak closely related Kalenjin languages of the East Sudanic family. With the exception of the Pokot who have been markedly less subject to European influence, the tribes are approximately equal in their present degree of acculturation. It is not feasible here to provide any detailed description of the four tribes (introductions to the tribes are available elsewhere). In the perspective appropriate to this discussion, although the four tribes are roughly alike in social structure, economy, and material culture, yet each has a different cultural repertory, each is an independent cultural system with both specific and general traits not common to the other tribes, and each differs in its patterning of the interpersonal conduct of everyday life.

For reasons essential to the research design of the overall project, it was necessary that information concerning attitudes, values, and personality attributes be elicited from a large number of respondents selected by probability sampling

techniques. It was also important that these persons be roughly equivalent in their lack of European acculturation; hence persons significantly influenced by European culture were excluded from the sample. All males included were heads of household and the females were the wives of these men. The respondent refusal rate was slightly under 5 percent.

The interview schedule included a picture test of values (Goldschmidt and Edgerton 1961), a Rorschach test, other projective materials and approximately 90 questions ranging over a variety of topics. Several of these questions concerned psychosis. Each respondent, male and female alike, was interviewed in private under highly standardized conditions. All interviews were conducted by the author in the respondent's own language through carefully trained, directed, and cross-checked interpreters. Despite sometimes difficult field conditions there was virtually no variation in the standard interviewing format. Post-interview validity procedures indicated that there was remarkably little systematic misunderstanding, misrepresentation, or withholding of information throughout the four tribes, and none of any importance in the material to be presented here.

Before questions about psychosis could be asked, it was obviously necessary to discover equivalent terms for psychosis in the languages of the four tribes. At first, this task appeared to be hopelessly formidable, but fortunately, there was ample time for pretesting and, in Swahili, there was an available *lingua franca* for the East African area. Swahili refers to madness as *wazimu*, or a mad man, *mwenye wazimu*; in both usages, spirit possession or witchcraft are implied as causative factors. However, the Swahili word *kichaa* seems to be closely equivalent to the English conception of severe mental disorder, or psychosis, and it has no necessary connotation of spirit possession or witchcraft (Koritschoner 1936). The word *kichaa* appears to be widely known and used in East Africa. Further, in the process of pretesting, words closely equivalent to *kichaa* were found in each of the four languages (Sebei, Pokot, Kikamba and Kihehe). Contrary to expectation based upon the findings of Brelsford (1950), no great profusion of terms for mental disorder was discovered. For example, Kihehe has several terms referring to psychosis but they differ primarily in terms of etiology not symptomatology. Pokot likewise has two major terms for psychosis but these, too, imply different causes rather than different symptoms. In some cases it was possible to find native doctors who knew finer distinctions in mental disorder, but the terms they knew were not commonly known or used. For example, two Pokot doctors distinguished between *kipoiyin* "a severe loss of sense" that is caused by a disease called *cheptugna*, and *yoiyon*, which is a mild and temporary depression and confusion caused by worry or grief. The first is immensely difficult to cure, the second is easily cured by removing the patient to a new location: "If you leave him at home with his worries, he will never recover." But the Pokot in general referred only to the term *kipoiyin* and this is the word used in my investigation. In all four tribes questions were always phrased using both the Swahili word *kichaa* and the local equivalent. The native doctors and other key informants agreed in all instances that these translations carried the general, nonspecific meaning of severe mental disorder implied by "psychosis."

In addition to the basic interview concerning conceptions of psychosis, a number of intensive ethnographic inquiries concerning psychosis were made with native doctors. The purpose of this paper is to present not a detailed analysis of the knowledge of the specialist (native doctor or diviner) about psychosis, but rather to examine the beliefs held by the ordinary members of those societies. Where appropriate, the beliefs of the specialists will be compared with the "commonsense" beliefs of the non-specialists.

## FINDINGS

Before turning to a discussion of conceptions of psychosis, it might be noted that only 7 respondents of the 505 interviewed mentioned psychosis as the most serious illness or affliction suffered by people in their area. It would also be helpful to know how many of the respondents in the four tribes have actually seen a psychotic person.

Except for the Kamba, virtually all of whom say they have seen psychotics, approximately half of the respondents have not actually seen someone who is psychotic. The large number of positive responses

**Table 1** "Have You Actually Seen a Psychotic?"

|     | Kamba | Hehe | Pokot | Sebei |
| --- | --- | --- | --- | --- |
| Yes | 122 | 57 | 65 | 64 |
| No | 4 | 66 | 63 | 64 |

**Table 2** "Have You Actually Seen a Psychotic?"

|     | Men | Women |
| --- | --- | --- |
| Yes | 187 | 121 |
| No | 66 | 131 |

(Chi square corrected for continuity, P<.001)

among the Kamba is difficult to explain (the Kamba themselves say, "We have a great many psychotics in our tribe"), but it is reasonably certain that this result is not an artifact of the interview situation. We might also note that there is a statistically significant tendency for women to have less contact with psychotics.

The reason for this difference is not clear. It may be that since men have travelled more extensively than women, they have had more opportunity to see psychotics, but this differential should be irrelevant as the question was clearly phrased to refer to psychotics seen in the respondents' own immediate neighborhood. In any case, since it was anticipated that not everyone would personally have seen a psychotic person, two questions were asked: (1) "How do psychotic people behave?" (2) "Have you actually seen a psychotic person right here in (name of area)?" (If yes) "Tell me how this person behaved." There were no statistically significant differences between the answers to these questions. That is, those behaviors attributed to psychotics in general are the same as those attributed to specific and personally seen psychotics. Furthermore, there were no significant differences between the answers of those respondents who had actually seen a psychotic and those who had not. Apparently, and not surprisingly, beliefs regarding psychotic conduct are known widely and are not confined to those persons who have themselves seen a psychotic.

The first of these beliefs to be examined here concerns the etiology of psychosis.

The results of Table 3 point to several matters of interest. First, it is clearly not the case, as some writers (Smartt 1956) have assumed, that *all* Africans see sorcery or witchcraft as the sole cause of psychosis as well as all other misfortune. In all four tribes examined here, there are alternatives. The Sebei and Pokot, in fact, take an extremely naturalistic view of psychosis; they tend to attribute the disorder to the presence of a worm in the frontal portion of the brain (this same phenomenon has been reported for West Africa). The worm (or, in some cases, worms) can be felt

**Table 3** "What Causes Psychosis?"

|  | Hehe | | Kamba | | Pokot | | Sebei | | Total |
|---|---|---|---|---|---|---|---|---|---|
|  | N | % | N | % | N | % | N | % | |
| Disease or illness | 0 | (.00) | 10 | (.08) | 52 | (.41) | 78 | (.60) | 140 |
| Witchcraft | 50 | (.40) | 70 | (.56) | 1 | (.01) | 18 | (.14) | 139 |
| God | 28 | (.23) | 1 | (.01) | 0 | (.00) | 2 | (.02) | 31 |
| Stress of Life | 1 | (.01) | 35 | (.28) | 0 | (.00) | 2 | (.02) | 38 |
| Heredity | 18 | (.15) | 3 | (.02) | 0 | (.00) | 3 | (.02) | 24 |
| Other | 0 | (.00) | 5 | (.03) | 0 | (.00) | 1 | (.01) | 6 |
| Don't know | 26 | (.21) | 2 | (.02) | 75 | (.58) | 24 | (.19) | 127 |

moving about and as it moves it deranges the victim. The worm does not usually enter the brain as a result of witchcraft (although 18 Sebei said that it does); more often it does so without human intervention. As one Sebei said: "Psychosis is a disease, you catch it for no reason." Another added: "Cattle get this disease just as people do." The Pokot, too, see psychosis as a naturally occurring phenomenon. For the Pokot, it is an unspecifiable disorder of the brain, sometimes of the "muscles in the head," and here too it occurs "for no reason."

The Hehe and the Kamba answer differently. They both attribute the cause of psychosis most often to witchcraft or sorcery. This differential may point to a meaningful difference between the "Bantu" and "Kalenjin" peoples, with the former said generally to attribute all misfortune to human malevolence (Evans-Pritchard 1937; Field 1960; Wilson 1959) and the latter emphasizing natural, non-magical explanations of this misfortune (Evans-Pritchard 1931; Gulliver 1955; Huntingford 1953a; Peristiany 1939). But even for the "Bantu" tribes, not all psychosis is due to witchcraft. For example, the Hehe implicate God, who is for them a powerful if remote force, and 18 Hehe said that psychosis is inherited in certain clans. The Kamba frequently contend that psychosis is the direct result of stress such as worry or fear or grief concerning the affairs of everyday life. Especially likely to cause psychosis for the Kamba are the shame of poverty, grief over the death of a beloved child, worry over personal incompetence, or excessive drinking—all can "tire the brain" and cause it to malfunction. And, of course, all tribes recognize the possibility of multiple causation of psychosis.

It might also be noted that with the exception of the Kamba, these people do not always claim to know what causes psychosis. In this lack of

certainty they do not differ from laymen (or specialists) in Western societies.

Now to turn to the conceptions of psychotic behavior operative in each of the four tribes. In response to the question "How do psychotics behave?" respondents gave answers that varied in length from a single behavior to as many as ten. Each behavior was tabulated separately and the catalogue of all such behaviors is shown in Table 4.

The most obvious aspect of the many behaviors ascribed to "psychosis," is the agreement between the four tribes. However, there are also some interesting differential emphases within each tribe. For example, the Sebei most often point to "going naked" as evidence of psychosis; also emphasized are such behaviors as shouting and screaming, talking nonsense, wandering, eating dirt and collecting trash. But the Sebei also give frequent mention to the violently aggressive acts of murder and assault. This dual picture of violent and benign psychotic behavior is consistent with the account of an elderly Sebei farmer: "There are two kinds of mads, those who merely talk nonsense and wander about foolishly and the wild ones who attack people and destroy things."

The Kamba also mention "going naked" more often than any other behavior, but the combined acts of murder and assault are even more frequent. Kamba nudity occurs among both sexes—a woman may lie naked in a path all day or a man may knock on a door, stand there naked, then laugh and run away. Kamba acts of violence can be violent indeed: a woman removed her husband's head with a large knife, then kicked it around like a soccer ball for all to see; a man killed seven people with a bow and arrow; a young woman disemboweled several cows before she could be restrained.

The Hehe also mentioned nudity frequently, but most often mentioned is a timorous retreat from

**Table 4**  Psychotic Behavior as Construed by Four East African Tribes*

| | Kamba | | Hehe | | Pokot | | Sebei | |
|---|---|---|---|---|---|---|---|---|
| | *N* | % | *N* | % | *N* | % | *N* | % |
| 1. Murder or attempted murder | 84 | (.14) | 38 | (.08) | 58 | (.14) | 30 | (.07) |
| 2. Serious assault | 72 | (.12) | 41 | (.09) | 11 | (.03) | 58 | (.13) |
| 3. Arson | 23 | (.04) | 3 | (.01) | 55 | (.13) | 8 | (.02) |
| 4. Destroys property | 37 | (.06) | 9 | (.02) | 26 | (.06) | 4 | (.01) |
| 5. Abuses people verbally | 22 | (.04) | 17 | (.04) | 17 | (.04) | 8 | (.02) |
| 6. Shouts, screams, cries, sings | 22 | (.04) | 11 | (.02) | 33 | (.08) | 53 | (.12) |
| 7. Runs wildly | 12 | (.02) | 18 | (.04) | 30 | (.07) | 17 | (.04) |
| 8. Steals openly | 27 | (.04) | 4 | (.01) | 21 | (.05) | 7 | (.02) |
| 9. Goes naked | 119 | (.20) | 57 | (.12) | 23 | (.06) | 65 | (.14) |
| 10. Suicide | 6 | (.01) | 9 | (.02) | 5 | (.01) | 2 | (.004) |
| 11. Sex misconduct | 5 | (.01) | 5 | (.01) | 2 | (.004) | 2 | (.004) |
| 12. Talks nonsense | 37 | (.06) | 21 | (.05) | 65 | (.16) | 53 | (.12) |
| 13. Wanders aimlessly | 27 | (.04) | 13 | (.03) | 15 | (.04) | 43 | (.09) |
| 14. Eats and smears feces | 18 | (.03) | 11 | (.02) | 8 | (.02) | 15 | (.03) |
| 15. Eats and smears dirt | 12 | (.02) | 2 | (.004) | 6 | (.01) | 32 | (.07) |
| 16. Wears or collects trash, leaves, etc. | 26 | (.04) | 8 | (.02) | 13 | (.03) | 33 | (.07) |
| 17. Sleeps and hides in the bush | 28 | (.05) | 183 | (.40) | 8 | (.02) | 8 | (.02) |
| 18. Injures self | 6 | (.01) | 1 | (.002) | 5 | (.01) | 11 | (.02) |
| 19. Catatonic stupor | 1 | (.001) | 3 | (.01) | 0 | (.00) | 1 | (.002) |
| 20. Acts like a child | 12 | (.02) | 2 | (.004) | 0 | (.00) | 4 | (.01) |
| 21. Climbs trees | 0 | (.00) | 0 | (.00) | 7 | (.02) | 1 | (.002) |
| 22. Hallucinations | 3 | (.004) | 1 | (.002) | 0 | (.00) | 1 | (.002) |
| 23. Shaves head and bites self | 0 | (.00) | 0 | (.00) | 0 | (.00) | 2 | (.004) |
| 24. Compulsive actions | 2 | (.003) | 0 | (.00) | 0 | (.00) | 2 | (.004) |

* The figures in Table 4 represent all mentions of behavior given in response to three questions: (1) "How do psychotics behave?" (2) "How else?" (3) "Have you actually seen a psychotic right here in (name of area)? How did this person behave?"
Due to rounding error, the percentages given do not total 100.

people to a solitary life in the bush. The Hehe also state that there are two types of psychotics—the violent and the passively fearful. One Hehe native doctor insisted that all Hehe psychosis begins with a period of violent excitement and confusion which is soon followed by foolish docility characterized by nudity, eating and smearing feces, talking nonsense and living alone in the bush. This latter trait of solitary withdrawal is a characteristic Hehe reaction not only in the heavily populated mountains where it is relatively safe, but also in the lowland plains where lions, leopards, hyenas and the like make sleeping in the open bush hazardous in the extreme.

The Pokot most often point to "talking nonsense" as evidence of psychosis, but both murder and arson are also often mentioned. The Pokot are particularly given to arson. A psychotic Pokot is very likely to set fire to a house, sometimes while the occupants are asleep inside. The Pokot, too,

speak of a difference between "wild" and "mild" psychotics, but do not seem to regard them as mutually exclusive types.

Aside from these few tribal differentia, the general pattern is remarkably similar for all four tribes; no tribe presents a catalogue of behaviors that is at marked variance with that of any other tribe. One notable emphasis in all the tribes is upon nudity. Certainly, nudity is a common feature of many Western psychoses, yet by Western criteria this African emphasis would appear to be extreme. Even the Pokot, whose men are typically nude, are horrified by nudity among women. For women in all four cultures and for men (excepting the Pokot) to expose the genitals is shameful and shocking, yet despite the horror expressed in all four tribes when a person "walks naked without shame," other sexual offenses in psychosis are very rare. Only two Sebei mentioned sexual behaviors—both mentioned mother-son incest followed by the son murdering the mother. Five Kamba mentioned sexual conduct; in every case the behavior was rape. Of five Hehe mentions, four were rape, and one Hehe woman said that psychosis causes a woman to want to have sexual relations with her own sons when they are asleep at night. Only two Pokot mentioned sexual misconduct, both saying that when a woman becomes psychotic, she will chase a man and prankishly attempt to pull his penis. This incidence of sexual behavior in psychosis—only 14 mentions out of a total of 1,926—is probably quite low by Western standards. Conversely, the amount of overtly violent behavior mentioned would appear to exceed Western-based expectations. The occurrence of violence in psychosis, combined with excitement and confusion, has been noted over much of Africa.

It is also noteworthy that hallucinations are so seldom mentioned (only 5 times in all). Since hallucinations are so characteristic of Western psychosis, this omission requires some comment. It is possible that hallucinations are not sufficiently visible to the observer of behavior to be included in his listing of psychotic behavior; it is, after all, not always possible to determine when someone is hallucinating. It is certain that both auditory and visual hallucinations do occur among patients in East African mental hospitals. Unless we assume that patients "learn" to hallucinate only after entering a hospital, then we must conclude that they also do so before being hospitalized. Efforts to question native doctors about this matter and to observe actual psychotics in the field were inconclusive—it would appear that hallucinations do occur but may be relatively infrequent.

The results contain some major surprises. The first is that the symptom picture given by over 500 respondents in four different tribes is quite similar to the clinical picture seen in mental hospitals throughout East Africa. Contrary to the contention that hospital admissions in East Africa reflect only those behaviors that lead to major law violation in the European legal system, it is apparent that the same behaviors that lead to hospitalization are the basis for native conceptions of psychosis. Furthermore, it is remarkable how alike these African conceptions of psychosis are to the Western European psychoses, particularly to the constellation of reactions known as schizophrenia. The Africans of these four tribes do not regard a single behavior as psychotic which could not be so regarded in the West. That is, they do not produce symptoms which are understandable as psychotic only within the context of their own cultures. What is psychotic for them would be psychotic for us.

## TREATMENT

Another important question concerns native conceptions of the appropriate treatment for psychosis. Table 5 presents the answers of the same 505 respondents to the question, "What should be done with a psychotic?"

**Table 5** "What Should Be Done with a Psychotic?"

| | Kamba | Hehe | Pokot | Sebei |
|---|---|---|---|---|
| Tie them, then have a doctor treat them | 121 | 48 | 20 | 37 |
| Tie them forever, no treatment | 1 | 2 | 8 | 16 |
| Beat them, nothing else | 0 | 0 | 0 | 3 |
| Tie them and let them starve | 1 | 0 | 9 | 17 |
| Let them wander until they die | 0 | 1 | 13 | 19 |
| Kill them | 0 | 2 | 15 | 9 |
| Nothing | 0 | 1 | 5 | 4 |
| Don't know | 3 | 69 | 57 | 23 |

Once again, there is a manifest difference between the Kamba and Hehe—who believe that psychotics should be given therapy—and the Sebei and Pokot—who are more inclined to treat psychotics harshly than they are to attempt to cure them. This differential reaction is consistent with the tribal beliefs concerning prognosis.

Clearly, the Kamba and Hehe tend to believe that the condition can be cured, at least temporarily, whereas the Sebei and Pokot generally regard psychosis as incurable. Since both sets of tribes are referring to an essentially similar catalogue of behaviors as psychosis, it is curious that such a disagreement should exist. Perhaps this difference derives from the relative efficacy of the

**Table 6** "Can Psychotics Be Cured?"

| | Kamba | Hehe | Pokot | Sebei |
|---|---|---|---|---|
| No | 1 | 12 | 58 | 71 |
| Yes | 84 | 36 | 9 | 19 |
| Sometimes | 27 | 13 | 10 | 20 |
| Temporarily | 10 | 0 | 0 | 0 |
| Don't know | 4 | 62 | 51 | 18 |

363

types of treatment practiced in the two sets of tribes.

The following case illustrates a prevalent form of treatment among the Kamba:

I am now an old man but I know about this madness. Mads (psychotics) can kill people for no reason. They also spoil things just like a baby. They have no responsibility. I was mad myself. There were no hospitals then. I knew I was mad—it felt like a fever. I thought everyone was a wild beast so I ran and hid in the bush because I was afraid of them. I was cured by a Kamba doctor. She divined the cause. It was caused by ancestral spirits so I was required to start taking snuff. She also said that from my mother's family must come snuff and beer. My father had to provide tobacco and beer. All of this was mixed and given to the ancestors. A goat was slaughtered too. A small strap of goat skin was put around my wrist in order for me to carry a small calabash containing snuff. I carried this always. I also had to wear a black cloth until it wore out. I was completely cured after some time.

In general, Kamba therapy combines drugs with magical treatment of this sort, but one very famous Kamba doctor employs a more dramatic technique. He places the psychotic in a large pit that has been filled with water. The pit is then covered over with green wood, then dry wood and leaves, which are ignited. The patient soon reacts to the intense heat by screaming. According to the doctor, "This proves that the treatment is powerful. He screams and screams but I do not release him for several hours. My patients are almost always cured."

The Hehe may also employ magical means to counter psychosis, but at least some Hehe doctors also maintain an impressive pharmacopoeia. These drugs are always administered with both religious and magical accompaniment but some of the drugs appear to have considerable pharmacological activity as tranquilizing agents. In general, the Hehe emphasize chemotherapy and the Kamba prefer magical psychotherapy or "shock" therapy.

No native doctor specializing in the treatment of mental disorders could be located among the Sebei, but several common therapies are widely known. In one well-known practice, assorted liquids are poured down the nose of the patient while he is tied securely to a granary or centerpost of a house. Other medicines are smoked and inhaled, or a patient may be immersed in a bath containing medicines. The most highly regarded technique, however, is reminiscent of Medieval Europe. A red hot iron is pressed against the forehead of the patient because the heat is thought to kill the insect which is the agent of his misfortune. One man (who

is still psychotic) had three scars to testify to the repeated use of the treatment where necessary. Still, the Sebei have little confidence in the efficiency of their cures. Indeed, as the following case indicates, they often call in foreign specialists.

Old Eriyeza is very mad indeed. He eats his own dung. He cannot even have intercourse with his wives. All day he hangs upside down from the roof of his house; he must be fed while he hangs this way. He has been mad this way for about four years now. Recently, his son called for a Pokot doctor to come and treat him. This doctor came and killed a bull, then squeezed some of its dung into some water. Eriyeza was made to drink this water but it did not help him. Then some medicine was poured down his nose. This did not help either. He still hangs upside down.

For their part, the Pokot have no more confidence in their doctors than the Sebei do in theirs. Two well-known Pokot doctors were contacted and their medicines and techniques seen. Medicines are given by mouth and occasionally through the nose. None is thought to be very effective, even by the doctors. The two most renowned cures are described by the native doctors who employ them:

To cure such a mad man you must sacrifice a goat. This is done to rid him of the evil spirits that are troubling him. Then he is put inside a fallen tree and the goat is killed on top of him and bleeds down upon him. Then he is covered with white mud. Then the goat meat is scattered in eight directions. He will be cured.

I am able to cure mads. I order the patient tied and placed on the ground. I then take a large rock and pound the patient on the head for a long time. This calms them and they are better.

While it is possible that the Kamba and Hehe actually have more effective therapeutic techniques than the Pokot and Sebei, it is more probable that the treatments among the four tribes alone do not differ sufficiently to account for the disagreement in belief concerning their efficacy. However, it may be that the answer can be found by consulting Table 1. The Kamba and Hehe tend to find a magical or supernatural etiology for psychosis. The Sebei and Pokot tend to regard it as an illness which is contracted for no reason. The Kamba-Hehe are combating magic, witchcraft or the ancestors; the Sebei-Pokot are contending with a disease. Since all four tribes are almost certainly attempting to treat the same generic schizophrenia-like disorder, it is strange that two tribes should think that they can cure it, while two believe that they cannot. No explanation can be given with confidence but it is at least possible that the Kamba-Hehe belief in magical causation requires concomitant belief in magical cure while the Sebei-Pokot belief in natural causation fosters belief in man's inability to control natural forces.

There is no evidence to indicate that Kamba-Hehe psychotics recover while Sebei-Pokot patients do not. All available data suggest that psychotics in all four societies, despite temporary remissions, tend to remain psychotic throughout their lives. However, there is a difference. For the Kamba-Hehe, a temporary remission is evidence of a cure; the return of symptoms need not be evidence for the continuation of the disorder; on the contrary, it is seen as evidence for a *new* case of witchcraft. The Sebei-Pokot do not have the advantage of similar reasoning.

## THE SOCIAL CONTEXT

A number of researchers have suspected that severe mental disorder in African tribal societies would be defined primarily in terms of serious antisocial conduct. The grounds for this argument apparently originate in the thought that primitive societies—as opposed to large urban, industrial societies—will define psychosis essentially in terms of those acts that disturb basic social processes and structures or violate vital cultural patterns, and will either tolerate less severe forms of social deviance altogether or simply define these behaviors as non-psychotic.

In order to examine this question, the 24 behaviors listed in Table 4 were ranked by the extent to which they would ordinarily be socially disruptive in these societies. Behaviors 1 through 4 were considered to be severely disruptive, 5 through 11 were considered mildly disruptive, and 12 through 24 only minimally so, or "eccentric." Obviously, this categorization is not adequate in every instance but it does provide a reasonably

accurate ranking. Table 7 indicates the results of categorizing the behaviors listed in Table 4 in this manner.

The Kamba and Pokot most often mention severely disruptive behavior, and even here only to the extent of 36 percent and 37 percent respectively. It is apparent that all four societies include in their definitions of psychosis a great many mild and non-disruptive behaviors. When the data are reanalyzed in terms of psychotic persons actually seen, the same pattern emerges: more people are described as being mild or eccentric than violently aggressive. The same pattern is also retained when each respondent's description of psychotic behavior is rated by the *most* disruptive behavior mentioned (i.e., if the respondent mentions three "eccentric" behaviors and one "severely disruptive" one, the description is scored as "severely disruptive"). Obviously, these African societies do not construe psychosis only in terms of flagrant, socially-disruptive actions. It should also be added that degrees of mental disorder less severe than psychosis are recognized in all four societies and these "neuroses" are characteristically defined in terms of socially benign or merely eccentric behavior.

But there is one essential feature of African psychosis. Respondent after respondent qualified his description of a psychotic behavior by saying "without reason." That is, murder as such is not psychotic—only murder *without some good reason* is psychotic. The same thing is true of every other behavior cited. Eating feces, collecting trash, living in the bush, going naked, and all the other behaviors, are not necessarily psychotic. Each behavior can occur in exceptional circumstances, such as in ceremonies, or as the result of injury or illness, etc., without any suggestion of psychosis. It is when they occur without good reason that they constitute evidence of psychosis. The implication is that the recognition of psychosis in these four societies is by no means an automatic or simple process. It involves considerable interpretation and

**Table 7** Psychotic Behaviors Presented in Table 4 as Ranked by Degree of Social Disruptiveness

|  | Kamba | | Hehe | | Pokot | | Sebei | |
|---|---|---|---|---|---|---|---|---|
|  | N | % | N | % | N | % | N | % |
| Severely Disruptive (Nos. 1–4) | (216) | 36 | (91) | 20 | (150) | 37 | (100) | 22 |
| Mildly Disruptive (Nos. 5–11) | (215) | 35 | (121) | 26 | (131) | 32 | (154) | 34 |
| Merely "Eccentric" (Nos. 12–24) | (172) | 29 | (245) | 54 | (127) | 31 | (204) | 44 |

negotiation in order to determine the "reason" why an action occurred, and consequently, what person, group, or supernatural force is to be held responsible, as well as to determine the kinds of compensatory actions required. Psychosis is but one possible "reason" to account for an action in question—other common reasons could include witchcraft, fever, drunkenness, negligence, or simply malicious intent. The point to be emphasized is that, except for chronic cases, psychosis is recognized, defined, and responded to through a process of interpersonal negotiation and jural consideration scarcely less complex than that which obtains in modern Western societies.

## SUMMARY AND CONCLUSION

Though brief and limited, this report has presented a number of findings concerning native conceptions of psychosis in four East African Societies. (1) Psychosis is not always attributed to witchcraft; it is often regarded as an illness occurring for no reason or the natural result of life stress. (2) Despite some differential tribal emphases (e.g., the Hehe emphasis on sleeping alone in the bush), the catalogue of behaviors constitutive of psychosis was surprisingly similar in all four tribes. (3) This catalogue of psychotic behaviors is not markedly at variance with Western symptomatology, especially for schizophrenia. (4) These African tribesmen stress the difference between aggressively acting-out and mildly withdrawn psychotics; however, it is not clear in all cases whether these are seen as exclusive types or simply stages within the same progressively less violent symptom pattern. (5) Psychotic behaviors as defined by unacculturated tribal members are virtually identical to those seen in the large, European directed, mental hospitals that were a part of medico-legal apparatus of Colonial East Africa. (6) Native treatment for psychosis is diverse but confidence in the effectiveness of this treatment seems to depend upon the accepted etiology of the disorder and, hence, whether or not a temporary improvement is counted as a cure. (7) Psychosis in these societies is not defined solely, or even principally, in terms of severe, socially disruptive conduct. (8) The process by which a person becomes socially recognized as a psychotic is a complex negotiation with moral and legal implications.

In conclusion, I would like to point to a fundamental question. In several disciplines, contention flourishes over the question of the effect of culture upon the etiology, incidence, symptomatology and treatment of mental illness. One view, often held by psychiatrists, is universalist. It argues that mental illness—especially psychosis—is essentially similar transculturally. An example of this view is expressed by E. B. Forster (1962:35), a psychiatrist with much practical experience in Ghana:

Psychiatric syndromes or reactions, by and large, are similar in all races throughout the world. The mental reactions seen in our African patients can be diagnosed according to Western textbook standards. The basic illness and reaction types are the same. Environmental, constitutional and tribal cultural background merely modify the symptom constellation. Basically, the disorders of thinking, feeling, willing and knowing are the same.

Traditionally, anthropologists have disagreed, arguing for the sovereign force of culture in determining the dynamics of mental illness. Hence, anthropologists tend to emphasize the transcultural dissimilarity of mental illness. However, the cultural determinist position does not always distinguish between the effect of culture upon mild mental illness, as opposed to psychotic disorders.

I would first insist that efforts to substantiate either position on the basis of existing knowledge are premature, because available cross-cultural data are both so fragmentary and uneven in quality as to render hopeless even the most heroically Procrustean efforts to stretch the evidence to fit *any* conclusion.

The data of the present study are a case in point. They can be employed to argue for the transcultural similarity of psychosis; indeed, I am impressed that the psychotic behavior mentioned in these four African tribes does not differ markedly from the psychotic behavior displayed on "backwards" of mental hospitals in this country and in Britain. Conversely, I would also admit that the psychotic behaviors described by these four African tribes not only differ between tribes in some significant ways but can also be interpreted as diverging from the Euro-American pattern of psychotic symptoms. Thus, the cultural determinist can also find support for his view. Although I am reluctant to perpetuate that most hackneyed of conclusions by calling for more research, in this instance that call is essential. We need fewer manifestos and expressions of faith, and more field data that tell us how non-Western peoples do in fact perceive and respond to severe mental illness.

Surely, the impasse between the cultural de-terminists and the universalists will not be broken by the partial data of this study. Indeed, the problem may only be exacerbated. But if that were to happen, it would be all to the good, for it is surely the case that anthropologists should re-examine this question in full seriousness. The question has serious implications not merely for psychiatry but also for the central concerns of anthropology. For, in the answer to the question of the extent to which the force of culture truly influences the frequency and the ways in which men become psychotic, we will learn something of importance about the nature of man, about the relations between men in societies, and, about culture.

# 41  Spirit Possession and Its Sociopsychological Implications Among the Sidamo of Southwest Ethiopia

## *John and Irene Hamer*

Anthropologists have long been intrigued with the phenomenon of possession. It is always a powerful and dramatic expression of the strength of spiritual and religious beliefs in a culture. The objective for the anthropologist in studying this fascinating behavioral manifestation is to relate it to the social structure and culture of the society. For the medical anthropologist, in addition, it is imperative to find the correlates between spirit-possession and the medical system. This study by John and Irene Hamer attempts, successfully in my view, to achieve both objectives. A significant cause of disease for the Sidamo is the incurring of the displeasure of spirits called *shatāna*, and when a disease seems otherwise inexplicable the victim knows that he/she will be possessed by his/her *shatāna*. Once possessed, the host must feed his spirit at intervals and in a manner prescribed by it, usually for the remainder of the person's life. The Hamers show that possession is used by males who have failed in the competition for wealth, status, and power, and that they use possession to attain those ends and psychologically for emotional release as well. Women,

Reprinted with abridgments from John and Irene Hamer, 1966, "Spirit Possession and Its Socio-Psychological Implications Among the Sidamo of Southwest Ethiopia," *Ethnology*, 5:392–408, with permission of the authors and *Ethnology: An International Journal of Cultural and Social Anthropology*.

all of whom are in a secondary, invidious position in the social structure, use possession for similar ends and as a compensating vengeance against oppressive spouses. The Hamers suggest interesting psychosomatic correlates of possession, comparing Sidamo spirit-possession manifestations with psychosomatic complaints in the West. Finally, a regional comparison is made with other groups in Ethiopia. A subsequent study by Lewis (1971) using a cross-cultural sampling of many societies tends to confirm the Hamers' study and to generate a series of remarkable propositions regarding the relationship between possession and social structure.

Since possession among the Sidamo is a frequent and expected emotional reaction to certain illnesses, the question arises as to whether it may be considered a behavioral disorder or "mental illness." We know that when a physical disorder (for example, pinta in certain areas of tropical America) becomes endemic it may no longer be defined by a society as a disease but as simply an expectable condition of life. The Hamers say persons who are inclined toward possession seem to be highly dependent, but what we do not know is the incidence of high dependency in the society, nor whether more highly dependent people become possessed than those who are not. These kinds of questions must supplant the more glib kinds of associations between emotional disorders and personal-social characteristics so frequently alleged in clinical psychiatry and psychology without reference to population, incidence, and other epidemiological factors.

The Sidamo are a Cushitic-speaking people found in southwestern Ethiopia, about 150 miles south of Addis Ababa.... They are organized into a number of segmentary, patrilineal clans in which political authority is completely in the hands of the elders, whose position is supported by a system of age grades. Little is known of the origins of these people other than that, according to data obtained from genealogies and mythology, they were closely associated with the Galla as recently as the sixteenth century. The Sidamo practice a mixed crop and livestock economy....

In this paper we wish to consider the phenomenon of spirit possession among the Sidamo as it relates to the social structure and beliefs about disease therapy and religion. Possession among these people is related to certain concepts pertaining to supernatural power and the healing quality of spirits. It is believed that the spirits which possess individuals have been sent by Magāno, the sky god. Furthermore, all unexplainable illnesses are attributed by the possessed to the dissatisfaction of these supernatural beings, and only through their appeasement can sickness be alleviated.

An important aspect of the social structure is the ability of an individual to show his superiority in one or a combination of attributes involving wealth, oratorical ability, or bravery. In addition, there is a noticeable ascribed sexual difference in the superior status accorded males over females. A person with one or more of these attributes is considered to have the ability to influence the lives of others. Considering that in the struggle for power and prestige there must be losers, either by ascription or by failure to achieve through one of the three attributes, there must be some cultural means of alleviating the sense of failure if social unity is to be preserved. It is our contention that spirit possession provides such a psycho-cultural outlet.

## SPIRITS

To appreciate the importance of spirits it is first necessary to see how the Sidamo conceptualize their position *vis-à-vis* the supernatural world. According to the religious mythology, the sky god creator was originally much closer to the people than he is today. It seems, however, that he became angry with mankind and returned to the sky, where he influences the course of events only in a distant and most indirect fashion. This sky god, Magāno, is seen as a punishing deity who seems in the main to be concerned with the giving and taking of life. Though they do not go so far as to suggest that Magāno sent the spirits, known as *shatāna* (sing. *shatāni*), to compensate for his aloofness, most informants were of the opinion that they had indeed been sent as his emissaries. The *shantāna* are thought to have an influence on such important aspects of everyday life as childbirth, health, and the reproduction of cattle. No specific form is ascribed to the *shatāna*, and the observer becomes aware of their presence only indirectly through the occurrence of unexplained illness, the dialogue which they carry on through the mouth of the possessed, and the jerking motion of the head and shoulders of the individual when the spirit enters his body.

The method of propitiating these spirits is analogous to that used in appeasing Magāno and the founders of the principal Sidamo clans. It is based on a pragmatic view of a supernatural world which people seek to manipulate for their own ends.... Since these spirits are believed to have the ability to bring and alleviate illness, as well as to control reproduction, an individual may be able to manipulate their actions in his favor by offering a comparable form of reciprocity. For example, when a possessed person becomes ill, the *shatāni* is asked if it brought the illness; if it replies in the affirmative, people agree to give it food if it will promise to heal the victim. When the spirit has fulfilled his end of the bargain, the men of the community gather to perform the ritual food offering.

...Some informants were of the opinion that females are more subject to possession than males, while others questioned any significant difference by sex. In our sample there were nearly as many men as women, 13 as compared with 16, who indicated they were subject to possession. Both men and women reported that they were more often possessed by male than female *shatāna*.

## POSSESSION

Possession can be considered from the standpoint of its onset and associated illnesses, ritual procedures, and the intensity and duration of the phenomenon. Regardless of when they first appear to the individual, *shatāna* are always preceded by an illness. It was the opinion of all informants, and substantiated by 23 subjects with spirits, that illnesses cannot be related to specific *shantāna*. The four most frequently reported disorders for possessed individuals of both sexes involved complaints of the head and nose, malfunctions of the gastrointestinal tract, fever, and rheumatic conditions. The high frequency of head, nose, fever, and intestinal disorders may be at least partially attributed to the contrasting heat, cold, and dampness of the highland environment, the lack of sanitary facilities, and the contact with malaria on journeys to the lowlands. Because of the expense of feeding *shatāna*, most informants reported that they initially resisted accepting possession. They nevertheless asserted unanimously that they began to get better, some even reporting complete recovery, as soon as they gave in and accepted the demands of the spirits.

The occurrence of a prolonged unexplainable illness is generally considered the first sign that a *shatāni* is seeking to possess an individual. Though the potential host at first resists possession, possibly for as long as several months, he eventually evinces a tendency to shiver and shake periodically. If one or both of his parents has been subject to possession, his kinsmen and fellow villagers became convinced that the spirit wishes to

368

be acknowledged and to pass on to the child. Generally the parent has died before such a transference occurs, though we recorded one instance where an old man passed on a *shantāni* to his daughter before his death. It was difficult to establish the criteria by which *shatāna* are transmitted when both parents have been hosts, but informants were of the opinion that the more powerful spirit would be the one passed on. In anticipation of possession in such cases, the men of the village assemble after dark in the hut of the patient and call the *shatāni* to the accompaniment of drumming and hand clapping. When the spirit begins to speak through the mouth of the patient, it first accepts responsibility for causing the illness, alleging that it wants "the child" to become its new host. It refers to the possessed as a horse (*forāsho*) if he is male, or a mule (*gāngo*) if female, and asks for the same measure of care and attention as is accorded these animals, in return for which it promises to protect the steed from future illnesses.

In cases when the patient is not the descendant of a parental host, or where there is uncertainty as to the connection between the physical disorder and the intervention of *shatāna* , it is possible to consult an expert, called *količa*, who understands the supernatural world and can verify the presence of a spirit as well as suggest a song to be used in summoning it. Such an expert, nearly always a male, is known to possess a powerful spirit which he has acquired either from his father or through dreaming and divination. In the latter case, the *shatāni* has appeared to him in a dream on several occasions, demanding that he serve as its host or face the alternative of death, and the dream has been confirmed by sacrificing a cow and examining the veins of its stomach lining. The *shatāna* of *količa* are more powerful than those of ordinary mortals; as one of these experts explained, "The distinction between our possession and that of the non-*količa* is the difference between the expert and the amateur." Indeed, they are considered potent enough to permit their hosts to predict the future as well as to cure disease. A *količa* has the ability to communicate with his *shantāni* at any time, though night is generally preferred, by beating upon his drum and singing the appropriate summoning song. These specialists in the supernatural are viewed by the community with a mixture of awe and fear. They have the power not only to diagnose and cure illness but also to provide solutions to personal and communal problems; and they are noted for their dire predictions of famines, epidemics, and interpersonal conflicts. They are

characterized by alternate periods of mysterious withdrawal from and close intermingling with other people.

Six of our 17 subjects indicated that, after prolonged illness, they had consulted a *količa* to determine whether a spirit wanted to possess them. Four of the six had parents with spirits, and two did not. The diagnostic procedures of the *količa* indicate that his role is primarily to provide confirmation of possession. His initial act is to summon his spirit, which speaking through him, asks a series of leading questions about the client's illness and life history. What follows is dependent on the results of this dialogue and on how much the *količa* knows of the client's background. If he is uncertain as to the cause of the illness, he may direct the client to return home and await the occurrence of a dream or make a sacrifice to his deceased father. If, on the other hand, he knows enough about the life of the client and his family, he may diagnose possession immediately. When a sacrifice has been prescribed, and the client recovers, it is evident that a *shantāni* was not involved. When recovery does not follow, the first occurrence of a dream sends the client back to the *količa*, who can now decide with confidence that a *shatāni* is involved. The specialist then teaches the client a song for calling spirits and advises him to return to his village, call the *shatāni*, and thereby determine its identity. For this service the client and his kinsmen provide him with a gift of money or food....

An ill person lies on a bed during the early stages of the procedure, but one who is not suffereing too much discomfort sits on a stool with the men, who are gathered around the fire. The spirit enters the head of the possessed and causes it to shake—at first gradually and then more violently until his whole body begins to shudder. It is believed that the spirit entering the head of the possessed rides him as one would ride a horse or mule. The sideways, to-and-fro motion of the head and shoulders does in fact resemble that of a rider traveling at a gallop. As the shaking becomes more pronounced, the neophyte may rise, move toward the fire, and quickly pick up and drop some hot coals. The men, however, catch him and return him to his seat beside the fire. Finally the spirit announces its presence through its host, either by making a whirring sound like an insect or simply speaking out. There follows a dialogue between the *shatāni* and one of the men who has been designated spokesman because of his knowledge of spirits. . . .

The spokesman may then ask what it is that the spirit wishes to be fed, and the latter may suggest the kind of food that it wishes to receive, at least once a year, if it is to keep the horse or mule in good health. Most informants reported that they had been instructed to feed their spirits an animal, such as a bull, ram, or a sheep, along with ensete flour, butter, and honey. A few stated that it was sufficient to provide only barley, butter, and honey at the annual feeding.

After the initial possession experience, the possessed has the spirits called only at the annual feeding, when their children or cattle are ill, or when they wish to give thanks for some auspicious occurrence such as the birth of a child. Except in emergencies, the calling procedure always requires singing and drumming by the adult male members of the community. The catalogue of *shatāna* songs is known to all, and during the course of an evening the men sing a number of general calling songs, climaxed by that associated specifically with the host's *shatāni*. If an unusual illness suddenly befalls a child of the possessed, and there is insufficient time for the men of the community to foregather, the spirit may be called by taking a special grass (*hortshā*), mixing it with butter and spices, and placing it on the head of the host. The latter then asks the spirit to enter and tell whether it has caused the child to become sick. . . .

As to the effect of possession on the individual, four out of ten informants reported that they lost consciousness when the *shatāni* first came upon them but became aware of what was going on as soon as it began to speak. The others, however, were completely cognizant of what was happening throughout the possession experience. The voice of a *shatāni* is recognized as being the same as that of the possessed, the only difference being that it is sometimes louder than usual and may be characterized by a noticeable hesitancy, almost a stutter. One woman stated that her spirit sometimes spoke in Gallenia, though she herself claimed not to understand this language. A majority of the informants reported that the *shatāni* always speaks in an angry and indignant manner which seems quickly to exhaust the vitality of its steed. It was in fact observed that after its departure the host was usually drenched with perspiration and so exhausted that he needed several days to recover.

Spirits exhibit considerable variation in supernatural power, which the Sidamo attribute to the noticeable differences in the degree to which they influence the lives of the possessed. Generally, spirits are considered to be the most potent at their time of origin, but there have been cases of seizure by older spirits who are recognized as more than usually strong. It is an indication of a powerful possession if the possessed remains behind the bamboo partition which divides the dwelling during the ritual, rather than mingling with the crowd around the fire. Criteria for the potency of a *shatāni*, in addition to the number of its accompanying spirits, include its ability to force people other than family members to serve as its steed, its demands for large gifts, and the making of prophesies.

A person may have a dream in which a spirit appears in the form of a neighboring host and asks to be served and fed. If he ignores this request, he is likely to suffer a severe physical illness or temporary insanity. To recover his health he must then not only fulfill the demands made in the dream but also go to the neighbor's compound accompanied by his close paternal relatives to beg the spirit to release him. He should remain with the host for a period of from several days to a month providing such services as cutting wood, preparing food, or working in the garden. At the end of this time he is considered to be cured and goes home, but he must return periodically with a small token of food as a sign of continuing respect for the spirit. It is said that the majority of people who are either afraid of or actually subject to this temporary form of possession are women. . . .

Traditionally, and even today for a majority of people, the only way to escape from a *shatāni* is through death. The spirit leaves its host just prior to his death, having indicated its intention to pass on to a favored child, who may be of either sex and who is alleged to be the one who has been most obedient and subservient to the possessed parent. Occasionally the spirit requests to be fed by both the possessed and this favorite child during the lifetime of the former.

Since World War II it has been possible to break the tie with one's *shatāni* by joining one of several European mission churches. When this happens, the spirits are believed to depart when the host stands before the congregation, renounces all *shatāni*, and professes a belief in Christian principles. Persons who experience this form of religious conversion acknowledge that they are motivated to do so through anticipation of a superior form of supernatural protection to be provided by Jesus Christ; they are convinced that they will never again experience the illness and pain formerly associated with their *shatāna*. Coincident with this belief, however, is a fear that to waver in the newly found faith or to neglect church duties is to invite the return of the *shatāna*.

Considering the socio-psychological functions of possession, it may seem strange that some persons should want to break their ties with a spirit. There is, however, always a certain amount of ambivalence toward accepting possession because of its association with ill health and the fear that if the spirit is not properly served the host will die. Moreover, unless others recognize the *shatāni* as powerful and are motivated to serve it, the feeding obligation can become expensive for the possessed and his immediate kinsmen.

## SOCIAL STRUCTURE

The extent to which prestige is based on the power to influence others provides the key to understanding the relations between social structure and possession among the Sidamo. Since there is considerable sexual difference in the way positions of influence are structured, we may begin by examining the situation among men.

At all levels of organization in which males are involved, prestige is partially based on seniority in chronological age. Deference must always be shown by a younger to an older male. In childhood younger brothers are expected to serve and obey older brothers. Initiation into the age-grade system, which can happen at any time between early childhood and late adolescence, is merely a preliminary to the circumcision ritual, which confers elder status on the individual years later. For a man to become an elder and live to a very old age is to acquire as much prestige as it is possible to obtain by ascription.

Since however, there are many other males with similar ascribed positions at all age levels, a man must achieve status in some way if he is to distinguish himself. One traditional means of acquiring fame was to show unusual bravery in battle or in attacking and subduing a leopard, lion, or other ferocious beast. There are still some old men, and even a few younger ones, who have achieved fame by killing an Arussi tribesman in a border skirmish. The usual means of achieving renown and influence today, though, is through the acquisition either of wealth or of oratorical expertise. A man is considered wealthy if he has a large number of cattle or combines a smaller herd with extensive fields of ensete and coffee. It is our impression that skilled orators tend also to be wealthy.

For men who aspire to fame and social dominance, but for one reason or another have no talent as warriors, orators, or farmers, spirit possession provides an alternative opportunity for achieving status. A person with a powerful spirit may accumulate wealth from gifts, and he has the potentiality of attracting large audiences when he undergoes possession, even if he is completely ignored in the assembly of elders. In the villages where field work was conducted, three of the four men with spirits were considered to be poor farmers, to possess few livestock, and to be inadequate public speakers, and two of them were also alleged to be cowards. Moreover, it was reported by some of the older men that two out of three known originators of powerful spirits in the last fifty years had lived in poverty prior to their possession experience. Within a few years of the initial appearance of their *shatāna*, they became wealthy and achieved fame throughout Sidamo. The followers of Shiffa, the original "horse" of the spirits Galāmo and Mārame, increased to the point that a large village of supplicants grew up around his residence.

Indirect evidence to the same effect was provided by informants who indicated that they wanted spirits so that people would serve them, or that they dismissed them when people stopped bringing food for the ritual feedings. One man frankly admitted that he had decided to become a Christian when he realized that he had few supplicants and was wasting much of his own property in feeding his *shatāna*.

The possession of women can best be understood by comparing their status with that of men. The Sidamo place so much stress on the importance of the male line and on patrilocal residence that a man, once he has paid bride-wealth, has virtually absolute rights to the services and procreative potential of his wife. A woman has no rights of inheritance from her affines or agnates. Consequently, in her old age, if her husband is dead and she has no sons, she must either rely on the generosity of her spouse's kinsmen or return to her own agnates, who may receive her reluctantly. During her marriage her husband may send her away at will and beat her whenever he pleases. She must always defer to him and his male agnates and must observe a variety of taboos; for example, she may not mention the name of her husband's father, she must avoid him and all his collateral male agnates, and she must look down at the ground when spoken to by a man. Even in their ritual greeting of men it is customary for women to demean themselves by referring to their position as of no more consequence that the earth upon which the men tread. The only aspects of a woman's role which serve to alleviate her subordinate position are her capacity for child-bearing and the dependence of her husband upon her for food preparation and labor.

Since a man can never admit to accepting the opinion or advice of a woman, one of the few ways she has of commanding the attention of her male affines, or of achieving wider renown, is through spirit possession. In possession, it is not she but the spirit temporarily using her as a host who arrests the attention of the men in the community. Hence a woman who achieves fame as the "mule" of a powerful spirit does not constitute a threat to male feelings of status superiority. In the name of her *shatāni* she can make demands on her husband and his male agnates for food and presents which would not be appropriate to her role as a woman and a wife.

Though a husband and his male kinsmen may resent the expense and inconvenience of feeding the woman's spirit, they usually accept the obligation in order to prevent conflict that could lead to divorce and the consequent costs and effort of obtaining another spouse. Failure to feed a possessed woman's spirit, moreover, provides her with an excuse for being ill and thus unable to serve her husband. One female informant even told of having "given in" after being admonished by her *shatāni* to leave her negligent husband. The significance of this indirect form of feminine manipulation for a man of limited resources can be seen from the fact that women married to wealthy men do not have spirits. Marriage to a man of wealth is considered ideal, because it guarantees a woman enviable gifts of clothing, food, land, and animals. Less successful men are often aware that their wives use possession to exploit their fear of losing the bridewealth, which is not returnable at divorce, and many humorous stories of such forms of exploitation are current throughout Sidamo. Several informants related instances of men who had become so infuriated with the whimsical demands of their spouses' spirits that they managed, by means of severe beatings, to frighten their wives into foregoing possession....

## PSYCHOLOGICAL ASPECTS

Failure by men as warriors, orators, or farmers, and by women in making desirable marriages, does not provide a sufficient explanation for the possession phenomenon. Not all unsuccessful persons acquire spirits, and it is necessary to examine certain psychological variables to account for the selective aspects of possession and its association with illness. Such an approach requires a consideration of psychological dependency and of the personality attributes of a certain type of psychosomatic debility....

The frequency with which children sought help, physical contact, and close proximity with adults and peers, as well as their rather obvious attempts to gain attention in the home, community, and testing situations, led the authors to conclude that dependency is generally encouraged in Sidamo....

In view of the dependency factor, it is not surprising that, when a parent has acquired a *shatāni*, it is the favorite son or daughter who becomes the host in the next generation. It was possible to obtain data on the approximate age at which spirit possession first occurred in 15 such subjects—six males and nine females. All of the males first underwent possession at around the onset of middle age, i.e., well after marriage and at about the age when the death of their parents is to be expected. Two of them specifically indicated that they had dreamed, after the death of the parental host, that the spirit wanted them and had shortly thereafter become ill. For males, possession thus appears to provide a substitute for the dependency relationship previously exhibited toward parents. It enables them periodically to focus upon themselves the concern of their male agnates and other members of the community, thereby rewarding them for their dependency on their *shatāna* manifested in the ritual feeding of the latter.

For favorite daughters, it is not death which disrupts the dependency relationship with the parents, but rather marriage and removal to the village of the husband. Of our nine female subjects, one had her first possession experience prior to marriage, six at the time of their marriage, one four years after her marriage, and one after the birth of her children. The physical separation of married women from their parents is intensified by the reluctance of their husbands to permit them to return for visits. Under these circumstances, acquiring a spirit enables a woman periodically to attract dramatic attention from her husband and other men in the community, who are ordinarily indifferent to her emotional needs. Possession thus provides a similar outlet for dependency in women as in men....

Psychosomatic factors seem frequently to be involved in illness associated with possession. Of 23 subjects who reported their symptoms, ten mentioned severe rheumatic disturbances involving stiffness, swelling, and aching of the joints. They asserted that, after accepting possession, they were able to resume their normal activities almost immediately, even in cases where they had been confined to their beds for prolonged periods. All of them maintained, moreover, that they experienced no recurrence of their rheumatic pains as long as their *shatāna* were fed on demand by their male agnates and other adult males of the community.

This information is especially interesting in the light of a number of studies which have indicated a relationship between psychosocial factors and rheumatoid arthritis in modern industrial societies. These researches, though their findings have not always been consistent, nevertheless reveal a tendency for arthritic patients to be excessively concerned over separation from a key parent and to be unusually self-sacrificing and willing to serve others (King 1955:287–302; Ludwig 1949:339; Scotch and Geiger 1962:1037–1067; Robinson 1957:344–345). Another study (Cobb and King 1958:466–476) goes so far as to indicate a connection between an arthritic condition and the stresses generated by frustrated occupational and educational ambitions. The rheumatic complaints of the Sidamo, with their postulated relationship to dependency and the striving for attention, reveal obvious similarities to the rheumatoid arthritis syndrome. Other illnesses associated with possession—gastro-intestinal disturbances, skin disease, fever, and head and nasal complaints—may also have a psychosomatic aspect, since rapid recoveries are similarly reported upon acceptance of the role of host to a spirit.

The state of helplessness that goes with disease tends to be rewarded by the community. Any form of sickness in Sidamo entitles the sufferer to an extraordinary amount of attention. Even in the case of a small child, kinsmen and friends of the parents from miles around congregate in the hut of the patient, bringing food and sharing it with him. This rewarding of dependency derives from childhood when parents regard the giving of food as the standard means of satisfying any attempt to attract attention or achieve closeness. To fail to respond with sustenance is tantamount to rejection, and is in fact employed by parents as a convenient form of punishment for small children. Since feeding has such important emotional connotations, it is not surprising that the Sidamo are reluctant to turn away strangers and even stray dogs who are hungry. If our hypothesis that possessed people show an unusual amount of dependency is correct, then it is understandable why the host of a spirit reverts to a state of helplessness characterized by conscious or unconscious somatic symptoms, and why *shatāna* complain of neglect which can only be compensated by feeding.

## REGIONAL COMPARISON

Despite the sparsity of data on spirit possession for Ethiopia as a whole, certain comparisons are possible between the *shatāna* of the Sidamo on the one hand and the *gari* of the neighboring Arussi and the *zar* spirits of the Amhara on the other. Five of the 15 spirits listed by Haberland (1963:514–516) as known to the Arussi are also recognized and accepted by the Sidamo. Three of these—Ilbesa, Mārame, and Borantiča—are admitted to be of foreign or even specifically Arussi origin. Golfē, however, is regarded as the daughter of Iyo, the mother of all traditional Sidamo spirits, and Fātimē is considered to be the daughter of Golfē. Messing (1957:619–627) lists four of the 31 *zar* spirits recognized by the Plateau Amhara as being Cushitic in origin, but none of them bear names or titles in any way resembling those of Sidamo *shatāna*.

Though the Sidamo, like the Arussi (Haberland 1963:511), conceive of the original *shatāna* as constituting a family, they do not attribute form, shape, or personality to their spirits. The Amhara, on the other hand, think of *zar* as invisible men and women with distinctive personalities and graded social positions within the supernatural world (Leiris 1934:96–103; Messing 1957:599–602). Both the Arussi and the Amhara dichotomize spirits as good or evil, but the Sidamo consider theirs as potentially possessing both characteristics, varying in their manifestations. In none of the three societies is the power of a spirit considered to be a constant, but the Sidamo and Amhara differ in their explanations of this fluctuation. Among the Amhara the power of a *zar* seems to vary with the prestige of particular cult leaders (Messing 1957:650–657), whereas the Sidamo believe that all *shatāna* are powerful when they first appear but gradually lose their potency.

For the Amhara and the Arussi, Messing (1957:605–606, 613, 645; 1959:331) and Haberland (1963:508–509), respectively, indicate that overt psychological manifestations such as epilepsy and hysteria are the preliminary signs of the onset of dissociation and that somatic disturbances such as headaches, sleeplessness, and intestinal disorders are of secondary importance. Among the Sidamo, however, it is the somatic complaints which mark the beginning of possession, the psychosocial aspects being much more covert.

There are also differences in the manifestations of personality dissociation. The Sidamo host shows none of the theatrical exhibitionism which Leiris (1958) has described for Amhara possessed by *zar* spirits, e.g., the conspicuous display of fine clothing and jewelry, boasting, and the violent whirling of the *gurri* dance. Nor do the Sidamo consider, as do the Amhara, that possession is symbolic of a form of coitus between the spirit and the host. In most manifestations of dissociation the Arussi seem to resemble the Sidamo more closely, although the latter lack the epileptic-like seizures involving violent trembling of the whole body, the covering of the host's head when the spirit begins to speak, and differences from ordinary speech in tonal quality and vocabulary which Haberland (1963:511–512) reports for the Arussi.

The three societies exhibit several points of similarity in the way in which individuals react to and maintain spirits. The potential hosts consistently resist possession at first, but once they have acquiesced they tend to remain under the power of the spirit for life. Acceptance of periodic personality dissociation appears to provide an indirect means for expressing aggression and dominating others, although this function seems peripheral to others among the Arussi and Amhara as compared with the Sidamo. There is a convergence in regard to the maintenance of spirits. In all three societies the host while in a state of trance is questioned by others as to the offenses which may have caused the spirit to bring the affliction upon him or his immediate kinsmen. The demands for appeasement which follow are uniformly high and involve some form of animal sacrifice as well as supplementary food offerings.

Why should the conceptualization, acquisition, and manifestation of spirits vary so much among three societies in such relatively close proximity to one another? At least part of the explanation is to be found in the differing social structures, functions, and historical development of the possession phenomenon in these societies. For the Amhara, the hierarchical ordering of *zar* spirits seems to be a supernatural projection of the highly stratified human social system with its nobility, bureaucracy, clergy, merchants, and peasants. The lack of such

stratification among the Sidamo and Arussi helps to explain their egalitarian view of the spirit world. Any Sidamo who is able to acquire a traditional spirit or introduce a new one can achieve success as a practitioner, whereas in the *zar* cult the doctors are full-time specialists. Nevertheless, we cannot assume that the cult situation as it exists in Gondar extends to the inhabitants of the countryside; most Amhara do not live in towns, and we do not know the extent to which *zar* concepts and practices are accepted in rural areas.

Messing (1957:644–646) has suggested that the *zar* cult represents the feminine side of Amhara society, and the Ethiopian church the masculine side. *Zar* adherents are mostly women of commoner status who join the cult because of their alienation from a man's world. Women of the nobility, like their feminine counterparts in Sidamo who have married wealthy men, never become possessed. The apparent function of the cult is thus to treat the hysterical and depressive symptoms resulting from status inferiority and to provide women with the necessary psychological strength to carry on their roles within the family and in certain accepted community occupations (Messing 1959:330). Though we have suggested that spirit possession is likewise associated with status inferiority among the Sidamo, it functions somewhat differently. Women are similarly subordinate to men and are able to gain temporary mastery over them through possession, but there exists no alternative structural means by which this subordination can develop into a cult for the expression of social alienation. Functionally, therefore, the *zar* cult serves to help a largely feminine clientele to accept a permanent status of subordination, whereas Sidamo possession provides men as well as women with a potential means for escaping from status inferiority.

Arussi possession also differs in function from that of the Sidamo. Haberland (1963:505–508) considers the extensiveness of the phenomenon among the Arussi to be relatively recent, resulting from a gradual mixing with foreigners and from contact with new religious beliefs. The form of personality dissociation has many of the attributes of a cult, with weekly assemblies of adherents gathering around a leader possessing a powerful spirit whose position is validated by the use of various symbolic artifacts obtained largely from Islam. Hence possession among the Arussi would appear to function as a means of accommodation to the conflicts and confusion arising from the pressures of acculturation. Since the Sidamo have also been subject to these pressures, first from the Amhara conquest and later from the Italian invasion, the question arises as to why personality dissociation does not function for them in the same fashion. The explanation would seem to be at least partially historical.

Cerulli (1934:1217) has suggested a Cushitic origin for spirit possession in Ethiopia. Though its origin among the Sidamo is indeterminate, it seems likely that it has considerable time depth. The mythology indicates an association of Abo and Iyo, the father and mother of all spirits, with the forest and water; it is just such a belief about nature as the source of spirits which Cerulli attributes to the early Cushites. Despite an admixture of recently incorporated spirits from other cultures, most of the older spirits seem to be of Sidamo origin.

The attitude of Sidamo informants in regard to the significance of spirit possession in a changing world is interesting. In contrast to the Arussi, among whom personality dissociation appears to be increasing in response to the pressures of acculturation, our informants were often emphatic in asserting, not only that possession has been declining in frequency, but that the spirits themselves have lost power since the coming of the Amhara and the Italians. Even the *količa*, the professionals who are called upon to divine the future and confirm the presence of *shatāna* in potential hosts, are widely regarded today as imposters who have lost all power to make predictions. There are those who believe that either Amhara or European Christianity, as the belief systems of more powerful conquering peoples, will ultimately replace traditional spirit possession. Nevertheless, it is apparent that personality dissociation still remains a satisfactory technique for many individuals in adapting to the frustrations and failures of their everyday existence.

# 42 Nubian Zar Ceremonies as Psychotherapy

## John G. Kennedy

In reporting on the zar cult in Ethiopia, Messing (1958) concluded that it was a "catch-all for many psychological disturbances, ranging from frustrated status ambition to actual mental illness," functioned as group therapy, offered in-group security and re-cognition to its devotees, cemented the social structure by pairing each patient with a spirit of comparable status in the spiritual hierarchy, and offered a means of social mobility for lower-class persons. More or less confirming Messing's earlier observations, John Kennedy's study of zar ceremonies among Nubians in Egypt more fully describes these rites, and intensively analyzes their social and psychological components. Here zar is used as a therapy of final choice to cope with a variety of emotional disturbances through abreaction and suggestion, possibly with greater and quicker effectiveness than Western psychotherapy.

Given the conditions of Nubian life, "It might even be suggested that dependence on the zar, shown by the lifetime linking with a spirit, is a viable and functional adjustment *under conditions of more or less perpetual stress*" [italics in original]. In other words, zar seems tailor-made to help Nubians deal with the kinds of stresses that are indigenous to their culture and social system. The zar ceremonies permit the freeing of repressed impulses which may be projected onto the patient's spirit and thus relieve the patient of the burden of unrelieved guilt. Having tried native and even Western healers, a Nubian in desperation turns to zar in order to gain symbolic purification through embracing these evil spirits, seeking salvation as it were through a pact with the devil. As with other saint cults in Nubia, zar permits a release of tensions produced in women in a sexist society. And thus, confirming Messing, we see it as a preservative of the status quo. Finally, Kennedy points to some implications for Western psychotherapy. Relevant studies will be found by the Hamers and Yap in this section and in Lewis (1971).

The term *zar*, referring both to a ceremony and a class of spirits, is usually associated with Ethiopia and may be of Amharic origin. However, the zar is also found the length of the Nile, from Alexandria to at least Khartoum in the Sudan. In Egyptian Nubia, the purpose of a zar ceremony is to cure mental illnesses through contact with the possessing spirits which cause such maladies. The evidence

Reprinted with abridgments from John G. Kennedy, 1967, "Nubian Zar Ceremonies as Psychotherapy," *Human Organization, 4*:185–194, with permission of the author and the Society for Applied Anthropology.

indicates that though the Nubians possess several methods for dealing with psychological disturbances, the zar is a last resort which has powerful therapeutic effects for several kinds of ailments. It seems particularly tailored for alleviation of the hysterias and anxiety-produced illnesses which seem to be related to the life conditions of Old Nubia. However, the technique also has been used in treatment of depressions and some obvious psychoses. This paper examines the form and content of the zar ceremony in an attempt to account for this therapeutic effectiveness. The analysis suggests that the concentration and combination of symbolic and emotional elements in such prolonged dramatic ceremonies might be studied for possible applications to the often fragmented, intellectualized therapeutic techniques of Western society.

## SETTING

The Egyptian Nubians comprised a racially mixed population scattered along the Nile in small villages between Aswan and Wadi Halfa. Administrative districts (*omodiyyas*) composed of 20 to 30 villages (*nagas*) probably corresponded originally to natural tribal divisions which were combined into larger linguistic and subcultural groups. Despite local cultural variation among these groups, all Nubians share a basically common cultural pattern.

Economically, Old Nubia depended on *dhurra* (sorghum) for its subsistence staple, its famous dates being a medium of exchange for procuring goods from other regions. For centuries an additional economic feature has been migrant labor in cities. This increasingly has become the main source of income since the first Aswan Dam was built in 1902. Successive raisings of the dam (1912 and 1933) were followed by marked reduction in the already limited resources of the region. This migratory feature of the economy meant that most young productive males, except for some in local government positions, were absent from Nubia. A 1961 census indicated roughly one male in the Nubian villages for every two females, but most resident males just prior to the relocation of 1963–64 were old retirees, children, or defectives of some kind.

The Nile Valley has been a corridor for many ethnic groups and cultural influences, but Nubia has been economically and politically marginal for centuries. Although the Nubians were converted from Jacobite Coptic Christianity to Islam in the 14th and 15th centuries, the doctrines of the Great Tradition have been mingled, as in so many parts of the world, with persisting folk beliefs and practices. Thus it is not surprising to find traces of pharaonic practices, Coptic survivals, and older popular Islamic rituals and beliefs, which like the zar have been integrated into the uniquely Nubian ceremonial pattern (Fernea and Kennedy 1966, Fernea 1967).

## THEORY AND PURPOSE OF THE ZAR

The zar ceremony is essentially a means of dealing with the demonic powers of evil (variously called *shaytan*, *afreet*, *ablees*, *jinn*, or *zar* spirits) who may cause illness. It is used only when other curing methods have failed. It is therefore in a sense an acknowledgment that the demons have won: the whole tone of the ceremony is one of propitiation and persuasion rather than coercion. Before trying the zar, most patients have already been to healers such as sheikhs of the *hegab* (charm makers) who use the Koran to exorcise jinn; they may also have visited diviners or other native doctors who use herbs, blood-letting, or various physical techniques. Sometimes too, they will have tried Western trained doctors. In resorting to the zar there are overtones of an alliance with evil powers. For if it is determined that demons are indeed causing the disorder, the patient becomes inextricably associated with the particular spirits for the rest of his life. He assumes a perpetual responsibility to satisfy this zar or jinn with a special performance at least once a year and incurs an obligation to attend the zar ceremonies of others. Orthodox opinion condemns the zar for dealing with devils, but opposition is not strong since jinn are mentioned in the Koran, some verses of which may be interpreted to connect them with illness.

Nubian disease theory recognizes many purely physiological illnesses; these are treated with a variety of herbs and physical manipulations. However, certain type of sickness which do not respond to such treatment are assigned supernatural causes. The evil eye of envy, the breaking of taboos, and sorcery all produce illness and are often associated with spirits. For instance, breaking a taboo is sometimes felt to bring a kind of automatic, almost mechanistic punishment, while at other times it is linked with a punishing spirit.

In Nubian theory, spirits, or jinn, are the most important causes of mental disease. The earth is believed to be inhabited by a host of invisible spirits that parallel the human population. Many are angels or good spirits; but the people seem more aware of demons descended from the devil that began propagating at the same time God created the prophet Adam. Although the demons tend to cluster in certain areas (such as along rivers or canals or in mountainous and desert regions) they are also quite mobile. They like to occupy rooms and houses while residents are absent. They are particularly fond of filth, garbage, and ashes; but they prefer to dwell in human bodies, and are thus always a threat to people.

It is possible to dispel demons by saying the first line of the *fatiha*, or opening of the Koran: people use this incantation frequently. Of course the jinn hover in unsuspected places and sometimes people forget to say the preventive words. Though there is an implicit idea of pollution and purification in all zar rituals, moral stigma is not necessarily bound up with mental or other disorders. It is said that an angry or aggressive and violent person is more susceptible and attractive to the jinn; nevertheless, blame for erratic behavior usually falls on the spirit rather than the individual.

## FORM AND VARIATION OF THE ZAR CEREMONY

Zar ceremonies vary considerably in detail according to personal idiosyncrasies of the practitioner or "sheikh of the zar," and according to the type of illness being treated. For example, a ceremony intended primarily to cure a seriously impaired psychotic is longer and more elaborate than one called by a trance-prone woman for the required annual placation of her zar spirit. Although some zars focus heavily on social, entertainment, and divination activities, their major concern is mental illness. Nevertheless, certain features are common to most of the ceremonies.

When a zar is requested, the *sheikh* (male) or *sheikha* (female) begins by asking questions about the patient. A sheikh of Ballana (who supplied our most complete information) said he first asks whether the ill person has an appetite and sleeps regularly. He also asks about behavioral symptoms. If the eating and sleeping habits of the patient

are not disturbed, he says that he usually decides the zar is not needed. After the initial interview comes the *attar* to establish a diagnosis by various forms of divination. For this the sheikh may receive ten piasters as a fee.

Some sheikhs go further in diagnosing some cases. If in doubt after the first interview, they may visit the patient a second time and ask for certain ingredients (henna, mastik, and clove) which are then ground up and dissolved in a potion which the patient must drink. He may also pass a special incense beneath the clothing of the sick person which has a powerful effect on certain types of jinn, who then cause the patient to quake uncontrollably and create a desire to dance. This means a zar is called for. Another kind of diagnosis, made during the zar ceremonies themselves, does not concern the principal patient. Instead, people in the audience request the spirit-possessed sheikh to tell them the causes and cures for ailments from which they or their families are suffering. Such requests are accompanied by ten piasters wrapped in a piece of the patient's clothing.

After the trouble has been diagnosed, a proper zar should be held for seven consecutive days, excluding Friday—since the jinn stay under cover on orthodox religious occasions. The ceremony may be restricted—because of financial inability, quick recovery, or mildness of illness—to two or three days, or even to one. A two-day zar usually occupies the afternoon and evening of one day, finishing at noon the following day. A full-scale seven-day ceremony goes from morning to evening each day, ending at noon on the seventh day.

The zar is primarily a female activity, though males often play the principal roles of leader and musicians. The hard core of any zar audience are women who have been cured and who are obligated to attend in order to placate their spirits. Each member of this zar cult group of initiates puts on at least one annual zar to keep her spirit satisfied. The remainder of the audience come to lend support to ill relatives or neighbors, to get an answer to some pressing question, or simply to be entertained.

Theoretically, anyone may attend the zar, but it is felt that men should not attend women's ceremonies, and *vice versa*. None of our informants had heard of a public zar with an all-male audience. (Our principal informant recalled several men he had treated secretly because they wished to avoid public admission of their belief in such practices.)

The place of the zar is usually a house with a very large room since the audience will number from thirty to a hundred or more women. A cleared "stage" area in the center is needed for the sheikh and his (or her) helpers, with enough room for the dancers. Doors and windows are closed and the only light comes from lanterns. Room temperature should be high since "the jinn are more likely to jump from the body when it is sweating."

On entering the room, each woman leaves her shoes at the threshold and places five or ten piasters on the sheikh's tambourine. All of those attending the zar wear new or clean clothing to please the "masters," as the spirits are sometimes called. The main patient usually wears a white gown (*galabeya*) and a white veil (*terha*). Her hands and body are dyed with henna, and her eyelids are blackened with kohl. She also wears as much gold jewelry as possible, is heavily perfumed, and sits like a bride, looking neither to left nor to right. If the patient is a man, he also is adorned as a bride. The sheikh usually has several costumes for changes during the performance according to the personalities and desires of various spirits. It is important to keep the room filled with the fragrance of incense and perfume and a censer is passed around the audience several times during the performance.

Music and dancing are invariable elements of the Nubian zar ceremony. An Arabic proverb is often quoted: "Songs are the life of the soul and music helps to heal the sick." Important qualifications of a zar specialist are his knowledge of special songs for summoning spirits and an extraordinary drumming ability. If the ceremony is small, a single *tar* (a kind of tambourine) may be used, but large performances require more *tars* and perhaps a *dabella* (another type of tambourine). The sheikh may also drum on a *tisht* (metal wash basin) which has an especially powerful effect on spirits.

The skeikh begins the ceremony with song and drumming. The form of the songs adheres to a typical Nubian pattern of verse and refrain, with the refrain often being the name of the spirit called. Each song is addressed to a different spirit. When a spirit associated with some person in the audience is called, that person begins to shake in her seat. Eventually she makes her way to the central dancing area, sometimes dancing and trembling till she falls exhausted to the floor. Before the spirit consents to leave, it usually demands special favors such as jewelry, new clothing, or expensive foods. It is the duty of the relatives and friends to gather round the prostrate woman and pacify the spirit. The patient may lie for some minutes on the floor "as if dead" with only her hands twitching before a special song by the sheikh brings her back to consciousness.

The audience's enthusiasm may be low at the beginning of a zar performance, or may flag at later points during long sessions. At such times the sheikh of the zar usually demonstrates his own supernatural abilities. He becomes possessed by a series of often quite different spirits, each demanding elaborate costume changes....

Fortune telling and prescribing cures for people in the audience are other frequent features of zar ceremonies. A typical example is a woman who asked what was ailing her infant son. The spirit replied that she had neglected her son by leaving him alone. In her absence a man passing by had given the boy the "evil eye." The prescription was to pass incense throughout the room in which the boy had been left alone and to rub a substance called *mahlab* over the bodies of both boy and mother. Many questions put to the spirits concern family members absent in Cairo or other cities. In one ceremony a woman was assured that some expected clothing had been sent and would soon arrive. Another was told that her son's injured hand had been healed, while a third was informed that her husband would find work soon. A worried wife was reassured by being told how to offset black magic (*amal*) which had been used to steal her husband who had not returned from his work in Suez for many months.

A final set of ritual actions of the Nubian zar involves animal sacrifice. The length of a zar depends as much on the desire and wealth of the person or family holding it as upon the condition of the patient; the timing and type of sacrifice is decided by the duration of the ceremony. If the sponsoring family is poor or if the zar is a relatively routine annual performance, the sacrifice may be a single cock or perhaps two pigeons. On the other hand, if the ceremony lasts the full seven days, several chickens may be killed on the first, third and fifth days; the final slaughter on the seventh will be a lamb or sheep. In a typical case, a white or black cock (according to the type of illness) is killed over the patient's head on the third day at exactly noon and the blood is smeared over her face, hands, and legs. In the evening or on the following day, this fowl is cooked and only the sheikh shares it with the patient. On the seventh day the patient ceremonially straddles the lamb (or sheep), holding the slaughtering knife in her hand. The animal's throat is then cut by the sheikh after five piasters have been placed in the animal's mouth. The hot blood of the sacrificial animal is rubbed all over the patient's face and body; some of the blood is mixed with cloves, henna, and water in a potion which the patient drinks.

The jinn is now said to be pacified, but the music and dancing continue while the animal is being cooked for the final ceremonial feast. As a conclusion, the patient leads the other possessed participants of the zar to the Nile where all bathe their faces and legs. Sometimes the patient is then advised to sit for 40 days in seclusion like a new bride.

## SOCIAL AND PSYCHOLOGICAL FUNCTIONS

For its audience, the zar obviously serves psychological and social needs beyond the therapeutic ones for which it is ostensibly held. Most significantly, it is primarily an adult female activity reflecting Nubian social conditions of sex-separation, low female status, restriction of women from religious participation, an unbalanced sex ratio, marital insecurity, and relative isolation.

As Moslems, the Nubians teach girls submissiveness to males and reinforce women's feelings of inferiority by permitting them only half the inheritance of men. They are further restricted by exclusion from the highly valued religious activities of the mosque. On all ceremonial and public occasions, men and women are grouped separately, and in daily life intersex communication is minimal. Women's marital choices are much more firmly regulated than those of men, and their premarital chastity is zealously guarded. Their activities, particularly any which take them outside the village, are closely supervised. Perhaps as important is the insecurity resulting from Islamic customs of easy divorce and polygynous marriage. Polygyny is not frequent, but its presence in the normative system is regarded by most women as a threat. This is especially true under conditions of migration where the convenience of having both a country and city wife sometimes detrimentally affects the economic resources of the country wife. Divorce is an even greater fear, and is commonly threatened by disgruntled husbands.

The anxieties of female status are further intensified by migrant labor conditions. In isolated villages populated predominantly by women and children with a few old men, and far from medical care and the diversions of a city, it is understandable that the women embrace zar ceremonies with enthusiasm. The same anxieties and frustrations that find relief in the zar also are expressed in other ritual activities, thus supporting the hypothesis that for the non-sick participant as well as for the sufferer, such ceremonies constitute a socially sanctioned "safety-valve." Women have elaborate saint cults in Nubia in which they petition spirits for many of the same things which are requested in the zar; return of husbands, marriage of children, marital goods, cures, and the like (Messiri 1969). They also have many special rituals centering on the "angels of the Nile" who can grant similar favors (Guindi 1967).

The wish-fullfillment aspects of the ceremonies give evidence of anxieties deriving from migration and isolation. Demands of the spirits are for items usually procurable only in urban areas. Typical questions put to the divining spirit are: "Is my husband being seduced by another woman in Cairo?" "When will my daughter marry?" etc. That the answers and prescriptions do have an anxiety-reducing effect which makes life more bearable for the ordinary non-sick woman was directly attested by several informants, and their relief in having their worries paid attention to was evident.

## PSYCHOTHERAPEUTIC ASPECTS

The zar provides an ideal situation for relief of persistent and regular anxieties and tensions arising from the Nubian life conditions. In much of the activity, in fact, it is difficult from our data to distinguish "normal" individuals from those who could be classified as mentally ill. The evidence seems to indicate that many, probably the majority, of the zar patients suffer from anxiety reactions or hysteria, although these symptoms are difficult to separate (Ewalt and Farnsworth 1963). The skeikh in his diagnosis places great importance on the patient's eating and sleeping difficulties. These symptoms are of course typical of the anxiety reaction neuroses, but manifestations of hysterical symptoms in the zar are even clearer. Psychiatrists attest that ". . . the quality that emerges as the most plausible single feature constant to all cases [of hysteria] is the tendency to dissociation." Dissociative states are one of the most outstanding characteristics of the zar ceremonies. Paralysis is another seemingly hysterical reaction described by many informants as being treated and cured by the zar. The hysterical nature of such paralysis is suggested by frequent reports that the cause was fright or fear stemming from a moral or ritual breach. Although we have no good epidemiological evidence for the Nubians, the data indicate that hysterical or hysteriform ailments are closely associated with the zar and may be the most frequent type of mental illness in the culture.

We may hypothesize that those who make up the central core of zar cult initiates tend to be rather unstable, emotional, and hysteria-prone persons. This seems plausible in view of the Nubian theory that possessed individuals are inescapably linked with their demons and must regularly placate them. It also accords well with clinical observations. The wish-fulfillment aspect of the zar performance also fits the hysteria syndrome and supports the idea that the ceremony is in some way a cultural form built around this type of ailment in response to precipitating conditions of endemic stress.

Direct evidence of the wish-fulfillment hypothesis is seen in the important part of the zar ceremony where the spirit possessing the entranced person demands material items. The demanded goods (jewelry, clothing, fancy goods, etc.) are all things which husbands should provide. On the other hand, the spirit often does not request material items, requiring instead such special activities as wearing a green veil. In some cases where jewelry or other material goods are demanded, they are given for a temporary pacifying of the spirit and returned after the ceremony. This can be interpreted as more of a demand for attention than for goods, or that the goods demanded symbolize a desire for attention. The response of the audience is an affirmation of social support and temporary indulgence of wish fantasy.

Although a majority of the active participants in the Nubian zar seem to suffer from anxiety and hysterical types of neuroses, in the eyes of the people themselves such individuals are not considered to be especially abnormal. Many come to the zar as audience participants rather than as patients. The people themselves feel that the depressive conditions which they call *wass wassa* are most frequently treated. Usually the precipitating event is the death of a close relative or a frightening encounter with a spirit. The specific manifestations of *wass wassa* (not always all occurring) are apathy, withdrawal from human company, minimal communication (with rational communication still possible), refusal to work, strong desire to die, lack of appetite, and sleeplessness. In these cases the zar is said to untie the depression.

Two common and frequently treated psychosomatic complaints are an unlocalized pain and an unaccountable wasting away and progressive weakening, accompanied by listlessness and loss of appetite. Both of these conditions are reported to be usually cured in the ceremony.

In Nubian nomenclature (Mahass dialect) mental disorders are classified in two main categories: *witti dowu* or *dowi* (big madness) and *witti kodoud* (small madness). Disturbances falling under *witti dowu* are the most serious and would probably be identified by Western psychiatrists as psychoses and chronic brain disorders. These are subcategorized according to the type of behavior exhibited, e.g., *witti atoji* (violent and dangerous). *Witti kodoud* refers roughly to what modern psychiatrists call neuroses. Though most of the psychic ailments brought to the zar seem to be neuroses, it is obvious that severe schizophrenias or other psychoses are also treated. The diagnostic techniques of the sheikhs provide a means of excluding the completely psychotic, noncommunicating individual. But motives of economic gain or the importuning of relatives sometimes prevail to allow the severely impaired into the zar, and surprising recoveries are sometimes said to occur.

One reported example of a remission from apparent schizophrenia was Sadiya, a woman now about 35 years of age from the village of Gustal. Shortly after the death of her mother (ten years prior to the report) Sadiya, who was then single and living in the same house with her father and siblings, awoke screaming one morning and ran from the house. Her father caught her and beat her, but to no avail. The neighbors brought her gifts and tried to calm her, but her speech was meaningless and jumbled and she would run frantically through the village laughing wildly. She remained in this hopelessly incapacitated condition for several months. Her father took her without result on long journeys to several famous sheikhs of the *hegab*, who agreed that she had the whispering disease, the most feared form of *witti dowu*. Finally, a seven-day zar was held for her and she recovered. She has been married for eight years, has two children and is considered normal by the community. The fieldworker was impressed by her rational, capable behavior.

Within the limits of their categories and experience, it appears that Nubian sheikhs can usually distinguish between minor neurotic symptoms such as hysteria, and psychotic or schizophrenic manifestations (*witti dowu*).

## EFFECTIVENESS OF THE ZAR TREATMENT

All systems of psychotherapy have as their major purpose the change of socially inadequate or unacceptable behavior patterns to adequate acceptable ones. Frank has perhaps defined therapeutic ends as clearly as anyone by speaking of symptom relief and improved functioning (Kiev 1964:27). At the same time, the great proliferation of differing psychotherapeutic methods and partial theories in the Western world, along with the fact that about the same proportion of individuals are cured no matter what system is used (Kiev 1964:5), suggests the need for more serious study of other culturally determined systems for treating mental illness.

The zar often does accomplish therapeutic aims of symptom relief and improved functioning, and it may be of interest to inquire into some of the reasons for its success. Part of its effectiveness can be attributed to such universal characteristics of therapy as emotional support, intellectual support, and emotional discharge (Alexander 1963:273–275). However, notable in the zar and practices of other non-literate societies is the lack of intellectual and insight approaches. Introspection, verbalization, or "working through" of early conflicts or traumas are absent. Writers who have noted this seem to feel that because of these lacks, the cures are not as effective as their Western counterparts. Devereaux, for example, makes the questionable generalization that remission without insight is not really a "cure." But Kiev points out, somewhat apologetically, that "although primitive therapies are fundamentally magical, that is, non-rational attempts to deal with non-rational forces, they often contain elements of rational therapy (Kiev 1964:10)." It is entirely possible that Prince's opinion that Western psychiatric techniques are not demonstrably superior to many indigenous Yoruba practices may apply to other non-Western systems (Prince 1964:116). Opler made a similar point concerning the indigenous therapeutic milieu developed in the Ethiopian zar and in Ute Indian dream analysis (Opler 1959:14).

The factors most often singled out for these emotional rather than rational insightful cures, are faith, suggestion, catharsis, and group support. In addition, Frank has shown that magical techniques give the patient a framework for organizing his vague distresses and heightening his sense of worth. Of course, these elements are also present in varying degrees in Western psychiatry, usually in combination with or subordinated to "intellectual" techniques administered in a two-person situation.

What seems critical in the case of the zar is that these emotional factors are combined and concentrated in a mutually reinforcing matrix which brings emotion to an exceptionally high pitch. This emotion-arousing, heightening, and intensification is effected through the dramatization of danger and awesome power in a ritually-constructed world where "society" is temporarily neutralized. The situation is so defined that restraints are removed, learned norms are stripped away, and repressed impulses allowed to reign. This is the kind of situation that a "rational" therapy would have great difficulty accomplishing through free association or other methods. Even psychodrama, which superficially seems to utilize similar techniques, appears "intellectual," artificial, and contrived by comparison. It is in this context that the elements which seem to account for the effectiveness of "primitive" therapy may be understood. This may be illustrated by some of these elements as they function in the zar.

*Faith.* Since it is omnipresent, belief alone is obviously not enough to account for the curative effects of the ceremonies. People believe in the supernatural causes of these illnesses, and they will try several methods in the same attitude of faith. This generally high level of faith in traditional curative practices is tempered by a practical skepticism since (though rationalizations are available), there is clear awareness that some people do not respond to treatment. In addition, everyone is aware of the opposition from religious orthodoxy and from those who ridicule with accusations of fakery. Furthermore, in some cases which have responded to treatment, the patient has been functioning too inadequately to establish the effectiveness of faith as a critical factor, at least at the outset. In most cases, however, the sheikh begins immediately during the diagnostic procedure to arouse and buttress the patient's faith. The diagnosis is really the beginning of the treatment: the sheikh works to reinforce the patient's belief by entering his weighty supernaturally given opinion of cause and possible cure. Faith is also intensified by the fact that possible causes such as evil eye, sorcery, and non-zar types of spirits have been eliminated by first trying other diagnostic and curing techniques appropriate to these causes. When he enters the zar, the patient knows that "this is it." At the same time, the sheikh may reduce the possibility of failure by excluding those whom he senses lack the faith to respond to the ceremony, or who are hopelessly beyond any sort of communication.

*Group Support.* The patient also has had constant group support. In contrast to the withdrawal response of people in some societies, the Nubians rally around a disturbed individual and try to keep him (and his jinn) continuously diverted. The belief is that he should be given good things to eat, like oranges and dates, and that two or three people should always be present to converse and carry on other activities with him. As in the case of faith, group support and attention are not unique to the zar, since they have been given from the beginning of the patient's trouble. What is different in the zar is their intensity and combination with each other and other powerful influences.

The essential point is that in the zar ceremony, both faith and group support are given new dimensions and a much higher intensity by the drama involved, by the association with powerful cultural forces through symbolism, and by the definition of the situation as one of supernatural power, outside the jurisdiction of social conventions and norms. The atmosphere is charged; the mood is set. People approach in a mood of exhilaration. Intensified anxiety, fear, and guilt derived from impending contact with dangerous and irresponsible spirits is mixed with anticipation of entertainment and escape from the daily humdrum. This is all enhanced by the requirement to remove the shoes, by the wearing of new or special clothing, and the special staging of the room. Therapeutic activities take place in this already-charged atmosphere, from which orthodox religion and God are excluded, social rules suspended, and where the forces of evil are in evidence.

*Symbolism.* The emotional effects of the zar are to a large degree dependent on stimulation by the symbolism employed. The symbols are those found throughout Nubian ritual signifying goodness, joy, purification, and protection from evil.

First, there is an attempt to make the occasion as happy as possible for the benefit of both spirits and patients. Much of the activity is patterned on the most joyful of Nubian ceremonial occasions, the wedding. The patient is dressed as a bride, adorned with henna and kohl, and performs some of the marriage rituals. Music and dancing in general are also most strongly associated with weddings. But all of the materials used have much more symbolic significance than as wedding items. Their uses in other rituals indicates that they evoke powerful emotions and associations. Henna, for example, is used on practically every ritual occasion, usually by women. When applied to the hands, feet, and body it is considered to create and enhance beauty. It is associated with purity, femininity, sexual pleasure, and protection from evil; it is used as a medicine for small cuts and as a skin cleanser. Its special effects on spirits are shown by its use on the flags on saints' tombs, and on the draped coffins inside them, its use in burial, and as an ingredient in purificatory incense.

The theme of purification runs through the entire symbolism of the zar. In addition to the purificatory meaning of henna, the ubiquitous incense and perfume are also thought to have a purging effect in that they entice out the polluting evil spirits. The potions drunk by the patient and the ritual cleansing in the Nile are acts of the same order. The color white required for clothing and for sacrificial animals has a purifying meaning, as does the sacrificial blood itself which, in addition, placates spirits.

While the purification symbols also have a protective meaning, other symbols and acts are more exclusively concerned with protection from harm, e.g., the color green associated with heaven, palm trees, and all good things, as well as the many uses of the numbers seven, three, and forty. For instance, the zar should last seven days. Seven dates are thrown on the sugar in divination or dropped on the patient's head, etc. Dates symbolize general goodness, wealth, and health in themselves, while the numbers signify good luck, protection, and the proper way to do things. Gold is another symbolic substance found throughout Nubian ritualism. It gives protection from the evil eye and spirits as well as signifying wealth and general Good. Animal sacrifice and the commensal eating of the ceremonial food *fatta* is also a common Nubian pattern. This food is associated with communal solidarity, generosity, and good will.

All of these symbols have a powerful emotionally evocative effect in themselves, increasing the intensification of faith and awareness of group support. They also represent familiar Nubian themes which, in addition to their magical potency, have a purging effect on subconscious guilts and give a sense of appropriateness and correctness to the occasion which probably harks back to pre-Islamic days. The marshalling of these symbols in the zar throws the weight of all positive Nubian traditional values on the side of the patient.

Such multidimensional cultural reinforcement is undoubtedly more powerful than "group support" alone, and goes much deeper than simple "faith." Not only is the patient bombarded with symbols and given powerful sociocultural support, but this is done dramatically and involves the violent acting out of roles by the practitioner and other members of the audience as well as by the ill person. The powers of suggestion are enhanced by the focus of attention on healer and patient as protagonists in this drama. The zar practitioner not only heightens belief and intensifies emotion by legerdemain; he himself also acts as a model for dissociative abreaction which under the hypnotic conditions of the zar is readily imitated. Several kinds of emotional discharge take place but the one aimed for in the zar is that of the hypnotic trance, which frees the patient from restraints imposed by both social norms and superego controls. The situation is defined as one in which ordinary norms do not hold; further, in trance and under temporary recognition as another identity, the patient is permitted even more freedom. It is not only that norms are suspended: there is an expectation of reversal, in itself lending an air of excitement and unpredictability to the performance which is appealing to all participants. Abreaction is often associated with the assuaging of guilt; it is of interest to note that, unlike cathartic techniques in many societies, the Nubian zar does not involve confessions. Responsibility is usually projected to the jinn rather than accepted by the individual, yet the purification emphases in the whole proceeding imply an underlying sense of guilt. This is also indicated in the whippings administered to mentally ill individuals in the zar and in other non-zar contexts. It may be inferred from the fact that simple-mindedness is sometimes considered to be caused by adultery of the parents. The idea that jinn are attracted to individuals who are angry and aggressive is also suggestive of a guilt association, especially since the Nubians have strong values of non-violence and non-aggressiveness. However, it is interesting that symbolic purificatory elements of the zar ceremony are carried out in an anti-religious, evil atmosphere; much of the acting out is anti-social or at least morally undesirable in other contexts. Thus in one sense the patient is allowed to act out his evil while powerful symbolism is being evoked to purge him of it. During it all he never admits guilt, but projects it onto spirit surrogates.

It should be pointed out that physiology plays a role in the abreactive aspect of the zar. The patient does not lie on a couch, but is emotionally stimulated by rhythm, music, and physical action to the point of emotional exhaustion. But the cathartic release is preceded by a tremendous *increase* of tension and anxiety. This seems to be as important for the inducement of trance as for catharsis. The patient is also to some degree manipulated, i.e., put through a course of symbolically important motor activities: he (or she) is dressed in special clothing, dates are dropped on his head; he is smeared with animal blood, smoked with incense, etc. All these actions are an attempt to "involve" the patient physically and emotionally as much as possible in the proceedings.

We may finally suggest the analogy of the zar—the whole atmosphere as well as the hypnotic trance—to a culturally staged dream. As in dreams the censoring superego is removed and repressed wishes are allowed free expression: the weak and subjugated dominate; the timid aggress; the repressed express strong sexual desires; males become females, and females males. It is as if these were implicit cultural recognitions of the effectiveness of "dream work" and an attempt made to simulate it through symbolic and dramatic means.

## CONCLUSION

In this analysis I have tried to single out those factors of the Nubian zar which could account at least partially for its curative effects on mental illness. It is clear that the essential emphases are on emotional rather than intellectual techniques. The "real world" is submerged; the world of fantasy, the subconscious, and the *id* are deliberately exploited. The processes involved seem more complex than such familiar explanatory catchwords as "suggestion," "group support," and "catharsis" would indicate. This suggests that more intensive research of such techniques as the zar might be of some use to Western theories of psychotherapy.

It seems that the problems most effectively treated by the zar are those of hysteria. This is not surprising since techniques of suggestion and abreaction are often used for such cases even in Western psychiatry. However, the zar may be a more effective technique than others since it combines a whole battery of methods, including hypnosis, which some psychiatrists feel should be investigated and further exploited in such ailments.

The symbolism and the removal of repression in the zar act to counteract precipitating environmental stress factors, especially if the stress is constant (non-removable). They may well be more effective techniques than most of the segmented and partial methods of present-day Western psychotherapy. It might even be suggested that dependence on the zar, shown by the lifetime linking with a spirit, is a viable and functional adjustment *under conditions of more or less perpetual stress.* The security and stability of such a lifelong relationship is not the sick dependence which may develop in a situation where stresses can be removed.

Different societies bring different types of stress systems to bear on their members, and Opler's (personal communication) comment on the zar is apropos.

This hysteriform acting out is not just a matter of thwarted wish-fullfillment and safety valves provided in the culture, but these folk-cult forms in psychiatry additionally offer group social supports which certainly counteract or take the place of isolation and private wish-fulfillment in a very active way. Psychoanalysts and family group therapists do not have such ready resources close at hand. The zar cult form is tailored to problems quite different epidemiologically from those we have in our own urban populations in the United States with their high incidence rates of paranoid schizophrenia.

It is undoubtedly true that these techniques are more appropriate and effective in the cultural settings in which they developed. Yet, the zar is apparently effective not only with hysterical and anxiety reactions but with depressive neuroses, psychosomatic ailments, and even some psychotic conditions. More research is needed to ascertain how effective such treatment is, but the data suggest that certain kinds of emotional strategies might be exploited by Western psychiatry much more than they have been. Social factors such as group support and family and milieu therapy are increasingly utilized in the West. The data from the zar suggest that cultural symbolism and drama might also be effective and that the ego-strengthening powers of faith, group support, suggestion and attention might be enhanced, focussed, and concentrated. The *wholeness* of the zar experience is also suggestive: it is not a piecemeal event like the daily or weekly one-hour session so typical of our own urbanized, fragmented existence. In the zar ceremony, seven days may be devoted by the group to intensive therapy. All of the techniques, many of which are singly employed in Western psychiatry, are brought to bear in one integrated context. Research might reveal that the emotional therapies discovered by so-called primitive peoples with their "irrational" belief systems have greater power to cope with some of the still dimly understood forces of the human psyche than do many of the methods still unable to escape from assumptions inherent in the model of rational man.

# XII
# The Patient: Status and Role

## The Position of the Afflicted in Society

The status and role of the healers in nonliterate societies have always been a source of interest for anthropologists and other observers because of their frequently outstanding personalities, the power and danger they symbolized, and the often critical part they played in the affairs of their communities. In fact, we probably know as much or more about this aspect of medical anthropology as about the functioning of whole medical systems. What about the persons who sought the help of these dramatic individuals and were the subjects of their ministrations? Sad to say, we know relatively little in detail about the role of the patient. This dysbalance also characterizes medical sociology in its research on the medical systems of Western societies. We know a good deal about patients as classes of people: socioeconomic classes, ethnic strata, categories of illness, and so on, but the behavior and social position of the patient, and the requirements of that position, especially within a cultural context, are still far less well-known empirically and theoretically than the role(s) of healers.

Rather early attention was paid to the question, although as a secondary factor in the patient-physician transaction, in a paper by L. J. Henderson (1935), "Physician and Patient as a Social System." Building on Henderson's formulations, Talcott Parsons, in a series of papers and books (1942, 1949, 1951, 1952, 1958), attempted to formulate a theoretical model that would both account for the physician-patient relationship and explain the status and role of each in society. As will be seen in my introduction to the first paper in this section, Parsons was apparently unaware of a pioneering statement on the status and role of the patient by the historian of medicine Henry E. Sigerist, in 1929. (True, this paper was published originally in German, but Parsons is very much at home in that language.)

In any event, Parsons' formulations are useful *if seen within their sociocultural frame of reference* and with recognition of certain limitations that I spell out below. Briefly, Parsons structures his model of the physician-patient relationship as a dyadic one, although he is aware of the implications of illness not only for the patient but for relevant others, including the patient's family, occupational group, and society. In fact, Parsons makes a direct analogy between the doctor as a parentlike, strong figure and the patient as a relatively weak, dependent, childlike figure (reduced to this state by the effects of illness). The doctor's role is characterized by permissiveness, support, scrupulous adherence to professional attitudes, and bestowal of conditional rewards (to propel the patient away from pathological dependency and illness and toward independence and wellness). The sick role requires the surrender of normal adult rights and obligations, the acceptance of a dependent, childlike status (Parsons called it a "sort of 'de-socialization'"), active participation in the therapeutic process (doing what the doctor orders), and the maintenance of motivation to get well (and relinquish the "secondary gains" of exemption from adult role responsibilities). That is, the patient must be willing temporarily to give up his usual work and other obligations, seek "technically competent help," and strive to "get well."

To maintain objectivity and prevent emotional complications, the patient-physician relationship must be "universalistic," "functionally specific," and "affectively neutral." In other terms, both roles are institutionalized categories that, despite the analogy with family roles noted previously, must adhere to a set of behavioral principles that are directly antethetical to those of the family. Indeed, in the society of the United States the increasing tendency has been to remove the family as completely as possible from the therapeutic process, which has led to frequent resort to hospitalization. This approach to therapy precludes family "interference," and places the patient almost completely under the control of the physician and his surrogates among the hospital staff. Two passages from Parsons' *The Social System* help to focus his argument:

> With respect to the first context [successful performance of the medical system in Western culture], the role of being sick as an institutionalized role may be said to constitute a set of conditions necessary to enable the physician to bring his competence to bear on the situation. It is not only that the patient has a need to be helped, but that this need is institutionally categorized, that the nature and implications of this need are socially recognized, and the kind of help, the appropriate general pattern of action in relation to the source of help, are defined. It is not only the sick person's own condition and personal reactions to what should be done about it which are involved, but he is placed in an institutionally defined framework which mobilizes others in his situation in support of the same patterns which are imputed to him, which is such an important feature of his role. The fact that others than the patient himself often define that he is sick, or sick enough for certain measures to be taken, is significant.

> ... Certain of the features of the role structure on both sides of the relationship are essential to bringing together the cultural and the situational elements of the action complex. It is possible to have a sick role, and to have treatment of illness institutionalized, where the role of therapist is not of the modern professional type. Treatment by kinsmen is a common example. But if, as in our society, the primary cultural tradition defined as relevant to health is science, it is not possible to have the role of therapist institutionalized in the same pattern terms as those of kinship. Hence in addition to the *sick* role we may distinguish the role of *patient* as the recipient of the services of a scientifically trained *professional* physician. The definition of the sick role as that of potential patient is one of its principal characteristics in our society (Parsons 1951:475–476)

Finally, Parsons also sees the sick role and the physician role as functioning as mechanisms of social control:

> The sick role is ... a mechanism which in the first instance channels deviance so that the two most dangerous potentialities, namely, group formation and successful establishment of the claim to legitimacy, are avoided. The sick are tied up, not with other deviants to form a "sub-culture" of the sick, but each with a group of non-sick, his personal circle, and, above all, physicians. The sick thus become a statistical class and are deprived of the possibility of forming a solidary collectivity. Furthermore, to be sick is by definition to be in an undesirable state, so that it simply does not "make sense" to assert a claim that the way to deal with the frustrating aspects of the social system is "for everybody to get sick" (Ibid.:477).

Parsons must be accorded recognition for having systematically laid out the sociological-cultural dimensions of the physician-patient relationship and of the two sets of roles in a more carefully and fully articulated fashion than anyone else in his time, and for having greatly aided in the investigation and analysis of these basic components of a medical system. Since his analysis extends in part to the medical system as a whole (through his treatment of the medical profession as a social system and as part of the larger social structure of contemporary society in the United States), Parsons has aided also in a better understanding of the functioning of that system. His students, and even his critics (I number myself among both), have built upon his foundations. However, for a medical anthropologist, although enormously helpful, Parsons' model poses serious problems and limitations. Among these are the following:

1. His model is heavily dependent upon that of psychotherapy in Western psychiatry, and more particularly the psychoanalytic version of that model. Although it is undoubtedly true, as Parsons states, that *all* medical treatment contains a significant element of psychodynamic principles and in actual practice application of these principles (however little the physician may be aware of them) frequently makes the difference in the success or failure of treatment, nevertheless the occurrence of physical illness brings with it a whole train of factors and consequences not involved in psychological disturbance, or at least very differently involved.

2. The Parsonian model is culture-bound and class-bound. It is culture-bound as even Parsons himself seems to be cognizant in a number of passages (for example, in the quotation given) in that it seems applicable mainly to the industrial capitalist society of the United States—though by implication perhaps to all of Western Europe as well. It is class-bound in that it is built upon the supposed features of the American middle-class family, itself an elusive, shifting, variable entity that may conform more to the social analyst's own familial traits than to any clearly definable social category. It will be patent to the readers of this book, in the papers in this section and elsewhere, that the model would have to be radically modified to be applicable to other cultures, and probably even to middle-class segments of other stratified societies. Even within the United States, application of the model to various class and ethnic groupings requires qualification. As an example, see Zola (1966).

3. Parsons' formulations are based upon an acceptance of normative assumptions of an ideal type of middle-class society, and of an idealized, almost "official" view of the American medical profession. Actually, Parsons' norms regarding medical practice and values in the United States represent the way in which the profession has defined itself. But as with all ideal values, these only approximate social-cultural reality, and the extent to which the ideal departs from the real in American medical practice is not spelled out. Parsons disposes of departures from his idealized norms by referring such behaviors to "peripheral," "marginal" groups and cults that represent "deviant" medical institutions on the fringes of American medical culture. But the deviations *within* the profession are unacknowledged. As so often happens, the "deviations" may, upon careful study, turn out to be the real norms, as Zola's (1966) study of symptomatology among American ethnic groups has shown.

4. Finally, Parsons perceives the sick role as a deviant one and sickness itself as a form of deviance. He sees the sick role as a societal mechanism for managing a temporary deviant condition by precluding the temptation to engage more permanently in this deviant status because of the relief it brings from the over-demanding obligations of a "well" or "normal" role. Clearly, if large numbers in a population sought to engage in such "deviant" behavior, it would undermine the social system. But, on the basis of an extensive study of the presenting complaints

of members of several ethnic groups in the city of Boston (Irish Catholic, Italian Catholic, Anglo-Saxon Protestant), another sociologist, Irving K. Zola (1966) reaches a rather different conclusion:

> Symptoms, or physical aberrations, are so widespread that perhaps relatively few, and a biased selection at best, come to the attention of treatment agencies.... There may even be a sense in which they are part and parcel of the human condition.... The empirical reality may be that illness, defined as the presence of clinically serious signs, is the statistical norm.

Thus in our heavily industrialized, urbanized society no less than in nonWestern and preindustrial societies, who a person is and where he is located in the social and cultural institutional structures strongly influence who presents an illness, or at least the signs that are interpreted as illness, for treatment. His ethnic and social statuses similarly help to determine which symptoms he characteristically regards as serious and which as minor or even routine, the nature and number of complaints, and so on.

Nevertheless, with all of these limitations (and additional ones we cannot spare the space for here), the Parsonian model of the patient's role and of its place in the medical system affords a convenient marker against which to compare the findings of observers of patients and medical systems in other cultures (and in the subcultures of our own society). As the reader explores the findings in the studies in this and other sections, he will begin to sense the need for a more universal model and theoretical underpinning. What is needed ultimately—and such studies as we present here are examples—is a body of cross-cultural sociomedical data that will enable the eventual construction of a truly culture-free paradigm. In tribute to Parsons it should be added that the new paradigm ought to offer at least as much explanatory significance as Parsons' model offers within the limitations I have described.

# 43 The Special Position of the Sick

## *Henry E. Sigerist*

Henry Sigerist was, in the opinion of many, perhaps the greatest historian of medicine. Certainly the range of his scholarship far exceeded that of most of his contemporaries or of those that followed him. Sigerist brought to his studies tremendous scope, careful scholarship in many languages, and above all a profound humanity that oriented his scientific efforts always toward the objective of improving the health and life of all people. His humanism and internationalism inclined him naturally toward the social

Reprinted with abridgments from Henry E. Sigerist, 1960, "The Special Position of the Sick," in *Henry E. Sigerist on the Sociology of Medicine*, Milton I. Roemer, ed., New York: MD Publications (originally published in German as "Die Sonderstellung des Kranken," *Kyklos, Jahrbuch des Instituts für Geschichte der Medizin in der Universität Leipzig*, 2:11–20, 1929; translated by Rowena Connell), with permission of Nora Sigerist Beeson and MD Publications, Inc.

sciences, and he, like Virchow, defined the practice of medicine as a social science and a human art. Sigerist was particularly attracted to anthropology, as was his illustrious colleague Erwin Ackerknecht, whose work was noted earlier in Sections I and VII. Sigerist's treatment of "Primitive and Archaic Medicine," which formed half of Volume I (1951) of his projected eight-volume *History of Medicine* (which was cut off by his death while writing Volume II) was the first attempt to encompass the whole field of what presently underlies medical anthropology in a coherent and intelligible fashion. Even with its limitations it remains a very useful introduction to the subject.

As I remarked in the introduction to this section, this paper by Sigerist is the first, full theoretical statement on the status and role of the afflicted person in society of which I am aware, antedating Parsons' first statement on the topic (1942) by 13 years, though unacknowledged. Dr. Milton Roemer brought it to the attention of English-speaking scholars in a two-volume anthology of selected writings by Sigerist in 1960 (the other volume was edited by Dr. Felix Marti-Ibañez [1960]), and I am delighted to reproduce it here in slightly abridged form.

But this paper is valuable not only because of its historical value but because it offers a brief essay on the status of the sick person in society which consists of both a sociological model and a historical model. Its attention to history and to the cultural dimensions of the role in succeeding historical epochs in Western civilization lend it a depth and dimensionality that are largely absent from the Parsonian view, although clearly Sigerist had not worked out the kind of fine-grained sociological analysis that Parsons accomplished subsequently. I do not know whether Parsons had read Sigerist's paper, although Parsons had long been interested in German social science as well as the sociology of medicine, but many of the ideas barely described here will be found directly or indirectly in Parsons' later extensive writings. This short statement by Sigerist offers an historical perspective that lends a whole new dimension and time-depth to our understanding of the sick role. Furthermore, even though largely confined to Western European society, Sigerist does indicate in passing that he is conscious of the importance of differences in the great Eastern civilizations. And he adds a transcultural dimension with his passing references to "primitive" societies. Thus, Sigerist broadens our understanding of the position of the patient in society and culture in time and in space.

A sick person occupies an admittedly exceptional position in society. At present, the work of the physician consists of the task of restoring to bodily health anyone afflicted with illness. This consists of treatment of the sick in such a way that all the parts of his body regain the form and function which they had before his illness. This restoration to health (*restitutio ad integrum*) is so much the desired goal that a doctor may consider his task completed when he succeeds in taking the sick man from his special position and restoring him to a useful place in society. A scar, deformities, a missing appendix, the aftereffects of a cured ailment do not matter, as long as they do not lastingly injure a man in his ability to work and to find pleasure....

The exceptional position which the diseased person holds in today's society has come about through a very complex development over a period of thousands of years. This status as it exists today can only be understood through historical analysis....

To begin with, the fact of illness means an interruption in the rhythm of his life. We all live in a specific rhythm, determined by nature, culture, and habit. Day and night alternate in an unending ebb and flow, and we ourselves conform to this rhythm with waking and sleeping, with work and rest. The custom of a weekly day of rest, which we derive from the East, has brought a definite pattern into our lives. The beginning and the end of daily work, the hours of meals, all these make up the rhythm of

our lives, which vibrates in a different tempo for city dweller, for farmer, for factory worker, for white-collar worker. (The pervasive influence of daily employment in producing a rhythm in life is a modern phenomenon of Western culture, which, for example, is unknown in the East, as a consequence, pathology takes a somewhat different form.)

An undisturbed rhythm means health. A change in the rhythm, perhaps when a farmer moves into the city and starts a city job, means a risk to health and produces altered conditions of illness and treatment.

Disease, then, strikes abruptly into this structure. It throws us off our accustomed track. It breaks the rhythm of our existence sharply. Night comes, and other men sleep. But sleep eludes the sick man. Mealtime arrives, but the stomach of the sick person refuses food altogether or makes strange demands at odd hours. The sick man, therefore, lives differently from the rest of society—from the healthy. In short, sickness isolates.

To be ill means to suffer—to suffer in a twofold sense. To suffer means to be passive. The sick man is cut off from the active life to the extent that he is even unable to procure his own food. He is literally helpless and is assigned to the care of other persons.

But to suffer also means to feel discomfort. Every disease has a certain amount of discomfort connected with it, which varies in intensity from individual to individual and from disease to disease. This discomfort is termed pain. Pain presupposes an organic unity and means that this unity has been broken. Through pain we become conscious of our bodily organs. Their proper functioning, to which we are accustomed, does not take place. Pain is a cry of alarm which tells us that in some specific part of our bodies a struggle is taking place. Pain is a mobilization order for the defenses of the body.

Pain sometimes becomes fear—even that greatest of all fears, the fear of death. Every serious illness is a reminder of death (*memento mori*). Disease breaks the rhythm of life and places a boundary to human existence. We feel that our life on earth is transitory. This feeling is aroused by many experiences, by the fading of nature in autumn or by the glimpsed immensity of the heavens on a clear summer night. Disease likewise forces us to recognize the place of destiny in our lives. It activates our spiritual sensitivity. It directs our gaze towards the eternal.

But, to return, we must consider the position of the diseased person in the individual cultures which have contributed to the structure of western civilization.

However, first a brief look at the special status of the sick among very primitive peoples.

[Let us consider]... a culture which has produced no sort of skilled medical practice, the Kubu of Sumatra. These are a generally intelligent people who carry on a difficult way of life in the primeval forest close to nature. Skin diseases and injuries to the skin occur frequently among them—so often that they do not find such conditions at all abnormal. The person suffering from such a disease is not considered a sick man among the Kubu. He lives as do the rest of his fellow tribesmen. It is a different matter with a serious illness, especially an illness accompanied by a fever. Perhaps a pox epidemic descends upon the countryside. The sufferer from such illness can no longer take part in the life of the tribe. Sickness isolates him so completely that he is left helpless and in pain, even by his relatives. He is shunned, as death is shunned.

Here we have the primitive attitude. The instinct for self-preservation on the part of the healthy is all powerful. The healthy man feels no social responsibility for the sick. Danger threatens from sickness as it does from death. Consequently, sickness is shunned. The attitude of the primitive man, therefore, marks the special status of the sick as one of complete isolation. The sick man is dead to society even before his physical death.

The Kubu native does not seek a cause for illness. He simply cuts off from society any person whom disease strikes. However, among primitive cultures which have reached a higher stage of development, one finds a strong urge to find cause and effect relationships. The sick man is a human being of a special type. His condition has a specific cause. He is ill, i.e., he has trouble and cannot live as other men do, because something has in some manner bewitched him. Another human being has cursed him with some sort of spell because he is an enemy or because the bewitched man has taken something belonging to the other man. Or perhaps it is something nonhuman which has done the evil: perhaps some god or spirit is displeased with the sick man. The sick man is therefore a victim. He has, on this account, a claim to the special attention and help of his fellow men. They try to discover the culprit. If he be another human being, they try to counteract his magic or punish him. If he be a god or demon, they try to placate him or exorcise him.

The place of the sick man is understood in this kind of culture to be a magicoreligious one. Prescribed actions must be performed in order to restore the sick man to the favor of the human witch or the nonhuman spirits. The diseased man is a victim of powerful and secret forces, which it is the task of the witch doctor to know and control. Thus he is shaman, priest, sorcerer, and physician rolled into one.

On a higher level, namely, in the Semitic culture group, there exists the attitude that the sick man is not an innocent victim but rather that he has deserved his suffering because of his wickedness. Sickness is punishment for sin. It is not the vengeance or spite of another human being or the blind ill will of some demon. Sickness is given by the just God, who is angry because of an outrage committed by the afflicted person. This view is specifically expressed in Babylonian medicine, which is, to be sure, nothing more than a primitive medicine of powerful proportions, with all the characteristic features of that genre. ...

The view of disease as a punishment for sin, which is contained in Babylonian literature, is also the dominant judgment voiced in the Old Testament. God has revealed his law. Whoever follows it piously will be blessed in this world. Whoever breaks the law will be punished. Every disease is a punishment. Every suffering is a suffering for sin—for the sins of the individual himself, for those of his parents, or for those of his relatives. This is a thought of brazen consequence, of clearest simplicity. This attitude is that which sets in such tragic relief the situation of Job, who suffered though he was a just and perfect man.

Nevertheless, sickness is not only punishment. It also serves to expiate sin. If a man becomes ill, he can thereby atone for his wrongdoings and find purification.

As a consequence of this view of disease as punishment, the sick man was marked with a certain stigma. He was not a guiltless victim. To be sure he suffers, but he has deserved his suffering because he has sinned. Through his sickness his sins become a matter of public knowledge. The diseased man is branded with his sinfulness. Thus sickness isolates him in an especially harsh manner.

This isolation became, in many cases, aggravated by the concept of ceremonial cleanliness. The man who would walk justly before God must be clean. A person became ceremonially unclean through any contact with an unclean person and through physiological processes, such as menstruation and childbearing. The man who had a discharge from the urinary passage was unclean. His bed, his chair, his saddle cloth, his excrement, in fact anything he touched, became unclean. In traveling he was to be kept away from any bed. And still more detailed are the proscriptions against lepers, which were the models for the medieval campaign against leprosy. Not only did the stigma of sin weigh heavily upon the leper, but society completed the punishment by the addition of total isolation.

The position of the sick in Greek society during classical times was of quite another type. The Greek world was a world of heath. Health appeared as the highest good. "The true aristocrat is he who enjoys a healthy body," says one of the earliest Attic proverbs. In one of the dialogues attributed to Plato it is demonstrated that it would be better to have little money and bodily health than to be ill and to possess all the wealth of kings. And in *Gorgias*, 452, Socrates says: "The highest blessing possible for a man to possess is the health of the body."

The physician, who preserves and restores health, was as a result a highly valued member of Greek society. Personal hygiene takes a high position from the very beginning of Greek civilization.

The ideal human being was a balanced man who was properly developed in body and soul, noble and handsome. On this point there is complete agreement, and such an ideal forms the completion of the Pythagorean life, among others.

Illness is, therefore, a great evil. It prevents a man from reaching his full development. Disease makes a man less worthy. The sick man, the cripple, the weakling are less worth-while men and can only be reckoned as such in the view of society. Their worth is determined solely in terms of the possibility for bettering their condition. A lifetime of sickness was completely despised. Antiquity offers no evidence of any provision for the care of the crippled. A sick man must become well again in order to count again as a worth-while person.

The physician is to help him to this end, and through the skill of the physician the state gives him aid. Nevertheless, if the position of the diseased man be hopeless, if the disease is incurable, then the physician's skill is useless for himself and for the patient, since the object desired by society, namely, health, is not to be attained. In Greek society there remains a certain stigma attached to the sick man. It is not, to be sure, the stigma of sinfulness but rather the stigma of being less worthy.

Stoicism sought to go beyond this classic Greek position, in that it understood health and sickness as two sides of the same coin, as two things of equal worth. Only virtue was a genuine good. Vice was the only genuine evil. But in its later development Stoicism conceded that, for the needs of the active life, these two sides of the coin were of differing values. Thus, health was something desirable and sickness undesirable. Chrisippus terms it madness not to desire health, wealth, and freedom from pain. An incurable disease was held to be a sufficient reason for suicide. Zeno hanged himself because of a broken finger.

The most important and decisive development in the special status assigned to the sick was introduced with Christianity.

Christianity came to the world as a religion of healing, as the glad tidings of a redeemer and of redemption. The world was sick with sin and in need of the cure of grace. This new teaching, in contrast to the other religions of the ancient world, which were religions for the healthy and just man, appealed to the sick, to the weak, to the crippled. It spoke of spiritual healing, but it also spoke of bodily healing. Did not Christ himself heal many of the sick? Sickness was no longer a stain, no longer a punishment for one's own sins or for those of others. Sickness did not make a man less worthy. On the contrary, sickness meant purification. Sickness was held to be a grace. Out of the pathos of suffering came an ethos. Disease is suffering, and it is through suffering that mankind is completed. Suffering is the friend of the soul. It develops spiritual strength. It turns the gaze of the human spirit towards eternity. Sickness has become the cross which the sick man carries, following in the footsteps of Christ.

To suffering humanity the Christian religion brought a great liberation. The sick man was freed from the stigma that had previously been attached to his condition. Disease must be completely suffered, for it was in the very fullness of suffering that a human soul found purification. To be sure suffering was painful, but pain itself had taken on a new meaning. It could be freely expressed. As Max Scheler put it, "The cry of the suffering creature, so long repressed, sounded again free and sharp throughout the universe."

Disease must be completely suffered, says the Christian ethic of suffering. Is there, then, no place for the physician? Does the physician have the right to shorten suffering? On this point, there runs throughout Christian literature the familiar refrain from Ecclesiastes 38:1: "Honor the physician because of necessity, for the Most High has created him." Quite another attitude, it must be admitted, from the Homeric "The physician possesses the skill properly belonging to the gods alone" or the Hippocratic phrase on the godlike-ness of the physician. Again and again. Christian writers feel the need to justify the physician, perhaps through the argument that he is a servant and instrument of God, or that the body is the earthly vessel of the immortal soul, and so on.

Disease is grace. The healthy can participate in this grace through association with the sick. Indeed, this was enjoined upon the healthy as a duty by the very word of Christ Himself: "I was sick and you visited me. Whatsoever you have done unto one of these, the least of my brethren, you have done it unto me."

The place of the sick in society was altered from its very foundation. Whereas disease in the entire course of previous historical development had sharply isolated the sufferer, in Christian times he was actually brought closer to his fellow men by the fact of his illness. The special status of the sick has become a privileged status. The diseased person is a man who has become a participant in the grace of God. To care for him is a Christian obligation, is positively beneficial to the salvation of the soul. The birth-hour of large-scale, organized care of the sick had come. The care of the ill is now the concern of the church. The bishop is in charge; the deacons and widows are his active agents. On Sundays, free-will offerings are collected for the sick and the poor of the church community. From the fourth century on, hospitals were constructed which were not founded on economic considerations, as had been the Roman slave and military hospitals. They were, on the contrary, a fine expression of Christian charity. From the sixth century on the monasteries above all cared for the sick, and St. Benedict of Nursia placed the care of the sick especially before the minds of his monks: "The care of the sick is to be attended to before all things."

However, medical care is not medicine. Medicine was regarded as a pagan science, against which the church at first inveighed and took active measures. Some two hundred Christian pupils of Galen were even excommunicated because of their occupation with pagan medicine. After all, Christ had healed without medicine, and the Epistle of James showed the proper Christian method of treatment: "Is any sick one among you? Then call the Eldest member of the Church to him, and let the Elder pray over him and anoint him with the holy oil in the name of the Lord, and the prayer of faith will help the sick

man." It almost seemed that the only portion of medical knowledge which would survive would be the practical suggestions for the care of the sick. But the process of reconciliation between Christianity and pagan science soon began, and Cassiodorus explained the rationale of this, pointing out the fact that pagan learning could be most properly and fittingly used in the service of God. On this basis the development of medicine for many centuries following was decided.

The position of the sick in society was thus raised to a privileged status, which is still true in Western civilization even to our own times. (It may be mentioned peripherally here that in India a development took place in which conditions of quite another kind produced a quite similar final effect. In the later Upanishads, suffering is seen as punishment for failing in an earlier incarnation. The teachings of Buddha concerning suffering lead in quite another direction. Even as the compassion taught by Buddha is similar to Christian charity, so the position of the sick was improved by it in a similar fashion. Any study of Indian medicine must first of all take into account the cultural tradition on the meaning of suffering.)

In fact, western society is now distinguished by its concern for the care of the sick. At first it was the church which acted as a pacesetter, showing the way to the secular authority in taking to itself the care of the sick. Individual orders of monks were founded for the specific purpose of caring for the sick. From the thirteenth century on, the Society of the Holy Spirit Hospitalers spread across Europe. The struggle against the widespread destructive diseases such as leprosy was organized on a large scale. Through this historical development it is possible to understand why even today the care of the sick still remains in religious hands or even more specifically in the hands of religious orders, even though the conditions which made such an assumption of responsibility necessary have now disappeared.

With the increasing importance of the towns, beginning in the fourteenth century, the town hospitals were founded. Private organizations such as the craft guilds provided for their members in time of trouble. More and more the provision for the care of the sick passed into secular hands.

The motive lying behind this development is not far to seek. To the medieval man the sick person was a man possessed of a special grace, who was to be supported from motives of Christian charity, and so the matter was judged in town councils. The sick were cared for as a matter of secular policy.

And the more the secular authority developed in the direction of the welfare state, towards an idea of the commonweal, the more contributions toward the care of the sick grew richer and larger, until at last in the course of time social security was its most striking expression.

We have now observed in brief outline the historical development of the special status of the sick as found in modern society, and it is hoped that the review has added to our understanding of this status. We must remark, however, that all the previously held attitudes of earlier times live on in modern society, more or less hidden. Strong as is the sense of social responsibility, there nevertheless remains buried in the subconscious of us all the desire to flee from the sick. Under normal conditions this feeling will rarely if ever come to the surface. But suppose a plague epidemic should descend upon Europe—fortunately, a thoroughly unlikely possibility—doubtless a mass exodus would take place. The flu epidemic of 1918 brought this attitude into sharp relief in the rigid isolationism of those regions, not yet infected, towards those which had been hard hit.

There is still a strong survival of the view of illness as punishment for sins. In the Christian Middle Ages and also in the Renaissance, catastrophes such as the plague or syphilis were termed sufferings for the purpose of punishment. And still today in certain segments of the population the syphilitic is a man who has been punished for his sins, and—which seems especially evil—has been punished in the part of the body with which he has committed the sin. The syphilitic often conceals his affliction. There is no lack of irony in the fact that the scientific expression still used by the physician is Lues insontium—the plague of the innocent. The stigma which falls upon the syphilitic also extends to skin diseases generally among large sections of the populace.

The idea that sin is a punishment also survives in the feeling of self-righteousness which many sick persons experience as a result of their suffering.

Finally, psychoanalysis has discovered that many diseases, like many accidents, occur very often as self-punishment for sins of thought, which society holds blameless.

The ancient valuation of the sick as men of lesser worth is still a current attitude. We grasp the hand of a man and notice that several fingers are missing. Our first instinct is to ask him sympathetically by what accident he came to lose them. We suppress the question, not only because we wish to spare him the recollection of a painful experience but also because we unconsciously feel that the injury should be judged both by him and by us to have made him somehow less than a whole man.

But the dominant attitude is that which recognizes the privileged position which the sick man enjoys. Certainly sickness still isolates men, in the sense that the daily routine of the sick man is entirely different from that of the healthy one. But this isolation does not remove him from the concern of mankind but rather brings him even closer to his fellows. The mother loves the sickly child more than she does her healthy children. In times of sickness husbands and wives draw closer together. The sick person occupies the central position in the attention of the family, for life revolves around him. Relationships which seemed entirely broken are made close again by sickness. Just as pain shows us that something we have always taken for granted has departed from us, so every disease which attacks an individual human being calls attention to his integral relationship to a social group. Society suffers in sympathy with the illness of one of its members and is moved to take every possible measure to prevent his loss. Even the poorest, the most abandoned, who has no one in this world to care about him, becomes a party to an intimate person-to-person relationship with at least one other man, the physician who comes to him as a service from the government.

Illness releases. It releases from many of the obligations of society, first, from school attendance, and generally from work duties. The sick person is relieved from many important concerns with which society demands that the healthy busy themselves. Yes, the sick man even becomes the object of duties, the recipient of special attention. Illness frees a man also from the performance of many occupations. It also lessens the degree of responsibility or removes it entirely, a viewpoint which has revolutionized the penal law from its foundations.

So far does the privileged position of the sick extend that the execution of a sentence of death upon a man is feared if he is ill. Several years ago in Greece the minister of a fallen cabinet was shot, and he captured the sympathy of the world because of the fact that he was very ill with typhus at the time of the attempted assassination.

Illness frees a man from the obligation to work. In other words, it places him in the ranks of the unemployed. In today's society, in which work is the absolute prerequisite for any kind of existence, in which supply and demand rule the labor market, the position of the sick worker must inevitably be a little dubious. His place does not really exist, in the sense that the sick man through becoming ill becomes an outsider to the economic order. The state enjoins upon its individual members who are economic liabilities that they put aside a part of their pay during their times of health as insurance against times of sickness. With this institution, the worker acquires a right to help and care. He cannot work, but he will, nevertheless, be paid—with money that he himself has earned. He is no more at the mercy of society, no longer a recipient of charity. The privileged position which he enjoys as a sick person is one which he has in a certain sense earned through his labor. The fact that the healthy and strong worker, who needs little insurance himself, permits a portion of his wages to be used to help the worker who is frequently ill is a fine expression of human solidarity.

The firmer the privileged position of the sick, the sooner will the inclination appear to take that position voluntarily, to escape from the struggle of living into sickness. This is by no means a rare occurrence. It appears at the root of a talent for becoming ill, which we call hysteria. The more intensive the struggle of existence, the more irritating the friction of modern life, the greater the demands of life will be upon the individual and the more frequently will occur the conditions which produce hysterical disorders. But one must avoid generalization. It is, above all, necessary to avoid using that vulgar word malingerer on every occasion. A man who has succumbed before the stress of life, who can find no other way to save himself than to flee into the safety of illness, is a wounded creature (even if there is no hysteria actually present), and he has called out for help.

When the opponents of social security bring up again and again, as an argument against it, the fact that the number of days of illness has increased since the institution of insurance, they overlook the fact that today, thanks to insurance, numerous cases of illness are treated which before would not have been. They overlook above all that, granted the fact that the number of days of illness has increased (more thanks to increased care), the state of health of people generally has become a great deal better and that the average life span has increased to an almost unbelievable degree.

The development of the modern state has brought a new feature into the position of the sick. In earlier times, sickness and health were matters of private concern, but now there is laid upon the individual a positive duty to be healthy. The law to stamp out venereal diseases, passed in 1927, is the

first step in this direction. Whoever spreads this type of disease, whoever, having contracted it, neglects to do all that is possible to be cured is an outlaw from society and as such subject to punishment. The stigma of sinfulness and the stigma of being less worthy have been in large measure removed from the sick, but a new burden has begun gradually to be placed upon them, and that is the stigma of at least being an antisocial human being and even in many cases a criminal.

Society has developed the special status of the sick into a far-reaching position of privilege. It has placed today within the power of almost every person the means to maintain health and to cure sickness. It can appropriately and rightly demand that the individual be conscious constantly of his obligation to the general welfare of society.

# 44 Status, Ideology, and Adaptation to Stigmatized Illness: A Study of Leprosy

## Zachary Gussow and George S. Tracy

The role of patient, especially in many seriously disabling illnesses, may be extremely difficult. Even so, in many cases if a patient recovers or temporarily overcomes the effect of a deadly disease, he may not only regain his status in the community but even become an object of admiration. In our society, individuals who have overcome the effects of disabling diseases such as cancer, diabetes, polio, and so on have frequently enhanced their status in the eyes of society. However, some diseases, in addition to actual or supposed impairment of the individual, carry with them an onerous burden of stigma, a social definition of disease that transforms the victim into a social outcast. Thus, for example, few persons in our society would freely admit to having had a venereal disease, because the resulting stigma could be too burdensome to conquer. Another disease with a long history of social disapproval is leprosy, and, as with most stigmatized diseases, it has been surrounded by complex mythology difficult for its victims to shake off. Not all victims of these culturally branded maladies

Reprinted with abridgments and with changes by the authors from Zachary Gussow and George S. Tracy, 1968, "Status, Ideology, and Adaptation to Stigmatized Illness: A Study of Leprosy," *Human Organization*, 27:316–325, with permission of the authors and the Society for Applied Anthropology.

accept their fate passively, however. As this unique study by Zachary Gussow and George Tracy shows, some of them attempt to struggle against the corrosive effects of stigma by assuming a *career patient status,* to use the concept of these authors. The characteristics of the disease complicate the career patient status of these victims, as the authors demonstrate, but do not deflect it.

To counter the opprobrious consequences of the conventional and medical theories of leprosy and of the stigma of the disease, the patients at this leprosarium create, as it were, a new subculture for themselves (and consequently new images or "impression management") by constructing their own theory of the disease and its stigma, in order to destigmatize their disability, and, of course, themselves. This process of destigmatization has a number of interesting social and psychological consequences in the efforts of these patients to legitimize their career patient status. Some of the implications for theories of stigma are also discussed. For a study of a group of former mental patients who decided to submit to the stigma of psychiatric hospitalization but band together for mutual support, see "The Culture and Social Organization of a Club of Former Mental Patients" (Landy and Singer 1961). See also Goffman (1963) for a provocative treatise on the management of stigma.

The social and psychological components of stigma have been the subject of a series of essays by Goffman (1959, 1963). His first interests in the subject were with "impression management," by which term he means the efforts made by people to create desired images about themselves in the face of the inescapable fact that whether a person wishes or not, his actions yield expressions about himself. Impression management is a way to "control the conduct of others, especially their responsive treatment" by controlling what they see and hear. In the later work Goffman focuses on persons characterized by stigma, or "undesired differentness," of which he identifies three general types: (1) physical disfigurement; (2) aberrations of character and/or personality; and (3) social categorizations such as race, nation, and religion (1963:1–5). Since stigma may be visible or invisible, known about or not, impression management yields two sub-types: (1) the management of social information about self, and (2) the management of tension in interpersonal encounters. The management of information is the main task of "discreditable" individuals—those possessing a deeply discrediting attribute which may not be known or immediately perceivable. The management of tension is the main task of the "discredited"—stigmatized individuals who can assume that their differentness either is already known or is immediately evident.

"The central feature of the stigmatized individual's situation in life... [lies in efforts to achieve] what is often, if vaguely, called 'acceptance'" by normals (1963:8). We are told that all the stigmatized can ever hope for is a "phantom acceptance" which provides the base for a "phantom normalcy" (1963:122). Much of Goffman's thesis postulates an array of "protective" and "defensive" management strategies used by stigmatized individuals in easing interaction with normals trying to cope with mortifying situations in the task of salvaging or retaining personal dignity despite some undesired and deeply discrediting attribute which, it would seem, nobody is ever completely willing to overlook or forget.

The stigmatized are involved in a basic dilemma. Not only are they denied real acceptance but, more importantly, they confirm the evaluation of their condition and remain stigmatized in their own eyes. Goffman's people are both *other-* and *self-*stigmatized and forever doomed. The basis for this dilemma lies in the fact that those stigmatized are apparently firmly wedded to the same identity norms as normals, the very norms that disqualify them. They may believe that the norms should not be used to their disadvantage. Nevertheless they concur with the norms and therefore view themselves as failures.

This theory offers no possibility of any serious attempt by stigmatized individuals to destigmatize themselves. None seem to engage in efforts to disavow the norms that impute discreditability. None apparently try to substitute other standards that might allow them to view their "stigma" as a simple and not especially discredited difference rather than as a failing. Nor does there seem to be much chance to move from a discredited to a less discredited or to an accepted deviant status. Surely there are other modes of adaptation. One is the development of stigma theories by the stigmatized—that is, theories that would explain or legitimize their social condition, that would attempt to disavow their imputed inferiority and expose the real and alleged fallacies involved in the dominant perspective.

Perhaps Goffman gives so little attention to this line of thought because he deals with single individuals in brief encounters with normals, usually in "unfocused gatherings." He seems less concerned with patients' efforts toward destigmatization in more permanent groupings, especially in social settings where they live together in more or less continuous interaction, where they are able to develop their own subculture, norms, and ideology, and where they possess some measure of control over penetrating dissonant and discrediting views from without (Glaser and Strauss [1964:675] who have also criticized Goffman for this limitation).

It is precisely these circumstances under which a *group* of "stigmatized" evolve their own stigma theory that interest us here. We are concerned with the meaning of this more or less consciously constructed perspective and its function in facilitating a linkage with the wider society. To this end, we conceptualize the *career patient status* as an alternative mode of adaptation to stigmatizing conditions and elucidate its ideological base in a stigma theory.

Our argument is developed in terms of problems faced and strategies employed by leprosy patients at the USPHS Hospital, Carville, Louisiana, in their efforts to delineate a viable social and psychological explanation for the widespread prejudice toward leprosy. The ideology and strategy presented below serve to provide patients with a means of attenuating self-stigma and altering other-stigma. From a description of this particular system of adjustment, it is possible to suggest some general characteristics of the career patient status and the conditions contributing to its development.

### GENERAL BACKGROUND AND METHODOLOGY

Leprosy has been little studied sociologically as either disease or stigma in the United States. Prior to 1961, when the senior author first undertook to study the illness and the hospital-colony at Carville, Louisiana, there had been only a few local psychological and epidemiological studies and no general sociological or social psychological research. (For earlier reports by the authors see Gussow 1964, Gussow and Tracy 1965; for subsequent reports see Gussow and Tracy 1969, 1970, 1971, 1972. For psychological and epidemiological studies see Lowinger 1959; Belknap and Haynes 1960; Johnwick 1971; Dimaya 1963.)

The USPHS Hospital at Carville is the only leprosarium in the continental United States. It was established in 1894 as the Louisiana Home for Lepers and came under PHS jurisdiction in 1921.

The resident patient population at Carville is relatively stable at slightly more than 300. In addition to the Carville hospital, there are at present four PHS leprosy out-patient clinics: one each in New Orleans; San Francisco; San Pedro, California; and Staten Island, New York. The total number of cases of leprosy in the United States is not known. The standardized estimate of 2,000 to 2,500 has been used for some time, but workers in the field believe this is somewhat low and estimate the number at two to three times the supposed figure. On a worldwide basis the prevalance is estimated at 12 to 16 million cases.

In this study, over 100 patients, Carville residents plus New Orleans and San Francisco outpatients, were interviewed. In addition, the study included patient group discussions, individual psychotherapy sessions, interviews with Carville staff members, recordings of staff meetings, and participant observation of hospital and colony life.

### SOME MEDICAL AND BEHAVIORAL CHARACTERISTICS OF THE DISEASE

Leprosy is a chronic communicable disease of the skin, eyes, internal organs, peripheral nerves, and mucous membranes. It can produce severe physical handicaps and disfigurement, especially when untreated. There are also a number of significant uncertainties regarding basic epidemiological questions of etiology, susceptibility, contagion, resistance, treatment, and societal reactions which limit treatment and rehabilitation. Five of these are especially relevant here.

(1) The mode of transmission is not thoroughly understood. Prolonged skin-to-skin contact with an active case is believed necessary for infection to take place. However, respiratory transmission has not been completely ruled out nor has the role of insect vectors. The idea that genetic factors may play a crucial role, particularly with repsect to susceptibility, is becoming increasing popular. The incubation period is prolonged and undetermined, apparently anywhere from a few months to many years (Badger 1964; USPHS Hospital 1960, 1961, 1963, 1964).

(2) The mycobacterium (*Mycobacterium leprae*) thought to be reponsible has not been cultivated *in vitro*. The disease resists experimental transmission in humans, leaving doubt about the identified organism, in addition to raising questions about

the relationship of host to organism (Carpenter and Miller 1964).

(3) Success of treatment is also uncertain. Medical authorities are reluctant to use the term "cure." Current drugs such as the sulfones introduced in the early 1940's, are more effective in general than earlier drugs but are useless with some patients and induce strong reactions in others. As a result, individuals do not know and cannot readily learn what disabilities may occur, or how long they may remain a potential communicable risk (Bushby 1964; USPHS Hospital 1963, 1964).

(4) Leprosy, in the United States at least, is rarely suspected as a likely diagnosis. Even today diagnosis based on a clinical examination alone, without the aid of a biopsy, is difficult. The disease is therefore frequently mistaken for other conditions, and patients may be treated for long periods for the wrong disease (USPHS Hospital 1963, 1964).

(5) The legal status of patients is unclear. Aliens are usually constrained to seek treatment at Carville or face the possiblity of deportation. State laws applying to U.S. citizens vary and are differentially enforced (Doull 1950; USPHS Hospital 1963, 1964). Criteria for "discharge" from Carville vary with disease classification, clinical judgment, rehabilitation potential, and assessment of patients' responsibleness. Indefinite outpatient treatment may be advised.

Additional insight into the nature of leprosy is provided by Skinsnes (1964), a pathologist who recently constructed a hypothetical disease expressing the ultimate in physical disablement and in eliciting extreme negative social and emotional responses. This hypothetical disease would: (1) be externally manifest; (2) be progressively crippling and deforming: (3) be nonfatal and chronic, running an unusually long course; (4) have an insidious onset; (5) have a fairly high endemicity, but not be epidemic; (6) be associated with low standards of living; (7) appear to be incurable; and (8) as a master-stroke, would have a long incubation period. This illness would expose the individual to protracted experience with pain, suffering and deformity, as well as social ostracism. Death would not be the frightening element; the major threat would be bodily deterioration and assault on the body-ego. Skinsnes notes the resemblance of leprosy to his hypothetical disease and concludes that "it appears reasonable to postulate that it is this complex and its uniqueness which is responsible for the unique social reactions to leprosy" (1964:15).

The popular view of leprosy portrays the disease in just such black terms. The very term evokes an image of a maximally ravaged, untreated victim. In addition to its depiction in fiction and film, this view is typically found in the fantasies and expectations of newly diagnosed patients. Like others in the general population, they usually possess little real information about the disease and have had little or no previous contact with persons known to have it. In fantasy and expectation leprosy is considered "highly" contagious, horribly deforming, painful, and eventually fatal. The stereotypic belief is widely held that bodily appendages literally fall off. Many individuals also think of it as a legendary disease or one associated only with tropical "jungle" life, and are astonished to learn that leprosy actually exists in industrial nations.

Perhaps best epitomizing the bleakness of the popular view is the fact that it excludes the idea of amelioration. New patients anticipate being banished "for life." Importantly, they rarely have to learn the advisability of concealing their disease. Even when they know little about leprosy, they invariably realize its stigma and begin to develop strategies for keeping this information from others. The notion of "high" contagion is usually strong. New patients are apt to take precautionary measures far in excess of anything suggested by medical authorities. The urgency with which some consent to immediate hospitalization even when there is no compelling medical or public health pressure further indicates their perception of the situation as "extreme."

The popular or "folk" view of leprosy seems to represent two levels of experience. In terms of deformity and societal reactions, though not in terms of contagion or fatality, the image comes close to describing actual leprosy in untreated cases of advanced deterioration, though not what it must be nor is in all or most cases. At another level the "folk" view represents a fantasy of the worst that can happen to one's body—a *fantasy of total maximal illness*. In fantasy the two darkest fates are to "lose one's mind" as in lunacy or to "lose one's body" as in leprosy. Both involve a loss of self, either psychic identity or body image. Given the unique combination of disease characteristics and the associated medical and social uncertainties, it is apparent that neither the fantasy of leprosy as total maximal physical illness nor extreme cases of the real disease are conducive to an optimistic outlook for patients.

397

## LEPROSY AS AN IDENTITY CRISIS

Diagnosis of leprosy with or without concomitant hospitalization, signals a sudden undesired transformation of the patient's life program. Many activities and relationships formerly engaged in must be modified or given up. The situation is further compounded by the chronicity of the disease and the need for continued prophylactic actions. The disease becomes the nucleus around which the patient's life program is transformed. The disease also sets boundaries which, for many patients, impose a severe truncation of their normal status and role activities. In this complex, self-and other-stigmatization are but two facets contributing to a major identity crisis.

A further complication in the crisis comes with the patient's realization that (1) while he has a serious condition (serious either as disease or stigma or both), he has not changed as a person, yet (2) society would now regard him as totally different. The patient fears that his condition will engender not only a discontinuity between his past and previously expected future, but also will create an incongruity between his self-identity and his social identity. As long as he can conceal his condition, he can, within limits, engage normally in behavior open to him on the basis of a social identity in which others do not know of his stigma. But once the condition is known, the patient is faced with the problem of "building a world," to use Goffman's phrase. He has to learn what from the past must be discarded and what is salvageable, which past activities and roles will facilitate adaptation, which will not, and what new behaviors need to be added.

Patients handle the discontinuity and dissonance between self and social identities in a variety of ways, and the kind and quality of their adjustment can be expected to vary according to their relation to others who hold different views about leprosy. In Goffman's treatment of single stigmatized individuals, interacting with normals in everyday encounters, the penetrating social norms remain continually in effect. Under these circumstances it is difficult for the stigmatized person to see himself differently than others see him for he continues to live, work, and play in social contexts that affirm the conventional standards.

We are concerned here, however, with situations in which the stigmatized develop and implement an ideology counter to the dominant one that stigmatizes them. They formulate a theory of their own to account for their predicament, to de-discredit themselves, to challenge the norms that disadvantage them and supplant these with others that provide a base for reducing or removing self-stigma and other-stigma. The most significant element for this to take place, it would seem, is a mutually reenforcing collectivity of like-stigmatized people, a subculture capable of maintaining effective immunity from the dominant code. Such collectivities may be of the urban homosexual variety or the rash of "hippie" movements which, although located physically within the larger society, nevertheless managed to set themselves apart, reenforcing each other's actions while setting some degree of social, emotional, and cognitive distance between themselves and their critics.

Such a collectivity is that formed by the leprosy patients at the USPHS Hospital in Carville. Originally (in its pre-sulfone days) an asylum, it is now a "quasi-open residential treatment community." (Nichols 1966) with a well-developed patient culture which has evolved a distinctive and coherent stigma theory of its own in isolation from the mainstream of American social routines.

## THE PATIENTS' THEORY OF STIGMA

A diagnosis of leprosy, followed by hospitalization or out-patient treatment, introduces the new patient to the known medical facts and to many of the misconceptions and uncertainties related to the disease. It is a common fact of our observation that new patients hold expectations which compare leprosy with Biblical notions and include the fantasy of "total maximal physical illness." Early in the introduction to their new career, patients learn that Biblical references and contemporary leprosy are associated only in historical myth and misconception. This aspect of the stigma theory attempts to de-mythologize leprosy by emphasizing the historical, social, and medical errors and confusions which surround it. The theory further argues that leprosy as now known is wholly undeserving of the social prejudice it arouses and elaborates the view that society's negative image arises not from the medical and physiological facts but from faulty Biblical exegesis based at best on poorly substantiated historical evidence and reasoning. Scientific and medical data are adduced to show that leprosy historically has been mistakenly identified with a wide variety of other skin and nerve conditions and that for centuries it has been a general catch-all category for any number of deforming illnesses that have afflicted mankind.

The theory also attempts to deal with contagion. Since there are a number of medical and scientific uncertainties relating to contagion, the theory encounters certain difficulties. Much is made of leprosy as a "mildly contagious" disease, but the epidemiology is uncertain; and the question is commonly raised that if it is only "mildly" contagious, how come so many people have it? At Carville it is routine to relate that in nearly three-quarters of a century only one employee ever contracted the disease and this man, it is pointedly added, was reared in the leprosy endemic area of Southern Louisiana. At times, the theory goes further and declares that in some regions leprosy may be considered a "non-communicable" disease.

In line with the theory, serious proposals are advanced to change the name of the illness to Hansen's Disease. The term "leper" in particular, but also the term "leprosy," is considered opprobrious and inappropriate except in the ancient, Biblical context. The present-day condition is termed "Hansen's Disease" or "so-called leprosy" in order to clarify the distinction between present reality and past symbol and myth.

The stigma or, perhaps more correctly, the destigmatizing theory is advanced in various ways. Almost without exception it plays a part in all printed or verbal presentations to the public by patients or their representatives. It appears in its most explicit form in the pages of *The Star*, a bimonthly journal published by the patients and distributed internationally. The theory is less a "line" in Goffman's sense than an ideological position. Unlike "codes" or "lines," it does not elaborate rules of conduct by which the stigmatized should guide themselves in their relations with normals so much as it provides a "world view." As ideology the theory is a highly formal explanation of the stigmatic nature of their illness which permits patients to minimize the notion that they are severely afflicted; it also provides them with readily available and, to them, provable evidence that society has wrongly labeled them.

The theory is a nativistic effort to redefine the disease and remove it from its hitherto eminent position as the idealized maximal horrible illness. It also supplies some measure of hope and certainty through the suggestion that the social and psychological problems patients face are due substantially to society's defective view of the disease. The basic assumption is that ostracism and

rejection will appreciably diminish and perhaps disappear when social misconceptions are corrected. The USPHS Hospital itself actively functions as a disseminator of the stigma theory by encouraging visitors through an established routine of planned programs. An average of 13,000 visitors annually tour the hospital.

Since the new patient usually had a somewhat nihilistic view of leprosy before his own socialization into the world of patients, the position that society is wrong about the disease is one he can convincingly endorse. Psychologically, the theory functions to drain energy, and often hostility, away from physical and medical aspects of the disease that are realistically distressing, about which little is presently known, and for which little or nothing can be done. Instead, the theory focuses attention on a punitive and misunderstanding society whose views, it contends, can be altered if sufficient effort is made to bring the "real" facts before the public and if the public makes an honest effort to replace their erroneous views with the idea that leprosy is "just like any other illness."

The theory understandably heavily emphasizes a social and historical perspective rather than the medical and physiological aspects of the disease, since it is an attempt to introduce a measure of certainty and optimism into an area of experience that is for many markedly uncertain, and for some less than hopeful. There is, however, a germ of truth in the theory. Leprosy is not of course, except in extreme conditions, the ultimate disease it is fantasied to be; nor is it the Biblical "disease."

Although incomplete as a social or historical explanation for the prejudices encountered, the theory has important value for patient adaptation and de-discreditation. Psychologically, leprosy patients typically exhibit a sense of total rejection by society and initially even by themselves. Interestingly, this sense of initial self-rejection sometimes offers the patient an opportunity to work out, or at least, work on, intrapsychic conflicts that may have antedated the illness. For some patients with a premorbid, diffuse self-identity, leprosy may ultimately have an integrating effect. For regardless of the discrediting nature of the disease, as an identity mark it cannot but impress upon the individual an acute awareness that if he did not know who he was before, there can be no question as to who he is now. In not wishing to accept this "who he is now," which might result in apathy and hopelessness, the stigma theory provides patients with an available rationale for reevaluating their discredited status and, additionally, for engaging in ego-satisfying and socially syntonic assertive actions....

Most patients...elect to conceal their leprosy identity from society. Many take up permanent residence at the hospital where they live, work, and sometimes marry. They protect themselves by "colonizing." They maintain the notion of society's ignorance and misconceptions about leprosy as a means of reconciling their own lowered self-esteem. Through exposure to and socialization by other patients they incorporate the stigma theory into their own world view.

## THE THEORY AS LEGITIMATION FOR CAREER PATIENT STATUS

A number of patients, apparently independently of severity or visibility of symptoms, reveal their condition to society in quite open ways. In the interest of altering the public image of leprosy, which they hold as bearing the major responsibility for their discredited status and predicament in life, these patients assume the stance of educators bringing specialized information about leprosy to the public. Such *career patients* engage in a number of activities which are legitimized through the elements of the stigma theory and carry the approval of the majority of other patients.

The following case history, abstracted from extensive interviews, illustrates some of the ways attitudes toward leprosy are reformulated and basic problems of revealing and educating are handled by those who are career patients.

The patient has been a fairly regular Carville resident since his first admission more than five years ago. He has a more benign and less contagious form of the disease. He has no visible symptoms and the disease seems dormant at present. The patient is below middle age and his general health is good. His present wife—they married since his admission to Carville—is a Carville patient with a severe form of the disease and requires continuous medical care. Both live together at the hospital, visiting outside for varying periods. He works sporadically both at Carville and at various jobs outside. He does not use an alias.

The patient's view of the disease has been modified considerably since his diagnosis. At that time he believed leprosy to be highly contagious, extremely painful, even fatal and that he would soon lose various body parts—nose, ears, toes, etc. He continuously tested for signs of atrophy and also experienced depressive moods including rumination about suicide. He carefully concealed knowledge of his disease from others, passing his symptoms off as due to a nonstigmatized condition. He was upset when the Carville staff did not endorse his

fantasy for total and immediate confinement. Now he believes leprosy is a minimal disease, especially when treatment is begun early. He ranks cancer, heart disease, tuberculosis, arthritis and rheumatism as worse than leprosy. He views genetic susceptibility as a prime factor in contagion. Now he never denies having leprosy and pointedly informs others of his true condition.

This patient is an active "educator" of the public and keeps himself informed about leprosy. He frequently talks to various groups as a leprosy patient and appears on television and radio. He is committed to generating more public interest in the disease and welcomes all questions and opportunities to discuss it. He acknowledges the existence of public fear, has personally experienced it, and feels that continuous efforts are necessary to overcome intractible public disinterest and fear. In order to correct erroneous public views and minimize the contagion factor, he paradoxically cites prevalence figures higher than those usually given by medical authorities.

Selective disclosing of information about leprosy is acknowledged by this patient: "There are many ways of telling people." When addressing the public, he sidesteps questions about and minimizes the problems of deformity to avoid reinforcing existing fantasies and misconceptions. In talking to Carville visitors, he feels the matter of deformity can be placed in perspective by pointing to the many patients who are not disfigured and by relating deformity to inadequacy of the older drugs, to the "oldtimers," and to those whose treatment was begun late. He links the maximal illness fantasy of leprosy and the stigma to the teachings of the churches and to writers and film makers who continue to hold erroneous ideas.

The patient cites his own experiences and marked shift in viewpoint as an example of the "conversion" anticipated in the public once an interest in and an understanding of the disease is created. He believes he has avoided developing a discredited self-identity through his education activities and the opportunities they have provided him in disclosing his leprosy identity. Concealers, he notes, have denied themselves this opportunity; their fear of exposure has altered their self-conception to that of an "outsider."

At present he is working outside Carville where his employer and his co-employees know all about him. He would not have it otherwise, he says. Informally he reveals his identity in almost all appropriate situations with only minor reservations.

In functioning as educational specialists the relationship of such patients to society undergoes an important shift. For some it furnishes them with a clear identity perhaps for the first time in their lives, providing them with altruistic service roles which, considering the fact the majority of patients at Carville are lower-class and rural, would not ordinarily be open to them. Some write articles and books, speak on the radio, appear on television or before community groups both out in the community and on patient-panels to Carville visitors. Two prominent career patients are Gertrude Hornbostel and Joey Guerrero, whose brief biographies appear in Stanley Stein's book *Alone No Longer* (1963). Stein himself is probably the most prominent current career patient. All who reveal are potential educators. However, the decision to reveal is usually made only after much thought and weighing of consequences. Only when the patient believes he can cope with the reactions he anticipates is he likely to decide on this alternative.

Some career patients, like the one cited above, bear little evidence of their condition. This may seem logical insofar as such patients present the best case for leprosy in face-to-face encounters with the public, serving as examples to contradict the "erroneous" public view of the disease and lending credence to the patients' special stigma theory of leprosy. At the same time, there is a paradox in that these individuals are the very ones who could most easily "pass" and thereby minimize social rejection. That they do not choose this path is a comment on the fact that stigma may provide the basis for a total self-conception.

An important limitation of the patient educator relates to the kind and amount of information he may freely impart to the public. His function decrees he present leprosy in a favorable light. To emphasize the medical and social uncertainties or elaborate on the pathological picture of the disease might intensify reactions rather than temper them. The picture of the disease he presents must be carefully designed not to alarm. Thus, in the case history above, the patient mentioned "there are many ways of telling people" and many ways of dealing with difficult and embarrassing questions about deformity. The management of information has its own pitfalls, however. To reveal too much may be self-defeating. At the same time what is presented cannot be so out of tune with reality that it is dismissed as an obvious effort to paint an overly optimistic picture. The situation is especially precarious in view of public ideas of the disease as "extreme." Emphasis is thus placed on correcting errors and misconceptions rather than on fully elaborating all the factual details of leprosy....

Career patients, when not engaged in public education activities outside of Carville, require a place to which they may retreat. Refuge is most readily available at the hospital itself. Individuals who have attempted to maintain the dual statuses of career patient and private citizen in outside

communities often, though not always, experience severe role conflicts. While "accepted" as public educators about leprosy, they find that this limited acceptance does not always qualify them for general social acceptance. Patient educators on tour often find it expedient to use an alias so that adverse publicity will not precede or follow them when they wish to settle down.

There are probably few individuals who can permanently tolerate feeling discredited without making efforts to alleviate or restructure their definition of self. Insofar as the career patient status is viable, it assists in this task. From discredited concealers whose safety lies in hiding their identity, such individuals take on a new and laudable, though somewhat marginal, position as educational specialists. Their self-esteem and social prestige are elevated. Their actions receive the approval of the hospital and others within the leprosy community and ultimately may be deemed worthy by society in general. Many patients are thus motivated to energetic and outgoing lives, and the public attitudes to which they address themselves are undoubtedly moved toward some increasing understanding and tolerance. However, it must be pointed out that *at the present time this status appears to be the only legitimate one the leprosy patient has available to him for life in open society*.

## FURTHER PERSPECTIVE ON STIGMA THEORIES AND CAREER PATIENTS

Though the destigmatizing ideology and the concept of career patient have been elaborated here in relation to leprosy, such statuses and ideologies are not limited to this illness alone. In mental illness, also, there is a stigma theory operating. Cumming and Cumming note that

[one] mechanism is redefinition of the situation so that the "public" is held to be ignorant and prejudiced about those who must go to mental hospitals. In this mechanism, only the initiated know that such people are not crazy at all, but only temporarily ill, or in need of a rest (1965:1).

The entire mental health movement is in a sense directed toward attenuating the stigma of mental illness. Such ideologies are present also in a number of other conditions, although in a more diffuse form. In alcoholism, for example, there is an attempt to shift public belief in "weakness of character" as a main component to a more acceptable emotional illness model. Similarly, urban homosexuals are active and vocal in their attempts to alter public views and stereotypes.

We offer the generalization that stigma theories tend to develop and achieve a more articulate, coherent, and viable form to the extent that four conditions obtain: (1) there is a basic inadequacy of the existing social model to deal with the many and complex dimensions of the total problem; (2) persons involved in the stigmatized condition are engaged in close and sufficiently prolonged interaction so that a subculture, with ideology and norms, may develop; (3) the stigmatized are sufficiently free of daily encroachment on their lives by dissonant public views; and (4) there are a few (or at least one thoroughly dedicated) of the "discredited" able to enunciate and disseminate a coherent "stigma theory" and willing to risk the concomitant exposure. These few can then, as "career patients," legitimately use the theory for their own adaptation and, more significantly, to effect a transformation in society's attitudes toward their deviant groups.

# 45 *Susto* Revisited: Illness as Strategic Role

## *Douglas Uzzell*

Using two concepts, that of sick role from the social sciences, and that of *susto* as a frequently described folk illness (see Rubel's selection in Chapter 12) or "culture-bound reactive syndrome" as Yap describes such emotional illnesses (in Chapter 38), Douglas Uzzell manages to offer new dimensions and broadened understanding of both concepts. This paper suggests that the sick role is a conscious choice made as a strategic alternative to the less rewarding sex and other roles of men and women in this Mexican Zapotec village. Thus, though Uzzell does not say so, one could say that the assumption of the sick role under these conditions brings not only the usual "secondary gains" of illness (relief from normal role requirements) but that in the sense that this was the reason for its selection, these rewards of the role may be seen as "primary." In converting the role for a given individual from the consensual fictions surrounding it to the reality of actual selection for action, the role performer also achieves an altered identity. This presents the need, as

Reprinted with abridgments from Douglas Uzzell, 1974, "*Susto* Revisited: Illness as Strategic Role," *American Ethnologist*, 1:369–378, with permission of the author and the American Anthropological Association.

Uzzell says, for medical anthropologists "not only ... of discovering the strategic merits and demerits of *susto* as a role, but also that of uncovering the dialectic by which the role comes to be assumed, and, once assumed, real."

*Susto* is the Spanish name of a disease that may be translated roughly as fright sickness. In detail its symptoms vary regionally throughout Latin America, but almost always they include listlessness, loss of appetite, and withdrawal from social interaction. Effects imputed to the illness may include death. Often it is treated by a *curandero* ("folk healer," a physician who does not have modern Western academic credentials) (Press 1971). Methods, difficulty, and cost of curing also vary regionally. As the name implies, the illness is supposed to be caused by severe fright. Usually, this is also associated with some form of soul loss. A number of writers have dealt with *susto* (e.g., Adams 1952; Adams and Rubel 1967; Fitzsimmons n.d.; Gillin 1948; O'Nell and Selby 1968; Rubel 1960, 1964).

Most literature on *susto* has primarily been descriptive. Rubel (1964), however, besides describing the illness complex and suggesting its distribution and range of variation, sets forth a number of hypotheses regarding its occurrence. A central hypothesis is the following: "In Hispanic-American societies, the *susto* syndrome will appear as a consequence of an episode in which an individual is unable to meet the expectations of his own society for a social role in which he or she has been ·socialized" (1964:280). Corollary to this, Rubel predicts that because males and females are differently socialized, the kinds of situations that lead to *susto* will vary according to sex (1964:280–281).

Although the quotation above may seem to imply the contrary, Rubel does not consider the causal episode necessarily to occur immediately before the onset of symptoms (personal communication). Folk etiologies sometimes telescope time, so that the causal episode may have occurred several years before the onset of symptoms.

O'Nell and Selby (1968) begin with Rubel's hypothesis, but do not concern themselves with the mechanism of becoming *asustado* (state of suffering *susto*, and by extension, the sufferer himself). They assume "that *susto* represents an important culturally and socially sanctioned avenue of escape for an individual suffering from intra-culturally induced stress" (1968:97). And they formulate the hypothesis that "The sex which experiences the greater intra-cultural stress in the process of meeting sex role expectations will evidence the greater susceptibility to *susto*" (1968:98).

Without precisely defining stress, O'Nell and Selby give convincing reasons for believing that in Zapotec villages in the Oaxaca Valley, (1) the social roles of women are more stressful than those of men, and (2) women are provided with fewer mechanisms for reducing stress than men are. If that is true, and if *susto* is indeed a response to stress, they argue, then more women than men should suffer *susto*. Using data gathered in two Zapotec villages in the Oaxaca Valley, the authors find that their hypothesis is, in fact, supported.

Fitzsimmons (n.d.) has recently taken a clinical approach to explaining *susto*. Working in a Zapotec village, he interviewed *asustados* during the course of their illnesses and supplemented the interviews with projective tests and (in at least one case) reports of medical and psychological examinations. Unfortunately, the case Fitzsimmons reports in the paper cited above is complicated by apparently severe amebic colitis and hepato amebiasis, which might account for the symptoms of *susto*. Nevertheless, Fitzsimmons' approach is welcome, if for no other reason than that it substitutes academic medical explanations for "folk" explanations of the illness and thus provides a fresh perspective.

From his different vantage point, Fitzsimmons argues that *susto* represents a "pathological" adaptation to anxiety, which, though necessarily partially effective, is ultimately costly, both because of physiological damage wrought by the sympathetic nervous system and because of the partiality of the adaptation, which renders it self-sustaining.

It is apparent from those studies that *susto* represents a form of deviance and that it is to be associated with something awry between the *asustado* and his society, whether we call that something stress, anxiety, or another term. In the remainder of this paper, I shall pursue further the social side of the phenomenon. Although I shall present data that may lead me to question some of O'Nell and Selby's conclusions, my purpose is not to dispute them, but simply to examine *susto* from a different analytical perspective, that of face-to-face interaction.

The study from which data presented in this paper are taken was conducted during the summer of 1968 in the village of San Andrés Zautla, Oaxaca, Mexico. With a population of about 1,300, Zautla is surrounded by Zapotec villages. It is not quite proper, however, to characterize Zautla as Zapotec. Linguistically and otherwise, it is in the process of becoming a Mexican peasant village without ethnic identity (see Dennis 1973; Uzzell n.d.). My study was not of *susto*, per se, but was a general inquiry into illness beliefs. I did, however, attempt to replicate O'Nell and Selby's study, and that attempt has led to the present discussion.

My study began with formal interviews during which I elicited names, symptoms, causes, and cures of as many illnesses as my informants could think of. After a great deal of information had been generated, informants were asked to perform several sorting tasks, sometimes with no criteria of distinction specified, and sometimes with criteria suggested by previous sortings such as dangerousness of the illness and cost of curing. Finally, a list of questions about illnesses was prepared and it was administered to two groups of school children (one in Zautla and one in the neighboring village of Santo Tomás Mazaltepéc where Selby had done his fieldwork) and to a sample of women who resided within the area of a sample census I had conducted previously (Uzzell n.d.).

Among other things, respondents were presented with a list of illnesses and were asked the number of people in their families, if any, who had suffered each, indicating whether the victim was a man, a woman, or a child. *Susto* was one of the illnesses in the list. Twenty-three cases were reported by a total of forty-seven respondents. As O'Nell and Selby's data would lead us to expect, considerably more women than men were reported to have suffered the disease (twelve women and four men) (Rubel 1964). However, seven children also were reported to have been *asustado*.

Of course, the fact that children suffer *susto* does not invalidate O'Nell and Selby's hypothesis, which confines itself to the occurrence of *susto* among adults. It does raise problems, however, with the larger notion of role-specific stress, and of *susto* as a response to it. Although I agree with O'Nell and Selby that demands on women in these societies are greater than those on men, I think that they would agree that childhood for either sex is less demanding than adulthood, so that we should expect that children would suffer *susto* least of all.

Two "explanations" present themselves. The first, which I suggested in my 1969 paper, is that because the actions of the *asustado* are generally passive, and because passivity is acceptable in women and children, but not in men, then being *asustado* is somewhat more deviant for men than for women and children. That notion is supported by my informants, who said that for a man to become *asustado* required a more frightening experience (e.g., almost drowning or being attacked by a mountain lion) than is necessarily required to make a woman or a child *asustado*. That, of course, tends to confirm Rubel's corollary mentioned above; however, he says that in only two of three villages he is now studying is a stigma attached to a man's being *asustado* (personal communication).

A second consideration, however, while possibly explaining why the rate of occurrence of *susto* among children is as high as it is, casts some doubts upon the adequacy of the first explanation. All the discussion so far has assumed that the *asustado* participates in defining himself as such. Part of Rubel's first hypothesis is that "People . . . not only choose to assume the sick role but also elect the kinds of symptoms by which to make manifest to others an absence of well-being" (1964:280). For children, though, especially for very young ones, it is adults, and not the victims, who make the diagnoses. This is further complicated by the fact that symptoms present in a child who is *asustado* may be identical to those associated with other illnesses, particularly *ojo* ("evil eye"). (The same may also be true of adults.) I shall return to this problem. Meanwhile, I should like to consider further the occurrence of *susto* among adults. But first a word is necessary to clarify what I shall mean when I speak of "roles."

Rubel, O'Nell and Selby (and I, in discussing their work) treat social "roles" as though: (1) they existed outside the mythic universe of the social scientist; (2) members of the subject society also used the concept (though perhaps under other names); and (3) the "roles" were uniformly perceived by the members. This, of course, is a strong and venerable concept in the social sciences. However, its strength springs from the same source as its weakness, as may be seen if we think of roles in dramas.

Everyone can recognize the title role in *Hamlet*. The part has certain lines and directions, and they, in turn, condition, and are conditioned by, the lines and directions that are given to the other roles. By understanding all the roles and their relationships to one another, presumably we can understand (or explain) the drama. In a world of diversity, one needs simple uniformity. Providing simplification is the strength of the concept of institutionalized roles. However, we also speak of actors creating roles, that is, impregnating the lines with their own

unique fictions. In a sense, *Hamlet* is *Hamlet*, whether the title role be played by Herrick or by Olivier, but in another sense, it is not. And in still another sense, *Hamlet* in all its richness of meaning and popularity is, in addition to the written lines and directions, not only all of its performances, but also all the millions of words of commentary that have been written about it.

When O'Nell and Selby discuss cultural phenomena in terms of roles, they are doing something akin to discussing the play without its performances, but with this important difference: it is they themselves who have written the script. Further, in asserting that the roles he writes also exist in the minds of the members of society, the social scientist implicitly assumes the position of member himself, and his analysis proceeds from that level. Now, whether or not the roles we (anthropologists) write are perceived that way by all, or indeed by any, of the members of a society (Wallace 1970), is beside the point. If our fiction is useful, it is justified. And one feels an essential rightness about, for example, what O'Nell and Selby say about sex roles in the villages they studied. Also, as far as I know, adult *susto* always involves withdrawal from certain kinds of activities. Thus it seems reasonable to assume that the *asustado* somehow finds those activities undesirable. What both Rubel and O'Nell and Selby do is claim that those activities the *asustado* withdraws from are written into certain roles. That line of reasoning is persuasive (though somewhat circular). But that does not really tell us much about *susto*.

What I should like to do now is somewhat similar to thinking of the performance of a drama rather than of the script itself. In doing this, I shall speak of roles, not necessarily as fixed and universal within a culture, but as fictions the member invents, however much he may borrow from what he perceives to be other members' fictions, and whatever the duration of the fiction (a lifetime or a bus ride). To elaborate (if not to overwork) the analogy with theatrical performances, we might think of improvisational theatre rather than the ordinary kind. But even in ordinary drama, the actor must see his role as a set of constraints within which he must create his own fiction, just as the improvisational actor must operate within constraints imposed by such things as size of stage, material for props, his own talents, and his fellow actors. The difference is one of degree. In that sense, then, we may think of *susto* as a role, and being *asustado* as its performance.

One of the striking things about *susto* among illness roles is that it is preeminently social, as opposed to cancer, for example, which may be performed in private. Most of *susto*'s external symptoms are activities that, in other contexts, might be ascribed to cantankerousness, hostility, or the like. And the way you know the *asustado* is cured is not that he stops coughing, bleeding, or complaining of pain, but that he begins to interact with other members differently. Indeed, *susto* might be considered in Goffman's terms as a kind of "misinvolvement" in a social interaction (1967:117–125).

Another interesting thing about *susto* as an illness role, at least in Zautla, is that although my informants considered it fairly dangerous (fatal if not cured), they repeatedly told me that it was cheaply and easily cured—a matter of a visit to a *curandero* whose fee would be two or three pesos, or a simple cure at home, accomplished by a member of the family. That contrasted sharply with most other illnesses in two ways. First, cost of curing appeared to be a function of the perceived dangerousness of the illness. Second, I was told that for most illnesses, the majority of people consult the *enfermera* ('nurse'), or for serious illnesses, a medical doctor, whereas *susto* usually is not treated by these people.

But the most important characteristic of *susto* as an illness role is its flexibility. Rubel (1964) argues that *susto* is a stable set of symptoms, causes, and cures, with at most, Indian and Ladino variations. It is, of course, necessary that he take that position in order to justify his epidemiology. And at his level of analysis—folk drama as a script written by anthropologists—I think he is correct. But in terms of performances, *susto* is a very loose script indeed.

This may, in fact, be true of most illnesses (contrary to an impression I once had from such studies as Frake's [1961] analysis of Subanun diagnostics). I have already mentioned my own failure to find consistency among beliefs of various informants. Having documented variance among Zinacantecans of what he calls "medical knowledge," Fabrega concludes,

In other words, knowledge about illness, at the level tapped by our study, is distributed unevenly in Zinacantan. This suggests that a critical posture should be adopted toward reports about the specificity of socio-culturally peculiar syndromes (Rubel 1964). Illness beliefs and natively construed health crisis episodes no doubt exist, and at a general level of measurement (e.g., the

mode) unique and consistent patterns can be demonstrated on certain dimensions. It appears, however, that subjects apply these beliefs rather loosely to certain dimensions and that, even on those dimensions where a strong consensus exists, subsets of the members of the cultural group manifest different responses (1971:38).

And this variability he also found to exist among curers. Unfortunately, Fabrega does not show the degree of variance (which he expresses in bits of information contained in a response) for *susto* (*espanto* in Zinacantan). I would predict, though, that *susto* should show a relatively high degree of uncertainty.

Even if members' knowledge of *susto* were perfectly uniform, however, there are other features that make it a very adaptable illness role. A key factor is the etiology. The causal episode is cut loose in time, so that one may seek his fright at large. This virtually assures that some kind of episode will be available to everybody, but more than that it gives enough latitude for the *asustado* to find a kind of episode that fits his overall personal fiction. The symptoms, also, are loosely defined: one withdraws, loses his appetite, and sleeps fitfully. Though death may lie at the end of such behavior, one can gauge its nearness and control the term (or equally important, the apparent projected term) of the illness. And moment by moment, the *asustado* may behave pretty much as he wishes.

And, finally, *susto* comes closer than any other illness in Zautla to providing a psychological explanation of deviant behavior. Selby has argued (n.d.b) that residents of Mazaltepéc do not normally use psychological explanations of deviant behavior. If a man is surly, for example, it is simply because he is a surly man. If that notion is correct (and I feel that it is, and that it applies to Zautla), then *susto* certainly stands out as exceptional. The *asustado* is not withdrawn because he is a withdrawn person (as some non-*asustados*—in other words, those who have not been defined as such—may indeed be), but because he is *asustado*. In passing, I might even suggest that etiologies and some forms of treatment of *susto* bear resemblance to psychoanalytic myths of cause and cure of "mental illness."

Those considerations cause me to reconsider my characterization of *susto* as a form of *misinvolvement* in interaction. As Goffman (1967) defines it, misinvolvement is destructive to interactions and may give co-participants offense. However, the *asustado* is allowed to do things with impunity that in other contexts would destroy interactions, give offense, and perhaps even invite physical punishment. It appears reasonable, then, to think of the playing of the role of *asustado* by one participant in an interaction in such a way that his co-participants recognize that he is playing that role, as establishing a context in which the *asustado*'s otherwise deviant acts not only become nondeviant, but are even required for maintenance of the interaction. Goffman says,

when an individual projects a definition of the situation and thereby makes an implicit or explicit claim to be a person of a particular kind, he automatically exerts a moral demand upon the others, obliging them to value and treat him in the manner that persons of his kind have a right to expect (1959:13).

The *asustado*'s playing the *susto* role successfully enables him to impose his own definition on the situation, a definition that gives his otherwise deviant acts legitimacy.

More than one paradox is implicit in this state of affairs. First, there is the phenomenon of legitimate deviance. Next, there is the curious development that *susto*, which is characterized by withdrawal from interaction, becomes a mechanism for maintaining interaction. Coupling these with the other anomalies of *susto* as an illness role, one begins to realize that *susto* is, in fact, a complex of reversals as complete as the "backward person complex" of North American Plains Indians.

As an illness role, adult *susto* has advantages over similar illnesses. Here are some examples. *Muina*, which may be caused by envy or unexpressed anger, reflects weakness (though sometimes desirable weaknesses) in the victim's personality. Also, *muina* does not necessarily involve withdrawal (it may be no more than chronic indigestion). The *muina* role sets one off as a passionate person, but it does not define situations in such a way as to give the victim interactional liberties. For adults in Zautla, *pasmo* most closely approximates *susto* in symptoms, but it involves the magical theft of the soul, usually of a man, by a woman. This doubles the passivity (from a masculine point of view) of the role, and also involves another human in the etiology. *Susto*'s causes may be as impersonal as those of whooping cough; and if one assumes the role, he may even be projecting himself as being at war with superhuman forces. The same would hold true for 'evil eye' (see Rubel 1960), although it appears to be strictly a child's disease in Zautla.

What I have been suggesting is that we consider adult *susto* as a role that may be assumed by an individual, primarily in order to impose his or her definition upon situations and thereby control the interactions. This implies dissatisfaction with existing definitions, but it does not necessarily imply "role stress' or perceived inadequacy to meet the demands of a role. Rubel (1960, 1964) gives us a nice example of a woman who he says has epileptoid symptoms. Perhaps the *asustado* identity is preferable to being identified as epileptic. Perhaps withdrawal is preferable to being beaten excessively (a little beating may be normative) by one's husband.

As for why more women than men suffer adult *susto*, two factors suggest themselves. First, becoming passive is a more extreme change of identities for men than for women, and it requires one of a smaller set of precipitating incidents. Second is the situs of interactions controlled by *susto*. The *asustado* typically remains at home, and it seems reasonable to assume that the situations he controls by virtue of his role are essentially household situations. Now in Zautla, men spend much less time in the house than women do, and when they are at home men normally dominate household interactions. There would usually, then, be fewer cases in which it would be strategically useful for men to adopt a *susto* role in order to gain dominance than there would be for women. The wonder, then, is not that more women than men suffer *susto*, but that men suffer it as much as they do!

It remains to make some observations about children's *susto*, which I have already suggested involves different roles than *susto* in adults. By children's *susto*, I mean *susto* in an individual who is too young to participate in the diagnosis. I should admit that some of the seven cases I mentioned earlier probably do not fit that definition.

The salient characteristic of children's *susto* is that adults diagnose it as such. That means that while the child plays the role, the adult invests it with meaning, so that it may still be seen as an extension of the adult's personal fiction. Alternative diagnoses of the same symptoms are 'evil eye' and various alimentary disorders. The latter are quite common due to the scarcity of supplements if the mother's milk is inadequate, the prevalence of intestinal parasites, and the severity of diet change at weaning.

It is my impression that 'evil eye' and *susto* are routinely invoked after other diagnoses and their remedies have failed. In other words, the symptoms of *susto* and 'evil eye' are distinctive by their persistence. 'Evil eye' is caused by another person. That person may covet the child, or may simply have "heavy" eyes. Or the agent may simply be in a state of increased bodily activity. Thus, it is dangerous for a father, just returned from the fields and hot from exertion, to play with his small children.

With only skimpy case histories available, I would suggest the following:

(1) that diagnoses of *susto* and 'evil eye' are invoked after other curing strategies have failed;

(2) that when a child is afflicted, a more rigorous etiology is employed than with adults (the traumatic experience must be recent);

(3) that 'evil eye' will be diagnosed when it is strategically desirable to place blame on a person, e.g., when a wife wants to place guilt on a husband or when there is a need to give concreteness to a sense of undesirability to another person;

(4) that *susto* will be diagnosed when a genuinely frightening episode is available and when a diagnosis of 'evil eye' would expose the mother or other responsible person to charges of negligence.

All of these hypotheses need to be tested with case histories, a feat that will be rendered the more difficult because infant mortality is quite high, and parents in Zautla resist discussing their dead children.

## CONCLUDING REMARKS

None of the above should be considered as a "debunking" of earlier studies. It is supplementary to clinical studies such as that of Fitzsimmons, and it is a necessary next step after the organizational work of Rubel and after O'Nell and Selby's unique attempt to test Rubel's hypotheses in the field. Rubel's level of analysis was the only one possible at the time it was carried out. O'Nell and Selby's operationalization of it has pointed the way to other levels, other anthropological myths to be created and explored.

There is a danger, when speaking of strategic roles, of making people appear totally rational and calculating. I have not meant to imply that the decision to play the *susto* role is conscious and straightforward—although, of course, it could be. How one comes to accept a given identity for oneself is a mysterious and intricate process that has long intrigued novelists and existentialist philosophers, while failing to interest most anthropologists (however, see Lévi-Strauss 1967). I imagine that the identity *asustado* is most commonly arrived at dialectically through negotiation with others—a number of clues being provided by people of varying authority for the actor, and he, assimilating the information in the clues, until at some point he concludes, "I am *asustado*."

Diagnosis by a *curandero* consecrates the identity and makes it public, like a marriage ceremony or a jury's verdict. And the diagnosis prescribes general guidelines for behavior of the *asustado* and of other actors in his life drama. The same is true for all illnesses and all other changes of identity; but socially, it is particularly important where actors can or will no longer weave the social fabric into recognizable patterns. The social task becomes one of generating enough redundancy in exotic behavior to make it intelligible.

In our society, psychologists, either directly or by shaping folk beliefs, channel certain kinds of deviant behavior into one of a half dozen or so categories, teaching the deviant how to be insane properly, and rewarding him by holding out the prospect of cure if he learns his lessons. One indication that this is a social solution to deviance is that similar patterns of behavior may be labeled as various illnesses with varying etiologies and prognoses, or as criminal, depending upon other social identities of the patient (cf. Akers 1968; Rosenhan 1973).

But there is a kind of "Catch 22" in all this that enormously complicates our problem of understanding. It proceeds from the fact, which has been stressed in this paper, that deviant adults may participate in their own diagnoses. As Wittgenstein (1963) argues, when I say that I have a pain, not, only is that statement not subject to direct verification by another person, but also it is absurd for me to ask myself whether the sensation I felt was really a pain or, say, an itch. The experience of pain, though, is far less problematic than the sensations experienced while one is *asustado*. Wittgenstein suggests that when a child cries and adults inquire if he has a pain, he learns that whatever sensation made him cry is pain, so that "the verbal expression of pain replaces crying" (1963:89). There are no such clear mechanisms for learning how to experience being *asustado*. Yet *susto* surely is a role that one both *assumes* and *experiences*. And at the point where assumption becomes experience, fiction becomes reality.

The problem I suggest for future research, then, turns out to be not only that of discovering the strategic merits and demerits of *susto* as a role, but also that of uncovering the dialectic by which the role comes to be assumed and, once assumed, real. Treatments such as that of Fitzsimmons, which translate one myth into another preexisting myth, and ethnological distinctions between "folk" beliefs and that which is scientifically verifiable, though probably necessary at early stages of our developing understanding, must ultimately give way before the realization that they (along with much of this paper) are spurious. What we are confronted with is not a problem of how folk beliefs correspond to a single reality, but one of how various realities go about being real.

# 46 Religious Conversion and Elimination of the Sick Role: A Japanese Sect in Hawaii

## Takie Sugiyama Lebra

Sickness carries its burdens but also, insofar as it is legitimated through the sick role as culturally defined, its benefits. But what happens when the cultural definition of the sick role works to cancel its legitimacy? In this study, Takie Sugiyama Lebra observes illness in a Japanese religious sect she calls Tenshō, which has healing as one of its major functions, as the sect seems to influence its members in Hawaii. In Tenshō, illness is symptomatic of spiritual power, but a spiritual attack of illness may indicate malign, benign, or neutral spiritual intent, so such illness may be interpreted in various ways. Sickness may also be taken as a sign of testing by the Supreme spirit, Kami. In Japan, traditionally heavy demands for social conformity stimulate heavy use of the sick role as a sanctioned release and as a masochistic attempt to induce guilt in others. Tenshō changes all this since in it illness inspires guilt and shame in the victim. Though still thought to be spirit-caused, illness is now held to be brought upon the victim by his own

Reprinted with abridgments and minor emendations by the author from Takie Sugiyama Lebra, 1972, "Religious Conversion and Elimination of the Sick Role," in William Lebra, ed., *Transcultural Research in Mental Health: Vol. II of Mental Health Research in Asia and the Pacific*, University of Hawaii Press, Chap. 19, pp. 282–292, with permission of the author and the University of Hawaii Press.

behavior. Thus, Tenshō views sickness as supernatural punishment for religious or social wrong conduct. The Tenshō convert experiences deep, painful guilt when ill, thus, in effect, denying the legitimacy of the sick role: "The only way he can expiate his guilt is to save [his suffering, deceased mother's] spirit, which is signified by his own recovery." Sickness represents a denial of the difficult Tenshō norms and of obligations of the member to sectarian comrades. Rewards of sect affiliation are economic, interactional, affectional, and tactile for converts who join because of their strong needs in these areas. Recovery is proof of the sect's reward system which is activated by the convert's prayers. When one is sick, one's sectarian colleagues avoid all contact with him for fear of contamination and sympathy for the patient is minimized. "...Change in desirability and change in legitimacy reinforce each other until the point is reached where the sick role is eliminated."

It seems safe to assume that every society has its definition of illness as a social role. The sick person as a role occupant can claim certain rights, such as the right to be exempted from work and other normal obligations and to be treated with "compassion, support, and help" (Parsons 1964:113). Precisely because illness is a social role, the contents of privilege vested in illness are likely to vary from one social system to another such that they are fitted into a particular system as a whole, of which the sick role is a part. When a new social system emerges, a new definition is likely to be given of the sick role. An emerging religious sect is most likely to carry its own definition of health and illness, as well as death, as an essential component of its culture. If healing takes place as a sectarian performance, it can be understood, I assume, in the light of the sectarian definition of the sick role.

I would like to explore possible relations between religious commitment and healing phenomena, with special attention to the redefined sick role. Religious commitment here specifically refers to conversion to a new sect which involves intense interaction between the candidate and proselytizer for conversion, exclusive membership in the sect, sustained participation in the sect's collective action, and rigorous conformity to the sectarian norms.

The sect studied is formally called Tenshō Kōtai Jingū Kyō, more commonly known as the Dancing Religion because of the outdoor collective dance, a part of its regular ritual which is most visible to the outside public. Here I shall abbreviate it as Tenshō. Tenshō emerged in postwar Japan under the leadership of a middle-aged farmer's wife, Sayo Kitamura, who came to be addressed as

Ōgamisama, great deity. In 1952, the first overseas division of the sect was established in Hawaii, and its membership is roughly estimated to have reached 500 as of 1965. The following analysis is based on a year-long field research (Lebra 1967) on Tenshō converts in Hawaii. The data were collected through interviews with 55 Honolulu members over 30 years old and through observation of collective activities at local branch meetings. Most interviewees had had direct contact with Ōgamisama, the self-appointed messiah, at one phase of conversion or another, which was made possible by her occasional visits to Hawaii or by the follower's pilgrimage to the sect's headquarters in Japan. Being either *issei* (Japan-born immigrants) or *nisei* (*issei*'s American-born children) including *kibei* (American-born returnees from Japan after growing up there), the informants all understood Japanese with varying degrees of literacy and bilinguality. As for class background, they were found distinctly lower in education and occupation than members of a Buddhist church in Honolulu. Among various reported evidences of salvation, healing was mentioned most frequently. Sixty percent of the informants who had been ill or whose family members had been ill or both ($N = 40$) declared that complete healing had taken place due to conversion; 20 percent claimed definite improvement. Post-conversion experience of healing was reported even more frequently in both interviews and weekly congregations. Whether one should accept such information as reliable or reject it as a wishful distortion, or whether conversion did not bring the opposite outcome (aggravation of illness or death) as well, does not affect our analysis. Our interpretation of the sectarian redefinition of the sick role should account for both the reported successful curing and unreported aggravation of illness.

As in many other religions, Tenshō ideology identifies illness as a sign of supernatural potency. Therefore, a brief review of Tenshō concepts of the supernatural is necessary. In my informants' vocabulary a variety of supernatural agents associated with illness were found. The supernatural being may be suprahuman, human, or infrahuman (e.g., dog spirit); it may be emitted from a dead person (a dead spirit) or a living person (a live spirit); and it may be familiar or strange to the person being possessed by it. It may be benevolent, malevolent, or neutral, and thus sickness may be taken as a sign of the disciplinarian intent of a fatherly supernatural, as an attack by a hostile spirit which is jealous or holding a grudge or

as a gesture of a dead person's spirit trying to call attention and solicit help from the living person.

The central supernatural figure in Tenshō is the Kami, specifically identified as Tenshō Kōtai Jin (the heaven-illuminating, great-ruling deity), who is claimed to have descended into Sayo Kitamura's abdomen and transformed her from a simple farmer into a third messiah after Buddha and Christ. Tenshō Kōtai Jin has partial identity with the Shinto Sun-Goddess, Amaterasu—a point which cannot be overlooked in understanding the conversion of the people of Japanese ancestry, particularly of *issei* and *kibei*. This supreme Kami causes sickness to give divine tests. However, sickness is usually associated more with lesser spirits, or both the Kami and lesser supernatural agents are believed to be jointly responsible for sickness.

A word about a semi-supernatural agent called *innen*. *Innen* is understood as a Karma chain, fate or bondage that is transmitted from one individual to another through consanguineal links in most cases but not always. *Innen* is the most frequently mentioned symbol to explain sickness, although, here again, *innen* may join the spirit of one or another dead person in causing illness.

Given the above cognitive orientation toward sickness, it follows that the sick role must be redefined. The following analysis focuses upon the evaluative change of the sick role. Evaluation of the sick role refers to judgment of sick-role occupancy in terms of good or bad. It falls into two categories. One is evaluative judgment by a collectively shared and sanctioned standard involving moral principles; the other refers to judgment by the evaluator's own emotional acceptability. The former is objective; the latter, subjective. These two standards of judgment are identified here as legitimacy and desirability.

## CHANGE IN LEGITIMACY

In Japan, where the individual is rigidly bound by role obligation as a member of a group, illness appears as a primary opportunity for release from obligation. Excessive legitimacy of the sick role seems to be necessitated to compensate for excessive demands for role conformity in daily life. This is shown by the overtolerance of the Japanese for the public figure who fails to fulfill his public responsibility because of illness as well as by the false pretense of being sick which the Japanese frequently resort to when they want to resign from a job. This tendency may be explained not only by the social function of sickness as suggested here but by the deep layer of personality system. The studies conducted by DeVos (1960) and DeVos and Wagatsuma (1959) delineated the Japanese conception of illness in connection with guilt. Illness is viewed as a sign of moral masochism which characterizes the behavior of Japanese women, particularly of the mother. The mother's illness as the physical expression of her self-sacrifice and self-blame for others' faults, the authors contended, induces guilt in the child, and the latter may also find in his own illness the desired expiation of his guilt. It may be said that the moral tone surrounding illness is so generalized that the sick person feels or appears righteous, and the people around him are compelled to feel guilty. Conversion to Tenshō brought about a radical change in this orientation. Illness, as such, has lost claim to legitimacy. It is not that what was described above as Japanese disappeared completely but that it was channeled in another direction.

In Tenshō, illness is looked upon as a signal of neglect of one's duty; it reflects or arouses guilt and shame in the sick person. This view is internalized in two ways: either through the relation between ego and the identified supernatural that is believed to be causing the sickness or through the relation between ego and Ōgamisama or fellow members or both.

Conversion reestablishes not only cognitive but also moral relations between the convert and the supernatural. Sickness is caused by a spirit, it is true, but the spirit's activation is partly contingent upon the sick person's action. The Kami, for example, gives more tests to those who neglect the duty to Him than to those who are faithful. The convert suffers from muscular pain because, as Ōgamisama interprets, he is greatly indebted to a deceased kin. As long as the latter's spirit continues to visit him and cause pain, he will feel guilty for not repaying the debt. Even hostile spirits such as *jashin* (a false deity), *inugami* (a dog spirit), and *ikiryō* (a live spirit) are supposed to be activated, at least in part, in response to ego's disposition or behavior. "*Jashin* comes from *janen* (wicked intent) [of the possessed]"; "to be possessed [by a spirit] is just as shameful as to possess [someone]." If a person is attacked by *ikiryō*, he must reflect that he has done something which made the *ikiryō* originator jealous or caused him to hold a grudge. Such retributive significance is clearly associated with *innen* as well; here is involved the idea that a person receives a certain *innen* as a reward or punishment for what he did in his present or previous life.

Moral masochism of the mother and the child's guilt toward her are both effectively mobilized toward denial of the legitimacy of sickness. The convert is reminded to recall his deceased mother who suffered all her life for the sake of her drunken husband and unfilial son. His guilt sometimes reaches the point that he bursts into tears. The only way he can expiate his guilt is to save her spirit which is signified by his own recovery. Righteousness is associated with being healthy.

The convert's moral obligation to the supernatural is effectively supported and controlled by his social relation to Ōgamisama and fellow members. Obligation to the supernatural seems to overlap with obligation as a member of Tenshō sect, as Ōgamisama's disciple, and as a *dōshi* (comrade) to other members. To become sick and unable to attend regular meetings is taken as a consequence of violating the sectarian norms. Among the norms are: renunciation of external religious memberships, symbols, and paraphernalia; minimization of social affiliations; minimization of nonreligious solution of problems such as medical treatment; and avoidance of worldly indulgence. These norms are difficult to follow. Particularly, renunciation of religious symbols such as ancestral altars, mortuary tablets, ashes and graveyards, and withdrawal from the family-inherited Buddhist and Shinto affiliation creates utmost conflict and, in some cases, results in family dissolution. Once the convert overcomes this conflict and becomes committed to the sectarian norms, he tends to dramatize his experience and to be intolerant of uncommitted fellow members whose sickness he sees as the Kami's punishment. It is interesting to note, in passing, that Tenshō emphasis upon guilt toward deceased kin and ancestors may be reinforced by the required destruction of their reminders such as tablets and altars.

To what extent sickness is associated with guilt depends upon internalization of sectarian norms. It is proposed here that the driving force for internalization of sectarian norms was provided by the deep sense of indebtedness to the proselytizers (Ōgamisama or members). The benefits ranged from tangible to interactional. Tangible benefits include provision of food, shelter, money, employment, professional services, and customers for traders. One informant was assigned a house by Ōgamisama's order which had belonged to her brother against the expressed wishes of her parents and siblings, not to mention the rule of patrilineal inheritance. Another claimed that Ōgamisama saved him from bankruptcy by giving advice on management of his business. Several informants benefited from the professional services of fellow members such as carpenters, painters, masseurs. By receiving such benefits, an initially uncommitted convert feels increasingly obligated to become a true Tenshō follower. Among other tangible benefits, the provision of marriage partners and children for adoption may be included. Locally, a number of new families emerged through Ōgamisama's matchmaking, in most cases between a local convert and a convert in Japan. The sense of indebtedness for tangible benefits is further strengthened by Ōgamisama's declaration that this religion demands no membership dues. This alleged pecuniary indifference on the part of the prophet seems an exceedingly important factor in generating the obligation of total compliance among the converts.

More important locally than tangible benefits are interactional benefits. The benefit here is derived from the behavioral capacity of the proselytizer, verbal and nonverbal, in public or private scenes, to initiate and maintain interaction. At the most physical level, it includes tactile interaction—patting or pressing parts of the candidate's body where a spirit is supposed to be located, such as shoulder, back, stomach; pulling the candidate by the hand to stand up; in exceptional cases, eating and sleeping with Ōgamisama. It is not coincidental that masseurs have been effective proselytizers, as numerous local cases indicate. At another level, interaction consists of expressive communication. This includes facial movements (Ōgamisama's radiant face, compassionate smile, frightening gaze, frown, tearful eyes) hand movements (pointing at a person, beckoning to him to come forward) head movements (nodding, shaking) and combined movements (bowing with folded palms in a prayer form, showing a smile of welcome for any candidate).

Verbal interaction is through either direct speech or correspondence. The benefactor may play an active role as a speaker or a passive role as an eager sympathetic listener. Most early converts have the treasured memories of what Ōgamisama said to them in their first encounter with her. The meaning of the verbalized content does not necessarily seem to count. Many did not understand Ōgamisama's particular dialect and yet felt as if struck by a thunderbolt. The effect of exposure to vocal stimulation from the whole congregation chanting the meaningless phrase is another example.

Another dimension of interaction may be added. While the interaction described above refers to Ōgamisama's or a member's action directly oriented toward the convert, this involves the introduction of a third party, individual or collective, into the interaction situation. First, a transmitter's role or a go-between role is played by the third person, as when Ōgamisama's favorable comment on a new convert is transmitted to the latter through a leader close to her. As the access to Ōgamisama decreases, reliance upon such a go-between increases in order to maintain interaction. In fact, this form of communication can be even more effective than a direct one in that the third person, with better knowledge of the potential or new convert, can adjust or modify the information to be transmitted. Secondly, in a public scene where the candidate is introduced to Ōgamisama in front of a large audience, the audience's responses can be utilized effectively to gratify the candidate. Ōgamisama fully used this social resource to flatter, approve, upset, or shame the candidate.

Tangible and interactional benefits presented by Ōgamisama or members, however trivial they may look, tend to have a tremendous impact in obligating a new convert and urging him to do whatever the Kami (that is, Ōgamisama) tells him. The way he comes to feel deeply obligated for a seemingly negligible benefit may reflect the degree of deprivation, material and social, which made him inordinately appreciative of the slightest favor offered. The scarcity value of the benefit, in other words, must have been high. This was confirmed by the fact that livelihood had been a serious problem for many converts and by the fact that still more converts had been lonely as a result of family disharmony, especially of marital friction or of family dissolution. Thus, they were hungry for human warmth. The process of becoming obligated may have been accelerated also by the Japanese cultural idiom surrounding the concept of *on*. Simply by labeling whatever is received an *on*, the convert may feel compelled to generalize it into an unpayable debt and to attempt to repay it at any cost.

When these benefits are accompanied, as they often are, by at least temporary relief from illness, the beneficiary becomes convinced that Ōgamisama is his lifesaver or, as informants put it, *inochi-no-onjin*, the *on*-person to whom he owes his life. To repay the *on*, he must become a further committed follower, and to be healthy is a sign of such commitment. As Ōgamisama says, "If you discipline yourself hard enough, you will enter the world where there is no need of doctors or drugs." Where there is any degree of ambivalence on the part of the convert, he is more likely to dramatize and publicly announce his experience of salvation, letting the audience know how deeply he is indebted to Ōgamisama for his life. Once committed to this extent, the convert must maintain his state of salvation (being healthy), not only as a moral obligation to the benefactor but to save face vis-à-vis fellow members. Thus, a deeply committed convert shows embarrassment and apologizes to Ōgamisama in his testimony when he falls ill.

As a human being subject to illness, Ōgamisama plays two roles. She takes a typically "exemplary" leadership role (Weber 1963) by stressing that she has attained absolute salvation and by telling her followers to emulate her. She says, "Come up where I am. How good I feel!" At the same time, she lets them know that she constantly suffers from all sorts of illness. It is here that moral masochism is fully displayed. And yet masochism does not lie so much in being sick as in ignoring sickness and working regularly like a healthy person. Ōgamisama takes pride in the fact that she has never had a single day off from the duty of preaching even when she was seriously ill. This form of masochism is demanded of the members. One of the local pilgrims to the headquarters testified that, while there, she had been scolded by Ōgamisama for using sickness as a reason for not attending the daily disciplinary meeting. She was told that she was indulging herself. Seventy-nine years old, this informant could not get out of bed because of pain and stiffness throughout her body. After learning of Ōgamisama's scoldings through a go-between, she made up her mind to attend the meeting and even participated in yard work to which all pilgrims were assigned.

It has been shown that the legitimacy of the sick role is denied to Tenshō members and that they are obligated, once ill, to recover as promptly as possible.

## CHANGE IN DESIRABILITY

With regard to the Japanese attitude toward illness, Caudill (1962) singled out the characteristically gratifying aspect of the sick role. Specifically, he noted that in Japan sickness provides an important social occasion for the emotionally

satisfying communication between the patient and the nursing person from which they are ordinarily inhibited. People in Japan, it was observed, like to go to bed with mild illnesses. Caudill related such expectation of communication through sickness to the Japanese tendency to live out emotions. Institutionalization of tsukisoi (subprofessional nurses attached to particular patients on a 24-hour basis), also studied by Caudill (1961), shows that such expectation of the sick role is not confined to home care but extended to the hospital situation. The desirability of the sick role described here is shared by the patient and the nursing person, and thus we can say that the function of sickness is socially integrative as well as ego integrative. If sickness justifies the wish to depend upon and be indulged by the attending person, it also legitimizes the wish to be depended upon and indulged upon by the patient. It may be recalled, in this connection, that many pure love stories widely read in Japan involve a love partner who is sick and sometimes fatally so. The socially integrative function of sickness can be seen not only in the form of reciprocity and communication between the patient and the attendant. Sickness further gratifies the wish for physical gregariousness with a larger group of people since relatives, friends, and other concerned people gravitate toward the patient to do mimai (inquiry after a sick person).

The general desirability of the sick role described here is also eliminated through Tenshō conversion. As the illegitimate aspect of the sick role is internalized by Tenshō converts, so is the undesirable expectation of it. Elimination of desirability can be analyzed from two points of view: change in expectation of dependency and gregariousness and vested interest in exemplary well-being.

Through conversion, sickness ceases to be an occasion for gratification of the wish for dependency and solidary gregariousness. Since sickness is believed to be caused supernaturally, recovery is expected to follow the ritual effort (prayer) of the sick person himself. The individuals around him, on the other hand, are supposed to stay away from him lest they should catch and carry with them the spirit causing the illness. This is one reason why Tenshō members are discouraged from attending secular funerals as well as visiting hospitals. Contact with a sick person is to be avoided, particularly by vulnerable members. Coupled with the realization of the supernatural causation, the conceptualization of sickness as illegitimate reduces sympathy for the sick. Such a cold attitude facilitates severing oneself from old secular obligations to sick people outside the sect, thus contributing to the autonomy of the sect. When a member becomes sick, he tends to express discontent with such forced isolation, as some informants indicated. However, this isolation seems only to reinforce the patient's wish to get well, to go back to the regular meeting, and to be approved by fellow members; the temporarily frustrated wish for solidary gathering is gratified through restored health. Ōgamisama strongly disapproves the desire for dependency and indulgence and stresses discipline and self-help even with sick followers, as we have observed before.

Desire to be sick is further inhibited by the fact that the convert has made a social investment in his well-being. First, commitment to sectarian norms involves self-sacrifice on the part of the convert in his secular interest which is likely to amount to an overpayment for whatever debt he owes to the sect. Not only does he cut himself off from secular ties, but he also positively contributes to the sect in money or kind on a voluntary basis. One important means to secure the payoff is to expand the sect and to make its prophecy—final salvation of the Kami's children and damnation of the rest of mankind on the coming day of judgment—come true. The convert has a vested interest in the successful recruitment of new converts. To demonstrate how the proselytizer himself has been saved is a most effective and generally used technique for persuasion. As living evidence of the experienced miracle, he must manage his front, as Goffman (1959) would phrase it, as a revitalized, young, healthy-looking man. His face is more persuasive than words. It is all too understandable that Tenshō emphasizes the importance of the facial look as the window of the soul. Such "face-work" (Goffman 1955) is constantly required when potential converts are within one's family. It is also necessary for self-defense when one's conversion has created family conflict, since any symptom of sickness on the part of the convert will give a reason for the family members opposed to Tenshō to attack him.

Social investment in well-being has further implications. Payoff for sacrifice is partly derived from the status obtained by the convert within the members' community. Particularly for those who are frustrated with status aspirations in the outside world, it seems crucial to assume and maintain a leader's status in the local branch. Here again, leadership is mainly exemplary in that the leader himself must look saved. Physical vulnerability will cost him the exalted status as well as his face.

The desirability of the sick role, or rather its undesirability, has been discussed with reference to both emotional pleasurability and calculated interest. We can see how change in desirability and change in legitimacy reinforce each other until the point is reached where the sick role is eliminated. This may account not only for Tenshō members' willingness to get well and to exaggerate healing miracles but also for actual instances of cures. At the same time, elimination of the sick role may be responsible for aggravation of illness, including sudden death, whenever recovery would have required physical and psychological rest more than anything else. Aggravation and death did occur frequently, though they were not reported as such. When death occurs, the survivors explain it this way: the deceased person was completely cured before he died, when he was dying, or after he died. The evidence of such a cure is found in the following situations: Ōgamisama's declaration such as, "Don't worry, your husband has now attained Buddhahood in heaven"; the corpse remaining soft and warm long after death occurred; the survivor's hallucination with the vision of the deceased appearing healthy; and the belief that all poisons were squeezed out of the body right before death occurred.

## QUALIFICATIONS

The preceding analysis was carried on with the assumption that Tenshō converts in Hawaii have redefined the sick role from a typically Japanese image into a less Japanese image. A close examination of interview materials, however, justifies this assumption only in part.

It is unlikely that Japanese culture, as the point of departure for redefinition of the sick role in legitimacy and desirability, applies to Hawaii's members of Tenshō completely. First, both legitimacy and desirability of the sick role in Japan are structurally supported by the availability of the nursing personnel as well as by economic security within a household. The multi-generational family system, together with solidary ties with collateral kin, will guarantee an attendant to a sick member and transference of economic responsibility in case the major breadwinner gets sick. Such security for emergency may be further provided by the mutual aid network in rural communities. In Hawaii, as far as my informants are concerned, the nuclear family, including single member households, was predominant and the mutual aid, systems, e.g.,

413

association of immigrants from the same provinces, were breaking down. Thus, the sickness of one member tends to be disastrous. The working wife may share economic responsibility but then is not available as a nurse. No wonder that many informants, especially male converts, expressed deep attachment to their mothers from whom they had been long separated and that Ōgamisama struck the responsive chord in their hearts when she reminded them of the unpayable debt to their mothers. No more surprising is the fact that Ōgamisama was identified as "like my mother or grandmother" or "someone even more missed."

Secondly, probably conditioned by such structural change of the family system and also by social contact with other ethnic groups, Hawaii's Japanese seem to have internalized some of the American compulsion for independence and autonomy. The informants recalled their sickness having caused depression and even suicidal attempts because the physical incapacity and forced dependency were too painful to bear.

It is now necessary to modify our assumption as to legitimacy and desirability of the sick role. Hawaii's members of Tenshō may have internalized the Japanese expectation of the sick role but lacked a structural basis for realizing it, and they may have learned two types of value regarding dependency—Japanese and American. What Tenshō did was to get rid of frustrations arising from the discrepancy between expectation and gratification, and it expelled ambivalence stemming from bicultural learning by demoting the Japanese expectation pattern. With all these qualifications, it is still clear that Tenshō brought about a change in the sick role which encouraged its total elimination. . . .

# XIII
## The Healers: Statuses and Roles

## Conceptions of Healing Statuses and Roles

It has not been so long ago that anthropologists and other observers of the medical systems of non-Western societies referred to their healers as "quacks," "charlatans," "magicians" (in the derogatory sense of the term), and similar epithets. These notions of healers in nonliterate societies as practitioners of essentially false medicine were embedded in a view of such human groups as being riddled with irrational thinking and perception and an overpowering dependence on magic; their members were said to possess, by Western standards, exceptionally high quotients of suggestibility. Although anthropology, and the subfield of medical anthropology, have begun radically to alter the transcultural perspective on such human activities, one may still find traces of these earlier views in the contemporary work of some medical anthropologists, physicians, and historians. Nevertheless, in recent times efforts have been made to refute the earlier concepts and to supplant them with a new appreciation for the cultural potentialities of preindustrial peoples, including the medical aspects of their lives and behavior. A critical feature in some of these studies is the key role of the healer.

The amount of ethnological attention to healers has been far greater than to their patients, as I noted in the preceding section. For the healer in these "exotic" societies was often himself or herself the most striking personage in the group. Even among those observers who derided the practices of healers, there was frequently great admiration for the knowledge and intellect (and for the "craftiness") of the individuals who occupied these statuses. Much of what I have to say here is exemplified in the accounts of healers in this section and in many of the other studies throughout this book. One point to be driven home at the outset is that contemporary observers of the statuses and roles of healers have been strongly impressed with the complexities both of the persons occupying these positions and of the degree of variation in the implementation of these roles. Clearly, the earlier accounts, although frequently rich in detail, were usually bent in the direction of a rather static, stereotyped delineation of the role(s) with scant margin for what we are now learning was great variability, both in the personalities of those individuals who became healers and in the ways in which each interpreted the statuses and roles he or she filled.

I shall attempt here to examine briefly some common concepts of healing roles, concentrating on the following dimensions: (1) generalization and specialization, (2) pathways to the healer's role, (3) the healer as sorcerer, (4) differentiation of the shaman's role, and (5) medical functions of the curer's role.

Anthropologists and others have conceptualized classically the role of the healer primarily as mediator between ordinary persons in their earthly environment and the spiritual world, attaining this position through special endowment, achievement, or spiritual selection (for example, Maddox 1923:22–71). The healer possesses special secret or semisecret knowledge, some of which may not even be shared with other healers. An archetypal concept for Maddox (in his pioneering book, *The Medicine Man*) and others (for example, Sigerist 1951; Stone 1932) is the American Indian notion of medicine as a very broad, complex belief including "... anything sacred, mysterious, or of wonderful power or efficacy ... clairvoyance, ecstasism, spiritism, divination, demonology, prophecy, necromancy, and all things incomprehensible .... the medicine man is not only the primitive doctor but he is the diviner, the rain-maker, the prophet, the priest, and in some instances, the chief or king. He is, in short, the great man of primitive times" (Maddox 1923:24–25). (The term *medicine man*, brought into the language by early European observers of American Indians, seems inappropriate, encompassing both too much and too little. For instance, the role of women as healers, largely obscured and possibly misinterpreted and distorted by male observers, is precluded by it [though Maddox (1923:72–90) does include a unique chapter titled "Medicine Women"]. As generics I have employed the terms *healer* or *curer* interchangeably in my remarks throughout this book, although there are connotative differences which need not be explicated here.)

The conceptualization implicit in Maddox's statement is that the curing roles of nonliterate and non-Western peoples tended to be highly generalized and usually were contrasted with the extreme degree of specialization in Western medicine. In fact, however, as Sigerist (1951:171ff) realized, specialization of healing roles is "by no means a phenomenon of late civilization but is frequently encountered among primitives." In many such communities there is often a variety of specialized healing roles, some of which are purely empirical and nonreligious in nature. In fact, in some of these societies, considering their crude level of technological capability, medical roles may seem overspecialized. Rivers (1927:43, 46), for example, notes much specialization of healing roles and treatment modalities in Melanesia, and Nurge (elsewhere in this volume) has described specialized healing roles in a fishing-agricultural village in Easten Leyte, Philippines. It is not yet clear to me whether medical role specialization is correlated in an absolutely linear fashion with technological and social structural complexity. What does seem apparent is that dependence solely on the general practitioner seems to be characteristic of hunting-gathering or foraging societies and some, but not all, horticultural societies. There does seem to be a growth in healing role diversification in herding and agricultural societies, and, of course, a profuse flowering into myriad specialties and subspecialties in industrial societies.

Recruitment into the healer's role may occur through one or more of a number of different means and pathways, greatly outnumbering those that are open to the Western scientific healer. Among these means and pathways are the following:

1. *Inheritance*: from parent to child or even within a hereditary priesthood.

2. *Selection by others*: by parents, relatives or other adults; by other healers; by tribal elders; by religious sodalities; by the spirits or gods.

3. *Self-selection*: by apprenticing oneself to a healer; by borrowing, buying, or stealing secret medical knowledge, rituals, and paraphernalia; by seeking entrance into a healing cult or guild; by study, observation, and practice, perhaps at first covertly for a long period before publicly declaring or being discovered as having

assumed the role (for example, some shamans in Zinacantan, Chiapas, Mexico [Fabrega and Silver 1973]).

4. *Undergoing a profound emotional experience*, involving symptoms that inspire awe and fear and signify spiritual power, and/or receiving a divine call through a dream, trance, or hallucination, sometimes induced through privation, torture, or drugs.

5. *Self-dedication to a healing cult*, having recovered from an illness to qualify for membership after a cult cure, as in American Indian medicine societies or African curing cults (see Turner 1964).

6. *Miraculous self-recovery* from a condition or experience that normally would kill or permanently disable, as recovery from being struck by lightning, being bitten by' a snake, falling off a precipice, or surviving a fatal disease or other lethal condition.

7. *Genetic, congenital, or acquired physical disability or deformity* such as various psychiatric symptoms, tics, epilepsy, blindness, misshapen face, body, limbs, or digits; a fixed penetrating stare or gaze.

8. *Exceptional personal traits* such as intelligence, emotional control to a high degree, proven judgment, musical or storytelling ability, or great courage in the face of attack or disaster.

One source of confusion to students of the healer's role is the often free interchange of the concepts of sorcerer and witch (see my discussion of this point in the introduction to Section VI.). This is particularly unfortunate not only because it is not always possible to know which phenomenon is being described but because it blocks a clear understanding of the role of the healer. In any case, some types of healers utilize sorcery. The result is that the power to cure or kill creates cognitive dissonance within the belief system of a society in the attitudes toward healer-sorcerers, and probably, though this is not well documented, in the attitude of the healer toward himself. Thus, some healers are sorcerers as well, and it is toward these that emotional ambivalence will be directed. Lieban's (1967) *Cebuano Sorcery* and Kiev's (1968) *Curanderismo* present two cases in point. Despite this ambivalence, it is my impression, yet to be empirically tested cross-culturally, that most healers tend to regard their power as a sacred trust and social obligation, and do not often resort to harmful magic. (See, for example, Hallowell 1942 and Handelman 1972.) Clearly the malign possibilities of sorcery are an ever-present suspicion in the minds of a people, and if their fears are stimulated too frequently they will not hesitate when pressed to punish, or even to execute an incorrigible healer-sorcerer. It should be emphasized that *some* healers, but not all, are sorcerers, and *some* sorcerers, but not all, are healers.

Another cause of confusion is the ambiguity surrounding the use of the concept of the shaman. As Loeb (1929) attempted to do, I would restrict the notion of shaman to describe only those healers, male or female, who receive their calling inspirationally from a divine source and are instructed directly in healing, divination, and prophecy by their spiritual contacts, frequently serving as the medium to communicate their utterances to the mundane world. Some writers loosely refer to inspirational and noninspirational shamans, but the latter, in my opinion, ought to be excluded from the concept.

Without at this time stepping too far into the often murky waters of debate in which the concept of shaman seems so often to be submerged, and without passing premature judgment by the application of such psychiatric labels as neurotic, psychotic, hysteric, schizophrenic, obsessive-compulsive, psychopathic, or epileptic to characterize the personality and behavior of shamans, I wish to offer this hypothesis: In some societies a deep emotional disturbance *may* be a characteristic of shamans and may even be a role requirement; in others, a shaman may undergo an intense emotional experience without having been, or becoming, emotionally disturbed; in yet other societies there may be a variety of personality types including *some* who may have undergone a neurosis or psychosis but used the process of becoming a shaman as a self-cure, and other shamans who never were even temporarily deranged (Edsman 1967; Eliade 1964). Murphy's (1964) significant finding among the St. Lawrence Eskimo is that a variety of personality types within the same society may enter the role of shaman but the critical factor is that shamans possess some exceptional quality to set them apart from the average community member. This special characteristic could be one or more psychiatric symptoms, a physical disability, a homosexual or transvestite bent, high intelligence, or something else. In any event, Murphy concluded that the St. Lawrence shamans were unusual persons, but whether or not they had a physical or mental disability, they all possessed a high degree of intelligence and of emotional control. Furthermore,

Psychiatric disorder was not necessarily a prerequisite for shamanism. The group of shamans that came to attention in the St. Lawrence study appeared to reflect the population as a whole in distribution of psychiatric symptoms. The well-known shamans were, if anything, exceptionally healthy in this sense (Murphy 1964:76).

These shamans tended to be outstanding persons, even leaders in the community, a point corroborated in the study by Murdock (1965) of a Tenino Indian shaman. The St. Lawrence Eskimo judged the proficiency of their shamans with such phrases as "really shaman," "sort of shaman," "partly shaman," and "foolish shaman," "...the last term being used for anyone considered a 'quack.'"

As Catherine Berndt (1964) shows, the combination of sorcery, healing, divination, and prophecy in the same person made for a potent social role, and the name for the healer-sorcerer in Western Arnhem Land, Australia, *margidbu*, glosses as "powerful man." In recent years, the tendency has been to slight the medical significance of the healer's role in favor of its sociological significance, particularly as an agent of conflict-resolution and a healer of social networks rather more than of ailing individuals as such.

Although welcoming these important analyses of the social structural role of the healer, it is an error to downplay the actual medical aspects of the role. For many cultures of the world where the curer's role has been seriously attenuated as a result of the impact of Western domination and the competitive advantages of the Western medical system (Landy 1974a), it is probably already too late to capture these precious cultural data. But for many other non-Western communities the healer's role shows amazing viability and adaptability in face of the Western challenge, as the studies in Section XIV testify.

Heretofore our information on the medical systems of nonliterate peoples has been mainly fragmentary because the focus of most ethnographers was on other parts of the cultural and social system, and ethnocentric bias tended to denigrate, overlook, and distort indigenous medical knowledge and practice. When the healer's role was acknowledged, the emphasis was on the magical rather than the medical features. In recent years some excellent studies have begun to emerge in which the focus has been placed upon the medical system and the healer's role. These studies have yielded a wealth of heretofore unsuspected and unrecorded data. The best of these studies have emphasized the medical as well as the religious and social functions of the healer's role, and what emerges is a picture of the healer and the medical system that we have seldom seen before. Occasionally, the research employs the skills of both an anthropologist and a physician, as in the study by Fabrega and Silver (1973) of the healers and healing systems of Zinacantan, Chiapas, Mexico.

(*Note*: Parts of the preceding have been adapted from Landy 1974b.)

418

# 47  The Exorcist in Burma

*Melford E. Spiro*

The folk Buddhism of Burmese religion recognizes four types of supernatural beings: ghosts, demons, witches, and *nats*, the latter a class of spirits that figure prominently in Burmese thought and beliefs and that use their great power to cause humans to suffer. Suffering of any kind, including illness, is caused by the ineluctable working out of one's *karma*, and such misfortunes originate in sinful desires. But as Melford Spiro shows in his fine study of Burmese supernaturalism from which this selection is taken, a more emotionally satisfying explanation is found not in the formal Buddhist creed but in the animistic folk beliefs that attribute illness to such supernaturals as witches and *nats*. The practitioners who operate as therapists in Burma are of many varieties. In this study Spiro concentrates mainly upon two, the exorcist and the shaman. We have selected Spiro's chapter on the former for inclusion here, although the reader will note that the exorcist is compared with the shaman along several dimensions.

The exorcist seems to cover a wide range of occupational positions tending mainly toward those of lower social status in the class system. The role is usually a part-time one combined with a full-time occupational role. In addition to many types of trades, a full-time medical practitioner or astrologer may also practice exorcism. Spiro examines the moral obligations of the exorcist-patient relationship as they revolve around the exorcist's responsibilities to the patient and vice-versa, as well as the exorcist's ethical obligations to other healing colleagues. The exorcist appears to enjoy a modicum of social prestige in direct proportion to his fame within the Buddhist context. Spiro makes a significant point regarding the exorcist's clientele: skepticism about a particular exorcist is directed toward the individual occupant of the status but not toward the role itself. (The reader may wish to compare this finding with the behavior of the skeptical shaman in Lévi-Strauss's essay in this section.) Unlike the shaman, the exorcist acquires power and competence not through spirit-possession but by apprenticing himself to a Buddhist master. Spiro concludes that the reward lies mainly in a measure of prestige and power, however momentary, so that "... this role serves as a compensatory mechanism for feelings of social and/or physical inferiority." For the full ethnographic and descriptive context of the medical and religious

Reprinted with abridgments from Melford E. Spiro, 1967, *Burmese Supernaturalism: A Study in the Explanation and Reduction of Suffering*, Englewood Cliffs, N.J.: Prentice-Hall, Inc., Chap. 13, "The Exorcist," pp. 230–245, with permission of the author. (Copyright © 1967 by Melford E. Spiro.)

system, the reader is referred to the study from which this selection has been taken and the more complete work, *Buddhism and Society* (Spiro 1970).

## DESCRIPTION OF THE ROLE

The Burmese call the supernatural practitioner with which this chapter is concerned an *ahtelan hsaya* ("Master of the Upper Path"). Among the many components which comprise the role-set of this practitioner, we are concerned here primarily with its exorcistic component. Among other things, the *ahtelan hsaya* possesses the power to expel harmful supernaturals from those whom they have possessed. Here, then, is a salient difference between the exorcist and the shaman. The shaman propitiates the harmful supernaturals, the exorcist (in principle, if not always in practice) controls them. The *ahtelan hsaya*, however, is not the only practitioner who possesses power to control harmful supernaturals. The same power is exercised by the *aulan hsaya* ("Master of the Lower Path"). The latter, it will be recalled, is a master witch who achieves his malevolent ends by compelling harmful spirits to execute his intentions.

Although this chapter is concerned with exorcistic power of the *ahtelan hsaya*, it should at least be noted that his power to control spirits is but one aspect of his more general power. Every *ahtelan hsaya* is a member of one of many quasi-Buddhist sects (*gaings*), all of which share the common aim of acquiring magico-religious power (Mendelson 1960, 1961a, 1961b, 1963a). In some instances it is religio-political power, to be attained through the restoration of the monarchy, which is sought. But in most instances what is sought is the power to become a *weikza*, the power, that is, to prolong life indefinitely, or at least until the arrival in 2,500 years of the future Buddha, Maitreya. Just prior to his arrival, the relics of the present Buddha, Gautama, will be recombined to form his physical body. By worshiping him, the *weikza* will automatically achieve nirvana. In the meantime, he has not only achieved a partial immortality, but he has acquired power to perform numerous supernatural feats.

The crucial means for becoming a *weikza* is through the practice of alchemy, and different sects specialize in different alchemic practices. The *ahtelan hsaya*, therefore, devotes much of his time and most of his economic resources to this occult practice. Although his *materia alchemica* may still be insufficiently powerful to enable him to become a *weikza*, they are yet powerful enough to combat harmful supernaturals. The *ins*, *datlouns*, and other objects used in the exorcistic seance are key ingredients of the *ahtelan hsaya*'s alchemic kit. Moreover, it is the power acquired from the alchemic (and other occult) practices of his sect, as well as the power derived from the *weikzas* associated with his sect, which, in part, permit him with impunity to have traffic with harmful supernaturals.

But his alchemic and occult practices are not the only source of his power. The *gaing* is a "quasi-Buddhist" sect, not only because one of its goals is the attainment of nirvana—and, in some instances of Buddha-hood—but because initiation into the sect requires a commitment to Buddhist discipline. The sect member must observe the moral precepts of Buddhism; he must practice Buddhist devotions; and he must engage in Buddhist meditation. These activities are not only the necessary—though not sufficient—means for the achievement of *weikza*-hood, but they are also a means for achieving control over harmful supernaturals. Through them he acquires the power which renders him less susceptible, if not immune, to attack from these malevolent beings. Moreover, by these activities he comes under the protection of the Buddhist "gods" (*devas*), and it is with their assistance that he is able to defeat the harmful supernaturals.

Exorcism, then, is but one of the occult powers which is acquired by membership in one of these sects. Not every sect member is an exorcist, but every exorcist is a member of, and acquires his power through membership in, a sect. Since only the exorcistic role of the *ahtelan hsaya* is relevant to our discussion of Burmese supernaturalism, I shall refer to him simply as an "exorcist."

Like the shaman, the exorcist is a part-time practitioner. Since, however, many exorcists are also traditional doctors (*hsei hsaya*), and since many combine both types of medical practice with astrology and other occult practices, it is possible that some urban exorcists are full-time practitioners. The city, whose population base provides a potentially large clientele, might well enable some exorcists who combine all of these therapeutic skills to devote full time to the practice of medicine and the occult. All the exorcists whom I know, however, both in rural and urban areas—even when they are also native doctors—are part-time specialists, deriving their main income from other occupations. These include, in my sample, an agricultural laborer, a canal guard, a night watchman, a truck driver, a police sergeant, and a Buddhist monk. In addition to these, I know two exorcists, both living in Mandalay, who, claiming to be *weikzas* as well as being claimants to the throne, are supported by the offerings of their followers.

Unlike the shaman, the exorcist, *qua* exorcist, does not participate in any cultus, nor is he an officiant of one. He may, *qua* animist, participate in the nat cultus; and he most certainly, *qua* Buddhist, participates in the Buddhist cultus. As an exorcist, however, he is exclusively devoted to the treatment of supernaturally caused illness and, particularly, of possession.

Although practiced as a part-time specialty, the exorcist role exhibits, if only in nascent form, most of the characteristics of professionalization. It not only requires specialized, achieved skills but it is also, in the words of contemporary role theory, functionally specific, affectively neutral, client-oriented, and universalistic. Since all but the last of these criteria have more or less the same meaning in any sociocultural context, it is only the latter, the universalistic, criterion which I should like briefly to discuss. This criterion, uniquely, raises certain moral dimensions of a professional relationship which can be culturally variable. Among these dimensions I should like to examine, through some simple examples, only four which arise in the exorcist-patient relationship.

The first dimension concerns the exorcist's responsibility for the patient. Here an unqualified rule is expected to govern the exorcist's behavior. Although an exorcist may refuse with impunity to treat a patient, once he has entered a case he must, unless he knows that he is inadequate to the task, see it through to completion. Let us take, as an example, the case of Kou Swe, the young man who was possessed by an *ouktazaun* spirit. After four hours of exorcism, it became apparent, to both the assembled group and the exorcist himself, that some dangerous forces had been unleashed which were too powerful for him to cope with; he was clearly frightened. Despite his fear, however, it was his professional duty to continue with the treatment, a duty which placed him in a painful dilemma. If he fulfilled his moral obligation and continued with the treatment, he would expose himself to serious physical danger. If, however, he discontinued the treatment on those grounds, he would lay himself open to the charge of unethical practice; and if he discontinued it on the grounds of inadequacy, he would be admitting his incompetence. Fortunately, his dilemma was resolved, and he was allowed to save face, when the headman and elders recommended that the most famous exorcist in the area be called into the case. With respect to the moral issue, theirs was a face-saving recommendation because it was not he, but they, the village authorities, who decided that he withdraw. Moreover, by recommending that a most distinguished exorcist be called in, his competence was not uniquely impugned; it was as if an ordinary physician in our society, faced with an especially vexatious case, were to turn for assistance to a famous specialist. (This attempted face-saving was not entirely successful. A few weeks later the exorcist informed me that he was forsaking exorcism—this, after I had heard a number of people suggest that he was, indeed, not very competent.)

A more serious example, in which an exorcist was in fact charged with unethical practice, arose in the case of Kou Aung, who was bewitched by his former wife. A few nights after an apparently successful exorcism, Kou Aung again became exceptionally violent, attacking even his friends and kinsmen with fists and knife. In great fear, his relatives invited his exorcist, who lived in another village, to resume his treatment. When they described the symptoms to the exorcist, it became quite obvious to me—I had driven them to his home—that he was as frightened as they. Saying that he could not resume his treatment unless the date were astrologically auspicious, he entered his house to consult his calendar. Emerging after a long delay, he reported that he could not accompany them to the patient's home because, according to his calendar, that day and the next were inauspicious; were he to treat the patient, both he and his patient would suffer serious trouble. He could, however, he hastened to add, return on the third day. In the meantime, he would give them some medicine which they could administer to the patient, and he would lend them his exorcist's wand by which they would be able to subdue the witch. Taking the medicine and the wand out of courtesy, Kou Aung's relatives returned to the car. As we drove away they all agreed that the exorcist's astrological explanation was a ruse, that by not accompanying them he had violated his professional duty. Regardless of the danger or inconvenience to him, the exorcist "must first of all have compassion (*myitta*) for the patient." Never again would they turn to him.

But the exorcist has still another responsibility to a patient. Just as he may not abandon a patient once he has begun the treatment, so—and this is the second rule—he may not commence treatment without permission of the patient or, if the latter is incompetent, of a responsible kinsman. Thus, in the case of Kou Swe, his exorcist, a close friend, could not treat him until he gave his consent. When a second exorcist was called into the case, he took no heed of Kou Swe's insistence that he did not wish to be treated by him—Kou Swe was in a state of great agitation and, hence, incompetent—but he would not proceed until he had first obtained permission from Kou Swe's wife. To treat a patient without permission would be laying oneself open to the charge of practicing the black arts, of being an *aulan hsaya* rather than, or in addition to, an *ahtelan hsaya*.

As the exorcist has a responsibility to the patient, the latter has a responsibility to the exorcist. Thus a third rule governing the exorcist-patient relationship is that a patient may not, in the course of treatment, seek a second exorcist without obtaining the permission of the first. And, as a corollary, there is still a fourth rule, one which governs the relationship between exorcists: one exorcist may not enter a case which has been, or is being, treated by another exorcist without the latter's consent. Thus, in the case of Kou Swe, it was necessary to obtain the permission of his first exorcist in order to bring in a second. And, when the latter arrived, he asked the former if he had his permission to enter the case. Similarly, in the case of Kou Aung, when his exorcist refused to treat him for three days, he made it clear that if this were not satisfactory, he would release the patient so that his relatives would be free to seek another therapist. When, in fact, they did obtain another, they immediately informed him that Kou Aung had been released by his former exorcist.

## RECRUITMENT TO THE ROLE

Not having conducted a systematic census of exorcists, I cannot say how prevalent they are, either within and among villages, or within and among regions. In the Yeigyi region, exorcists are to be found in some, but not in all villages, and in Yeigyi itself, a village of five hundred people, there are two. Although the average exorcist does not, *qua* citizen, enjoy exceptional prestige, neither does he suffer the mild contempt that is frequently the fate of the shaman. Moreover, there is less skepticism concerning his skills, for only half of those in Yeigyi who expressed skepticism about the power of shamans were skeptical of the power of exorcists. And there is also a greater demand for them—while only seven Yeigyi households (out of eighty-two) had used shamans, thirty-three had used exorcists.

Putting it more positively, it would not be inaccurate to state that the exorcist, *qua* exorcist—here, again, he differs from the typical shaman—enjoys the respect of his fellows. In the case of a famous exorcist, the respect is commensurately greater. This is not surprising when it is remembered that almost all the elements in his elaborate symbol system are Buddhist, and that with these symbols the exorcist has the ability to tap the great reservoirs of beneficent power contained in Buddhism. Symbolic of this respect is the obeisance which the patient, in the form of ritual prostration, offers him during the ceremony. In Burma, this is the highest possible form of respect.

This is not to say that all exorcists are viewed as powerful or that all are regarded as equally powerful; it is to say, however, that there is very little skepticism about the efficacy of the role. Thus, in the case of Kou Swe, although there developed considerable skepticism concerning the power of his first exorcist, skepticism of the man generated no skepticism concerning the role: instead of suggesting that some alternative technique be used to deal with the case, it was suggested, rather, that a more powerful exorcist be called in. Moreover, when an exorcist in whom people have faith meets with apparent failure, they are prepared to follow him in attributing the fault to some technical error in the performance of the role rather than to question its efficacy. Thus, when the *ouktazaun* returned to haunt Kou Swe only a few brief days after a second exorcist had conducted an apparently successful ceremony, the villagers agreed with the exorcist that the ceremony had not, after all, been entirely unsuccessful because, although the *ouktazaun* had returned, she was obviously afraid to enter Kou Swe's house. They also accepted as reasonable the exorcist's explanation for his partial failure, *viz.*, when he ordered her not to return, he neglected to include her subordinates in his injunction. (It was the latter who had returned on horseback to Kou Swe's house.) In his second attempt, he would—and, in fact, he did—forbid her subordinates, as well as the *ouktazaun* herself, to return.

It is fair to say, then, that whatever may be the impediments to recruitment to the exorcist's role, they do not consist of negative cultural evaluation, of skeptical attitudes, or of the absence of a clientele.

On the other hand, although not suffering from social or cultural disabilities, neither does the exorcist, *qua* citizen, enjoy any special prestige. The respectful attitude shown him while performing his professional role does not spill over into his nonprofessional life. Except for very famous exorcists, whose fame is a tribute not only to their exorcistic skills, but also to their general reputation as powerful *ahtelan hsayas*, the position of the exorcist in the prestige hierarchy of the village is unaffected by his professional role. Typically, as we shall see below, village exorcists are recruited from humble stations in the social structure, and their relatively low prestige—as day laborers, tenant farmers, and so on—is not enhanced by their practice of exorcism.

Although the exorcist, *qua* citizen, receives no special respect by virtue of his occult skills, he is nonetheless treated somewhat differently from his fellows. Since the power of the exorcist to control nats or witches is morally ambiguous—the same power that can be used to protect people from their harm can be used to compel them to harm people—one can never be entirely confident that an exorcist, appearing to be an *ahtelan hsaya*, is not really an *aulan hsaya*. And, indeed, at least some villagers believe that the two exorcists in Yeigyi practice both roles. Few people, therefore, would wish to insult an exorcist or to incur his anger. In general, it is deemed wise to be somewhat circumspect in his presence, to treat him with a certain amount of deference.

Although the ambiguity of magical power is conducive to a certain ambivalence toward the exorcist, none of the exorcists whom I know viewed this as a deterrent to their own recruitment to the role. Hence, unlike the shaman who is involuntarily recruited to her role by being "called" by a nat who has fallen in love with her, the exorcist enters his role entirely voluntarily. And, unlike the shaman, for whom spirit possession is a necessary qualification for role recruitment, the exorcist is recruited by studying as an apprentice at the feet of a Master.

At this point, unhappily, my data almost completely fail me; I know next to nothing about this apprenticeship. The following meager information must suffice. If the apprentice lives with his Master, he can acquire the necessary knowledge within six months; otherwise it may take many years. During his apprenticeship, he not only learns the techniques of exorcism, but he becomes subject to Buddhist discipline as well. He must practice meditation, recite and observe the Buddhist precepts, say his beads, and so on. At the same time, he acquires magical power by making and swallowing many *ins*, and by becoming tattooed (which, in effect, means covering parts of his body with *ins*). He is also instructed in the various taboos which as an exorcist he must observe. Among other things he may not eat beef; he may not eat food used either in a funeral or at a wedding feast, or which has been offered to the nats; he may not drink intoxicating liquor; he may not walk under a ladder or under a house in which a woman is in labor.

Upon satisfying his Master of his competence, the apprentice, before he is permitted to practice, must be able to answer the following questions in the affirmative and to swear that his answers are true. "Do you believe in the Buddha unconditionally? Are you willing to eat the food granted to you by the Buddha (i.e., will you remain content with whatever you may have)? Are you willing to go anywhere the Buddha may direct you? Can you remain anywhere the Buddha may send you?" If the recruit can truthfully answer these questions in the affirmative, all that remains before he can begin his practice is the ritual laying on of hands, by which the magical power of the Master is transferred to the apprentice. When this is completed, and with the acquisition of the exorcist's wand, the apprentice has become an exorcist.

## A MOTIVATIONAL EXPLANATION OF THE EXORCIST

Although the exorcist is remunerated for his work, typically the fee is too small and his practice too limited for economic considerations to play an important part in his recruitment motivation. There are, of course, exceptions to this generalization, and these exceptions, as in the case of affluent shamans, are found in urban areas. I know Buddhist monks who—or whose monasteries—have become wealthy through their exorcistic practice. I know, too, of at least one layman, a bus driver, whose monthly income from his practice is K300 (about $65), a substantial income in Burmese terms. In the typical rural case, however, the exorcist's income does not exceed a few kyat a month....

On the basis of my very limited sample, I would suggest that the two dominant motives for recruitment to the exorcist role are status anxiety and power. Almost without exception, the exorcists I have known were recruited from humble origins and from occupations yielding low incomes and little prestige. Many of them, moreover, suffer from some kind of physical disability; they tend to be very short or very ugly or partially lame or partially blind. It would seem, then, that this role serves as a compensatory mechanism for feelings of social and/or physical inferiority. To be sure, a lowly night watchman, although an exorcist, remains (as we have seen) a lowly night watchman. But in performing his professional role, he has his brief moment of glory. He may, as did the watchman whom I know, allude to his humble occupation even during an exorcistic ceremony—"I am not a Master, I am only a watchman"—but nevertheless it is he who continuously occupies stage front and center. Indeed, the allusion to his humble, nonceremonial status may be interpreted in two ways: on the one hand it betrays his status anxiety—"I am merely a humble person"—but on the other hand it reflects his momentary triumph—"although I am a mere watchman, it is I to whom you have come for assistance."

The exorcist's desire for esteem and admiration is satisfied not only during the ceremony, but also in its prelude and aftermath. When he talks, everyone listens; what he says is attended to with care; when he shares his esoteric knowledge—"There are six types of wishes, and each type, in turn, has eleven subtypes"—they are visibly impressed. Outside of this context, he may be nothing.

But power must surely be as strong as prestige in the exorcist's motivational system. From his normally humble position, the exorcist can seldom command; and if he commands, he is seldom obeyed. In the exorcistic ceremony, however, it is he who dominates the situation throughout. What he asks for, he is given; when he tells the patient to prostrate himself before him, it is done. And his power, unlike the power of even political authority, extends to the supernaturals as well. They too must obey him. When he orders them to leave the patient, they leave. It is little wonder, then, that the exorcist, *qua* exorcist, exhibits a manner, a flourish, and a confidence that is lacking in his role as cowherd, transplanter, or guard....

## A CULTURO-HISTORICAL EXPLANATION OF THE EXORCIST ROLE

### Historical Reconstruction of the Role

In attempting to elucidate the "meaning" of the exorcist role, viewed within the entire context of Burmese supernaturalism, we must note the curious fact that this role has apparently ("apparently," because our historical information is unsatisfactory) undergone, even within the brief span of the last one or two hundred years, some important changes.

Sangermano, one of the few early writers to describe Burmese exorcism, refers to the exorcist as a "physician," a neutral term which tells us nothing about his therapeutic technique. Sangermano does tell us, however, that in some cases the "physician" would invite a shaman to enter a case which he was treating. Bidding her to perform a ritual dance (a "devil dance"), she would become possessed by the nat who had victimized the patient, and, using her as a medium, the "physician" would then interrogate the nat....

Thus in this earlier period, in contrast to the contemporary scene, it was a shaman, rather than the patient, who served as the exorcist's medium.

Sir George Scott, writing about one hundred years later, gives two accounts of exorcism and the exorcist.

...In any event, the term, *ahtelan hsaya*, is found in neither of Scott's accounts. According to his later account, the exorcist achieved his aims by beating the supernatural (i.e., by beating the patient, whom the supernatural has possessed), by choking him with a rope, or by threatening to kill him. If none of these techniques was effective, the exorcist called upon a shaman who, by her dancing, induced the supernatural to leave the body of the patient and to enter her body. It was then that the exorcist questioned the supernatural in order to discover what might be done to appease him. Again, as in Sangermano's description, it was a shaman, rather than the patient, whom the exorcist used as his medium.

Turning to a description of healing ceremonies among tribal societies in Burma and in traditional Burmese Mon society, one might speculatively reconstruct three historical changes in Burmese exorcism. These putative changes consist in a shift from the importance of the shaman to the importance of the exorcist, and, with that, in a shift from practitioner-possession to patient-possession, and from an animistic emphasis to a Buddhist

emphasis. Let us first, however, look at these additional data.

Among certain of the hill tribes in Burma (those in the "northern division"), when illness is caused by spirit possession, a "spirit medium" is called upon to treat the patient....

Here then, it is a shaman, not an exorcist, who performs the ceremony; moreover, it is the shaman who goes into trance; and, finally, if the patient goes into trance, it is spontaneous, rather than deliberately induced by the practitioner.

Among the Talains (the Burmese Mon), the preferred treatment was for the patient himself, rather than the shaman (but at the instigation of the shaman, or "spirit doctor," as O'Riley designates her), to perform the "spirit dance." Only if the patient was too old or too sick did the shaman perform the dance. (For a marvelous description of this dance, see O'Riley 1850:594–95, 596–97.) Again, as in the case of Burmese tribal societies, it is a shaman rather than an exorcist who performs the ceremony, but, as in the case of contemporary Burmese exorcism, it is preferably the patient, rather than the practitioner, who becomes possessed.

On the basis of these data, one might offer the hypothesis that contemporary techniques of Burmese exorcism represent relatively recent innovations, and that the exorcist as we know him—the *ahtelan hsaya*—is a relatively recent phenomenon in the history of Burmese psychotherapy. Using some (but not all) Burmese tribal practice and Mon historical data to establish a historical baseline for a historical reconstruction, one might speculate that exorcism was initially practiced in Burma by female shamans. From the former, but only to some extent from the latter, data, it might be suggested that the therapeutic technique consisted in inducing the offending spirit to leave the patient and to possess the exorcist himself. If this is, in fact, a true baseline, then, on the basis of the meager historical evidence available to us at this time, it can be inferred that three significant changes have occurred in the historical development from shamanistic to exorcistic therapy. First, there has occurred a change in the sex of the therapist from female to male. Second, there has occurred a change in therapeutic technique—from a self-induced trance in, and thereby possession of, the therapist, to a therapist-induced trance in, and thereby possession of, the patient. Third, there has occurred a change in the cultural content and meaning of therapy—from expulsion of the offending spirit by the power of the therapist, to exorcism of the spirit by the power of "Buddhism."

Since shamanism continues to exist—although the shamans have been stripped of their former exorcistic function—it would seem that the roles of shaman and exorcist represent parallel historical developments. That is, although the exorcist appears to be a later development than the shaman, it seems that rather than evolving from the shaman, he, instead, superseded the shaman. It is also clear from eighteenth-century Mon data, as well as from nineteenth-century Burmese data, that this supersedence was gradual rather than sudden, and that the consequent changes in therapy—from female to male therapist, and from therapist possession to patient possession—did not occur simultaneously. Thus, in the case of the Mons, although exorcism was conducted by a female shaman, preferred practice was to have the patient rather than the therapist become possessed. In the case of the Burmese, even after the male exorcist superseded the female shaman therapeutic practice, in difficult cases at least, consisted in the exorcist's inducing the offending spirit to possess a shaman of his (the exorcist's) choosing. But whatever the details of the historical sequence may have been, the following broad trend may be suggested: originally the function of the (female) shaman, the treatment of supernatural possession has become the exclusive monopoly of the (male) exorcist.

If, in cultural terms, the ascendance of the exorcist over the shaman represents, as I think it does, the triumph of magical Buddhism over magical animism, in therapeutic terms it represents the triumph of verbal over ecstatic, and of patient-centered over practitioner-centered therapy. It is not at all clear, however, why these different therapeutic roles could not have existed side by side. In Ceylon (like Burma, a Theravada society) both types of therapists, the shaman and the exorcist, exist side by side (Pieris 1953:115–116).

## Cultural Status of the Role

Although the above reconstruction of the historical relationship between the shaman and the exorcist, being highly speculative, is open to many questions, there is little question about the contemporary cultural relationship between these two roles. The cultural features which characterize the exorcist as a type are readily distinguishable from those which characterize the shaman as a type, and these distinguishable features offer some important insights into the cultural status of the

exorcist, especially within the context of a Buddhist culture.

In a series of very important papers, Mendelson (1960; 1961a; 1961b) has suggested that the quasi-Buddhist Burmese sects (*gaings*) to which all exorcists belong represent an interstitial magico-religious area which both separates animism from Buddhism and, at the same time, bridges the gap between them. Following on Mendelson's thesis, I would suggest that the exorcist, who as we have seen learns his role in the process of acquiring membership in one of these sects, is an exemplification of his thesis. Just as the belief system of the sect bridges the gap between animism and Buddhism, so the exorcist, whose therapeutic role, it will be recalled, is but one component of the role-set of the *ahtelan hsaya*, is the cultural mediator who bridges the gap between the animistic practitioner (the shaman) and the Buddhist practitioner (the monk). Indeed, speculating somewhat beyond the available data, it might be suggested that the exorcist, standing between the shaman and the monk, represents those Hindu-Mahayanist elements which, even today, continue to inform much of the (Theravada) Buddhism of Burma.

Let us turn, then, to those cultural differences between the shaman and exorcist which, in their configuration, serve to distinguish these two magico-religious types. These differences include their relationship to, and their method of interacting with, the nats, the *devas*, and Buddhism.

*Relationship to the Nats.* For the shaman, nats are powerful beings whose power, with respect to human beings, is ambiguous. On the one hand, the nats can be solicited for various kinds of human benefits; the shaman officiates in a cult, both private and collective, which invokes their assistance. On the other hand, the nats may also harm human beings, and their malevolent power cannot be countered; one can only acquiesce in it. Hence, the shaman performs propitiatory rituals which, rather than combating their power, attempt to induce the nats to remove their harm.

The exorcist, like the Buddhist monk, seldom seeks the assistance of the nats. Unlike the monk, however, who is prohibited from any traffic with nats, the exorcist interacts with the nats, without, however, acquiescing in their power or attempting to propitiate them. Instead, he engages them in combat, attempting not only to remove their harm, but also, unlike the shaman, to drive them away or to exorcise them. And this latter feat he accomplishes by the use of Buddhist power. Here, then, one clearly sees the interstitial position of the exorcist. Like the shaman he recognizes the power of the nats, but like the monk he does not invoke it. Like the monk, too, he recognizes the superior power of Buddhism, but unlike the monk he utilizes this power to counter the nats (Scott and Hardiman 1900: V.1)

It should be added, of course, that the shaman, having no access to power other than that afforded by animism, has no choice but to acquiesce in the power of the nats. The exorcist, in whose role a variety of historical traditions intersect, has access to many different sources of power. This was dramatically symbolized in the example of the exorcist who, arriving for an exorcistic sèance, was dressed in white to symbolize both his strict observance of the Buddhist precepts and, implicitly, the power of these precepts. Strapped to his side—he was a police sergeant—was a police revolver, symbolizing the power of the state. In one hand he held his exorcist's wand, which contains occult power, while with the other he fingered his rosary, which contained Buddhist-derived power. Armed with these different kinds of power, he then proceeded to invoke still another source of power, that of the Hindu-derived *devas*, in order to do battle with the evil nat.

*Method of Interacting with Nats.* Although both shaman and exorcist are specialists in dealing with troubles caused by nats—the former by acquiescing in their power, the latter by combatting it—their ritual methods of interacting with nats are quite different. The shaman, concerned to know the reasons for an offending nat's anger, asks her nat spouse to possess her, and while she is in a trance state, she serves as his medium. The exorcist, wishing to speak with an offending nat, asks him to possess the patient, who, while in a trance state, serves as the nat's medium. Employing Loeb's (1929) distinction, it may be said that the shaman is a person *through* whom the nats speak, while the exorcist is one *with* whom they speak. Although differing, then, from the Buddhist monk, who does not engage in any traffic with nats, the exorcist differs from the shaman, as well, by eschewing a shamanistic (ecstatic) technique, and by adopting a Buddhist (verbal) technique in his interaction with the nats.

*Relationship to the* Devas. In addition to the power he acquires through Buddhist magic, the exorcist most importantly attempts to acquire the assistance of the benevolent Buddhist supernaturals, or *devas*. Although all *devas* enjoy their present celestial bliss by virtue of good karma acquired in former existences, Buddhists, it will be recalled, distinguish between a large class of unnamed and undifferentiated *devas* who do not interact with the human world, and a small class of named, individualized *devas* who render assistance to human beings. The latter class comprises the gods of the Hindu pantheon—which the Buddhists can and do identify as Hindu gods, and it is the *devas* of this class who, by name, are invoked by the exorcist. Just as it is true that these *devas*, having been incorporated into the Buddhist cosmological system, are part of Buddhism, so it is also true that to ritually invoke their aid clearly reflects a Hindu, rather than a Buddhist, conception and practice. Nevertheless, since on the one hand, the shaman, as an animistic practitioner, recognizes neither Buddhism nor its Hindu-derived elements, and since, on the other hand, the exorcist believes that by invoking the *devas* he is invoking Buddhist power, the exorcist again occupies an interstitial, essentially Hindu, position between animism and Buddhism.

*Relationship to Buddhism.* Here the difference between the two roles is clear-cut. The exorcist qualifies for and practices his role as a devout Buddhist. He must not only practice Buddhist precepts in his daily life—should he violate them, the *devas* will not render their assistance—but the content and symbolism of the exorcistic ceremony, as we have already seen, are almost exclusively Buddhist. The recitation of the Buddhist precepts, the Buddhist rituals of the dissemination of love and of the sharing of merit, the worship of the Buddha, and so on, constitute the core of the ceremony. None of this holds for the shaman. Shamanistic performances are devoid of Buddhist content or of Buddhist symbolism; they are exclusively animistic. Indeed, the shamanistic performance is not only devoid of Buddhist elements, but the shaman and her performance alike may violate important Buddhist precepts. Thus, the consumption of liquor is a prevalent feature of shamanistic performances, and the sexual "immorality" of shamans is common gossip. In short, whether in the performance of her role or in her personal life, the shaman violates or is believed to violate, two of the five Buddhist precepts.

Here, as in the first three features by which the exorcist is distinguished from the shaman, the role of the exorcist in mediating the difference between animism and Buddhism is salient. As a salvation religion, Buddhism is exclusively concerned with otherworldly goals. All Buddhist discipline—

morality, meditation, and ritual—has as its aim the attainment of nirvana; and, in normative terms, the Buddhist monk practices this discipline exclusively for the attainment of this otherworldly goal. Like the monk, the exorcist, too, practices Buddhist discipline, but his aim—unlike the monk's, but identical with the shaman's—is the attainment of this-worldly rather than otherworldly goals. Hence, in combining the goals of animism with the discipline of Buddhism, the exorcist again exemplifies his interstitial position between these two traditions. In using Buddhist rather than animist means for the attainment of his goals, he asserts the primacy of Buddhist over animist power. At the same time, since his goals are those of animism, he subverts the essence of these Buddhist means by converting them from religious discipline into magical technology.

On all these dimensions, then, the exorcist stands midway between the shaman and the monk. Neither sacred nor profane, he is rather sacred *and* profane; neither this-worldly nor otherworldly, he is both this-worldly *and* otherworldly; neither Apollonian nor Dionysian, he is both Apollonian *and* Dionysian. In short, by incorporating both animist and Buddhist elements within one role, the exorcist has become the cultural mediator between the polar cultural traditions of Buddhism and animism. As a mediator one might suggest that he has been an important factor in maintaining their polarity. For just as the public nat cultus may have served to protect the integrity of Buddhist worship from the incursions of Tantric elements, so the exorcist may serve to protect the integrity of the Buddhist monk from the incursions of shamanistic practices.

# 48 The Development of a Washo Shaman

## *Don Handelman*

There are some detailed, documented accounts of the life careers of healers in ethnographic literature. Most often, even those careers that are rather well and fully described seem essentially to provide

Reprinted with abridgments from Don Handelman, 1967, "The Development of a Washo Shaman," *Ethnology*, 6:444–464, with permission of the author and *Ethnology: An International Journal of Cultural and Social Anthropology*.

descriptive life-history materials. Though these are of some use in the archives of ethnographic data, they are limited in their usefulness by lack of inferences or implications drawn by the ethnographers. In other words, a theoretical perspective is absent. This study by Don Handelman of the career of a Washo Indian healer named Henry Rupert is unique in many respects, for not only is the documentation rich and full (much had to be omitted here) but as the biography unfolds the author draws implications, large and small, of their meanings, both empirically and theoretically. In addition, and in contrast to Romano's study of a Mexican healer (1965), we find that this Indian shaman is an innovator, a potential cultural broker, as Handelman suggests. Indeed, far from being a cultural conservative, although he draws freely on traditional ritual and knowledge, Henry Rupert easily, even enthusiastically, maintains himself open to new ideas, whatever their provenience. Thus, in his career Rupert embraces a number of new spirit-helpers and curing techniques that come from other cultures and uses them to his own advantage, and even in advanced age does not hesitate to cast aside traditional methods he had been using for half a century.

As Handelman demonstrates, though Rupert takes dreams and visions quite seriously, he is neither neurotic nor psychotic, as some theories of shamanism insist. Rupert rejects sorcery and witchcraft, or at least their antisocial aspects (Handelman 1972). And not only has Rupert traveled far and wide seeking new knowledge, but, as the author notes here, and more fully in another paper (1967), his practice is not confined to his own people but extends to a variety of ethnic categories beyond the boundaries of his culture. Handelman's biography may be compared with such studies as John Gillin's (1956), "The Making of a Witch-Doctor," and with those by Edgerton in this section and by Romano (1965) which I describe in the introduction to Press' "The Urban Curandero" (Chapter 51).

This paper presents the life history of the last shaman among the Washo Indians of western Nevada and eastern California. This man, Henry Rupert, presents us with a unique case of the development of a shamanic world view through time. More specifically, he offers us an opportunity to examine the shaman as an innovator and potential innovator, especially with respect to the curing techniques and personal ideology relating him to the supernatural, the natural environment, and other men. While the anthropological literature is replete with descriptions of shamanic rituals and cultural configurations of shamanism in particular societies, as well as functional explanations purporting to explain the existence of shamanic institutions, little attention has been paid to the shaman as an innovator, although the idea was presented by Nadel (1946), exemplified by Voget (1950) in a somewhat different religious context, and briefly touched upon by Murphy (1964:77). Henry Rupert exemplifies the shaman as a creative innovator and potential "cultural broker," and his life history will be presented as an essentially chronological sequence of events, situations, and ideas.

In the period before White contact, the Washo occupied territory between Lake Tahoe, on the border of present-day California and Nevada, and the Pine Nut Mountains east of Reno and Carson City; in the north their territory extended to Honey Lake, and in the south to Antelope Valley (Merriam and d'Azevedo 1957; Downs 1963:117). In terms of social organization, the Washo were composed of three bands, although the family, sometimes nuclear and sometimes extended, was the primary unit of social organization; and the family unit decided the yearly round of hunting and gathering activities, sometimes under the leadership of antelope shamans and rabbit "bosses." A high prevalence of witches and sorcerers has also been reported among the aboriginal Washo (Leis 1963; Siskin 1941) in much the same configuration as has been reported for the neighboring Northern Paiute (Park 1939; Whiting 1950), with all shamans suspect as potential sorcerers. With increasing White occupation of their territory during the late nineteenth century, their seasonal round was disrupted, and the Washo settled around White habitations and ranches, working as seasonal laborers, ranch hands, lumberjacks, and domestic servants. It was into this disrupted cultural milieu, and disorganized social situation, that Henry Rupert was born.

## THE BECOMING AND BEING OF A SHAMAN

Henry Rupert was born in 1885, the son of Pete Duncan and Susie John, both Washo, in Genoa, Nevada. Genoa was an area of lush farm and ranch land amidst the arid Nevada semi-desert which had been first settled by Mormon emigrants from Utah. In the shadows of Job's Peak, a 9,000-foot mountain in the Sierra Nevada range, the Mormons had farmed the desert and transformed it into the rich grassland it still is today. When Henry Rupert was still very young, about two to three years old, his father deserted the family. Henry did

not meet his father again until he was twenty years old and his father, a complete stranger, was working as a handyman in a Chinese restaurant in Carson City. By this time Pete Duncan had remarried; and father and son remained strangers until Pete Duncan died.

Henry's mother, Susie John, worked as a domestic servant for a ranch in Genoa. Most of her time was taken up with her domestic chores, and Annie Rube, Henry's older sister, organized and managed the family household and acted as the family disciplinarian. Her husband, Charley Rube, worked as a ranch hand and fisherman, but he was also an antelope shaman, a man who in aboriginal times was entrusted with the task of "singing" antelope to sleep during the annual Washo antelope drives. Near the encampment of Henry Rupert's family lived Henry's mother's sister's husband, Welewkushkush, and his wife. Until the age of eight, when he was taken to school, Henry divided most of his time between Genoa during the winter and the shores of Lake Tahoe during the summer, usually in the company of either Charley Rube or Welewkushkush.

During his early years, Henry had a series of dreams which he still remembers with clarity, and which probably marked him early as having shamanic and mystic potential. As he describes the situation, he would go to sleep on the ground inside the family lean-to and dream of a bear who came and stood in the lean-to opening and stared at him. When he looked at the bear, it would vanish, and then Henry would fly up into the sky toward the moon. This dream recurred frequently over a fairly long period. As a youngster, Henry was also subject to spells of dizziness and fainting. These spells also occurred at bedtime, and both the lean-to and ground would whirl around in a circular motion. Henry would then tell his family to go outside the lean-to and build large fires to stop the ground from whirling about. However, no one paid any attention to his demands, and after awhile he would recover.

Welewkushkush, a well-known shaman among the Washo, was already between 60 and 70 years old when Henry was born, and on a number of occasions Henry was able to watch him healing. During one of these curing sessions, Henry observed Welewkushkush dance in a lean-to fire barefoot and emerge unscathed. Not surprisingly, the youngster respected his uncle greatly both for his curing feats and for his generous kindly attitude and demeanor toward his patients, relatives, and acquaintances. Henry maintains that he harbored similar feelings of respect toward his brother-in-law, Charley Rube, and that the same general attitudes prevailed in his family relationships. He was never severely disciplined at any time, and only his sister, Annie Rube, scolded him. Nevertheless, even within this milieu, Henry exhibited strong feelings of hostility and aggression, as well as independence. . . .

During these early years Henry had few friends. He spent much time by himself wandering over desert and mountain for days at a time, living off the land when he could, and going hungry when he could not. Given the laissez-faire attitude within his family, he had to report to no one, nor did he even have to be home at regular intervals. While not self-sufficient, he was able and independent. On one occasion, he "hopped" a freight train to Sacramento to see what lay on the other side of the Sierra Nevada Mountains. He also exhibited a boundless curiosity about the natural world around him, a world filled with strange forces and beings, and their existence was often manifested to him. He still remembers sleeping in an abandoned campsite one night and seeing a object which resembled a cloud pass close by his body while he was awake, and wondering what it represented. On another occasion, while walking down a deserted path at dusk he saw a white object ahead of him. As he walked forward, it moved. When he stopped, the object also halted. He began to sweat heavily and was extremely frightened. Finally he gathered his courage, walked up to the object, and found an old night shirt flapping in the evening breeze. Yet he wondered that the object flapped only when he walked forward, and stopped when he desisted. Such incidents were not simple coincidences; they suggested an importance and significance that he was not yet able to unravel.

In 1892, at the age of seven, Henry received the first conscious intimation of what his future powers might be. A relative of his mother died; his mother was deep in mourning and quite despondent. Henry dreamt of the event which would follow, and the event came to pass during that winter. His mother went from the family encampment to a slue on the frozen Carson River, and there she attempted suicide by trying to break through the ice and drown herself. But the ice was too thick, and her attempt failed. This was the first time that Henry began to feel that he too might be gifted in the manner of his beloved uncle, Welewkushkush.

Without becoming unduly analytic at this point, it is pertinent to indicate that during these first eight years of Henry Rupert's life many of the elements which resulted in his becoming a shaman were present. During these early years Henry was a Washo, but a Washo who camped on the fringes of the dominant White society upon whom his mother depended for her livelihood. He spoke no English, only Washo; his mother worked as a menial, a domestic servant; and his father had forever deserted the family encampment. There is little doubt that these factors engendered much hostility in Henry. Yet, because of the great degree of freedom allowed him, much of this hostility was dissipated in his extensive and lengthy wanderings, which at times almost take on the attributes of a rudimentary vision quest. As a child of a culturally disrupted and socially disorganized Indian group, he differed little from many other Indian children in the area, but even at this early age his dreams, visions, and fantasy world were beginning to coalesce around the conception that he might have unusual abilities. Also, he had no peers with whom to identify. His models of socialization and learning were much older and more important; they included a shaman and an antelope shaman, both very well versed in Washo lore and tradition. Both of these men, and in fact his whole family, presented him with models of behavior based on kindness and sympathy, and to a lesser extent understanding. The aforementioned incident involving the puppy was apparently the one occasion that Henry's hostility was expressed within the family milieu, and even here it was met with sympathy. Up to the present time, Henry Rupert exhibits strong loyalties and deep affection toward his immediate family, their children, and grandchildren. . . .

Some ten miles north of Genoa and two miles south of Carson City is the Stewart Indian School. Today it is a boarding school primarily for Indian children from the Southwest, but in 1893 it was a center for the "forced acculturation" of Indian children from the Great Basin under the supervision and control of the United States Army. As part of its pacification program in the area, the Army required all Indian children to attend and board at Stewart until they had completed the equivalent of an eighth grade education. Children held back by their parents were forcibly removed from their families by the cavalry. At the age of eight, Henry Rupert was taken from Genoa to Stewart, where he lived until the age of 18. It was here that he received the "power dream" which marked him as a potential shaman; here, too, he met his future wife, and here he began to formulate the basis of his philosophy of healing and his rationale for becoming a shaman, both of which were to be greatly expanded in later life.

At Stewart Henry experienced an environment vastly different from that of his years of freedom and independence. Stewart was highly regimented and often brutal. This was Henry Rupert's first sustained contact with White society. Discipline was harsh, and every effort was made at forced acculturation. Order was maintained with a rawhide whip and detention cells. Children were not allowed to return home for short respites until they had completed three full years at Stewart. Classes were held in the mornings and in the evenings. In the afternoons the children were taught a trade. If a child was late for meals, he did not eat. Here also, Henry was introduced to White religion through a profusion of Catholic, Baptist, Methodist, and Anglican proselytizers. All the children were forcibly baptized. Every morning, before breakfast, the children attended services. At breakfast, prayers were sung in Latin. On Sundays the children went to church in the morning, and in the evening they attended Bible classes and sang hymns. Some proselytizers even came on Saturdays and preached all afternoon.

The day after Henry arrived he ran away, but he was quickly returned. All told he ran away three times. The second time he was severely whipped on his bare back. However, Henry did well in school, and learned to set newspaper type. He found a friend in the school cook, who often gave him extra food to supplement the bare school rations. He also developed his own techniques for maintaining some symbolic degree of independence.... One of Henry's strongest assets was his ability to absorb selectively those aspects of White culture which he felt were beneficial to him; thus he was able to master academic subjects, notably reading and writing, and learn an occupation, while resisting Christianity, regimentation, and alcohol.

In 1902, at the age of seventeen, Henry experienced his power dream, the event which marked him with certainty as shamanic material and which conferred certain abilities upon him. He described it to me as follows:

I was sleeping in the school dormitory. I had a dream. I saw a buck in the west. It was a horned buck. It looked east. A voice said to me: "Don't kill my babies any more." I woke up, and it was raining outside, and I had a nosebleed in bed.

Henry interpreted the dream in the following way. The conjunction of buck and rain suggested that he could control the weather, since the buck was the "boss of the rain." The buck was standing in the west, but looking east. The Washo believed that the souls of the recently dead travel south but that, soon after, the souls of those who have been evil turn east. The buck looking east was interpreted as a warning against developing certain potentialities which could become evil. The voice in the dream was that of a snake warning against the indiscriminate taking of life; previously Henry had killed wildlife, insects, and snakes without much concern. The rain, as he awakened, indicated that his major spirit power would be water. Awakening with a nosebleed placed the stamp of legitimacy upon the whole experience, since the Washo believed that this kind of physical reaction is necessary if the dream is to confer power. The fact that his spirit power was to be water was unusual, since most Washo shamans had animate rather than inanimate objects as their spirit helpers. Thus, while water baby was a fairly common spirit helper, water was not. In addition, weather control was highly unusual among the Washo, being more prevalent among both the Northern Paiute and the Shoshone.

The dream stressed certain potentials, specifically a Washo calling, that of shaman. It also confirmed the validity of Henry's early behavioral models, Welewkushkush and Charley Rube, and their philosophy in living in harmony with the natural world. In so doing, it de-emphasized those aspects of White society and culture which contradicted Washo values and behavioral expectations, but it did not forbid Henry the continuation of his quest for knowledge in the White world. Rather, it suggested that he pick and choose his way in relation to earlier models, thus serving as both a warning and a promise of greatness. That it was a power dream was congruent with Henry's aspirations and expectations concerning himself and his future.

At this transition point in Henry's life, shortly before he left the Stewart School, the dream served as a guidepost which integrated both his childhood years and his years at the school. His indecisions regarding the future were resolved, and his aspirations of becoming a shaman were crystallized. But his ideology of healing remained inchoate, for he had not yet acquired the requisite shamanic techniques. He felt the need to help his people when they were ill, but he knew not how. Nevertheless, he was aware and insightful, and in learning through what he called the "law of nature" he set the stage for years of thought and introspection, aware also that discoveries came slowly: "One little thing may come every eight or ten years; you can't grab it in one bunch."

When Henry graduated from Stewart, he took a job as a typesetter with the Reno Evening Gazette, and he lived in Reno for most of the next ten years. During this period he mastered hypnotic techniques and began curing. But the most immediate power conferred on him by his power dream was control of the weather, and in 1906 he exercised this power for the first time. During that summer, Henry went to visit his family in Genoa. While there, he used to hang his pocket watch over his bed. One evening, before retiring, he had a vision in which snow slowly, but completely, covered the face of the watch. That winter the snowfall was very heavy and too deep to enable him to cut firewood. One day, Henry concentrated on removing the snow. That night and all the next day it rained, resulting in fairly widespread flooding. Although he told no one of what he had done, his older sister, Annie Rube, accused him of causing the floods.

In the winter of 1908 he once again called down the rain, but in doing so he lost this power forever. The winter was again difficult, and one day he constructed a medicine bundle, and dropped it into the Truckee River, which flows through Reno. That evening the weather turned warm and it rained. However, in tying his medicine bundle, Henry used the buckskin from his shamanic rattle and replaced the buckskin on the rattle with a length of thread. This offended the spirit of the buck, the "boss of the rain," and Henry was never again able to control the weather. . . .

In 1907, Welewkushkush suggested that Henry hire another shaman to help him train and control his powers. The Washo believed that when the power, or spirit helper, first comes to a shaman he becomes ill, and that the novice shaman then hires an older experienced shaman to teach him how to extrude and control the intrusive spirit-power. Although Henry had experienced only a nosebleed in 1902 and did not consider this as a "sickness," he followed his uncle's advice and hired the well-known Washo shaman Beleliwe, also known as Monkey Peter. The experienced shaman could also help the novice to renounce his power, if such was the latter's desire. I do not know what the customary period of time was between the power dream and the hiring of another shaman to control the power, but in Henry's case some five years elapsed.

Beleliwe, instead of giving Henry specific advice, told him what he could accomplish with his power.

He spoke of the two old women who had first brought the power of healing to the Washo, and he warned that the power of blood is evil. He also described some of the feats which shamans could accomplish, citing the cases of an old woman who had walked up the perpendicular side of a cliff, of Welewkushkush who had walked under the waters of Lake Tahoe without drowning, and of Southern Washo who danced in campfires. Then he told Henry: "All kinds of sickness will look pretty tough, but it will melt; it seems like you can't do anything with it, but it will melt." However, the actual content of the shamanic ritual had to be learned by observing other shamans at work. Significantly, Henry's attitudes toward Beleliwe were very similar to his attitudes toward Welewkushkush—respect and admiration for both their personal attributes and their work. He told me, "Beleliwe was a great man; he knew more than the rest put together." While Henry's feelings toward Welewkushkush changed somewhat during the next few years, Beleliwe's stature continued to grow. And when Lowie visited the Washo in 1926, Henry not only wished him to meet Beleliwe, but referred to him as a philosopher (Lowie 1939; 321).

Henry performed his first successful cure in 1907. A brother of Frank Rivers had died of alcohol poisoning. His mother was deeply grieved and became very depressed. A White doctor was called in but was unable to calm the woman. A few days later Henry, as he was passing by, heard the old woman crying. He went in, washed her face, and prayed for her. She recovered. It is significant that this first cure was performed on the mother of his best friend—within a milieu where his confidence would be bolstered. It is also significant that Henry's family, with the exception of Welewkushkush, knew nothing of his shamanic power or his achievements with weather control until after this first cure. His reticence is an example of the self-doubt that always plagued him—doubt in his abilities and fear that he would not find the answers his curiosity demanded—but which drove him to greater efforts.

In his first cure, Henry used techniques generally similar to those utilized by other Washo shamans. Traditional Washo curing rituals required a shaman to work for three consecutive nights from dusk to midnight, and a fourth night until dawn. In the course of the ritual, repeated every night, Henry used tobacco, water, a rattle, a whistle, and eagle feathers. He began by smoking, praying, washing the patient's face with cold water, and sprinkling all his paraphernalia with cold water. He then blew smoke on the patient and prayed to come in contact with water. A peace offering followed, in which he paid for the health of the patient by scattering grey and yellow seeds mixed with pieces of abalone shell around the body of the patient; the seeds symbolized food, and the shells symbolized money. Next he chanted, prayed, and again blew smoke on the patient and sprinkled his paraphernalia with cold water. Arising, he walked about blowing his whistle, attempting to attract the disease object or germ from the body of the patient and into his own body, whence it might be repulsed and captured by the whistle. Then he sat down again and blew a fine spray of cold water over the body of the patient. This ended the first half of the curing ritual, which was repeated each night.

At some time during the course of the ritual, Henry would receive visions relating both to the cause of the illness and the prognosis. They usually involved either the presence or absence of water. Thus a vision of damp ground suggested that the patient was ill but would live a short while; muddy water suggested that the patient would live but would not recover completely; ice suggested that Henry must break through the ice and find water; burning sagebrush suggested that the patient would die quickly unless Henry could stamp out the fire. Over the four-night period the content of these visions, or occasionally dreams, tended to change. Thus, Henry might see a fire or a burned-over hillside on the first night, damp ground on the second, muddy water on the third, and on the fourth night a stream of clear, cold water or the Pacific Ocean rolling over the Sierra Nevada. The portent of the vision of the fourth night overrode those of the visions seen on the previous nights.

During 1907–08, Henry Rupert acquired his second spirit helper, a young Hindu male. He used, at infrequent intervals, to visit a high school in Carson City which contained the skeleton of a Hindu, and on one of these visits the spirit of the Hindu "got on" Henry. Since the Hindu was a "White power," this precipitated a major conflict in Henry's fantasy world and in the most important area of his life, his healing. As a spirit helper, the Hindu demanded to be used in curing sessions. Henry's problem was how to reconcile the opposing demands of his Indian and Hindu spirit helpers. The confrontation and its resolution came in a dream:

I saw this in a dream. The Hindu's work says: "You will do great things if you make us the leader in this kind of work." The two Indian women say no: "We started this

with Henry Rupert; we were the first. He (the Hindu) has no right here; this work belongs to us." I didn't know what to make of it. I pondered on it for a long time. Finally I decided, and I told them what I decided: "We all do the same work; let's help each other and be partners." And that is the way it works today; nobody is the leader. The Hindu wanted to be the leader in this kind of work. The two women said no. I fixed it.

This dream dramatically illustrates the basic conflict between opposing themes in Henry Rupert's life: his desire to expand his potentials for learning and healing by utilizing non-Indian resources and his desire to follow the childhood models he loved and respected. His resolution of this conflict was highly sophisticated; he utilized a more complex level of conceptualization and synthesis in which both opposing themes were subsumed under a common rubric, that of healing, which applied to both categories of spirit helpers. This rubric was neither Washo nor "White" but constituted an ethic which cross-cut different ethnic and racial categories. I prefer the term "ethic" to "principle" because the synthesis had definite moral connotations of aiding and succouring others, and because to Henry the fact that he had become a healer was more important than either his being born a Washo or his forays into non-Indian knowledge. It was the Hindu who first gave Henry his insights into the components of the "law of nature" and offered him the code of living which has since followed: to be honest, discreet, and faithful; to be kind and do no harm. These conceptions often ran counter to the behavior of traditional Washo shamans, but they were consistent with the models of Welewkushkush, Charley Rube, and Beleliwe. The ethic of healing which Henry developed was an integrated and complete synthesis; he was never troubled again by this kind of acculturative conflict.

After Henry acquired the Hindu spirit helper a number of changes occurred in his curing techniques—the first of his innovations of which I am aware. Before beginning a cure, he would now place a handkerchief on his head to represent the Hindu's turban, and when he blew water on the patient he prayed to the Hindu to come and rid the patient of his illness. He also began to place his hands on the patient's head, chest, and legs in a symbolic attempt to encompass the whole being of the patient with his power. He also began to envision himself differently while curing; while sitting by the side of the patient he saw himself as a skeleton with a turban on its head moving quickly around the body of the patient.

Henry did not perform his second cure until 1909, two years later. It was this cure which established him as a legitimate shaman among the Washo. The patient was a Washo whose family was camping on the Carson River near Minden, Nevada. This man had been treated by both shamans and White doctors without success, although the doctors had diagnosed his case as typhoid fever. Henry, although as a novice shaman he had been consulted as a last resort, was successful in curing the patient....

Welewkushkush suggested that Henry would receive no aid if he pursued his interest in the knowledge of White society and implied that he would become ill if he continued; the two worlds, Indian and non-Indian, must remain separate in terms of both intellect and affect. But the ethic of curing which Henry had synthesized from Indian and non-Indian elements prevailed over Welewkushkush's thinly veiled warning. His independence established Henry as a mature adult prepared to continue to develop his own philosophy of living and ultimately to restructure Washo cosmogony.

In October, 1910, Henry married Lizzie, a Northern Paiute woman whom he had first met at the Stewart Indian School. Her father, Buckeroo John, a ranch hand and maker of rawhide lariats, had been a devotee of Jack Wilson, the apostle of the 1890 Ghost Dance. Buckeroo John did not approve of Henry as a prospective bridegroom, nor did he think highly of Henry's curing abilities. It was nevertheless, significant that Henry should take a Paiute wife at a time when intermarriage was infrequent and generally viewed with disfavor, especially by shamans and other conservative Washo. The union produced four children, three of whom today live with their offspring in the same community as Henry. After his marriage, Henry returned to work with the Reno Evening Gazette, melting linotypes [metal castings—Ed.]. But he soon came to suspect that the lead fumes were poisoning him, and he returned with his family to Genoa, where he worked as a ranch hand until 1924. During this period he continued his healing, becoming increasingly well known.

In 1924, with all their children away at school in Stewart, by now operated by the Bureau of Indian Affairs, Henry and Lizzie decided to leave Genoa. Rather than choosing Dresslerville, the major Washo community of that time, Henry decided on Carson Colony, 40 acres of land bought for the Washo in 1916 but unoccupied except for a few transient Northern Paiute and Shoshone families.

In making this move, Henry isolated himself physically—and later also socially, when Lizzie died of tuberculosis in 1933 despite Henry's attempts to cure her. He became more of a recluse with greater opportunity to meditate the problems of healing. "Rupert, the sophisticated young Washo...was a mystic credited with shamanistic ambitions," says Lowie (1939:321) of him at this time.

Henry also worked hard, planting and raising an acre of strawberries as well as a flock of turkeys. In the Depression years he earned as much as $100 a week during the summer months, and his flock of turkeys was later sold for $5,000. He also spent many evenings digging a large irrigation pond, which he later filled with goldfish.

But these were essentially years of thought, introspection, and self-examination. As a child, and later as a novice shaman, Henry had learned the tenets of traditional Washo religion. This included a conception of a spirit world populated by the departed souls of all animate beings which had populated the natural world. The spirit world resembled the natural world; it had the same people and a comparable round of activities. The age of a person in the spirit world was that at which he had died. The spirits of evil persons were segregated in one section of the spirit world, but they underwent no particular punishments because of their earthly transgressions. The spirits or ghosts of animate beings were feared as potential causes of illness because of their ability to intrude into the bodies of the living or to project inanimate disease-producing objects into them. When an individual died, consequently, his dwelling and possessions were burnt so that his ghost would be unable to retrace his path to the natural world.

The Washo had no coherent religious philosophy or theology, but they did have a number of creation myths and creator figures. Among the latter were the two old women who fought the Hindu in Henry's dream. However, these creator figures played but little part in the placation of the supernatural. In this respect the Washo dealt with the ghosts of animate beings, and these had the same motivations as living Washo, including revenge for present or past misdeeds and curiosity which brought them back to the world of the living. Hence, for example, parents avoided striking or spanking a child for fear of angering a dead relative, whose ghost might kill the child to punish the parents (Downs 1966:60).

In the process of evolving a general ethic of healing, Henry Rupert reformulated some of the traditional conceptions of Washo cosmology. According to his new formulation, the substance and composition of the spirit world is very similar to electric waves or pulses of energy. These are everlasting and everpresent, and all objects in the natural world are also partially composed of them. To Henry, therefore, spirit and mind are the same, both being composed of what he called "ethereal waves." When an individual dreams, his "mind-power" travels to the spirit world, remaining connected to his material body by a thin lifeline of energy. If this thin thread of energy breaks, the individual's "mind-power" is unable to return to its material shell, and death results. According to Henry, when a person dies his departing spirit or "ego" remains temporarily encased in a weak body shell, the "astral body," but within one month the "astral body" falls away and the "pure" ego or spirit returns to the spirit world.

The spirit world itself has three planes—the first a "coarse" level, the second a finer level, and the third was the finest or purest level. Normally, when a person dreams, his spirit or mind-power travels to the first level. Passage into the second level, either in dreams or death, is impossible unless the individual has been pure in mind and heart and has followed "the law of nature." The third level is the domain of "God," "creator," and "omnipotent life." All spiritual life from the highest to the lowest is a manifestation of some kind of energy which has its ultimate source in the third level of the spirit world. This energy is an essence found in all animate life and inanimate objects in the natural world and may, in Henry's terms, be called "soul," "ego," "spirit," or "mind-power." The same energy is also the essence of all spirits, in which it coalesces into certain forms found in the natural world, thereby forming a connecting link between the natural and spirit worlds. While there is no actual separation of good and evil spirits in the hereafter, only those spirits which are "purer" in essence can reach the second level. No spirits, however, can reach the third level, the ultimate energy source.

We thus find, in conjunction with Henry's general ethic of healing, a general conception of "power" or "energy" which is the basis of healing. Henry makes no distinction between the miracles performed by the Old Testament prophets, those performed by Christ and his disciples, the healing powers of shamans, and his own work, since the basis of the power is in every case the same, though manifested at different times and in different social situations. All of these people learned to tap the same source of energy and to channel it for purposes of curing and miracle-working. This power or energy is not, however, ethically neutral. It is positive and "good," and this accounts for Henry's disavowal of witchcraft and sorcery, which will be described later. Henry is aware that his conceptions are an act of faith. As he stated to me: "In my line of work I see it that way. Nobody told me this. Nobody can prove it. That is what I believe ... the power is everpresent; it never wears out."

Because Henry's ethic of curing was based on contact with the supernatural or paranatural, it was necessary for him to develop some conception of a general source of power for curing. His personal restructuring of the spirit world did not rest on a dichotomy of good and evil but rather on a conception of differing degrees of "good." In his ideology, no person or spirit could be completely evil, thus precluding belief in active malevolent supernatural agencies. It was no longer conceivable that ghosts, for example, could cause illness by intruding their spirit essence into humans. All mind-power derived from the same source, and both the source and the power it represented were beneficent and could not be utilized for malevolent designs. Consequently, traditional Washo beliefs in malevolent ghosts, witchcraft, and sorcery no longer had a place in Henry's world view. However, while human ghosts could not cause illness, the spirits of animal life and inanimate objects could and did.

How did Henry explain this possible contradiction? Everything, animate and inanimate, has some form of life, "ego," or "soul." All living things require water as a minimal basis for existence. So, for example, when feathers are not sprinkled with water at regular intervals, they take water from the person owning them, "drying" him out and making him ill. Henry did not consider this a malevolent action, but he held that a person who transgressed, consciously or through ignorance, was accountable, since if the feathers were given water, the patient would recover. In one case I recorded, that of an old man who could neither speak nor eat, Henry had the following diagnostic vision on the fourth night of the curing session. He was sitting at the eastern end of a valley hiding from a whirlwind. Seeing it coming straight toward him, he was frightened and hid in the willows. The whirlwind stopped in front of him, and a magpie flew out and lit on a nearby willow. After he emerged from the trance state, Henry was told by relatives that the patient had at one time made feather headdresses and that he still kept a trunk of them in a deserted cabin. Henry said to me:

The trunk of feathers made him sick. I prayed to the feathers and the birds not to be angry; he thought he was doing right, but he didn't give them water. I said: "I will give you water; don't dry this fellow up." Next day he spoke and was okay....

As Henry's fame as a healer spread he began to receive patients from a wide variety of ethnic groups. Though not common, it was unknown for Washo shamans to treat Northern Paiute and Shoshone patients, but Henry treated these and Hawaiian, Filipino, Mexican, and White patients as well. In this trans-cultural healing he was successful, doubtless because his ethic of healing gave him increased confidence in dealing with non-Indians. His status as a healer grew continuously, and he became known and respected as a successful shaman from the Shoshone Yomba reservation in central Nevada to Mexican enclaves in Sacramento. His increasing renown attracted non-Indian patients who had exhausted other alternatives....

In 1942, at the age of 57, when Henry Rupert was working as a general handyman and night watchman at the Stewart Indian Agency, he decided to retire to Carson Colony and devote full time to healing. He was acutely aware that "reality" in healing and living is a matter of relative perception, psychological set, and social situation. The Hindu spirit helper had told him: "What appertaineth unto one, another knoweth not." And on one occasion he stated to me: "You don't know what I am talking about, and the same is true for anybody who reads this thing you write. What is real for me is not real for you." As an example, he cited an occasion when he was walking across a bridge over the Truckee River in Reno. He saw a woman who wailed to him that her son had fallen into the river and pleaded with him to save the boy. Henry was about to plunge into the water when the woman's daughter appeared and told him that her mother had periodic hallucinations and there was no one in the water. Henry concluded: "It was real for that woman; she thought her son was in the water; but it isn't real for me. What I know is real for me, but it isn't real for anybody else."

We must remember, in considering the phenomenological basis of Henry's conception of "reality," that he was an adept hypnotist cognizant of the importance of gaining and holding a patient's attention during a curing session by the use of such instruments as a rattle and eagle feathers. "I use

them," he told me, "only to gain the attention of the sick person, nothing more...."

"Suggestions" made by the shaman in the context of the curing session are clearly an important factor in the efficacy of certain cures. A case in point was that of a young Washo who was brought to Henry. He had been unable to walk for a week and believed that he was stricken with polio. Henry worked on him for a few hours and then, during a rest period, told the young man that he did not have polio. He cited a personal experience of his own as an example. When he was working in Reno he had attended a medicine show, where he was examined and told that he had "heart trouble due to indigestion." Henry bought a bottle of medicine and drank some of it, after which his heart began to beat quickly and his breathing became irregular, but he then threw the bottle away and felt normal. After this illustration he again told his patient that he did not have polio, that his muscles were simply overworked, and that he should forget the matter. A week later the patient returned, saying that he had followed Henry's advice and felt fine.

In the course of his meditations and his dialogues with the spirit world, Henry also consciously restructured traditional Washo conceptions about the acquisition of shamanic power. The traditional Washo belief system required that an individual receive shamanic power involuntarily, through a dream or vision, after which he had the choice of either accepting or rejecting the power. While shamanic power tended to run in particular families, where children were socialized in an environment charged with the importance of dreams and the supernatural interpretations of events, shamanic power was never conciously transmitted from one person to another. Only after receiving power did a novice shaman hire an experienced practitioner to help him master and control it.

To Henry, however, living by "the law of nature" meant being closely attuned to the forces that created and controlled all beings and things of the world. Since power derived from a common pool of "energy," anyone who could tap this pool could use the resultant power for purposes of healing. In order to accomplish this, however, an individual had to possess certain personal qualities; he had to be honest, faithful, and discreet and live a pure life. It is significant that Henry first learned this possibility of the transmission of power from the Hindu, a non-Washo and non-Indian spirit helper. According to Henry:

Anybody could learn it, but you have to come under these three things, and be like a recluse, and follow the law of nature. You can't be happy-go-lucky. If you live by nature, you can understand a little of nature and help nature do her work. I had to live just so to get what I was looking for. You can't get it by being foolish. I got it just by thinking. It took me over sixty years to learn that. If I had a teacher, I could have learned that in a month.

Even if a person was not pure enough to tap the power source himself, he might still borrow another's power for the purpose of effecting minor cures. Henry lent his power at least twice, once to a sister and once to a daughter-in-law, with the clear understanding that their use of the power was only temporary.

During the years when Henry was developing his own philosophy of healing and conceptions of cosmology he also continued patiently to search for new techniques and more efficacious curing methods. But he had little success until 1956, when, at the age of 70, he undertook to cure George Robinson, a Hawaiian, who had married a distant relative of his and was living in Hayward, California. Robinson was also a curer and had been a personal friend for a number of years. Henry regarded him with much the same affection and respect in which he had earlier held Welewkushkush and Beleliwe....

In return for being cured, Robinson made Henry a gift of some of his power, in the form of a Hawaiian spirit helper named George. Although George lived in a volcano in Hawaii, his power was at its maximum in the vicinity of Henry Rupert's home. Consequently, Henry now preferred to cure at home and would no longer journey to visit patients except in emergency cases. Henry received from George a new set of instructions. The most important of these—"Everything comes quick and goes away quick,"—emphasized the speed and efficacy of the new Hawaiian techniques. The content of Henry's dream themes also changed. He saw a dead and desiccated chicken which returned to life, and the skeletal remains of a horse which also came alive. Robinson had claimed that he could bring the dead back to life, and these dreams showed Henry knew that this ability might also be his.

A curing session utilizing the techniques now took place in daylight, and it lasted no longer than four hours and sometimes as little as a few minutes, depending on the nature of the ailment. Henry no longer needed visions of diagnosis or prognosis, and he could also eliminate chants, the blowing of smoke and water on the patient, and the use of the whistle to capture disease objects. Instead the patient was asked the location of the pain or swelling and was seated in a chair facing west, the direction of the Hawaiian Islands. Standing behind the chair, Henry twice called upon George for help, each time placing his fingers on the patient's neck, with thumbs on spine, for about ten seconds. Then, with his hands again on the patient's neck, he called out: "Wake up my body, wake up my nerves and circulate my blood; let my whole body be normal; let my heart beat, my speech, my eyesight, and my breathing be normal; and give me strength." Next, standing in front of the patient, he stated: "This person says he was sick here; he had pains here; it's not there now; it's gone." Then he placed his hand on the "pain spot" for some five seconds and asked the patient to take a deep breath and move his head from side to side. Usually the pain departed, but sometimes it moved to a different part of the body, in which case Henry again invoked George and repeated the procedure three or four times. Then, placing his left hand on top of the patient's head and his right hand at the patient's feet, he called to George: "Please mend this." Finally, he removed his hands and said: "We will close this."

According to Henry, the key to these techniques is contained in the following statement by his Hawaiian spirit helper: "We help nature, and nature does the rest." The above is a description of "Hawaiian curing" in its simplest form, as applied by Henry to ailments which he regarded as easy to cure.

Henry did not discard his previous techniques completely. Though he worked for briefer periods in his cures, for severe ailments he would use both the Hindu and George, and would search for visions of prognosis involving the presence or absence of water, as well as employing his newer methods. In effect, he had developed a set of functionally streamlined curing techniques, involving less reliance on ceremonial artifacts, from which he could pick and choose according to the nature of the ailment. At the advanced age of 70, Henry relinquished willingly, without personal conflict, techniques that he had used for almost 50 years.

George posed no problems of integration for Henry. As a spirit helper, his power derived from the same general source as that of the Hindu, water, and the two old Indian women, and his curing functions were incorporated into Henry's general ethic of healing which overrode ethnic, racial, and cultural differences. The potential for innovation had not ended. From George he learned of a new way to stop bleeding in serious wounds quickly by placing his hands on the wound. However, the occasion to test this technique has not yet arisen, and Henry has doubts, not unreasonable or neurotic, as to his capacity to utilize it:

I am kind of afraid of it; I don't have enough confidence. I have the idea it can't be done. I don't try it because I don't have enough confidence.

Today, Henry Rupert lives quietly in Carson Colony, continuing to cure, meditate, and tend a flourishing orchard in the desert. The Washo, despite their traditional fear and mistrust of shamans, regard Henry in a different light, recognizing, perhaps indirectly, the changes he represents. Leis (1963:60) states:

Only one [shaman] remained when we studied the Washo . . . and he was trusted and not feared by anyone. In other words, the sole remaining shaman was "good" as opposed to the "bad" Indian doctors who practiced witchcraft.

My own experiences confirm this completely.

Exactly what the social consequences of Henry's personal innovations are likely to be is uncertain. It is clear that the Washo have little knowledge of either the extent or content of these innovations, although they recognize that he does not doctor in the traditional Washo manner. At present there are no budding young shamans among the Washo, and it is unlikely that future shamans would take the traditional path to gaining supernatural power. Although Henry does not proselytize, he offers an alternative, but the regimen and qualities required are either unappealing or rare. Nevertheless, the potentiality exists, and this could open a fascinating new chapter on shamanic healing among the Washo.

## CONCLUSIONS

The most striking fact, in this life history, to me, is the coherence and integration of the innovations considered. The conceptions, both of an ethic of healing and of a coherent cosmology, are congruent with each other. Within this framework, Henry has been able to incorporate heterocultural spirit helpers, new techniques of curing, and proficiency in trans-cultural curing, as well as to explore the possibility of transmitting and teaching his healing abilities. Although his childhood

models have greatly influenced his development, he has been able to resist their strictures and to reconceptualize his thinking on sorcery and witchcraft as causes of illness in terms of his reinterpretation of Washo cosmology. Throughout the material presented run themes of curiosity, experimentation, and perseverance, balanced by uncertainty of success. Henry's personality unfolds, through the years, slowly and positively with few contradictions. It takes the form of learning, testing, and integration, of working for maximal organization of all potentials within the framework of sophisticated general principles flexible enough to admit defeat in areas where spirit helpers are unable to operate. Thus Henry has recognized, through experience, the illnesses he cannot treat, and has accepted these limitations while delving into potentially more fruitful areas.

It is highly inadequate to suggest that Henry Rupert adopted shamanism as a neurotic defense against personal aggression and instability, or simply that he made a successful adjustment to the acculturative situation in which he lived. The shaman has often been analyzed and typed as a neurotic or borderline psychotic who performs valuable social functions in a deviant role to which he is shunted to meet his own neurotic needs (cf. Kroeber 1940; Radin 1937:108; Spencer and Jennings 1965:151; Boyer 1962:233; Lantis 1960:164; Devereux 1956, 1957:1043, 1961a:1088, 1961b:63–64.) The neurotic defense of the shaman is conceptualized as unstable, transitory, and inadequate; the experience of becoming a shaman is also often described as a revitalization experience.

These conceptions are not applicable in the case described. Henry Rupert presents us with a case of continuous psychological development, growth, and innovation throughout his individual life span. His first innovations included both a complex philosophical statement about the nature of the supernatural and natural worlds and a sophisticated approach to transcultural curing. All his other innovations were integrated into this psychological matrix, and this has remained stable through time and space. While his uncertainties and fears are considerable, Henry knows that one cannot face the unknown with certainty, unless it be rooted in rigidity. While man is fallible, Henry believes that the only path to knowledge is through experimentation, and his fears have never stopped him from experimenting.

Unfortunately, in anthropology, we have few ways of describing or analyzing the ego strength or ego integrity of individuals in the cultures we deal with, and ordinarily this does not concern us. We have good evidence of both social disorganization and psychological disturbance among acculturating peoples, and we can tentatively suggest that in many ways cultural processes have overwhelmed individual defenses in these cases by destroying traditional alternatives and failing to provide new ones. But what of the creative individual? What of the individual with great ego strength who is able to choose and combine traditional and new alternatives, not merely integrating them but developing new syntheses which may be both personally satisfying and socially transmissible? Of such persons and the roles they play we know little. And the same is true of the shaman who, as Nadel has suggested, can play a creative and innovative role. In the case of Henry Rupert we gain a glimpse of what the quality and content of such a synthesis can be in an acculturative situation.

Despite the fact that his epistemology of mental illness is developed within a belief system that emphasizes witchcraft and moral magic, and although he has become expert in dealing with such supernatural considerations, he is primarily a pragmatic psychopharmacologist. His devotion to empiricism in botany and pharmacology, while unusual among his people, may nevertheless have historical antecedents among the Hehe, and may be more common throughout African ethnopsychiatry than has yet been recognized. This African psychiatrist—like so many of the men who built Western psychiatry—serves to remind us that even within a supernatural belief system the beginnings of science may emerge.

Thus, this curer has managed to achieve the difficult feat of transcending his own culture, as Edgerton points out, by placing his reliance mainly upon a secular, empirical methodology while continuing to incorporate, without depending upon, the magical and religious prescriptions of the indigenous medical system. Such an accomplishment is the mark of the significant innovator in any culture. Compare this healer with the Washo Indian innovating shaman (Chapter 48) and the Mexican-American "renovating" folkhealer in Romano (1965).

# 49 A Traditional African Psychiatrist

## Robert B. Edgerton

Conventionally in the ethnographic literature, indigenous healers are called either by the native term or with a neutral one (healer, curer, practitioner) or by rather more lurid names (see the introduction to this section). But seldom are terms used, with the occasional exception of the generic and ambiguous "doctor," that label native medical practitioners with the names that are also used for the Western medical specialties. Thus, for example, a "bone-setter" would be called an orthopedist, an herbalist would be termed a pharmacist or pharmacologist, and so on. Thus, the title of this paper by Robert Edgerton is a refreshing departure. What is even more delightful is that the qualifier (if there need be one at all) is not "primitive" but the more meaningful and less pejorative "traditional." Like many contemporary Western psychiatrists, this healer leans heavily upon the use of drugs and has a high degree of botanical and pharmacological knowledge, mingled with magic, to be sure. But as Edgerton says in the abstract of the original version,

Reprinted with abridgments from Robert B. Edgerton, 1971, "A Traditional African Psychiatrist," *Southwestern Journal of Anthropology*, 27:259–278, with permission of the author and the *Journal of Anthropological Research*.

...Before any considered opinion on the nature of traditional African medicine or "psychiatry" can be reached, we not only need more research from additional areas of Africa, but research which adopts additional perspectives. The following report is offered because its practitioner, a Hehe of Tanzania, is a specialist in psychiatry, and his beliefs and practices, particularly as they emphasize botanical and pharmacological empiricism, complement our knowledge of African ethnopsychiatry as it is practiced in other parts of Africa.

The Hehe are a Bantu-speaking people located in the Southern Highlands Region of Tanzania, formerly Tanganyika. Their territory stretches from the Great Ruaha River on the north and west to the escarpment of the Kilombero Valley on the south and east....

The Hehe, who now number over 200,000, live in dispersed homesteads which are organized into neighborhoods. A homestead is typically occupied by a man, his wife or wives, and their children. It is surrounded by its fields of maize, millet, beans, cassava, and squash and by small numbers of cattle, sheep, and goats. Each Hehe neighborhood is bound together by ties of kinship and friendship, by ceremonial activities, and by cooperative work parties. In addition to the strong ties of kinship, the Hehe recognize a hierarchy of lesser and greater chiefs who possess considerable traditional authority and have obligations to the British administration (see also Brown and Hutt, 1935, Nigmann 1908, Winans 1965).

When the Hehe fall ill, as they often do, they may attribute their misfortune to any of several sources: to natural phenomena such as worry, impure water, or faulty inheritance, to witchcraft, or to legitimate retribution for the violation of Hehe norms. If the source of illness is seen as natural, a Hehe may seek help from a European-trained physician or medical helper in a nearby town. But even for "natural" illnesses, the patient is likely also to seek out a traditional doctor—an *mbombwe*—and where the source of illness is other than natural, he is certain to do so. There are many such doctors (the Swahili term is *mganga*) throughout Hehe territory, and their advice is continually sought. Some, of course, are more highly regarded than others. The best known native doctor in the Iringa area was a man whom I shall name Abedi. Unlike most traditional Hehe doctors who attempt to treat any disorder, Abedi is a specialist in mental disorders—he is a Hehe psychiatrist.

## ABEDI'S TRAINING

Abedi was the headman (*jumbe*) of an area near Iringa until early in the 1950's when he encountered some sort of difficulty with the British administration. Accused of malfeasance, he left the post in 1955 and turned to full-time practice as an *mbombwe*. Abedi was born around 1910 to a man who had been a renowned *mbombwe*, a doctor to the King, Mkwawa, himself. Thus Abedi's father had access to the traditional medicine not only of the royal clan and court of the Hehe, but also from those neighboring tribes whom the Hehe conquered. Abedi's mother was also an *mbombwe*, who, like Abedi, was known as a specialist (her specialty was female disorders).

Abedi's formal training as an *mbombwe* did not begin until he was an adult, by which time his father was quite elderly. Abedi learned primarily from his father, but also studied with his mother who gave him intensive instruction in botany. Much of his training was highly practical, giving attention to the method of diagnosis and treatment, observation of symptoms, collection of plants and roots, knowledge of inherited disorders, etc. But an equal emphasis was placed upon the supernatural. Abedi inherited his father's *lyang'ombe*, a small metal object that appeared to be an old European belt buckle. Through prayer, the *lyang'ombe* could be imbued with God's power to cure. Abedi learned to pray to God (*Nguluvi*), to practice divination, to discover the cause of witchcraft, to defend against witchcraft, and to employ magic. His father also gave him protection against the malevolence of witches, who might be angered because he cured those whom they had sickened, by rubbing a secret medicine (*gondola*) into a series of cuts (*nyagi*)....

Abedi's specialization in mental illnesses began during his apprenticeship when he first hallucinated ("hearing voices of people I could not see") and ran in terror to hide in the bush. He was discovered and returned to his father's care, but lay ("completely out of my senses") for two weeks before being cured. The cause was diagnosed as witchcraft and since the cure, Abedi has never been sick again. This experience initiated Abedi's interest in mental illness, and the subsequent mental disorders of his sister and his wife reinforced it. At different times, both women became violently psychotic, but Abedi quickly cured them both. These two cures not only heightened Abedi's interest in psychiatric phenomena, but they led to his reputation as a skillful psychiatrist.

## DIAGNOSIS, ETIOLOGY, AND PROGNOSIS

...Seeking treatment from Abedi in his office often requires interrupting him in the course of preparing his medications, but he always greets a patient warmly as he asks him (and the usual family members or kinsmen who attend him) to be seated by the fireplace before he begins his diagnostic routine.

In proceeding with his diagnosis, Abedi must keep in mind his nosology of disorders (the catalogue of illness categories that he knows), the signs and symptoms, and the patient's biography—including past illnesses and, especially, antagonists who might want to bewitch him. In short, Abedi is concerned with the entire social context of the patient and his illness—a context which Abedi enters and typically alters—for while successful treatment pleases some, it may displease others (Winans and Edgerton 1964).

In a general way, Abedi recognizes a great variety of illnesses such as impotence, venereal infections, infertility, stomach and bowel ailments, respiratory disorders (including pneumonia and asthma), orthopedic malfunctions, and fevers. He also recognizes more specific diseases such as tracoma, tetanus, malaria, and smallpox. While he may choose to treat all such disorders with specific medications he has developed for that purpose, it is only when the disorders are "mental" (when the locus of disorder, in his perspective, is in the mind) that his diagnosis categories achieve any prognostic differentiation. Indeed, his categories of mental illness are defined by criteria that are based far less upon symptoms than they are upon etiology and prognosis.

Hehe men and women who live in the area near Abedi typically described mental illness in behavioral terms, perceiving its onset as sudden, with aggressive behavior that can result in human injury, but rapidly "cooling" to a fearful and stuporous retreat from human interaction (Edgerton 1966). They made no distinctions among psychotics. Abedi's views of mental illness were more complex. He recognized two symptoms as being indicators of excessive worry: headache and stomach pain. He felt that both responded well to removal of the source of worry and to his herbal medications. For extreme cases, he recommended that the patient move away from his neighborhood for a prolonged vacation with kinsmen. He denied, however, that worry was a common cause of psychotic conditions. He also recognized epilepsy by its *grand mal* seizures, and mental retardation by the fact that intellectual ability was deficient from birth. Mental retardation he deemed untreatable, but he felt that epilepsy, which he said was an inherited condition, was curable by medication if treatment were begun in the first few days after the initial seizure....

In his diagnostic search for symptoms, Abedi never touches the patient. He observes carefully, although usually unobtrusively and he carefully questions the patient and any available kinsmen or friends. The questioning is often lengthy, involving what appears to the patient (or kinsmen) to be nothing more than an exchange of pleasantries and a concern for mutual acquaintances. In reality, it appeared that Abedi was probing carefully for an understanding of the social context of the illness. Who might be an enemy? What is the patient fearful about? Has he had a similar problem before? Do such illnesses run in his family?

Following the period of informal conversation, Abedi initiates his formal divinatory procedures. He begins by praying to *Nguluvi* to give him the power to see the cause of the sickness and to understand what ought to be done. He then takes out his *lyang'ombe*, kisses it to imbue it with God's power, and begins to divine by means of his *bao*. The *bao* is a paddle-shaped board about eight inches long and three inches wide, with a groove in which a small wooden cylinder is rubbed running diagonally along its upper surface. Abedi places the board on the ground, puts the *lyang'ombe* on its narrow end, and holds both objects down with his foot. He then sprinkles water on the groove and begins rubbing the wooden cylinder in it. As he manipulates the *bao*, he chants in a low liturgical voice interrupted from time to time by a question he addresses to the *bao*. As the water in the groove dries up, the counter moves less easily and at some point it will stick. This is taken as an affirmative answer to the last question addressed to the *bao*. As long as the counter moves freely, the answers to questions addressed to it are usually taken to be negative. In any case of illness, Abedi asks five preliminary questions: Did the patient commit adultery? Did he steal? Did he borrow money and refuse to repay it? Did he quarrel with someone? Did he actually have a fight with someone? In some instances, the answer to all the questions is negative. This indicates that the patient has become ill for no good reason and hence the cause is natural. Or, it means that effective counter magic must be made against the evil person who has performed magic or witchcraft against the patient without cause. This Abedi determines by further questions. He then asks specific questions about his ability to cure the patient, alternating "yes" and "no" questions until the *bao* answers. Finally he asks about the effectiveness of various medicines until the *bao* selects for him the medicine favored by God.

Throughout the investigations and supplications Abedi takes great care, for both he and his patient realize that the treatment of illness is dangerous, involving as it does not merely natural phenomena but such critical matters as moral magic, witchcraft, spirits, and the like. All realize that a faulty diagnosis endangers the doctor as well as the patient.

## TREATMENT

Although Abedi's treatment routine varies somewhat depending upon the diagnosis he reaches, for almost all of the "mental illnesses" that he recognizes (*mbepo, lisaliko,* etc.), his treatment follows a prescribed course. First, the patient must be made tractable. Only a few patients are quiet enough that Abedi will begin their treatment without subjecting them to some degree of restraint. Most patients are agitated and difficult to manage, and they are either tied sitting to the center post of Abedi's office or, if treated at home, they are shackled to a bed. Next, all patients are purged. For this purpose Abedi maintains a ready supply of purgatives and emetics. The emetic is administered first; if the patient will not cooperate by swallowing the medication, a liquid preparation, his nose is held until he is compelled to swallow. If vomiting should not quickly ensue, Abedi assists by tickling the patient's throat with a feather. As soon as vomiting has taken place, a purgative is given with almost universal success within a few hours. Once purged, the patient is allowed to rest but is usually permitted only water until Abedi's specific medications have been prepared and administered.

As we have seen, Abedi's *bao* has already identified the appropriate medications, but it may take Abedi several hours, or even overnight, to prepare the prescriptions. In some cases, the necessary ingredients have already been collected, ground into powder, and stored, but in other instances Abedi must sort out the correct mixture of leaves, roots, patent medicines, and other substances before mixing them. Occasionally, he must actually go out to collect the ingredients. Some medications cannot even be selected until Abedi has gone to a crossroad (a place where village footpaths intersect or, ideally, trisect), stood naked at midnight, and used his magical powers to "see" the correct medicine (the *bao* is not involved in this form of divination). Sometimes the medication must be mixed at the crossroad as well, and in rare circumstances, the patient must ingest the medicine at the same crossing. Where selection of a medication has proven particularly difficult, and where the cause of the psychosis has been diagnosed as witchcraft, the patient himself may be made to act as an oracle in the selection of his own medication. This is done by burning a mass of *Cannabis sativa*, covering the patient with a blanket, and forcing him to inhale the smoke for a period of an hour or more. The patient identifies the person who has bewitched him, and by answering Abedi's questions with "yes" or "no," selects an effective medicine.

Once assured that the medication of choice is known and available, Abedi "cooks" it by boiling the powdered ingredients over a fire in full view of the patient and his kinsmen. Most of the resulting medications are taken as liquids, usually drunk in a glass of tea. A few medications are rubbed on the skin as ointment, others are rubbed into shallow linear incisions, and a few are inhaled. Before the medicine is actually given, Abedi offers 'a brief *sotte voce* prayer for the success of the medicine and spits once or three times upon the patient's head as a blessing for good luck. Doses of medicine are repeated at varying intervals until a cure is effected. Abedi accepts no payment for his treatment (except a small retainer for house calls) until such time as the patient has recovered....

## DISCUSSION

Abedi's therapy for "mental" illness is often, perhaps even usually, rewarded by the remission of symptoms. There are obvious reasons why this pattern of apparent remission should not be construed as a "cure." For one thing, the symptoms presented by Abedi's patients are so diverse as to challenge the therapeutic arsenal of any doctor, African or Western. What is more, while my four week study of his practice revealed striking success in the remission of symptoms, it would be naive to suppose that failures could not have been hidden from me had Abedi chosen to do so. Finally we have no way of knowing how often the symptoms would have vanished under differing treatment or with no treatment at all. We do know, however, that rapid and seemingly complete recovery from apparently psychotic conditions has been reported from several parts of Africa (Collis 1966:25). Any discussion of the efficacy of Abedi's treatment must await properly designed research of the sort begun in West Africa by Collis (1966). The purpose of this discussion is to compare Abedi's treatment routine with principles of treatment reported from other parts of Africa and to ask why his therapeutic practices have taken their particular form.

Analyses of "primitive medicine" from Ackerknecht (1943) to Frank (1961) have emphasized the role of suggestion in treatment. Recently, Kiev (1964) concluded that two universals of non-Western psychiatry were suggestion and confession. Others have expanded this list to include faith, catharsis, group support, and suggestion (Kennedy MS). Let us examine the role of each of these in Abedi's psychiatric practice.

### Faith

By faith I mean the generalized expectation on the part of the patient that treatment of the sort offered by the traditional doctor *can* be effective. These expectations are difficult to determine and research reports regarding them are generally superficial. The Hehe data are also superficial, although here at least some quantification and comparison is possible For example, 36 of 123 Hehe respondents in a neighborhood near Abedi's office said that psychotic patients could be cured, 12 said that they could not, and 75 were unsure. This degree of expressed faith was much greater than that shown by the Pokot of Kenya or the Sebei of Uganda, but less than that indicated by the Kamba of Kenya (Edgerton 1966:416). We can probably conclude that while the Hehe have some faith in psychiatric treatment they also maintain ample skepticism. Turning now to Abedi, who is certainly the most highly regarded doctor in this area, we see that even where his ability is concerned, a degree of what might be considered skepticism remains. For example, in the case presented earlier of serious and prolonged illness, the boy's parents were in no hurry to see a native doctor and while they had heard of Abedi's reputation, they had no blind faith in his ability. They, as did others, began their contact with Abedi by testing him—could he identify the sick boy and his illness? And all patients withhold payment until a cure has taken place (a practice which is as unusual in Africa as in the West). Thus while Hehe patients approach Abedi with some faith in his reputation as a doctor, most enter treatment with an attitude that combines hope and doubt. For his part, Abedi does nothing to foster or require a testimonial of faith before treatment begins. Instead he is content to rely upon his treatment itself.

### Catharsis

For the Hehe, as for other African peoples, catharsis through confession is a commonplace. In childbirth, as in many forms of illness, both Hehe patient and spouse or other kinsmen must confess and apologize for wrongful thoughts or acts before birth or recovery can take place (Winans and Edgerton 1964). Nevertheless, Abedi makes virtually no use of catharsis in his practice. He never asks a patient or kinsman to act out any hidden desire and only very infrequently do his questions to the *bao* elicit any sort of confession from a patient. Asked about this anomaly, Abedi said, "Talking cures nothing. Medicines cure."

### Group Support

There are reports from several African societies that point to the importance of group support in the treatment of mental illness. In West Africa, for example, group support may be supplied by religious cults (Prince 1964), secret societies (Dawson 1964), or by elaborate "discharge" ceremonies that ritualize the patient's cleansing of illness, death, and rebirth into a new life (Prince 1964). Elsewhere, the patient may receive support by moving from one area and social network to another. Among the Ndembu of Northern Rhodesia, the patient's kinsmen may join with hostile persons in what amounts to group therapy, complete with catharsis and social reintegration (Turner 1964).

While Abedi permits kinsmen of his patients to be present throughout his diagnosis and treatment he does nothing to solicit group support. As with his disavowal of confession, this neglect of group concern is remarkable, for just such group support is a regular feature of childbirth and the recovery from many illnesses. As with catharsis, other Hehe doctors I knew did require that their patients undergo treatment within a larger social nexus.

### Suggestion

Research on African psychiatric practice has emphasized the role that suggestion plays in treatment. For example, Prince (1964:110), writing about the Yoruba, refers to a "continuous barrage of suggestions at all levels from the most intellectual to the most concrete and primitive." Others have attributed whatever success the African therapies may have entirely to suggestion, noting that Africans are highly suggestible (Collis 1966, Laubscher 1937, Turner 1964). There can be no doubt that suggestion plays an important part in Abedi's practice, and yet Abedi makes little or no use of a variety of practices widely employed in Africa to heighten suggestibility or to implant specific ideas. For example, Abedi never alters his own personality to indicate special powers, nor does he claim direct communication with supernatural powers through dissociation or possession. Neither does he employ special effects through legerdemain or ventriloquism. He makes no attempt at indirect communication by means of allegory, simile, traditional, or sacramental stories. He never gives commands, nor does he attempt to change his patient's consciousness through hypnosis, drumming, or dancing to exhaustion (cf. Whisson 1964). What is more, he utilizes none of the many versions of body contact common in Africa such as rubbing, sucking, bathing, or such stressful ones as whipping, burning, or steaming.

Kennedy (MS) and others have noted the significance of dramatic rituals and powerful symbolism in psychiatric practice in Africa and throughout the non-Western world. For example, Gelfand (1964) notes the flamboyant regalia of Shona "medicine men"; the Yoruba, Luo, and Ndembu all enact potent rituals in the service of therapy. However, Abedi's use of ritual is minimal, being confined almost entirely to a few ritual acts on the first day of treatment. Others have noted that non-Western psychiatrists rely upon settings so suffused by religious or magical symbolism that they are set apart from the ordinary world (Kennedy MS). Again, nothing could be more prosaic than the settings in which Abedi works.

Abedi's principal uses of suggestion lie in his appeals for supernatural guidance or power and in his utilization of potent medications. Although Abedi's frequent prayers for divine assistance are understated and humble, they nonetheless must serve to impress patients, as must also the divine and magical power that resides in his *lyang'ombe*. And, of course, the *bao* is an impressive divinatory device, especially when it reveals information about the patient that would seem to be inaccessible to Abedi by normal means. It is possible that Abedi maintains an "intelligence system" in the form of boys who inform him of matters relevant to actual or prospective patients, but I saw no evidence that he did so. Abedi's knowledge of magic and his occasional visits to crossroads and the like must also contribute to the supernatural aura that he is able to establish.

Probably of equal importance, however, is the placebo effect of Abedi's medications. Several of his preparations contain copper sulphate which has the impressive property of turning from blue-green to white when heated. The patients whom I watched during their first exposure to this transformation were visibly startled. Similarly, his infrequent but copious use of *Cannabis sativa* may produce impressive psychological changes, and the reliable effects of his standard emetics and purgatives must alike create in a patient a sense of the dramatic power of Abedi's medications. The resulting alteration of psychological and bodily states should produce a heightening of suggestibility. Such effects from the use of herbal remedies by African doctors have been widely noted (e.g., Collis 1966, Gelfand 1964, Kiev 1964, Prince 1964). However, in recognizing the prominent place of suggestion in Abedi's use of drugs, we should not overlook the possibility that some of his medications possess specific psychopharmacological action that may have value in the treatment of mental illness (Gelfand 1964).

## ABEDI AS PHARMACOLOGIST

Abedi's pharmacopoeia is extensive. In addition to emetics, purgatives, and his specific preparations for mental illness or epilepsy, he keeps on hand many drugs for gastro-intestinal disorders, as well as a variety of aphrodisiacs for men, and, for women, various drugs specific for infertility, miscarriage, menorrhagia, and the like. Most of the botanical knowledge that underlies his drugs was inherited from his father and mother, but some knowledge was purchased and some preparations were purchased ready-made (e.g., copper sulphate). I collected seven preparations said to be specific for mental illness or epilepsy. Of these, several were described by Abedi as (and were seen by me to have the apparent effect of) soporifics or tranquilizers. Of these, the most potent was called *mwini....*

Abedi's empirical knowledge of the botany of Hehe territory was considerable, and so was his pharmacological skill in preparing and administering these medications. For example, several of these plants contain violent emetics and purgatives which can produce death in overdose (Mathias 1965:87). Yet, of over 120 Hehe questioned, none had heard of so much as an accusation that Abedi's medications had ever killed a patient. Recall, too, that Abedi refused to increase the standard dosage of his emetics and purgatives when they did not have an immediate effect upon the boy in the previous case. In the mixing of each medication, Abedi takes care to prepare and measure each ingredient, and he does so with the secular manner of a pharmacist, not that of a magician. Yet his preparations are not confined to the leaves and roots of plants with at least potential psychopharmacological effect. He often adds to his medicine such magical substances as the aforementioned copper sulphate, powdered rock from the sea coast, corn flour, the blood of a black cock, and the urine or powdered bones of a sheep. Abedi insists that these latter substances are as essential to certain of his medications as the plant components. In this sense, he is not without full commitment to the Hehe world of supernatural belief. But other medications contain only leaves and roots. For these, no magic in preparation, content, or administration is employed. Abedi's pharmacopoeia has its supernatural elements, but they are relatively few, and may be relatively unimportant.

Neither is there evidence that he regularly employs his medications in the manner of a charlatan. To be sure, we can point to the fact that he feels the need for copper sulphate, which he says that he regards as just another vital ingredient, and that he sometimes uses *Cannabis sativa* to evoke witchcraft accusations from his patients. But unlike doctors among the Yoruba, he does not use hallucinogenics to worsen a patient's condition simply in order to achieve a spectacular treatment success 'by withdrawing the toxin (Prince 1964:118). Nor does he employ *Datura* to evoke confessions of witchcraft or to induce psychosis, although he knows of its properties, is aware that it grows in many accessible places, and knows that other "medicine men" in Tanzania, including those among the nearby Mtumbi, use it for those purposes (Lienhardt 1968:75–76). He said, "*Datura* can cause madness but it cannot cure it." I agree with Lienhardt (1968:74) that the medications used or sold by many a *mganga* in Tanzania are known to be useless by the so-called doctor himself. Abedi stands apart from fraud. He believes in the efficacy of his medications.

Demonstrating that Abedi is a serious empiricist about his medications is one thing; demonstrating that the medicines have any specific effect upon the central nervous system is quite another. The final word here must await complete pharmacological analysis, of course, but we might note that Abedi's treatment regime follows that of the Yoruba of Nigeria—emetics and purgatives followed by a drug that seems to induce sleep and tranquility. For the Yoruba, this drug is *Rauwolfia*, the source of reserpine (Prince 1964:Hordern 1968). Abedi's "tranquilizing" drugs, especially the one he calls *mwini*, were observed to induce both sleep and, following sleep, tranquility. These effects may be a product of verbal suggestion, but if this is so, then the suggestion must be very subtle, for I have witnessed the use of this drug on ten occasions, and on none of these occasions could I detect any verbal suggestion that would lead to sleep or tranquility. My Hehe-speaking interpreter also failed to discover any such cues. On the other hand, this drug (and others he employs) *could* have soporific or tranquilizing effects since Abedi's pharmacopoeia included 19 alkaloid-producing plant families.

Although the pharmacological analysis of *mwini* has proven difficult in research with laboratory animals, psychopharmacological activity (some of it soporific) has been noted. The drug had a quieting effect upon mice, reducing their activity noticeably. It also doubled the barbiturate sleeping time (modern tranquilizers will increase it six or seven times). Because of difficulties in acquiring

sufficient quantities of the plant and in developing techniques for the assay of this plant material, a more active fraction from the plant could not be obtained. The plant involved was *Limosella major* Diels, a member of the Scrophulariaceae. The family has not been noted for its medicinal properties.

## CONCLUSION

In his practice as a traditional African psychiatrist, Abedi not only must, but does, live within the belief systems of his culture, and these beliefs center around the etiological and prognostic significance of magic and witchcraft. Abedi diagnoses and treats mental disorders within the constraints posed by this supernatural system, constraints that emphasize his vulnerability to danger in equal measure to that of his patients. He believes in supernatural causes of illness, and he excels in discovering and in thwarting such causes. At the same time, however, he recognizes natural causes of illness and he seeks medication that will cure, not merely impress. He has stated this conviction, and his actions have given his convictions legitimacy. Only extensive botanical and pharmacological research can determine to what extent he has succeeded in locating medications whose successes are due to specific action and not to the placebo effect. If future analyses should show that the medications have specific actions upon the central nervous system, it would be an error to conclude that such action is a fortuitous product of the more or less random collection of leaves and roots. Abedi, and other Hehe doctors before him, have believed not only in supernatural causation and treatment of illness, but also in herbal remedies.

For example, Mkwawa, the King, and members of his court, were highly pragmatic men who displayed a keen interest in innovation. Their empiricism was especially notable in regard to botany. Mkwawa imported several plants to his kingdom from other parts of East Africa, seeking not only better medicinal plants but better food sources and even superior shade trees. He also experimented with cross-breeding cattle. At the same time, Mkwawa and his court retained their traditional beliefs in witchcraft, divination, and the like. Abedi's father, as physician to Mkwawa, was a member of this elite, among whom traditional belief in supernatural causation coexisted with an intense pragmatic interest in natural cause and effect (Collis 1966, Gelfand 1964, Mathias 1965).

Years of empirical effort have yielded Abedi's pharmacopoeia and his knowledge of it. It would be surprising indeed if his medications did not possess some specific pharmacological effectiveness.

In comparison to traditional doctors in other parts of Africa, as well as among the Hehe, Abedi is notable for his secular approach to medicine. He does not reject the supernatural beliefs or practices of his culture. On the contrary, he excels in their use. But he does attempt to go beyond them by formulating principles of natural causation and by empirically discovering chemical cures. In this sense, he has transcended his culture, and such transcendance is an achievement for any man. Yet, whether Abedi's success in treating mental illness has anything to do with the pharmacological action of his drugs or not, he possesses the essential attitude of a scientist—a belief in natural causes and effects, and an empirical method of seeking out causal relationships. His story is worth recording simply because he has made the effort to find useful drugs, to continue the beginnings of science within a pre-scientific system of medicine.

There is nothing necessarily contradictory about Abedi's continuing commitment to a world of supernatural cause and effect. As Koestler (1963) has pointed out, such beliefs were very much a part of the lives of Kepler, Galileo, Newton, and others who nevertheless brought about scientific revolution. Abedi is no Newton either in intent or accomplishment, but neither is he simply a magician-herbalist. He believes that supernatural practices are necessary but not sufficient for a cure. Only medicines are sufficient, and he is devoted to the discovery of more effective chemical agents. Abedi's own words best reflect this quest: "I became a doctor to cure people. Medicines cure, nothing else works. I have some very strong medicines, but I always hope to find better ones. I would like to be able to travel to a place where roots stronger than those around here grow. My medicines cure some things. If I had stronger roots I could cure more." Abedi undoubtedly undervalues the importance of suggestion in his practice of psychiatry, just as he no doubt overvalues the efficacy of his medications. His commitment to empiricism is botanical, not psychological.

Abedi is not the first of his kind in pre-scientific societies: curare, quinine, digitalis, atropine, reserpine, and many other valuable drugs attest to that. The dominant presence of a scientific ethos does not exclude magical practices in modern Western psychiatry. This we realize all too well. We should remind ourselves that the dominance of a supernatural ethos in non-Western psychiatry does not exclude the presence of beliefs and practices that are of significance for science.

# 50 The Sorcerer and His Magic

## Claude Lévi-Strauss

Like Victor Turner, whose analysis of symbolism in the divination process among the Ndembu was presented in Section V, Claude Lévi-Strauss is interested in the symbolic functions of the actors and systems in sociocultural processes. However, he moves somewhat beyond, or at least outside, a purely symbolic analysis by invoking psychoanalytic, as well as cultural-linguistic concepts, to provide answers to his problems. In this paper, Lévi-Strauss asks not so much how or why sorcery works, but what are the processes by which it is invoked, believed in, and maintained? If the accusation of sorcery is consensual, how can the accused demonstrate his innocence? What about the role of skepticism on the part of subjects and sorcerers, patients and healers? Since the sorcerer is aware that he is utilizing sleight-of-hand, how does he retain his own faith in the system? Using examples from three different ethnographies, including his own field research in South America, Lévi-Strauss concludes that individual experiences "remain intellectually diffuse and emotionally intolerable unless they incorporate one or another of the patterns present in the group's culture. The assimilation of such patterns is the only means of objectivizing subjective states, of formulating inexpressible feelings, and of integrating inarticulate experiences into a system." This explanation insists upon the indispensability of the cultural dimension that is so absent from Freudian analysis. In the three cases presented we learn that subjects, objects, and users of sorcery all are at least somewhat consciously aware that they are using, manipulating, rationalizing, and maintaining the system of magic, and in doing so they are also corroborating, validating, and reinforcing it.

Reprinted with abridgments from Claude Lévi-Strauss, 1963, *Structural Anthropology*, New York: Basic Books, Inc., Chap. 9, "The Sorcerer and His Magic," pp. 167–185, with permission of the author, Basic Books, Inc., Publishers (Copyright © 1963), and The Penguin Press, England (Copyright © 1968). (First published as "Le Sorcier et sa magie," in *Les Temps Modernes*, 1949, 41:3–24; translated from the French by Claire Jacobson and Brooke Grundfest Schoepf.)

Lévi-Strauss assumes the sorcerer to be a neurotic, although in a footnote not reproduced here, he adds that he later became aware of his error in doing so. Nevertheless, one could substitute for *disorders* the word *roles* and still find insightful the following statement:

> Because of their complementary disorders, the sorcerer-patient dyad incarnates for the group, in vivid and concrete fashion, an antagonism that is inherent in all thought but that normally remains vague and imprecise. The patient is all passivity and self-alienation, just as inexpressibility is the disease of the mind. The sorcerer is activity and self-projection, just as affectivity is the source of symbolism. The cure interrelates these opposite poles, facilitating the transition from one to the other, and demonstrates, within a total experience, the coherence of the psychic universe, itself a projection of the social universe.

Though Lévi-Strauss assumes a rather more passive posture for the patient than I would be willing to grant, his analysis, as a whole, assists greatly in understanding the operation of magic in a sociocultural system. Furthermore, he responds to a question frequently asked by students (and other intelligent laymen), namely, doesn't anyone ever question or challenge the system itself? The answer is, of course. But challenge and challenger, as in the case of the skeptical Kwakiutl shaman, become transformed in the process so that far from removing foundation stones in the edifice of magic, these challenges become cement for strengthening the system.

...There is no reason to doubt the efficacy of certain magical practices. But at the same time we see that the efficacy of magic implies a belief in magic. The latter has three complementary aspects: first, the sorcerer's belief in the effectiveness of his techniques; second, the patient's or victim's belief in the sorcerer's power; and, finally, the faith and expectations of the group, which constantly act as a sort of gravitational field within which the relationship between sorcerer and bewitched is located and defined. Obviously, none of the three parties is capable of forming a clear picture of the sympathetic nervous system's activity or of the disturbances which Cannon called homeostatic. When the sorcerer claims to suck out of the patient's body a foreign object whose presence would explain the illness and produces a stone which he had previously hidden in his mouth, how does he justify this procedure in his own eyes? How can an innocent person accused of sorcery prove his innocence if the accusation is unanimous—since the magical situation is a consensual phenomenon? And, finally, how much credulity and how much

skepticism are involved in the attitude of the group toward those in whom it recognizes extraordinary powers, to whom it accords corresponding privileges, but from whom it also requires adequate satisfaction? Let us begin by examining this last point.

It was in September, 1938. For several weeks we had been camping with a small band of Nambicuara Indians near the headwaters of the Tapajoz, in those desolate savannas of central Brazil where the natives wander during the greater part of the year, collecting seeds and wild fruits, hunting small mammals, insects, and reptiles, and whatever else might prevent them from dying of starvation. Thirty of them were camped together there, quite by chance. They were grouped in families under frail lean-tos of branches, which give scant protection from the scorching sun, nocturnal chill, rain, and wind. Like most bands, this one had both a secular chief and a sorcerer; the latter's daily activities—hunting, fishing, and handicrafts—were in no way different from those of the other men of the group. He was a robust man, about forty-five years old, and a *bon vivant*.

One evening, however, he did not return to camp at the usual time. Night fell and fires were lit; the natives were visibly worried. Countless perils lurk in the bush: torrential rivers, the somewhat improbable danger of encountering a large wild beast—jaguar or anteater—or, more readily pictured by the Nambicuara, an apparently harmless animal which is the incarnation of an evil spirit of the waters or forest. And above all, each night for the past week we had seen mysterious campfires, which sometimes approached and sometimes receded from our own. Any unknown band is always potentially hostile. After a two-hour wait, the natives were convinced that their companion had been killed in ambush and, while his two young wives and his son wept noisily in mourning for their dead husband and father, the other natives discussed the tragic consequences foreshadowed by the disappearance of their sorcerer.

Toward ten that evening, the anguished anticipation of imminent disaster, the lamentations in which the other women began to join, and the agitation of the men had created an intolerable atmosphere, and we decided to reconnoiter with several natives who had remained relatively calm. We had not gone two hundred yards when we stumbled upon a motionless figure. It was our man, crouching silently, shivering in the chilly night air, disheveled and without his belt, necklaces, and arm-bands (the Nambicuara wear nothing else). He allowed us to lead him back to the camp site without resistance, but only after long exhortations by his group and pleading by his family was he persuaded to talk. Finally, bit by bit, we extracted the details of his story. A thunderstorm, the first of the season, had burst during the afternoon, and the thunder had carried him off to a site several miles distant, which he named, and then, after stripping him completely, had brought him back to the spot where we found him. Everyone went off to sleep commenting on the event. The next day the thunder victim had recovered his joviality and, what is more, all his ornaments. This last detail did not appear to surprise anyone, and life resumed its normal course.

A few days later, however, another version of these prodigious events began to be circulated by certain natives. We must note that this band was actually composed of individuals of different origins and had been fused into a new social entity as a result of unknown circumstances. One of the groups had been decimated by an epidemic several years before and was no longer sufficiently large to lead an independent life; the other had seceded from its original tribe and found itself in the same straits. When and under what circumstances the two groups met and decided to unite their efforts, we could not discover. The secular leader of the new band came from one group and the sorcerer, or religious leader, from the other. The fusion was obviously recent, for no marriage had yet taken place between the two groups when we met them, although the children of one were usually betrothed to the children of the other; each group had retained its own dialect, and their members could communicate only through two or three bilingual natives.

This is the rumor that was spread. There was good reason to suppose that the unknown bands crossing the savanna belonged to the tribe of the seceded group of which the sorcerer was a member. The sorcerer, impinging on the functions of his colleague the political chief, had doubtless wanted to contact his former tribesmen, perhaps to ask to return to the fold, or to provoke an attack upon his new companions, or perhaps even to reassure them of the friendly intentions of the latter. In any case, the sorcerer had needed a pretext for his absence, and his kidnapping by thunder and its subsequent staging were invented toward this end. It was, of course, the natives of the other group who spread this interpretation, which they secretly believed and which filled them with apprehension. But the official version was never publicly disputed, and

until we left, shortly after the incident, it remained ostensibly accepted by all (Lévi-Strauss 1955:Ch. 29).

Although the skeptics had analyzed the sorcerer's motives with great psychological finesse and political acumen, they would have been greatly astonished had someone suggested (quite plausibly) that the incident was a hoax which cast doubt upon the sorcerer's good faith and competence. He had probably not flown on the wings of thunder to the Rio Ananaz and had only staged an act. But these things might have happened, they had certainly happened in other circumstances, and they belonged to the realm of real experience. Certainly the sorcerer maintains an intimate relationship with the forces of the supernatural. The idea that in a particular case he had used his power to conceal a secular activity belongs to the realm of conjecture and provides an opportunity for critical judgment. The important point is that these two possibilities were not mutually exclusive; no more than are, for us, the alternate interpretations of war as the dying gasp of national independence or as a result of the schemes of munitions manufacturers. The two explanations are logically incompatible, but we admit that one or the other may be true; since they are equally plausible, we easily make the transition from one to the other, depending on the occasion and the moment. Many people have both explanations in the back of their minds.

Whatever their true origin, these divergent interpretations come from individual consciousness not as the result of objective analysis but rather as complementary ideas resulting from hazy and unelaborated attitudes which have an experiential character for each of us. These experiences, however, remain intellectually diffuse and emotionally intolerable unless they incorporate one or another of the patterns present in the group's culture. The assimilation of such patterns is the only means of objectivizing subjective states, of formulating inexpressible feelings, and of integrating inarticulated experiences into a system.

These mechanisms become clearer in the light of some observations made many years ago among the Zuni of New Mexico by an admirable fieldworker, M. C. Stevenson (1955). A twelve-year-old girl was stricken with a nervous seizure directly after an adolescent boy had seized her hands. The youth was accused of sorcery and dragged before the court of the Bow priesthood. For an hour he denied having any knowledge of occult power, but this defense proved futile. Because the crime of sorcery was at that time still punished by death among the Zuni, the accused changed his tactics. He improvised a tale explaining the circumstances by which he had been initiated into sorcery. He said he had received two substances from his teachers, one which drove girls insane and another which cured them. This point constituted an ingenious precaution against later developments. Having been ordered to produce his medicines, he went home under guard and came back with two roots, which he proceeded to use in a complicated ritual. He simulated a trance after taking one of the drugs, and after taking the other he pretended to return to his normal state. Then he administered the remedy to the sick girl and declared her cured. The session was adjourned until the following day, but during the night the alleged sorcerer escaped. He was soon captured, and the girl's family set itself up as a court and continued the trial. Faced with the reluctance of his new judges to accept his first story, the boy then invented a new one. He told them that all his relatives and ancestors had been witches and that he had received marvellous powers from them. He claimed that he could assume the form of a cat, fill his mouth with cactus needles, and kill his victims—two infants, three girls, and two boys—by shooting the needles into them. These feats, he claimed, were due to the magical powers of certain plumes which were used to change him and his family into shapes other than human. This last detail was a tactical error, for the judges called upon him to produce the plumes as proof of his new story. He gave various excuses which were rejected one after another, and he was forced to take his judges to his house. He began by declaring that the plumes were secreted in a wall that he could not destroy. He was commanded to go to work. After breaking down a section of the wall and carefully examining the plaster, he tried to excuse himself by declaring that the plumes had been hidden two years before and that he could not remember their exact location. Forced to search again, he tried another wall, and after another hour's work, an old plume appeared in the plaster. He grabbed it eagerly and presented it to his persecutors as the magic device of which he had spoken. He was then made to explain the details of its use. Finally, dragged into the public plaza, he had to repeat his entire story (to which he added a wealth of new detail). He finished it with a pathetic speech in which he lamented the loss of his supernatural power. Thus reassured, his listeners agreed to free him.

This narrative, which we unfortunately had to abridge and strip of all its psychological nuances, is still instructive in many respects. First of all, we see that the boy tried for witchcraft, for which he risks the death penalty, wins his acquittal not by denying but by admitting his alleged crime. Moreover, he furthers his cause by presenting successive versions, each richer in detail (and thus, in theory, more persuasive of guilt) than the preceding one. The debate does not proceed, as do debates among us, by accusations and denials, but rather by allegations and specifications. The judges do not expect the accused to challenge their theory, much less to refute the facts. Rather, they require him to validate a system of which they possess only a fragment; he must reconstruct it as a whole in an appropriate way. As the field-worker noted in relation to a phase of the trial, "The warriors had become so absorbed by their interest in the narrative of the boy that they seemed entirely to have forgotten the cause of his appearance before them." And when the magic plume was finally uncovered, the author remarks with great insight, "There was consternation among the warriors, who exclaimed in one voice: 'What does this mean?' Now they felt assured that the youth had spoken the truth." Consternation, and not triumph at finding a tangible proof of the crime—for the judges had sought to bear witness to the reality of the system which had made the crime possible (by validating its objective basis through an appropriate emotional expression), rather than simply to punish a crime. By his confession, the defendant is transformed into a witness for the prosecution, with the participation (and even the complicity) of his judges. Through the defendant, witchcraft and the ideas associated with it cease to exist as a diffuse complex of poorly formulated sentiments and representations and become embodied in real experience. The defendant, who serves as a witness, gives the group the satisfaction of truth, which is infinitely greater and richer than the satisfaction of justice that would have been achieved by his execution. And finally, by his ingenious defense which makes his hearers progressively aware of the vitality offered by his corroboration of their system (especially since the choice is not between this system and another, but between the magical system and no system at all—that is, chaos), the youth, who at first was a threat to the physical security of his group, became the guardian of its spiritual coherence.

But is his defense merely ingenious? Everything leads us to believe that after groping for a subterfuge, the defendant participates with sincerity and—the word is not too strong—fervor in the drama enacted between him and his judges. He is proclaimed a sorcerer; since sorcerers do exist, he might well be one. And how would he know beforehand the signs which might reveal his calling to him? Perhaps the signs are there, present in this ordeal and in the convulsions of the little girl brought before the court. For the boy, too, the coherence of the system and the role assigned to him in preserving it are values no less essential than the personal security which he risks in the venture. Thus we see him, with a mixture of cunning and good faith, progressively construct the impersonation which is thrust upon him—chiefly by drawing on his knowledge and his memories, improvising somewhat, but above all living his role and seeking, through his manipulations and the ritual he builds from bits and pieces, the experience of a calling which is, at least theoretically, open to all. At the end of the adventure, what remains of his earlier hoaxes? To what extent has the hero become the dupe of his own impersonation? What is more, has he not truly become a sorcerer? We are told that in his final confession, "The longer the boy talked the more absorbed he became in his subject....At times his face became radiant with satisfaction at his power over his listeners." The girl recovers after he performs his curing ritual. The boy's experiences during the extraordinary ordeal become elaborated and structured. Little more is needed than for the innocent boy finally to confess to the possession of supernatural powers that are already recognized by the group.

We must consider at greater length another especially valuable document, which until now seems to have been valued solely for its linguistic interest. I refer to a fragment of the autobiography of a Kwakiutl Indian from the Vancouver region of Canada, obtained by Franz Boas (1930:Pt. II).

Quesalid (for this was the name he received when he became a sorcerer) did not believe in the power of the sorcerers—or, more accurately, shamans, since this is a better term for their specific type of activity in certain regions of the world. Driven by curiosity about their tricks and by the desire to expose them, he began to associate with the shamans until one of them offered to make him a member of their group. Quesalid did not wait to be asked twice, and his narrative recounts the details of his first lessons, a curious mixture of pantomime, prestidigitation, and empirical knowledge, including the art of simulating fainting and nervous fits,

the learning of sacred songs, the technique for inducing vomiting, rather precise notions of auscultation and obstetrics, and the use of "dreamers," that is, spies who listen to private conversations and secretly convey to the shaman bits of information concerning the origins and symptoms of the ills suffered by different people. Above all, he learned the *ars magna* of one of the shamanistic schools of the Northwest Coast: The shaman hides a little tuft of down in a corner of his mouth, and he throws it up, covered with blood, at the proper moment—after having bitten his tongue or made his gums bleed—and solemnly presents it to his patient and the onlookers as the pathological foreign body extracted as a result of his sucking and manipulations.

His worst suspicions confirmed, Quesalid wanted to continue his inquiry. But he was no longer free. His apprenticeship among the shamans began to be noised about, and one day he was summoned by the family of a sick person who had dreamed of Quesalid as his healer. This first treatment (for which he received no payment, any more than he did for those which followed, since he had not completed the required four years of apprenticeship) was an outstanding success. Although Quesalid came to be known from that moment on as a "great shaman," he did not lose his critical faculties. He interpreted his success in psychological terms—it was successful "because he [the sick person] believed strongly in his dream about me." A more complex adventure made him, in his own words, "hesitant and thinking about many things." Here he encountered several varieties of a "false supernatural," and was led to conclude that some forms were less false than others—those, of course, in which he had a personal stake and whose system he was, at the same time, surreptitiously building up in his mind. A summary of the adventure follows.

While visiting the neighboring Koskimo Indians, Quesalid attends a curing ceremony of his illustrious colleagues of the other tribe. To his great astonishment he observes a difference in their technique. Instead of spitting out the illness in the form of a "bloody worm" (the concealed down), the Koskimo shamans merely spit a little saliva into their hands, and they dare to claim that this is "the sickness." What is the value of this method? What is the theory behind it? In order to find out "the strength of the shamans, whether it was real or whether they only pretended to be shamans" like his fellow tribesmen, Quesalid requests and obtains permission to try his method in an instance where the Koskimo method has failed. The sick woman then declares herself cured.

And here our hero vacillates for the first time. Though he had few illusions about his own technique, he has now found one which is more false, more mystifying, and more dishonest than his own. For he at least gives his clients something. He presents them with their sickness in a visible and tangible form, while his foreign colleagues show nothing at all and only claim to have captured the sickness. Moreover, Quesalid's method gets results, while the other is futile. Thus our hero grapples with a problem which perhaps has its parallel in the development of modern science. Two systems which we know to be inadequate present (with respect to each other) a differential validity, from both a logical and an empirical perspective. From which frame of reference shall we judge them? On the level of fact, where they merge, or on their own level, where they take on different values, both theoretically and empirically?

Meanwhile, the Koskimo shamans, "ashamed" and discredited before their tribesmen, are also plunged into doubt. Their colleague has produced, in the form of a material object, the illness which they had always considered as spiritual in nature and had thus never dreamed of rendering visible. They send Quesalid an emissary to invite him to a secret meeting in a cave. Quesalid goes and his foreign colleagues expound their system to him: "Every sickness is a man: boils and swellings, and itch and scabs, and pimples and coughs and consumption and scrofula; and also this, stricture of the bladder and stomach aches. . . . As soon as we get the soul of the sickness which is a man, then dies the sickness which is a man. Its body just disappears in our insides." If this theory is correct, what is there to show? And why, when Quesalid operates, does "the sickness stick to his hand"? But Quesalid takes refuge behind professional rules which forbid him to teach before completing four years of apprenticeship, and refuses to speak. He maintains his silence even when the Koskimo shamans send him their allegedly virgin daughters to try to seduce him and discover his secret.

Thereupon Quesalid returns to his village at Fort Rupert. He learns that the most reputed shaman of a neighboring clan, worried about Quesalid's growing renown, has challenged all his colleagues, inviting them to compete with him in curing several patients. Quesalid comes to the contest and observes the cures of his elder. Like the Koskimo, this shaman does not show the illness. He simply incorporates an invisible object, "what he called the sickness" into his head-ring, made of bark, or into his bird-shaped ritual rattle. These objects can hang suspended in mid-air, owing to the power of the illness which "bites" the house-posts or the shaman's hand. The usual drama unfolds. Quesalid is asked to intervene in cases judged hopeless by his predecessor, and he triumphs with his technique of the bloody worm.

Here we come to the truly pathetic part of the story. The old shaman, ashamed and despairing because of the ill-repute into which he has fallen and by the collapse of his therapeutic technique, sends his daughter to Quesalid to beg him for an interview. The latter finds his colleague sitting under a tree and the old shaman begins thus: "It won't be bad what we say to each other, friend, but only I wish you to try and save my life for me, so that I may not die of shame, for I am a plaything of our people on account of what you did last night. I pray you to have mercy and tell me what stuck on the palm of your hand last night. Was it the true sickness or was it only made up? For I beg you have mercy and tell me about the way you did it so that I can imitate you. Pity me, friend."

Silent at first, Quesalid begins by calling for explanations about the feats of the head-ring and the rattle. His colleague shows him the nail hidden in the head-ring which he can press at right angles into the post, and the way in which he tucks the head of his rattle between his finger joints to make it look as if the bird were hanging by its beak from his hand. He himself probably does nothing but lie and fake, simulating shamanism for material gain, for he admits to being "covetous for the property of the sick men." He knows that shamans cannot catch souls, "for . . . we all own a soul"; so he resorts to using tallow and pretends that "it is a soul . . . that white thing . . . sitting on my hand." The daugher then adds her entreaties to those of her father: "Do have mercy that he may live." But Quesalid remains silent. That very night, following this tragic conversation, the shaman disappears with his entire family, heartsick and feared by the community, who think that he may be tempted to take revenge. Needless fears: He returned a year later, but both he and his daughter had gone mad. Three years later, he died.

And Quesalid, rich in secrets, pursued his career, exposing the impostors and full of contempt for the profession. "Only one shaman was seen by me, who sucked at a sick man and I never found out whether he was a real shaman or only made up. Only for this reason I believe that he is a shaman; he does not allow those who are made well to pay him. I truly never once saw him laugh." Thus his original attitude has changed considerably. The radical negativism of the free thinker has given way to more moderate feelings. Real shamans do exist. And what about him? At the end of the narrative we cannot tell, but it is evident that he carries on his craft conscientiously, takes pride in his achievements, and warmly defends the technique of the bloody down against all rival schools. He seems to have completely lost sight of the fallaciousness of the technique which he had so disparaged at the beginning.

We see that the psychology of the sorcerer is not simple. In order to analyze it, we shall first examine the case of the old shaman who begs his young rival to tell him the truth—whether the illness glued in the palm of his hand like a sticky red worm is real or made up—and who goes mad when he receives no answer. Before the tragedy, he was fully convinced of two things—first, that pathological conditions have a cause which may be discovered and second, that a system of interpretation in which personal inventiveness is important structures the phases of the illness, from the diagnosis to the cure. This fabulation of a reality unknown in itself—a fabulation consisting of procedures and representations—is founded on a threefold experience: first, that of the shaman himself, who, if his calling is a true one (and even if it is not, simply by virtue of his practicing it), undergoes specific states of a psychosomatic nature; second, that of the sick person, who may or may not experience an improvement of his condition; and, finally, that of the public, who also participate in the cure, experiencing an enthusiasm and an intellectual and emotional satisfaction which produce collective support, which in turn inaugurates a new cycle.

These three elements of what we might call the "shamanistic complex" cannot be separated. But they are clustered around two poles, one formed by the intimate experience of the shaman and the other by group consensus. There is no reason to doubt that sorcerers, or at least the more sincere among them, believe in their calling and that this belief is founded on the experiencing of specific states. The hardships and privations which they undergo would often be sufficient in themselves to provoke these states, even if we refuse to admit them as proof of a serious and fervent calling. But there is also linguistic evidence which, because it is indirect, is more convincing. In the Wintu dialect of California, there are five verbal classes which correspond to knowledge by sight, by bodily experience, by inference, by reasoning, and by hearsay. All five make up the category of knowledge as opposed to conjecture, which is differently expressed. Curiously enough, relationships with the supernatural world are expressed by means of the modes of knowledge—by bodily impression (that is, the most intuitive kind of experience), by inference, and by reasoning. Thus the native who becomes a shaman after a spiritual crisis conceives of his state grammatically, as a consequence to be inferred from the fact—formulated as real experience—that he has received divine guidance. From the latter he concludes deductively that he must have been on a journey to the beyond, at the end of which he found himself—again, an immediate experience—once more among his people (Lee 1941).

The experiences of the sick person represent the least important aspect of the system, except for the fact that a patient successfully treated by a shaman is in an especially good position to become a shaman in his own right, as we see today in the case of psychoanalysis. In any event, we must remember that the shaman does not completely lack empirical knowledge and experimental techniques, which may in part explain his success. Furthermore, disorders of the type currently termed psychosomatic, which constitute a large part of the illnesses prevalent in societies with a low degree of security, probably often yield to psychotherapy. At any rate, it seems probable that medicine men, like their civilized colleagues, cure at least some of the cases they treat and that without this relative success magical practices could not have been so widely diffused in time and space. But this point is not fundamental; it is subordinate to the other two. Quesalid did not become a great shaman because he cured his patients; he cured his patients because he had become a great shaman. Thus we have reached the other—that is, the collective—pole of our system.

The true reason for the defeat of Quesalid's rivals must then be sought in the attitude of the group rather than in the pattern of the rivals' successes and failures. The rivals themselves emphasize this when they confess their shame at having become the laughingstock of the group; this is a social sentiment *par excellence*. Failure is secondary, and we see in all their statements that they consider it a function of another phenomenon, which is the disappearance of the *social consensus*, re-created at their expense around another practitioner and another system of curing. Consequently, the fundamental problem revolves around the relationship between the individual and the group, or, more accurately, the relationship between a specific category of individuals and specific expectations of the group.

In treating his patient the shaman also offers his audience a performance. What is this performance? Risking a rash generalization on the basis of a few observations, we shall say that it always involves the shaman's enactment of the "call," or the initial crisis which brought him the revelation of his condition. But we must not be deceived by the word *performance*. The shaman does not limit himself to reproducing or miming certain events. He actually relives them in all their vividness, originality, and violence. And since he returns to his normal state at the end of the séance, we may say, borrowing a key term from psychoanalysis, that he *abreacts*. In psychoanalysis, abreaction refers to the decisive moment in the treatment when the patient intensively relives the initial situation from which his disturbance stems, before he ultimately overcomes it. In this sense, the shaman is a professional abreactor.

We have set forth elsewhere the theoretical hypotheses that might be formulated in order for us to accept the idea that the type of abreaction specific to each shaman—or, at any rate, to each shamanistic school—might symbolically induce an abreaction of his own disturbance in each patient. In any case, if the essential relationship is that between the shaman and the group, we must also state the question from another point of view—that of the relationship between normal and pathological thinking. From any non-scientific perspective (and here we can exclude no society), pathological and normal thought processes are complementary rather than opposed. In a universe which it strives to understand but whose dynamics it cannot fully control, normal thought continually seeks the meaning of things which refuse to reveal their significance. So-called pathological thought, on the other hand, overflows with emotional interpretations and overtones, in order to supplement an otherwise deficient reality. For normal thinking there exists something which cannot be empirically verified and is, therefore, "claimable." For pathological thinking there exist experiences without object, or something "available." We might borrow from linguistics and say that so-called normal thought always suffers from a deficit of meaning, whereas so-called pathological thought (in at least some of its manifestations) disposes of a plethora of meaning. Through collective participation in shamanistic curing, a balance is established between these two

complementary situations. Normal thought cannot fathom the problem of illness, and so the group calls upon the neurotic to furnish a wealth of emotion heretofore lacking a focus.

An equilibrium is reached between what might be called supply and demand on the psychic level—but only on two conditions. First, a structure must be elaborated and continually modified through the interaction of group tradition and individual invention. This structure is a system of oppositions and correlations, integrating all the elements of a total situation, in which sorcerer, patient, and audience, as well as representations and procedures, all play their parts. Furthermore, the public must participate in the abreaction, to a certain extent at least, along with the patient and the sorcerer. It is this vital experience of a universe of symbolic effusions which the patient, because he is ill, and the sorcerer, because he is neurotic—in other words, both having types of experience which cannot otherwise be integrated—allow the public to glimpse as "fireworks" from a safe distance. In the absence of any experimental control, which is indeed unnecessary, it is this experience alone, and its relative richness in each case, which makes possible a choice between several systems and elicits adherence to a particular school or practitioner.

In contrast with scientific explanation, the problem here is not to attribute confused and disorganized states, emotions, or representations to an objective cause, but rather to articulate them into a whole or system. The system is valid precisely to the extent that it allows the coalescence or precipitation of these diffuse states, whose discontinuity also makes them painful. To the conscious mind, this last phenomenon constitutes an original experience which cannot be grasped from without. Because of their complementary disorders, the sorcerer-patient dyad incarnates for the group, in vivid and concrete fashion, an antagonism that is inherent in all thought but that normally remains vague and imprecise. The patient is all passivity and self-alienation, just as inexpressibility is the disease of the mind. The sorcerer is activity and self-projection, just as affectivity is the source of symbolism. The cure interrelates these opposite poles, facilitating the transition from one to the other, and demonstrates, within a total experience, the coherence of the psychic universe, itself a projection of the social universe.

Thus it is necessary to extend the notion of abreaction by examining the meanings it acquires in psychotherapies other than psychoanalysis, although the latter deserves the credit for re-discovering and insisting upon its fundamental validity. It may be objected that in psychoanalysis there is only one abreaction, the patient's, rather than three. We are not so sure of this. It is true that in the shamanistic cure the sorcerer speaks and abreacts *for* the silent patient, while in psychoanalysis it is the patient who talks and abreacts *against* the listening therapist. But the therapist's abreaction, while not concomitant with the patient's, is nonetheless required, since he must be analyzed before he himself can become an analyst. It is more difficult to define the role ascribed to the group by each technique. Magic readapts the group to predefined problems through the patient, while psychoanalysis readapts the patient to the group by means of the solutions reached. But the distressing trend which, for several years, has tended to transform the psychoanalytic system from a body of scientific hypotheses that are experimentally verifiable in certain specific and limited cases into a kind of diffuse mythology interpenetrating the consciousness of the group, could rapidly bring about a parallelism. (This group consciousness is an objective phenomenon, which the psychologist expresses through a subjective tendency to extend to normal thought a system of interpretations conceived for pathological thought and to apply to facts of collective psychology a method adapted solely to the study of individual psychology.) When this happens—and perhaps it already has in certain countries—the value of the system will no longer be based upon real cures from which certain individuals can benefit, but on the sense of security that the group receives from the myth underlying the cure and from the popular system upon which the group's universe is reconstructed.

Even at the present time, the comparison between psychoanalysis and older and more widespread psychological therapies can encourage the former to re-examine its principles and methods. By continuously expanding the recruitment of its patients, who begin as clearly characterized abnormal individuals and gradually become representative of the group, psychoanalysis transforms its treatments into conversions. For only a patient can emerge cured; an unstable or maladjusted individual can only be persuaded. A considerable danger thus arises: The treatment (unbeknown to the therapist, naturally), far from leading to the resolution of a specific disturbance within its own context, is reduced to the reorganization of the patient's universe in terms of psychoanalytic interpretations. This means that we would finally arrive at precisely that situation which furnishes the point of departure as well as the theoretical validity of the magico-social system that we have analyzed.

If this analysis is correct, we must see magical behavior as the response to a situation which is revealed to the mind through emotional manifestations, but whose essence is intellectual. For only the history of the symbolic function can allow us to understand the intellectual condition of man, in which the universe is never charged with sufficient meaning and in which the mind always has more meanings available than there are objects to which to relate them. Torn between these two systems of reference—the signifying and the signified—man asks magical thinking to provide him with a new system of reference, within which the thus-far contradictory elements can be integrated. But we know that this system is built at the expense of the progress of knowledge, which would have required us to retain only one of the two previous systems and to refine it to the point where it absorbed the other. This point is still far off. We must not permit the individual, whether normal or neurotic, to repeat this collective misadventure. The study of the mentally sick individual has shown us that all persons are more, or less oriented toward contradictory systems and suffer from the resulting conflict; but the fact that a certain form of integration is possible and effective practically is not enough to make it true, or to make us certain that the adaptation thus achieved does not constitute an absolute regression in relation to the previous conflict situation.

The reabsorption of a deviant specific synthesis, through its integration with the normal syntheses, into a general but arbitrary synthesis (aside from critical cases where action is required) would represent a loss on all fronts. A body of elementary hypotheses can have a certain instrumental value for the practitioner without necessarily being recognized, in theoretical analysis, as the final image of reality and without necessarily linking the patient and the therapist in a kind of mystical communion which does not have the same meaning for both parties and which only ends by reducing the treatment to a fabulation.

In the final analysis we could only expect this fabulation to be a language, whose function is to provide a socially authorized translation of phenomena whose deeper nature would become once again equally impenetrable to the group, the patient, and the healer.

# 51 The Urban Curandero

## *Irwin Press*

The large literature on *curanderismo* in Latin America tends to emphasize a relatively few traits as featuring the role of the curer in those areas, leading to what Irwin Press, the author of this article, calls a "peasant-derived stereotype" that may be adequate for the relatively limited range of possibilities in the rural context, but is limiting and misleading when applied to urban folk curers. This study of a large city in Colombia demonstrates an amazing variety of curers available to the city dweller, most of them attracting a massive clientele, including even rural inhabitants who may come long distances to avail themselves of their services. Press proposes that in approaching the study of folk medical practitioners in cities, the orienting concept of "urban curing complex" be used as a way of opening up the full spectrum of possibilities rather than dependence upon the constricted peasant model of curers and their practice. Although this is not the first study of folk curers in urban areas (sociologists and anthropologists have studied them in New York City and elsewhere), it provides medical anthropologists with a theoretical model for future research into this important area.

Similar to Press' point is one made by Octavio Romano (1965) that the stereotypical, unidimensional portrayal of healers in ethnological literature suggested relatively rigid, almost caricatured personalities and statuses with scant room for individual achievement and variation, and not much more for specialization and differentiation (see other papers in this section and my introduction). Romano postulates that the healer's role carries with it two charismatic and complementary components: the role may be strengthened and maintained with little change through reinforcing effects of the individual healer's personality, or it may be changed through the innovating consequences of his personality. In Mexican-American culture (as in all cultures), there are competing strains toward cooperative maintenance of the social order and individual autonomy and expression. Atomistic tendencies are reinforced by the traditional emphasis on independence, mistrust, and uncooperativeness, especially in the male role, whereas the traditional emphasis on the healer role is one of communal responsibility, service, and cooperativeness. The healer, in choosing his role, ideally rejects the traditional male role imperatives, and closes off any alternative except that of complete dedication to the commonweal. Romano describes a ten-status hierarchical social structure for

Reprinted in abridged form from Irwin Press, 1971, "The Urban Curandero," *American Anthropologist*, 73:742–756, with permission of the author and the American Anthropological Association.

healers, from the lowest one of a bent toward healing competence to the most revered, powerful, and respected international, religious, formal saint. His analysis is built around the biography of Don Pedro Jarmillo, a legendary 19th-century Mexican healer in Southwest Texas, whose fame spread far beyond the borders of his own community, and who reached a mythological level and became apotheosized after his death, having achieved the ninth hierarchical level of an international religious folk-saint.

His grave became a shrine to which pilgrimages were made from great distances by Mexican-Americans of all social levels to beseech his aid in medical and other problems. Don Pedro's power beyond death continues to the present time, influencing the behavior of contemporary healers in his direction of ascetic, selfless, loving devotion to his calling. Romano compares Don Pedro's career with the model of the charismatic leader of Max Weber and concludes that though the model seems generally applicable to this saintly curer, it departs from the model in two respects: this healer's role, though clearly charismatic, was conservative not radical and not so much innovating as renovating.

## I

As though illness and requirements of the sick role were everywhere of a more or less homogeneous order, *the* curandero has become an institution in the Latin Americanist's repertoire; a veritable homage to the peasant milieu which represents Latin America at its "purest."

This development is certainly justifiable, given the contributions to anthropology of peasant-derived (particularly Latin American) studies and the necessity for bringing order to a complex and important psycho-social phenomenon. At base, too, such exotica as evil eye, sorcery, *susto* and other illnesses have tended to be especially attractive to the anthropologist. However, while providing needed insight into an important and unusual phenomenon, a continuum of (for example) *susto* studies such as those of Gillin (1948:1957), Foster (1951), Rubel (1964), O'Nell and Selby (1968) and others inadvertently fosters the impression that a "real" curandero is almost continually involved in collaborating with patients in a series of intimate psycho-social dramas.

It is difficult not to notice a developing stereotype of *the* curandero's style and function. More mundane illness is generally relegated to a minor position, and a wide range of practitioners is ignored or assigned to some residual category such as "marginal" or "limited." As derived from a sample of both urban and rural studies which attempt to describe or synthesize curer typologies for various areas of Latin America, such stereotypic curer style consists in: the use of confession as a therapeutic device (Kiev 1968:28; Adams and Rubel 1967:350); performance or diagnosis "familiar" to the patient (Rubel 1966:194; Clark 1959:207; Gutierrez 1961:71, 76; Saunders 1958:547–548; Kiev 1968:127); manifest concern for reintegration of the patient into his community (Adams and Rubel 1967:349; Romano 1965:1165; Saunders 1958:547–548); a lengthy diagnostic and/or curative performance (Clark 1959:216; Kiev 1968:125–126); active involvement of family or friends in the diagnosis and/or cure (Adams and Rubel 1967:349; Clark 1959:208; Saunders 1958:547–548); no fees, low fees, non-specified fees or fee ritualization (Adams and Rubel 1967:349; Romano 1965:1153; Rubel 1966:194; Madsen 1964:430; Gutierrez 1961:74; Clark 1959:208)....

Such approaches provide little leeway for understanding and classifying curers who are not of an "either-or" type—who combine stereotypic and non-stereotypic elements of style; who may exhibit "socio-ritual concern" only occasionally or when not treating such mundane complaints as arthritis; or who may take a clear, yet minimal interest in the socio-ritual state of the patient.

Perhaps above all, reliance upon a stereotype (particularly a peasant-derived one) or catch-all classification decreases sensitivity to the social, cultural and physical environment in which healers operate. Differing psychological foundations, illness lore, community structure, sanctioning devices and—not least important—differing sanitary habits, immunities and disease contacts would all seem to require shifts in the style and competence of healing personnel.

## II

Adams and Rubel implicitly suggest that the likelihood of greater curer specialization in Mesoamerica increases with increase in acculturation of the community (1967:347). The variety both of functions urban curanderismo may fill, and of the dual manners in which physicians and curers may be utilized has been suggested by Rubel (1960), Press (1969) and others. In particular, it would seem, the potential coexistence of hospitals, pharmacies, patent medicines, physicians, emergency centers, ambulance service, herbalists,

curanderos, "spiritists," homeopaths, naturopaths, osteopaths, etc., makes the urban milieu dramatically more competitive and open to idiosyncratic healer behavior than the peasant or rural.

In sum, we would anticipate increased diversity of curer style and function in the more urban milieu, reflective of a more heterogeneous range of psychological, social, subcultural, and somatic patient needs.

Existing accounts of urban curers suggest such diversity, yet provide little basis for generalization. All focus upon elements of the peasant-oriented stereotype, resulting usually in cursory concern for "other" types, or for other elements of their focal curer's stylistic repertoire. The variety of typologies reflects this uneven concern.

Romano identifies his South Texas "type" curer on the bases of charisma and "communality" or social concern. He ignores other types. Subsequently, he subdivides his curandero population on the bases of fame and success, giving the impression that curers differ little in other respects. His types range from household member, through neighbor and community curer to regional and "international" (in this specific case, "border") curers (1965:1153). Rubel, reporting on a south Texas community of 15,000, identifies essentially one type of curer, largely on the basis of the source of his calling (gift of God, dreams), and makes little reference to stylistic differences among curers. He utilizes degree of experience, however, to differentiate his remaining "types"—housewives and neighborhood curers (1966:200). Kiev's San Antonio (Texas) curandero is a "religious healer" who employs stereotypic elements and utilizes techniques which Kiev views as familiar to modern psychiatric medicine (1968:30–31). Other types of curers are ignored, as Kiev distinguishes simply between the religious curer and herbalists who are "paid specialists in herbs" (1968:32). Clark's typology from San Jose, California, also involves a sweeping dichotomy. It separates the highly personalistic "curandera" (her informants were female) from all other curers, whom she lumps as "marginal" practitioners (1959:211). The locus of her study is a much larger urban area than that described by Romano or Rubel, and it is of interest that she notes the existence of more healer-related roles including herbalists, chiropractors and homeopaths.

Not far south of the Mexican border, in the large city of Torreon, Kelly notes four healer categories: (1) "witches (brujas, hechiceras, curanderas)" who fit many aspects of the stereotype list and who may cause as well as cure illness (1965:25); (2) spiritualistic mediums who also diagnose and treat and who may also cause illness. Kelly further notes the existence of other spiritualistic mediums who do not cure, but rather specialize in problems of luck. Kelly differentiates spiritualistic mediums from curanderas on the basis of the spiritualist's traffic with supernatural spirits and their use of much religious symbolism "and ritual" (1965:27); (3) herbalists (generally full-time); and (4) "subprofessionals" such as massagers, midwives, and specialists in fallen fontanel (1965:38). Kelly distinguishes curanderas from spiritualists on the apparent basis of power source and her types (3) and (4) from each other and from (1) and (2) on implicit and unclear bases....

In sum, while it is likely that curers represent a more complex and environmentally dependent phenomenon than hitherto suggested, the constrained focus of existing approaches is unconducive to understanding either this complexity or relationship.

## III

... In the course of searching out and categorizing Bogota curers, the deficiency of present curer models became apparent. With little difficulty, a rather "stereotypic" curandera was located in a Bogota suburb. She showed considerable "socioritual" concern for her patients, cured sorcery, evil-eye and *susto*, charged but little, prescribed ritual as well as herbal cures, took a relatively personal approach to the curative session, etc. However, she received, at most ten patients weekly—scarcely sufficient for the study's purpose. On the other hand, three far less stereotypic curers treated upwards of 400 patients weekly among them. These, then, had to supply the required patient sample....

\* \* \*

Pablo Gato's office is located in one of the poorest established barrios of Bogota. At one end of a second floor balcony is Gato's consultation room. At the other end are his herb room and steaming kitchen-laboratory. There are rarely fewer than 20 patients stretched along the balcony, and the number is replenished as the day wears on.

Gato's office opens at seven a.m. A half-dozen patients have spent the night on his balcony so as to be sure of an early turn. The average wait is four hours. Approximately 90 percent of his patients are lower and lower middle class. Most were born outside of Bogota, though a simple majority reside in the city itself. Patients may be accompanied by one or two family members. Most usually, family accompany only those too young or feeble to make the journey by themselves. During their long wait, patients freely discuss their problems, swap impressions of curers, physicians, and home remedies they have used.

Each patient enters in privacy and sits next to Gato. Gato wears a spotted suit, white shirt and tie. He is a stout and partially crippled man of 63. His speech is slurred. His eye glasses are thick and distorting. On a desk before him are a book of orations and a cluttered array of bottles containing patients' urine. There are several pink upholstered chairs, a pink sofa, and a coffee table with doilie. In the corner is a tall statue of San Martin de Porres, patron saint of the sick and poor. On its head is Gato's black homburg. Gato's office days are Tuesday and Friday—the "days" of S. Martin.

The sessions last from five to ten minutes. Gato greets each patient with a smile and a friendly "how are things?" He diagnoses by laying on of hands, taking wrist pulse, examining urine, and listening to patients' symptoms. Urinalysis is conducted by the addition of a "bismuth solution." The darker the urine and resulting precipitate, the more likely a case of sorcery. Patients who cannot come in person may send their urine with a friend or kinsman. During and after the patient's statement of symptoms and/or suspicions, Gato's hands move from patient's wrist to temples, to back of neck, to knee, to forehead. Of the five or ten minutes' total consultation, however, *rarely* are more than two or three given to conversation with the patient. Regardless of the case involved, only minimal information is required by the curer. If the patient exhibits an initial suspicion of sorcery, Gato usually concurs. On subsequent visits, verbal interchange may shrink to a minute or disappear entirely.

All patients then make a "petition"—a responsive recitation of an oration led by Gato, two or three words at a time. This consumes the remainder of the office consultation. The petition-oration consists in obscure references and phrases, juxtaposed with Catholic prayers and perhaps a word or two specific to the patient's complaint. Patients do not refer among themselves to their visits as "visits" or "consultations," but rather as "petitions," thus at least verbally ritualizing this portion of their treatment.

456

Gato claims to have learned his trade from "Indians" and improved it through books. All ills seem to be represented among his patients. Gato claims ability to cure sorcery, *susto*, evil eye, and non-magical illnesses including cancer and obesity. He can bring back errant spouses, find lost persons or objects, end bad luck, and endow good. On occasion, he himself functions as sorcerer in sending evil against enemies of his patients. A quarter of his patients he diagnoses as suffering from a "natural" illness. A quarter suffer from bad luck or abandonment. The remaining half he diagnoses as suffering from sorcery, *susto*, evil eye, or *duende* (ghostly malice). Gato "lumps" symptoms and arrives at a diagnosis of but one or two underlying causes. It is important to note that Gato does not dispense herbals during or immediately following each diagnosis and petition, but rather waits until perhaps a half dozen patients have been seen and are waiting by his herb room. For the average patient, an hour might pass between petition and dispensation of medicine.

Gato charges but a nominal sum for consultations. Patients with complaints which also require herbals, are charged but a peso (six U.S. cents) per visit (or "petition"); for the herbals, however, they must pay from 30 to 150 pesos or more. Patients receiving petitions only (for bad luck, say) are charged far higher prices. Always, however, these sums are of some apparently symbolic significance: for example 100.01 for the first petition, 5.05 pesos the second, 100.01 the third, etc. As centavos are almost non-existent, Gato solemnly provides the patient with a penny which the patient, with equal solemnity, returns to Gato with 100 pesos of his own. Payment is thus ritualized and appears to be part of the cure. Patients are generally asked to return in odd-numbers of visits, up to 33 times. Diagnostic-petition payments are made at the time of diagnosis, formally "closing" the consultation. Payment for herbals is thus conceptually separate and made later, following dispensing.

Patients suffering from sorcery, bad luck, and abandonment are often required to bring votive candles. Gato lights these on an altar in his herb room on which are a cross, human skull, and portraits of saints. Clearly visible, too, are glossy candid snapshots of individuals with pins stuck through the chest, victims of Gato's sorcery on behalf of patients. Gato usually gives additional advice at this time (stay away from pork, liquor, etc.) and may sell blessed rings (or bless the patient's) for good luck. Ritual prescriptions (such as attendance at 33 masses) are made only during the initial petition. Where non-supernatural illness is diagnosed, it is most always due to an imbalance or upset of the patient's "nature" (*naturaleza*). Indeed, Gato calls himself a practitioner of "the Mother Science, Naturalistic Flower."

Gato sees upwards of seventy patients on each of his two weekly consulting days. Payments (consultations and herbals combined) appear to average 70 pesos ($4.20), and patients with failing businesses may pay thousands for a turn of luck. A conservative estimate puts Gato's gross income at $800 per week.

\*   \*   \*

Delfino Pacheco—"The Curer of San Martin de Porres" as he is referred to by his patients—lives in a poor community within fifteen minutes of Bogota. As at Gato's, a line of up to thirty patients stretches from the consulting room. Here, too, the line and inevitable delays demand an entire day of the patient. In addition to the front three or four of the line, there are four or five patients sitting on a bench and awaiting (or loudly recovering from) potent green ear, eye, or nose drops. One or two crying cripples are having their limbs massaged with the same fluid. There is no privacy here. A dozen others can clearly hear each patient's complaint. On two walls hang dozens of crutches and braces left by patients who walked from the office after massage. Another wall is occupied by framed testimonials. On the forewall hang pictures of San Martin de Porres. Below the pictures is a desk beside which sits a female secretary.

Pacheco, the curer, is short, dapper, and in his early forties. He wears a neat, blue suit and a dark blue fedora which he never removes in the office. Each hand sports several large gold and gem-stone rings.

Pacheco was born with a special diagnostic power in his hands. He learned to cure, he claims, from Indians in the jungles of Ecuador. Following his apprenticeship, he claims to have toured the world, curing as he went. Kings were at his feet. At last he came to Bogota, to place himself "at the service of the public."

Standing before his desk, Pacheco takes the patient's left hand and asks him to recount his symptoms. He may ask a question or two, though always directed toward symptoms, never etiology or suspected cause. Conversation lasts a minute at most. Pacheco then reiterates the symptoms aloud, and for each named his secretary plucks a slip of paper from a pigeon-hole in a box on the desk. From five to eight slips are pulled. Each contains directions for the preparation of some simple (generally herbal) concoction specific to one symptom. When the patient names but one or two symptoms, Pacheco invariably "divines" others to bring the number up to an average of six. As with Gato, Pacheco rarely misses when he announces that the patient has headache, "dizziness from time to time," pains "in the mouth of the stomach" and diarrhoea. His patients, it should be noted, can suffer *only* from among the thirty symptoms contained in his recipe collection—"gall bladder," head pain, back pain, stomach pain, fever, etc.

Unlike Gato, the Curer of San Martin de Porres does *not* recognize supernatural or social causality. Should a patient insist upon suffering from sorcery, Pacheco asks him to leave. Simple *sustos* (which do not involve soul-loss) and *aires* are, however, admissible.

Pacheco, too, charges a minimal fee for the diagnostic consultation—a mere peso per slip of paper. Many patients also receive drops, for which a nominal charge is also made. Upon leafing through his prescriptions, the patient finds that most can be prepared from simple herbs and familiar home ingredients. There is almost always one symptom, however, requiring some exotic ingredient which, fortunately, can be purchased conveniently in a pharmacy which Pacheco maintains (along with two pharmacists) behind his office. These ingredients (certain holy wine, exotic animal blood, etc.) cost patients from thirty to several hundreds of pesos. Drops aside, Pacheco does not dispense or receive money for medicinals or personally massage. Pacheco may require the patient to return several times, each time to receive refills and additional slips of paper. That one of six or seven recipes should demand an exotic substance is not considered unreasonable by patients. That it should cost a good deal confirms its efficacy. The prestige derived from paying high medicinal costs in Colombia has been noted by Guiterrez (1961:36) and the Reichels (1961:312).

*     *     *

"The Bishop" had been a lay friar for many years. During this time he corresponded with a European school of homeopathy and began to receive patients. In addition to the prescription and preparation of homeopathic remedies he began to take an interest in "iris diagnosis," a well-known naturopathic technique wherein the condition of body organs can be ascertained from striations of the eye's iris. When his fame was high, The Bishop left the Church and set up an office of his own. Several years later he married and established a practice in a fashionable upper middle-class neighborhood. Though a licensed homeopath, he has no shingle on his door.

Some ten to 15 patients, of a wealthier class than those at Gato's or Pacheco's, sit in a neat, tiled waiting room. The Bishop prefers that patients make appointments several days in advance. His office looks "medical": diploma, neat desk, glass-fronted laden bookcases, file cabinet, charts, dentist chair.

The Bishop is a short, rotund, and pleasant man in his late forties with a physician's look and manner. He wears a white half-frock coat over a clean suit.

Upon entering the consulting room, a white-frocked nurse takes a history of previous illness and treatment, which she places in a manila folder and files. The patient sits in the dentist's chair while The Bishop asks question about symptoms. He then directs light into the patient's eye while peering at the patient's iris through a six or eight inch diameter lens. Seen through the patient's end, The Bishop's eye is omnipresent: huge, intimidating, invincible.

The Bishop dispenses injections, and most patients receive a prescription for homeopathic medicines. According to ex-patients, his repertoire also includes cures such as beef-broth body rubs. He may personally massage the infirm. Consultation, though more frequently expensive than consultation with Gato or Pacheco, again costs less than the medicinals. Most of these can only be purchased across town at a homeopathic pharmacy owned by The Bishop.

Ex-patients declare that The Bishop can cure all ills, even magical. Several "miraculous" cures are attributed to him. Offhand, his style would seem to place him apart from Gato or Pacheco. The patient, however, is the final arbiter of style and classification, and he constantly names The Bishop in conjunction with more "familiar" types. It has been noted in the Colombian countryside and specifically recorded by the Reichel-Dolmatoffs in Aritama to the north, that curers examine the pupils of a patient's eyes "because they are said to show whether the disease is due to a very potent witchcraft" (1961:289). Intentionally or not, The Bishop appears to be looking for just such a sign.

It cannot be said that The Bishop is representative of all homeopaths in Bogota. Another visited has modest, unkempt offices in a poor barrio. A shingle hangs on his door. His dispensary shelves are cluttered with herbals and nostrums in various-sized apothecary jars with cork stoppers and faded Latin labels. In an ill-fitting, stained suit, the elderly homeopath diagnoses by questioning and by cursory examination on an examination table. He himself prepares and dispenses medicines, charging once for all. His charges are low and his patients few. He does not treat supernatural illness as such or utilize spectacular techniques.

\*     \*     \*

On the fringe of Bogota, in the dirt-street back section of a fashionable suburb, live two sisters-in-law. Their offices are a block apart. The better known of the two, "Serafina's Daughter," is the daughter of a well-known curandera, Serafina. Indeed, many patients come to her unaware that the old lady has been dead for over three years. The daughter has managed to surmount this obstacle; she receives advice from her dead mother "who appears in my mirror in the form of a dove." Lately, the mother has been less communicative. "She got mad. Said it wasn't fitting for her to deal continuously with living people. So I only call upon her when evil spirits have made me ill. They are constantly at me, jealous of my ability to heal." Regardless of the evil spirits, however, and though she unambiguously believes in the operation of supernatural forces such as sorcery, Serafina's Daughter will not treat supernaturally caused illness. She deals instead with grippe, abortions, pregnancy, childbirth, sinusitis, asthma, and other "natural" problems, including *sustos*. "My sister-in-law, up the hill, knows how to deal with sorcery and luck."

Outside the office, slowly sweeping the street, is the curer's retarded brother. An elderly female helper is necessary in that Serafina's Daugher also is both somewhat retarded and very hard of hearing. The helper interprets the daughter's words, shouts into her ear and speaks for her. "She's a virgin," explains the helper, glancing toward the daughter, "yes, a real virgin." The daughter, who is in her early thirties, concurs.

Diagnosis is made by looking at the patient and examining urine. A single cause is derived from the various symptoms. Most usually, symptoms and diagnoses are matter of fact (grippe, asthma, etc.). Cure involves the writing of simple herbal prescriptions or preparation of compounds which she gives to the patient. Total cost per consultation (including herbals) rarely exceeds ten pesos. She claims to have learned to cure from her mother, who had books on curing. "Illiterates can't learn to cure," comments the daughter of Serafina.

Sofia, the sister-in-law, lives up the hill in a better, neater house. She is a woman in her late forties, tiny and alert. She had married old Serafina's son. "A mistake," she explains. "They're all feebleminded idiots in that family. All except the old lady, who I learned to cure from. I have a lot of trouble from them. I've suffered from the *envidia* of my sister-in-law. My neighbors are envious of me too. I'm constantly sick from their machinations."

Sofia claims to cure all ills. Cancer, TB, evil eye, all cases of sorcery, and luck problems. She will accept urine specimens and can diagnose stay-at-homes if brought their urine. She generally diagnoses by listening to complaints and is more than ready to press patients about their enemies. For natural illness, she prescribes home remedies (calcium water, rich broths, etc.). She believes that good nutrition and tranquility are major parts of a good cure. Supernatural illness is due to evil eye, sorcery, or failure to recite a prayer properly. Evil eye can be cured by the Church only. A "recanta" (lit. rechanting) is required in which a priest re-baptizes the patient. Sofia can direct patients to priests who will perform this cure. Other supernatural illnesses, once their cause is determined, can be cured through recitation of certain "novenas" to certain saints. Her often lengthy diagnosis may involve a detailed elicitation of social and ritual background experiences of the patient.

To make ends meet, Sofia grows corn beside her house. Her cures rarely involve more than a thirty peso charge. Neither she nor her sister-in-law are successful in terms of patient case-load. Neither sees more than ten patients weekly.

\*     \*     \*

By no means do these five curers exhaust the types available to patients in Bogota. In terms of diagnosis alone, for example, there are curers in Bogota who determine illness through: examination of a personal object brought by the patient; examination of skin discolorations and/or hair patterns; various divination techniques including interpretation of oil stains and coffee grounds; and use of "pseudo-scientific or scientific instruments." The manner of establishing payment is equally varied and includes: setting a fixed, unvarying sum for all patients; setting varying sums depending upon treatment and patient wealth; accepting payment only for treatments used, while claiming to refuse any "personal" honorarium; acceptance of non-cash gifts only; relegating treatment to assistants who then charge the fee. There are also curers who receive no fee whatsoever for their services, but who are supported by a "congregation" or "followers."

Still other individuals specialize in mass cures. With a number of patients present, one such curer requests each to place a personal identification number (telephone, address, social security) on a piece of paper which is deposited in a bowl. Before the assembly, the curer "sends the notes to God" with prayer. God will be able to identify and thus locate and cure each supplicant through the number provided. Another "group curer" delivers special injections to patients before an audience. If the patient has faith in God, the injection will cure any ill. If not, the patient will die forthwith. God himself diagnoses. Surviving patients feel especially blessed in having publicly demonstrated to themselves and others a faith in God. Neither of the "group curers" charges a set fee. Rather, they accept donations.

Should patients prefer "auto-curative" means to consultation with a healer, there are a number of "do-it-yourself" methods available. The Church of Saint Ignacius of Loyola promises health from its curative waters. A long line of individuals—each with his bottles—stretches from the spigot (kept behind bars) to the church entrance. The water can cure illness or make unruly sons more responsible around the house.

An important recourse, too, is the wealth of saintly images throughout Bogota's churches. No rural parish offers the variety of problem-specific saint-images that are available in a large city.

Of herb venders there are many. Each public market sports one or more and each is ready to diagnose and prescribe. Most herb venders also sell lucky charms and amulets, particularly for protection of children against evil-eye. *Many* individuals, it should be stressed, get no further than the local herb-vender in their search for a cure. Natural remission of symptoms often occurs while the "patient" is still taking simple herbal remedies.

Patent medicines are numerous, as are pharmacies, and offer an array of nostrums unavailable to rural dwellers.

Lastly, at market and street bookstalls dozens of books are available on a variety of pertinent subjects. Typical are pamphlets on herbs and their uses, family hygiene, occult arts (curing and sorcerizing) and, perhaps most abundant of all, ready-made prayers and orations to particular saints for good luck, exorcism and cure of a variety of highly specific conditions.

## IV

The wide array of non-medical services available to the Bogotano—most particularly the remarkable heterogeneity of the curer fraternity—is readily apparent. This heterogeneity may be seen in a number of diverse elements, some of which include: degree of privacy of the consultation; source of the calling ("Indians," apprenticeship, correspondence, books, etc.); diagnostic or curative power source (curer himself, God, dead kin, medicinals, etc.); use of religious identification (orations, prescription of masses, curer's name, "faith injections," etc.); diagnostic technique; curative technique; recognition of supernatural or social causality; manner in which consultation is separated (if at all) from cure; etc. One may readily conclude that far more "folk-medical" services are available to the urban dweller here than are available to most peasants. Indeed, it is of direct interest to note that almost half of Gato's and Pacheco's patients are rural dwellers willing to travel up to six hours for city treatment.

The healers described are not "specialized" practitioners who "concern [themselves] with particular situations" (to utilize Adams' and Rubel's rather ambiguous definition of the "limited" practitioner). Each is a generalist who treats a variety of problems, socio-ritual or not. Their specialization is primarily of style and technique.

While the Bogota group exhibits a number of characteristics common to Latin American curanderismo, it cannot be satisfactorily described in terms of the stereotype discussed earlier.

Pacheco treats a wide variety of complaints, uses many common herbs or plants, identifies himself with the protection of a saint and makes it clear that his "power" to diagnose by touch is not a natural one. At the same time, he limits his interest to symptoms rather than cause or etiology. He specifically refuses to take an interest in the "socio-ritual" state of his patients. Gato recognizes and treats problems of a "socio-ritual" nature. However, beyond a quick elicitation of symptoms and suspicions, his interest in the social or psychological etiology of his patients' complaints is at best perfunctory. He will not probe with a patient for situations and individuals likely to have influenced the course of an illness. Once sorcery has been ascertained (a matter of minutes—the patient has suspicions, or Gato "reads" it in his urine), if the patient cannot immediately think of a likely enemy he is asked not to return until he does. It must be stressed that many patients come to Gato with "mundane" complaints which are treated as such. Furthermore, regardless of the cause ("weak blood" or sorcery), physical discomfort is at least partially treated with herbals.

All of the generalists described treat large numbers of "mundane" complaints which neither patients nor curers view as bearing social, ritual or psychological significance. All, excepting (on occasion) the curandera Sofia, spend little time with patients—a matter of five to ten minutes in most instances. None of the curers requires the active participation or presence of additional personnel such as family or community representatives in the curative process. All, excepting the group types, charge explicit fees, and these may be extraordinarily high.

It cannot be said, furthermore, that the urban curer's style affords a greater across-the-board rapport with patients than does that of physicians. In a recent study, Ordoñez, Cohen, and Samora conclude that only a minority of Bogota outpatients and physicians claim to experience difficulty in communicating with one another (1968:190). With respect to the "familiarity" of curers' technique, many of the concoctions prepared by them are unknown to their patients. Certainly Gato's oration and The Bishop's overall diagnostic technique are out of the ordinary. An informative statement comes from a patient at Pablo Gato's office. He was asked why he had traveled four hours by bus to Bogota. Were there no curers in his own rural community? "Sure," he answered. "But the herbs and prayers he uses, *we* use in our own house. Why bother seeing him? Now, I come to Don Gato and, man, I don't understand a thing he says or know what it is he gives me to drink."

## V

The variations and combinations of stylistic elements manifest by the curers are numerous. Much as we might desire a neat or familiar breakdown, to force the Bogota group into a limited number of categories would be to obscure this surprising heterogeneity and hamper the search for any common denominators which may underly it. Too many inconsistencies—from both

our own and the patients' point of view—would be involved in classifying, say Gato and Sofia, as "real" or "socio-ritual" curers and lumping the remainder as "limited" or "marginal."

The difficulty in deriving an easy categorization of Bogota curers is shared by their patients. Gato, Pacheco and The Bishop are variously referred to as "doctor," *botánico*, "curandero," and "homeopath" (Gato claims to use elements of homeopathy in prescribing herbals and several texts are visible to patients in his dispensary). It is interesting to note that patients most often refer to Gato as a *botánico*, as he himself encourages. In addressing him, however, patients will almost invariably use the term "doctor." In Bogota a *botánico* has the dual ability to diagnose illness and subsequently (in addition to any other techniques) prescribe and prepare a variety of herbal-vegetable curatives. In so doing, he is distinct from a "simple" herb-seller with a market stall, whose *primary* function is to purvey raw ingredients and various magical or ritual objects and who only *secondarily* might diagnose and prescribe. As a *botánico*, however, Gato is also nomenclaturally distinct from the *tegua*, who is thought to exist in isolated rural or bush areas where he treats "Indians" or "backward" people largely for sorcery. Now, Gato is well known for curing sorcery. He utilizes a number of exotic, "nonmechanical" techniques such as oration, candle burning, destruction of sorcery-contaminated clothing, "pin-sticking," etc. His patients are quite aware of this, regardless of the label applied to him. That he is classified as a *botánico* reflects less his use of herbals than the desire of his patients to identify the curer—and themselves—as modern and urban. By the same token—and such mundane considerations may exert important influence over urban stylistic manifestations—Gato is less likely to face difficulties with police and medical authorities if he identifies himself in minimally provocative terms.

Just as nomenclature used by patients or curers may not necessarily reflect the curer's major stylistic (and functional) identity, so too the variety of stylistic elements which constitute this identity may preclude patients' categorizing of curers along invariant lines. Gato, for example, in private session, with use of exotic recitations, and with a reputation for effectiveness in treating sorcery, would appear to be of a different genre from Pacheco. Patients *do* view them as differing—but *not* necessarily for these reasons. One patient, who had consulted both, was asked why he preferred

Gato. "Because Pacheco treats each separate symptom. Gato, on the other hand, treats you only once, for everything. He treats you for what you've got." To this patient, stylistic elements other than supernatural or "socio-ritual" concern take precedence in his own perception, classification and choice of curer. Yet other reasons account for the almost twenty-to-one preference of patients for Pacheco over Sofia (who is far more "stereotypic").

Thus, when we take into account the full range of curer stylistic manifestations which might conceivably create an important impression upon a patient, we realize how limiting are those bases of categorization which rely upon but few selected elements. "Socio-ritual" concern and other "stereotypic" phenomena become but several among a wealth of potential variables which a curer may exhibit. The existence of such variability has been central to our argument thus far. Its extent may be more fully appreciated when presented, as below, in the form of an inventory of stylistic elements (and sub-elements or variables) exhibited by all curers and which are capable of perception by their patients (let alone by anthropologists).

**Curer Stylistic Inventory**

(1) *Reputation of the healer* (degree of success, types of illness he is reputed to cure, any gossip, etc.)

(2) *Personal and environmental impressionistic phenomena* (healer's sex, name, dress, office and location, religious associations, medical v. non-medical appearance, etc.)

(3) *Origin of curer's vocation as claimed* (promise, dreams, forced possession by supernatural forces, altruistic desire, etc.)

(4) *Origin of the curer's ability or knowledge* ("Indians," apprenticeship, correspondence, self-teaching, observation, dreams, etc.)

(5) *Power source of the cure* (curer himself, medicinals, supernatural, patient's own faith or will, etc.)

(6) *Personnel involved in the cure* (curer and patient only, family, community representatives)

(7) *Diagnostic technique* (questioning, patient confession, divination, pulsing, examination, etc.)

(8) *Socio-cultural identification of the cure* ("Local," "foreign," medical, non-medical, lower or middle class, *ladino*, *indio*, etc.)

(9) *Curing technique* (tremendous variation possible, among which are herbals, ritual manipulation, patient confession of transgression, external manipulation such as egg rubbing, etc.)

(10) *Degree of specialization of the curer* (here a three-way grid might be required on which were plotted: causes or etiological courses recognized by the curer; symptoms recognized and treated; and treatments utilized. Combinations and permutations are many)

(11) *Manner of establishing payment* (donation, fee-setting, fee ritualization, compartmentalization, etc.).

...If carefully drawn, curer categorizations could provide us with important insights into the manner in which illness and related experiences are perceived and differentiated. This is but part of the picture. *A holistic approach to curanderismo* may provide other, broader insights into the range of health values and facilities available and the manner in which they reflect and accommodate the socio-cultural milieu in which they operate. By way of illustration, in applying such a holistic approach it is possible to derive the following tentative statements about curanderismo (here taken to include the entire range of curative phenomena including "auto-curative") in Bogota and those who utilize it.

(1) The considerable number and heterogeneity of curative phenomena suggest a population itself heterogeneous in both social and somatic needs. The curer is under less pressure than his rural counterpart to conform to a narrow body of expectations. He is free to develop as idiosyncratic a style as he wishes. This heterogeneity is clearly capable of accommodating a wide variety of social, sub-cultural, economic, psychological, and somatic needs.

(2) Almost all of the curers described—certainly the more well known and successful—utilize medicinals in addition to any other curative techniques. Gato's use of both herbals and supernatural manipulation in treatment of sorcery suggests that physical discomfort, regardless of cause, is viewed in the city as possessing elements strictly susceptible to "mechanical" manipulation. Economic demands, unpredictable work hours, dispersal of "significant others," etc., make complex, time-consuming "socio-ritual" treatment impractical. Public support by government and/or dominant classes of "modern" medical practice could make the use of more conspicuous, "exotic" aspects of curanderismo detrimental to self-image and social mobility. Belief in supernatural causality is more easily retained in such circumstances if it is describable or at least partially treatable by

"modern" or mechanical means. It is suggestive to note that among Mexican Americans in San Jose, California, sorcery may result in a "medical" illness such as flu (Clark 1959:199).

(3) The curers are all relatively brief and impersonal in their approach. As compared with the "typical" peasant community practitioner, the curer, here is an independent agent who rarely knows the patient, his family or his often small and dispersed network of significant others. As such, he can do little more than reinforce patients' initial suspicions, impersonally divine or otherwise diagnose cause (urine analysis as sorcery-indicator, for example). In either case, the curer has little to do with development of an etiological brief. Complicated etiologies, causes and treatments, furthermore, do not appear to be *required* of the city curers. If illness is indeed the cue for a social drama of sanction, cultural identity, escape from responsibility, etc., the city curer is *not* a principal actor nor is his office the stage. The patient himself has a large responsibility for reporting diagnostic and curative events to others, and for choosing and developing the socially relevant aspects of his problem.

(4) None of the curers requires the presence or participation of persons other than the patient. At most, a spouse, child, or parent of the patient will be present at the diagnostic and curative sessions. Often, the patient comes alone. Again, we are led to the conclusion that development of the important social and psychological elements of illness, and the casting of parts to be played by others, occur *outside* the more or less mechanical diagnostic-curative session. The number of significant others necessary (let alone available) in the city for development and validation of the sick role appears to be limited.

(5) The availability of diverse "auto-curative" means for self-treatment (including herbalists, holy water, oratory books, images, etc.) suggests an active, rather than passive, submissive response to illness. Furthermore, this suggests a less than total reliance upon the incumbents of authoritative healing roles.

(6) With few exceptions, the Bogota curers are professionals for hire, are viewed as such, and charge a fee. Alone, the two group types accept donations only. These two alone cure within an implicit *framework of public religious ritual*. As such, their relationship to patients is more one of "shepherd-flock" than "professional-client." It is suggested that the "shepherd-flock" mode, and acceptance of donations rather than set fees, is

more common where the curer performs in a ritual-associated role, or where he is viewed as a public servant, or where he exercises virtual monopoly over important health and/or ritual resources. These latter curer roles are more common in peasant than urban milieus. Ritual associated curers, on the other hand, are not uncommon in cities, and the public-spectacle faithhealer (often Protestant) is probably better known to urban than to isolated peasant populations....

Bogotanos readily compartmentalize curer consultation from dispensation of remedies. As with physicians and drugs, it is possible that urban patients view the curer and his cure as related, but not identical.

## VI

The broader implications of this holistic approach and these conclusions are readily apparent. Rather than a particular urban curer "type," what is suggested is the existence of an *urban curanderismo complex* which in variety and quality of *overall* services offered, appears to accommodate peculiarly urban needs. This complex embraces: heterogeneity of healer style and curative recourses, pecuniarity, brevity, impersonality, consultative isolation from significant others, reliance upon mechanical (though not necessarily "natural") manipulation of diagnosis and/or cure, and patient self-reliance. Like Goode's "polar ideal typology" of religion and magic (1951:152–155), the complex is more a model for elicitation and analysis of data than a description of any necessarily existing phenomenon. It necessarily implies the existence of an "opposite," in this case "rural" (peasant, tribal, etc.), pole or complex. Each of the elements is necessarily of a relative nature, in that there is no clear stylistic point, for example, at which a curer becomes "impersonal."

This relativity must be emphasized. When compared with the day-long, highly personal and community-involved cures described by Gillin (1948) or, for that matter, with the intricate and extensive social diagnoses performed by Turner's Ndembu curer (1964), *all* of the urban curers described in the Latin American literature appear to be of a very different order. Thus, the performances of Clark's "folk curers" who may "sometimes" deal with a patient for "an hour or more" (1959:216) could hardly be viewed as strikingly personal. Yet her curers are still more personalistic than certain of those described in south Texas and New Mexico who may attend large numbers of patients in a single session and can hardly spend more than several minutes with each (Rubel 1966:188–189). Similarly, Romano's "regional" and "international" curers are well known and receive large numbers of patients with whom they spend short time. The more successful of Lieban's Cebu City (Philippines) curers may treat upwards of 75 patients in a single afternoon (1967:94).

In terms of diagnosis, curers in these above instances can rarely do more than quickly accept patients' suspicions, mechanically divine, pulse, or otherwise reach a diagnosis without involving the patient in lengthy, personal analysis. It is perhaps logical to conclude that the more effective and patronized (i.e., successful) the curer, the more he must approximate the urban model if he is to treat all the patients in his increasing case-load. . . .

Clearly, the concept of an "urban curanderismo complex" requires further examination. Especially needed are approaches which provide broader description of curers and auto-curative services, perhaps along the lines of the stylistic inventory presented earlier. Rather than studies which focus upon any particular curer "type," or attempts to delimit sweeping categories of practitioners, what is needed is more flexible reporting of both the range of curer types *and* their relative importance within the curing complex they serve. Curanderismo is a two-way street. Just as healers reflect the illnesses and values of the patients they treat, so, too, certain aspects of illness and health practice must necessarily shift to become susceptible to the kinds of healers and services available. In sum, a flexible and holistic approach toward curanderismo, particularly under urban or acculturating conditions, will provide deeper understanding of the dynamics of illness-associated behaviors and the socio-cultural milieus in which they are manifest.

# XIV
## Healers and Medical Systems in Social and Cultural Change

### The Impact of Sociocultural Change and Acculturation on Healers and Medical Systems

The impassioned revolutionary, Franz Fanon, in *The Wretched of the Earth*, concludes his book with this plea:

Come, then, comrades; it would be as well to decide at once to change our ways. We must shake off the heavy darkness in which we were plunged and leave it behind.... We must leave our dreams and abandon our old beliefs and friendships of the time before life began. Let us waste no time in sterile litanies and nauseating mimicry.... The European game has finally ended; we must find something different. We today can do everything, so long as we do not imitate Europe, so long as we are not obsessed by the desire to catch up with Europe.... Yet it is very true that we need a model, and that we want blueprints and examples.... European achievements, European techniques and the European style ought no longer to tempt us and to throw us off our balance.... But if we want humanity to advance a step further, if we want to bring it up to a different level than that which Europe has shown it, then we must invent and we must make new discoveries. If we wish to live up to our peoples' expectations, we must seek the response elsewhere than in Europe.... For Europe, for ourselves and for humanity, comrades, we must turn over a new leaf, we must work out new concepts, and try to set afoot a new man (Fanon 1966: 252–255).

Fanon's cry is representative of the ethos and the attitude of developing societies around the world straining to organize themselves technologically to reap some of the benefits of the Industrial Revolution while hoping to avoid the often brutal costs in human lives and suffering and dehumanization. Having thrown off the iron collar of colonialism they are aware of the advantages of industrial development, and often this is accompanied by a grudging admiration for the great strides in the West in improving living standards of large segments of populations. But the emerging nations are also aware of the social problems that all industrial societies face—and have always faced, even in the most prosperous eras. They do not forget their bitter heritage of subordination, exploitation, and deculturalization and they want to revive their ancestral cultures within the context of the modern world. They admire the material culture of industrial civilization, but they do not wish to become Europeanized or Americanized.

The Western countries, and the larger and militarily stronger Eastern ones, have for decades been engaged in various forms of technical assistance to their former

465

colonies, partly perhaps to expiate their guilt over past injustices to them, but probably and more importantly, because they wish to continue to influence these areas, sell them goods, receive their raw materials, and pull them if possible into active alliances or at least neutrality in the international power struggle. Whatever the reasons, more often than not, the efforts of the industrially developed nations to change the behaviors and attitudes of the developing nations, or introduce technological changes in them without awareness of the sociocultural concomitants and consequences, have resulted in a surprising number of failures in public health and medicine, educational systems, agricultural practices, family planning, and other areas of culture. I have always been impressed to find in the many manuals written for American health and medical workers and others involved in programs of overseas assistance (for example, Arensberg and Niehoff 1964, Foster 1962, Goodenough 1963, Mead 1955, Paul 1955, Saunders 1954, Spicer 1952) that a preponderance of the case studies used as teaching examples are essentially biographies of failures. These programs are often, indeed usually, motivated by high ideals on the part of the fieldworkers thus engaged who often include anthropologists among their number. Yet even anthropologists do not seem able in most instances to avoid what Goodenough (1963) calls the "pitfalls of cultural ignorance," One wonders whether anthropology and the other social sciences are capable of even crude predictions of the consequences of applied anthropology programs, whether in medicine and health, or in other aspects of social life. A quarter-century ago Alexander Leighton (Foreword, Spicer 1952:9–11) was convinced that social science "can be of considerable help" in applied programs. But, he says, "A more significant question is the morality of attempting to manipulate human beings. Should anyone try to change peoples' ways?" Leighton succinctly summarizes the assumptions and the problems that face such efforts:

1. Millions of men, women, and children all over the world desire more freedom than they now possess from starvation, disease, and physical insecurity.
2. These people under stress, together with others who are more fortunate, are aware of the technological power and efficiency of the West and would like to have some, if not all, of these advantages.
3. The people who desire such improvements have little perception of the complex human difficulties involved. They want change, but have very incomplete ideas of the cost to their way of life.
4. The members of Western society who introduce the changes are also incompletely aware of consequences.

It seems justifiable to assume, therefore, that the technological experts in public health, land improvement, industrialization, and similar fields (together with the administrators of such programs) have some responsibility for the human relations involved in their work. For instance, although the people of a society may want to be free of disease, they may have to be led to appreciate many subgoals, such as cleanliness in the house, which are not in their original perception related to the main problem. On the other hand, they may also have to be led away from ruthless adoption of Western sanitary regulations, which would be far more disruptive to their way of life than any gain they could possibly derive.

Although one feels admiration for Leighton's keen respect for the complexity of the issues involved, after reading Frantz Fanon's words one is impelled to ask: Are any people in the world today (with the possible exceptions of some very small-scale societies in Oceania) in the mood to be led toward or away from anywhere, even for their own health and profit? Probably not.

The changes taking place in these societies today are not only the result of acculturation and the influences of dominant industrial cultures. They are also, as they have always been, in part the result of evolutionary change occurring from within the social system and culture; all societies always change, whether or not in response to external influences. In the sense that no society is now and probably

466

has not for a long time been free of direct or indirect foreign influence, all change that results in new social, cultural, and technological forms may be said to be ultimately evolutionary or, as the case may be, revolutionary.

It should be apparent, though one would not always know it from reading the manuals on directed culture change alluded to previously, that the hunger for change and a better and healthier life exists not only in the "developing" nations but in large segments of the societies of "developed" nations as well. Increasingly such social-ethnic units and strata are demanding changes, and like the former colonial dependencies, they are not eager to ape the behaviors of dominant social strata of their own countries. These groupings, the objects of all sorts of state aid at all levels, still seem as stubbornly to resist reformative efforts as the smaller nations of the world. But this does not mean that they do not want reform; they do, but on their own terms.

The papers that follow, and many that preceded, illustrate that healers and healing systems are responding to the conditions of change in many ways and that the consequences are not always negative and destructive. The challenges of change and of powerful competing systems often result in the near-submergence of traditional healers and medical systems. But just as often they afford opportunities as much as threats, and the indigenous systems and personnel respond in adaptive, and not infrequently in innovative ways. The traditional systems, which may have been fading out, often will experience a revitalization and exist competitively, and sometimes more successfully (in terms of adoption by the population), with the scientific medical system. Sometimes this seems to be a process of individual healers perceiving ways in which they can salvage, even strengthen, their traditionally conservative roles or actually create new syntheses. Sometimes whole groups will be involved, as in the revival of Ayurvedic medicine in India. And sometimes the central government will promulgate by decree policies that both revive and strengthen traditional healers and medicines and also invent or reinvent whole new roles and healing techniques, as in the case of contemporary China and its barefoot doctors. These changes are taking place not only in small-scale societies and nations but also in large-scale, powerful, and populous societies and nation-states.

As so, as Fanon's statements suggested at the beginning of this introduction, the Third World (in terms of population, at least, something of a misnomer) has come to "turn over a new leaf, . . . work out new concepts, and try to set afoot a new man."

In medical anthropology the task ahead will be to create models for understanding changes and evolution in medical systems as a whole, in which healing roles represent just one locus of investigation. The studies in this section and throughout the volume have made significant contributions toward that objective.

# 52 Role Adaptation: Traditional Curers Under the Impact of Western Medicine

## David Landy

Despite frequent attention to the healer's role by anthropologists, only recently have attempts been made to conceptualize the role in order to build models for more systematic analysis. This is also true of studies of healing roles within the context of change resulting from culture contact and from internal evolutionary change. In this essay I have attempted to examine the effects on the curer's role of the contest between indigenous systems of medicine and the Western medical systems. Adaptation of the curing role under acculturation and change in a series of selected societies is considered and a typology is derived of the curer's role as "adaptive," "attenuated," or "emergent." The concept of role adaptation, which to my knowledge is used here for the first time, has been adapted from a model of role strain suggested by the sociologist William Goode. The notion is related to such associated ideas as that of cultural broker, role analogue, and role ambiguity, and I propose that it may contribute to a model for the analysis of healing role adaptation under acculturation and perhaps suggest models for the study of other roles in culture change. Although the three broad modes of adaptation seem to me to subsume all the possibilities, I do not preclude either that other possibilities will not be discovered as further research takes place, or that the present typology cannot be refined; indeed, it is my hope that other medical anthropologists will attempt in their findings to do just that.

What may be useful in the present study is that it further indicates the point made in a number of studies in this volume that healing roles have been much too stereotyped by anthropologists in the past, and that there is a great measure of flexibility in the interpretation and implementation of these roles. Though my conclusion in this paper is that the healer's role is essentially conservative, and I do not wish to change that notion as yet, papers in this and other sections of the book show that it is subject to much change, and indeed may be one of the more sensitive roles to the pressures for change in any social system. For most societies it is certainly a key role since the healer is dealing with matters of life and death, and what happens to the curer may be an important barometer of what is going on in the total process of sociocultural change.

Reprinted with abridgments and changes by the author from David Landy, 1974, "Role Adaptation: Traditional Curers Under the Impact of Western Medicine," *American Ethnologist*, 1:103–127, with permission of the American Anthropological Association.

The functions of the curer's role in a tradition-directed society facing the challenge of a technologically more powerful medical system may be studied from many points of view. This paper will be confined to a consideration of certain theoretical aspects in the adaptation of the curer's role to changes accompanying acculturation threats and opportunities. Data are taken from a variety of studies by anthropologists and others. My objective is to place the changing role of the curer into substantive and theoretical perspective and to contribute to a model for the study of role adaptation under conditions of culture change....

Perhaps the closest approach to our concern with adaptation of the traditional healer's role in acculturation appears in the work of Alland (1970:155–178) on the medical system of the Abron of the Ivory Coast; reference to Alland's material appears later in the present study. Several studies in the compilations of Kiev (1964) and Middleton (1967) deal in part with the problem, though not within the context of the concept of role adaptation or role theory.

## THE ROLE CONCEPT IN ANTHROPOLOGY

....In the past decade some anthropologists have... begun to rethink the concept of role as providing an important key to what Goodenough terms the "cultural organization of social relationships" (Barth 1963, 1966; Banton 1965; Benedict 1969; Coult 1964; Freilich 1964, 1968; Goodenough 1965; Keesing 1970; Southall 1959). Certain studies in political anthropology have focused on changing functions of chiefs and other political roles (e.g., Swartz, Turner, and Tuden 1966), and in economic anthropology on changing functions of entrepreneurs, traders, and other economic roles (e.g., Barth 1963, 1966; Belshaw 1955; Helm, Bohannan, and Sahlins 1965).

Among the more stimulating formulations, and most relevant to my notion of role adaptation, have been those explorations around the notion of the "cultural broker," beginning with the seminal paper by Wolf (1956) on the mediating functions of the politician-broker role between local and national institutions in Mexico; Geertz's (1960) incisive analysis of the cultural broker role of the Javanese *kijaji* as Moslem religious teacher and nationalist politician; and the more recent work in Mesoamerica of Hunt (1968) and Press (1969) to which subsequent reference will be made. It will be seen that in some ways the more adaptive traditional curer roles incorporate important aspects of the cultural broker's role, though in some respects the curer's role departs from the broker model.

Press' (1971) very useful study of curers in an urban South American city calls attention not only to basic differences in the curing role in rural and peasant communities as contrasted with urban ones, but the fact that the culture and multiplex social organization of cities provide opportunities for a wide variety of curers to flourish. While in complete agreement with Press' major points, it must be asserted that many rural and peasant cultures contain a fair degree of variation in curing roles, though not nearly as broad as in urban cultures. Reference in this paper to *the* curing role refers only to specific instances in specific societies and makes no assumption about either stereotyped role models or lack of variation in role types. . . . [Cf. Chapter 51—Ed.].

## CONCEPTUAL AND THEORETICAL ASSUMPTIONS

The use of the role concept in social science has been primarily structural-functional (role performance, role-taking, role-modeling, role expectations, etc.), as recent comprehensive surveys clearly indicate (Biddle and Thomas 1966; Sarbin and Allen 1968). Processes of role change have been studied primarily as chronological modifications occurring, as in the socialization process, when the person assumes new roles as he reaches new age grades and therefore new social horizons. Research has also dealt with sex role changes due to status changes, as in the changing roles of women, or socialization into occupational roles in industrial organizations.

But in the case of role change in response to the stimulus of competing values and technology of another, economically more potent culture, this question has seldom been handled except in terms of conflict and strain, and these are seen as almost inevitably arising from culture contact. (Exceptions in economic and political anthropology were noted previously.) Indeed some writers seem to assume that a concomitant of acculturation will be personality disturbance, and by implication role conflict. It will be seen in the present essay that in the case of the curer the contact situation may be actually or potentially conflictual, but it may also possess possibilities for role adaptation insofar as

elements of ideology and behavior patterns of the impinging culture are adopted to enhance therapeutic efficacy, and even to strengthen the curer's status in his own society. Some curers may resemble marginal men caught in an insoluble dilemma between the drag of the culture of orientation (what Belshaw [1955] calls the entrepreneur's "home group" culture) on the one hand, and the pull of the culture of reference—that of scientific Western medicine—on the other. But frequently the curer maintains his position strongly in his membership group while borrowing liberally from Western medicine, without necessarily identifying with the reference group, in which realistically he accepts the fact that the doors to membership are closed, and without losing his psychological and social stability through fruitless floundering between the two cultures.

We define role adaptation as the process of attaining an operational sociopsychological steady-state by the occupant of a status or status set through sequences of "role bargains" or transactions among alternative role behaviors. In situations of rapid culture change, alternative behavior possibilities, expectations, rewards, and obligations will originate both within and without the indigenous social system. All individuals in any sociocultural system are confronted with "over-demanding" total role obligations (Goode 1960:485 passim) but must manage to equilibrate role relationships and role sets through continual bargaining and consensuses with other actors in the system, and consequently reduce role strain. Therefore, the instance of the traditional curer's role under potential stress from the demands and temptations of the competing medical systems represents an extension of Goode's theory of role strain (cf. also Banton 1965:Chs. 2, 3).

I make the following assumptions: (1) The curer's place in his society originally was relatively secure until threatened by the pressures of culture change. His personality may or may not have been in phase with the behavioral norms of his own sociocultural system, but his status was traditional and prescribed, though not invariably ascribed.

(2) Prior to contact, in addition to ameliorating the effects of illness and disease, the curer's activities were oriented toward enhancing and/or reinforcing his social position. Although role prescriptions were traditional, he would still have to rationalize nonsuccess, and ordinarily he would have to compete with other curers in the number and profundity of his achievements. . . .

(3) Nevertheless, a measure of security was

present in that role performance expectations were shared with other members of the society, and competition originated primarily from within the group and presented a relatively known range of possibilities. To some extent competing performances could be gauged, anticipated, and controlled. Sources of role strain probably were fewer than in the post-contact period, and possibilities for successful interpersonal transactions in the interest of reduction of role strain and achievement of role adaptation probably were greater (Goode 1960:491).

(4) The curing role could be a full-or part-time one, but prestige in one role tended to be linked to prestige in others, so that status in any tended to reinforce the power of all (Goode 1960:491–493). This follows from the notions of role sets, status sets, and status sequences (Merton 1957).

Analysis of role adaptation of curers in selected societies undergoing acculturation has suggested a model of adaptation possibilities in which the data may be grouped into three categories: adaptive, attenuated, and emergent curing roles.

## ADAPTIVE CURING ROLES

Erasmus (1952) found in Quito, Ecuador, as has been discovered by many other investigators, that those illnesses thought to be supernaturally caused were referred to indigenous practitioners, those that had a mundane origin and were thought to respond to common remedies were treated at home, and certain others of nonsupernatural origin such as tuberculosis and appendicitis were referred to the modern physician, "folk" practitioners agreeing that the latter referral was appropriate. Usually the victim of illness first tried home remedies, then a folk curer, and only when these two possibilities failed did he consult the physician. As Erasmus (1952:417) shows, a division of role responsibility has been arranged tacitly between the traditional curer and the physician.... [Cf. Chapter 29—Ed.].

In the village of Sherupur in North India, Gould (1957) differentiated between what he called "village medicine" and "doctor medicine." He conceptualized these as two systems of treatment in constant interaction. Village medicine was used primarily to treat "chronic nonincapacitating dysfunctions" ("conditions manifesting drawn-out periods of suffering, sometimes cyclical in character, usually not fatal ... and only partially debilitating, enabling the sufferer to maintain a semblance

of his daily routine" [Gould 1957:508]). Doctor medicine was solicited mainly for "critical incapacitating dysfunctions" ("ailments... involving sudden and often violent onset, and rather complete debilitation with reference to some aspects of the individual's routine" [1957:508]). The people tended to make choices on the basis of what Gould terms "folk pragmatism." Choice of scientific over folk medicine was related directly to "(a) economic well-being, (b) formal education, and (c) occupational and spatial mobility" (1957:515). Since there is a wide range of chronic nonincapacitating dysfunctions for which modern medicine can prescribe no specific, and since many critical incapacitating dysfunctions may respond to different remedies, including the therapy of time, it seemed probable that native medicine would continue to thrive in a structure complementary to scientific medicine.

Nurge's (1958) study of an agricultural fishing village in eastern Leyte, Philippine Islands, differs somewhat in its conclusions from Erasmus and Gould, since "the relationship between a treatment and its effect is usually far from obvious, is often obscure, and at best is amazingly complex" (Nurge 1958:1170). She felt that neither Eramus nor Gould could be certain that disease entities that they defined in Western scientific terminology were clearly apprehended by their subjects. As she stated the case for this Filipino village, "the individual does not grapple with a disease, but with a discomfort or malaise which he may describe as being itchy, disturbing, or painful. It is not measles or bronchitis or tuberculosis but an unhappiness and a dis-ease which the patient brings to specialists and which the curer or physician defines for the patient" (Nurge 1958:1169–1170)....

Nurge describes the functions of five types of indigenous curers, and, like Gould and Erasmus, sees them functioning in a cultural system in effective interaction with modern medicine. [Cf. Chapter 14—Ed.].

After additional fieldwork Gould (1965) elaborated on his earlier work by recasting his findings within the cognitive structure and world view of the indigenous culture. That people in Sherupur made pragmatic choices did not mean that they had achieved an understanding, let alone acceptance, of scientific medicine, but simply that they had availed themselves selectively of its technology. He appears to approach the view of his critic, Nurge, when he says, "the acceptance of scientific medicines... resulted in no material changes in basic folk cognitive structure. These experiences were filtered through the screen of this cognitive system and converted into meanings which did no violence to it" (Gould 1965:204).

The implications of Gould's findings for the role of the traditional curer coping with the competition of Western medicine are that

The more modern medicine becomes entrenched in, say, the domain of the critical incapacitating dysfunctions, the more indigenous practitioners stabilize their control over the treatment of chronic nonincapacitating dysfunctions. The latter even adopt the paraphernalia of modern medicine in order to intensify their psychological impact on their patients.... The routinized impersonality now so intrinsically a component of the modern professional role probably intensifies and helps promote the consolidation of this defensive reaction (1965:207–208).

Gould has made a significant contribution to the study of comparative medical systems by indicating the need to differentiate the technical from the scientific since they do not necessarily coexist. (For example, in such complex preindustrial societies as those of ancient India and China, huge areas of culture were highly technological, as the superbly developed Indian surgery and the Chinese irrigation systems, but they rested on a substructure of essentially empiricist and spiritual beliefs regarding the nature of man and the universe.) Thus, also, the traditional healer is seen not merely as passive receptor of modern science and technology, but as incorporating technocultural agent and as creator of new technocultural syntheses. The curing role is not only changed, but resynthesized. [Cf. Chapter 55—Ed.].

Many detailed descriptions are available of the role of Navaho singers, diagnosticians, and herbalists, as well as of the reactions of the Navaho to modern medical practice (Leighton and Leighton 1945). More recently in the work of Adair (1963) and others we are beginning to learn of the adaptation of traditional Navaho curers to contemporary scientific medicine. Rosenthal and Siegel (1959:148) pointed out that they have "often tried, unsuccessfully, to make new magical songs for the white man's tuberculosis, measles, influenza, and syphilis." Adair and the Leightons indicate that most Navaho still trust traditional curers even while selectively utilizing "white medicine," and occasionally they were permitted to hold a sing in a hospital or clinic, usually after Western medical treatment had been given (see also Kluckhohn and Leighton 1962). Adair (1963) reports that in the Many Farms community there were fifty-five curers or singers "among our clinic

population—one for every two and one-half camps, or one for every forty-one people." Adair points out that Navaho curers respect White doctors, acknowledge their superiority in some areas, and cannot understand why their respect is not reciprocated. Diagnosticians (hand tremblers) are still usually the first professionals to be consulted and they in turn advise "their patients to go to the clinic in certain circumstances, rather than to the medicine men" (1963:246). After extensive interviewing and psychological testing of thirty Navaho informants, Adair (1963:248) concludes:

There was general agreement... that both types of medicine were essential for Navaho health needs, and that it was best to follow the advice of the hand trembler. There are 73 diagnosticians in the area, more than one to every two camps.... This large number of diagnosticians reflects the important role they play in the Navaho society, as decision-makers between alternate means of curing.

Adair points out that patients with injuries or suffering from acute, sudden disease attacks "are readily brought to the clinic," while those suffering from illnesses developing more slowly and less well-defined are assumed to have broken a taboo and usually are treated by the singer, a finding reminiscent of those of Erasmus and Gould....

Among the highly acculturated Cherokee Indians of the southeastern United States, Fogelson (1961) has found a strong persistence of traditional medical beliefs and practices compounded with many Christian elements, and the role of the conjurer-curer still surprisingly viable. The Cherokee syllabary, originally an instrument of progressive change in the early nineteenth century, has functioned as a conserving force, since it affords the conjurer a means of transcribing sacred formulas formerly transmitted orally through a priestly hierarchy. One result, strengthened by geographic isolation until comparatively recently, has been for an increase in secretiveness and interconjurer rivalry, and a rigidifying and freezing of practices and beliefs current in the early 1800's. As elsewhere, some functions and related artifacts have changed in modern times, with hunting, fishing, and agricultural magic fading out, but divination, sorcery, and curing by the conjurer persisting and being used simultaneously with scientific medicine by modern Cherokee. "The impact of Western medicine on Cherokee theory and practice can be seen to involve partial assimilation, the accentuation of differences where the two theories are irreconcilable, and an overall feeling that the two systems are complementary, rather than fundamentally contradictory" (Fogelson 1961:222).

A study of the medical system of a Philippine town (Lieban 1960, 1962) illustrates again the role of the curer as control agent and the process of cultural and role adaptation and resynthesis. Illnesses of supernatural origin remain in the province of the local curers, and while physicians may be consulted for illnesses of more earthly etiology, it is felt that treatment by them of supernaturally caused maladies actually may exacerbate them. What we may term the medical mythology is altered, so that the traditional chameleon-like, dangerous, illness-producing spirits called *ingkantos* that may be unpredictably invisible or exist in any organic or nonorganic form, including that of humans, have assumed new powers and functions.

To the people of the barrios, ingkantos appear to represent, *inter alia*, glittering and inaccessible wealth and power beyond the local community. The individual who sees and interacts with an ingkanto can, through fantasy, bring temptation within reach, or succumb to it. However, such experiences are considered hazardous and often are thought to lead to illness or death. This pattern of thought and behavior associated with beliefs about ingkantos and their influences appears to support social equilibrium in the community by dramatizing and reinforcing the idea that it is dangerous to covet alluring, but basically unattainable, wealth and power outside the barrios. In this way, the value of accepting the limitations of barrio life and one's part in it is emphasized. Furthermore, if someone has a relationship with a dazzling ingkanto and becomes ill, it is the manambal [indigenous healer], a symbol of barrio service and self-sufficiency, who restores the victim to health and reality (Lieban 1962:309).

The local healer had always acted as an agent to control overly lusty appetites. To this traditional function is now added that of controlling the expression of newly acquired tastes as well. The healer represents the leveling pressures of the community so that "part of an individual's wealth is siphoned off to kinsmen and neighbors.... In this perspective illness attributed to *ingkantos* can be seen as helping to reconcile the individual to social reality by demonstrating that it is a mistake to overindulge personal desires" (1962:311). The healer frequently functions in a dual role as sorcerer and must be capable of the kind of cognitive adjustment that will smoothly incorporate both roles.

The contrastive roles of sorcerer and healer may be assimilated by scheduling each for the appropriate situation, whether that be service for health or service for "justice" [the rationalization underlying vengeance sorcery]. Even in situations where role contradictions are most sharply focused—when X, the healer, treats someone whose illness the same X, as sorcerer, was responsible for—the apparent discrepancy in behavior can be explained by resorting in turn to relevant values of the roles involved (Lieban 1960:132).

This presents an interesting example of role adaptation of the curer, since he must operate in at least two different roles and clusters of ideas and behaviors that are cognitively dissonant (Rosenthal and Siegel 1959: Banton 1965: Ch. 7). He must adapt the apparently contradictory indigenous roles of healer and sorcerer while preserving and extending his status as healer and control agent in his contest with modern medicine.

In the southern Caribbean islands of Trinidad and Grenada, Mischel (1959) found that healing functions of the Shango cult curer operated within the context of a tendency for people to "affiliate themselves with several different religious organizations [and] many of them visit both the bush healer and the legitimate [*sic*] doctor in times of illness" (Mischel 1959:407). The Shango cult is itself "an amalgam of old Yoruba beliefs and New World Roman Catholicism" (1959:408), and cult leader-healers derive their powers directly from the gods, but resort to medications and advice derived in part from older cult members and in part from such sources as Napoleon's *Book of Fate*, prayer books, the Bible, and the *Home Physician's Guide*. Scientifically trained physicians and clinics are over-burdened, refer patients in "severe mental stress" to mental hospitals, and tend to treat only physical complaints. By contrast, the cult healer will treat any type of ailment using differential diagnosis and therapy; where he fails after several attempts he will "often refer his patient to an older or generally more prestigeful leader" (1959:411), and where ills appear for which he recognizes that the cult treatment has no cure, fractured limbs for example, he will refer the patient to a physician.

In Trinidad the physician feels modern medical facilities are available, dismisses the Shango healer as pagan, and will not refer patients to him. But in Grenada, with inadequate medical facilities, the physician frequently refers psychic or psychosomatic disorders to a cult curer. From the viewpoint of the people, the modern physician is perceived as a person of a different social class and culture whose financial and social prestige and technical abilities are recognized, but not his scientific knowledge. The "bush" healer is seen as a trustworthy sharer of one's own culture, with a direct tie to the spirit world, and a broad range of curing powers. The patient may be a passive participant in the curing process, and does not have to try to recover as is required of the European or American sick role (Parsons 1951; Parsons and Fox 1958). Especially in the case of lower-class Negroes whose channels of social advancement are blocked, the sick role becomes a source of social recognition, and "the longer the illness, the broader the symptoms, the more the patient may gain in the way of attention and unquestioning acceptance of his limitations with respect to work and other duties" (Mischel 1959: 417). The indigenous curer thus serves, in contrast to the Philippine case, not so much to dampen newly acquired appetites as to assuage them in acceptable and unpunishing ways. And he assumes the major responsibility in the therapeutic relationship.

In Southern Ghana, despite some utilization of Western medicine and hospitals, indigenous healers are handling the bulk of ailments, physical and mental, in all social classes, and a differentiation cannot be made between literate and illiterate (presumably more and less acculturated) patients, either in kinds of medical problems or frequency of use of native curers. These inferences derive from a study by Jahoda (1961) and are strengthened because of the care with which he investigated sociocultural background factors of the clientele, as well as the nature of presenting symptoms and complaints. More men than women seem to consult and utilize services of indigenous healers, probably because the brunt of acculturative pressures is felt most poignantly in the demands placed on male role performance, and channels of social mobility and role enhancement are more open to men than to women. While complaints of a group of mental hospital patients contained a frequent overlay of "magical" problems such as "accidental contact with dangerous 'juju,'" most emotional problems centered around interpersonal conflicts at home and at work that seem directly related to the acculturative impact on role requirements.

Jahoda's study of 315 adult cases that were handled by his five healer informants reveals that 54 percent dealt with physical complaints of which more than half were concerned with venereal disease and gynecological problems, 12 percent were classified as "mental," 18 percent as "job, love, and marriage," and 16 percent as "protection

and ritual." (I made these extrapolations by converting percentages in Table 1 of Jahoda [1961:248] back into whole numbers and taking means of the rows.) It could be speculated that a large proportion of the latter two categories would be looked upon as emotional disturbance by Western-trained psychiatrists. The majority of cases under "job, love and marriage" concern problems connected with social and occupational mobility.

In addition to traditional healers, a new type has emerged "involving the adoption of some of the external trappings of the Western medical man and pharmacist" (Jahoda 1961:254), who dispenses herbal remedies in an affectively neutral manner and tends not to become as closely involved with the patient as the traditional healer. Furthermore, a number of healing churches have sprung up that cater to, and recruit on the basis of, a broad range of illnesses summarized by Jahoda as "barrenness, sickness, difficulties in life, worry caused by witches" (Jahoda 1961:255), and which approach the role of the traditional healer in the intensity and closeness of the therapist-patient relationship. . . .

Alland's (1970) investigation of the Abron medical system and its several curing roles compared their fate *vis-à-vis* Western medical practitioners. Major Abron curing roles are those of the nonprofessional curer, essentially a lay herbalist and user of charms; the *kparese*, a priest with powerful magico-religious curing functions, who operates both as diviner-diagnostician who may refer a diagnosed patient to a specialist, and as healer; the *sise*, a secular curer, employing magical and empirical techniques, standing "halfway between the nonprofessional curer and the kparese" (Alland 1970:167), working in symbiotic complementarity with the *kparese* since the *sise* is not trained in divining and depends upon the *kparese* for referrals; and the *sogo*, a Moslem sorcerer who is sometimes used and usually feared. Facing this indigenous array of healers stand the Western trained physician, few in number, not always accessible; the *médecin africain*, Africans with a two-year special course in medicine at the University of Dakar, more numerous and more accessible; the nurse, frequently accessible but with very limited training and competence; and the missionary doctor. To the Abron, the *médecin africain*, the physician, and the nurse are all classed as "doctor" which "further dilutes the doctor role in the eyes of his Abron patient" (1970:178). The more analogous and viable indigenous roles are those of the *sise* and *kparese*, the former because his approach to medicine is similar to the Western approach, the latter because he is, as the missionary doctor, priest and curer rolled into one. Thus the *kparese* actually may use the *médecin africain* and Western physician for referrals, but he feels understandably threatened by the missionary, "a conflict," says Alland, "the missionary welcomes." The Abron will use Western practitioners if available, but do not hesitate to use their own practitioners, and, for magically caused or prolonged illnesses, prefer them.

In the face of incessant pressures of immigration and social-cultural change, the healing role of the Yemenite Jewish *mori* persists, though in a somewhat narrowed orbit (Hes 1964). For centuries he functioned as "a teacher, a judge, a religious leader, a ritual slaughterer, and a healer" (1964:364) but as the Jews of Yemen slowly and resistantly adapted to life in Israel, with a curtailing of the traditionally authoritarian father's role (and expansion of the social importance of wives and children), as schools displaced his role as teacher, courts took over his function as judge, and physicians and clinics his role as healer, he adapted to these losses, while maintaining his traditional roles as healer of supernaturally caused disease, especially mental illness, and as counselor in times of emotional stress and social uncertainty. Indeed in these roles he has maintained his community status and not only older Yemenites but even acculturated, educated younger ones continue to use him to help cure emotional stress, or resort to him when the ministrations of medical psychiatry have failed. As Hes (1964:382) states it, "Although stripped of many of his traditional functions, the mori in Israel still provides an important source of psychotherapeutic help for persons suffering from emotional problems and troubles in living. This kind of help is adapted specifically to the needs of his fellow men and could not be easily supplied in more effective ways from any other source." Surrounded by ways of life they do not fully prefer and economic and social discrimination, the Yemenite Jews cling to their traditional beliefs, and only the *mori* understands them and knows how to negotiate the believer back to health within their terms.

## ATTENUATED CURING ROLES

As the powerful scientific medical and economic system spreads its influence, the curer may choose to continue in his traditional role and ignore the attrition in clientele due to competitive services. This implies, in effect, his voluntary acceptance of diminished prestige because he now yields his influence to more powerful competitors that threaten to render his own role completely obsolete. The social position of a Tuscarora curer with whom I lived was in part anchored to the fact that he was a clan chief and member of the tribal council (Landy 1958) and in part to the fact that he still prepared his remedies and performed his treatments, not only for many Indians, but for middle-and lower-class Whites from Niagara Falls and Buffalo. He charged modest amounts for his potions and services and did not depend upon them for a living (his wife owned a small store on the reservation) but he had resigned himself to only a moderate amount of prestige, no special powers beyond those of diagnosis and prescription, and to the reality of the state health clinic on the reservation and the physicians and hospitals in the city. He expressed deep discouragement over his inability to interest a younger man to train as his successor and predicted that the traditional role of curer would terminate with his death.

Among the Anang, an Ibibio group of southeastern Nigeria (Messenger 1959), traffic is heavy among native healers in patent medicines and other forms of treatment, but an increasing number of persons are visiting physicians and hospitals where, paradoxically, treatment is less expensive than among indigenous curers. Anang women, attracted by efficient obstetrical services, preceded men in changing their medical allegiance. Here the traditional curer would seem not to have been able effectively to adapt his role, and perhaps the most prevalent form of therapy is the sale of commercial remedies.

Bantu curers in South Africa of a variety of types, all of whom are called *izinyanga*, were studied in Durban and Johannesburg by Bloom (1964) and compared with lay Africans of varying degrees of literacy and urbanization. As in the West Indies, they refer difficult cases to presumably more qualified Bantu specialists, and as in many places, they handle a broad range of diseases, with special competence in the treatment of emotional and hysterical states. They were found to rely more heavily than most laymen on "traditional, hereditarian, magical explanations," and to serve as "a conservative force in African society and therefore as repositories of traditional beliefs" (Bloom 1964:66, 94). Bloom goes on to say, "The *izinyanga* respond to the pressures of urbanization largely by clinging to their traditional beliefs but also, paradoxically, by trying to incorporate into these certain elements derived from urban experience" (1964:69). Apartheid only seems to whet the appetites of the Bantu for Western ways and this author feels that as soon as racial restrictions are removed there will be "a complete assimilation of modern ideas and a withering away of traditional beliefs that are no longer functionally significant" (1964:94), and, one would conclude, consequent obsolescence of the traditional curer's role. Role adaptation here seems to have decreasing support because of rapidly changing beliefs among the laity and the curer's role is subject to much strain, uncertainty, and attenuation.

One type of parallel, but dependent, coexistence was the case of the Negro midwife in parts of the rural southern United States who took over many of the obstetrical accoutrements of the modern town physician, utilized his sponsorship as protection against the threat of dislicensing by public health agents, and for a long time enhanced and preserved her place in the indigenous social system (Mongeau, Smith, and Maney 1961). Her role after several decades, however, became weakened and decayed as recruiting into the apprenticeship system failed because younger female relatives acquired formal education and entered other occupations, as the older White town physicians who functioned as protectors and sanctioning agents died out, as contemporary physicians sought not to change but outlaw midwifery, and as hospitals and clinics grew in influence.

Still another type of marginal coexistence is the kind of parallel but competitive role of the subprofessional nurse or *tsukisoi* in Japan, a combination domestic and mother-figure who ministers to, and sleeps in with, the mental patient (Caudill 1961). Caudill sees the *tsukisoi* role as directly reflective of the mother's function in the Japanese family and social structure, as in conflict with the nurse and psychiatrist, though her role is legitimated by both professionals, as therapeutic but also possibly maltherapeutic, and probably slated for drastic change.

## EMERGENT CURING ROLES

While some curers have adapted their roles successfully to the demands of acculturation and others have become so battered as to be attenuated and in danger of extinction, the contact situation may stimulate new, emergent roles. This happened among the Manus, a technologically primitive people of New Guinea when first observed by Mead (1930), with no special curing roles who treated most injuries and illnesses by family members within the household but referred some to the "doctor boys" appointed by the administration of the Australian Trust Territory. By the time of Mead's (1961) restudy doctor boys were being used as agents of control by the central government, and the efforts of the charismatic, Western-oriented leader, Paliau, to encourage the use of modern medicine by setting up his own hospitals and "screening" presenting symptoms were interpreted by physicians and government officials as hiding patients and therefore "subversive" (Mead [1961:264–265]). Nevertheless, some individuals had apparently become part-time local practitioners

who collect huge fees for using counter-magic.... The tendency to blame disease, whenever it is intractable, on a source wholly external to the society, and to reserve tractable and curable diseases for confession, reform, and medicine, may well grow. These attributions of sorcery to work boys from other areas are justified on the grounds that other peoples may not have "thrown everything away yet," and by the statements of the inability to help made by European physicians and employers who send hopeless cases home to their villages to die (1961:286).

Thus, in a sociocultural system in which apparently there had been no traditional curing specialists, the impact of Western medicine in fact seemed to give rise to them. In this formerly preindustrial but rapidly acculturating society, medical system and curing role thus resemble only in part solutions reached in other spheres of culture. A new synthesis both of sociocultural system and of curing role begins to appear, with Western medicine fertilizing, rather than starving, the emerging practitioner's role.

Another new medical role, emerging side-by-side with both the still strong traditional curing roles on the one hand, and those of the scientific medical system on the other, is that the Navaho health worker or health visitor (Adair 1960; Adair and Deuschle 1957; Deuschle and Adair 1960; McDermott et al. 1960). This role was created by the Cornell University health project as a way of contacting isolated Navaho and mediating, linguistically and medically, between them and the clinic. The role seems to have fallen mainly to Navaho who were more or less marginal to local groups, either because of formal education and high aspiration levels, or because they had been away in White society and were out of touch with the native culture. Unfortunately we are not told whether the role was ever filled by indigenous curers, but it proved strategic in securing increased acceptance of modern medicine by the people.

A healer may invent or discover a revolutionary new medical method that places him in a potently competitive position *vis-à-vis* modern medicine. In McCorkle's (1961) brief study of chiropractic we learn that the method was discovered by one D. D. Palmer in rural Iowa in 1895. Palmer, "a sometime general storekeeper and magnetic healer," cured the hearing impairment of a man by snapping a displaced vertebra back into place. He extended this curing technique to others with great success, and thereby evolved a single-cause disease theory that all ailments are due to obstructions between the brain and body organs, the spine being the principal transmission tract. As McCorkle (1961:22) describes it,

Healing is by manual "adjustment" of the spine, supplemented by massage, and by advice as to diet and rest, the latter defined as proper amounts of sleep, not as taking to one's bed. *All* medicines are denounced as "drugs" and therapy may involve "withdrawal" from "drugs" formerly used by the patient. Surgery and preventive medicine are rejected as violations of the sanctity of the human body. Appeals, delivered verbally and through pamphlets written to relate chiropractic theory to specific diseases and ailments, are to the "common sense" of the mechanically minded Mid-western patient.

The widespread and continued success of this emergent indigenous healer appears to be due to the precision with which he fitted his theory and practice into the existing social structure and value system. Especially in the Midwestern family-type farm, the major relevant characteristics are: extensive mechanization, frequent injuries, and "aches and pains" (perhaps related to working in all kinds of weather), work as a primary value, pragmatic world view (a thing is good if it works), deep belief in "the good work of God and in the sanctity of the human body," the healing power of the laying on of hands, and belief in natural remedies. The role of the chiropractor, therefore, has been not simply competitive, but parallel in its development and spread to modern medicine. McCorkle does not describe the prestige and power of these healers in their communities but it is likely they are rewarded with both trust and wealth.

Finally, we may see an instance of an emergent curing role that involves aspects and functions of several preceding roles, that of the Puerto Rican spiritist medium. Rogler and Hollingshead (1963) found widespread belief in spiritism and utilization of mediums in all urban social strata, being most pervasive in the lower class, and rationalized in scientific terms in the upper class. For the former, especially, beset by "the intimate trials, strife, and personal turmoil that enmesh the members of a socially and economically deprived stratum... its function is to discharge the tensions and anxieties generated in other areas of social life" (Rogler and Hollingshead 1961:654). These investigators believe that most lower-class schizophrenics will receive group therapy from a spiritist medium before, during, after, or instead of seeing a psychiatrist, and they see this emergent curing role in competition with modern medicine as having many assets.

In addition to the presumed advantages of group psychotherapy as practiced in clinical settings, spiritualist sessions are coterminous with the values, beliefs, aspirations, and problems of the participants. No discontinuity in social contacts is required for partici-pation. Little social distance separates the afflicted person from the medium, but, in contrast, visiting a psychiatrist involves bringing persons together who are separated by a vast social gulf. The others in the session are often neighbors, and so the spiritualist and her followers form a primary group where problems are discussed in a convivial setting, classified, interpreted, and rendered understandable within a belief system that is accepted even by those who profess not to believe in it.... Participation in a spiritualist group serves to structure, define, and render behavior institutionally meaningful that is otherwise perceived as aberrant (1963:657–658).

These authors claim that the spiritist also serves a protective function since going to a clinic or psychiatrist places the person in the category of *loco*, which is stigmatized and highly feared, while anyone may visit the medium regardless of the severity of his affliction (see also Landy 1965:42–44 passim; Seda Bonilla 1969).

## INTERPRETATION AND DISCUSSION

...In any society the process of healing involves to some degree what Freidson (1959, 1960, 1961, 1970) has conceptualized as the interaction of the lay referral system with the professional medical system. Freidson postulates that the process by which a case for curing reaches beyond the stage of home treatment involves a concentric series of decision-making diagnoses by the patient himself, by family members, friends, and then, in ever-widening circles of referral, various types of lay, religious, and medical agents. Even in New York City where Freidson's studies took place, the process could be short-circuited at the door of an indigenous ethnic curer before reaching a physician or clinic. Only at that point did the lay system come into contact with the professional medical system. The indigenous medical role may carry as much and at times more, power, prestige, and responsibility as the medical role in Western society (Sigerist 1951:161–180). Therefore the label of "professional" should not be confined to scientifically trained personnel, though obviously the ideology, technology, and recruitment of personnel of scientific medicine are different in many respects from that of nonscientific medicine. In culture contact and change, then, the formulations of Freidson can be extended to include two potentially contesting medical systems in contact with each other and with the indigenous referral system.

We have seen that the indigenous medical system frequently contains its own professional referral system, as in the instance of the Ecuadorian urban folk curer, the Bantu *izinyanga*, the Abron *kparese*, the Navaho hand trembler, or the West Indian Shango religious curers, and that sometimes the indigenous professional referral system maintains a degree of cooperative interaction with the scientific professional referral system, and sometimes it does not, as in the relatively independent activities of the Yemenite *mori*, the Japanese *tsukisoi*, and the curers in the Leyte fishing village. Such factors as numbers, cost, and location of Western medical services, as well as ability to recognize and tolerate the indigenous medical system, undoubtedly set the limits and conditions permitting such cooperative interaction. Primarily it is the local curer who borrows elements from Western medicine rather than vice versa, although many "primitive" botanicals have been incorporated or synthesized. In his role adaptations to culture change, the traditional healer not only incorporates, but elaborates, Western elements. Furthermore, re-synthesis flows in the other direction when customary ceremonies and fetishes become used for new functions, especially to relieve some of the tensions and anxieties of acculturative pressures, as in West Africa, for example, the Anang Ibibio and Ashanti.

The indigenous curing role may exist in complementarity to the scientific medical system in a variety of ways, from almost complete isolation to almost total interaction. In endeavoring to strengthen his role relationships, the traditional curer may make grudging or happy accommodations to as many Western medical elements as he feels he must. Generally this means, as in most instances cited herein, that he becomes, or remains, an advocate of conservative beliefs, and if change is sharply accelerated, may find himself perhaps fatally lagging his lay fellows. When this occurs, his role adaptations have become ineffective since the basis for his prescribed role relationships is broken, and it is likely that his role is slated for oblivion, as in the instance of the Tuscarora curer. Furthermore, even if a dependent relationship is worked out under the protection of the scientific medical system, as the Southern rural Negro midwife had evolved under the town physician, when the external supports are removed (the dying out of the older physicians as patrons, the attack of public health and medical authorities) and the internal means of recruitment to the role dry up (young women preferring other careers), the role soon crumbles away.

Another possibility is that at the bidding of the donor culture (Manus doctor boys, Navaho health workers) a new medical or quasi-medical role is created, usually in order to bring about change and acceptance more quickly and efficiently, though, as among the Manus, new indigenous healers also may arise. Still another possibility is that a new role is created, due to the ingenuity of native practitioners or laymen (Midwest U.S. chiropractor, Puerto Rican spiritist, many varieties in urban Bogota), which operates completely independently of, and offers vigorous competition to, the scientific medical system, I do not know whether the point has been investigated, except by Adair (1960), but it is likely that such powerful, emergent curing professions contain many practitioners who utilize this occupational channel to circumvent blocked mobility, and that some of these individuals possess capabilities that, given education and training, might equip them for entering the scientific medical system.

Although he may be a change agent and innovator, the effect of any of the role adaptations we have cited nevertheless places the traditional curer in the position of a cultural conservative. Not only is he a conserver of old ways, but his social control functions in a situation of culture change seem largely to be those of assuaging or holding the lid on rising aspirations and containing the discontent of his people, as the Filipino *barrio* and

Shango curers. This may not be his intent, but it appears to be a consequent of his role imperatives. Hunt (1968) has made a strong case for the basically conservative role functions of the cultural broker in Mexico.

We attempt to document the following propositions: (a) the mestizos in the rural areas of Oaxaca form an important group of cultural brokers [Hunt uses the Spanish term *agentes* as a preferred equivalent]; (b) these brokers act mainly as promoters of the status quo, that is, they are conservatives and do not induce change in the indigenous segment [the Indian culture]; and (c) the functions of these mestizo brokers are not so much to maintain open interaction among the [cultural] segments as to preserve cultural distance (Hunt 1968:600; translation mine).

In a sense, the curer, even more than such cultural brokers as teachers, entrepeneurs, and politicians, has a crucial stake in the maintenance of the indigenous culture, for the more closely it begins to approximate the donor culture, the more vulnerable his role becomes. Adaptation for role preservation consists in selecting only those changes that will preserve his role while at the same time minimally disturbing his already intruded culture. A possible exception might be the case of the leader-curer Handsome Lake in the re-vitalization of nineteenth century Iroquois culture. Even here, however, he was interested not so much in changing his culture to approximate White, Christian, capitalist culture as in remaking it in an image that would allow a greater probability of survival against the thrusts of White society while at the same time strengthening those components which had become frayed under acculturative pressures, and returning to his people a sense of pride and ethnic identity (Wallace 1966:31–33, 211–213 passim, 1961b).

On the psychological level it may be assumed that if role adaptation to cultural stress is to be achieved, it must be accompanied by cognitive change or by what Wallace (1956a, 1956b, 1956c, 1957, 1961a, 1961b, 1961c, 1966) terms "mazeway resynthesis." Depending upon the pace of culture change, the curer may have to undergo continual adaptation, not only socially in seeking constant realignment of interpersonal relationships, but psychologically in assimilating or redirecting the ever-increasing flow of new ideas, values, and technology, in learning rewarding paths in the changing external maze, and in repressing some paths in his internal mazeway while adding on others. His personality inventory would include a tolerance of cognitive dissonance, a capacity to "compartmentalize" (Goode 1960) dissonant values and role requirements. In applying his theory to the case of the individual facing a suddenly catastrophic change in his environment following such disasters as tornadoes, floods, fire, or bombardment, Wallace (1957:26) says

There is first of all a considerable reluctance ("drag") to changing the old way, because of its symbolic satisfying value. As the old way, however, leads to less and less reward, and as frustrations and disappointments accumulate, there are set in motion various regressive tendencies, which conflict with the established way and are inappropriate to the existing maze. The individual can act to reduce his discomfort by several means: by learning a new way to derive satisfaction from the maze; by encapsulating the regressive strivings in a fantasy system; and by reifying to himself his current way and maze, regarding a major portion of it as dead, and selecting (from either traditional or foreign regions, or both) part of the existing mazeway as vital, meanwhile mourning the abandoned (or abandoning) portion.

The traditional curer who achieves a viable role adaptation not only retains the indigenous community as his major membership group but also retains it as his basic reference group, as in the examples of the curers of Sherupur and the Cherokee conjurer-curer. It is from the culture of his membership group that he draws his sanction as healer, and from the maintenance of its values and practices that he retains the legitimation of his role. We may speak of the scientific medical system as representing only his secondary reference culture, since his identification with its values is partial and he draws upon its practices only insofar as his clientele may demand them or he may safely select those that augment his therapeutic repertory without diminishing his charisma. He may even enhance his diagnostic capabilities by utilizing the scientific system for referral of those cases he clearly recognizes to be beyond his capabilities. Insofar as such cases may be identifiably terminal, the apparent failure of the modern medical system to alter the course of death actually may enhance his position in the local community while discrediting his competitor.

The curer's status does become attenuated, however, when the expectations of his community are such that the technology, if not the values, of scientific medicine is perceived by them as so clearly superior that they distinctly prefer it to their own, as the Anang women who prefer scientific obstetrics, or the Tuscarora who increasingly use the state clinic. Role strain and role conflict follow, and the curer's status may become so hopelessly compromised that role adaptation is impossible of fulfillment and the status of curer becomes marginal and headed for extinction. Since only viable or partly viable curing roles are most readily perceived by the anthropologist, we do not, unfortunately, have very much or very useful data on circumstances under which the role becomes marginal or obsolete, and this process is little understood. I suggest the following alternatives (and others could be hypothesized as well):

(1) The curer accepts a marginal status, though perhaps maintaining some recognition and gratification through hostile means, such as sorcery.

(2) The curer attempts to denigrate scientific medicine by associating it with an oppressor group. If this occurs in a period of rising nationalism, his efforts may succeed since his medicine may not seem as potent as scientific medicine, but it will be associated with "good" values and the other with "bad" ones.

(3) The curer surrenders or radically modifies his status and attempts to capture a substitute status, perhaps even as an adjunct to the Western physician or clinic. This has occurred with mutual benefit in Western Nigeria where native healers may be called in as adjunctive therapists in difficult cases of psychoneuroses (Lambo 1956; Leighton, Lambo, et al. 1963).

(4) The curer becomes unable, or unwilling, to adapt to a marginal role and his sufferings from status deprivation may drive him not only to alienation from his traditional role but from the society which has rejected that role. The result may be behavioral deviance, including the possibility of neurosis or psychosis, or even self-exile as he in turn rejects the society. At least in part these alternatives, and others as well, could be cast into the framework of alternative modes of deviance suggested by Merton (1957) in his essay on "Social Structure and Anomie," though I suspect the model would have to be modified.

As for the new emergent curing or quasi-medical roles, it may be predicted that they also are likely to be thrust into competitive stress and strain with their analogues within the Western medical system, especially such paramedical roles as those of nurse, attendant, medical technician, etc. Structural strains certainly seem characteristic of all paramedical roles in Western medical systems. In urban settings where population size and heterogeneity

encourage many variations in role performance and technique, curers may compete with each other (Press 1971).

A well-established general principle of sociocultural change is that those values and practices will be most easily transferred which are most consonant with the ideology and behavioral standards of the host culture. Proceeding from this premise, Alland (1970:157 passim) hypothesizes that those impinging new roles for which "analogue roles' exist in the host culture will be most easily accepted. His example, to which we earlier alluded, was that of the missionary doctor and his analogue, the Abron *kparese*.

The process of change is influenced not only by the relationship between new elements and existing theories and the reward value of certain behavior, but also by similarities and differences between role systems in donor and receptor populations. When analogous roles exist in two different behavioral systems, change need only involve a shift in the content of existing roles. When no such analogues exist, change may require the adoption of an entirely new role or set of roles. What I am suggesting is that analogue roles act as templets for behavior and have the effect of facilitating and directing change (Alland 1970:157–158).

The *kparese* was most threatened by the missionary doctor's role and seemed most vulnerable to displacement precisely because his role was pervasive, encompassing "the entire religious life of the Abron" and not only the medical system, so that the missionary is predicted by Alland to "have much greater success [than the secular physician] in the long run in the introduction of Western medical practice in Abron culture" (1970:178). Although the *sise* (secular curer) provides an analogue to the secular physician's role, his role is likely to be retained since it is semantically classed with that of the doctor, *médicin africain*, and nurse as "doctor" (see earlier discussion), and many critical substances considered essential in curing are not obtainable in the Western medical system. However, Alland does not suggest that the *kparese*'s role is slated for complete obsolescence and one could wonder what might happen to a *kparese* who adopted Christianity and parts of the Western physician's technical and pharmacological repertory. Perhaps it should also be assumed that those roles that provide no, or a negative, analogue to the Western medical roles stand the greatest chance of survival and are least in need of change in the interest of adaptation, for example, that of the Moslem sorcerer.

Press (1969) suggests in the instance of the cultural broker role of a teacher in Yucatan that his role-set is strengthened as it embodies larger numbers of mutually dependent roles from both cultures, thus rendering his "total configuration" "the more ambiguous" (1964:214). Press seems to be saying that in such a case role viability, and by implication role adaptability, are strengthened by the incumbent taking on visible, essential, and needed roles or role characteristics, of both the host and the contacted culture. He suggests that "As the bicultural passes from one behavioral complex or role-set to another . . . it is possible that he is clearly identified at one time or place, and viewed ambiguously at another" (1969:216) and that this very ambiguity increases role adaptability. Thus, insofar as the indigenous curer attempts to innovate, adopting elements of Western medicine, he increases the ambiguity of his role but also the possibility of its adaptation to the acculturation situation. Indeed he could increase what is already fundamentally ambiguous in his traditional role, since it has been recognized that the medical role in Western medicine (Davis 1960; Parsons 1951), and, I assume, in non-Western medicine, is fraught with ambiguity precisely because the healer in any society deals with "real" uncertainty in scientific and clinical knowledge, with the uses to which uncertainty is put by the healer and his patient, and by the fact that such uncertainty derives from the basic ambiguities inherent in all serious phenomena that threaten life, such as disease and illness.

Associated with the uncertainty and ambiguity of the phenomena with which the curer deals are the factors of unpredictability and uncontrollability. As Aberle (1966:221 passim) has shown

it is through the unpredictable and uncontrollable that man most experiences power, whether in the world of nature or of man, that he endows with power that which or those who help him cope with the helplessness that results from these experiences, and . . . due consideration of amounts and kinds of unpredictability and uncontrollability may help to order a variety of beliefs and acts relating to supernatural power.

The curer's role is endowed with power precisely because it stands at the interstices of religion, magic, and the social system. As Aberle (1966:228–229) further states:

Magic is a technique used to try to achieve empirical ends when empirical techniques provide inadequate prediction and control; religion is action that deals with the inevitable, unpredictable, and uncontrollable gap between the normative and the existential order; charismatic figures are unpredictable, do things other people cannot do, and force decisions in spite of lack of information; divinatory techniques use the unpredictable to predict the unpredictable.

As the course of disease becomes more controllable (prevention, public health measures), more predictable (medical intervention with miracle drugs, scientific surgery) and less uncertain, the curer's role faces its greatest challenge. Its survival, of course, is heavily dependent in the acculturation situation on the ability of its incumbents to increment their power through adoption of what might, in indigenous terms, seem to be Western "magic." But he soon learns that most serious diseases may still be essentially unpredictable and uncontrollable, and in this basic uncertainty lies the probability of successful role adaptation. For he should come to know that uncertainty is often no less for his scientific competitors than for himself.

There are many relevant questions that could not be handled in this paper. Thus, it is apparent that the ultimate usefulness of the notion of role adaptation will depend upon the clarity with which future investigators may be able to define the social and cultural conditions under which role adaptation will succeed or fail. The relationship of this concept to new ways of conceptualizing the notion of role, for example in the work of Goodenough (1965) and Keesing (1970) should be examined. I am aware, for example, of the point that both of these scholars make regarding the social identity component of role, and the fact that, because a role is operative mainly in terms of the various alters with which a particular ego interacts, it is misleading to speak of *the* curing role, or even *a* curing role. A curer necessarily enacts his role differently with each class of alters (men, women, children, nurses, other curers, chiefs, etc.). Another important factor completely ignored here is that of the "impression management" aspects of role, since, as Goffman (1959) has shown, this is basic to defining and understanding the way in which roles are in fact effectively negotiated.

The relationship of role adaptation to the notion of cultural broker also needs further exploration. Most, though not all, instances of cultural brokers, especially in Mexico (Wolf 1956; Hunt 1968; Press 1969), are those of bicultural Mestizos, who in a basic sense stand outside the indigenous (in this case, Indian) culture, while the curer is indigenous to his cultural system. Furthermore, especially for shamans and other religious curers (some are mainly empirical lay practitioners), there is a strong element of a calling and of religiosity in the curing role which is of course completely absent from those teachers, entrepreneurs, and politicians who frequently are the focus of analyses in terms of the cultural broker concept. It is also clear that field studies in depth of role adaptation of the curer confronting the Western medical system need to be undertaken to a much greater extent than they have been heretofore.

In his essay on role Southall (1959:17) has said: "What is required is a type of theoretical formulation applicable to the analysis of highly heterogeneous situations, influenced alike by the ubiquitous international exchange economy and by the presence of persons from markedly contrasting social matrices, Western and industrial on the one hand, nonliterate, peasant and 'folk' on the other." I propose role adaptation as one such formulation. As I have attempted to use it here, I believe it permits the possibility of more fully understanding the changing role of the traditional curer in the confrontation between the "markedly contrasting social matrices" mentioned by Southall. I suggest also it may be applied usefully as well to other changing roles in traditional societies moving toward industrialization and what many, perhaps ethnocentrically, have called "modernization."

# 53 The Hierarchy of Resort in Curative Practices: The Admiralty Islands, Melanesia

## *Lola Romanucci-Ross*

This is a study of what happens to the choice of medical treatment in the acculturative situation of the people of Manus, who were made famous in ethnological literature by the early studies of Margaret Mead (1930, 1961) and Reo Fortune (1935). It is of especial interest since the Manus accept—indeed, assiduously

Reprinted with abridgments from Lola Romanucci-Ross,* 1969, "The Hierarchy of Resort in Curative Practices: The Admiralty Islands, Melanesia," *Journal of Health and Social Behavior*, 10:201–209, with permission of the author and the American Sociological Association.

*Written as Lola Romanucci Schwartz.

strive for—most aspects of European-American culture, having been completely Christianized around 1930. And yet European medicine actually seems to be losing ground at the present time. Dr. Romanucci-Ross' concept of the "hierarchy of curative resort" is reminiscent of the lay and professional medical referral systems concepts of the medical sociologist, Eliot Friedson (1960, 1961) to which Romanucci-Ross refers in a footnote omitted here. There was also a hierarchy of resort in the traditional culture as to which illnesses were to be empirically treated and which were to be magically treated. Somewhat paradoxically, then, not only is European medicine often the treatment of last resort (when it is frequently doomed to failure because the patient has become terminally untreatable), but attributions of sorcery as the cause of illness have greatly increased from earlier times. Thus, the picture portrayed of Manus medical acculturation is quite different from other areas where the indigenous and Western medical systems find some points of complementarity and contact; in the Manus, the two systems actively compete, and which system is chosen depends more upon the natives' classification of the moral component of the specific illness than upon their perception of what each medical system can do. There is, as Romanucci-Ross says, a kind of loyalty to traditional sicknesses. The paper is highly suggestive of the kind of thoughtful analysis required to deal with problems of changing medical systems and acculturation.

## INTRODUCTION

Through several studies of Manus culture ranging over a period of thirty-five years, one is struck by the Manus desire, particularly since World War II, for total acculturation to the European-American life styles, but also by the occasionally dissonant counter-acculturative behavior that is found in the area of medical treatment. It is not a matter of distrust of European doctors, but rather a critical use of European medical resources that seem to fall in patterns of acculturative and counter-acculturative sequences in a manner that at first glance puzzle the observer. This indeterminacy of resort for cures constitutes a marked contrast to the relatively uncritical enthusiastic acceptance of European-American solutions to other life crises, large and small, individual or political, economic and even religious (where change keeps its direction towards acculturative acceptance of Western Christianity). Food preferences, dress, education, party behavior, and, in fact, the general structuring of daily events is dictated by what is known and what is available of European-American cultural adaptations.

In this paper I will examine the following:

(1) The Manus state of acceptance and resistance to European medicine, its agents and its theories concerning etiology in the crises that concern medical practice. European theories embody the dominant views in the socio-cultural systems of European origin that are committed to an attitude that is naturalistic. Manus presuppositions about cause and explanation used to be grounded in notions of causality centered on ghost-ancestor supernatural powers or similar powers from the living through magic and sorcery.

(2) The nature of acculturative and counter-acculturative sequences in a hierarchy of resort of curative practices. These will be investigated through several cases that serve well as paradigms from among the many that could be cited. This hierarchy of resort is viewed as providing the alternative choices for treatment of illness that eventually are given preference and become available to all.

(3) A hierarchy of resort in curative practices can be shown to have existed in the old culture also. In those times it was a function of whatever sanctioning was both required and capable of implementation so that the socio-moral system could be kept in an equilibrium state. The contact culture (European-American), though its influence was felt primarily in other areas, has made it possible to shift the notions of blame for illness, as will be demonstrated.

(4) The geographical area in which the Manus native may contract illnesses has expanded to include the New Guinea mainland, New Britain, New Ireland, etc., through opportunities provided by the Australian Administration and businesses for study and work. Hostility has been displaced from its former targets, neighboring tribes and possible marauders, to other linguistic and cultural groups on the outer fringes of the Territory of Papua and New Guinea. This opportunity for attribution of serious disease to native sorcery abroad relates to the greatly increased spatial mobility of natives and interpersonal fears are proportional to perceived cultural and spatial differences.

(5) Disease must be considered as categories in the language of analysis, or as categories defined by the language of the native culture; this distinction is highly relevant to understanding the resort hierarchy.

(6) To the native, European medical practice is not understood as a theory or explanation; it is lower level descriptive, incomplete, and does not admit of multiple etiology in a bio-social-moral frame. With this belief Manus natives categorize illnesses rather than cures.

(7) On the boundaries of juxtaposed ethno-theoretical systems in contact, large areas are distinguished by easy access and other areas feature occasional shifts from easy access to periodic impermeability. Medical practice in Manus in its dealing with life crises from birth to death is a case in point, and characterized by its open-closed features.

## CULTURES IN CONTACT AND PARADIGMS OF RESORT BEHAVIOR

The Admiralty Islands (which include Manus) are a small archipelago about 150 miles north of New Guinea and about the same distance from the Bismarck Archipelago (of which it is sometimes seen as a Western extension). The total population of the Admiralties recently reached 20,000. This paper draws upon cases of illness recorded incidentally in the journals of events of four expeditions: by Fortune and Mead in 1928, by Mead and T. Schwartz in 1953–1954, by T. Schwartz, myself, and Mead in 1963–1966, and by T. Schwartz in 1967 (Mead 1930, 1956; Fortune 1935, L. R. Schwartz 1966; T. Schwartz 1961, 1962, 1963, 1968). Some detailed cases described by Fortune (1935) and Mead (1930) before conversion of the Manus to Christianity, are used as background for subsequent change. Forty-one cases were recorded in our notes since 1953. Although these were not uniformly or systematically collected and quantitative tabulation does not seem warranted, the following observations are offered based on this extensive and varied record.

Sightings of the Admiralty Islands probably date to the 16th century. More intensive contacts, trade with ships and landing parties may not have taken place until the latter part of the 18th century and the beginning of the 19th century. German Administration was lightly established in 1884; this was followed by Australian Administration after 1914. The islands were occupied by the Japanese and then by the Americans during World War II and this was followed by the Australian Administration under a United Nations trusteeship to the present. Pacification of the area is said to have been effected by 1911. Mission activities began about the turn of the century. The Manus people of the south coast were converted, almost en masse, around 1930. The process of conversion was largely completed during the early 1930's among the Roman Catholic, Lutheran Evangelical, and Seventh Day Adventist Missions. There has been some recent activity by Jehovah's Witnesses and Bahai as well.

Some European medical services have been available to natives at least since the establishment of German Administration. The system of so-called indirect rule, later adopted with little modification by the Australians, was laid down at that time. A village headman was appointed or recognized for each village; a second official was also formalized, one who was thought of as a person of greater contact experience to assist the headman and act as translator. Thirdly, most larger villages had a health official known in pidgin English as "doctor-boy." Though this is still the term of address, the health officials have been referred to as "aid post orderlies" since World War II. At first they had only a few medicines, mainly quinine and materials for treating wounds and tropical sores. Their training was usually brief but some acquired experience as hospital orderlies. Almost all Europeans dispensed some medicines, either through orderlies, or directly at mission, plantation, and administrative centers. European doctors were present during this century, with regularity by the 1930's, at which time a hospital with ward facilities was maintained by the Australian Administration. During this period the disease load of the native population was probably enormously increased by introduced disease agents. Several devastating epidemics can be established from native accounts, among them dysentery and influenza. Tuberculosis probably rose throughout this period to its present high prevalence; about one in forty persons in the Admiralties was actually under treatment in 1966. Virtually the entire native population was infected with malaria according to a World War II survey.

World War II greatly affected the availability of medical services. Little had been provided under the Japanese occupation. But the Admiralties became one of the largest American bases in the South Pacific. Large base hospitals and an abundance of medical supplies were established with treatment facilities for natives. This coincided for the first time with the availability of antibiotics, sulfa drugs and penicillin as well as more effective anti-malarials. A great many natives were treated at American hospitals, though regular medical services were resumed by 1945 under the re-established Australian Administration. The American establishment was rapidly reduced and phased out by 1948 but the level of medical services and supplies remained greatly above the pre-war level, based partly on war-surplus supplies and materials and on staffing by European refugee doctors.

European medicine had never completely carried the field in competition with native medical theory and practice. The war and the immediate post-war period of improving medical service represented the high point in native acceptance and use of European medicine. I believe this acceptance has declined since then. I will discuss the state of acceptance and resistance to European medicine, its agents and its theory. Native and European systems co-exist; they do not only complement each other but they compete (see Friedson 1960). In many cases which we have observed, native practitioners weaken the position of the local A.P.O.s. Where natives turn to curers as first resort in serious illness (or after home remedies), many, who might have been saved by early treatment die later in a hospital or are sent home as apparent failures of European medicine. The often prolonged treatments by a series of native practitioners weaken programs of control of such disesases as TB and leprosy. On the native side, quite apart from the self-interest of curers who collect high fees, I have found in many discussions a sense of loyalty, not so much to native cures, as to *native illness:* the *"sick belong ground"* that lies beyond the pale of European medicine, knowledge, and power; an exceptional knot of resistance to a technology otherwise acknowledged as superior and invested with the highest prestige.

I would like to briefly allude to a small number of cases among these observed since 1953 to illustrate some of the variety of native handling of health crises. In 1953, Ted Schwartz observed a case in the company of a white plantation manager and the local A.P.O. A boy of seven, Tano, had a high fever in intermittent convulsions. His frightened parents reported the very sudden onset of the illness and their turning to the A.P.O. for help. Medical treatment was attempted on the guess that it might be cerebral malaria. The boy appeared to be near death and occasional dirging began when, during the first night the village leader took charge in an attempt to diagnose some ill feeling or moral infraction between the parents or within the family. Such feelings were confessed and rectified in a hand-shaking ceremony between husband and wife. When the boy did not respond, the attempt to save him moved to hymn singing and prayer addressed to God and Jesus. The boy did not regain consciousness. During a series of terrible convulsions it was decided among assembled relatives that this was caused by the spirit of one who had died in violence. The boy had been in a place of "blood," as it is called. His convulsions were the result of an attempt by the spirit to shake the soul stuff out of the boy. An exorcist was called from a nearby Manus village. This exorcist specialized in working a charm by passing a burning coconut husk around the patient. This was the last resort. The boy died shortly after receiving this treatment. The village leader, who in this case was also preacher in his village's branch of the Native Christian Separatist Church, absented himself during this treatment and angrily condemned it as acculturatively regressive. The boy was buried with prayer in the manner of this church; the religious rationale for his death was reasserted, but it was the final ghostly explanation, in spite of failure of the cure, that persisted.

This case is paradigmatic of the acculturative hierarchy of resort. European medicine was the treatment of first resort. This was followed by "confession and rectification" in the manner established in the Paliau Church adaptation of native Christianity. Following this, hymns and prayer in the manner of their earlier mission experience was attempted. Finally, the last in this sequence of resort, a pre-Christian diagnosis and cure which persisted in spite of reassertion of the Paliau Church doctrine. I speak of an acculturative sequence when European medicine is the first resort, or, if the sequence starts with more recent, modern modes, and the trend is toward earlier cultural modes of treatment and explanation. I speak of counter-acculturative sequence where the first resort is to an earlier mode, and the trend, in the event of failure, is then to seek more recently introduced modes.

Many cases show a counter-acculturative sequence. One is the case of Matawai, a man for whom an extraordinary sequence of treatments by native practitioners began during the war. He had become a victim of sorcery while away at work in Rabaul (New Britain) among foreign natives. After first and continuing resort to various herbalists and exorcists he was treated unsuccessfully in the American Army, and later in an administration hospital. I have no idea of a diagnosis. He describes periods of vomiting incredible quantities of blood that brought him near death, or so he thought. These were followed by periods of remission attributed to herbal and exorcistic treatments. His father took him from curer to curer. Not returning

to medical treatment again, he continued this odyssey to foreign curers in New Ireland, New Britain, and, finally, in 1967 to Buka in the Solomon Islands whence he returned pronouncing himself finally cured, having acquired part of the means of cure himself.

More typically, the counter-acculturative sequences begin with a serious illness treated for awhile with home remedies (herbs, hot leaf applications, etc.), then on to one, or a series of curers, and finally to a hospital in last resort for medical treatment with the illness in an advanced state. Such cases must sometimes be cured, but most of those that came to our attention died in the hospital or were sent home to die, pronounced incurable. In 1967, Ted Schwartz, suspecting a counter-acculturative trend, checked through all recent major illnesses and deaths in Pere village, and found all, without exception, to fall in this category. In cases of death from cancer and TB, where medical treatment and hospitalization was finally resorted to, the European diagnosis was not accepted as complete. Native explanation: sorcery. Of two cases of asthma, one took the acculturative sequence seeking medical relief repeatedly, though convinced of sorcery, then abandoning this for a series of treatments by a native curer from among the bush people of Manus. The other refused medical treatment, sought cures in Manus and New Ireland for possible sorcery, then, in a later episode, accepted the explanation and implied remedy that he was punished by the ghosts of his own lineage for having permitted his sister to live illicitly in his house with her lover. Having expelled the pair, but finding no relief, he went back to the sorcery theory and continued to refuse to seek medical treatment. Many other examples of both types could be given covering a full range of native explanations and practices. Of the 41 cases recorded, I have noted that of the recent ones we have in the 1963–1967 period there were 25 cases (total), of which 8 percent were acculturative, and 92 percent counter-acculturative. In the group of 16 cases recorded in the 1953–1954 period, 36 percent were acculturative and 64 percent were counter acculturative. Counter-acculturation seems to have gained in this area of decision making. Though this cannot be established quantitatively on the basis of a set of cases collected incidentally as we worked on other problems, our own conviction is supported by the analysis which follows of the changing contexts of health crises, native explanations, and resort to cures.

We certainly took careful notations in all serious

cases in which there was concern for the life of the sick person. Many minor cases in which treatment is sought and cure effected I might not have noted, except in passing—to mention in my diary perhaps that my morning clinic took so much time, or brought to my attention needed material. Sores, wounds, malaria, pneumonia, and TB or leprosy cases detected in mass surveys were usually submitted for medical treatment, often by threat of government sanctions.

## CHOICES AND THEIR MEANINGS

These illustrative cases exhibit sets and sequences of alternatives of diagnostic interpretations and curative practices. Adair (1963), studying a similar situation among the Navajo, adapts Linton's (1936) concepts of intrasocietal universals and alternatives. According to Linton and Adair, ideas or practices that are well established in a tradition are seen as universals, manifested by all, or available to all within a given society. In change such universals are replaced by others but there is a period in which the new is added to the old in competitive alternativity until a new universal emerges. I wish to go further suggesting that such sets of alternatives may be ordered in hierarchies of resort, where sequences of one, or usually more alternatives may be resorted to as the illness passes from one phase to another when cure is not forthcoming. First resort is taken as a superficial index of the acculturative stance of the group or individual. A last resort is reached as earlier choices are exhausted. However they may be ordered, the alternatives are not equal, nor have we exhausted the matter if we could describe a distribution of frequencies and probabilities among them. The alternatives represent greatly different meanings to the chooser. They refer to different phases in the acculturative process and acculturative history of the group. Considered synchronically, each "choice" has a different socio-moral function.

Further, we may note that we go not from universals (in the intra-social sense) to alternatives, but rather it is noted that one set of alternatives is transformed into another. Traditional explanations of illness now constitute one internally rearranged sector of a much expanded range of alternatives. Cursing by an aggrieved relative is still considered, sometimes in new forms as when one's child fails examinations or loses a job. Sorcery attribution is now far more common for grave illnesses among adults than it was in the period

reported by Fortune (1935). It seems no longer to be used for illnesses of children and it is not expected from within the group or close at hand, but almost exclusively from foreign natives. Moral illness, attributed to punishment by the ghost of one's own lineage, while still occasionally diagnosed in this manner, have now mostly been shifted to the alternatives derived from native Christianity in the contact culture (see Fortune 1935:344–345).

The alternatives of diagnosis and cure which appear in Mead's and Fortune's cases from 1928 may also have constituted a hierarchy of resort. The allocation of cases among alternatives then may be seen from Fortune's discussion to have been a product of balance between the distribution of moral burden and the need for sanctioning events furnished by health crises. The 1928 diagnoses and cures may be seen as a set of alternatives of differing frequencies conditioned by moral requirements. As Manus society was then post-contact but pre-Christian, undergoing the effects of such drastic changes as pacification, there might have been an acculturative component even then to the hierarchies of resort though this is less apparent than the socio-moral ordering.

We have indicated the components of (T) the traditional set of alternatives. Another set derives from the contact (C) culture in two levels: (1) native versions of Christianity influenced by mission membership; (2) native Christianity further differentiated in acculturative cults and movements and a separatist church. Moral illness is now mainly treated on this level. In place of the traditional moral concerns with a puritanical sexual ethic and the fulfillment of ceremonial and economic obligations, moral illness is now mostly attributed to bad feelings, anger, jealousy, intransigence, exclusive concern over individual interest, etc., between husband and wife especially and relatives generally. These are punished directly by God through illness, death and misfortune. European medicine (E) is generally not understood as a theory or explanation. It is impersonal and amoral, therefore it is incomplete and descriptive rather than explanatory. It states that a person died of a brain tumor but does not say why this happened to him or "hudunit." On this basis it is not morally applicable as a sanctioning event.

Many sequences of T, C, and E are possible, and some cases for most of them could be found in our records. A few comments may further clarify the relations among them. Ideally, in an acculturative hierarchy, C should occur medially as it does in the Tano case. Actually it may occur in any position, often occurring simultaneously with E. This is one of the indications of the weakness of the position of European medicine even when it is the first resort. E tends not to occur alone as C and T do, but to be taken as supplementing the others. For example, European medicine will not work unless accompanied by moral rectification or by exorcism. E often stands alone or with home remedies in cases involving sores, wounds, or malaria and pneumonia, but only when there has been no delirium, loss of consciousness, marked weight loss or convulsions, all of which imply soul pathology. ECT is not symmetrically the reverse of TCE for the above reasons, and also because, in many counter-acculturative sequences, an E of last resort that does not result in a cure reverts to C or T before death, or as a posthumus explanation of death. Natives may think of Christian explanations and religious cures as European but tend not to do so. Nativized Christianity is well assimilated into the native version of the contact culture.

The cases to which we refer have been selected as instances of the etic category of "health crisis." In native conception these would be subsumed under a much broader emic category of "mishaps" which included not only matters of the organic and mental health of human beings but also their general well being or misfortune. All events under this emic category, good or bad, depended, at least in part, on the intervention of animate beings, other persons, aided by magic or their spirit familiars, non-human spirits, ghosts, and in the contact-culture, by God. Even among the Catholic natives, Mary is rarely referred to in health crises and the saints play no role. This is in contrast to other areas of Catholic influence. This broad class of mishaps included not only such disorders as sickness and death, but constipation, prolonged labor or delayed afterbirth, infertility, insanity, any unusual loss of weight or loss of teeth, loss of hair or its premature graying, impaired motivation and accidents, such as being struck by a falling coconut, loss of a canoe, bad luck in fishing or gambling, etc. One might seek a personal cause in some animate being for any of these, as well as for conspicuous good fortune, long life, large family, etc. This broad category was internally differentiated in terms of the alternatives of resort for remedy and specific explanation. This division stems primarily from confining resort to outside, specialist curers of acute illness where death could result.

Reversible illness has played a major role in the native system of externalized moral sanctions in that each such event contains both the punishment in the illness, the judgment in the diagnosis, and the reward for rectification in the cure. Infant mortality, once extremely high, potentially imposed too great a moral burden on the parents to examine, analyze and confess their guilt, and often, as Fortune has suggested, where illness verged on death, sorcery rather than sin became the explanation of last resort. The cause of death could be displaced from close relatives, living and dead. In the shift to native Christianity, infant deaths are commonly attributed to sins, as they are now defined, with God as the usual agent, except in those dramatic circumstances such as Tano's death where an older mode of explanation is the last resort. Even in epidemics of infant gastroenteritis, individual diagnosis of parental sin is sought.

For adults, other than the aged for whose death no specific explanation seems necessary, sorcery seems now to be an extremely common explanation for death and sudden or prolonged illness of dramatic symptomatology. Moral lapses and attack by spirits not under the direction of other human beings are among the alternatives occasionally considered as causes of illness. Almost all recent deaths and grave illnesses in our record are attributed to sorcery. In the earliest acculturative stage reported by Fortune (1935) and Mead (1956), such deaths (explained during the illness as moral sanctions by the ghosts of the sick person's own lineage) were displaced, after death, upon the motivated anger, vengeance or malice of ghosts of other lineages. In the shift to sorcery among the alternatives in the traditional sector of the present hierarchy of resort, the displacement distance is increased.... Sorcery is still possible from other Admiralty Islands natives, particularly the people of the interior, but the main focus of anxiety is now on the circle of foreigners defined by overseas natives of the Bismarck archipelago, the Solomons, and New Guinea. This expansion of the Manus area of interaction occurred under the pacification, greatly increased mobility and labor migration made possible under colonial administration. Though the zone of displacement has shifted outward, now, as before, the sorcerers and the curers are sought from the same zone. The white man is completely out of the system, neither affected by, nor able to cure native illnesses. The foreign native is close enough to participate in the same ethno-theoretical system, but he is distant enough spatially and culturally to inspire fear of his powers and prestige for his cures. Though the foreign native zone serves for the displacement of hostility, fear, resentment and responsibility for these deaths, the natives of the Admiralty Islands have increasingly to live, work and attend schools in this same zone. The Manus, who has always been an itinerant consumer of curative services, now travels, when local curers fail, along the network of his relatives working overseas, to specialists whose high fees enhance the hope of cure. In European medical channels, where treatment is free, there is also a correlation of gravity of illness, distance of treatment center, and the prestige of hope of cure.

After nearly a century under European administration with increasing intensity of contact and experience with European medicine, and while the latter had considerable success in reducing mortality, it has by no means become the treatment of first resort in cases of considered serious illness. The counter-acculturative sequence which exhausts native cures before turning to European medicine if ever, seems still to be the most prevalent. Use of European medical services in first resort or first after home remedies, in cases considered grave, has probably decreased for the indications mentioned above.

In native thinking it seems as if it is not so much the treatment that is dichotomized into native and European, but the illnesses themselves. Some, such as ordinary non-grave attacks of malaria, may be susceptible to European medicine. Others may be aided by European medicine, while native treatment gets at the cause. But in grave and dramatic illnesses, only rectification or exorcism will help. Some writers, such as Erasmus (1961) explain the differential success and failure of European medicine in competition with native cures and explanations primarily on "observed frequencies" of success. It is thought that where medical treatment is quickly effective, dramatic and evident, it will prevail over others. The explanation has some validity but it is incomplete. The native specialist curer, like the European hospital, also sees mainly serious cases of which many die or are unrelieved. The curer has his explanation for failure. In one such explanation it is said that there are two kinds of sorcery, one curable and remissable, the other incurable. The latter reveals itself in the intractability of an illness or the death of a patient. The incurable form is known as Nam. It originates in the Admiralties rather than in the foreign zone. Foreign sorceries are also often not cured, though theoretically they can be cured if the right curer is consulted before death results, hence the near inexhaustibility of the search for cure by native means as long as life remains. But beyond explanations based on a calculus of curative

efficacy, there is the social and cultural context of death and disease, diagnosis and cure, and their place in the pluralistic contact culture. The European and native modes of response to health crises are not comparable to each other—not equal functional substitutes. They derive from opposed ethno-theoretical systems. The separation of the curative and moral functions that has evolved in European cultures in the general trend toward institutional dissociation is not transmitted by mission Christianity. For the native, illness is still a socio-moral crisis, a sanctioning event for which these is still no convincing substitute.

I have the impression, difficult to demonstrate, but derived from my discussions about illness with natives, that there is a nativistic loyalty to native diseases—their "*sick belong ground*" which lie beyond the sphere of European knowledge and power. Here is an area in which an older world view adapts and persists for those who have known the past to which it belonged, and, to judge by our work with school children and teachers, European medicine has a long period of competition ahead for primacy in the hierarchy of resort.

# 54 Humoral Medicine in Guatemala and Peasant Acceptance of Modern Medicine

## Michael H. Logan

The tendency of peoples in many parts of the world to subscribe to the humoral theory of medicine and physiology is perhaps most dramatically illustrated in the folk beliefs of Latin American societies and particularly among peasants. This paper by Michael Logan briefly reviews the history of the humoral theory, its basic premises and the way it functions among Guatemalan peasants, and presents an analysis of humoral classification as a cognitive system as well as a comparison of the hot-cold medical beliefs of Guatemalans with those of Puerto Ricans. Logan suggests that many of the problems that plague modern physicians attempting to bring Western scientific medical care to such peoples could be solved if these practitioners

Reprinted with abridgments from Michael H. Logan, 1973, "Humoral Medicine in Guatemala and Peasant Acceptance of Modern Medicine," *Human Organization*, *32*:385–395, with permission of the author and the Society for Applied Anthropology.

would try to understand and appreciate indigenous beliefs, determine whether and where such beliefs impede the administration of medical care, and work out a course of healing action that will utilize the traditional medical system by casting prescriptions within the boundaries of its categories. Useful appendixes of classifications of foods, medicinal plants, and proprietary and prescribed medicines according to the hot-cold categories have been omitted here but can be found in the original source.

Many Indian and Ladino peasants of highland Guatemala classify foods, medicinal plants, illnesses, and now modern medicines according to a conceptual scheme of opposition between the qualities of hot and cold. Belief in the humoral scheme of medicine influences an individual's selection and assessment of medical treatment. When prescribed treatment ignores the humoral concept, or creates unacceptable contradictions between modern and native philosophies of health, such treatment is likely to be less effective than if native concepts were incorporated into the prescribed therapeutic program.

The concept of humoral medicine has received considerable attention in the anthropological study of folk cultures. The history and diffusion of humoral medicine has been dealt with adequately (Foster 1953; Hart 1969); methodological procedure for recording data on humoral classifications has been outlined (Foster and Rowe 1951); and descriptive accounts of the humoral theory of disease are present in the ethnomedical literature of Mexico (Currier 1966; Foster 1967; Ingham 1970; Lewis 1960; C. Madsen 1965; W. Madsen 1955; Mak 1959; Redfield and Park 1940), Guatemala (Adams 1952; Cosminsky 1972; Douglas 1969; Gillin 1951; Gonzales 1969; Woods 1968), Costa Rica (Orso 1970); Richardson and Bode 1971), Puerto Rico (Landy 1965; Mintz 1956; Wolf 1956), South America (Gillin 1947; Reichel-Dolmatoff and Reichel-Dolmatoff 1961; Simmons 1955; Valdızan 1922; Wellin 1955), Latin Americans in the United States (Clark 1959; Kiev 1968; W. Madsen 1964; Padilla 1958; Rubel 1960; Saunders 1954), the Philippines (Hart 1969), Burma (Spiro 1967), India (Opler 1963), and England (Tillyard 1944). Although anthropologists have concerned themselves with describing the humoral theory of disease, "the direct implications of this theory for understanding and treating patients who subscribe to it have rarely been examined" (Harwood 1971:1153).

In this presentation I will discuss (1) the history and structure of humoral medicine; (2) the function of humoral medicine among the peasantry of Guatemala; (3) the cognitive system underlying humoral classifications; and (4) how commitment to humoral medicine can impede effective medical treatment. From my discussion and comparison of data with those collected and reported by Alan Harwood in the *Journal of the American Medical Association*, I hope to present conclusions from which I will be able to provide useful and practical suggestions for those interested in the ethnomedicine and public health of Latin American culture areas.

...The three peasant populations included in this research, and referred to specifically in this presentation, are the Cakchiquel and Tzutuhil Maya, and the monolingual Spanish-speaking class of Ladinos.

## HISTORY AND STRUCTURE OF HUMORAL MEDICINE

The science of treating illness and maintaining health by prescribing elements or foods with the qualities of hot and cold first appears in the writings of Greek scholars, notably Hippocrates. It is interesting to note, however, that the striking similarities between the Hippocratic doctrine and the centuries older Yin-Yang philosophy of ancient China might suggest a center of origin other than that of the Mediterranean area (cf. Hart 1969; Lessa 1968).

Humoral science diffused from Greece and Rome to the Arabic world and was introduced into Iberia with the Moorish occupation of that region (Foster 1953). Expansion of the Spanish empire during the sixteenth century brought the doctrine to aboriginal America, and through acculturation in the conquest and colonial periods, humoral medicine was incorporated into Indian and Mestizo world views of health and, to this day, humoral medicine remains an integral part of peasant culture.

According to the Hippocratic theory, "there were four primary and opposite fundamental qualities, the hot and the cold, the wet and the dry... these met in binary opposition to constitute the Essences or Existences which entered in varying proportions into the constitution of all Matter" (Singer 1928:33). The four humors—blood, phlegm, black bile, and yellow bile—possessed these fundamental qualities. Each humor had its complexion: blood, hot and wet, yellow bile, hot and dry; phlegm, cold and wet; black bile, cold and dry (Foster 1953:202). The health or "complexion" of an individual could only be maintained as long as the body's natural and requisite equilibrium between hot and cold, wet and dry was not upset.

The humoral qualities of hot and cold do not refer to actual temperature changes produced by cooking nor to pungent tastes as found in peppers. Similarly, the terms wet and dry do not pertain to water content. They refer, rather, to the constitutional essence or innate character of a given item or personal state of being. Natural objects, foods, and illnesses possess these symbolic qualities and can alter the health of an individual through contact, consumption, or contagion. For example, overconsumption of hot foods increases the body's normal content of heat and, if excessive, provokes ailments thought to be hot in nature. Treatment, therefore, would call for equalizing the body's temperature balance and restoring neutrality by consuming principally cold foods and medicines.

In the New World, the Hippocratic theory of humoral medicine was simplified as a result of cultural trait selection. The qualities of moisture became less significant in diagnosis and treatment, while the temperature dichotomy grew in importance and came to dominate the Latin American version.

## FUNCTION OF HUMORAL MEDICINE IN GUATEMALA

The assumption that one's life is affected by the ever-present qualities of hot and cold is widely held in Guatemala, and the peasant's belief in the reality of the humoral qualities serves as a principle guiding his daily behavior. The natural world and its elements possess these qualities and continuously threaten to upset the individual's internal balance between hot and cold. It is believed that the body is a self-regulating system which strives to maintain its temperature balance, but if exposed to sources of heat and cold of an intensity or duration which it is incapable of handling, illness or death will develop as a result of temperature imbalance.

Children are particularly susceptible to extremes in temperature. In one village, for example, the death of a six-month-old infant was attributed to the "coldness" of penicillin given the infant by her godparent (*padrino*). The child's mother, an Indian, in an attempt to aid her daughter asked the child's godparent, a Ladino from a neighboring town, to help in any way he could. Responding to the mother's plea, the godparent purchased penicillin and a syringe, and unknowing to the parents of the child, injected the infant with 2 c.c. of penicillin (probably 100,000 units) and afterwards instructed the parents to give the child several pills which he had also purchased. That night, only hours after the injection and first series of tablets, the child died. The godparent, upon returning to visit the household the following morning, was shocked to hear of the child's death and explained to the despondent mother that he had given the child an injection of penicillin in hope of saving the child's life. (The remaining tablets, along with the empty syringe, were presented to me by the mother. The pills contained penicillin.) Although the godparent acted in good faith, the amount of the drug given was excessive and it is likely that the child was allergic to penicillin. This fact, however, was never realized by the parents of the deceased. They maintained that it was the additional cold produced by the penicillin that brought death to their child, who had been suffering from severe diarrhea for over two weeks. All agreed that the child was simply too weak to combat the excessive cold created by both the penicillin and diarrhea. Maintaining an even balance between hot and cold is an essential prerequisite for health: a prerequisite rarely sustained.

Heat may "overwhelm" the body as a consequence of strenuous labor, radiation from a cooking fire, emotional or sexual excitement, intoxication, exposure to "evil eye," overconsumption of hot foods, or from contracting an illness regarded as being "heat induced," for example, fever. Cold may overtake the body from careless use of cold medicines, foods and beverages, exposure to "evil winds," bathing while one is hot, or from having an illness with symptoms of diarrhea or chills, both of which are "cold induced."

It would be inappropriate for a patient suffering from fever to employ a medicine known locally to be hot. The equal qualities of heat existing between the illness and the medicine would not only make the medicine ineffective, but harmful. On several occasions, as reported to me by staff members at the Behrhorst Clinic, hospitalized patients running high fevers refused to take the prescribed vitamin and protein supplements given to them daily. Rather, the patients hid the pills under their pillows or secreted them elsewhere in the room. Upon questioning, a few confessed that it would be best not to use vitamins at that time because vitamins, like their fever, are *katan*, or very hot. Taking or continuing to use a hot medicine in this case would worsen the patient's condition, supposedly by increasing the level of heat in his body. Therefore, the only appropriate choice of remedies, according to the patient's frame of reference, would be those consisting of medicines and foods cold in nature. Vitamins were temporarily rejected by patients as long as their fevers continued, because vitamins were not considered to be an appropriate medicine for treatment of fever.

Commitment to the humoral philosophy functions as a directive of behavior, and the effect upon behavior is relative to the degree of commitment. Most significantly, belief in this system of disease etiology influences the individual's diagnosis of illness and choice of diet and medical treatment.

## COGNITIVE SYSTEM OF HUMORAL CLASSIFICATION

Patterns of hot-cold classification vary considerably throughout Meso-America (Adams and Rubel 1967; Currier 1966; Foster 1953, 1967; Ingham 1970; Lewis 1960; Redfield 1934, 1940). The cognitive system underlying various classifications, however, remains constant and is universal. It is based on the assumption that elements exist naturally in a state of binary opposition and the effect of one element upon the other equalizes the valence of each. Taken as such, this theorem is simplistically understood. One must ask: What conceptual criteria segregate elements into opposing qualities? How are new elements defined and incorporated into preexisting structures?

In an attempt to answer these questions, I start with a "given": categorization is based upon binary opposition. Logically, then, each element must fulfill specific, culturally known criteria by which it is defined as being either hot or cold. Therefore, if the definitional criteria underlying classification can be successfully elicited and tested empirically, then our current understanding of the effect of humoral medicine upon modern therapeutic programs will be significantly improved.

I find that the following criteria are operative in the binary classification of foods and medicinal plants: color, sex, origin, nutritive value, physiological effect, and medical use. It should be added that the first criterion, color, is significant only in reference to foods, the domain here used to briefly illustrate the suggested criteria.

*Color*: Generally speaking, darker colored flesh, for example, beef, is hot, but lighter toned meats, such as pork and fish, are cold.

*Sex*: Female items are hot, while males are cold. Thus, hens are hot but roosters are not.

*Origin*: A by-product typically retains the temperature quality of its source—flour and bread are cold because their source is cold. Moreover, aquatic products, like most subterranean animals and low-lying plants, are cold, whereas organisms more exposed to the direct heat of sunlight are generally hot.

*Nutritive value*: Most fruits and vegetables are cold, although those believed to be unusually nutritious, such as avocados and peanuts, are hot.

*Physiological effect*: Foods that affect an individual by producing an allergic response are thought to be hot, and so is the disease. Hives, for example, is classified as being hot; but those foods which consistently provoke symptoms of diarrhea or other cold reactions are defined as being cold.

*Medical use*: Dietary items traditionally consumed to treat a cold ailment are typically hot; and those used to treat a hot ailment are typically cold. Thus, chocolate for chills and lemonade for fevers.

Definitional criteria involved in classifying illnesses include: etiology, therapeutic prescription, individual sensation, and affected organs and body substances.

*Etiology*: When etiology is known, the ailment is equal in temperature to that of the cause. One "overcome" by evil eye, for example, will manifest an illness also hot in nature.

*Therapeutic prescription*: Instructing a patient to omit hot foods from his diet—say peppers and liquor—inadvertently isolates a temperature quality for the illness equal to that of the restricted foods. In this case, the illness would be hot because the forbidden foods are hot.

*Individual sensation*: In general, when a patient has a sensation of being "chilled" or "heated" due to abnormal metabolic temperature, his condition is categorized equally to that of his sensation. If chilled, the condition is cold; if feverish, the condition is hot.

*Affected organs and body substances*: Lastly, illnesses affecting specific organs or body substances are of the same temperature quality of the organ or substance. Hepatitis, for example, is hot because it involves a pathogenic condition of the liver, which also is thought to be hot.

Temperature classification of modern medicines is based upon a single, dominant criterion: establishing contrast with illness. Regardless of the color, physical properties, or means of administration, a medicine is classified opposite to the culturally known temperature quality of the illness or symptoms for which it is to be employed. Aspirin is hot because it is believed to be highly effective in treating cold-induced ailments, such as head colds or rheumatism; but Alka Seltzer is cold because it is preferred for treating fever and stomach inflammation, both of which are hot.

Medicines not yet known to a patient will, upon introduction, be classified according to the above assumption that a medicine, if it is to be effective, must be of an opposite quality of the known disorder, because equal qualities between illness and medicine only aggravate a patient's condition. Furthermore, this assumption also holds true for classifying an unknown illness. For example, if a culturally known medicine is prescribed to treat an unknown illness, the illness will be classified in the opposite temperature grouping of the prescribed medicine. Therefore, the use of Aspirin defines "migraine" as being cold.

Term-frame test questions (Goodenough 1965) were used in 40 of the several hundred informant interviews to test the validity of the contrasting illness-medicine criterion. While frame components and given terms (known) were addressed in the informant's language, test-terms were pronounced in English and occasionally were fictitious to insure their "unknown" character....

Use of the term-frame method established sufficient data to now conclude that modern medicines are classified opposite to the temperature quality of the illnesses for which they are to be used.


## THE HUMORAL CONCEPT AND IMPROVING MEDICAL TREATMENT

When physicians or medical aids prescribe medicines or dietary regimens that conflict with a patient's belief in the humoral concept, the successful treatment of that patient can be adversely affected. Comparison of data from Puerto Rican patients in New York City (Harwood 1971) shows significant similarities in patient behavior between Guatemalans and Puerto Ricans.

Guatemalan and Puerto Rican patients display almost equivalent behavioral patterns in response to treatment of specific disorders. That is, when a conflict arises between the temperature qualities of a patient's condition and the prescribed medication, the patient will typically reject the medication. For example, in both Guatemalan and Puerto Rican samples, vitamins are rejected in treatment of illnesses producing high fevers. Fruit juices rich in citric acid are rejected in treatment of the common cold. On the other hand, preferential use of foods in accordance with humoral theory may prove beneficial, as with selecting a restricted diet of hot foods like chicken-broth and peanuts to treat infant diarrhea, a frequent symptom of malnutrition (Logan 1972).

To illustrate behavioral patterns for patients who adhere to the humoral concept, two charts have been constructed giving (1) the temperature classification for various symptoms, diseases, and treatment regimens and (2) expectable patient behavior or reaction to prescribed treatment. The Guatemala data were elicited from intensive interviews with field informants and from consultation with patients and medical personnel at the Behrhorst Clinic. Data were verified by employing various methods, namely term-frame construction (Goodenough 1965), named information-slips (Berlin 1968), paired comparisons (Berlin 1968), and triads test (Romney and D'Andrade 1964). The data presented here concerning Puerto Ricans were extracted from Harwood's study. His data were derived from three sources (1971:1154): observations of medical practices in 64 Puerto Rican households; responses to a questionnaire concerning postpartum practices, and infant care administered to 27 mothers; and anecdotal reports from medical personnel at the Martin Luther King, Jr., Neighborhood Health Center.

When patient behavior differed in the two study groups—as with selection of medication to treat fever—it is found that this variation is caused by a difference in the way the two groups classify the medicine prescribed in therapy. Fever is classified as a hot illness by both groups. Puerto Ricans also consider penicillin to be hot and, therefore, will not take this medicine to treat fever but instead will use cold substances in therapy. Guatemalans, on the contrary, judge penicillin to be a cold medicine and therefore accept this drug for treatment of fever.

**Table 1** Important Symptoms in Native Illness Classification

| Symptoms | Symptom Classification | | Prescribed Treatment | Treatment Classification | | Expectable Behavior | |
|---|---|---|---|---|---|---|---|
| | Guat. | P.R. | | Guat. | P.R. | Guat. | P.R. |
| Chills | C | C | Penicillin | C | H | Reject | Accept |
| Fever | H | H | Penicillin | C | H | Accept | Reject |
| Chronic cough (no blood) | C | —* | Penicillin; tetracycline | C | — | Reject | — |
| Chronic cough (blood) | H | — | Penicillin; tetracycline | C | C | Accept | Reject |
| Common cough | C | C | Citrus fruits | C | — | Reject | Reject |
| Nonproductive cough | H | — | Penicillin; citrus fruits | C | — | Accept | — |
| Productive cough | C | — | Penicillin; citrus fruits | C | — | Reject | — |
| Sinus pains | C | C | Menthol | H | — | Accept | — |
| Hoarseness | C | C | Gargle (hot salt water) | H | — | Accept | — |
| Wheezing | C | — | | — | — | — | — |
| Rash | H | H | Creams | C | — | Accept | — |
| Black urine | H | — | Aspirin; no alcohol | H | H | Reject | — |
| White stools | C | — | Aspirin; no alcohol | H | H | Accept | — |
| Diarrhea (no blood) | C | H | Entero-leina | H | — | Accept | — |
| Diarrhea (blood) | H | H | Entero-leina | H | — | Reject | — |
| Constipation | C | H | Fruits; greens | C | C | Reject | Accept |
| Indigestion | H | C | Alka-Seltzer | C | — | Accept | — |
| Menstrual pain | C | C | Aspirin | H | H | Accept | — |
| Urinating pain | H | — | Penicillin | C | H | Accept | — |
| Penis discharge | H | — | Penicillin | C | H | Accept | — |
| Joint and body pains | C | C | Vicks Vapor Rub | H | H | Accept | Accept |
| Paralysis | C | C | Aspirin | C | H | Accept | Accept |
| Vomiting | C | — | Alka-Seltzer | C | — | Reject | — |
| Heartburn | H | — | Alka-Seltzer | C | — | Accept | — |
| Weakness | C | — | Vitamins; sucros | C | H | Accept | — |
| Sweating | H | — | Cold compress | C | — | Accept | — |
| Fainting | C | — | Vitamins; sucros | H | — | Accept | — |
| Burns | H | H | Creams | C | C | Accept | Accept |
| Cuts | H | H | Creams | C | C | Accept | Accept |

*Dashed lines indicate data not available.

**Table 2** Diseases Recognized by Natives and Medical Doctors

| Disease | Disease Classification | | Prescribed Treatment | Treatment Classification | | Expectable Behavior | |
|---|---|---|---|---|---|---|---|
| | Guat. | P.R. | | Guat. | P.R. | Guat. | P.R. |
| Common Cold* | C | C | Citrus fruits | C | C | Reject | Reject |
| Influenza* | H | —** | Penicillin | C | H | Accept | — |
| Tuberculosis (no blood) | C | — | Penicillin | C | H | Reject | — |
| Tuberculosis (blood) | H | — | Penicillin | C | H | Accept | — |
| Whooping cough* | C | — | — | — | — | — | — |
| Bronchitis* | C | — | Penicillin | C | H | Reject | — |
| Pneumonia* | C | — | — | — | — | — | — |
| Laryngitis* | C | C | Gargle (hot salt water) | H | H | Accept | — |
| Asthma* | C | — | Ethedrine | H | — | — | — |
| Measles* | H | H | Aspirin; vitamins | H | H | Reject | — |
| Chicken pox | H | H | Aspirin, vitamins | H | H | Reject | — |
| Hepatitis | H | — | Alcohol and spices prohibited | H | — | Accept | — |
| Tenesmus | H | C | Diuretics; potassium (fruits) | C | C | Accept | Reject |
| Dysentery* | H | H | Penicillin; tetracycline | C | H | Accept | Reject |
| Intestinal worms* | C | — | Lombiz-sante (T.M.) | H | — | Accept | — |
| Rheumatic fever | — | C | Penicillin | C | H | — | — |
| Rabies* | H | — | — | — | — | — | Accept |
| Typhoid | H | — | Penicillin | C | H | Accept | — |
| Syphilis | H | — | Penicillin | C | H | Accept | — |
| Rheumatism* | C | C | Aspirin; Vicks | H | H | Accept | Accept |
| Meningitis | C | — | Penicillin | C | H | Reject | — |
| Ulcers | H | — | Milk; bread | C | C | Accept | — |
| Malnutrition (with diarrhea) | C | — | Vitamins; sucros | H | H | Accept | — |

*Diseases recognized by natives.
**Dashed lines indicate data not available.

Similarly, we find that Puerto Ricans reject penicillin when employed to treat diarrhea, because both the illness and the medicine are hot. Guatemalans, however, accept penicillin as treatment for dysentery (presence of blood) because the temperature quality of the illness is hot while that of the medicine is cold. Although their treatment-behavior varies at times, as we have seen, it is, nonetheless, predictable and consistent to humoral theory.

From the above data it becomes obvious that patient behavior is predictable as long as, and to the degree with which, the appropriate temperature qualities are known for both the patient's illness and the prescribed medicine. By knowing these, a physician would be capable of forecasting expectable patient behavior and therefore devising a therapeutic program suitable to the patient's medical and ideological needs. This can be done by (1) selecting medicines and foods of the opposite temperature quality of that of the patient's condition, but if this cannot be done without jeopardizing the clinical effectiveness of treatment, then by (2) "neutralizing" the essential medicines and foods by jointly prescribing "placebo" elements of an appropriate temperature category to restore the necessary opposition between the patient's condition and essential medication.

In treating cases of malnutrition, for example, adequate sources of protein and vitamins can usually be derived from either hot-or cold-classified foods. Care should be given to select a therapeutic diet consisting of foods opposite in temperature to the dominant symptom. If diarrhea is persistent, hot foods are appropriate; if symptoms of fever or skin rash are manifest, then cold foods are preferable. Several medical students from Columbia University, who were participating in the Behrhorst program in Guatemala, confessed to me that they could not understand why patients, including those who were not hospitalized, refused to eat some of the foods prescribed in therapeutic diets. At time, vegetables or fruits were left on the plate, while beef, beans, and coffee were consumed. Invariably, these patients displayed symptoms reported to be cold. When patients had symptoms confessed to be hot, a reverse in eating patterns was observed.

Foods and medicines may be "neutralized" by combining element of opposing temperature qualities. Guatemalan peasants recognize the principle of neutralization and use it to their advantage, as do Puerto Ricans (Harwood 1971). Frequently I observed individuals adding sugar (*panela*) to fruit juice recommended to them by physicians. When asked why sugar was added, the predominant reply was "to heat the juice," and therefore render it safer to drink when afflicted with a cold illness. Similarly, vitamins, sugar water, chocolate, or Incaparina might be used to "heat" penicillin, thus making it more acceptable to the patient to treat general diarrheal symptoms resulting from enterobacterial infection. Harwood reports several cases where the neutralization of foods and medicines resolved the contradiction of opposing temperature qualities. Postpartum mothers, for example, added tea and barley water to "cool" evaporated milk formula and therefore protect their infants from the "heat" of this prescribed food (Harwood 1971:1156).

## SUGGESTIONS FOR MEDICAL PERSONNEL

Contact between modern and traditional forms of medicine is characteristically marked by discrepancies and contradictions in theories of health specific to each form of medical knowledge. Physicians working with patients from cultures other than their own must realize that discrepancies and contradictions left hidden, or patently ignored, hinder optimal therapeutic success. Ethnographic examples abound that illustrate how ineffective modern therapeutic programs can be when medical personnel fail to gain a thorough understanding of the principles and concepts of traditional medicine that govern the behavior of their patients.

Coexistence of modern and folk systems of medical practice is a persistent feature of peasant societies undergoing acculturation in the expansion of Western science and culture. Acculturation in medical beliefs, however, frequently has not kept pace with changes that have occurred in other aspects of folk society. As a result, patients may overtly appear to be "progressive" in dress and speech, but in respect to basic premises of health, they often adhere to traditional beliefs. The general pattern that prevails, then, at least in much of Latin America, is that modern medicine does not replace or significantly alter patterns of folk medicine, but serves as an additional system employed concurrently with traditional forms of medical practice (Douglas 1969; Gonzales 1966; Holland 1962; Press 1971; Simmons 1955).

The probability of a physician changing a patient's belief in humoral medicine in the course of often infrequent and impersonal treatment sessions is exceedingly low. It is far more productive, in a pragmatical sense, to accept and work within the existing system of humoral beliefs than to simply impose modern medicine upon native concepts and trust that patients will comply to prescribed medical regimens despite contradictions arising between the different forms of medical theory.

To improve the efficiency of patient care under the present conditions of health services in Guatemala and elsewhere in rural Latin America, physicians are urged to continue employing medicines and dietary regimens known to be clinically effective, while at the same time, attempting to construct therapeutic programs sympathetic to, and compatible with, their patients' belief in the humoral doctrine.

For optimal success in achieving this goal, I feel the following conditions must be met: (1) the physician should gain an understanding and appreciation of local ethnomedical theories; (2) the physician should interview the patient concerning his humoral classification of foods, illnesses, and medicines; (3) the physician should then determine if the patient's beliefs undermine the prescribed treatment; and if so, (4) the physician should try to construct a medical regimen which is agreeable to both the physician and the patient.

Finally, it should be noted that many other investigators have demonstrated convincingly that folk theories of health often challenge, and sometimes cancel, the general effectiveness of modern therapeutic programs (Paul 1955). The commitment of Guatemalan peasants to the humoral concept illustrates the usefulness of incorporating the patient's theory into the doctor's practice.

# 55 Modern Medicine and Folk Cognition in Rural India

## Harold A. Gould

One of the early observers of acculturational changes in the medical system of a non-Western culture was Harold Gould whose paper of 20 years ago (Gould 1957) was noteworthy not only for the problem he focused upon but for his keen analysis of the local medical system and its way of coping with disease and

Reprinted with abridgments from Harold A. Gould, 1965, "Modern Medicine and Folk Cognition in Rural India," *Human Organization*, 24:201–208, with permission of the author and the Society for Applied Anthropology.

choosing medical treatment within the traditional or the Western system. Gould briefly summarizes the findings of that paper in the first section of the present selection, then goes on to present a further and fuller analysis as a result of additional fieldwork in the North Indian village of Sherapur. This study is unique for emphasizing the ways in which both illness and choice of treatment modalities are screened through the cognitive perceptual sieve of the local culture and for its emphasis on differences in the perception of illness and treatment not only by culture but within a culture and even among individuals. In other words, the etiology of a disease is influenced not only by the indigenous theory but by who happens to be sick, a point of supreme significance in a society as complex and as rigidly stratified as that of India.

But the paper is also unique in describing in some detail how a partially medically trained field ethnologist, who assumes the role of participant observer on a profound and intimate level, finds himself not only being called upon for medical remedies but, in fact, assuming an active interventionist role in health crises. In so doing, of course, his presence becomes a vital factor in the medical system, at least while he is there, and probably for a time after his departure. Whatever may be the reader's judgment of this active intervention, Gould presents what I consider to be a compelling and insightful analysis of the factors involved in the confrontation of the traditional and modern medical systems and concludes with some suggestions for agents of change in medical and other cultural practices.

In an earlier paper dealing with the impact of technological change on the medical practices of some villagers in North India, I conceptualized a distinction between chronic nonincapacitating dysfunctions and critical incapacitating dysfunctions. By chronic nonincapacitating dysfunctions were meant.

conditions manifesting drawn-out periods of suffering, sometimes cyclical in character, usually not fatal (or fatal by slow degrees), and only partially debilitating (enabling the sufferer to maintain a semblance of his daily routine) (Gould 1956).

Critical incapacitating dysfunctions were marked by

the opposite inventory of symptoms: that is, maladies involving sudden and often violent onset, and rather complete debilitation with reference to some aspects of the individual's routine.

Since scientific medicine had proved popular with the villagers only with respect to the critical incapacitating dysfunctions, I concluded that, a competition between folk and scientific medicine has been occurring in Sherupur [pseudonym for the village studied] through which each has come to serve a distinct class of ailments within a general range of culturally perceived maladies.

The basic insight, then, which led to this way of interpreting the place which scientific medical practices had come to occupy in this peasant community was that victims of illness only turned to doctors of modern medicine when they were desperate and when to their way of thinking the help the doctor could render was demonstrably quicker and/or more effective than indigenous approaches. The other side of this was that for some kinds of illness scientific procedures were either dubiously effective or nonexistent and that in these instances peasants unabashedly used and recognized as superior indigenous, nonscientific therapeutic systems and their underlying conceptualizations. The villagers were, in short, pragmatists who resorted to whatever systems of medicine were available and seemed valuable to them.

## MEDICAL PRACTICES AND COGNITIVE PROCESSES

Intervening years have not altered the conviction that at the level of therapeutic practices this dichotomous characteristic of contemporary medicine in Sherupur is a real and viable feature of its social life, nor that a kind of rustic pragmatism is a root mechanism which facilitates such a dichotomy. However, an opportunity to do three additional years of field work in India between 1959 and 1962, some of which time was spent revisiting Sherupur, has helped make it clear that a number of modifications and refinements in my original contribution are necessary.

Perhaps the main deficiency in my original essay was the failure to recognize the important relationship obtaining between medical practices and cognitive orientation. It was indeed true that the people of Sherupur exercised a rustic pragmatism whereby some diseases were more readily treated by scientific than by folk therapies; however, further field work make it equally clear that the acceptance of modern medical help for critical incapacitating dysfunctions involved no concomitant conversion to scientific thoughtways concerning the causation and etiology of diseases. The germ theory was just as much a mystery in

Sherupur in 1961 as it had been in 1954 or in the centuries prior to the advent of European rule. When I attempted to explain the germ theory to one of Sherupur's more informed citizens in 1961, I realized that the language itself is so undeveloped in this domain of experience that the task was semantically hopeless. In Hindustani, one could only depict germs as tiny insects, an imagery which certainly failed to convey the reality to a listener who knew no English and was unschooled in any science whatsoever.

## THE PERSONAL EQUATION AND THERAPY

Another factor which received inadequate attention in my initial study was the role which the personal relationship plays in the peasant community. To the peasant, trustworthy relationships are personal relationships between individuals who by virtue of caste, kinship, and community ties share common values and are consequently bound together with a system of mutually enforceable obligations. This is one of the great gaps separating modern medical practitioners in India from their potential peasant clienteles. The former are rarely able, because rarely inclined, to establish the kind of rapport that would win acceptance of *themselves* in the villages; yet without this acceptance there is little hope of gaining much acceptance there of what they represent professionally. What Parsons (1952) has called the "functionally specific" relationship, where personal considerations are held in abeyance, remains incomprehensible and, therefore, suspect to a peasant because it is structurally alien to him. Speaking of another North Indian village in this connection, Marriott has said:

The people of Kishan Garhi thus recognize three great social realms—that of kinship and family, which is an area controlled by limitless demands and mutual trust; that of the village and caste, which is an area in part controlled by particular obligations and formal respect; and that of the outside world, of government and market place, which is an area controllable only by money and power—things which the villager scarcely possesses (Marriott 1955).

## DISEASE ETIOLOGIES AND THERAPEUTIC APPROACH

Still another factor that proved to be important was the complexity of disease etiologies. One may

**Table 1**    "Disease Situations" in Relation to Form of Therapy Received by People in Sherupur

| Type of Illness | Independently Chosen | | Personal Tie with Anthropologist | |
|---|---|---|---|---|
| | Indigenous Therapy | Scientific Therapy | Accepts Medicine from Anthropologist | Induced by Anthropologist See Doctor |
| *Chronic Nonincapacitating Dysfunctions* | | | | |
| Chronic Asthma | 1 | — | — | — |
| Mild Fever, Cough, Cold | 8 | — | 8 | — |
| Old Age Aches and Pains | 4 | — | 1 | — |
| "Weakness" (Ambulatory) | 6 | — | — | — |
| Early or Chronic TB | 2 | — | — | — |
| Stomach and Bowel Disorder | 9 | — | 6 | — |
| Sprains, Cuts, Bruises | 3 | — | 2 | — |
| Cutaneous Infections | 6 | — | 3 | — |
| Uterine Discharge | 1 | — | 1 | — |
| Anemia | — | — | 2 | 2 |
| | (40) | (—) | (23) | (2) |
| *Critical Incapacitating Dysfunctions* | | | | |
| Asthmatic Complications | — | 1 | — | — |
| Severe TB | — | 1 | — | — |
| Severe Dysentery | — | — | 2 | 1 |
| Cholera | — | 1 | — | — |
| Smallpox | 6 | — | 1 | — |
| Embedded Testicles | — | 1 | — | — |
| Ulcerous Cutaneous Infections | — | — | 9 | — |
| Severe Sprains, Cuts, Bruises | — | — | 2 | — |
| Severe Foreskin Infection | — | — | 2 | 1 |
| Eye Infections | — | — | 23 | — |
| Multiple Insect Bites | — | — | 1 | — |
| Rheumatic Filaria | — | — | 1 | 1 |
| | (6) | (4) | (41) | (3) |
| Total | 46 | 4 | 64 | 5 |

not simply attach a name to a malady and, on this basis, assign it a single place in a neat classificatory scheme. Illnesses strike people who are different from one another both organically and psychologically; they strike persons who are members of particular sociocultural systems, each with its particular cognitive world. The same disease, scientifically defined, may strike an ultraconservative person who rigidly adheres to indigenous medicine at all costs or a liberal-minded person who as uncritically turns to a modern medical practitioner. It may strike a person with a strong constitution, on the one hand, or a person with a weak one, on the other, with the result that it may constitute a chronic nonincapacitating dysfunction to the one and a critical incapacitating dysfunction to the other. A given illness may fall within the ambit of what is defined in a culture as the realm of divine ordination and may, therefore, be singled out for special supernatural treatment. In short, what a disease *is* will be inevitably conditioned by a very complicated set of factors which must be conceptually disentangled as carefully as possible by the observer.

In order to illustrate these and other points, let us turn now to data obtained during my latest visits to Sherupur. Table 1 ... summarizes some aspects of therapeutic activities in the village which may serve as a point of departure for the discussion to follow.

Experience made it plain this time that only when allowance was made for my presence in Sherupur could a comprehensive inventory of sickness and medical therapy be compiled. The total amount of time I spent in this community of 750 people was approximately ten months spread at intervals over a three year period. During these interludes of residence, I myself entered actively into the cognitive world and the action pattern system of the population through the roles I came to play in the treatment of the sick. The table reveals the consequences of this. Where choices of therapy were made independently, which usually meant when I was absent from the village, the pattern was about the same as was indicated in my earlier article; especially is this the case if we ignore smallpox which, although a critical incapacitating dysfunction, is a special problem, as will be shown later. But where I was a factor in therapeutic-choice-situations, a radical departure from the former pattern occurred.

The primary variable accounting for this difference was, of course, the personal relationship *per se*. The kind of person I was, with the kind of powers and resources at my disposal, became an aspect of the structure of village medicine in Sherupur. Once I had become accepted and trusted in Sherupur, even people suffering from critical incapacitating dysfunctions who sought relief through scientific medical procedures nevertheless preferred to use me as an intermediary between themselves and scientific medicine rather than directly approach its professional practitioners. Part of the reason for this was that I was there in Sherupur whereas doctors were at least a mile-and-a-half distant. But this is only part of the story because, as my reputation spread, people began coming to me from other villages that were sometimes closer to a hospital or clinic than to my residence. It should be noted here that I had received some training as a medic during World War II. This proved useful not only in coping with certain kinds of illness, but also in making me aware of the necessity for never attempting to treat any malady personally which I suspected to be outside my competence. In such instances I would take the sufferer to a doctor or else consult with a doctor on the person's behalf. Throughout my stay in the community I maintained close working relationships with doctors who were personal friends as well as ones who were associated with various state and central government health schemes. In short, I tried to recognize my personal limitations in the field of medicine and to operate strictly within them. This careful delineation of the role I was prepared to play in Sherupur seems to have helped me to quickly gain the villagers' confidence. They knew what to expect from me, what they could *depend* upon in case of trouble.

Certainly one of the most striking facts which emerged from the tabulations is that in one-third of all the recorded instances of chronic nonincapacitating dysfunctions, victims accepted medicines from me, an avowed advocate of scientific therapy. This is the most important manifestation of all of the preference for personal relationships. For it is doubtful whether my scientific medicines helped any of these cases any more than did indigenous remedies, and I believe the villagers were themselves fairly well aware of this. Their main reason for approaching me for such maladies was a mixture of the mystical and the honorific. It was their way of saying that they accepted me as an esteemed member of the community, on a par with other esteemed members of the community, who was expected to give aid and comfort in times of crisis; who was expected to provide reassurance through words and deeds because I possessed certain half-understood powers capable of bringing about good results. As Carstairs (1955) has pointed out, it is important in village medicine that there be someone at hand who vitally matters, who can proclaim that things will have a favorable outcome. That, in Sherupur, persons like this are indeed valued in the areas of sickness is attested not only by the general results in the tables but also by incidents such as the following, which occurred frequently. After a number of people had received help from me, a woman summoned me and requested that I purchase a glass bangle for her infant daughter and place it myself on the child's wrist. She believed this would ward off illness in the future after I had departed from Sherupur. The diffuse powers I represented in this woman's eyes must be made to linger on after my departure.

What was said previously about problems of disease diagnosis also stands out in the tables. One cannot merely determine that a subject suffers from, say, asthma and then inflexibly conclude that, in terms of treatment, it is a case which can be assigned to the category of chronic nonincapacitating dysfunctions. Asthma may be mild or severe, or it may be mild at times and severe at other times in the same individual. It may alternate within very circumscribed limits of severity for years and then change its pattern profoundly, as when a heart complication develops. Just such a case as this in Sherupur was Badari, a member of a cultivator and dairying caste known as Ahir. He had served in World War II as a private soldier and afterwards had returned to the village and resumed farming. He developed an asthmatic condition which he treated with indigenous remedies despite the fact that his condition had been diagnosed by an army doctor. For years he continued this therapeutic pattern until eventually complications from an enlarged heart began to seriously incapacitate him. When this happened, Badari went to a doctor for further diagnosis and treatment. Ultimately he died from the heart condition.

From the standpoint of folk cognitive structure, this Ahir had not suffered from one malady, but two. One was a chronic ailment best handled by folk medicine, the other was a critical ailment best handled by scientific medicine as understood by the peasant. Some rather vague continuity was perceived between the two phases of Badari's illness, to be sure; that is, people said that one thing had more or less led to the other. Essentially, however, it was held that there had been two disease situations, each calling for a therapeutic approach that was valid for its appropriate domain. True, the latter of the two therapies had failed, but this was not seen as being a result of the prior failure of the former.

Looking now at the critical incapacitating dysfunctions, it is clear that the most frequent complaints in this category were eye infections and skin diseases involving painful ulceration or scabbing. One reason why I was so often approached for these disorders is that penicillin eye ointment and both penicillin and sulfa-based skin ointments achieved in most cases truly dramatic results, probably due to the fact that the villagers had acquired no prior tolerances for these drugs. Again, however, this must be seen in conjunction with the personal relationship. For once learning of the power of penicillin and sulfa they could have easily and cheaply purchased these drugs on their own. But it was important that I be the agent of dispensation; my person was somehow intertwined with the medicines. This was not simply because they could obtain free medicines from me either, because some who could pay willingly did so when I asked them to. In other words, my medicines and I had become integral parts of certain disease situations. In this sense, the acceptance of scientific medicines from me, and from doctors too for that matter, resulted in no material changes in basic folk cognitive structure. These experiences were filtered through the screen of this cognitive system and converted into meanings which did no violence to it. One therefore wonders whether it is correct to say that the villagers accepted modern technology or that they converted modern medical technology into folk medicine. One wonders, furthermore, whether more can be expected as long as the peasant social system survives intact to maintain the fabric of folk culture.

## PRIMITIVE MEDICINE IN THE FOLK SETTING

Smallpox illustrates the degree to which still essentially primitive cognitive orientations may remain an integral part of the folk orientation to some diseases. Smallpox is quite obviously a critical incapacitating dysfunction in every sense of the word. It is a great killer that is deeply feared by the peasantry. Yet this illness is deemed an entirely religious matter. It is thought that a goddess named *Bhagoti Mai* (also called *Sitala Mai* and *Sitala Mata*) causes smallpox and that the only way to expunge her influence is by performing religious rituals. If an individual household is struck by the disease, a senior member will place an offering of water contained in a clay cup before a *Nim* tree. One *Nim* tree is enshrined as the abode of *Bhagoti Mai* in Sherupur but a worshipper may not necessarily place his offering before that particular tree. In individual cases, different *Nim* trees are employed which suggests that it is the tree's symbolic importance as a source of curative power (many remedies are prepared from its bark and leaves) that is decisive. If the disease reaches epidemic proportions, however, a Brahman priest is engaged to perform more elaborate rituals at the site of the *Bhagoti Mai* shrine.

It is almost impossible to get peasants to accept vaccination to prevent smallpox or to accept any medicines once they have contracted it. Modern medicines have very little effect, as a matter of fact, once a person contracts smallpox. Consequently the modern medical practitioner is not able to counter the powerful religious aversions to treatment with a powerful cure of his own. This may help to make smallpox one of the last serious diseases to be brought under control by public health programs in India.

## A CASE OF SMALLPOX IN SHERUPUR

A case in which I was deeply involved will illustrate many of the problems connected with smallpox and, at the same time, will afford insight into a number of the other questions that have been raised throughout this discussion, especially pertaining to cognitive orientation and acceptance of change.

During early 1961, the ten-year-old son of a very poor, illiterate low-caste family with whom I had been close friends for many years contracted a bad cough. His parents consulted me and I consulted a doctor in their behalf. It was decided that a course of sulfa drugs and aspirin would adequately deal with the condition. It seemed to be only a bad cold. Shortly after initiating this therapy I left the village for several days. When I returned friends informed me that Balaka Ram (the boy's name) had grown gravely ill in my absence and the parents were extremely worried. The parents, however, had not summoned me upon my return so I rushed at once to their small dwelling at the edge of Sherupur.

When I reached the place, the door was closed and some of the other young children of the household were sitting disconsolately about in the front compound. When I asked where the parents were, the children were evasive. Finally, I learned from them that their mother had shut herself up inside the house with Balaka Ram and had left word for me that my assistance was not required. I knocked on the door, however, and when there was no response I pushed it open and entered. Lying on a stringed cot and covered by a blanket I found Balaka Ram and his mother. It was clear that the child was desperately ill. His fever was very high and he was weak and incoherent. His mother, however, kept insisting that everything was all right and that my help was not needed. This agitated me greatly so I went to search for Balaka Ram's father who, I thought, as head of the household would be more reasonable.

It was only after locating Balaka Ram's father that I learned what the trouble was. They believed he was suffering from smallpox and that all one could do under the circumstances was make the boy abstain from eating and perform religious rites. I insisted that a doctor be summoned at once and Balaka Ram's father finally reluctantly agreed, largely because my status and our friendship made it impossible for him flatly to refuse.

By the time I returned with a doctor, the boy's father had been joined by his wife, his two adult sisters and his aged mother. The mother had been abandoned many years ago by her husband and had been the family's head ever since. She was very strong-willed, energetic, aggressive, and outspoken. In the interim this old matriarch had clearly assumed control of her family and was now leading the group that barred the entry of the doctor and me into the house where Balaka Ram lay. The argument that ensued centered around the issue of whether the doctor should be allowed to intervene in an illness that called for religious measures alone. The women became frenzied and shouted and wailed that to permit injections, or even an examination, would further anger *Bhagoti*

*Mai* and then she would kill Balaka Ram for certain.

After much effort, I convinced the old matriarch and her daughters and daughter-in-law that they could safely permit an examination of Balaka Ram by the doctor provided he promised to administer no medicines of any kind. The doctor made his examination and concluded that this was not a case of smallpox but of pneumonia and bronchitis made worse by the fast which the child had been compelled to endure. But by now the doctor had become extremely truculent over the reception he had received at the hands of people whom he deemed social inferiors and ignorant savages. He had called the grandmother an old hag and had berated the whole family for their blind superstition which prevented them from getting the help required to save this boy's life. After the examination and some further refusal by Balaka Ram's domestic group to accept modern medicine, the doctor departed in anger from Sherupur and vowed to have no further dealings with the case.

Once the doctor had departed, I continued talking to the old woman and the rest of the family. At one point, after Balaka Ram's grandmother repeated her conviction that this was an exclusively supernatural matter, I countered by asking her how she could be so certain that God works only in one narrow way. Here I was quite consciously attempting to awaken in her rustic mind some of the implications of Hindu pantheism. Is it not true, I asked her, that God is to be found in everything and that he acts in many different ways? He lives in the earth, does he not, and in the *Nim* tree, and in animals, and even in the walls of this house. May he not also live in the doctor and work through his medicines? Could she be sure this might not be so, I asked. Would it not be wise to do the religious rites and then also let the doctor and me help through medicines?

To my amazement, the old woman suddenly burst into tears, knelt down and touched my feet and commenced telling me with great emotion that she was just an ignorant old woman who tried to do her best. She thanked me for what I was trying to do and agreed to let the doctor's medicines be tried. Meanwhile the rituals would be performed. I was delighted, of course, because I knew that Balaka Ram did not have smallpox and would undoubtedly recover now. It seemed to me unimportant whether modern medicine or *Bhagoti Mai* got the credit so long as the boy survived.

The doctor refused to return to Sherupur, as he had vowed he would never do, but he was willing to prescribe the appropriate medicines, mainly pentid-sulfa tablets, cough medicine, and proper diet. We decided to attempt no hypodermics because of the religious fears concerning them, for it had to be remembered that Balaka Ram's family still believed him to be suffering from smallpox. In time the boy recovered completely and it was doubtless one of the few times, if not the first time, in the history of Sherupur that anyone had accepted modern medical therapy for what was believed to have been a case of smallpox.

## SOME OBSERVATIONS ON THE SMALLPOX CASE

In this incident, then, many different things stand out. First, the villagers' conceptualization of the causes and cure of smallpox are firmly rooted in the typical primitive cognitive orientation, where, as Simmons (1960) says,

medical beliefs and practices seem to be well integrated with the religion and morality of the group and play a prominent role among the mechanisms of social control.

Others, similarly rooted, include snake bite, evil eye and bewitchment. *Bhagoti Mai* strikes because moral transgression has occurred; religious rites and fasting alone can correct this condition. The rituals performed have been assimilated into the corpus of Hinduism, but the cognitive foundations remain aboriginal—*viz*, disease is intermeshed with the supernatural and with social control. Recall that in the direct encounter between scientific and primitive world views which my intervention in Balaka Ram's case engendered, refusal to accept modern medical aid was based upon the belief that *Bhagoti Mai* would be made angrier and would inflict more severe misfortune on the household. At the same time, this encounter revealed how under ordinary conditions a scrupulous differentiation is made and maintained between the spheres of competence of the various medicines employed in the villages. Violation of these functional boundaries, particularly where the extreme poles of scientific and supernatural world views are brought into direct conflict, can generate severe anxiety and extremely volatile reactions.

Second, the power of the personal relationship has been demonstrated through two of its consequences in this case. On the one hand, its strength was sufficient, where combined with great perseverance and appropriate status, to facilitate partial overriding of the most powerful religious sanctions against the use of scientific medicine. On the other hand, in its absence, the professional relationship exercised by itself proved to be utterly inoperable. The doctor whom I had summoned wished to be accepted on the basis of his professional proclivities alone. In essence, he demanded of these villagers an immediate and uncompromising conversion to the ideologies of modern science and modern social structure with disastrous results for the goals which his professional training had equipped him to achieve. Villagers do not understand or trust the professional relationship because they are not in any meaningful sense members of the culture in which the sanctions and premises underlying such a relationship form integral aspects of the socialization process.

It seems to me that observations of this kind have vast overtones for efforts nowadays being directed at helping and changing the so-called underdeveloped peoples of the world. For one question naturally arises if there is any general validity to what has been said here. How can one design institutions and train personnel able to bring to the peasantry and the aboriginal the innumerable material advantages which flow from modern technology, whose very nature requires the professional type (and here I refer to a whole person and not just a technical skill), in a manner which enables the agents of this new technology to simultaneously establish the deep personal ties with those to be benefitted which they alone trust. At least this is the problem as long as the peasantry persists as a structural phenomenon towards whom the members of the modern world feel they have a mission. At the point where technological change dissolved the peasantry, of course, the problem would no longer have any meaning because then there would be a single world view in which disease and medical therapy enjoyed the same sets of premises among all categories of the population and in which social interaction was keyed to mutually intelligible roles set in compatible social institutions.

A third point is the strength of the pragmatic impulse. The old woman, once her religious resistance had been modified, rather automatically moved to the position that henceforth *both* religious rites *and* scientific medicine would be utilized in dealing with Balaka Ram's illness. There was no notion on her part that one thing must be rejected on behalf of the other. The underlying dictum always seems to be:

Try anything that is available and culturally legitimate.

Fourth, we must reiterate that in folk medicine, just as in scientific medicine, there are always problems about correct diagnosis. The canons employed by peasants for identifying illness are not invariably successful even with respect to purely indigenous maladies. With smallpox, villagers believe that the stool reveals by its texture and color the presence of the disease. In Balaka Ram's case, this was the main symptomatological tenet of his kins' adamant refusal to accept the doctor's conclusion that the child was suffering from pneumonia and not smallpox. Linked with their mistaken interpretation of symptoms was the general mood of the community, however. Smallpox was fairly rife in Sherupur at the time and there was no doubt a consequent tendency to believe that any illness whose symptoms remotely resembled those believed to be associated with smallpox was indeed an instance of *Bhagoti Mai's* wrath. The point is, at any rate, that peasants can be objectively wrong in determinations made about the nature and cause of sickness as defined by their own extranaturalistic and supernaturalistic premises. Partly this is because these premises include no basis for the articulation of critical mechanisms such as ideally, at least, are the essence of the scientific method. But failure of diagnosis also occurs in the domain of folk medicine for a reason that is common to scientific medicine as well, *viz*, the complexity of disease etiologies. Declares Nurge:

Diseases do not exist as categories which can be identified, named and brought for treatment according to the classification ... especially to the layman, symptoms are confusing, are interpreted naively, and are subject to frequent reinterpretation. A particular malaise is not quickly and accurately identified by either a villager or anthropologist (Nurge 1958).

Yet in this very ambiguity inherent in symptomatology may also lie one of the strengths of both folk and primitive medicine. From an objective standpoint, wrong diagnoses are undoubtedly being made constantly in folk and primitive sociocultural settings. Disease classifications ordinarily aid this tendency by their vagueness; they will subsume under the heading of a particular named malady, on the basis of superficially understood symptoms, a multitude of objectively distinct diseases ranging in severity from the easily curable to the incurable. Take the illness called fever (*bookār*) in Sherupur; it can cover everything from a slight case of flu to pneumonia and worse. You take medicines for fever and it can be pointed out that most people recover after taking the appropriate indigenous medicines. Some die of fever, of course, but the number are few compared to those who recover which means to the peasant that in most cases the medicine he employs is efficacious. In other words, indigenous medicines have a wide mark to shoot at which virtually guarantees the appearance of success no matter what their chemical composition. It is well known that the same logic operates in the modern world with respect to the sale of remedies for headaches, colds, neuralgia, etc.

## SOME ACTION IMPLICATIONS

Conclusions that might be useful for public health workers and programs are difficult to draw because so much remains unknown or at most half-understood about primitive and folk world views when they encounter modern technology and the sociocultural systems that accompany it. One thing seems clear, however. Mechanisms like rustic pragmatism are often valuable as pathways for the acceptance of many modern health *practices*, but transformations in *thoughtways* concerning sickness and debilitation should not be expected to accompany such acceptance readily or indeed, in many instances, ever. This, at least, must be regarded as axiomatic as long as technological change and economic development do not proceed far enough to achieve the *structural elimination* of peasantries and primitives.

The reactions to the incursion of scientific health procedures can be remarkable sometimes at both the general and the specific levels. What Simmons (1960) characterizes as "defensive reactions" to modern medical technology are very striking. In essence the more modern medicine becomes entrenched in, say, the domain of critical incapacitating dysfunctions, the more indigenous practitioners stabilize their control over the treatment of chronic nonincapacitating dysfunctions. The latter even adopt the paraphernalia of modern medicine in order to intensify their psychological impact on their patients. There is one in Sherupur who administers many of his indigenous compounds with a hypodermic syringe and his business has boomed since he began doing this. In Simmons' words:

> The explicit delimitation of the domain of popular medicine by the people is in part a defensive reaction to their acculturation experience. The illnesses placed in the domain and defined as inaccessible to the ministrations of modern medicine represent precisely those popular medical beliefs that have been ignored or attacked most consistently by the representatives of modern medicine with whom the people have come in contact, beliefs which the former in no case have taken seriously.

The routinized impersonality so intrinsically a component of the professional role probably intensifies this defensive reaction. For it stems as much from fear and misunderstanding of the *persons* who possess professional medical skills as from the content of these skills. Often I found peasants wanting very much to receive modern medical treatment but avoiding doing so because it necessitated their attending an outpatient clinic or being admitted to a hospital. It is hard to describe the aversion the peasants feel to the institutional structures in which modern medicine is presented to them and into which they are compelled to enter if they are to be treated. For them the *social experience* is the crucial variable, the very aspect which from the standpoint of the ideology of modern social interaction is not supposed to be allowed to stand in the way of maintaining good health. But the peasant sees hospitals and clinics as places where he will be compelled to wait endless hours in congested anterooms, castigated and mocked by officious attendants, and finally examined and treated by a doctor who will show no personal interest in him whatsoever. This is the main reason why people in Sherupur preferred to get medicines from me and to be seen by doctors whom I personally brought into the village for the purpose, for here medicine was being integrated into patterns of social interaction which they understood and which did not drain from them every ounce of their self-respect as the price for being benefited by what the modern world has to offer....

Rapid modernization of non-modern thought-ways respecting sickness and its treatment is going to require, it seems to me, a series of gradual culture changes that cut both ways. That is, changes must be made in the professional role which reflect awareness of the nature of primitive and peasant cognitive and social structure. Without them efforts to achieve any fundamental shifts by peasants and primitives toward values that the

modern world cherishes appear doomed. The challenge is to find ways of creating an institutionalized approach to public health in the underdeveloped societies which incorporates *into a single role* the technical qualifications conferred by professional training and the interpersonal skills needed for dealing with primitives and peasants in their own institutional terms which successful anthropological training confers.

# 56 The Barefoot Doctors of China: Healers for All Seasons

*Peter Kong-ming New and Mary Louie New*

In the preceding papers on the adaptation and nonadaptation of healers' roles in the face of culture change and acculturation, none of the ethnographic studies cited was based upon the unique case of contemporary China under Communist hegemony. China's case is in a class completely by itself for a number of reasons, among which we may list the following: It has the largest population of any country in the world, well over 800 million persons, representing one fourth of the entire human race. It has the oldest civilization in the world. It is the largest Communist-ruled country in the world. The measures taken by its government since 1949 are unparalleled in any country, Communist, capitalist, or the various mixed economies of the Third World. Peter and Mary New are among the few social scientists from the United States to visit the People's Republic of China as part of a group of American academics of Chinese descent who were invited by the Chinese government to observe aspects of the Chinese health delivery systems. The group's attention centered upon the "barefoot doctors," and this report, one of many, has been especially rewritten for this volume by the authors. While in China, the group made a film about the barefoot doctors (available through Diane Li, Department of Communications, Stanford University).

Clearly, the barefoot doctor's role may be classified under the rubric of "emergent" healing roles as outlined in my paper on role adaptation of healers under acculturation. But, as the News' paper makes obvious, this role is quite unlike that of any healing role noted in my study. China's situation is the most

Adapted, rewritten, and abridged by the authors especially for this book from Peter Kong-ming New and Mary Louie New, 1975, "The Links Between Health and the Political Structure in New China," *Human Organization, 34*:237–251, with permission of the authors and the Society for Applied Anthropology.

revolutionary in its startling innovations; yet, just as startling are its deliberate policies of preserving much of the traditional culture, encouraging traditional ways (though in the context of the new cooperative Communist society rather than the old, family-centered society), and, at the same time, introducing many elements of Western science and technology, including medicine. What will emerge—is emerging—is an unprecedented blend of the old and new, unlike anything that has been experienced previously anywhere.

The News not only inform us about this exciting new healing role but place it in economic, political, and historical perspective, and then demonstrate that though it may be ingeniously invented to cope effectively with the problems of health care in the People's Republic of China, the barefoot doctor concept cannot be torn from its political-economic-historic context and transported to other quite different societies and cultures—at least, not without concomitant revolutionary structural changes in the society.

## INTRODUCTION

Since the establishment of the People's Republic in 1949, China has undergone some dramatic changes, not the least of which is in the area of health delivery and health care. Earlier visitors to China (Fox 1957) were somewhat skeptical that the changes would represent any significant progress in health care. Since 1972, more health professionals have visited and reported on the recent advances in health delivery systems (see, in particular, Dimond 1971a, 1971b; Sidel and Sidel 1973; Horn 1972a, 1972b). In these and other reports, physicians and public health workers are most impressed with various technical medical advances, such as the use of acupuncture as analgesia, limb reimplantations, treatment of burns, and the like, and with the use of paramedical workers in large numbers in preventive and primary health care (Quinn 1973; Wegman, Lin, and Purcell 1973; Geiger 1972, 1973; Pickowicz 1973; Levin 1973). For the most part, they have described the specific training and skills that are required to carry out these tasks; in some instances, they have discussed their applicability in Western societies (Gringras and Geekie 1973; McGill Medical Journal 1973), with suggestions that Western cultures such as ours may well adopt the use of barefoot doctors in large numbers as well (Sidel and Sidel 1973: 203–207).

In the United States, we are particularly prone to try various measures in health care because we are basically in a quandary as to what is best. Just within the past decade we have tried to settle on some feasible methods, such as neighborhood health centers, health maintenance organizations, regional medical programs, professional services review organizations, training of physicians' associates, nurse-practitioners, and now national health insurance schemes. Thus, it is not surprising to find that many are attracted to the potentials of transporting the barefoot doctors concept across the Pacific and instituting this program in the United States.

What we fail to recognize is that the introduction of barefoot doctors in China cannot be seen in isolation from the historical and current social contexts. The current successes of the barefoot doctors, within the prevailing conditions of the political and health systems, can also be contrasted with other Third World countries, such as Cuba (Danielson 1973, 1975a, 1975b; Navarro 1972; Stein and Susser 1972), Kenya (Thomas 1971, 1975) Ghana (Stromberg 1975), Nigeria (Onoge 1975), and Tanzania (Gussow and Gussow 1975; Tschannerl 1975; Raikes 1975). Historically, these Third World countries, including China (Crozier 1968), relied heavily on health care systems "imported" from other countries. In some instances, these systems were imposed on the countries by the colonial powers which were administering the countries. When the countries became independent, it took a longer period for them to rid themselves of any colonial vestiges that still prevailed in the area of health care. For instance, in some of the African nations such as Kenya, Nigeria, and Ghana, the former colonial models continue to dominate health care delivery. However, all of these countries are well aware that new ways must be found to introduce health care which is consonant with the existing realities of the country (Ingman and Thomas 1975; Van Etten 1972; Nyerere 1969). Of all these countries, China and Cuba (Morgan 1974) made conscious efforts radically to alter the health structure by infusing political ideologies into health care.

For centuries, China has had a long tradition of healers who used indigenous methods to cure various ailments. Because accessibility to Western medicines and treatment was only available to a relatively few, traditional healers continued to flourish even into the 1930s and 1940s (Crozier 1968). In the 1930s, there was a vigorous attempt on the part of the Western trained physicians to declare the practices of traditional healers illegal. The success of the Government of the People's Republic in introducing nearly 1 million barefoot doctors obviously raises the question of how China was able to eliminate, within one generation, various forms of traditional healers and yet not create insurmountable conflicts between these healers and the barefoot doctors of the current generation.

At present, data are not yet available to answer this question fully. There can be only some speculations based on our recent visit to the People's Republic. In the final part of this paper, we attempt to speculate on this in light of Landy's (1974) discussion of role adaptation as it applies to healers and barefoot doctors. It could be said that the barefoot doctor represents one form of role adaptation whereby he becomes the "healer for all seasons."

It is also our contention that only by examining the barefoot doctor movement in its historical, social, and comparative aspects can we gain a better insight into its appropriateness for our Western culture. The conclusion that we reach is that in the United States, the Chinese concept of barefoot doctors could not survive. At the same time, this examination can help us appreciate the broader qualities of a way of life that we may choose to strive toward if we are to achieve any gains in the quality of health care in the near future.

## BAREFOOT DOCTORS (BMD)

Various estimates place the number of barefoot doctors at 1 million or higher. When Chairman Mao's directive of June 26, 1965, was issued, to the effect that health care should be provided in rural areas, BMD's already existed in different parts of China. Norman Bethune, a Canadian physician, who served with the Eighth Route Army of the People's Liberation Army (PLA), is credited with training these medical assistants in the 1930s (Sidel 1972). The PLA also helped train some of the first groups in later years. With the 1965 directive, the training of BMDs was hastened, with the goal of having one barefoot doctor per thousand population, throughout China. In general, barefoot doctors were residents in their respective communes or urban neighborhood areas prior to their training. Some of these barefoot doctors may have already learned some skills, such as acupuncture or the use of herbal medicines, when they were traditional healers. Subsequent to their training, they were usually assigned back to their home communities. At present, the distribution of the barefoot doctors in the six communes visited varied

from 1.3 to 3.5 per thousand population (New and New 1975a : 106–107).

The singular striking fact in the education of the BMDs is that their prior schooling and their training may vary from three months to two years. Unlike paramedicals in the United States, especially physician's assistants or nurse-practitioners (see Godkins, Stanhope, and Lynn 1974), once BMDs are trained, they return to their local communities. Thus, there is a great deal of attention paid to local conditions and the intensity of training depends on local capabilities. Further, the range of functions of the BMDs varies according to local needs.

For example, in urban areas such as Peking, with abundant hospitals and schools as well as fully trained physicians, a BMD may have minimum formal training (two or three months' duration) and be closely supervised. In the Hsi-ch'ang-an Street Neighborhood, Peking, we met an older woman BMD who was barely literate. She carried out first-aid type duties with neighborhood children and also handed a certain amount of herbal drugs to patients. At the same time, a physician from Peking Hospital No. 2 was present during part of the day to supervise her activities. When we spoke to the physician and the BMD, the former mentioned that the BMD was encouraged to begin doing some independent diagnosis of patients who were subsequently checked by the physician. In addition, the BMD went to a nearby hospital one afternoon a week to receive additional training.

At the other end of the spectrum, we met BMDs who had two years of training, performed vasectomies and minor surgery (one BMD even brought along his patient whose neck tumor was removed by him). These BMDs would return to school for 30-day periods during the year for further training and specialization in obstetrics, internal medicine, and pediatrics. In every sense of the word, the BMDs are primary physicians who care for the patients in their regions.

Thus, it is not quite accurate to equate BMDs with paramedicals, as their range of duties and length of training vary. There is an increasing attempt to standardize the knowledge required. However, even here, attention is paid to local conditions. There are at least two regional editions of the *Instructional Manual for Barefoot Doctors* with instructions on diagnosis and treatment of common ailments, and the use of herbs and acupuncture (see Pickowicz 1973, for topics covered by manuals).

What this brief description of the training and duties of BMDs illustrates is the importance of supporting links of changes that have occurred in the rest of the country which encourage its development. We now examine other concurrent changes that have gone on in other areas: education, the integration of Chinese and Western medicine, cooperative health plans, family planning, and the organization of urban areas and communes.

## EDUCATION

After receiving his training, the BMD works in his community, whether this be a commune, a factory, or a neighborhood health clinic and sometimes even in a hospital during the rest of the year. However, during this time, he (or she) is expected to work part of the time as a farmer or a factory worker. At regular intervals, he returns to a hospital or a medical school to receive further training. While working as a BMD, if he is unsure about certain procedures, he may receive immediate training from a physician to whom he has referred his patient (for details, see Wang 1974).

The philosophy of integrating theory and practice pervades all areas of higher education. The goals of education received a thorough review during the Cultural Revolution (1965–1968) when schools, among other endeavors, were closed. Long periods of schooling, away from the people, is no longer acceptable (details in New and New 1975b).

Concurrent with the changes at the college and medical school level, which is also three years (Dimond 1971b), there are now five years of primary school and two years of middle school (all schooling is on an eleven-month basis) for all children. In a few cities, some primary schools have six grades and there are some high schools with two more years added. In one medical school, the chairman of the Party Committee mentioned that he believed that medical training needs to be lengthened a bit because there is too much material to be covered. What this swing back to the old system portends is difficult for us to discover. Nevertheless, there is a constant search by various people to reach some kind of balance between adequate training and yet not delay the process of serving the people.

The process of recruitment for individuals to attain higher education has also been changed. Although the exact process of gaining admission is unclear, it seems that criteria for admissions are based on the following: the individual should be in his or her twenties, single, in good health, have completed at least middle school education, and possess an acceptable ideological background. For persons who wish to become BMDs, it is not entirely necessary that they have middle school education; however, with compulsory education, the current young people undoubtedly will have minimal educational requirements. A particular unit of organization will nominate these individuals to receive further training in universities or hospitals. The universities, in turn, usually accept the nominees, based on these criteria.

Once the people in these units have made a collective decision as to who should go, then at the college level, there is the constant emphasis of "helping each other." If the barefoot doctor trainee or the medical student is not doing well, it is up to everyone to help that person to get through—a collective responsibility is assumed by students and instructors alike—so that the people "out there" could be served and not be forgotten. Hence, the practical must never be slighted.

## INTEGRATION OF CHINESE AND WESTERN MEDICINE

As far as medical training and practice is concerned, barefoot doctors and other health personnel learn both Chinese and Western medicines. Crozier (1968) has pointed out that because of the antagonistic views that Western-trained physicians and politicians had toward traditional Chinese medicine in the late nineteenth and early twentieth century, Chinese medicine had been on the wane. After the liberation, Chairman Mao urged health practitioners to pay more attention to Chinese medicine, through a combination of ideological push to respect the legacy of Chinese medicine and scientific scrutiny of the worth of these medicines. At the same time, this was also practical; herbal medicines are cheap to produce and, in line with the "self-sufficiency" ideology, herbs can be grown locally for use by practitioners. From 1954, medical schools began to teach both Chinese and Western medicine, but this went into a decline. It was not until the Cultural Revolution, especially with the June 26, 1965, directive, that Chinese medicine regained its importance in all spheres of health care: in the medical curriculum, in hospitals, in clinics, and certainly in the medicine bags of BMDs.

Pickowicz (1973) mentioned that 131 pages of the 591-page *Instructional Manual for the Barefoot Doctors* are devoted to common Chinese herbal medicine and another 30 pages describe methods of new acupuncture. In most BMD clinics, herbal medicines are very much in evidence in medicine chests or in large wicker baskets, along with Western medicines. Hospitals and clinics in communes and cities also dispense herbal medicines along with Western medicines.

With the integration of Chinese and Western medicines, there is now also a de-emphasis of licensing of practitioners: (1) the Government believes that licensing encourages the maintenance of a corps of elites; (2) it also restricts the mobility of health practitioners into other types of work. Thus, at the Liaoning School of Chinese Medicine, for instance, nearly half of the current medical students were BMDs.

## COOPERATIVE HEALTH PLANS

As we had indicated earlier, BMDs are usually recruited from among the ranks of peasants in communes. Once they are trained, they return to their communes to work. Ideally, one third of their time is spent in agricultural labor, one third is spent in various health clinics placed throughout the commune, and the remaining third of their time is spent in field and home visits. Communes pay for their services through funds that they collect from their residents. We should mention that physicians and nurses on the communes are paid by the Central Government. Since 1962, various communes began to implement cooperative health plans.

Each commune determines the sums that it should collect from its residents, varying from U.S. 60 cents to 75 cents per person. Communes contribute an equal amount (for details, see New and New 1975a:108).

The manner in which health insurance is implemented seems to best illustrate local autonomy. The amount that each individual pays into the local health insurance varies according to the fiscal solvency of that commune. For instance, in the Evergreen Commune, when the cooperative health plan was drawn up, prior to 1972, it was estimated that the amount would be 3.00 *yuan* per person (U.S. $1 = 2 *yuan* in 1973), with half the amount paid by the brigade. However, after a year's experience, that commune found that too much money was being collected. Thus, for the

following year, the amount was reduced to 2.50 *yuan* per person. In addition, most health clinics collect a nominal registration fee of 10 *fen* (five cents) for each patient.

Not all communes have cooperative health plans. Since 1969, when the cooperative health plan campaign started in Liaoning Province with 34 million prople, 95 percent of the 16,000 brigades in 1,330 communes have adopted the plan. Sixty percent of these brigades have well-equipped clinics. The remaining brigades which do not have the health plans may be either too poor or they are fairly well off so that members can afford to pay for their own health needs.

## FAMILY PLANNING

At the national policy level of family planning, a number of excellent papers have appeared in recent years so that we will not attempt to summarize the position of the Government (see for example, Chen 1973a; Aird 1973; Orleans 1973). At the local level, BMDs play a significant role in persuading residents to practice family planning (Chen 1973b; Wang 1974).

Party Committee members mentioned that prior to marriage, no contraceptive information is supplied to single persons. In fact, as many young people have told us, there is very little premarital sex practiced—the drop in venereal disease (Horn 1972a, 1972b) is one direct evidence of this. Ideally, the age of marriage is around 27 for men and 24 for women. At the time of marriage, the couple is asked to fill out a family planning form, stating the desired number of children (see New and New 1975b). BMDs would personally deliver contraceptive pills to married women. Clinical tests are now being carried out on once-a-month injections and pills (Faundes and Lukkainen 1972). BMDs are trained to insert intrauterine devices and perform vasectomies and records are also kept locally on this information. From the various communes and urban areas visited, we note the crude birth rates are dropping, varying from 5.28–24.0 per thousand.

The attempt to lower the birth rate is not achieved solely through the raising of age at the time of marriage. A steady stream of slogans is directed toward the residents: girls are just as valued as boys; now, because of the declining infant mortality, both girls and boys are as likely to survive. In addition, when women marry, they keep their family names and their children may adopt the father's or mother's name as surname, or even choose another surname for themselves.

## ADMINISTRATIVE ORGANIZATION OF COMMUNES AND URBAN AREAS

Although most of the barefoot doctors work on communes, they are also present in factories, where they are known as "worker-doctors" and in urban neighborhood areas, where they are known as "red guard doctors" (for more details, see Wang 1974). The BMDs work within the urban municipalities (which are further subdivided into districts, streets, and neighborhood areas) or in rural areas (further subdivided into prefectures, counties, communes, brigades, and work teams). Each of these subdivisions may carry out certain autonomous decisions regarding health care (see, Towers 1973:125–126, 1974).

In this type of tightly organized society, decisions can go on at both levels on a number of issues, some at the Central Government level and some at the local level. China has adopted the ideology of "participatory democracy by centralism." As far as we could tell, key issues are directed from above. Thus, the June 26, 1965, directive, that there shall be health care in all rural areas, was decided at the Central Government level, but how this decision is to be implemented is pretty much left to the people in the communes. Depending on the local capabilities, they have to figure out how many residents should be trained as BMDs, how long this training might take, how the BMDs are to be deployed, the number of health clinics that should be established in the communes, the size of the hospital that might be built, how medical expenses are to be met, and a host of other relevant questions.

As far as barefoot doctors are concerned, their work is always linked to the larger health networks available to them. When asked whether they can seek the help of others if they need help from more competent sources, BMDs from a number of different communes have mentioned that there are others who help in different ways. A typical incident was mentioned by one BMD:

One day, one of my patients was quite sick and I gave her some pills, but I didn't know whether they were the right pills or whether I had diagnosed the case properly. So, I was quite worried that I might have given her too much medication. I took her to a medical center nearby and asked the physician whether I had done the right thing. The physician asked me to stay overnight at the hospital and study the case together. He checked her over and taught me some procedures and we watched her progress. The physician assured me that I had done the right thing and the following day I returned to the commune much relieved.

Physicians seem quite willing to help the BMDs over such hurdles and spend time with them when necessary. Undoubtedly, the spirit of "helping each other" is fostered by the fact that as medical students, they have to spend a certain length of their training (usually the last six months) on communes so that they could better understand the needs of the people. Instructors in medical schools and students go out to communes in mobile teams to treat residents and to give further training to BMDs and other health workers—teams are out one month of the year. At times, they work in factories or on communes as workers just so that they do not lose sight of the needs of the people.

As a specific illustration of the health linkages, the August 1 Commune in Shen Yang has a total of 26 barefoot doctors, assigned to each of the 15 brigades (some are even on production teams, of which there are 73). At the commune level, there is a small 30-bed hospital with 38 health personnel working there, including 12 physicians (3–5 of whom have university training, as opposed to the others who had middle school education and then became physicians), 10 nurses, four BMDs, and 12 technical staff. At the city level, the commune health personnel have the backup of larger hospitals, such as one of the hospitals affiliated with Liaoning School of Chinese Medicine—there is another medical school in Shen Yang which teaches mainly Western medicine, as well as a School of Public Health which specializes in two-year training courses for BMDs. The Liaoning School of Chinese Medicine has a 400-bed hospital and over 1,500 staff personnel, many of whom are with the medical school.

The August 1 Commune started with six BMDs in 1965 with two more added in 1970, another five added in 1971, and 12 more in 1972–1973. There are now eight women and 18 men undertaking basic health care for nearly 21,000 commune residents. They are part of the 38,000 BMDs in Liaoning Province which has 34 million people, who work in 1330 communes and other urban locations, backed by 6,100 Chinese medicine physicians, 15,000 university graduated physicians, 14,000 physicians with less than university training, and 26,000 nurses. Their patients who need acute care can enter hospitals with a total of 94,000 beds (as compared with 8,900 beds before 1949).

In the context of the entire commune and the administrative structure of the country, one can begin to appreciate the strength behind the BMD movement. The innovation of the single BMD instance is woven among other concurrent changes in the entire society. Lu (1973) has made this perceptive comment:

In order to understand the self-conception and behavior of the people in the present Chinese society..., it is necessary to know how the Chinese perceive their success or failure fulfilling the social expectations in the performance of their *new* social roles.... The transformation of the individual, the cultivation of a "new person"...is one of the objectives of the Cultural Revolution in China. It is recognized that the development of a new "self" among the individuals is indispensable to the building of a new society and at the same time the building of a new society is a precondition for the development of a new "self."

## DISCUSSION

In Landy's (1974) discussion of the role adaptation of traditional curers under the impact of Western medicine, he posits that "the curer's status does become attenuated...when the expectations of his community are such that the technology, if not the values, of scientific medicine is perceived by them as so clearly superior that they distinctly prefer it to their own..." (Landy 1974:119). In China, if anything, the curer's status, we suggest, may have been shifted from an ill-defined (or purposely hazy) role to one which has high saliency. To a superficial observer (and we quickly admit to being such), the Government may seem to have eliminated, in one stroke, all the traditional healers. In fact, we speculate, this has not been the case. The traditional curers may have been drawn within the orbit of "scientific medicine," which the Government defines as partly traditional and partly Western medicine. Thus, to remain as a curer, the Government has assigned him a role within the health scheme only if he undergoes more health training as well as ideological realignment. At the same time, the Government literally "swamps" the populace with BMDs who are also trained in both Chinese and Western medicines, as are the new physicians. Thus, by fiat, it is possible that the Government prevented any potential role strains and role conflicts, although we did allude to some in the early 1950s and 1960s when Western-trained physicians were not entirely pleased with

the prospect that BMDs were going to be trained in such large numbers. At the same time, through the deliberate policy of "leveling" the Chinese physician (Record 1974) the Government is sending large numbers of BMDs into medical schools so that upward mobility is assured for many. Conflicts arise, we hypothesize, if curers perceive that they are operating in a sphere where they are not recognized, where they have no opportunity to move into an integrated health approach (see, Lee 1975:57–58), and where they are blocked from learning the "other" approach should they desire.

In China the formulation of health care policy by the Central Government seems to permit a large degree of flexibility and autonomy of implementation according to conditions in local communities. We ourselves do not have any information as to whether this is indeed the case with the traditional curers and much more data must be collected. In the few weeks we were in China, we could not be sure whether we saw the idealized forms of delivery of health care or whether in reality what we have described or surmised actually works. (For the analogue of our experience, in politics, see Whyte 1974.) Further, it is difficult to know *how* different aspects function. The problem of obtaining research data of the types that we in the Western world are accustomed to has been brought up by innumerable groups that have visited China (see, for instance, Kessen 1974; Orleans 1974; Li 1974; Cheatham et al. 1973).

There are undoubtedly shortcomings in relying so heavily on barefoot doctors to carry out primary health care. Based on Western standards, one can raise any number of questions as to whether they are properly trained, know their limitations, and other related questions (Hsu 1974). These are problems of which even the Chinese are well aware. However, we do need to bear in mind the type of health system which China had prior to 1949: a lack of health personnel and facilities, a lack of coordination, and a generally benign neglect of a large proportion of Chinese who were in rural areas. If one were to compare China with other Third World countries, many problems were similar. Rationally, the Chinese Government since 1949 may not have consciously decided to change the entire political and health structure just so that barefoot doctors could be introduced as a viable entity. Indeed, pieces and parts of health activities were introduced at various time periods, such as the times when family planning would be pushed (Aird 1973; Orleans 1973; Chen 1973a) or patriotic health campaigns would be emphasized. Whether by design or not, we feel that the Cultural Revolution of 1965–1968 became the single most important impetus to change a vast number of policies in all areas. In terms of change, the "litany" from various workers usually began with, "Before the Revolution (1949)..." or "Before the Cultural Revolution (1968)...," certain old ways gave away to new ways of doing things. Given certain total political structural changes, our view is that the concept of barefoot doctors was able to be nurtured to its fullest capabilities.

To the casual observer, the notion of instituting barefoot doctors in the United States seems beguiling. We are now attempting to solve our health delivery problems by training all sorts of paramedical personnel such as physician's assistants or nurse-practitioners who could relieve physicians in various parts of the rural areas, so why should we not flood the countryside with BMDs as well? What we attempt to show in this paper is that the training, per se, of BMDs may not be difficult to achieve. However, the implementation of such a large number of BMDs must be accompanied by societal structural changes as well. Thomas (1974 and 1975), for instance, has shown that in Kenya, a large number of medical assistants are also at work. However, the colonial antecedents of Kenya remain as an obstacle to the effective use of its medical assistants.

We believe that one of the keys to the success of BMDs in China lies not in the area of technical and operational innovations but in the way that China manages the delicate balance of mass participation and central directives by having their citizens accept the ideological position of the Government (see, Record 1974). Even though on many issues, the desired decision is made fairly clear by the Central Government, citizens still have an opportunity to discuss the merits (or demerits) of the position and see how these decisions can be implemented, given the local resources or predilections. Numerous citizens whom we encountered seem to be genuine in their feeling that they have a stake in the progress of the country and they have certainly internalized the ideology of "serve the people" to the exclusion of any personal gains.

In the United States, citizen participation is meeting a great deal of resistance, partly because of the dominant elite structure (New, Hessler, and Cater 1973). In various sectors of health care, elitism is not giving away to mass participation. The result is that clashes occur frequently, and no one party wants to be accountable for the faults that arise within the system. In China, most citizens feel that they are sharing in some major and minor decisions. By deliberating in the actions they take, we believe that they are also arriving at some form of collective accountability. The "blame," for instance, of not achieving the desired lower birth rate, is not directed to some other party but rather to themselves. As the chairman of the Party Committee in the Man Fan Commune mentioned to us, "We must do better." The end result of "doing better" is quite evident for those who have seen the progress of China's health care.

A second lesson that we have learned is that health conduct cannot be isolated from political factors. Although the interrelationship of various sectors of society is hardly novel, somehow when we discuss health matters, we almost take it for granted that health care is a neutral entity and can be transported from one society to another. The ideology and the supporting political structures of China could hardly be transposed. If we were to adopt BMDs among the health personnel, we would have to radically alter the prevailing ideologies that maintain our professional dominance (see Ronaghy and Solter 1974).

What is so intriguing about barefoot doctors is that as we describe their activities in health, we are also looking inward to reflect on the strengths and weaknesses of our health system and of the larger political structure that maintains this system. As Chin (1973:113) has stated:

In China health behavior is more accurately described as health conduct. The older connotation... of "conduct," meaning moral behavior, is appropriate here because health acts are "political." For China and the "New Man" no act is devoid of political factors, which define the purposes and direction of the society. Thus health conduct is moral conduct laced together by the cognition, ideologies, actions, and spirit of the socialist state and of the socialist citizen.

# 57 Pluralism and Integration in the Indian and Chinese Medical Systems

## Charles M. Leslie

The final paper in this section by Charles Leslie is a comparison of the medical systems of modern India and China from the point of view of the integration of indigenous and Western elements in these systems. However, this essay moves beyond the levels of analysis of the preceding papers in that it places these two countries of Asia—the most populous in the world, containing nearly half of the world's people between them—in perspective not only in terms of their history and present societies but of their place in the world social order. The paper deals mainly with India, the country with which Leslie is most familiar on the basis of several years of ethnographic research there, but the comparisons with China are apt and timely. This paper adds to our knowledge of innovation and conservatism in the medical systems of India as shown in the preceding study by Gould, and of China in the preceding study by the News.

Leslie takes off from the fundamental distinction made in the concepts of society and culture in anthropology to apply them to a consideration of comparative medical systems. Thus, we can view a medical system as a cultural system (concepts, theories, normative practices, consensual modes of perception) and a social system (organization of roles and role relationships in institutional structures). Although both of these systems are subsumed in the earlier definitions of medical system and medicine that I offered in the introductory statement to Section IV of this volume, Leslie's statement represents an important conceptual advance and aids in sharper theoretical analysis of medical systems.

Another important conceptual advance herein is the notion that the medical systems of complex societies are at least as complex as the social systems and cultures of which they are a part. Therefore, applying this thinking to our own society, our medical system can be seen as consisting of a great deal more than the organization of scientific medical institutions. It also consists of, and is in competition with, many other traditional types of healers and healing as well as

Adapted, abridged, and rewritten by the author especially for this book from Charles M. Leslie, 1976, "Pluralism and Integration in the Indian and Chinese Medical Systems," Chap. 24 in *Medicine in Chinese Cultures*, ed. by E. Russell Alexander, Arthur M. Kleinman, and Peter Kunstadter, Washington, D.C.: The John E. Fogarty International Center, National Institutes of Health, with permission of the author and The John E. Fogarty International Center, National Institutes of Health.

modern nonmedical (as defined in the United States) healers (clinical psychologists, Christian Scientists). Similarly the medical systems of India and China reflect in large part their pluralistic social systems and cultures. In both cases, though perhaps more forcefully in the People's Republic of China, we find traditional healing and healers being encouraged, legitimated, and integrated into the total medical system, and in both cases against the initial (and probably lingering) resistance of physicians and institutions trained in Western or Western-oriented medicine. The statistics of numbers of native healers in India, as those of China supplied in the preceding article by the News, strongly reinforce the arguments of both Leslie and the News. Thus, unlike our Western medical systems, in Asia (countries other than India and China are also included in Leslie's argument) "professionalized indigenous medicine is not in practice isolated from cosmopolitan medicine," as Leslie suggests. Both the Indian and Chinese systems are not free of conflict between the modern and traditional elements, though in the latter case the conflict may be more submerged through the various forms of direct and indirect official persuasion and coercion. Leslie's essay, with its far-ranging but conceptually innovative perspective, seems a fitting note on which to complete this section and conclude the book.

The demand of laymen in Western countries for acupuncture and other Chinese medical treatments, and the desire of physicians to learn about them, have been stimulated by descriptions of traditional medicine in the People's Republic of China. I am skeptical about this Western enthusiasm for Chinese medicine. The economic and cultural reasons for the use of indigenous medicine in China should be distinguished from its potential contribution to medical science. Only fringe practitioners in Western countries hope to use the theories of the Five Elements, of *yin* and *yang*, or the meridians. These theories belong in the domain of historians and cultural anthropologists. From this perspective, research in China would provide valuable data to compare to the persistence of both humoral and magical theories of disease in Chinese communities elsewhere (Caudill 1975; Otsuka 1975; Topley 1970, 1975; Unschuld 1973, 1975). Although useful medications have been derived from the traditional Asian pharmacopoeias, few new discoveries are likely to come from this direction. Dr. Francisco Guerra writes:

The value of the native systems of medicine lies in the cultural elements . . . a great mass population is tied down to the use of native pharmacopoeias chiefly for economic reasons, because native pharmacopoeias are cheaper than the products of the West (Guerra 1969:252).

The sociology of Chinese medicine has greater potential value for the rest of the world than Chinese medical theories, acupuncture, or herbals. And this is particularly true because China has provided a new model for the modernization of medical systems. Two main features of the model are the large-scale use of practitioners with little formal training, and the legitimization of indigenous traditions which, from a scientific perspective, were thought to be obsolete by giving them a major role in state-sanctioned medical bureaucracies. The model is most relevant, therefore, to societies with more limited resources than those of industrialized countries, and with dual systems of indigenous and cosmopolitan medicine. The countries of South Asia meet these criteria, and planners in these countries will surely compare their medical systems to the Chinese model. The task of this paper is to describe a conceptual approach for making such comparisons, and to present relevant data from India.

The common Western image of contemporary Asian medical systems pictures a small number of institutions for "Western medicine" as an alien enclave in an amorphous structure of indigenous folk curers whose practice is limited to traditional medications and shamanistic rites. Against this background the image of an extensive, bureaucratically rationalized system that integrates indigenous and cosmopolitan medicine in China is enormously appealing. Both images should be treated as models rather than as descriptions of actual systems. It would be naïve to assume that either model corresponds to social reality. The first model is based upon limited observation, and the second is an ideal of Chinese health planners. We lack systematic research on the social organization and health cultures of laymen and specialists in the People's Republic, but in Taiwan, Hong Kong, Malaya, Thailand, and Burma the variety of practitioners and the diverse forms of therapy available to laymen in those societies indicates that a similar variety probably exists in China. To discuss this fact we use concepts that contrast sacred to secular medicine, Chinese to Western medicine, scientific to folk medicine, and the institutionalized medicine of specialists to the diffuse medicine of popular culture. These concepts divide phenomena in different ways but they all predicate the pluralistic character of these medical systems. For comparative purposes we must clarify different approaches to medical pluralism, and define the process that shapes its character in modern times.

The distinction that social scientists make between culture and society is useful for the comparative study of medical systems. As a cultural system medicine is an organization of concepts, theories, and normative practices. It is a way of perceiving and thinking about health and illness coded in the traditions of a society. As a social system medicine is a set of occupational roles, role relationships, and institutional structures. It is part of the division of labor, more or less differentiated from other activities. From this perspective a medical system is a system of specialist roles. Laymen use the system but are outside it, and the primary desiderata for learning how a medical system works is to learn what access laymen have to it. In New York city, for example, Puerto Rican laborers, Chinese shopkeepers, Jewish clerks, and Christian Scientist schoolteachers have access to different kinds of curers.

Although the pluralistic health cultures of laymen are readily acknowledged in our own society, we ignore the corresponding pluralism of our medical system when we talk about it as if it were only the structure of hospitals, clinics, colleges, and other agencies of "modern" or "scientific" medicine. These institutions of cosmopolitan medicine dominate the prestige hierarchy and legal structure of practice. Their representatives brand other forms of curing as "irregular" or "fringe" medicine, thus putting them ideologically outside of *the* medical system. From a realistic sociological perspective, however, specialists in clinical psychology, yoga, chiropractic, homeopathy, espiritismo, curandismo, faith healing, health foods, or Chinese herbals are part of the overall, pluralistic medical system of our society. Millions of people regularly consult these kinds of specialists, and at some points in their lives most American citizens probably resort to one or another of them.

The medical systems of all complex societies are socially and culturally pluralistic, but the professionalization of cosmopolitan medicine, which has progressed rapidly in this century, is an effort to reduce the degree and to govern the nature of medical pluralism. A struggle exists in the medical division of labor throughout the world in which advocates of cosmopolitan medicine attempt (1) to standardize the curricula for training health specialists, (2) to reserve the legal practice of medicine to individuals with the requisite training, (3) to enforce a hierarchy of medical authority dominated by doctors who form a self-governing profession with the right to define and to supervise the work of paramedical specialists. (4) to limit access of laymen or of other kinds of curers to the technology of cosmopolitan medicine, and (5) to eliminate or narrowly restrict all other forms of medical practice.

The actual systems of different countries are compromise structures of cosmopolitan medical workers and of other kinds of health specialists, and the models of them projected by their critics or admirers are ideological tools in the struggle to gain or keep power, and to control their course of development. The ideological conflicts in modern medical systems have been extensively analyzed in the history and sociology of medical reform in the United States and other Western countries, but they are also an essential element in the less-known sociology of "Western" medical institutions in societies of the developing world. An American observer with long experience in India described a characteristic aspect of these conflicts in this manner:

Medical education in India was based on the dogma that the early British educators were working in a complete vacuum of medical ignorance. British doctors essentially ignored or ridiculed the quackery of indigenous practitioners....(Indian) doctors found security in accepting the professional culture of Western medicine in toto. As a result, it proved to be hard for Indian doctors to select and adapt those parts of the Western medical culture that were relevant to the country's needs while, at the same time, compensating for feelings of social inferiority imposed on them by representatives of the British Raj (Taylor 1968:154).

As an organized professional group, cosmopolitan medical doctors in India have opposed governmental recognition and the support of indigenous medical institutions. But this policy has never been fully successful, or fully supported by all members of the profession, and laymen from all social classes, religious communities, castes, and ethnic and occupational groups resort to practitioners of indigenous medicine. Although the People's Republic of China has gained wide publicity for its extensive use of indigenous medicine, the scale of utilization of indigenous medicine in India is probably as great as that of China. Approximately 150,000 physicians now practice cosmopolitan medicine in India, but an estimated 400,000 physicians, many of them unregistered, practice indigenous medicine there. The indigenous systems are Ayurveda, which is based upon Sanskrit texts; Yunani, or Greek medicine, based upon Arabic and Persian texts; and Siddha, a tradition of humoral medicine in South India.

A dual system of professionalized indigenous and cosmopolitan medicine exists in India, with parallel institutions for research, education, and practice. In 1972, the state boards of indigenous medicine had registered 257,000 practitioners, of which about 93,000 had at least four years of formal training. There were 95 cosmopolitan medical colleges, compared to 99 Ayurvedic colleges, 15 Yunani colleges, and one college for Siddha medicine. Many of the indigenous medical schools were small and ill-equipped, but 26 of them were affiliated with universities and 10 offered postgraduate training. Two research institutes for indigenous medicine awarded between 35 and 45 Ph.D. and D.A.M. (Doctor of Ayurvedic Medicine) degrees annually. Also, in 1972 the state and central governments supported entirely or in part 185 hospitals and 9,750 dispensaries for indigenous medicine. The Indian government allocated 160 million rupees for indigenous medical institutions in the fourth five-year-plan, but in contrast to cosmopolitan medicine, where 75 percent of the physicians were in government service, more than one half of the registered physicians of indigenous medicine were fee-for-service private practitioners.

Homeopathic medicine is also widely practiced in India, and, for legislative purposes, it is often associated with the indigenous systems. Dr. S. M. Bhardwaj has described a process that he calls "the naturalization of homeopathy" in India during the nineteenth century. He argues that homeopathy first appealed to the new urban elite as a "modern" system. Its basic ideas were readily understandable and were soon made accessible in Indian languages to "even moderately literate people." The rise of nationalist sentiments, its German origin, and the opposition to it by the British-dominated cosmopolitan medical profession prevented homeopathy from acquiring the stigma of colonialism. Unlike the advocates of cosmopolitan medicine, the advocates of homeopathy were sympathetic to indigenous medical practices and tried to show that the principles of Ayurveda were consistent with homeopathy. Finally, Bhardwaj writes:

Although homeopathy was not an indigenous system, its practitioners were closely empathetic with the Indian ethos. Homeopathy...had an aura of mysticism and spiritualism about it. Hahnemann speaks of energies such as "vital powers," "dynamic powers," and "moral powers." These beliefs were not lost on the Indian homeopathic physicians. Many of them consciously tried to bring religious ideas into homeopathy. Dr. A. C. Bhaduri claimed that according to the vedanta philosophy minute doses are best suited for the cure of diseases.... Whether the logic of harmonization between Hinduism and homeopathy was faulty or not is not the issue. It is important that the homeopaths saw no conflict between their system of medicine and their religious and cultural beliefs even though the system was clearly imported from the West (Bhardwaj 1973:292).

Most registered homeopathic practitioners are registered jointly with practitioners of Ayurvedic and Yunani medicine, although separate state Boards of Homeopathic Medicine are now being formed. The fourth five-year-plan allocated 15 million rupees for this purpose, and 47 institutions offered homeopathic training in 1972 (Ministry of Information 1972). Even so, training is often acquired through correspondence courses that thinly disguise the selling of credentials (Montgomery 1975).

To describe the main area of full time professionalized medical practice in India we can imagine a continuum with one pole among the highly trained specialists who engage in scientific research and teaching at the more prestigious cosmopolitan medical schools, and the other pole among registered practitioners who may have a high-school education of a few years in college, and who have taken a correspondence course in homeopathy, studied the brochures of companies that manufacture indigenous and cosmopolitan medications, and perhaps served as an apprentice to another physician with similar or more formal institutional qualifications to practice Ayurvedic, Yunani, or cosmopolitan medicine. Most of the physicians who have completed full courses of training in the college for indigenous and cosmopolitan medicine fall between these poles. If we could measure their beliefs and practices, I believe that they would form a continuous series.

The point that I want to make is that professionalized indigenous medicine is not, in practice, isolated from cosmopolitan medicine, although separate colleges, hospitals, professional associations, and governmental agencies exist for the different systems. Ayurvedic and Yunani concepts of health and illness are coded into the domestic culture, cuisine, religious ritual, and popular culture of physicians trained in cosmopolitan medicine, and indigenous medical practitioners often used cosmopolitan medicines or instruments such as the thermometer and stethoscope. Well known Ayurvedic and Yunani physicians will have brothers, sons, or other kinsmen who are cosmopolitan medical doctors—or we could put this the other way around and say that many cosmopolitan medical practitioners have kinsmen who practice indigenous medicine. Thus, despite the bureaucratic structure that I have labeled a "dual system" of professionalized indigenous and cosmopolitan medicine, a large measure of cultural syncretism and social integration exists. In fact, different forms of medicine are sometimes brought together in a single bureaucratic complex. For example, in Varanasi, a city on the Ganges River midway between Delhi and Calcutta, the Institute for Medical Science of Banaras Hindu University awards degrees in Ayurveda and in cosmopolitan medicine. Outpatient clinics and wards for research and teaching both systems are located in the university hospital. In the same city, a large privately endowed hospital has outpatient clinics for homeopathy, Ayurveda, and cosmopolitan medicine, along with inpatient facilities for Ayurvedic and cosmopolitan medicine.

The continuum I have described between scientific specialists in India and an amalgam of popular culture physicians more or less corresponds to the distribution of practitioners from barefoot doctors to hospital specialists that recent visitors have described in the People's Republic of China (Sidel and Sidel 1973). But the essays on Taiwan, Hong Kong and other Chinese communities in *Medicine in Chinese Cultures* (Alexander et al. 1976) tell us about shamanistic and other kinds of religious and folk medical practice that are not reported in the model of New China. Since these forms of practice are an important dimension of medical pluralism, we need to locate the continuum I have described in relation to folk medicine and to religious curing. For this purpose, I have used a chart in another essay (Leslie 1973)

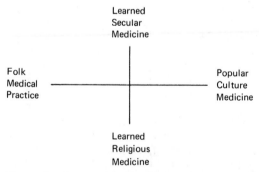

**Figure 1.** Conceptual axes of folk and popular culture medicine and of learned secular and religious medicine.

(Figure 1) with one axis to indicate a continuum between folk practices based upon the ways of thought and traditional technology of illiterate rural and urban people, and the popular culture medicine communicated through advertising, schoolbooks, and other mass media. A second axis perpendicular to this one has at opposite poles learned, secular scientific practice and learned religious curing.

We can locate regions of practice in the conceptual space of such a chart, marking the different regions with letters and based upon various studies of the Indian medical system, indicate the pattern of full-time practitioners by dots. I indicate the pattern of part-time practitioners in another chart, distinguishing full-time practice as one that accounts for at least one half of the practitioner's income. The continuum of full-time physicians who practice Ayurvedic, Yunani, homeopathic, and cosmopolitan medicine, or some combination of these traditions, is shown between regions (A) and (C) of Figure 2. These physicians are employed in governmental health services and in private practice, and form the majority of registered, institutionally trained practitioners. But some physicians of this kind regularly practice in clinics attached to religious institutions, or themselves adopt forms of religious curing. They form a continuum with other kinds of practitioners such as astrologers, diviners, priests, and holy men whom laymen consult for health problems, and who acquire some knowledge of indigenous medicine, homeopathy, or cosmopolitan medicine which they use in association with their religious activities. Some of these specialists acquire considerable reputations for supernatural curing and become,

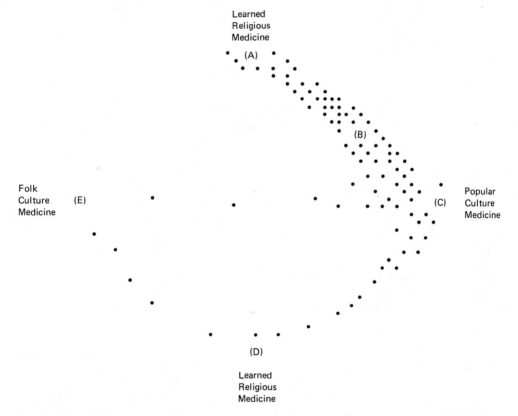

**Figure 2.** Regions of medical practice and the pattern of full-time practice in contemporary India: (A) Physicians with M.D. and Ph.D. degrees engaged in advanced research and teaching at a prestigious cosmopolitan medical college. (B) Physicians with degrees in indigenous medicine and with Bachelor or Licentiate degrees in cosmopolitan medicine, who teach at an Ayurvedic or Yunani medical college affiliated with a university. (C) Physicians who have completed a correspondence course in homeopathic medicine, and have other limited training in indigenous or cosmopolitan medicine. (D) Religious scholars or learned priests with reputations for unusual healing powers. (E) Bonesetters, midwives, and other individuals with reputations for traditional skills to handle common problems.

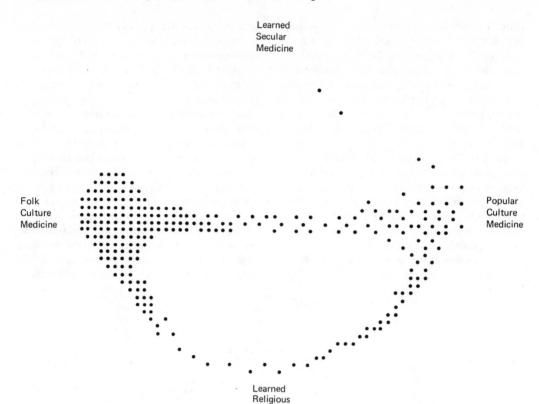

**Figure 3.** The pattern of part-time medical practice in contemporary India.

by our definition, full-time medical practitioners. The pattern of their distribution is shown between regions (C) and (D). A similar continuum of priests, holy men, and astrologers who practice forms of shamanistic curing, links folk culture medicine to learned religious medical practice, and is shown between regions (D) and (E) of Figure 2.

Part-time practitioners far outnumber full-time practitioners in the Indian medical system. In 1965, a community development block in the Punjab with 80,000 people had 59 full-time and 300 part-time indigenous medical practitioners (Taylor 1974). In the same year, a district in South India with a population of 120,000 had six doctors, 30 full-time practitioners of Ayurvedic and Yunani medicine, and 598 part-time practitioners (Neumann 1971). Almost all folk medicine is practiced as a part-time specialty by midwives, bonesetters, and individuals who know a remedy for rashes, fever, diarrhea, or other forms of indisposition. As these practitioners add aspirin, antibiotic ointments, and commercially prepared Ayurvedic and Yunani medicines to their repertory, they form a continuum with numerous part-time practitioners

of popular culture medicine. And as folk and popular culture practitioners deal with snake bites, or maladies attributed to supernatural causes, they form continua with learned religious medicine. These patterns are shown in Figure 3.

This way of looking at the Indian medical system does not emphasize the table of organization of professionalized medicine, beginning with the Ministry of Health and working down to the Primary Health Centers, nor does it start with the biomedical categories of pathology and epidemiology. These two approaches are the familiar ones of health planners, cosmopolitan medical specialists, and social scientists. They are essential for some purposes, but because they dominate our ways of thinking about medical systems they inhibit attention to the pluralistic structure of these systems and distort our understanding of the way they work. We characteristically look at our own and other medical systems from a statist perspective, and one biased by the categories and professional interests of cosmopolitan medicine.

Since part-time practitioners are rarely registered with state boards for indigenous or cosmopolitan medicine, they are not officially a part of the Indian medical system. Yet, if one superimposed the chart showing their distribution on the chart of full-time practitioners, and tried at the same time to represent their proportions, then one would have to show from 10 to 20 part-time practitioners for every full-time practitioner. And if one tried to distinguish registered from unregistered full-time practitioners, at least one half of them would probably be unregistered. The survey already mentioned for a district in South India found three unregistered for every registered full-time practitioner (Neumann 1971). They, too, form a dimension of the medical system that a state oriented perspective frequently ignores, and that the professional ideology of cosmopolitan medicine relegates to the limbo of "quack medicine."

Indigenous and cosmopolitan medicine are not officially integrated in India as they are in China in a state-sponsored hierarchy of medical institutions, but the continua of practitioners that I have described indicate a substantial *de facto* integration between different regions of the Indian medical system. The integration of indigenous and cosmopolitan medicine is even more obvious when one adopts the perspective of laymen, for throughout Indian society they utilize whatever forms of medical knowledge and practice are available to them. They are less concerned with whether therapy is indigenous or foreign, traditional or modern, than with how much it will cost, whether or not it will work, how long it will take, and whether the physician will treat them in a sympathetic manner. They are also often concerned with the ways that different kinds of diagnosis and treatment attribute illness to a moral flaw of the patient or some other person, or to forces for which they are not responsible. In these respects, laymen everywhere are pretty much alike. They differ only in the knowledge they draw upon to resolve these issues, and the kinds of specialists they have access to.

Conflicts between indigenous and cosmopolitan medicine occur primarily between practitioners of these systems who compete for positions and legitimacy within state-sanctioned medical bureaucracies. Since the official integration of indigenous and cosmopolitan medicine in China has been achieved by denying the kind of professional autonomy that cosmopolitan medical practitioners have attained in India, it is unlikely that this aspect of the model presented by the People's Republic will appeal to them. But the *de facto* integration that already exists will continue to evolve. The patterns that I have described are a momentary "compromise structure" that will change as the kind and number of practitioners change, as various different kinds of medical practitioners act as pressure groups to influence policies of the Indian government (Brass 1973). Still, our analysis should be useful to anyone who seeks to describe and compare the pluralistic structures of the medical systems of complex societies in different parts of the world.

# References

ABEGGLEN, JAMES G., 1958 The Japanese Factory. New York: The Free Press.

ABERLE, DAVID F., 1952 Arctic Hysteria and Latah in Mongolia. Transactions of the New York Academy of Sciences **14**:291–297.

———, 1966 Religio-Magical Phenomena and Power, Prediction, and Control. Southwestern Journal of Anthropology **22**:221–230.

ABSE, D. WILFRED, 1959 Hysteria. *In* American Handbook of Psychiatry. Silvano Arieti, ed. New York: Basic Books, Inc. **1**:272–292.

ACKERKNECHT, ERWIN H., 1942 Primitive Medicine and Culture Pattern. Bulletin of the History of Medicine **12**:545–574.

———, 1942 Problems of Primitive Medicine. Bulletin of the History of Medicine **11**:503–521.

———, 1943 Primitive Autopsies and the History of Anatomy. Bulletin of the History of Medicine **13**:334ff.

———, 1943 Psychopathology, Primitive Medicine and Primitive Culture. Bulletin of the History of Medicine **14**:30–67.

———, 1945 Malaria in the Upper Mississippi Valley, 1860–1900. Supplement to the Bulletin of the History of Medicine No. 4. Baltimore.

———, 1945 On the Collecting of Data Concerning Primitive Medicine. American Anthropologist **47**:427–432.

———, 1945 Primitive Medicine. Transactions of New York Academy of Sciences, Series 2, **8**:26–37.

———, 1946 Contradictions in Primitive Surgery. Bulletin of the History of Medicine **20**:184–187.

———, 1946 Natural Diseases and Rational Treatment in Primitive Medicine. Bulletin of the History of Medicine **19**:467–497.

———, 1947a Primitive Surgery. American Anthropologist **49**:25–45.

———, 1947b The Role of Medical History in Medical Education. Bulletin of History of Medicine **21**:135–145.

———, 1948 The Eskimo. Ciba Symposia **10**:1 July–August.

———, 1949 Medical Practices of the South American Indians. *In* Handbook of South American Indians. J. Steward, ed. Washington, D.C.: Smithsonian Institute **5**:621–643.

———, 1953 Rudolf Virchow. Madison: University of Wisconsin Press.

———, 1958 Primitive Medicine's Social Function. Miscellanea Paul Rivet. Mexico.

———, 1959 A Short History of Psychiatry. New York: Hafner Publishing Co., Inc.

———, 1965 History and Geography of the Most Important Diseases. New York: Hafner Publishing Co., Inc.

———, 1971 Medicine and Ethnology: Selected Essays. Baltimore: The Johns Hopkins Press.

ACSADI, GY., and J. NEMESKERI, 1970 History of Human Life Span and Mortality. Budapest: Akademiai Kiado.

ADAIR, JOHN, 1960 The Indian Health Worker in the Cornell Navaho Project. Human Organization **19**:59–63.

———, 1963 Physicians, Medicine Men, and Their Navajo Patients. *In* Man's Image in Medicine and Anthropology. Iago Galdston, ed. New York: International Universities Press.

519

————, and KURT DEUSCHLE 1957 Some Problems of the Physicians on the Navaho Reservation. Human Organization 16:19–23.

ADAM, W. Y., 1964 Post Pharoanic Nubia in Light of Archaeology, I. Journal of Egyptian Archaeology 50:102–120.

————, 1965 Post Pharoanic Nubia in Light of Archaeology, II. Journal of Egyptian Archaeology 51:160–178.

ADAMS, RICHARD N., 1953 An Analysis of Medical Beliefs and Practices in a Guatemalan Indian Town. Guatemala: Instituto Indigenista Nacional de Guatemala (also publ. 1953 by Pan American Sanitary Union).

————, 1957 Cultural Surveys of Panama-Nicaragua-Guatemala-El Salvador-Honduras. Washington.

————, and ARTHUR J. RUBEL 1967 Sickness and Social Relations. In Handbook of Middle American Indians. Austin: University of Texas Press 6:333–356.

AGUIRRE BELTRÁN, GONZALO, 1946 La Problación Negra de Mexico, 1519–1810. Mexico City.

AIRD, J. S., 1973 Population Problems, Theories, and Policies. In China: A Handbook. Y. L. Wu, ed. New York: Praeger Publishers, Inc.

AKERS, RONALD L., 1968 Problems in the Sociology of Deviance: Social Definitions and Behavior. Social Forces 46:4.

ALEXANDER, FRANZ, 1963 Fundamentals of Psychoanalysis. New York: W. W. Norton & Co.

————, and SHELDON T. SELESNICK 1966 The History of Psychiatric Thought and Practice from Prehistoric Times to the Present. New York: Harper & Row, Publishers, Inc.

ALLAND, ALEXANDER, JR., 1964 Native Therapists and Western Medical Practitioners Among the Abron of the Ivory Coast. Transactions of the New York Academy of Sciences 26:714–725.

————, 1966 Medical Anthropology and the Study of Biological and Cultural Adaption. American Anthropologist 68:40–51.

————, 1967 Evolution and Behavior. Garden City, N.Y.: Natural History Press (Doubleday).

————, 1969 Ecology and Adaptation to Parasitic Diseases. In Environment and Cultural Behavior. A. P. Vayda, ed. Garden City, N.Y.: Natural History Press (Doubleday).

————, 1970 Adaptation in Cultural Evolution: An Approach to Medical Anthropology. New York: Columbia University Press.

ALLISON, A. C., 1954 Malaria and Sickle-Cell Anemia. British Medical Journal 1:290.

————, 1960 Genetic Factors in Resistance to Malaria. Annals of the New York Academy of Sciences 91:710–729.

ALPERS, M., 1970 Kuru in New Guinea: Its Changing Pattern and Etiologic Elucidation. American Journal of Tropical Medicine and Hygiene 19:133–137.

ALTMANN, STUART A., and JEANNE ALTMANN, 1970 Baboon Ecology. Chicago: University of Chicago Press.

ALVAREZ, W. C., 1937 The Emergence of Modern Medicine from Ancient Folkways. Annual Report of the Smithsonian Inst., 409–30.

AMERICAN GEOGRAPHICAL SOCIETY OF NEW YORK, 1953 Study in Human Starvation. Two sets of annotated maps.

ANDERSON, J. E., 1963 The People of Fairty. National Museum of Canada, Bulletin 193.

ANDERSON, JAMES E., 1965 Human Skeletons of Tehuacán. Science 148:497.

ANDERSON, ODIN W., 1958 Infant Mortality and Social and Cultural Factors. In Patients, Physicians, and Illness. E. G. Jaco, ed.: New York, The Free Press.

ANDREWES, SIR C., 1964 Viruses of Vertebrates. Baltimore: The Williams & Wilkins, Co.

ANGEL, J. LAWRENCE, 1946 Skeletal Changes in Ancient Greece. American Journal of Physical Anthropology 4:69–97.

————, 1967 Palaeodemography and Evolution. Paper presented at the 66th annual meeting, American Anthropological Association, Washington, D.C.

————, 1972 The Bases of Paleodemography. American Journal of Physical Anthropology 30:427–438.

ANONYMOUS, 1943 Food and Health of Eskimo and Lapps. British Medical Journal ii:207.

ANONYMOUS, 1968 Arbovirus Studies in Bush-Bush Forest, Trinidad. American Journal of Tropical Medicine and Hygiene 17:219–298.

APPLE, DORRIAN, ed., 1960 Sociological Studies of Health and Sickness: A Source Book for the Health Profession. New York: McGraw-Hill, Inc.

APTEKAR, H., 1931 Anjea: Infanticide, Abortion, and Contraception in Savage Society. New York:

ARENSBERG, CONRAD M., and ARTHUR H. NIEHOFF, 1964 Introducing Social Change: A Manual for Americans Overseas. Chicago: Aldine Publishing Co.

ARMELAGOS, GEORGE J., 1967 Man's Changing Environment. In Infectious Diseases: Their Evolution and Eradication. A. Cockburn, ed.

Springfield, Ill.: Charles C Thomas, Publisher.
———, 1969 Disease in Ancient Nubia. Science **163**:255–259.
———, JAMES H. MIELKE, and JOHN WINTER, 1971 Bibliography of Human Paleopathology. Research Reports No. 8. Department of Anthropology, University of Massachusetts/Amherst.
———, JOHN DEWEY, P. MAHLEV, J. MIELKE, K. OWEN, and D. P. VAN GERVEN, 1972 Bond Growth and Development in Prehistoric Populations from Sudanese Nubia. Journal of Human Evolution **1**:89–119.
ARTAMONOV, M. I., 1965 Frozen Tombs of the Scythians. Scientific American **212**:101–119.
ASHBURN, P. M., 1947 The Ranks of Death—A Medical History of the Conquest of America, F. D. Ashburn, ed. New York: Coward-McCann, Inc.
BADGER, L. F., 1964 Epidemiology. Leprosy in Theory and Practice. R. G. Cochrane and T. F. Davey, eds. Baltimore: The William & Wilkins Co.
BAHNSON, CLAUS B. et al., 1974 Behavioral Factors Associated with the Etiology of Physical Disease. American Journal of Public Health **64**:1033–1056.
BANTON, MICHAEL, 1965 Roles: An Introduction to the Study of Social Relations. New York: Basic Books, Inc.
BARBER, THEODORE X., 1961 Death by Suggestion: A Critical Note. Psychosomatic Medicine **23**:153–155.
BARNES, S. B., 1969 Paradigms—Scientific and Social. Man **4**:94–102.
BARNETT, HOMER G., 1953 Innovation: The Basis of Cultural Change. New York: McGraw-Hill, Inc.
BARNETT, S. A., 1964 Psychogenic Death from Stress in Mammals. Viewpoints in Biology **3**:203–218.
BARNOUW, VICTOR, 1974 Culture and Personality, · Homewood, Ill.: Dorsey Press (rev. ed.).
BARRACK, BRUCE, 1956 Syphilis and Yaws. Archives of Dermatology **73**:510–515.
BARTH, FREDRIK, 1963 Introduction. *In* The Role of the Entrepreneur in Social Change in Northern Norway. Fredrik Barth, ed. Oslo: Norwegian Universities Press.
———, 1966 Models of Social Organization. Occasional Paper No. 23. Royal Anthropological Institute of Great Britain and Ireland.
BASCOM, WILLIAM R., 1946 Ponape: A Pacific Economy in Transition. Honolulu: U.S. Commercial Co. (mimiographed).

BASEDOW, HERBERT, 1932 Diseases of the Australian Aborigines. Journal of Tropical Medicine and Hygiene **35**:177–278. London.
BATES, MARSTON, 1953 Human Ecology. *In* Anthropology Today, A. L. Kroeber, ed. Chicago: University of Chicago Press.
———, 1959 The Ecology of Health. *In* Medicine and Anthropology, Iago Galdston, ed. New York: International Universities Press.
BAUER, RAYMOND A., ed., 1966 Social Indicators. Cambridge, Mass., The MIT Press.
BEALS, ALAN R., and BERNARD J. SIEGEL, 1966 Divisiveness: Conflict Within the Group. Stanford, Cal.: Stanford University Press.
BECH, V., 1962 Measles Epidemics in Greenland 1951–1959. American Journal of Diseases of Childhood **103**:252.
———, 1965 The Measles Epidemic in Greenland in 1962. *In* Seminar on the Epidemiology and Prevention of Measles and Rubella. (Archiv für die gesamte Virusforchung.) New York: Springer Publishing Co., Inc.
BECK, WILLIAM S., 1961 Modern Science and the Nature of Life. London: Penguin Books.
BEECHER, HENRY K., 1959 Measurements of Subjective Responses: Quantitative Effects of Drugs. New York: Oxford University Press.
BELKNAP, H. R., and W. G. HAYNES, 1960 A Genetic Analysis of Families in Which Leprosy Occurs. Unpublished M.D. Thesis. New Orleans, Louisiana. Tulane University School of Medicine.
BELSHAW, CYRIL S., 1955 The Cultural Milieu of the Entrepreneur: A Critical Essay. Explorations in Entrepreneurial History **7**:146–162.
BENEDICT, BURTON, 1969 Role Analysis in Animals and Men. Man **4**:203–214.
BENEDICT, RUTH, 1934 Anthropology and the Abnormal. Journal of Genetic Psychology **10**:59–82.
———, 1934 Patterns of Culture. Boston: Houghton-Mifflin.
———, 1940 Race, Science and Politics. New York: The Viking Press, Inc.
BENNETT, DAVID W., 1975 The Response to Pain: An Analysis of Cultural Determinants. Unpublished paper, Department of Anthropology, University of Massachusetts/ Boston.
BENNETT, F. J., and A. MUGALULU-MUKIIBI, 1967 An Analysis of People Living Alone in a Rural Community in East Africa. Social Science and Medicine **1**:97–115.
BENNETT, JOHN W., HARVEY L. SMITH, and HERBERT PASSIN, 1942 Food and Culture in

521

Southern Illinois—A Preliminary Report. American Sociological Review 7:645.

BERLIN, BRENT, D. E. BREEDLOVE, D. E. BREEDLOVE, and P. H. RAVEN, 1968 Covert Categories and Folk Taxonomies. American Anthropologist 70:290–299.

BERNDT, CATHERINE H., 1964 The Role of Native Doctors in Aboriginal Australia. In Magic, Faith, and Healing. Ari Kiev, ed. New York: The Free Press.

BERNDT, RONALD M., 1964 Warfare in the New Guinea Highlands. American Anthropologist 66:183–203.

———, 1966 The Concept of the Tribe in the Western Desert of Australia. In Readings in Australian and Pacific Anthropology. I. Hogbin, and L. R. Hiatt, eds. Melbourne: Melbourne University.

———, and C. H. BERNDT 1964 The World of the First Australians. Sydney, Australia: Ure Smith.

BERREMAN, GERALD D., 1966 Anemic and Emetic Analyses in Social Anthropology. American Anthropologist 68:346–354.

BERTELSON, A., 1905 Neuro-patologiske Meddelelser fra Grønland. Bibliotek for Laeger. København, Denmark. pp. 109–135, 280–335.

BHARDWAJ, S. M., 1973 Early Phase of Homeopathy in India, Asian Profile 1:281–296.

BHATT, P. N., M. K. GOVERDHAN, M. F. SHAFFER, C. D. BRANDT, and J. P. FOX, 1966 Viral Infections of Monkeys in Their Natural Habitat in Southern India. American Journal of Tropical Medicine and Hygiene 15:551–560.

BIDDLE, BRUCE, and EDWIN J. THOMAS, 1966 Role Theory: Concepts and Research. New York: John Wiley & Sons, Inc.

BIDDLE, M., 1965 Excavation at Winchester, 1964. Antiquaries Journal 45:230–266.

———, 1967 Health in Medieval Winchester: The Evidence from Excavations. In Infectious Diseases: Their Evolution and Eradication. T. A. Cockburn, ed. Springfield, Ill.: Charles C Thomas, Publisher.

BILBY, J. W., 1923 Among Unknown Eskimos. Philadelphia: J. B. Lippincott Co.

BILLINGTON, B. P., 1960 The Health and Nutritional Status of the Aborigines. Records of the American–Australian Scientific Expedition to Arnhem Land: 2. Anthropology and Nutrition. C. P. Mountford, ed. Melbourne: Melbourne University Press.

BIRDSELL, JOSEPH B., 1957 Some Population Problems Involving Pleistocene Man. Cold Spring Harbor Symposia on Quantitative Biology 22:47–69.

———, 1968 Some Predictions for the Pleistocene Based on Equilibrium Systems Among Recent Hunter-Gatherers. In Man the Hunter. R. B. Lee, and I. DeVore, eds. Chicago: Aldine Publishing Co.

BIRKET-SMITH, KAJ, 1929 The Caribou Eskimo. Fifth Thule Expedition 5:1.

———, 1935 The Eskimos. New York: E. P. Dutton & Co., Inc.

BLACK, FRANCIS L., 1975 Infectious Diseases in Primitive Societies. Science 187:515–518.

BLACK, ROBERT H., 1959 Haptoglobins and Haemoglobins in Australian Aborigines. Medical Journal of Australia 1:175–176. Sydney.

BLACKWOOD, BEATRICE, 1935 Both Sides of the Buka Passage. Oxford: The Clarendon Press.

BLIX, M., 1884 Experimentelle Peitrage zur Losung der Frage über die specifische Energie der Hautnerven. Leitschrift für Biologie 20:141–160.

BLOCH, IWAN, 1901 Der Ursprung des Syphilis. Jena. Verlag von Gustav Fisher.

BLOOM, LEONARD, 1964 Some Psychological Concepts of Urban Africans. Ethnology 3:66–95.

BLUM, RICHARD H., 1962 Case Identification in Psychiatric Epidemiology: Methods and Problems. Milbank Memorial Fund Quarterly 40:253–289.

———, and EVA BLUM, 1965 Health and Healing in Rural Greece, Stanford Cal.: Stanford University Press.

BLUMBERG, B. S., ed., 1962 Proceedings of the Conference on Genetic Polymorphisms and Geographic Variations in Disease. New York: Grune & Stratton, Inc.

BOAS, FRANZ, 1907 The Eskimo of Baffin Land and Hudson Bay. Bulletin of the American Museum of Natural History 15.

———, 1930 The Religion of the Kwakiutl. Columbia University Contributions to Anthropology X:II:1–41. New York.

———, 1938 Invention. In General Anthropology, Boas et al. Chap. 6.

———, 1940 Race, Language and Culture. New York: Macmillan Publishing Co., Inc.

BODIAN, D., 1955 Emerging Concepts of Poliomyelitis Infections. Science 122:105–108.

BOHANNAN, PAUL, 1961 Review of Search for Security, by M. J. Field. American Anthropologist 63:435–436.

BONFIL BATALLA, GUILLERMO, 1966 Conservative Thought in Applied Anthropology: A Critique. Human Organization 25:89–92.

522

BOGORAS, WALDEMAR, 1909 The Chukchee. Publications of the Jesup North Pacific Expedition, 7, part 2.

BORAH, WOODROW W., 1951 New Spain's Century of Depression. Ibero-Americana No. 35.

BORAH, WOODROW W., and S. F. COOK, 1960 The Population of Central Mexico in 1548. Ibero-Americana No. 43.

———, and ———, 1963 The Aboriginal Population of Central Mexico on the Eve of the Spanish Conquest. Ibero-Americana No. 45.

BOSERUP, ESTER, 1965 The Conditions of Agricultural Growth. Chicago: Aldine Publishing Co.

BOUFFARD, G., 1909 Autopsie d'un cas do goundou chez le cynocephale. Bulletin de la Société de Pathologie Exotique 2:216–220.

BOUGHEY, A. S., 1973 Ecology of Populations (2nd ed). New York: Macmillan Publishing Co., Inc.

BOURGUIGNON, ERIKA, and A. HASS, 1965 Transcultural Research and Culture-Bound Psychiatry. Paper presented at Meeting of the Western Division of the American Psychiatric Association, Hawaii.

BOURGUIGNON, ERIKA and L. PETTAY, 1964 Spirit Possession and Cross-Cultural Research. Proceedings of the 1964 Annual Spring Meeting of the American Ethnological Society. J. Helm, ed. New York: American Ethnological Society.

———, and ———, 1965 The Self, the Behavioral Environment and the Theory of Spirit Possession. Context and Meaning in Cultural Anthropology. M. E. Spiro, ed. New York: The Free Press.

BOWERS, JOHN Z., 1965 Medical Education in Japan. New York: Harper & Row, Publishers, Inc.

BOWMAN, JAMES E., 1967 G-6-P-D Deficiency and Malaria. The Lancet. May 27:1158.

BOYDEN, S. V., 1970 The Impact of Civilization on the Biology of Man. University of Toronto Press.

BOYER, L. B., 1962 Remarks on the Personality of Shamans. The Psychoanalytic Study of Society. W. Muensterberger and S. Axelrad, eds. New York: International Universities Press.

Bradford's History of Plimouth Plantation from the original manuscript, 1928 Boston: Commonwealth of Massachusetts, Wright and Potter.

BRASS, P., 1973 The Politics of Ayurvedic Education: A Case Study of Revivalism and Modernization in India. Politics and Education in India. L. Rudolph and S. Rudolph, eds. Cambridge, Mass.: Harvard University Press.

BRAY, R. S., 1963 The Exoerythrocytic Phases of Malaria Parasites. International Review of Tropical Medicine 2:41.

BRELSFORD, W. V., 1950 Insanity Among the Bemba of North Rhodesia. Africa 20:46–54.

BRIFFAULT, R., 1935 Birth Customs. Encyclopedia of the Social Sciences 2:565–568.

BRIGGS, JEAN L., 1970 Never in Anger; Portrait of an Eskimo Family. Cambridge, Mass.: Harvard University Press.

BRILL, A. A., 1912 Piblokto or Hysteria Among Peary's Eskimos. Journal of Nervous and Mental Disease 40:514–520.

BROCK, J. F. and M. AUTRET, 1952 Kwashiorkor in Africa. World Health Organization Monograph. Series No. 8.

BRONTE-STEWART, B., and O. E. BUDTZ-OLSEN, JOAN M. HICKLEY, and J. F. BROCK, 1960 The Health and Nutritional Status of the King Bushmen of South-West Africa. South African Journal of Laboratory Clinical Medicine 6:187–216.

BROTHWELL, DON R., 1961 The Palaeopathology of Early British Man: An Essay on the Problems of Diagnosis and Analysis. Journal of the Royal Anthropological Institute 91:318–344.

———, 1971 Paleodemography. In Biological Aspects of Demography. W. Brass, ed. London: Taylor and Francis.

———, and A. T SANDISON, 1967 Diseases in Antiquity: A Survey of Diseases, Injuries, and Surgery in Ancient Populations. Springfield, Ill.: Charles C. Thomas, Publisher.

BROWN, G. G., and A. McD. HUTT, 1935 Anthropology in Action. London: Oxford University Press.

BROWN, JANET W., 1975 Native American Contributions to Science, Engineering and Medicine. Science 189:38–40.

BROWN, ROGER, 1958 Words and Things. New York: The Free Press.

BRUCE-CHWATT, L. J., 1965 Paleogenesis and Paleo-epidemiology of Primate Malaria. Bulletin of the World Health Organization 32:368–387.

BRYANT, A. T., 1970 Zulu Medicine and Medicine Men. Capetown, South Africa: C. Struik.

BUCK, PETER H., 1932 Ethnology of Manihiki and Rakahanga. Bishop Museum Bulletin 99.

BUETTNER-JANUSCH, JOHN, 1959 Natural Selection in Man: the ABD(H) Blood Group System. American Anthropologist 61:437–456.

———, 1966 Origins of Man. New York: John Wiley and Sons.

BURLING, ROBBINS, 1962 Maximization Theories

and the Study of Economic Anthropology. American Anthropologist 64:802–821.

BURNET, F. M., 1946 Virus as Organism. Cambridge, Mass.: Harvard University Press.

———, 1963 The Integrity of the Body. Cambridge, Mass.: Harvard University Press.

BURNET, MACFARLANE, and DAVID O. WHITE, 1972 Natural History of Infectious Disease. 4th ed. Cambridge, England: Cambridge University Press.

BURTON, LLOYD EDWARD, and HUGH HOLLINGSWORTH SMITH, 1975 Public Health and Community Medicine for the Allied Medical Professions. 2nd ed. Baltimore: The Williams & Wilkins Co.

BUSHBY, S. R. M., 1964 Chemotherapy. Leprosy in Theory and Practice. R. G. Cochrane and T. F. Davey, eds. Baltimore: The Williams & Wilkins Co.

BUTLER, SAMUEL, 1961 EREWHON. New York: Signet Books, Inc.

CALLEN, E. O., and T. W. M. CAMERON, 1970 A Prehistoric Diet Revealed in Coprolites. The New Scientist July. 7, 35–40.

CAMERON, T. W. M., 1956 Parasites and Parasitism. London: Methuen Co. Ltd.

CANCIAN, FRANK, 1965 Economic and Prestige in a Maya Community: the Religious Cargo System in Zinacantan. Stanford: Stanford University Press.

CANNON, WALTER B., 1929 Bodily Changes in Pain, Hunger, Fear and Rage: An Account of Researches into Function of Emotional Excitement. New York: Appleton-Century-Crofts.

———, 1942 Voodoo Death. American Anthropologist 44:169–181.

CARDOZO, A. REBECCA, 1970 A Modern American Witch-Craze. In Witchcraft and Sorcery. Max Marwick, ed. Harmondsworth, Middlesex, England: Penguin Books.

CARLSSON, GOSTA, 1966 The Decline of Fertility: Innovation or Adjustment Process. Population Studies 20 (2):149–174.

CARLUCCIO, C., J. A. SOURO, and L. G. KOLB, 1964 Psychodynamics of Echo-Reactions, Archives of General Psychiatry 10:623–629.

CARNEIRO, ROBERT L., and DAISY, F. HILSE 1966 On Determining the Probability Rate of Population Growth During the Neolithic. American Anthropologist 68:177–181.

CAROTHERS, J. C., 1959 Culture, Psychiatry, and the Written Word. Psychiatry 22:307–320.

CARPENTER, C. M., and J. N. MILLER, 1964 The Bacteriology of Leprosy. Leprosy in Theory and Practice. R. G. Cochrane and T. F. Davey, eds. Baltimore: The Williams & Wilkins Co.

CARPENTER, EDMUND S., 1953 Witch Fear Among the Aivilik Eskimos. American Journal of Psychiatry 110:194–199.

CARRASCO, P., 1960 Pagan Rituals and Beliefs Among the Chontal Indians of Oaxaca. Anthropological Records 20:87–117.

CARROLL, JOHN ALEXANDER, and MARY WELLS ASHWORTH, 1957 George Washington, Vol. VII. New York: Charles Scribner's Sons (completing biography begun by Douglas Southall Freeman).

CARR-SAUNDERS, A. M., 1922 The Population Problem. Oxford, England: Clarendon.

CARSTAIRS, G. MORRIS, 1955 Medicine and Faith in Rajasthan. Health, Culture, and Community. Paul Benjamin, ed. New York: Russell Sage Foundation.

CARTER, HENRY ROSE, 1931 Yellow Fever. An Epidemiological and Historical Study of Its Place of Origin. Laura Carter and Hampton Wade, eds. Baltimore: The Williams & Wilkins Co.

CASELEY-SMITH, J. R., 1959 The Haemotology of the Central Australian Aborigine, 11. White and Differential Counts; Eosinophil Counts and Casoni Tests. Australian Journal of Experimental Biology and Medical Science 37:481–488.

CASSEL, JOHN, R. PATRICK, and D. JENKINS, 1960 Epidemiological Analysis of the Health Implications of Change: A Conceptual Model. Annals of the New York Academy of Sciences 84:938–949.

CAUDILL, WILLIAM, 1953 Applied Anthropology in Medicine. Anthropology Today. A. L. Kroeber, ed., University of Chicago Press.

CAUDILL, W., 1958 Effects of Social and Cultural Systems in Reactions to Stress. Memorandum to the Committee on Preventive Medicine and Social Science Research. Pamphlet 14.

———, 1961 Around the Clock Patient Care in Japanese Psychiatric Hospitals: the Role of the Tsukisoi. American Sociological Review 26:204–214.

———, 1962 Patterns of Emotion in Modern Japan. Japanese Culture: Its Development and Characteristics. R. J. Smith and R. K. Beardsly, eds. Chicago: Aldine Publishing Co.

———, 1975 The Culture and Interpersonal Context of Everyday Health and Illness in Japan and America. Asian Medical Systems. C. Leslie, ed. Berkeley: University of California Press.

CAWTE, JOHN E., 1965 Ethnopsychiatry in Central Australia: Traditional Illness in the Eastern

Aranda People. British Journal of Psychiatry **111**:1069–1077.

CERRULLI, E., 1934 Zar. Encyclopedia of Islam **4**:1217. London:

CHAMISSO, ADELBERTUS DE, 1824 Cetaceorum maris Kamtschatici imagines, ab Aleutis e ligno fictas, adum-bravit recensuitque. Verhandlungen der Kaiserlichen Leopoldinisch-Carolinischen Akademie der Naturforscher **12**:249–263. Bonn.

CHAPMAN, W. P., 1944 Measurements of Pain Sensitivity in Normal Control Subjects and in Psychoneurotic Patients. Psychosomatic Medicine **6**:252–257.

———, and C. M. JONES, 1944 Variations in Cutaneous and Visceral Pain Sensitivity in Normal Subjects. Journal of Clinical Investigation **23**:81–91.

CHAPPLE, ELIOT D., 1970 Culture and Biological Man: Explorations in Behavioral Anthropology. New York: Holt, Rinehart and Winston, Inc.

CHEATHAM, T. E. et al., 1973 Computing in China: A Travel Report. Science **12**:134–140.

CHEN, P. C., 1973a China's Population Program at the Grass Roots Level. Studies in Family Planning **4**:219–227.

———, 1973b Population Planning: Policy Evolution and Action Programs. Public Health in the People's Republic of China. M. E. Wegman et al., eds. New York: Josiah Macy, Jr., Foundation.

CHILDE, V. GORDON, 1936 Man Makes Himself. London: Watts and Co.

CHIN, R., 1973 The Changing Health Conduct and the "New Man". Public Health in the People's Republic of China. M. E. Wegman et al., eds. New York: Josiah Macy, Jr., Foundation.

CHODOFF, PAUL, and HENRY LYONS, 1958 Hysteria. American Journal of Psychiatry **114**:734–740.

CHOMSKY, NOAM, 1957 Syntactic Structures. The Hague: Mouton and Co.

CHOU, W. C., 1973 To Create a New Chinese Music Idiom. Drama Section, New York Times, September 9.

CHRISTIE, E. B., 1909 The Subanun of Sindangan Bay. Manila Bureau of Science, Division of Ethnology Publications 6.

CIANFRANI, THEODORE, 1960 A Short History of Obstetrics and Gynecology. Springfield, Ill.: Charles C Thomas.

CLARK, G. W., 1953 A Vitamin Digest. Springfield, Ill.: Charles C Thomas, Publisher.

CLARK, MARGARET, 1959 Health in the Mexican-American Culture. Berkeley: University of California Press. (orig. 1958)

CLARK, W. E. LE GROS, 1949 A History of the Primates. London: British Museum.

CLELAND, J. B., 1928 Disease Among the Australian Aborigines. Journal of Tropical Medicine and Hygiene **31**: 53–59, 66–70, 141–145, 157–160, 173–177.

CLEMENTS, FORREST E., 1932 Primitive Concepts of Disease. University of California Publications in American Archeology and Ethnology **32**: 185–252.

CLUNE, FRANCIS J., 1973 A Comment on Voodoo Deaths. American Anthropologist **75**:312.

COATNEY, G. R., 1968 Simian Malarias in Man. American Journal of Tropical Medicine and Hygiene **17**: 147–155.

COBB, STANLEY, and SIDNEY H. KING, 1958 Psychosocial Factors in the Epidemiology of Rheumatoid Arthritis. Journal of Chronic Diseases **7**:466–475.

COCKBURN, T. AIDAN, 1959 The Evolution of Infectious Diseases. International Review of Medicine **172**:493–508.

———, 1960 Infectious Diseases and the Population of East Pakistan. In Seminar on Populations. Karachi: Government of Pakistan.

———, 1961 The Origin of the Treponematoses. Bulletin of the World Health Organization **24**:221–228.

———, 1961 Epidemic Crisis in East Pakistan, 1958. Public Health Reports **75**:26–36.

———, 1963 The Evolution and Eradication of Infectious Diseases. Baltimore: The Johns Hopkins University Press.

———, 1967 Infectious Diseases: Their Evolution and Eradication. Springfield, Ill.: Charles C Thomas, Publisher.

COCKBURN, AIDAN, ROBIN A. BARRACO, THEODORE A. REYMAN, and WILLIAM H. PECK, 1975 Autopsy of an Egyptian Mummy. Science **187**:1155–1160.

COLBY, BENJAMIN N., and PIERRE L. VAN DEN BERGHE, 1969 Ixil Country: A Plural Society in Highland Guatemala. Berkeley: University of California Press.

COLLIS, ROBERT J. M., 1966 Physical Health and Psychiatric Disorder in Nigeria. Transactions of the American Philosophical Society **56**:5–45.

COLSON, ANTHONY C., 1969 The Prevention of Illness in a Malay Village: An Analysis of Concepts and Behavior. Ph.D. dissertation. Stanford University.

———, and KAREN E. SELBY, 1974 Medical Anthropology. Annual Review of Anthropology **3**:245–262.

COLUMBUS, FERDINAND, 1959 The Life of the Admiral Christopher Columbus by His Son Ferdinand. Benjamin Keen, trans. New Brunswick, N.J.: Rutgers University Press.

COMMUNICABLE DISEASE CENTER, U.S. PUBLIC HEALTH SERVICE, 1965 Chimpanzee-Associated Hepatitis. Hepatitis Surveillance Report No. 23.

CONKLIN, H. C., 1962 Lexicographic Treatment of Folk Taxonomies. In Problems in Lexicography. F. W. Householder and S. Bloomington Saporta, eds. Indiana University Research Center in Anthropology, Folklore, and Linguistics.

————, 1964 Ethnogeneaological Method. In Explorations in Cultural Anthropology. W. H. Goodenough, ed. New York: McGraw-Hill Book Co.

COOK, SHERBURNE F., 1946 The Incidence and Significance of Disease Among the Aztecs and Related Tribes. Hispanic American Historical Review XXVI: 320–335.

————, 1955 The Epidemic of 1830–1833 in California and Oregon. University of California Publications in American Archeology and Ethnology 43: 303–326. Berkeley.

————, and WOODROW W. BORAH, 1960 The Indian Population of Central Mexico, 1531–1610. Ibero-Americana No. 44.

COON, CARLETON S., 1948 A Reader in General Anthropology. New York: Harper & Row, Publishers, Inc.

COOPER, JOHN M., 1933 The Cree Wiitiko Psychosis. Primitive Man 6: 20–24.

————, 1933 The Northern Algonkian Supreme Being. Primitive Man 6: 41–111.

————, 1934 Mental Disease Situations in Certain Cultures: A New Field for Research. Journal of Abnormal and Social Psychology 29: 10–17.

————, 1935 Magic and Science. Thought 10: 357–373.

COSMINSKY, S., 1972 Decision Making and Medical Care in a Guatemalan Indian Community. Ph.D. dissertation. Brandeis University, Waltham, Massachusetts.

COULT, ALLAN D., 1964 Role Allocation, Position Structuring, and Ambilineal Descent. American Anthropologist 66: 29–40.

CROIZIER, RALPH, 1968 Traditional Medicine in Modern China. Cambridge, Mass.: Harvard University Press.

CROMBIE, ALISTON, 1969 Discussion. Medicine and Culture. F. N. L. Poynter, ed. London: Wellcome Institute of the History of Medicine.

CROSBY ALFRED W., 1967 Conquistador y Pestilencia: The First New World Pandemic and the Fall of the Great Indian Empires. HAHR XLVII: 321–337.

————, 1972 The Columbian Experience: Biological and Cultural Consequences of 1492. Westport, Conn.: Greenwood Press.

CROTTY, J. M., and R. C. WEBB, 1960 Mortality in Northern Territory Aborigines. Medical Journal of Australia 2: 489–492.

CUMMING, ELAINE, and JOHN CUMMING, 1957 Closed Ranks: An Experiment in Mental Health Education. Cambridge: Harvard University Press.

CUMMING, JOHN, and ELAINE CUMMING, 1965 On the Stigma of Mental Illness. Community Mental Health Journal 1: 135–143.

————, and ————, 1966 Ego and Milieu. New York: Atherton Press, Inc.

CUMMINS, S. L., 1939 Primitive Tuberculosis. London: John Bale Medical Publications.

CUNNINGHAM, CLARK E., 1970 Thai "Injection Doctors": Antibiotic Mediators. Social Science and Medicine 4: 124.

CURRIER, RICHARD L., 1966 The Hot-Cold Syndrome and Symbolic Balance in Mexican and Spanish Folk Medicine. Ethnology 5: 251–263.

CURTIN, PHILIP, 1968 Epidemiology and the Slave Trade. Political Science Quarterly LXXIII: 190–216.

CURTIS, M. R., W. F. DUNNING, and F. D. BULLOCK, 1933 Genetic Factors and Malignant Tumors. American Journal of Cancer 17: 894–923.

CUSSLER, MARGARET, and MARY L. DE GÈVY, 1952 Twixt the Cup and the Lip. New York: Twayne Publishers, Inc.

DALL, W. H., 1870 Alaska and Its Resources. Boston: Lee and Shepard.

DANIELSON, R., 1973 Cuban Health Organization: History and Development. Ph.D. dissertation. University of Pittsburgh.

————, 1974 The Cuban Health Area and Polyclinic: Organizational Focus in an Emerging System. Inquiry. Supplement 12: 86–102.

————, 1975 Cuban Health Care in Process: Models and Morality in the Early Revolution. In Topias and Utopias in Health. S. Ingman and A. Thomas, eds. The Hague: Mouton & Co.

DARWIN, CHARLES, 1906 6th ed. The Origin of Species. London: John Murray. (First published in 1858).

DAVENPORT, WILLIAM, 1960 Jamaican Fishing: A Game Theory Analysis. New Haven: Yale University Publications in Anthropology 59.

DAVID, FRED, 1960 Uncertainty in Medical

Prognosis: Clinical and Functional. American Journal of Sociology **66**:41–47.

DAVIS, KINGSLEY, 1955 Institutional Patterns Favoring High Fertility in Underdeveloped Areas. Eugenics Quarterly **2**:33–39.

———, 1960 Social Impediments to Health and Longevity. *In* Human Society. New York: Macmillan Publishing Co., Inc.

———, 1967 Population Policy: Will Current Programs Succeed? Science **158**:730–739.

———, and JUDITH BLAKE, 1956 Social Structure and Fertility: An Analytic Framework. Economic Development and Cultural Change **4**:211–235.

DAWSON, JOHN, 1964 Urbanization and Mental Health in a West African Community. *In* Magic, Faith, and Healing. Ari Kiev, ed. New York: The Free Press.

DEEVEY, C. S., 1960 The Hare and the Haruspex: A Cautionary Tale. *In* Man Alone. Eric Josephson and Mary Josephson, eds. New York: Dell Publishing Co., Inc.

DEEVEY, EDWARD, JR., 1968 Discussion. *In* Man the Hunter. R. B. Lee and I. DeVore, eds. Chicago: Aldine Publishing Co.

DEMENY, PAUL, 1968 Early Fertility Decline in Austria-Hungary: A Lesson in Demographic Transition. Daedalus **97**:502–522.

DENNIE, CHARLES C., 1962 A History of Syphilis. Springfield, Ill.: Charles C Thomas, Publisher.

DENNIS, PHILIP ADAMS, 1973 An Inter-Village Land Feud in the Valley of Oaxaca, Mexico. Ph.D. dissertation. Cornell University.

DERUISSEAU, L. G., 1940 Ancient Pediatrics. Ciba Symposia **2**, (5).

DEUSCHLE, KURT, and JOHN ADAIR, An Interdisciplinary Approach to Public Health on the Navajo Indian Reservation: Medical and Anthropological Aspects. Annals of the New York Academy of Sciences **84**:887–904.

DEVEREUX, G., 1956 Normal and Abnormal: The Key Problem of Psychiatric Anthropology. *In* Some Uses of Anthropology, Theoretical and Applied. J. B. Casagrande and T. Gladwin, eds. Washington, D.C.: Washington Anthropological Society.

———, 1957 Dream Learning and Individual Ritual Differences in Mohave Shamanism. American Anthropologist **59**:1036–1045.

———, 1961a Mohave Ethnopsychiatry and Suicide: The Psychiatric Knowledge and the Psychic Disturbances of an Indian Tribe. Bulletins of the Bureau of American Ethnology **175**:1–586.

———, 1961b Shamans as Neurotics. American Anthropologist **63**:1088–1090.

———, 1963 Primitive Psychiatric Diagnosis. *In* Man's Image in Anthropology and Medicine. Iago Galdston, ed. New York: International Universities Press.

DEVEREUX, GEORGE, 1967 A Typological Study of Abortion in 350 Primitive, Ancient, and Pre-Industrial Societies. *In* Abortion in America. H. Rosen, ed. Boston: Beacon Press.

DE VOS, GEORGE, 1960 The Relation of Guilt Towards Parents to Achievement and Arranged Marriage Among the Japanese, Psychiatry **23**:287–301.

———, and HIROSHI WAGSTSUMA, 1959 Psychocultural Significance of Concern Over Death and Illness Among Rural Japanese. International Journal of Social Psychiatry **5**:5–19.

DEWEY, JOHN R., 1968 Metric Assessment of Osteoporotic Bone Loss in Meroitic X-Group and Christian Archeological Populations from Sudanese Nubia. Ph.D. thesis. University of Utah.

DIAMOND, STANLEY, 1963 The Search for the Primitive. *In* Man's Image in Medicine and Anthropology. Iago Galdston, ed. New York: International Universities Press.

DIAZ, BERNAL, 1956 The Bernal Diaz Chronicles. Trans. by Albert Idell. New York: Doubleday Dolphin Books.

DIAZ DE YSLA, RUY, 1542 Tractado llamado fructo de todos sanctos: contra el mal serpentino. Sevilla.

DIMAYA, N., 1963 An Analytical Study of the Self-Concept of Hospital Patients with Hansen's Disease. Unpublished Ph.D. dissertation. Detroit, Michigan. Wayne State University, School of Social Welfare.

DIMOND, E. G., 1971a Medical Education and Care in the People's Republic of China. Journal of the American Medical Association **218**:1552–1556.

———, 1971b Acupuncture Anesthesia. Journal of the American Medical Association **218**:1558–1563.

DOBELL, C., 1926 Intestinal Protozoa of Monkeys. Annual Report, Medical Research Council. London: Her Majesty's Stationery Office.

DOBKIN DE RIOS, MARLENE, 1972 Visionary Vine: Psychedelic Healing in the Peruvian Amazon. San Francisco: Chandler Publishing Co.

DOBZHANSKY, THEODOSIUS, 1950 Evolution in the Tropics. American Scientist **38**:209–221.

———, 1951 Genetics and the Origin of Species. 3rd ed. New York: Columbia University Press.

———, 1962 Mankind Evolving. New Haven: Yale University Press.

DOHRENWEND, BRUCE P., and B. S. DOHRENWEND, 1965 The Problem of Validity in Field Studies of Psychological Disorder. International Journal of Psychiatry 1:585–605.

DOLLARD, J., 1949 The Acquisition of New Social Habits. In The Science of Man in World Crisis. R. Linton, ed. New York: Columbia University Press.

DOLMAN, C. E., 1964 Botulism as a World Health Problem. In Botulism: Proceedings of a Symposium. K. H. Lewis and K. Cassel, eds. Cincinnati: U.S. Public Health Service.

DOOB, LEONARD W., 1965 Psychology. In The African World. R. A. Lystad, ed. New York: Praeger Publishers, Inc.

DORE, RONALD P., 1958 City Life in Japan. Berkeley: University of California Press.

DOUGLAS, MARY, 1970 Purity and Danger: An Analysis of Concepts of Pollution and Taboo. Harmondsworth, England: Penguin Books (orig. 1966).

———, 1970 Thirty Years After Witchcraft, Oracles and Magic Among the Azande. In Witchcraft Confessions and Accusations. M. Douglas, ed. London: A.S.A. Monograph 9.

DOUGLAS, W. 1969 Illness and Curing in Santiago Atitlan. Ph.D. dissertation. Stanford University. Stanford, California.

DOULL, J. A., 1950 Laws and Regulations Relating to Leprosy in the United States of America. International Journal of Leprosy 18:145–154.

DOWNS, JAMES F., 1961 Washo Religion. Anthropological Records 16:365–385.

———, 1963 Differential Response to White Contact: Paiute and Washo. In The Washo Indians of California and Nevada. W. L. d'Azevedo, ed. Salt Lake City.

———, 1966 The Two Worlds of the Washo. New York: Holt, Rinehart and Winston, Inc.

DREIZEN, S., R. M. SNODGRASSE, H. WEBB-PEPLOE, and T. D. SPIES, 1958 The Retarding Effect of Protracted Undernutrition on the Appearance of the Postnatal Ossification Centers in the Hand and Wrist. Human Biology 30:253–264.

DUBOIS, ABBE J., 1906 Hindu Manners, Customs and Ceremonies. London: Oxford University Press.

DUBOIS, CORA, 1941 Attitudes Toward Food and Hunger in Alor. In Language, Culture, and Personality. Leslie Spier et al., eds. Mensha, Wis.: Sapir Memorial Publication Fund.

DUBOS, RENÉ, 1959 Mirage of Health. New York: Harper & Row, Publishers, Inc.

———, 1965 Man Adapting. New Haven: Yale University Press.

DUGAL, L. P., and G. FORTIER, 1952 Ascorbic Acid and Acclimatization to Cold in Monkeys. Journal of Applied Physiology 5:143–146.

DUGUID, CHARLES, 1963 No Dying Race. Adelaide, Australia: Rigby Ltd.

DUMOND, DON E., 1965 Population Growth and Cultural Change. Southwestern Journal of Anthropology 21:302–324.

———, 1972 Population Growth and Political Centralization. In Population Growth: Anthropological Implications. B. Spooner, ed. Cambridge, Mass.: MIT Press.

DUMONT, L., and D. F. POCOCK, 1959 Contributions to Indian Sociology, No. III. The Hague: Mouton & Co.

DUNN, FREDERICK L., 1965 MSI Ecology, Acculturation and Parasitism in the Orang Asli of Malaya. Paper presented at meetings of Southwestern Anthropological Association, UCLA, Los Angeles. Unpublished.

———, 1965 On the Antiquity of Malaria in the Western Hemisphere. Human Biology 37:383–393.

———, 1966 Patterns of Parasitism in Primates. Folia Primatiologica 4:329–345.

———, 1968 Epidemiological Factors: Health and Disease in Hunter-Gatherers. In Man the Hunter. Richard B. Lee and Irven DeVore, eds. Chicago: Aldine Publishing Co.

———, n.d. Ecological Simplification, Parasitism and Primate Evolution. Paper presented at American Association for the Advancement of Science Meetings. Berkeley: Manuscript No. 2, Unpublished.

———, and J. M. BOLTON, 1963 The MIF Direct Smear (DS) Method in the Study of Intestinal Parasitism in Malay Aborigines. Singapore Medical Journal 4:175–176.

DURAND, JOHN D., 1967 A Long-range View of World Population Growth. Annals of the American Academy of Political and Social Science 369:1–8.

———, 1972 The Viewpoint of Historical Demography. In Population Growth: Anthropological Implications. B. Spooner, ed. Cambridge, Mass.: The MIT Press.

EATON, JOSEPH W., and ALBERT J. MAYER, 1953 The Social Biology of Very High Fertility Among the Hutterites: The Demography of a Unique Population. Human Biology 25:206–264.

EDGERTON, ROBERT B., 1966 Conceptions of Psychosis in Four East African Societies. American Anthropologist **68**:408–425.

———, ed. 1969 On the "Recognition" of Mental Illness. *In* Changing Perspectives in Mental Illness. Stanley C. Plog and Robert B. Edgerton, eds. New York: Holt, Rinehart and Winston, Inc.

EDSMAN, CARL-MARTIN, ed., 1967 Studies in Shamanism. Stockholm: Almquist & Wiksell.

EHRENREICH, BARBARA, and DEIDRE ENGLISH, 1973 Witches, Midwives, and Nurses: A History of Women Healers. Old Westbury, N.Y.: The Feminist Press.

EHRSTROM, M. CH., 1951 Medical Investigations in Northern Greenland. Acta Medica Scandinavica **140**:239–253.

ELBERT, S. H., 1947 Trukese–English and English–Trukese Dictionary. Pearl Harbor Naval Military Government. Honolulu.

ELGOOD, CYRIL, 1951 A Medical History of Persia and the Eastern Caliphate. Cambridge: Cambridge University Press.

ELIADE, MIRCEA, 1946 Shamanism: Archaic Techniques of Ecstasy. New York: Pantheon Books, Bollingen Series LXXVI.

ELKIN, A. P., 1964 The Australian Aborigines. Sydney, Australia: Angus and Robertson.

ELLENBERGER, H. F., 1951 Der Tod aus Psychischen Ursachen bei Naturvolken ("voodoo death"). Psyche **5**:333–344.

EMORY, H. L., 1946 Soybean Milk-Substitute as Used on Okinawa. U.S. Navy Medical Bulletin **46**:616–618.

ENGLEMANN, G. J., 1884 Labor Among Primitive Peoples. St. Louis.

ERASMUS, CHARLES J., 1961 Man Takes Control. Minneapolis: University of Minnesota Press.

———, 1952 Changing Folk Beliefs and the Relativity of Empirical Knowledge. Southwestern Journal of Anthropology **8**:411–428.

ERASMUS, DESIDERIUS, 1965 The Colloquies of Erasmus. trans. Thompson, Craig R. Chicago and London: University of Chicago Press.

ERST VERSLAG VAN VET ONDERZOCK NAAR DE PDANTEN STOFFEN VAN NEDERLANDSCH INDIE., 1890 Batavia: Hoofstuck.

EVANS-PRITCHARD· E. E., 1937 Witchcraft, Oracles, and Magic Among the Azande, London: Oxford University Press.

———, 1965 Theories of Primitive Religion. London: Oxford University Press.

EWALT, J. R., and D. L. FARNSWORTH, 1963 Textbook of Psychiatry. New York: McGraw-Hill, Inc.

EWING, H. E., 1924 Lice from Human Mummies. Science **60**:389–390.

———, 1926 American Lice of the genus *Pediculus*. Proceedings of the United States National Museum **68**:1–30.

EYESENCK, H. J., 1955 A Dynamic Theory of Anxiety and Hysteria. Journal of Mental Science **101**:28–51.

EYLES, D. E., 1963 The Species of Simian Malaria. Journal of Parasitology **49**:866–887.

FABREGA, HORACIO, and DUANE METZGER, 1968 Psychiatric Illness in a Small Ladino Community. Psychiatry **31**:339–351.

FABREGA, HORACIO JR., 1971 Some Features of Zinacantecan Medical Knowledge. Ethnology **10**:1–24.

———, 1972 Medical Anthropology. *In* Biennial Review of Anthropology. B. J. Siegel, ed. Stanford, Cal.: Stanford University Press.

———, and DANIEL SILVER, 1970 Some Social and Psychological Properties of Zinacanteco Shamans. Behavioral Science **15**:471–486.

———, and ———, 1973 Illness and Shamanistic Curing in Zinacantan: An Ethnomedical Analysis. Stanford, Cal.: Stanford University Press.

FAERGEMAN, P., 1963 Psychogenic Psychoses. London: Butterworth.

FANON, FRANZ, 1966 The Wretched of the Earth. New York: Grove Press, Inc.

FASAL, PAUL, E. FASAL, and L. LEVY, 1967 Leprosy Prophylaxis. Journal of the American Medical Association, **199**:905.

FAUNDES, A., and T. LUKKÄINEN, 1972 Health and Family Planning Services in the Chinese People's Republic. Studies in Family Planning. Supplement **3**:165–176.

FEINSTEIN, ALVAN R., 1967 Clinical Judgment. Baltimore: The Williams & Wilkins Co.

FENWICK, A., 1969 Baboons as Reservoir Hosts of Schistosoma Mansoni. Transactions of the Royal Society of Tropical Medicine and Hygiene **63**:557–563.

FIELD, MARK G., 1957 Doctor and Patient in Soviet Russia. Cambridge, Mass.: Harvard University Press.

FIELD, M. J., 1937 Religion and Medicine of the Gá People. London: Oxford University Press.

———, 1960 Search for Security: An Ethnopsychiatric Study of Rural Ghana. London: Faber & Faber, Ltd.

FIENNES, R., 1967 Zoonoses of Primates. Ithaca: Cornell University Press.

FINDLEY, P., 1933 The Story of Childbirth. New York.

FIRTH, RAYMOND, 1940 The Analysis of Mana: An Empirical Approach. Journal of the Polynesian Society **49**: 483–510.

———, 1957 Health Planning and Community Organization. Health Education Journal **15**: 118–125.

———, 1959 Acculturation in Relation to Concepts of Health and Disease. *In* Medicine and Anthropology. Iago Galdston, ed. New York: International Universities Press.

FISCHER, ANN, 1963 Reproduction in Truk. Ethnology **2**: 526–540.

———, and JOHN L. FISCHER, 1961 Culture and Epidemiology: A Theoretical Investigation of Kuru. Journal of Health and Human Behavior **2**: 16–25.

FISCHER, J. L., 1957 Totemism on Truk and Ponape. American Anthropologist **59**: 250–265.

FITZGERALD, OTHO W. S., 1948 Love Deprivation and the Hysterical Personality. The Journal of Mental Science **94**: 701–717.

FITZSIMMONS, CHARLES I., n.d. A Case Study of Susto in the Zapotec Pueblo of Teotitlan del Valle, Oaxaca, Mexico: A Theoretical Appraisal of Folk Illness as an Adaptation to Culturally Induced Psychological Stress. Unpublished Manuscript.

FLECK, A. C., and F. A. J. IANNI, 1958 Epidemiology and Anthropology: Some Suggested Affinities in Theory and Method. Human Organization **16**: 38–41.

FOGELSON, RAYMOND D., 1961 Change, Persistence, and Accommodation in Cherokee Medico-Magical Beliefs. *In* Symposium on Cherokee and Iroquois Culture. W. N. Fenton and J. Gulick, eds. Bureau of American Ethnology Bulletin **180**: 215–225.

FORD, CLELLAN S., 1945 A Comparative Study of Human Reproduction. New Haven: Yale University Publications in Anthropology **32**: 1–111.

———, 1964 A Comparative Study of Human Reproduction. New Haven: Yale University Publications in Anthropology No. 32 (orig. 1945), Reprinted by HRAF Press.

FORTUNE, REO., 1935 Manus Religion. Philadelphia: Philosophical Society.

FOSTER, GEORGE M., 1951 Some Wider Implications of Soul-Loss Illness Among the Sierra Popoluca. *In* Homenaje a Don Alfonso Casa, Mexico.

———, 1953 Relationships Between Spanish and Spanish American Folk Medicine. Journal of American Folklore **6**: 201–219.

———, 1953 Use of Anthropological Methods and Data in Planning and Operation. Public Health Reports **68**: 848.

———, 1955 Guidelines to Community Development Programs. Public Health Reports **60**: 19.

———, 1958 Problems in Interculture Health Practice. Pamphlet 12. New York: Social Science Research Council.

———, 1962 Traditional Cultures and the Impacts of Technological Change. New York: Harper & Row, Publishers, Inc.

———, 1967 Tzintzuntzan: Mexican Peasants in a Changing World. Boston: Little, Brown and Co.

———, 1972 The Anatomy of Envy: A study of Symbolic Behavior. Current Anthropology **13**: 165–186.

———, 1974 Medical Anthropology: Some Contrasts with Medical Sociology. Medical Anthropology Newsletter **6** (1): 1–6.

———, and J. H. ROWE, 1951 Suggestions for Field Recording of Information on Hippocratic Classification of Diseases and Remedies. Anthropological Society Papers **5**: 1–3.

FOULKES, EDWARD F., 1972 The Arctic Hysterias of the North Alaskan Eskimo. Anthropological Studies No. 10, American Anthropological Association.

FOX, JOHN P., CARRIE E. HALL, and LILA R. ELVEBACK, 1970 Epidemiology: Man and Disease. New York: Macmillan Publishing Co., Inc.

FOX, RENEÉ, 1968 Illness. *In* The International Encyclopedia of Social Sciences. New York: The Free Press.

FOX, T. F., 1960 Medical Care in China Today. Journal of Public Health **50**: 28.

———, 1975 The New China: Some Medical Impressions. The Lancet **9**: 935–939, **16**: 995–999, **23**: 1053–1057.

FRACASTORO, GIROLAMO, 1935 Frocastor, Syphilis or the French Disease, a Poem in Latin Hexameters. Trans. Wynne-Finch, Heneage. London: William Heinemann Medical Books, Ltd.

FRAKE, CHARLES O., 1957 Litigation in Lipay: A Study in Subanun Law. Bangkok: Proceedings of the Ninth Pacific Science Congress.

———, 1957 The Subanun of Zamboanga: A Linguistic Survey. Bangkok: Proceedings of the Ninth Science Congress.

———, 1961 The Diagnosis of Disease Among the Subanun of Mindanao. American Anthropologist. **63**: 113–132.

———, 1962 The Ethnographic Study of Cognitive Systems. Anthropology and Human Behavior,

Washington, D.C.: The Anthropological Society of Washington.

FRANCIS, THOMAS, JR., 1959 The Epidemiological Approach to Human Ecology. The American Journal of Medical Sciences **237**:677–684.

FRANK, JEROME, 1961 Persuasion and Healing. Baltimore: The Johns Hopkins Press.

FRAZER, JAMES G., 1951 The Golden Bough. (original published in 1890; first abridged by author in 1922). New York: Macmillan Publishing Co., Inc.

FREEDMAN, MAURICE, 1956 Health Education: How It Strikes an Anthropologist. Health Education Journal **14**:18–24.

———, 1957 Health Education and Self-Education. Health Education Journal **15**:78–83.

FREEDMAN, RONALD, 1961–62 The Sociology of Human Fertility. Current Sociology **10–11**:35–121.

FREIDSON, ELIOT, 1959 Specialties without Roots: The Utilization of New Services. Human Organization **18**:112–116.

———, 1960 Client Control and Medical Practice. American Journal of Sociology **65**:374–382.

———, 1961 The Organization of Medical Practice and Patient Behavior. American Journal of Public Health **51**:43–52.

———, 1970 Profession of Medicine: A Study of the Sociology of Applied Knowledge. New York: Dodd, Mead & Co.

FREILICH, MORRIS, 1964 The Natural Triad in Kinship and Complex Systems. American Sociological Review **29**:529–540.

———, 1968 The Anthropological Use of Role. Paper presented to the American Anthropological Association meetings. Seattle.

FREUD, ANNA, 1954 The Ego and the Mechanisms of Defense. London: Hogarth.

FREUD, SIGMUND, and J. BREUER, 1895 The Psychic Mechanism of Hysterical Phenomena. *In* Selected Papers on Hysterical and Other Psychoneuroses, 3rd ed., transl. by A. A. Brill. Nervous and Mental Disease Publishing Co.

———, 1920 My Views on the Role of Sexuality in the Etiology of the "Neuroses." Reprinted in Selected Papers on Hysteria and Other Psychoneuroses, Freud, Sigmund, (3rd enlarged ed.). Translated by A. A. Brill. Nervous and Mental Disease Publishing Co.

———, 1933 New Introductory Lectures on Psycho-Analysis. New York: W. W. Norton Co.

———, 1936 The Problem of Anxiety. Trans. H. A. Bunker. New York: W. W. Norton Co.

FRIBOURG-BLANC, A., G. NIEL, and H. H.

MOLLARET, 1963 Note sur quelques aspects immunologiques du cynocéphale africain. Bulletin de la Société de Pathologie Exotique **56**:474–485.

———, and H. H. MOLLARET, 1968 Natural Treponematosis of the African primate. Primates in Medicine **3**:110–118.

FRIED, MORTON H., 1968 Introduction to Chapters 5, 6, and 7, *in* Readings in Anthropology—Cultural Anthropology, Vol. 2 (2nd ed.). New York: Thomas Y. Crowell & Co.

FRIEDMAN, M., R. H. ROSEMAN, and V. CARROLL, 1958 Changes in the Serum Cholesterol and Blood Clotting Time in Men Subjected to Cyclic Variation of Occupational Stress. Circulation **17**:852–861.

———, and ———, 1959 Association of Specific Overt Behavior Pattern with Blood and Cardiovascular Findings. Journal of the American Medical Association **169**:1286–1296.

FRY, G. F., and J. G. MOORE, 1970 Enterobius Vermicularis: 10,000-Year-Old Infection. Science **166**:1620.

FUCHS, STEPHEN, 1964 Magic Healing Techniques Among the Balahis in Central India, *in* Ari Kiev (ed.): Magic, Faith, and Healing. New York: The Free Press.

FUNKE, 1879 Der Tastsinn und die Gemeingefühle. Handbuch der Physiologie der Sinnesorgane. L. Hermann, ed.

FERNEA, ROBERT, and J. G. KENNEDY, 1966 Initial Adaptions to Resettlement: A New Life for Egyptian Nubians. Current Anthropology **7**.

FERNEA, ROBERT, ed., 1966 Symposium on Contemporary Nubia. New Haven, Conn.: Harflex.

GADJUSEK, D. C., 1963 Kuru. Transactions of the Royal Society of Tropical Medicine and Hygiene **57**:151–166.

GALDSTON, IAGO, ed., 1959 Introduction. Medicine and Anthropology. New York: International Universities Press.

———, ed., 1963 Retrospect and Prospect. *In* Man's Image in Medicine and Anthropology. New York: International Universities Press.

GARNHAM, P. C. C., 1963 Distribution of Simian Parasites in Various Hosts. Journal of Parasitology **49**:905–911.

GARRISON, F. HARRISON, 1914 An Introduction to the History of Medicine. Philadelphia.

———, 1933 Quackery and Primitive Medicine. New York Academy of Medicine Bulletin pp. 601ff.

GEERTZ, CLIFFORD, 1960 The Javanese Kijaji: The Changing Role of a Cultural Broker.

Comparative Studies in Society and History **2**:228–249.

———, 1960 The Religion of Java. New York: The Free Press.

———, 1962 The Growth of Culture and the Evolution of Mind. *In* Theories of the Mind. Jordan Scher, ed. New York: The Free Press.

———, 1963 Agricultural Involution. Berkeley: University of California Press.

GEIGER, H. JACK, 1972 Putting China's Medicine in Perspective . Medical World News **14**:43–49.

———, 1973 A Pragmatic Approach to Medicine. Medical World News **14**:22–25.

GELFAND, S., 1964 The Relationship of Experimental Pain Tolerance to Pain Threshold. Canadian Journal of Psychology **18**:36–42.

GELLHORN, ERNST, 1970 The Emotions and the Ergotropic and Trophotropic Systems. Psycholische Forschung **34**:48–94.

———, and G. N. LOOFBOURROW, 1963 Emotions and Emotional Disorders: A Neurological Study. New York: Harper & Row Publishers, Inc.

———, and WILLIAM F. KIELY, 1973 Autonomic Nervous System in Psychiatry. Joseph Mendels, ed. New York: John Wiley & Sons, Inc.

———, and ———, 1972 Mystical States of Consciousness: Neurophysiological and Clinical Aspects. Journal of Nervous and Mental Disease **154**:399–405.

Genetics and Infection. 1969 British Medical Journal **2**:317–318.

GIBBS, C. J., and D. C. GAJDUSEK, 1970 Kuru: Pathogenesis and Isolation of Virus. American Journal of Tropical Medicine and Hygiene **19**:138–318.

GIBSON, G., 1972 Chinese Medical Practice and the Thoughts of Chairman Mao. Social Science and Medicine **6**:67–93.

GILLIN, JOHN P., 1947 Moche: A Peruvian Coastal Community. Publications of the Institute of Social Anthropology. Washington, D.C.: Smithsonian Institute.

———, 1948 Magical Fright. Psychiatry **11**:387–400.

———, 1948 The Ways of Men. New York: Appleton-Century-Crofts.

———, 1951 The Culture of Security in San Carlos. Middle American Research Institute, publication 16. New Orleans: Tulane University Press.

———, 1956 The Making of a Witch-Doctor. Psychiatry **19**:131–136.

GILLMAN, J., and T. GILLMAN, 1951 Perspectives in Human Malnutrition. New York: Grune & Stratton, Inc.

GLADWIN, THOMAS, and SEYMOUR B. SARASON, 1953 Truki Man in Paradise. Viking Fund Publications in Anthropology **20**:1–655.

GLASER, BARNEY G., and AHSELM L. STRAUSS, 1964 Awareness Contexts and Social Interaction. American Sociological Review **29**:669–679.

GLASS, D. V., 1972 General Introduction. Population and Social Change. D. V. Glass and Roger Revelle, eds. London: Edward Arnold.

GLICK, LEONARD B., 1963 Foundations of a Primitive Medical System: The Gimi of the New Guinea Highlands. Unpublished doctoral dissertation, University of Pennsylvania.

———, 1967 Medicine as an Ethnographic Category: The Gimi of the New Guinea Highlands. Ethnology **6**:31–56.

———, 1968 Possession in the New Guinea Highlands. Transcultural Psychiatric Research **5**:200–205.

———, 1972 Sangguama. Encyclopedia of Papua and New Guinea. Melbourne.

GLUCKMAN, MAX, 1955 The Judicial Process Among the Barotse of Northern Rhodesia. Manchester, England: Manchester University Press.

GODKINS, T. R., W. D. STANHOPE, and T. N. LYNN, 1974 Current Stratus of the Physician's Assistant in Oklahoma. Journal of Oklahoma Medical Association **67**:102–107.

GOFFMAN, ERVING, 1955 On Face-work. Psychiatry **18**:213–231.

———, 1959 The Presentation of Self in Everyday Life. Garden City, N.Y.: Anchor Books.

———, 1963 Stigma, Englewood Cliffs, N.J.: Prentice-Hall, Inc.

———, 1967 Interaction Ritual. Garden City, N.Y.: Doubleday & Co., Inc.

GOLDENWEISER, A. A., 1922 Early Civilization. London.

GOLDSCHEIDER, A., 1884 Die Specifische Energie der Gefühesnerven der Haut. Monatschruft für Prakätsche Dermatologie **3**:283.

GOLDSCHMIDT, WALTER, and ROBERT EDGERTON, 1961 A Picture Test of Values. American Anthropologist **62**:26–47.

GOLDSTEIN, MARCUS S., 1957 Skeletal Pathology of Early Indians in Texas. American Journal of Physical Anthropology **15**:299–311.

———, 1963 The Paleopathology of Human Skeletal Remains. *In* Science in Archaeology. Don Brothwell and Eric Higgs, eds. New York: Basic Books, Inc.

GONZALES, NANCIE SOLIEN, 1966 Health Behavior in Cross-Cultural Perspective: A Guatemalan Example. Human Organization 25:122–125.

———, 1969 Beliefs and Practices Concerning Medicine and Nutrition Among Lower-Class Urban Guatemalans. In The Cross-Cultural Approach to Health Behavior. L. R. Lynch, ed. Rutherford, N. J.: Fairleigh Dickinson University Press.

GOODE, WILLIAM J., 1951 Religion Among Primitives. New York: The Free Press.

———, 1960 A Theory of Role Strain. American Sociological Review 25:483–496.

GOODENOUGH, WARD H., 1951 Property, Kin, and Community on Truk. Yale University Publications in Anthropology 46:1–192.

———, 1956 Componential Analysis and the Study of Meaning. Language 32:195–216.

———, 1963 Cooperation in Change: An Anthropological Approach to Community Development. New York: Russell Sage Foundation.

———, 1965 Rethinking "Status" and "Role": Towards a General Model of the Cultural Organization of Social Relationships. In The Relevance of Models for Social Anthropology. Max Gluckman and Fred Eggan, eds. A.S.A. Monographs. London: Tavistock Publications, Ltd.

———, 1965 Yankee Kinship Terminology: A Problem in Componential Analysis. American Anthropologist 67:259–287.

GORDON, JOHN E., 1952 Ecological Investigation of Disease. New York: Milbank Memorial Fund.

———, 1958 Medical Ecology and the Public Health. American Journal of the Medical Sciences 235:337–359.

GOULD, HAROLD A., 1957 The Implications of Technological Change for Folk and Scientific Medicine. American Anthropologist LIX: 507–516.

———, 1965 Modern Medicine and Folk Cognition in Rural India. Human Organization 24:201–208.

GOUROU, P., 1956 The Quality of Land Use by Tropical Cultivators. In Man's Role in Changing the Face of the Earth. W. L. Thomas, ed., Chicago: University of Chicago Press.

GOWAN, J. W., 1948 Inheritance of Immunity in Animals. Annual Review of Microbiology 2:215–254.

———, 1951 Genetics and Disease Resistance. In Genetics in the 20th Century. New York: Macmillan Publishing Co., Inc.

GRAHAM, SAXON, 1963 Social Factors in Relation to the Chronic Illness. In Handbook of Medical Sociology. H. E. Freeman, S. Levine, and L. G. Reeder, eds. Englewood Cliffs, N.J.: Prentice-Hall, Inc.

GRAHAM, D. T., S. WOLF, and H. G. WOLFF, 1950 Changes in Tissue Sensitivity Associated with Varying Life Situations and Emotions. American Journal of Allergy 21:478–486.

GRAMSCI, A., 1971 Selections from Prison Notebooks. Q. Hoare and G. N. Smith, eds., trans. London: Lawrence and Wishart.

GREEN, D. L., and GEORGE J. ARMELAGOS, 1972 Mesolithic Population from Wadi Halfa. University of Massachusetts, Department of Anthropology Research Reports No. 11.

GREENE, D. L., G. W. EWING, and GEORGE J. ARMELAGOS, 1967 Dentition of a Mesolithic Population from Wadi Halfa, Sudan. American Journal of Physical Anthropology 27:41–56.

GREENWOOD, MAJOR, 1935 Epidemic and Crowd Diseases. New York: Macmillan Publishing Co., Inc.

GREGG, ALAN, 1956 The Future Health Officer's Responsibility: Past, Present and Future. American Journal of Public Health 46:1384–1389.

GREULICH, W. W., and S. I. PYLE, 1959 Radiocarbon Atlas of Skeletal Development of the Hand and Wrist. Stanford, Cal.: Stanford University Press.

GRINGRAS, G., and D. A. GEEKIE, 1973 China Report. Canadian Medical Association Journal 109:150A–150P.

GUERRA, F., 1964 Maya Medicine. Medical History 7:31.

———, 1969 Discussion. In Medicine and Culture. F. N. L. Poynter, ed. Publications of the Wellcome Institute of the History of Medicine. XV (n.s.).

GUILLOUD, N., 1965 Paralytic Poliomyelitis Among Primates. Florida: Communicable Disease Center. U.S. Public Health Service. Poliomyelitis Surveillance Report, No. 286.

GUINDI, FADWA, 1967 Rituals of the River in Dahmit. In Symposium on Contemporary Nubia. R. Furnea, ed. New Haven, Conn.: Harflex.

GUINEE, V. F. et al., 1963 A Collaborative Study of Measles Vaccines in Five United States Communities. American Journal of Public Health 53:645–651.

GUITERAS-HOLMES, C., 1961 Perils of the Soul. New York.

GULLIVER, PHILIP H., 1955 The Family Herds. London: Routledge and Kegan Paul, Ltd.

GUSSOW, ZACHARY, 1960 Pibloktoq (Hysteria) Among the Polar Eskimo: An Ethnopsychiatric Study. Psychoanalytic Study of Personality I: 218–236. New York: International Universities Press.

———, 1963 A Preliminary Report of Kayak-Angst Among the Eskimo of West Greenland: A study in Sensory Deprivation. International Journal of Social Psychiatry 9: 9–18.

———, 1964 Behavorial Research in Chronic Disease: A Study of Leprosy. Journal of Chronic Diseases 17: 179–189.

———, and G. S. TRACY, 1965 Strategies in the Management of Stigma: Concealing and Revealing by Leprosy Patients in the United States. (mimeographed).

———, and ———, 1969 Disability, Disfigurement, and Stigma. A Brief Overview. Proceedings of the Leonard Wood Memorial Seminar on Combating Stigma Resulting from Deformity and Disease. New York: Leonard Wood Memorial for the Eradication of Leprosy.

———, and ———, 1970 Stigma and the Leprosy Phenomenon: The Social History of a Disease in the Nineteenth and Twentieth Centuries. Bulletin of the History of Medicine 44: 425–449.

———, and ———, 1971 The Use of Archival Materials in the Analysis and Interpretation of Field Data: A Case Study in the Institutionalization of the Myth of Leprosy as "Leper." American Anthropologist 73: 695–709.

———, and ———, 1972 The Phenomenon of Leprosy Stigma in the Continental United States. Leprosy Review 43: 85–93.

———, and A. R. GUSSOW, 1974 Health Services and Decolonization in Tanzania. Paper presented at the annual meeting of the Society for Applied Anthropology. Boston, Massachusetts. (Mimeo).

GUTHE, THORSTEIN, 1960 The Treponematoses as a World Problem. British Journal of Venereal Diseases 36: 67–77.

GUTIERREZ, VIRGINIA DE PINEDA, 1961 La Medicina Popular en Colombia; Razones de su Arriago. Monografias Sociological, No. 8. Bogota: University Nacional de Colombia.

GWEE, A. L., 1963 Koro—A Cultural Disease. Singapore Medical Journal 4: 119–122.

HABERLAND, E., 1963 Galla Süd-Aethiopiens. Stuttgart.

HACKETT, C. J., 1963 On the Origin of Human Treponematoses. Bulletin of the World Health Organization 29: 7–41.

HAHON, N., 1961 Pox and Related Poxvirus Infections in the Simian Host. Bacteriological Reviews 25: 459–476.

HALDANE, J. B. S., 1957 Natural Selection in Man. Acta Genetica et Statistica Medica (Basel) 6: 321–332.

HALL, K. R. L., and IRVEN DeVORE, 1965 Baboon Social Behavior. In Primate Behavior. I. DeVore, ed. New York: Holt, Rinehart and Winston, Inc.

HALLIDAY, JAMES L., 1948 Psychosocial Medicine. New York: W. W. Norton & Co., Inc.

HALLOWELL, A. IRVING, 1934 Culture and Mental Disorder. Journal of Abnormal and Social Psychology 29: 1–9.

———, 1935 Primitive Concepts of Disease. American Anthropologist 37: 365–368.

———, 1939 Sin, Sex, and Sickness in Saulteaux Belief. British Journal of Medical Psychology XVIII: 191–197.

———, 1940 Aggression in Saulteaux Society. Psychiatry 3: 395–407.

———, 1942 The Role of Conjuring in Salteaux Society. Philadelphia: University of Pennsylvania Press.

———, 1946 Some Psychological Characteristics of the Northeastern Indians. In Man in Northeastern America. Frederick Johnson, ed. Andover Papers of the Robert S. Peabody Foundation for Archeology 3.

———, 1947 Myth, Culture, and Personality. American Anthropologist 49: 544–556.

———, 1950 Values, Acculturation and Mental Health. American Journal of Orthopsychiatry 20: 732–743.

———, 1954 The Ojibwa Self and Its Behavioral Environment. Explorations 2: 105–165.

———, 1955 Culture and Experience. Philadelphia: University of Pennsylvania Press.

———, 1960 Ojibwa Ontology, Behavior and World View. In Culture in History. S. Diamond, ed. New York: Columbia University Press.

———, 1963 Ojibwa World View and Disease. In Man's Image in Medicine and Anthropology. Iago Galdston, ed. New York: International Universities Press.

———, 1971 The Role of Conjuring in Salteaux Society. New York: Octagon Books.

HALPERN, JOEL M., 1963 Traditional Medicine and the Role of the Phi in Laos. Eastern Anthropologist 16: 191–200.

HANDELMAN, DON, 1972 Aspects of the Moral Compact of a Washo Shaman. Anthropological Quarterly 45: 84–101.

HARDY, J. D., HAROLD G. WOLFF, and H. GOODELL, 1940 Studies on Pain. A New Method for

Measuring Pain Threshold: Observations on the Spatial Summation of Pain. Journal of Clinical Investigation **19**:649–657.

——, ——, and ——, 1952 Pain Sensations and Reactions. Baltimore: The Williams & Wilkins Co.

HARING, DOUGLAS, ed., 1956 Personal Character and Cultural Milieu. Syracuse: Syracuse University Press (3rd rev. ed.).

HARLEY, GEORGE WAY, 1941 Native African Medicine, with Special Reference to Its Practice in the Mano Tribe of Liberia. Cambridge, Mass.: Harvard University Press.

HARNER, MICHAEL J., ed., 1973 Hallucinogens and Shamanism. New York: Oxford University Press.

HARRIS, MARVIN, 1964 Patterns of Race in the Americas. New York: Walker and Co., Inc.

HART, DONN V., PHYA ANUMAN RAJADHON, and RICHARD J. COUGLIN, 1965 Southeast Asian Birth Customs: Three Studies in Human Reproduction. New Haven, Conn.: HRAF Press.

——, 1969 Bisayan Filipino and Malayan Humoral Pathologies: Folk Medicine and Ethnohistory in Southeast Asia. Southeast Asia Program, data paper no. 76. Ithaca: Department of Asian Studies, Cornell University.

HARTLAND, E. S. et al., n.d. Birth. Hastings Encyclopedia of Religion and Ethics **2**:635–643.

——, 1909 Primitive Paternity. London: Publications of the Folklore Society LXIII.

HARWOOD, ALAN, 1971 The Hot-Cold Theory of Disease: Implications for Treatment of Puerto Rican Patients. The Journal of the American Medical Association **216**:1153–1158.

HASAN, KHWAJA A., 1975 What Is Medical Anthropology? Medical Anthropology Newsletter **6**(3)7–10.

HASSAN, FEKRI A., 1973 On Mechanisms of Population Growth During the Neolithic. Current Anthropology **14**(5):535–540.

HAYGARTH, J., 1793 A Sketch of a Plan to Exterminate the Casual Smallpox from Great Britain and to Introduce General Inoculation. London.

HEGNER, R., and H. J. CHU, 1928 Evolutionary Significance of the Protozoal Parasites of Monkeys and Man. Quantitative Review of Biology **3**:225–244.

——, and ——, 1930 Protozoal Infections of 44 Wild Philippine Monkeys. American Journal of Hygiene **12**:62.

HELGASON, T., 1964 Epidemiology of Mental Disorders in Iceland. Acta Psychiatrica Scandinavia Supplement, **73**.

HELM, JUNE, PAUL BOHANNAN, and MARSHALL D. SAHLINS, eds., 1965 Essays in Economic Anthropology. Proceedings of the American Ethnological Society. Seattle, Wash.: University of Washington Press.

HENDRICKSON, G. L., 1934 The "syphilis" of Girolamo Fracastoro with Some Observations on the Origin and History of the Word "Syphilis." Bulletin of the History of Medicine **2**:515–546.

HENRY, LOUIS, 1961 Some Data on Natural Fertility. Eugenics Quarterly **8**:81–91.

HENSCHEN, FOLKE, 1966 The History of Geography of Disease. Trans. Joan Tate. New York: Delacorte Press.

HES, JOSEF PH., 1964 The Changing Social Role of the Yemenite Mori. In Magic, Faith, and Healing. Ari Kiev, ed. New York: The Free Press.

HILLIS, W. D., 1961 Infectious Hepatitis from Chimpanzees. American Journal of Hygiene **73**:316.

HIMES, NORMAN E., 1970 Medical History of Contraception. New York: Schocken Books (orig. 1935, The Williams & Wilkins Co.).

HIRSCH, A., 1883 Handbook of Geographic and Historical Pathology. London: New Sydenham Society.

HOBSON, W., ed., 1965 The Theory and Practice of Public Health. 2nd ed. London: Oxford University Press.

HOCHSTRASSER, DONALD L., and JESSE W. TAPP, JR., 1970 Social Anthropology and Public Health. In Anthropology and the Behavioral and Health Sciences. O. VonMering and L. Kasden, eds. Pittsburgh: University of Pittsburgh Press.

HOEPPLI, R., 1959 Parasites and Parasitic Infections in Early Medicine and Science. Singapore: University of Malaya Press.

HOLCOMB, RICHMOND, 1936 Ruiz Díaz de Isla and the Haitian Myth of European Syphilis. Medical Life **43**:270–316, 318–364, 415–470, 487–514.

——, 1944 Letter to the editor, dated 14 March. American Journal of Syphilis, Gonorrhea and Venereal Disease **28**:515.

HOLDRIDGE, L. R., 1965 The Tropics, a Misunderstood Ecosystem. Association for Tropical Biology Bulletin **5**:21–30.

HOLLAND, WILLIAM R., 1962 Highland Maya Folk Medicine: A Study of Culture Change. Ph.D. dissertation. Tuscon: University of Arizona.

HOLLANDER, E., 1939 A Clinical Gauge for Sensitivity to Pain. Journal of Laboratory and Clinical Medicine **24**:537–538.

HOLM, GUSTAV, 1914 Ethnographic Sketch of the

Angmagsalik Eskimo. *In* The Ammassalik Eskimo. William Thalbitzer, ed. Meddelelser om Grønland **39**:1.

HONIGFELD, GILBERT, 1964 Non-specific Factors in Treatment. Diseases of the Nervous System **25**:145–156, 225–239.

HONIGMANN, JOHN J., 1959 The World of Man. New York: Harper & Row, Publishers, Inc.

———, 1960 Review of M. K. Opler, ed., Culture and Mental Health. American Anthropologist **62**:920–923.

———, 1967 Personality in Culture. New York: Harper & Row, Publishers, Inc.

———, and IRMA HONIGMANN, 1959 Notes on Great Whale River Ethos. Anthropologica **1**:106–121.

HOOTON, ERNEST A., 1930 The Indians of Petos Pueblos. New Haven: Yale University Press.

———, 1946 Up from the Ape. New York: Macmillan Publishing Co., Inc.

HORDERN, ANTHONY, 1968 Psychopharmacology: Some Historical Considerations. *In* Psychopharmacology: Dimensions and Perspectives. C. R. B. Joyce, ed. London: Tavistock Publications, Ltd.

HORN, J. S., 1972a Away With All Pests: An English Surgeon in People's China, 1954–1969. New York: Bantam Books, Inc.

———, 1972b Building a Rural Health Service in the People's Republic of China. International Journal of Health Services **2**:377–383.

HORTON, ROBIN, 1970 African Traditional Thought and Western Science. *In* Witchcraft and Sorcery. Max Marwick, ed. Harmondsworth, Middlesex, England: Penguin Books.

HOWE, P. E., n.d. Growth of the Adolescent Child as Affected by Restricted Nutrition. (Manuscript).

———, and M. SCHILLER, 1952 Growth Responses of the School Child to Changes in Diet and Environmental Factors. Journal of Applied Physiology **5**:51–61.

HOWELL, NANCY, (In Press) The Population of the Dobe Area !Kung Bushman (Zun/Wasi). *In* Kalahari Hunter-Gatherers. R. B. Lee and I. DeVore, eds. Cambridge, Mass: Harvard University Press.

HRDLIČKA, A., 1941 The Eskimo Child. Annual Report of the Smithsonian Institute. Washington, D.C.: U.S. Government Printing Office.

———, 1945 The Aleutian and Commander Islands. Philadelphia: Wistar Inst. of Anatomy and Biology.

HSU, FRANCIS L. K., 1952 Religion, Science, and Human Crises. London: Routledge and Kegan Paul, Ltd.

———, ed. 1972 Psychological Anthropology. Cambridge, Mass.: Schenkman Publishing Co. (new ed.).

HSU, R. C., 1974 The Barefoot Doctors of the People's Republic of China—Some Problems. New England Journal of Medicine **291**:124–127.

HUARD, PAR P., 1956 La syphilis vue par les médicins Arabo-Persians, Indiens et Sino-Japonais du XV and XVI siecles. Histoire de la Médicine **6**:9–13.

HUARD, PIERRE, 1969 Western Medicine and Afro-Asian Ethnic Medicine. *In* Medicine and Culture. F. N. L. Poynter, ed. London: Wellcome Institute of the History of Medicine.

———, and MING, WONG, 1968 Chinese Medicine. New York: McGraw-Hill, Inc.

HUBBLE, DOUGLAS, 1969 Discussion. Medicine and Culture. F. N. L. Poynter, ed. London: Wellcome Institute of the History of Medicine.

HUDSON, E. H., 1963 Treponematosis and Anthropology. Annals of International Medicine **58**:1037–1048.

———, 1964 Treponematosis and African Slavery. British Journal of Venereal Disease **40**:43–52.

———, 1965 Treponematosis and Man's Social Evolution. American Anthropologist **67**:885–901.

———, 1965 Treponematosis in Perspective. Bulletin of the World Health Organization **32**:735–748.

HUGHES, CHARLES, 1958 Anomie, the Ammassalik, and the Standardization of error. Southwestern Journal of Anthropology **14**:352–377.

———, 1963 Public Health in Non-Literate Societies. *In* Man's Image in Medicine and Anthropology. Iago Galdston, ed. New York: International Universities Press.

———, 1965 Under Four Flags: Recent Culture Change Among the Eskimo. Current Anthropology **6**:3–69.

———, 1968 Ethnomedicine. *In* International Encyclopedia of the Social Sciences. New York: The Free Press.

———, and JOHN M. HUNTER, 1970 Disease and Development in Africa. Social Science and Medicine **3**:443–493.

HULL, R. N., J. R. MINNER, and C. C. MASCOLL, 1958 Simian Viruses. American Journal of Hygiene **68**:31.

HULL, R. N., and A. NASH, 1960 Experimental Immunization Against B Virus. American Journal of Hygiene **71**:15.

HULSE, FREDERICK S., 1955 Technological Advance

and Major Racial Stocks. Human Biology 27:184–192.

HUMBOLDT, ALEXANDER VON, 1811 Political Essay on the Kingdom of New Spain. Trans. from French by John Black. New York.

HUNT, ROBERT, ed., 1967 Personalities and Cultures. Garden City, N.Y.: Natural History Press. (Doubleday).

———, 1968 Agentes Culturales Mestizos: Estabilidad y Cambio en Oaxaca. América Indígena 28:595–609.

HUNTINGFORD, G. W. B., 1953 The Nandi of Kenya. London: Routledge and Kegan Paul, Ltd.

———, 1953 The Southern Nilo-Hamites. London: International African Institute.

HUTT, A. McD., and G. BROWN, 1935 Anthropology in Action. London: Oxford University Press.

HUTT, F. B., 1963 Comment in Genetic Systems Involved in Disease Susceptibility in Mammals. A. Motulsky, ed. Genetic Selection in Man. Third Macy Conference on Genetics. J. W. Schull. Ann Arbor: University of Michigan Press.

HUTTEN, ULRICH VON, 1540 Of the Wood Called Guaiaeum. London. Thomas Bertheletregii.

INGHAM, JOHN M., 1970 On Mexican Folk Medicine. American Anthropologist 72:76–87.

INGMAN, S., and A. THOMAS, eds. 1975 Topias and Utopias in Health. The Hague. Mounton & Co.

ISENBERG, MAX, 1940 Syphilis in the Eighteenth and Early Nineteenth Centuries. Medical Record 152:456–460.

IVANOVSKY, A., 1923 Physical Modifications of the Population of Russia Under Famine. American Journal of Physical Anthropology 6:331–353.

JACO, E. GARTLEY, 1958 Introductory: Medicine and Behavioral Science. In Patients, Physicians, and Illness. E. G. Jaco, ed. New York: The Free Press.

JAHODA, GUSTAV, 1961 Traditional Healers and Other Institutions Concerned with Mental Illness in Ghana. International Journal of Social Psychiatry 7:245–268.

JANNSENS, PAUL A., 1970 Palaeopathology: Diseases and Injuries of Prehistoric Man. London: John Baker Publishers, Ltd.

JARCHO, J., 1934 Postures and Practices During Labor Among Primitive Peoples. New York.

JARCHO, SAUL, 1964 Some Observations on Diseases in Prehistoric America. Bulletin of the History of Medicine 38:1–19.

———, ed. 1966 Human Paleopathology. New Haven: Yale University Press.

JASPERS, K., 1962 General Psychopathology. Trans.

M. W. Hamilton and J. Hoenig. Manchester: Manchester University Press.

JEANSELME, ED, 1931 Traité de la syphilis. Paris. G. Doin et Cie.

JELLIFFE, D. B., 1956 Cultural Variation and the Practical Pediatrician. Journal of Pediatrics 49:661–671.

———, WOODBURN, J., F. J. BENNETT, and E. F. P. JELLIFFE, 1962 The Children of the Hadza Hunters. Tropical Pediatrics 60:907–913.

JENNESS, DIAMOND, 1922 The Life of the Copper Eskimo. Canadian Arctic Expedition. Ottawa.

———, 1959 The People of the Twilight. Phoenix Books. Chicago: The University of Chicago Press, (copyright 1928 by Macmillan Publishing Co., New York).

JOCHELSON, WALDEMAR, 1905–1908 The Koryak. Publications of the Jesup North Pacific Expedition, 6.

———, 1910 The Yukaghir and the Yukaghirized Tungus. Publications of the Jesup North Pacific Expedition, 9.

JOHNSON, H. M., 1964 The Kahuna Hawaiian Sorcerer. Archives of Dermatology. 90:530–535.

JOHNSON, L. C., and N. L. CORAH, 1963 Racial Differences in Skin Resistance. Science 139:766–767.

JOHNSTON, FRANCIS E., and CHARLES E. SNOW, 1961 The Reassessment of the Age and Sex of the Indian Knoll Skeletal Population: Demographic and Methodological Aspects. American Journal of Physical Anthropology 19:237–244.

JOHNWICK, E. B., 1961 A Reply to Lowinger's Article on Leprosy and Psychosis. International Journal of Leprosy 29:110–111.

JONES, IVOR H., 1968 Subincision Among Australian Western Desert Aborigines. British Journal of Medical Psychology.

JOOS, M., 1958 Semology: A Linguistic Theory of Meaning. Study in Linguistics 13:53–70.

JOS, EMILIANO, 1942 Centenario de Fernando Colón: en fermedad de Martín Alonso. Revista de Indias 3:85–110.

JUNG, CARL, 1928 Contributions to Analytical Psychology. New York: Harcourt Brace Jovanovich.

———, 1928 Two Essays on Analytical Psychology. New York: Dodd, Mead & Co.

JUNOD, H. A., 1927 The Life of a South African Tribe. London. Two volumes.

KALLMAN, F. J., 1959 The Genetics of Mental Illness. In American Handbook of Psychiatry. S. Arieti, ed. New York: Basic Books, Inc.

537

KAPLAN, BERT, 1961 Studying Personality Cross-Culturally. New York: Harper & Row, Publishers, Inc.

KAPLAN, DAVID, and ROBERT MANNERS, 1972 Culture Theory. Englewood Cliffs, N.J.: Prentice-Hall, Inc.

KARDINER, A., 1959 Traumatic Neurosis of War. In American Handbook of Psychiatry. vol. 1. A. Arieti, ed. New York. Basic Books, Inc.

KATZ, SOLOMON H., and ANTHONY WALLACE, 1974 An Anthropological Perspective on Behavior and Disease. American Journal of Public Health 64: 1050–1052.

KAUFMAN, WILLIAM, 1952 Self-Inflicted Food-Induced Allergic Illness. Annals of Allergy 10: 308–323.

———, 1954 Some Psychosomatic Aspects of Food Allergy. Psychosomatic Medicine 16: 12–36.

KEBLE, S. A., G. J. CHRISTOFINIS, and W. WOOD, 1958 Natural Virus B. Infection in Rhesus Monkeys. Journal of Pathology and Bacteriology 76: 189–199.

KEESING, ROGER M., 1970 Toward a Model of Role Analysis. In A Handbook of Method in Cultural Anthropology. Raoul Naroll and Ronald Cohen, eds. Garden City, N.Y.: Natural History Press.

KELLY, G., 1955 The Psychology of Personal Constructs. New York: W. W. Norton & Co., Inc. vol. 1.

KELLY, ISABEL, 1965 Folk Practices in North Mexico. Austin: University of Texas Press.

KENNEDY, JOHN G., 1969 Psychosocial Dynamics of Witchcraft Systems. International Journal of Social Psychiatry 15(3): 165–178.

KENYON, F. E., 1966 Hypochondriasis: A Survey of Some Historical, Clinical, and Social Aspects. International Journal of Psychiatry 2: 308–334.

KENYON, KATHLEEN M., 1960 Archeology in the Holy Land. New York: Praeger Publishers, Inc.

KESSEL, J. F., 1928 Intestinal Protozoa of Monkeys. Zoology 31: 275–306.

KESSEN, W., 1974 An American Glimpse of Children of China. Items 28: 41–44.

KEYS, A., 1950 The Residues of Malnutrition and Starvation. Science 112: 371–373.

KIDSON, Malcolm A., 1967 Psychiatric Disorders in the Walbiri, Central Australia. Australian New Zealand Journal of Psychiatry 1: 14–22.

KIELY, William F., 1974 From the Symbolic Stimulus to the Pathological Response: Neurophysiological Mechanisms. International Journal of Psychiatry in Medicine 5: 517–529.

KIEV, Ari, ed., 1964 Magic, Faith, and Healing: Primitive Psychiatry Today. New York: The Free Press.

———, 1964 The Study of Folk Psychiatry. In Magic, Faith and Healing. Ari Kiev, ed. New York: The Free Press.

———, 1966 Obstacles to Medical Progress in Haiti. Human Organization 25: 10–15.

———, 1968 Curanderismo: Mexican-American Folk Psychiatry. New York: The Free Press.

KILBOURNE, E. D., 1968 Recombination of Influenza A Viruses of Human and Animal Origin. Science 160: 74.

KING, STANLEY H., 1955 Psychosocial Factors Associated with Rheumatoid Arthritis. Journal of Chronic Diseases 2: 287–302.

———, 1963 Social Psychological Factors in Illness. In Handbook of Medical Sociology. H. E. Freeman, S. Levine, and L. G. Reeder, eds. Englewood Cliffs, N.J.: Prentice-Hall, Inc.

KLUCKHOHN, CLYDE, 1944 Navaho Witchcraft. Papers. Peabody Museum of American Archaeology and Ethnology.

———, 1962 Navaho Witchcraft. Boston: Beacon Press. (orig. 1944)

———, HENRY A. MURRAY, and DAVID M. SCHNEIDER, eds., 1953 Personality in Nature, Society, and Culture. (rev. ed.) New York: Alfred A. Knopf, Inc.

———, and DOROTHEA LEIGHTON 1962 The Navajo. Garden City. N.Y.: Natural History Press. Doubleday. (1st pub. 1947).

KOLATA, GINA BARI, 1974 !Kung Hunter-Gatherers: Feminism, Diet, and Birth Control. Science 185: 932–934.

KORITSCHONER, H., 1936 Ngoma Ya Sheitani. An East African Native Treatment for Psychiatric Disorder. Journal of the Royal Anthropological Institute 66: 209–219.

KOSA, JOHN, AARON ANTONOVSKY, and IRVING K. ZOLA, eds., 1969 Poverty and Health: A Sociological Analysis. Cambridge, Mass.: Harvard University Press.

KRECH, DAVID and RICHARD S. CRUTCHFIELD, 1948 Theory and Problems of Social Psychology. New York: McGraw-Hill, Inc.

KRETSCHMER, ERNST, 1934 Textbook of Medical Psychology. Trans. E. B. Strauss. London: Chatto & Windus.

KROEBER, ALFRED L., 1899 The Eskimo of Smith Sound. Bulletin of the American Museum of Natural History, 12.

———, 1948 Anthropology. (New rev. ed.). New York: Harcourt Brace Jovanovich, Inc.

————, 1952 Psychosis or Social Sanction. *In* The Nature of Culture. Chicago: University of Chicago Press.

————, 1957 Ethnographic Interpretations. University of California Publications in American Archeology and Ethnology 47:191–204.

KROGMAN, WILTON M., 1940 The Skeletal and Dental Pathology of an Early Iranian State. Bulletin of the History of Medicine 8:28–48.

————, 1939 Medical Practices and Diseases of the Aboriginal American Indians. CIBA Symposia 1:11–18.

————, 1935 Missing Teeth and Skulls and Dental Caries. American Journal of Physical Anthropology 20:43–49.

KRUPINSKI, J. et al., 1967 A Community Health Survey of Heyfield, Victoria. Medical Journal of Australia 1:1204–1211.

KRZWICKI, LUDWIK, 1934 Primitive Society and Its Vital Statistics. Trans. H. E. Kennedy and A. Truszkowski. London: Macmillan and Co.

KUCZYNSKI-GODARD, M. H., 1945 Estudio Familiar Demografico-Ecologico en Estancias Indias de la Altiplano del Titicaca. (Ichupampa). Lima, Peru: Ministerio de Sálud Publica.

KUHN, THOMAS S., 1970 The Structure of Scientific Revolutions. Chicago: University of Chicago Press. 2nd ed. (orig. published in 1962).

KUHN, U. S. G., L. J. BROWN, and V. H. FALCONE, 1968 Seroreactivity of Human Primates in Treponemal and Nontreponemal Antigen Tests for Syphilis. WHO VDTRES 68. Geneva: World Health Organization.

KUNSTADTER, PETER, 1960 Culture Change, Social Structure, and the Use of Medical Care by the Residents of the Mescalero Apache Reservation. Paper presented at annual meeting of the American Anthropological Association. Minneapolis.

————, 1969 Fertility, Morality, and Migration of Hill and Valley Populations in Northwestern Thailand. Paper presented at annual meeting of the American Anthropological Association. New Orleans.

LACEY, JOHN L., 1967 Somatic Response Patterning and Stress: Some Revision of Activation Theory. *In* Psychological Stress: Issues in Research. M. H. Appley and R. Trumball, eds. New York: Appleton-Century-Crofts.

LAMBERT, W. E., E. LIBMAN, and E. G. POSER, 1960 The Effect of Increased Salience of a Membership Group on Pain Tolerance. Journal of Personality 38:350–357.

LAMBO, T. ADEOYE, 1956 Neuropsychiatric Observations in the Western Region of Nigeria. British Medical Journal 2:1388–1394.

————, 1962 Malignant Anxiety. Journal of Mental Science 108:256–264.

LAMBRECHT, F. L., 1964 Aspects of Evolution and Ecology of Tsetse Flies and Trypanosomiasis in Prehistoric African Environment. Journal of African History V:1–24.

LANDES, RUTH, 1938 The Abnormal Among the Ojibwa Indians. Journal of Abnormal and Social Psychology 33:14–33.

————, 1938 The Ojibwa Woman. New York: Columbia University Press.

LANDY, DAVID, 1958 Tuscarora Tribalism and National Identity. Ethnohistory 5:250–285.

————, 1960 Exploration in Residential After-Care of Psychiatric Patients: A Men's Halfway House. International Journal of Social Psychiatry 6:132–149.

————, and SARA E. SINGER, 1961 The Social Organization and Culture of a Club for Former Mental Patients. Human Relations 14:31–41.

————, 1965 Tropical Childhood: Cultural Transmission and Learning in a Puerto Rican Village. New York: Harper & Row Torchbooks (orig. 1959 University of North Carolina Press).

————, 1974a Role Adaption: Traditional Curers Under the Impact of Western Medicine. American Ethnologist 1:103–127.

————, 1974b Concepts of the Healer's Role. Paper presented at Symposium on Theoretical Foundations of Medical Anthropology. American Anthropological Association, Mexico City.

LANE, JOHN E., 1920 A Few Early Notes on Syphilis in the English Colonies in North America. Archives of Dermatology and Syphilis 2:215–219.

LANGNESS, L. L., 1964 Some Problems in the Conceptualization of Highlands Social Structures. American Anthropologist 66:162–182.

————, 1965 Hysterical Psychosis in the New Guinea Highlands. Psychiatry 28:258–277.

LANNING, EDWARD P., 1967 Peru Before the Incas. Englewood Cliffs, N.J.: Prentice-Hall, Inc.

LANTIS, MARGARET, 1946 The Social Culture of the Nunivak Eskimo. Transactions of the American Philosophical Society, New Series, 35:3. Philadelphia: The American Philosophical Society. New Series, 35:3. Philadelphia: The American Philosophical Society

————, 1959 Alaskan Eskimo Cultural Values. Polar Notes. (Occasional Publications of the Stefansson Collection). Hanover, N. H.: Dartmouth College Library.

————, 1960 Eskimo Childhood and Interpersonal Relations. Seattle: University of Washington Press.

LAS CASAS, Bartolomé de 1876 Historia de las Indias. Madrid: Imprenta de Miguel Ginesta.

LASKER, GABRIEL W., 1947 The Effects of Partial Starvation on Somatotype: An Analysis of Material from the Minnesota Starvation Experiment. American Journal of Physical Anthropology 5:323–333.

LAUBSCHER, B. J. F., 1937 Sex, Custom, and Psychopathology: A Study of South African Pagan Natives. London: Routledge and Kegan Paul, Ltd.

LAUGHLIN, WILLIAM S., 1961 Acquisition of Anatomical Knowledge by Ancient Man. In The Social Life of Early Man. S. L. Washburn, ed. Viking Fund Publications in Anthropology No. 31:150–175.

————, 1963 Primitive Theory of Medicine: Empirical Knowledge. In Man's Image in Medicine and Anthropology. Iago, Galdston, ed. New York: International Universities Press.

LEACH, EDMUND R., 1961 Golden Bough or Gilded Twig? Daedalus 90:371–387.

LEAKEY, LOUIS S. B., 1959 A New Fossil Skull from Olduvai. Nature 184:491–493.

LEBEUF, J. P., 1955 Sociology as the Basis of Health Education. Health Education Journal 13:232–236.

LEBRA, TAKIE SUGIYAMA, 1967 An Interpretation of Religious Conversion: A Millenial Movement Among Japanese-Americans in Hawaii. Ph.D. dissertation. University of Pittsburgh.

————, 1970 Logic of Salvation: The Case of a Japanese Sect in Hawaii. International Journal of Social Psychiatry 16:45–53.

LEDERBERG, JOSHUA, 1970 Government Is Most Dangerous of Genetic Engineers. Washington Post. July 19.

LEE, DOROTHY D., 1941 Some Indian Texts Dealing with the Supernatural. The Review of Religion. May.

LEE, RICHARD B., 1965 Subsistence Ecology of !Kung Bushmen. Unpublished Doctoral Dissertation, Department of Anthropology, University of California, Berkeley.

————, 1968 What Hunters Do for a Living, or, How to Make Out on Scarce Resources. In Man the Hunter. R. B. Lee and I. DeVore, eds. Chicago: Aldine Publishing Co.

————, 1972 Population Growth and the Beginning of Sedentary Life Among the !Kung Bushmen. In Population Growth: Anthropological Implications. B. Spooner, ed. Cambridge, Mass: The M. I. T. Press.

LEE, R. P. L., 1975 Health Services System in Hong Kong: Professional Stratification in a Modernizing Society. Inquiry. Supplement, 12:51–62.

LEE, RICHARD B., and IRVEN DeVORE, eds., 1968 Man the Hunter. Chicago: Aldine Publishing Co.

LEGAN, MARSHALL SCOTT, 1971 Hydropathy in America: A Nineteenth-Century Panacea. Bulletin of the History of Medicine 45:267–280.

LEIGHTON, ALEXANDER H., 1961 Remarks. Milbank Memorial Fund Quarterly 30:486.

————, ADEOYE T. LAMBO, CHARLES C. HUGHES, DOROTHEA C. LEIGHTON, JANE M. MURPHY, DAVID B. MACKLIN, 1963 Psychiatric Disorder Among the Yoruba. Ithaca, New York: Cornell University Press.

————, and DOROTHEA C. LEIGHTON, 1945 The Navajo Door. Cambridge, Mass.: Harvard University Press.

LEIGHTON, DOROTHEA C., 1956 The Distribution of Psychiatric Symptoms in a Small Town. American Journal of Psychiatry 112:716–723.

————, JOHN S. HARDING, DAVID B. MACKLIN, ALLISTER M. MacMILLAN, ALEXANDER H. LEIGHTON, 1963 The Character of Danger. New York: Basic Books, Inc.

LEIRIS, M., 1934 Le Culte des Mars à Gondar. Aethiopica 3:96–103.

————, 1958 La Possession et ses Aspects Theatraux Chen les Ethiopiens de Gondar. Paris.

LEIS, PHILIP E., 1963 Washo Witchcraft: A Test of the Frustration-Aggression Hypothesis. In The Washo Indians of California and Nevada. W. L. d'Azevedo, ed. Salt Lake City: University of Utah Press.

LEON, C. A., 1965 El "Espanto": Sus Implicaciones Psiquiatricas. Transcultural Psychiatric Research 2:45–48. (abstract). (Lecture to Second Latin-American Congress of Psychiatry, Mexico)

LESLIE, CHARLES, 1967 Professional and Popular Health Cultures in South Asia: Needed Research in Medical Sociology and Anthropology. In Understanding Science and Technology in India and Pakistan. W. Morehouse, ed.

————, 1969 Modern India's Ancient Medicine. Trans-action 68:46–55.

————, 1969 Traditionalism and Modernization in Asian Health Cultures. New Orleans: Paper presented at annual meeting of the American Anthropological Association.

————, 1975 The Ambiguities of Medical

Revivalism in Modern India. *In* Asian Medical Systems. Charles Leslie, ed. Berkeley: University of California Press.

LESSA, WILLIAM A., 1968 Chinese Body Divination: Its Forms, Affinities, and Functions. Los Angeles: United World.

LESTER, DAVID, 1972 Voodoo Death: Some New Thoughts on an Old Phenomenon. American Anthropologist **74**: 386–390.

LEVIN, K., 1973 Medicine and Chinese Society. *In* Modern China and Traditional Chinese Medicine. G. B. Risse, ed. Springfield, Ill.: Charles C Thomas, publisher.

LeVINE, ROBERT A., 1973 Culture, Behavior, and Personality. Chicago: Aldine Publishing Co.

LÉVI-STRAUSS, CLAUDE, 1955 Tristes Tropiques. Paris.

———, 1967 The Sorcerer and His Magic. *In* Structural Anthropology. Garden City. N.Y.: Doubleday & Co, Inc.

LEWIN, KURT, 1952 Group Decision and Social Change. *In* Readings in Social Psychology. Swanson, Newcomb, Hartley et al., eds. New York: Holt, Rinehart and Winston, Inc.

LEWIS, IOAN M., 1971 Ecstatic Religion: An Anthropological Study of Spirit Possession and Shamanism. Harmondsworth, Middlesex, England: Penguin Books, Ltd.

LEWIS, OSCAR, 1955 Medicine and Politics in a Mexican Village. *In* Health, Culture, and Community. Benjamin D. Paul, ed. New York: Russell Sage Foundation.

———, 1960 Tepotzlan, Village in Mexico. New York: Holt, Rinehart and Winston, Inc.

LEWIS, T., 1942 Pain. New York: Macmillan Publishing Co., Inc.

LEWIT, E., 1947 A Preliminary Report on a Study of 4,000 Czechoslovakian Children. London Medical Women's International Journal **54**:41–44.

LI, V. H., 1974 Making the Whole Greater Than the Sum of Its Parts. Comments on Chinese Studies and Visits to China. Memo.

LIEBAN, RICHARD W., 1960 Sorcery, Illness, and Social Control in a Philippine Municipality. Southwestern Journal of Anthropology **16**: 127–143.

———, 1962 The Dangerous Ingkantos: Illness and Social Control in a Philippine Community. American Anthropologist **64**: 306–312.

———, 1962 Qualification for Folk Medical Practice in Sibulan, Negroes Oriental, Philippines. Philippine Journal of Science **91**: 511–521.

———, 1966 Fatalism and Medicine in Cebuano Areas of the Philippines. Anthropological Quarterly **39**: 171–179

———, 1967 Cebuano Sorcery: Malign Magic in the Philippines. Berkeley: University of California Press.

———, 1974 Medical Anthropology. *In* Handbook of Social and Cultural Anthropology. Chicago: Rand, McNally & Co.

LIENHARDT, PETER, ed. and trans., 1968 The Medicine Man. Swifa ya Ngurumali. Oxford: Clarendon Press.

LIN, T., 1953 A Study of Mental Disorders in Chinese and Other Cultures. Psychiatry **16**: 313–336.

LINDEMANN, ERICH, 1950 An Epidemiological Analysis of Suicide. Epidemiology of Mental Disorder. New York: Millbank Memorial Fund.

LINNE, S., 1957 Technical Secrets of American Indians. Journal of the Royal Anthropological Institute **87**: 149–164.

LINTON, RALPH, 1945 The Cultural Background of Personality. New York: Appleton-Century-Crofts.

———, 1936 The Study of Man. New York: Appleton-Century-Crofts.

———, 1945 The Science of Man in the World Crisis. New York: Columbia University Press.

LISKER, RUBEN et al., 1965 Studies on Several Genetic Hematological Traits of the Mexican Population. American Journal of Human Genetics **17**: 179–187.

LISKER, RUBEN et al., 1966 Studies on Several Genetic Hematological Traits of Mexicans. Blood **27**: 824–830.

LIVINGSTONE, FRANK B., 1958 Anthropological Implications of Sickle-Cell Gene Distribution in West Africa. American Anthropologist **60**: 533–562.

———, 1960 Natural Selection, Disease, and Ongoing Evolution, as Illustrated by the ABO Blood Groups. *In* The Processes of Ongoing Human Evolution. G. W. Lasker, ed. Detroit: Wayne State University Press.

———, 1966, 1967 Abnormal Hemoglobins in Human Populations. Chicago: Aldine Publishing Co., Inc.

LLOYD, P. C., 1968 Africa in Social Change. New York: Praeger.

LLOYD-STILL, R. M., 1940 Remarks on the Aetiology and Symptoms of Young-dah-hte with a Report on Four Cases and Its Medico-Legal Significance. Indian Medical Gazette **75**: 88–93.

LOEB, E. M., 1929 Shaman and Seer. American Anthropologist **31**: 60–84.

LOGAN, MICHAEL H., 1972 Humoral Folk Medicine: A Potential Aid in Controlling Pellagra in Mexico. Ethnomedizin 1:397–410.

LOWIE, ROBERT H., 1939 Ethnographic Notes on the Washo. University of California Publications in American Archeology and Ethnology 36:301–352.

LOWINGER, P., 1959 Leprosy and Psychosis. American Journal of Psychiatry 116:32–37.

LU, Y. C., 1973 Social Values and Psychiatric Ideology in Revolutionary China. Paper presented at the American Sociological Association. New York. Mimeo.

LUCIER, CHARLES V., JAMES W. VAN STONE, and DELLA KEATS, 1971 Medical Practices and Human Anatomical Knowledge Among the Noatak Eskimos. Ethnology 10:251–264.

LUDWIG, A. O., 1949 Emotional Factors in Rheumatoid Arthritis: Their Bearing on the Care and Rehabilitation of the Patient. Physiotherapy Review 29:338–350.

LYNCH, F. X., 1949 An Mga Asuwang: A Bicol Belief. Philippine Social Sciences and Humanities Review XIV:401–427.

MACAURTHUR, SIR W., 1958 The Plague of Athens. Bulletin of the History of Medicine 32:242–246.

MACDONALD· GEORGE, 1965 On the Scientific Basis of Tropical Hygiene. Transactions of the Royal Society of Tropical Medicine and Hygiene 59:611–620.

MACFARLANE, A. D. J., 1970 Definitions of Witchcraft. In Witchcraft and Sorcery. Max Marwick, ed. Harmondsworth, Middlesex England: Penguin Books.

MACLEAN, CATHERINE M. U., 1966 Hospitals or Healers? An Attitude Survey in Ibadan. Human Organization 25:131–139.

———, 1969 Traditional Healers and Their Female Clients: An Aspect of Nigerian Sickness Behavior. Journal of Health and Social Behavior 10:172–186.

MACLEOD, WILLIAM C., 1925 Certain Mortuary Aspects of Northwest Coast Culture. American Anthropologist 27:122–142.

MADDOX, JOHN LEE, 1923 The Medicine Man: A Sociological Study of the Character and Evolution of Shamanism. New York: Macmillan Publishing Co.

MADSEN, C., 1965 A Study of Change in Mexican Folk Medicine. Middle American Research Institute, publication 25. New Orleans: Tulane University Press.

MADSEN, WILLIAM, 1955 Hot and Cold in the Universe of San Francisco Tecospa, Valley of Mexico. Journal of American Folklore 68:123–139.

———, 1964 The Mexican Americans of South Texas. In Case Studies in Cultural Anthropology. New York: Holt, Rinehart and Winston, Inc.

———, 1964 Value Conflicts and Folk Psychiatry in South Texas. In Magic, Faith, and Healing. Ari Kiev, ed. New York: The Free Press.

MAGUIGAD, L. C., 1964 Psychiatry in the Philippines. American Journal of Psychiatry 121:21–25.

MAK, C., 1959 Mixtec Medical Beliefs and Practices. American Indigena 19:125–150.

MAINGARD, J. F., 1937 Some Notes on Health and Disease Among the Bushmen of the Southern Kalahari. In Bushmen of the Southern Kalahari. J. D. Jones et al., ed. Johannesburg: University of Witwatersrand Press.

MALINOWSKI, BRONISLAW, 1922 Argonauts of the Western Pacific. Routledge and Kegan Paul, Ltd.

MANN, ALAN E., 1968 The Paleodemography of Australopithicines. Ph.D. thesis, University of California, Berkeley. University Microfilms 69-3652.

MANN, G. V., O. A. ROELS, D. L. PRICE, and J. M. MERRILL, 1962 Cardiovascular Disease in African Pygmies: A Survey of the Health, Status, Serum Lipids, and Diet of Pygmies in Congo. Journal of Chronic Diseases 15:341–371.

MANN, I. 1957 Possible Origins of Trachoma in Australasia. Bulletin of the World Health Organization 16:1165–1187.

MANSON-BAHR, PHILIP H., 1966 Manson's Tropical Diseases. Baltimore: The Williams & Wilkins Co.

MARCHOUX, E., and F. MESNIL, 1911 Osteite Hypertrophique Generalisee des Singes avec Lesions Rappelant le Goundou. Bulletin de la Société de Pathologie Exotique 4:150–155.

MARETT, J. de la R., 1936 Race, Sex, and Environment. London: Hutchinson's Scientific and Technical Publications.

MARETT, R. R., 1914 The Threshold of Religion. London. 2nd ed.

MARRIOTT, MCKIM, 1955 Little Communities in Indigenous Civilization. In Village India. M. Marriott, ed. American Anthropological Association. Memoir no. 83:171–222.

———, 1955 Western Medicine in a Village of Northern India. In Health, Culture, and Community. B. D. Paul, ed. New York: Russell Sage Foundation.

542

MARSH, GORDON H., and WILLIAM S. LAUGHLIN, 1956 Human Anatomical Knowledge Among the Aleutian Islanders. Southwestern Journal of Anthropology 12:38–78.

MARSHALL, LORNA, 1960 !Kung Bushman Bands. Africa 30:325–355.

MARTI-IBAÑEZ, FELIX, ed., 1960 Henry E. Sigerist on the History of Medicine. New York: MD Publications.

MARWICK, MAX G., ed., 1970 Witchcraft and Sorcery. Harmondsworth, Middlesex, England: Penguin Books.

———, 1967 The Sociology of Sorcery in a Central African Tribe. In Magic, Witchcraft, and Curing. J. Middleton, ed. New York: Natural History Press (Doubleday).

———, 1965 Sorcery in the Social Setting. Manchester, England: Manchester University Press.

MATHIAS, MILDRED E., 1965 Medicinal Plant Hunting in Tanzania. In Ecology and Economic Development in Tropical Africa. David Brokensha, ed. Berkeley: Institute of International Studies, University of California.

MAUSNER, JUDITH S. and ANITA K. BAHN, 1974 Epidemiology: An Introductory Text. Philadelphia: W. B. Saunders Co.

MAXCY, K. A., ed., 1941 Papers of Wade Hampton Frost, M.D. New York.

MAY, JACQUES M., 1960 The Ecology of Human Disease. Annals of the New York Academy of Sciences 84:789–794.

MCCORKLE, THOMAS, 1961 Chiropractic: A Deviant Theory of Disease. Human Organization 20:20–22.

MCCRACKEN, ROBERT D., 1971 Lactase Deficiency: An Example of Dietary Evolution. Current Anthropology 12:479–517.

MCDERMOTT, WALSH, KURT DEUTSCHTE, JOHN ADAIR, HUGH FULMER, and BERNICE LOUGHLIN, 1960 Introducing Modern Medicine in a Navajo Community 131:197–280.

MCGILL MEDICAL JOURNAL, 1973 Reflections After China: An Interview with Gustave Gringras. McGill Medical Journal 42:8–11, 15.

MCKEOWN, THEODORE, R. G. BROWN, and R. G. RECORD, 1972 An Interpretation of the Modern Rise of Population in Europe. Population Studies 26(3):345–381.

MCKINLEY, KELTON R., 1971 Survivorship in Gracile and Robust Australopithecines: A Demographic Comparison and a Proposed Birth Model. American Journal of Physical Anthropology 34:417–426.

MEAD, MARGARET, 1924 Coming of Age in Samoa. New York: William Morrow Co., Inc.

———, 1930 Growing Up in New Guinea. New York: William Morrow & Co., Inc.

———, 1930 Social Organization of Manu'a. Honolulu: Bernice P. Bishop Museum Bulletin 76:1–218.

———, 1949 Male and Female. New York: William Morrow & Co., Inc.

———, 1950 Sex and Temperament in Three Primitive Societies. New York: Mentor Books, New American Library.

———, ed. 1955 Cultural Patterns and Technical Change. New York: Mentor Books, New American Library (original edition pub. by UNESCO).

———, 1961 New Lives for Old: Cultural Transformation, Manus 1928–1953. New York: Mentor Books, New American Library (1st pub. 1956).

MECHANIC, DAVID, 1962 The Concept of Illness Behavior. Journal of Chronic Diseases 15:189–194.

———, 1968 Medical Sociology. New York: The Free Press.

MEDAWAR, PETER B., 1960 The Future of Man. New York: Basic Books, Inc.

MEEHAN, J. P., A. M. STOLE, and J. D. HARDY, 1954 Cutaneous Pain Threshold in the Native Alaskan Indian and Eskimo. Journal of Applied Physiology 6:397–400.

MEENAN, P. N., M. R. BOYD, and R. MULLANEY, 1962 Human Influenza Viruses in Domestic Animals. British Medical Journal 1:86–90.

MENDELSON, E. Michael, 1960 Religion and Authority in Modern Burma. The World Today 16:110–118.

———, 1961 A Messianic Buddhist Association in Upper Burma. Bulletin of the School of Oriental and African Studies 24:560–580. University of London.

———, 1961 The King of the Weaving Mountain. Royal Central Asian Journal 48:229–237.

———, 1963 Observations on a Tour in the Region of Mount Popa, Central Burma. France-Asie 179:786–807.

MERRIAM, ALAN, and WARREN L. D'AZEVEDO, 1957 Washo Peyote Songs. American Anthropologist 59:615–641.

MERSKEY, H., and F. G. SPEAR, 1964 The Reliability of the Pressure Algometer. British Journal of Social and Clinical Psychology:3:130–136.

MERTON, ROBERT K., 1957 Social Theory and Social Structure. New York: The Free Press (rev. ed.).

———, 1967 On Theoretical Sociology. New York: The Free Press.

MESSENGER, JOHN C., JR., 1959 Religious Acculturation Among the Anang Ibibio. *In* Continuity and Change in African Cultures. William R. Bascom, and Melville J. Herskovits, eds. Chicago: University of Chicago Press.

MESSING, SIMON, 1957 The Highland-Plateau Amhara of Ethiopia. Unpublished Ph.D. dissertation. University of Pennsylvania.

———, 1958 Group Therapy and Social Status in the Zar Cult of Ethiopia. *In* Culture and Mental Health. M. K. Opler, ed. New York: Macmillan Publishing Co., Inc.

MESSIRI, NAWAL, 1967 The Sheikh Cultin Dahmit Life. *In* Symposium on Contemporary Nubia. R. Fernea, ed. New Haven, Conn: Harflex.

METZGER, DUANE, and GERALD WILLIAMS, 1963 Tenejapa Medicine I: The Curer. Southwestern Journal of Anthropology 19:216–234.

MIDDLETON, JOHN, 1953 The Kikuyu and Kamba of Kenya. London: International African Institute.

———, ed., 1967 Magic, Witchcraft, and Curing. Garden City, N.Y.: Natural History Press (Doubleday).

———, and E. H. WINTER, eds., 1963 Witchcraft and Sorcery in East Africa. London: Routledge and Kegan Paul Ltd.

MILLER, N., 1928 The Child in Primitive Society. New York.

MILLER, WALTER B., 1958 Lower Class as a Generating Milieu of Gang Delinquency. Journal of Social Issues 14:5–19.

MINDELEFF, COSMOS, 1898 Navaho Houses. Bureau of American Ethnology Reports 17:475–517.

MINISTRY OF INFORMATION, 1972 India: 1971–1972. New Delhi: Ministry of Information.

MINTZ, SIDNEY W., 1956 Cañamelar: The Subculture of a Rural Plantation Proletariat. *In* The People of Puerto Rico. J. Steward, ed. Urbana: University of Illinois Press.

MIRSKY, JEANETTE, 1937 The Eskimo of Greenland. *In* Co-operation and Competition Among Primitive Peoples. Margaret Mead, ed. New York: McGraw-Hill Book Co., Inc.

MISCHEL, FRANCES, 1959 Faith Healing and Medical Practice in the Southern Caribbean. Southwestern Journal of Anthropology 15:407–417.

MITCHELL, H. H., and E. EDMAN, 1951 Nutrition and Climactic Stress. Springfield, Ill.: Charles C Thomas, Publisher.

MONARDES, NICOĹS, 1577 Joyfull Newes Out of the Newe Founde Worlde. John Frampton, trans. London: Willam Norton.

MONGEAU, BEATRICE, HARVEY L. SMITH, and ANN C. MANEY, 1961 The "Granny" Midwife: Changing Roles and Functions of a Folk Practitioner. American Journal of Sociology 66:497–505.

MONTAGU, ASHLEY, 1949 Embryological Beliefs of Primitive Peoples. Ciba Symposia 10:994–1008.

———, 1962 The Fallacy of the "Primitive." Journal of the American Medical Association 179:962–963.

MONTANDON, GEORGE, 1937 La Civilization Ainou et les Cultures Arctiques. Paris: Payot.

MONTGOMERY, EDWARD, 1973 Ecological Aspects of Health and Disease in Local Populations. Bernard J. Siegel, Alan R. Beals, and Stephen A. Tyler, eds. Annual Review of Anthropology. Palo Alto, Calif.: Annual Reviews, Inc. 2:30–35.

———, 1975 Systems and the Medical Practitioners of a Tamil Town. *In* Asian Medical Systems. C. Leslie, ed. Berkeley: University of California Press.

MOODIE, ROY L., 1923 Paleopathology: An Introduction to the Study of Ancient Evidences of Disease. Urbana: University of Illinois Press.

MOORE, OMAR KHAYYAM, 1957 Divination—A New Perspective. American Anthropologist 59:69–74.

MOOSE, ROBERT J., 1911 Village Life in Korea.

MORGAN, R., 1960 Host Cell Factors and Virus Virulence. *In* Virus, Virulence, and Pathogenicity. Ciba Foundation Symposium 4. London. Churchill.

MORGAN, T., 1974 Cuba. New York Times Magazine. December 1:27ff.

MORICE, A. G., 1901 Déné Surgery. Transactions of the Canadian Institute 7:15–27.

MORISON, SAMUEL ELIOT, 1942 Admiral of the Ocean Sea, a Life of Christopher Columbus. Boston: Little, Brown, and Co.

MORRIS, JEREMY N., 1964 Uses of Epidemiology. rev. ed. Edinburgh: Livingstone.

MORSE, DAN D., R. BROTHWELL, and P. J. UCKO, 1964 Tuberculosis in Ancient Egypt. American Review of Respiratory Diseases 90:425–541.

MORTON, R. S., 1966 Venereal Diseases. Baltimore: Penguin Books.

MOTULSKY, ARNO G., 1960 Metabolic Polymorphisms and the Role of Infectious Diseases in Human Evolution. *In* The Processes of Ongoing Human Evolution. G. W. Lasker, ed. Detroit: Wayne State University Press.

MOUQUET, A., 1929 Osteite Hypertrophique Rappelant le Goundou Chez un Cercocebus

Aethiops Vivant. Bulletin de la Société de Pathologie Exotique **22**:918–922.

———, 1930 Presentation d'un Squelette de Cercocebe Atteint de Goundou des Singes. Bulletin de la Société de Pathologie Exotique **23**:918–922.

MOWRER, O. H., 1938 Preparatory Set (Expectancy): A Determination Motivation and Learning. Psychological Review **XLV**:62–91.

———, 1939 A Stimulus-Response Analysis of Anxiety and Its Role as a Reinforcing Agent. Psychological Review **554**.

———, 1940 Preparatory Set (Expectancy): Some Methods of Measurement. Psychological Monographs **LII**:1–2, 39.

MUNGER, ROBERTS, 1949 Guaiacum, The Holy Wood from the New World. Journal of the History of Medicine and Allied Sciences **4**:196–229.

MURDOCK, GEORGE P., 1949 Social Structure. New York: Macmillan and Co., Inc.

———, 1959 Africa: Its People and Their Culture History. New York: McGraw-Hill, Inc.

———, 1965 Tenino Shamanism. Ethnology **4**:165–171.

———, et al., 1945 Outline of Cultural Materials. New Haven: Yale Anthropological Studies.

MURPHY, JANE M., 1964 Psychotherapeutic Aspects of Shamanism on St. Lawrence Island. In Magic, Faith, and Healing. A. Kiev, ed. New York: The Free Press.

———, and A. LEIGHTON, 1965 Approaches to Cross-Cultural Psychiatry. Ithaca: Cornell University Press.

MURPHY, ROBERT C., 1958 From Indian to Negro in the Columbian Choco. In Race Individual and Collective Behavior. Edgar T. Thompson and Everett Hughes, eds. New York.

MURPHY, ROBERT F., 1958 Mundurucú Religion. University of California American Archeology and Ethnology **49**:1–154.

NADEL, S. F., 1946 A Study of Shamanism in the Nuba Mountains. Journal of the Royal Anthropological Institute **76**:25–37.

———, 1954 Nupe Religion. London: Oxford University Press.

NAG, MONI, 1962 Factors Affecting Human Fertility in Nonindustrial Societies: a Cross-Cultural Study. New Haven: Yale University Publications in Anthropology 66.

———, 1972 Economic Value of Children in Agricultural Societies: Evaluation of Existing Knowledge and an Anthropological Approach. In The Satisfactions and Costs of Children:

Theories, Concepts, Methods. J. T. Fawcett, ed. Honolulu: East–West Center.

———, 1973 Anthropology and Population: Problems and Perspectives. Population Studies **27**(1):59–68.

NASH, MANNING, 1965 The Golden Road to Modernity. New York: John Wiley & Sons.

NAVARRO, V., 1972 Health, Health Services, and Health Planning in Cuba. International Journal of Health Services **2**:397–432.

NEEDHAM, JOSEPH, and LU GWEI-DJEN, 1969 Chinese Medicine. In Medicine and Culture. F. N. L. Poynter, ed. London: Wellcome Institute of the History of Medicine.

NEEL, JAMES V., 1962 Diabetes Mellitus: A "Thrifty" Genotype Rendered Detrimental by "Progress". American Journal of Human Genetics **14**:352–362.

———, 1970 Genetic Aspects of the Ecology of Disease in the American Indian. In The Ongoing Evolution of Latin American Populations. F. M. Salzano, ed. Springfield, Ill.: Charles C Thomas, publisher, In Press.

———, 1970 Lessons from a "Primitive" People. Science **170**:815–822.

———, F. M. SALZANO, P. C. JUNGUEIRA, F. KEITER, and D. MAYBURY-LEWIS, 1964 Studies on the Xavante Indians of the Brazilian Mato Grosso. American Journal of Human Genetics **16**:52–140.

———, A. H. P. ANDRADE, G. E. BROWN, W. C. EVELAND, J. GOODBAR, W. A. SODEMAN, G. H. STROLLERMAN, E. D. WEINSTEIN, and A. H. WHEELER, 1968 Further Studies on the Xavante Indians IX. American Journal of Tropical Medicine and Hygiene **17**:486–498.

———, W. R. CENTERWALL, N. A. CHAGNON, and H. L. CASEY, 1970 Notes on the Effect of Measles and Measles Vaccine in a Virgin-Soil Population of South American Indians. American Journal of Epidemiology.

NELSON, G. S., 1960 Schistosome Infections as Zoonoses in Africa. Transactions of the Society of Tropical Medicine and Hygiene **54**:301; 316.

NEUMANN, A., et al., 1971 Role of Indigenous Medicine Practitioners in Two Areas of India: Report of a Study. Social Science and Medicine **5**:137–149.

NEW, PETER K., RICHARD M. HESSLER, and P. B. CATER, 1973 Consumer Participation and Public Accountability. Anthropological Quarterly **46**:196–213.

NEW, PETER K., 1974a Barefoot Doctors and

545

Health Care in the People's Republic of China. Ekistics **38**:220–224.

———, 1974b Barefoot Doctors and Health Care in the People's Republic of China. Eastern Horizon **13**:7–19.

———, and MARY L. NEW, 1974 China's Barefoot Doctors: Health Care By and For the People. Dartmouth Alumni Magazine **66**:22–25.

———, and ———, 1975 Republic of China: The Barefoot Doctor. Inquiry, Supplement **12**:103–113.

———, and ———, 1975 The Links Between Health and Political Structure in New China. Human Organization **34**, (3).

NEWELL, KENNETH W., 1957 Medical Development Within a Maori Community. Health Education Journal **15**:83–89.

NEWMAN, PHILIP, 1964 "Wild Man" Behavior in New Guinea Highlands Community. American Anthropologist **66**:1–19.

NEWMAN, LUCILLE F., 1970 Cultural Factors in Family Planning. Annals of the New York Academy of Sciences **175**:833–846.

———, 1972 The Anthropology of Birth. Sociological Symposium No. 8, Childbirth and Infancy. Department of Sociology and Anthropology, Western Kentucky University.

———, 1972 Birth Control: An Anthropological View. Addison-Wesley Modules in Anthropology No. 27, 1–21.

NICHOLS, D. S., 1966 The Function of Patient Employment in the Rehabilitation of the Leprosy Patient. Unpublished M.A. thesis. Baton Rouge, Louisiana, Dept. of Sociology, Louisiana State University.

NICHOLS, L., and A. NIMALASURIYA, 1939 Adaption to a Low Calcium Intake in Reference to the Calcium Requirements of a Tropical Population. Journal of Nutrition **18**:563–577.

NIGMANN, E., 1908 Die Wahehe. Berlin. Ernst Siegfried Mittler und Sohn.

NORTHROP, F. S. C., 1963 The Neurophysiological Meaning of Culture. *In* Man's Image in Medicine and Anthropology. I. Galdston, ed. New York: International Universities Press.

NOVAKOVSKY, STANISLAUS, 1924 Arctic or Siberian Hysteria as a Reflex of the Geographic Environment. Ecology **5**:113–127.

NURGE, ETHEL, 1958 Etiology of Illness in Guinhangdan. American Anthropologist **60**:1158–1172.

NYERE, JULIUS K., 1969 Essays in Socialism. Dar-es-Salaam: Oxford University Press.

ODUM, EUGENE P., 1959 Fundamentals of Ecology

(2nd ed.). Philadelphia, London: Saunders Co.

O'NELL, CARL W., and HENRY A. SELBY, 1968 Sex Differences in the Incidence of Susto in Two Zapotec Pueblos: An Analysis of the Relationship Between Sex Role Expectations and a Folk Illness. Ethnology **7**:95–105.

ONOGE, O. F., 1975 Capitalism and Public Health— A Neglected Theme in Africa. *In* Topias and Utopias in Health. S. Ingman and A. Thomas, eds. The Hague: Mouton & Co.

OPLER, MARVIN K., 1956 Culture, Psychiatry, and Human Values. Springfield, Ill.: Charles C Thomas, Publisher.

———, 1959a Culture and Mental Health. New York: Macmillan Publishing Co., Inc.

———, 1959 The Cultural Backgrounds of Mental Health. *In* Culture and Mental Health. M. K. Opler, ed. New York: Macmillan Publishing Co. Inc.

———, 1959 Dream Analysis in Ute Indian Therapy. *In* Culture and Mental Health. M. K. Opler, ed. New York: Macmillan Publishing Co. Inc.

———, 1961 Ethnic Differences in Behavior and Health Practices. *In* The Family: A Focal Point for Health Education. I. Galdston, ed. New York: New York Academy of Medicine.

———, 1961 On Devereux's Discussion of Ute Shamanism. American Anthropologist **63**:1091–1093.

———, 1963 The Cultural Definition of Illness in Village India. Human Organization **22**:32–35.

———, 1963 The need for New Diagnostic Categories in Psychiatry. Journal of the National Medical Association **2**:133–137.

———, 1967 Culture and Social Psychiatry. New York: Atherton Press, Inc.

OPPENHEIMER, JANE M., 1967 Essays in the History of Embryology and Biology. Cambridge, Mass.: The M.I.T. Press.

ORDONEZ PLAJA, ANTONIO, L. M. COHEN, and J. SAMORA, 1968 Communication Between Physicians and Patients in Outpatient Clinics. Milbank Memorial Fund Quarterly **46**:161–213.

O'RILEY, EDWARD, 1850 On the Spirit (Nat or Dewah) Worship of the Talines. Journal of the Indian Archipelago and Eastern Asia **4**:591–597.

ORLEANS, L. A., 1973 Population Dynamics. *In* Medicine and Public Health in the People's Republic of China. J. R. Quinn, ed. Washington, D.C.: U.S. Government Printing Office.

———, 1974 Chinese Statistics: The Impossible Dream. The American Statistician **28**:47–52.

ORSO, E., 1970 Hot and Cold in the Folk Medicine

of the Island of Chira, Costa Rica. Working Paper, Institute of Latin American Studies. Baton Rouge, La.: Louisiana State University.

ORTNER, S., 1973 Sherpa Purity. American Anthropologist 75:49–63.

OTSUKA, Y., 1975 Chinese Traditional Medicine in Japan. *In* Asian Medical Systems. C. Leslie, ed. Berkeley: University of California Press.

OVIEDO Y VALDES, GONZALO FERNANDEZ, 1851 Historia de la Indias. Madrid: Imprenta de la Real Academia de la Historia.

———, 1959 Natural History of the West Indies, trans. Sterling A. Stoudemire. Chapel Hill N.C.: University of North Carolina Press.

OZTÜRK, ORHAM M., 1964 Folk Treatment of Mental Illness in Turkey. *In* Magic, Faith, and Healing. Ari Kiev, ed. New York: The Free Press.

PADILLA, ELENA, 1958 Up from Puerto Rico. New York: Columbia University Press.

PALES, L., 1930 Paleopathologie et pathologie comparative. Paris: Masson.

PANUM, P. L., 1940 Measles in the Farce Islands. New York: Frans Hatcher, Delta Omega Society.

PAOLI' A. D., 1965 Schistosoma Haematobium in the Chimpanzee. American Journal of Tropical Medicine and Hygiene 14:561–565.

PARK, GEORGE K., 1963 Divination and Its Social Contexts. The Journal of the Royal Anthropological Institute 93:195–209.

PARK, WILLARD, 1938 Shamanism in Western North America. New York: Harper & Row Publishers, Inc.

PARKER, SEYMOUR, 1960 The Wiitiko Psychosis in the Context of Ojibwa Personality and Culture. American Anthropologist 62:603–623.

PARSONS, ELSIE CLEWS, 1913 The Old-Fashioned Woman. New York.

PARSONS, TALCOTT, 1942 Propaganda and Social Control. Psychiatry 5, (4) November.

———, 1949 Essays in Sociological Theory, Pure and Applied. New York: The Free Press.

———, 1951 The Social System. New York: The Free Press.

———, 1953 Illness and the Role of the Physician. *In* Personality in Nature, Society and Culture. C. Kluckhohn, and H. A. Murray, eds. 2nd ed. New York: Alfred A. Knopf Inc.

———, 1955 The American Family: Its Relationship to Personality and the Social Structure. *In* Family, Socialization, and Interaction Process. T. Parsons and R. F. Bales, eds. New York: The Free Press.

———, 1958 Definitions of Health and Illness in the Light of American Values and Social Structure. *In* Patients, Physicians, and Illness. E. G. Jaco, ed. New York: The Free Press.

———, 1963 Introduction. *In* The Sociology of Religion, Max Weber. Ephraim Fischoff, trans. Boston: Beacon Press.

———, 1963 Social Change and Medical Organization in the United States: A Sociological Perspective. Annals of the American Academy of Political and Social Science 346:21–34.

———, 1964 Social Structure and Personality. New York: The Free Press.

———, 1964 Some Reflections on the Problem of Psychosomatic Relationships in Health and Illness. *In* Social Structure and Personality. T. Parsons, ed. London: The Free Press.

———, 1966 Societies: Evolutionary and Comparative Perspectives. Englewood Cliffs, N.J.: Prentice-Hall, Inc.

———, and RENEÉ FOX 1958 Illness, Therapy, and the American Family. *In* Patients, Physicians, and Illness. E. G. Jaco, ed. New York: The Free Press.

PASQUEL, LEONARDO, ed., 1960 La Ciudad de Veracruz. (2 vols.) Tucubaya, Mexico.

PAUL, BENJAMIN D., 1955 Health, Culture, and Community: Case Studies of Public Reactions to Health Programs. New York: Russell Sage Foundation.

———, 1963 Anthropological Perspectives on Medicine and Public Health. Annals of the American Academy of Political and Social Science 346:34–43.

PAUL, HUGH, 1964 The Control of Diseases (Social and Communicable). 2nd ed. Baltimore: The Williams & Wilkins Co.

PEARSALL, MARION, 1963 Medical Behavioral Science: A Selected Bibliography of Cultural Anthropology. Social Psychology, and Sociology in Medicine. Lexington: University of Kentucky Press.

PEARY, ROBERT E., 1910 The North Pole. New York: Frederick A. Stokes Co.

PELTO, GRETEL H., and PERTTI J. PELTO, 1976 The Human Adventure: An Introduction to Anthropology. New York: Macmillan Publishing Co., Inc.

PENFIELD, W., 1961 Oriental Renaissance in Education and Medicine. Science 141:1153.

PERISTIANY, J. G., 1939 The Social Institutions of the Kipsigis. London: Routledge and Kegan Paul, Ltd.

PETERSEN, WILLIAM, 1969 Population. 2nd ed. London: Macmillan.

547

———, 1975 A Demographer's View of Prehistoric Demography. Current Anthropology **16**:227–246.

PHILLIPS, J., 1960 Agriculture and Ecology in Africa. New York: Praeger Publishers, Inc.

PICKOWICZ, P. G., 1973 Barefoot Doctors in China: People, Politics, and Para medicine. *In* Modern China and Traditional Chinese Medicine. G. B. Risse, ed. Springfield, Ill.: Charles C Thomas, Publisher.

PIERIS, RALPH, 1953 The Brodie Papers on Sinhalese Folk Religion. University of Ceylon Review **11**:110–128.

PI-SUNYER, ORIOL, 1957 Historical Background to the Negro in Mexico. Journal of Negro History **XLII**:237–246.

PIZZI, T., and H. SCHENONE, 1955 Trichuris in an Inca. Tropical Medicine and Hygiene Notes **4**:6–7.

PLOG, STANLEY C., and ROBERT E. EDGERTON, eds., 1969 Changing Perspectives in Mental Illness. New York: Holt, Rinehart and Winston, Inc.

PLOSS, H., and M. BARTELS, 1927 Das weib in der Natur und Völkerkunde. Berlin. 3 vols.

POLGAR, STEVEN, 1962 Health and Human Behavior: Areas of Interest Common to the Social and Medical Sciences. Current Anthropology **3**:159–205.

———, 1963 Health Action in Cross-Cultural Perspective. *In* Handbook of Medical Sociology. H. E. Freeman, Sol Levine, and L. G. Reeder, eds. Englewood Cliffs, N.J.: Prentice-Hall, Inc.

———, 1964 Evolution and the Ills of Mankind. *In* Horizons of Anthropology. S. Tax, ed. Chicago: Aldine Publishing Co.

———, 1971 Preface. *In* Culture and Population. S. Polgar, ed. Cambridge, Mass: Schenkman Publishing Co., Inc.

———, 1972 Population History and Population Policies from an Anthropological Perspective. Current Anthropology **13**(2):203–211.

POLSON, STEVEN, 1968 Health. *In* International Encyclopedia of the Social Sciences. New York: The Free Press.

POLUNIN, IVAN, 1953 The Medical Natural History of Malayan Aborigines and their Medical Investigation. Medical Journal of Malaya **8**:55–174.

POPHAM, ROBERT E., 1954 Trepanation as a Rational Procedure in Primitive Surgery. University of Toronto Medical Journal **31**:204–211.

POSER, E. G., 1963 Some Psychosocial Determinants of Pain Tolerance. Read at XVIth International Congress of Psychology, Washington, D.C.

POWELL, ROBIN D. et al., 1968 Effects of Glucose-6-Phosphate Dehydrogenase Deficiency Upon the Host: Drug-Malaria Parasite Interactions. Military Medicine **131**:1039–1056.

PRESS, IRWIN, 1969 Ambiguity and Innovation: Implications for the Genesis of the Cultural Broker. American Anthropologist **71**:205–217.

———, 1969 Urban Illness: Physicians, Curers, and Dual Use in Bogotá. Journal of Health and Social Behavior. **10**:209–218.

———, 1971 The Urban Curandero. American Anthropologist **73**:741–756.

PRICE, D. L., G. V. MANN, O. A. ROELS, and J. M. MERRILL, 1963 Parasitism in Congo Pygmies. American Journal of Tropical Medicine and Hygiene **12**:383–387.

PRIESTLY, HERBERT I., 1923 The Mexican Nation, A History. New York.

PRINCE, RAYMOND, 1964 Indigenous Yoruba Psychiatry. *In* Magic, Faith, and Healing. Ari Kiev, ed. New York: The Free Press.

PUSEY, WILLIAM A., 1933 The History of Epidemiology of Syphilis. Springfield, Ill.: Charles C Thomas, Publisher.

QUINN, J. R., ed., 1973 Medicine and Public Health in the People's Republic of China. Washington, D.C.: U.S. Government Printing Office.

QUISENBERRY, WALTER B., 1960 Sociocultural Factors in Cancer in Hawaii. Annals of the New York Academy of Science, No. 7, **84**:795–806.

QUISUMBING, EDUARDO, 1951 Medicinal Plants of the Philippines. Republic of the Philippines Department of Agriculture and National Resources. Technical Bulletin No. 16. Manila: Republic of the Philippines Bureau of Printing.

RADCLIFFE-BROWN, A. R., n.d. Sanctions. Encyclopedia of the Social Sciences.

———, 1933 The Anadaman Islanders. 2nd ed. Cambridge: Cambridge University Press.

RADIN, PAUL, 1957 Primitive Religion. New York: Viking Press, Inc. (Orig. published in 1937, also 1967 ed.).

RAIKES, A., 1975 Medical Education in Transition: Tanzania. *In* Topias and Utopias in Health. S. Ingman and A. Thomas, eds. The Hague: Mouton & Co.

RASMUSSEN, KNUD, 1932 Intellectual Culture of the Copper Eskimos. Report of the Fifth Thule Expedition, 1921–1924, Vol. 9.

RAVEN, H. C., 1950 The Anatomy of the Gorilla, New York: Columbia University Press.

RAZZELL, P. E., 1974 An Interpretation of the Modern Rise of Population in Europe—A Critique. Population Studies **28**(1): 5–17.

READ, KENNETH E., 1925 Nama Cult of the Central Highlands, New Guinea. Oceania **23**: 1–25.

———, 1954 Cultures of the Central Highlands, New Guinea. Southwestern Journal of Anthropology **10**: 1–43.

READ, MARGARET, 1966 Culture, Health, and Disease. London: Tavistock Publications, Ltd.

RECORD, J. C., 1974 Leveling the Chinese Physician: "Permanent Revolution" and the Medical Profession in the People's Republic of China. Paper presented at the annual meeting of the American Sociological Association. Montreal. Mimeo.

REDFIELD, ROBERT, 1934 Chan Kom, A Maya Village. Chicago: University of Chicago Press.

———, 1956 Peasant Society and Culture. Chicago: University of Chicago Press.

———, and M. P. Redfield, 1940 Disease and Its Treatment in Dzitas, Tucatan. Contributions to American Anthropology and History. Carnegie Institute of Washington, D.C. Publication No. 523.

REICHEL-DOLMATOFF, GERARDO, and ALICIA REICHEL-DOLMATOFF. 1961 The People of Aritama. London: Routledge and Kegan Paul, Ltd.

———, and ———, 1963 The People of Aritama: The Cultural Personality of a Columbian Mestizo Village. Chicago: University of Chicago Press.

REICHENBACH, HANS, 1951 The Rise of Scientific Philosophy. Berkeley: University of California Press.

REYNOLDS, BARRIE, 1963 Magic, Divination, and Witchcraft Among the Barotse of Northern Rhodesia. London: Chatto & Windus.

RHODES, A. J., and C. E. VAN ROOYEN, 1962 Textbook of Virology for Students and Practitioners of Medicine. Baltimore: The Williams & Wilkins Co.

RICHARDS, A. I., 1939 Land, Labour, and Diet in Northern Rhodesia. Oxford: Oxford University Press.

RICHARDS, I. A., 1929 Practical Cricitism. New York: Harcourt Brace Jovanovich, Inc.

RICHARDSON, M., and B. BODE, 1971 Popular Medicine in Puntarenas, Costa Rica: Urban and Societal Features. Middle American Research Institute, Publication 24. New Orleans: Tulane University Press.

RICHTER, CURT P., 1957 On the Phenomenon of Sudden Death in Animals and Man. Psychosomatic Medicine **19**: 191–198.

RILEY, MATILDA W., 1963 Sociological Research: A Case Approach. New York: Harcourt Brace Jovanovich, Inc.

RIN, H., 1965 A Study of the Aetiology of Koro in Respect of the Chinese Concepts of Illness. International Journal of Social Psychiatry **11**: 7–13.

RIVERS, W. H. R., 1900 A Geneological Method of Collecting Social and Vital Statistics. Journal of the Royal Anthropological Institute of Great Britain and Ireland **30**: 74–82.

———, 1906 The Todas. New York and London: Macmillan Publishing Co., Inc.

———, 1914 The History of Melanesian Society. vol. 2. Percy Sladen Trust Expedition to Melanesia, Publication No. 1. Cambridge, England: Cambridge University Press.

———, 1914 Kinship and Social Organization. London School of Economics and Political Science. Studies No. 36. London. Constable.

———, 1926 Psychology and Ethnology. London: Routledge and Kegan Paul, Ltd. New York: Harcourt Brace Jovanovich, Inc.

———, 1927 Medicine, Magic, and Religion. London: Kegan Paul, Trench, Trubner & Co. (orig. ed. 1924).

ROBERT, J. M., 1930 Coutumes des Wafipa. Manuscript.

———, 1949 Croyances et coutumes Magico-Religieuses des Wafipa Paines. Tabora: Tanganyika Mission Press.

ROBERTS, DEREK F., 1952 An Ecological Approach to Physical Anthropology: Environmental Temperatures and Physiological Features. Actes du IV Congrés International des Sciences Anthropologiques et Ethnologiques. Vienne. Tome **I**: 145–148.

ROBINSON, C., 1957 Emotional Factors and Rheumatoid Arthritis. Canadian Medical Association Journal **77**: 344–345.

ROBINSON, J. T., 1963 Adaptive Radiation in the Australopithecines. *In* African Ecology and Human Evolution. F. C. Howell and F. Bourliere, eds. Viking Fund Publications in Anthropology **36**: 385–416.

ROEMER, MILTON I., 1954 Health Service Organization as a Task in Applied Social Science. Canadian Journal of Public Health **45**: 133–145.

———, 1959 Social Science and Organized Health Service. Human Organization **18**: 75–77.

———, ed. 1960 Henry E. Sigerist on the Sociology of Medicine. New York: MD Publications.

ROGLER, LLOYD H., and AUGUST B. HOLLINGSHEAD, 1961 The Puerto Rican Spiritualist as a Psychiatrist. American Journal of Sociology 67:17–22.

ROHEIM, GEZA, 1953 The Evil Eye. Yearbook of Psychoanalysis 9:283.

ROMANO, OCTAVIO V., 1960 Donship in a Mexican-American Community in Texas. American Anthropologist 62:966–976.

———, 1965 Charismatic Medicine, Folk-Healing and Folk-Sainthood. American Anthropologist 67:1151–1173.

ROMNEY, A. KIMBALL, and ROY G. D'ANDRADE, 1964 Cognitive Aspects of English Kin Terms. American Anthropologist 66:146–170.

RONAGHY, H. A., and S. SOTLER, 1974 Is the Chinese "Barefoot Doctor" Exportable to Rural Iran? The Lancet June 29:1331–1333.

RONEY, JOHN G. JR., 1966 Palaeoepidemiology: An Example from California. In Human Palaeopathology. New Haven: Yale University Press.

———, 1959 Paleopathology of a California Archeological Site. Bulletin of the History of Medicine 33:97–109.

RONGY, A. J., 1937 Childbirth: Yesterday and Today. New York:

ROSEN, GEORGE, 1963 The Evolution of Social Medicine. In Handbook of Medical Sociology. H. E. Freeman, S. Levine, and L. G. Reeder, eds. Englewood Cliffs, N.J.: Prentice-Hall, Inc.

———, and E. WELLIN, 1959 A Bookshelf on the Social Sciences and Public Health. American Journal of Public Health 50:441–454.

ROSENHAN, D. L., 1973 On Being Sane in Insane Places. Science 179:4070.

ROSENTHAL, T., and B. J. SIEGEL, 1959 Magic and Witchcraft: An Interpretation from Dissonance Theory. Southwestern Journal of Anthropology 15:143–167.

ROTH, JULIUS A., 1956 What Is an Activity? Etc.: A Review of General Semantics 14:54–56.

———, 1957 Ritual and Magic in Control of Contagion. American Social Review 22:310–314.

ROTH, M., 1963 Neuroses, Psychoses, and the Concept of Disease in Psychiatry. Acta Psychiatrica Scandinavia 39:128–145.

ROTHENBERG, A., 1964 Puerto Rico and Aggression. American Journal of Psychiatry 120:962–970.

ROUSSELOT, R., and A. PELLISSIER, 1952 Pathologie du Gorille. Bulletin de la Société de Pathologie Exotique 45:568–574.

ROWE, JOHN HOWLAND, 1950 Thoughts on Knowledge and Ignorance. Kroeber Anthropological Society Papers, No. 2:6–8.

RUBEL, ARTHUR J., 1960 Concepts of Disease in Mexican-American Culture. American Anthropologist 62:795–814.

———, 1964 The Epidemiology of a Folk Illness: Susto in Hispanic America. Ethnology 3:268–283.

———, 1966 Across the Tracks. Austin: University of Texas Press.

RUCH, T. C., 1959 Diseases of Laboratory Primates. Philadelphia: W. B. Saunders.

RUFFER, M. A., and A. R. FERGUSON, 1911 Smallpox in an Egyptian Mummy. Journal of Pathology and Bacteriology 15:131.

RUFFER, M. A., and G. E. SMITH, 1910 Pathological Disease in an Egyptian Mummy. Zur Historischen Biologie der Krankheit. Berlin: Sandhoff and Sticker.

RUFFER, M. A., 1921 Studies in Paleopathology of Egypt. Chicago: University of Chicago Press.

RUHN, H-J., 1968 Parasites and the Phylogeny of the Catarrhine Primates. In Taxonomy and Phylogeny of Old World Primates with References to the Origin of Man. B. Chiarelli, ed. Torino. Rosenberg and Sellier.

RUSSELL, J. C., 1958 Late Ancient and Medieval Population. Transactions of the American Philosophical Society. 48, pt. 3.

SABIN, ALBERT B., 1952 Nature of Inherited Resistance to Viruses Affecting the Nervous System. Proceedings of the National Academy of Sciences 38:540–546.

SAHLINS, MARSHALL D., and ELMAN R. SERVICE, eds., 1960 Evolution and Culture. Ann Arbor: University of Michigan Press.

SAL Y ROSAS, F., 1958 El mito de Jani o Susto de la medicina indigena del Peru. Revista de la Sanidad de Policia 18:167–210.

SAMUELS, R., 1965 Parasitological Study of Long-Dried Fecal Samples (Contributions of the Weatherill Mesa Archeological Project). Memoirs of the Society of American Archeology 19:175–179).

SANDERS, WILLIAM, 1953 The Anthropology of Central Vera Cruz: Huastecos, Totonacos y sus vecinos. Ignacio Bernal and Eusebio Davalos Hurtado, eds. Mexico.

SANGREE, WALTER H., 1970 Tribal Ritual, Leadership, and the Mortality Rate in Irigue, Northern Nigeria. Southwestern Journal of Anthropology 26:32–39.

SANGERMANO, VICENTIUS, 1893 The Burmese Empire a Hundred Years Ago. Westminster: A. Constable.

SAPIR, EDWARD, 1916 Time Perspective in Aboriginal American Culture: A Study in Method.

Canada, Dept. of Mines, Geological Survey, Memoir 90, Anthropological Series No. 13. Ottawa: Government Printing Bureau.

SARBIN, THEODORE R., and VERNON L. ALLEN, 1968 Role Theory. In The Handbook of Social Psychology. Gardner Lindzey and Elliot Aronson, eds. Reading, Mass.: Addison-Wesley Publishing Co., Inc.

SAUCIER, JEAN-FRANCOIS, 1972 Correlates of the Long Post-partum Taboo: A Cross-Cultural Study. Current Anthropology 13:238–249.

SAUL, LEON J., and C. BERNSTEIN, JR., 1948 The Emotional Settings of Some Attacks on Urticaria. In Studies in Psychosomatic Medicine. F. Alexander, ed. New York.

SAUER, CARL O., 1966 The Early Spanish Main. Berkeley and Los Angeles: University of California Press.

SAUNDERS, LYLE, 1954 Cultural Difference and Medical Care: The Case of the Spanish-Speaking People of the Southwest. New York: Russell Sage Foundation.

———, 1958 Culture and Nursing Care. In Patients, Physicians and Illness. E. G. Jaco, ed. New York: The Free Press.

———, 1958 Healing Ways in the Spanish Southwest. In Patients, Physicians and Illness. E. G. Jaco, New York: The Free Press.

SCARPA, ANTONIO, 1967 Introduction. Ethnoiatria 1:2–4.

SCELLE, GEORGES, 1910 The Slave-Trade in the Spanish Colonies in America: The Asiento. The American Journal of International Law 4:612–661.

SCHALLER, GEORGE, 1963 The Mountain Gorilla: Ecology and Behavior. Chicago: University of Chicago Press.

SCHIEFF, J. M., 1858 Lehrbuch der Physiologie 1:228.

SCHILDER, P., 1938 Comments Reported in the Section on Culture and Personality. American Journal of Orthopsychiatry 8:46–47.

SCHMIDT, KARL E., 1964 Folk Psychiatry in Sarawak. In Magic, Faith and Healing. A. Kiev, ed. New York: The Free Press.

SCHNEIDER, K., 1959 Clinical Psychopathology. New York: Grune & Stratton.

SCHOFIELD, F. D., A. D. PARKINSON, and D. JEFFEY, 1963 Observations on the Epidemiology, Effects and Treatment of Tinea Imbricata. Transactions of the Royal Society of Tropical Medicine and Hygiene 57:214–227.

SCHOFIELD, F. D., 1970 Some Relations Between Social Isolation and Specific Communicable Diseases. American Journal of Tropical Medicine and Hygiene 19:167–169.

SCHRAER, H., and M. T. NEWMAN, 1958 Quantitative Roentgenography of Skeletal Mineralization in Malnourished Quechua Indian Boys. Science 128:476–477.

SCHULL, W. J., ed., 1963 Genetic Selection in Man. Third Macy Conference on Genetics. Ann Arbor: University of Michigan Press.

SCHULTZ, ADOLF H., 1950 The Specializations of Man and His Place Among the Catarrhine Primates. Cold Springs Harbor Symposium on Quantitative Biology 15:37–53

SCHWARTZ, LOLA ROMANUCCI, 1963 Morality, Conflict, and Violence in a Mexican Mestizo Village. Doctoral dissertation. Ann Arbor: University of Michigan, Microfilms.

———, 1966 Conflicts Fonciers a Mokereng, Village Matankor des Iles des Amiraute. L'Homme, revue francaise d'Anthropologie 6:32–52.

———, 1969 The Hierarchy of Resort in Curative Practices: The Admiralty Islands, Melanesia. Journal of Health and Social Behavior 10:201–209.

SCHWARTZ, THEODORE, and MARGARET MEAD, 1961 Micro-and Macrocultural Models for Cultural Evolution. Anthropological Linguistics 3:1–7.

———, 1962 The Paliau Movement in the Admiralty Islands, 1946–1954. Anthropological Papers of the American Museum of Natural History. New York.

———, 1963 Systems of Areal Integration: Some Considerations Based on the Admiralty Islands of Northern Melanesia. Anthropological Forum. 1.

———, and LOLA ROMANUCCI, 1968 Inebriate Behavior in Melanesia. Manuscript.

SCIENTIFIC COUNCIL FOR AFRICA SOUTH OF THE SAHARA (CSA), 1956 In Nutritional Research in Africa South of the Sahara. London: CCTZ/CSA Pub. No. 19.

SCOTCH, NORMAN, 1960 A Preliminary Report on the Relation of Sociocultural Factors to Hypertension Among the Zulu. Annals, New York Academy of Sciences 84:1000–1009.

———, 1963 Medical Anthropology. In Biennial Review of Anthropology. B. J. Siegel, ed. Stanford, Cal.: Stanford University Press.

———, and H. GEIGER, 1962 The Epidemiology of Rheumatoid Arthritis. Journal of Chronic Diseases 15:1037–1067.

SCOTT, E. M., R. C. WEIGHT, and B. T. HANAN, 1955

Anemia in Alaskan Eskimo. Journal of Nutrition **55**:137–149.

SCOTT, SIR JAMES GEORGE, and HARDIMAN, 1900–1901 Gazeteen of Upper Burma and the Shan States. Rangoon: Government Printing Office **1–5**.

SCRIMSHAW, NEVIN S., 1953 Excerpt of address published in Proceedings of Food and Nutrition Board **12**:24, May 1952. Journal of the American Dietetic Association **29**:133.

————, C. E. TAYLOR, and J. E. GORDON, 1959 Interactions of Nutrition and Infection. American Journal of the Medical Sciences **237**:367–403.

————, and C. TEJADA, 1970 Pathology of Living Indians as Seen in Guatemala. *In* Handbook of Middle American Indians. T. Dale Stewart, ed. Austin: University of Texas Press.

————, M. BIHAR, F. VITERI, G. ARROYANE, and C. TEJADA, 1957 Epidemiology and Prevention of Severe Protein Malnutrition (Kwashiorkor) in Central America. American Journal of Public Health **47**:53–62.

SCULLY, VIRGINIA, 1970 A Treasury of the American Indian Herbals. New York: Bonanza Books.

SECQUES, F., 1929 Un Cas Diagnostique Goundou Chez le Gorille. Revue de Medecine et Hygiene Tropicale **21**:50–53.

SEDA-BONILLA, EDUARDO, 1969 Interaction Personalidad en Una Communidad de Puerto Rico. San Juan, Puerto Rico: Ediciones Juan Ponce de León.

SELBY, HENRY A., 1974 Zapotec Deviance. Austin: University of Texas Press.

SELYE, HANS, 1956 The Stress of Life. New York: McGraw-Hill, Inc.

SEMINAR ON THE EPIDEMIOLOGY AND PREVENTION OF MEASLES AND RUBELLA. 1965 Archiv für die Gesamte Virusforschung. New York: Springer.

SERVICE, ELMAN R., 1966 The Hunters. Englewood Cliffs, N.J.: Prentice-Hall, Inc.

SHATTUCK, G. C., 1951 Diseases of the Tropics. New York: Appleton-Century-Crofts.

SHELTON, AUSTIN J., 1965 The Meaning and Method of Ifa Divination Among the Northern Nsukka Ibo. American Anthropologist **67**:1441–1455.

SHERMAN, KATHERINE, 1956 Spring on an Arctic Island. Boston, Mass.: Little, Brown and Co.

SHILOH, AILON, 1958 Middle East Culture and Health. Health Education Journal **16**:232.

————, 1961 The System of Medicine in the Middle East Culture. Middle East Journal **15**:277.

————, 1963 Conceptual Progress Toward Structuring the Universal Pattern of Medicine. Health Education Journal **21**:47.

————, 1965 A Case Study of Disease and Culture in Action: Leprosy Among the Hausa of Northern Nigeria. Human Organization **24**:140–147.

————, 1967 Programming the Integration of Chinese Traditional and Modern Medicine. Health Education Journal **26**:37.

————, 1968 The Interaction of the Middle Eastern and Western Systems of Medicine. Social Science and Medicine **2**:235–248.

SHIROKOGOROFF, S. M., 1935 Psychomental Complex of the Tungus. London: Routledge and Kegan Paul, Ltd.

SHWAY YOE (Sir James George Scott), 1896 The Burman: His Life and Notions. Reprinted 1963. New York: W. W. Norton & Co.

SHRYOCK, RICHARD HARRISON, 1947 The Development of Modern Medicine: An Interpretation of the Social and Scientific Factors Involved. New York: Alfred A. Knopf, Inc.

SIDEL, VICTOR W., 1972 The Barefoot Doctors of the People's Republic of China. New England Journal of Medicine **286**:1292–1300.

————, and R. SIDEL, 1973 Serve the People: Observations on Medicine in the People's Republic of China. New York: Josiah Macy, Jr., Foundation.

SIGERIST, HENRY E., 1941 Medicine and Human Welfare. Yale University Press.

————, 1951 A History of Medicine: Primitive and Archaic Medicine, Vol. 1. New York: Oxford University Press.

SILVER, DANIEL, 1966 Zinacanteco Shamanism. Unpublished Ph.D. dissertation, Harvard University.

SIMMONS, LEO W., and HAROLD G. WOLFF, 1954 Social Science in Medicine. New York: Russell Sage Foundation.

SIMMONS, OZZIE G., 1955 Popular and Modern Medicine in Mestizo Communities of Coastal Peru and Chile. Journal of American Folklore **68**:57–71.

————, 1958 Social Status and Public Health. Pamphlet No. 13. New York. Social Science Research Center.

————, 1960 Popular and Modern Medicine in Mestizo Communities of Coastal Peru and Chile. *In* Sociological Studies of Health and Sickness. Dorrian C. Apple, ed. New York: McGraw-Hill, Inc.

————, 1963 Social Research in Health and

Medicine: A Bibliography. *In* Handbook of Medical Sociology. H. E. Freeman, S. Levine, and L. G. Reeder, eds. Englewood Cliffs, N.J.: Prentice-Hall, Inc.

SIMONDS, PAUL E., 1974 The Social Primates. New York: Harper & Row, Publishers, Inc.

SIMPSON, GEORGE, G., 1962 Comments on Cultural Evolution. *In* Evolution and Man's Progress. H. Hoagland and R. W. Burhoe, eds. New York: Columbia University Press.

SINCLAIR, A., 1957 Field and Clinical Survey Report of the Mental Health of the Indigenes of the Territory of Papua and New Guinea. Port Moresby: Government Printer.

SINGER, RONALD, 1962 The Significance of the Sickle-Cell in Africa. The Leech **XXII**:152–161.

SISKIN, E., 1941 The Impact of the Peyote Cult Upon Shamanism Among the Washo Indians. Unpublished Ph.D. dissertation. Yale University.

SKINSNES, O. K., 1964 Leprosy Rationale. New York: American Leprosy Mission, Inc.

SLATER, E., 1965 Diagnosis of Hysteria. British Medical Journal **1**:1395–1399.

SLOBODKIN, L. B., 1961 Growth and Regulation of Animal Populations. New York: Holt, Rinehart and Winston, Inc.

SMARTT, C. G. F., 1956 Mental Maladjustment in the East African. Journal of Mental Science **102**:441–466.

SMITH, C. A., 1954 Effects of Maternal Undernutrition Upon the Newborn Infant in Holland. Journal of Pediatrics **30**: 229–243.

SMITH, CHARLINE G., 1970 Culture and Diabetes Among the Upland Yuma Indians. Ph.D. dissertation. University of Utah.

SMITH, G. E., and JONES F. WOOD, 1910 Report on Human Remains. Archaeological Survey of Nubia. Report for 1907–1908. Cairo. Ministry of Finance.

SNODGRASSE, R. M., S. DREIZEN, C. CURRIE, G. S. PARKER, and T. D. SPIES, 1955 The Association Between Anomalous Ossification Centers in the Hand and Wrist, Nutritional Status and Rate of Skeletal Maturation in Children Five to Fourteen Years of Age. American Journal of Roentgenology, Radium Therapy, and Nuclear Medicine **74**:1037–1048.

SNOW, J., 1936 Snow on Cholera. New York: Commonwealth Fund.

SOUTHALL, AIDEN, 1959 An Operational Theory of Role. Human Relations **12**:17–34.

SPENCER, ROBERT F., 1949–1950 Primitive Obstetrics. Ciba Symposium **11**:1158–1188.

SPENCER, ROBERT F., and JESSE D. JENNINGS, 1965 The Native Americans. New York.

SPENGLER, J. L., 1960 Population and World Economic Development. Science **131**:1497–1502.

SPICER, EDWARD H., 1952 Human Problems in Technological Change: A Casebook. New York: Russell Sage Foundation.

SPIRO, MELFORD E., 1966 Religion: Problems of Definition and Explanation. *In* Anthropological Approaches to the Study of Religion. M. Banton, ed. London.

———, 1967 Burmese Supernaturalism: A Study in the Explanation of Suffering. Englewood Cliffs, N.J.: Prentice-Hall.

———, 1970 Buddhism and Society: A Great Tradition and Its Burmese Vicissitudes. New York: Harper & Row Publishers, Inc.

SPOONER, BRIAN, 1970 The Evil Eye in the Middle East. *In* Witchcraft Confessions and Accusations. M. Douglas, ed. London: A.S.A. Monograph 9.

SPOONER, BRIAN, ed. 1972 Population Growth: Anthropological Implications. Cambridge: MIT Press.

SPRADLEY, JAMES J., ed. 1972 Culture and Cognition: Rules, Maps, and Plans. San Francisco: Chandler Publishing Co.

SPUHLER, JAMES N., 1959 The Evolution of Man's Capacity for Culture. Detroit: Wayne State University Press.

SRINIVAS, M. N., 1952 Religion and Society Among the Coorgs of South India. Oxford: Oxford University Press.

Stanford Observer 1974 China's Barefoot Doctors: A Lesson for Law Students. Stanford University, January 3ff.

STEARN, E. W., and A. E. STEARN, 1945 The Effect of Smallpox on the Destiny of the Amer-Indian. Boston: Bruce Humphreys.

STEFANSSON, VILHJALMUR 1914 The Stefansson–Anderson Arctic expedition of the American Museum: Preliminary Ethnological Report. Anthropological Papers of the American Museum of Natural History **14**:part 1.

———, 1956 The Fat of the Land, New York: Macmillan Publishing Co., Inc.

STEGGERDA, M., and B. KORSCH, 1943 Remedies for Diseases as Prescribed by Maya Indian Herbdoctors. Bulletin of the History of Medicine **XIII**:54–82.

STEIN, STANLEY, 1963 Alone No Longer. New York: Funk & Wagnalls.

STEIN, Z., and M. SUSSER, 1972 The Cuban Health System: A Trial of a Comprehensive Service in a

Poor Country. International Journal of Health Services **2**:551–566.

STERN, BERNHARD J., 1959 Historical Sociology: Selected Papers. New York: The Citadel Press.

STERNBACH, R. A., and B. TURSKY, 1965 Ethnic Differences Among Housewives in Psychophysical and Skin Potential Responses to Electric Shock. Psychophysiology **1**:241–246.

STEVENS, H., 1965 Jumping Frenchmen of Maine. Archives of Neurology **12**:311–314.

STEVENSON, MATILDA C., 1905 The Zuni Indians. 23rd Annual Report of the Bureau of American Ethnology. Washington, D.C.: Smithsonian Institute.

STEWARD, JULIAN H., 1955 Theory of Culture Change. Urbana: University of Illinois Press.

STEWARD, T. DALE, and ALEXANDER SPOEHR, 1952 Evidence of the Paleopathology of Yaws. Bulletin of the History of Medicine **26**:538–553.

———, 1958 Stone Age Skull Surgery: A General Review, with Emphasis on the New World. In Smithsonian Report for 1957, Washington.

———, 1962 Comments on the Reassessment of the Indian Knoll Skeletons. American Journal of Physical Anthropology **20**:143–148.

STONE, ERIC, 1932 Medicine Among the American Indians. New York: Paul B. Hoeber (reprinted 1962, New York: Hafner Publishing Co. Inc.).

STREHLOW, T. G. H., 1965 Culture, Social Structure, and Environment in Aboriginal Central Australia. In Aboriginal Man in Australia. R. M. Berndt, and C. H. Berndt, eds. Sydney: Angus and Robertson.

STRODE, G. K., 1951 Yellow Fever. New York: McGraw-Hill, Inc.

STROMBERG, J., 1974 Community Involvement in Solving Local Health Problems in Ghana. Inquiry, Supplement **13**:148–155.

STRONG, J. P., H. C. McGILL, and J. H. MILLER, 1961 Schistosomiasis Mansoni in the Kenya Baboon. American Journal of Tropical Medicine and Hygiene **10**:25–32.

STURTEVANT, WILLIAM C., 1964 Studies in Ethnoscience. American Anthropologist **66**:99–131.

SUCHMAN, EDWARD A., 1968 Epidemiology. In International Encyclopedia of the Social Sciences. New York: The Free Press **5**:97–101.

SUMNER, WILLIAM GRAHAM, and ALBERT G. KELLER, 1927 The Science of Society. New Haven. Yale University Press.

SUSSMAN, ROBERT W., 1972 Child Transport, Family Size, and Increase in Human Population During the Neolithic. Current Anthropology **13**(2):258–259.

SWANSON, GUY E., 1960 The Birth of the Gods. Ann Arbor: University of Michigan Press.

SWARTZ, MARC, VICTOR TURNER, and ARTHUR TUDEN, eds. 1966 Political Anthropology. Chicago: Aldine Publishing Co.

SYME, S. LEONARD, and LEO G. REEDER, 1967 Social Stress and Cardiovascular Disease. Milbank Memorial Fund Quarterly **45**(2), pt. 2.

SZASZ, THOMAS S., 1961 The Myth of Mental Illness. New York: Hoeber-Harper.

TAEUBER, IRENE B., 1958 The Population of Japan. Princeton: Princeton University Press.

TAX, SOL, 1950 Animistic and Rational Thought. Kroeber Anthropological Society Papers, No. **2**:1–5.

TAYLOR, CARL E., 1968 The Health Sciences and Indian Village Culture. In Science and the Human Condition in India and Pakistan. Ward Morehouse, ed. New York: Rockefeller University Press.

———, 1975 The Place of Indigenous Medical Practitioners in the Modernization of Health Services. In Asian Medical Systems. C. Leslie, ed. Berkeley: University of California Press.

———, and MARIE-FRANCOISE HALL, 1967 Health, Population and Economic Development. Science **157**:651–657.

TAYLOR, E. L., 1955 Parasitic Helminths in Medieval Remains. Veterinary Record **67**:216–218.

TAYLOR, HERBERT C., Jr., and LESTER L. HOAGLIN, JR., 1962 The "Intermittent Fever" Epidemic of the 1830's on the Lower Columbia River. Ethnohistory **9**:160–178.

TEICHER, MORTON I., 1960 Windigo Psychosis Proceedings of the 1960 Annual Spring Meeting of the American Ethnological Society. V. F. Ray, ed. New York: American Ethnological Society.

THOMAS, A. E., 1971 Adaptation to Modern Medicine in Lowland Machakos, Kenya: A Controlled Comparison of Two Kamba Communities. Ph.D. dissertation. Stanford University.

———, 1974 Oaths, Ordeals, and the Kenyan Courts: A Policy Analysis. Human Organization **33**:59–70.

———, 1975 Health Care in Ukambani, Kenya: A Socialist Critique. In Topias and Utopias in Health. S. Ingman and A. Thomas, eds. The Hague. Mouton & Co.

Thompson-McFadden Pellagra Commission 1913 First Progress Report. American Journal of the Medical Sciences **191**.

THORNE, F. C., 1944 Startle Neurosis. American Journal of Psychiatry **191**:105–109.

TILLYARD, E. M. W., 1944 The Elizabethan World Picture. New York: Macmillan Publishing Co., Inc.

TODD, T. W., 1927 Skeletal Remains of Mortality. Scientific Monthly **24**:481–496.

TOPLEY, M., 1970 Chinese Traditional Ideas and the Treatment of Disease: Two Examples from Hong Kong. Man(n.s.). **5**:421–437.

———, 1975 Chinese Traditional Etiology and Methods of Cure in Hong Kong. *In* Asian Medical Systems. C. Leslie, ed. Berkeley: University of California Press.

TOWERS, G., 1973 City Planning in China. Journal of the Royal Town Planning Institute **59**:125–128.

TRAUTMAN, J. R., E. B. JOHNWICK, O. W. HASSELBLAD, and C. I. CROWTHER, 1965 Social and Educational Aspects of Leprosy in the Continental United States. Military Medicine **130**:927–929.

TSCHANNERL, J., 1975 Contemporary Health Planning Trends in Tanzania. *In* Topias and Utopias in Health. S. Ingman, and A. Thomas, eds. The Hague: Mouton & Co.

TSCHOPIK, HARRY, 1951 The Aymara of Chucuito, Peru: Magic. Anthropological Papers of the American Museum of Natural History **44**:133–308.

TUCKER, A., and M. BRYAN, 1956 The Non-Bantu Languages of North-Eastern Africa. London.

TUFT, LEWIS, 1949 Clinical Allergy. Philadelphia: Lea & Febiger.

TURNBULL, COLIN M., 1965 Wayward Servants: The Two Worlds of the African Pygmies. Garden City, N.Y.: Natural History Press (Doubleday).

———, 1968 Discussion. Man the Hunter. R. B. Lee, and I. DeVore, eds. Chicago: Aldine Publishing Co.

TURNER, VICTOR W., 1961 Ndembu Divination: Its Symbolism and Techniques. Manchester: Manchester University Press. Rhodes–Livingstone Institute Paper No. 31.

———, 1964 An Ndembu Doctor in Practice. *In* Magic, Faith, and Healing. Ari Kiev, ed. New York: The Free Press.

———, 1964 Betwixt and Between: The Liminal Period in Rites de Passage. *In* Symposium on New Approaches to the Study of Religion. J. Helm, ed. Seattle: Proceedings of the American Ethnological Society.

———, 1964 Witchcraft and Sorcery: Taxonomy versus Dynamics. Africa **34**:314–325.

———, 1966 Colour Classification in Ndembu Ritual. *In* Anthropological Approaches to the Study of Religion. M. Banton, ed. London: Tavistock Publications.

———, 1967 The Forest of Symbols. Ithaca, N.Y.: Cornell University Press.

———, 1968 The Drums of Affliction: A Study of Religious Processes Among the Ndembu of Zambia. Oxford: Clarendon Press and the International African Institute.

———, 1969 The Ritual Process: Structure and Anti-Structure. Chicago: Aldine Publishing Co., Inc.

UNSCHULD, P., 1973 Die Praxis des Traditionellen Chinesischen Heilsystems. Weisbaden: Franz Steiner Verlag.

———, 1975 The Social Organization and Ecology of Medical Practice in Taiwan. *In* Asian Medical Systems. C. Leslie, ed. Berkeley: University of California Press.

U.S. Public Health Service Hospital 1960 Annual Reports. Carville, Louisiana.

———, 1961 Annual Reports. Carville, Louisiana.

———, 1963 Syllabus of Lecture Notes. Fourth Seminar on Leprosy in Collaboration with American Leprosy Missions, Inc. Mimeograph. Carville, Louisiana.

———, 1964 Syllabus of Lecture Notes. Fifth Seminar on Leprosy in Collaboration with American Leprosy Missions. Inc. Mimeograph, Carville, Louisiana.

United States Department of Health, Education, and Welfare 1959 Patients in Mental Institutions, 1950 and 1951. Washington: National Institutes of Health.

———, 1967 Illness Among Indians. Washington.

UZZELL, DOUGLAS, n.d. San Andres Zautla: Progressing Downward. Unpublished manuscript.

———, 1969 A Preliminary Look at Determinants of Illness Beliefs in a Mexican Village. Paper presented at the joint Meeting of the Southern Anthropological Society and the American Ethnological Society. New Orleans.

VALDIZAN, H., 1922 La Medicina Popular Peruana. Imprenta Torres Aguirre.

VALLOIS, HENRI V., 1937 La Duree de la vie chez Phomme. Anthropologie **47**:5–6.

VAN DER KROEF, J. M., 1958 Indonesian Social Psychological Considerations. Amsterdam: Van der Peet.

VAN DER LEEUW, G., 1938 Religion in Essence and Manifestation. New York.

VAN DER SCHALIE, HENRY, 196 Egypt's New High

555

Dam—Asset or Liability. The Biologist **42**:63–70.

————, 1969 Control in Egypt and the Sudan. Natural History, February special supplement, 62–65.

VAN ETTEN, G., 1972 Toward Research on Health Development in Tanzania. Social Science and Medicine **6**:335–352.

VARRON, A. G., 1939–1940 Medieval Hygiene. Ciba Symposium **1**:213–214.

VEITH, ILZA, 1966 The Yellow Emperor's Classic of Internal Medicine. Berkeley: University of California Press.

VOGEL, VIRGIL J., 1970 American Indian Medicine. Norman: University of Oklahoma Press.

VOGET, FRED, 1950 A Shoshone Innovator. American Anthropologist **52**:53–63.

VOGT, EVON Z., 1966 Los Zinacantecos. Mexico, D.F.: Instituto Nacional Indigenista.

WALLACE, ANTHONY F. C., 1956a Mayeway Resynthesis. Transactions of the New York Academy of Sciences, Series 2, **18**:626–638.

————, 1956b Revitalization Movements. American Anthropologist **58**:264–281.

————, 1956c Stress and Rapid Personality Changes. International Record of Medicine and General Practice Clinics **169**:761–774.

————, 1957 Mayeway Disintegration: The Individual's Perception of Sociocultural Disorganization. Human Organization **16**:23–27.

————, 1958 Dreams and Wishes of the Soul: A Type of Psychoanalytic Theory Among the Seventeenth Century Iroquois. American Anthropologist **60**:234–248.

————, 1959 The Institutionalization of Cathartic and Control Strategies in Iroquois Religious Psychotherapy. In Culture and Mental Health. Marvin K. Opler, ed. New York: Macmillan Publishing Co., Inc.

————, 1961a Religious Revitalization: A Function of Religion in Human History and Evolution. Pamphlet. Institute on Religion in an Age of Science. Boston.

————, 1961b Cultural Composition of the Handsome Lake Religion. Symposium on Cherokee and Iroquois Cultures. William N. Fenton, and John Gulick, eds. Bureau of American Ethnology Bulletin **180**:139–151.

————, 1966 Religion: An Anthropological View. New York: Random House, Inc.

————, 1970 Culture and Personality. 2nd ed. New York: Random House, Inc. (1st ed. 1961).

————, 1972 Mental Illness, Biology and Culture. In Psychological Anthropology. F. L. K. Hsu, ed.

Cambridge, Mass.: Schenkman Publishing Co.

WANG, W. L., 1973 Health Education in the People's Republic of China. Paper presented to the Annual Meeting of the American Public Health Association, San Francisco, Calif. (Mimeo.)

————, 1974 Health Education and Family Planning in the People's Republic of China. International Journal of Health Education, Supplement, **17**:1–25.

WARDWELL, WALTER, I. MERTON HYMAN, and CLAUS B. BAHSON, 1964 Stress and Coronary Heart Disease in Three Field Studies. Journal of Chronic Diseases **17**:73–84.

WARWICK, R., 1964 Medical Report. Eburacum. London: Her Majesty's Stationery Office.

WASHBURN, SHERWOOD L., 1957 Australopithecines: The Hunters or the Hunted? American Anthropologist **59**:612–614.

————, 1959 Speculations on the Interrelations of the History of Tools and Biological Evolution. In The Evolution of Man's Capacity for Culture. J. N. Spuhler, arranger. Detroit: Wayne State University Press.

————, 1965 An Ape's Eye View of Human Evolution. In Symposium on the Origin of Man. Paul I. DeVore, ed. New York: Wenner-Gren Foundation for Anthropological Research, Inc.

WATSON, JOHN B., ed., 1964 New Guinea: The Central Highlands. American Anthropologist **66**:iv, pt. 2.

————, and HAROLD E. NELSON, 1967 Body-Environment Transactions: A Standard Model for Cross-Cultural Analyses. Southwestern Journal of Anthropology **23**:292–309.

WAX, MURRAY, and ROSALIE WAX, 1964 Magic and Monotheism. In Symposium on New Approaches to the Study of Religion. J. Helm, ed. Seattle: Proceedings of the American Ethnological Society.

WEAVER, S. M., 1971 Smallpox or Chickenpox: An Iroquoian Community's Reaction to Crisis, 1901–1902. Ethnohistory **18**:361–378.

WEAVER, THOMAS, 1968 Trends in Research and Medical Education. In Essays on Medical Anthropology. T. Weaver, ed. Southern Anthropological Society. Athens: University of Georgia Press.

————, 1970 Use of Hypothetical Situations in a Study of Spanish American Illness Referral Systems. Human Organization **29**:140–154.

WEBER, MAX, 1948 The Theory of Social and Economic Organization. New York:

————, 1963 The Sociology of Religion. Boston: Beacon Press.

WEBSTER, L. T., 1932 Experimental Epidemiology. Medicine **11**:32.

WEBSTER, H., 1942 Taboo. Stanford.

WEGMAN, M. E., T. Y. LIN, and E. F. PURCELL, eds., 1973 Public Health in the People's Republic of China. New York: Josiah Macy, Jr., Foundation.

WEYER, EDWARD M., 1932 The Eskimos. New Haven: Yale University Press.

WEINSTEIN, E. A., 1932 Cultural Aspects of Delusion. New York.

WEISMAN, ABNER I., 1966 Syphilis: Was It Endemic in Pre-Columbian America or Was It Brought Here from Europe? New York Academy Medical Bulletin **42**:284–300.

WEISS, KENNETH M., 1973 Demographic Models for Anthropology. Memoirs of the Society for American Archaeology No. 27.

WEITLANER, R. J., 1961 La Ceremonia Ilamada. Levantar la sombra. Typescript.

WELLIN, EDWARD, 1955 Maternal and Infant Feeding Practices in a Peruvian Village. Journal of the American Dietetic Association **31**:889.

————, 1955 Water Boiling in a Peruvian Town. In Healing, Culture, and Community. B. Paul, ed. New York: Russell Sage Foundation.

WELLS, CALVIN, 1967 Pseudopathology. In Disease in Antiquity: A Survey of Diseases, Injuries, and Surgery in Ancient Populations. Springfield, Ill.: Charles C Thomas, publisher.

————, 1964 Bones, Bodies, and Disease: Evidence of Disease and Abnormality in Early Man. London: Thames and Hudson.

WERBNER, RICHARD P., 1973 The Superabundance of Understanding: Kalanga Rhetoric and Domestic Divination. American Anthropologist **75**:1414–1440.

WHARTON, R. H., A. B. C. LAING, and W. H. CHEONG, 1963 Studies on the Distribution and Transmission of Malaria and Filariasis among Aborigines in Malaya. Annals of Tropical Medicine and Parasitology **57**:235–254.

WHITE, ABRAHAM, 1950 Role of the Adrenal Cortex in Immunity. Journal of Allergy **21**:273–281.

WHITE, LESLIE, 1949 Ethnological Theory. In Philosophy for the Future. R. W. Sillers, ed.

————, 1959 The Evolution of Culture. New York: McGraw-Hill, Inc.

WHITE, William A., 1929 Outlines of Psychiatry. Washington, D.C.: Nervous and Mental Disease Publishing Company.

WHITING, Beatrice B., 1950 Paiute Sorcery. New York: Viking Publications in Anthropology, No. **15**:1–110.

WHITING, JOHN W. M., 1941 Becoming a Kwoma. New Haven: Yale University Press.

————, 1964 Effects of Climate on Certain Cultural Practices. In Explorations in Cultural Anthropology. Essays in Honor of G. P. Murdock. W. Goodenough, ed. New York: McGraw-Hill Inc.

————, 1968 Discussion., Man the Hunter. R. B. Lee, and I. DeVore, eds. Chicago: Aldine Publishing Co.

————, and IRVIN L. CHILD, 1953 Child Training and Personality. New Haven.

WHITNEY, HARRY, 1911 Hunting with the Eskimos. New York: The Century Co.

WHYTE, M. K., 1973 Bureaucracy and Modernization in China: the Maoist Critique. American Sociological Review **38**:149–165.

————, 1974a Small Groups and Political Rituals in China. Berkeley: University of California Press.

————, 1974b Stratification and Destratification in the People's Republic of China. Paper presented at annual meeting of the American Sociological Association, Montreal, Canada.

WIESENFELD, S. L., 1967 Sickle-Cell Trait in Human Biological and Cultural Evolution. Science **157**:1134–1140.

WILLIS, R. G., 1967 The Head and the Loins. Man **2**:519–534.

————, 1968 Changes in Mystical Concepts and Practices Among the Fipa. Ethnology **7**:139–157.

WILLMOTT, W. E., 1960 The Flexibility of Eskimo Social Organization. Anthropologica **2**:52.

WILLOUGHBY, R. R., 1935 Magic and Cognate Phenomena: An Hypothesis. In A Handbook of Social Psychology. Carl Murchison, ed. Worcester, Mass.:

WINANS, EDGAR V., and ROBERT B. EDGERTON, 1964 Hehe Magic Justice. American Anthropologist **66**:745–764.

————, 1965 The Political Context of Economic Adaptation in the Southern Highlands of Tanzania. American Anthropologist **67**:435–441.

WITTGENSTEIN, LUDWIG, 1963 Philosophical Investigations. New York and London: Oxford University Press.

WOLF, ERIC R., 1956 Aspects of Group Relations in a Complex Society. American Anthropologist **58**:1065–1078.

————, 1956 San Jose: Subculture of a Traditional Coffee Municipality. In The People of Puerto

Rico. J. Steward, ed. Urbana: University of Illinois Press.

———, 1967 Types of Latin American Peasantry. *In* Tribal and Peasant Economies. G. Dalton, ed. New York.

———, 1959 Sons of the Shaking Earth. Chicago: University of Chicago Press.

WOLFF, BERTHOLD B., 1964 The Relationship of Experimental Pain Tolerance to Pain Threshold: A Critique of Gelfand's Paper. Canadian Journal of Psychology. **18**:249–253.

———, 1967 Some Behavioral Mechanisms of Human Pain. IIIrd Symposium IX: Pharmacology of Pain. IIIrd International Pharmacological Congress, 1966. London: Pergamon Press.

———, and A. A. HORLAND, 1967 Effect of Suggestion Upon Experimental Pain: A Validation Study. Journal of Abnormal Psychology **72**:402–407.

———, and M. E. JARVIK, 1964 Relationship Between Superficial and Deep Somatic Thresholds of Pain with a Note on Handedness. American Journal of Psychology **77**:589–599.

———, and M. E. JARVIK, 1965 Quantitative Measures of Deep Somatic Pain: Further Studies with Hypertonic Saline. Clinical Science **28**:43–56.

———, T. G. KANTOR, M. E. JARVIK, and E. LASKA, 1966 Response of Experimental Pain to Analgesic Drugs. II, Codeine and Placebo. Clinical Pharmacology and Therapeutics **7**:323–331.

———, N. A. KRASNEGOR, and R. S. FARR, 1965 Effects of Suggestion. Upon Experimental Pain Response Parameters. Perceptual and Motor Skills **21**:675–683.

———, and SARAH LANGLEY, 1968 Cultural Factors and Response to Pain: A Review. American Anthropologist **70**:494–501.

WOLFF, ROBERT J., 1965 Modern Medicine and Traditional Culture: Confrontation on the Malay Peninsula. Human Organization **24**:339–345.

WONG, K. CHIMIN, and WU LIEN-TEH, 1936 History of Chinese Medicine. Shanghai. National Quarantine Service.

WOOD, CORINNE SHEAR, 1975 New Evidence for a Late Introduction of Malaria into the New World. Current Anthropology **16**:93–104.

WOOD, JONES F., 1929 Man's Place Among the Mammals. London: Arnold, Edward.

WOOD, W., and F. T. SHIMADA, 1954 Isolation of Strains of Virus B from Tissue Cultures of Cynomolgus and Rhesus Kidney. Canadian Journal of Public Health **45**:509–518.

WOODBURN, J. C., 1959 Hadza Conceptions of Health and Disease. One day symposium on attitudes toward health and disease among some East African tribes. Kampala, Uganda: East African Institute of Social Research, Makerere College.

WOODBURN, JAMES, 1968 Discussion. Man the Hunter. R. B. Lee, and I. DeVore, eds. Chicago: Aldine Publishing Co.

WOODS, CLYDE, 1968 Medicine and Culture Change in San Lucas Toliman: A Highland Guatemalan Community. Ph.D dissertation. Stanford, Cal.: Stanford University.

World Health Organization 1946 Constitution of the World Health Organization. Geneva: World Health Organization.

———, 1963 Conference on Medicine and Public Health in the Arctic and Antarctic. Technical Report Series No. 253. Geneva.

———, 1964 Research in Population Genetics of Primitive Groups. Technical Report Series, No. 279.

———, 1965 Manual of the International Statistical Classification of Diseases, Injuries and Causes of Death. 8th revision, section V. Geneva.

WRIGLEY, E. A., 1968 Mortality in Pre-Industrial England: The Example of Colyton, Devon, over Three Centuries. Daedalus **97**: 546–580.

———, 1969 Population and History. New York: McGraw-Hill, Inc.

WYMAN, LELAND C., 1936 Navaho Diagnosticians. American Anthropologist **38**:236–246.

WYNDER, ERNEST L., JEROME CORNFIELD, P. D. SCHROFF, and K. R. DORAISWAMI, 1954 Study of Environmental Factors and Cancer of the Cervix. American Journal of Obstetrics and Gynecology **68**:1016–1052.

WYNNE-EDWARDS, V. C., 1962 Animal Dispersion in Relation to Social Behavior. Edinburgh: Oliver and Boyd.

YASKIN, JOSEPH C., 1937 The Psychobiology of Anxiety. Psychoanalytic Review **XXIV**: supplement p. 53.

YAP, POW MENG, 1951 Mental Diseases Peculiar to Certain Cultures: a Survey of Comparative Psychiatry. The Journal of Mental Science **97**:313–327.

———, 1952 The Latah Reaction. Journal of Mental Science **98**:515–564.

———, 1958a Hypereridism and Attempted Suicide in Chinese. Journal of Nervous and Mental Disease **127**:34–41.

————, 1958b Suicide in Hong Kong, with Special Reference to Attempted Suicide. London: Oxford University Press.

————, 1960 The Possession Syndrome: A Comparison of Hong Kong and French Findings. The Journal of Mental Disease **106**:114–138.

————, 1962 Words and Things in Comparative Psychiatry, with Special Reference to the Exotic Psychoses. Acta Psychiatrica Scandinavia **38**:163–169.

————, 1965 Kora-A Culture-Bound Depersonalization Syndrome. British Journal of Psychiatry **111**:43–50.

————, 1965 Phenomenology of Affective Disorder in Chinese and Other Cultures. *In* Transactional Psychiatry. A. V. S. de Reuck and R. Porter, eds. London: Ciba Foundation.

ZAGUIRRE, J. C., 1957 Amuck. Journal of the Philippine Federation of Private Medical Practitioners **6**:1138–1149.

ZBOROWSKI, MARK, 1952 Cultural Components in Responses to Pain. Journal of Social Issues **8**:16–30.

————, 1969 People in Pain. San Francisco: Jossey-Bass.

ZIGAS, V., and D. C. GAJDUSEK, 1957 Kuru. Medical Journal of Australia **2**:745–754.

ZOLA, IRVING K., 1966 Culture and Symptoms: An Analysis of Patients' Presenting Complaints. American Sociological Review **3**:615–630.